# ENCYCLOPEDIA OF
# POLITICS

## *The Left and The Right*

# ENCYCLOPEDIA OF
# POLITICS

*The Left and The Right*

VOLUME 1: *The Left*

GENERAL EDITOR

Rodney P. Carlisle, Ph.D.

RUTGERS UNIVERSITY

A SAGE Reference Publication

SAGE Publications

Thousand Oaks ▪ London ▪ New Delhi

*Volume 1 Cover Photo:* President Lyndon B. Johnson signs the Civil Rights Act of 1964 on July 2, 1964, as Martin Luther King, Jr. looks on. Credit: LBJ Library Photo by Cecil Stoughton.

*Volume 2 Cover Photo:* President Gerald Ford (center, right) and former presidential candidate Ronald Reagan (center, left) show solidarity at the Republican National Convention, August 19, 1976. Credit: Courtesy Gerald R. Ford Library.

*For information:*

Sage Publications, Inc.
2455 Teller Road
Thousand Oaks, California 91320
E-mail: order@sagepub.com

Sage Publications Ltd.
1 Oliver's Yard
55 City Road
London EC1Y 1SP
United Kingdom

Sage Publications India Pvt. Ltd.
B-42, Panchsheel Enclave
Post Box 4109
New Delhi 110 017  India

Printed in the United States of America

**Library of Congress Cataloging-in-Publication Data**

Encyclopedia of politics: The left and the right / Rodney P. Carlisle, general editor.
    p. cm.
Includes bibliographical references and index.
ISBN 1-4129-0409-9 (cloth)
    1.  Right and left (Political science)—Encyclopedias. 2.  Political science—Encyclopedias.
I. Carlisle, Rodney P.
JA61.E54 2005
320'.03—dc22

                                                                                            2005002334

This book is printed on acid-free paper.

05   06   07   08   10   9   8   7   6   5   4   3   2   1

| GOLSON BOOKS, LTD. STAFF: | | SAGE PUBLICATIONS STAFF: | |
|---|---|---|---|
| *President and Editor:* | Geoff Golson | *Acquiring Editor:* | Rolf Janke |
| *Managing Editor:* | Laura Laurie | *Editorial Assistant:* | Sara Tauber |
| *Design Director:* | Kevin Hanek | *Production Editor:* | Denise Santoyo |
| *Copy Editor and Proofreader:* | Martha Whitt, Lori Kranz | *Proofreader:* | Doris Hus |
| *Indexer:* | Gail Liss | *Production Artist:* | Michelle Lee Kenny |

# ENCYCLOPEDIA OF
# POLITICS

## VOLUME 1 CONTENTS
## *The Left*

ALSO SEE VOLUME 2: *The Right*

# Introduction

## The Left and The Right

ALTHOUGH THE DISTINCTION between the politics of the left and the right is commonly assumed in the media and in treatments of political science and history, the terms are used so loosely that the student and the general reader are often confused: What exactly are the terms *left* and *right* supposed to imply? In this two-volume encyclopedia, we have assembled over 450 articles on individuals, movements, political parties, and ideological principles, with those usually thought of as left in the left-hand volume and those considered on the right, in the right-hand volume.

The terms *left* and *right* are derived from the political divisions in the French Constituent Assembly, formed during the French Revolution in 1790. Sitting on the right of the assembly were those who favored the preservation of the monarchy and a more moderate course of change, the Girondins, while on the left in the assembly sat those who wished to overthrow the existing system and establish a more egalitarian republic, the Jacobins. The terms *left* and *right* stuck, with the left usually representing the radicals of politics and the right representing the conservatives. Over the next century, with the rise of utopian socialism and later, Marxism, those proposing conversion of the means of production from private property to social property held in common were regarded as leftists, while those seeking to preserve the status quo were regarded as rightists. The terms passed into common parlance and became handy labels, both for serious students of politics, and for use by publicists, politicians, and observers.

For those involved in politics, the terms soon became heavily charged with overtones. By the middle of the 19th century, many followers of Karl Marx took pride in regarding themselves as further to the left and would often designate their own fractional group or wing of the party as the Left Socialists. Of course, as propaganda, such a label was not always useful, for it would suggest that those belonging to the left group were out at the fringe of opinion with only a few adherents. For this reason, V.I. Lenin designated his small wing of the Russian Socialist Party as the majority wing (even though it only held a majority at one brief meeting in 1903), or "Bolshevik" in Russian. Through most of the 20th century, with the rise of international communism, headed by the Communist (Bolshevik) Party in the Soviet Union, extreme leftism tended to be associated with adherence to the international communist movement, while extreme rightism tended to be associated with politicians who made a career of denouncing the international communist movement. The Bolshevik Party officially changed its name to the Communist (Bolshevik) Party in March 1918.

In countries operating under democratic constitutions, like the United States, Canada, Great Britain,

New Zealand, and various other republics and constitutional monarchies, the terms *left* and *right* were used to describe parties and politics of the center that addressed domestic issues, rather than the role of international communism. That is, leftism became associated with liberals who endorsed a wide variety of programs designed to mitigate the harsh effects of capitalism, such as programs of social welfare, unemployment compensation, a progressive income tax (that is, one that taxed higher incomes at a higher proportion than lower incomes), provision of health services to the poor, and more equal educational opportunities. Those who were conservative, who believed that the economic status quo should not be tampered with, and that free market conditions should be allowed to operate without too much government interference, were generally regarded as rightists. Often, those on the right believed that while government should allow the free enterprise system to operate without interference, they were quick to demand that government use its authority to impose and enforce a moral code on the general population. From the point of view of those who owned property, of course, maintenance of law and order and protection of property were the major and proper role of government.

While such distinctions appear simple enough to apply to the politics and movements of many nations around the world, they often tend to oversimplify the complexities of politics. Individual political leaders and political movements often defied easy categorization. For example, in the United States, in Eastern Europe, and in Latin America, "populist" leaders arose in the late 19th and through the early and mid-20th centuries. While populism in each context and in each era was somewhat different, it usually represented an appeal for social reform and egalitarianism which seemed radical and leftist, but it also often incorporated a reactionary thrust that was opposed to modernization and was often quite nationalistic and ethnically exclusive, ideas usually associated with the right. Often a leader with a populist agenda was accused by some of his enemies of being a right-wing reactionary, and by other enemies as being a left-wing radical. And in some cases, both charges made perfect sense.

In the United States, some historians have evaluated the Progressive movement, which espoused many of the social programs usually considered as part of the left, as springing from a reactionary response to the "status revolution" of the early 20th century. That is, many of the Progressives were salaried professionals like clerics, lawyers, journalists, teachers, and govern-

ment employees who were distressed not only at the dominance of society by newly rich big-business leaders, but also upset by perceived threats to their own status posed by new immigrants, radical ideologues, city political bosses, and labor-union leaders. For such reasons, many Progressives endorsed the movement to establish Prohibition, which they saw as a moral reform designed to restore America to its moral standards, and as an attack on the habits of immigrants and the dominance of the liquor interests in politics. So Prohibition of alcohol, which was an attempt to enforce conformity to a moral code, and thus appears to be authoritarian and right-wing to many observers, was supported by many whose views sprang from reactionary motives, but who also endorsed left-leaning social programs.

One movement that grew out of populist concepts in Europe was fascism. In Italy, Germany, Spain, Portugal, and other countries, popular leaders proposed a mix of ideas that were drawn from socialism, and adopted radical methods to establish a nationalistic, exclusive, elitist-operated authoritarian state. Although usually regarded and classified as parties of the right, fascist parties reflected both leftist and rightist ideas and methods. However, with their broad popular appeal and social agendas, fascist parties did not resemble the conservative, status-quo oriented parties of the traditional right. Often, the issue was one of perspective, or even more simply, one of name-calling. Thus, the Communist Party of the United States in the early 1930s often denounced advocates of pro-labor positions who did not work with the Communist Party as "social fascists" and lumped them with the right wing in their propaganda literature.

In local settings around the world, other issues cut across the clear logic of left and right distinctions. For example, in many countries, movements for ethnic autonomy, independence, or unification with a group outside of the territorial boundaries of the state confused the picture, often leading to great conflicts. Those trying to form a nation out of ethnic groups dispersed among several states were known as "irredentists" after the 19th-century Italian unification movement that sought to bring the *irridenta* or "unredeemed" Italians into a state headed by the house of Savoy out of Piedmont. Serbian irridentist nationalists in territories controlled by Austria-Hungary sought to unite with Serbia, and it was a group of such nationalists who assassinated Archduke Franz Ferdinand in 1914, setting off World War I.

In Spain, during the 1930s, separatists in the Basque northwest and Catalonians in the northeast of the country joined in the civil war. While they were nationalists, and thus might be regarded as rightists, in fact, they joined with a coalition largely consisting of parties of the left to defend the existing government, against a revolution led by the army, which sought to impose a fascist regime. Spanish politics in the 1930s, while often described in terms of left and right, posed a great many problems for those who sought to understand it in those terms. The leftists and separatists were known as Loyalists or Republicans because they supported the existing republic; the fascists, monarchists, and the army officers, supported by Catholic Church leaders, were known as the Insurgents.

Elsewhere, irredentists, separatists, and nationalists used radical methods to achieve nationalistic goals. Such groups included the Irish, as well as separatists in countries as far afield as Sri Lanka (Ceylon), Kurdistan, the Caucausus regions of the Russian Federation, and the French-controlled island of Corsica. In the United States, the radicalism mixed with nationalist rhetoric of American black nationalists seemed to defy a simple classification of left or right. In South Africa, the policy of racial exclusion and imposition of a white-dominated regime adopted many ideas and principles that seemed to reflect the fascist doctrines of Germany's Nazi Party, at the same time, maintaining an electoral, republican form of government for the controlling white minority. The South African doctrine of apartheid, or separateness, was viewed by most observers as an ideology of the right.

These political, social, and ethnic complications often lead to confusion of terminology, and even to some heated debates among experts. In fact, when individual politicians and their positions are studied closely, the individual's career may defy simple categorization. For many individuals who participated in politics over several decades, their radical-populist ideas seemed increasingly dated as the world changed around them, and they appeared, in the new context, as hopelessly conservative and backward-looking. Thus, while William Randolph Hearst may have seemed a radical in 1912 when he supported municipal ownership of utilities and labor-endorsed candidates, by the 1930s, he was regularly denounced as a right-winger for his opposition to the New Deal of Franklin Roosevelt and for his strident anti-communist rhetoric.

Other leaders and politicians with populist ideas in the United States often found themselves voting with very conservative colleagues in legislatures on specific issues. The cross currents that appeared to be at work during the Progressive era, which led many otherwise left-oriented politicians to endorse moral authoritarian views like Prohibition, continued through much of the 20th century and into the 21st century. By the late 20th century in the United States, both sides of the abortion issue cast their views in terms of liberties or personal rights. On one side were arrayed those who believed in "freedom of choice" or "a woman's right to choose," while those opposed regarded themselves as defending "the right to life." Opposite sides of this heated social debate couched their position in terms of liberty. By generally accepted convention, the right-to-life advocates were regarded as right wing; however, some of the most dedicated members of that side of the argument adopted radical means to achieve their goals, such as picketing abortion clinics, or in a few cases, even bombing them.

In this encyclopedia, we have made some decisions following the generally accepted convention of whether a movement or individual should be treated as falling on the left or right side of the political spectrum. Often, the views and positions of the individual or movement make such a classification rather clear-cut or obvious. In other cases, the placement is far more complex or problematic, and we have suggested the reasons for the complexity, reflecting among others, the ones outlined here.

Not a day goes by in the media or in a history or political science classroom that the terms *left* and *right* are not employed to describe an historical or contemporary aspect of politics. Rather than assuming such terms are universally understood or acknowledged, as editors we have attempted to make the distinction clearer, albeit with the caveats mentioned above.

Although our emphasis is on the modern era, we have included many movements, political leaders, and thinkers from the 19th and early 20th centuries. And although each contributor offered his or her own interpretative slant, we have attempted to achieve a tone of balance, presenting the information with objectivity rather than advocacy. In the broad spectrum of politics, it is our hope that the articles of the *Encyclopedia of Politics: The Left and The Right*, contributed by academics and scholars from all over the world, help further the understanding of political science and historical movements.

RODNEY P. CARLISLE, PH.D., GENERAL EDITOR
PROFESSOR EMERITUS, RUTGERS UNIVERSITY

# Reader's Guide

This list is provided to assist readers in locating article entries on related topics.

## People on the Left
Anthony, Susan B.
Bellamy, Edward
Bentham, Jeremy
Breitman, George
Browder, Earl
Carmichael, Stokely
Carter, James E.
Carville, James
Cleaver, Eldridge
Clinton, William J.
Coxey, Jacob
Croly, Herbert
Debs, Eugene V.
Deng Xiaoping
Douglass, Frederick
Du Bois, W.E.B.
Duclos, Jacques
Dunayevskaya, Raya
Engels, Friedrich
Flynn, Elizabeth Gurley
Foster, William Z.
Freidan, Betty
Fromm, Erich

Ghandi, Mahatma
Gilman, Charlotte Perkins
Gitlow, Benjamin
Goldman, Emma
Gorbachev, Mikhail
Guevara, Che
Hall, Gus
Hammett, Dashiell
Harrington, Michael
Hayden, Tom
Haywood, William D
Hillman, Sidney
Hillquit, Morris
Hobbes, Thomas
Hollywood Ten
Hopkins, Harry
Hume, David
Humphrey, Hubert H.
Jefferson, Thomas
Johnson, Lyndon B.
Kefauver, Estes
Kennedy, John F.
King, Martin Luther, Jr.
La Follette, Robert
Lenin, Vladimir I.
Lincoln, Abraham
Lippmann, Walter
Lloyd, Henry Demarest

Locke, John
Long, Huey
Lovestone, Jay
Malcolm X
Marcuse, Herbert
Marx, Karl
Moore, Michael
Mott, Lucretia
Muste, Abraham J.
Nader, Ralph
Nearing, Scott
O'Neil, Thomas P.
Orwell, George
Paul, Alice
Randolph, A. Philip
Reed, John
Roosevelt, Eleanor
Roosevelt, Franklin D.
Rousseau, Jean-Jacques
Sacco and Vanzetti
Schlesinger, Arthur M., Jr.
Stanton, Elizabeth Cady
Steinem, Gloria
Stevenson, Adlai E.
Thomas, Norman M.
Thompson, Hunter S.
Trotsky, Leon
Truman, Harry

Wallace, Henry A.
Washington, George
Wilson, Woodrow
Wright, Frances

**People on the Right**
Ali, Noble Drew
Bennett, William J.
Bilbo, Theodore G.
Borah, William E.
Buchanan, Patrick J.
Buckley, William F., Jr.
Burke, Edmund
Bush, George H.W.
Bush, George W.
Churchill, Sir Winston
Coolidge, Calvin
Coughlin, Charles E.
Coulter, Ann H.
Dewey, Thomas E.
Dos Passos, John
Drudge, Matt
Eisenhower, Dwight D.
Ford, Gerald R.
Garvey, Marcus
Gingrich, Newt
Goldwater, Barry
Harding, Warren G.
Hearst, William Randolph
Hitler, Adolf
Hoover, Herbert
Hoover, J. Edgar
Khomeini, Ruhollah
La Guardia, Fiorello H.
Landon, Alfred M.
Limbaugh, Rush
Lincoln, Abraham
Lind, Michael
Lindbergh, Charles A.
Luce, Henry R.
Mises, Ludwig von
Nietzsche, Friedrich
Nixon, Richard M.
Rand, Ayn
Reagan, Ronald
Roosevelt, Theodore
Shockley, William B.
Sowell, Thomas
Taft, Robert A.
Taft, William H.
Thatcher, Margaret

Washington, Booker T.
Will, George F.
Willkie, Wendell

**Countries/Regions: Left Politics**
Africa
Argentina
Asia
Australia
Austria
Brazil
Canada
Chile
China
Czech Republic
Egypt
France
Greece
India
Indonesia
Iran
Ireland
Israel
Italy
Japan
Korea, North
Korea, South
Mexico
Middle East
Nigeria
Peru
Poland
Russia, Post-Soviet
Saudi Arabia
Singapore
South Africa
South America
Soviet Union
Spain
Sweden
Switzerland
Turkey
Uganda
Ukraine
United Kingdom
United States

**Countries/Regions: Right Politics**
Africa
Argentina
Asia

Australia
Austria
Brazil
Canada
Chile
China
Czech Republic
Egypt
France
Greece
India
Iran
Iraq
Ireland
Israel
Italy
Japan
Korea, South
Mexico
Middle East
Nigeria
Peru
Poland
Russia, Post-Soviet
Saudi Arabia
Singapore
South Africa
South America
Soviet Union
Spain
Sweden
Switzerland
Turkey
Uganda
Ukraine
United Kingdom
United States

**Leftist "Isms"**
Abolitionism
Anarchism
Anarcho-Syndicalism
Bicameralism
Bolshevism
Communism
Communitarianism
Despotism
Environmentalism
Fabianism
Feminism
Fourierism

Liberalism
Maoism
Market Socialism
Marxist Humanism
Populism
Postmodernism
Québec Separatism
Saint-Simonism
Socialism
Socialist Realism
Stalin and Stalinism
Syndicalism
Third Worldism
Titoism
Zionism

**Rightist "Isms"**
Agrarianism
Black Nationalism
Black Separatism
Capitalism
Colonialism
Conservatism
Corporatism
Corsican Separatism
Darwinism
Despotism
Elitism
Falangism
Fascism
Feudalism
Fundamentalism
Imperialism
Isolationism
Libertarianism
McCarthyism
Monarchism
Nationalism
Orientalism
Pan-Africanism
Patriotism
Peronism
Prohibitionism
Sabbatarianism
Totalitarianism
Ultramontanism
Unilateralism
Zionism

**Leftist Political Issues**
Abolitionism

Alienation
Anarchism
Anarcho-Syndicalism
Anti-Globalization
Bicameralism
Campaign Finance
Communism
Communitarianism
Cultural Diversity
Democracy
Desegregation
Environmentalism
Human Rights
Ideology
Liberalism
Lobbying
Market Socialism
Media Bias, Left
Politically Correct
Political Economy
Polls and Pollsters
Social Democracy
Socialism
Socialist Realism
Stalin and Stalinism
Vietnam War
Voting, Unrestricted
Welfare and Poverty

**Rightist Political Issues**
Balance of Power
Capitalism
Censorship
Conservatism
Corporatism
Darwinism
Despotism
Education
Ethnic Cleansing
Fascism
Foreign Policy, U.S.
Fundamentalism
Globalization
Healthcare
Ideology
Isolationism
*Laissez-Faire*
Libertarianism
Lobbying
Manifest Destiny
Media Bias, Right

Polls and Pollsters
Realpolitik
Segregation
States' Rights
Technocracy, Inc.
Theocracy
Totalitarianism
Unilateralism
Vietnam War
Welfare and Poverty
Xenophobia

**Leftist Laws**
Abortion/Pro-Choice
American Civil
    Liberties Union
Animal Rights
Bill of Rights
Censorship
Church and State Separation
Civil Liberties
Civil Rights
Constitutional Amendments
Consumer Rights
Death Penalty Elimination
Desegregation
First Amendment
Freedom of Information
Gun Control
Healthcare
Human Rights
Immigration
Lobbying
New Deal
Social Security
Supreme Court
Voting, Unrestricted
Welfare and Poverty

**Rightist Laws**
Anti-Abortion/Pro-Life
Censorship
Courts and Law
Healthcare
Immigration Restriction
Lobbying
Martial Law
Second Amendment
Segregation
States' Rights
Supreme Court

## Leftist Political Parties

African National Congress
American Civil Liberties Union
Black Panthers
Catholic Worker
Christian Democracy
Communist Party, Soviet
Democratic Party
Green Party
Greenback Party
Labour Party, UK
Liberal Party, Australia
Liberal Party, Canada
Liberal Party, Hong Kong
Liberal Party, UK
PRI (Mexico)
Progressive Party
Socialist Party, U.S.
Socialist Workers' Party, UK
Suffragists
Workers Party
Workingmen's Party

## Rightist Political Parties

American Party

British National Party
Conservative Party, UK
Kuomintang
Republican Party

## Leftist Political Movements

Abortion/Pro-Choice
Affirmative Action
Anarcho-Syndicalism
Animal Rights
Anti-Globalization
Bolshevism
Civil Rights
Consumer Rights
Death Penalty Elimination
Democracy
Desegregation
Environmentalism
Feminism
Gay and Lesbian Movements
Gun Control
Human Rights
Niagara Movement
Palestine Liberation Organization
Postmodernism

Protests
Solidarity
Students for a
    Democratic Society
Suffragists
Zionism

## Rightist Political Movements

Anti-Abortion/Pro-Life
Basque and
    Catalan Separatism
Black Nationalism
Black Separatism
Bruder Schweigen
Christian Coalition
Globalization
Isolationism
John Birch Society
Kuomintang
*Laissez-Faire*
Militia Movements
Manifest Destiny
Prohibitionism
Segregation
White Citizens' Councils

# Timeline of Politics

**509 B.C.E.**

Tarquin, the last king of Rome, is deposed as the empire becomes a republic.

**410 B.C.E.**

In his comedy, *Lysistrata*, Aristophanes depicts an ancient world in which civil disobedience is prevalent; the women in the warring cities of Athens and Sparta conspire to deprive all men of sexual intercourse for the duration of the war. Moreover, the Athenean women stage one of the first recorded sit-ins by occupying the Parthenon, blocking access to the state treasury where the war chest is housed.

**1215**

King John signs the Magna Carta, the first document of human rights in English history, and a first step in a centuries-long struggle to end feudalism.

**1771**

Robert Owen, who would come to be known as the father of British socialism, is born.

**1776**

Great Britain's 13 North American colonies declare independence, proclaiming to be the United States of America. Britain, who had begun their colonization of North America at Jamestown, Virginia, more than 100 years earlier, did not recognize the American independence until after the Revolutionary War, when the Treaty of Paris affirmed the young nation's independence.

**1792**

*A Vindication of the Rights of Women* by Mary Wollstonecraft is published. The book would later inspire women's right activists Lucretia Mott and Elizabeth Cady Stanton.

**1793**

The division between Jacobins on the left and Girondists on the right in the meetings of the French Legislative Assembly creates the left-right terminology, reflected in later association of the left with radicals and the right with conservatives.

**1803**

The United States acquires the Louisiana Territory from France for $15 million. The acquisition, known as the Louisiana Purchase, doubles the geographic extent of the country.

**1804**

After executing one of his fellow governing consuls for suspicions regarding a plot to assassinate him, Napoleon Bonaparte declares himself emperor of France.

## 1825

On a visit to the United States, Robert Owen establishes one of the first secular experimental communities, New Harmony, Indiana.

## 1827

In his "Notes on the State of Virginia," former U.S. President Thomas Jefferson remarks on the purity of agrarian society: "Corruption of morals in the mass of cultivators is a phenomenon of which no age nor nation has furnished an example."

## 1840

Pierre-Joseph Proudhon, considered the father of modern anarchism, publishes his pamphlet, *What Is Property?*, in which he argues that, "Property is profit stolen from the worker, who is the true source of all wealth."

## 1841

George Ripley establishes Brook Farm, a secular community near Boston, Massachusetts. Later, Brook Farm is transformed into a Phalanx, following the ideas of French utopian socialist, Francois Fourier.

## 1844

The Rochdale Society of Equitable Pioneers, a group consisting of seven socialists, establishes a cooperatively owned venture known as the Rochdale Equitable Co-operative Society Ltd.

## 1848

Liberal uprisings take place in many German cities, including the capital of Prussia, Berlin. In response to the violence, Prussian King Frederick William IV promises a constitution and an elected assembly.

## 1848

Karl Marx and Friedrich Engels publish *The Communist Manifesto*, which would serve as the inspiration for future communist revolutions.

## 1849

Henry David Thoreau is credited with theorizing the practice of civil disobedience in his essay "Resistance to Civil Government," in which he explains his refusal to pay taxes as an act of protest against slavery and the U.S.-Mexican War.

## 1849

The first challenge to Northern U.S. segregation occurs when a black Bostonian sues the city for the right to send his daughter to the nearest public school, rather than across town to the all-black school. Despite the case being unsuccessful, it sparks public debate, and six years later the state of Massachusetts passes a law desegregating the state's public schools.

## 1853

The American Party, or more commonly known as the Know-Nothings due to its members' insistence that such a party did not exist, is founded on the basis of removing political power from immigrants and the politicians who court them.

## 1861

Following the election of Republican Abraham Lincoln, which angered Southerners due to Lincoln's position on slavery, South Carolinians open fire on Fort Sumter, sparking the American Civil War. Upon the war's completion, the Thirteenth Amendment to the Constitution is signed, abolishing slavery. The Fourteenth Amendment extends citizenship to African Americans and the Fifteenth Amendment prohibits the denial of the right to vote on the grounds of race or previous servitude.

## 1864

Meeting in Paris, labor leaders, Marxists, and various socialists from across Europe create the First International Federation of Working Men, known as the First International. Karl Marx becomes a member of the executive committee of the First International.

## 1871

Following the transfer of power of France's capital city, Paris, to the Prussian government, the city undergoes a short-lived communistic transformation known as the Paris Commune.

## 1883

The first modern government-supported welfare program is created in Germany, where legislation is introduced giving accident insurance to workers.

## 1889

Two international workers' congresses convene in Paris, France, one consisting of Marxists and one consisting of non-Marxist labor leaders. They agree to merge, forming the Second International, announced on July 14, on the 100th anniversary of the storming of the Bastille by peasants and workers during the French Revolution.

## 1890

Wyoming, the second-lowest populated state with nearly 100,000 people, becomes the first U.S. state to grant women's suffrage. As a territory, Wyoming had extended the right to vote to women in 1869.

## 1895

In a speech that would later come to be known as the Atlanta Compromise, Booker T. Washington suggests that in order to alleviate racial tensions, blacks should assume a subservient role in society, embarking on vocational careers. The proposal was widely accepted between both races, but social activists such as W.E.B. Du Bois challenged it as a form of accommodation.

## 1898

A 19-year-old Leon Trotsky helps to found the Russian Social Democratic Labor Party (RSDLP). Arrested by the regime in power, he is exiled to Russian Siberia.

## 1903

At a meeting of the RSDLP, the more elitist branch that holds the party should be open only to dedicated revolutionaries rather than to all sympathetic socialists, led by V.I. Lenin, holds a slim majority. The RSDLP splits into the Bolshevik Party and the minority Menshevik Party.

## 1905

Russian workers in the city of St. Petersburg protest outside of Tzar Nicholas II's winter palace. The massacre that followed sparked the Revolution of 1905.

## 1910

The National Association for the Advancement of Colored People (NAACP) is founded, with W.E.B. Du Bois as executive secretary; he edits its magazine, *Crisis*, for more than 20 years, advocating the extension of civil rights to African Americans.

## 1911

The most successful American Progressive Party is created, first being named the National Progressive Republican League, and then, under the leadership of former President Theodore Roosevelt, the Progressive Party, or more popularly, the Bull Moose Party.

## 1912

The South African government passes the Native Lands Act, which forbids blacks from owning or leasing land in white-designated areas. The African National Congress, whose future members would include President Nelson Mandela, launches a petition campaign in protest.

## 1912

Theodore Roosevelt runs for the presidency of the United States on the Progressive Party ticket, splitting the Republican vote. As a consequence, Woodrow Wilson, Democrat, is elected president. Eugene Debs, the Socialist, wins nearly one million popular votes.

## 1913

Noble Drew Ali founds the Moorish American Science Temple, which states in its doctrine of beliefs that peace on earth can only come when each racial group has its own religion.

## 1913

American citizens first begin to pay income taxes, which in time become the largest source of federal government revenues.

## 1913

The term *protest march* is originated as Mahatma Ghandi and his followers organize a march to protest restrictions imposed on Indians in South Africa.

## 1914

The Archduke Franz Ferdinand, heir to the Austrian Empire, is shot by a group of Serb gunmen in Sarajevo, Bosnia-Herzegovina, an area which was just added to the Austrian Empire. The incident is the spark that set off World War I.

## 1914

Marcus Garvey founds the Universal Negro Improvement Association (UNIA) in Jamaica; in 1916, he moves to the United States and extends branches of the organization in many cities; his Black Star shipping line is created to establish black business connections with the Caribbean and Africa.

## 1915

Activist A. Philip Randolph co-founds *The Messenger*, "the first radical Negro magazine."

## 1917

In February, the tzar of Russia, Nicholas II, abdicates and a Provisional Government is formed; Alexander Kerensky, a socialist lawyer, emerges as prime minister by the summer.

## 1917

In October and November, the Bolsheviks stage a coup that throws out the Provisional Government and establishes the Soviet rule; Lenin and Trotsky emerge as the leaders of the new regime.

## 1919

John Reed publishes *Ten Days That Shook the World*, giving a rare first-hand account of the Bolshevik takeover of Russia in November 1917.

## 1919

Third International, the third iteration of an international communist movement, is created following the International Communist Conference, in which Soviet leader Vladimir Lenin stresses the importance of worldwide communism.

## 1919

Great Britain, France, Italy, and Japan, and later Germany and the USSR, form the League of Nations at the Paris Peace Conference. The United States does not ratify the treaty or the covenant of the league.

## 1919

One of the worst race riots in United States history erupts in Chicago when a black swimmer passes an imaginary territorial line in Lake Michigan and floats into the white swimming area, where he is murdered.

## 1920

The 19th Amendment to the United States is passed; it grants all adult American women the right to vote.

## 1920

In response to the Red Scare, in which nearly 10,000 suspected communists were detained by the U.S. government, the American Union Against Militarism (AUAM) and other progressive groups band together to form the American Civil Liberties Union (ACLU).

## 1924

Soviet leader Vladimir Lenin dies following a massive stroke. Josef Stalin succeeds him in power, and by 1928 has outlawed Trotsky and assumed dictatorial powers.

## 1924

Robert M. La Follette is chosen to be the representative of the Progressive Party in the 1924 U.S. Presidential election. La Follette manages to garner five million votes, or about 4 percent of the voting public, but only takes the 13 electoral college votes of Wisconsin. La Follette's sons would continue the progressive movement after the election by founding the Wisconsin Progressive Party.

## 1930

Over a 110-year period, the United States receives approximately 60 percent of all the world's immigrants.

## 1932

During a visit to Miami, U.S. President-elect Franklin D. Roosevelt is shot at by anarchist Giuseppe Zangara. FDR survives the assassination attempt, but the mayor of Chicago, Anton Cermak, is fatally wounded.

## 1933

Upon his inauguration and as a result of the Great Depression, Franklin Roosevelt enacts his New Deal policies, which become the largest and most liberal restructuring of the U.S. government in history.

## 1933

Having only been chancellor of Germany for a few months, Adolf Hitler is given the legislative right by the German Parliament, the Reichstag, to rule by decree, making him the absolute ruler of the German people.

## 1935

The first widespread use of the term *apartheid* emerges during the political campaign of the South African Herenigde Nasionale party, which uses the African-originated word as a slogan. When the party comes into power nearly a decade later, it begins to systematically implement the race restriction policies associated with the term.

## 1935

In the United States, the National Industrial Recovery Act is declared unconstitutional on the grounds that Congress had delegated law-making authority to nonelected corporate and labor leaders. In response, Franklin Roosevelt and Congress move to the so-called Second New Deal, which attempts reform through regulation reform rather than through direct economic administration.

## 1935

As the labor movement in the United States gains strength, Congress passes the National Labor Relations Act, requiring that employers bargain with labor unions.

## 1935

As part of the Second New Deal, the United States Congress enacts the Social Security Act, establishing the retirement system of Social Security as well as national public welfare for dependent children.

## 1939

The membership of Hitler Youth, an organization created by Hitler three years earlier in order to mold young citizens of the Third Reich, has risen to an estimated eight million young people.

## 1940

The America First Committee is established with help from aviator Charles Lindbergh. The committee becomes nonexistent within a year, but its message of noninvolvement in World War II had attracted 800,000 members.

## 1943

Despite being forced out of office due to the failures of Italy in World War II, Benito Mussolini is installed as leader of German-occupied Northern Italy, where he wages a civil war against anti-fascists until the culmination of World War II.

## 1945

At the end of World War II, Europe falls into Western and Eastern spheres of influence, predicating the decades of Cold War between the United States and the Soviet Union.

## 1948

Zionist leaders declare the state of Israel, thus creating a Jewish nation in British-controlled Palestine, in the center of the Arab Middle East.

## 1948

Mahatma Ghandi, considered a champion of nonviolent civil disobedience, is murdered by Hindu nationalist extremists as he attends a prayer meeting in the Indian city of New Delhi.

## 1948

In the United States, former Vice President Henry Wallace runs for president on the Progressive Party ticket; he receives support from the Communist Party of the United States, but wins no electoral college votes. Harry Truman defeats Thomas Dewey in a surprise victory despite the division of the American political left.

## 1949

Mao Zedong is victorious in his quest to make China a communist nation, defeating the nationalist forces of the Kuomintang.

## 1952

French intellectual Alfred Sauvy coins the term *third world*, a concept that originated during the worldwide decolonization process that began in the aftermath of World War II.

## 1953

Nikita Khrushchev replaces Josef Stalin as premier of the Soviet Union. Khrushchev, looking to alleviate the dissent caused by Stalin's brutal regime, denounces Stalin's rule in a speech to a closed meeting of the 20th Party Congress in 1956, leading to uprisings in Poland and Hungary in that year.

## 1954

Martin Luther King, Jr. begins his career as the leader of the civil rights movement and plans the Montgomery, Alabama, bus boycott.

## 1954

In the aftermath of the *Brown vs. Board of Education* ruling, which began desegregation in America's public schools, Robert P. Patterson forms the White Citizen s' Council, whose purpose is to preserve segregation regardless of the *Brown* ruling.

## 1956

Egyptian leader Gamal Abdel Nasser attempts to nationalize the Suez Canal in order to fund expansionist policies. In response, Israel, Great Britain, and France attack to seize the canal. A United Nations resolution ends the conflict.

## 1957

Martin Luther King, Jr., along with a number of black leaders from 10 states, founds the Southern Christian Leadership Conference (SCLC) in response to growing protests among African Americans. The group's main focus is to preach nonviolent civil disobedience.

## 1960

Ramon Mercader, who had assassinated exiled Soviet leader Leon Trotsky nearly 20 years earlier on Josef Stalin's orders, returns to the Soviet Union following his incarceration in Mexico and is awarded the title of "Hero of the Soviet Union."

## 1960

The Ba'ath Party, whose members would include future leader Saddam Hussein, seizes power in Iraq after launching a military coup and assuming the title of the National Council of Revolutionary Command.

## 1961

President Dwight D. Eisenhower, during his final speech as president, draws the world's attention to the concept known as the military-industrial complex. He describes it as the relationship between the military and industrialists who profit by manufacturing arms and selling them to the government.

## 1962

Tom Hayden founds the Students for a Democratic Society (SDS) after he writes the "Port Huron Statement," an essay that called for participatory democracy based on nonviolent civil disobedience.

## 1964

The Civil Rights Act is passed, which guarantees equal access to commercial establishments, travel facilities, housing, employment, and all government benefits without regard to race.

## 1964

In response to the widespread loss of power among conservatives in the United States's national political arena, the American Conservative Union (ACU) is founded. Within 10 years, membership would rise to an estimated 45,000 people.

## 1965

The Voting Rights Act is passed in the United States, providing a system of guarantees to ensure that the right to vote would not be denied on the basis of race, sex, belief, or social status.

## 1969

Following a series of violent conflicts that occurred between homosexuals and New York City's police department that came to be known as the Stonewall Riots, the Gay Liberation Front is formed.

## 1970

The Christian Identity Movement (CIM), first founded in 1840, begins to take on a new set of beliefs and adopts the term *Zionist Occupation Government* (ZOG), which CIM members describe as a conspiracy for Jewish world-domination.

## 1979

Saddam Hussein, who would remain in power for nearly 25 years before an invasion ousted him, becomes the leader of Iraq.

## 1979

The Islamic Revolution, led by the Ayatollah Khomeini, breaks out in Iran, bringing theocratic reform to the Arab nation.

## 1984

Ronald Reagan wins a second term of the U.S. presidency over Democratic candidate Walter Mondale with the largest electoral margin in history, signifying the success of rightist politics in America.

## 1991

The Union of Soviet Socialist Republics is officially dissolved, having collapsed under the liberal policies of Mikhail Gorbachev.

## 1993

A member of the anti-abortion group Rescue America kills Dr. David Gunn, an abortion provider at the Pensacola Women's Medical Services Clinic. In response, Congress passes the Freedom of Access to Clinic Entrances Act (FACE).

## 2000

In one of the most contested presidential elections in history, Republican George W. Bush is declared the winner of the election over Democrat Al Gore. A split between the left and right in the country is further widened.

## 2001

Al-Qaeda terrorists hijack and crash four planes in the United States, causing the worst foreign attack on U.S. soil in modern times. President George W. Bush responds with an invasion of Afghanistan, where the terrorists cells were trained and equipped.

## 2003

Citing a new doctrine of preemptive war, the United States and Great Britain invade Iraq and topple dictator Saddam Hussein.

## 2005

George W. Bush is inaugurated for a second term as president, continuing a far-right, conservative U.S. administration.

# List of Contributors

Aksu, Esref
Independent Scholar, Turkey

Artaraz, Kepa
University of Derby
United Kingdon

Barnhill, John
Independent Scholar

Basista, Jakub
Jagiellonian University
Poland

Baugess, James S.
Columbus State Community
College

Beech, Matt
University of Southampton,
United Kingdom

Belton, Patrick
Oxford University
United Kingdom

Böttger, Jörg
Independent Scholar, Germany

Burgess, Amanda
Wayne State University

Callaghan, Clare
Independent Scholar

Callahan, Kevin J.
Saint Joseph College

Canefe, Nergis
York University, Canada

Carlisle, Rodney P.
General Editor

Charskykh, Igor
Donetsk National University
Ukraine

Çolak, Yilmaz
Eastern Mediterranean University
Turkey

Cronin, D. Steven
Mississippi State University

Cundiff, Kirby R.
Northeastern State University

Davidov, Veronica
New York University

De Leon, Josie Hernandez
Laurentian University, Canada

Desnoyers, Ronald C., Jr.
Roger Williams University

DeWiel, Boris
University of Northern British
Columbia, Canada

Dorey, Peter
Cardiff University, United Kingdom

Downs, William M.
Georgia State University

Fettmann, Eric
Independent Scholar

Finley, Laura L.
Independent Scholar

Fowler, Russell
University of Tennessee
Chattanooga

Friedman, Monroe
Eastern Michigan University

Green, Gary S.
Christopher Newport University

Greenfield, Norman
Independent Scholar

Greven, Thomas
Freie Universität, Germany

Gutzman, Kevin R.C.
Western Connecticut State
University

Guy, James John
University Collge of Cape Breton
Canada

Hemmerle, Oliver Benjamin
Chemnitz University, Germany

Hicks, Gloria J.
University of Wymoming

Hill, Tony L.
Massachusetts Institute of
Technology

Holst, Arthur
Widener University

Karp, Janusz
Jagiellonian University, Poland

Kerby, Rob
Independent Scholar

Keskin-Kozat, Burçak
University of Michigan

Kimmel, Leigh
Independent Scholar

Magill, Dana
Texas Christian University

Martin, Geoffrey R.
Mount Allison University,
Canada

McBride, David W.
University of Nottingham
United Kingdom

McNaylor, Mitchell
Our Lady of the Lake College

Monje, Scott C.
Independent Scholar

Morley, Ian
Ming Chuan University, Taiwan

Murphy, John F., Jr.
American Military University

Nascimento, Amos
Methodist University of Piracicaba
Brazil

Nesbitt-Larking, Paul
Huron University College, Canada

Olivares, Jaime Ramón
Houston Community College,
Central

Orlov, Stanislav
University of Toronto, Canada

Orr, Shannon K.
Bowling Green State University

Pirani, Pietro
University of Western Ontario

Power, Margaret
Illinois Institute of Technology

Prono, Luca
University of Nottingham
United Kingdom

Purdy, Elizabeth
Independent Scholar

Rein, Sandra
Athabasca University, Canada

Roberts, Jason
George Washington University

Rolph, Stephanie R.
Misssissippi State University

Sant, Toni
New York University

Silver, Lindsay
Brandeis University

Spencer, Mark G.
Brock University, Canada

Steverson, Leonard A.
South Georgia College

Tranmer, Jeremy
University of Nancy 2, France

Tucker, Aviezer
Australian National University

Upchurch, Thomas Adams
East Georgia College

Uttam, Jitendra
Jawaharlal Nehru University
India

Vuic, Jason C.
Ohio State University

Waskey, Andrew J.
Dalton State College

Weathers, Kimberley Green
University of Houston

Wertz, James
American University

Wolin, Sheldon
Independent Scholar

Wood, Andrea Molnar
Boston College

Wood, William R.
Boston College

Zyla, Benjamin
Royal Military College of Canada

# List of Articles

# Volume 2: Right

# ENCYCLOPEDIA OF
# POLITICS

## VOLUME 1: *The Left*

# The Left

## Abolitionism

THE ABOLITIONIST movement lasted for a century in Western Europe and the Americas and resulted in ending the transatlantic slave trade and the practice of humans owning other humans. Slavery has a long past as an integral part of ancient civilizations. After the fall of the Roman Empire, Europe abandoned slavery for serfdom. But in 1442, Portuguese ships brought African slaves first to Europe, but then mainly to the Americas to work in the plantations, in what were regarded as unhealthy climates. The Europeans brought Africans to the New World, thinking it was similar to the slaves' native West Africa. Between the 15th and 19th centuries, traders brought about 15 million slaves to the Americas.

For an Enlightenment thinker of the 18th century, the idea of slavery was irrational. The violation of the rights of one person for the benefit of another was unacceptable. Human beings had the right to determine their own destinies and were too valuable to be the property of others. Thus, Enlightenment philosophers proclaimed that slavery should be abolished. All major religious groups had historically practiced slavery, but within each group there were dissenters. Some abolitionists split from their slavery-accepting churches and established denominations of their own. Quakers and evangelical religious groups began challenging slavery as

un-Christian. The rise of moral disapproval allowed reformers such as Granville Sharpe to win a legal case in 1772 for the abolition of slavery in Great Britain. The English Court Chief Justice Lord Mansfield wrote a judgement, which is historically called the Charter of Freedom. In his decision, Mansfield wrote, "England is a soil whose air is deemed too pure for slaves to breathe in." West Indian Englishmen could no longer bring their slaves to England.

Abolitionists attempted to outlaw slavery in the plantation areas of South America, the West Indies, and the U.S. South. Between 1777 and 1804, all American states north of Maryland outlawed slavery. France abolished slavery in 1794 during the French Revolution, restored slavery under the empire in 1802, and abolished it for good during the revolutionary fervor that spread through Europe in 1848. Great Britain officially abolished slavery in the British Empire in 1833, and the Royal Navy enforced the ban on the slave trade.

### U.S. ABOLITION

Historians point out that France and England legislated slavery away relatively easily because for them it was a colonial and not a home issue. In the United States, it was a domestic problem, the social and economic underpinning of half of the states, especially after the market for cotton skyrocketed. The United States had

1

outlawed the importation of slaves in 1808, but smuggling continued through the early years of the Civil War. Having outlawed the trade, abolitionists focused on the emancipation of slave populations. However, After Eli Whitney's invention of the cotton gin and the northern textile revolution, Enlightenment idealism gave way to economic reality: slavery was highly profitable in cotton country and cotton was the fiber of the New England textile industry. Abolitionists rejected the economics of slavery, citing the moral arguments against holding another human in bondage.

Abolitionist clergy included Theodore Dwight Weld and Theodore Parker. Writers included John Greenleaf Whittier, James Russell Lowell, and Lydia Maria Child. Free-black former slaves included William Wells Brown and Frederick Douglass. Early in the 19th century, the abolitionists accepted the concept of gradualism; that is, gradually freeing the slaves with, perhaps, relocation to Africa. Arthur and Lewis Tappan led the gradualists, but the movement passed them by in the 1830s.

David Walker published *David Walker's Appeal* in 1829, smuggling it into the South in the linings of sailors' clothing. He invoked the Declaration of Independence, citing the right of revolution, and he urged slave insurrection. White Southerners passed laws prohibiting the teaching of reading and writing to African Americans. During the 30 years before the Civil War, abolitionists demanded immediate action. White and black abolitionists created local and national organizations, published attacks on a moral and political evil, and inflamed passions while trying to enlighten northern whites and make slavery a national issue.

William Lloyd Garrison, publisher of *The Liberator* from 1831 through 1865 and founder of the American Anti-Slavery Society (1833–70), supported Walker but was a pacifist, and preferred moral suasion. His rhetoric was incendiary, though, and demanded immediate emancipation and full legal equality. Southerners blamed his newspaper for Nat Turner's uprising (1831), even though Garrison denounced the action. Slave revolts such as Turner's, which killed 55 whites, led Southerners to tighten their legal and extralegal controls over the system and to stifle discussion of abolition. Abolitionists increased their pressure.

Abolitionist rejection of the legality of slavery threatened the economic and social system of the South and the integrity of the Union. The U.S. Constitution allowed states to determine whether to authorize or prohibit slavery within their borders. Abolitionists attempted to impose a national standard on a state's rights. They encountered hostility from distrustful Northerners alarmed at their extremism. Still, the movement grew. Abolitionists flouted the Fugitive Slave Law of 1850, which obligated the states to support each other's slave laws, by spiriting slaves to freedom through the Underground Railroad. Mob violence grew as the movement became more visible. The 1838 Anti-Slavery Convention of American Women saw 3,000 white and black women gather in Philadelphia, Pennsylvania. The speakers could not be heard over the noise of the anti-abolitionist mob outside. The women left under a barrage of stones and insults, and the crowd burned the hall the next day.

In the 1840s, leadership moved to escaped slaves such as Douglass, who rejected Garrison's reading of the Constitution as pro-slavery. For Douglass, the constitutional power to regulate slavery included the power to outlaw it. Garrison and Douglass split, but the movement persisted.

The opening of the west raised the stakes in the 1840s and 1850s. Northerners accepted slavery as a Southern right but opposed its spread into the west. Southerners needed slavery to spread to maintain political parity for their system; they could not afford to let free states outnumber slave states. Some historians believe they overreached with the Fugitive Slave Law. As ruthless slave catchers returned runaways, Northern public opinion shifted toward the abolitionists. Harriet Beecher Stowe's *Uncle Tom's Cabin* (1852) further strengthened the abolitionist cause by its graphic depiction of the horrors of the system.

John Brown's 1859 raid on Harper's Ferry, Virginia, convinced the South that the Northern fanatics would stop at nothing. The rise of the American Republican Party, which promoted policy against the spread of slavery, intensified Southern concern. Southerners feared the election of Abraham Lincoln would kill their way of life.

Abolitionists worked together, but that did not necessarily mean that whites regarded African Americans as equals. Whites who would eagerly abolish slavery could not bring themselves to regard blacks as equal. Black abolitionists tended to want equal rights. Male abolitionists were not totally comfortable with women in the movement. Women boycotted slave-produced goods and raised money through food sales and fairs. Women's abolitionist activism led, by the 1830s, to debates over whether women should be involved in "men's" activities. Women abolitionists were prominent in the Seneca Falls (New York) Convention of 1848, which first organized the women's movement.

Maria Stewart, a black woman, wrote and spoke against slavery and she eased the way for African American women such as Frances Ellen Watkins Harper, Sojourner Truth, and Harriet Tubman.

Abolitionists persisted through the Civil War because the Emancipation Proclamation applied only to those slaves behind Confederate lines. True abolition came after the war with ratification of the Thirteenth Amendment. In the aftermath of U.S. abolition, Latin American slave states began to emancipate, with Cuba and Brazil freeing slaves from 1880 to 1886 and from 1883 to 1888, respectively.

POLITICS OF SLAVERY

Abolitionism, as an extension of the Enlightenment principle of natural rights, represented a radical challenge to the economic and political status quo, and as such, it was an essentially radical doctrine. Indeed, those members of the American Republican Party who were the strongest advocates of abolition (rather than just opposed to the extension of slavery into new territories of the west), were known by enemies and friends alike as Radical Republicans. However, the vision for the former slaves, held by the Radical Republicans and most abolitionists, was that they would become free wage-laborers.

Defenders of slavery and Marxists alike pointed out that so-called free laborers in capitalist society often suffered conditions that were worse than those of slaves. Society made no formal provisions to prevent the starvation of the unemployed, the injured, or the orphans of such workers. By contrast, many slave owners made such provisions for slaves. Thus abolitionism, while radical from the perspective of the slave owners, was essentially conservative in so far that it was supportive of the capitalist wage system.

**SEE ALSO**
*Volume 1 Left:* Anthony, Susan B.; Stanton, Elizabeth Cady; Constitutional Amendments; Douglass, Frederick.
*Volume 2 Right:* United States; Lincoln, Abraham; Republican Party.

**BIBLIOGRAPHY**
Herbert Aptheker, *Abolitionism: A Revolutionary Movement* (Twayne Publishers, 1989); Paul Finkelman, ed., *Antislavery* (Garland, 1989); Stanley Harrold, *American Abolitionists* (Longman, 2001); Richard S. Newman, *Transformation of American Abolitionism* (University of North Carolina Press, 2002); Jean R. Soderlund, *Quakers and Slavery* (Princeton University Press, 1985); WGBH PBS, "Africans in America," www.pbs.org (March 2004).

JOHN BARNHILL, PH.D.
INDEPENDENT SCHOLAR

# Abortion/Pro-Choice

FEW WORDS IN THE HISTORY of the United States have caused more controversy than *abortion*. Abortion is an issue that encourages absolutist views on both sides. Pro-choice advocates argue that abortion rights deal with the right of women to control their own bodies. Anti-choice advocates claim that abortion is murder under all circumstances. Other views are more moderate. Some anti-choice may accept rape, incest, fetal deformity, and threats to maternal mortality as valid exceptions to a total ban on abortions. Some pro-choice advocates may oppose late-term abortions. The battle for control of the issue has been waged in homes, family-planning clinics, the streets, and in administrative offices, courts, and legislatures at both the state and national levels.

Conservatives who believe that government should uphold traditional sanctions against the taking of human life have asserted that the killing of any fetus at any age represents a violation of the inherent right to life. The anti-abortion position has attracted support from religious conservatives who believe that abortion represents only one symptom of moral decay in modern culture. On the other hand, liberals have been attracted to the pro-choice position precisely because they believe that the realm of personal moral choice includes control over reproduction. Furthermore, by freeing women from the obligation to have unwanted children, they see the extension of abortion rights as a step in the direction of the liberation of women. However, the division between conservatives and liberals on this issue often cuts across conservative-liberal alignments on other issues. Thus, for example, opposition to abortion can be found among both men and women who are active in labor union causes, while pro-abortion advocates can be found among otherwise conservative Republicans in the United States.

When the U.S. Constitution was written in 1787, abortion was accepted as a matter of course, and few people considered it a legal issue. Over the next few decades, newspapers regularly carried ads for various methods to induce abortion. During the mid-19th century, the medical profession led the move to limit abortion in order to gain control over women's health issues and to shut midwives out of the birthing process. As a result, many states banned abortions after "quickening," the point at which the mother first felt the fetus move. In 1873, Congress passed the Comstock Law, which was designed to prevent the transfer of materials that Anthony Comstock viewed as obscene. This included not only ads related to abortion, but also all information concerning birth control.

In 1945, Alan Guttmacher, a physician and a birth control advocate, devised a plan to cut down on the number of botched abortions. Guttmacher developed the idea of therapeutic abortions that were performed in hospitals by licensed medical personnel to protect the physical and psychological health of pregnant women. Hundreds of hospitals responded by appointing committees to determine whether women requesting abortions met the "therapeutic" standard.

The national media drew attention to the abortion debate in 1962 when it was discovered that a number of American women who had participated in medical tests had received the drug Thalidomide. This drug, which had been used routinely in Europe, was responsible for an epidemic of birth deformities that ranged from babies born without arms and legs to serious internal deformities. In Europe, 5,000 such babies were born. Sherri Finkbine, the mother of four children and the host of the children's television show *Romper Room*, took the medication without knowing she was pregnant. Finkbine ultimately obtained an abortion in Switzerland after being harassed and threatened by local anti-abortion advocates and being vilified around the country. The abortion battle heated up again four years later during a German-measles epidemic in San Francisco, California. Ninety percent of babies born to mothers who had been exposed to measles were born with significant birth defects. Sates began to pass more liberal abortion laws.

## GRISWOLD v. CONNECTICUT

In the 1960s, the reenergized women's movement made reproductive issues an essential element of women's rights, targeting states that banned access to birth control. For years, women and the medical community had tried to challenge such laws in Connecticut but failed to meet requirements of "standing" (having a personal stake in the case) and "ripeness" (being relevant at the time the case reached the courts). As a result, birth con-

trol advocates, including Mrs. Charles Tiffany and Mrs. Thomas Hepburn (the mother of actress Katharine Hepburn), planned a test case that would meet technical requirements. A physician and a clinic director were convicted and fined, and the Supreme Court agreed to hear the case.

On June 7, 1965, in a 7-2 decision, the court held in *Griswold v. Connecticut* (381 U.S. 479) that the right to privacy, which had never before been articulated by the court, provided the basis for a constitutional right to birth control for married people. Advocates of judicial restraint were appalled, arguing that the court was making laws rather than interpreting them. In 1972, the court extended the right to single people in *Eisenstadt v. Baird* (405 U.S. 438), a case brought by a doctor, which had been prohibited from distributing birth control to patients whose lives were jeopardized by pregnancy.

## ROE v. WADE

In 1969, Norma McCorvey discovered that she was pregnant. McCorvey already had a five-year-old daughter, who was being brought up by her mother in Texas. She was prevented from having an abortion in Texas, despite her false statement that she had been raped. McCorvey met Sarah Weddington and Linda Coffee, two young lawyers who were looking for a test case to challenge the 19th-century law that limited women's reproductive choices in Texas. Although they had little legal experience, Weddington and Coffee were enthusiastic about helping women take control of their lives.

In 1971, McCorvey's case reached the Supreme Court as *Roe v. Wade* (410 U.S. 113). Due to two vacant seats and the magnitude of the case, the court ordered rearguments for the following year. Weddington and Coffee challenged the Texas law on the grounds that it violated a woman's right to privacy according to the Ninth Amendment, the Due Process Clause of the Fifth Amendment, and the Equal Protection Clauses of the Fourth and Fourteenth Amendments. On January 22, 1973, the court handed down the decision, which built on the right to privacy guaranteed in *Griswold*. The court determined that a woman has a constitutional right to obtain an abortion. The court suspended both the "standing" and "ripeness" requirements on the basis that the outcome of the case would affect other women who were pregnant or who might become so.

Chief Justice Warren Burger assigned Harry Blackmun to write the decisions in *Roe v. Wade* and a companion case, *Doe v. Bolton* (410 U.S. 179), which overturned Georgia's law restricting abortions to hospitals accredited by special committee. Blackmun, who had a background in medical law, provided for access to abortion based on the development of the fetus. In the first trimester (1 to 11 weeks), abortions were considered to be solely the decision of the woman and her physician.

During the second trimester (12 to 24 weeks), in which "quickening" occurred, states were given some freedom to restrict access to abortion. In the final trimester (25 weeks to birth), states were considered to have a substantial right to protect a fetus that had a chance of surviving outside the mother's womb. Blackmun contended that denying access to abortions throughout a woman's pregnancy violated the Due Process Clause of the Fourteenth Amendment, denying a woman her constitutional right to privacy.

The court's decision in *Roe* sent a wake-up call to anti-abortion advocates, who began to lobby for a constitutional amendment to ban all abortions. In 1980, Ronald Reagan campaigned with a promise to end abortions. In 1985, in *Thornburgh v. the American College of Obstetrics and Gynecology* (476 U.S. 747), the Supreme Court came within one vote of overturning *Roe*. Over the next few years, with the intention of stacking the court, (appointing conservative judges), the Reagan and George H. W. Bush administrations used views on abortion as a litmus test for choosing Supreme Court nominees.

## ABORTION FUNDING

Abortion opponents determined to use any available method to chip away at the right to choose. In Congress, Senator Jesse Helms (R-NC) and Representative Henry Hyde (R-IL) introduced what became known as the Hyde Amendment, banning the use of Medicare funds for abortion services and limiting reproductive choices of poor women. The bill was reintroduced in every session of Congress from 1976 onward. In 1980, the Supreme Court upheld the Hyde Amendment in *Harris v. McRae* (448 U.S. 297) and allowed states to ban state-funded abortions in *Williams v. Zbaraz* (448 U.S. 358).

Abortion opponents in Congress also convinced their colleagues to further restrict reproductive rights by targeting clinics receiving funds under Title X of the Public Health Services Act, which had funded family planning research, education, and health services since 1970. Congress banned abortions funded through Title X early in the abortion debate. In the 1990s, they decided to go further, banning recipients of Title X funds from even using the word "abortion." Clinic workers were required to read a prepared statement, which said "this project does not consider abortion an appropriate method of family planning and therefore does not counsel or refer for abortion."

A number of groups banded together to fight the enforcement of the Title X ban. Civil libertarians and medical personnel objected to the "gag rule" on the grounds that it violated freedom of speech. Physicians argued that the ban prevented them from providing a full range of medical services. Civil rights advocates believed the law discriminated against poor women, who were predominately African American and Hispanic. Pro-choice advocates saw it as one more nail in the coffin of abortion rights.

In 1991, in *Rust v. Sullivan* (500 U.S. 173), the court upheld the law in a 5-4 decision. After *Rust*, Congress passed the Wyden-Porter bill, standing by their original plans for Title X funds. A Bush veto of the bill was upheld by a narrow margin. After entering the White House in January 1993, Bill Clinton issued an executive order that called for new guidelines for Title X, effectively negating the *Rust* decision.

## CLINIC ACCESS

Pro-choice advocates have often been frightened by the constant presence of protestors outside family planning clinics. Protestors insisted that the First Amendment gives them to right to keep up their campaign of intimidation. As courts continued to uphold abortion rights, protestors became more hostile to clinic staff and clients. Their activities took the form of stalking, assault, battery, kidnapping, bombing, chemical attacks, and death threats. In 1993, in *Bray v. Alexandria Women's Health Clinic* (506 U.S. 263), the Supreme Court refused to accept the argument that the protests violated the civil rights of the staff and clients of family planning clinics. Pro-choice advocates were stunned with the *Bray* decision, believing that protestors would become even more violent. They did.

On March 10, 1993, Michael Griffin of the Rescue America anti-abortion group killed Dr. David Gunn, an abortion provider at the Pensacola Women's Medical Services Clinic in Florida. After Gunn's death, Congress passed the Freedom of Access to Clinic Entrances Act (FACE), enacting both criminal and civil penalties for obstructing and damaging family planning clinics and interfering with those engaged in giving or receiving services. Despite the new law, on July 29, 1994, Paul Hill, a former minister, killed Dr. John Britton and James Barrett, a volunteer escort, at a Pensacola clinic.

*A pro-choice coalition group, Georgians for Choice, displays their protest signs demanding abortion be kept legal. Such pro-abortion advocacy grew out of reaction to anti-abortion advocates making progress to have the U.S. Supreme Court overturn the legality of abortion.*

Insisting that their actions were protected by the First Amendment, protestors continued their Florida campaign. At one clinic, they threw butyric acid at the facilities and repeatedly stalked clinic staff. Protestors gathered personal information about clinic staff from license plates and used it to harass staff and their families and neighbors. In response, Florida established buffer zones to keep protestors away from abortion clinics. Such laws required protestors to stay at least 36 feet away from clinics at all times. When the law was challenged in *Madsen v. Women's Health Clinic* (512 U.S. 753) in 1994, the court did an about-face and acknowledged Florida's legitimate interest in protecting the right of those seeking services at family planning clinics. In 1997, in *Schenck v. Pro-Choice Network of Western New York* (519 U.S. 357), the court upheld a law requiring abortion protestors to remain at least 1,500 feet from abortion clinics but struck down so-called floating zones that gave clinic staff greater protection.

During the 1990s, pro-choice advocates decided to go after anti-abortion protestors by making the actions of the protestors so costly that it would deter violence at family planning clinics. Strategists chose the Racketeer Influenced and Corrupt Organizations Act (RICO), which had been passed in 1970 as part of an effort to prevent those engaged in organized crime from benefiting economically from acts of violence. Under RICO, defendants faced punitive damages as well as criminal penalties.

In 1994, in *National Organization for Women v. Scheidler* (510 U.S. 249), the Supreme Court unanimously upheld the right to use RICO to prevent attacks on family planning clinics. However, in 2003, in *Scheidler v. NOW* (537 U.S. 393), in an 8-1 decision, the court threw out a $250,000 award levied against abortion opponents, stating that abortion protests did not amount to "extortion" under the terms of RICO.

## WEBSTER v. REPRODUCTIVE HEALTH SERVICES

By the early 1990s, pro-choice advocates and court watchers around the country had become convinced that the Reagan/Bush judicial appointees were ready to overturn *Roe*. Anti-choice advocates won a resounding victory in 1989 with *Webster v. Reproductive Health Services* (492 U.S. 490), which allowed states to control access to abortion as long as they did not outlaw abortions entirely. The liberal wing of the court voted to overturn all aspects of Missouri's restrictions on abortion. Blackmun, the author of *Roe*, wrote in an unpublished opinion: "I rue this day. I rue the violence that has been done to the liberty and equality of women. I rue the violence that has been done to our legal fabric and to the integrity of the Constitution. I rue the inevitable loss of public esteem for this Court."

## PLANNED PARENTHOOD OF SOUTHEASTERN PENNSYLVANIA v. CASEY

In a surprise move on June 29, 1992, the Supreme Court announced its decision in *Planned Parenthood of Southeastern Pennsylvania v. Casey* (505 U.S. 833), allowing both pro-choice and anti-abortion advocates to claim success. Casey specifically stated that the court stood by *Roe*. Nevertheless, the court also upheld certain aspects of Pennsylvania's restrictive abortion laws, including informed consent in which a woman seeking an abortion was given information material geared toward convincing her not to have an abortion and a 24-hour waiting period before abortions could be performed. The court overturned the spousal consent provision of the law that required a married woman to notify her husband before obtaining an abortion.

Guided by Justice Sandra Day O'Connor, the court backed away from the trimester system established by Blackmun in *Roe*, replacing it with the "undue burden" test, which recognized that states have a substantial interest in protecting an unborn fetus while stipulating that no state could place an "undue burden" on a woman's access to abortion. Many pro-choice advocates believed that the 24-hour waiting period placed an undue burden on women who lived in areas where abortion services were not readily available. They offered the fact that 80 percent of all counties in the United States have no abortion providers because physicians have become afraid to perform the procedures.

## POST-CASEY

While pro-choice advocates felt less threatened after *Casey*, the battle over abortion rights continued, gathering new heat after Congress passed the Partial-Birth Abortion-Ban Act, criminalizing the procedure known as intact dilation extraction. Clinton had twice vetoed similar bills. Liberals saw the act as a back-door method of limiting *Roe*. The Department of Justice began to subpoena records of abortions at hospitals and clinics. Judges in New York, California, and Nebraska temporarily halted the release of the records, calling the law "vague" and "unconstitutional." Pro-choice advocates were also dismayed by Congressional approval of the Unborn Victims of Violence Act in early 2004 that made it separate crimes to harm a pregnant woman and an unborn fetus, which was defined as "a member of the species *homo sapiens*, at any stage of development, who is carried in the womb." Pro-choice advocates saw it as another way to limit reproductive rights.

**SEE ALSO**

*Volume 1 Left:* Civil Liberties; Feminism; Friedan, Betty; Steinem, Gloria; Supreme Court.
*Volume 2 Right:* Anti-Abortion / Pro-Life; Supreme Court; Feminism.

**BIBLIOGRAPHY**

Ellen Alderman and Caroline Kennedy, *The Right to Privacy* (Alfred A. Knopf, 1995); Jules Archer, *Breaking Barriers* (Viking, 1991); Mary Boyle, *Re-thinking Abortion* (Routledge, 1997); Barbara Hickson Craig and David M. O'Brien, *Abortion and American Politics* (Chatham, 1993); Marian Faux, Roe v. Wade: *The Untold Story of the Landmark Supreme Court Decision that Made Abortion Legal* (New American Library, 1988); Carl Hulse, "Senate Outlaws Injury to Fetus during a Crime," *New York Times* (March 26, 2004); J. Ralph Lindgren and Nadine Taub, *The Law of Sex Discrimination* (West, 1993); Leslie J. Reagan, *When Abortion Was a Crime: Women, Medicine, and Law in the United States* (University of California Press, 1997); Susan Saulny, "Trials Open across Nation on Abortion-Procedure Ban," *New York Times* (March 30, 2004); James F. Simon, *The Center Holds* (Simon & Schuster, 1995).

ELIZABETH PURDY, PH.D.
INDEPENDENT SCHOLAR

# Affirmative Action

BY THE MIDDLE of the 1960s, it had become obvious that the state of the African American underclass in the United States needed to be addressed. Measures were required to attempt to mend some of the problems that

African Americans faced. The American public had become exposed to a new civil rights movement with leaders rallying black masses to take action against an oppressive and racist society. A sympathetic President Lyndon Johnson signed the Civil Rights Act on July 2, 1964, in an attempt to help eradicate acts of racial discrimination, but it seemed primarily to address overt acts of personal prejudice.

Affirmative action programs have their legal basis in the Civil Rights Act of 1964. Although the first executive order enforcing affirmative action was not issued until September 1965, the act marked a major new commitment toward outlawing racial and sexual discrimination. Johnson defined his policy in a speech to Howard University students on June 4, 1965, in which he declared that institutionalized racism was preventing African Americans from attaining equal rights. Institutional racism is the concept that underlying structural forces prevent African Americans from gaining equality with whites.

Civil rights leaders Malcolm X and Stokely Carmichael were the earliest activists to publicly denounce institutional racism and its effects on the black masses, identifying such factors as inferior education due to segregated schools as constituting institutional racism. To rectify this problem, Johnson advocated protection of minority group rights over individual rights, which led to affirmative action programs.

The basis of affirmative action programs was that while blacks were legally equal to whites, because of segregation, they were still trapped in the lowest societal class and faced many obstacles in order to rise in society. Thus, for America to truly treat African Americans equally, blacks were entitled to certain privileges that incorporated them into various professions and places of higher education. Such programs have proven to be successful, but nonetheless have undergone extreme criticism from conservative opponents who claim that such programs are "reverse racism."

Restitution has been one of the basic principles that define affirmative action programs. Proponents of restitution believe that African Americans should be compensated for their victimized pasts. Slavery lasted for almost 250 years in America and when it was abolished, it was then replaced by legalized segregation to facilitate the economic and political control of the freed slaves. Lynching became a common mistreatment of blacks at the end of the 19th century and served to further enforce racial injustice. While segregation was legally abolished by 1968, the positive effects would not be felt by African Americans unless further actions were taken

to integrate them into better jobs, higher education, and middle class society. Affirmative action programs thus focused on giving priority to a small percentage of African Americans who displayed the qualities and potential to excel in school or at work, and who otherwise would have been overlooked in favor of white candidates.

## LEGAL INTERPRETATIONS

Opposition to affirmative action programs increased in the 1970s and 1980s and can be seen in landmark court decisions such as *Regents of the University of California v. Bakke*. In this case, a white student was denied admission to the Medical School at the University of California, whereas minority students with lower grades and test scores secured admission based on race. The court ruled in favor of the student, claiming that the admissions policy of the school practiced reverse discrimination by using a quota system. Such a system reserved a set number of places only for minority students. However, the court did not rule that race could not be an issue in determining admissions, which would lead to further interpretations of admissions policies.

This monumental decision effectively defined various affirmative action programs as reverse racism. It banned all programs that used inflexible quota systems. The court's reversal of policy reflected America's profound ambivalence toward racism. Conservative public figures played upon white resentment toward minorities, claiming that African Americans received preferential treatment rather than having to work hard to gain success. Such resentment was a potent force due to the economic crises and restructuring that shook the United States in the 1970s. Black demands seemed to pose a direct threat to already discouraged white job seekers. White hostility toward African Americans intensified in the 1980s. Racial violence surfaced again as "skinhead" white supremacist movements appeared in numerous cities. White proponents of affirmative action anticipated that these programs would only last for a short period of time and would end once the last existing discriminatory aspects of society had been eradicated. But this point was lost in the heat of the moment.

By the start of the 1980s, many Americans believed that affirmative action programs were no longer necessary. Throughout the 1970s, a small but noticeable number of African Americans had risen out of the lower class, secured better jobs, and entered the middle class. A small percentage of blacks had gained admission into schools of higher education. A few conspicuous African American success stories in the news media, combined with the abolition of legalized segregation, persuaded much of white America that racist practices had been curtailed and that widespread affirmative action was no longer required. However, at the same time, while there was a slight increase in the black middle class, conditions for lower-class African Americans were steadily growing worse. Their employment was concentrated in unskilled jobs in the old industrial sectors and de-industrialization eliminated these positions.

In 1980, the Supreme Court supported the affirmative action policy in *Fullilove v. Klutznick*. The court rejected a contractor's claim against a federal requirement stating that 10 percent of the work on federal projects must be assigned to minority firms. The case of *Bob Jones University v. United States* in 1983 witnessed another victory for affirmative action proponents. The court ruled that if a university practices discriminatory admissions policies, then it should forfeit its tax-exempt status, as this amounted to a form of federal aid, and consequently constituted state action governed by the Fourteenth Amendment. These liberal rulings would soon face conservative criticism. From 1981 to 1991, four of the next five appointed Supreme Court Justices shared conservative views.

The 1980s marked a stark deterioration of affirmative action policies as conservative Republican Presidents Ronald Reagan and George H.W. Bush occupied the White House for 12 consecutive years. After a few important Supreme Court victories on behalf of these programs, the Supreme Court began to rule against affirmative action policies.

In 1984, the Supreme Court ruled in *Firefighters Local Union v. Stotts* that an affirmative action program that attempted to protect black workers from a disproportionate amount of redundancies was not valid. In this instance, the court underlined the importance of proving that a direct act of discrimination against African Americans had occurred in order for such a countervailing policy of preferential treatment to apply. The following year, in *Wygant v. Jackson Board of Education*, the Supreme Court ruled that societal discrimination on its own would not be enough to justify an affirmative action program.

In 1995, even though Democratic President Bill Clinton supported affirmative action, the conservative courts continued to make the implementation of such policies an arduous task. In *Adarand Constructors v. Pena*, the Supreme Court made it more difficult to justify the use of affirmative action by ruling that only a "compelling interest" would allow the government to support a race-based decision.

## UNIVERSITY ADMISSIONS

In the early 2000s, the Supreme Court strayed from its past rulings on affirmative action in regard to admissions to universities. In the University of Michigan court case in 2003, *Grutter v. Bollinger*, the Supreme Court made a major ruling in favor of the University of Michigan's Law School admissions policy. The law school used race as one of many secondary factors that it considered in determining which students to accept for admission. The court based its decision on the fact that race was only used as one of many secondary factors. The law school used a points-based admissions program, and Native Americans, Latinos, and African Americans all received 20 points because they were categorized as underrepresented minorities. Other groups that received preferential points included children of alumni, poor rural students, and students whose parents had donated money to the school. Race alone could not gain a student acceptance.

The law school's strong academic reputation served to defend the school's claim that it only accepted minority students who showed promise to reach academic success and fulfill their degrees without any undue problems. In addition, the university argued successfully that a more diverse student body precipitates a better learning environment, with more ideas and perspectives to add to discussions. Many major businesses wrote in support of the policy, claiming that more minority students are needed to bring diversity to an ever-increasing global marketplace. These points were taken into great consideration when the court made its ruling.

The argument for some liberals is that there are many other factors that determine an applicant's fate that are also nonacademic in nature, such as musical abilities, athletics, whether she is the child of alumni, or whether the family is a financial contributor to the university. Liberals point to the case of President George W. Bush, whose grades and test scores fell short of the standard when he applied to Yale University. Yet because his family had a long history as Yale alumni, the future president was admitted. The point is that there are many factors besides race and academic merit that determine a student's application, and that race is a valid factor when considered alongside others.

A final argument of proponents for affirmative action programs in university admissions programs is the belief in the importance of a diverse student body.

Thus, the admission of promising minority students who otherwise would have been denied a place at the institution if the admissions policy was solely based on test scores and grade point average is justified. This results in black graduates being able to receive better jobs and add cultural diversity to the marketplace.

Within the American political context, affirmative action programs have been advocated by liberal Democrats and opposed by conservative Democrats and Republicans.

**SEE ALSO**

**BIBLIOGRAPHY**

Francis J. Beckwith and Todd E. Jones, eds., *Affirmative Action: Social Justice or Reverse Discrimination?* (Prometheus Books, 1997); Gertrude Ezorsky, *Racism and Justice: The Case for Affirmative Action* (Cornell University Press, 1996); Manning Marable, *How Capitalism Underdeveloped Black America* (South End Press, 2000); Manning Marable, *Beyond Black and White: Rethinking Race in American Politics and Society* (Verso Books, 1996); Russell Nieli, ed., *Racial Preference and Racial Justice: The New Affirmative Action Controversy* (Ethics & Public Policy Center, 1990); "The Progress of Black Student Matriculations at the Nation's Highest-Ranked Colleges and Universities," *The Journal of Blacks in Higher Education* (Autumn, 1998); "Why There Has Been No Progress in Closing the Black-White SAT Scoring Gap," *The Journal of Blacks in Higher Education* (Winter, 1998–99); "The Persisting Myth that Black and White Schools are Equally Funded," *The Journal of Blacks in Higher Education* (Winter, 1998–99); "Naked Hypocrisy: The Nationwide System of Affirmative Action for Whites," *The Journal of Blacks in Higher Education* (Winter, 1997–98).

DAVID W. MCBRIDE
UNIVERSITY OF NOTTINGHAM, ENGLAND

# Africa

PRIOR TO WORLD WAR II, only three countries in Africa could claim independence: Liberia, Egypt, and Ethiopia. By the second half of the 20th century, the process of decolonization took hold on the continent as former European colonies gained independence. The new countries of Africa adopted a variety of forms of government, some emulating their former colonial structures, others embracing socialism, and many falling into states of tribal totalitarianism.

THE LEFT IN AFRICA

Indeed, the ideology behind the independence movements varied considerably. Within Angola, Zimbabwe, and Mozambique, the inspiration was radically communist and imported into the continent. By contrast, in the conservative Kenya of Jomo Kenyatta and Daniel arap Moi, a more culturally linked nationalist ideology emerged after independence, around the Harrambee movement. This was an attempt to harness already existing communal work practices among Kenya's tribes to the goal of nation-building.

Africans involved in the communist "national liberation movements," spearheaded by the Soviet Union's quest to export Marxist-Leninism, underwent indoctrination in camps with like-minded revolutionaries. From 1976, such Marxist African national liberation movements as the ANC (African National Congress) were receiving training in camps sponsored by Yasser Arafat's PLO (Palestine Liberation Organization) in southern Lebanon. Conservative writers like Jillian Becker Claire Sterling asserted that the Soviet Union was funding the training camps. Training camps were also alleged to exist in Colonel Muammar Quaddafi's Libya.

After liberation, some progressive countries in Africa embraced socialism as their guiding force. Quaddafi would bring his own brand of socialism to Libya through his *Green Book*. But his administration, while supporting terrorism in the Middle East and territorial aggrandizement at the expense of Chad to the south, did not devote its energies fully to socialism at home. Besides, Quaddafi's *Green Book* presented an imperfect guide; at best, it was an ad hoc socialist manifesto geared toward maintaining his personal power.

Perhaps the most significant, if lesser known, example of socialism in Africa was Senegal during the long administration of Leopold Senghor, who was the country's first president (1960–80). He espoused a philosophy called Negritude, emphasizing the uniqueness of African culture, which found receptive listeners in the United States as well as in France. Senghor cultivated his progressive form of African socialism, which combined socialist thought with the tribal heritage of the country. According to African historian David P. John-

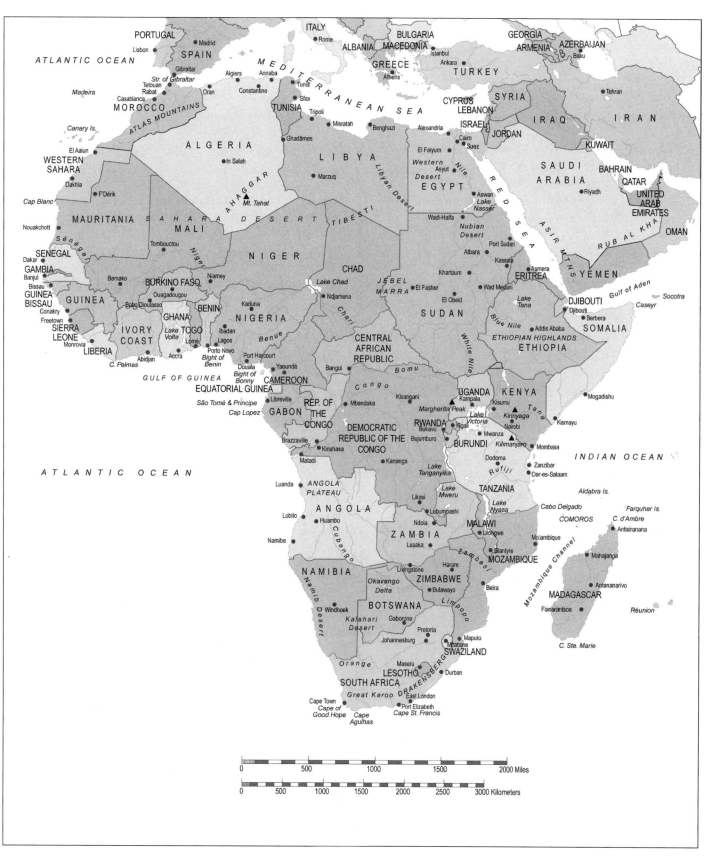

The continent of Africa has seen its share of leftist movements, some homegrown, as in Egypt, others imported from communist regimes abroad into countries such as Angola and Mozambique. In the 2000s, Africa faced issues of tribal genocide and Islamic extremism, particularly in Sudan—a close geographic neighbor to the Arab nations of the Middle East.

son, "in the so-called passive revolution of 1976, Senghor responded to economic and political stagnation by introducing greater political and economic freedom. However, Senegal's economic crisis persisted, and, bowing to popular discontent, Senghor retired from office in 1980, one of the few African rulers to voluntarily relinquish power." Senghor also brought a sense of unity to a country where both Christianity and Islam were represented next to traditional tribal beliefs. The introduction of new economic planning in 1994 led to a reduction in socialism in the state economy and better economic growth began in 2001.

Another example of socialism emerged in Algeria, Like Senegal, Algeria was part of the former French Empire and this reflects the impact that socialism had had upon the French intellectual ferment since the 1830s. Algeria's war for independence against the French began in November 1954, when the National Liberation Front (FLN) began its struggle against the colonial government that lasted until Algerian independence in 1962. One of the most noteworthy of FLN commanders was Houari Boumedienne. In 1965, he led a military coup against President Ahmed Ben Bella and succeeded in establishing an Islamic socialist state. However, Boumedienne was able to avoid the fanatic Islamism as seen in the movements of al-Qaeda, Hamas, Hizbollah, and the Islamic Jihad.

Through force of character, Boumedienne governed Algeria with no formal position until he was elected president in 1976. His form of socialism, unlike Senghor's experiment in Senegal, led to strong economic growth in Algeria. When he died in 1978, Boumedienne was on the verge of establishing a unique North African Socialist Federation. After his death, the FLN continued in power with its socialist agenda. However, in the period from 1991 to 1992, the nullification of elections in which more extreme Islamists in the Islamic Salvation Front (FIS) showed a strong electoral presence led to a civil war that plagues Algeria into the 2000s. At least some 70,000 lives have been lost thus far.

As the fight for independence raged in Algeria, both Morocco and Tunisia gained independence from France in 1956. In Morocco, King Hassan II and in Tunisia, Habib Bourguiba, chairman of the Neo-Destour Party, would both govern their countries with a liberalism little seen in Africa.

In the country of South Africa, leftist movements help topple the apartheid regime. During the 19th century in South Africa, a brutal series of colonial wars, climaxing with the destruction of the Zulu kingdom in 1879, had reduced the original black inhabitants to a state of subjugation to the minority white population. This system was institutionalized as apartheid—the rigorous separation of the races. Blacks could work in the cities and contribute to the growth of the wealth of the white ruling class, but they were compelled to live in segregated and often poverty-stricken townships.

As a result of apartheid, an indigenous African National Congress (ANC) party was formed with a strong communist leaning. The extreme right-wing National Party took power in 1948, making apartheid the official policy of the country. Because of massacres against blacks committed by apartheid forces, the ANC formed its military wing, the Umkhonto we Sizwe (MK, or Spear of the Nation), in December 1961. For more than 30 years, the struggle between the ANC and the apartheid regime dominated South Africa, until apartheid was abolished in 1991. In the democratic elections that followed, former ANC leader Nelson Mandela was elected the country's first black president. With a successful and peaceful transition of government, the ANC left behind much of its leftist ideology in favor of a capitalist system.

## FOREIGN MERCENARIES

The 1960s was a decade of turmoil in Africa, in which numerous countries revolted against European colonial rule. Leftist revolutionary movements, staffed with mercenaries from faraway communist nations such as Cuba, often ruptured these emerging African nations, and this was perhaps most apparent in Angola and Mozambique.

With help from Algeria, full-scale resistance to Portuguese rule had begun in 1963 in Angola. However, intramural warfare between the two independence movements, the MPLA and FNLA, hampered the struggle against the Portuguese, who had exploited the country—as Mozambique—since the early 16th century. However, by 1968 the MPLA was in control of the country. The MPLA had a political advantage over the FNLA because of its links to the international ideological left. At the same time, an anticolonial struggle was being waged by another communist group in Mozambique, FRELIMO, a sign that the independence movements had become part of the "wars of national liberation" that Soviet Premier Nikita Khrushchev had vowed to support throughout the world.

After 10 years of sporadic warfare and major political changes in Portugal, Mozambique became independent on June 25, 1975. FRELIMO quickly established a one-party Marxist state. By 1975, both

Angola and Mozambique were independent states but fated for continued internal strife.

During the same era, under Gamal Abdel Nasser, Egypt played a major role in developing socialist thought among the arabs of Africa. In 1942, Nasser founded the secret Society of Free Officers, which fought against political corruption and foreign domination of Egypt, and in 1952 Nasser led an army coup that deposed King Farouk. In 1956, he was elected, unopposed, president of the republic of Egypt. His nationalization of the Suez Canal in 1956 precipitated a short-lived, abortive invasion by Great Britain, France, and Israel.

In 1967, Nasser precipitated war with Israel by dissolving United Nations peacekeeping forces in the Sinai and blockading the Israeli port of Elat. He resigned from office following Egypt's disastrous defeat, but massive demonstrations of support forced his return. During his period of rule, Nasser instituted a program of land reform and economic and social development known as Arab socialism, which sought to unify Arabic Africans under a unique leftist doctrine. Nasser helped reestablish Arab national pride, which had been undermined by many decades of Western domination.

In foreign affairs, Nasser originally assumed a neutralist position, seeking support from both the East and the West to bolster his position in the Middle East. After his nation's military defeat in 1967, however, Nasser became increasingly dependent on the Soviet Union for military and economic aid. Nasser died in 1970, but the secular and leftist-leaning government structures he left behind endure in Arabic Africa.

The decades that followed saw Marxist-Leninist or communist rulers take hold in Africa. For example, Zimbabwe gained independence under Robert Mugabe, who would spend the decade cementing his harsh Marxist rule in the country and pursuing a persecution of the white settlers who had been the economic mainstay of the national economy for decades.

In another case, the long-festering feud in the Sudan between the Muslim government in Khartoum and the Christians and animists in the south broke out into civil war. The Muslims had been involved in secretly bringing back the slave trade, selling southern blacks in the old slave markets of Yemen and Saudi Arabia. The southerners were united in the Sudan People's Liberation Army, another communist-inspired nationalist movement.

By the 1990s, Africa saw the fragile independent nation states threatened by both tribalism and the rise of Islamic extremism. These forces involved extreme cases of genocidal conflict, with tribalism gone amok especially in Burundi and Rwanda, where hundreds of thousands of people were killed. In most cases, the continent's national experiments with leftist ideologies were not conduits to peaceful growth, but rather aggravators of existing conflicts. As the millennium dawned in 2000, it brought mixed hope for stability in Africa.

## SEE ALSO

*Volume 1 Left*: African National Congress; Egypt; Third International; Nigeria; South Africa; Uganda.
*Volume 2 Right*: Africa; Apartheid; Black Nationalism; Egypt; South Africa; Nationalism.

## BIBLIOGRAPHY

Roy Gutman and David Rieff, eds., *Crimes of War: What the Public Should Know* (Norton, 1999); Reference Information, www.clickafrique.com (July 2004); Alistair Horne, *A Savage War of Peace: Algeria, 1954–62* (Viking, 1978); James R. Davis, *Fortune's Warriors: Private Armies and the New World Order* (Douglas and McIntyre, 2000); Organization of African Unity, www.itcilo.it (July 2004); Metropolitan of Dar Es Salaam, www.rc.net (July 2004); Joseph S. Nye, *Peace in Parts* (Rowman and Littlefield, 1987); U.S. Library of Congress Studies: Angola, http://lcweb2.loc.gov (July 2004); Bill Berkeley, *The Graves Are Not Yet Full* (Perseus, 2001); John F. Murphy, Jr., *Sword of Islam: Muslim Extremism from the Arab Conquests to the Attack on America* (Prometheus, 2002); Karl Maier, *Into the House of the Ancestors: Inside the New Africa* (Wiley, 1998).

JOHN F. MURPHY, JR.
AMERICAN MILITARY UNIVERSITY

# African National Congress

THE AFRICAN NATIONAL Congress (ANC) led the struggle against apartheid in South Africa. The ANC was formed in 1912 to oppose the political and civil exclusion of Africans from the Union of South Africa, which was created in 1910 when the British colonies and the Boer Republics joined together to form one nation.

During its early years, the ANC advocated nonviolence, the defense of political rights for Africans, and nonracialism—the belief that the peoples of South Africa were to be viewed as one, regardless of skin color. For example, in response to the 1912 Natives' Land Act, which said that blacks could no longer own or lease land in white areas, the ANC launched a petition campaign in protest. In 1912 and 1913, women supporters of the ANC launched the antipass campaign to publicly condemn the restrictive Pass Laws, which required African and Colored (the official designation of mixed race people in South Africa) to carry passes and to buy permits if they wanted to live outside of black-designated areas. The activists refused to carry the passes, an offense for which some were arrested.

In the 1940s, a group of young ANC activists, including the future leaders Nelson Mandela, Walter Sisulu, and Oliver Tambo, criticized the cautious tactics and conciliatory politics of the ANC leadership. They created the ANC Youth League in 1944 and called on the organization to adopt more aggressive tactics and assertive politics. Instead of focusing on nonracialism, their Manifesto emphasized Africanism, which stressed the need for Africans to liberate themselves.

In 1948, the National Party made apartheid, the official separation of the races, the law of the land. In response, the ANC, along with the South African Indian Congress, launched the Defiance Campaign in 1952. It called upon Africans to nonviolently defy the apartheid laws, such as the passbook law or the curfew law, which made it illegal for Africans to stay in white parts of the city past curfew, unless they were domestic servants. Accepting arrest and jail as the expected outcome of their decision to break the apartheid laws, the ANC transformed imprisonment from a stigma to a badge of honor. By the end of 1952, 8,500 people of all races had proudly gone to jail for freedom.

The increasing brutality of apartheid, combined with the emergence of groups of anti-Apartheid whites, such as the Congress of Democrats, and the unflinching support of the Communist Party of South Africa convinced the ANC that it should pursue a nonracialist political strategy. The 1955 Freedom Charter strongly reflects that perspective, and remained the key ANC document during its fight against apartheid. The charter states, "That South Africa belongs to all who live in it, black and white, and that no government can justly claim authority unless it is based on the will of the people."

The apartheid state met the attempts by the ANC to end apartheid and improve their lives with repression and violence. In 1960, it banned the ANC, forcing many of its leaders, including Mandela, to go underground to avoid arrest. Believing that nonviolent resistance was futile, the ANC launched armed struggle in South Africa in 1961. It formed Umkhonto we Sizwe (Spear of the Nation), the armed wing of the ANC, headed by Mandela and Joe Slovo of the South African Communist

Party. The apartheid government arrested the ANC leaders, convicted them of sabotage in the famous Rivonia trial of 1964, and sentenced them to life imprisonment on Robben Island. In his stirring speech to the court, Mandela said, "I have cherished the ideal of a democratic and free society in which all persons live together in harmony and with equal opportunities. It is an ideal which I hope to live for and to achieve. But if needs be, it is an ideal for which I am prepared to die."

The imprisonment of its top leaders weakened the ANC, which declined in visibility and membership. Then, in June 1976, students in Soweto opened the next round of anti-apartheid struggle, protesting the educational system. The police responded with bullets and by 1977 they had killed 700 young people. Many young people fled South Africa and joined the ANC military training camps in surrounding African nations. Mass opposition to apartheid spread from the African, Indian, and colored communities to include a number of whites as well. To channel this upsurge in anti-apartheid sentiment, the ANC formed the United Democratic Front in 1983, which consisted of 300 organizations. Spear of the Nation accelerated its attacks, protests increased, and the worldwide anti-apartheid movement exerted enormous financial and political pressure on the apartheid government.

Many Western countries, including the United States, had imposed various degrees of economic sanctions against the apartheid government. In 1990, the government gave in and dissolved the ban against the anti-apartheid organizations and, in February, it released Mandela, who was now the worldwide symbol of the anti-apartheid movement. Elections were held in 1994 in which people of all races were allowed to vote and Mandela was overwhelmingly elected the president of South Africa.

The ANC, in its battle against apartheid, had some similarity to the movement for civil rights in the United States. As an organization fighting for the recognition of equal rights, it shared liberal ideals. At the same time, more radical members of the ANC identified with the broader African anticolonial national liberation struggles sweeping the continent.

**SEE ALSO**

*Volume 1 Left:* South Africa; Africa.
*Volume 2 Right:* Apartheid; South Africa; Colonialism.

**BIBLIOGRAPHY**

Stephen M. Davis, *Apartheid's Rebels* (Yale University Press, 1987); Heidi Holland, *The Struggle: A History of the African*

*National Congress* (George Braziller, 1990); Amanda Kemp, Nozizwe Madlala, Asha Moodley, and Elaine Salo, "The Dawn of a New Day: Redefining South African Feminism," *The Challenge of Local Feminisms* (Westview Press, 1995); Nelson Mandela, *The Struggle Is My Life* (IDAF Publications, 1990); David Mermelstein, *The Anti-Apartheid Reader* (Grove Press, 1987).

MARGARET POWER
ILLINOIS INSTITUTE OF TECHNOLOGY

# Alienation

IN KARL MARX's political theory, alienation is the process through which workers became estranged from their milieu and are rendered powerless through the capitalist division of labor, which cripples the laborer by opposing the functions of the body against the functions of the mind. In "The Eighteenth Brumaire of Louis Bonaparte," Marx goes as far as claiming that this alienation deprives humankind of its very capacity for volition: "Men make their own history, but not of their own free will; not under circumstances they themselves have chosen but under the given and inherited circumstances with which they are directly confronted."

Marx developed the theory of alienation particularly in his early writings, such as "Contribution to a Critique of Hegel's Philosophy of Right" and *The Economic and Philosophical Manuscripts*. Marx specifically focused on the experience of alienation in modern bourgeois society and he fleshed out his understanding of the process through his critique of Georg W.F. Hegel. According to Hegel, people create a culture by means of their actions, which are the expression of the spirit. Such culture eventually becomes an entity alien from the people who produce it. Giving a materialist base to Hegel's mystical conception, Marx insisted that it was human labor that created culture and history: "Precisely because Hegel starts from the predicates of universal determination instead of from the real subject, and because there must be a bearer of this determination, the mystical idea becomes this bearer." What Hegel called the spirit was, according to Marx, a human product.

Thus, the history of humankind is marked by a paradox: people increasingly control nature yet they becomes alienated from and dominated by forces of their own creation. In a capitalist system of production,

"man's own deed becomes an alien power opposed to him, which enslaves him instead of being controlled by him." The worker is forced to deny rather than affirm himself in his work, thus capitalist labor amounts to "the loss of his self." Religion becomes the human response to alienation in material life.

According to Marx, the labor process is an objectification of human powers. Yet, workers are unable to relate to their product as an expression of their own essence and thus fail to recognize themselves in their product. This lack of recognition is the basis for alienation. The specific form of labor characteristic of bourgeois society, wage labor, corresponds to the most profound form of alienation. Since wage workers sell their labor power to earn a living, and the capitalist owns the labor process, the product of the workers' labor is, in a very real sense, alien to the worker as it becomes the property of the capitalist and not of its maker. Workers cannot say: "I made that; this is my product." Workers' alienation worsens during the regime of industrial capitalism where workers are attached to a machine and are themselves a mere unit along an assembly line, performing a meaningless task which is only part of a larger process: "He becomes an appendage of the machine, and it is only the most simple, most monotonous, and most easily acquired knack, that is required of him."

Marx described the concept of alienation as fourfold: workers are alienated from work, from the objects they make, from their fellow workers, and from their potential for creative production. This is because labor is a commodity that can be bought and sold under capitalist economic relations. Employers also control the means of production, and the cooperation between workers is destroyed as is their creativity in the name of a higher and more effective production.

In Marx's later writings, the concept of alienation is subsumed under the idea of "fetishism of commodities." In *Capital*, Marx argues that social relations between human beings become relations between things. "In order, therefore, to find an analogy, we must have recourse to the mist-enveloped regions of the religious world. In that world the productions of the human brain appear as independent beings endowed with life, and entering into relation both with one another and the human race. So it is in the world of commodities with the products of men's hands. This I call the fetishism which attaches itself to the products of labor, so soon as they are produced as commodities, and which is therefore inseparable from the production of commodities. This fetishism of commodities has its origin, as the foregoing analysis has already shown, in the peculiar social character of the labor that produces them."

Marx's prescription to overcome alienation is, of course, the transformation of the economic system from capitalist to socialist. In socialist economies, work and products are no longer commodities and the rigid distinction between mental and physical work breaks down, thus allowing the full development of every worker's potential. Thanks to a socialist system of production, class distinctions disappear and society becomes a genuine community, "in which the free development of each is the condition of the free development of all." Communism is thus the "positive transcendence of all estrangement" and it considers "accumulated labor . . . but a means to widen, to enrich, to promote the existence of the laborer."

## SEE ALSO

*Volume 1 Left:* Marx, Karl; Communism; Socialism.
*Volume 2 Right:* Capitalism.

## BIBLIOGRAPHY

Istvan Meszaros, *Marx's Theory of Alienation* (Prometheus, 1986); Bertell Ollman, *Alienation: Marx's Conception of Man in Capitalist Society* (Cambridge University Press, 1973); Wolfgang Schirmacher, ed., *German Socialist Philosophy* (Continuum Publishing, 1997); Lawrence H. Simon, ed., *Karl Marx: Selected Writings* (Hackett Publishing, 1994).

LUCA PRONO, PH.D.
UNIVERSITY OF NOTTINGHAM, ENGLAND

# American Civil Liberties Union

WHILE EUROPEANS fought in the early years of World War I, the United States remained neutral, at least in theory. America had a long tradition of isolationism and opposition to war in general, European wars in particular. Led by President Woodrow Wilson, the United States drifted closer and closer to backing Britain, then entered the war on the side of Britain and France. In reaction, antiwar protesters organized the American Union Against Militarism (AUAM). Founders included Crystal Eastman, Jane Addams, Paul Kellogg, Oswald Garrison Villard, and others. At the same time as it brought the United States into the European war, the government enacted a series of repressive laws, including the Espionage Act, that made antiwar speech and draft resistance into crimes. The AUAM established a Civil Liberties Bureau (CLB) to protect the rights of conscientious objectors and other antiwar elements to express their views, however unpopular. And the Free Speech League, which dated from the 19th century, continued its long-standing objections to censorship of any sort.

Heading the CLB, later the National Civil Liberties Bureau (NCLB), was Roger Baldwin, who gained his experience from working with the Free Speech League. Baldwin committed himself completely to the organization and the cause: he went to jail for resisting the draft, serving nine months in 1918. On release, he joined the Industrial Workers of the World (IWW), a radical socialist union. Baldwin's bureau extended its services beyond war opponents, taking on the cases of socialists and IWW when their rights were trampled in the mad rush of war hysteria. The AUAM and the Free Speech League faded, leaving the NCLB to face the postwar Red Scare without their resources.

## RED SCARE

When the war was over, the anti-German hysteria of the war years gave way to anticommunism, which had begun with the 1917 Russian Revolution. Wilson's attorney general, A. Mitchell Palmer, decided that communists were going to overthrow the government so he appointed J. Edgar Hoover as special assistant in the war against communism. Using the 1917 Espionage Act and the 1918 Sedition Act, they attacked leftist organizations. On the second anniversary of the Russian Revolution, November 7, 1919, they rounded up more than 10,000 suspected communists and anarchists. There was no evidence of a revolution in the making, but the government held many of the suspects without due process for a long time. Eventually, the government let most of them go, but it did deport 248 people to Russia, including the socialist Emma Goldman. Again, in January 1920, Palmer seized alleged communists and anarchists. Many of the 6,000 rounded up in these raids were members of the IWW. Again, these people were held indefinitely without trial. The NCLB in 1920 took legal action that forced the Justice Department to release antiwar activists and to slow the deportations.

The Red Scare ignited the civil liberties movement because of the excesses of Palmer and his zeal to stamp out radicalism in postwar America. As the Red Scare exhausted itself in 1920, prominent progressives from all walks of middle-class life awoke to an awareness of how vulnerable civil liberties had been to destruction during the years between 1917 and 1920. Survivors of the AUAM and other concerned progressives came together to create the American Civil Liberties Union (ACLU) in 1920. Founders included legal experts such as Felix Frankfurter and Clarence Darrow and progressive reformers, some socialist, such as Addams of Hull House, education reformer John Dewey, and socialists Upton Sinclair and Norman Thomas. Also among the founders were historian Charles Beard, feminist and antiwar activist Crystal Eastman, and Florence Kelley, Lillian Wald, Oswald Garrison Villard, Paul Kellogg, and Elizabeth Gurley Flynn. Baldwin was director, a position he held for nearly three decades.

The United States in 1920 was somewhat deficient in guaranteeing civil liberties. Antiwar speakers and socialists were still in jail under the wartime acts. The government was deporting aliens without due process and without cause other than their unpopular (that is, socialist) views. Women lacked the vote. And there was not even a comprehension that rights belonged to outsiders such as the poor, the mentally ill, prisoners, and homosexuals. Eugenics had not yet crested. And the Supreme Court had not yet read the First Amendment as a guarantor of free speech in the modern sense.

Racial discrimination was still spreading, with even Wilson resegregating the federal government, and anti-black violence, including lynching, riots, and attacks on returned servicemen, breaking out. Although lynching had diminished during the war, the first year after the war's end saw the lynching of more than 70 African Americans, including 10 soldiers still in uniform. Mob violence between 1919 and 1922 resulted in 239 lynchings. Other white-on-black violence increased too, and it often went unpunished.

## MUCH WORK TO DO

Under Baldwin, the ACLU fought for free speech as a necessity for correcting society's flaws. He rejected free speech in the areas of personal expression, for example pornography, which freethinkers felt should not be regulated. He kept the ACLU on the radical course of opposing the draft and war and any suppression of civil liberties. He defended the rights of radical socialists such as Goldman to believe and say as they wished while keeping the ACLU at arm's length from their more radical ideas. Some of the ACLU's accomplishments during subsequent decades included:

In 1925, the ACLU and Clarence Darrow defended John T. Scopes in his case against Tennessee's anti-evo-

lution law, a free speech case. In the 1930s, the ACLU followed the Supreme Court's move to greater protection of free speech as called for by Justices Louis D. Brandeis and Oliver Wendell Holmes. As late as the 1940s the ACLU was still sensitive enough to the political climate that it purged its board of communists.

In 1939, when Mayor Frank ("I am the law") Hague of Jersey City took on the power to silence radical speech, the ACLU fought him in the Supreme Court, winning a court ruling that public places belong to the people, not the government, and the people could speak there as they chose. In 1941, the ACLU won *Edwards v. California*, overturning the California law prohibiting the transport of indigents into the state. In 1942, the ACLU supported the 110,000 Japanese Americans who were relocated from the West Coast inland to concentration camps. Hysterical government decision-making in the aftermath of Pearl Harbor lead to a violation of the rights of Japanese Americans, two-thirds of whom were native-born citizens of the United States. In 1943, the ACLU was there when the court ruled in *West Virginia v. Barnette* that Jehovah's Witnesses could not be compelled to salute the flag. *Smith v. Allwright* (1944) gave Texas African Americans the right to vote in the state's white primary. *Shelley v. Kramer* (1948) overturned restrictive covenants that had barred the sale of houses to blacks.

In the 1950s, as the Cold War replaced World War II, loyalty oaths became popular with federal and state governments. School teachers commonly had to swear that they were not communists or members of "subversive" organizations. The ACLU fought the oaths through the decade. In 1952, the case of *Burstyn vs. Wilson* stopped New York State from censoring the movie *The Miracle* for sacrilege. The First Amendment prohibited state interference in religion. In 1954, the ACLU was there when on May 17 the Supreme Court ruled in *Brown v. The Board of Education* that segregation in public schools was unconstitutional because it violated the Fourteenth Amendment.

Not until the 1960s did the ACLU catch up with the freethinkers of the late 19th century. Then, finally, it began backing an absolute right of free speech that included pornography as well as political expression by such hate groups as the American Nazi Party.

In 1973, the ACLU was first to call for the impeachment of President Richard Nixon for violations of civil liberties. That same year, the ACLU won its efforts in the states to overturn anti-abortion laws; the Supreme Court ruled in *Roe v. Wade* and *Doe v. Bolton* that the right to privacy extends to childbirth and abortion. In

1981, the evolution issue came back in Arkansas, when the ACLU fought a state effort to require creationism in biology textbooks as an equal theory to evolution. The ACLU won because the judge agreed that creation science was not science but religion, disallowed by the separation of church and state.

In 1989, the issue was flag desecration, which first Texas then the federal government attempted to criminalize. The courts supported the ACLU and symbolic political speech in 1991. Another free speech case, *R.A.V. v. Wisconsin*, struck down local law that attempted to prohibit display on public or private property of any symbol (for example, a burning cross) that "arouses anger, alarm or resentment in others on the basis of race, color, creed, religion, or gender." Another case, *Ladue v. Gallo* (1994), affirmed that a town could not bar a homeowner from placing on his property a sign opposing the Persian Gulf War.

In 1997, the Supreme Court overturned the 1996 Communications Act ban of "indecent" speech. Before the ACLU there had never been a free speech defense that succeeded in the Supreme Court. The ACLU changed this. Major free speech and press victories came in the case of the Jehovah's Witnesses, denied the right to distribute their literature in Georgia. The ACLU also won the *Ulysses* (James Joyce's controversial novel) censorship case and guaranteed Henry Ford's right to distribute antiunion literature.

The activities of the ACLU have long been controversial, and organizations such as Reclaim America accused the ACLU of confusing liberty with license to destroy the Christian moral fabric of the country and imposing an atheist agenda. Into the 2000s, the ACLU provides legal expertise, including attorneys, in civil rights cases. Its mission is to uphold the civil liberties and constitutional rights of every person in the United States regardless of race, religion, creed, or other category. The cause is not always popular, but the responsibility is there to protect everyone, whether the Ku Klux Klan or the Nation of Islam. The issue is not the beliefs but the right to assemble and express, just as Baldwin committed the organization to back in the 1910s.

**SEE ALSO**

**BIBLIOGRAPHY**

American Civil Liberties Union, "Defending the Bill of Rights," www.aclu.org (March 2004); ACLU of Illinois, "A Brief History," www.aclu-il.org (March 2004); Coral Ridge Ministries, "The ACLU: A Wolf in Sheep's Clothing," www.reclaimamerica.org (2001); PageWise, "ACLU History," http://arar.essortment.com (2002); D.M. Rabban, *Free Speech in Its Forgotten Years* (Cambridge University Press, 1997).

JOHN BARNHILL, PH.D.
INDEPENDENT SCHOLAR

# American Civil War

IN THE EARLY 1860s, the political lefts within the American political spectrum were the Radical Republicans, who opposed President Abraham Lincoln for his political moderation in regard to emancipation and political liberties. In 1861, seven southern states in the United States, apprehensive of the latest political policies of the Republican Party in relation to the institution of slavery, seceded, or left, the Union to form the Confederate States of America. The states essentially protested the threatening idea that Republican President Lincoln, once elected, would initiate policies leading to the abolition of slavery. The commencement of hostilities signaled the beginning of an intense debate within the political spectrum. On the one side, the Democrats were divided between the War Democrats or those who opposed the conduct of the war but supported the war effort and the "Copperheads," who opposed the war as well as Lincoln.

After the 1860 presidential elections, Radical Republicans assumed a prominence in the halls of Congress. Many were appointed to key committee assignments that were important for the conduct of the war. Some of these appointments included Thaddeus Stevens (Ways and Means), Owen Lovejoy (Agriculture), James Ashley (Territories), Henry Winter Davis (Foreign Relations), George W. Julian (Public Lands), Elihu Washburne (Commerce), and Henry Wilson (Judiciary).

The ideology of the Radical Republicans shifted to the left. Many, like Stevens, believed that Lincoln had not proposed a sufficiently radical program for the abolition of slavery. They believed that Lincoln was essentially a moderate who could propose plans that could forever abolish slavery from the Union. Many came to believe in the radical notion that African Americans should be afforded equal civil and political rights as the Anglo population—an idea that confirmed the notion

*Thaddeus Stevens, a leftist Radical Republican, did not believe Abraham Lincoln went far enough with the abolition of slavery.*

that they were indeed radical. Moreover, their ideology involved the notion that once the war commenced, Lincoln should have made the war one of slavery rather than unionism. From its inception, Lincoln, in speech after speech, had declared the war a struggle over unionism rather than the abolition of slavery. Radical Republicans chided Lincoln over his seemingly moderate tone. For these Republicans, who hailed mostly from the Northeast, Lincoln's policies were not meant to punish the seceded states. Rather, Lincoln sought to incorrectly integrate the southern states back into the Union fold. Thus, the ideology of the Radical Republicans during the war pointed to a criticism of Lincoln's policies as moderate and inconsistent with the ideology of the party.

The Radical Republicans' most fervent attack occurred in 1861. On August 30, 1861, Major General John C. Fremont, commander of the Union Army in St. Louis, declared that all slaves owned by Confederates in Missouri were free. Lincoln was furious at Fre-

mont for having acted without authorization of the president as well as essentially emancipating the slaves without Lincoln's authority. Many within the Radical Republican camp cheered the move. But Lincoln, concerned for maintaining the crucial border states on the side of the Union by not making the war over slavery, was in a precarious situation. Lincoln fired Fremont and the Radical Republicans became disenchanted at the president's conservatism on the controversial issue of emancipation.

The Radical Republicans also became incensed in May 1862 over Lincoln. On May 9, 1862, General David Hunter authorized the liberation of all slaves in Union hands in South Carolina. He proceeded to sanction the first African-American regiment in South Carolina. Lincoln was also angry over Hunter's unilateral decision. Lincoln reassigned Hunter and in the process alienated many radicals within the party.

The radicals' growing opposition in the early stages of the war dissipated after Lincoln's 1863 Emancipation Proclamation. As the war winded down and it became apparent that the Union would win the war, the radicals looked to the postwar period. The debate evolved into one over the issues of the freed population and the political and economic makeup of the conquered territories. On December 8, 1863, President Lincoln issued a Reconstruction Plan. Also known as the 10 Percent Plan, Lincoln offered pardons and restoration of property to Confederates who took an oath of allegiance to the Union and agreed to accept emancipation. His plan proposed a formula by which loyal voters of a seceded state could begin the process of readmission into the Union. Clearly, the Lincoln plan was meant to integrate the conquered southern states into the Union fold at a lesser cost. The radicals were unhappy with the presidential plan.

On July 2, 1864, Congress passed a reconstruction bill, known as the Wade-Davis Bill. By 1864, the radicals had decided that their goal was universal freedom and harsh punishment for the South. Many radicals simply did not trust the "loyal" southerners to maintain their pledges. The radicals, especially approaching the 1864 election, entered into an alliance with the War Democrats and promulgated their own plans. The Wade-Davis Bill resulted from that liberal alliance. Sponsored by Benjamin F. Wade and Henry W. Davis, the bill provided for the appointment of provisional military governors in the seceded states. When a majority of a state's white citizens swore allegiance to the Union, a constitutional convention would be called. Each state's constitution was to be required to abolish slavery, repudiate secession, and disqualify Confederate officials from voting or holding office. In order to qualify for the franchise, a person would be required to take an oath that he had never voluntarily given aid to the Confederacy. Lincoln's pocket veto of the bill presaged the struggle that was to take place after the war between President Andrew Johnson and the Radical Republicans in Congress.

## SEE ALSO

*Volume 1 Left:* United States; Civil Rights; Lincoln, Abraham.
*Volume 2 Right:* Lincoln, Abraham; American Civil War.

## BIBLIOGRAPHY

Eric Foner, *Reconstruction: America's Unfinished Revolution* (HarperCollins, 1988); Harold Hyman, ed., *The Radical Republicans and Reconstruction, 1861–70* (Macmillan, 1967); Stephen Oates, *Abraham Lincoln: The Man Behind the Myths* (HarperPerennial, 1994).

JAIME RAMÓN OLIVARES, PH.D.
HOUSTON COMMUNITY COLLEGE, CENTRAL

# American Revolution

FROM A LEFT POINT of view, the outcome of the American Revolution is ambiguous, although leftists tend to see revolutions and revolutionary process per se as progress. From a Marxist view, the American Revolution symbolizes the transfer of power from the feudal era (with a mercantilistic economy) to the bourgeois (with a capitalist economic system).

The revolutionaries of 1776 therefore were mainly bourgeois traders in cities and owners of larger plantations in rural areas. Their aim was not in the first place to establish a democracy, but to change the economic conditions from the restrictions set by the English colonial authority to the demands of an emerging capitalist system in the New World. In France in 1789, despite all the economic interest of the French bourgeoisie, there was a real clash between monarchists and republicans.

The main representatives of the American Revolution (starting with George Washington) were nearly identical with the ruling class in Britain—with the sole exception that the ruling class in Britain, via taxes and control of export/import licenses, wanted to exploit the colonies, including the ruling class of the colonies. Thereby, some of the most important American revolu-

tionaries became revolutionary not by democratic conviction but by chance. In fact, Washington himself had fought for the British just a few years before 1776.

When the delegates from the colonies met in Philadelphia, Pennsylvania, in 1776, they were unlikely revolutionaries in a social sense. They represented the ruling class of the colonies and would have been much less successful and inspiring without a small number of bourgeois intelligentsia within and outside of the Continental Congress (for example, Thomas Jefferson and Thomas Paine). That many of the revolutionaries took the revolutionary side by chance may be demonstrated by the infamous traitor Benedict Arnold, who first served the revolutionary forces well, but then helped the British; better financial compensation was one of the reasons for this change of heart. For many revolutionaries, the economic deal they could make with the Revolution was personally much more decisive and convincing than any idealistic goals like "no taxation without representation" or self-determination in a democratic way.

Many of the foreign sympathizers of the American Revolution (for example, the French Marquis de Lafayette) came for idealistic reasons to help the emerging American republic fight against the British military might. France, however, as the major and decisive foreign ally of the new American entity, came for strategic interests within the contest of colonialist competition, not to support any ideals of some Americans assembled at Philadelphia. The U.S. Constitution of 1787 is seen as the most important achievement of the revolutionary republic. But this Constitution did not create a democracy, not even one for all the white males in the population. It excluded women, African Americans, Native Americans, and gave any essential power only to white people with a certain amount of property. It took the American republic nearly 200 years to give and to guarantee at least the right to vote to all adult inhabitants of the country.

A leftist could argue that democracy in Britain at the time was at least as equally developed as that in the emerging U.S. system, only the people involved in the decision-making process shifted from rich Englishmen to rich Americans. The majority of the population in the former colonies was left out of any power before and after the revolutionary period from 1776 to 1787. The most ill treated victims of the new American republic were the African Americans who were brought by force to the Americas to serve as slave labor.

One could argue that in the case of continuing British rule, slavery might have been discontinued well before the 1860s. The antislavery movement in Europe and especially in Britain was much more influential in the early 19th century than in the United States. A shame for the founding fathers is that despite the words about "all men are created equal," they allowed slavery to be an integral part of the American republic.

The other main victims of the American Revolution were the Native Americans, who were more ruthlessly expropriated by the American republic than by any colonial ruler. In fact, the natives in the 18th century had generally preferred the French colonialists, because the French colonial approach was more inclined to guarantee certain rights and self-rule to the natives, whereas the British, and especially the Americans under British rule, had expanded much more ruthlessly at the cost of the natives for years.

Leading figures of the American Revolution could be accused of personal duplicity, for example Jefferson, who spoke out at occasions against slavery, but owned slaves himself. During the presidency of John Adams, the former revolutionaries did not take the side of the French Revolution, but tried something like an equidistance from France and Britain. The Adams presidency was also overshadowed by various assaults on the civil liberties (of the ruling white males), and it took the presidencies of Jefferson and Jackson to make those liberties safe.

After such a harsh perspective, it has to be said that, even from a left position, the American Revolution that succeeded was better than an American Revolution which could have collapsed. Despite all insufficiencies, it was a starting point for liberty, which enabled, from a left point of view, a much more emancipatory French Revolution of 1789. To say it in the words of Jefferson, who pointed out in his last letter of June 24, 1826 (concerning the coming of the 50th Anniversary of the Declaration of Independence): "May it be to the world, what I believe it will be (to some parts sooner, to others later, but finally to all), the signal of arousing men to burst the chains under which monkish ignorance and superstition had persuaded them to bind themselves, and to assume the blessings and security of self-government."

**SEE ALSO**

**BIBLIOGRAPHY**

Bernard Bailyn, *The Ideological Origins of the American Revolution* (Belknap Press, 1992); Joseph J. Ellis, *Founding Brothers* (Knopf, 2000); John E. Ferling, *A Leap in the Dark: The Struggle to Create the American Republic* (Oxford University Press, 2003); Leonard W. Levy, *Jefferson and Civil Liberties: The Darker Side* ( Ivan R. Dee, 1989); James W. Loewen, *Lies My Teacher Told Me* (Touchstone, 1995); Conor Cruise O'Brien, *The Long Affair: Thomas Jefferson and the French Revolution, 1785–1800* (University of Chicago Press, 1996); Michael Pearson, *Those Damned Rebels: The American Revolution as Seen through British Eyes* (Da Capo Press, 2000); Larry E. Tise, *The American Counterrevolution: A Retreat from Liberty, 1783–1800* (Stackpole Books 1998); David Waldstreicher, *Runaway America: Benjamin Franklin, Slavery, and the American Revolution* (Hill & Wang 2004); Gordon S. Wood, *Radicalism of the American Revolution* (Vintage Books, 1993).

OLIVER BENJAMIN HEMMERLE, PH.D.
CHEMNITZ UNIVERSITY, GERMANY

# Anarchism

ANARCHISM IS A MODERN political theory that holds that all forms of government or authority are oppressive and therefore should be abolished in order to attain equality and justice based on free contractual agreements between individuals and groups. The etymology of the word *anarchism* is derived from the Greek word *anarchos* (anarchy), meaning rule by nobody or having no government.

Central to anarchist thought is the belief that all forms of authority and oppression—state, church, patriarchy/sexism, economic and environmental exploitation, racism, national chauvinism, and conventional morality—are artificial and detrimental to the fulfillment of human potential. Anarchists contend that society is natural and people are good but power is corrupting. Therefore, the highest stage of humanity is the freedom of individuals to express themselves and to live together in harmony on the basis of creativity, cooperation, and mutual respect.

Through history, there have been as many forms of anarchism as anarchist thinkers. Anarchists have been socialists, nonsocialists, and even antisocialists. Anarchists have envisioned social change via peaceful means, while a small minority has called for violence and revolution. In short, there is much diversity of opinion within anarchist thought over issues such as the individual versus the community, ecology versus technology, and the nature of gender roles.

The origins of anarchist thought stem back to the ancient world. The Greek Zeno of Citium, founder of Stoic philosophy, argued that individuals should resist the will of the state and instead be governed by individual morality. The Chinese philosopher Lao-Tzu, founder of Taoism, stressed the importance of individualism and creativity and the danger of government and social conventions. In medieval Europe, anarchism was closely connected to utopian, millenarian religious movements such as the Gnostic heresies and the Anabaptists of the Reformation. Jean-Jacques Rousseau's 1753 *Discourse on the Origin of Inequality* offered the notion of natural man in a state of "anarchist primitivism" until humans were fettered by civilization. William Godwin's 1793 *Enquiry Concerning Political Justice* comes closest to modern anarchism in its critique of government and a vision of a rational free society devoid of private property and the family.

The French writer Pierre-Joseph Proudhon is generally regarded as the father of modern anarchist theory. In his famous 1840 pamphlet, *What Is Property?*, Proudhon argued that property was profit stolen from the worker, who was the true source of all wealth. Proudhon propagated the doctrine of mutualism, a program for maintaining a socially regulated system of small landholdings through the administration of mutual aid. Whereas Proudhon hoped for a gradual evolution of society toward anarchic organization, the Russian aristocrat Mikhail Bakunin preached that isolated acts of political terror would spur people on toward social revolution. Moreover, Bakunin believed that individual liberty could only be safeguarded within a communal setting and thus developed the idea of anarchist communism.

The French philosopher Georges Sorel added a dimension to Bakunism by propagating a cult of violence and the myth of the general strike as a revolutionary tactic. The scientist Peter Kropotkin used Darwinian evolution theory in his 1897 book, *Mutual Aid*, to assert that cooperation equaled or even surpassed individualism in nature. Leo Tolstoy, a Russian novelist, is considered a Christian anarchist who believed in nonviolence and the renunciation of all worldly values.

Anarchism as a political force started with Bakunin in his tireless propaganda efforts and his opposition to the "authoritarian socialism" of Karl Marx in the 1860s and 1870s. In the 1880s and 1890s, anarchism was associated with a wave of assassinations of heads of states (not all committed by anarchists), including Russian Tzar Alexander II in 1881, the French President Sadi Carnot in 1894, and the American President William McKinley in 1901. In the United States, many crimes were blamed unjustly on anarchists, such as the bomb thrown during the Haymarket Square Riot in Chicago in 1886. The deportation of anarchists, including Emma Goldman and Alexander Berkman, were also ordered. Anarchism's only real mass following was in Latin countries including Spain, Portugal, Italy, and South and Central America in the form of the militant organized labor movement anarcho-syndicalism. Anarchists played roles in many failed attempts of general strikes, aborted peasant uprisings, revolutionary movements in Russia in 1905 and 1917, and in the Spanish Civil War (1936–39) until their defeat by fascist General Francisco Franco.

As an organized movement, anarchism since the 1930s has been largely marginal, although it remains important as a philosophical perspective and a political tendency. Anarchist thought has been further developed since the 1960s in various directions, including anarcha-feminism, anarcho-capitalism, post-structuralist anarchism, and anti-globalist anarchism and is associated with prominent intellectuals such as Noam Chomsky. Anarchist activism in modern times has taken the form of visible protests against globalization, environmental degradation, and militarism. In the United States, right-wing, militia-type anarchist movements have also emerged, which oppose taxation and governmental rule by those deemed "socially undesirable" ethnic groups.

**SEE ALSO**

*Volume 1 Left:* Anarcho-Syndicalism; Anti-Globalization. *Volume 2 Right:* Libertarianism; Feminism.

**BIBLIOGRAPHY**

Albert Fried and Ronald Sanders, eds., *Socialist Thought: A Documentary History* (Columbia University Press, 1992); James Joll, *The Anarchists* (Harvard University Press, 1980); Todd May, *The Political Philosophy of Poststructuralist Anarchism* (Pennsylvania State University Press, 1994).

KEVIN J. CALLAHAN, PH.D.
SAINT JOSEPH COLLEGE

# Anarcho-Syndicalism

ALTHOUGH ANARCHISM and syndicalism constitute two distinct philosophies and bases of activity, they also enshrine particular points of commonality and similarity sufficient to meld them into a discrete political doctrine and movement known as anarcho-syndicalism.

It was in France during the late 19th century and early 20th century (until World War I), and in Spain until the Spanish Civil War, that anarcho-syndicalism proved most popular or influential, although Italy, the United States (via the Industrial Workers of the World, IWW, formed in 1905), and parts of Latin America have also proved receptive to anarcho-syndicalism at various junctures.

## ASSAULT ON CAPITALISM

Syndicalism sought to organize the "exploited" proletariat on the basis of various industries or crafts, both in order to secure short-term material improvements for workers and peasants, and to prepare for a longer-term assault on capitalism and the state (which ultimately served and protected the interests of the bourgeoisie). Through direct action—most notably in the form of a general strike—some anarchists viewed syndicalism as a valuable channel through which to establish links with the rapidly expanding working class and educate them into the alleged virtues of anarchist principles and practice, and in so doing, warn them against relying on socialist parties and parliamentary activity to liberate them. The former, if they obtained political power, would invariably become the new rulers of the proletariat and peasantry.

Anarcho-syndicalists would eventually be able to point to the 1917 Bolshevik Revolution and its tragic aftermath as evidence of the danger of relying on vanguard socialist parties to lead and liberate the workers, while relying primarily on parliamentary activity would merely serve to enslave and integrate the organized working class into the extant capitalist system, with concessions to workers and trade unions only granted on terms, and in circumstances, judged appropriate by the bourgeoisie and "their" state. For anarcho-syndicalists, therefore, the genuine emancipation and liberation of the working class could only be achieved by the activities of the workers and peasants themselves; revolution had to be a bottom-up, not a top-down, activity.

Anarcho-syndicalists deemed the occupational or craft federations (syndicates) to provide the best model for the decentralized and ultra-democratic society (based on mass participation and direct democracy) for which they were ultimately striving: "Federal forms of organization corresponded to anarchist principles, and

so the syndicates could be seen as the embryos of a new, stateless social order," David Miller explained.

Closely linked to this, syndicalism tended to formally reject established political institutions and processes, partly because these seemed to entail organizational rigidity and the centralization of political power, and partly because established political parties and institutions seemed to weaken the apparent revolutionary potential of the proletariat through a twin process of subordination to, and integration into, the wider politico-economic system.

This eschewal of "bourgeois politics" was therefore highly attractive to some anarchists, for whom radical socialist parties, while espousing the (anarchist) goal of a classless and completely egalitarian society, often relied on the concept of a tightly organized, highly centralized, Leninist-vanguard party to lead the proletariat in overthrowing capitalism. To anarchists, this was likely to result in the replacement of one elite and its subordination of the workers by another, irrespective of the egalitarian or emancipatory rhetoric deployed.

Consequently, anarcho-syndicalism fully supported forms of direct action by workers and peasants, with the general strike envisaged as the workers' ultimate revolutionary weapon against capitalism and the bourgeois state. For anarcho-syndicalists, it is the general strike that is ultimately to herald the overthrow of capitalism and thereby secure liberation of workers and peasants from wage-slavery. In these respects, the emphasis of anarcho-syndicalism was on economic direct action to pursue fundamental socio-economic change, rather than relying on more conventional modes of political activity. In the words of a prominent French anarchist, Emile Pouget: "The aim of the syndicates is to make war on the bosses and not to bother with politics."

Anarcho-syndicalists were most active in the 1930s and were regarded by the Soviet Comintern as deviationists, that is, as deviating from the Moscow-approved communist parties around the world. In Spain, the anarcho-syndicalists organized into a strong political force, the CNT, which worked in an uncomfortable alliance with other groups of the left in supporting the Loyalist cause during the Spanish Civil War, 1936–39.

## SEE ALSO

Volume 1 Left: Anarchism; Communism; Socialism.
Volume 2 Right: Capitalism; Laissez-Faire; Libertarianism.

## BIBLIOGRAPHY

James Joll, *The Anarchists* (Methuen, 1979); Peter Marshall, *Demanding the Impossible: A History of Anarchism* (Fontana,

1993); David Miller, *Anarchism* (J. M. Dent, 1984); Rudolf Rocker, *Anarcho-Syndicalism* (Pluto Press, 1989 reprint); George Woodcock, *Anarchism* (Pelican Books, 1963).

PETER DOREY
CARDIFF UNIVERSITY, UNITED KINGDOM

# Animal Rights

IN THE LATE 17th century, English philosopher John Locke introduced the concept of "natural rights," arguing that human beings had the right to life, liberty, and property ownership. Since these rights were given by the Creator, no government or individual could take them away. Proponents of animal rights believe that Locke's rights should be extended to nonhumans as well. Decidedly on the left of the political spectrum, they argue that all animals were created not for the use of humans but for themselves.

Advocates of animal welfare may accept the benefit that humans receive from animals, but they demand humane treatment of animals in all circumstances. Animal welfare advocates object strenuously to the practice of "intensive rearing" on factory farms where animals are too closely confined, kept indoors for their short lives, and "doctored" with various antibiotics to keep down possible infections. Over five billion animals are slaughtered each year in the United States alone.

Within the animal rights and animal welfare movements, there are various strains of thought. For instance, some advocates of animal rights object to factory farming but are willing to accept traditional animal agriculture as necessary to the well being of humans. Many animal rights activists, on the other hand, argue with some truth that if people had to kill animals before they could eat them, the incidence of meat eating would drop dramatically. They oppose both hunting and trapping. Other animal rights advocates are opposed to testing cosmetics on animals but see the benefits of using animals in medical research.

At opposite poles are the activists who reject all use of animals for human needs, even disapproving of the extermination of pests such as cockroaches and rats, and those individuals who believe in animal rights as theory but who are unwilling to commit to a particular position on what they mean by the concept.

Some animal rights advocates, known as abolitionists, go so far as to compare the lot of animal to that of slaves, who have been historically oppressed with no hope of freedom.

While animal rights supporters may vary in commitment to the cause, they tend to share certain characteristics. Most of them are white, full-time professionals with high levels of education. They are predominantly female. They are likely to be between 30 and 45 years of age and live in cities and towns rather than in rural areas. Nearly 60 percent of animal rights activists have no children, and about half have never been married. As might be expected, animal rights supporters tend to own animals as pets, sometimes several animals. Approximately 87 percent of those involved in the animal rights movement refuse to eat meat.

Animal rights advocates offer various "proofs" of animal intelligence to show that animals should be leading lives free of human interference. There is some irony in the fact that many of these "proofs" were gathered through medical experimentation. Honeybees, with brains only one-millionth the size of humans', have been shown to have complex mental abilities. Even though their brains are only the size of walnuts, parrots are capable of learning and understanding human speech. While the memory of elephants has become part of common folklore, these huge mammals are also capable of self-consciousness and have the ability to communicate and even to solve problems. Orangutans have demonstrated humanlike behaviors that include deceitfulness and pretending. Some orangutans have learned thousands of words in sign language. A gorilla scored between 70 and 95 on human-child intelligence tests. The bond between dogs and humans has been documented for hundreds of years, and no dog owner doubts the ability of canines to show emotion and to react to potential danger. Even cats, notoriously independent creatures, have saved the lives of their human owners.

## HISTORY OF ANIMAL RIGHTS

Early interest in animal rights can be traced to Plutarch (circa 46–120) and Porphyry (232–305), who believed that it was morally wrong to inflict unnecessary suffering on any creature. Rationalist thinkers, however, dismissed this argument. René Descartes (1596–1650) and Immanuel Kant (1724–1804), for example, insisted that animals had no moral worth at all because they had no consciousness of self. Even at a time when the animal rights movement was almost invisible, the British House of Commons introduced in 1809 the first animal rights bill in recorded history. During the late 19th and early 20th centuries, the animal rights movement regained its momentum.

Among the large body of literature on animal rights, the works of philosophers Peter Singer and Tom Regan and veterinarian Bernard Rollin stand out as contributing the greatest understanding of why animals deserve rights. The publication of Peter Singer's *Animal Liberation* in 1975 marked the official beginning of the contemporary animal rights movement. Singer offered a philosophical argument for the moral treatment of animals and issued a call for major reforms in the ways that animals are used and treated. In 1981, in *Animal Rights and Human Morality*, Bernard Rollin demanded that humans take responsibility for the way animals are treated. In 1983, Tom Regan further expanded the argument for animal rights in *The Case for Animal Rights*. The works of Singer, Regan, and Rollin were motivating forces in the renewed activism of the animal rights movement that began in the 1970s and gained momentum throughout the 1980s and 1990s.

As early as 1966, the U.S. Congress passed the Animal Welfare Act, giving the U.S. Department of Agriculture (USDA) the responsibility of enforcement. The law has since been strengthened six times. The 2002 version of the bill established minimum standards for the care of animals used in commerce, research, sales, and entertainment. These standards cover proper housing, handling, sanitation, nutrition, water, exercise, veterinarian care, and protection from extreme weather. Animal rights advocates maintain that the law contains too many exceptions, including the fact that agricultural animals are not included and that retailers are only bound by the law if they sell exotic or zoo animals or regulated birds. The USDA has the authority to punish violations of the law with cease-and-desist orders, fines, and suspension and revocations of licenses. State and local governments also have separate laws that govern the ownership, care, and use of animals

## CONTEMPORARY MOVEMENT

Animal rights extremists have been accused of being terrorists in the United States and in Europe. In Great Britain, for example, such groups have been given a lifetime ban that prevents their protesting outside Huntington Life Science, Britain's largest research laboratory. The ban also includes the homes of all Huntington employees. In the United States, animal rights extremists have become known as "home-grown terrorists." Their activities range from harassment such as shoving animal excrement through mail slots, putting rape alarms in letter boxes at night, sending unwanted emails, blocking phone lines, and frightening children to damage to property and destruction of research, including placing paint stripper on cars, destroying records and equipment, and setting fire to buildings.

Opponents of animal rights point out that when extremists break into buildings and destroy research and equipment, they are not merely "rescuing exploited animals" but are eliminating the possibility that human beings will benefit from studies, such as those conducted on Sudden Infant Death Syndrome (SIDS), which kills approximately 5,000 infants each year. When the Animal Liberation Front broke into the lab of Professor John Orem at Texas Tech on July 4, 1989, his work on SIDS was brought to a grinding halt. After People for the Ethical Treatment of Animals (PETA) went undercover at the lab of psychologist Edward Taub in 1981, he spent five years before being cleared of all charges. Essential time was lost from his research on the rehabilitation of stroke victims.

As justification for extreme activism on the behalf of animals used in research, animal rights supporters have documented a number of atrocities conducted in the name of science, including the snapping of wings of mallard ducks in order to examine the self-evident theory of whether or not this animal could survive in the wild. Monkeys have been addicted to drugs, deafened, intentionally brain damaged, dipped in boiling water, and even shot. Pigs have been blowtorched to study burns.

The scientific community argues that such tests are necessary because scientists are limited in their options for learning about medical conditions, drugs, devices, and procedures. They argue that saving human lives is more important than saving animal life. Animal rights supporters insist that alternate, albeit more expensive, methods could be used. Computer simulation, for example, has proved useful in a number of cases. Even some scientists admit that unnecessary duplication of testing results in unnecessary deaths of animals.

While animal rights activists are passionate about their cause and may be willing to engage in what many see as crimes, they devote more attention to civil disobedience and public education. For example, PETA, which is the most visible of all animal rights groups in the United States, declared April 17 World Day for Lab Animals to alert the public to the mistreatment of animals. They hold rallies, engage in research, write legislation, lobby legislatures, commit to animal rescue, recruit celebrity involvement from such luminaries as Paul McCartney, Michael Stipe, and the Indigo Girls, and hold special events such as Rock Against Fur. PETA considers itself successful for such activities as stopping the slaughter of baby seals in Canada and convincing General Motors to refrain from using pigs and ferrets in crash testing.

Other well known animal rights groups include the Humane Society, Anti-Vivisection League, World Wildlife Fund, Trans-Species Unlimited, In Defense of Animals, Gorilla Foundation, Primarily Primate, Humane Farming Association, Farm Animal Reform, Alliance for Animals, Citizens to End Animal Suffering and Exploitation (CEASE), Whale Adoption Project, and Digit Fund.

## SEE ALSO

*Volume 1 Left:* Human Rights; Locke, John; Liberalism.
*Volume 2 Right:* Conservatism; United States.

## BIBLIOGRAPHY

"The Animal Welfare Act," www.aphis.usda.gov (July 2004); Paola Cavalieri, *The Animal Question* (Oxford University Press, 2001); Jean Bethke Elshtain, "Why Worry about Animals?" Robert K. Miller, ed., *The Informed Argument: A Multidisciplinary Reader and Guide* (Harcourt Brace Jovanovich, 1992); Ken Midkiff, "Animal Rights and Wrongs," www.sierraclub.org (July 2004); Lyle Munro, *Compassionate Beasts: The Quest for Animal Rights* (Praeger, 2001); "PETA Criticizes University of North Carolina's Treatment of Lab Animals," *Herald Sun* (May 13, 2004); "Playing Terrorists," *Economist* (April 17, 2004); "PETA's Mission Statement," www.peta.org (July 2004); Tom Regan, *The Case for Animal Rights* (University of California Press, 1983); Tom Regan, *The Struggle for Animal Rights* (International Society for Animal Rights, 1987); Bernard Rollin, *Animal Rights and Human Morality* (Prometheus, 1981); Peter Singer, *Animal Liberation: A New Ethics for Our Treatment of Animals* (Random House, 1975); Steven M. Wise, *Drawing the Line: Science and the Case for Animal Rights* (Perseus, 2000); Steven M. Wise, *Rattling the Cage: Toward Legal Rights for Animals* (Perseus, 2000).

ELIZABETH PURDY, PH.D.
INDEPENDENT SCHOLAR

# Anthony, Susan B. (1820–1906)

SUSAN BROWNELL ANTHONY was born into a devout Quaker family in Adams, Massachusetts. The second of eight children of Daniel and Lucy Anthony, she learned to read and write at the age of three. In 1826, the Anthonys moved to Battensville, New York, where Susan attended a local school. She later attended a home school before being sent to boarding school near Philadelphia, Pennsylvania.

Following the economic panic of 1837, the Anthonys declared bankruptcy. Consequently, Anthony took a teaching position in 1839 at Quaker Eunice Kenyon's boarding school in New Rochelle, New York, where she taught for one year. By 1845, her family's financial situation had improved, and her father purchased a farm in Rochester, New York. Anthony lived there until accepting a position in 1846 as the headmistress of female students at Canajoharie Academy. She taught there for two years, earning $110 a year, her first paid position.

Anthony entered the ranks of reformers through the temperance movement. Raised a Quaker, her family believed drinking liquor was sinful. She first joined the Daughters of Temperance while working at Canajoharie Academy, helped found the Women's State Temperance Society of New York in 1848, and became president of the Rochester branch of the Daughters of Temperance in 1849. When the Sons of Temperance refused Anthony the right to speak at the state convention in 1853 because she was a woman, she left the meeting and called her own. She founded the Women's State Temperance Society with Elizabeth Cady Stanton, whom she met in 1851 at an abolitionist meeting. Anthony and Stanton resigned from the organization after being criticized for their interest in women's rights.

The Anthony family became active in the abolitionist movement after moving to Rochester. Antislavery Quakers met at their farm almost every Sunday, where individuals such as Frederick Douglass and William Lloyd Garrison joined them on occasion. In 1854, Anthony devoted herself to the antislavery movement and became an agent in 1856 for the American Anti-Slavery Society.

Anthony and Stanton petitioned Congress for a constitutional amendment guaranteeing universal suffrage for former slaves and women. In 1863, Anthony and Stanton organized the Women's National Loyal League and petitioned for the Thirteenth Amendment outlawing slavery. She campaigned for the Fourteenth and Fifteenth Amendments, advocating full citizenship for former slaves and women, including the right to vote. Following the Civil War in 1865, Anthony concentrated almost exclusively on women's issues and women's suffrage.

Anthony and Stanton campaigned for more liberal divorce laws in New York. Largely due to their efforts,

*Susan B. Anthony was an early suffragist, abolitionist, and feminist who demanded equal rights for blacks and women in America. She posed for a photograph (above) by S.A. Taylor at the turn of the 19th century—sometime in the period of 1880 to 1906.*

the New York State Married Women's Property Bill became law in 1860. This allowed married women to own property, keep their own wages, and retain custody of their children. In 1866, Anthony and Stanton founded the American Equal Rights Association. Two years later, they began publishing the liberal weekly *The Revolution*, with the motto, "Men, their rights, and nothing more; women, their rights, and nothing less." The newspaper advocated an eight-hour day and equal pay for equal work. In the 1890s, Anthony served on the board of trustees of Rochester's State Industrial School and raised $50,000 in pledges to ensure the admittance of women to the University of Rochester; they were first admitted in 1900.

Anthony believed "that the right women needed above every other was the right of suffrage." In 1854, she traveled to all of New York's counties and around the country promoting women's suffrage legislation. The western United States, however, was more receptive to the idea of women's suffrage than other regions of the country. In 1890, Wyoming became the first state in the nation to allow women the right to vote. Utah and Colorado followed in the next decade. Anthony spent eight months campaigning for suffrage in California in 1896, but the measure failed.

On November 1, 1872, Anthony persuaded election inspectors in Rochester to register her to vote. She led a group of women, including three of her sisters, to vote in the presidential election. Two weeks later, she was arrested and charged with casting an illegal vote in a federal election. Anthony refused to pay her streetcar fare to the police station because she was "traveling under protest at the government's expense." She was arraigned and refused to pay for bail. She applied for *habeas corpus* but her lawyer paid the bail, keeping the case from reaching the Supreme Court. At her trial the judge instructed the jury to find her guilty without discussion. He fined her $100, compelled her to pay courtroom fees, but did not imprison her when she refused to pay the fine.

She explained, "May it please your honor, I will never pay a dollar of your unjust penalty." No attempt was made to force her to do so and the fine remains unpaid to this day. Afterward, she campaigned earnestly for a federal women's suffrage amendment through the National Woman Suffrage Association (1869–90) and the National American Woman Suffrage Association (1890–1906).

Anthony gave her last public speech on her 86th birthday and ended by declaring, "Failure is impossible!" Less than a month later, on March 13, Anthony died in her Rochester home. Ten thousand mourners attended her funeral. Anticipating her death some years earlier, Anthony requested: "When there is a funeral, remember that there should be no tears ... go on with the work." In 1920, 100 years after Anthony's birth, the Nineteenth Amendment to the U.S. Constitution was ratified, extending the vote to women.

Anthony's unrelenting campaign for women's rights can be seen as an extension of Enlightenment doctrine of equal rights. She criticized the male establishment for its acceptance of slavery, the exploitation of the poor by the liquor interests, the persecution of women through unjust marriage and divorce laws, and the exclusion of women and blacks from suffrage. Anthony clearly belonged on the radical side of mid- and late-19th century politics in America.

**SEE ALSO**

*Volume 1 Left:* Stanton, Elizabeth Cady; Suffragists; Constitutional Amendments; Voting, Unrestricted.
*Volume 2 Right:* Feminism.

**BIBLIOGRAPHY**

Rheta Childe Door, *Susan B. Anthony: The Woman Who Changed the Mind of a Nation* (Frederick A. Stokes, 1928); Ann D. Gordon, ed., *The Selected Papers of Elizabeth Cady Stanton and Susan B. Anthony* (Rutgers University Press, 1998); Judith E. Harper, *Susan B. Anthony: A Biographical Companion* (ABC-CLIO Publishers, 1998); Linda K. Kerber and Jane Sherron De Hart, *Women's America: Refocusing the Past* (Oxford University Press, 1995); S. Michele Nix, ed., *Women at the Podium: Memorable Speeches in History* (Harper Resource, 2000); Judith and William Serrin, ed., *Muckraking: The Journalism That Changed America* (The New Press, 2002);

Geoffrey C. War, *Not for Ourselves Alone: The Story of Elizabeth Cady Stanton and Susan B. Anthony* (Alfred A. Knopf, 1999).

DANA MAGILL
TEXAS CHRISTIAN UNIVERSITY

# Anti-Globalization

FIRST INVESTIGATED by Canadian scholar Marshall McLuhan in 1964 and then further explored during the 1970s, globalization is the process by which world populations become increasingly interconnected, both culturally and economically. Proponents consider it a positive process in the long run, though short-term globalization can cause dire effects in specific populations. Anti-globalization is globalization's antithesis: The globalization process from the left-wing perspective is often perceived as alienating, as creating standardization throughout the globe and reinforcing economic inequalities between developed and underdeveloped countries.

Advanced capitalism, enhanced by technological developments such as the internet and electronic business transactions, is seen as stretching social, political, and economic activities across the borders of communities, nations, and continents. The process of globalization increases the stream of trade, investment, migration, and cultural communication. Global connections and circulation of goods, ideas, capital, and people have deepened the impact of distant events on everyday life. Thus, globalization entails two related phenomena: the development of a global economy and the rise of a global culture.

Critics of globalization point out that the new global economy involves a discrepancy between a huge displacement of production workers, often to developing countries where labor is cheaper, child labor can be exploited, and workers' rights may be nonexistent. Big corporations assign the material tasks of producing their goods to third world contractors whose only aim is to send back the order on time and preferably under budget, no matter how many underpaid hours their workers put in. Meanwhile the corporations' headquarters, where all the marketing strategies and the commercial directives are issued and where the well-paid jobs are, firmly remain in the West. Far left anti-globalization forces have theorized that large corporations, which are accountable only to their shareholders, are perceived to have replaced governments and effectively become global entities unto themselves. This condition has been called "corporate rule." In her anti-global manifesto *No Logo* (2000), Canadian journalist and activist Naomi Klein exposes the "unbranded points of origin of brand-name goods," stressing the exploitative nature of transnational corporations, the leading actors in the globalization process:

"The travels of Nike sneakers have been traced back to the abusive sweatshops of Vietnam, Barbie dolls' little outfits back to the child laborers of Sumatra, Starbuck's lattes back to the sun-scorched coffee fields of Guatemala, and Shell's oil back to the polluted and impoverished villages of the Niger Delta." In addition, while supporters of neoliberal global economics claim that lifting trade barriers and tariffs will necessarily favor poorer countries, critics counter that weaker economies are not yet ready to compete with the more industrialized countries. Labor movements and trade unions are particularly concerned that economic globalization will increasingly shift manufacturing jobs from advanced countries to economies where labor is cheap. According to the perverse logic of capital, corporations have engaged in a competition to seek out the cheapest production location.

Yet, as Klein points out, "the triumph of economic globalization has inspired a wave of techno-savvy investigative activists who are as globally mined as the corporations they track." Since the mid-1990s, the number of public investigations in corporate crime has increased exponentially, so much so that American Studies Professor Andrew Ross dubbed the period between 1995–96 as "The Year of the Sweatshop." Corporations involved in this massive exposure of exploitative labor practices included Gap, Wal-Mart, Guess, Nike, Mattel, and Disney.

In addition, several human rights groups such as Amnesty International, PEN, and Human Rights Watch and green organizations are investigating the links between transnational corporations and totalitarian regimes in developing countries. Before the mid-1990s, Western investments in the third world were considered as a first step to fight poverty. By the end of the 1990s, corporate investment in the third world included alliances with many governments in the developing world, alliances predicated on human rights violations.

Anti-globalization forces propose that totalitarian governments are willing to protect profitable investments by disregarding human rights violations against their people by corporations, while Western corporations accept the political repression and the elimination of all opposition organized in some countries in order to protect their own global marketability.

Therefore, to anti-global activists, the equation between increased foreign investment and increased democracy in developing countries is a blatant lie. On the contrary, they point out, "Big Business" frequently relies on local police and armed forces to control demonstrations and to evict or move peasants from lands needed by foreign conglomerates. Nobel Prize winner Aung San Suu Kyi, who was imprisoned for six years following the refusal of the Burmese military regime to acknowledge her overwhelming victory in the 1990 election, explicitly condemned the foreign companies operating in Burma and profiting from institutionalized forced labor: "Foreign investors should realize there could be no economic growth and opportunities in Burma until there is agreement on the country's political future."

## KEN SARO-WIWA

Still more important for the development of the human rights critique of global economy was the execution in 1995 of Nigerian author Ken Saro-Wiwa, who had taken a leading position in the Ogoni people's campaign against the human and ecological destruction of the Niger Delta due to Royal Dutch/Shell's oil-drilling. The Nobel Prize nominee and his Movement for the Survival of the Ogoni People (MOSOP) had blamed the Nigerian dictator, General Sani Abacha, for the murder and torture of thousands Ogoni to silence their protest of Shell's exploitation of their land. Yet, they had also denounced with equal force Shell's use of Nigerian police forces as a private militia and its financial backing for a totalitarian regime. At his trial, that would end with the death penalty, Saro-Wiwa told the court that "Shell is here on trial. ...The company has, indeed, ducked this particular trial, but its day will surely come."

The Saro-Wiwa incident was a powerful catalyst for the emergence of anti-globalization activism, as it showed the interconnection among issues of social justice, environmental exploitation, and labor policy. In addition, because Saro-Wiwa was a writer, his trial was also perceived by many literary authors as a denial of the freedom of self-expression. Nadine Gordimer went as far as saying that "to buy Nigeria's oil under the conditions that prevail is to buy oil in exchange for blood. Other people's blood; the exaction of the death penalty on Nigerians." Saro-Wiwa's execution showed that movements with different aims and partially different constituencies could join forces on an anti-global agenda. As Naomi Klein makes clear, "In Saro-Wiwa, civil liberties came together with anti-racism; anti-capitalism with environmentalism; ecology with labor rights. The bright yellow bulbous logo of Shell—Saro-Wiwa's Goliath of an opponent—became a common enemy for all concerned citizens." Appropriately, it was Saro-Wiwa's brother who summarized the multiple significances of the author's execution: "In this case, at the twilight of the 20th century, Shell has been caught in the triangle of ecosystem destruction, human rights abuse, and health impairment of the Ogoni people."

## CULTURAL IMPERIALISM

Parallel to economic globalization is the phenomenon of cultural globalization. Its supporters claim that the rise of a global culture entails multiculturalism and a hybridization of national cultures. Yet, critics of cultural globalization point out its darker side, claiming that cultural globalism destroys all local traditions and regional distinctions, creating in their place a homogenized world culture.

According to this view, human experience everywhere is under threat of becoming essentially the same. Everywhere in the world people shop in similar malls, eat the same chicken nuggets at McDonald's restaurants, drink Starbucks coffee, watch the hottest TV shows or the ultimate Hollywood blockbuster, or listen to the latest report from the same news channels. Not surprisingly, the disparaging name for this phenomenon is "McDonaldization," because anti-global activists perceive that the spread of McDonald's restaurants entails a parallel spread of uniform values.

What is passed off as world culture, its detractors claim, is really the Americanization of world culture. Local cultures are replaced by a uniform and single culture, dictated by the same powerful corporations that control the global economy. Though there is much evidence for this cultural imperialism, Arjun Appadurai cautions us not to underestimate the power of local cultures to react to this phenomenon. He also stresses that there are various alternative fears to that of Americanization: "it is worth noticing that for the people of Irian Jaya, Indonesianization may be more worrisome than Americanization, as Japanization may be for Koreans, Indianization for Sri Lankans, Vietnamization for Cambodians, Russianization for the people of the Baltic republics," and adds "one man's imagined community is another man's political prison."

Anti-global theorists stress how corporations have hijacked culture and education through their aggressive marketing practices. Hidden behind slogans that stress the rhetoric of the global village (Levi's "a world-wide style culture" or IBM's "solutions for a small planet"), cultural choices are narrowing in the face of corporate censorship, and public space is increasingly occupied by brand advertising. While the production of goods is contracted to underpaid workers who may be assembling computers but do not know how to operate them, the campaigns that market these products are decided in the offices of the developed West.

Anti-global activists have said that the real work of corporations does not lie so much in manufacturing as in the marketing process, in the production of an image for their brands. Scott Bedbury, head of marketing at Nike and later Starbucks, has explained the process through which corporations associate an image to their products: "A great brand raises the bar—it adds a greater sense of purpose to the experience, whether it's the challenge to do your best in sports and fitness or the affirmation that the cup of coffee you're drinking really matters." Corporations have thus become producers of lifestyles.

## UNIFORMITY

In spite of appealing multiethnic images and slogans that stress the consumers' right to choose what they please, cultural globalization does not welcome diversity. On the contrary, the process is predicated on a considerable reduction of available choices, so much so that Klein has pointed out "the odd double vision of vast consumer choice coupled with Orwellian new restrictions on cultural production and public space." Independent shops are replaced by chain stores and "options for unbranded alternatives, for open debate, criticism and uncensored art—for real choice—are facing new and ominous restrictions." To sustain their claims that globalization has to fight local traditions and regional tastes, critics of globalization quote Theodore Levitt's essay "The Globalization of Markets." In his program for global marketing, Levitt distinguishes between multinational corporations, which adapt in different ways to the countries where they operate "at high relative costs," and global corporations, which remain always the same in all regions of the globe.

Levitt celebrates the achievement of the global corporation: it "operates with resolute consistency—at low relative costs—as if the entire world (or major regions of it) were a single entity; it sells the same things in the same way everywhere. Ancient differences in national tastes or modes of doing business disappear."

SEATTLE 1999

The anti-globalization movement was thrown from the fringes to the center of political debate thanks to the protests in Seattle against the World Trade Organization in November 1999. Since then, major financial and commercial summits of the G8, the International Monetary Fund, the World Economic Forum and the World Bank were disrupted by mass demonstrations in the streets of Washington D.C., Genoa (Italy), and Prague (Czech Republic).

In the activists' view, Genoa was a particularly significant example of state violence and the need of authorities to build fortresses to protect their debates, which mirrors the international creation of a global security state where rich nations are safely fenced off against poor countries. The decision of the right-wing Italian government to ban certain parts of the city to the demonstrators gave rise to popular anger. Riots exploded throughout the city and evidence suggests they were fomented by the police, which infiltrated armed criminals within the demonstrators' ranks. The Italian police also shot and killed Carlo Giuliani, a 23-year-old demonstrator.

Since January 2001, annual counter-meetings have been held at the World Social Forum in Porto Alegre, Brazil, under the slogan "Another World Is Possible." Anti-global activists have attracted sympathies of left-wing political parties such as the Brazilian Workers' Party (PT) and the Italian Party of Communist Refoundation (PRC) and Left Democrats (DS). Alternative media and communication networks have been established to turn the internet, one of the tools that makes globalization feasible, into a powerful anti-global weapon.

Yet, perhaps, as many important activists have pointed out, the label of anti-global is an ironic misnomer for people who are closely tied together across nationality, race, class, and gender. To the corporate world, anti-global activists are arguing for fragmentation and radical power dispersal. This attitude is best represented in the words of the Zapatista spokesperson Subcomandante Marcos, whose movement is taken as an ideal blueprint for many anti-global militants: "Marcos is gay in San Francisco, black in South Africa, an Asian in Europe, a Chicano in San Ysidro, an anarchist in Spain, a Palestinian in Israel, a Mayan Indian in the streets of San Cristobal, a Jew in Germany, a Gypsy in Poland, a Mohawk in Quebec, a pacifist in Bosnia, a single woman on the subway at 10 at night, a peasant without land, a gang member in the slums, an unemployed worker, an unhappy student and, of course, a Zapatista in the mountains."

SEE ALSO

*Volume 1 Left:* Protests, Left; Democratic Party.
*Volume 2 Right:* Globalization; Republican Party; Hegemony.

BIBLIOGRAPHY

A. Appadurai, *Modernity at Large: Cultural Dimensions of Globalization* (University of Minnesota Press, 1996); Z. Bauman, *Globalization: The Human Consequences* (Columbia University Press, 1998); M. Hardt and A. Negri, *Empire* (Harvard University Press, 2002); F. Jameson and M. Miyoshi, *The Cultures of Globalization* (Duke University Press, 1998); N. Klein, *No Logo* (Flamingo, 2000); N. Klein, *Fences and Windows: Dispatches from the Front Lines of the Globalization Debate* (Flamingo, 2002); J. Mander and E. Goldsmith, *The Case against the Global Economy* (Sierra Club Books, 1996); W. I. Robinson, *Promoting Polyarchy: Globalization, U. S. Intervention, and Hegemony* (Cambridge University Press, 1996); A. Ross, *No Sweat: Fashion, Free Trade, and the Rights of Garment Workers* (Verso, 1997); A. Ross and K. Ross, *Anti-Americanism* (New York University Press, 2004); G. Ritzer, *The McDonaldization of Society: An Investigation into the Changing Character of Contemporary Social Life* (Pine Forge Press, 1996); J. Smith, R. Pagnucco, and C. Chatfield, eds., *Transnational Movements and Global Politics* (Syracuse University Press, 1997); J. Stiglitz, *Globalization and Its Discontents* (W. W. Norton, 2003); J. Tomlinson, *Globalization and Culture* (University of Chicago Press, 1999).

LUCA PRONO, PH.D.
UNIVERSITY OF NOTTINGHAM, UNITED KINGDOM

# Argentina

THE LEFT IN ARGENTINA includes different groups that have reacted against traditional reactionary forces. These elements can be seen in social movements starting in the 1880s until the return to democracy in 1983. However, these movements also had the counterpoint of several crises in 1922, 1952, 1956, 1959, 1962, 1966 and 1975, characterized by military coups d'etat. Thus, the left in Argentina is represented by its attempts to react to the constant challenges of the right.

After Argentine independence in 1810, groups continued to struggle to establish a constitution and to lead revolts whenever their interests were contradicted by the ruling elite. After the conservatism of President Guillermo Rosas and the Paraguay War between 1865 and 1870, younger intellectuals began to advocate a new movement in Argentine history, which would be called the "generation of the 1880s." At the same time, immigrants who came from Europe brought their socialist and anarchist experiences, while the military middle class questioned traditionalism and adopted positivism in order to propose the modernization of the country.

One important result of the 1880s is the foundation of the Radical Civic Union Party (Unión Cívica Radical) in 1891. The Socialist Party was founded in 1896. Anarchists articulated their forces with groups that founded the Workers Federation (FORA). However, the influence of these groups was better felt during a series of crises between 1907 and 1913, which were recorded by the leftist newspaper *La Crítica*. These groups were motivated even more by World War I and the Russian Revolution.

Within this context, the election of Hypólito Yrigoyen as president in 1916 became a historical mark for the left in Argentina. Yrigoyen and the Unión Cívica Radical performed a series of social reforms that provoked the reaction of the right. Yrigoyen was reelected in 1928, but the political situation had worsened and a military coup took him out of office. The articulation between the army and Catholic groups was responsible for the imposition of an authoritarian nationalism from 1930 to 1943.

One of the most peculiar and important phenomena in politics in Argentina is the nationalist populism of Juan Perón, which can be related to both the right and the left. Peronism was able to involve liberals, socialists, and the labor movement for its causes—at the same time that it had the support of oligarchism, integralism, fascism, and authoritarianism. Perón was part of the government that assumed power in 1943, had spent some time in Europe, and was influenced by the experiences he observed in Spain, Italy, France, and Germany.

Moreover, he became an advocate of the "shirtless masses" (*descamisados*) and the working class in Argentina. Based on this political platform, he was elected in 1946 and began to promote a series of measures akin to socialist ideas. What brought him closer to the left was his alliance with the worker's movement. Furthermore, Perón upheld a very liberal agenda in opposition to the Catholic Church, which then provoked a reaction

against his government, leading to another coup by the military in 1955.

The 1960s started with the impact of the Cuban Revolution, Marxism, and anti-Peronism. The guerrillas promoted by the Argentinean Ernesto Che Guevara in Bolivia motivated several groups. However, it was only after 1966 that these movements began to express their ideas and actions more radically—motivated also by yet a new coup by the military. In 1968, leftist groups led a series of protests in the streets. In 1969, the General Union of Workers called a general strike and university students in Cordoba organized a demonstration, which became known as Cordobazo.

These initiatives continued until 1975. Sectors of the church, related to Liberation Theology, sided with the poor and made vindications on their behalf. The Peronist Youth became a radical arm of Peronism, from which other groups also originated, such as the Fuerzas Armadas Peronistas, the Descamisados, the Armed Revolutionary Forces, and Armed Forces for Liberation. Some of their actions included the kidnapping and murder of important politicians and businessmen. But the most famous of them were the Montoneros, who continued to support the guerrillas.

Political parties, guerrillas, and those influenced by the action of human rights groups began to question the military modus operandi. Between 1976 and 1983, a Dirty War promoted by the military government murdered some 40,000 Argentineans suspected of opposing the government. The movement, Madres de la Plaza de Mayo, a group of mothers of those who disappeared (*desaparecidos*), conducted daily manifestations and brought more attention to the oppression of the military dictatorship. This group was supported by human rights organizations, such as the Movimiento Ecuménico por los Derechos Humanos (MEDH) and the Nobel Peace Prize winner Adolfo Pérez Esquivel. After the humiliating defeat of the Argentinean army by the British in a war over the possession of the Falkland/Malvinas Islands in 1982, there was a call for the return to a democratic government and for putting the military leaders on trial. The election of President Raul Alfonsin in 1983 marked the coming to power of a mitigated left, which is described as a political humanism.

Politics in democratic Argentina has been developed according to partisan lines, whereby the main protagonists are radicalism and Peronism. After the long period of neoliberalism under President Carlos Menem (during the 1990s) and a series of economic crises, President Nestor Kirchner was elected and adopted a new form of populism. Since these crises have brought about a series of social problems and the spread of poverty, new groups have turned toward the left, including the *piqueteros*—people unemployed or sympathetic to socialist causes, who led public manifestations in the streets of Argentinean cities and actions against globalization at the beginning of the 21st century, leaving an open venue for the left in Argentina.

## SEE ALSO

*Volume 1 Left:* Guevara, Che; Socialism; Communism; South America; Populism.
*Volume 2 Right:* Argentina; Peronism; South America.

## BIBLIOGRAPHY

Aldo Buntig, *El catolicismo popular en América Latina* (Buenos Aires, Bonnum, 1969); Enrique Dussel, *Historia de la Filosofía y Filosofía de la Liberación* (Nueva América, Bogotá, 1994); Richard Gillespie, *Soldados de Perón: Los Montoneros* (Buenos Aires, Grijalbo, 1987); Daniel James, *Resistance and Integration. Peronism and the Argentine Working Class, 1946–76* (Cambridge University Press, 1988); David Rock, *Argentina, 1516–1987: From Spanish Colonization to Alfonsin* (University of California Press, 1987); Luis A. Romero, *Breve Historia Contemporánea de la Argentina* (Buenos Aires, FCE, 1994).

AMOS NASCIMENTO
METHODIST UNIVERSITY OF PIRACICABA, BRAZIL

# Asia

ASIA IS THE LARGEST of the six continents, occupying a third of the world's land space and containing about two-thirds of the world's population. In Greek mythology, Asia was a water-nymph, the daughter of Oceanus and Tethys; the continent Asia was supposedly named after her. According to one version, fabulous Asia was a wife of Prometheus. Another legend allegorizes her as mother of Prometheus and Atlas. Asia may have been the leader of the Okeanides, who carried rain to the Asian mainland.

Notions of Asia as an integrated unit reflect an inherently Western view of the world, but even in ordinary language, Asia designates large geographic areas that house diverse political entities and their people, with drastically different cultures and religions, and unevenly developed (or undeveloped) economies and political systems. In reality, Asia is too immense, complex, and diverse to only allow a cursory view of it.

The continent of Asia is defined by subtracting Europe and Africa from the Eurasia-African great land masses. Asia is bordered on the southwest by Africa in the Suez. The boundary between Asia and Europe runs through the Dardanelles, the Sea of Marmara, the Hellespontus, the Black Sea, the Caucasus humps, the Caspian Sea, the Ural River, and the Ural Mountains to Novaya Zemlya. About 50 states and bodies politic have Asian locations in whole or in part.

## EASTERN DESPOTISM

Three of four large communities that arose between 8000 and 6000 B.C.E. and generated the first states were situated in the Asian major river valleys of the Tigris, the Indus, and the Huang Ho. The fourth one, in the Nile in Africa, was close to Asia. That is why Asia embodied what became known as the ancient societies of the East and become synonymous with the East (or Orient). Asia has seen the rise and fall of many civilizations, from Akkaida in Mesopotamia to the Moghal empire in India. The states of the ancient East were the earliest slave-owning ones. They differed from the later Greece and Rome of antiquity.

In the East, the slaves were not the main productive force of the society. They were not producers of material goods. The people who were formally considered free were employed in agriculture and handicraft. The land in the East belonged to the state or was a state-communal or common property. The political system in Asia had a special form of Eastern despotism, that is, the inhabitants of the state were absolutely rightless before the authority.

The causes of such peculiarities can be explained by the existence of the commune system, the root of leftist political philosophy in Asia. The overwhelming number of inhabitants of the ancient East were engaged in agriculture. "The communal conditions for real appropriation through labor such as the irrigation systems (very important among the Asian peoples) ... will then appear as the work of the higher unity—the despotic government—which is poised above the lesser communities," wrote Karl Marx in *Pre-Capitalist Economic Formations*.

In that way, the state tightened its grip over the commoners or cultivators and they practically lost their freedom. They were applied in constructing complicated irrigation systems, sanctuaries, and other megastructures. Unlike the slaves, it was a costless work force that needed neither to be dressed nor fed. In Asia the state had its special sphere of governing, the superintendency of public works. Such a system needed a considerable bureaucratic apparatus. "An economic function devolved upon all Asiatic governments, the function of providing public works," Marx added. The centralized state system of managing the economy came round.

So, the full division of society into an exploiting and an exploited class, a general form of slavery, and a fully developed state-apparatus of force were the most important features of this Asiatic mode of production theory.

## EASTERN STAGNATION

There were no private feudal fees (manors) in the East. The territory of the state was the common fief of the ruling class. The state was seeking for appropriation as much surplus produce as possible. Such a political system was called "total slavery" by Marx. In academic writings it is also called Eastern despotism. That sustainable system existed unchanged for many centuries. The economic development of Asian countries almost stopped. The European peoples could outproduce the countries of the East in economic development; this phenomenon came to be known as the Eastern Stagnation.

The main reason for it was the fact that the individual interests were subordinated to the social interest, that is, the interest of the commune, caste, and the state. The stationary character of Asia "is fully explained by two mutually dependent circumstances: 1) the public works were the business of the central government; 2) beside these, the whole empire, not counting the few larger towns, was resolved into villages, which possessed a completely separate organization and formed a little world in themselves. I do not think one could imagine a more solid foundation for the stagnation of Asiatic despotism," Marx wrote in a letter to Friedrich Engels. Private initiative is impossible without free possession. That is why any entrepreneur initiative was dejected. The commune implies a large number of traditions when every action is predetermined by the customs and strict rules.

There is no assent among left-wing scholars concerning the issue of Asiatic mode of production. On the one hand, Marx is the principal inventor of the term. On the other hand, some neo-Marxists, especially Gunder Frank, argue that there is no basis for the latter-day European denigration of Asians as having allegedly had and been held back by some Asian mode of production (Marx), or hydraulic/bureaucratic society (Wittfogel) or the lack of rationality or even irrationality

(Weber, Sombart); but rather a redistributive (Polanyi), or some other traditional (Lerner, Rostow) society.

In the 16th to 18th centuries, the East, represented by the developed and civilized societies like China, India, and Japan, was not poorer than Europe. Moreover, it was much richer. Gunder Frank sees the reasons for Asia's further lagging behind in the fact that Europeans managed to use "American money" (the gold robbed in America) against it.

## COLONIALISM AND DECOLONIZATION

Either as a result of Asian economic and social backwardness, or because the Europeans outproduced Asians through the industrial revolution, almost all Asia was subjected to imperial control by European nations.

The European colonization in Asia started from the formation of closed administrative enclaves in alien territories. Those autonomous territories imitated the parent state and were closely connected with and supported by it. Such enclaves could be formed and were created only by the representatives of such countries in which private entrepreneurial activity was officially flourishing. That is why the economic colonies as trade factories were formed almost only by Europeans. The Portuguese were the first in Ceylon (1505) and Macau (1557). In the late 16th and early 17th centuries, the English, the Dutch, and the French began to undertake colonization of Asia through the agency of chartered companies.

The Dutch and the British East India Companies, at least up to the 17th century, retained the capitalist enterprises with certain administrative functions. The right to wage wars and have armies made the companies authoritative political powers commensurable with the local state units. European merchant venturers differed greatly from local tradesmen in their intention for self-organizing under the support of the mother country. They constantly broadened their free rein and sphere of control. In that way, the colonial trade was being transformed into colonial political expansion, which could already be felt in India in the 18th century and became evident across the whole of Asia in the 19th century.

From the point of view of the colonized peoples, colonialism was a brusque interference of the foreign self-seeking minority backed by force of arms. Those interventions were aimed at getting profit from the trade and making the indigenous population work for the use of invaders. The trade, accompanied by the exploitation of aboriginals, was not a European invention.

The economic strategy essential for the relationship between colonies and great powers was known as mercantilism (a government regulatory trade strategy for accumulating state wealth and power by encouraging exports and discouraging imports). Colonies were desirable in this respect because they guaranteed exclusive access to unused markets and sources of cheap raw materials and direct sources of precious metals. Each European great power was determined to monopolize as many overseas mercantile opportunities as possible.

The conquering of a number of Asian territories was a bloody process. The second wave of imperialism washed over the world, including Asia, beginning in the 1870s and extending until the outbreak of World War I. In 1916, the leader of Russian Marxists, Vladimir Lenin, argued that military expansion abroad was naturally produced by the monopoly stage of capitalism. Lenin put forward the idea of self-determination of the oppressed colonial peoples. He concluded that the movement of national liberation as natural ally of the working-class struggle against imperialism was the only way to put an end to capitalism.

Liberals regarded the new imperialism not as a product of capitalism as such, but rather as a response to certain maladjustments within the capitalist system that could be corrected. The history of capitalist colonial exploitation of India, Indonesia, Indochina, among others, made the necessity for their eventual national liberation evident. Nevertheless, impartially, Europe's colonial penetration into Asian countries operated as a progressive force. The external capitalist influencing them could serve to break stagnant social forms that blocked further development and provide the material preconditions for historical advance.

## ANTI-IMPERIALISM

The climate of opinion changed definitely toward anti-imperial when the 1918 Versailles peace settlement that ended World War I embraced the principle of national self-determination under pressure of U.S. President Woodrow Wilson. Though the idea did not become an immediate reality, the territories previously controlled by defeated Germany and the Ottoman Empire were transferred under League of Nations auspices to countries that would govern them as mandated territories pending their eventual self-rule. In the Middle East, France got the mandate for Syria, and Britain assumed it for Iraq and Transjordan and Palestine.

Since the beginning of the 20th century, Asian nationalist and leftist parties started parliamentary and underground struggles against the colonial administrations. Asian participants (Wang Min, Katoyama Sen, and others) were some of the most active in the Comintern or Third International (1919–33), which was organized around communist ideology to protect Soviet Russia internationally and to help the communist parties in other countries to take power, without regard to nationality. Owing to capitalist influence from the West, Asian working classes developed into the wide social basis for anti-imperialist movements that brought their countries to independence after World War II.

The initial aggressor of World War II in Asia was Japan, which joined Germany and Italy in the Tripartite Alliance. Imperial Japanese occupied large territories of Indochina in September 1940. On December 7, 1941, it attacked the main American Pacific naval base, Pearl Harbor, and then moved on Hong Kong, Malaya, and the Philippines. Huge areas of East and Southeast Asia as well as most of Oceania fell under Japanese imperial control. In the decisive battle at Midway in 1942, U.S. forces repelled the Japanese and thereafter the Allies began to drive Japanese imperialism back, eventually defeating the country in August 1945.

After the end of World War II, imperialism was viewed with growing international hostility. The peoples of Asia, inspired by half a century of ideological and political redefinition around a new nationalism, revolted after 1945. The local political leaders who dominated the region both during and after the war promoted state-based nationalisms that broke with and were hostile to existing identities but served their objective of taking control of the bureaucratic systems of the prewar colonial states and using them to fulfill modernizing agendas. Colonialism and the United Nations Charter were increasingly recognized as incompatible, though independence was often slow and sometimes marked by prolonged conflict and war, like the colonial wars in Indochina that were waged by the French (1945–54) and the Americans (1965–73) against Vietnam.

The Cold War often complicated and hindered the transition to independence, but on the other hand the imperialist countries were weakened by the confrontation with the Soviet Union and its bloc. The colonial empires in Asia were the first to fall down. British India acquired the status of dominion in 1947, divided into Indian Union and Pakistan. Burma gained independence in 1948. Indonesia became free from Holland in 1949 and Malaya from Britain in 1957. Most Asian countries became a core of the nonalignment movement (NAM), which strengthened their political independence. Though NAM was officially formed in 1961, the starting point for it was the Bandung Conference (1955, Java), with leading roles taken by Sukarno (Indonesia), Jawaharlal Nehru (India), and Chou Enlai (People's Republic of China). After independence, everything was set for what Bandung called new developmentalism: independence, modernization, and industrialization. The strategic alliance between this movement and the Soviet Union enabled the latter to escape isolation.

## ASIA AND MODERNIZATION

When explaining the concept of modernization, its three main characteristics are usually presumed: 1) replacement of agrarian labor by industrial; 2) differentiation of the society into various spheres (economic, political, jural, cultural); and 3) shaping of the autonomous personality as the subject of society. The formation of this distinctiveness is taking place in a different way in the East, where the personality is formed in the framework of some corporation or other (commune, caste, ummah, sangh).

The modernization in Asia differs substantially from the Western one. It began later than in the West. The impetus for Asian modernization was exogenous. Western adepts of the modernization theory consider the countries of the first modernization wave the core of the world unity that was formed as the result of modernization. The orientalists who recognize modernization theory do agree that the world unity was formed at that period, but they are reluctant to accept the existence of its center.

The role of the political factor in Asian modernization was more significant than in the West. More often than not it was determinative. That was not surprising. The initial point for spontaneous modernization was weak; because of the people's social differentiation, activity was lower than in the West, and national unity was weaker. Traditionalist conservatism was stronger. The colonial inheritance aggravated the situation. Hence, the important role of political power when the impulse comes from the state. The role of the state as an organizer of modernization was more important the later a traditional society dashed toward industrialization.

Such a phenomenon as developmental authoritarianism is connected with this. There exist many ways of implementing authoritarianism. The developmental type is distinguished among others due to its orientation to the progress guided by political power. Unlike

political democracy, developmental authoritarianism is defined by the following characteristics: 1) The domination of state power over society; 2) the supremacy of executive power over the other branches of power; and 3) strict limitations (in different forms) over legal opposition. These features are characteristic of any authoritarianism, including the developmental type. But at some stage, those traits evolve into relatively soft rationalized forms. Authoritarianism really seeking modernization cannot help looking for social pillars beyond the traditional ruling groups and broadening its support.

The height of authoritarian power in the political life of third-world Asian countries was from the 1960s to the 1970s. But on the threshold of the 1980s, a tendency for transition from authoritarian to more democratic forms of government occurred. The causes lie probably in the fact that any authoritarian rule, even the most enlightened, contains shortcomings in terms of adequate reflection of society's interests and the autonomy of personality. As for developmental authoritarianism, it is a case study of solving the economic and social tasks of modernization while undermining the ground of its own existence, whether it likes it or not.

## SEVEN REVOLUTIONS OF THE RISING EAST

For a half century of postcolonial development, the leading Asian countries gained worldwide success owing to seven interlocked revolutions that, according to Richard Halloran, became a source of Asia's new power. They are:

1) industrial revolution, which generated the dramatic economic growth achieved by Japan in the 1970s and 1980s; the four "East Asian tigers" (Korea, Taiwan, Hong Kong, and Singapore) in the 1980s and mid-1990s; and the three "aspiring tigers" (Thailand, Indonesia, and Malaysia) until the middle of 1997; and the revolutions which underlay Chinese and Indian leaps forward in the 1990s;

2) political revolution of the growing middle classes seeking a stronger say in the political system and the new generation of leaders;

3) demographic revolution in which young, educated, healthy people operate steel mills, telecommunication networks, and railroads, constituting up to 70 percent of the population;

4) green revolution in agricultural technologies that meant the ability of key Asian countries to feed themselves and even export some grain and rice;

5) revolution in nationalism, finding expression in greater national resilience, confidence, and self-assur-

ance, gained with economic achievements and increased prosperity and sometimes adverting to traditional religions as expression of patriotism;

6) revolution in internationalism, which turned Asians into more outward looking people, as trade and new technology seekers who want to achieve more from the world, and know how to do it in different ways, including demanding a greater voice in the United Nations;

7) revolution in military power or the acquisition of military strength because economic progress has provided the funds and now Asia has seven of the world's eight largest armed forces. China, India, and Pakistan are authorized nuclear powers while some others have nuclear weapons unofficially.

Asia is developing faster and becoming more powerful than the rest of the world. "Now the long-feared Asiatic colossus takes its turn as world leader, and we—the white race—have become the yellow man's burden. Let us hope that he will treat us more kindly than we treated him," expressed Gore Vidal in *The Decline and Fall of the American Empire* (1992).

One of the most controversial reasons that has been considered as the basis of Asian countries' achievements in the last quarter of the 20th century was that the success sprang from so-called Asiatic values, which were contrasted to Western values.

## ASIATIC VALUES

A vigorous discussion in the 1990s on the universal nature of rights and values, and whether these are compatible with the ethics and concepts of rights inherent in Asian peoples, has attracted the interest of national leaders and political scientists. According to Lee Kuan Yew (Singapore) and Mohadhir Mohammad (Malaysia), Asiatic values comprise collectivism and group interests instead of individuality; reliability toward community instead of individual rights and freedom; paternalistic, family-oriented, consensual, and clientelist political action instead of pluralism and democracy. Other attributes of Asian values include respect and acceptance of authority and social order; rating personal relations higher than personal qualities; harmony and consensus instead of discourse and confrontation, conflict, and competition; higher rating of ethics and morality before law.

Asian values also comprise business ethics: diligence, hard work, thrift and frugality, self-discipline, obedience, and patience. The rhetoric on specific Islamic values is similar. The defenders of the universality

of human rights and liberal opponents of the Asian values approach cite the fact that the most active prophets of Asian communitarianism are the top politicians from the region who pick and choose freely from other cultures, adopting whatever is in their political interest.

"They seem to have no qualms about embracing such things as capitalist markets and consumerist culture. What troubles them about the concept of human rights, then, turns out to have little to do with its Western cultural origin," explains Xiaorong Li, an expert on Asian values philosophy. Many practices that are considered traditionally Asiatic are, in fact, quite recent inventions, often deliberately constructed to serve particular ideological ends. The so-called Asian view creates confusion by collapsing community into the state, and the state into the current regime.

When such equations are drawn, any criticisms of the regime become crimes against the nation-state, the community, and the people. The Asian view, with its stand for "limited democracy" in Asian countries, relies on such a conceptual maneuver to dismiss individual rights that conflict with the regime's interest. Contrary to Asian values, individual freedom is not intrinsically opposed to and destructive of community. Free association, free expression, and tolerance are vital to the well-being of communities. In a liberal democratic society, a degree of separation between the state and civil society provides a public space for the flourishing of communities, Xiaorong Li argues. She calls the claim of the Asian view, that economic development rights have a priority over political and civil rights, a false dilemma.

The oppressors, according to human rights activists in Asia, are pursuing the aim of amassing wealth for themselves, and their declared project of enabling people to "get rich" may increase the disparity between the haves and the have-nots. Moreover, the most immediate victims of oppression—those subjected to imprisonment or torture—are often those who have spoken out against the errors or the incompetence of authorities who have failed to alleviate deprivation, or who in fact have made it worse.

National development is an altogether different matter from securing the economic rights of vulnerable members of society. Of course, such reasoning goes too far for those in Singapore, Malaysia, and Beijing, who saw a dangerous rebel in every democrat. These observations will be also disliked by unscrupulous Western businessmen, who prefer the combination of big money, weak unions, and authoritarian government to aggregate growth rates and amass profit. Some people argue that West and East do not nearly speak the same

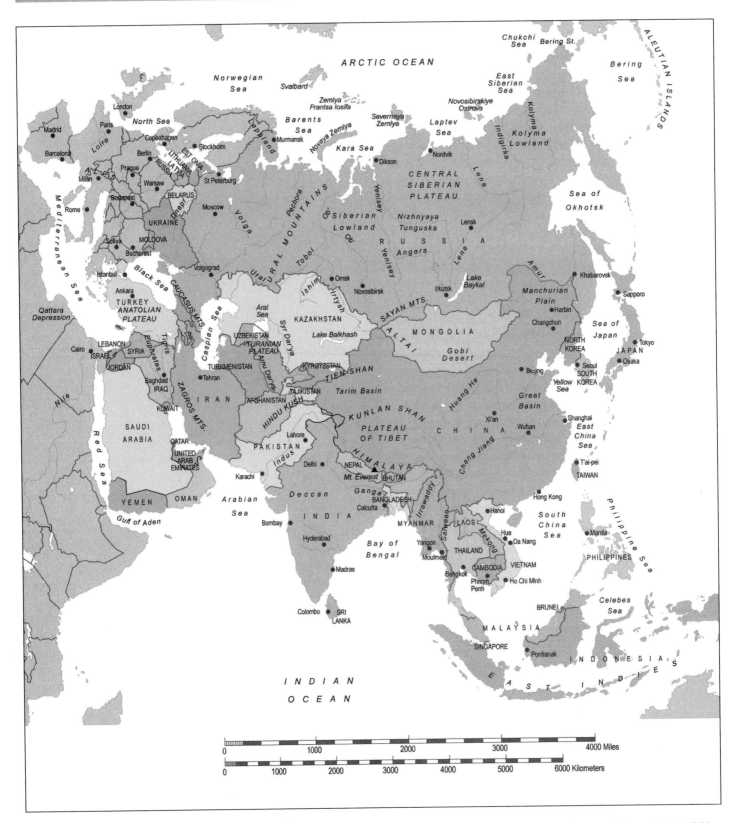

Asia has had a political left long associated with a communal structure, where the group's needs come ahead of the ambitions of the individual, but much debate has ensued as to why.

language, even when it is English. The discussed peculiarities of Asian capitalism were not an advantage but rather the course of serious damage manifested in the financial crisis of 1997–98.

## ASIAN FINANCIAL CRISIS

Triggered by the collapse of Thailand's baht currency on July 2, 1997, four economies that had high positive Gross Domestic Product (GDP) growth for several years before experienced negative growth (between 5 and 12 percent) in 1997 and 1998. Asset values in these crisis countries—Thailand, South Korea, Malaysia, and Indonesia—plummeted by about 75 percent due to currency depreciation, deflated equity, and property valuations. Averaging over the four economies, an asset worth $100 in June 1997 was worth only $25 a year later

Because of the currency crisis, East Asia had lost some $500 billion of purchasing power. Even those countries that were not in quite the same position as those four faced enormous difficulties. The crisis seriously endangered the livelihood of millions of people, causing untold misery and suffering. Massive ecological harm has also been done to the region.

While each country had its own peculiar characteristics, most leftist investigators blame crony and opaque manners of doing business in Asia most of all. The privileged groups of moguls operated in a close network consisting of themselves, the government, and the bureaucracy, receiving cheap loans and offering gifts, bribes, and rapid growth in return. This was built on borrowed money.

In Indonesia, for example, it was the friends and family of the nation's leader, President Suharto, who seemed to be the beneficiaries of such relations. Asian governments tended to give advantage to local firms, which obtained cheaper, state-subsidized supplies of capital while foreign firms were denied full market access. There was a general problem of over-lending with huge pyramids of bad debts, over-investment, and in some cases over-production. When the baht collapsed, international investors took flight and withdrew their capital. When capital is pulled out, it can cause a country to collapse completely. Enormous wealth has gone from East Asia as a result.

The explanation of what happened from the left point of view is evident. In the years of Cold War, the dictators of the region were the U.S. allies in combating communism. They were allowed to maintain their dictatorships and were supported in developing their illiberal crony capitalism or following the dependent capitalist development path. Central to U.S. strategy in the Asian financial crisis was the imposition of a specific neoliberal model of Asian economic restructuring. In the context of the crisis, state-directed and controlled forms of political economy have been pressured to liberalize. The transnational corporations and international banks supported such form of structural adjustment. The IMF presented the question as if there was no alternative to the orthodoxy of Wall Street and the so-called Washington consensus. The positive dimension of this ideology was that it gave identity and political direction to the processes of power, class formation, and restructuring. It was the crisis in favor of neoliberalists that resulted in shifting from state capitalism toward more free market systems, based on investor interests and the maximization of shareholder value. Neoliberals claim this system is more efficient. "What they fail to emphasize is how deregulation, privatization, and liberalization are a means of strengthening a particular set of class interests, principally the power of private investors. Structural adjustment allows for a redistribution of claims on future profit flows that enable foreign capital to gain power and control over regional development patterns," says Stephen Gill in *Monthly Review* (March, 1999).

## INTERNATIONAL RELATIONS IN ASIA

Owing to its surpassing size and number of inhabitants, Asia has always been an important continent in geopolitical terms. Constantly the major scene of international cooperation and conflicts, Asia was home to most wars of the last six decades: the Korean War (1950–53), three Arab-Israeli wars (1948–49, 1967, 1973), Jordan-Palestine armed conflict (1970), Vietnam-France war (1945–54), Vietnam and U.S. war (1965–73), three India-Pakistan armed conflicts (1947, 1965, 1971), China-India war (1962), China-Vietnam war (1979), Iran-Iraq war (1980–88), Indonesia and East Timor conflict (1975–2002), Lebanon-Israel-Syria (1976, 1982–83), the war in Afghanistan with the Soviet Union (1979–89) and American interventions, repelling the Iraqi occupation of Kuwait (1991), followed by the second Iraq-U.S. war with international participation (2002–).

Asian countries are members of a huge number of international organizations and also have their own regional cross-border institutions and forums. The most known among them are: the Association of Southeast Asian Nations (ASEAN); ASEAN Regional Forum (ARF); the Shanghai Forum of three Central Asian countries, China and Russia; and the Economic Cooperation Organization, which is comprised of the five Central Asian countries: Azerbaijan, Turkey, Iran, Afghanistan, and Pakistan. In Asia, there are 27 of 57 members of the Organization of the Islamic Conference (OIC); 8 of 11 members of the Organization of Petroleum Exporting Countries (OPEC); and 12 of 21 members of the Arab League.

**SEE ALSO**

*Volume 1 Left:* China, India, Japan; Communitarianism.
*Volume 2 Right:* Asia, China, India, Japan.

**BIBLIOGRAPHY**

Fernand Braudel, *Civilization and Capitalism* (Harper and Row, 1982); Timothy Brook, ed., *The Asiatic Mode of Production in China* (Sharpe, 1989); Michael Davis, ed., *Human Rights and Chinese Values* (Oxford University Press, 1995); Alan Dupont, "Is There any Asian Way?" *Survival* (v.1/38, 1996); Stephen Gill, "The Geopolitics of the Asian Crisis," *Monthly Review* (March 1999); Jurgen Habermas, "Modernity versus Postmodernity," J. C. Alexander and S. Seidmann, eds., *Culture and Society. Contemporary Debates* (Cambridge University Press, 1990); Karl Marx, *Pre-Capitalist Economic Formations* (International Publishers, 1964); Umberto Melotti, *Marx and the Third World* (Macmillan, 1972); David Kelly and Anthony Reid, eds., *Asian Freedoms: The Idea of Freedom in East and Southeast Asia* (Cambridge University Press, 1998); Brendan O'Leary, *The Asiatic Mode of Production: Oriental Despotism, Historical Materialism and Indian History* (Blackwell, 1989); Joseph S. Nye, Jr., "The Case for Deep Engagement," *American Foreign Policy 1997–98* (Dushkin-Brown & Benchmark, 1997); Richard Robison, Mark Beeson, Kanishka Jayasuriya, and Kim Hyuk-Rae, *Politics and Markets in the Wake of the Asian Crisis* (Routledge, 1999); Amartya Sen, "Our Culture, Their Culture," *The New Republic* (April 1, 1996); Han Sung-Joo, ed., *Changing Values in Asia* (Japan Center for International Exchange, Tokyo, 1999); Julian Weiss, *The Asian Century* (Reed Business Information, 1989); Karl August Wittfogel, *Oriental Despotism* (Yale University Press, 1957).

IGOR CHARSKYKH
DONETSK NATIONAL UNIVERSITY, UKRAINE

# Australia

AUSTRALIA HAS A FEDERAL SYSTEM of government, which means there is both a national and a second level of government, the state and territorial authorities. It is a liberal democratic government and its structure is a hybrid, reflecting the influence of both the British parliamentary model and the American presidential model. The British queen is the head of state and the governor general represents the monarch in her absence (which is most of the time). The head of state is a mostly symbolic position. The national parliament is bicameral, with a House of Representatives and a Senate. Like a parliamentary system, there is a blending of the legislative and executive branches; there is cabinet solidarity and responsible government; there is strict party discipline. Australia has a written constitution. The date of elections is not fixed, but there is a maximum length to a term (and different terms for both houses) and an election must be called before the end of the term. The individual states also have constitutions and these documents may be amended in most parts by the state legislature without the express consent of the people.

The Australian party system is theoretically a multi-party system. In actuality, it is a strong bipolar party system, essentially a two-party system. The Liberal Party is a center-right party and the National Party is also a center-right party and together they act as a coalition to counter the center-left Labor Party. All of the main parties differ more with respect to social policy than economic policy.

The Australian Labor Party (ALP) is the oldest party in Australia politics, dating back to 1891 and formed in the colonies prior to federation. In the first election in the Commonwealth of Australia, the ALP elected 16 members to the House of Representatives and 8 members to the Senate. The ALP first formed the government in May 1904 (in a parliamentary system, the party that wins the most number of seats forms the government, and it is the leader of that party who becomes the prime minister). This Labor government, however, was a minority government (this means that although the ALP won a plurality of seats, it did not win a majority of the seats, and this is an inherently unstable government) and the government only lasted three months.

Australia's ALP was the first successful labor party in the world. By 1915, it had formed the national government three times and it had governed in all the states, even if only for a brief time. The last Labor government lasted a record 13 years (from 1983 to 1996), and at the time of its defeat, Australia was left in a sound economic position. Australia had experienced over four years of sustained economic growth, low inflation, stable interest rates, and more than 2 million new jobs had been created.

The ALP was historically committed to socialist economic policies, including national wage fixing and a strong welfare system. The ALP did not try to nationalize private enterprise. There was an attempt to nationalize the banking system in the 1940s, but the High Court of Australia ruled this move was unconstitutional. Since the 1970s, under party leader Gough Whitlam, the ALP moved from describing itself as socialist to social democratic. In the 1980s, during the ALP's 13-year domination of national politics, the party pushed for the privatization of government enterprises and the deregulation of many tightly controlled industries—measures more closely identified with conservative politics, on the right side of center.

Over its long life, the ALP has suffered several splits within the party. In 1915, the party was divided over the issue of World War I conscription. In 1931, different economic remedies for the Depression split the party. In 1954, the party was fractured over the threat of communism. An anti-communist faction split to form the Democratic Labor Party (DLP), although this party ceased to exist after the 1974 national election. Into the 2000s, there are two factions within the ALP. The dominant faction is the Labor Right, dedicated to economic liberalism and social conservatism. The weaker faction is the Socialist Left, advocating interventionist policies and socialist economic policies.

The ALP's party constitution describes the party as "a democratic socialist party" that has "the objective of the democratic socialization of industry, production, distribution and exchange, to the extent necessary to eliminate exploitation and other anti-social features in these fields." The constitution lists goals that include: the redistribution of political and economic power; the social ownership of Australia's natural resources; the maintenance of and support for a competitive, nonmonopolistic private sector; the recognition and encouragement of the right of labor to organize; the abolition of poverty and the achievement of greater equality in the distribution of income, wealth, and opportunity; equal access and rights to employment and education; the recognition and protection of fundamental political and civil rights including freedom of expression, the press, assembly and association, conscience and religion, and the right to privacy; the elimination of both discrimination and exploitation on the grounds of class, race, sex, sexuality, religion, political affiliation, national origin, citizenship, age, disability, regional location, economic or household status; and recognition and encouragement of diversity of cultural expression and lifestyle within the Australian community.

Australia's left-wing politics, in practice and history, have not veered far from the center as the former British colony follows much in the political footsteps of its progenitors, the United States and Canada.

**SEE ALSO**

*Volume 1 Left:* Communism; United Kingdom; Labour Party, UK.
*Volume 2 Right:* Colonialism; Capitalism; Australia.

**BIBLIOGRAPHY**

Australian Labor Party, "History," www.alp.org.au (April 2004); Australian Labor Party, "National Constitution," www.alp.org.au (April 2004); Owen E. Hughes, *Australian Politics* (Palgrave Macmillan, 1995); Peter Beilharz, *Transforming Labor: Labor Tradition and the Labor Decade in Australia* (Cambridge University Press, 1994).

AMANDA BURGESS
WAYNE STATE UNIVERSITY

# Austria

THE AUSTRIAN LEFT, consisting of the Austrian Social Democratic Party (SDAP until 1934, SPO since 1945) and a fringe communist party (KPO), is intriguing because it calls into question the facile polarities of political terminology such as left versus right, working class versus middle class, and revolutionary versus reformist. In many ways, the Austrian left is somewhat of a paradox.

Rooted in the working-class movement of the 19th century, the SDAP/SPO has produced prominent leaders primarily from middle-class and often Jewish origin. Influenced by revolutionary Marxism, the SDAP/SPO has always been inspired by a strong ethical, democratic, and humanitarian spirit. At various junctures in its past, the Austrian left has found itself as a reformist movement with revolutionary pretensions (SDAP from 1889–1918), an establishment force defending the status quo (SDAP from 1918–34 and SPO from 1945 until today), and an outlawed party forced into exile and resistance (SDAP and KPO from 1934–45). Perhaps the best way to describe the Austrian left is a political movement dominated by the SDAP/SPO that has constantly negotiated a middle course between absolute political and economic ideals such as individualism versus collectivism, capitalism versus communism, and nationalism versus internationalism. In its efforts to forge an "Austro-reformist" or "third way" approach to past and contemporary problems, the SPO is sustained by its commitment to unity (the reason why the KPO has been a marginal force in Austrian politics) and its pragmatic orientation.

The capable leader and middle-class Jewish doctor Victor Adler founded the SDAP in 1889. Under Adler's stewardship, the SDAP placed a premium on party unity and organization, combining a revolutionary rhetoric with reformist actions or simply a revisionist Marxism. The SDAP led a successful campaign to institute universal male suffrage for parliamentary elections in 1905 and later extended the vote for women in 1919. Intellectuals such as Karl Renner and Otto Bauer have made important contributions to 20th-century socialist thought, which some scholars have identified as "Austro-Marxism." Theorizing on the role of nationality within culturally diverse political realms, Renner advocated for cultural autonomy of ethnic groups within a supra-national state, while Bauer envisioned the peaceful coexistence of national cultures in a united states of Europe. Bauer, who emphasized the party's Marxist orientation and its class-based politics, was the SDAP's most influential personality during the political turbulence of the 1920s and 1930s as Austria's fledgling First Republic (1919–34) set up by the SDAP crumbled under the onslaught of right-wing reactionary and fascist movements.

The shining light of these years was the municipal socialism of Red Vienna, which led to the construction of workers' apartments, hospitals, parks, schools, and recreational centers. Renner steered the party toward reformism by joining in coalition governments with bourgeois parties in the 1940s and 1950s in order to erect a social welfare state. Renner also moved the party beyond its working-class base to include middle-class salaried employees, culminating with the 1958 party program which heralded Austrian socialism as "the party of all those who work for a living." The 1960s was a period of malaise for the SPO until the ascension to power of a man of international stature, Bruno Kreisky. Kreisky rejuvenated the SPO by paying lip service to lofty socialist ideals of a classless society while governing from the center as Austria's prime minister from 1971–83, when the SPO enjoyed an absolute majority in parliament. The Kreisky governments placed great emphasis on quality-of-life issues such as education and the environment while aiming for greater economic performance and full employment. Franz Vranitzky—the first party chairman of working-class background (although he made a career as a banker)—led the SPO as party leader and prime minister in the 1980s and 1990s. Vranitzky embraced the privatization of state-owned industries amid complaints that the party became dominated by technocrats and a form of "pinstripe socialism."

Today, the SPO is a flexible left-of-center party committed to reforming the welfare state in order to preserve it. As a result, the Austrian left offers itself as a viable political alternative between American-style liberal capitalist democracy and collectivistic authoritarian communism.

## SEE ALSO

*Volume 1 Left*: Socialism; Communism; Germany.
*Volume 2 Right*: Austria; Fascism; Germany.

## BIBLIOGRAPHY

Helmut Gruber, *Red Vienna: Experiment in Working-Class Culture, 1919–34* (Oxford University Press, 1997); Charlie Jeffery, *Austrian Socialism in the Provinces 1918–34: Beyond Red Vienna* (Fairleigh Dickinson University Press, 1995); H. Pierre Secher, *Bruno Kreisky: Chancellor of Austria, A Political Biography* (Dorrance Publishing, 1994); Melanie A. Sully, *Continuity and Change in Austrian Socialism: The Eternal Quest for the Third Way* (Columbia University Press, 1982).

KEVIN J. CALLAHAN, PH.D.
SAINT JOSEPH COLLEGE

# B

## Bellamy, Edward (1850–1898)

EDWARD BELLAMY WAS born on March 26, 1850, in Chicope, Massachusetts. His father was a Baptist minister and his mother was the daughter of a minister. Both parents could trace their families to 17th-century New England roots. Bellamy appears to have had a relatively comfortable childhood, although his youth was overshadowed by the American Civil War.

In 1867, he attempted to enter the U.S. Military Academy at West Point, only to be rejected. After this disappointment, he studied literature for a year at Union College in Schenectady, New York, before making a trip to Europe. There, he studied the prosperous state china works in Dresden, Germany, and contrasted the conditions of its workers with the squalor experienced by England's working poor. Appalled by life in the English urban slums, he called the lot of factory workers "English serfdom." He became determined to make changes in society to better the lives of the poor but did not know how to go about it.

In 1869, Bellamy returned to the United States and studied law in a Springfield, Massachusetts, law firm, following the custom common at the time of "reading the law" under an experienced lawyer rather than studying at a law school. In June 1871, Bellamy was admitted to the bar and opened his law office, but after taking a single case he abandoned the legal profession and turned his hand to journalism. Bellamy took a position at the *New York Evening Post*, then went back to Springfield to write book reviews and editorials for the *Springfield Daily Union*. He also wrote short stories and began placing them in various magazines and began writing novels, although his first four novels were undistinguished and known only to specialists. The first, *Dr. Heidenhoff's Process* (1880), was notable only in its use of symbols, which was reminiscent of the work of Nathaniel Hawthorn. The second, *Mrs. Ludington's Sister* (1884), was a romance about psychic phenomena.

By 1887, Bellamy left journalism to pursue a literary career full-time. This was no small move for a man who had married in 1882 and had his first child in 1884. Perhaps driven by the need to support his family by his writing, in 1888 he produced the one novel by which he has entered the history books.

On the surface, *Looking Backward* is a rather simplistic romance of a young man of the time who falls into a hypnotic sleep similar to suspended animation. When the protagonist awakens in the year 2000, he discovers a utopian society in which all social problems have been eliminated and everyone is healthy, happy, and well educated. The exploration of this society's workings in meticulous detail is the real meat of the novel, and the admittedly thin plot merely serves as a vehicle for presenting Bellamy's political ideas. The vision propounded in *Looking Backward* inspired the founding of more than 150 Bellamy clubs. These groups were dedicated to the realization of Bellamy's ideals through social reform legislation and the presentation of his work to others. Bellamy called his movement "Nationalist," since it involved the nationalization of all real estate and the use of the resulting rents to create a social-welfare fund, but it had very little to do with the usual meaning of the term *nationalist*. Rather, it was a form of socialism, although distinct from communism (Marxist socialism). From 1891 to 1894, Bellamy used his journalistic experience to edit a weekly paper, the *New Nation*, for the movement.

In 1897, Bellamy published *Equality*, a sequel to *Looking Backward*, but was unable to equal the force or the appeal of the original. *Equality* was the last book he wrote, as his health was failing. He subsequently traveled to Denver, Colorado, to be treated for consumption (tuberculosis), a disease common among intellectuals of the time. When the treatment was unsuccessful, he returned to his native home, where he died on May 22, 1898.

**SEE ALSO**

*Volume 1 Left:* Socialism; Communism; Unions.
*Volume 2 Right:* United Kingdom; Capitalism.

**BIBLIOGRAPHY**

Harold Bloom, *Classic Science Fiction Writers* (Chelsea House, 1995); Sylvia E. Bowman, *Edward Bellamy* (Twayne, 1986); John L. Thomas, *Alternative America: Henry George, Edward Bellamy, Henry Demarest Lloyd, and the Adversary Tradition* (Belknap Press, 1983).

LEIGH KIMMEL
INDEPENDENT SCHOLAR

# Bentham, Jeremy (1748–1832)

KNOWN AS THE FATHER of utilitarianism, English philosopher Jeremy Bentham was born on February 15, 1748, in Spitalfields, London, England, to Jeremiah and Alicia Grove Bentham. Bentham's father was a prosperous attorney, and he devoted a good deal of time to the education of his son, who had begun reading his father's books at the age of three. His father banned Bentham from reading for amusement, forcing him to focus on such subjects as history, Greek, and Latin. Bentham was sent to Oxford's Queens College at the age of 12.

Jeremy Bentham, a founder of utilitarianism, believed government should provide the greatest good for the greatest number of people.

Because he had become financially independent after his father's death, Bentham could follow his own pursuits, and he was interested in reform.

Bentham began his reform activities by publishing an attack on William Blackstone's *Commentaries on the Laws of England*. Blackstone was somewhat of a monarchist and approached the law from a scientific rather than from a human perspective. Bentham added critiques of politics and society to his resume and began advocating major social reforms, which included prison reform, accessible education, animal rights, and relief for the poor. In a period when rights of suffrage were generally extended only to white males of a certain economic status, Bentham supported suffrage for all males who met reasonable age, soundness of mind, and residency requirements. He also demanded that homosexuality be decriminalized.

In 1789, Bentham published his influential work, *An Introduction to the Principles of Morals and Legislation*. Over the next 30 years, powerful people in Europe began to listen to Bentham, and 19th-century public administration policies began to show his influence. This influence continued for the next two centuries, impacting economic theory, cost theory, decision theory, public choice theory, and benefit analysis.

Bentham rejected the notions of natural law and contract theory espoused by many of his contemporaries and articulated in the Declaration of Independence in the United States in 1776 and in 1789 in the Rights of Man in France. Instead, Bentham was drawn to utilitarianism, also known as philosophical radicalism. While the first inkling of the philosophy can be traced to Aristotle, Bentham was most influenced by the more contemporary works of Joseph Priestly, who first used the term "the greatest happiness for the greatest number."

Bentham also studied David Hume before forming his own theory of utilitarianism, which he based on the notion that human beings are governed by two sovereigns, pain and pleasure. To utilitarians, the way to achieve happiness was to maximize pleasure while minimizing pain, resulting in the motto: "the greatest good for the greatest number." Bentham identified four classes of pain and pleasure: physical, political, moral, and religious.

The measure of any society, Bentham argued, was the sum of the happiness of all individuals who made up the society. Morals, which were ideal only if they were universally accepted, served the purpose of promoting the good of the greater society. The goal of any society was to promote utility, which, Bentham contended, was determining public policies according to how they augmented happiness and diminished pain. Laws were judged solely on their utility in accomplishing this purpose. The responsibility of government was to protect individuals from needless suffering and to promote wealth among an abundant population. As a classical liberal, Bentham argued that each individual was the best judge of deciding what his happiness entailed, and government was obligated to allow individual routes to happiness.

Bentham and economist James Mill were close friends, and Mill sent his young son, John Stuart, to be tutored by Bentham. Unlike Bentham, Mill also considered women when determining how happiness could best be achieved. He argued that utilizing only half of the population cheated government and society. Mill also differed from Bentham in his views on population control, becoming a strong believer in birth control methods.

Bentham died in 1832 at the age of 84. Eccentric to the end of his life, Bentham donated his body to University College London for medical research. According to his will, Bentham wanted future generations to remember "the founder of the greatest happiness system of morals and legislation." Following his instructions, Bentham's fully dressed skeleton, with cane in hand, topped by a wax head made in his likeness, has resided in a cabinet in the main building of University College London since 1850. According to popular legend, Bentham is regularly wheeled out to attend meetings of the College Council.

In the 18th- and 19th-century contexts, Bentham's philosophical radicalism was liberal, but with the development of the clash between capitalism and socialism in the 20th century, Bentham's concepts became increasingly associated with conservative rational justifications for free trade capitalist systems, in which the rights of the individual against the government were asserted.

**SEE ALSO**

*Volume 1 Left:* Hume, David; Liberalism; United Kingdom; Political Economy.
*Volume 2 Right:* Conservatism; United Kingdom; Capitalism.

**BIBLIOGRAPHY**

Charles Milner Atkinson, *Jeremy Bentham: His Life and Work* (Augustus McKeeley, 1969); Jeremy Bentham, *An Introduction to the Principles of Morals and Legislation* (Clarendon Press, 1879); David E. Ingersoll and Richard K. Matthews, *The Philosophic Roots of Modern Ideology: Liberalism, Communism, Fascism* (Prentice-Hall Publishers, 1986); "Jeremy Bentham," www. cepa.newschool.edu (May 2004); "Jeremy Bentham," www.ucl.ac.uk (May 2004); John Taylor, ed., *The Classical Utilitarians: Bentham and Mill* (Hackett Publishing, 2003).

ELIZABETH PURDY, PH.D.
INDEPENDENT SCHOLAR

# Bicameralism

WHEN THE FOUNDERS of the American confederation attended the Constitutional Convention in 1787, they were told the mind of the people of America was made up on the principle of having a legislature with more than one branch.

The bicameral form of government that America knows has its roots in the century preceding the American Revolution. This is when the people of England rose in a civil war to put an end to the absolutism of the rule by the Stuart kings and brought the king down to be the king-in-parliament. This now meant the actions of the king were dependent on the approval of two branches of parliament.

Dividing forms of governments into rule by one (monarchy), by the few (aristocracy), or by the many (democracy) reaches back to Polybius, a noted Greek philosopher. He insisted that unless each of these forms of government was not balanced by the other two, a government could degenerate into tyranny, oligarchy, or mob rule.

Bicameralism offered security against corruption and ambition. It was noted that in a republican government having two chambers, each chamber would keep the other's doings under close and suspicious watch. However, those founding fathers who penned the Constitution were not of one mind on the idea of having a Senate and House of Representatives. In the end, men like James Madison vigorously stated in *The Federalist Papers* that acceptance of the need for equal representation in the Senate for the states would be unavoidable if the nation were to be successful.

Federal states, such as the United States and Germany and others, have a two-chamber structure of government for accommodating territorial representation. There is an argument for the benefit of a bicameral system, such as a protection against the tyranny of the majority. There can also be an argument against bicameralism based on the tyranny of the minority. It is interesting to note that many of the drafters at the Constitutional Convention only saw U.S. Senators as agents of the state legislatures and defenders of the residual powers of the states. The Seventeenth Amendment took this power away from the states and gave it to the people.

It might be interesting to put forward the proposition that, in fact, the U.S. Constitution was deliberately designed to prevent the unfettered expression of the people's will, and in fact goes against the premise of one person, one vote. It could be said that the document that set up the bicameral system was meant to prevent true democracy in America, and has, in fact, set up a system based on minority rule.

As an example one only has to look at the confirmation of Supreme Court Justice Clarence Thomas, and how the small and unequal representation found in the current bicameral system has infected the judicial and executive branches. The U.S. Senate did confirm the appointment with a margin of four votes. The Senators who voted against the appointment represented 7 million more voters than those who voted for the appointment.

**SEE ALSO**
*Volume 1 Left:* Democracy; United States.
*Volume 2 Right:* Monarchism; Elitism.

**BIBLIOGRAPHY**
"Federal States That Use Either the Bicameral or Unicameral Systems," www.spea.indiana.edu/pdp/analyses (May 2004); Samuel C. Patterson and Anthony Mughan, eds., *Senates: Bicameralism in the Contemporary World* (Ohio State University Press, 1999).

NORMAN GREENFIELD
INDEPENDENT SCHOLAR

# Bill of Rights

IT WOULD NOT BE unfair to state that, had there been no U.S. Constitution in 1787, there would have been no Bill of Rights in 1791. The Constitutional Convention had been summoned to meet in the national capital of Philadelphia, Pennsylvania, in May 1787 to provide a more effective government for the young United States. Of the 29 delegates, all were white and male, no women or people of color were among them. The Articles of Confederation, given to the states for ratification in 1777, were simply fraying apart. The delegates, almost all of whom had been in the American Revolution in one capacity or another, were faced with a national crisis.

Domestically, the American states were beginning to act like the ancient Greek city states, erecting trade barriers among themselves. In 1786, revolutionary veteran Daniel Shays had led a brief rebellion in Massachusetts. Shays' Rebellion, in fact, was perhaps the most important single reason for summoning this Constitutional Convention. Externally, although the Treaty of Paris in September 1783 had recognized American independence, there was little that the new government could do to enforce its terms. The treaty had established the western boundary of the United States as "a line to be drawn along the middle of the said river Mississippi," however, the British in Canada were still actively abetting the Native American tribes in blocking American expansion to the Mississippi—as they had during the war.

At the same time, Spain, which had been an ally in the war, had grown alarmed at American expansion toward its territories in what is now Louisiana, Texas, and the southwest. Spain attempted to block American use of the mouth of the Mississippi by its control of New Orleans. On October 10, 1784, George Washington wrote to Governor Benjamin Harrison of Virginia: "I need not remark to you, sir, that the flanks and rear of the United States are possessed by other powers, and formidable ones, too."

The Constitutional Convention, however, diverged into two radically opposing camps. One group envisaged the answer in a strong central government, and became known as the Federalists. Their opponents, the Anti-Federalists, advocated a more decentralized government. The problem they faced was best put by the Federalist James Madison in what became known as the *Federalist Letter 51*: "You must first enable the government to control the governed; and in the next place oblige it to control itself." The question posed by Madison was one known to all. The revolution had had its origins, after all, in growing American resistance to the tyranny of England's King George III and his sycophant ministers in London, England. The Virginia Plan called for representation based on population, which, however, made the smaller states fear being outvoted and overwhelmed in the new government they were framing. The small states countered with the New Jersey Plan, which urged that representation be equal for all. However, the impasse was to a large extent broken when, on July 16, each state was given the same number of votes in the Senate, balancing the numerical superiority of the larger states in the House of Representatives. This measure was often referred to as The Great Compromise. James Madison stated the outcome when he observed: "As soon as the smaller states had secured more than a proportional share in the proposed government, they became favorable to an augmentation of its power."

Clearly, the convention had succeeded admirably in fulfilling the first part of Madison's prime concern in *Federalist Letter 51*: "You must first enable the government to control the governed." However, the second article had been virtually ignored, "and in the next place oblige it to control itself." Indeed, had it not been for the Virginian George Mason, the entire question of the individual rights of American citizens might have been subsumed under the vague terms of Article IV, section 2 of the 1787 Constitution, paraphrased as: The citizens of each state shall be entitled to all privileges and immunities of citizens in the several states. However, Mason had been the author of a declaration of civil rights in Virginia and carried his public advocacy with him to Philadelphia.

On July 26, 1787, he declared that he had "for his primary object, for the polestar of his political conduct, the preservation of the rights of the people." In short, Mason was critically concerned with what he felt was "the natural propensity of rulers to oppress the people." Roger Sherman of Connecticut and Elbridge Gerry of Massachusetts supported Mason in his democratic mission. Mason's most explicit declaration was he had "wished the [constitutional] plan had been prefaced with a bill of rights." Gerry had already raised the ire of the Federalists like Alexander Hamilton of New York by being a vociferous critic of their plan for a standing army to be the main pillar of the new Federal government.

In his *Observations on the New Constitution*, Gerry observed, "freedom revolts at the idea, when the Divan, or the Despot, may draw out his dragoons [light cavalry] to suppress the murmurs of a few." Mason possessed a focus in his reasoning that made him the chief spokesman for those who wanted what was, in fact, a bill of rights to guard Americans from their own government and its possible restriction of their liberty. Christopher Collier and James Lincoln Collier summed up his philosophy in their *Decision in Philadelphia: The Constitutional Convention of 1787*: "he was ... a determined and consistent libertarian who was concerned that no government meddle in the lives of its citizens."

## TYRANNICAL ARISTOCRACY

The main argument for a bill of rights was not so much to defend individual rights as conceived of today, or the rights of groups that have felt discrimination and hostility such as African Americans. Instead the argument flowed out of Mason's concern that without a bill of rights, the Constitution could lead to a "monarchy, or a tyrannical aristocracy." This was inextricably tied to the matter of a standing army. Here the debate became heated. Charles Pinckney would later say in South Carolina that "[the] dignity of a government could [not] be maintained, its safety insured, or its laws administered without a body of regular forces to aid the magistrate in the execution of his duty." Still, at the convention in Philadelphia, Mason had said that "[you] could no more execute civil relations by military force than you can unite opposite elements, than you can mingle fire with water."

However, all delegates, keeping in mind the threats that plagued the young nation, in more or less degree accepted the idea of a regular army. The perceptive Madison stated that if an army was indeed necessary, then "the calamity must be submitted to." While conceding the obnoxious necessity of a regular army, delegates like Mason sought a counterbalance in the militias of the states. It had been the militias, often derided by regular army officers, upon which the states had depended for defense against the British and marauding pro-British Tories (Loyalists) when the main Continental Army was in the field. Numerically at least, the militias, under the control of each state governor, were a force to be respected.

Walter Millis wrote in *Arms and Men: A Study of American Military History* that at the height of the American Revolution in 1780 there were some 41,760 Continental soldiers—and about 43,076 militiamen. In the end, both Federalists and Anti-Federalists compromised on the issue of the militia. While the Federal Congress would make laws for "organizing, arming, and disciplining" the militias, their control (except in time of war or emergency) would still remain in the hands of the states.

However, the question of individual rights now had to be addressed because, even in the case of the militias, the federal power still had partial control. Indeed, had it not been for the efforts of a small band of the Anti-Federalists, the Constitutional Convention may have adjourned without assuring the civil rights of the citizens. Now it was up to them to ensure that the people could be defended from their own government. Sherman of Connecticut offered the opinion that the "the state declarations of right are not repealed by this constitution; and being in force are sufficient." Future court decisions may have upheld this, in fact, because Article IV also states that "full faith and credit shall be given in each state to the public acts, records, and judicial proceedings of every other state." But there would have been no equal protection of rights throughout the Union.

Already, there had been problems in business with tariffs among the middle Atlantic states, and there was even more to be concerned about with problems in the most combustible of all commerce: Ideas. Therefore, Sherman, Gerry, and Mason were adamant that the convention would provide for a bill of rights that would equably serve the inhabitants of all the United States. Therefore, in a dramatic move, Edmund Randolph of Virginia, Mason, and Gerry announced definite reservations about signing the document—unless provision was made for a second Constitutional Convention to frame a bill of rights. Gerry flatly refused to sign it without one. Finally, the second assembly was promised, and the Constitution was signed by all.

When the Constitution was given to the states for the necessary ratification, the lack of a bill of rights drew some of the sharpest criticism. Melancton Smith of New York state, possibly in collaboration with Richard Henry Lee, the hero of the Revolutionary War, in his *Letters from the Federal Farmer*, published in the *Poughkeepsie* (New York) *Country Journal* in October 1787, perhaps most cogently stated the argument for a bill of rights. Harkening back to the Declaration of Independence, observed Smith, "There are certain unalienable and fundamental rights, which in forming the social compact, ought to be explicitly ascertained and fixed ... these rights should be made the basis of every constitution." In the Virginia debates, Lee, according to the National Archives and Records Administration, "despaired at the lack of provisions to protect 'those essential rights of mankind without which liberty cannot exist.'" The writer of the Declaration, Thomas Jefferson, generally in favor of the new government, wrote to Madison that a bill of rights was "what the people are entitled to against every government on earth."

The National Archives and Records Administration goes on to state that: "By the fall of 1788, Madison had been convinced that not only was a bill of rights necessary to ensure acceptance of the Constitution but that it would have positive effects. He wrote, on October 17, that such "fundamental maxims of free government" would be "a good ground for an appeal to the sense of community" against potential oppression and would "counteract the impulses of interest and passion."

In July 1788, New Hampshire became the ninth state to ratify the Constitution, thus putting it into effect. With the functioning of the new government, the Congress now became the arena in which the battle for the bill of rights would be fought. Madison proposed a bill of 17 amendments to the Constitution, designed to protect the liberties of the people. It was perhaps one of the rare times in history when a government freely debated what would really be limitations placed upon its own power. Presented with the 17 amendments, the Senate trimmed the number to 12, and both houses of Congress, the House of Representatives and the Senate, agreed on that number. In October 1789, President Washington submitted a list of the 12 amendments for ratification by the 13 states. Eventually, the 12 amendments were reworked into 10, combining them into a more succinct and explicit document promoting human liberty.

On December 15, 1791, three-fourths of the states, the number needed to achieve ratification, had voted to approve the Bill of Rights. Mason's dream of a guarantee for American civil liberties had become a constitutional reality.

Designed as an embodiment of Enlightenment ideas of individual rights, the provisions of the 10 amendments have been invoked by partisans of both left- and right-wing positions. In the late 20th century, defense of the right to bear arms, as stated in the Second Amendment, has been advocated by conservatives.

## SEE ALSO

*Volume 1 Left:* Constitutional Amendments; First Amendment; American Revolution.
*Volume 2 Right:* National Rifle Association; Second Amendment; American Revolution.

## BIBLIOGRAPHY

Frederic Austin Ogg, *The Opening of the Mississippi* (Cooper Square, 1968); "The Bill of Rights: Archiving Early America," www.earlyamerica.com (May 2004); Ernest R. May, ed., *The Ultimate Decision: The President as Commander in Chief* (Braziller, 1960); Ralph Ketcham, ed., *The Anti-Federalist Papers and the Constitutional Convention Debates* (Mentor Books, 1986); National Archives and Records Administration, "The Charters of Freedom," www.archives.gov (May 2004); Christopher Collier and James Lincoln Collier, *Decision in Philadelphia: The Constitutional Convention of 1787* (Ballantine, 1786); Leonard Kriegel, ed., *Essential Works of the Founding Fathers* (Bantam, 1964); John A. Garatty, *The American Nation: A History of the United States* (Harper and Row, 1966); Richard A. Kohn, *Eagle and Sword: The Beginnings of the Military Establishment in America* (Free Press, 1975); John F. Murphy, Jr., "The U.S. Army, 1783–1815," Independence Hall National Historic Park (1991); Walter Millis, *Arms and Men: A Study of American Military History* (Mentor Books, 1956).

JOHN F. MURPHY, JR.
AMERICAN MILITARY UNIVERSITY

# Black Panthers

THE BLACK PANTHER Party for Self-Defense, later simply the Black Panther Party (BPP), was a radical left organization founded in Oakland, California, in 1966, by Huey P. Newton and Bobby Seale, students at Merritt Junior College. The two student activists were influenced by the Black Power movement and the views of Malcolm X of the Black Muslims.

After the assassination of Malcolm X and the Watts, California, riots of 1965, Newton, Seale, and David Hilliard met together to sketch the outlines of their organization. They took the black panther from the Lowndes County, Alabama, Freedom Organization because the animal represented power. They added self-defense to contrast themselves with the nonviolence of the mainstream civil rights movement.

The BPP platform called for social, economic, and political equality in a remade American society. The platform also called for freedom, self-determination, full employment, restitution for slavery, housing, education, exemption from military service, an end to police brutality, release of wrongly convicted black prisoners, trial of blacks by blacks, and a United Nations-supervised plebiscite that would allow African Americans to determine their own destiny. The Panthers opposed racism and classism and the Vietnam War.

The Panthers and other Black Power advocates were disenchanted with the nonviolence of Martin Luther King, Jr., and the mainstream civil rights movement, The Black Panthers indulged in violent rhetoric and violent actions, primarily against the police. But they also provided neighborhood services. Panther patrols reduced the incidence of police abuse of residents. They also distributed food, provided health care, and established educational facilities in the poor communities. The Panthers became a national organization.

The violence and the reputation it produced overshadowed the positive community efforts. The Panther uniform—black berets, leather jackets, and firearms—increased the image of militancy. Eldridge Cleaver, Panther minister of information, ran for president of the United States in 1968. His party was the Peace and Freedom Party and his running mate was Jerry Rubin of the Youth International Party (Yippie). Later, Cleaver led the organization.

Because the Black Panthers espoused the right of black self-defense against racist authorities, they were constantly in conflict with local police and the Federal Bureau of Investigation (FBI). The Panthers' armed patrols and their willingness to join with white revolutionary activists led the FBI to establish a covert intelligence team (COINTELPRO) to keep the groups from uniting and increasing their influence. The FBI infiltrated local offices, used informants, and raided local offices, leading to shootouts in California, New York City, and Chicago. Panthers were killed, including Mark Clark and Fred Hampton, state leader in Illinois. After an Oakland, California, shootout left a policeman dead,

*Huey P. Newton, cofounder of the Black Panther Party, whose community service mission was overshadowed by violent advocacy.*

United States," but it was a clear needle in the white skin of complacent racism.

**SEE ALSO**
*Volume 1 Left:* Malcolm X; King, Martin Luther, Jr.; United States.
*Volume 2 Right:* Black Nationalism; Black Separatism; Hoover, J. Edgar.

**BIBLIOGRAPHY**
Black Panther Party, "Legacy," www.blackpanther.org (March, 2004); Ward Churchill and Jim Vander Wall, *Agents of Repression* (South End Press, 1990); Eldridge Cleaver, *Soul on Ice* (Laurel/Dell, 1992); Philip S. Foner, ed., *The Black Panthers Speak* (Da Capo Press, 2002); Charles E. Jones, ed., *The Black Panther Party (Reconsidered)* (Black Classic Press, 1998); Huey P. Newton with J.H. Blake, *Revolutionary Suicide* (Writers and Readers, 1995); Susan Robinson, "The Black Panther Party," *Gibbs Magazine,* www.gibbsmagazine.com (March 2004).

JOHN BARNHILL, PH.D.
INDEPENDENT SCHOLAR

Newton went to jail for manslaughter in 1967. Supporters began a Free Huey movement, and a California appeals court overturned the conviction in 1971. By the end of the 1960s, more than 20 Panthers were dead, others were in prison, and Cleaver had fled the United States to avoid arrest.

Newton changed the direction of the party after his release, emphasizing the building of community programs and de-emphasizing violent confrontation. He established a free breakfast program for children. The Panthers also established free clinics and gave away clothing and food. The group organized rent strikes and campaigned against crime and drug abuse. Seale won about 40 percent of the vote when he ran for mayor of Oakland in 1973. The party was in decline by then, victim of internal conflict as well as external attack. Most of the founders were gone one way or another.

The Panthers fell apart as an effective community organization by 1970 because of death, incarceration, and ongoing conflict with the FBI and police. Even as it lingered into the early 1970s, the BPP remained a symbol of the turbulence of the 1960s, a period when Americans became aware that their society was not quite as ideal as they thought. Probably, the Black Panther Party was never, as FBI chief J. Edgar Hoover once said, "the greatest threat to the internal security of the

# Bolshevism

"BOLSHEVIK" AND "BOLSHEVISM" derive from the Russian word that means "majority." In historical terms, Bolshevik was first employed to describe people associated with a splinter group formed in 1903 within the Russian Social Democratic Labor Party (a Marxist organization formed in Minsk, Russia, in 1898), a group formed at the party's congress in London, England, when many of the organization's leaders decided to support the ideas of a young intellectual, Vladimir Lenin. Those in the party who did not support Lenin were known as the Mensheviks, or "minority," and were led by Julius Martov. Arguably, the most famous of the Bolsheviks was its first leader, Lenin, a revolutionary heavily influenced by the work of Karl Marx. The term "Bolshevik" also has a derivative meaning and is often employed to mean communist. It is often used in this particular context by those of the right as a derogatory adjective for those belonging to the left of the political center.

Historically at least, the Bolsheviks are most famous for their overthrow of Tzar Nicholas II and the Kerensky government in 1917, the brutal assassination of the Russian royal family in 1918, and the subsequent establishment of the communist political system in Russia and its sister states—a system based on the economic and social theories of Marx. With Lenin appointed as the first leader of the Soviet Union, the Bolsheviks changed the name of the Russian Social Democratic Labor Party to the All Russian Communist Party in 1918, and by 1936 this name had become the Communist Party of the Soviet Union. As such, the Bolsheviks were able to embark on a course of power that existed from 1917 up to the fall of communism in Russia in the August coup of 1991 when the Communist Party of the Soviet Union was banned by Boris Yeltsin.

While internationally the Bolsheviks are often seen as purely Russian in nature, their actual composition was not so straightforward. Many of the original Bolsheviks were, for example, not only Russians but also many were of Jewish descent, particularly those of high status in the Russian Social Democratic Labor Party before 1917, and they were drawn toward Bolshevik ideas due to the oppression of non-Russian states within the Russian Empire. The participation of many Jews in the Russian Revolution and subsequent development of the Communist Party in Russia has led enemies of the Bolsheviks to theorize that communism is a political system that benefits Jewish interests. Arguably the most famous proponent of this notion was Adolf Hitler, who proclaimed in Nazi Germany a Bolshevik-Jewish conspiracy, which proclamation ultimately led to millions of Jews being killed in concentration camps in Europe during World War II. In reality though, many Jews were removed from Russian power and society by Josef Stalin, the communist leader after Lenin, during his Great Purges of the 1930s.

The ruthless policies and international aspirations of the Bolsheviks won them many opponents around the world. Their brutal disposition of the Russian royal family in 1918 drew much contemporary criticism, for instance. In addition, the Bolsheviks, after the Russian Revolution, often employed equally violent means to deal with enemies. For example, the Bolsheviks invigorated the Soviet state security force (Cheka) once power had been obtained, and the problem of dealing with unwanted political opponents was solved through the opening of labor camps in the remote north of the country and in Siberia. After the death of Lenin in 1924, and during the leadership of Stalin, these labor camps were developed into the infamous gulag prison structure within which up to 10 million people were held in the 1930s and early 1940s. Many prisoners in

the system did not live to see freedom again, and many, including intellectuals, disappeared within the highly controlled penal system. Additionally, state or class enemies such as the kulaks, a peasant social class, were forcefully moved and resettled in remote rural areas. Such a system provided a means to remove people from society without having to deal with the problem of execution.

## SEE ALSO

*Volume 1 Left:* Communism; Soviet Union; Lenin, Vladimir; Russian Revolution.
*Volume 2 Right:* Soviet Union; monarchism.

## BIBLIOGRAPHY

Robert Service, *Lenin: A Biography* (Harvard University Press, 2002); Robert Service, *A History of Twentieth-Century Russia* (Harvard University Press, 1999); Bertrand Russell, *Practice and Theory of Bolshevism* (Unwin Hyman, 1962).

IAN MORLEY
MING CHUAN UNIVERSITY, TAIWAN

# Brazil

THE HISTORY OF the left in Brazil shows that it has changed its focus from the idea of republicanism to those of communism, socialism, and, finally, democracy. With the democratic election of Luís Inácio "Lula" da Silva as president in 2002, leftist politics became mainline in Brazil, albeit in a form that involved a series of compromises. This shows that left and right are variables in Brazilian politics, while the constant since 1822 is the politics of conciliation.

The left in Brazil has been the defender of civil rights, national identity, social-economic development and democracy, while opposing the political right. It can neither be reduced to political parties nor simply related to positions such as liberalism, Marxism, communism, or socialism or to leftist political groups such as anarchism, Trotskyism, modernism, and postmodernism. It is a movement looking to address the social changes in Brazilian history.

Brazil became a colony of Portugal in 1500. Independence came in 1882, but the country adopted a monarchic regime that lasted until 1889. During this time, Brazilian politics was bipartisan, with conservatives and liberals committing to the center, in what became known as the politics of conciliation. Although leftist movements arose during the 19th century and were involved in the struggles for independence, abolition of slavery, republicanism, and universal suffrage, their impact was felt much later. Only in the 20th century, after the Declaration of the Republic in 1889, can one better identify the left in Brazil.

Leftist groups were active in the 1920s, leading to the founding of the Brazilian Communist Party (PCB) in 1922, the movement for modern art, and the attempt at a communist rebellion by Antonio Carlos Prestes in 1929. The 1930s were rather marked by the hegemony of conservative movements blessed by the populist dictatorship of Getulio Vargas. After World War II, left intellectual movements began to discuss the modern national identity, culture, tensions between rural and urban life, and economic models for Brazil. However, with the military coup d'etat in 1964, Leftist social movements, student groups, political parties, and even guerrillas went underground.

The 1970s witnessed the impact of liberation theology and the Base Christian Communities, while the 1980s marked the founding of the Worker's Party, the growth of the women's movement, the intellectual role of universities, concern with human rights, widespread reaction against militarism, and the movement Diretas Já! (Presidential Elections Now!). The 1990s showed democracy at work, first with the impeachment of a populist president accused of corruption and then with the election of a social-democrat. All this led to the 21st century, which started with the election of a socialist president from the Worker's Party, thus giving a definitive leftist character to Brazilian politics and including newer themes in political debates, such as diversity, environmental issues, poverty, and social responsibility.

Marxist thinking has played a clear role in developing the left in Brazil. Intellectuals such as Caio Prado, Jr., Nelson Werneck Sodré, and Florestan Fernandes proposed a bourgeois revolution and dedicated several studies to Brazilian problems, using Marxism as an important tool for their analyses. Later on, programs of the Brazilian Institute of Higher Studies (ISEB) addressed the socioeconomic situation of the poor and the peasantry. Similar initiatives can be seen also in the Hunger Aesthetics (Estética da Fome) of Gláuber Rocha and Augusto Boal and others interested in the quest for national identity. A more applied approach of leftist thinking can be represented by the theories of economic development and dependency put forth by Celso Furtado and Fernando Henrique Cardoso, who analyzed the relation between center and periphery as a paradigm for the analysis of the Brazilian situation. A corollary of these analyses can be seen in the literacy program and the Pedagogy of the Oppressed of Paulo Freire.

These initiatives reflect also international changes in Soviet politics and the Cuban Revolution in 1961, which led to founding of the Communist Party of Brazil (PCdoB) in 1962, the election of a leftist president, and a series of initiatives by workers, students, church groups, and others. However, all these initiatives were then frustrated by a military coup in 1964, which limited politics to a bipartisan system represented by the National Alliance for Renovation (ARENA) on the right and the Brazilian Democratic Movement (MDB), theoretically on the left. The military government did not pass without opposition, even though leftist parties, movements, or leaders had been censored, forbidden, and persecuted. As a result, artists, religious groups, university intellectuals and students, as well as women groups and unions created a new tradition of leftist militancy. Through them, democracy and human rights became key concepts of the Brazilian politics in the 1980s.

## POLITICAL ARTS

Theater and music were an important vehicle for disseminating progressive ideas in a very encrypted way that was nevertheless understood by the Brazilian youth at the time. Singers such as Chico Buarque, Milton Nascimento, Elis Regina, and others and playwrights such as José Celso and Plínio Marcos are among the representatives of this process. Liberation theology was also a main force during this time, bringing Marxism and religion together in order to address the social situation of the country. Priests and theologians such as Helder Camara, Paulo Arns, Hugo Assmann, and Rubem Alves contributed in this process, but Leonardo Boff and his book *Church, Charisma and Power* became the symbol of these initiatives.

At the same time, Carlos Nelson Coutinho, Fernando Henrique Cardoso, Leandro Konder, José Gianotti, and Marilena Chauí led Marxist intellectuals at the universities in São Paulo and Rio de Janeiro, coming to the public sphere to criticize authoritarianism and defend democracy. In the same way, the National Union of Students, which had been forbidden since 1964, reunited thousands of students at the University of Piracicaba while the theater of the Catholic University in São Paulo became the temple of student resistance. The women's movement complements this scenario.

But it was above all the founding of the Worker's Party (PT) in 1980 that inaugurated a new moment in

Brazilian politics. PT was able to embrace the above-mentioned initiatives, bringing them together with groups and organizations such as the powerful Central Worker's Union (CUT), the Landless Movement (MST), the working class, and the poor. This marked a clear shift to democracy in 1986, motivated dissidents from the MDB to found the Social-Democratic Party of Brazil (PSDB) in 1988, and influenced partisan politics in the 1990s.

At the beginning of the 21st century, left-wing parties represented a wide portion of the political spectrum in Brazil, albeit not as a whole block, but as a series of small parties and groups that have been classified as extreme left, left, and center left. The example for the extreme left is the Party for the Working Cause (PCO). Traditional leftist parties, such as the communist parties (PCB and PCdoB), have developed their positions and adapted themselves to the perestroika in the Soviet Union. The Democratic Worker's Party (PDT) continued to claim the inheritance of the populism from Getulio Vargas and Leonel Brizola and maintained connections with the Socialist International, but lost a great part of its former appeal. Other smaller leftist parties such as the Brazilian Socialist Party (PSB), founded in 1947 and characterized by its lower-middle-class and evangelical constituency, the Popular Socialist Party (PPS), and the Unified Socialist Worker's Party (PSTU) complement this spectrum. Most of these groups supported the Worker's Party (PT), gained some representation in Congress, but also adapted their politics to new situations, coming to oppose PT.

The so-called center left is formed by larger parties that were able to adapt their discourses, compromise on certain economic issues—such as the impact of globalization, the dependency on the International Monetary Fund and the need for internal reforms, and established alliances with parties of the center right. This was somewhat the case of the Worker's Party (PT), of the Social-Democratic Party of Brazil (PSDB), and the Party of the Brazilian Democratic Movement (PMDB).

**SEE ALSO**

*Volume 1 Left:* Socialism; South America; Guevara, Che; Communism.
*Volume 2 Right:* Brazil; South America; Fascism.

**BIBLIOGRAPHY**

Maria Helena Moreira Alves, *State and Opposition in Military Brazil* (University of Texas Press, 1985); Boris Fausto, *A Concise History of Brazil* (Cambridge University Press, 1999); Fernando H. Cardoso and Enzo Faletto, *Dependency and Development in Latin America* (University of California Press, 1979); Ronald Chilcote, *Brazil and Its Radical Left: An Annotated Bibliography on the Communist Movement and the Rise of Marxism, 1922–72* (Kraus International Publications, 1980); Thomas Skidmore, *Politics in Brazil, 1930–64: An Experiment in Democracy* (Oxford University Press, 1967).

AMOS NASCIMENTO
METHODIST UNIVERSITY OF PIRACICABA, BRAZIL

# Breitman, George (1916–1986)

BORN IN A WORKING-CLASS neighborhood in Newark, New Jersey, George Breitman's formal involvement in leftist politics started when he was barely out of his teens. His father's early death forced his older sister to quit school and support their family. She joined the Young Communist League and was a strong influence in the development of Breitman's political beliefs. His first job after graduating from high school was as a construction laborer with the Civilian Conservation Corps (CCC), and later, with the Works Progress Administration (WPA).

In 1935, he became a part of the American Trotskyist movement as a member of the Spartacus Youth League and shortly thereafter, as a member of the Workers Party. By the time he was 20 years old, he had been arrested for inciting a riot in Burlington, New Jersey as a member of the Workers Relief and WPA Union. He was also active in the Workers Alliance, an organization of the unemployed.

In 1938, Breitman became a founding member of Socialist Workers' Party (SWP). He was elected to its national committee in 1939; he was only 23 years old. In 1940, in the first of four tries, he ran as SWP candidate for senator from New Jersey. In 1941, he became the editor of *The Militant*, the weekly paper of the SWP. In 1942, he ran again as SWP candidate for Senator. While still an editor of the paper, he was drafted and sent to Europe in 1943. In Europe, he took the opportunity to link up with several European Trotskyists and to help rebuild the Fourth International.

At the same time, his meritorious service during the war was recognized by the French government, which awarded him in 1945 the Croix de Guerre avec Etoile de Bronze (War Cross with Bronze Star) for exceptional service rendered during the operations for the liberation of France.

After the war, he resumed his editorship of *The Militant*, and held this position until the early 1950s. He also found time to run again as SWP candidate for senator from New Jersey in 1948 and then in 1954. Thereafter, Breitman moved to Michigan and worked as a proofreader from the mid-1950s to the late 1960s. As part of his organizing work, he became a member of the International Typographical Union and the leader of the Detroit, Michigan, branch of the SWP. While there, he ran as SWP candidate for presidential elector for Michigan in 1960 and 1964. He also initiated the Friday Night Socialist Forum (later called the Militant Forum), an open discussion group that appealed to many activists, including those from the labor, student and African American movements. During this period, Breitman wrote using several pseudonyms, for example, Philip Blake, Chester Hofla, Anthony Massini, Albert Parker, and John F. Petrone.

Breitman regarded race as an aberration of capitalism and in 1953, wrote that the "negro question" was not about segregation and self-determination, but about integration. He looked at the African American problem as a working-class problem, where the crucial criterion is economic, and not the geographic concentration (that is, the South) of the population. Not surprisingly, it was also during this period that he edited *Malcolm X Speaks: Selected Speeches and Statements* (1965).

Breitman then returned to New York and took over the management of SWP's Pathfinder Press. As editor, he published for Pathfinder the 14-volume *Writings of Leon Trotsky*, which covered the period of Trotsky's exile from the Soviet Union in 1929 until his assassination in 1940 in Mexico. Other books he edited and/or wrote for Pathfinder were *The Struggle against Fascism in Germany* (1971); *Spanish Revolution 1931–39* (1973); *The Socialist Workers Party in World War II: Writings and Speeches* (1975); *The Crisis of the French Section 1935–36* (1977); and *Leon Trotsky on Black Nationalism and Self-Determination* (1978).

In 1984, along with several hundred members, he was expelled from the SWP for establishing the Fourth Internationalist Tendency, which aimed to unify American supporters of the Fourth International. Brietman's group criticized the John Barnes leadership of the SWP as "progressively adopt[ing] a Castroist methodology and outlook instead of a Trotskyist one." The purge eventually led to the decline of the party membership. On April 19, 1986, Breitman died of a heart attack in New York City. In his obituary, his friends described this man who was uncompromising in his beliefs as "writer, organizer, and revolutionary."

**SEE ALSO**

*Volume 1 Left*: Communism; Communist Party, Soviet; Trotsky, Leon; Socialist Workers' Party, UK.
*Volume 2 Right*: Capitalism; Ideology; United States.

**BIBLIOGRAPHY**

"George Breitman Papers 1928–86," Tamiment Library, Robert F. Wagner Labor Archives, Elmer Holmes Bobst Library, New York University, http://dlib.nyu.edu:8083 (May 2004).

Josie Hernandez de Leon
Laurentian University, Canada

# Bridges, Harry (1901–1990)

ALFRED RENTON BRIDGES (he was later named Harry by American sailors) was born in Melbourne, Australia, in 1901. His father worked for a real estate company and sent his son to collect rents from tenants, some of whom were unable to pay. This was a formative experience for Bridges as he became aware of poverty and decided that he did not want to enter the same line of work as his father. His growing interest in politics was reinforced by the fact that two of his uncles were members of the Australian Labour Party.

Bridges worked as a clerk when he left school, but he really wanted to go sea. He left Melbourne and finally settled in San Francisco, California, in 1920. In 1922, he began to work on the waterfront as a longshoreman. Longshoremen endured particularly harsh conditions. Wages were poor, accidents were commonplace, and competition was fierce to be given work by the foreman at the daily "shapeup." In 1919, longshoremen had taken strike action in favor of improved wages and conditions, but the owners had isolated them, blacklisted activists, and destroyed their union, the International Longshoremen's Association (ILA), in San Francisco. Bridges was involved in two abortive attempts to re-establish an ILA local, but it was not until 1933 that he and his colleagues succeeded. Most of the San Francisco longshoremen then joined the ILA, seduced by Bridges's proposals for a union local controlled by its members and capable of producing unity of action.

The new ILA local in San Francisco strengthened the position of more militant elements elsewhere on the West Coast. In 1934, the ILA's West Coast convention voted for immediate negotiations with the owners for the recognition of the union and for an agreement on improved conditions covering the whole of the coast. As a result of the owners' refusal to negotiate, the union voted to take strike action, expanding their demands to include the abolition of the "shakeup." The ILA received the support of other workers, including the Marine Workers Industrial Union, who struck in support. Bridges played a major role in the unfolding events, leading the Joint Marine Strike Committee, which ran the strike. The strike was conducted in a situation of extreme tension in San Francisco. On one occasion, two picketers were killed and over 100 injured as the police charged them. Martial law was declared and the national guard was called in. A general strike was subsequently called in San Francisco but soon collapsed after armed vigilantes attacked workers and the police arrested more than 300 activists. The longshoremen called off their strike, but most of their demands were subsequently met by an arbitration board.

During the strike, Bridges had faced intimidation by employers, been threatened with deportation, and was accused of being a communist. He famously refused to either confirm or deny the accusation, but he openly took advice from the Communist Party, which was heavily involved in the strike. As a result of the strike, Bridges became a major figure in the ILA and in union politics in general on the West Coast. In 1937, he left the ILA to found the International Longshore and Warehouse Union (ILWU) and participated actively in the emergence of the Congress of Industrial Organizations (CIO). He remained president of the ILWU for the following 40 years. However, the union's radical credentials, Bridges's close relationship with the Communist Party, and his support of the Soviet Union created problems for all concerned. The ILWU was expelled from the CIO after World War II, while Bridges was twice arrested on charges of being a secret member of the Communist Party and was again threatened with deportation.

Bridges's radical convictions always remained intact. He believed that there were fundamental differences of interest between social classes and that temporary improvements in workers' conditions were of limited value if no attempts were made to bring about radical social and economic change. Nevertheless, he was pragmatic enough to adapt to changing circumstances. In 1960, he signed the Mechanization and Modernization Agreement with maritime employers. This compromise allowed employers to use machinery and to reduce the number of longshoremen but guaranteed improved pay and conditions for the remaining workers. Bridges and the ILWU did not limit themselves to purely economic issues, and the union became well known for its support for progressive causes, opposing racial discrimination in the United States, the Vietnam War, and oppressive regimes in Central and South America. The ILWU also provided inexpensive health insurance and medical care for its members and used its members' pension funds to build housing for low-income workers. After his retirement, Bridges remained active, becoming president of the California Congress of Seniors. He died in 1990, but the ILWU continues to exist to this day.

**SEE ALSO**

*Volume 1 Left:* Unions; Socialism; Communism.
*Volume 2 Right:* Capitalism; Republican Party; McCarthyism.

**BIBLIOGRAPHY**

David Brody, *Workers in Industrial America: Essays on the 20th Century Struggle* (Oxford University Press, 1980); Charles P. Larrowe, *Harry Bridges* (Lawrence Hill, 1992); ILWU, www.ilwu19.com (May 2004); Sidney Lens, *The Labor Wars* (Doubleday, 1973); Robert H. Zieger, *American Workers, American Unions, 1920–85* (Johns Hopkins University Press, 1986).

JEREMY TRANMER
UNIVERSITY OF NANCY 2, FRANCE

# Browder, Earl (1891–1973)

EARL BROWDER WAS secretary-general of the Communist Party of the United States of America (CPUSA) from 1930 to 1944 and president of the communist political association (1944–45) that briefly replaced the party on the political scene. Eventually condemned by Josef Stalin and other communist leaders of the Iron Curtain countries as a social democrat, Browder led the CPUSA to its greatest size and, allegedly, directed a ring of spies for the Russian secret police and military intelligence.

Browder, the eighth son of a schoolteacher, was born in Wichita, Kansas. His childhood was plagued by his large family's poverty and ill health. Browder's father was disabled and debts forced the 10 children of the family to leave elementary school. Earl worked as a cash boy for the Wallenstein & Cohen Dry Goods

Company and, when he was 15, he joined the Socialist Party of America. He later secured a job as bookkeeper for the Potts Drug Company and started to attend the meetings of the Kansas City union of bookkeepers and accountants. Like many socialist party members, Browder condemned World War I in several public speeches and this caused him to be imprisoned twice for his opposition to the draft and for his continuing campaign (1917–18 and 1919–20).

In 1921, Browder left the Socialist Party and joined the American Communist Party, which had been founded in 1919. Browder quickly moved up the party's hierarchy. He first organized an American delegation to the first Congress of the Red International Labor Unions, held in Moscow, the Soviet Union, in 1921. In the mid-1920s, he became responsible for the organization of illegal Chinese trade unions fighting the Kuomintang government in China. Following Stalin's removal of Jay Lovestone as secretary of the CPUSA, Browder, together with William Z. Foster and William W. Weinstone, formed the troika that led the party until 1932, the year he became the sole secretary-general.

Browder was the party's presidential candidate in 1936 and in 1940, though with limited success. As secretary general, he had the difficult task of managing in the American political arena the shifting policies of the Soviets from the creation of the Popular Front against Fascism and Nazism (1933–39) to their Non-Aggression Pact with Hitler (1939). During the Popular Front period, Browder defined communism as the summary of American radical traditions, enlarging the party membership to 82,000 and including many immigrants and African Americans. It is during these years that, according to several scholars, Browder started to form and manage a ring of spies.

According to Allen Weinstein and Alexander Vassiliev, Browder was a pivotal figure in Soviet espionage as he was the one to handpick all Soviet "sources, couriers, and group handlers" with the exception of atomic espionage agents. He was able to turn communist sympathizers into spies, convincing them that handing government documents to the American Communist Party was ethically different than passing them directly to the Soviet secret services.

The release of the Venona files, comprising the decryptions of almost 3,000 intercepted Soviet intelligence cables, and the opening of the Eastern Bloc archives have also shed new light on the role of Browder's family in Soviet espionage in the United States. James Ryan has documented that at least six of his family members helped him in his covert actions.

The end of the Popular Front put the party in a difficult moral and political position and membership did not rise again until the German invasion of the Soviet Union in 1941. Browder's career, however, was never to rise again. Because of the claims in his "Teheran Thesis" that capitalism and communism could peacefully co-exist, he lost his position as party secretary. His theory that big business could contribute to defeat fascism and restore wealth in the postwar world made him a suspect social democrat.

In 1946, after being criticized by leaders in the Soviet Union, Browder was expelled from the American Communist Party and his death in 1973 failed to evoke emotion in the national and international communist press.

## SEE ALSO

*Volume 1 Left:* Communism; Cominform; Stalin and Stalinism; Third International (Comintern).
*Volume 2 Right:* Capitalism; McCarthyism; Hoover, J. Edgar.

## BIBLIOGRAPHY

John Earl Haynes and Harvey Klehr, *Venona: Decoding Soviet Espionage in America* (Yale University Press, 1999); James G. Ryan, *Earl Browder: The Failure of American Communism* (University of Alabama Press, 1997); James G. Ryan, "Socialist Triumph as a Family Value: Earl Browder and Soviet Espionage," *American Communist History* (v.1/2, 2002); Allen Weinstein and Alexander Vassiliev, *The Haunted Wood: Decoding Soviet Espionage in America* (Random House, 1999).

Luca Prono. Ph.D.
University of Nottingham, United Kingdom

# The Left

## Campaign Finance

ACCORDING TO A well-known expression, money has always been "the mother's milk of politics." Joseph Israel Tarte, a 19th-century Canadian political fundraiser, once declared "elections are not won with prayers." Political organizations and political campaigns require large-scale financial resources in order to succeed. Party organizations need to be staffed, accommodated, and equipped. In a political campaign, the costs of advertising, marketing, events, tours, and related activities have become enormous. Political friends need to be rewarded and activated, enemies must be targeted, and the neutrals persuaded. Each of these activities costs money. In the American federal election of 2000, the presidential candidates, between them, spent over $600 million, while Congressional candidates spent in excess of a further billion dollars.

Although in both Canada and the United States campaign finance reform has been quite bipartisan, the effort to reduce the special influence of generous contributors has usually been viewed as favoring liberal candidates rather than conservative ones who are regarded as having more access to wealthy contributors.

The relationship between money and politics has been ethically questionable from the start. In the 19th and early 20th centuries, bribery, graft, clientelism, patronage, kickbacks, and other forms of corruption were commonplace among parties, leaders, and the moneyed elite everywhere in the Western world. However, it was not until the 1960s and 1970s that serious action was taken to stop these practices. In both Canada and the United States, growing political efficacy and declining levels of trust in public officials combined to promote bold legislative initiatives in campaign finance reform at the federal level. The Federal Election Campaign Act (FECA) (1971, amended in 1974 and 1979) established the broad parameters of contribution, expenditure, and reporting regulation in the United States, while the Election Expenses Act (1974) set up the rules for campaign finance in Canada.

The concept of campaign finance is distinctly American. Relative to other polities, notably those in Western Europe, political competition in the United States is focused on the candidate and the campaign. In Europe, political finance has been more closely associated with support for political parties both in election campaigns and between elections. Large-scale fundraising is less critical in Europe because public broadcasters provide adequate free time and there is a range of other subsidies to political parties, such as free or reduced rates of postage and public financial support for party organizations. Recent changes to the Canada Elections Act, which came into effect in January 2004, have Europeanized the nature of party financing in Canada. Substantial new public monies will now be available to registered Canadian parties, based on the number of votes they received in the previous election.

The political culture of liberal individualism, suspicion of government, and the power of First Amendment rights have prompted Americans to reject limitations regarding the raising and spending of money. In a landmark Supreme Court decision, *Buckley v. Valeo* (1976), mandatory limits on campaign spending were declared unconstitutional in a decision that equated the spending of money with freedom of speech. Despite this, the decision upheld the rights of governments to set limits to campaign donations. The Supreme Court acknowledged that excessive donations by an individual or political committee might well be associated with corrupt practices or at least have the appearance of such association. By the same token, corporations and unions have been unable to make direct contributions to campaigns under federal law for a long time.

Of growing concern to American citizens has been the power of so-called soft money in politics. Soft money lends support to candidates and campaigns beyond the parameters of state regulation. Such contributions can be used for issue advocacy, even when such statements effectively are an endorsement of a particular candidate or party.

There is a wide range of other campaign-related expenditures not covered by the FECA that soft money can purchase. Soft money raised by the Republicans and Democrats in 2000 was over $450 million. The 2002 Bipartisan Campaign Reform Act (BCRA) extended federal campaign finance regulations to cover certain aspects of soft money donations and expenditures. While it has so far been upheld in the courts, it has not taken political operatives long to find ways of avoiding its limitations.

**SEE ALSO**

*Volume 1 Left:* United States; Democratic Party.
*Volume 2 Right:* Republican Party; United States.

**BIBLIOGRAPHY**

Anthony Corrado, ed., *Campaign Finance Reform: Beyond the Basics* (Century Foundation Press, 2000); Arthur B. Gunlicks, ed., *Campaign and Party Finance in North America and Western Europe* (Westview Press, 1993); U.S. Government, *21st Century Complete Guide to the Federal Election Commission* (CD-ROM) (Progressive Management, 2003).

PAUL NESBITT-LARKING, PH.D.
HURON UNIVERSITY COLLEGE

# Canada

DIFFERENCES IN IDEOLOGY play a negligible role in Canadian politics. A party's position often depends less on its official principles than on whether it is in or out of government. Also, federal and provincial politics are quite disconnected. This was shown in the 1990s when the Liberal Party was able to build a majority government largely on the basis of Ontario seats but could not control the Ontario provincial legislature. The parties of the left run the gamut from the mainstream Liberal Party through the smaller but occasionally influential New Democratic Party and the secessionist Parti Québécois to the peripheral Communist Party of Canada.

LIBERAL PARTY

The Liberals are Canada's "government party," having ruled for two-thirds of the 20th century. The party does not espouse a coherent theory of society, parliament, power, or policy. Its specific positions have evolved with changing circumstances, issues, and public attitudes. Run from the top down, it can become distant from its regular members and society at large after prolonged periods in power. It has also been able to renew itself, often by scouring its "extra-parliamentary wing" for ideas after its occasional electoral defeats.

The Liberal Party had its origins in 19th-century reform movements, even before Canadian independence. In that century, in near permanent opposition, it championed responsible government, provincial rights, free trade, closer ties with the United States (continentalism), and the interests of the working class.

In the 20th century, the party built a powerful nationwide coalition on the basis of regional power brokerage, an expansionary role for government, accommodation of English and French Canadians, patronage, and a highly pragmatic approach to policy, sometimes stealing Conservative causes. W. L. Mackenzie King (1921–26, 1926–30, 1935–48) used ambiguity to maintain a diverse coalition, and the party won a reputation for competence and compromise. Later, the Liberals' position in the west dissipated, and the party relied heavily on its strength in central Canada.

Social welfare programs initiated under King were expanded under Lester Pearson (1963–68) and Pierre Elliot Trudeau (1968–79, 1980–84). Trudeau also opposed Québec separatism while seeking to tie Québec to a new Canadian constitution, implement bilingualism, and promote Canadian French within the party and federal

*Canada has favored practical leftist governments over holding to a particular party ideology. Important factors for any Canadian government are how it deals with Québec separatism and the superpower neighbor to the south, the United States.*

government. The parties switched positions on continentalism in the 1970s, and the Liberals took a nationalist stance against the establishment of a free-trade area with the United States. By the time of Jean Chrétien (1993–2003), the party appeared to be the mirror image of its earlier self. Attuned to the public mood, Chrétien grumbled about the United States and the North American Free Trade Agreement (NAFTA), although he did not undo it, and prided himself on achieving a smaller government bureaucracy, fiscal responsibility, and balanced budgets. On social issues, however, he spoke in favor of gay marriage and the legalization of marijuana, positions that did not garner broad support.

## NEW DEMOCRATIC PARTY

The New Democratic Party (NDP) was formed in 1961 through the merger of the Co-operative Commonwealth Federation (CCF) and the Canadian Labour Congress. The CCF, a largely western-based progressive party formed in 1932, had never held power nationally, but it did govern Saskatchewan (1944–61), where it pioneered publicly financed hospitalization. The strength of the CCF caused the Liberal Party to shift to the left for a time in the 1940s, and in close collaboration with reform-minded Liberals, the CCF and NDP influenced the development of the Canadian welfare state.

More ideologically consistent than the major parties, the NDP is a member of the Socialist International and advocates a mixed economy, government planning, industrial democracy, "public" ownership (including cooperatives, crown corporations, and state enterprises) where necessary to sustain employment and services, and pacifism in foreign affairs. The evolution of CCF and NDP thinking can be followed through a series of formal statements: the Regina Manifesto (1933), the Winnipeg Declaration (1961), the New Party Declaration (1961), and the New Regina Manifesto (1986).

The New Democrats win on average just over 15 percent of the vote in national elections, but given the winner-take-all electoral system, it averages less than 9 percent of the seats in the House of Commons. Its influence is greatest during minority governments. The NDP has formed several provincial governments (British Columbia, 1972–75, 1991–2001; Saskatchewan, 1961–64, 1971–82, 1991–); Manitoba, 1969–77, 1981–88, 1999–); Ontario, 1990–95).

## PARTI QUÉBÉCOIS

The Parti Québécois (PQ) was formed in 1968 through the merger of two existing movements. It distinguished itself from earlier Québec secessionist organizations by its ability to attract voters, in part due to its more moderate stance on secession. The PQ was willing to wait until the population was ready for independence and willing to negotiate "sovereignty-association." The latter allowed for an economic union with the rest of Canada after independence, thus lessening the threat of disruption. (The party avoided the question of whether Canada would agree to it.) The PQ assumed social democratic stances on policy issues and attained observer status in the Socialist International.

The PQ has formed provincial governments in Québec (1976–85, 1994–2003). It made French the only official language of Québec and reformed insurance, family law, and the civil code. Its referenda on independence, in 1980 and 1995, failed, although the second was close (50.6 percent to 49.4 percent). The failures created dilemmas for the party, which had to govern within the federation it had denounced and try to extract budgetary resources from it. Party leaders occasionally argued over whether, when, or how to renew the secession issue. The PQ lost voters among hard-line secessionists and also among the working class, as it felt compelled to roll back public-sector wages. It gained other votes, however, as the general public wearied of the secession debate and grew increasingly middle class.

## COMMUNIST PARTY OF CANADA

The Communist Party of Canada (CPC) was formed in Guelph in 1921 and has operated at times under different names. The party adhered to the Communist International, which had sent three representatives to its inaugural meeting. The Royal Canadian Mounted Police subjected it to raids and arrests. Starting in the 1930s, however, it elected several city and provincial officials and one member of the House of Commons. The CPC also organized labor unions and recruited volunteers for the Republican forces in the Spanish Civil War. The party suffered from its close identification with the Soviet Union, especially after Igor Gouzenko, a Soviet embassy clerk, revealed the names of Canadians engaged in espionage in 1945. Splinter groups have included the Communist League, inspired by Leon Trotsky and later by Fidel Castro, and the Communist Party of Canada (Marxist-Leninist), which took its inspiration from Mao Zedong.

### SEE ALSO

*Volume 1 Left:* Québec Separatism; Liberal Party, Canada.
*Volume 2 Right:* Canada; Conservatism.

### BIBLIOGRAPHY

R. Kenneth Carty et al., *Rebuilding Canadian Party Politics* (University of British Columbia Press, 2000); Graham Fraser, *René Lévesque and the Parti Québécois in Power* (McGill-Queens University. Press, 2001); Hugh G. Thorburn and Alan Whitehorn, eds., *Party Politics in Canada* (Prentice Hall, 2001); Alan Whitehorn, *Canadian Socialism: Essays on the CCF-NDP* (Oxford University Press, 1992).

SCOTT C. MONJE, PH.D.
INDEPENDENT SCHOLAR

# Carmichael, Stokely (1941–1998)

STOKELY CARMICHAEL WILL be remembered for his role in the civil rights movement during the 1960s. Born in the Port of Spain, Trinidad, Carmichael moved to the United States in 1952 and attended high school in New York. He entered Howard University in 1960 and soon after joined the Student Nonviolent Coordinating Committee (SNCC), a pioneering civil rights activist group infused with the principles of nonviolence.

In 1961, Carmichael became a member of the Freedom Riders, a group of black and white volunteers who sat next to each other as they traveled through the Deep South, challenging existing racial discrimination and practices. Local police were unwilling to protect these passengers and in several places they were beaten up by white mobs. During one such protest in Mississippi, Carmichael was arrested and jailed for 49 days.

A similar single-man protest was carried out in June 1966 by James Meredith, who started The March Against Fear in order to assert the right of all African Americans to move across the South unmolested. Meredith wanted to prove that he could conquer his own fear, and that of others, by walking safely from Memphis, Tennessee, to Jackson, Mississippi. Meredith also hoped to encourage locals along the way to take the risks to register to vote and participate in the primary elections. He was shot soon after starting his protest, but Carmichael, along with other civil rights campaigners including Martin Luther King, Jr., and Floyd McKissick, decided to complete the march in Meredith's name.

## BLACK POWER

The March Against Fear became important for Carmichael as well as for the civil rights movement itself. Having been arrested for the 27th time, Carmichael made his famous "Black Power" speech upon his release. It was also this year that Carmichael became chairman of SNCC, marking a decisive change in the organization's founding philosophy by bringing Black Power to prominence. The goal of Black Power was to empower a strong racial identity for African Americans.

In his speech, Carmichael called for black people to unite, to recognize their heritage, and to build a sense of community. He also advocated that African Americans should form and lead their own organizations. Black Power also encouraged a separation from white society, arguing that black people should write their own histories and form their own institutions. This empowered African Americans by promoting feelings of self-worth and by showing that they were strong enough to thrive without the support of white institutions.

The ideas contained in the speech were institutionalized with the publication of a book of the same title

he coauthored with Charles Hamilton (*Black Power*). At this point it is possible to discern a split in the civil rights movement. In particular, leaders of civil rights groups such as the National Association for the Advancement of Colored People (NAACP) and Southern Christian Leadership Conference (SCLC) rejected Carmichael's ideas and accused him of black racism. This controversy was compounded by Carmichael's criticism of King and his ideology of non-violence. The split was made permanent when Carmichael joined the Black Panther Party, where he became an honorary prime minister.

The radicalization of the sector of the civil rights movement represented by the Black Panthers followed a parallel path to the radicalization that characterized young people, students, and the New Left in general in the late 1960s. Their opposition to the Vietnam War gave all these disparate groups a common bond and raison d'etre. However, Carmichael moved away from the Black Panthers because of their links with white radicals and began to advocate a return to Africa. He himself moved to Guinea with his wife in the early part of the 1970s, where he wrote the book *Stokely Speaks: Black Power back to Pan-Africanism*. There, he adopted the name Kwame Ture, working as an aide to Guinea's prime minister, Sekou Toure. Carmichael died of cancer on November 15, 1998.

Carmichael's politics, particularly his stand against the Vietnam War and his support for direct action in achieving integration, would classify him as a political leader of the left. In his cry for black power, he also associated with those on the left who sought more power for the politically dispossessed. However, his personal emigration to Africa reflected his acceptance of the essentially rightist ideology of ethnic nationalism.

**SEE ALSO**
*Volume 1 Left*: Black Panthers; Civil Rights; Desegregation.
*Volume 2 Right*: United States; Segregation.

**BIBLIOGRAPHY**
Coretta Scott King and Nathan Huggins, *Stokely Carmichael: Civil Rights Leader* (Chelsea House, 1996); Jacqueline Johnson, *Stokely Carmichael: The Story of Back Power* (Silver Burdett, 1990); Stokely Carmichael, *Ready for Revolution: The Life and Struggles of Stokely Carmichael (Kwame Ture)* (Vertigo, 2003); Stokely Carmichael and Charles Taylor, *Black Power: Politics of Liberation in America* (Penguin, 1969).

KEPA ARTARAZ, PH.D.
UNIVERSITY OF DERBY, UNITED KINGDOM

# Carter, James E. (1924–)

WHEN JIMMY CARTER was elected the 39th president in 1976, his Democratic victory over incumbent Gerald Ford seemed to symbolize the end of a political episode dominated by Republicans and tainted by the Watergate scandal. But Carter's one-term administration, regarded by some scholars as a considerable failure, became just an interruption in an extended period of conservative rule. Nevertheless, his post-presidency commitment to international peace and human rights recast his legacy as a well-respected humanitarian and diplomat across the globe.

Born on October 1, 1924, in the small community of Plains, Georgia, Carter was the eldest son of Lillian Gordy and James Earl Carter, a Georgia landowner and businessman. Carter was exposed to politics early in his life: his father had served on the school board (and would later be elected to the state legislature). Although his family had considerable prominence in the Plains community, like many rural families during the Great Depression, the Carters were not wealthy. However, the family held an abundance of land, enough to build a business based on the crops of cotton and especially peanuts. Growing up on his family's Southern farm, Carter lived in a society dominated by racial segregation. Yet, both his mother's liberal influence and his religious convictions tempered his views on race.

A motivated and successful student, Carter attended Plains High School and in 1941 enrolled in Georgia Southwestern College. After one year, he transferred to the Georgia Institute of Technology in Atlanta before being admitted to the U.S. Naval Academy in Annapolis, Maryland. Graduating from Annapolis in 1946, Carter was assigned to a postwar naval position and went on to serve a seven-year term of service with the navy.

Carter's academic career and rise in the naval ranks nurtured his sense of ambition, which put him somewhat in conflict with his parents, particularly his father, who lived out his life in Plains working within the family peanut business. When the elder Carter fell ill and died in 1953, his son reevaluated his choices and decided to return to Plains and rebuild the family's peanut business. Like his father, Carter became active in community affairs. A devout Baptist whose faith was an important component of both his private and public persona, Carter served as deacon to the local church. He also worked at the library, on the hospital authority, and on behalf of an unsuccessful referendum to consolidate the county schools. By 1960, Carter was one of

*Jimmy Carter's leftist human rights aspirations were in stark contrast with the realities of the Cold War.*

Plains' most well respected residents and leaders. Given his drive and commitment to civic duty, it was not long before friends encouraged him to consider a run for political office.

In 1962, Carter was elected to the Georgia Senate. Though he lost his first gubernatorial campaign in 1966, he won the next election and became the governor of Georgia on January 12, 1971. Carter was one of a new group of Southern governors identified by their moderate racial views and reform initiatives. Upon taking office, he promised to lead Georgia into an era of racial equality and economic and social justice. He made good on his word by taking measures to increase the number of African American state employees during his tenure. And foreshadowing some of his presidential activities, Carter also worked for greater environmental and consumer protection and for tax, welfare, and judicial reform, as well as an increase in services for the mentally ill.

Despite his gubernatorial success, political observers were surprised with Carter's 1974 announcement that he would seek the Democratic nomination for president in 1976. But Americans embraced the religious Southerner. Carter's campaign statement, "I will never lie to you," comforted those who had become skeptical of government in the wake of the Watergate scandal and Vietnam. The blend of Carter's cultural conservatism, his commitment to civil rights, and his moderate economic views brought him support from not only conventional Democrats, but also from African Americans and southern whites, who identified with his upbringing. In a narrow election, Carter defeated Republican incumbent Gerald R. Ford.

With Carter's ascendancy to the White House in 1977, liberals had high hopes for the resurgence of the Democratic Party. Many expected that the Democratic agenda fostered by Lyndon Johnson's Great Society would be rediscovered under Carter. Yet, although Carter had promised to make liberal government work, he was ultimately trapped between high expectations on the left and harsh criticisms from the right, and became somewhat isolated politically. But even against such challenges, Carter's administration enjoyed crucial successes on both foreign and domestic fronts. At home, Carter's achievements included significant environmental protection legislation, including the Alaska National Interest Lands Conservation Act, the 1978 Comprehensive Energy Act, and the 1980 Waste Cleanup Act. Carter also created the Cabinet-level Departments of Education and Energy.

Carter's major foreign policy accomplishments included the Panama Canal Treaties, the 1978 Camp David Summit Meeting between President Anwar Sadat of Egypt and Prime Minister Menachem Begin of Israel, which resulted in the Camp David Accords, and the establishment of American diplomatic relations with the People's Republic of China in 1979. Arguing that the United Nations should make the treatment of political prisoners and dissidents a matter of international concern, Carter also initiated a human rights campaign, a cause that he would be praised for and identified with. Despite the achievements of Carter's administration, both the failing economy and the Iran Hostage crisis—in which he failed to gain the release of American diplomatic personnel held hostage in Iran—seriously undermined his political future. In the 1980

presidential election, while Carter dwelt on the "malaise" affecting America, Republican Ronald Reagan offered America "a new morning" and decisively defeated him.

After leaving office, Carter returned to Georgia and continued his passionate advocacy of peace and human rights. In 2002, he was awarded the Nobel Peace Prize in recognition of his decades of service toward advancing democracy, international peace, and human rights and for promoting economic and social development worldwide.

**SEE ALSO**

*Volume 1 Left:* Democratic Party; Liberalism; United States. *Volume 2 Right:* Reagan, Ronald; Republican Party; Conservatism.

**BIBLIOGRAPHY**

Jimmy Carter, *An Hour before Daylight: Memories of a Rural Boyhood* (Simon and Schuster, 2001); Gary M. Fink and Hugh Davis Graham, eds., *The Carter Presidency: Policy Choices in the Post-New Deal Era* (University Press of Kansas, 1998); Erwin C. Hargrove, *Jimmy Carter as President: Leadership and the Politics of the Public Good* (Louisiana State University Press, 1988); Burton I. Kaufman, *The Presidency of James Earl Carter, Jr.* (University Press of Kansas, 1993); Victor Lasky, *Jimmy Carter: The Man and the Myth* (Richard Marek Publishers, 1980); Kenneth Morris, *Jimmy Carter: American Moralist* (University of Georgia Press, 1996); "Biography of Jimmy Carter," Jimmy Carter Library and Museum, www.jimmy-carterlibrary.org (July 2004).

LINDSAY SILVER
BRANDEIS UNIVERSITY

# Carville, James (1944–)

JAMES CARVILLE has been described as a grandmaster at the chessboard of politics by at least one historian. With Paul Begala, Carville set the communications strategy for Bill Clinton's 1992 presidential victory. Born in Carville, Louisiana—a town named for his grandfather—and famed for his blunt, hard-driving style, the "Ragin' Cajun" is credited with focusing the Clinton campaign's easy-to-understand expression of its political priorities.

Carville's first campaign work occurred while he was still a student at Ascension Catholic High School in

1959. He worked on a Louisiana state legislature race, distributing literature and posting signs for candidate Price LeBlanc. In 1962, Carville graduated from high school and began college at Louisiana State University (LSU). He left after a couple of years and joined the U.S. Marines. After his two-year service expired, Carville returned to LSU to complete his college degree. Between finishing his undergraduate degree and returning for his law degree, Carville worked as a high school science teacher. From 1973 to 1979, he practiced law in Baton Rouge, Louisiana.

Carville began his formal, professional campaign work in 1980. Over the next 10 years, he worked on many campaigns, including those of Robert P. Casey in the 1986 and 1990 Pennsylvania gubernatorial elections and Harris Wofford in the 1991 Pennsylvania senatorial election. In 1989, he and his long-standing collaborator, Begala, formed Carville and Begala, a political consulting firm. The 1991 Wofford campaign highlighted their approach to politicking.

Wofford had begun the election polling 47 points behind his opponent, Richard Thornburgh, a former Pennsylvania governor and attorney general under Ronald Reagan. Carville and Begala helped Wofford win the election by focusing his campaign on a few topics, such as health insurance, which were critical for the everyday voter, matters that transcended political ideologies. This sharp, seemingly nonpartisan approach led Wofford to victory and brought Carville and Begala national prominence as campaign strategists for Democrats seeking office.

The then-governor of Arkansas, Clinton, was one of several Democrats seeking the Democratic presidential nomination. Right after the Wofford election, Carville and Begala agreed to work with Clinton, bringing their laserlike style of campaign strategy and message development to the eventual Democratic nominee. This discipline helped Clinton secure the nomination and survive many political flashfires, such as those of Gennifer Flowers, who accused Clinton of having an affair with her, and of Clinton's student status, which kept him ineligible for the draft during the Vietnam War.

Ultimately, although both Carville and Begala were working on the campaign, Carville spearheaded the campaign's move to the top of the polls by articulating its focus on the economy and on the costs of incumbent George H. W. Bush's promises about no new taxes. Carville's blunt phrasing, "It's the economy, stupid," captured the ordinary voter's concerns about Bush and became the rallying cry of the successful campaign.

After Clinton won the 1992 election, Carville continued to serve as a media adviser for the president. During the Whitewater investigations of 1996–98, Carville staunchly defended the president even though he no longer had a formal role with the White House.

In 2004, Carville retained his prominence as a media adviser and campaign consultant for Democrats. He worked with Gould Greenberg Carville NOP (GGC NOP), a consulting group that assists corporations with their media and polling strategic development. He was also a cohost, with Paul Begala, Robert Novak, and Tucker Carlson, of the Cable News Network's (CNN) *Crossfire*, a political debate program on current topics. Carville has also written numerous books on campaign strategy as well as two autobiographical works. Carville and his wife, Mary Matalin, the Republican campaign strategist and adviser to Vice President Richard Cheney, live in Virginia.

Although Carville's career has not been characterized by a commitment to any ideology, his active support for and advice to the leading liberal Democrat of the 1990s places him on the liberal side of the American political spectrum.

**SEE ALSO**

*Volume 1 Left:* Media Bias, Left; Clinton, William J.; Democratic Party.
*Volume 2 Right:* Media Bias, Right; Bush, George H. W.

**BIBLIOGRAPHY**

James Carville and Mary Matalin, with Peter Knobler, *All's Fair: Love, War, and Running for President* (Random House, 1994); Peter Golomon, Thomas M. DeFrank, et al., *Quest for the Presidency 1992* (Texas A&M University Press, 1994); Cable News Network, "James Carville," www.cnn.com (May 2004); "GGC NOP: James Carville," Gould Greenberg Carville NOP, www.greenbergresearch.com (May 2004); Howard Kurtz, *Spin Cycle: Inside the Clinton Propaganda Machine* (The Free Press, 1998).

CLARE CALLAGHAN
INDEPENDENT SCHOLAR

# Catholic Worker

THE CATHOLIC WORKER, both the movement and the newspaper, was founded in 1933 by Dorothy Day and Paul Maurin. The movement brought together the passionate Catholicism and personal strengths of each: Day converted to Catholicism in 1927 and for over a decade had been a journalist and freelance writer concerned with social justice; Maurin was a French immigrant with a vision of ideal Catholic social activism. Day provided the logistical development of the Catholic Worker movement and newspaper, but Maurin provided its theoretical and intellectual ideals.

The newspaper, envisioned as a journal for advocating social change, began first, but the formal Catholic Worker movement quickly followed. The first issue targeted unemployed workers and informed them about race relations, housing, strikes, and schools run by various labor union movements. Sympathetic volunteer editors supplemented Day's own editorial and journalistic contributions, but Day remained the lead editor until her death in 1980.

## RADICAL CATHOLICS

Priced at a penny, the periodical was targeted to many different audiences, such as the disenfranchised poor, the unemployed, lay Catholics exploring the social teachings of the faith, and the religious leadership. Its articles covered news related to labor and social movements but also included reviews, essays, and editorials that helped provide analysis of events and advocacy of the Catholic Worker approach to social problems. Finally, the *Catholic Worker* included contributions of artwork and quotes from church authorities, such as popes and theologians, which grounded the paper in the Catholic tradition.

This grounding was necessary, because the *Catholic Worker* advocated such a radical approach. The paper helped build up a coherent and consistent belief system that established the Catholic Worker movement as a legitimate, but radical, part of the Catholic social theology. The movement's radicalism lies in its practices. The attempt to have a radical approach to the Gospel, or to live out a close, literal reading of the Gospel as the foundation of society, has a long legacy; the medieval St. Francis of Assisi, for example, promoted one such approach through his embrace of poverty.

The Catholic Worker movement was the first American Catholic approach. It began when Maurin brought a couple of impoverished friends to the newspaper's offices to share meals. Day quickly realized that an editorial commitment to helping the needy could only exist if there were a practical commitment as well. Thus, sharing a few meals with these friends at the main office of the *Catholic Worker* became the first of the national network of the Catholic Worker Houses of Hospitality, which provided meals, sleeping accommodations, and other assistance to the needy.

The Catholic Worker movement followed some simple principles, all advocated in the periodical as well. Maurin provided the first three: 1) roundtable discussions to help inform those without formal learning and to help ground those with formal learning; 2) Houses of Hospitality to provide places of social justice and service; and 3) farming communes to feed and train the unemployed. In addition, each House of Hospitality formed the spiritual center for a group of workers and of guests. All residents, whether workers or guests, were expected to share the ideal of voluntary poverty. This meant wearing donated clothes, receiving no salaries for work done at the house, and relying on donations to pay bills such as rent and utilities.

More broadly, the Catholic Worker movement became the first Roman Catholic group in America to articulate pacifism. Day argued that pacifism could be reconciled with the Catholic Worker concerns of social and labor justice, because war absorbed resources that could be used for social justice, because war is about defending possessions, which violates the Worker anti-materialist principles; and because workers could use their powers of boycott and strike to show their opposition to war. During World War II, the *Catholic Worker* newspaper openly encouraged men not to register for the draft. Furthermore, Catholic Workers assisted men of any religious belief in avoiding the draft. Day, and therefore the Catholic Workers, took similar positions during the Korean and Vietnam wars as well.

The Catholic Worker movement and newspaper have had a profound and ongoing effect on American Catholicism in particular, and on American social reform in general. For American Catholicism, the Catholic Workers demonstrate a radical, Gospel-driven response to contemporary American society, providing a channel through which ordinary American Catholics can live out the Gospel ideals of poverty and assistance. The newspaper helped articulate 20th-century social reforms, clearly grounding them in the rich Catholic intellectual tradition and thereby engaging the Catholic Church in the work. Above all, though, the movement promoted pacifism in the face of war and brought the Catholic Church to reconsider its "just war" doctrines.

## SEE ALSO

*Volume 1 Left:* Church and State Separation; Welfare and Poverty.
*Volume 2 Right:* Coughlin, Charles; Religion.

**BIBLIOGRAPHY**

Rosalie Roegle Troestes, ed., *Voices from the Catholic Worker* (Temple University Press, 1993); Mel Piehl, *Breaking Bread: the Catholic Social Worker and the Origin of Catholic Radicalism in America* (Temple University Press, 1982); Nancy L. Roberts, *Dorothy Day and the Catholic Worker* (State University of New York Press, 1984); Anne Klejment and Nancy L. Roberts, *American Catholic Pacifism: The Influence of Dorothy Day and the Catholic Worker Movement* (Praeger, 1996).

CLARE CALLAGHAN
INDEPENDENT SCHOLAR

# Censorship

FREEDOM OF BELIEF and conscience are essential to democracy; censorship threatens the free exchange of ideas that allows democracy to flourish. English philosopher John Stuart Mill summarized the liberal view of censorship in his essay, "On Liberty" (1869): "If all mankind, minus one were of one opinion, and only one were of the contrary opinion, mankind would be no more justified in silencing the one than he, if he had the power, would be justified in silencing mankind." Like Mill, most liberals are afraid that the one person who is silenced might be the one who discovers a universal truth or solves a scientific problem or writes a book, a song, or a poem that will stand the test of time.

The purpose of censorship is always to stop someone from saying, printing, or depicting something that is seen as dangerous or which threatens societal norms. Censors seek to place limits on words, images, ideas, symbols, signs, books, music, and art. The danger in censorship is that the censor sets herself up as the judge of what is permissible and what is not. When government acts as censor by prohibiting criticism of its actions or by blocking the flow of information, it lays the foundation for tyranny. In response to national and state efforts to infringe on civil liberties, the U.S. Supreme Court has become known, sometimes ironically, as the guardians of liberty. The court has cautioned in cases such as *FCC v. Pacifica Foundation* (438 U.S. 726 438 U.S. 726, 1978) that finding speech offensive is no reason for suppressing it.

The First Amendment to the U.S. Constitution states, "Congress shall make no law abridging the freedom of speech or of the press." Yet, by 1789, Congress had passed the first Sedition Act, which prohibited all criticism of the government. During the Civil War, Abraham Lincoln rode roughshod over the First Amendment. During World War I, Congress passed the Second Sedition and Espionage Acts, which restricted criticism of the government or of the war effort and established criminal penalties for any speech or writing that was considered "disloyal."

Efforts to censor speech during World War II centered around the Smith Act of 1940, which established severe penalties for anyone who advocated the overthrow of the government by force or violence. Following World War II, the Cold War and McCarthyism led to the passage of the McCarran or Communist Control Act of 1954 over President Harry Truman's veto, censoring freedom of association by making membership in the Communist Party illegal. During the 1960s, there was an unusual amount of tolerance for free speech that encompassed civil rights, women's rights, the anti-war effort, and student protests. As might be expected, a conservative backlash followed in the 1980s with the election of Ronald Reagan. The religious right launched an all-out effort to censor books, art, web sites, movies, signs, and television programming.

The abortion issue provides an excellent example of what happens when conservatives attempt to limit speech/action with which they disagree. The Reagan and George H.W. Bush administrations became so successful in censoring even the use of the word *abortion* that Congress passed a law banning the use of the word in clinics that received Title X funds. In 1991, in *Rust v. Sullivan* (500 U.S. 173), the conservative court upheld this limitation on the speech of medical and family planning personnel. President Bill Clinton overturned the case with an executive order, and Congress turned his actions into federal law.

Even though liberals dislike censorship on principle, some limits may be acceptable. In *Schenck v. United States* (249 U.S. 47, 1919), Justice Oliver Wendell Holmes identified what has become the classic acceptable infringement on free speech: "the most stringent protection of free speech would not protect a man in falsely shouting fire in a theatre and causing a panic." Many liberals also favor censorship of pornography on the grounds that it is harmful and likely to incite violent actions against women and children and hate speech because it infringes on human dignity.

## SUPREME COURT TESTS

From the beginning, the Supreme Court has been called upon to determine what speech should be censored and which is protected by the First Amendment. Normally, verbal expression known as "pure speech" is accorded the most protection. When pure speech involves action of some sort, it becomes known as "speech plus." Some liberal absolutists, such as Justices Hugo Black and William Douglas, believed that when the First Amendment said Congress should make no law abridging freedom of speech it meant that "no law was no law." For most justices, however, determining the line between protected speech and unprotected action has not always been easy. Early in the 20th century, during one of the most radical periods in U.S. history, the Supreme Court began to rely on tests to judge what was protected and what could be constitutionally censored.

In *Schenck v. United States*, Justice Holmes developed the Clear and Present Danger Test, which judged "whether the words used are used in such circumstances and are of such a nature as to create a clear and present danger that they will bring about the substantive evils that Congress has a right to prevent." Substantive evils were generally defined as trying to overthrow the government, inciting to riot, and destruction of life and property. On the basis of the Clear and Present Danger Test, convictions of most radicals were upheld. Rejecting the Holmes test, the court opted for the Bad Tendency Test, which allowed government to restrict speech that threatened public health, safety, and morals.

By the early 1940s, the court had drifted toward the Preferred Preference Doctrine, first articulated in *Jones v. City of Opelika* (319 U.S. 105) and eight companion cases, declaring that "freedom of press, freedom of speech, freedom of religion are in a preferred position." In *Thomas v. Collins* (323 U.S. 516, 1945), the court acknowledged that First Amendment freedoms are "indispensable" to democracy. By the 1950s, the justices were inclined to use the Balancing Doctrine, which weighed First Amendment freedoms against other constitutional protections. In 1951, in *Dennis v. United States* (341 U.S. 494), the court opted for the Hand Test developed by Judge Leonard Hand, which attempted to determine "whether the gravity of the 'evil,' discounted by its improbability, justifies such invasion of free speech as is necessary to avoid the danger."

The liberal reform mood of the 1960s escalated social tensions to the point that the Supreme Court needed new guidelines for determining acceptable censorship of speech. In *Brandenburg v. Ohio* (395 U.S. 444), in 1969, the court announced the Imminent Danger Test. On this guideline, states were allowed to enact laws that censored speech only "where such advocacy is directed to inciting or producing imminent lawless action and is likely to incite or produce such action."

## SYMBOLIC SPEECH

Throughout the history of the United States, individuals and governments have attempted to censor the ways that individuals express their beliefs through the use of symbols. Few issues have invoked more wrath than those concerning the American flag. In *West Virginia v. Barnette* (319 U.S. 624, 1943), the court overturned a mandatory flag salute. In 1974, in *Spence v. Washington* (418 U.S. 405), the court upheld the right of a war protestor to hang a flag upside down outside his dorm window. Fifteen years later, the court overturned the conviction of Gregory Johnson for burning an American flag on the steps of the Republican headquarters building to protest the policies of the Reagan administration.

In *Texas v. Johnson* (491 U.S. 397), Justice William J. Brennan spoke for a narrow majority when he wrote "We do not consecrate the flag by punishing its desecration, for in doing so we dilute the freedom that this cherished emblem represents." In response to the decision, Congress passed the Flag Protection Act of 1989, which was overturned the following year in *United States v. Eichman* (496 U.S. 310). In early 2004, the court heard arguments in which an atheist parent challenged the practice of requiring his child to recite the pledge to the flag that includes "under God."

During the Vietnam War era, the issue of symbolic speech took on new meaning. While the court leaned toward a tolerant interpretation of freedom of speech during this period, the justices were unwilling to accept what they saw as flouting the interests of the U.S. government. For instance, in *United States v. O'Brien* (391 U.S. 367), the court held that burning draft cards was not protected by the First Amendment. In the landmark case *Tinker v. Des Moines* (393 U.S. 503), the court protected the rights of high-school and junior high-school students to wear black armbands to protest against the war.

## CONSERVATIVE CENSORSHIP

The efforts of religious conservatives to censor anything in which they do not believe have a long history in the United States. In 1925, for example in what became known as the Scopes or "Monkey" Trial, conservative opposition to teaching evolution in the schools received national attention when high-school science teacher

John Scopes was arrested in Tennessee for teaching evolution. The Supreme Court addressed the creation/evolution argument in 1968 in *Epperson v. Arkansas* (393 U.S. 97) in which the court reiterated its position that "there is and can be no doubt that the First Amendment does not permit the State to require that teaching and learning must be tailored to the principles or prohibitions of any religious sect or dogma."

Censors have frequently targeted media of all kinds. In *Jenkins v. Georgia* (418 U.S. 153, 1974), the court held that state law should be used to determine whether material was "patently offensive." Three years later in *Smith v. United States* (431 U.S. 291), the justices held that national standards should apply when censorship of books and movies was in question. In 1978 in *FCC v. Pacifica Foundation*, the court stated that "of all forms of communication, broadcasting has the most limited First Amendment protection," because it enters homes where children may be exposed to it.

Liberals and conservatives have long debated whether music should be censored; and if so, on what grounds. The popularity of rock and roll in the 1950s and 1960s launched a then-unprecedented censorship effort. Many people thought that the genre was obscene, anti-establishment, anti-family, and communist-generated. During the 1970s, censors targeted anti-war songs and those, such as Peter Paul and Mary's "Puff the Magic Dragon" and the Beatles' "Yellow Submarine," which were thought to promote the marijuana drug culture.

In the 1980s and 1990s, songs were censored for a range of reasons. For instance, Garth Brooks's "The Thunder Rolls" and Martina McBride's "Independence Day," which highlighted domestic violence, were censored by those who insisted they promoted violence. Even the bland Backstreet Boys, who appealed mostly to teenage girls, were declared "indecent" and "inappropriate." Censorship often has the reverse effect as in the case of 2 Live Crew's "As Nasty as They Wanna Be," which climbed in the charts in 1990 after being declared obscene. After the events of September 11, 2001, one radio chain banned anything that might be construed as "insensitive." Censored songs included Metallica's "Seek and Destroy," AC/DC's "Shot Down in Flames," and Carole King's "I Feel the Earth Move."

The conservative mood of the Reagan era also led to a concentrated attack on the arts. Conservatives were so irate over the fact that the National Endowment for the Arts had funded the "erotic" works of photographer Robert Mapplethorpe that they attempted to cut all funds for art that offended their sensibilities. The attack included the funding for public television, fueled by rumors that nonhuman characters on popular children's television shows were gay. In the same vein, Vice President Dan Quayle attacked the decision of fictional television journalist Murphy Brown to have a child even though she was not married because it challenged typical "family values."

Censors have frequently targeted books. Banned books have included the Bible, *The American Heritage Dictionary*, *The Autobiography of Benjamin Franklin*, *Catcher in the Rye*, *Huckleberry Finn*, *I Know Why the Caged Bird Sings*, *Bury My Heart at Wounded Knee*, and *To Kill a Mockingbird*. During the Reagan era, conservative fervor gave the religious right new ammunition to go after books that threatened their beliefs.

In the late 20th century, conservatives targeted a series of children's books by English author J. K. Rowling. The Harry Potter series about an orphaned wizard who attends Hogwarts, a school of magic, has been called "anti-Christian" and "disturbing." Liberals laud the fact that so many children and adults are reading the books that Rowling has become the first author in history to become a billionaire from her writing. Even the Vatican defended the Harry Potter books, and the Gatehouse Research Project suggested that all kids should read the books because they promoted family, friends, and community. An Australian researcher presented a paper in 2004 in which she argued that the books have given teenagers an alternative to suicide by teaching them positive ways of dealing with depression.

## PRESS CENSORSHIP

Since the first newspaper appeared in the American colonies, certain individuals wanted to censor anything with which they disagreed. Government officials have frequently attempted to stop newspapers from publishing what might be damaging to national security or political careers. However, the Supreme Court has consistently rejected prior restraint by opting to respond to written matter after it is published. In 1931, in *Near v. Minnesota* (283 U.S. 697), for example, the court stated unequivocally that the Constitution protected the press from prior restraint. In 1971, the Richard M. Nixon administration attempted to block the *New York Times* and the *Washington Post* from publishing the Pentagon Papers, which detailed U.S. policy in Vietnam. In *New York Times v. United States* (403 U.S. 713), the court refused, insisting that prior restraint is acceptable only in cases where the government can prove an overwhelming responsibility for doing so.

At times, the press is censored in order to protect the right of individuals to a fair trial. In *Estes v. Texas* (381 U.S. 532, 1965), the court reversed the conviction of Billy Sol Estes, finding that broadcasting the trial violated Estes's Fourteenth Amendment rights. Likewise, in *Sheppard v. Maxwell* (384 U.S. 333, 1966), the court overturned the conviction of Dr. Sam Sheppard, who was accused of murdering his pregnant wife, because of the adverse pretrial publicity that created a circuslike atmosphere and denied Sheppard's right to a fair trial. Nevertheless, in *Nebraska Press Association v. Stuart* (427 U.S. 539, 1976), the court found gag orders unconstitutional.

Censors have frequently targeted teachers and students. In 1968, in *Pickering v. Board of Education* (391 U.S. 563), the court upheld a teacher's right to publish a letter critical of the way that her employers spent school funds. In *Papish v. University of Missouri Curators* (410 U.S. 667, 1968), the court held that college newspapers should be free from censorship. Nevertheless, in *Hazelwood School District v. Kuhlmeir* (484 U.S. 260, 1988), the court held that teachers and students in public schools have no First Amendment freedoms while at school.

## ASSEMBLY

The First Amendment protects the free speech right of assembly. During the 1950s and 1960s, the right to peaceful assembly was severely tested during the civil rights movement. While protestors led by Dr. Martin Luther King, Jr., took a pledge of nonviolence, violence often erupted as white supremacists sought to prevent protestors from assembling. Alabama and Mississippi arrested thousands of protestors for exercising their constitutional rights. In 1958, in *N.A.A.C.P. v. Alabama* (357 U.S. 449), the court held that Alabama could not force the National Association for the Advancement of Colored People (NAACP) to release its membership rolls. Even though most liberals support the right to peaceful assembly, a conflict may arise when the protestors are Nazis or Ku Klux Klansmen.

## UNPROTECTED SPEECH

The Supreme Court has consistently held that slander, libel, obscenity, "fighting words," and threats to public safety are open to censorship. Slander and libel laws protect individuals from having others say or write things that are untrue about them. In 1964, in *New York Times v. Sullivan* (376 U.S. 254), the court held that pub-

*An illustration of Huckleberry Finn from an early edition of Mark Twain's novel, a work that would still be censored 100 years later.*

lic figures cannot recover damages unless they can prove that erroneous information was presented with "actual malice" and "with knowledge that it was false or with reckless disregard of whether it was false or not." In *Hustler Magazine v. Falwell* (485 U.S. 46, 1988), the court used Sullivan to decide that Jerry Falwell could not collect damages for a lampoon that appeared in the magazine because "the State's interest in protecting public figures from emotional distress is not sufficient to deny First Amendment protection to speech that is patently offensive and is intended to inflict emotional injury when that speech could not reasonably have been interpreted as stating actual facts about the public figure involved." For several decades, the Supreme Court struggled with how to define obscenity. Before the late 1950s, the justices relied on the Hicklin Test, which was developed by an English judge in 1868 in *Queen v. Hicklin* (L.R. 3 Q.B. 360), identifying obscenity by whether the work was judged to have any redeeming social value. Then, in *Roth v. United Sates* (354 U.S. 476) in 1957, the court attempted to define obscenity in relation to "contemporary community standards" that judged whether "the dominant theme of the material taken as a whole appealed to the prurient interests." During this period, the justices gathered with their law clerks on what became known as "Dirty Movie Day" to view each movie that had been declared "obscene" on a case-by-case basis. In 1971, in *Cohen v. California* (403 U.S. 15), Justice John Harlan expressed the crux of the obscenity dilemma by acknowledging that "while the particular four-letter word being litigated here is perhaps more distasteful than most others of its genre, it is nevertheless often true that one man's vulgarity is another's lyric."

In *Miller v. California* (413 U.S. 15), the Supreme Court established a three-tier test for obscenity that would serve as a guideline for future cases:

> Whether the "average" person, applying contemporary community standards, would find that the work taken as a whole appeals to the prurient interest;
>
> Whether the work depicts or describes in a patently offensive way sexual conduct as specifically defined by applicable state law;
>
> Whether the work taken as a whole lacks serious literary, artistic, political, or scientific value.

"Fighting words" were declared unprotected forms of speech in *Chaplinsky v. New Hampshire* (315 U.S. 568) in 1942. Words classified as "fighting words" have included: adulterer, alcoholic, bigamist, cheat, deadbeat, fascist, gay, hypocrite, Nazi, spy, and villain; as well as racial, religious, and ethnic epithets. Many local communities have enacted hate crime laws to prevent crimes that target specific groups for violence. Such a law passed by St. Paul, Minnesota, was challenged in 1992 in *RAV v. City of St. Paul* (505 U.S. 377), when a local youth claimed that his right to burn a cross inside the fenced yard of a black family living in a predominantly white neighborhood was protected by the First Amendment. The court struck down the law on the grounds that it was overly broad.

The court has determined in hundreds of cases that there is no Constitutional right to incite to riot, disturb the peace, or attempt to overthrow the government (sedition). In *Schenck v. United States*, the court used the Clear and Present Danger Test to determine that Schenck had no constitutional right to send anti-war letters to men eligible for the draft. In his dissent to *Abrams v. United States* (250 U.S. 616) in 1919, Justice Oliver Wendell Holmes argued that the only acceptable limits on speech action arose from the threat of immediate danger.

In 1925, in *Gitlow v. New York* (268 U.S. 652), the court decided that freedom of speech and press applied to the states as well as to the national government. In a significant concurring opinion in *Whitney v. California* (274 U.S. 357, 1927), Justice Louis Brandeis summed up a new position on seditious speech: "Fear of serious injury cannot alone justify suppression of free speech and assembly. Men feared witches and burnt women. It is the function of speech to free men from the bondage of irrational fears. To justify suppression of free speech there must be reasonable ground to fear that serious evil will result if free speech is practiced. There must be reasonable ground to believe that the danger apprehended is imminent. There must be reasonable ground to believe that the evil to be prevented is a serious one."

There is always the danger that when government is allowed to censor in the name of national security it will invade the civil liberties of the innocent as well as the guilty. In October 2001, in the wake of the September 11 , 2001, terrorist attacks, Congress passed the USA Patriot Act (P.L. 107-56). The law gave the executive branch unprecedented powers, including electronic and physical surveillance, warrantless searches, privacy violations, and suspension of the right to due process, equal protection, a speedy trial, habeas corpus, and legal counsel.

Critics of the act argue that it violated the First, Fourth, Fifth, Sixth, Eighth, Ninth, and Fourteenth Amendments. In early 2004, the Supreme Court agreed to hear a series of cases arising from the actions of the George W. Bush administration, including the incarceration of 600 detainees at Guantánamo Bay, Cuba, who had been held without due process.

**SEE ALSO**

*Volume 1 Left:* First Amendment; Civil Liberties; Supreme Court; Freedom of Information.
*Volume 2 Right:* Reagan, Ronald.

**BIBLIOGRAPHY**

Harry M. Bracken, *Freedom of Speech: Words Are Not Deeds* (Praeger, 1994); Martina Cloonan and Reebee Garofalo, *Polic-*

ing Pop (Temple University Press, 2003); Owen M. Fiss, Liberalism Divided: Freedom of Speech and the Many Uses of State Power (Westview, 1996); Joel B. Grossman and Richard S. Wells, Constitutional Law and Judicial Policy Making (Longman, 1988); Bob Horbert, "A Justice's Sense of Privilege," New York Times (April 12, 2004); Joseph J. Hemmer, Jr., Communication Law: The Supreme Court and the First Amendment (Austin and Winfield, 2000); Peter Irons, Brennan v. Rehnquist: The Battle for the Constitution (Alfred A. Knopf, 1994); Sheila Seuss Kennedy, Free Expression in America: A Documentary History (Greenwood, 1999); Ken I. Kersch, Freedom of Speech: Rights and Liberties under the Law (ABC/CLIO, 2003); Nan Levinson, Outspoken Free Speech Stories (University of California Press, 2003); Juhani Rudanko, The Forging of Freedom of Speech: Essays on Congressional Debates on the Bill of Rights and on the Sedition Act (University Press of America, 2003); Wojciech Sadurski, Freedom of Speech and Its Limits (Kluwer, 1999); Steven H. Shiffin, Dissent, Injustice, and the Meaning of America (Princeton University Press, 1999); Thomas Tedford, Freedom of Speech in the United States (Random House, 1985); Elder Witt, The Supreme Court and Individual Rights (Congressional Quarterly, 1988).

ELIZABETH PURDY, PH.D.
INDEPENDENT SCHOLAR

# Central America

CENTRAL AMERICA IS A small region that links North and South America, bordering Mexico to the north and Colombia to the south. Its seven countries— Belize, Guatemala, El Salvador, Honduras, Nicaragua, Costa Rica, and Panama—constitute a very rich mixture of history, land, and cultures. This history, however, has been marked by high levels of violence and today, with notable exceptions, Central American societies are still characterized by extreme levels of social inequality, poverty, and injustice. The 20th century has seen left-wing revolutionary movements develop in some Central American countries to counteract the worst excesses of political repression with little long-lasting effect.

Although the region currently known as Central America has been inhabited for thousands of years, little is known of the cultures that dominated the area with exception perhaps of the Maya civilization. The Maya ruled in parts of current Guatemala, Belize, and southern Mexico. Although this civilization had begun to decline from the 14th century onward, the arrival of the Spanish conquerors in the 16th century marked the beginning of exploitation of the existing population. Initially led by Christopher Columbus, Spanish conquerors arrived in America with dreams of El Dorado, the mythical city of gold and riches. However, Central America did not prove to be a source of mineral wealth to the same extent as Mexico to the north and Peru to the south. As a result, although Central America was settled by the new masters from Spain, it remained largely a region of the vice-royalty of Mexico, then called Nueva España (New Spain), and received the name of Guatemala. At this time Guatemala consisted of five republics: Guatemala, El Salvador, Honduras, Nicaragua, and Costa Rica. Current Panama was at the time part of Colombia and only became independent in 1903, whereas Belize was declared a British colony and only became independent in 1981.

Independence for the various Central American republics came in the first part of the 19th century. Just as Spain was involved in European wars and under the invasion of Napoleon's forces, its grip on Central America loosened. By 1823, the five republics had declared their independence from Spain, and more significantly, from Mexico. This political move was led by Creoles, a new middle class of people born in the republics but of Spanish descent. Although attempts were made to maintain the republics of Central America united, by 1839 they had separated into five independent nations. Much of the rest of the 19th century was marked by political attempts to regain the lost unity with little suc-

The cultivation of coffee (above) and other agricultural products has resulted in leftist reaction against the exploitation of workers.

cess. Warring factions, divided between liberals and conservatives, succeeded each other in power with coup after coup. Besides political and social unrest, this period was also characterized by increasing foreign interventions and the threats to the territorial integrity of Central America.

In particular, Britain and the United States fought for preeminence in the area because of Central America's land and agricultural resources. The political hegemony of the United States consolidated toward the end of the 19th century. With it came a transformation of Central America's economies toward the production of coffee and bananas principally to supply the export market. The social consequences of this transformation were an increase in the levels of land concentration in a few hands, the rise of socioeconomic inequalities, and the increasing exploitation that stems from these.

## GUATEMALA

Guatemala is typical of Central America's repressive politics that emerge from a seriously dislocated society. By the mid 1920s, a series of transformations had ensured that only a small minority of the population (around 7 percent) and large foreign multinationals owned all the agricultural land. The successive expropriations, which had over the decades affected mainly the natives, automatically converted them into a source of mass cheap labor. Added to this was the foreign ownership of all the country's infrastructure; electricity supply—the main export port of Puerto Barrios—and the railways that linked the coffee and banana plantations to it. The biggest foreign multinational in Guatemala was the Boston-based United Fruit Company (UFCO).

The high level of Guatemala's dependency on international markets meant that the country was severely hit by the 1929 economic crash. The large rise in unemployment, wage cuts, and political repression that were used by successive governments to deal with popular demands sowed the seeds of revolutionary politics that would have a presence in Guatemala for the next four decades. The democratic revolution of 1944 saw a reformist government come to power with a program to implement serious social reform with a large-scale welfare program and legislation to improve the working conditions of the majority. The victory of Jacobo Arbenz in 1950 quickened the pace of social reform but was immediately seen by UFCO as a threat to its economic interests. Making the most of political contacts in Washington, D.C., and the Central Intelligence

Agency (CIA)—Secretary of State John Foster Dulles and his brother Allen, CIA director, were partners in UFCO's legal counsel—plans were soon in place to replace the democratically elected government with right-wing military leader Castillo Armas. From 1954 onward, the previous land reforms were reversed and a campaign of terror was launched against dissidents by successive military governments.

The low level industrialization that took place in the 1960s and 1970s did not do anything to alleviate the socioeconomic division and the level of exploitation of Guatemalan society. The periodical cycles of violence in Guatemalan society continued to increase, reaching their peak in the 1980s. In opposition to the government forces—the military and their death squads that terrorized the peasant population—stood only a number of guerrilla movements.

In the 1990s, with the return of civilian governments, the signing of a formal ceasefire and the awarding of the Nobel Peace Prize to indigenous leader Rigoberta Menchú in 1992, there were signs of an improving situation. However, the Guatemalan conflict left tens of thousands dead or "disappeared" and many more displaced, mainly poor peasants of Mayan descent, while the perpetrators continued to enjoy immunity from prosecution.

## NICARAGUA

A similar process of adaptation to the global coffee market and foreign ownership of land and infrastructure took place in Nicaragua and was managed by the direct intervention of the U.S. military in the country between 1909 and 1931. The main opposition to the United States and its friendly governments came from Augusto Sandino. His guerrilla army fought the Nicaraguan National Guard and the U.S. marines between 1927 and 1933, setting up agricultural cooperatives in the territory that was under his control and proving that a small army could inflict serious damage to the opposition. The war proved both economically and politically costly to the United States, which decided to extricate itself from the conflict, while retaining political control of the country through a friendly dictator, the head of the National Guard, Anastasio Somoza. Sandino was assassinated by Somoza in 1934, and Somoza installed the Somoza dynasty's reign of tyranny for the next four decades.

The Somoza family ran Nicaragua as their private estate, appropriating land and industry and even siphoning foreign aid sent in the wake of the 1972 earthquake that devastated the capital, Managua. Opposition to the Somoza regime was formally founded by student leaders and former fighting partners of Sandino who formed the Sandinista Front of National Liberation (FSLN) in 1961. Their opposition only triumphed in 1979 when, after Somoza's assassination of a prominent opposition journalist, the country went on a general strike. The national guard's repression that killed more than 5,000 FSLN sympathizers was replied with further demonstrations, strikes and, in June 1979, a final offensive of FSLN guerrilla forces in all parts of the country. Finally encircled by FSLN forces, Somoza agreed to go into exile to the United States and the Sandinista revolutionary movement was installed in government.

Taking their cue from the 1959 Cuban Revolution, the Sandinistas set out to nationalize Somoza's land and assets. This immediately put 40 percent of the national wealth in the hands of the state. The Sandinistas also passed legislation to implement land reform, create peasant cooperatives, and deal with the worst effects of four decades of dictatorship, namely high levels of poverty, illiteracy, and disease. However, these gains were soon offset by the covert war launched by the United States soon after the presidential election of Ronald Reagan in 1981. Using Honduras and Costa Rica to launch their attacks on Nicaragua, U.S.-funded counter-revolutionary military groups proved a drain on resources that Nicaragua could ill afford. At the same time, the United States put pressure on international aid agencies and banks not to lend to an impoverished Nicaragua struggling to meet payments on debts accumulated by the Somoza dynasty. In 1985, economic pressure was escalated with a trade embargo that lasted for the next five years and helped finally crush Nicaragua's economy. Elections held in 1990 gave the victory to a broad coalition of opposition parties and the FSLN stopped fighting. More than 14 years later in 2004, the economic recovery promised to Nicaraguans after the war has not materialized and the country remains one the poorest of Latin America.

## EL SALVADOR

The history of El Salvador is closely linked to that of Nicaragua in more ways than one. The country's extreme social and economic divisions at the time of independence continue to the current day. The unequal distribution of land is such that a small elite of 1 percent of the population—the so-called Fourteen Families—owns 77 percent of the land. In a country where coffee exports constitute most of the national wealth, this unequal land distribution—itself the result of forced expropriation from the native population in the 19th century—condemns the vast majority of the landless peasants to a life of misery.

The result has traditionally been a severe social dislocation with high levels of illiteracy, births outside marriage, and alcoholism. Also, El Salvador's total dependency on the international coffee market brought a severe economic crisis after 1929 in exactly the same way as happened to Nicaragua. Finally, these two countries' histories are linked by the radical nature of the political reactions that have emerged in the 20th century in response to this situation and the ruthless nature of army-inspired death squads that have terrorized the population and killed tens of thousands.

In 1932, Farabundo Martí, a close ally of Augusto Sandino, launched a failed revolt that resulted in his assassination. The cycles of poverty and violence that characterized other countries repeated themselves in El Salvador with successive right-wing governments kidnapping, torturing, and murdering thousands. By the late 1970s, many in El Salvador thought that the country had no option but to follow the same course as Nicaragua with an all-out assault on the government. The Farabundo Martí Front of National Liberation (FMLN) began such assault in 1980 after a popular archbishop who championed the plight of the poor was murdered in front of his congregation. The war between the FMLN guerrillas and the U.S.-funded army lasted officially until 1992, when a United Nations-mediated peace accord was signed and the FMLN became an opposition party. However, later governments have passed legislation to protect those responsible for decades of human rights abuses and the levels of extreme violence.

## HONDURAS, BELIZE

The political development of Honduras in the 20th century has been greatly enmeshed with developments elsewhere. Having been at the political and economic mercy of the United States and the banana industry, Honduras has not been able to develop or sustain great radical or left-leaning politics. When the 1930s economic Depression took hold of the country, the political resolution was to be found in military dictatorship. Indeed, much of the century has been dominated by successive military regimes and only modest land reforms have been peacefully achieved between 1962 and 1980. In the 1980s, when most of Central America was focused on the Sandinista revolution in Nicaragua, Honduras was used by America as the focus of policy and strategic operations in the region. This included using Honduran territory to launch covert military operations against Nicaragua. Mass protests and anti-U.S. political unrest took place during the late 1980s, but these could not be channeled into formal left politics.

In the case of Belize, foreign domination has historically had Britain as the main culprit. As a result, leftist politics have traditionally been associated with the country's desire for self-determination and independence, a movement that achieved success in 1981.

## PANAMA, COST RICA

At the other end of Central America, Panama and Costa Rica have had different historical developments, though not less influenced by foreign powers. In the case of Panama, revolutionary sentiments in the country only came to fruition during the 1903 civil war in Colombia when Panama managed to achieve independence from Colombia with the help of the United States. The price for that help would come in the form of the Panama Canal, which the United States financed and built, and U.S. political domination.

Twentieth-century political life in Panama has been dominated by the military and any leftist politics can only be associated with leaders who have developed some form of anti-imperialist ideology, such as Omar Torrijos and Manuel Noriega. Although neither of them were democrats, the former led the country between 1968 and 1981, conducting public works and social programs on a grand scale. Noriega, however, very soon became despotic and was removed from office after a U.S. invasion in 1989.

Costa Rica, on the other hand, has had a much more peaceful and democratic political life during the 20th century that has resulted in progressive social achievements for its population. Since the first democratic elections took place in the country in 1889, there have been few lapses. Leftist politics in the country have been dominated by the United Christian socialist party, created by President Rafael Angel Calderón Guardia in 1940. The ideology represented by this faction of Costa Rican political life is responsible in part for a constitution, approved in 1949, that gave women and blacks the vote and abolished the army.

## SEE ALSO

*Volume 1 Left:* South America; Socialism; Communism.
*Volume 2 Right:* Central America; United States.

## BIBLIOGRAPHY

Rose Spalding, ed., *The Political Economy of Revolutionary Nicaragua* (Westview, 1987); James Dunkerley, *Power in the Isthmus: A Political History of Modern Central America* (Verso, 1988); Leslie Bethell, *Central America since Independence* (Cambridge University Press, 1991); Jenny Pearce, *Promised Land: Peasant Rebellion in Chalatenango, El Salvador* (Monthly Review Press, 1985); Stephan Webre, *José Napoleón Duarte and the Christian Democratic Party in Salvadoran Politics, 1960–78* (Louisiana State University Press, 1979).

KEPA ARTARAZ, PH.D.
UNIVERSITY OF DERBY, UNITED KINGDOM

# Chile

FOR MOST OF THE 20th century, the two dominant parties of the Chilean left were the Communist and Socialist parties. Although both shared a Marxist perspective and declared the establishment of socialism to be their goal, they had distinct origins, membership, and programs.

For most of its history, the Chilean left used elections and the democratic process to achieve its aims. The 1970 election of socialist Salvador Allende to the presidency appeared to confirm this decision, but the 1973 military coup that overthrew him and ushered in 17 years of military dictatorship under the command of General Augusto Pinochet challenged it.

The Communist Party of Chile formed in 1922 under the leadership of Luis Emilio Recabarren. The development of the Communist Party (CP) reflected the increased militancy and organization of workers, especially in the northern nitrate mines. Like other CPs around the world, the Chilean CP affiliated with the Third International, thus allying itself with the Soviet Union. In 1932 socialists, led by Air Force Commander Marmaduque Grove, established the Socialist Republic. Following their defeat, they created the Socialist Party (SP) of Chile in 1933. Unlike the CP, the SP's roots were more middle class than working class and it favored independence from the USSR.

Both parties worked in the Popular Front governments (1936 to 1952) and members were elected to parliament, held ministerial positions, and worked in government institutions. However, as the Cold War intensified in the late 1940s, the U.S. government urged President Videla of Chile to break with the CP, which he did. The CP was forced underground and many of its members were sent to prison camps.

The 1959 Cuban revolution, rising expectations, growing frustration with the ruling parties, and the perception that the left could secure a better life for them, led to increased support among Chileans for the left in the 1960s. In 1969, the CP and the SP, along with other smaller leftist parties, formed the Popular Unity (UP) coalition, which elected Salvador Allende as president in 1970. The Movement of the Revolutionary Left (MIR) supported Allende, but rejected elections and the UP's "Peaceful Road to Socialism" as the path to power.

Allende and the UP ruled Chile from 1970 to 1973. Their program called for a redistribution of wealth to the workers, peasants, and poor; the nationalization of large-scale Chilean industry and foreign-owned, especially U.S., corporations; and the increased democratization of society. Both the Chilean elite and the U.S. government opposed Allende's victory and worked to undermine his government. They sabotaged the economy and supported the 1973 military coup that overthrew it in 1973.

The military dictatorship (1973 to 1990) attempted to exterminate the left. It imprisoned, tortured, murdered, "disappeared," and exiled over a hundred thousand Chileans and other nationalities. Weakened by the repression, many Chilean leftists sought refuge abroad, while others remained in Chile and resisted the dictatorship. The left worked to reconstitute itself within Chile and abroad; it also attempted to help Chileans survive the fear and economic losses that resulted from the dictatorship's terror reign and implementation of a neoliberal economic model. Breaking with its reliance on elections, the CP formed the Manuel Rodríguez Patriotic Front, a guerrilla organization, to fight the dictatorship; among other actions, it unsuccessfully attempted to assassinate Pinochet in 1986.

In the 1980s, much of the left joined with the centrist Christian Democratic Party to form the Concertación, which defeated Pinochet in the 1988 plebiscite he called on his rule and then won the 1989 presidential elections. In 2000, Ricardo Lagos, a Socialist and member of the Concertación, was elected president. The years of dictatorship and repression, much of the left leadership's exile in Europe and exposure to social democracy, and the collapse of the socialist model internationally transformed much of the Chilean left. Instead of calling for the construction of socialism in Chile, Lagos has continued the neoliberal economic policies initiated by Pinochet; at the same time his gov-

ernment has taken steps to end the poverty in which a high percentage of Chileans still live.

**SEE ALSO**

*Volume 1 Left:* Argentina; Brazil; South America.
*Volume 2 Right:* Capitalism; Fascism; Peronism.

**BIBLIOGRAPHY**

Pamela Constable and Arturo Valenzuela, *A Nation of Enemies: Chile under Pinochet* (W. W. Norton, 1991); Carmelo Furci, *The Chilean Communist Party and the Road to Socialism* (Zed Books, 1984); Brian Loveman, *Chile: The Legacy of Hispanic Capitalism* (Oxford University Press, 2001); Margaret Power, *Right-Wing Women in Chile: Feminine Power and the Struggle against Allende, 1964–73* (Pennsylvania State University Press, 2002); *Unidad Popular, Programa Básico de la UP* (Santiago: Impresora Horizonte, n.d.).

MARGARET POWER
ILLINOIS INSTITUTE OF TECHNOLOGY

# China

THE OVERTHROW of the Manchu (Qing) Dynasty in 1911 in China led to the establishment of the Chinese Republic in 1912 by Sun Yat-sen. As Sun wrote in his autobiography, "in 1912 I assumed office, and ordered the proclamation of the Chinese Republic, the alteration of the lunar calendar, and the declaration of that year as the First Year of the Chinese Republic."

However, actual power was wrested from Sun by General Yuan Shih-k'ai, the first of the *tuchuns* (warlords) whose armies would plague China like locusts for over a decade. The period had searing impact on Sun, whose republic was paid scant attention to by the Western powers or Japan. At the Versailles Peace Conference in 1919 after World War I, the United States in fact took Japan's behalf. This was a diplomatic paradox that Sun did not enjoy. It became clear to him that the "Western way" was not the path for China to follow, although, having lived in Hawaii and been influenced much by American missionaries, this had been his original intent.

In 1919, the May Fourth Movement exploded as a protest against exploitation and victimization of China by the Great Powers. In a very real way, the May Fourth Movement was the birth of strong Chinese nationalism—and Communism. Thus, by 1920, a significant shift occurred in Sun and his Kuomintang, or Nationalist Party. C.P. Fitzgerald wrote in *The Birth of Communist China* that "it was clear that the Western way was not the solution, and tacitly it was abandoned, even by the revolutionary element."

In 1917, Vladimir I. Lenin had successfully led the Russian Communist or Bolshevik Party to power in Russia, toppling the three-centuries-old Romanov Dynasty. To the Chinese, there were obvious parallels to their own overthrow of the Manchu rule. Also, in 1919, Bolshevik Russia was attempting to fight counterrevolutionary generals, backed by the same countries that had exerted influence in China, from overturning the 1917 Revolution.

At the same time, it was Lenin's intention to launch a worldwide Communist revolution, and naturally, China, exploited by the Great Powers, posed a likely objective. In July 1921, the first indigenous Chinese Communist Party was formed by Chinese Marxists aided by the Russian Gregor Voitinsky. The Chinese communists approached Sun, who accepted their overtures for a "united front," or alliance, especially since with the alliance came the promise of desperately needed foreign aid from Russia, now the Soviet Union. Moreover, Sun had a strong ideological attraction toward Russia and communism. In 1923, a formal pact was made between the Communist International (Comintern), which had been set up to export communism, and the Kuomintang.

However, in 1925, Sun died, leaving in power his chosen successor, Chiang Kai-shek. Chiang lacked the ideological attraction to communism that animated Sun and saw the alliance only in the most pragmatic of terms. Sun, on the contrary, wrote before he died in "A Message to Soviet Russia" that "you are at the head of the union of free republics—that heritage left to the oppressed peoples of the world by the immortal Lenin." (Lenin had died in 1924.) Josef Stalin, the General Secretary of the Russian Communist Party, and by 1925 de facto ruler of the Soviet Union, cabled the Kuomintang to honor Sun; promises of continued assistance immediately followed.

With Soviet military assistance, Chiang carefully built his army to begin the reconquest from the warlord clique. The Soviet mission was led by Mikhail Borodin and included leading Red Army advisers. In July 1926, Chiang was able to begin his Northern Expedition to unite the country by force. Within a year, he felt strong enough to strike at the communists, who had been for him only a means to an end. He had found Western backers more to his liking and had personally embraced Christianity as a Methodist. In April 1927, he struck at the Communist Party in Shanghai, long one of its Chinese strongpoints. Using the narcotics-dealing Green Gang as his storm troopers, Chiang had hundreds of communists killed and beheaded: many of their heads festooned Shanghai telephone poles in wooden cages. Chiang's Kuomintang force joined in the purge.

## THE PURGE OF NANKING

In 1928, Chiang's Soviet-trained army successfully completed the Northern Expedition by entering Beijing. Now, he turned his energies to his "extermination campaigns" against the communists. Li Lisan, the leader of the Chinese Communist Party, survived the Shanghai purge, but his adventurous nature concerned dedicated revolutionaries like Zhou Enlai. In September 1930, Wang Ming replaced him as head of the party, with Mao Zedong still waiting in the wings. Wang was one of the elite "Twenty-eight Bolsheviks" who had received training in Moscow. Yet in January 1931, his fear of assassination caused him to flee to Moscow. Although still technically head of the party, de facto control passed to Mao Zedong.

The purge at Nanking began a major effort by Chiang Kai-shek to destroy the Communists as his main rivals for power in China. Moreover, the Western powers to whom he looked for aid now expected that of him as well. After Wang Ming had fled to Moscow, Mao Zedong, who had entered revolutionary politics in 1912 while still studying at the First Normal School of Hunan to be a teacher, had emerged as leader of those communists who remained behind in China. By September 1934, Kuomintang agents had routed the last of the communists from Shanghai, including Kang Sheng, the leader of the party secret service. In October 1934, Mao in the party sanctuary in Kiangsi decided on a massive retreat to remove the party and its Red Army from the blows of Chiang's extermination campaign. The communists began the Long March to far away Shensi.

Mao and his men arrived in Shensi (Shanxsi) exactly one year after their departure. Anne Freemantle wrote in *Mao Zedong: An Anthology of his Writings*, "of the army that had left Kiangsi on October 6, 1934, 100,000 strong, barely 20,000 remained." In December 1935, the Red Army was refreshed enough to march to Yenan where, for 11 years, Mao made his communist base.

While the war was going on between the communists and Kuomintang, the Japanese Kwantung Army had successfully taken over the province of Manchuria in 1931–32. The Japanese had renamed it Manchukuo and put on its throne as a Japanese puppet Pu Yi, who had been a child emperor at the time of the revolution in 1911. Behind the scenes, Doihara Kenji, a Japanese agent, was in real control of Manchuria and exploited it for the interests of Japan's "Greater East Asia Co-Prosperity Sphere."

Chiang Kai-shek remained steadfast in his determination that the communists—not the Japanese who were invading and raping China—were his real enemy. Mao and the communists, however, retained hope in the United Front idea, which had proven to work well during the life of Sun Yat-sen. Chiang was kidnapped in December 1936 at Sian by the "Young Marshal," Chang Hseuh-liang. The "Young Marshal's" troops had fought bravely against the Japanese in Manchuria, without any Kuomintang support. Chang was the instigator of the Sian (Xi'an) Incident. He kidnapped the Chinese Nationalist leader, Chiang Kai-shek, and forced him to end the civil war against the Chinese Communists and form a united front against the Japanese invaders.

In July 1937, in the skirmish at the Marco Polo Bridge outside Beijing, Japan initiated a full-scale attempt to conquer China. Faced by a severe threat, both Kuomintang and Nationalists drew together against the Japanese enemy. While Chiang fought a more traditional war against the Japanese, Mao favored a style of war that embraced both conventional and guerrilla strategy. As Mao wrote, "regular warfare plays the principal role and guerrilla warfare a supplementary one ... if the enemy neglects to take this into account, he will certainly come to grief."

## THE PEOPLE'S REPUBLIC

While the Japanese were defeated in September 1945, the situation between the Communists and the Kuomintang had already begun to deteriorate. In spite of mediation efforts by American General George C. Marshall, open war broke out between the two factions. In 1946, Mao formed his People's Liberation Army out of the Eighth Route Army and the New Fourth Army. With some one million dedicated soldiers, he defeated Chiang, who fled to the island of Taiwan, which had been regained from Japan. In October 1949, Mao proclaimed the People's Republic of China in Beijing, the capital.

For the first time since the turn of the century, mainland China was truly united. As the U.S. Library of Congress Study on China observed, "The period of officially designated 'transition to socialism' corresponded to China's First Five-Year Plan (1953–57). The period was characterized by efforts to achieve industrialization, collectivization of agriculture, and political centralization."

The First Five-Year Plan stressed the development of heavy industry on the Soviet model. Soviet economic and technical assistance was expected to play a significant part in the implementation of the plan, and technical agreements were signed with the Soviets in 1953 and 1954. For the purpose of economic planning, the first modern census was taken in 1953; the population of mainland China was shown to be 583 million, a figure far greater than had been anticipated.

Among China's most pressing needs in the early 1950s were food for its burgeoning population, domestic capital for investment, and purchase of Soviet technology, capital equipment, and military hardware. To satisfy these needs, the government began to collectivize agriculture. Despite internal disagreement as to the speed of collectivization, which at least for the time being was resolved in Mao's favor, preliminary collectivization was 90 percent completed by the end of 1956. In addition, the government nationalized banking, industry, and trade. Private enterprise in mainland China was virtually abolished.

By 1956, Mao felt strong enough politically to launch the Hundred Flowers Campaign, in which he attempted to bring the country's intellectuals into the party camp as they had been in the days of the 1919 May Fourth Movement. However, rough criticism of the party caused him to curtail the experiment and launch his Anti-Rightist campaign. In 1958, the Second Five-Year Plan was announced as the Great Leap Forward, with the goals of fostering industrial growth and promoting industrialization. Yet, the Great Leap Forward was an economic failure. In early 1959, the party admitted that the favorable production report for 1958 had been exaggerated.

By 1961, Mao had begun to lose power in the party to those who took a more rightist view of development, including Liu Shaoqi and Deng Xiaoping. Yet Mao, having survived the political crisis during the Long March, struck back with the Socialist Educational Movement, taking strength from the generation of young Chinese who had grown up under communism. Mao started the Great Cultural Revolution, in which he used young Red Guards to wrest back control of the country from the rightists. Deng was imprisoned, and his son was killed. Soon, almost all Chinese youth seemed to be carrying the Little Red Book, *The Quotations from Chairman Mao Zedong*. His policy, as chosen from selected quota-

*Mao Zedong used Marxism-Leninism to build a communist China that today embraces capitalism. Mao's portrait was ubiquitous.*

mand of the political scene," the Library of Congress notes.

Relations darkened between China and the Soviet Union, which had provided great material assistance for the development of the People's Republic. Part of the problem lay in the fact that Soviet Premier Nikita Khrushchev (who governed Soviet Russia until 1964) and Mao both contested for the mantle of the true heir of Karl Marx and Vladimir Lenin. Furthermore, in 1964, Mao authorized the first Chinese atomic explosion, based on the work of Chinese scientists who had studied in the United States. This caused much concern in Russia, whose strategic plans had always counted on a massive conventional assault in case of war with China.

## NIXON AND MAO

By 1969, relations with the Soviet Union had deteriorated to the point that war almost erupted along the disputed Ussuri River. Mao, feeling confident in power again, made the last great gamble of his career. Using a political fluidity only seen among communist leaders like Lenin, Mao began normalization of relations with the United States. The process was greatly facilitated by Edgar Snow, Mao's old friend. Snow, an American journalist, had visited Mao in Yenan and had written *Red Star over China*, which had made Mao and the communists known to thousands of Americans.

In September 1972, President Richard M. Nixon visited the People's Republic and in the Shanghai Agreement recognized the People's Republic as the authentic Chinese state, leaving the Kuomintang regime in offshore Taiwan in a political limbo where it languishes today.

In April 1973, Deng Xiaoping was brought back to power in China Thus, political stability returned to China—Mao's last act as the country's Great Helmsman. In September 1976, Mao died, leaving a mixed legacy behind him. What Mao wrote in 1945 might stand as an epitaph for himself and his ideology: "We stand for self-reliance. We hope for foreign aid but cannot depend on it; we depend on our own efforts, on the creative power of the whole army and the entire people."

With Zhou Enlai also dying in January 1976, China had been stripped of her two most visible leaders within less than a year. Before dying, Mao chose the compromise candidate Hua Guofeng to lead the country, hoping to heal the rift he had caused in the Cultural Revolution. However, his wife, Jiang Qing, and a group

tions from his earlier works, put the revolutionary fervor into a new generation. "Our point of departure," he declared, "is to serve the people whole-heartedly and never for a moment divorce ourselves from the masses ... the organs of the state must practice democratic centrism, they must rely on the masses and their personnel must serve the people."

In an evolution of the self-criticism that had begun at Yenan, urban workers and professors were sent out into the countryside to work with the toiling peasants. However, the program became unstable and seemed to be heading toward anarchy. The People's Liberation Army was called in to stabilize the situation. "It was not until after mid-1968 that Mao came to realize the uselessness of further revolutionary violence. Liu Shaoqi, Deng Xiaoping, and their fellow revisionists and 'capitalist roaders' had been purged from public life by early 1967, and the Maoist group had since been in full com-of leftists known together as a the Gang of Four (Jiang, Zhang Chunqiao, Yao Wenyuan, and Wang Hong Wen), attempted to seize power after Mao's death. However, the moderates stopped the coup and put China on the moderate course it has followed into the 21st century. Deng Xiaoping became the effective ruler of China in the place of Hua. Under Deng, China followed what were known as the Four Modernizations: industry, agriculture, national defense, and science and technology. However, the government set itself against what reformist Chinese called the Fifth Modernization: Democracy.

In January 1979, Deng visited the United States to meet with President Jimmy Carter. As Carter noted in his memoirs, Deng spoke of how "the Chinese had come to realize that the danger from the United States was less and less, while the Soviet Union was a greater concern." While economic issues were not a serious problem, Deng was more cautious when Carter pressed for more human rights in China. Carter noted that Deng said, "in the Chinese system, these liberties had to approached very cautiously."

## TIANANMEN SQUARE

Seen in retrospect, the Deng-Carter meeting in many ways set the pattern for American-Chinese relations for the next quarter century. Deng pursued an economic policy of modernization that would turn China into the leading power of Asia, a position it had not held for a century. Concerning the issues of Tibet and Taiwan, he avoided confrontation with the United States with the "one country, two systems" approach, implying that, if Taiwan were to return to union with China, its political and social system could be incorporated without change. However, he proved as ruthless at retaining power as had Mao.

Although by 1989 he had relinquished most formal party posts, he authorized the brutal attack on the democracy demonstrators in Tiananmen Square on June 4, 1989, in which thousands may have been killed. (Ironically, the democracy demonstrations had been set in motion by the visit to Beijing of Soviet Premier Mikhail Gorbachev, who was in the process of liberalizing the Soviet Union.) Continued reports from Xinhua, the Chinese press agency, blamed agitators from Taiwan for helping to instigate the movement to destabilize the Beijing government.

Deng died in February 1997, with power already safely transferred to President Jiang Zemin. According to Jiang, speaking at the memorial service for Deng,

"We must continue under the guidance of Comrade Deng Xiaoping to follow the road of reform and socialist modernization."

In June 1997, Hong Kong was returned to China by the United Kingdom ending a 99-year lease, under the "one, country, two systems" philosophy. However, by the sixth anniversary of the handover, it seemed that the freedoms that Hong Kong's citizens had enjoyed under British rule were being eroded. Agence France Press reported that "Hong Kong will mark its sixth anniversary under Chinese rule on July 1 with a huge protest march over proposed national security legislation which many fear will restrict fundamental freedoms."

The Chinese government continues to push ahead with economic liberalization, even as it resists political reform. Fifteen years after the massacre at Tiananmen Square, it remained to be seen how long it will be before the Fifth Modernization—Democracy—comes to China ... 75 years after it was first introduced as a political goal in the May Fourth Movement of 1919.

## SEE ALSO

Volume 1 Left: Communism; Cominform; Third International; Soviet Union; Maoism.
Volume 2 Right: Soviet Union; China.

## BIBLIOGRAPHY

"The Life Of Deng Xiaoping," www.cbw.com (July 2004); "Massive Protest to Mark Anniversary of Hong Kong's Handover from Britain," AFP (Agence France-Presse, July 2004) Richard Heller, "The Young Marshal," www.clarity-4words.co.uk (July 2004); U.S. Library of Congress Country Studies: China, http://lcweb2.loc.gov (July 2004); Stuart R. Schramm, ed., Quotations From Chairman Mao Zedong (Bantam Books, 1972); Franz Schurmann and Orville Schell, Imperial China, Republican China, and Communist China (Vintage, 1967); Barbara W. Tuchman, Stilwell and the American Experience in China (Bantam, 1972); General Tao Hanzhang, Yuan Shibing, trans., Sun Tzu's Art of War: The Modern Chinese Interpretation (Sterling, 1990); Anne Freemantle, Mao Zedong: An Anthology of His Writings (Mentor Books, 1962); Winberg Chai, Essential Works of Chinese Communism (Bantam, 1972); C. P. Fitzgerald, The Birth of Communist China (Penguin Press, 1952); Harold R. Isaacs, The Tragedy of the Chinese Revolution (Stanford University Press, 1951); Don Lawson, The Eagle and the Dragon: The History of U.S.-China Relations (Crowell, 1985).

JOHN F. MURPHY, JR.
AMERICAN MILITARY UNIVERSITY

# Christian Democracy

CHRISTIAN DEMOCRACY CAN be defined as a political philosophy, founded on Christian principles that inspire movements and political parties. Although Christian Democracy is a worldwide movement, it is in Europe that the philosophy has been the most successful: Christian Democratic parties have frequently been in power in five major European countries (Austria, Belgium, Germany, Netherlands and, until recently, Italy), while the European Popular party (the European federation of Christian Democratic parties) dominates the European parliament together with the socialists.

Usually described as a pragmatic and opportunistic catch-all party, ideologically located between liberalism and collectivism, Christian Democracy is instead characterized by peculiar elements that define its distinctiveness from other political ideologies. The most distinctive feature of Christian Democracy is its endless tension toward integration, compromise, accommodation, and pluralism between social and interest groups with possibly opposed interests. The central concept of Christian Democratic ideology not only reflects a multidimensional approach and flexibility but also facilitates the coexistence of such a plurality of views and interests. In particular, an element common to all European Christian Democratic parties has been their capacity to successfully conjugate the Christian notion of equality and redistribution of wealth among individuals with the precepts of modern capitalism.

In what has been defined as social capitalism, European Christian Democratic parties have been able to synthesize a basic commitment to capitalist market relations with the need to correct its detrimental effects. In this perspective, Christian Democratic ideology can be considered a religiously inspired model of social reform which is both social and capitalist, that is, recognition of liberal values, such as private property, but subject to social obligations. European Christian Democratic parties traditionally support religious values, stress the special place for the family in society, and are generally in favor of extending privileges to churches, particularly in the realm of education. At the international level, Christian Democratic parties have been enthusiastic supporters of economic and political regional integration in Europe, laying the foundations for the establishment of the European Union.

Historically, Christian Democratic parties and movements trace their ideological origins to the response of Catholics to 19th-century liberalism. Liberalism attacked the prerogatives of the Catholic Church in areas such as education, marriage, and official state recognition. In Italy and France, liberals traditionally perceived the Catholic Church as an obstacle to the formation of the modern democratic state. In France, the church was associated with reactionary forces for its long-standing alliance with the Bourbon monarchy. In Italy, hostility toward the church was mainly based on the Vatican's opposition to the process of national unity carried out by Piedmonts. In Germany, Chancellor Otto von Bismarck, after the German unification in 1871, started a campaign against Catholicism, called Kalturekampf, forcing Catholics to organize themselves to defend the church and its institutions.

In reaction to liberal attacks, the church counterattacked, moving in two directions. On one hand, the church reaffirmed its position against democracy, rejecting the foundations of political modernity, such as representative democracy and modern liberties, as clearly stated in the 1864 pontifical encyclical, *The Syllabus of Errors*, in which Pope Pius IX condemned the doctrines of liberal democracy. On the other hand, the church started to mobilize Catholics and organize them in mass organizations in order to counterbalance liberal forces. In particular, the church was able to take advantage of those Catholic institutions, such as parishes, confraternities, and other devotional societies of Catholics that, although already in existence since the end of the French Revolution, never became a decisive political force because they had never been arranged in one, organized movement.

The aim of the church's strategy was not participation in the political process, but rather isolation within society. By isolating Catholics within the liberal state, "the church hoped to shield them and itself from anticlerical legislature and secularization," explains historian Stathis N. Kalyvas. Moreover, isolation also meant the possibility for the church to control these mass organizations and, at the same time, to proclaim its independence from external influences. Although statutory provisions excluded politics from the activity of Catholic institutions, Catholic mass organizations gradually began to change and evolved into hybrid organizations that combined elements of religious institutions and interest groups. In particular, an increasing number of Catholics started to proclaim the need for more participation in the political decision making process.

By the turn of the century, the church had changed its strategy and started to use the institutional tools provided by the democratic state more efficiently. Until that moment, the church had applied a strategy to limit the damage made by liberal forces against the prerogatives of the clergy. Now, the church decided to move from a defensive position to an offensive one, by allying itself with anti-liberal political forces to use them to influence the political agenda. Conservative forces fought at the institutional level for the promulgation of pro-Catholic laws or in protection of Catholic privileges. In exchange, the Church would have supported them electorally by using its well-developed net of mass organizations to mobilize the Catholic vote. The most classic example of such an alliance was the Gentiloni Pact, in which Italian Conservative forces signed a seven-points contract with representatives of Catholic organizations (controlled by the church) in the 1913 Italian elections.

## THE CATHOLIC VOTE

Despite the refusal of the church to accept an institutionalization of Catholic associations and groups, parties supported by the Catholic vote were successful in several countries (such as in Italy in 1913 where, out of 310 conservatives elected at the parliament, 228 candidates won because of the Catholic vote), thus accelerating the unsolicited process of emancipation of Catholic groups from the control of the church to the establishment of independent confessional parties in major European countries, such as the Zentrum in Germany and the Popular Party in Italy.

Despite their political inexperience, confessional parties were able to score astonishing successes in the elections in which they were presenting their own candidates. In countries such as Italy and Germany, where parties openly in favor of the church had never gained electoral success independently from other political forces, confessional parties not only consolidated their position in the domestic political scene—such as in Germany and Italy where respectively the Zentrum and the Popular Party became the second largest parties—they did so at the expense of the Liberals.

Despite their political accomplishments, the church did not welcome the formation of confessional parties. The Vatican looked with suspicion upon their formation, if not with preoccupation. Due to independent growth outside the church's control, these parties were seen as competitors rather than as allies. For the Vatican, confessional parties reduced the range of the church's political action and diminished its bargaining capacity in society.

Moreover, the church perceived confessional parties as competitors in the representation of Catholic interests. For this reason when, with the resurgence of dictatorial regimes in Germany and Italy, the Vatican

was offered the opportunity to obtain concessions over education and state's recognition for the Pope's withdrawal of support for the Zentrum in Germany (1933) and Popular Party in Italy (1923), the Vatican accepted, determining the end of confessional parties in these countries. Emblematic is the case of don Luigi Sturzo, founder and leader of Popular Party, who was forced by Pope Pio XI to resign from the Italian parliament, disband the party, and go into exile.

The end of World War II saw the resurgence of Catholic political movements and the establishment of modern Christian Democratic parties in all major European countries. From the ashes of confessional parties, such as the Zentrum in Germany and the Popular Party in Italy, new Catholic political formations re-emerged, this time stronger than their predecessors. These new Catholic parties found more conducive conditions in the aftermath of World War II to establish themselves as legitimate political forces. First, the Church renounced its antagonism for liberal democratic values as well as for the formation of Catholic political parties. Fear of communism played a relevant role in the Vatican's decision to support Christian Democratic parties, seen as a barrier to the expansion of the communist ideology and political power in Western European countries. Second, Christian Democratic parties gained legitimacy in the United States by becoming instrumental in the creation and support of democracy in Europe after the war.

## ITALIAN CHRISTIAN DEMOCRACY

In Italy, the Christian Democratic Party (DC) was the principal governing party from 1945 to 1994. Founded clandestinely in 1942 during the Fascist regime by members of the dissolved Popular Party, the DC soon became the leading political force in Italy. Alcide De Gasperi, its most important leader, was prime minister from 1945 until 1953. The DC set the foundations of the newly established Italian republic, anchoring the country to Western institutions, such as the North Atlantic Treaty Organization (NATO) and the European Community. During this period, the DC was strongly supported by the church in contraposition to the Italian Communist Party (PC), the largest in Western Europe.

However, after following a centrist strategy characterized by a contraposition between the center and the left, the DC felt the need to open itself to new political forces, in particular to the Socialist Party (PS) that, after the Soviet invasion of Hungary in 1956, had broken its relationships with the PC. However, it was not until

1963 that the formation of a center-left coalition emerged in Italy, when the PS officially became a member in the government led by the DC. Since the second half of the 1960s, the DC experienced a sizeable electoral decline that forced it to gradually open the government coalition to other political forces, increasing its dependency on them. This process of decline reached its climax in 1983 when, as the result of a dramatic loss, the DC obtained only 33 percent of the electorate vote (the lowest ever scored by the Catholic party since its foundation), opening the way to the first government led by a socialist. Causes of such decline are manifold.

First, the DC experienced an internal fragmentation in several heterogeneous factions, representing the different souls of the party, who were generally more intent on fighting each other than on promoting a common strategy. Second, the PC started to increase its popular support, at least until 1987, at which point the PC began to lose ground. Finally, political scandals, the inefficiency of the institutions and the deep economic crisis put the DC's leadership in Italy into question. Despite such decline, the DC remained the main force in the coalition, and its leadership unchallenged.

This radically changed in the early 1990s, when the disclosure of nationwide cases of corruption involving politicians and private companies delegitimized the entire DC elite. What seemed to be a localized political scandal soon developed into a nationwide phenomenon (so called Tangentopoli, or Bribe City) that drew in political parties, public agencies, and large public and private firms. By the end of 1993, many members of the DC had received an *avviso di garanzia*, official notification that they were under investigation by the magistrates, while its most distinguished leaders, such as Aldo Forlani and Giulio Andreotti, were also accused of collusion with the Mafia.

In reaction to these scandals (followed by a dramatic decline in electoral support), the party was reorganized into a new political formation in 1993, the Italian Popular Party (PPI), recalling its predecessor of the 1920s. The PPI was not the only group to emerge from the DC breakup. The Catholic right wing found its own voice in the Christian Democratic Center (CCD). In 1994, the CCD joined Silvio Berlusconi's Polo alliance, while the PPI adhered to the left coalition, signaling the end of unity of the Catholic electorate.

## GERMAN CHRISTIAN DEMOCRACY

In Germany, the Christian Democratic Party (CDU) became, along with the Social Democrats, one of the mainstays of postwar German politics. Although some of its leaders, such as Konrad Adenauer, had been affiliated with the Catholic Zentrum, the CDU detached itself from previous Catholic political organizations for the significant Protestant participation and leadership. The CDU, in partnership with its Bavarian cousin the CSU, ruled without a break until 1969, when the CDU lost the election against the Social Democratic Party (SPD).

During this period, the CDU was led by two charismatic figures: Adenauer (chancellor and Catholic) and Ludwig Erhard (minister of economy and Protestant). Adenauer set the foundations for the reconstruction of the German state after World War II and brought Germany back within "the concert of nations." Erhard was the father of the economic "miracle" experienced by the German economy that resulted in the country becoming one of the dominant economic powers in the world.

After 20 years of leadership, the CDU lost the elections, mainly due to its political rigidity towards the Soviet Bloc, in particular on issues related to the diplomatic relationships between West Germany and East Germany. Despite its attempts to regain popular support, the CDU did not return to office until 1982 under the leadership of Helmut Kohl. Kohl ruled in Germany from 1982 to 1998, when he lost the election to Gerhard Schroeder and the SPD. Under Kohl's leadership, the CDU administered the historical unification of the two Germanys.

**SEE ALSO**

*Volume 1 Left:* Germany; Italy; Liberalism; Church and State Separation; Socialism.
*Volume 2 Right:* Germany; Italy; Religion.

**BIBLIOGRAPHY**

Gregory Baum and John Coleman, eds., *The Church and Christian Democracy* (T. & T. Clark Publishers, 1987); David Hanley, ed., *Christian Democracy in Europe: A Comparative Perspective* (Pinter Publishers, 1994); Stathis N. Kalyvas, *The Rise of Christian Democracy in Europe* (Cornell University Press, 1996); Carolyn M. Warner, *Confessions of an Interest Group: The Catholic Church and Political Parties in Europe* (Princeton University Press, 2000); Thomas Kselman and Joseph A. Buttigieg, eds., *European Christian Democracy: Historical Legacies and Comparative Perspectives* (University of Notre Dame Press, 2003).

PIETRO PIRANI
UNIVERSITY OF WESTERN ONTARIO, CANADA

# Church and State Separation

CLAIMS CONNECTING or separating religion and politics exist both on the left and right. Therefore, some key historical, philosophical, and political elements are necessary to understand how the left approaches this issue. The long history of this topic has included discussion on theocracy, civil war, tolerance, separation of political powers, anti-clericalism, and civil religion, as well as the right to freedom of religion or freedom from religion.

A theocracy is a political system of religious leaders whose power supposedly comes from a deity, as found in ancient Egypt and the European Middle Ages. But this system imposes a dogma without clarifying the source of its legitimacy, thus creating conflicts among people of different beliefs.

Religious conflicts led to the Thirty Years War in Germany and the persecution of dissenters by the Church of England. While the Catholic Church was able to maintain its theocratic power in Europe for centuries, this situation changed with the Protestant Reformation, which backed the formation of secular nation-states aligned to either Papist or Reformed views.

Thus, on the eve of the English Civil War, Thomas Hobbes developed his political theory, defending a separation of the national state from the Roman Catholic Church, thereby seeking to avoid civil war. In *Leviathan*, he proposed total obedience to a local sovereign as a form of separation of the English state from the Roman Church, although he did not oppose the Church of England.

John Locke formulated his views around the separation of political powers and the principle of toleration. In 1689, he argued that religious freedom should be guaranteed in the private sphere. In his view, religion should not be imposed upon the individual by the state, because a church is a voluntary association of free people with shared beliefs. For Locke, intolerance, not religion, was the reason for conflicts, and religious freedom was a natural right.

The separation of church and state was further supported by the critique of religion during the Enlightenment, which questioned religion and upheld reason. Several methods were employed such as affirming the scientist as a *secundus deus*, embracing paganism and substituting Christian values for other cultural references, or promoting anti-clericalism and anti-Catholicism in favor of lay leadership. As a result, the French Declaration of the Rights of Man and Citizen of 1789 stressed the principle of *laïcité* on political matters. Rousseau, however, argued that society could not survive without religion, and therefore it needed "the dogmas of civil religion." But these dogmas would create a new problem: intolerance. Later secularism became the characteristic antidote to the dangers of religion and eventually Nietzsche would advocate the "death of God."

In the 20th century, there have been instances of a breakdown in this separation. For instance, the Argentine president had to receive a sanction by the Pope before taking office, while Iran and Afghanistan installed conservative Islamic states. The left, while supporting the division between church and state, has often combined religion and politics. In the 1960s, African American churches were associated with the civil rights movement and the Latin American Base Communities followed liberation theology to oppose military rule. In the 1980s, a church movement against political authoritarianism in East Germany, Demokratie Jetzt, served as prelude to unification and its leaders became influential politicians.

This issue is at the core of founding institutions in the United States. The Mayflower Compact of 1620 marks the initial step toward a commitment to freedom of religion, but this did not necessarily mean an end to intolerance. Therefore, Thomas Jefferson followed Locke in proposing freedom of religion in the following terms: "All persons shall have full and free liberty of religious opinion; nor shall any be compelled to frequent or maintain any religious institution."

But as sociologist Robert Bellah demonstrated in 1967, American "civil religion" remains a constant in the United States, for almost every president has used the language of Christianity and incorporated prayers, worship, and sermons in his agenda. The election of Jimmy Carter in 1976, Ronald Reagan in 1980, and George W. Bush with the support of the Christian right and the Moral Majority have motivated new debates. As these movements began to interfere in individual rights (promoting anti-abortion groups), in the school curriculum (questioning evolutionary theories), and in university campuses (opposing the study of Arab or Muslim cultures), some groups have attempted to build a better defense for the separation of church and state.

This explains why John Rawls defended political liberalism and rejected metaphysics, insisting that a "well-ordered democratic society is neither a community nor, more generally, an association" similar to a medieval society. In view of the pluralism and religious dimension advocated by communitarian critics of liberalism, Rawls proposed a neutral and political conception of justice.

However, the Congressional Act on International Religious Freedom (1998), the terrorist attacks against New York City and Washington, D.C. (2001), and the Faith-based and Community Initiative by Bush (2001) have added fuel to the debate. While the right insists on the motto "Religious freedom is a cornerstone of our Republic, a core principle of our Constitution, and a fundamental human right," the left argues that freedom from religion is necessary, based on a broad interpretation of the First Amendment. This latter position has been advocated by groups such as the American Civil Liberties Union, the Freedom from Religion Foundation, and the Americans United for the Separation of Church and State.

**SEE ALSO**

*Volume 1 Left:* Carter, James E.; Liberalism: Locke, John; Hobbes, Thomas.
*Volume 2 Right:* Religion; Christian Coalition; Bush, George W.

**BIBLIOGRAPHY**

Robert Bellah, "American Civil Religion," *Daedalus. Journal of the American Academy of Arts and Sciences* (Winter 1967); Edwin Gaustad, *Faith of Our Fathers: Religion and the New Nation* (Harper & Row, 1987); Philip Hamburger, *Separation of Church and State* (Harvard University Press, 2002); John Locke, *Letter Concerning Toleration* (Prometheus Books, 1990; A. P. Martinich, *The Two Gods of Leviathan: Thomas Hobbes on Religion and Politics* (Cambridge University Press, 1992).

AMOS NASCIMENTO
METHODIST UNIVERSITY OF PIRACICABA, BRAZIL

# Civil Liberties

The term *civil liberties* is often used interchangeably with *civil rights*. However, many theoreticians make a distinction between liberties as protections against government actions and rights as things one is permitted to do. In this schema, civil liberties are negative freedoms, while civil rights are positive ones.

In the United States, the Constitution and Bill of Rights are important sources of legislation on both civil rights and civil liberties. One of the key principles established in the Constitution is that of due process. This concept gives the individual protection from the arbitrary exercise of government power through court procedures that protect the accused and requirements the government must satisfy in order to deprive a person of life, liberty, or property.

The Bill of Rights constitutes the first 10 amendments to the Constitution, and was passed as part of the conditions for ratification in many states. These amendments were intended to provide a balance against the encroachments of a strong federal government feared by the anti-Federalists.

The First Amendment is one of the best known and most often cited parts of the Bill of Rights and secures several key civil rights and liberties. The first part ensures that the government cannot create a state church or prevent people from belonging to other religious groups, thus ensuring freedom of conscience. The rights of freedom of speech, press, peaceful assembly, and petition ensure that the government cannot silence dissenting voices. The framers of the Constitution believed in the Enlightenment principle that a variety of opinions was essential to the functioning of a democratic society by enabling decision makers to see all sides of an argument.

The Second Amendment, dealing with the militia and the right of individuals to own weapons, has become an intense point of controversy, with gun control advocates arguing that it was intended only to refer to the organized militia, such as modern National Guard units, and gun control opponents regarding the term *militia* as referring to all able-bodied citizens. The Third Amendment proscribes the practice used by the British government during the early part of the Revolutionary War, by which individual homeowners had to provide room and board for occupying soldiers. However, given the heavily mechanized nature of modern armies, dependent upon professional support and logistics trains that would make such arrangements impractical, the amendment has largely become of historical interest only. One need only try to imagine a suburban family trying to put up an M1A1 Abrams main battle tank and its crew to understand why.

The Fourth through Eighth Amendments provide key limits on the government's police power and establish important judicial procedures to protect the accused. Police may search a suspect's home only after obtaining a warrant, a document signed by a judge and clearly describing both the specific premises to be searched and the persons or objects being sought. With an exception for military tribunals, no one may be tried for major offenses unless they have been indicted by a grand jury, and a person who has been acquitted cannot be retried for the same offense. No one can be compelled to testify against him or herself, and key criteria of a fair trial are enumerated. The rights of civil litigants to a jury trial are also established, as are limits on the scope of punishment.

The Ninth and Tenth Amendments protect the rights of individuals and states from encroachments by the federal government, concluding the Bill of Rights. However, many later amendments also were passed to establish or protect civil rights as American society evolved. Three amendments, the Thirteenth, Fourteenth, and Fifteenth, were passed immediately after the American Civil War and made the principles won by blood during that conflict into the law of the land.

The Thirteenth Amendment formally abolished slavery, while the Fourteenth Amendment established the principle of equal protection under the law for all persons and the Fifteenth defined the right of former slaves to vote. The Nineteenth Amendment, passed in 1920, established the right of women to vote, and the Twenty-sixth Amendment established a citizen's 18th birthday as the minimum age to qualify to vote. The latter was passed in 1970 and was largely a response to the Vietnam War, in which young men could be sent to fight and die for their country before they were old enough to have a say in its governance.

## AFRICAN AMERICANS AND WOMEN

However, the mere fact that a given right or liberty was established in the written law of the land does not necessarily ensure that it will be available in practice. The struggle of African Americans for equality has been a well-known case in point. Although slavery had been abolished and their right to vote and to have equal standing before the law had been secured through constitutional amendments, those laws did not change the attitudes of their white neighbors, who were still accustomed to regarding them as inferiors. After the conclusion of the Reconstruction era, in which the federal government sought to enforce social change, white-dominated state governments rapidly eroded those rights through a set of practices commonly known as Jim Crow.

By various legal and economic manipulations, African Americans were prevented from registering to vote and effectively consigned to the bottom rungs of the socioeconomic ladder. Although they were no longer legally property, they had little choice about their circumstances of employment or any real hope of bettering themselves.

This situation prevailed until World War II, when American thinkers began to notice the uncomfortable hypocrisy of deploring the crimes of the Holocaust and the Nazi racial policies that led to the extermination camps while supporting segregation and legal subordination of African Americans at home. This shift of consciousness led to the first tentative calls for social change, including President Harry Truman's order that the U.S. armed forces be racially integrated and the *Brown v. Board of Education* decision against school segregation. However, these were small steps against an enormous injustice.

As African Americans began pushing aside the barriers that had prevented them from participating fully in civil life, women began to look closely at their own condition and wonder if it was time to make similar changes. Although women had enjoyed the vote since 1920, they were routinely paid less than men, excluded from certain jobs, refused credit without a male cosigner, and otherwise subject to discrimination. The late 1960s and the 1970s saw a powerful movement taking on successive forms of discrimination, from equal pay for equal work and the end of formal gender-based job discrimination to comparable worth (the idea that jobs involving similar levels of skill and responsibility should be paid similarly) and the fight against sexual harassment.

The experiences of both African Americans and women show a common pattern in the history of civil liberties; namely, such rights and liberties are extended to a succession of more marginalized groups. While the First Amendment protections of religion were originally conceived in terms of protecting the rights of various Christian denominations and grudgingly extended to the Jewish faith, it has since come to be extended to include practitioners of a number of previously despised minority faiths, including East Asian religions, Native American spiritual traditions, Wicca, and other Earth-based religions. The development of the idea that the Constitution guarantees a right of privacy was critical to several groups' progress, particularly gays and lesbians, but women and religious minorities as well. Persons with disabilities have been able to go from shunned pariahs and pitiful beggars to productive citizens, and the 1990 passage of the Americans with Disabilities Act (ADA) served to cement the concept of reasonable disability access as critical to disabled persons' ability to exercise their basic civil liberties.

While proponents of each successive extension to a new minority have considered it the natural and healthy evolution of civil society, opponents have scorned the activists as going to ridiculous extremes in search of battles. This has been particularly true in the case of gays and lesbians, largely because of the debate over whether sexual orientation is inherent (like race and gender) or a willful lifestyle choice.

Even when society agrees in principle to a given minority's civil rights and liberties, this does not always result in agreement as to the appropriate methods of securing those rights and liberties. Affirmative action, the practice of going to extra effort to bring members of formally excluded groups into jobs and other situations previously closed to them, is one example. There have been frequent accusations of lowered standards, for instance incompetent workers being hired and then being impossible to fire because of the risk of discrimination suits. Members of majority groups have brought reverse discrimination suits, claiming that they were passed over solely because of their membership in the majority group. By the 1990s, court cases began to limit affirmative action, often on the basis that it had done its work and was no longer needed.

The history of civil liberties has not always been one of growth. Times of national peril have often led to restrictions, even severe ones such as the Alien and Sedition Acts, President Abraham Lincoln's suspension of *habeus corpus*, or the internment of Japanese Americans during World War II. After September 11, 2001, there have been strong concerns about the potential of the USA Patriot Act to permanently and destructively curtail civil liberties, particularly if the War on Terrorism creates a perpetual state of crisis.

When civil liberties are threatened, a number of organizations have come to their defense. The American Civil Liberties Union (ACLU) is the most well known of these, but others include Amnesty International and the National Association for the Advancement of Colored People (NAACP). Government agencies such as the Equal Employment Opportunity Commission (EEOC) are charged with seeing that laws regarding civil liberties are enforced.

### SEE ALSO

Volume 1 Left: NAACP; American Civil Liberties Union; Nader, Ralph.
Volume 2 Right: Republican Party; United States; Anti-Abortion / Pro-Life.

### BIBLIOGRAPHY

Alan M. Dershowitz, *Shouting Fire: Civil Liberties in a Turbulent Age* (Little, Brown, 2002); Richard C. Leone and Greg Anrig, Jr., eds., *The War on Our Freedoms: Civil Liberties in an Age of Terrorism* (Public Affairs, 2003); Debbie Levy, *Civil Liberties* (Lucent Books, 2000); Aryeh Neier, *Taking Liberties: Four Decades in the Struggle for Rights* (Public Affairs, 2003); James D. Torr, ed., *Civil Liberties* (Greenhaven Press/Thomson-Gale, 2003); Samuel Walker, *In Defense of American Liberties: A History of the ACLU* (Southern Illinois University Press, 1999).

LEIGH KIMMEL
INDEPENDENT SCHOLAR

# Civil Rights

THE CIVIL RIGHTS MOVEMENT is founded on the belief that equality should be available to all Americans regardless of race. While the modern civil rights movement is most closely associated with the 1950s and 1960s, its foundations were laid in the late 17th century. By the 18th century, opposition to slavery was widespread. When Thomas Jefferson wrote the Declaration of Independence in 1776, he included an antislavery provision but was forced to remove it in order to win southern support for independence. In 1787, during the writing of the Constitution, Gouvenor Morris attempted to constitutionally abolish slavery. Again, the southern states refused to agree.

By the 19th century, opponents of slavery banded together in various antislavery societies. William Lloyd Garrison, the founder of the American Antislavery Association, brought national attention to the abolitionist movement in his newspaper, *The Liberator*. Frederick Douglass and Sojourner Truth, both former slaves, became eloquent spokespersons for abolition. In 1839, the publication of Theodore Weld's *American Slavery as It Is: Testimony of a Thousand Witnesses* brought the horrors of slavery to life as nothing had done before. Inspired by Weld's book, in 1851 Harriet Beecher Stowe published *Uncle Tom's Cabin*, a fictional account of slavery, which further galvanized the abolitionist movement.

Some slaves turned to the courts for assistance. For instance, a slave named Dred Scott argued that he should be declared legally free because he had traveled to the free state of Illinois with his owner. In 1857, in *Dred Scott v. Sanford* (60 U.S.393), the Supreme Court held that because Scott was "chattel," he was not a citizen and had no right to sue. The case was also important because the court determined that the Missouri

Compromise of 1820, which had sought to maintain a balance between free and slave states, was unconstitutional.

## CIVIL WAR AND RECONSTRUCTION

In 1860, Republican Abraham Lincoln was elected president. In his inaugural address, Lincoln attempted to avert war by declaring: "In your hands, my dissatisfied fellow countrymen, and not in mine, is the momentous issue of civil war. The government will not assail you. You have no oath registered in Heaven to destroy the government, while I shall have the most solemn one to preserve, protect and defend it." Lincoln was not an abolitionist, but he believed that slavery was a threat to the Union. Angered by Lincoln's election, the Civil War began when South Carolinians fired on Fort Sumter, on April 12, 1861. The following year, Lincoln issued the Emancipation Proclamation, freeing slaves in the seceded states. Four years later, the Thirteenth Amendment abolished slavery in the rest of the United States.

In April 1865, President Lincoln was assassinated, plunging the country into chaos. Vice President Andrew Johnson, a Democrat with southern sympathies, was neither strong nor wise enough to lead the nation through reunification. The election of General Ulysses S. Grant in 1868 reenergized Reconstruction, but it heightened tensions in the South where Grant was hated for his participation in the war.

After the Supreme Court overturned the Civil Rights Act of 1866, Congress made the passage of the Fourteenth and Fifteenth Amendments requirements for Southern redemption. The Fourteenth Amendment (1868) established rights of citizenship, while the Fifteenth Amendment (1870) granted suffrage to black males. The compromise election of Rutherford B. Hayes in 1876 brought Reconstruction to an abrupt end, and the Fourteenth and Fifteenth Amendments were virtually useless for the next five decades. In 1896, in *Plessy v. Ferguson* (163 U.S. 537), with only a single dissenting vote, the Supreme Court upheld the separate but equal doctrine that had become prevalent in the South.

## THE ROOSEVELT YEARS

During the early part of the 20th century, industrialization changed life in the United States. Large numbers of blacks left the rural areas of the South and migrated to cities in the North. The emergence of a black middle class created a strong reform climate within the black community, and white reformers further strengthened the civil rights movement. Black writers such as Langston Hughes and Richard Wright told the world about racism.

When the stock market crashed on Black Tuesday, October 29, 1929, it sent the United States into a major Depression. The Depression hit African Americans disproportionately hard because they had fewer resources to cushion their losses. Franklin D. Roosevelt was elected president in 1932 by promising to turn the country around. His New Deal program reached out to blacks as well as to whites. As a result, blacks deserted the Republican Party. The Supreme Court, liberalized by Roosevelt, began to look more closely at discriminatory laws and practices.

First Lady Eleanor Roosevelt was a civil rights activist, and she wielded considerable power in bringing national attention to discrimination. The first lady even took on the Daughters of the American Revolution, who objected to a concert planned at Constitution Hall to showcase the talents of black opera singer Marian Anderson. Refusing to cancel the concert, Eleanor Roosevelt simply moved it to the steps of the Lincoln Memorial. On Easter Sunday, April 9, 1939, some 75,000 attendees and millions of radio listeners heard Anderson's performance.

During the early 1930s, the eyes of the nation focused on the case of the Scottsboro Boys, which began in Alabama on March 24, 1931, when a group of nine young black men was falsely accused of raping two white women on a train. All-white juries sentenced eight of the men to death. The ninth, only 13 at the time, was sentenced to life in prison. In 1932 in *Powell v. Alabama* (287 U.S. 45), the Supreme Court overturned the convictions on technical grounds and ordered Alabama to retry them. Three years later, in *Norris v. Alabama* (294 U.S. 587), the court overturned the new convictions, stating that all-white juries violated the Fifth Amendment's guarantee of a jury by one's peers. This did not end the trials, however. Over a period of years, each of the young men spent from 6 to 19 years in prison, despite the fact that one of the women admitted the rapes had never taken place.

By the early 1940s, the National Association for the Advancement of Colored People (NAACP), founded in 1908, had appointed Charles Houston as the director of its Legal Defense and Education Fund. Houston was successful in challenging white primaries that limited the participation of blacks in the South, restrictive covenants that legalized discrimination in housing, and

*President Dwight Eisenhower signs the 1957 Civil Rights Act, which triggered further civil rights legislation over the next decade.*

discriminatory practices that denied blacks access to law and medical schools.

During the 1940 presidential election, both the Democratic and Republican parties wooed black voters in the North. In the South, however, many blacks were prevented from voting by grandfather clauses, white primaries, single-member voting districts, poll taxes, and literacy and constitutional understanding tests. In addition to legal tactics, some southern states prevented blacks from registering to vote by threats, intimidation, and intrusions into voter registration.

World War II was a turning point for African Americans in a number of ways. Large numbers of black men distinguished themselves in service to their country. While many of them experienced racism, the military also opened doors that had previously been closed. The G.I. Bill provided economic assistance to black veterans, which in turn expanded employment opportunities.

Civil rights activists of the period called for the elimination of job discrimination, anti-lynching laws, the abolition of poll taxes and white primaries, and the eradication of all Jim Crow laws that promoted the separate but equal doctrine. In 1944, Swiss economist Gunnar Myrdal published *An American Dilemma: The Negro Problem and Modern Democracy*, which focused worldwide attention on the economic problems of discrimination in America.

## THE EISENHOWER YEARS

By the mid-1950s, Thurgood Marshall had joined Charles Houston in a concentrated attack on segregation. Early battles had centered on ending discrimination in higher education, but Marshall attacked segregation in elementary schools in 1953 with *Brown v. Board of Education* (347 U.S. 483). Brown was actually a set of five cases that sought to end racial inequalities in the public school system. After hearing rearguments on *Brown* in 1954, a unanimous court, now led by Chief Justice Earl Warren, held that public schools must be integrated with "all deliberate speed."

The aftermath sent shockwaves throughout the South, leading to increased incidences of violence against African Americans. Eisenhower was forced to call out federal troops and nationalize the state national guard to maintain control. Some states shut down schools rather than integrate them. The Warren Court followed the *Brown* decision with a number of other cases that held that racial discrimination was a violation of the equal protection clause of the Fourteenth Amendment.

*Thurgood Marshall headed the drive for school integration and later became the first black Supreme Court justice.*

Nothing demonstrated the horrors of racial prejudice more than attacks on black children. In the summer of 1955, a 14-year-old boy named Emmett Till visited his uncle Reverend Mose Wright in Money, Mississippi. Till was from Chicago, Illinois, and was unfamiliar with the subservient behavior required of blacks in the South in the early 1950s. Because Till had whistled at a white woman, he was taken from his uncle's house by a group of white racists that included Roy Bryant and J. W. Milam.

After torturing and killing Till, his attackers weighted his body with parts of a cotton gin and threw him in the Tallahatchie River. Till's mother allowed *Jet* magazine to publish the horrific pictures of her son's mutilated body so that the world could see the effects of racism. An all-white jury acquitted Bryant and Milam. In March 2004, new evidence uncovered by a filmmaker led to demands for charges against other participants.

## THE KENNEDY YEARS

On December 1, 1955, Rosa Parks refused to give up her seat on a Montgomery, Alabama, bus to a white passenger. After she was arrested, Dr. Martin Luther King, Jr., led a bus boycott that forced the bus company to integrate. Adhering to his philosophy of nonviolence, King led the civil rights movement to protest discrimination through passive resistance, with sit-ins, protest marches, court challenges, and a steady campaign to call national attention to civil rights violations.

In 1960, Democrat John Kennedy, who had been molded in the Roosevelt tradition by his father, determined to make America more egalitarian. Kennedy appeared on national television in support of civil rights after southern governors tried to block integration. His brother, Attorney General Robert Kennedy, was also committed to civil rights, taking an active role in ending discrimination. The fact that the Kennedy brothers came to the assistance of King helped to place the majority of African Americans solidly in the Democratic fold. Kennedy established the Kerner Commission, which documented that two separate and unequal societies existed in the United States.

The civil rights movement brought blacks and white liberals together to fight discrimination. In 1961, a group of integrated civil rights workers launched Freedom Riders Summer to challenge segregation in interstate transportation, which had been found unconstitutional. When riders were attacked and arrested, they were replaced with others. At the urging of Attorney General Kennedy, in September 1961 the Interstate Commerce Commission ordered the immediate integration of all interstate facilities.

## THE JOHNSON YEARS

In 1963, Vice President Lyndon Johnson became president after the assassination of John Kennedy. Johnson promoted civil rights in a number of ways. His War on Poverty alleviated the poverty of many blacks, particularly those in the rural South. Johnson's legacy includes the 1967 Supreme Court appointment of Thurgood

*Martin Luther King, Jr. (foreground), meets with President Lyndon Johnson at the White House to discuss civil rights.*

Marshall, the first African American to serve on the court. Johnson also introduced the concept of affirmative action, which was designed to level out inequities by requiring employers to hire and promote more minorities, even if it meant implementing a quota system. Higher education developed affirmative action programs to make their programs more reflective of society as a whole. Affirmative action generated hostility among many whites who claimed reverse discrimination.

In 1964, Johnson proposed the Civil Rights Act of 1964. It was the most sweeping civil rights legislation in

*Lyndon Johnson signs the Civil Rights Act of 1964, a landmark in legislative attempts to improve the quality of life for African Americans and other minority groups by lessening racial discrimination in schools, housing, and voter registration.*

American history, targeting all aspects of discrimination. Titles I and VIII were designed to end voter discrimination; Title II banned discrimination in places of public accommodation; Title III prohibited segregation of public facilities; Title IV built on the Brown decision to ban segregated educational facilities, and Title VI ended discrimination in all federally assisted programs. Title VII proved to be one of the most controversial aspects of the act because it ended discrimination in employment on the basis of race, color, sex, religion, and national origin. Title V set up procedures for the Civil Rights Commission to investigate violations of the aspects of the law.

Despite the fact that voter discrimination was banned by the 1964 act, several southern states refused to allow blacks to vote. This practice, which had begun during Reconstruction, had become more fervent during the civil rights movement. On January 12, 1963, Medgar Evers, an employee of the NAACP, had been killed for trying to register black voters in Mississippi.

Six months later civil rights workers James Chaney, Michael Schwerner, and Andrew Goodman were killed by white racists for the same reason.

After King won a Nobel Peace Prize in 1964, he decided that the civil rights movement should become more aggressive about voter discrimination. King planned a march from Selma, Alabama, to the state capital in Montgomery. Local politicians and police officers attacked and arrested hundreds of marchers, leading to what became known as Bloody Sunday. On March 6, 1965, the attacks became so violent that Jim Reeb, a Unitarian minister, was killed.

Even though the death of Till and the four young girls killed in the bombing of a Birmingham church had not motivated white America to end racial discrimination, Reeb's death did. It ended the period where white moderates watched without doing anything to end the violence. Congress passed the Voting Rights Act of 1965, which allowed federal registrars to take over the voter registration process in areas where past discrimination had been well documented and to oversee the polls on election day. The act also empowered the Civil Rights Commission, created in the Civil Rights Act of 1957, to investigate charges of voter irregularities. The attorney general of the United States was given the power to bring challenges to courts on behalf of victims of voter discrimination.

While the civil rights movement is most closely associated with the nonviolence of Martin Luther King, some black leaders believed that violence was the only way to end blatant discrimination. Malcolm X, a Black Muslim, gathered thousands of followers in support of violent protests. The Black Panthers, founded by Huey Newton and Bobby Seale, also received a good deal of national attention.

## THE NIXON, FORD, AND CARTER YEARS

In 1968, Republican Richard Nixon campaigned on a promise to make America more responsive to the needs of the "silent majority." His plans included overturning the liberal reforms of the Kennedy/Johnson administrations. Busing had become one of the most explosive issues of the day, and Nixon determined to appease conservative parents by returning to neighborhood schools. After Nixon was forced to resign in August 1974 over the Watergate scandal, Gerald Ford was more open to civil rights. As a member of Congress, Ford had voted for civil rights measures, but only after conservatives had mitigated their impact.

The election of Jimmy Carter brought mixed reactions from African Americans. In truth, Carter was much more liberal than most southern Democrats. In his hometown of Plains, Georgia, Carter had refused to join the White Citizen Council, and he had supported civil rights as governor of Georgia. Although black votes gave Carter the necessary margin to win the election, his efforts to open up economic opportunities for blacks were stymied by the economic problems he had inherited. During his administration, the gap between the median wages of blacks and whites widened and the unemployment of blacks increased.

## THE REAGAN YEARS

In the election of 1980, Republican Ronald Reagan appealed to conservative whites by promising to end affirmative action, which he called reverse discrimination. He crippled the civil rights movement dramatically by appointing a conservative as head of the Civil Rights Commission and archconservative Clarence Thomas to the Equal Opportunity Employment Commission. As a result, few challenges to discriminatory practices were successful. Thomas was able to challenge civil rights laws when George H. W. Bush appointed him to the Supreme Court in 1991 amid charges against Thomas of sexual harassment.

Reagan tried unsuccessfully to block attempts to renew the Voting Rights Act. Bob Dole, a Kansas Republican, managed to limit the impact by allowing courts to consider the "totality of circumstances" rather than specific acts of voter discrimination. Blacks suffered enormous economic losses under Reagan, and his cuts to social programs disproportionately affected minorities. Reagan's impact on the Supreme Court ensured that his conservatism would outlive his presidency. His appointment of justices Sandra Day O'Connor, Antonin Scalia, Anthony Kennedy, and David Souter, as well as the elevation of William Rehnquist to chief justice, reshaped the Supreme Court, resulting in a major assault on affirmative action in the late 1980s.

## THE POST-REAGAN YEARS

While the Burger and Rehnquist courts softened the impact of civil rights legislation, they were not able to return the country to the pre-civil rights era. In 1991, Congress passed a new civil rights bill to undo the damage to affirmative action instigated by a conservative court. Since that period, the Supreme Court has become more centralized, providing more protection for civil rights. The election of Democrat Bill Clinton provided further support for civil rights, partially through the appointment of two liberal justices to the Supreme Court.

**SEE ALSO**

*Volume 1 Left:* Human Rights; King, Martin Luther, Jr.; Malcolm X; Civil Liberties; NAACP.
*Volume 2 Right:* United States; Supreme Court; Reagan, Ronald.

**BIBLIOGRAPHY**

Simon Booker, Jr., "Nation Horrified by Murdered and Kidnapped Youth," *Jet* (August, 1991); Lee Cokorinos, *The Assault on Diversity: An Organized Challenge to Racial and Gender Justice* (Rowman and Littlefield, 2003); Michael D. Davis and Hunter R. Clark, *Thurgood Marshall: Warrior at the Bar, Rebel on the Bench* (Birch Lane, 1992); "The Ghost of Emmett Till," *New York Times* (March 22, 1994); James Goodman, *Stories of Scottsboro* (Pantheon Books, 1994); Joel B. Grossman and

Richard S. Wells, *Constitutional Law and Judicial Policy Making* (Longman, 1988); Kermit Hall, et al, *American Legal History: Cases and Materials* (Oxford University Press, 1991); Steven F. Lawson, *Running for Freedom: Civil Rights and Black Politics in America since 1941* (McGraw Hill, 1991); Donald G. Nieman, *Promises to Keep: African-Americans and the Constitutional Order, 1776 to the Present* (Oxford University Press, 1991); Juan Williams, *Eyes on the Prize: America's Civil Rights Movement, 1954–65* (Penguin, 1987); Elder Witt, *The Supreme Court and Individual Rights* (Congressional Quarterly, 1988).

ELIZABETH PURDY, PH.D.
INDEPENDENT SCHOLAR

# Cleaver, Eldridge (1935–1998)

ELDRIDGE CLEAVER became known as an African American left-radical activist and writer. In his young days, he was convicted of an assault and was paroled in 1966 after eight years of imprisonment. Cleaver joined the leftist, anti-establishment nationalist group Black Panthers Party (BPP) based in Oakland, California, and owing to his notoriety as a writer for the New Left journal *Ramparts*, he became the information minister, or BPP spokesman.

In late 1960s, he was the most notorious proponent of the Black Power Doctrine, according to which blacks must organize politically and militarily for dealing with white society from a position of strength. Cleaver also played a critical role in introducing, advertising, and defining the black community free social programs that the BPP launched to improve public safety, political education, and economic outreach, including protesting against police brutality and rent eviction and informing welfare recipients of their legal rights. Hundreds of black ghetto youths across the nation were attracted to the BPP and its programs, the most famous of which was armed patrolling of neighborhoods.

Cleaver's book *Soul on Ice* was published in 1968. It contained essays he had written earlier in jail. The author showed the cold, dark, and oppressive underside of the American dream; the hypocrisy and racism of 1960s American society have been stigmatized in the book. In one essay, Cleaver described his rape of white women (after previously raping a number of black ones for a drill) as an insurrectionary liberation act. "It delighted me that I was defying and trampling upon the white man's law ... defiling his women," he wrote. As Cleaver was not prosecuted for rape after publishing the essay, it has remained unclear if what he described was true to fact or an account of complete fiction. There was definitely revenge in his heart, sending waves of consternation through white America. Some historians believe the rape issue was his manner of "black-macho-rebel" self-imaging. In this way, he also powerfully challenged James Baldwin's less reactionary model for the African American intellectual.

In 1968, the same year Cleaver ran for U.S. president on the ticket of the Peace and Freedom Party, he was wounded after a shootout between Black Panthers and police in Oakland. "That was the first experience of freedom that I had," Cleaver said about the incident. Faced however with a murder charge, he jumped bail and fled the United States for a life of exile in Algeria, Cuba, and North Korea, where he thought he had had a chance to witness Marxism up close in action. Abroad, he gave up many of his previous political viewpoints. "After I ran into the Egyptian police and the Algerian police and the North Korean police and the Nigerian police and Idi Amin's police in Uganda, I began to miss the Oakland police," he said.

Later, Cleaver went to France and in 1975, returned to the United States. He asserted he had experienced a "religious conversion" and styled himself as an anti-communist and born-again Christian. The murder charge was dropped and Cleaver was placed on probation for an assault. He described his conversion in his book *Soul on Fire* (1978). But the public took almost no notice of it. In 1986, Cleaver sought the Republican nomination for the U.S. Senate in California but was not successful.

Cleaver remained committed in his dedication to fostering progressive social changes but became much less radical and much more politically correct. In an interview conducted in the spring of 1997, he condemned the black bourgeoisie as corrupt and immoral like the white bourgeoisie. He declaimed against the assimilationist ethic of the black American middle class. At the same time, Cleaver spoke in favor of political and economic support of women. "Our Creator never wasted his or her time creating a second class person," he said and suggested that there were a lot of women in America who were qualified to be U.S. president and people should not rely on the Old Boy political network, which is racist and misogynistic.

The fact that Cleaver hasn't become one more black Messiah is not unconnected with the successful Federal Bureau of Investigation (FBI) investigation program against him and other BPP leaders, which was most intensive at the time of Panthers' highest popularity, but also continued even after Cleaver's death (see for example Robert Fulford's column about Cleaver in *Globe and Mail*, April 3, 1999). For his legacy of nonconformity and struggling against social and racial injustice, Eldridge Cleaver could be thought of as a hero of American leftist radicals.

### SEE ALSO

*Volume 1 Left:* Civil Rights; Malcolm X; King, Martin Luther, Jr.; Black Panthers.
*Volume 2 Right:* Black Separatism; Black Nationalism; Hoover, J. Edgar.

### BIBLIOGRAPHY

Eldridge Cleaver, *Soul on Ice* (McGraw-Hill, 1968); Eldridge Cleaver, *Soul on Fire* (Word, 1978); Stuart A. Kallen, ed., *Sixties Counterculture* (Greenhaven, 2001); Robert Scheer, ed., *Eldridge Cleaver, Post Prison Writings* (Random House, 1968); Kathleen Rout, *Eldridge Cleaver* (Twayne Publishers, 1991).

IGOR CHARSKYKH
DONETSK NATIONAL UNIVERSITY, UKRAINE

# Clinton, William J. (1946–)

WILLIAM JEFFERSON CLINTON was born William Jefferson Blythe IV in Hope, Arkansas. His father died prior to his birth, and he adopted the last name of his stepfather, Roger Clinton, whom his mother, Virginia Kelley, would later remarry. Clinton received his education at Georgetown, Oxford, and Yale universities and became governor of Arkansas in 1978 at the age of 32.

He lost his governorship in 1982, before regaining the position in 1986 and holding it until his bid for the presidency. In 1992, he successfully defeated the incumbent candidate, Republican George H.W. Bush, to become the 42nd president of the United States. Clinton's presidency lasted two terms, as he successfully defeated Republican candidate Bob Dole in the 1996 election and became the first Democrat to win reelection since the 1940s.

Clinton brought a new hybrid of mostly liberal Democratic policy mixed with some conservative Republican doctrine to his presidency. On the liberal side, his universal healthcare proposals epitomized the left, while his welfare reform package reflected conservative concerns. Though a Democrat through and through,

Clinton managed to steal the thunder of the right wing on occasion and fold it into his administration's policies.

His presidency was marked by allegations of misconduct, especially in his private life, and he became the second president in U.S. history to be impeached. However, as leftist commentators suggest, the charismatic president, with genuine political skill, was able to overcome these potentially politically fatal events and guided America through a period of economic prosperity, unrivaled by either his predecessor or his successor. During his tenure, more than 20 million new jobs were created in the United States.

Clinton's presidency was confronted with a Republican-controlled U.S. Congress during his first term. Nonetheless, he was able to achieve many successful acts, largely in part to his conservative liberal views and ability to appeal to moderate conservatives. The Brady Bill, passed during the first term in November 1993, stated that there would be a waiting period when purchasing a gun, thus allowing authorities to run background checks on buyers. A month later, he signed the North American Free Trade Agreement (NAFTA), which helped to bring about freer trading conditions with Mexico and Canada.

While Clinton found much success in his first term, the Whitewater land investment scandal came to the public's attention. Beginning in 1994, Clinton appointed an independent counsel to determine whether he had committed any wrongdoing regarding a sale of land in Arkansas while he was governor. The final conclusion of the investigation, which would ultimately not be decided until September 2000, was that Clinton was cleared of any wrongdoing.

Clinton gave particular attention to acts of violence and crime. In September 1994, he passed the 1994 Crime Bill, which increased the rights of the victims and established more severe penalties for criminals. Partially though through these measures, the crime rate in America dropped in each of Clinton's eight years in office. In 1995, Clinton was able to successfully fend off Republicans in budget negotiations, even though partisan opposition meant that the government was actually shut down for a limited time. His defiance of the Republicans gained him public approval and boosted his popularity in the wake of his reelection campaign. In April 1996, his administration was marked by the successful passage of an increase in the minimum wage, which affected over 10 million workers. This rise in minimum wage was the highest increase in American history (reflecting Clinton's liberal side).

Clinton's second term in office led to his impeachment. Synonymous with the Clinton administration is the Monica Lewinsky scandal. After successfully brushing aside claims of extramarital affairs prior to his election in 1992, the president could not avoid this scandal. The Lewinsky affair first made national headlines in January 1998 with Clinton emphatically denying an affair with Lewinsky. The Lewinsky investigation was led by longtime Clinton nemesis, independent counsel Kenneth Starr, who had earlier led the investigation into the Whitewater issue.

On August 17, 1998, Clinton testified in front of a grand jury that he had not conducted a sexual relationship with Lewinsky. Starr's official report would give great detail of Clinton's affair with Lewinsky but raise no substantial reason that would justify impeachment. The impeachment issue was based on whether Clinton's dishonesty in a court of law was grounds for removal from office. While the Republican-controlled House of Representatives voted to impeach the president, he was able to remain in office after the Senate voted against his removal.

It is in Clinton's political survival after being impeached that his centrist Democratic acumen prevailed. While the First Lady, Hillary Clinton, proclaimed "a vast right-wing conspiracy" was out to get her husband removed from office, Clinton continued with the business of state and garnered high public approval ratings. Clinton had truly piqued the right, not only with liberal policies and usurping some conservative ones, but mainly with a loose sense of personal morals that ran wholly against the grain of moralism in groups like the Moral Majority and the Christian Coalition.

Clinton's legacy, while always attached to the Lewinsky scandal, should also be remembered for its ability to sustain a strong American economy. Clinton also brought prestige to America overseas, especially with his work in helping to end conflict in Northern Ireland and Kosovo. Clinton will also be remembered for steering his leftist policies toward the center of American politics, often robbing Republicans of their own programs in the United States.

**SEE ALSO**

*Volume 1 Left:* Democratic Party; United States.
*Volume 2 Right:* Republican Party; United States; Christian Coalition.

**BIBLIOGRAPHY**

William C. Berman, *From the Center to the Edge: The Politics and Policies of the Clinton Presidency* (Rowman & Littlefield, 2001); Florian Bieber and Zidas Daskalovski, eds., *Understanding the War in Kosovo* (Frank Cass, 2003); Joseph R. Blaney, *The Clinton Scandals and the Politics of Image Restoration* (Praeger, 2001); Robert Busby, *Defending the American Presidency: Clinton and the Lewinsky Scandal* (Palgrave, 2001); Lewis Gould, *The Modern American Presidency* (University Press of Kansas, 2003).

DAVID W. MCBRIDE
UNIVERSITY OF NOTTINGHAM, UNITED KINGDOM

# Cominform

THE COMMUNIST Information Bureau (Cominform) was established in September 1947 to fill the vacuum that the dissolution of the Third International (also known as the Comintern) had created in the communist world. Under Soviet leadership, Cominform set out to institutionalize frequent and transparent information exchanges among its members. As such, it did not have any pronounced economic, political, or military agenda. Membership was voluntary, and decisions were nonbinding. In addition to the ruling communist parties in seven Eastern European states (Bulgaria, Czechoslovakia, Hungary, Poland, Romania, the Soviet Union, and Yugoslavia), two prominent Western European communist parties became members of Cominform: those of France and Italy.

It is possible to identify two significant phases in Cominform's short period of existence. The first phase, between 1947 and 1950, would define Cominform's main characteristics. The bureau was formed as and would remain an exclusively European undertaking; and Cominform would soon become a symbolic tool for the Soviet Union to assert its supremacy within the post-World War II communist world. The second phase, between 1950 and the dissolution of the organization in 1956, saw Cominform's gradual decline due to changing geopolitical realities.

It was no coincidence that Cominform's membership was exclusively European. In the immediate aftermath of the war, nowhere else but Europe was communism capable of redefining and reestablishing itself as an organized internationalist movement. Communism, in its capacity as the archrival of Nazism and fascism, had an appeal to large societal segments in Europe. Furthermore, in the presence of emerging U.S. initiatives for Europe's restructuring, the Soviet Union gave utmost priority to establishing a dedicated alliance in its historical sphere of influence along the western frontiers. There were, however, two major handicaps along the way. First, the recent war trauma had paved the way for serious ideological divisions within the communist camp. Second, the Soviet Union was neither physically strong enough to impose its will on all "dissenters," nor absolutely certain as to which dissenters could be tolerated more than others, should compromise prove necessary.

The situation in the Balkan Peninsula presented itself as particularly sensitive. Cominform was born, in part, as a Soviet-led reaction to novel reinterpretations of communism as exemplified in Yugoslavia and in Bulgaria. Furthermore, the strong historical, cultural and religious ties among several Soviet and Balkan peoples aside, the peninsula was strategically located between the Soviet Union and the Mediterranean Sea. Against this backdrop, Soviet leader Josef Stalin could not tolerate the emergence of what he considered a "revisionist" alliance between the Yugoslav and Bulgarian communist parties, not to mention the equally difficult case of Albania. The proposals for the establishment of a Balkan Federation were even more threatening from the Soviet perspective. Such unification in the Balkans might create an alternative hegemony in the communist world. In its first three years, therefore, Cominform was used by Stalin as an instrument for harassing undesired rival alliances in communist Europe. Several Cominform opinions and resolutions were orchestrated by the Soviet Union to criticize the revisionist approaches in other countries, in particular Yugoslavia.

The third and last conference of Cominform was held in November 1949. Until its dissolution in 1956, the bureau remained almost completely idle. One reason for this was Yugoslavian leader Josip Tito's perseverance in pursuing his own line of communism despite all Soviet opposition. In the meantime, following Mao Zedong's communist takeover in China, suddenly a more dangerous rival had appeared for the leadership of the communist world. Soon after, the onset of the Korean War largely diverted Stalin's attention away from what was going on in the Balkans. The Korean War finally came to an end in 1953, but Stalin died the same year.

Meanwhile, other crises were emerging in such places as Hungary and the Suez Canal. Moreover, Yugoslavia was well on its way to forming, together with Egypt and Indonesia, the non-aligned movement. Under these circumstances, the Soviet leadership realized that Cominform's existence did more harm than good to Soviet interests. On the one hand, a compromise had to be reached between the Soviet Union and Yugoslavia. The very existence of Cominform, with its institutionalized anti-Yugoslav stance, now presented a barrier to the peaceful coexistence of the two communist states. On the other hand, a loose information network, the Soviet Union understood, could not serve the communist project well. Eventually, Cominform was brought to an end with Khrushchev's rise to power in Moscow.

### SEE ALSO

*Volume 1 Left:* Third International (Comintern); Soviet Union; Communist Party, Soviet.
*Volume 2 Right:* Balance of Power.

### BIBLIOGRAPHY

I. Banac, *With Stalin against Tito: Cominformist Splits in Yugoslav Communism* (Cornell University Press, 1988); F. Claudin, *The Communist Movement: from Comintern to Cominform* (Monthly Review Press, 1975); G. Procacci, ed., *The Cominform: Minutes of the Three Conferences, 1947/1948/1949* (Fondazione Giangiacomo Feltrinelli, 1994).

ESREF AKSU
INDEPENDENT SCHOLAR

# Communism

IN 1870, Napoleon III had led his nation into the disastrous Franco-Prussian War against the expansionist Prussian state. In spite of his pretensions to be a conqueror like his uncle, the first Napoleon, Napoleon III's army was woefully unprepared for modern warfare and Napoleon III himself was taken as a prisoner of war.

In the face of the Prussian Army, the people of Paris rose up against the invaders. Marx wrote in *The Civil War in France*, "But Paris armed was the revolution armed. A victory of Paris over the Prussian aggressor would have been a victory of the French workmen over the French capitalist and his state parasites." A republic had been proclaimed in September 1870 in Paris, under Leon Gambetta.

Adolphe Thiers and his middle-class supporters organized a counter-government at Versailles for France and—with German support—declared war on the workers in Paris, who declared their regime the Paris Commune. The Paris Commune was the first true workers' republic in history. Thiers surrendered to Prussia in February 1871 in order to declare war against Paris. On March 18, the Commune was declared: "The proletarians of Paris, amidst the failures and treasons of the ruling classes, have understood that the hour has struck for them to save the situation by taking into their own hands the direction of public affairs."

Marx observed that "The communal regime, once established in Paris and the secondary centers, with the old centralized government in the provinces, has to give way to the self-government of the producers." The commune was a model for the soviets, or councils of workers, soldiers, and sailors that would later arise during the Russian Revolution of 1905. With brute force, Thiers's Versailles army attacked Paris. On May 21, the shooting began and after seven days (*la semaine sanglante*, the "bloody week"), Paris had become again the capital of a bourgeois France.

From then on, the communist movement was hounded by the police forces of the European monarchies, which either imprisoned or forced into hiding their opponents. For a generation, the working class was exploited ruthlessly in Europe, as the same governments exported their exploitation to the rest of the world in imperialist expeditions. Marx wrote, "Imperialism is the ultimate form of the state power which nascent middle class society had finally transformed into a means for the enslavement of labor by capital."

Imperialism only exacerbated the rivalry of the Great Powers of Europe. In 1905, Revolution broke out in Russia after a series of defeats in the war against Japan in 1904 and 1905. By June 1905, rebellion was widespread in Russia, symbolized by the mutiny aboard the *Potemkin*, of the Black Sea Fleet of Tzar Nicholas II, of the Romanov Dynasty. By September, Russian workers had gained their first broad experience in the arena of political action, and they had been aided by a number of revolutionary groups sworn to work for the overthrow of the Romanovs.

Chief of these were the two branches of the Marxist Social Revolutionary Party: the Mensheviks and the Bolsheviks. It was the Bolsheviks, under Vladimir I. Lenin, who would make the greatest mark. Swiftly, Lenin and his comrade Leon Trotsky moved to bring the soviets and their delegates of workers, peasants, and sailors, under their sway. Although Marx had considered Russia too backward for a revolution, Lenin and Trotsky would prove him wrong. Russia was ripe for revolution.

Within less than a decade, the Great Powers of Europe were locked in World War I. In August 1914, France, Great Britain, and Russia were locked into three years of war. The Russian Army suffered catastrophic losses.

## RUSSIAN REVOLUTION

It began on February 23, 1917, with demonstrations to celebrate the proletarian International Women's Day. The marchers, many from the Putilov Factory with their wives. began to sing the *Marseillaise*, the song of the French Revolution of 1789. They cried "Down With the Tzar" and "Give Us Bread." Trotsky wrote: "Thus the fact is that the February revolution was begun from below, overcoming the resistance of its own revolutionary organizations, the initiative being taken of their own accord by the most oppressed and downtrodden part of the proletariat—the women textile workers, among them no doubt many soldiers' wives."

On March 2, the tzar abdicated the throne, bringing three centuries of Romanov rule and exploitation to an end. In his place sat the Provisional Government of the liberal Prince Georgi Lvov. In July, he was replaced by his Minister of Defense. Alexander Kerensky, when threatened by a counterrevolutionary coup by General Lavr Kornilov. On August 29, Kerensky declared himself commander in chief and appealed to the Russian soviets for help against Kornilov.

However as Robert Service wrote in *Lenin: A Biography*, Kerensky had "turned in panic to the parties of the soviets, including the Bolsheviks, to support him by sending out agitators to persuade Kornilov's troops to obey the Provisional Government and allow Kornilov to be detained in custody." Seeing the uncertainty that governed Russian political affairs, Lenin used the centralism of his Bolsheviks to press for power. They had effectively become the main spokesmen for the soviets, representing workers, soldiers, sailors, and peasants. The soviets had been reformed during February. By October 1917, Lenin and his Bolsheviks would oust Kerensky from power and declare Russia the first communist state.

## COMINTERN

As Lenin's successor (after 1924), Josef Stalin, enforced Moscow's form of communism through the Communist International (Comintern), communists in other countries would inevitably be forced to adopt Soviet help if they hoped to achieve and remain in power. A major exception to this trend was World War II, when indigenous communists came to power in Eastern Europe beginning in 1944 in the wake of the T-34 tanks of Stalin's Red Army. An early form of indigenous communism was the Spartacist movement in Germany in the aftermath of World War I. In November 1918, the German Left Socialists, or Spartacists, led by Rosa Luxembourg and Karl Liebknecht, attempted to form a "soviet republic" in Berlin

Within China, the Communist International would reap unanticipated success with the Nationalist, or Kuomintang Party of Sun Yat-sen. Bitterly disappointed with what he felt was the betrayal of China at the Versailles Peace Conference in 1919 by the Western Powers, Sun turned for aid to Soviet Russia, the other "international outcast." In 1905, coincidentally the year of the first Russian Revolution, Sun developed what Jonathan D. Spence described as the Three Principles of the People, "Sun sought to combine the fundamental aspects of nationalism, democracy and socialism." The close alliance of the Kuomintang with the Chinese Communist Party would continue until Sun's successor, Chiang Kai-shek, attacked the communists in 1927.

For over 20 years, a virtual state of civil war existed in China until the communists triumphed under Mao Zedong in October 1949. When Mao seized power, he did not prove as faithful a disciple of Soviet communism as had Sun Yat-sen. By 1960s, when Nikita Khrushchev was Russian premier, the dispute also became nationalistic, as Mao refused to subordinate what he perceived as Chinese interests like the development of atomic power to Soviet Russian control. Into the 21st century, China has altered but still refused to surrender the vision of political communism that had first been imagined by Mao.

## TITOISM

During the years after World War II, like Mao, Josip Broz Tito, who had led communist partisans against the Germans in World War II, forged an intensely nationalist communism in Yugoslavia. This was so in spite of the fact he had spent 1935 working in the main offices of the Comintern in Moscow. Tito deliberately forged a path for Yugoslavia that did not embrace the Cold War hostility of Russia's socialist camp toward the United States as did neighboring Romania and Bulgaria. Indeed, he openly embraced Western, including American aid. A united Yugoslavia, largely his own creation, survived his death in 1980 by only a dozen years, to fracture in a bloody civil war after 1992.

Perhaps the most interesting variant of modern communism was Eurocommunism. It had its origins in the reaction of the European Communist parties to the shocking invasion of Czechoslovakia by the Soviet Union and its Warsaw bloc East European allies in August 1968. Taking advantage of the American preoccupation in Vietnam, the Soviets under Premier Leonid Brezhnev crushed the Czech attempt at liberalizing communism under Czech Premier Alexander Dubcek. European communists in Western Europe realized that their only real hope of ever achieving political power lay in distancing themselves from the iron-fisted foreign policy of Moscow. Eurocommunism, which attempted to carry on Dubcek's idea of "socialism with a human face," found its most outspoken leader in Enrico Berlinguer, leader of the Italian Communist Party until his death in 1984.

G.R. Urban explained the political hopes of Eurocommunism: "The debate should be open toward the future; it should sketch out a pluralistic way forward along which Communists, Socialists, Social Democrats and all those of Christian and liberal inspiration who are agreed on the necessity for the structural transformation of society on Socialist lines can advance towards the creation of a new Europe." However, the fall of communism in 1989, and the collapse of the Soviet Union in 1991, brought the experiment in Eurocommunism to an end.

With the collapse of the Soviet Union, China, North Korea, Cuba, and Zimbabwe in southern Africa remained perhaps the strongest and least reformed of communist states. In Cuba under Castro, and North Korea under Kim, the cult of personality, which once flourished around Stalin in Russia remains well and alive.

## SEE ALSO

Volume 1 Left: Third International (Comintern); Soviet Union; Marx, Karl; China.
Volume 2 Right: Capitalism; United States; Balance of Power.

## BIBLIOGRAPHY

G.R. Urban, ed., Eurocommunism (Bantam, 1978); "Josip Broz Tito, Premier of Yugoslavia," www.cnn.com (July 2004); Henry M. Christman, ed., Essential Works of Lenin (Bantam, 1966); Nigel Ferguson, The Rise and Demise of the British World Order and the Lessons for Global Power (Basic Books, 2002); Roy Medvedev, Let History Judge: The Origins and Consequence of Stalinism, Colleen Taylor, trans. (Vintage Books, 1971); Bruce Lincoln, The Romanovs: Autocrats of all the Russias (Dial Press, 1981); Edmund Wilson, To the Finland Station: A Study in the Writing and Acting of History (Anchor Books, 1953); Sergei Starikov, Roy Medvedev, and Philip

Mironov, *The Russian Civil War*, Guy Daniels, trans. (Knopf, 1978); David Remnick, *Lenin's Tomb: The Last Days of the Soviet Empire* (Vintage, 1994); Arthur P. Mendel, *Essential Works of Marxism* (Bantam, 1965).

JOHN F. MURPHY, JR.
AMERICAN MILITARY UNIVERSITY

# Communist Party, Soviet

FEW POLITICAL institutions in history have had the impact of the Soviet Communist Party. For over seventy years, it governed Russia, then the Soviet Union, only one of two Superpowers in the modern world. More than that, the Soviet Communist Party, as the Bolshevik Party, also seized power in Russia in 1917, bringing to an end three centuries of rule by the Romanov Dynasty.

The Bolshevik Party began as part of the Social Democratic Labor Party, which had its first Congress, or meeting, in Minsk, Russia, in 1898. From the beginning, its avowed goal was the overthrow of the Romanovs. Robert Service wrote in his *Lenin: a Biography*, the party "envisaged that a revolution would be led against the Romanov monarchy by the working class and would result in the establishment of a democratic republic. Yet all but one of the Congress participants were arrested within a few weeks. A functioning party had yet to be created."

With its program, the Social Democratic Labor Party firmly established itself as a Marxist party, placing itself on the foundations of Marxism as laid out by Karl Marx and Friedrich Engels in *The Communist Manifesto* of 1848. In it, Marx and Engels declared that "the Communists disdain to conceal their views and aims. They openly declare that their ends can be attained only by the forcible overthrow of all existing social conditions. Let the ruling classes tremble at a Communistic revolution. The proletarians have nothing to lose but their chains. They have a world to win. Working Men of All Countries, Unite!"

The Social Democrats built upon a revolutionary tradition in Russia that began as early as the 1870s, with such groups as the Populists. D.M. Sturley, in *A Short History of Russia*, wrote of how "under the influence of Alexander Herzen and N.G. Chernyshevsky, students and professional people went out to preach revolutionary socialism to the peasants in the countryside. The peasants were quite unresponsive: they wanted land not ideas." When revolution came to Russia, it would be through the working class, as Marx and Engels proclaimed. While the experiment of the Populists, or Narodniks, from the Russian word for "the people," failed, they later provided much of the leadership for the more radical revolutionary movements like "Land and Freedom" (1876) and "The Peoples' Will" (1879), as Sturley noted. It was on these last groups that the later Bolshevik Party based its program of action.

WHAT IS TO BE DONE?

In 1881, Tzar Alexander II was assassinated, in spite of the reforming character of his reign. His son, Alexander III, instituted an era of repression that would continue after his death in 1894. In March 1887, the revolutionaries attempted an assassination plot against them; one of those executed for complicity in the plot was Alexander Ulyanov. His younger brother, Vladimir, was severely traumatized by the event. As Vladimir I. Lenin, he would found the Bolshevik Party. Lenin made his contribution to the movement's ideology first in "What Is To Be Done?," which was published in 1902. Lenin wrote: "they relied on a theory which in substance was not a revolutionary theory at all [and which made it impossible] to link up their movement inseparably with the class struggle that went on within developing capitalist society."

After the foundation of the party in 1898, Lenin, who had been in exile for political activities in Siberia, became a leading member and editor of the journal *Iskra*, or *The Spark*.

In July 1903, the Social Democratic Labor Party would meet in Brussels, and like many revolutionary parties, met with a severe split within its ranks. The schism led to virtually two parties, the Menshevik, or minority group, and Lenin's Bolshevik, or majority, wing. It was at the Brussels Congress that Lenin split politically with Leon Trotsky, who had worked with him on *Iskra*. However, their personal relationship seemed untouched and they would be political allies again. Lenin was determined to make himself supreme in the Russian revolutionary movement. At this time, he exemplified the comments of Crane Brinton in *The Anatomy of Revolution*: "the ruthlessness, in the proper service of the ideal, went while they were alive into the making of their leadership."

In 1904, Russia, then under Tzar Nicholas II, who had ascended the throne in 1904, went to war with Japan over imperialist spheres of influence, including

*Vladimir Lenin addresses a crowd of followers at the Bolshevik headquarters in November 1917. Along with Leon Trotsky, Lenin was a principal founder of the Communist Party and its Union of Soviet Socialist Republics. (Painting by Vladimir Sechow.)*

Korea and Manchuria. Russia suffered devastating reversals on the battlefield, which led to the Russian Revolution of 1905. When it broke out in January, Lenin was in Geneva, and the uprising took him completely by surprise

David Shub wrote in *Lenin* that on October 13 "a strange new 'government' appeared in St. Petersburg, the Soviet [of] Workers' Deputies." The vice-chairman of this soviet, or council, was Trotsky. Both Lenin (who would not return until November) and Trotsky now renewed their political alliance: their personal friendship appears to have been undimmed.

Tzar Nicholas eventually reacted with the brutality that would turn so many against him. The "Black Hundreds" were summoned again. Thousands were executed or imprisoned; early Russian film shows the repression carried out by the troops. Trotsky was arrested with other members of the soviet, but Lenin had traveled to Finland on December 24, five days before the final insurrection was crushed in Moscow, with the Moscow garrison reinforced, as Shub wrote, by the "crack [Semenovsky] Guards and artillery from St. Pe-

tersburg." Lenin would remain in exile from Russia until 1917.

When World War I broke out in August 1914, Lenin was living in what was then Austria-Hungary and, as a Russian, was an enemy alien. Even more, as he wrote on August 7, "the local police suspects me of spying." Eventually, he was released from custody and allowed to leave for Switzerland, which followed its traditional policy of neutrality during the war. As in the war with Japan, Russia suffered terribly, with an autocratic government unable to prosecute a modern war.

SPONTANEOUS DEMONSTRATIONS

When on February 23, 1917 (March 8 in our modern calendar), demonstrations broke out in the capital city of St. Petersburg among the workers, many from the Putilov factory, Lenin and the Bolsheviks were in exile and caught totally by surprise at the spontaneous movement. Seeing an opportunity to seize power after the failed attempt of 1905, they set their eyes on taking over the rebellion to use it for their own political ends.

The tzar was in his front line headquarters when the disorders broke out. As Trotsky would write in *The History of the Russian Revolution*: "On February 25, a telegram came from the Minister of War that strikes were occurring in the capital, disorders beginning among the workers, but measures had been taken and there was nothing serious. In a word: 'It isn't the first time, and won't be the last!'" All efforts to suppress the growing rebellion failed, because the troops of the St. Petersburg garrison were in sympathy with the demonstrators, including the regiments of the elite Imperial Guard.

A new provisional government took power under the liberal—and ineffectual—Prince Georgi Lvov. Nicholas, who had been a well-meaning if ineffectual ruler, ended the three-century-old Romanov dynasty with his abdication from power on February 28 (March 13).

Meanwhile, Lenin watched with keen interest the inability of the provisional government to control the anarchy growing throughout the country. It was the opportunity he had been waiting to exploit. Real power lay with the soviets, which had been the main ally of his Bolsheviks in 1905.

## COMRADE LENIN

Lenin arrived in the Finland Station in St. Petersburg—now Petrograd—on April 3. He was greeted by Nicholai Chkheidze, president of the Petrograd Soviet, who said, "Comrade Lenin! In the name of the Petrograd Soviet and of the whole revolution, we welcome you to Russia." Resolutely, Lenin set forth the Bolsheviks as the only party to lead the Revolution.

Four days later, he published his "April Theses" in the Bolshevik newspaper, *Pravda*. He stressed his most important points in Theses Four and Five: "It must be explained to the masses that the Soviet of Workers' Deputies is the only possible form of revolutionary government and that, therefore, our task is, while this government is submitting to the influence of the bourgeoisie, to present a patient, systematic, and persistent analysis of its errors and tactics, an analysis especially adapted to the practical needs of the masses."

And in Thesis Five: "Not a parliamentary republic—a return to it from the Soviet of Workers' Deputies would be a step backward—but a republic of Soviets of Workers, Agricultural Laborers, and Peasants Deputies throughout the land, from top to bottom."

From April 24 to April 29, Lenin held a conference of his Bolshevik Party to map plans for assuming control not only of the government, but of Russia as well. A few days later, his old comrade Leon Trotsky would arrive; earlier, Josef Stalin had come to Russia. While working together under Lenin in the Revolution, a later power struggle between them would threaten to destroy the revolutionary state that Lenin would build. In June, the first All-Russian Congress of the Soviets would meet—an opportunity that Lenin did not miss as a means of exerting power over the armed workers, soldiers, and sailors, who he already conceived of as the fighting vanguard of his "proletarian revolution."

Although Lenin would be forced to exile in Finland again on August 9, Alexander Kerensky would have to turn to the soviets to battle the attempted coup d'etat of General Lavr Kornilov in September. Only they commanded the loyalty of enough soldiers and sailors to defeat Kornilov. On August 29, Kerensky appointed himself the new commander-in-chief to deal with the uprising. With the help of the soviets, the putsch was crushed. On September 1, Kornilov was imprisoned.

After the uprising, it became clear that the Bolsheviks and Lenin formed the main threat to Kerensky's provisional government. Yet, while Lenin and his party loyalists moved to consolidate their control over the soviets, Kerensky did nothing to stop them. With Lenin in Finland, it was Trotsky, coordinating for him in Petrograd, who laid the foundations for the coming Bolshevik surprise.

The last real threat to Lenin's plans lay in the meeting of the Democratic Conference, which took place on September 14. This was the last chance to build a coalition that could have united opposition to the Bolsheviks. But as John Reed wrote in *Ten Days That Shook the World*, "there were seventeen [party] tickets in Petrograd, and in some of the provincial towns as many as forty." Against this fragmented opposition, Lenin presented a united front. When the Conference ended in parliamentary bickering, the last real political opposition to the Bolsheviks collapsed. With the failure of the Congress, Lenin began to plan with the Petrograd Bolsheviks, with Trotsky the main strategist, to seize power in the vacuum left by the failed assembly.

## THE BOLSHEVIK SURPRISE

On October 7, Lenin secretly returned to Petrograd. Reed described the Red Guard, the revolutionary troops on which Lenin would call: "a huddled group of boys in workmen's clothes, carrying guns with bayonets, talking nervously together." But they were dedicated to the soviets.

When, on the night of October 18, Kerensky decided to move against Lenin, he had to go back to the front to seek troops. By then it was too late. On October 25, supported by the revolutionary Red Guards, Lenin and his Bolsheviks seized power. Lenin issued a proclamation from his headquarters at the Smolny Institute decreeing the end of the provisional government. The Winter Palace, home of the defunct administration, was stormed by troops loyal to him and the Bolsheviks. The next day, supported by the Council of Soviets, Lenin took power. Reed helped distribute printed flyers which neatly summed up in one line the Bolshevik triumph: "The Provisional Government is deposed."

Once in power, Lenin moved to establish himself and the Bolshevik Party as the only real source of control in Russia. Unlike in parliamentary governments such as in England or the United States, where a political party would take control of a government after winning an election, Lenin made sure that the Bolsheviks, now more properly called the Communists, were the government in Russia. Within the Soviet Union (as it now would be called), a constitution was promulgated in July 1918. As Basil Dmytryshyn wrote in *USSR: A Concise History*, "the constitution declared socialism to be the state program not only in Russia but throughout the world as well." Power in the new state flowed directly down from Lenin through the party to the rest of the country.

## WAR COMMUNISM

During the Civil War that raged from 1917 to 1921, Lenin used the "centralism" of the Bolshevik Party as the main organizing force against both foreign powers like the United States, England, and Japan who intervened to end the Revolution and the counter-revolutionary "White" generals like Anton Denikin or Baron Peter Wrangel who sought to destroy the Bolshevik's Red Army. From November 1918, the "Supreme Leader" of the Whites was Alexander V. Kolchak of the Black Sea Fleet. From the beginning, the Whites were handicapped by competing ambitions and a dreadful lack of coordination of their offensives.

On the other hand, Lenin was favored in having the talents of Trotsky, who served him as commissar for Military and Naval Affairs. Trotsky and his Red Army defeated each White effort in turn. But as the Civil War worsened, Lenin instituted a policy of pitiless terror toward any he and the party deemed an "enemy of the people." In December 1918, Lenin had the Sovnarkom,

the omnipresent Council of People's Commissars, the main organ of the new state, decree the establishment of the V-Cheka, the All-Russian Extraordinary Commission for Combating Counter-revolution and Sabotage.

Its chief was the expatriate Pole Feliks Dzerzhinsky. Soon, its agents, the Chekists, followed Lenin's orders to institute a reign of terror. When a village refused to meet the demands of "War Communism" in supplying the Red Army, Chekist squads would machine gun the entire village. By March 1921, all enemies of the Revolution had been crushed in the former Russian Empire by Trotsky's Red Army. Lenin, speaking at the Tenth Congress of the Communist Party on March 8, 1921, could say, "The last of the hostile armies has been driven from our territories."

Now, Lenin faced his greatest struggle: rebuilding a land and people ravaged by seven years of war. Indeed, the first challenge came at Ninth Communist Party Congress, which from March to April 1920 challenged the centralization of authority that had taken place during the Civil War. Lenin, never a slave to revolutionary ideology, tactically maneuvered to thwart the danger from within his own party. Now, during the Tenth Party Congress in 1921, the sailors of the Kronstadt naval base, who had manned the cruiser *Aurora* the day of the attack on the Winter Palace, rebelled. Although Trotsky put down the revolt ruthlessly in March, it was clear to Lenin that his new government was in jeopardy.

Famine stalked the land: many Russians became cannibals to survive. Lenin responded with almost a counterrevolution of his own. Beginning in the same month, the "War Communism" began to be drastically dismantled by the Tenth Party Congress, some of whose delegates had actually been in the attack on Kronstadt. The New Economic Policy (NEP) was introduced, which began to bring capitalism back to the new socialist state. Nevertheless, Lenin in his "On Party Unity" declaration at the Tenth Party Congress emphasized the centralism of the party. He wrote that "fractionalism of any kind ... shall entail absolute and immediate expulsion from the party."

Just as the new communist state began to emerge, Lenin became seriously ill in December 1921. His health continued to deteriorate. While still alive, he saw the power struggle begin that almost ripped his new state apart, between Trotsky and Stalin. Stalin had spent the Revolution and Civil War years cultivating allies within the party. However, as Roy Medvedev wrote in *Let History Judge: The Origins and Consequences of Stalinism*, "in 1922, Stalin was the least prominent figure in the Politburo," the governing body of the party.

But, on May 26, 1922, Lenin suffered a stroke and gradually lost control of the state and the party. Stalin moved to fill the power vacuum, as Lenin did so with Kerensky in October 1917.

Gradually, Lenin turned against Stalin, who openly insulted Lenin's wife, N.K. Krupskaya. In one secret letter, cited by Medvedev as being written between the end of 1922 and 1923, Lenin said that "Comrade Stalin, on becoming General Secretary [of the party], concentrated enormous power in his hands, and I am not sure he always knows how to use his powers carefully enough." Clearly, he was beginning to see Trotsky as his heir. In March 1923, he would suffer another stroke. On January 1, 1924, Lenin died, apparently from a massive heart attack. Instead of the USSR's future being in the ever-inventive mind of Lenin, the country would soon be in the ruthless hands of Stalin.

## RISE OF STALIN

By 1927, Trotsky was purged from the party, and Stalin would be the undisputed leader, or *vozhd*, of both the party and the state. By this time, the party had taken on the organizational form which, with few variations, would continue until the fall of the Communist Party regime in Russia in 1991. As Philip G. Roeder wrote in *Soviet Political Dynamics: Development of the First Leninist Polity*, "all party members must belong to a primary party organization (called a cell until 1939), which is usually organized in his or her place of work." Roeder commented "the role (or function) of the Communist Party in Soviet society has been central to the transformation of that society. As the ultimate authority on Marxism-Leninism, the party propounds the dogmas that legitimate the policies of the Soviet regime and defines its objectives."

In actuality, as seen in the reign of Stalin, the party was very much at the control of the leader. In 1934, Stalin initiated a series of political purges that completely vitiated the party leadership and body of the membership. He especially wanted to remove the "Old Bolsheviks," those senior party members who had served under Lenin and (at least in his eyes) had a similarly valid claim to party leadership. [It should be noted here that this article does not discuss the governmental organization of the Soviet system, but exclusively that of the Communist Party. Although the party controlled the Soviet state, the Soviet government and Communist Party existed as two different political units.]

The annual Communist Party Congress was the meeting in which—invariably presided over by the general (or first) secretary—the party membership was given a view of the state of the country and the party. In a very real way, it functioned as the Russian version of the State of the Union address which the president of the United States delivers each January.

It was in the Twentieth Party 1956 meeting that Nikita Khrushchev officially denounced the excesses of Stalin, who had died in 1953. (Drafts of his speech, however, had been circulated to the press earlier.) The Party Rules in force in 1988 noted in Article 31 that the Party Congress "is the supreme body of the Communist Party of the Soviet Union."

Under Stalin, the real power in the party began to reside in the office of the general secretary. Roeder observed that "actual power has gravitated with time toward the Secretariat and Politburo [Political Bureau] as the Congress and Central Committee have come to play less vital roles in the direction of the party." Although having lost real power in the party, the Central Committee presided over the party between Party Congresses. The Party Rules declared that the Central Committee "directs all the activity of the party and of local party agencies ... [and] creates various agencies, institutions, and enterprises of the party and directs their activity."

When the Central Committee had proved too unwieldy to cope with the civil war, the Politburo was officially created at the Eighth Party Congress in March 1919. Party decisions in the Politburo were expected to be made by consensus. However, during Stalin's era the *vozhd* made the decisions. Roeder points out that, aside from Stalin "only four of the other nine Politburo members in 1931" survived the purges he initiated three years later. By the time the Stalinist frenzy had abated, perhaps the best idea of the total number of victims—executed or imprisoned—would come from Stalin himself. Dmytryshyn said that at the Eighteenth Party Congress in March 1939, Stalin admitted that membership in the party from 1934 to 1939 "dropped from 1,874,488 to 1,588,852" members. From 1952 to 1966, the Politburo was known as the Party Presidium.

## KHRUSHCHEV AND GORBACHEV

After the death of Stalin in March 1953, the Politburo began to reassert some authority within the party organization. Although he was ultimately succeeded by Nikita Khrushchev in 1957, the latter never held the same power as had his *vozhd*. Indeed, when Khrushchev (who served as first secretary) was overthrown, it was largely due to dissatisfaction with his economic and foreign policy within what was collectively called the party leadership. Decisions were reached within the Politburo by consensus and with the help of essential advisers, as Roeder noted, including "members of the Central Committee, the state apparatus, the Academy of Sciences, as well as other experts and affected parties."

On March 10, 1985, Mikhail Gorbachev became general secretary. Within the first year of his taking office, he had the impetus for reform to push him beyond the range of the troglodytes in the party, armed forces, and secret police who still yearned for the days of Stalin, "The Boss."

In 1986, Gorbachev began a massive attempt to reconstruct the Soviet economy at the Party Congress in February. One of the facts that emerged was that, Stephen Kotkin notes, defense expenditures amounted to "a stunning 20 to 30 percent" of the Soviet annual budget. This was at a time when, increasingly exposed to the Western economy, Soviet citizens wanted a more consumer-based lifestyle.

Indeed, Gorbachev opened the era of *perestroika*, the attempt to radically reconstruct Russia's economy, and of *glasnost*, wherein the government would mount an "open door" campaign to open up the dark past of the Soviet Union. Fearing that the Communist Party might not be able to carry out his *perestroika*, at the July 1988 Party Congress, Gorbachev unveiled a plan to bring back the soviets, by which the party had first swept into power in 1917.

In effect, Gorbachev was now hoping for support for his new revolution "from the bottom up." However, as Kotkin points out in *Armageddon Averted: The Soviet Collapse*, by attempting to marginalize the Party Central Committee and bureaucracy, Gorbachev was also undermining the government that kept the Soviet Union together. The sheer size of the Communist Party could have made it an effective means for reform, but Gorbachev may have been concerned with the influence of the "Stalinists" who were against him; if so, indeed his fears would prove prescient.

In 1989, he attempted to open a Congress of People's Deputies, another step away from the centralism of the old Soviet Union. As the Library of Congress Country Study on Soviet Russia states, "In 1989 the Congress of People's Deputies stood at the apex of the system of soviets" and was the "highest legislative organ in the country." Created by amendment to the Constitution in December 1988, the "Congress of People's Deputies theoretically represented the united authority of the congresses and soviets in the republics. In addition to its broad duties, it created and monitored all other government bureaucracies."

However, the "old guard," which desired a reversal of course, attempted a coup on August 19, 1991, when Gorbachev and his wife, Raisa, were on holiday in the Crimea. On the same day, the old guard military officers and KGB set in motion a plan to seize power from Boris Yeltsin in Moscow. After two days of near chaos, the planned putsch collapsed, and its ringleaders, especially KGB chief Vladimir Kryuchkov and Defense Minister Marshal Dmitri Yazhov, were arrested on August 21. As David Remnick assessed the failed attempt: "the conspirators had launched the putsch to save the Soviet empire and their positions in it. Their failure was the finishing blow."

However, after the coup, Gorbachev was eclipsed by Yeltsin, whose brave stand against the coup in Moscow had marked him as the leader of the evolving Russian state. At the end of August, Gorbachev resigned as general secretary of the Communist Party. In September 1991, the Congress of People's Deputies met for the last time. The Union of Soviet Socialist Republics was officially dissolved, in its place would exist the federated Commonwealth of Independent States. Gorbachev, the last general secretary of the Communist Party of the Soviet Union, would be the first to enjoy a peaceful retirement.

## SEE ALSO
*Volume 1 Left:* Soviet Union; Communism; Lenin, Vladimir; Gorbachev, Mikhail; Stalin and Stalinism.
*Volume 2 Right:* Totalitarianism; Soviet Union.

## BIBLIOGRAPHY
"Vladimir Lenin's Biography Page," www.acerj.com (July 2004); D.M. Sturley, *A Short History of Russia* (Harper, 1964); "Primary Documents: Lenin's April Theses, April 1917 Updated," www.firstworldwar.com (July 2004); Robert V. Daniels, *Red October: The Bolshevik Revolution of 1917* (Scribner's, 1967); Richard Pipes, *The Russian Revolution* (Vintage, 1990); Leon Trotsky, *The History of the Russian Revolution*, Max Eastman, trans., www.marxists.org (July 2004); Henry M. Christman, ed., *Essential Works of Lenin* (Bantam, 1966); Edmund Wilson, *To the Finland Station: A Study in the Writing and Acting of History* (Anchor Books, 1953); Sergei Starikov and Roy Medvedev, *Philip Mironov and the Russian Civil War* (Knopf, 1978); Roy Medvedev, *Let History Judge: The Origins and Consequence of Stalinism* (Vintage Books, 1971); Philip G. Roeder, *Soviet Political Dynamics: Development of the First Leninist Polity* (Harper and Row, 1998); Basil Dmytryshyn, *USSR: A Concise History* (Scribner's, 1978); W. Bruce Lincoln, *Red Victory: A History of the Russian Civil War* (Touchstone Press, 1989;) David Remnick, *Lenin's Tomb: The Last Days of*

*the Soviet Empire* (Vintage, 1994); Robert Service, *Lenin: A Biography* (Harvard University Press, 2000); Thedore H. von Laue and Angela von Laue, *Faces of a Nation: The Rise and Fall of the Soviet Union, 1917–91* (Fulcrum Publishers, 1996).

JOHN F. MURPHY, JR.
AMERICAN MILITARY UNIVERSITY

# Communitarianism

COMMUNITARIANISM is characterized by an appeal to the idea of community as means to criticize liberal political theory. According to communitarians, the liberal emphasis on abstract individual rights disregards collective values and the relation between individuals and communities. This quest for community can be found in several countries, especially the United States. Part of its appeal lies in its ambiguity, since community has also been a key concept for conservatives, libertarians, communists, and Marxists.

This idea of community can be traced to Roman political theory, which defined *communitate* as the commonality or spontaneous consensus of individuals within a group. A similar term, *communis*, was used to translate the Greek word *koinonia* and was applied to denote the church community or the Catholic Church as Communitorium. This explains theological concepts, such as communion and excommunication.

The same concept was found in libertarian, communist, utopian, Marxist, and conservative positions in the 19th century. Pierre-Joseph Proudhon, Jean-Baptiste Fourier, and Henri de Saint-Simon insisted on the idea of community. Karl Marx spoke of a "community of producers" (Produzentengemeinschaft) in *Das Kapital*. The same plurality is present in the United States in Henry Thoreau's *Walden*, and in the works of pragmatists like Charles S. Peirce, William James, Herbert G. Mead, and John Dewey, who used terms such as *scientific community* and *moral community*.

One of the main German conservative thinkers, Ernst Jünger, considered the German Army during World War I as "the community on the front" (*Frontgemeinschaft*). A similar slogan was used by national socialism. However, a totally different meaning was ascribed to this term by the priests who created the pacifist movement Communauté in France, as well as by members of the Base Christian Communities in Latin America during the 1970s. Later, Robert Nisbet de-

fended a "quest for community" as a basic category for social and political philosophy, while Robert Bellah diagnosed a "loss of community" in the United States, as a result of individualism.

While the concept of community was present in the debate between conservatives and liberals, it is now found in the debate between communitarians and liberals. Some communitarians argue that the liberal emphasis on a general concept of justice leads to an inadequate view of community that jeopardizes a socially oriented state politics.

Michael Sandel criticizes Johan Rawls's theory of justice and political liberalism for pretending to be "universal" while also relying on the essentialist concept of "person" as individual, thereby ignoring moral, cultural, and political collectivity. Bellah, known for his sociology of civil religion and his plea for communitarianism in the study *Habits of the Heart*, followed Emile Durkheim and observed how ontological individualism eroded morality. He proposes social realism with emphasis on values "common to the biblical and republic nations." Like Jean-Jacques Rousseau, he defends a form of "civil religion," but does not guard against its side effect: intolerance. His Dukheimian conceptions are not related to a clear political condition, and so remain ambiguous.

A similar appeal to community was made by Michael Walzer in the book *Spheres of Justice*, as he observed the need for communal solidarity, attention to different "shared meanings," lower indexes of social disintegration, and a respect for the values and conceptions of good in different communities. Walzer denounced reducing all this to a single standard. Using the example of Medicaid, he showed the failure of liberal distributive justice and advocated that the members of different communities should decide about their own good. He also criticized the Protestant emphasis on individuality, which generally disregards communion or communication with others.

Alasdair MacIntyre raised a sophisticated and controversial position in the same direction and was labeled a conservative, due to his turn to Thomism and his emphasis on liturgical traditions. However, he started his career in the 1960s, discussing morality, Marxism, theology and secularism. In *After Virtue*, published in 1981, he questioned the very concept of morals, defended the heterogeneity of morals, and claimed that morality "presupposes a sociology" that relates values to concrete communitarian contexts. He pointed out that this is forgotten in modern liberal democracies. In *Whose Justice? Which Rationality?* from 1988, MacIntyre reaffirmed that a particular community is determined by a cultural tradition that provides identity for its members so that rationality and justice are contingent on a specific tradition. Since these values are not universal, the project of Enlightenment is doomed to fail. As an alternative, he goes back to three traditions: Aristotelianism, the Christian theology of Augustine and Thomas Aquinas, and the Scottish Enlightenment.

In general terms, communitarians have questioned some liberal assumptions, especially individualism, economic and political liberalism, and conceptions such as justice, autonomy, and rationality. However, Friedrich von Hayek noted an analytical differentiation between forms of liberalism. Therefore, communitarians can be understood as criticizing different aspects of the liberal agenda.

Communitarian ideas have been taken as a program by several groups inspired by new forms of conservatism. Amitai Etzioni has created an international communitarian project. Moreover, as part of his "compassionate conservatism," George W. Bush has utilized the concept of community as well. This, taken together with a positive consideration of religion, has reinforced the suspicion that communitarianism is a form of conservatism. Another criticism is that communitarian ideas can be used to justify nationalism and other forms of separatism. Furthermore, Walzer has given ammunition to critics with his defense of "just wars." Nevertheless, there is a critical intention in these thinkers, since they emphasize community to criticize metaphysics and abstraction, reject perfectionism and neutrality, value a plurality of cultures, question individualism, and access the negative impacts of these views on society.

While recent communitarian thought has tended to represent a conservative critique of liberal society, many 19th- and 20th-century communitarian idealists established communes that represented a form of utopian and radical critique of the mainstream society. While Karl Marx regarded such utopian schemes as impractical, his criticisms of individualistic and capitalistic society reflected many shared values with the communitarian idealists.

### SEE ALSO

*Volume 1 Left:* Communism; Marx, Karl; Liberalism; Fourierism.
*Volume 2 Right:* Conservatism; Libertarianism.

### BIBLIOGRAPHY

Robert Bellah, R. Madsen, W. Sullivan, A. Swidler, and S. Tipton, *Habits of the Heart: Individualism and Commitment in American Life* (University of California Press, 1985); Enrique Dussel, *Ética Comunitaria: Liberta o Pobre!* (Petrópolis, Vozes, 1986); Will Kymlicka, *Liberalism, Community and Culture* (Clarendon, 1991); Alasdair MacIntyre, *Whose Justice? Which Rationality?* ( University of Notre Dame Press, 1988); Stephen Mulhall and Adam Swift, *Liberals & Communitarians* (Blackwell, 1992); John Rawls, *Political Liberalism* (Columbia University Press, 1993); Michael Sandel, *Liberalism and the Limits of Justice* (New York University Press, 1982); Michael Walzer, *Spheres of Justice: A Defense of Pluralism and Equality* (Basic Books, 1983).

AMOS NASCIMENTO
METHODIST UNIVERSITY OF PIRACICABA, BRAZIL

## Constitutional Amendments

THE DOCUMENT signed in Philadelphia, Pennsylvania, in 1787 was structured to check abuses of government in a number of ways and to make it flexible enough to survive without constantly being rewritten. Over 10,000 constitutional amendments have been introduced in Congress, but both houses have approved only 33. Amendments that were never ratified by the states include the Equal Rights Amendment (ERA), statehood for Washington, D.C., and a ban on child labor. The Constitution has been changed only 27 times, and nearly half of the amendments were adopted in the first 15 years of government operation. Six additional amendments were ratified between 1913 and 1933 in response to the Progressive movement. The liberal mood of the 1960s and early 1970s resulted in four new amendments; but since 1971, only one amendment has received the necessary support to become part of the Constitution.

The fact that the amending process is difficult and lengthy makes it less likely that amendments will be passed in response to emotional issues such as abortion and flag burning. Originally, the Supreme Court decided that constitutional amendments only limited the national government; but through the process of incorporation, the court has also been restricted from interfering in basic rights. Conservatives in Congress continue to attempt to use the amending process to restrict individual rights. Liberals, on the other hand, have consistently argued against amendments that limit individual rights or those that restrict the ability of politicians to perform their responsibilities.

Article V of the Constitution details a two-step amending process of proposal and ratification with two options in each case. In order to be successful, a proposal requires a two-thirds vote in each house of Congress. The method by which state legislatures in two-thirds of the states call for a constitutional amending convention has never been used. If a proposed amendment wins the two-thirds vote needed, it is sent to state legislatures for ratification and must be ratified by three-fourths of the states. The only constitutional amendment adopted by a ratifying convention in three-fourths of the states was the Twenty-First Amendment, which repealed the Eighteenth Amendment (Prohibition). Most proposed amendments now have a seven-year deadline for ratification.

When the liberal Federalist constitution was sent to the states for ratification, conservative anti-Federalists tried to block its passage because they believed that a strong central government would threaten the sovereignty of the 13 individual states. James Madison, Alexander Hamilton, and John Jay published *The Federalist Papers* to allay their fears. While they could not block ratification of the Constitution, the anti-Federalists were successful in forcing the inclusion of a Bill of Rights. When Congress met for the first time, Madison introduced 12 amendments from the over 200 that were submitted. Ten of those became the Bill of Rights, which was designed according to the classical liberal belief that government should be limited in order to protect the "inalienable rights" of individuals.

## BILL OF RIGHTS (1791)

The First Amendment guarantees freedom of religion, speech and press, the right to peaceable assembly, and the right to petition the government for redress of grievances. Generally, liberals are opposed to any kind of restriction on First Amendment freedoms. Freedom of religion is guaranteed through the Establishment Clause, which bans Congress from creating a state religion, and the Free Exercise Clause. The Free Exercise Clause leaves individuals free to practice their own religions or to choose no religions. In 1802, in a letter to the Danbury Baptist Church of Virginia, Thomas Jefferson established the "wall of separation" that has become the foundation of freedom in religion in the United States.

In 1971, in *Lemon v. Kurtzman* (403 U.S. 602), the Supreme Court established a three-tier test that is used to test for separation of church and state: whether the law has a secular purpose; whether the primary purpose of the law is neither to advance nor inhibit religion; and whether the law avoids excessive entanglement between church and state.

Supreme Court justices tend to take one of three positions on the wall of separation: strict separation, which allows limited interference between church and state; strict neutrality, which refuses to accept no interaction between church and state; and the accommodationist approach, which allows some support of religion as long as no one religion is promoted over another.

While liberals endorse the concept of freedom of speech, there have always been some limits. Courts have been asked to determine what acceptable limits are by identifying when thought turns into speech and then into action. Over the course of its history, the Supreme Court has determined that unprotected forms of speech are: slander, libel, obscenity, sedition, inciting to riot, disturbing the peace, and "fighting words." Slander/libel are saying/printing something about someone with malice and a total disregard for truth. Obscenity has been defined according to a three-tier test in *Miller v. California* (418 U.S. 915, 1974), which depends on judging the work as a whole to determine whether it is "patently offensive" or if it appeals to the "prurient" (perverted) interests and applying contemporary community standards to determine whether it has any redeeming social value. Inciting to riot and disturbing the peace deal with public safety, and sedition is trying to overthrow the government with the means and intent to bring it about. Fighting words, such as racial epithets and religious slurs, are those that are likely to cause a violent reaction.

Because a free press is central to democracy, courts have tended to allow the American press a lot of leeway in its interpretation of the First Amendment. Normally, the court will not allow prior restraint or gag orders. With few exceptions, journalists are not forced to reveal their sources or turn over personal notes to police. Freedom of assembly has generally been interpreted to mean that Americans have an innate right to protest through speeches, marches, parades, political rallies, and other peaceful means of protest. The right to petition the government for redress of grievances gives American citizens the right to sue in federal courts, making the United States one of the most litigious nations in the world.

Positions on the Second Amendment tend to be emotional, with conservatives claiming that the amendment guarantees the right to own guns, even assault rifles. Liberals, on the other hand, argue that the Second Amendment must be taken in the context of the time that it was written. The amendment states "A well regulated militia, being necessary to the security of a free state, the right of the people to keep and bear arms, shall not be infringed." At the time the amendment was written, there was no police force or National Guard, and Congress only received the right to raise a military with the ratification of the Constitution. State militias were made up of private citizens who grabbed their own guns to respond to crises.

During the Revolutionary War, British troops frequently commandeered private homes for their own purposes. To prevent such intrusions on privacy, the Third Amendment (1791) bans the national government from quartering soldiers in private homes during peacetime and only in limited circumstances during wartime. Rarely litigated, this amendment seems almost irrelevant in modern times. However, it has been cited as one of the amendments that provide a constitutional right to privacy.

The Fourth, Fifth, and Sixth Amendments (1791) all deal with rights of persons accused of crimes. Liberals tend to favor broad interpretations of rights for persons accused of crimes, while conservatives are more likely to argue that such interpretations allow criminals to avoid punishment. From the early 1950s to the late 1960s, the Warren Court was successful in extending rights of the accused, incorporating aspects of the Constitution so that they also limited state governments for the first time. It was not until the 1980s, under Chief Justice William Rehnquist, that the court began to reverse the Warren Court's actions, allowing police officers greater leeway in the arrest and interrogation of prisoners and permitting what many liberals consider "unconstitutional" evidence to be used in courts.

The Fourth Amendment protects Americans from "unreasonable searches and seizures." This protection requires law officers to show probable cause before obtaining search warrants. Warrants must describe "the place to be searched, and the persons or things to be seized." The Fifth Amendment guarantees the right to a jury trial except in military and admiralty courts, establishes protections against double jeopardy, assures that no person can be forced to incriminate themselves in a court of law, mandates that no one shall be "deprived of life, liberty, or property, without due process of law; and mandates that "just compensation" shall be provided in cases in which the government takes over private property for public use (eminent domain). Guarantees in the Sixth Amendment include the right to a speedy trial, an impartial jury of one's peers, the right for the accused to confront witnesses, the right of

subpoena, and the right to counsel. It was not until *Gideon v. Wainwright* (372 U.S. 335) in 1963 that the Supreme Court held that the right to counsel forced states to provide lawyers for those who could not afford them in all criminal cases.

The Seventh Amendment (1791) extends the right to jury trials in civil as well as criminal cases. The Eighth Amendment has become one of the most controversial amendments because it prohibits the government from imposing "cruel and unusual punishment" and from requiring excessive bails and fines. Liberals have argued that the death penalty is always "cruel and unusual punishment," while conservatives believe that it is not and defend the death penalty as a way to deter crime.

While the first eight amendments provide specific protections from government interference into individual liberties, the Ninth Amendment (1791) retains unspecified rights for the people. James Madison included the amendment because he was afraid that conservatives might claim that no individual rights existed other than those specified in the first eight amendments. Before 1965, the Ninth Amendment was rarely used; but in *Griswold v. Connecticut* (381 U.S. 479, 1965), a case that protected the right of married people to obtain birth control, the court articulated the right to privacy for the first time. In 1973 in *Roe v. Wade* (410 U.S. 113), the court held that the right to privacy was derived from the Ninth Amendment as well as the First, Fourth, Fifth, and Fourteenth Amendments and that the right to privacy provided Constitutional protection for the right to obtain abortions.

While the abortion issue has been the most controversial application of the Ninth Amendment, privacy also became an issue in determining what individuals could do in their own homes. In 1986 in *Bowers v. Hardwick* (478 U.S. 186), the court upheld Georgia's sodomy law, determining that the right to privacy did not extend to homosexual behavior. Justices Blackmun, Brennan, Marshall, and Stevens, who made up the liberal bloc on the Supreme Court, charged that the decision was not based on fundamental rights but on an attempt to stamp out homosexuality. Ironically, Justice Potter, who cast the deciding vote in *Hardwick*, later admitted that he was wrong. In 2003, in a 6-3 decision in *Lawrence v. Texas* (02 U.S. 102), the court overturned *Hardwick* on the grounds that sodomy laws violated the Due Process Clause of the Fourteenth Amendment.

The American political system is a federal system, which means that powers are divided and/or shared between the national and state governments. The Tenth Amendment specifies that "powers not delegated to the

United States by the Constitution, nor prohibited by it to the states, are reserved to the states respectively, or to the people." When the two rights come into conflict, liberals are more likely to side with the national government, while conservatives favor state governments. The pull from left to right has meant that the court sends mixed signals.

Overall, the courts have been more inclined to side with the states, but during Franklin Roosevelt's presidency, the Supreme Court began to side with the national government as Roosevelt used unprecedented powers to bring the country out of depression and to deal with the issues of World War II. In 1976, in *National League of Cities v. Usery* (426 U.S. 833), the court held that the Commerce Clause does not empower Congress to enforce the minimum-wage and overtime provisions of the Fair Labor Standards Act (FLSA). In 1985 in *Garcia v. Metropolitan Transit Authority* (469 U.S. 528), the court overturned *National League of Cities*. In 1995, in *United States v. Lopez* (514 U.S. 549), the court reiterated that congressional power over interstate commerce does have limits and followed *Lopez* with a series of 1997 cases in which the court sided with states.

## STRUCTURAL AMENDMENTS

The Eleventh Amendment (1795) addressed the issue of whether individuals of other states or foreign countries could sue states in federal courts without the states' permission. The amendment was a direct response to *Chisholm v. Georgia* (2 U.S. 419, 1793), in which the Supreme Court determined that the Constitution did not specifically ban such suits. The states rebelled against *Chisholm* by ratifying the Eleventh Amendment, banning such suits. In 1821 in *Cohens v. Virginia* (6 Wheat 264, 1821), the court held that such individuals could sue states in federal district courts without their permission but on narrow constitutional grounds. The Eleventh Amendment does not prevent individuals from suing individual governmental officials, and in the 1970s in response to a number of successful lawsuits that led to damage awards and retroactive benefits, several states initiated the "Eleventh A" to argue that the Eleventh Amendment prohibited individuals from suing states without their permission.

Provisions in the original Constitution provided for electors to cast their votes for president and vice president on the same ballot. The person with the most votes became president, and the person with the next number of votes became vice president. The system worked until 1796 when John Adams, a conservative, received the most votes, and Thomas Jefferson, a liberal became vice president. Jefferson resigned the vice presidency because he found it so difficult to work with people who held such opposite views. In the election of 1800, Jefferson and Adams again faced one another, with Adams coming in third after Jefferson and Aaron Burr, who tied.

Despite the fact that Jefferson was the designated presidential candidate, Burr refused to accept the vice presidency. According to the Constitution, when no presidential candidate receives a majority of the electoral votes, the House of Representatives chooses the president. However, the House was controlled by Federalists who wanted neither of the liberal candidates to win. Jefferson ultimately won on the 37th ballot. To remedy the situation, Congress proposed the Twelfth Amendment (1804), requiring that electors vote separately for president and vice president. Opponents argued that the amendment would make the office of the vice president irrelevant since that election was tied to the president's. It did minimize the office so that in practice vice presidents are active or idle according to the whims of individual presidents.

## CIVIL RIGHTS AMENDMENTS

During Reconstruction, Congress proposed the Thirteenth, Fourteenth, and Fifteenth Amendments, which became known as the Civil Rights Package. The amendments were designed to bring former slaves into the American political system. Abraham Lincoln introduced the Thirteenth Amendment, which abolished slavery throughout the United States, in his annual address to Congress in 1861. The amendment was ratified in 1865 by pressuring southern states to ratify the amendment as a provision of unification.

The most litigated of all constitutional amendments, the Fourteenth Amendment (1868) is often called the "Second American Constitution." It was written by liberal reformers who wanted to ensure that former slaves were given basic rights of citizenship. The Fourteenth limits state rather than national actions. The Fourteenth Amendment specifies that "All persons born or naturalized in the United States, and subject to the jurisdiction thereof, are citizens of the United States and of the state wherein they reside." The amendment prohibits states from abridging the "privileges or immunities" of American citizens and promises that government cannot "deprive any person of life, liberty, or property, without due process of law;

nor deny to any person within its jurisdiction the equal protection of the laws."

The Equal Protection Clause has been used to prevent the passage of laws that discriminate on the basis of race, color, sex, religion, and national origin. Once Reconstruction ended, equal protection had little value as a protection against racial injustice. However, in the 1950s and 1960s, the amendment became the major weapon in reforms of the civil rights and women's movements. The Due Process Clause is most often used to protect the rights of persons accused of crimes, solidifying the protections of the Fourth, Fifth, Sixth, and Eighth Amendments.

After the Civil War, liberal reformers fought for suffrage for African American males with the passage of the Fifteenth Amendment (1870). The amendment guarantees that "the right to vote shall not be denied or abridged by the United States or by any state on account of race, color, or previous condition of servitude." Because women were not included in the amendment, a bitter division occurred between supporters of the movement and the leaders of the women's movement.

## INCOME TAX, ELECTION OF SENATORS

Before the passage of the Sixteenth Amendment (1913), the national government was dependent on states for revenue. By giving Congress the power to levy income taxes, the burden shifted to the people. The amendment specifically overturned *Pollock v. Farmer's Loan and Trust Company* (158 U.S. 601, 1895), in which the court held that the Constitution gave Congress no power to tax the American people.

The Framers were reluctant to place the power of choosing members of the Senate in the hands of the people. The Constitution provided for state legislatures to submit nominations to the House of Representatives, who then chose two senators from each state. As the concept of popular democracy expanded, the public rebelled. Reformers maintained that allowing the House to choose senators fostered corruption and interference by special interest groups. The Seventeenth Amendment (1913) placed the responsibility for electing senators with the people, who choose two senators to represent each state.

## PROHIBITION AND REPEAL

During the late 18th century, the Prohibition movement gained momentum as the number of saloons grew.

Shopkeepers suffered as more and more men spent their money in these saloons. The women's movement supported temperance because women and children were often beaten by drunken husbands and were sometimes left without food or shelter because their husbands had spent their wages drinking and/or gambling at the local saloon. The Prohibition Party, the Anti-Saloon League, and the Women's Christian Temperance Union were successful in 1919 in gaining support for the ratification of the Eighteenth Amendment.

The amendment banned the "sale, or transportation of intoxicating liquors" throughout the country. The result was disastrous. Speakeasies surfaced in every town and city, and organized crime flourished. Prohibition was repealed with the Twenty-First Amendment in 1933.

## WOMEN'S SUFFRAGE (1920)

Beginning with the Seneca Falls Convention in 1848 until the ratification of the Nineteenth Amendment, women and their allies waged a long battle to win the vote. Women marched, petitioned, orated, fasted, and submitted to arrest to call attention to their cause. Leaders of the movement divided into two camps, disagreeing over whether success was more likely through a state-by-state campaign or through a national amendment. World War I proved to be the turning point because it gave women the opportunity to perform what had long been considered jobs suitable only for men. The war also recruited President Woodrow Wilson, who did a complete about-face and lobbied Congress for women's suffrage.

The original Constitution provided for the terms of the president and Congress to begin in March. Since elections were held the first Tuesday in November, office holders were "lame ducks" for several months. A lame duck is a politician who will not be returning to office when a new term starts, and conventional wisdom dictates that a lame duck is less accountable than a politician who has to face reelection. To cut down on the period that a national politician can be a lame duck, the Twentieth Amendment (1933) stipulates that terms of the president and vice president begin at noon on January 20, and Congress begins new sessions at noon on January 3.

## CONSERVATIVE RESPONSE TO FDR

Technically, the purpose of the Twenty-Second Amendment (1951), which limits the president of the

United States to two full terms or to 10 years for vice presidents who succeed to office, was to prevent a concentration of presidential power. In reality, the Twenty-Second Amendment was the result of Republican pressure to prevent the possibility of another Democratic president from winning four elections as Franklin Roosevelt (FDR) had done. During the impeachment trial of Bill Clinton, liberals supported a move to overturn the Twenty-Second Amendment so that he could run for president again if he had been removed from office. Opponents of the restriction on presidential terms argue that it may require the country to change leaders in the midst of a crisis and that it infringes on the right of the people to choose.

## REFORMS OF THE 1960s AND 1970s

Citizens of Washington, D.C., were not given the right to vote for president until the Twenty-Third Amendment in (1961). Since the number of electors is based on population, the capital was given three electoral votes, equal to the number of the smallest state. The Twenty-Fourth Amendment (1964) banned poll taxes in national elections in response to the civil rights movement, and *Harper v. Virginia Board of Electors* in 1966 abolished all poll taxes.

The Twenty-Fifth Amendment (1967) articulated the order of presidential succession enacted by Congress in 1947. The vice president is first in line, followed by the speaker of the House, and the president pro tempore of the Senate. In the absence of these individuals, members of the Cabinet are designated as stand-ins, beginning with the oldest Cabinet position to the newest, until a special election is held. The amendment also provided solutions to two problems that had evolved over the course of the years. The office of the vice presidency had been vacated 18 times with no constitutional provision for filling the vacancy. The Twenty-Fifth Amendment allows the president to choose a new vice president, subject to confirmation by both houses of Congress. The first time this happened was when Vice President Spiro Agnew resigned in 1973 after being charged with income tax evasion. He was replaced by Gerald Ford, who then became president after Richard Nixon resigned in August 1974.

The Twenty-Fifth Amendment also provides a method for dealing with presidential incapacities. Physical incapacities of the president may be addressed by the president informing the speaker of the House and the president pro tempore of the Senate that he will be unable to perform his duties for a specified period, temporarily transferring his powers to the vice president who would serve as acting president. This provision could have been invoked when Ronald Reagan was shot or when he had cancer surgery; but he declined to do so on both occasions.

Before the Twenty-Fifth Amendment, no provisions existed for dealing with mental incapacities of the president. For instance, Woodrow Wilson was incapacitated by a stroke in 1919, with over a year left in his term. Democratic leaders and Edith Wilson (Wilson's wife) hid his incapacities from the Republicans who had taken control of Congress. The Twenty-Fifth Amendment stipulates that members of the executive department may notify congressional leaders if they believe the president is unable to perform his duties. At that point, the vice president becomes acting president.

Powers will revert to the president on notification that he is able to resume powers. If the vice president and executive department disagree that he is ready to resume powers, Congress will hold a hearing to determine the president's ability to continue in office. This provision has never been in invoked, but when former Republican senator Howard Baker was asked to accept the position of chief of staff after the resignation of Donald Regan, he seriously considered invoking the provision. Baker determined that the president was not really in charge at the White House, but Republican leaders discouraged Baker from invoking the provision because it would have been fatal to Republican political aspirations for the 1988 election.

The Twenty-Sixth Amendment (1971), changing the voting age from 21 to 18 in all states, was first introduced in 1942 by Jennings Randolph, a West Virginia Democrat, who believed that it was unfair to ask Americans who had no political voice to serve in World War II. During Vietnam, the issue resurfaced, and the amendment was ratified as a response to the reformist mood of the times.

## CONGRESSIONAL PAY

The passage of the Twenty-Seventh Amendment is unique in American history. It was first introduced by James Madison on June 8, 1789, as the Second Amendment; but by 1873 only seven states had ratified it. Even though the amendment contained no ratification limits, it virtually disappeared from consideration until George D. Watson, a young congressional aide in the Texas legislature, became irate that Congress continued to raise their salaries even when the economy was in recession. He brushed off the lost amendment and waged a 10-year battle to pass the Twenty-Seventh Amendment, which specifies that congressional raises will only be effective after an election. On May 7, 1992, the Michigan legislature ratified the amendment, giving it the necessary three-fourths approval.

## SEE ALSO

*Volume 1 Left:* First Amendment; United States; Liberalism; Bill of Rights.
*Volume 2 Right:* Second Amendment; United States; Conservatism.

## BIBLIOGRAPHY

Richard B. Bernstein, *Amending America: If We Love the Constitution So Much, Why Do We Keep Trying to Change It?* (Random House, 1993); David J. Bodenhamer, "Lost Vision: The Bill of Rights and Criminal Procedures in America," David E. Kyvig, ed., *Unintended Consequences of Constitutional Amendments* (University of Georgia Press, 2000); John D. Feerick, *The Twenty-Fifth Amendment: Its Complete History and Application* (Fordham University Press, 1992); Joel B. Grossman and Richard S. Wells, *Constitutional Law and Judicial Policy Making* (Longman, 1988); Kermit Hall et al., *American Legal History: Cases and Materials* (Oxford University Press, 1991); David E. Kyvig, ed., *Unintended Consequences of Constitutional Amendments* (University of Georgia Press, 2000); David M. O'Brien, *Constitutional Law and Politics, Volume 1: Struggles for Power and Government Responsibility* (Norton, 1991); David M. O'Brien, *Constitutional Law and Politics, Volume 2: Civil Rights and Civil Liberties* (Norton, 1991); John R. Tushnet, *Abortion: Constitutional Issues* (Praeger, 1992); John R. Vile, The *Constitutional Amending Process in American Political Thought* (Praeger, 1992); Elder Witt, *The Supreme Court and Individual Rights* (Congressional Quarterly, 1988).

ELIZABETH PURDY, PH.D.
INDEPENDENT SCHOLAR

# Consumer Rights

FOR MANY YEARS, a foundation of America's efforts to protect its consumers has been a set of four consumer rights that have played a special role in the origins and development of the consumer movement in the post-World War II era. The significance of these rights derives from their inclusion in a "Bill of Consumer Rights" in President John F. Kennedy's Special Message on Protecting the Consumer Interest that was transmitted to Congress on March 15, 1962. This was the first communication of its kind by an American president, and it provided direction for the fledgling consumer movement of the time. The four rights are: 1) The right to be informed, 2) The right to choose, 3) The right to safety, 4) The right to be heard.

## THE RIGHT TO BE INFORMED

This right represents a basic economic interest of consumers. It has two principal components. The first is to safeguard the public against negative or harmful types of consumer information, while the second is to encourage the presence of positive or helpful types of consumer information.

Looking first at the safeguarding function, it is not always clear what distinguishes harmless information from harmful information. For example, an advertising claim for a particular product or service may be literally true but the Federal Trade Commission (FTC) may nonetheless find the information to be deceptive if it falsely implies that the claim holds only for the advertised product or service, and not for any others. Thus, while knowing what the advertising claim says is important, it is also important to know how the claim is interpreted by consumers.

Moving next to positive or helpful consumer information, relevance applies to three consumer activities (purchase, use, and disposal), but most attention has been given by far to purchase decisions. And here the concern is with making sure that consumers have available enough of the appropriate kinds of product or service information to enable them to make the buying decision that is right for them. Some common examples of information that has been mandated by government to facilitate consumer purchase decisions are simple annual interest on consumer loans, unit pricing on consumer products, and nutritional quality for foods and food products.

In attempting to satisfy the right of consumers to be informed, government is confronted with several practical problems. One is that much of the purchase information that consumers rely upon is provided by the businesses that sell products to them, and these businesses are sometimes more interested in providing persuasive information to consumers than in providing useful information. Another problem is that, practically speaking, there may be very limited opportunities for useful information to be presented in that literally thousands of consumer products are sold in packages that sit on store shelves, with little available package space to provide useful information to interested consumers.

## THE RIGHT TO CHOOSE

Historians who consider this consumer right find themselves shifting back to the end of the 19th century when the Sherman Antitrust Act was passed to control the large corporations of that time, which often exercised monopoly control over the marketplace. At first, the government effort was concerned with protecting small companies from their larger and more economically powerful competitors, but later efforts focused more on fostering competition as a legitimate goal in its own right. This means making certain that there were sufficiently large numbers of companies in an industry to assure that competition can occur and, indeed, does occur.

One intended result of these government efforts by such federal agencies as the Justice Department and the FTC was a more economically healthy marketplace for consumers, with prices controlled by competitive practices rather than monopolistic practices. Under such circumstances, consumers should have real value choices in what they purchase in the marketplace, with the prices they pay being determined by the quality of the goods that they purchase, rather than by the pricing practices of one or more corporations that dominate the market.

Often, however, this ideal situation is not realized. To illustrate, airline fares at certain American airports are often heavily influenced by a dominant airline at the airport, and, likewise, cable television rates are often determined by the dominant carrier in the community.

## THE RIGHT TO SAFETY

This right is concerned with protecting consumers from products that are hazardous to their health or safety. The right has been responsible for many laws and regulations that protect consumers when they can not be expected to protect themselves (due often to lack of knowledge or sophistication). These protections have led to regulations for such consumer commodities as food, drugs, cosmetics, automobiles, and household appliances.

Some of the safety measures consist of warnings, such as cancer warnings on cigarette packs. While these measures have led to few objections from American consumers since such warnings can be heeded or ignored at the consumer's discretion, a rather different

public response has been found for safety measures that require consumers to act in a certain manner, such as buckling their seatbelts. Lawmakers, in these instances, may appear to be dictatorial; they claim they are simply protecting consumers from themselves, or perhaps more accurately, from their own lesser instincts. While certain consumers, like some motorcycle riders forced to wear helmets, bridle at what they see as legislative paternalism, most consumers accept these practices as a legitimate use of government policy.

Other safety issues concern the importance of incorporating safety in the design of consumer products to protect users as well as nonusers who may be affected by accidents involving the product. To illustrate, automobile manufacturers of sport utility vehicles (SUVs) have been criticized for creating larger and more powerful vehicles that, in a crash with an ordinary automobile, are more likely to cause serious injury to the automobile's occupants than would an ordinary car or station wagon.

## THE RIGHT TO BE HEARD

The fourth right on the Kennedy list is perhaps the most controversial. And the controversy has to do with 1) whose voice or voices have a right to be heard, and 2) by what audience or audiences? The second question seems easier to answer than the first in that many observers see a need for government policymakers to hear what consumers have to say about relevant policy issues as well as regulatory proceedings. Still others believe that producers and retailers of consumer goods and services should be listening to the voice of consumers to help with the shaping of corporate policy as well as the resolution of customer complaints registered by individual consumers.

The first question, however, also poses major problems in that since everyone is a consumer, everyone can claim that her voice should be heard. But, since everyone cannot be polled, there is a practical need to limit participation to a small subset of all consumers. Normally, this small subset would consist of the acknowledged leaders in the field, but the consumer movement is often said to lack the recognized leaders to effectively speak for it.

Having a right to be heard is not the same as having a right to dictate to others what they must do. So be it a boycott campaign or a customer complaint, not all voices will trigger the desired response. Nonetheless, a right to be heard serves the function of legitimizing the consumer voice in matters affecting consumers.

How well does Kennedy's proclamation on consumer rights in 1962 manifest itself in the early years of the 21st century? There are two schools of thought here. On the one hand, many consumers and consumer advocates would undoubtedly say that there is much to cheer about. New government agencies to protect consumers now exist at federal, state, and local levels, and they have been active to help assure that the rights of consumer information, consumer choice, and consumer safety are respected in the United States. And their efforts have been helped by such nonprofit organizations as Consumers Union, publisher of *Consumer Reports*, and the Consumer Federation of America. Academic organizations, such as the America Council on Consumer Interests, have provided valuable research and educational supports. Finally, a variety of volunteer organizations have used consumer boycotts and other instruments of consumer protest to voice their concerns to corporate America about a wide variety of issues including high prices, environmental protection, and animal rights.

On the other hand, other consumers and consumer advocates would see things differently. They would argue that the last 40 years have witnessed extraordinary changes, with advances in technology leading the way. In their view, the result for many consumers has been an almost overwhelming amount of new information and choices in the marketplace. Consumers are constantly reminded to buy a myriad of new products and services as well as new versions of existing products and services.

According to this second viewpoint, for many consumers the result, ironically, is not a need for more information and choices, but a need for less; and not a need for more safety (since this may not be possible), but a need to learn how to live with less. Interestingly, many of these consumers do have a real need to be heard in the halls of government and the corridors of corporations. And the message many of them would like to deliver is simply that they need help in identifying the proper paths to cope successfully with the economic and psychological stresses of life in the 21st century.

## SEE ALSO

*Volume 1 Left:* Nader, Ralph; Kennedy, John F.
*Volume 2 Right:* Capitalism; *Laissez-Faire.*

## BIBLIOGRAPHY

Stephen Brobeck, ed., *Encyclopedia of the Consumer Movement* (ABC-CLIO, 1997); Monroe Friedman, *Consumer Boycotts* (Routledge, 1999); E. Thomas Garman, *Consumer Economic Issues in America* (Dame, 2002); Neva Goodwin, Frank Ackerman, and David Kiron, eds., *The Consumer Society* (Island Press, 1997); Robert Mayer, *The Consumer Movement* (Twayne, 1989); Kenneth J. Meier, E. Thomas Garman, and Lael R. Keiser, *Regulation and Consumer Protection* (Dame, 1998).

MONROE FRIEDMAN
EASTERN MICHIGAN UNIVERSITY

# Coxey, Jacob (1854–1951)

JACOB COXEY, reformer and activist, was born north of Harrisburg, Pennsylvania, the son of a sawmill engineer. Raised in a Democratic family, he joined the Greenback Party in 1877, which began his activist career for currency reform. In 1881, he moved to Massillon, Ohio, where he invested in various business ventures and entered politics. He ran unsuccessfully for the Ohio Senate on the Greenback ticket in 1885, but he remained undeterred.

During the economic panic that began in 1893, Coxey decided to lead a march of the poor and unemployed on the nation's capital. In language and format familiar to legislators, he framed a set of bills he believed could alleviate the suffering caused by the panic. He wanted the national government to fund a Good Roads Bill, which required the secretary of the treasury to issue $500 million of legal tender currency for all debts public and private in small denominations and place the bills in fund known as the General County Road Fund System of the United States. Under Coxey's proposal, after the government inaugurated the projects, it was to spend the sum of $20 million a month, pro rata. The proposed bill required the paying of laborers at the rate of not less than $1.50 per day, for common labor, and not less than $3.50 per day for team and labor. The duration of the workday was eight hours. He also wanted a Non-Interest Bearing Bond Bill, providing any state or local unit of government in need of improvements with necessary funds.

On Easter Sunday, March 25, 1894, accompanied by a group of newspaper reporters and loyal supporters, Coxey and the marchers, known as the Commonweal of Christ, began the march, traveling 15 miles a day. By the end of April, when the marchers arrived on the edge of the nation's capital, they numbered approximately 500. On May 1, the marchers reached the city. Upon mounting the capital steps, police arrested Coxey and gave him a 20-day jail sentence for carrying banners (he was wearing a flag lapel badge) and issued a fine for walking on the Capitol Building's grass. The Congress remained insensitive to the plight of the marchers, who stayed in town until August. Coxey, upon his return to Massillon, ran on the Populist ticket for a seat in the House of Representatives but received only 21 percent of the vote.

Coxey spent the rest of his life running for office and suffering defeats. In 1897, he ran for governor of Ohio on a platform based on his 1894 agenda as well as pensions for old soldiers, the direct election of the president and senators, and right of voters to use the initiative and referendum. After publishing the story of his experiences in *Coxey's Own Story* in 1916, he ran for the U.S. Senate, and in 1932, he ran as the Farm-Labor candidate for president, receiving only 7,309 votes. The Farm-Labor Party nominated him again in 1936, but he chose not to run. The exception was in 1931, when at age 77 he received the nomination of the Massillon Republicans and won a single term as mayor. The traditional city council fought him continually, and his party chose not to nominate him for a second term.

On May 1, 1944, the 50th anniversary of the great march, Coxey, then 90 years of age, completed the protest speech he attempted to deliver on the Capitol steps a half-century earlier with the permission of House Speaker Sam Rayburn and Vice President Henry Wallace. By 1944, the government-sponsored public work projects no longer contained the stigma of socialism or radicalism. Jacob Sechler Coxey died in Massillon, Ohio, in 1951 at the age of 97. Coxey's populist ideas and his march on Washington earned him a place in the history of the popular left in the United States, although by the 1940s, much of his platform had been incorporated into the politics of the New Deal.

**SEE ALSO**

*Volume 1 Left:* Democratic Party; Greenback Party.
*Volume 2 Right:* Capitalism; *Laissez-Faire.*

**BIBLIOGRAPHY**

Donald L. McMurry, *Coxey's Army: A Study of the Industrial Army Movement of 1894* (University of Washington Press, 1968); Carlos A. Schwantes, *Coxey's Army: An American Odyssey* (University of Nebraska Press, 1985).

JAMES S. BAUGESS
COLUMBUS STATE COMMUNITY COLLEGE

# Croly, Herbert (1868–1930)

HERBERT CROLY WAS a journalist and writer best known for his work *The Promise of American Life*, which was widely influential in political and intellectual circles in the early 20th century. Theodore Roosevelt borrowed the phrase "the new nationalism" from Croly's book and made it his political campaign slogan in 1912. Croly was also one of the founders and editors of the *New Republic*, an American left-of-center, liberal magazine still a powerful voice almost a century later. Croly was an active supporter of Roosevelt's Progressive Party, and as editor of the *New Republic*, supported Woodrow Wilson's policies during World War I.

Croly was born the son of two prominent journalists. His father was David Croly, for years the editor of the *New York World* and influenced by the French philosopher Auguste Comte, who called for the melding of religion and science. Many scholars believe that Croly's son, Herbert, was likewise influenced by Comte. Croly's mother, Jane Cunningham Croly, was a life-long journalist who wrote for the *New York Times* as well as the *New York World* on a variety of political and economic issues.

Croly attended classes at the City College of New York, then left to attend Harvard University where he came under the influence of philosophers such as William James and Josiah Royce. Croly left Harvard in 1888 due to his father's deteriorating health and helped with his father's publications. Upon his father's death in 1889, Croly inherited his father's journal, the *Real Estate Record and Builder's Guide*. For two years, he served as editor, using the journal to write about social and economic issues. Croly returned to Harvard in the 1890s, only to drop out after a nervous breakdown.

From 1905 to 1909, Croly wrote *The Promise of American Life*, published to wide acclaim. Influential figures from Roosevelt to Judge Learned Hand to Senator Henry Cabot Lodge praised the book. Croly explored the idea of nationalism, tracing the concept back to the Founding Fathers period. Croly praised the nationalist policies of Alexander Hamilton while disparaging the states' rights and *laissez-faire* policies of Thomas Jefferson. Croly advocated combining the nationalist ideas of Hamilton with the democratic sentiment of Jefferson.

In surveying American history from 1787 through the early 20th century, Croly found most political figures to be wanting with the exception of Abraham Lincoln and Roosevelt. To Croly, Lincoln and Roosevelt were the ideal politicians because they were ardent nationalists who were able to appeal to the people. In the period from 1910 to 1912, Croly became more active in American politics, ardently supporting Roosevelt when he ran unsuccessfully for the Republican nomination against President William Howard Taft, as well as Roosevelt's third party campaign as the Progressive Party's candidate. Croly helped shape Roosevelt's policies for regulating corporate trusts in the 1912 campaign.

In 1913, Croly wrote *Progressive Democracy*, which built on the ideas expounded in *Promise of American Life*, continuing to advocate nationalism while also supporting a strong executive. The work was highly critical of Wilson, Roosevelt's primary political opponent. In 1914, in the pages of the *New Republic*, Croly, along with Walter Lippmann were initially supportive of Roosevelt, but gradually became more sympathetic to Wilson as a result of the reforms such as the Clayton Antitrust Act enacted by his administration.

At the outset of World War I, Croly and the editors of the *New Republic* argued for neutrality. However, with the sinking of the *Luisitania* by German submarines, which resulted in the deaths of 128 Americans, Croly supported American intervention. For the most part, Croly supported the Wilson administration's wartime policies from U.S. entry into the war in April 1917 until the war's end in November 1918. On the other hand, Croly was critical of what he perceived to be the Wilson administration's violation of civil liberties. Croly criticized the Espionage and Sedition Acts, which he believed were used to crack down on domestic opposition to the Wilson administration. Yet, Croly consistently supported Wilson's wartime policies, believing that a better world would result from the war.

To Croly's disappointment, the war's outcome did not bring the better world that he desired. He was disillusioned with the Versailles Treaty, which he felt was vindictive and power politics at their worst. Through the 1920s, Croly continued to work for the *New Republic*, but now there was a sense of disillusionment that was not present before in his work. Croly was critical of the policies and scandals of the Warren Harding and Calvin Coolidge administrations. In 1928, Croly supported the Democratic presidential candidate Alfred E. Smith, only to see Smith lose to Republican Herbert Hoover; in the race, Croly believed Smith was unfairly attacked for his Catholic religion. He died May 17, 1930.

Croly's blend of nationalism and social liberalism aligned him with the slightly left-of-center Progressive Party and its candidates, and in his last years, his evolution into a liberal critic of the Republican administra-tions of the 1920s was consistent with his earlier political and social viewpoints.

**SEE ALSO**

*Volume 1 Left:* Lippmann, Walter; Media Bias, Left; Wilson, Woodrow; Progressive Party.
*Volume 2 Right:* Buckley, William F., Jr.; *National Review*; Media Bias, Right.

**BIBLIOGRAPHY**

Herbert Croly, *The Promise of American Life* (Macmillan, 1910); Charles Forgey, *The Crossroads of Liberalism: Croly, Weyl, Lippmann and the Progressive Era, 1900–25* (Oxford University Press, 1961); Edward A. Stettner, *Shaping Modern Liberalism: Herbert Croly and Progressive Thought* (University of Kansas Press, 1993).

JASON ROBERTS
GEORGE WASHINGTON UNIVERSITY

# Cultural Diversity

FOR MANY on the political left, cultural diversity is not just a fact about the modern world but a central value, an ideal that combines two important themes of leftist thought. The first is the belief that we are not just self-interested individuals competing for economic satisfaction. More importantly, we are members of communities or cultures that shape our individual identities. The second theme is the idea of progressive social growth in which each culture is seen as a self-creative communal entity that must be allowed to develop in its own unique way. Hence the freedom to participate in the creative development of one's unique culture is a key ideal on the political left.

Although today we think of the peoples of the world throughout history in terms of their cultures, the idea of culture is a relatively recent idea. Before modernity began in about the 17th and 18th centuries, people in Europe saw themselves not as participants in various cultures but as members of competing religions. With the secularizing trends of early modernity, social scientific ideas began to replace religious terms in the self-understanding of Europeans. The idea of culture was first defined by Edward Tylor (1832–1917), the English founder of cultural anthropology. In the opening lines of *Primitive Culture* (1871), Tylor first described it as "that complex whole which includes knowledge, belief, art, morals, law, custom, and any other capabilities and habits acquired by man as a member of society."

However, Tylor did not believe in cultural diversity, neither as a fact nor as a political value. He thought of culture as synonymous with civilization and that all "higher cultures" would come to share similar standards. In contrast to Tylor's cultural universalism, the political ideal of cultural diversity holds that each society should be allowed to develop its own unique standards. This self-developmental idea came from continental Europe with German thinkers like the philosopher Johann Herder (1744–1803) and the poet Johann Goethe (1749–1832), who emphasized the idea of self-creative uniqueness for individuals and groups.

In the 20th century, the influence of this idea led many thinkers to abandon the distinction between higher and lower cultures. Hence today's political ideal of cultural diversity emerged from the synthesis of a pair of earlier European ideas, the Romanticist belief in self-creativity and the original anthropological idea of culture.

The idea of self-creativity as the core value of cultural diversity is articulated in UNESCO's Universal Declaration on Cultural Diversity (United Nations, 2002). It asserts that "culture should be regarded as the set of distinctive spiritual, material, intellectual and emotional features of society or a social group, and … encompasses, in addition to art and literature, lifestyles, ways of living together, value systems, traditions and beliefs." While this definition is similar to that of Tylor, UNESCO goes further to argue that "diversity is embodied in the uniqueness and plurality of the identities of the groups and societies making up humankind." Accordingly, the declaration calls for all nations to guarantee self-creative freedoms such as the rights of artistic expression and intellectual self-development.

One of the most frequently cited authors on the subject today is the philosopher Charles Taylor. He argues that individual self-creativity is among the central goals of what he calls the "ethic of authenticity" but this can only occur through dialogue with others. Similarly, cultural groups do not develop in isolation from each other but can only acquire their sense of uniqueness through interaction with other groups. Taylor believes that for individuals and for groups, the autonomous development of unique identities always requires symbolic acknowledgements from others. Only by being recognized as unique beings can we develop authentic individual and communal identities.

When the ideal of cultural diversity is sought as a policy goal within a single nation, the result is usually called multiculturalism. Canada has been a leader in multicultural policies in recent decades, followed by Australia. In Canada, these policies arose by extension from its original French-English biculturalism, to give official recognition to Aboriginal peoples and immigrant groups. The United States does not yet have an official policy of multiculturalism at the federal level.

## ISSUES IN CULTURAL DIVERSITY

Although it is one of the most widely recognized values in politics today, the ideal of cultural diversity is not without its critics including, some within the political left. Among the latter are Todd Gitlin, who argues that an overemphasis on diversity can lead to the breakdown of social solidarity, and the feminist, Susan Moller Okin, who sees traditional cultures as patriarchal and misogynistic. However, most of the critics of cultural diversity and multiculturalism are on the political right. They tend to see the idealization of non-Western cultures as motivated by anti-Americanism and anti-capitalism and by the desire to deny the accomplishments of modern civilization.

Conceptually, the tensions within the idea of cultural diversity can be seen in the fact that it developed within the traditions of thought of one particular culture, that of post-Enlightenment Europe. This raises questions about whether the ideal is self-consistent. For example, in its future development there are two alternative paths that the ideal of cultural diversity may take. One path leads to the globalization of the concept, such that everyone in the future will come to share a single cosmopolitan set of liberal values including the ideals of cultural diversity and multiculturalism. This would lead paradoxically to the end of cultural diversity through the rise of a global monoculture of liberal cosmopolitanism. The other path leads to a world in which liberal cosmopolitans are just another cultural group coexisting with others who do not share such values. Ironically, the latter scenario, in which many of the peoples of the world reject liberal values like cultural diversity, seems to describe a world that is culturally more diverse than the former.

### SEE ALSO

### BIBLIOGRAPHY

Todd Gitlin, *The Twilight of Common Dreams* (Metropolitan Books, 1995); Amy Gutmann, ed., *Multiculturalism and the*

*Politics of Recognition* (Princeton University Press, 1994); S.M. Okin, *Is Multiculturalism Bad for Women?* (Princeton University Press, 1999); United Nations Educational, Scientific and Cultural Organization (UNESCO), *Cultural Diversity: Common Heritage, Plural Identities* (UNESCO, 2002); C. Taylor, *The Ethics of Authenticity* (Harvard University Press, 1992).

BORIS DE WIEL, PH.D.
UNIVERSITY OF NORTHERN BRITISH COLUMBIA

# Czech Republic

THE TWO DOMINANT left-wing parties in the Czech Republic, since its creation in 1993, have been the Communist Party of Bohemia and Moravia and the Social Democratic Party. The first is the unreformed continuation of the totalitarian Communist Party that ruled Czechoslovakia (that was divided at the end of 1992 into the Czech and Slovak Republics) from 1948 to 1989. The Social Democrats won the elections of 1998 and 2002 and formed coalition governments under the premiership of Milos Zeman and Vladimir Spidla.

The Communist Party has won the support of about 20 percent of population in recent years, a rise from a steady 13 percent prior to 2000. This makes it the strongest unreformed Communist Party in any European Union country. Much of the support for the Communist Party is drawn from population sectors that became disaffected following the transition from communist command economy: workers in the large heavy industries and mines in northern Bohemia and Moravia who lost their jobs without government subsidies and following new pollution control regulations; pensioners who spent most of their lives in an apparently egalitarian environment and react with envy and resentment to the increasing visible gap in income that followed economic reforms and growth; unemployed young people; and residents of the border areas with Germany who settled in the homes of Sudeten Germans who were expelled from Czechoslovakia in 1946 and fear German claims for their homes following unification with Europe.

Another source of support for the Communist Party comes from the former higher echelons of the Czechoslovak Communist Party that ran that country under communism and still dominate the now-privatized national economy and the middle to high state bureaucracy.

Prior to World War II, communism and other leftist ideologies built on the egalitarian traditions of the Czech village communities that survived when farmers became urban industrial workers and on the leftist sympathies of the intelligentsia. These tendencies were strongly reinforced by the British and French betrayal of democratic Czechoslovakia to Adolf Hitler's Germany in the Munich accords of 1938. After the liberation of most of Czechoslovakia by the Red Army, the Communist Party emerged as the strongest political force. In February of 1948 they took over the government and abolished democracy in a fairly popular revolution, although how popular is disputed.

The 1950s were marked by the imposition of the Stalinist model on Czechoslovakia, marked by terror, labor camps, persecution of political opponents, anti-Semitism, and the settling of scores within the communist elite through show trials and executions. The 1960s witnessed an attempt to liberalize communism and institute "Communism with a human face" under the leadership of Alexander Dubcek. The losing, orthodox, wing of the Communist Party then invited a Soviet invasion in 1968 that put an end to the "Prague Spring." About half a million members of the Communist Party who were involved with liberal reforms were expelled from the party and replaced by new members loyal to the orthodox communists, who, then in the process of "normalization" during the 1970s, placed their loyalists in all positions of power in the state, its security forces, industries, bureaucracy, and educational institutions.

Few of the "reform communists" led by 1968 foreign minister Jiri Hajek, joined independent socialists, liberals and conservatives and artists and intellectuals to form the dissident human rights movement of Charter 77. Since the Communist Party was purged of all reformist elements after 1968, it was unable to reform itself and become a party of the democratic left after the fall of communism in 1989, like the former communist parties in Poland and Hungary. Consequently, it is excommunicated in Czech politics, none of the mainstream parties can enter into a coalition with it, and much of its support is a protest vote against mainstream parties. The communists have opposed Czech integration into the North Atlantic Treaty Organization (NATO), the European Union, and the economic reforms that followed the collapse of the communist command economy.

The Czech Social Democratic Party entered Czech politics after the split of Civic Forum, the broad protest movement that brought down communism, in 1991. Following the 1996 elections, it has become one of the largest two political parties. A series of corruption scandals, a collapse in the value of the crown, and a split within the ruling Civic Democratic Party led to the collapse of the center-right coalition in 1997. The independent President Vaclav Havel, formerly a leader of Charter 77, moved in to fill the political vacuum by appointing a technocratic government. The 1998 elections resulted in parity between the two main parties. To preempt the continued dominance of Havel and the smaller potential coalition partners, the two main parties reached a coalition agreement named "opposition agreement" to distribute power between them. This agreement allowed the formation of the first Czech Social Democratic government in 1998.

The state of the economy prevented the Social Democratic government from fulfilling its promises to increase welfare and pensions. Instead, it was forced to reduce government subsidies and initiate restructuring of the economy and increased unemployment. It continued and expanded the privatization of state enterprises, most importantly the banks, and introduced a "clean hand" program that failed to significantly reduce the corruption of Czech politicians and bureaucrats. The economic restructuring bore fruits and the economy improved. Despite the expectations of the right-wing Civil Democratic Party, the Czech voters did not punish the Social Democrats in the 2002 elections for the transition pains, and Zeman's successor, Spidla, became prime minister in a coalition government with the centrist Christian-Democrats and right-wing Freedom Union Party. Spidla's government was successful in concluding the financial and other negotiations necessary for the Czech Republic to join the European Union in May 2004.

Within the context of the European Union, the Social Democrats will attempt to move the Czech Republic in the direction of a European welfare state. It will have to face the challenges of lingering high levels of political corruption, low revenues in comparison with Western European countries that limit the level of transfer payments that the government may make, and the reluctance of Western European nations to transfer funds to the new members of the European Union.

**SEE ALSO**

*Volume 1 Left:* Communism; Socialism; Soviet Union; Stalin and Stalinism; Titoism.
*Volume 2 Right:* Totalitarianism; Soviet Union.

**BIBLIOGRAPHY**

Rick Fawn, *Czech Republic: A Nation of Velvet* (Harwood, 2000); Robin E. H. Shepherd, *Czechoslovakia: The Velvet Revolution and Beyond* (Palgrave, 2000); Aviezer Tucker, *The Philosophy and Politics of Czech Dissidence from Patocka to Havel* (Pittsburgh University Press, 2000).

AVIEZER TUCKER
AUSTRALIAN NATIONAL UNIVERSITY

# The Left

## Death Penalty Elimination

AS OF 2004, 38 states plus the U.S. military and federal government have the death penalty in their criminal codes. In 1972, the Supreme Court declared a moratorium on executions in the case of *Furman v. Georgia* but stopped short of declaring capital punishment itself cruel and unusual. At that time, the court held that the way death sentences were assigned was arbitrary and capricious. States were required to revise the way death sentences were imposed. Most did and now use a bifurcated trial process, where a jury determines the defendant's guilt in the first phase and decides between a life sentence and execution in the second phase. The bifurcated system was declared constitutional in the case *Gregg v. Georgia* and executions resumed in 1976.

The federal courts historically have only imposed death sentences for treason. In 1988, executions of those convicted of involvement in drug-kingpin conspiracies were added, and in 1994, 60 additional offenses were added as part of the Omnibus Crime Bill. In a controversial practice, the United States also executes foreign nationals. Currently, there are 122 foreign nationals from 31 nations awaiting execution. Many countries will not allow their citizens to be prosecuted in the United States, instead extraditing them and trying them at home, unless there is a guarantee by the U.S. government they will not receive a death sentence.

From the perspective of the left in American politics, one primary reason the death penalty should be eliminated is that it is not effective as a deterrent. Internationally, there is no data supporting the death penalty as a deterrent. Despite being the only Western democracy with the death penalty, the United States is the leader of the industrialized world in homicide rates. Likewise, few studies have shown a decrease in homicides in states having the death penalty compared to states that do not. Similarly, those states that have more recently added or reinstated the death penalty, New York, for instance, have not shown a decrease in homicide rates either. If there were to be a deterrent effect it would most likely appear in Texas, as that state uses the death penalty far more frequently than others. In some years, Texas conducts over half of the nation's executions. Yet no studies have found the death penalty to be a deterrent in Texas. The few studies that have shown a deterrent effect are often methodologically flawed or fail to control for important factors, such as crime trends in general. Several major studies have even shown a "brutalization" effect, or an increase in homicides after a well-publicized execution.

Leftists stress, moreover, the death penalty is not cost-effective. Studies conducted in several states have demonstrated capital punishment is far more costly than life sentences without parole. For instance, it is estimated that New York will spend over $20 million

*Eighteen people, including a 17-year-old, were executed in this gas chamber at the Oregon Department of Corrections.*

more each year now that is has reinstated the death penalty. The cost of having the death penalty in Indiana is 38 percent greater than having life in prison without parole as the maximum sentence. North Carolina spends $2.16 million more per execution than for a life sentence without parole, Florida spends an additional $51 million per year to keep the death penalty, and executions in California each cost $32 million. Federally, trial costs almost quadruple when the attorney general authorizes seeking the death penalty. The huge cost is due to the enormous amount required for trial preparation for both the guilt phase and the penalty phase, the costs of appeals, and the costs of running and maintaining death row. While clearly it would be cheaper to execute offenders immediately upon conviction, to do so is inconsistent with any notion of justice in a democratic society and threatens the integrity of the entire judicial system.

Another argument for elimination of the death penalty is that it is racially biased. Numerous studies have found that, even when controlling for all important factors, African American men who kill white victims are far more likely to receive a death sentence. Since the death penalty was reinstated in 1976, 12 white defendants who have killed black victims have been executed, compared to 185 black defendants who killed white victims. While there have been no executions for rape since 1964, and the practice was condemned by the Supreme Court in 1977, the vast majority of those occurring prior to this year were African American males. Of the 455 men who were executed for rape prior to the 1977 case, 405 them were black. Blacks currently constitute 42 percent of death row inmates, far greater than their representation in the population.

Compounding the racial bias of the death penalty is the fact that it disproportionately impacts those of lower socioeconomic status. Indigent defendants are guaranteed representation, but the quality of their court-appointed attorneys is sometimes questionable. Even the most dedicated and skilled public defenders are overburdened and underpaid. In Ohio, for instance, there is a huge shortage of attorneys qualified to represent the defense in capital cases. One county has only one qualified person. Research has demonstrated that defendants with court-appointed attorneys are significantly more likely to be convicted and to receive death sentences. Appellate courts have the ability to overturn convictions or remand cases back to lower courts for a retrial in cases where the defendant received incompetent counsel, but infrequently do so. They have stated that there is no constitutional guarantee to effective counsel. In deciding this, they have affirmed cases where the defense counsel fell asleep during trial and where attorneys were clearly drunk during legal proceedings.

"DR. DEATH"

Another argument is that the imposition of the death penalty is arbitrary. It varies tremendously depending on geography. According to a 1999 study, prosecutors in upstate New York were nine times more likely to seek capital convictions than prosecutors downstate. This is despite the fact that upstate New York is much less densely populated and consequently has lower murder rates. Prosecutors, who are almost always elected, may be more likely to seek the death penalty in certain counties. Sometimes they have made campaign promises to be tough on crime, other times their office has recently lost a number of high-profile murder cases and they need a capital conviction to restore public confidence. Georgia had a prosecutor dubbed "Dr. Death" because in the span of three years he secured four death sentences in a county that had none in the prior 10 years. In Harris County, Texas, one district attorney has sent more men to their death than any other district attorney in America.

Jurors in one locale may also be more inclined to impose death sentences than in others. Further, jurors in capital cases may be more likely to assign death sentences due to the selection process. Jurors in capital cases must be "death qualified" during voir dire. Thus, all potential jurors who admit they could never assign a death sentence are eliminated, leaving only those who would at least consider it. Some research suggests these people are more conviction-prone to begin with.

In recent years, much attention has been focused on death row inmates who were wrongly convicted. Faulty eyewitness testimony, jailhouse snitches, improper police and prosecutorial procedures, and DNA tests have lead to the release of 112 people in 25 states from death row. Former Illinois Governor George Ryan vacated his state's death row as he was leaving office in 2000 based on studies showing the system of imposition to be flawed. Other states have instituted or are considering moratoriums. Despite the recent attention to the issue of wrongful conviction, few are aware that over 20 people have been wrongly executed. Anti-death penalty advocates maintain these flaws cannot be fixed.

Most liberals in America agree the death penalty teaches violence: It is state-sanctioned murder. Since the state is intended to represent the will of the people, it is important that the public is in favor of capital punishment. Opinion polls have found some support, with great variation depending on how the questions are asked. When given the choice of death or life in prison without parole, many favor the latter. When the option of life in prison without parole and with some form of restitution is presented, less than 50 percent favor the death penalty. Some people express concern that "life in prison" does not actually mean offenders will remain in prison for the remainder of their existence. Several states do, however, define life in prison without parole as at least 25 years. Support for the death penalty varies by race, gender, income, and political party. Generally, racial minorities are less supportive of the death penalty, as are females, those in lower-income groups, and Democrats.

The United States is the only democratic nation to have the death penalty and is in the company of countries with atrocious human rights records, such as Uganda and Pakistan. Further, several states still allow the execution of those who committed their crime as juveniles, a practice in violation of the United Nations Convention on the Rights of the Child as well as six other major international instruments. Currently there are 75 people on death row who were assigned death sentences as juveniles, representing about 2 percent of the approximately 3,500 death row residents. Several studies have found the juvenile death penalty even more arbitrary and capricious, more racially biased, and even more subject to error than capital punishment for adult offenders. The Supreme Court has agreed to hear a Missouri case challenging use of the death sentence with juveniles in 2004.

Until 2003, the United States allowed the execution of mentally retarded people. This practice was also generally condemned worldwide. Executions of the mentally ill, but not retarded, persist and are problematic, given the number of inmates suffering from mental illness. Estimates of the number of mentally ill inmates approach 20 percent, with 5 percent actively psychotic. One study of over 700 death row inmates found 34 percent had been treated for a psychiatric problem. Historically, prison officials have even medicated inmates in order to make them mentally competent to stand trial as well as to be executed.

## HUMANE OR INHUMANE?

Some assert the death penalty is humane; that offenders feel very little based on the scientific methods in use today. However, liberals contend all of the methods in recent or current use have significant flaws and are far from humane. One study found that one out of every nine or ten executions was botched. Execution by hanging can leave the offender decapitated if careful consideration is not given to weight ratios. Because of the emotion involved in cold-bloodedly shooting someone, marksmen on firing squads have been known to miss the target's heart.

A study of 39 executions by firing squad found it took victims between 15 seconds and 29 minutes to die. The gas chamber takes minutes to actually kill the offender as well, in effect torturing them as they die. Electrocutions have gone awry as well, with offenders even catching fire and essentially burning alive. The method of choice in most states now is lethal injection, but it too is not without its problems. Even small errors in dosage can result in paralysis so that the offender watches himself asphyxiate. Some anti-death penalty advocates maintain support for the death penalty would be significantly reduced if executions were performed in public, as then citizens would see how horrible they truly are.

Similarly, death row is a dehumanizing, torturous environment. Inmates generally spend 22 to 23 hours per day confined to their cells, approximately the size of a normal household bathroom. Death row inmates are typically denied even the meager privileges other inmates enjoy. There is some encouraging news for death-penalty abolitionists, however: In 2004, a judge ruled Mississippi's death row to be cruel and unusual and mandated reforms.

Finally, death penalty critics assert that to execute criminals is immoral. Some interpret religious doctrine to allow the death penalty. The most frequently cited argument is the biblical "eye for an eye" notion. Many scholars, however, have maintained that this phrase had nothing to do with execution and most major religions prohibit killing. Further, while advocates assert executions are necessary to provide family and close friends of murder victims a sense of closure, there is no clear consensus that the death penalty indeed provides closure. Murder Victims Families for Reconciliation is one organization created by victim's families to work for elimination of the death penalty.

**SEE ALSO**

Volume 1 Left: Bill of Rights; Human Rights; Liberalism.
Volume 2 Right: Republican Party; Conservatism.

**BIBLIOGRAPHY**

Jim Dwyer, Peter Neufeld, and Barry Scheck, *Actual Innocence: When Justice Goes Wrong and How to Make It Right* (Signet, 2001); Robert Johnson, *Death Work: A Study of the Modern Execution Process* (Wadsworth, 1998); Robert J. Lifton and Greg Mitchell, *Who Owns Death? Capital Punishment, the American Conscience, and the End of Executions* (Perennial, 2002); Dan Malone and Howard Swindle, *America's Condemned* (Andrews McMeel Publishing, 1999).

LAURA L. FINLEY, PH.D.
INDEPENDENT SCHOLAR

# Debs, Eugene V. (1855–1926)

EUGENE V. DEBS WAS born in Terre Haute, Indiana. His career made him one of the best known American socialist critics of the capitalist system. Unlike most European and American socialist thinkers, Debs avoided obtuse theory or hair-splitting about the timing of the socialist revolution. He kept his ideas simple and accessible to a wide audience and within the American traditions of utopianism, individualism, political democracy, and radical reform.

Debs left school to support his immigrant parents by scraping and painting railroad cars, so when he got the chance, he took a much better job as a locomotive fireman. The job was dangerous, so when his mother asked him to quit, he took a job with a wholesale grocer. He became active in local politics and the Brotherhood of Locomotive Firemen. After reviving the union, he used it as his springboard to local politics, and he won the office of city clerk twice, beginning in 1879. His one term as state legislator began in 1885, but he became disillusioned by the process and by the lack of interest in his ideas. His legislative efforts, all unsuccessful, involved elimination of racial distinctions, women's suffrage, and compensation for railroad workers.

He returned to union work, still a conventional trade unionist who believed that organization and persuasion would bring class harmony. Debs came to reject craft unions because those unions rejected the unskilled, weakening worker solidarity and allowing management to divide and conquer workers. He left the Brotherhood in 1892, forming the American Railroad Union (ARU), an industrial union open to all regardless of craft or skill level. He led the ARU in a sympathy strike when the Pullman Sleeping Car company workers protested wage reductions in 1894. With the ARU refusing to handle trains carrying Pullman cars, the national railroad system stopped. The attorney general brought in federal troops to end the strike. In the resulting violence, dozens died. Debs was prosecuted for obstruction of the mails and contempt of court because he and others defied a court order to end the strike. Debs became a founder of the Industrial Workers of the World (IWW) in 1905.

His conviction in 1894 jailed him for six months and made him a hero to the Left, a national figure, and a reluctant socialist. He supported the Populists and William Jennings Bryan in the 1896 presidential. After that loss, he acknowledged his socialism, and ran for president himself on the American Socialist Party ticket in 1900. He ran in every election but one between 1900 and 1920. His first campaign won him less than 87,000 votes. Four years later his total was over 400,000, and his 1908 effort was only slightly better. In 1912, the party peaked with over 900,000 votes, roughly 6 percent of the vote. In 1916, Debs ran for Congress again as an anti-war candidate. His speeches against the war inevitably meant he ran afoul of the federal anti-sedition laws against such speeches. For violating the Espionage Act, he received a 10-year sentence. He served from 1919 until President Warren Harding commuted his sentence to time served in 1921. In the 1920 election, Debs captured 913,664 votes, his largest count but only 3 percent of the electorate.

Debs was a reformer in the American tradition of Ralph Waldo Emerson, Robert Owen, and John Brown. His homegrown socialism alienated old-style theoretical socialists. For him, it was a means of preserving the humanity and dignity of workers. It had to have tangible outcomes such as workers' compensation, pensions, sick leave, an eight-hour workday, and social security. In subsequent decades after his death, the United States would catch up with the dreams of Debs.

## SEE ALSO

*Volume 1 Left:* Socialism; Socialist Party, U.S.; Social Security; Unions.
*Volume 2 Right:* Capitalism; *Laissez-Faire.*

## BIBLIOGRAPHY

Bernard J. Brommel, *Eugene V. Debs: Spokesman for Labor and Socialism* (Charles H. Kerr, 1978); Eugene V. Debs, *Walls and Bars* (Charles Kerr, 1973 reprint); Eugene V. Debs Foundation, "Personal History," www.eugenevdebs.com (March 2004); Marc Horger, "Eugene Debs: Competing Visions for America," www.1912.history.ohio-state.edu (March 2004); Nick Salvatore, *Eugene V. Debs: Citizen and Socialist* (University of Illinois Press, 1982); Marguerite Young, *Harp Song for a Radical* (Alfred Knopf, 1999).

JOHN BARNHILL, PH.D.
INDEPENDENT SCHOLAR

# Democracy

A DEMOCRACY can be described as a type of government in which members of the public take part in the governing process. This inclusion can take different forms; it may be direct or it may be indirect. The term *democracy* is also employed to be a means of measurement of how much influence people (within a nation or state) have over their government. In the modern world, the notion of what exactly constitutes a democracy varies widely, as do the types of democracy used in political systems across the world.

The word *democracy* comes from the Greek language: *demos* meaning "the people"; *kratein* "to rule" or "people to rule." In Greek, therefore, the term literally means "rule by the people." While many people across the world are familiar with what a democracy is, these same people are also familiar with political systems of a somewhat different nature. Different governmental forms include, for instance, a plutocracy (a governmental system where wealth is the basis of power), or a dictatorship (a government headed by a dictator, a totalitarian or authoritarian leader). Given the broad familiarity with democracy and its almost global acceptance, other governmental forms are seen in negative terms, sometimes in terms of oppression and brutality. Hence a dictatorship is also known as misrule or a kleptocracy (a government that rules solely to enrich its rulers and to maintain their rule).

In order for a democracy to exist, criteria must be met. These include, by way of example, freedom of speech, human rights, the right to elect a government through free and just elections, the freedom of assembly, freedom from discrimination and, finally, the rule of law. Given these elements, it may be said that democracy is a means not only to promote social good and freedoms but also is a method to limit tyranny. That is, democracy is a means to limit the abuse of power as well as provide for fair government.

While acknowledged as not being a perfect form of government, a democracy, as Sir Winston Churchill once said, is "the worst form of government except for all those others that have been tried." At the core of the democratic principle is the rule that if the majority are in agreement then the opinions of the minority are overruled.

Governments employing the principle of democracy can effectively be split into two types. First, there are those governments that are seen as direct democracies and those viewed as indirect democracies. Direct democracy can simply be described as being a system of politics whereby all citizens are permitted to influence policy through means of a direct vote (a referendum) on any given issue of importance. An indirect democracy describes a method of governance consisting of elected representatives. There are a number of different indirect democracies, such as a delegative democracy and a representative democracy. A representative democracy refers to a system where people elect government officials who then make decisions on their behalf. In a delegative democracy representatives are elected and are then expected to act solely on the behalf of the constituents.

In a delegative form of democracy, constituents have the authority to recall a representative should they be unhappy with a delegate's particular political position on a specific matter. In a representative democracy, the process of recall is often more difficult to achieve as the representative is given elected authority to make decisions on the behalf of the electoral voters, and constituents usually must wait for the next election to replace the representative The right of who can and who cannot vote (also known as suffrage) is of great significance to the success of a democracy. Throughout history, the consistency of the voting population has shifted from place to place and culture to culture. New Zealand was the first modern democratic society to give women the right to vote (1893) although there are examples of women voting in other societies. The Iroquois Native Americans in North America gave women the right to vote on issues in possibly the 12th century.

Another important matter in a democratic society is the selection process of candidates for government. In societies such as the United States and the United Kingdom, candidates are chosen by the main political parties according to party regulations. In Iran, by contrast, candidates are selected not on party lines but by religious authorities. In early 2004, the selection process was brought into question within Iran's politics after candidates of a more liberal nature were not given permission by the nation's ruling religious council to stand in the national elections.

In addition, during the history of particular countries, legislation is often introduced to limit who can stand as a candidate for office, not to mention excluding vast segments of a population from voting. South Africa's apartheid regime, which excluded nonwhite citizens from the electoral process during the 20th century, is a strong example of how politics can be employed to limit the democratic process.

**SEE ALSO**

*Volume 1 Left:* Suffragists; United States; United Kingdom; Voting, Unrestricted.
*Volume 2 Right:* Republican Party.

**BIBLIOGRAPHY**

Robert Alan Dahl, *On Democracy* (Yale University Press, 2000); David Held, *Models of Democracy* (Stanford University Press, 1997); Gabriel Almond et al., *European Politics Today* (Pearson Longman, 2001).

IAN MORLEY
MING CHUAN UNIVERSITY, TAIWAN

# Democratic Party

THE DEMOCRATIC PARTY is America's oldest and largest political party and, in terms of history, its most successful. However, the party has been in considerable decline since 1980, perhaps earlier. The party traces its origins to 1792, when Thomas Jefferson wrote a letter to Alexander Hamilton outlining the philosophical differences between Jefferson and his followers, who came to be known as the anti-Federalists, and the Federalists, who were led intellectually by Hamilton, and in the political sphere, by George Washington.

Although the 1792 presidential election was a nearly unanimous ratification of George Washington's reelection, when Washington stepped aside four years later, the United States had formed two distinct parties, the Federalists and anti-Federalists. The Federalists narrowly held the presidency in the 1796 election, but it would be their last hurrah. John Adams, the man who had wanted to be king, was a weak president and an even weaker political leader. There was also a distinct geographic pattern in the electoral vote, with Adams sweeping New England, and taking most of the middle Atlantic states, while anti-Federalist Jefferson carried every state in the south and almost every southern elector. This is a geographic pattern that would be key to the Democratic Party's success for 180 more years.

In an 1800 rematch between the two, Jefferson's party, now called the Republican Party (usually referred to in history as the Democratic-Republican Party or the Jeffersonian Republicans to avoid confusion with the modern Republican Party), Jefferson held his southern base and also carried New York, which gave him a majority. The Democratic-Republicans soon expanded well beyond their southern base. Jefferson's reelection in 1804 was a major sweep, the Federalists carrying only Connecticut and Delaware and getting two votes from Maryland electors. The next series of elections were a time of one-party dominance of the presidency. The Democratic-Republicans elected three great presidents (all Virginians, as it happened) to two terms each: Jefferson, James Madison, and James Monroe. Meanwhile, their Federalist opponents are barely footnote characters in history: Charles Pinckney, DeWitt Clinton, and Rufus King. During most of this time, the Federalist Party lacked a substantial caucus in Congress. By 1820, the party had effectively ceased to exist, and Monroe was reelected without opposition. The lone vote against him in the electoral college came from a New Hampshire elector who believed Washington should be the only president ever elected unanimously.

Up until then, presidential candidates were chosen by the congressional party caucus, and state legislatures had shown little difficulty in ratifying their choices. By 1824, however, popular vote for the presidency was gaining favor across the country as the means of selecting presidential electors, rather than legislative vote. The Democratic-Republican caucus in Congress chose William H. Crawford of Georgia as the presidential candidate that year. This choice was not well received by many legislatures or by the many partisans in the larger party who felt they would make a superior candidate. So, the party fractured, and three candidates better known than Crawford ran: John Quincy Adams, son of the former president (who might have had a leg up having come in second in the electoral college in 1820), Andrew Jackson, hero general of the War of 1812, and Henry Clay.

Although only 356,038 popular votes were cast nationwide, Crawford, the official party candidate, came in last. He carried only his home state and Virginia, plus a few scattered electoral votes from other states. Jackson won a plurality of the popular vote, 43 percent, and won electoral votes in all regions of the country except New England. Adams, with 31 percent of the popular vote, swept New England's electoral votes, took more than two-thirds of New York's electoral votes, and received scattered electoral votes from other states, including Illinois and Louisiana, which were then the frontier. Clay carried the electoral votes of Ohio, Kentucky, and Missouri. With no majority in the electoral college, the election was left to the House of Representatives. Clay withdrew in favor of Adams, and Adams was elected on the first ballot. (Strangely enough, John C. Calhoun won a majority of votes in the electoral college to become vice president.)

The presidency of Adams was a watershed moment for the Democratic Party. Jackson and his supporters, who had prevailed in the popular vote, pressed for a series of reforms within the party to put greater emphasis on the popular vote and to deemphasize the congressional caucus nominations. They also took to calling themselves Democrats rather than Republicans. Adams and Clay and their supporters called themselves National Republicans to distinguish themselves from the Jacksonian Republicans (or was it Jacksonian Democrats? The problem was obvious.) What was left of the Federalist Party joined with Adams. The 1828 election, which some herald as the birth of the modern Democratic Party, was practically a rehash of the 1800 Jefferson landslide, only with more western states (in what is now called the Midwest and the South). The National

Republicans were once again reduced to a New England rump with a scattering of electoral votes from the Middle Atlantic states. Jackson won a majority of the popular vote, which was then over a million.

## 1832 THROUGH 1852 ELECTIONS

The 1832 election, another landslide for Jackson, spelled the demise of the National Republican Party. The party essentially dissolved and was supplanted by the Whig Party, or more precisely, by Whigs. There really was no Whig Party, that is, no national organization and not even a national ticket. So in the 1836 election, the Democratic-Republican Party (in the last election with that name formally) ran Martin Van Buren against a collection of Whigs who each ran regional campaigns: William H. Harrison in the Midwest, Daniel Webster in the Northeast, Hugh L. White in the south, and W. P. Magnum in the Carolinas. Against such a disorganized field, Van Buren had no problem winning a majority in both the electoral and popular votes.

The next series of elections can be better explained by twists of fate and a popular predilection for military heroes than any coherent set of party platforms. Whigs learned from their previous imbroglio and formed a true national party for the 1840 election, which they won mostly on the popularity of their war-hero candidate, Harrison, and his slogan "Tippecanoe and Tyler Too." It was an accident of fate that restored the Democrats to power in 1844. Harrison had died one month after becoming president, the first time a chief executive had died in office, and Vice President John Tyler refused to be sworn in as acting president, as the Constitution dictates (and which every other vice president to succeed to the presidency has ignored). Some saw this as usurpation of the presidency, and Tyler was a most hated man throughout his presidency.

The Whig Party chose Clay in 1844, and a renegade effort to launch a Democratic Tyler candidacy separate from the main party was an abysmal failure. The Democrats regained the White House with James K. Polk in a narrow popular vote. Having spent most of his term fighting the Mexican War, Polk had no desire for a second term, and instead, the public chose a hero from that war, Zachary Taylor, who happened to be running for the Whigs. Taylor also died in office, and his successor, Millard Fillmore, proved to be an ineffective president. He led on the first ballot at the 1852 Whig convention but lost to Winfield Scott on the 53rd ballot. Democrat Franklin Pierce won a narrow popular majority but won all but four states in the electoral college. Pierce was another ineffective president who let the slavery issue get out of control by admitting Kansas and Nebraska not as balanced free and slave territories (something presidents and Congresses had been careful to do throughout western expansion), but with local referenda to decide the issue; and by seeking conquest of Cuba by force, if necessary. Pierce lost renomination to James A. Buchanan (although Pierce too had led on the first ballot.)

Buchanan won the election but the all-consuming questions of slavery, the Union, and states' rights were now front and center. A third party, the Republican Party, had formed, and it quickly moved into second place in its first presidential election, leaving the Whigs (running the same Fillmore they had discarded four years earlier) with only Maryland's electoral votes. The north-south pattern that would be key in U.S. presidential politics for 104 years was revealed: the nascent Republicans had swept New England and five states along the northern tier: New York, Ohio, Michigan, Wisconsin, and Iowa. The Democrats won everything else.

## CIVIL WAR YEARS

Buchanan won a tinder box, and he spent his presidency trying in vain to keep north and south together. He refused to seek reelection, and he was not successful in his chief goal: Seven states seceded during his tenure. The Democratic Party fractured again in 1860. The official party convention adjourned without choosing nominees. In separate conventions held simultaneously in Baltimore, Maryland, the northern faction nominated Stephen C. Douglas of Illinois, who took second in the popular vote (29 percent to Republican Abraham Lincoln's 40 percent) but won the electoral votes of only Missouri and part of New Jersey. The southern faction supported Democrat John C. Breckinridge, who won most of the states that soon seceded. A fourth party, the Constitutional Union Party, took no position on slavery but pledged to keep the Union together. Not surprisingly, it captured the electoral votes of three border states: Virginia, Kentucky, and Tennessee.

The 1864 election was almost a non-happening for the Democrats. With their most reliable territory gone from the country, their candidate was only able to carry Kentucky, Delaware, and New Jersey. In another twist of fate, the country soon had a Democratic president again, as Lincoln, in a bipartisan gesture, had chosen Democrat Andrew Johnson as his running mate. Lincoln was assassinated only six weeks into his second term. But Congress was in no mood for bipartisanship and feuded with Johnson to the point of impeaching him. He was acquitted by only one vote in the Senate. He sought the Democratic nomination in 1868 but was defeated.

Thus began a long period in the wilderness for Democrats. In the period from 1868, when war hero Ulysses S. Grant won his first landslide, to 1932, when the country tired of Herbert Hoover's inability to end the Great Depression, only two Democrats were elected president: Grover Cleveland to nonconsecutive terms in 1884 and 1892, and Woodrow Wilson in 1912 and 1916. But these victories can be attributed more to Republican weakness than Democratic strength. Many progressive Republicans were dismayed at the party's choice of James G. Blaine, whom many saw as a tool of machine politics, and they openly supported Democrat Cleveland, who was an anti-machine former sheriff from Buffalo, New York. Wilson was able to win against the paradigm of the era when the Republican Party fractured in 1912 and former Republican President Theodore Roosevelt ran against Republican incumbent William H. Taft.

## FRANKLIN DELANO ROOSEVELT

In 1932, the country was desperate for an end to the Depression, which was ushered in by the stock market crash of October 1929, but was at its height in 1930 and 1931. Many people voted Democratic for the first time in 1932, because even though they didn't know what Franklin D. Roosevelt (FDR) would do to end the Depression, they knew it would be more than the hapless Hoover had done. Roosevelt's victory restored the Democrats to power writ large, and most significantly, it was a broad national landslide, with Hoover carrying only a few states in the northeast. (During the Democrats' long losing period, the party was usually reduced to its "solid south" and whatever scattered states in the rest of the country it could win by championing locally popular populist ideas.)

Roosevelt's election was the first of five consecutive Democratic victories. During Roosevelt's tenure, the Democrats became the majority party of the United States, a position they have yet to relinquish in the electorate after more than 70 years, despite the Republican Party's being the greater electoral force of the recent period. More significantly, the Democrats gained an iron lock on Congress under Roosevelt that lasted until 1994, with only a few sparse interruptions in the intervening 62 years.

In presidential politics, the Democrats have been less successful since Roosevelt, with the parties alternating in power more than either of them having a lock. When Roosevelt's hand-picked successor, Harry S Truman, chose to retire in 1952, the country picked another war hero, Republican Dwight D. Eisenhower. After two terms in office, Eisenhower was the first president forced to retire under the Twenty-Second Amendment, which Republicans had pushed through in order to not have a repeat of FDR's multiple terms. The Democrats nominated John F. Kennedy, who defeated Vice President Richard M. Nixon to become the first Catholic president. More significantly, the 104-year paradigm of north and south was broken, with several southern states going Republican and the Democrats capturing many states in the traditionally Republican northeast. This paradigm was completely upended in 1964, after the Democrats (who had opposed freeing the slaves) enacted civil rights laws for blacks, which the Republicans, the party formed to free the slaves, had opposed.

That year the Republican won only his home state and five states in the Deep South, four of which had not gone Republican since Reconstruction. This split, a reverse of the traditional geographic divide in American politics, has governed presidential elections ever since. Indeed, the only Democrats to win in the subsequent period have been southerners Jimmy Carter and Bill Clinton, who were able to neutralize the growing Republican tendency of the south and do well enough in the rest of the country to win.

## PARTY PROBLEMS

The problems of the Democratic Party are more than geographic. The core of the electoral dynamo that FDR put together was organized labor, whose members could be counted on to vote as a bloc and whose leaders learned to be careful not to demand too much of Democrats in power. With the civil rights movement of the 1960s, other groups were empowered politically— not only African Americans, but also women, the young, the poor, Hispanics, recent immigrants, gays, lesbians, and other traditionally disenfranchised groups. All of these groups gained power within the Democratic Party at the expense of organized labor, which has also seen its base of members shrink due to the decline of domestic industrial activity.

The Democratic Party has become less solid as its agenda has consisted less of pan-progressive ideas like the 40-hour work week and unemployment insurance, and contained more esoteric planks pertaining only to isolated factions within the party. While the Republican Party also has divisions, this party makes more sense when viewed as a coalition of entrepreneurs who push a pro-capitalist agenda of less taxes and government spending and social conservatives who seek constitutional amendments on issues like abortion and school prayer. While such a coalition is at times unstable, it is less uneasy than the Democratic Party, which cannot be conceived of as coalition of as few as two factions.

The Democratic Party has also been hampered by its use of proportional representation in its governance, whereby a faction that has 19 percent of the attendees at a meeting gets 19 percent of the delegates to the next level of convention. This reform was implemented in the 1970s as an alternative to the winner-take-all politics that prevailed previously (and still does in the Republican Party) as a means of making the party more inclusive of traditionally underrepresented groups. While it has accomplished that end famously, many in the party criticize it as the cause of disharmony within the party when a political minority as small as 15 percent can obstruct the will of the majority. It is not surprising that those who would like to reform the party are unable to get those elected under the 15-percent threshold to agree to a higher threshold.

## THE 2000 ELECTION

The 2000 presidential and congressional elections were very close to being ties, with the Senate splitting 50-50 and the House of Representatives breaking nearly as closely. Some historians believe the identity of the true winner of the 2000 presidential election may never be known. In such an environment, it is essential for political parties to mobilize every vote they can. For the Democrats, this is a supreme challenge, because in addition to the problems imposed by geography and the difficulty of uniting a party that is practically designed to be fractious, the Democrats have the problem of splinter voting more than do Republicans. The third party candidacy of Ralph Nader in 2000 drained Democratic votes in key states. From the liberal side of politics, it is certain that Democrat Al Gore would have won the 2000 election had Nader not been a factor.

Third party candidates in modern history have done more to make elections unwinnable for Democrats than Republicans, such as George Wallace in 1968 and John Anderson in 1980. Indeed, if Eugene J. McCarthy had been on the ballot in 1976, he would have taken the 2000 votes by which Carter beat Republican

Gerald R. Ford—and Ford would have carried New York and won the election. So the issue of Democratic voters being less committed to the party than Republicans are to theirs, is a serious problem for Democrats. If there is hope for the Democratic Party, it is that emerging minority groups in the country (Hispanics, Asians) lean more heavily Democratic than other voters.

America's oldest party, while shakily holding to its claim of being the majority party, is at a critical juncture in the first decade of the 21st century. If the Republican Party becomes the majority party again after more than 70 years, with the Democrats' historical role as the party of the south having been eviscerated, the future of the party will be in serious question.

## IDEOLOGY

As the American political system evolved, the parties tended to be organizations for the election of candidates, rather than alliances of ideologically similar adherents seeking representation in a parliamentary system. For this reason, the Democratic, Whig, and Republican parties reflect far less ideological consistency than major European parties.

Nevertheless, it is fair to say that since Roosevelt's dominance of the party and the construction of a coalition of voters representing labor and minorities during his ascendency, the Democratic Party has been associated on a national level with liberal positions, while the Republican Party has generally tended to be associated with conservative positions. From an international perspective, however, both parties are centrist.

### SEE ALSO

### BIBLIOGRAPHY
Kristi Andersen, *The Creation of a Democratic Majority, 1928–36* (University of Chicago Press, 1979); William N. Chambers, *The Democrats, 1789–1964: A Short History of a Popular Party* (Van Nostrand, 1964); Scott C. James, *Presidents, Parties, and the State: A Party System Perspective on Democratic Regulatory Choice* (Cambridge University Press, 2000); John B. Judis and Ruy Texeira, *The Emerging Democratic Majority* (Scribners, 2002); *Of the People: The 200-Year History of the Democratic Party* (General Publishing Group, 1992); Kevin Phillips, *The Politics of Rich and Poor: Wealth and the American Electorate in the Reagan Aftermath* (Random House, 1990); Ronald Radosh, *Divided They Fell: The Demise of the Democratic Party, 1964–96* (The Free Press, 1996); Robert A. Rutland, *The Democrats: From Jefferson to Clinton* (University of Missouri Press, 1995); Stephen Skowronek, *The Politics Presidents Make: Leadership from John Adams to Bill Clinton* (Belknap Press, 1997); Theodore H. White, *America in Search of Itself: The Making of the President 1956–80* (Harper & Row, 1982).

TONY L. HILL
MASSACHUSETTS INSTITUTE OF TECHNOLOGY

# Deng Xiaoping (1904–1997)

DENG XIAOPING WAS a Chinese communist, paramount leader, and political thinker whose reformist ideas and administrative abilities enabled mainland China to overcome the Maoist economic stagnancy and to develop one of the largest and fastest-growing economies in the world. He joined the Communist Party of China in 1924 and took an active part in anti-Kuomintang (nationalist capitalist party) struggle. After the Communists gained power in 1949, he occupied high offices in Chinese leadership. He was known as a skillful manager and a very convincing pragmatist. "It doesn't matter what color the cat is. It is of the utmost importance that it mouses well," Deng said of private ownership in agriculture. He was repressed twice during the Maoist Cultural Revolution but came back after Mao Zedong's death in 1976 and hustled aside Mao's successor, Hua Guofeng, by posting his own comrades as the top officials.

The reforms Deng was able to put into practice from 1979 to 1994 envisaged decollectivization and implementing a family-contracting system in agriculture, approving profit as the decisive factor in industry performance and attracting private capital including foreign investments. It took 10 years before Deng's motto took root: that to get rich is not only glorious but revolutionary as well.

The main long-term aim of the Chinese people, according to Deng, is to turn China into a strong, prosperous, democratic, and modern socialist state. The path to this aim consists of three steps. The first step (1980–90) involved doubling the gross domestic product (GDP) and solving the feeding and clothing problems of the

Chinese people. The second step (1991–2000) was aimed at surpassing $1 trillion GDP with $1,000 per capita and achieving the "relative flourishing." These tasks have been fulfilled successfully as of 2004, but not without serious tensions. The student and dissident movement (widely known as Tiananmen Square protesters) has been harshly repressed with thousands people murdered and arrested on Deng's orders in 1989. The military was used against those who demanded reaching the formally declared goal of democratization quicker than it was officially scheduled. "China is too big a ship to afford zigs," Deng asserted.

For Deng, the stability in the country of 1.2 billion people was the main criterion of correctly realized national interests. From Deng's point of view, China should follow the authoritarian-pluralist model for several decades. The third step is planned for 2000–50 and envisions achieving the developed countries' level of wealth and implementing the main tasks of the Four Modernizations (of agriculture, industry, science and technology, and the military). The latter entails the policy of economic effectiveness and openness, including free economic zones of development.

One of Deng's achievements was the 1984 agreement with Britain that Hong Kong would be handed over to China in 1997, as Britain's 99-year lease was expiring. Deng agreed that China would not interfere with Hong Kong's capitalist system for 50 years. This "one country, two systems" approach was developed by Deng to entice Taiwan into a reunion with mainland China. Success crowned his ambition in Hong Kong and the former Portuguese colony of Macao (Aomin), but not in dealing with hard-line Taiwan.

The two main problems of contemporary international relations, according to Deng, are peace and development. The first one is the problem of the East-West dimension. The second implies North-South relations. International conditions are favorable for a new world order formation that tends to multipolarity, based on the principles of peaceful coexistence, interstate relations on national interests, and combating hegemonism at the global and regional level. Deng insisted national interests be defined by the nature of the Chinese socialist state and be the highest priority of the country's foreign policy. By national interests, he meant sovereignty, security, economic development, international status, and dignity. Thanks to Deng's wording, China is unique in defining dignity as national interest.

Deng's concept of socialism with Chinese characteristics came from the blend of Vladimir Lenin's doctrine and the East Asian Tigers' capitalist experiences

Deng Xioaping revolutionized the Chinese economy by introducing capitalism into the socialist system.

(the quick rise and fall of east Asian economies). Typically, social innovations have been tried out by local leaders (of Shanghai, Guangdong, and others). If successful and promising, these reforms were supported by Deng and introduced nationally. Some economists have argued that the bottom-up approach of Deng's reforms, in contrast to the top-down approach of Mikhail Gorbachev's Soviet *perestroika* (liberalization), was the key factor in the China's success. Other experts insist that the triumph of Deng's reforms was secured to a greater extent by a different priority: unlike the Soviet Union break-up, China began with and focused primarily on economics, leaving the political system almost untouched. Stable political structure cemented by the Chinese Communist Party has assured gradualness of reforms, immovability of proven economic effectiveness, and manageability of the most populated country in the world.

## SEE ALSO

*Volume 1 Left:* China; Socialism; Maoism; Gorbachev, Mikhail.
*Volume 2 Right:* Capitalism; *Laissez-Faire*; Hegemony; United States; Nixon, Richard M.

## BIBLIOGRAPHY

*People's Daily*, "Selected Works of Deng Xiaoping," http://english.peopledaily.com.cn (July 2004); New China

News Agency, "Official Biography of Deng Xiaoping," www.cbw.com (July 2004); Michael Ying-Mao Kau and Susan H. Marsh, eds., *China in the Era of Deng Xiaoping: A Decade of Reform* (M.E. Sharpe, 1997); Maurice Meisner, *The Deng Xiaoping Era: An Inquiry into the Fate of Chinese Socialism, 1978–94* (Hill & Wang, 1996); Michael E. Marti, *China and the Legacy of Deng Xiaoping: From Communist Revolution to Capitalist Evolution* (Brasseys, 2002)

IGOR CHARSKYKH
DONETSK NATIONAL UNIVERSITY, UKRAINE

# Desegregation

SINCE RECONSTRUCTION after the American Civil War, civil rights advocates have worked toward racial parity in the United States. When the Civil Rights Amendments were passed after the Civil War, it appeared that the country was on the road to fulfilling the promise of equality set forth in the Declaration of Independence in 1776. The Thirteenth Amendment (1864) completed the abolition of slavery; the Fourteenth Amendment (1868) guaranteed equal protection and due process of the laws for all Americans; and the Fifteenth Amendment (1870) extended suffrage to African American males. However, the effectiveness of the Fourteenth and Fifteenth Amendments was stymied after the contested election of 1876 when Republican Rutherford B. Hayes agreed to end Reconstruction if Southerners would support him over Samuel B. Tilden, the Democrat who had won the popular election.

Because of its power to interpret the Constitution, the Supreme Court has played a major role in the history of desegregation in the United States. In 1857, in *Dred Scott v. Sanford* (60 U.S.393), The Supreme Court determined that slaves had no right to citizenship, because they were property. In effect, the Fourteenth Amendment overturned *Dred Scott*. Then in 1880, in *Strauder v. West Virginia* (100 U.S. 303), the court held that the Fourteenth Amendment was specifically created to ensure that African Americans had the same civil rights as whites. Despite this assurance, many states passed "Jim Crow" laws that legalized the practice of "separate but equal." Such laws allowed legal separation of the races in education, transportation, public facilities, public accommodations, and housing. Separatist mania led to such travesties as the Florida law that required separate storage facilities for textbooks for black and white students, and the South Carolina law that prohibited black and white textile workers from looking out the same window.

In 1892, civil rights activists challenged the practice of segregation in transportation in New Orleans, Louisiana. Homer Plessy was chosen to bring the suit because he was seven-eighths white and one-eighth black. When Plessy sat in a whites-only section of a railcar, he was arrested. In 1896, in *Plessy v. Ferguson* (163 U.S. 537), the Supreme Court upheld the separate but equal doctrine. As the sole dissenter, Justice John Harlan wrote that separate but equal was "inconsistent with the guaranty given by the Constitution to each state of a republican form of government."

It took another 40 years for the Supreme Court to swing toward Harlan's position. In 1938, in *United States v. Carolene Products* (304 U.S. 144), Justice Harlan Stone published what has been called the most significant footnote in the history of the Supreme Court, opening the door for desegregation by acknowledging that the Fourteenth Amendment had some application to the states. Stone suggested that "legislation which restricts those political processes which can ordinarily be expected to bring about repeal of undesirable legislation" should be "subjected to more exacting judicial scrutiny under the general prohibitions of the Fourteenth Amendment than are most other types of legislation." Over the next several decades, the courts began to chip away at legal discrimination, declaring that classes created on the basis of race were inherently "suspect" and would be henceforth examined with "strict scrutiny."

Congress passed weak civil rights bills in 1957 and 1960, but it was not until 1964 that Congress threw the weight of the federal government into ending segregation in public accommodations, public facilities, education, and employment. The bill gave the Civil Rights Commission the authority to investigate cases of discrimination and the attorney general of the United States the power to challenge discriminatory practices in court. It stipulated that federal funds would be withheld from programs that practiced discrimination. After the passage of the bill as the Civil Rights Act of 1964, riots broke out in New York, New Jersey, Chicago, Los Angeles, Michigan, and Philadelphia with enormous injury to persons and property.

## TRANSPORTATION AND ACCOMMODATIONS

As early as 1900, African Americans launched boycotts aimed at ending segregation on streetcars in several southern cities, but they did little to curb open discrimination. All this changed on December 1, 1955, when Rosa Parks, a black seamstress, refused to give up her seat on a bus in Montgomery, Alabama. After her arrest, Dr. Martin Luther King, Jr., the pastor of Dexter Avenue Baptist Church, led a successful boycott that forced the bus company to integrate and spurred nationwide protests and hundreds of challenges to laws that permitted segregation in transportation.

In 1961, a small integrated group launched Freedom Ride Summer to challenge segregated bus stations. They planned to travel from Washington, D.C., to Louisiana, with stops at major cities along the way. The Freedom Riders encountered little active resistance until they reached Anniston, Alabama. In Anniston, an angry mob set fire to a Greyhound bus, forcing the civil rights workers to climb out of the back window. After this incident, violence and resistance continued to escalate. Whenever Freedom Riders were injured or arrested, new riders arrived to continue the battle. By the end of the summer, 328 Freedom Riders had been arrested and sent to southern penitentiaries. On September 22, the Interstate Commerce Commission (ICC) banned segregation in interstate transportation.

On February 1, 1960, a group of students staged a sit-in at a lunch counter in Greensboro, North Carolina, and refused to leave until they were served. Over the next two decades, thousands of sit-ins were staged around the country. In Title II of the Civil Rights Act of 1964, Congress guaranteed that "All persons shall be entitled to the full and equal enjoyment of the goods, services, facilities, privileges, advantages, and accommodations of any place of public accommodation ... without discrimination or segregation on the ground of race, color, religion, or national origin." The Supreme Court rejected a challenge to Title II in *Heart of Atlanta Motel v. United States* (379 U.S. 241, 1964), stating that the Constitution gave Congress the right to regulate interstate commerce.

## SCHOOL DESEGREGATION

Because integrating the public schools proved to be one of the most difficult aspects of desegregation, the National Association for the Advancement of Colored People (NAACP) decided to challenge segregated schools in the federal courts. As the director of the NAACP's Legal Defense and Education Fund, Charles Houston and Thurgood Marshall traveled the country looking for cases to challenge discriminatory laws. In 1938, Houston accepted the case of Lloyd Gaines, a

qualified African American student who was denied admission to the law school of the University of Maryland. The state offered to pay for Gaines to attend law school in a nearby state. In *Missouri v. ex Rel Gaines v. Canada* (305 U.S. 337), Houston challenged segregation as a violation of the equal protection clause of the Fourteenth Amendment. The Supreme Court agreed and ordered Missouri to admit blacks to its all-white law school. In response, Missouri and five other states established all-black law schools.

By 1950, federal courts had begun to take a firm stand against segregated colleges and universities. In *Sweatt v. Painter* (339 U.S. 629), the court held that the black law school established by the University of Texas did not provide equal opportunities to African American students. On the same day, in *McLaurin v. Oklahoma State Regents* (339 U.S. 637), the court overturned the practice of internally segregating a black student from his white classmates. The justices held that requiring McLaurin to sit outside the classroom and isolating him in the library and lunchroom unfairly impaired his right to an equal education.

After convincing the courts to agree that segregation at higher educational levels was unconstitutional, Marshall, who had succeeded Houston as director of the NAACP's Legal Defense Fund, decided to challenge segregation in elementary schools. He achieved success with five cases that were bundled together under *Brown v. Board of Education* (347 U.S. 48, 1954). The cases challenged segregated schools systems in Kansas, South Carolina, Virginia, Delaware, and Washington, D.C. On May 17, 1954, speaking for a unanimous Supreme Court, Chief Justice Earl Warren concluded "that in the field of public education the doctrine of 'separate but equal' has no place. Separate educational facilities are inherently unequal." Marshall later said that the *Brown* decision "awakened the Negro from his apathy to demanding his right to equality." Because the Supreme Court was fully aware of the impact of Brown, they scheduled arguments on its implementation the following year. In *Brown II* (349 U.S. 294), the court ordered desegregation to commence with "all deliberate speed."

States responded to *Brown* with massive resistance and open defiance. A campaign was launched to impeach Warren, who some people claimed was a communist. States accused the federal government of trampling on their sovereignty. Alabama tried to nullify the decision, claiming that the decision was not binding. State legislatures passed laws that turned public schools into private facilities and provided tuition grants for white children to attend private schools. Some states instituted the "freedom of choice" policy, which allowed parents to determine where their children went to school. Segregated private academies appeared almost overnight. Segregationist governors promised to do everything in their power to prevent the desegregation of Southern schools, including closing down the schools if necessary. In some areas, African American children received no public education for several years.

In 1957, Central High School in Little Rock, Arkansas, was integrated. President Dwight Eisenhower, who had been harshly criticized for not actively implementing *Brown*, was forced to use federal troops to restore order and to nationalize the Arkansas National Guard. Ernest Gaines, a senior, was the only one of the nine black students who attended Central High to graduate from the school. Three months after graduation ceremonies, Governor Orval E. Faubus closed down the public school system in Arkansas. In 1958, in *Cooper v. Aaron* (358 U.S. 1), the Supreme Court ordered Arkansas to continue desegregating its schools.

When Prince Edward County, Virginia, abandoned their school system in June 1959, the court ordered the system reinstated in *Griffin v. Prince Edward County School Board* (377 U.S. 218 and 375 U.S. 391, 1964). The justices stated emphatically that "'the time for mere 'deliberate speed' has run out." The court ordered all segregated schools to develop a desegregation plan that "promises realistically to work, and promises realistically to work now." Five years later, Justice Hugo Black stated unequivocally in *Alexander v. Holmes County Board of Education* (396 U.S. 1218, 1969) that there was "no longer the slightest excuse, reason, or justification for further postponement" of desegregation. "In my opinion, wrote Black, "the phrase 'with all deliberate speed' should no longer have any relevancy whatsoever in enforcing the constitutional rights of Negro students."

## SCHOOL BUSING

A number of desegregation methods were introduced to promote desegregation. Attendance zones and gerrymandering, for example, drew lines to include quotas of blacks and whites in each school district. No issue was more volatile than busing, which involved transporting students to designated schools in order to achieve racial

*In 1957, nine black students enrolled at Central High School in Little Rock, Arkansas. Governor Orval Faubus ordered the Arkansas National Guard to stop the students from entering the school. President Eisenhower sent federal troops to escort the students (above).*

parity. By 1970, some 40 percent of the nation's students were being bused to schools outside their own neighborhoods. Parents objected strenuously to taking children from neighborhood schools and busing them miles away to meet numerical quotas for integration. The busing issue became such a hot political topic that Richard Nixon promised in the 1968 election that he would put an end to the practice. In 1969, Chief Justice Earl Warren retired from the Court and was replaced by Warren Burger, who agreed with Nixon that busing should be discontinued.

In 1971, in *Swann v. Charlotte-Mecklenburg* (402 U.S. 1), the court addressed differences in state-sponsored (*de jure*) segregation, and segregation that occurred unintentionally from housing patterns (*de facto*). The court unanimously agreed that busing could be used to remedy the unconstitutional practice of de jure segregation. Thee years later, in *Milliken v. Bradley* (418 U.S. 717, 1974), the court held that busing could not be used to remedy de facto segregation.

Over the next few years, opposition to busing became more entrenched. In 1982, in *Crawford v. Board of Los Angeles Board of Education* (458 U.S. 527), with only Marshall dissenting, the Supreme Court upheld California's Proposition 1, an anti-busing constitutional amendment. However, in *Missouri v. Jenkins* (495 U.S. 33, 1990), the court upheld a tax increase to fund a court-ordered busing program. That same year, in *Board of Education of Oklahoma City Public Schools v. Dowell* (498 U.S. 237), the court allowed the Oklahoma City school board to end a 13-year busing program even though the city's schools were not completely integrated. The practice of busing children to promote desegregation was essentially dead, and school desegregation was in jeopardy.

In 1992, in *Freeman v. Pitts* (503 U.S. 467), the court upheld the decision of a federal district judge to return control of desegregation programs in Atlanta's De Kalb County (Georgia) to the local school board, despite the fact that the schools were still segregated. In 2003, in *Grutter v. Bollinger* (02 U.S. 241), the court again upheld narrowly drawn affirmative action programs, rejecting the claim of a white student that the University of Michigan's law school affirmative action program violated the equal protection of the Fourteenth Amendment. On the same day, in *Gratz v. Bollinger* (02 U.S. 516), the court rejected an affirmative action policy drawn up by the College of Literature, Science, and the Arts at the University of Michigan, holding that it violated the Fourteenth Amendment because the policy was not narrowly drawn.

## REVERSE DISCRIMINATION

In order to comply with laws and court decrees and to promote diversity, many colleges and universities developed affirmative action programs that used different formulas for the admission of black and white students. Angry white students who felt they had been rejected in favor of less qualified black students claimed reverse discrimination. The first challenge, *DeFunis v. Odegaard* (416 U.S. 312, 1974), was declared moot (irrelevant) because the plaintiff was in his last semester of law school when the case reached the Supreme Court. Four years later, the justices heard arguments in the case of Alan Bakke, who had been denied admission to the medical school of the University of California because of an affirmative action program. In *University of California Regents v. Bakke* (438 U.S. 265, 1978), the court upheld narrowly drawn affirmative action programs but agreed that Bakke had been discriminated against by the special admissions policies used in the medical school. *Bakke* was significant because it legitimized the concept of reverse discrimination, which came close to overturning affirmative action during the conservatism of the late 1980s and early 1990s.

## EMPLOYMENT DISCRIMINATION

Civil rights advocates also targeted discrimination in employment, and Title VII of the Civil Rights Act of 1964 banned racial discrimination in employment. Over the next four years, the Equal Employment Opportunity Commission (EEOC) received over 40,000 complaints, and hundreds of lawsuits were filed. In 1971, in *Griggs v. Duke Power Company* (401 U.S. 424), the court struck down the use of all employment practices that were designed to keep from hiring and promoting minorities unless they were related to job performance. The court stated that it would consider both the motivation and the consequences of such practices and placed the burden of proof on the employer to defend discriminatory practices. Two years later, in *McDonnell Douglass Corporation v. Green* (411 U.S. 792, 1973), the court specified that racial bias existed if the complainant belonged to a racial minority and if the individual applied for a position for which she was qualified but was rejected despite the fact that the employer continued to take applications.

By 1976, the mood of the Supreme Court had begun to shift; and in *Washington v. Davis* (426 U.S. 229), the court placed the burden on African Americans to prove that the Washington, D.C. Police Department had intentionally designed tests to discriminate against blacks. The following year, in *Teamsters v. United States* (431 U.S. 324), the court upheld the seniority system even though it discriminated against blacks who had not been employed before Title VII opened up employment opportunities.

## AFFIRMATIVE ACTION

In order to comply with orders to end employment discrimination, employers around the country instituted affirmative action programs. By the mid-1970s, white employees were challenging these programs on the basis of reverse discrimination. In 1976, in *McDonald v. Santa Fe Trail Transportation* (427 U.S. 273), the court maintained that Title VII banned discrimination in employment of all races. Nevertheless, in *United States Steelworkers v. Weber* (443 U.S. 193, 1979), the court upheld private affirmative action programs. In 1980, in *Fullilove v. Kultznick* (448 U.S. 448), the court upheld the Public Works Act of 1977, which set aside 10 percent of all federal contracts for minorities. Likewise in 1987, in *United States v. Paradise* (480 U.S. 149), the court upheld an affirmative action program that required the state of Alabama to hire and promote one black police officer for every white hired or promoted until racial parity had been achieved.

In a series of cases in 1989, conservatives on the Supreme Court came close to outlawing affirmative action. In *City of Richmond v. J.A. Croson* (488 U.S. 469), the court overturned a 30 percent set-aside program for minority contractors in Richmond, Virginia. Justice Sandra Day O'Connor contended that numerical remedies based on race were inherently "suspect" and would be strictly scrutinized. In *Martin v. Wilks* (490 U.S. 755, 1989), the court allowed the Birmingham Fire Department to back away from decades of affirmative action. Deciding that only the original participants were bound by court-ordered remedies for blatant discrimination, the court gave permission for current employees to challenge affirmative action on the grounds of reverse discrimination. In *Lorance v. AT&T* (490 U.S. 900, 1989), the court held that women and minorities who discover that they have been discriminated against by the seniority system have 300 days to file suit.

In *Ward's Cove Packing Company v. Atonio* (490 U.S. 642), the court rejected the solid evidence presented by employees who documented that minorities were relegated to nonskilled jobs that paid less. Rejecting the evidence, the court held that the absence of minorities "reflects a dearth of qualified non-white applicants."

Even more damaging was the court's insistence that "the burden of proof remains with the plaintiff at all times." From the perspective of proponents of desegregation, the court's actions totally negated the intent behind the Civil Rights Act of 1964, which allowed the federal government to bring suit because individuals were at a distinct advantage when pitted against large companies that employed teams of lawyers. In 1991, Congress passed the Civil Rights Act of 1991, reiterating the original intent of the 1964 act.

## SEE ALSO

*Volume 1 Left*: Civil Rights; Supreme Court.
*Volume 2 Right*: Segregation; Shockley, William; Supreme Court.

## BIBLIOGRAPHY

Lucius J. Barker and Twiley W. Barker, Jr., *Civil Liberties and the Constitution* (Prentice Hall, 1990); Charles Bullock and Charles Lamb, *Implementation of Civil Rights Policy* (Brooks-Cole, 1984); Michael D. Davis and Hunter R. Clark, *Thurgood Marshall: Warrior at the Bar, Rebel on the Court* (Birch Lane, 1992); Joel B. Grossman and Richard S. Wells, *Constitutional Law and Judicial Policy Making* (Longman, 1988); Kermit Hall et al., *American Legal History: Cases and Materials* (Oxford University Press, 1991); Henry Hampton and Steve Fayer, *Voices of Freedom: An Oral History of the Civil Rights Movement from the 1950s through the 1980s* (Bantam, 1990); Steven F. Lawson, *Running for Freedom: Civil Rights and Black Politics in America since 1941* (McGraw Hill, 1991); Benjamin Muse, *Ten Years of Prelude: The Story of Integration since the Supreme Court's 1954 Decision* (Viking, 1964); Donald G. Nieman, *Promises to Keep: African Americans and the Constitutional Order, 1776 to the Present* (Oxford University Press, 1991); Juan Williams, *Eyes on the Prize: America's Civil Rights Years, 1951–65* (Penguin, 1987); Elder Witt, *The Supreme Court and Individual Rights* (Congressional Quarterly, 1988).

ELIZABETH PURDY, PH.D.
INDEPENDENT SCHOLAR

# Despotism

DESPOTISM CONNOTES autocracy, the absolute rule of one or a select group and exercise of power without imposed limits. The word is closely associated with a host of other concepts, including tyranny, domination, absolutism, dictatorship, oppression, and servitude. In politics, it refers to a specific model of governance regarding the ability to make others do what one wants them to do despite their possible opposition.

Despots come into a position of power in a number of different ways: seizing power through inheritance (the cases of Roman emperors Caligula and Nero), through military means and then legitimizing their position once in power (the case of Roman emperor Augustus), through revolution and bloodshed (Josef Stalin following Vladimir Lenin in the newly founded Soviet Union), through bids for power supported by the religious or other key establishments in the society (Alexander the Great of ancient Macedonia).

But despotism was not always regarded as a dangerous political practice and was once considered a liberal concept. Its dubious reputation today is related to the fact that the word *demokratia* (democracy) did not even exist before the 5th century. Furthermore, the ambiguities around the meaning of the word *tyrant* were part and parcel of ancient Greek politics. In effect, tyranny practically meant a "transitional government" in the Greek city-state that emerged in times of crisis, one that served to weaken an overbearing and exclusivist aristocratic government, one that can manage rapid economic change and enlarge the range of citizenship.

According to Aristotle, for instance, tyrants were commonly champions of the many and the poor against the few and the rich—a definitively leftist or liberal view. Despots or tyrants were thus seen as the engines of transformation, who initiated a shift from oligarchy to democracy. It is only later in history that tyranny and despotism began to be associated with evil and cruelty guarded by a narrow, unchecked, and more often than not class-based rule. Still, the ancient tyrants themselves also had class ties: many of them had aristocratic origins and sought further fame, fortune, and power. Their main difference perhaps was that they wanted to weaken the rule of older, more traditional aristocracies.

In other words, ancient forms of tyranny had a lot to do with the internal class feud within the aristocracy, although the tyrants opted for populism while the settled aristocrats tended to favor elitism. This characteristic was generally maintained by later instances of despotism in history.

Plato's tyrant is, by definition, a person governed solely by desire and hence totally out of balance as he or she is indifferent to both reason and honor. Whereas the philosopher-ruler pursues rationality and prioritizes justice and well-being of the society, the tyrant is portrayed as someone chasing after his or her own satisfac-

tion. This characterization of tyranny is also present in the writings of Aristotle, Tacitus, and later on Niccolo Machiavelli. Meanwhile, neither Plato nor Aristotle defined despotism as the opposite of freedom. Their problems with despotism or a particular despot were related more to the issues of virtue, excellence, and justice.

Similarly, Baron de Montesquieu, an early liberal, described despotism as part and parcel of the rule of French monarchs, that is, an integral part of the political system. It was only in the 19th century that despotism assumed a decidedly negative face. In particular, founding fathers of sociology were deeply troubled by what they identified as new forms of tyranny, despotism, and what they perceived as the iron hand of the burgeoning modern life: the city, bureaucracy, and technology.

Alexis de Tocqueville, for instance, was ever so worried about the invisible tyranny of modern life in society without the existence of an identifiable tyrant to blame. The common ground among differing definitions is that the despot does not have to answer to anyone and does not seem to have a moral compass that can legitimize this ultimate exercise of power. A derivation of this simplified formula for despotism is that it is a model of governance composed of unwilling subjects and ran according to arbitrary rules. Hence, in observing a despotic system, there is marked concern about the well-being of the polity at large, as well as rulers' lack of consideration for general interest and absence of mechanisms of control over the actions of the government. These concerns, in turn, are expected to be taken care of via democratic rule.

In summary, although despotism may meet at least some of the basic physical needs of a society, from Plato to Hannah Arendt, there is consensus among political thinkers that it is the least conducive form of human governance to fulfill what may be called higher human needs. Despotism forces the political aspirations of the human nature to be shunned, to be kept away from the public realm by way of silencing opposition and refusing to provide a platform of interaction between the rulers and the ruled. Surrounded by a loyal army, police force, militia, secret police, and spies and informers, from ancient times onward, despots need protection from their own people to sustain their rule.

Interestingly, this need for protection from one's own people also constitutes the very factor that makes despotism a highly fragile political model that can only be maintained for a limited period of time and at a great cost.

SEE ALSO
*Volume 1 Left:* Liberalism; Democracy.
*Volume 2 Right:* Despotism; Totalitarianism.

BIBLIOGRAPHY
Hannah Arendt, *The Origins of Totalitarianism* (Meridian Books, 1958); Eric Carlton, *Faces of Despotism* (Scholars' Press, 1995); Roger Boesche, *Theories of Tyranny from Plato to Arendt* (University of Pennsylvania Press, 1996); Sheldon Wolin, *Politics and Vision: Continuity and Innovation in Western Political Thought* (Little & Brown, 1960); Karl Wittfogel, *Oriental Despotism: A Comparative Study of Total Power* (Vintage Books, 1981).

SHELDON WOLIN
INDEPENDENT SCHOLAR

# Douglass, Frederick (1818–1895)

STATESMAN, WRITER, humanitarian, and diplomat, former slave Frederick Douglass was known and respected throughout the world. He never knew his white father and only saw his mother rarely. Douglass was brought up by his grandmother on a Maryland plantation. The Christian faith that Douglass learned as a child remained with him throughout his life, and he often peppered his speeches with quotes from Scriptures. He was particularly drawn to the Golden Rule: "Do unto others as you would have them do unto you."

At the age of eight, Douglass was bought by a liberal Baltimore family, Hugh and Sophia Auld. His mistress began teaching Douglass to read, but she backed away when her husband reminded her that it was against state law to do so. Douglass secretly continued his education with the aid of young, white playmates. Reading opened a new world to Douglass, awakening a keen intellect and insight. At 16, Douglass was thought to need "breaking," so he was sent to Edward Covey, a well-known "slave breaker." The experience made Douglass even more determined to escape his bondage.

From 1836 to 1838, Douglass worked as a caulker in Baltimore, Maryland, where he married Anna Murray, a free black. In 1839, at 21, Douglass escaped to New York by way of New Bedford, Massachusetts. He began attending meetings of the Massachusetts Antislavery Society. On August 16, 1841, under guard, Douglass spoke publicly for the first time at a Nantucket, Massachusetts, anti-slavery rally, attended by noted abolition-ists William Lloyd Garrison, Elizabeth Cady Stanton, Lucretia Mott, Wendell Phillips, and Parker Pillsbury. Stanton would later write that Douglass reminded her of a powerful and majestic prince. Douglass became an antislavery agent, lecturing throughout the North. Afraid of the impact that Douglass had on his listeners, his detractors spread rumors that he had never been a slave. In response, Douglass published his first autobiography, *My Bondage and My Freedom.* In 1846, while in Europe, friends negotiated his freedom.

Douglass spent several years in close association with his mentor William Lloyd Garrison, the leading abolitionist of the day. Douglass originally accepted Garrison's belief that the U.S. Constitution was pro-slavery. However, as Douglass's views expanded, he began to feel that reform could come by using the Constitution to work within the existing political system. In 1847, Douglass and Garrison severed their ties. Douglass moved to Rochester, New York, and began publishing his own newspaper, the *North Star,* often contradicting opinions expressed in Garrison's *Liberator.* The following year, Douglass attended the first women's rights convention in Seneca Falls, New York, and defended the radical notion of female suffrage in the *North Star.* In 1852, at a Fourth of July celebration, Douglass gave what became one of his best-known speeches. He reminded his audience of several hundred that while the Founding Fathers had freed themselves from British tyranny, they had continued to accept a greater tyranny within their own borders.

Anna, Douglass's wife, never learned to read, and she was often reluctant to travel with Douglass. On his tours, Douglass became friends with two white sisters, Julia and Eliza Griffiths. People whispered that Douglass and Julia were involved in an interracial relationship, and Douglass's opponents used the relationship rumors to attack his legitimacy. Douglass began to spend time with Gerrit Smith, the cousin of Elizabeth Cady Stanton and an ardent abolitionist. The two men were threatened with arrest for assisting John Brown, a white abolitionist who was hanged in 1859 for leading a slave rebellion at Harper's Ferry, West Virginia. Douglass had indeed given Brown money that had been collected for his cause, but he refused to join him in the rebellion. After Brown's arrest, Douglass escaped to Europe by way of Canada.

Although Douglass was opposed to violence on principle, he believed that the Civil War was necessary to end slavery. In 1863, he became an official recruiter for the 54th Massachusetts Volunteer Regiment. When Douglass discovered that black soldiers were being discriminated against, he protested directly to President Abraham Lincoln.

During Reconstruction, President Andrew Johnson asked Douglass to serve as the commissioner of the Freedman's Bureau. He refused that position, as well as a proposal to move to a southern state and run for Congress. After founding the *New National Era*, a Washington, D.C., weekly, Douglass agreed to serve on a committee investigating the possible annexation of Santo Domingo, which had been suggested as a location for African Americans who chose to relocate.

In the years before the Civil War and during the period immediately after, Douglass had continued to work closely with the leaders of the women's rights movement, particularly with Stanton and Susan B. Anthony, who were close friends. However, during the battle over the Fifteenth Amendment, which granted suffrage to black males but not to females of either race, the friendship and political ties were ruptured for over two decades.

Free-love advocate Victoria Woodhull convinced Douglass to run as vice president on the Equal Rights Party ticket in her unsuccessful bid for the presidency in 1872. Two years later, Douglass was named president of the Freedman's Savings and Trust Company. In 1877, Douglass was appointed U.S. marshal for Washington, D.C. In 1881, he took a position as Recorder of Deeds for the nation's capital.

Douglass expected to be shunned when Democrat Grover Cleveland was elected in 1884. A staunch Republican, Douglass praised President and Mrs. Cleveland for treating him and his second wife cordially on a White House visit. Douglass was grateful because many friends and supporters had deserted him when he married Helen Pitts, a white woman, after Anna's death. When Republican Benjamin Harrison succeeded Cleveland in the 1888 election, he offered Douglass the positions of charge d'affaires for Santo Domingo and minister resident and consul-general to Haiti. Douglass spent the last four years of his life quietly and was eulogized around the world after his death on February 20, 1895.

Douglass, by opposing slavery and then accepting political patronage positions within both Republican and Democratic administrations, set the stage for African American acceptance of integration as a path toward racial justice and equality. In this fashion, his earlier career as a radical, like that of many of his contemporaries, was easily transformed into a policy of accommodation and integration into the existing class structure. Thus, while he might be viewed as a radical

critic of the system in his youth, he moved to the center in his later years.

**SEE ALSO**

*Volume 1 Left:* Abolitionism; Stanton, Elizabeth Cady; Suffragists; American Civil War.
*Volume 2 Right:* American Civil War.

**BIBLIOGRAPHY**

Frederick Douglass, *My Bondage and My Freedom* (University of Illinois Press, 1987); Frederick Douglass, *Narrative of the Life of Frederick Douglass, an American Slave* (New American Library, 1968); Sharon R. Krause, *Liberalism with Honor* (Harvard University Press, 2002); William S. McFeely, *Frederick Douglass* (W.W. Norton, 1991).

ELIZABETH PURDY, PH.D.
INDEPENDENT SCHOLAR

# Du Bois, W.E.B. (1868–1963)

WILLIAM EDWARD BURGHARDT Du Bois was a sociologist, author, historian, activist, poet, editor, professor, social reformer, and activist for racial equality. One of the great intellectual and inspirational forces of his era, he was viewed differently by various black leaders. To Martin Luther King, Jr., he was considered an "intellectual giant"; to Booker T. Washington, he was an irritant; to Marcus Garvey, he was a pawn of the white power structure. Although his numerous books, articles, and other writings showed some diversion in thought over his 60 years of writing, his strivings were always directed toward the betterment of social conditions for African Americans.

Du Bois was born in the small mountain community of Great Barrington, Massachusetts. Although he possessed a heritage that consisted of an African, Dutch, French, and Huguenot lineage, throughout his life he preferred the label of African American (or, using the common terms in his day, "Negro" or "colored").

People in his hometown realized that the youngster was intellectually gifted and helped send him to Tennessee's Fisk College, although his dream was to attend prestigious Harvard University. At Fisk, Du Bois wrote for the school newspaper and developed his skills as a public speaker. While in Tennessee, he was also exposed to an increased amount of racism, which in-

*W.E.B. Du Bois used metaphorical imagery to explore the plight of African Americans in U.S. society.*

cluded lynching and other forms of violence and discrimination against blacks. After graduating from Fisk, Du Bois fulfilled his dream of attending Harvard, where he received his master's degree and, after attending school in Europe, his Ph.D., becoming the first African American to receive a doctorate from Harvard. After a short-term teaching assignment at a small religious college, he became an instructor of sociology at the University of Pennsylvania, where he published one of the great urban studies of the day, *The Philadelphia Negro*.

The next 13 years were spent as a sociology professor at Atlanta University, an African American institution in Georgia. In 1903, he published one of the most influential books on race relations of the 20th century, *The Souls of Black Folk*. This work was a compilation of essays that used poetry, political thought, philosophy, history, sociology, and personal commentary. Through the use of thought-provoking metaphorical imagery, Du Bois introduced his readers to terminology such as the "color-line," the invisible barrier that separates blacks and whites; the "veil," the screen that obscures an un-

derstanding of the problems of black people; and "double-consciousness," a socio-psychological battle that comes from being both black and American. It was in this work that his burgeoning ideas on social activism and reform became evident.

In 1905, Du Bois gathered a group of black leaders together on the Canadian side of Niagara Falls to form an advocacy group for the rights of blacks. This group was formally incorporated in 1906 under the name The Niagara Movement. The movement lasted five years and, though not in itself a major catalyst of change, it was the precursor to a much more powerful movement, the National Association for the Advancement of Colored People (NAACP). Du Bois served as an officer and as the editor of the organization's publication *The Crisis*, which became one of the nation's premier journals.

Du Bois had one powerful adversary during the early 1900s in Booker T. Washington. Washington believed that better social and economic conditions for blacks should be achieved through vigorous technical training in order to slowly assimilate into white society. In contrast, Du Bois felt that African Americans should obtain academic, rather than vocational education, and not passively wait for change. In fact, Du Bois called on the top 10 percent of the leaders in the black community (whom he called "the talented tenth") to occupy important positions that would help improve conditions for African Americans. Du Bois returned to Atlanta University after his editorship of *The Crisis*. He continued to write and publish vigorously and, in 1919, he became the chief organizer of the Pan-African Congress, a convention of people who supported Pan-Africanism, an ideology of Black Nationalism that advocated the reinforcement of ties to Africa. Du Bois made his first trip to that continent in 1923 and the experience seems to have changed his perspective on racial issues. He began to study the writings of Karl Marx and came to believe that a socialist system provided greater chances of achieving equality for black Americans than one based on capitalistic principles.

Du Bois continued to write and be a force in social reform up until his declining years. In 1963, due to frustration over the lack of progress toward racial equality in America, he joined the Communist Party and moved to Ghana, where he became a citizen. In that same year, Du Bois died at age 95. His influence on race relations has been immense and his ideas and numerous writings are the source of continuing discourse in the field.

In reviewing his ideology, his advocacy of integration and racial equality in his early days put him on the left end of the spectrum of black advocacy as compared to the position of Washington. However, in the 1930s, as editor of *The Crisis,* DuBois fell afoul of the organization's leadership by advocating an early form of affirmative action that suggested federal funding be directed, not on racially impartial grounds, but with specified amounts to programs for African American people. In that sense, his break with the NAACP grew out of the fact that on race issues, he found himself on the right end of the spectrum, accepting some separatism. In his adoption of socialist ideals and his decision to join the Communist Party, he clearly migrated to the left in the last years of his life.

## SEE ALSO

*Volume 1 Left:* Desegregation; King, Martin Luther, Jr. *Volume 2 Right:* Black Nationalism; Black Separatism; Washington, Booker T.

## BIBLIOGRAPHY

W.E.B. Du Bois, *The Autobiography of W.E.B. Du Bois: A Soliloquy on Viewing My Life from the Last Decade of Its First Century* (International Publishers, 1968); W.E.B. Du Bois, *Dusk of Dawn: An Essay toward an Autobiography of a Race Concept* (Schocken, 1968); David Lettering Lewis, *W.E.B. Du Bois: The Fight for Equality and the American Century* (Henry Holt, 2000); William M. Tuttle Jr., ed., *W.E.B. Du Bois* (Prentice Hall, 1973).

LEONARD A. STEVERSON, PH.D.
SOUTH GEORGIA COLLEGE

# Duclos, Jacques (1896–1975)

JACQUES DUCLOS, the leader of the French Communist Party (PCF) during much of the 20th century, symbolized the struggles of the French people. Born in 1896, Duclos joined the Marxist French Communist Party in the 1920s. He favored an anarcho-syndicalist worldview of the role of social revolution. Duclos believed that the PCF symbolized an expression of working-class grievances and frustrations. From 1926 to 1932, Duclos served as a member of the Chamber of Duties as well as on the Party's Central Committee.

During the 1920s, the French government curtailed many civil liberties. There were frequent arrests, fines, and the seizure of the party's daily newspaper. Duclos recounted how he played a cat-and-mouse game with authorities to evade arrest. In 1927, the government arrested Duclos as a congressional member of the seditious Communist Party. He was sentenced to 30 years in prison. Fortunately, the Chamber of Duties passed a bill releasing all imprisoned deputies. This law only applied to when the chamber was in session so that when the session expired, Duclos had to flee Paris in the middle of the night.

In early 1931, during the height of the Great Depression, Duclos was once again arrested. While serving his jail time, he achieved the prestigious position of party secretary and member of the political bureau. Duclos spearheaded a drive to recruit additional members to the party. At the Seventh Party Congress, Duclos could boast of an increase in membership, though not to the extent that he wished. He believed that the unemployment and social dislocation caused by the Depression would bolster membership, however, this never came to fruition. Duclos also came to the realization that in order for the PCF to succeed politically, it needed to reach across political lines, dispense with the ideology of revolution, and create a broad-based coalition—an idea that would be fulfilled as Duclos led the communists to join the Popular Front government of the late 1930s. The time of peace, however, was about to end.

In 1941, Adolf Hitler brutally invaded France and established a "puppet" government. Duclos spearheaded the French resistance to the foreign aggressors. During the German occupation, the PCF was deemed an illegal party. Duclos not only led the party from France but he also edited the underground resistance newspaper, *L'Humanité,* that was the sole source of information during the occupation. Duclos edited 46 issues during the war, advocating "action" against the ruling classes as well as against the fascists. Duclos and the Communist Party underground were persecuted and jailed by the Nazi-allied Pétain/Laval government. Duclos escaped arrest on numerous occasions. In 1942, Duclos helped to establish the communist-based resistance groups, Front National and Frances-Tireurs, which formed the militant wing of the Communist Party. It was becoming evident that Duclos and the party would act as the internal resistance to the Nazi occupation while the more liberal forces would provide the external resistance. As the war concluded, Duclos and the communists assumed a leadership role in the transition governments.

When the Soviet Communist Party decided to get rid of Earl Browder, the head of the Communist Political Association (the form that the American party took during and immediately after World War II), the policy was announced by way of an article written by Duclos and published in the journal *Cahiers de Communism*. Known as the Duclos Letter in the United States, the article condemned "Browderism" and the American communists' continuation of popular front tactics as "right wing deviationism." Obediently, the Communist Political Association in the United States called a leadership meeting, and with only Browder dissenting, the group reorganized as the Communist Party and suspended Browder from office. William Z. Foster took charge. In this way, the Duclos Letter became the means by which official Stalinist policy was communicated to the American party.

After the war, Duclos sought to place the Communist Party in the vanguard of the new French regime. He resisted the Gaullist Fifth Republic, reaching such an extent that he was jailed in 1952. From 1945 to 1948, he served in the National Assembly, serving as the vice president from 1946 to 1952. He reached his greatest popularity when in 1961, he ran for president on the PCF ticket and garnered 21.5 percent of the popular vote, running a close third in the balloting.

**SEE ALSO**

*Volume 1 Left:* France; Communism; Socialism; Cominform; Anarcho-Syndicalism.
*Volume 2 Right:* France.

**BIBLIOGRAPHY**

M. Adereth, *The French Communist Party: A Critical History (1920–84), from Comintern to the Colors of France* (Manchester University Press, 1984); Edward Mortimer, *The Rise of the French Communist Party, 1920–47* (Faber & Faber, 1984); Ronald Tiersky, *French Communism, 1920–72* (Columbia University Press, 1974).

JAIME RAMÓN OLIVARES, PH.D.
HOUSTON COMMUNITY COLLEGE, CENTRAL

# Dunayevskaya, Raya (1910–1987)

RAYA DUNAYEVSKAYA WAS the founder and national chairwoman of News and Letters and one of the key philosophical forces behind the development of Marxist Humanism both within the United States and internationally. Dunayevskaya emigrated to the United States from Ukraine in 1922 with her parents, and even at a young age associated with the Communist Party. By 1928, Dunayevskaya found herself (along with many others) expelled from the Communist Party for "Trotskyist sympathies." Between 1928 and 1937, Dunayevskaya worked across the United States for a number of progressive organizations and causes, including the Spartacus Youth League and the Washington Committee to Aid Agricultural Workers.

In 1937, Dunayevskaya accepted an invitation to serve as Leon Trotsky's Russian language secretary in Mexico. Dunayevskaya returned to the United States in 1938 and continued to work and organize on behalf of Trotsky. However, in 1939, Dunayevskaya broke with Trotsky's assessment that the "Soviet Union was a workers' state, though degenerate," and began the process of developing her own philosophical understanding of the nature of the Soviet Union. In 1940, Dunayevskaya joined the new Workers Party (WP) and in 1941(as Freddy Forest) circulated an article entitled "The Union of Soviet Socialist Republics Is a Capitalist Society" in the internal bulletin of the WP. She would subsequently collaborate with C.L.R. James and Grace Lee Boggs, forming a tendency within the WP known as the State Capitalist Tendency (later the Johnson/Forest Tendency).

By 1955, not only had Dunayevskaya left the WP (which ceased to exist in 1949), but she also broke with Johnson and formed an independent organization known as the News and Letters committees, an organization which survives her death. From 1955 to 1987, Dunayevskaya published numerous articles, actively chaired the organization, contributed weekly philosophic bulletins, and authored three books. Having undertaken a study of Vladimir Lenin's *Philosophic Notebooks* in 1953 and subsequently G.W.F. Hegel's *Logic*, Dunayevskaya worked out a new philosophic understanding of Marx rooted in Hegel's dialectic and Karl Marx's own assertion of the need for a New Humanism. Over the course of her lifetime, she furthered her understanding of Marx's works and what she saw as a "double movement" between theory and practice.

Dunayevskaya's assessment of the state capitalist nature of the Soviet Union, her assertion of a humanist Marxism, and her success leading a revolutionary organization in the United States marks her as a unique figure in the history of the American left. Her works have been overlooked by academics and radicals, yet within her texts emerges a vision of a "new society" that is free. Her writings remain pertinent today and her insights into important social movements, such as the civil rights movement, youth movements, women's movements, and workers' movements, as forces of revolution stand in stark contrast to dogmatic assertions, theories, and dialectics proclaimed under the banner of Marxism.

## SEE ALSO

*Volume 1 Left:* Marxist Humanism; Praxis Group; Workers Party.
*Volume 2 Right:* Capitalism; United States; Totalitarianism.

## BIBLIOGRAPHY

Raya Dunayevskaya, *Marxism and Freedom: From 1776 until Today* (Pluto Press, 1975); Raya Dunayevskaya, *Philosophy and Revolution* (Lexington Books, 1989); Raya Dunayevskaya, *Rosa Luxembourg, Women's Liberation, and Marx's Philosophy of Revolution* (Bookman Associates, 1991); Terry Moon, "Raya Dunayevskaya," *Women Building Chicago: 1790–1990* (Indiana University Press, 2001); News and Letters, www.newsandletters.org (March 2004).

SANDRA REIN
ATHABASCA UNIVERSITY, CANADA

# The Left

# E

## Egypt

THE MODERN HISTORY of Egypt can be said to have begun with the opening of the Suez Canal in November 1869. The canal, largely the creation of the Frenchman Ferdinand de Lesseps (who would later attempt the first Panama Canal), opened Egypt to much new investment in the commercial waterway and its related industries. The canal, for example, would be the shortest maritime route between the Mediterranean and the Red Sea, the Persian Gulf, and the Indian Ocean beyond. Indeed, the canal was built during a period of progressive thought in Egypt, as the ruling Khedive Ismail attempted to bring Egypt out of the years of backwardness caused by the rule of the Ottoman Empire. However, ironically, Ismail's dreams of modernization were thwarted by their cost. Hostile pressure from Germany, Austria, England, and France forced the Ottoman Sultan Abdul Hamid to force Ismail to abdicate in favor of his son Tewfik.

The obvious influence of foreign governments in Egypt greatly exacerbated the internal problems of modernization and the debt. With the government seen as being corrupt, nationalist thinking began to coalesce around followers of Jamal al-Din al-Afghani, who, as Peter Mansfield wrote in A History of the Middle East, "was one of the most powerful intellectual influences in 19th-century Islam." The nationalist leader became

Colonel Arabi Pasha, one of the first of the modernizing military officers who would have such an impact in modern history. The London Times quoted him on September 12, 1881, as saying "the army, we must remember, is the only native institution which Egypt now owns." Unfortunately, a developing Egyptian nationalism was not on the agenda of England, which had bought the debt-ridden Ismail's Suez Canal Company shares in November 1875. In September 1882, at Tel-el-Kebir, British General Sir Garnet Wolseley crushed Arabi's force and the compliant Tewfik dissolved his own army to prevent further resistance.

The British conquest led to the establishment of what the British called "the veiled protectorate" in the time of Evelyn Baring, later Lord Cromer. Theoretically, Tewfik still reigned, but the British ruled, as shown by the troop garrison now in the country and the use of Alexandria as a main port in the Mediterranean for the British fleet. The British Royal Navy had, in fact, bombarded Alexandria before the invasion under Wolseley. Cromer served as the imperial proconsul, the true "power behind the throne." A.P. Thornton, in The Imperial Idea and Its Enemies: A Study in British Power noted that the anti-imperialist sociology pioneer Herbert Spencer felt such "militarism was just another aspect of the rebarbarization of the nation."

Before long, Baring found himself embroiled in a revolt in the Sudan, which had been the subject of ineffective and corrupt Egyptian rule since 1820. As in Egypt itself, with political avenues blocked, popular disaffection among the Sudanese expressed itself in Mohammed Ahmed, who styled himself the Mahdi, "the Expected One" of Allah. After leading it astray in the desert, the Mahdi's Ansar army crushed an Egyptian army under former British General William Hicks at El Obeid.

Prime Minister William Gladstone of the Liberal Party was reluctant to carry on the imperial burden that his Conservative Party rival Benjamin Disraeli had taken on when he had secured Ismail's shares in the Suez Canal in 1875. Rather than commit an entire British army to the Sudan, Gladstone sent Charles George "Chinese" Gordon to evacuate the Egyptians from the capital of Khartoum. Ignoring orders, Gordon was killed in Khartoum in January 1885. British and Egyptian forces would impose Anglo-Egyptian rule on the Sudan again in 1898, after the Sudanese had been ruled by the nationalist Mahdist regime since 1885.

In spite of attempts by Baring and his successors to rationalize Egyptian administration, the record of their "veiled protectorate" was at best spotty. Brigandage in the countryside, which had vexed Egypt since the days of the Pharaohs, still remained a constant threat. In fact, Peter Mansfield, in *The British in Egypt*, wrote that the British were "pained and mystified by the steady increase in crime during the occupation." Furthermore, in their imperialist zeal, they succeeded in severely undermining the authority of the *omdehs*, the village mayors, who administered justice in consultation with the *qadis*, or authorities in the Islamic law, or *sharia*. Thus, not only was the problem of growing crime not resolved, but nationalist feelings were offended by circumventing the ancient system of law-giving.

In spite of Arabi's defeat in 1882, nationalism continued as a potent force in Egyptian life. Since Wolseley and his Highlanders had proven armed resistance futile at the battle of Tel-el-Kebir in 1882, Egyptian nationalists took their cause into the legislative assembly. Bruce B. Lawrence wrote in *Shattering the Myth: Islam Beyond Violence*, "the nationalist movement coalesced around Sa'd Zaghlul [who] founded the opposition Wafd Party that reflected an elision of political independence with dedication to Islam." Any real strides toward asserting independence were cut short when the authoritarian Ottoman Empire threw in its lot with Imperial Germany in World War I when the letter went to war with England in November 1914. Egypt, astride the Suez Canal, became the most strategic point in the British Empire. It was from the banks of the Nile that British

General Sir Edmund Allenby launched his conquest of the Ottomans in Palestine and Syria in 1917–18.

## EGYPTIAN INDEPENDENCE

After World War I, Egyptian nationalism rose up again after being repressed during the war. Rioting erupted for national determination in 1919. The leaders were Zaghlul Pash, Ismail Sidky Pasha, and Mohammed Mahmoud Pasha. Fortunately for both, the British and the Egyptians, the imperial proconsul was Allenby, who had for his era a highly sophisticated view of the growth of Egyptian self-determination. Independence, in fact was granted in 1922, but as Lawrence remarked, "British control of defense and foreign affairs persisted." Thus, in spite of promises to the contrary, the veiled protectorate endured in Egypt. However, nationalist political parties kept their faith in the parliamentary system as the avenue to press for full freedom.

King Fuad, the first monarch of a technically independent Egypt, was succeeded by his son King Farouk in 1936. In that year, another treaty was negotiated between England and Egypt, but true independence remained a chimera. Article VIII provided a blueprint for the British to immediately seize power again if warranted by concerns for imperial defense.

When England went to war in World War II, Farouk declared Egyptian neutrality in response to the unequal treaty of 1936. However, as Mansfield remarked, "the outbreak of war with Germany [in September 1939] caused Britain to invoke Article VIII which, in placing all Egypt's facilities at its disposal, implied the virtual re-occupation of the country." Frustrated in their attempts to gain independence through parliamentary means, nationalists formed groups like the Green Shirts, who attacked politicians they felt were betraying Egypt by being partisans of the Empire. Among these nationalists were the future presidents of Egypt: Gamal Abdel Nasser and Anwar Sadat. Hassan al-Bana in 1928 had already founded the Islamic nationalist group the Muslim Brotherhood, which became the fountainhead of all later groups that blended nationalism and Islamic beliefs.

During the war, Farouk was clearly pro-Italian and a supporter of Italy's Fascist Duce Benito Mussolini, the strongest ally of Adolf Hitler's Nazi Germany. Farouk, in spite of his belief in Egyptian independence, refused to realize that the Germans and Italians would impose a rule far harsher on Egypt than the British. Consequently, British Ambassador Miles Lampson acted drastically. On February 2, 1942, Lampson and General

R.G.W.H. Stone, the commander of the British garrison in Egypt, approached the royal Abdin Palace with a column of British troops and armored cars. Brushing aside any Egyptian opposition, Lampson confronted Farouk in his study. Lampson provided the monarch with a choice: either make Nahas Pasha, the head of the Wafd Party and a supporter of the war effort, prime minister—or abdicate the throne. King Farouk agreed to call Pasha to power.

After the war, Farouk and his supine capitulation to Lampson led to his being toppled from his throne in the Free Officers Association coup of 1952. Although General Mohammed Naguib was the figurehead, Gamal Abdel Nasser held the real power and from 1954, Nasser followed a line of direct rule.

However, Nasser's attempts to invigorate the Land of the Pharaohs were in many ways frustrated by his own extreme nationalism. He embroiled Egypt in two costly wars with Israel, in 1956 and 1967, which were military disasters. Although his seizure and nationalization of the canal in 1956 had made him highly popular, the Egyptian peasant, or *fellahin*, still worked under dire economic conditions. Daniel Lerner wrote in *The Passing of Traditional Society: Modernizing the Middle East* that as early as 1958, the year Nasser established his United Arab Republic with Syria, Egypt was "linking the goals of popular welfare and national grandeur ... in a land inadequately prepared for either, has led to soul-searching and bold enterprises."

## NASSER'S LEFT

Nasser's nationalistic bold enterprise of socialism was profound. As early as 1952, according to the U.S. Library of Congress, he announced a list of nationalizations that cut more deeply into the private sector than any that had occurred in any country outside of Eastern Europe. The decrees nationalized all private banks, all insurance companies, and 50 shipping companies and firms in heavy and basic industries. The nationalization program continued in successive waves through 1962 and 1963 and involved £E7 billion (approximately $14 billion) in shared and private assets being transferred to public ownership by 1966.

The decrees also included legislation such as taxing high incomes at the rate of 90 percent. Half of all seats in parliament and on all elective bodies and worker-management boards were reserved for peasants and workers. In 1964, Nasser released a draft constitution that functioned until 1971, which emphasized freedom, socialism, and unity.

Internally, Nasser suppressed all opposition, from Islamic extremists to minorities like Greeks and Jews, the latter two of which left Egypt in droves. Externally, Nasser's foreign policy was disastrous. In 1956, in an attempt to free Egypt from foreign control, he nationalized the Suez Canal but ironically set off the Suez Canal Crisis. Egypt was defeated in the war, as it would be after the June 1967 war, which he also precipitated. Paradoxically, Nasser weakened Egyptian sovereignty even more by his dependence on the Soviet Union. As a socialist, he had aligned Egypt more with the Soviet Communist Party than with the Western democracies. Although Nasser strove for nonalignment, the reality was that he was under Moscow's thumb.

When Anwar Sadat succeeded Nasser after Nasser's death in September 1970, he continued the campaign against Islamic groups, seeing them also as obstacles to modernization. But, with a regime that stifled political dissent, the Islamic groups became the only real opposition force in Egypt. At the same time, he freed Egypt from its dependence on the Soviet Union, risking Moscow's ire for Egyptian freedom of action. Three years after Nasser's death, Sadat launched the October 1973 war against Israel. Although defeated, he used the good showing of his army as a negotiating tool in seeking peace with Israel. In September 1978, at the Camp David accords, Sadat negotiated with Israeli Prime Minister Menachem Begin the first peace treaty between Israel and an Arab state. However, Sadat's bravery in making peace with Israel exacerbated his unpopularity with the Islamic militants, who viewed him as a modern, misguided Pharaoh. In October 1981, he was assassinated by army militants while watching a parade.

Into the 2000s, the chronic Egyptian struggle with Islamic extremism is rooted in the inability of the government to provide adequate opportunities for its citizens. According to Lawrence, the fundamentalists come from the ranks of those who "have had sufficient education to perceive another reality than the one they daily confront." Islamic groups cite continued government repression as a reason for their continued war against the government—and current alliance with al-Qaeda.

According to the United States Institute of Peace (USIP), "The revelations of the leaders of al-Gama'a al-Islamiyya [the Islamic Group] in Egypt confirm this point of view. A careful reading of the statements of this group's leaders in *Al-Ahram al-Duwali* (published in Cairo in February/March 2002) clearly indicates the role of humiliation and state violence in pushing the group toward violence in the 1980s and 1990s." Hosni

Mubarak, who succeeded Sadat, was almost killed by them in June 1995. Egyptians still believe that the Mubarak regime, like those that preceded it, is incapable of any real reform. This is demonstrated in the expectation of many Egyptians that when Mubarak retires, he will be succeeded by his son Gamal.

**SEE ALSO**

Volume 1 Left: Socialism; Soviet Union; Africa; Middle East.
Volume 2 Right: Egypt; Africa; Middle East.

**BIBLIOGRAPHY**

Peter Mansfield, A History of the Middle East (Penguin, 1991); A.P. Thornton, The Imperial Idea and Its Enemies: A Study in British Power (Anchor Books, 1959); Philip Magnus, Gladstone (Dutton, 1964); Daniel Lerner, The Passing of Traditional Society: Modernizing the Middle East (The Free Press, 1958); Lord Kinross, Between Two Seas: The Creation of the Suez Canal (Morrow, 1969); Neil Macfarquhar, "Who after Mubarak?" The Hindu (December 26, 2003); M.J. Williams, "The Egyptian Campaign, 1882," Brian Bond, ed., Victorian Military Campaigns (Praeger, 1967); Anthony Nutting, Gordon of Khartoum (Clarkson Potter, 1966); Winston S. Churchill, The River War (Award Books, 1964); United States Institute of Peace (USIP), "Islamic Extremists: How Do They Mobilize Support?" www.usip.org (July 2004).

JOHN F. MURPHY, JR.
AMERICAN MILITARY UNIVERSITY

# Electorate, African American

AFRICAN AMERICAN VOTING behavior has always been different from the rest of the electorate in the United States. Blacks essentially became a subgroup in the electorate with the passage of the Fifteenth Amendment to the Constitution, which provided that no male citizen could be denied the right to vote on account of race. Blacks instantly became a powerful voting bloc in the former slave states of the reconstructed American South. Since it was the Republican Party that had freed the slaves, made them citizens, given them the vote, and taken a hard line with the southern states in Reconstruction, blacks naturally voted and ran as Republicans in large numbers. A few were even elected.

Soon, Congress relaxed its hard line with the states, and the southern states imposed segregation. The voting rights African Americans had accrued under the Fif-

teenth Amendment were essentially nullified by tax and residency requirements and by literacy tests. Particularly burdensome was the "grandfather" rule, which excused a potential voter from the necessity of taking the literacy test if his grandfather had voted. This provision allowed illiterate whites to vote, while requiring all blacks to take the literacy test. Even after 1920, when many southern blacks passed through elementary and secondary educations, literate black voters were denied the right to register through fraudulent application of the test. In some states, African Americans who sought to register for the first time were told they had to pay poll taxes for all previous elections in which they had been of voting age but failed to register. Even though the tax might be only one or two dollars per election, the accumulated bill for $20 to $50 was sufficient to prevent many from registering. In some counties, other tax bills, such as dog licenses and other charges, were presented to prevent registration.

Despite these restrictions, in several districts in the south, African American congressmen and other officials continued to serve in office and be re-elected through the 1870s and 1880s. From 1899 to 1901, George H. White, a black attorney from North Carolina, served as the only black member of Congress. He won his post through a coalition of Republican and Populist Party voters. After 1901, no blacks served in Congress until 1928. On the national level, Republican administrations continued to appoint black men to important positions in the Treasury Department, in the city government of Washington, D.C., and as ministers to the black-governed republics of Haiti and Liberia.

It was not much better for blacks in the north. In most cities, party "machine" politics dominated, and blacks were mostly useful only to the machines for delivering votes, not for participating in the process as equals. Even in nonmachine cities, African Americans were condescended to by the political elite. However, in several areas, particularly in Chicago and New York City, machine politicians treated the black vote as they had other ethnic voting blocks. In 1928, Oscar De Priest was elected from Chicago to serve in the 71st Congress on the Republican ticket. He was reelected in 1930 and 1932. Following in De Priest's footsteps, black congressmen began to be elected in both Republican and Democratic urban congressional districts through the 1930s.

Although Franklin Roosevelt's New Deal included no civil rights legislation, the Democratic party during the 1930s began to increasingly attract African American voters through programs directed at resolving the problems of unemployment and poverty and through a

| AFRICAN AMERICANS | Total | Total Population | | | | | | | | | | U.S. citizen | | |
|---|---|---|---|---|---|---|---|---|---|---|---|---|---|---|
| | | Reported registered | | Not registered | | Reported voted | | Did not vote | | | | Reported registered | Not registered | Not a citizen |
| | | Number | Percent | Number | Percent | Number | Percent | Number | Percent | | | Number | Number | Number |
| BOTH SEXES | | | | | | | | | | | | | | |
| Total 18 years and over | 24,445 | 14,304 | 58.5 | 10,141 | 41.5 | 9,695 | 39.7 | 14,750 | 60.3 | | | 14,304 | 8,608 | 1,533 |
| 18 to 24 years | 3,930 | 1,555 | 39.6 | 2,375 | 60.4 | 760 | 19.3 | 3,171 | 80.7 | | | 1,555 | 2,134 | 241 |
| 25 to 44 years | 10,478 | 5,850 | 55.8 | 4,628 | 44.2 | 3,778 | 36.1 | 6,700 | 63.9 | | | 5,850 | 3,751 | 877 |
| 45 to 64 years | 7,207 | 4,820 | 66.9 | 2,387 | 33.1 | 3,606 | 50.0 | 3,601 | 50.0 | | | 4,820 | 2,055 | 333 |
| 65 to 74 years | 1,618 | 1,197 | 74.0 | 421 | 26.0 | 923 | 57.0 | 695 | 43.0 | | | 1,197 | 375 | 46 |
| 75 years and over | 1,212 | 883 | 72.8 | 330 | 27.2 | 629 | 51.9 | 584 | 48.1 | | | 883 | 294 | 36 |
| MALE | | | | | | | | | | | | | | |
| Total 18 years and over | 10,811 | 5,758 | 53.3 | 5,053 | 46.7 | 3,815 | 35.3 | 6,996 | 64.7 | | | 5,758 | 4,240 | 813 |
| 18 to 24 years | 1,835 | 621 | 33.8 | 1,214 | 66.2 | 303 | 16.5 | 1,532 | 83.5 | | | 621 | 1,072 | 142 |
| 25 to 44 years | 4,663 | 2,336 | 50.1 | 2,327 | 49.9 | 1,430 | 30.7 | 3,234 | 69.3 | | | 2,336 | 1,846 | 481 |
| 45 to 64 years | 3,232 | 2,006 | 62.1 | 1,227 | 37.9 | 1,477 | 45.7 | 1,755 | 54.3 | | | 2,006 | 1,061 | 165 |
| 65 to 74 years | 684 | 503 | 73.5 | 182 | 26.5 | 385 | 56.3 | 299 | 43.7 | | | 503 | 172 | 10 |
| 75 years and over | 396 | 292 | 73.8 | 104 | 26.2 | 221 | 55.7 | 176 | 44.3 | | | 292 | 88 | 16 |
| FEMALE | | | | | | | | | | | | | | |
| Total 18 years and over | 13,634 | 8,546 | 62.7 | 5,088 | 37.3 | 5,879 | 43.1 | 7,755 | 56.9 | | | 8,546 | 4,368 | 720 |
| 18 to 24 years | 2,096 | 934 | 44.6 | 1,161 | 55.4 | 457 | 21.8 | 1,639 | 78.2 | | | 934 | 1,062 | 99 |
| 25 to 44 years | 5,814 | 3,513 | 60.4 | 2,301 | 39.6 | 2,349 | 40.4 | 3,466 | 59.6 | | | 3,513 | 1,905 | 396 |
| 45 to 64 years | 3,975 | 2,814 | 70.8 | 1,160 | 29.2 | 2,129 | 53.6 | 1,846 | 46.4 | | | 2,814 | 993 | 167 |
| 65 to 74 years | 933 | 694 | 74.4 | 239 | 25.6 | 538 | 57.6 | 396 | 42.4 | | | 694 | 203 | 36 |
| 75 years and over | 816 | 590 | 72.4 | 226 | 27.6 | 408 | 50.0 | 408 | 50.0 | | | 590 | 205 | 20 |

Note: 'Not registered' includes 'did not register to vote,' 'do not know,' and 'not reported.' 'Did not vote' includes 'did not vote,' 'do not know,' and 'not reported.'

The table above, from the U.S. Census Bureau, shows November 2002 data (in thousands) on voting and registration by African Americans, broken down by sex and age, in the United States. The 2002 cycle did not include a presidential election.

number of symbolic political actions. It was not until after World War II that African Americans began to achieve notable political success in the north. In 1946, President Harry S Truman appointed a Civil Rights Commission, and its 1947 report, *To Secure These Rights*, set an agenda for enfranchisement and expansion of rights. Although Congress refused to enact the proposals, Truman was able to implement several through executive order, for example, his 1948 order ending segregation in the U.S. Army.

With the civil rights movement of the 1950s and 1960s, blacks began to achieve meaningful political power. The Twenty-Fourth Amendment, which bars poll taxes, was passed in 1964. The Voting Rights Act of 1965, enacted with bipartisan political support, was the first federal act since Reconstruction designed to guarantee the vote to blacks. It has been renewed and expanded several times, and its provisions also apply to redistricting. It has been extended to apply to some northern cities and states where blacks have traditionally been electorally disadvantaged.

Since the 1950s, blacks have become the single most solid bloc within the Democratic Party. This is quite jarring to those Republicans who believe blacks should be in their camp because of the 19th-century pattern in which Republicans worked to enfranchise blacks, while the Democratic Party in the south became dedicated to denying black suffrage. Also bringing African Americans into harmony with the Democratic Party is the fact that blacks primarily live in inner cities, which since 1970 have become increasingly the domain of the Democratic Party. Surveys during election cycles consistently show that over 90 percent of blacks vote Democratic. They are also more loyal to the party than other voters. When John Anderson in 1980 and Ralph Nader in 2000 ran third-party presidential bids that siphoned white Democratic votes, black voters remained foursquare behind the Democratic candidate, and those third-party candidates achieved little success in black voting districts.

Black voters appear to make a connection to the Democratic Party platform that transcends the presence of prominent blacks in other parties. For example, Ezola Foster ran for vice president in 2000 with Patrick Buchanan, but this appears to have been a cipher in terms of black vote. George W. Bush appointed blacks to high-profile posts in his first administration—notably Secretary of State Colin Powell and National Security Adviser Condoleezza Rice—but polling among blacks shows these appointments have made very little impact in drawing blacks to vote Republican, or even to vote Republican in 2004, despite the fact that such appointments carry with them far more responsibility for national security issues than any cabinet posts held by blacks in former administrations.

Some pundits argue that high preference for the Democratic Party among blacks is a function of socioeconomic status, in that poorer voters, regardless of race, tend to prefer the Democratic Party. This is an argument, however, that is not supported by the majority of facts as black support for the Democrats is much higher than for voters of comparable income of other races. Nevertheless, particular Republican black politicians have continued to work to break the linkage between race and party, claiming that the black vote is taken for granted by Democratic politicians and that if it were made clear that the vote had to be earned, blacks would be in a better position to win more gains for racial justice and equality.

**SEE ALSO**

*Volume 1 Left:* Electorate, Hispanic; Democratic Party.
*Volume 2 Right:* Republican Party; Bush, George W;

**BIBLIOGRAPHY**

David Lublin, *The Paradox of Representation* (Princeton University Press, 1997); Keith Reeves, *Voting Hopes or Fears* (Oxford University Press, 1997); Carol M. Swain, *Black Faces, Black Interests* (Harvard University Press, 1995); Hanes Walton, *African American Power and Politics* (Columbia University Press, 1997).

TONY L. HILL
MASSACHUSETTS INSTITUTE OF TECHNOLOGY

# Electorate, Hispanic

HISPANIC AMERICANS are increasing in importance as a voting group. Unlike African Americans, who have been part of the country since colonial times, Hispanic people have only been a significant presence since the start of the 20th century, when the first Puerto Rican refugees began arriving after the Spanish-American War (1898). This was even before the state with the greatest Spanish presence, New Mexico, was admitted to the union.

Hispanics have been carefully cultivated by both parties in recent years, in part because they have been less overwhelmingly attached to the Democratic Party than blacks. It is also significant that they hold the balance of power in some large and key states: California, Texas, and Florida. In the 1980s, California was a swing state in national elections, but in the 1990s, the state became increasingly Democratic and is now perhaps too far into the Democratic column for Republicans to be competitive there. Part of the explanation for this is the state's increasing Hispanic population, and that Hispanic voters have become more likely to identify with Democrats during this time because of some noisy and obtrusive moves on the part of Republicans to exclude "illegal immigrants" (nearly all of them Hispanic) from the mainstream of California life and to make English the official language of the state, restricting the services made available in both English and Spanish in the process.

While Texas is not a competitive state in national politics, being solidly Republican, it is no accident that Republicans there, including former Governor George W. Bush, have taken steps to cultivate the Hispanic vote for their party rather than see it go inexorably to the Democrats as in California.

Florida is one of the fastest growing states, and Hispanics (primarily Cubans) have been one of the incipient demographic groups there for several decades. Florida also held the balance of power in the 2000 presidential election (infamously), and both parties were very careful in their treatment of south Florida's large Cuban community. The seizure of young Elian Gonzalez, son of a Cuban refugee mother who was deported to his father in Cuba in 1999, had large ramifications for the Cuban vote in 2000.

In the first decade of the 21st century, Hispanics are a growing part of the electorate in almost every state and community in the United States. This is due not only to lax immigration laws and enforcement but also to the willingness of immigrants from Mexico and other places in Latin America to travel far and wide to do the kinds of jobs that other Americans are no longer interested in, such as working in food processing plants.

One important ramification of this increased Hispanic presence is that it makes the Republican Party less likely to pursue policies of immigration restrictions and crackdowns on illegal aliens, two policies that have been staples of Republican platforms and fundraising appeals for decades. As long as about a third of Hispanic voters are choosing Republicans, as polls indicated in 2000 and 2002 (by contrast, not even 10 percent of blacks vote Republican), and in so many key states, Hispanics have an edge in the political process that other

| HISPANIC (of any race) | Total | Reported registered Number | Reported registered Percent | Not registered Number | Not registered Percent | Reported voted Number | Reported voted Percent | Did not vote Number | Did not vote Percent | U.S. citizen Reported registered Number | U.S. citizen Not registered Number | Not a citizen Number |
|---|---|---|---|---|---|---|---|---|---|---|---|---|
| **BOTH SEXES** | | | | | | | | | | | | |
| Total 18 years and over | 25,162 | 8,196 | 32.6 | 16,966 | 67.4 | 4,747 | 18.9 | 20,415 | 81.1 | 8,196 | 7,405 | 9,561 |
| 18 to 24 years | 4,825 | 1,005 | 20.8 | 3,820 | 79.2 | 390 | 8.1 | 4,435 | 91.9 | 1,005 | 1,928 | 1,892 |
| 25 to 44 years | 12,860 | 3,718 | 28.9 | 9,142 | 71.1 | 1,970 | 15.3 | 10,890 | 84.7 | 3,718 | 3,432 | 5,711 |
| 45 to 64 years | 5,586 | 2,436 | 43.6 | 3,151 | 56.4 | 1,603 | 28.7 | 3,983 | 71.3 | 2,436 | 1,486 | 1,665 |
| 65 to 74 years | 1,131 | 635 | 56.1 | 496 | 43.9 | 490 | 43.3 | 641 | 56.7 | 635 | 322 | 174 |
| 75 years and over | 760 | 402 | 53.0 | 357 | 47.0 | 295 | 38.8 | 465 | 61.2 | 402 | 238 | 120 |
| **MALE** | | | | | | | | | | | | |
| Total 18 years and over | 12,855 | 3,783 | 29.4 | 9,072 | 70.6 | 2,225 | 17.3 | 10,630 | 82.7 | 3,783 | 3,811 | 5,261 |
| 18 to 24 years | 2,666 | 437 | 16.4 | 2,229 | 83.6 | 153 | 5.7 | 2,513 | 94.3 | 437 | 1,041 | 1,188 |
| 25 to 44 years | 6,676 | 1,741 | 26.1 | 4,935 | 73.9 | 964 | 14.4 | 5,712 | 85.6 | 1,741 | 1,793 | 3,143 |
| 45 to 64 years | 2,684 | 1,141 | 42.5 | 1,542 | 57.5 | 726 | 27.1 | 1,957 | 72.9 | 1,141 | 749 | 794 |
| 65 to 74 years | 528 | 283 | 53.7 | 245 | 46.3 | 238 | 45.1 | 290 | 54.9 | 283 | 157 | 88 |
| 75 years and over | 301 | 180 | 60.0 | 120 | 40.0 | 143 | 47.6 | 158 | 52.4 | 180 | 72 | 49 |
| **FEMALE** | | | | | | | | | | | | |
| Total 18 years and over | 12,307 | 4,413 | 35.9 | 7,894 | 64.1 | 2,522 | 20.5 | 9,785 | 79.5 | 4,413 | 3,595 | 4,300 |
| 18 to 24 years | 2,159 | 568 | 26.3 | 1,591 | 73.7 | 237 | 11.0 | 1,922 | 89.0 | 568 | 887 | 704 |
| 25 to 44 years | 6,184 | 1,977 | 32.0 | 4,207 | 68.0 | 1,006 | 16.3 | 5,178 | 83.7 | 1,977 | 1,639 | 2,568 |
| 45 to 64 years | 2,902 | 1,294 | 44.6 | 1,608 | 55.4 | 877 | 30.2 | 2,025 | 69.8 | 1,294 | 737 | 871 |
| 65 to 74 years | 603 | 351 | 58.3 | 251 | 41.7 | 252 | 41.8 | 351 | 58.2 | 351 | 166 | 86 |
| 75 years and over | 459 | 222 | 48.4 | 237 | 51.6 | 151 | 33.0 | 307 | 67.0 | 222 | 166 | 71 |

Note: 'Not registered' includes 'did not register to vote,' 'do not know,' and 'not reported.'  'Did not vote' includes 'did not vote,' 'do not know,' and 'not reported.'

The table above, from the U.S. Census Bureau, shows November 2002 data (in thousands) on voting and registration by Hispanics (all races), broken down by sex and age, in the United States. The 2002 cycle did not include a presidential election.

minority groups lack. No other minority group is as efficacious in setting the agenda in both political parties.

### SEE ALSO

*Volume 1 Left:* Electorate, African American; Democratic Party; Civil Rights; Johnson, Lyndon B.
*Volume 2 Right:* Republican Party; Bush, George W.

### BIBLIOGRAPHY

Louis Desipio, *Counting on the Latino Vote* (University of Virginia Press, 1996); Jorge Ramos, *The Latino Wave* (HarperCollins, 2004).

TONY L. HILL
MASSACHUSETTS INSTITUTE OF TECHNOLOGY

# Electorate, World Demographics

IN MOST COUNTRIES around the world, voting is the way in which citizens express policy preferences, giving those individuals who participate a choice in who governs them and how they do so. Democracies, in particular, cannot survive without a citizenry that is willing to exercise rights of suffrage. Leftist or liberal parties are generally in favor of government interference in the economy to protect the quality of life for individuals. They also tend to be reformist in nature. Liberal parties are likely to be concerned with equality and may advocate the redistribution of income in order to bring this about. In most countries, parties of the Left are usually in favor of implementing high taxes to support social programs, promoting occupational safety regulations to protect workers, and encouraging collectivism such as that practiced by labor unions.

Liberal parties are also likely to take similar stands on issues such as law and order, foreign policy and defense, civil liberties, and civil rights. For instance liberals are more likely to insist on rights for those accused of crimes, equality before the law, and gun control than are conservatives, who take opposite positions. On foreign policy and defense issues, liberals are likely to be anti-war, anti-nuclear weapons, and prefer to spend tax dollars on social programs rather than on increased defense budgets. While liberals are rarely pro-war in general, they may express support for wars perceived as necessary for self-defense and/or the promotion of democracy and may approve of global involvement in countries where human rights issues have been violated. Liberals tend to be strongly opposed to restrictions on civil liberties and civil rights because they interfere with the individual's innate right to preserve human dignity.

Generally, groups that have been historically discriminated against, such as minorities, women, ethnic and religious minorities, the poor, manual laborers, and homosexuals tend to cluster on the left side of the political spectrum. Intellectuals may also form a major part of the political base of leftist political parties. This group usually includes scholars, writers, artists, and entertainers.

Most liberals endorse the ideas promoted by John Locke, a founder of classical liberalism, who believed that each individual owns the fruits of his or her own property. They also accept Locke's contention that certain inalienable rights belong to the individual and that no government can take those rights away. As a result, liberal parties tend to be strong on individual rights and reject the conservative tendency to institute government policies that restrict those rights. As liberals, Locke's supporters have traditionally been dedicated to working within the existing political system to achieve their goals. Liberals are generally not anti-capitalism, but they are against the exploitation that sometimes accompanies politics in capitalistic societies. Karl Marx, a founder of communism, represented the extreme left position. He argued that the bourgeoisie (property owners) exploited the proletariat (the working class) by usurping their labor. Marx believed that the alienated proletariat would rise up against the bourgeoisie and initiate a worldwide revolution to overthrow capitalism.

## LIBERAL PARTIES

Most countries maintain one or more parties that are distinctly liberal and reformist. In the United States, for example, the liberal party is the Democratic Party, which has been associated with the social welfare state since Franklin Roosevelt's New Deal program of the 1930s. The Democrats also support religious tolerance, government regulation, and environmental issues. They are strong supporters of individual rights, including reproductive freedom, freedom of speech and conscience, and criminal rights. In Canada, the reform party is the Liberal Party, which controlled Canadian politics throughout most of the twentieth century, beginning with the administration of William Lyon Mackenzie King for much of the period between 1921 and 1948. Like the American Democrats, Canada's Liberal Party instituted a social welfare state. Unlike the

Democrats, who failed to win popular support for universal health care, the Liberal Party successfully instated this program in Canada. Ireland's Fianna Fáil has traditionally represented leftist politics. Fianna Fáil takes credit for the progressivism that has taken place in the country since Ireland gained its independence from Great Britain. In multiparty systems, two or more leftist parties may form alliances with other liberal parties to put together a coalition government and/or retain representation in national legislatures.

## VOTING BEHAVIOR

While some kinds of voting behaviors are unique to given countries or to particular electoral systems, most countries share certain influences on voting behavior. Scholars often use these characteristics to explain why voters choose to vote at all and why they vote in certain ways. Political efficacy, the idea that voting makes a difference, tends to play an important role in voting behavior. Individuals who consider themselves as either strongly liberal or highly conservative are likely to have high political efficacy because they see voting as a way to influence government. Such individuals tend to identify strongly with political parties that represent their own ideologies because ideology is interwoven with a person's personal value system.

Some scholars have found that socioeconomic status is the best overall predictor of whether a person will vote or not. The three most influential impacts on voting behavior are education, income, and age. Education often plays a major part in voting because it affects many of the other characteristics associated with likelihood of voting, such as access to informational resources and a high sense of political involvement.

Education also helps to shape political views, making a person less likely to be an independent voter. Education also has a major impact on the way that people vote. For instance, intellectuals are likely to have achieved high levels of education, which predisposes individuals to hold leftist political views. At the other end of the spectrum, those with the least level of education are also likely to be liberal, but they are less likely to vote than the more educated.

Income is also likely to make citizens feel they have a stake in politics. The wealthiest individuals tend to be conservative, preferring that government abstain from interfering in the economy in order to protect the economic interests of the wealthy. While the poorest element of any society is not likely to vote, the poor tend to hold leftist political views. During the early days of the Industrial Revolution, class conflicts were present in most Western democracies, and left-wing politics flourished. For instance, socialism and communism were briefly popular among extreme left-wingers in the United States during the 1920s and 1930s.

Developing countries and new democracies may still be experiencing class struggles in the 21st century. As countries mature politically, realignment may take place. For instance, the Social Democrats achieved new prominence in the Czech Republic in the early to mid-1990s by adopting positions that were more clearly egalitarian, while conservatives strongly opposed the liberal shift. In 1998, Miloš Zeman, of the Czech Social Democratic Party, was elected prime minister, heading up a minority government. In 2002, the CSSD joined other leftist minorities parties in a coalition government.

Class also achieved new significance in post-communist Russia. As conservatives expressed support for a free market economy, liberals promoted government involvement in the economy to protect those who remained at the lower end of the economic scale. As a result, the lower class became more predominately leftist in their political attitudes, and a number of left-wing parties flourished. The most prominent of these were Rodina, the left-wing populist party, and the Liberal Democratic Party of Russia. At the extreme left, the Communist Party retained the Russian presidency.

Those who do manual labor have historically been more likely to vote for liberal parties, particularly in countries where strong divisions among classes exist, such as in the United Kingdom. Some scholars believe that incidences of class voting have declined in those countries without rigid class lines. In the United States, for example, with its relatively open class system, most people classify themselves as "middle class," regardless of their socioeconomic status. Since the 1980s, blue-collar workers in the south have been more likely to support conservative politics. Class may also be an indicator of reformist attitudes that are usually linked to the Left. Historically, the middle class has been the most politically involved group of citizens, originating most reform movements.

Age has also been found to be a significant influence on voter turnout in most countries. Some studies have found it be the most reliable indicator of political participation. Young people are the least likely group of eligible voters to exercise their right of suffrage in countries around the globe. Some political scientists believe that parties have not been effective in appealing to younger people who are still forming their political attitudes, which are due only in part to the views expressed by parents, friends, teachers, churches, or media. As young people become educated and exposed to leftist ideas, they may become more liberal than they were previously. Once young people do decide to support a party in a number of elections, they tend to remain loyal unless a major event jolts those loyalties. Such events may include economic depressions, wars, and rebellions against authoritarian regimes.

A swing to the left might result from such events because economic depressions are likely to signal increased government involvement in the economy; protests against protracted wars may signal a rise in radicalism; and rebellions against either far-right or far-left authoritarian regimes are likely to be initiated by liberal reformers. As a rule, participation in politics rises as a person matures, with the middle-aged being the most likely to vote in every society. When people become older and perhaps more infirm and less mobile, political participation may decline. There is no indication that political perspective changes drastically after a person reaches middle age.

## RELIGION AND WOMEN

Religion is of major significance in some countries, while it plays a negligible role in voting behavior in others. In the United States, for example, where religion is more closely associated with the Republican Party than with the Democratic Party, religion plays a key role in determining levels of partisanship. Other countries where religion is an important factor in determining voting behavior are Germany, Hungary, Mexico, the Netherlands, Poland, Taiwan, Ukraine, and the United Kingdom. Those who consider themselves highly religious are more likely to be conservative, while those who support religious toleration are more likely to be liberal. What is meant by the involvement of religion with politics may differ from country to country. In the United States, for example, religious attitudes may affect decisions on social issues but they would never be the deciding factor in a national election. In countries such as those in Latin America where there is no separation of church and state, religious leaders may head up governments.

In Denmark and Norway, women are more likely to vote than men in large part because both governments have initiated political environments that have promoted women's rights. Beginning in the 1980s, women have made up approximately half of the Norway's government officials. Around 60 percent of the country's college graduates are female. Nevertheless, the Norwegian government has met conservative opposition to its plan to require that women make up at least 40 percent of board members of all corporations. Since 1987, the government of Denmark has worked toward promoting gender equality through legislation, affirmative action, and the appointment of the Minister of Gender Equality. In 2000, Denmark's legislature passed the Equal Status Act, designed to further promote equality of the sexes.

Recent election trends in the United States have also shown that women are voting in larger numbers than are men in national elections. Since the last quarter of the twentieth century, both the United States and Western Europe have witnessed a gender gap, wherein woman are increasingly more likely to vote for liberal parties. Some scholars contend that the gender gap is due in large part to women's movements and to the changing social status of women. The fact that many women decide to forego marriage or that they become single again through divorce or widowhood has also had an impact on changing roles of women. Many women may decide not to have children or to have children without being married. All of these changes have promoted independent, generally leftist trends, in the political attitudes of women.

The greatest gap between the voting behavior of men and women is found in Switzerland, where women only received the right to vote in all elections in 1991. The right-wing Swiss People's Party believes that women have no role in politics and should stay home to care for their families. As a result, the Swiss parliament boasts only three women to sixty men. Those who advocate women's rights, therefore, support the Social Democrats. In countries such as Poland, Hungary, and Romania, males are more likely to vote than females because these societies are still strongly patriarchal. Women in these countries are less likely to support liberal parties.

However, these countries have witnessed emerging women's movements since the 1990s. In Poland, for instance, the Parliamentary Group of Women (PGK), made up chiefly of representatives from the Democratic Left Alliance, has become active in promoting women's rights and interests. Such women's organizations tend to promote leftist politics because they challenge the patriarchal status quo championed by conservatives. Females have no right to vote at all in the United Arab Emirates, and Kuwait only made the first move toward female suffrage in May 2004.

Race or minority status may also be a major influence on leftist voting behavior. In the United States, for instance, whites are more likely to vote than blacks. In South Africa, where a conservative minority white population dominated a liberal majority black population before the end of apartheid, the reformist African National Congress was forced to go underground in order to develop strategies for fighting apartheid. Easily identifiable leaders such as Nelson Mandela were jailed for decades by the conservative government. In April 1991, South Africa's first free elections brought the African National Congress to power, rallying 62.6 percent of the total vote.

## POLITICAL PARTIES

High levels of partisanship make voting choices easier because party leaders have already selected candidates who are representative of the party's ideologies and partisan goals. In some countries, such as the United Kingdom, the chief executive is chosen by virtue of being the leader of the party in power, as with Prime Minister Tony Blair who headed the Labour Party. In the United States, on the other hand, where partly lines are less clearly defined, the chief executive is voted on by the nation at large but becomes official only after the electoral college votes. These votes differ only rarely, as they did in the election of 2004 when Democrat Al Gore won the popular vote, but the electoral college named Republican George W. Bush the winner. While partisanship has been on the rise in the United States since the 1980s, many Americans vote for a president who is of the opposite party.

Opponents of two-party systems like those operating in the United Kingdom, Australia, New Zealand, France, Sri Lanka, and the United States argue that choices are always limited and are less representative of the people because such parties must appeal to such a broad range of voters. Because of the need for extensive appeal, parties in two-party countries may not be as distinctly leftist or rightist as those in multiparty systems, which some say better represent minority interests. Some scholars claim that there is little difference in the left and right in the United States because, while program initiatives may change as power in government shifts between the two parties, the overall structure of the government and basic rights of citizenship remain the same. The same could be said of Indonesia for different reasons. In this Muslim nation, both leftist and centrist parties are forced to make major concessions to rightist parties supported by Islamic parties as well as the power centers of the country's military and police forces.

In multiparty systems, small parties may form alliances to gain more support. This has been true in Australia, where the National Party and the Liberal Party have formed a permanent alliance against the larger parties. Some critics of multiparty systems argue that they are likely to be dominated by socialist and or communist parties. In Austria, for example, the two largest parties are the Communist (KPO) and the Socialist (SPO).

In countries where extreme left parties dominate, the largest base of opposition usually comes from rightist Christian parties. In Belgium, for instance, the Socialist Party represents the Left, while the Christian Socialist Party supports the Right. Social Democrats are the liberal parties in a number of countries, including Austria, Denmark, Finland, Sweden, Switzerland, and Germany.

In Latin America, government officials have historically come to power through military coups rather than free and fair elections. As a result, voters have not always had a choice between liberal and conservative candidates. Of course, the same was true in communist countries where one party was predestined to retain authority.

## SEE ALSO

## BIBLIOGRAPHY

Gabriel A. Almond and Sidney Verba, eds., *The Civic Culture Revisited* (Sage, 1989); Douglas J. Amy, *Behind the Ballot Box: A Citizen's Guide to Voting Systems* (Praeger, 2000); Geoffrey Brennan and Loren Lomasky, *Democracy and Division: The Pure Theory of Electoral Preference* (Cambridge University Press, 1993); Ian Budge and Dennis J. Farlie, *Explaining and Predicting Elections: Issues, Effects, and Party Strategies in 23 Democracies* (Allen and Unwin, 1983); CAWP, "Sex Differences in Voter Turnout," www.cawp.rutgers.edu (July 2004); Gary W. Cox, *Making Votes Count: Strategic Coordination in the World's Electoral Systems* (Cambridge University Press, 1997); Ivor Crane, "Electoral Participation," David Butler et al., *Democracy at the Polls: A Comparative Study of Competitive National Elections* (American Enterprise Institute for Public Policy Research, 1981); Russell J. Dalton, *Citizen Politics: Public Opinion and Political Parties in Advanced Industrial Democracies* (Chatham House, 1996); Mark N. Franklin, *Voter Turnout and the Dynamics of Electoral Competition in Established Democracies since 1945* (Cambridge University Press, 2004); Mark N. Franklin et al., *Electoral Change: Response to Evolving Social and Attitudinal Structures in Western Countries* (Cambridge University Press, 1992); Ian Gorvin, *Elections since 1945: A World Wide Reference Compendium* (Longman, 1989); M. Martin Harrop and William L. Miller, *Elections and Voting: A Comparative Introduction* (Macmillan, 1987); Institute for Democracy and Electoral Assistance, "Voter Turnout: A Global Survey," www.idea.int (July 2004).

ELIZABETH PURDY, PH.D.
INDEPENDENT SCHOLAR

# Engels, Friedrich (1820–1890)

Friedrich Engels was born the eldest son of a textile industrialist in Braman, Germany. Engels's life is closely associated with another German national, Karl Marx. Together they wrote the highly influential work *The Communist Manifesto* (1848), a piece of literature which had a profound impact on politics and society in Russia, China, and other places in the 20th century.

As a young man, Engels was sent to Manchester, England, to manage a cotton factory that his father owned. Upon his arrival in the city, Engels was shocked to see the widespread poverty and poor living conditions endured by the working population. As the first industrial nation, England, with its towns and cities, saw the growth of manufacturing industry as progress, despite the often horrific social conditions that working people lived in due to being economically restrained by the forces of capitalism employed by factory owners.

Such was the effect of the early-Victorian Manchester society upon Engels that he wrote *The Condition of the Working Class in England in 1844*, a piece of social commentary about Manchester's social and economic life. At about the same time, he began to write for *Franco-German Annals*, a journal edited in Paris, France, by Marx. But on January 25, 1845, while the pair was working on a piece entitled "The Holy Family," Marx was deported from France and went to Belgium, a European nation that permitted a greater freedom of expression at that time. To assist with the burden of leaving France, Engels used the royalties from *The Condition of the Working Class in England in 1844* to support the Marx family.

Furthermore, Engels drafted the financial support of other sympathizers to allow Marx the means to study so as to develop his economic and social theories. In July 1845, Engels brought Marx to England and by spending time in Manchester and meeting with

Chartists, including the worker movement's leader, George Harney, Marx and Engels were able to further develop their philosophies.

Between January 1846 and February 1848, Engels and Marx continued their close friendship and exclusively gave their time to developing the social, economic, and philosophical notions that are today known as socialism. For example, in January 1846, the pair established the Communist Correspondence Committee; in 1847 they spent time working on a paper, based on Engels's essay "The Principles of Communism," which was to be published as *The Communist Manifesto* in February 1848. Opening with the line "The history of all hitherto existing society is the history of class struggles," Marx and Engels argued that history is not so much about great individuals or conflicts between nations but rather the story of social classes and their struggles with each other. They noted that the composition and form of social classes had altered throughout history, yet by the 19th century the most important classes were the bourgeoisie (the factory owners) and the proletariat (the factory workers). To solve social injustices and to end poverty and oppression in society, the book suggested the proletariat should overthrow the capitalist system and the bourgeoisie, and thus create a classless society.

The period immediately following the publication of the manifesto, from March 1848 to 1849, was turbulent for Engels and Marx. In March 1848, they were expelled from Belgium and moved to Cologne, Germany, in so doing establishing a radical newspaper *New Rhenish Gazette*, which led to their expulsion from Germany; they finally moved to England in 1849. Despite pressure from Prussian authorities on the British government (under the leadership of Prime Minister Lord John Russell) to expel Marx, the attempt by the Prussians was unsuccessful. However, forced to live solely off the money Engels could raise, the Marx family lived in poverty. As a consequence, Engels returned to Germany to work for his father to provide further income for Marx.

In the following years, Engels continued to write. In 1850, *The Peasant War in Germany* was published, and other books included *Revolution and Counter-Revolution in Germany*; *Ludwig Feuerbach and the End of Classical German Philosophy*; *Anti-Dühring*; *Origins of the Family, Private Property, and the State*; and *Dialectics of Nature*. Following the death of Marx in 1883, Engels devoted his time to translating and editing the works of his close friend. Engels died in London, England, August 5, 1890.

**SEE ALSO**
*Volume 1 Left:* Marx, Karl; Socialism; United Kingdom; Germany; Soviet Union; China.
*Volume 2 Right:* Capitalism; *Laissez-Faire.*

**BIBLIOGRAPHY**
Friedrich Engels, *Condition of the Working Class in England in 1844* (Allen & Unwin, 1950 reprint); Friedrich Engels, *The Principles of Communism* (Monthly Review Press, 1952 reprint); Karl Marx and Friedrich Engels, *The Communist Manifesto* (Prometheus Books, 1988 reprint).

IAN MORLEY
MING CHUAN UNIVERSITY, TAIWAN

# Environmentalism

THE LATE 19th and early 20th centuries witnessed growing concern in the United States over the fate of pristine wilderness areas, particularly in western states, as well as the need for conservation of such areas throughout the country. In 1854, Henry David Thoreau's *Walden* advocated a return to a more simple and natural existence. John Muir's travels and writings in the late 19th century were instrumental in setting aside large areas of land for preservation, most notably Yosemite National Park. Muir was also a cofounder of the Sierra Club.

Others, such as Gifford Pinchot, appalled at the rapid exploitation of resources, advocated the need for conservation through the "wise-use" and management of wilderness areas. By the beginning of the 20th century, the concerns of conservationists and preservationists such as Muir and Pinchot were addressed in part by Theodore Roosevelt in the creation of the U.S. Forest Service. Although this new agency did effectively counter much of the wanton destruction of natural wilderness areas, it has historically sided with conservationists and the disagreement between the two sides over preservation and conservation continues in various forums up to the present day.

The period between World War I and the end of World War II saw a marked decrease in public concerns over the state of America's wilderness areas. Such areas were increasingly earmarked for the war efforts and other privatized uses. The economic boom following World War II brought forth rapid technological and industrial growth, increasing consumption, and most no-

*Greenpeace environmental activists try to stop a fishing vessel from operating in the Dogger Bank Marine Preserve (North Sea) by attaching a big plastic buoy to the boat's net.*

tably the rise of an automobile culture. With these changes, however, came few concerns over the environmental effects of such progress. By the end of the late 1950s and early 1960s, with little regulation concerning the use of petrochemicals, automobile and industrial emissions, nuclear power, and increased consumption, serious environmental degradation was occurring not only in America's wilderness areas or its slums, but in all areas of American life.

In the context of burning rivers, polluted air and water, chemical poisonings, and nuclear radioactivity, Rachel Carson published her now seminal book, *Silent Spring*. Although not solely responsible for the already growing concern over environmental degradation, Carson's bestselling work linked growing environmental problems to the multiplying health problems of Americans, as well as to the problems facing all living creatures in an increasingly polluted and toxic ecosystem. In the years immediately following her work, environmental concerns flourished. Importantly, as historian Adam

Rome has argued, these increasing concerns were undoubtedly linked to other political and social changes in the 1960s, including the rise of the New Left, the increasing disenchantment of middle-class women, and the growth of student counterculture movements. By the latter 1960s, the environmental movement was able to distinguish itself clearly enough to draw some 20 million Americans to the first Earth Day in April 1970.

Throughout the late 1960s and 1970s, environmental groups such as the Sierra Club and Audubon Society were so successful in gaining public support that they sponsored and influenced significant legislative environmental protections on the federal, state, and local levels. The most important of these were the Water Quality Act of 1965 and the Clean Water Acts of 1966 and 1972, the Wilderness Act of 1964, the National Environmental Protection Act of 1969, and the establishment in 1970 of the Environmental Protection Agency. These "mainstream" environmental groups utilized public support to effect change through policy. Other groups and movements, however, moved toward more personal or "direct" types of involvement and action.

Often labeled as "radical" by both adversaries and mainstream environmentalists, movements such as Ecofeminism and Deep Ecology, as well as organizations like Earth First! and Greenpeace, sought to counter environmental problems through acute changes in personal lifestyles, philosophies, and direct environmental actions such as protests, "monkeywrenching," and civil disobedience. While these groups and organizations, with the exception of Greenpeace, have remained largely on the fringe of the environmental movement, it is arguable that they have succeeded in legitimizing the agendas of more mainstream environmental organizations.

Although opposition to environmentalism is not new, by the 1980s the environmental movement was facing sophisticated corporate public relations campaigns and numerous legal challenges, as well as the largely unsympathetic Ronald Reagan administration. Numerous grassroots movements, such as the Wise Use Movement, actually funded through corporate and conservative interests, challenged the gains and philosophies of environmentalism as unpatriotic and out of touch with the American public. Multinational corporations began spending millions of dollars on public relations designed to make their activities appear environmentally friendly, all the while seeking to depose large segments of recently passed environmental legislation. With the election of the George W. Bush administration, many of the most important pieces of environmental legislation passed over the last half century were challenged, including the Clean Air and Clean Water Acts, as well as numerous regulations concerning the use of toxic chemicals and logging.

Although polls indicate that public support for environmental issues remains high in the United States and Europe, the environmental movement and its gains are facing serious problems in the near future. The rededication of resources and public attention to the War on Terrorism and national security have shifted funding and visibility away from environmental issues on a domestic level. Over the last two decades, western environmentalists have also faced increasing opposition from developing countries, who seek to modernize and are often opposed to stringent environmental regulations.

On the other hand, environmentalists have made important inroads into building alliances with indigenous communities, labor, urban nonwhite communities, and other groups seeking to broaden the scope and definition of environmental justice. Anti-systemic movements such as those opposed to the International Monetary Fund and World Trade Organization have successfully integrated environmentalism as a key component in their calls for global social justice. The growing global imbalance of resources and wealth will be perhaps the single biggest issue facing environmentalists in the next century, and environmentalism must continue to pursue alliances with like-minded movements and organizations if it is to successfully counter the challenges it currently faces.

**SEE ALSO**

*Volume 1 Left:* Democratic Party; Anti-Globalization.
*Volume 2 Right:* Globalization; Reagan, Ronald.

**BIBLIOGRAPHY**

Robert Gottlieb, *Forcing the Spring* (Island Press, 1993); Adam Rome, "Give Earth a Chance: The Environmental Movement and the Sixties," *The Journal of American History* (v.90/2, September, 2003); Victor Scheffer, *The Shaping of Environmentalism in America* (University of Washington Press, 1991); Jacqueline Vaughn Switzer, *Green Backlash* (Lynne Rienner, 1997).

WILLIAM R. WOOD
BOSTON COLLEGE

# The Left

## Fabianism

GREAT BRITAIN, with its high level of industrialization, commerce, and colonization, had become the world's political superpower in the 19th century. Although the country was home to some of the richest sociopolitical doctrines, including Thomas Hobbes's totalitarianism, John Locke and Adam Smith's liberalism, Edmund Burke's conservatism, and Jeremy Bentham's utilitarianism, the monumental societal changes in the British Empire were creating new intellectual challenges in this period.

As a consequence, at least four influential sociopolitical approaches flourished on British soil almost simultaneously: communism as theorized by Karl Marx and Friedrich Engels, utilitarian liberalism as reinterpreted by John Stuart Mill, social Darwinism as proposed by Herbert Spencer, and finally Fabianism—a brand new and eclectic political program—promoted by a diverse group of British intellectuals. This last philosophy would remain the most "local" of the new sociopolitical approaches. It would not, in any significant way, find a place for itself beyond Britain. Furthermore, while doctrine preceded organization in the other three cases, Fabianism emerged as the attitude developed by a prior organization, namely the Fabian Society.

The Fabian Society was founded in 1883 by a group of concerned intellectuals, including Frank Podmore

and Edward Pease, who were influenced by utopian thinking and found it necessary to explore possibilities for ethical reform in Britain. The society's rise to prominence came with the membership of writer George Bernard Shaw in 1884, followed by Sidney Webb in 1885 and such influential names as Emmeline Pankhurst, H.G. Wells, Beatrice Potter (later Webb), Graham Wallas, Annie Besant, and Leonard Woolf at around the same time. The name Fabian was derived from Quintus Fabius Maximus, the notable Roman general of the Second Punic War. Fabius was famous for avoiding full engagement with Carthaginians, preferring to weaken them by harassing operations. In a similar vein, the Fabian Society believed that success required a piecemeal approach, social appeal, and patience. These ideas were systematically elaborated in the famous *Fabian Essays* of 1889 and later popularized in more than 200 *Fabian Tracts*.

Fabians were professed socialists and the society was clearly placed on a socialist basis in their policy statement in 1887. However, not only did early Fabianism stand in sharp contrast with Marxism, but also it had little to do with revisionist versions of the Marxian movement, namely variants of continental social democracy. Fabianism completely refused the Marxist idea that the transformation of society could be achieved by revolution. Instead, the idea of evolution was promoted. Socialism, Fabians believed, would

*George Bernard Shaw brought notoriety to the socialist intellectuals of the United KIngdom's Fabian Society in 1844.*

the Fabian Society and the Labour Party, and today the society continues to serve the Labour Party as a supportive yet critical think tank.

**SEE ALSO**
*Volume 1 Left:* Labour Party, UK; Socialism; Social Democracy.
*Volume 2 Right:* United Kingdom; Conservative Party, UK.

**BIBLIOGRAPHY**
P. Beilharz, *Labour's Utopias: Bolshevism, Fabianism, Social Democracy* (Routledge, 1992); M. Cole, *The Story of Fabian Socialism* (Heinemann, 1961); R. C. Macridis, *Contemporary Political Ideologies: Movements and Regimes* (Winthrop Publishers, 1980); A.M. McBriar, *Fabian Socialism and English Politics, 1884–1918* (Cambridge University Press, 1966).

ESREF AKSU
INDEPENDENT SCHOLAR

come as the natural sequel to the full realization of universal suffrage and representative government. Sidney Webb, their main theorist of the "inevitability of gradualness," for instance, regarded the social reforms of the 19th century (for example, factory, mines, housing, and education laws) as the beginnings of socialism.

Equally fundamental was the society's rejection of the Marxian theory of value in favor of David Ricardo's law of rent and other views on utility. On the other hand, Fabianism, especially in its early years, did not identify itself with the working class the way continental social democracy did. Yet, the help of the Fabian Society in the creation and development of the British Labour Party is undeniable; the Society saw no inconsistency in having members associated with diverse political organizations. By the same token, while several European socialists opposed their government's involvement in the World War I, the majority of the Fabians gave explicit support to British participation in the war.

In general, there was a detectable pragmatic aspect to Fabianism. Permeation appeared as the cardinal Fabian principle in every sphere of activity. Fabianism did not find it useful to distinguish between socialists and nonsocialists, because the aim was to influence as many institutions as possible, as much as possible, and as smoothly as possible. Following World War II, a tighter relationship progressively developed between

# Feminism

AT ITS CORE, feminism is an ideology based on equality. Feminist ideology demands that women be granted legal, political, and social rights that have been denied throughout history. While feminist scholars have identified a number of different types of feminism, individuals who are consciously feminist tend to be either liberal or radical. Both liberal and radical feminists believe that patriarchy is the cause of inequality, but they disagree on how to deal with the problems caused by inequities. Liberal feminists are committed to using the existing political system to implement reforms, while radical feminists are willing to eliminate the existing system if it interferes with their goals. Unconscious feminists are those who accept the goals of feminism without identifying with feminist ideology.

Feminists believe that the patriarchal system divided males and females into the public and the private worlds. The public world of men invested them with the power to make decisions for themselves and for others. Women were relegated to the private world in which they had no power.

In 1675, William Blackstone solidified English common law in *Commentaries on the Laws of England.* Blackstone's work codified the concept of coverture, which controlled the lives of women in England and America for centuries. *Femme sole* provided a legal basis for limited rights for single women. *Femme covert*, on the other hand, stipulated that a married woman was "covered" by her husband, with no separate legal identity. Property that a woman owned before marriage or that she inherited afterward belonged to her husband, and he could do with it as he wished. Guardianship of children was also in the hands of fathers, who could will the guardianship of children away from their mothers. Women could not sue or be sued. They could not testify in court or serve on juries. They could not have bank accounts.

In many jurisdictions, a man had the right to "punish" his wife by beating her with a board as long as the size of the board was no thicker than his thumb. Hence, the "rule of thumb." Divorce laws were unheard of, and women were forced to remain married to drunken, abusive, or absent husbands. Women had no control of their own bodies. They were legally bound to be receptive to their husband's sexual appetites. Knowledge of birth control was sketchy and generally illegal. Many women gave birth year after year until their bodies simply gave out. The bodies of female slaves were considered "property," and female slaves were often raped. Slave children could be taken from their mothers and sold, never to be seen again.

Poor women and slaves received little or no education, and the education of middle- and upper-class women was often limited to basic skills and so-called feminine arts. Without education and job skills, single women were often dependent on male relatives for their very livelihood. Even after women began to be educated, many professions such as law and medicine were closed to them. Without the right to vote, women had no political voice, so there was little they could do to change the patriarchal system that controlled their lives.

## EARLY FEMINISM

In the United States, one of the first written examples of feminism appeared in a letter from Abigail Adams to her husband, John, attending the Second Continental Congress. She wrote, "I desire you would remember the ladies and be more generous and favorable to them than your ancestors," and threatened to foment a rebellion to free women from male tyranny. Adams and the other Founding Fathers dismissed her words, and the new government granted rights only to white males.

By the early 19th century, women in the United States and England were awakening to the injustices of political systems that ignored their rights. In 1792, in response to the increased attention to the rights of man in

the United States, England, and France, Mary Wollstonecraft published *A Vindication of the Rights of Woman*. She introduced the unprecedented idea that women often acted silly and dependent because they were socialized into doing so, not because such behavior was innate. Wollstonecraft suggested that education was the key to awakening the true nature of women, who would then be treated as rational beings rather than as emotional beings. Wollstonecraft influenced the feminist views of English philosopher/economist John Stuart Mill, the first male philosopher to openly endorse the rights of women. In 1869, in *The Subjection of Women*, Mill wrote that the nature of woman was like a tree that had been forced to grow in a certain way rather than allowing it to follow its own instincts. Like Wollstonecraft, Mill believed that women were capable of rationality and acknowledged their right to equality.

## FIRST WAVE

Surprisingly, two sisters from Charleston, South Carolina, were among the first to openly challenge the idea that women were destined to remain in the private world of hearth and home. Ardent abolitionists Sarah and Angelina Grimké ignored laws forbidding women to speak in public and spoke out for the right for women and slaves to be free. Margaret Fuller also openly acknowledged her feminist views. In 1845, Fuller, a transcendentalist, published *Woman in the Nineteenth Century*, which became a manifesto for First Wave feminists.

Women in the First Wave were familiar with the works of Wollstonecraft, Mill, and Fuller. The early movement arose among abolitionist women who were appalled at the discrimination of women within the anti-slavery movement. As a result, Elizabeth Cady Stanton and Lucretia Mott organized the Seneca Falls Convention in 1848, calling for an end to coverture and demanding female suffrage, reproductive rights, and greater access to education and employment. Susan B. Anthony also took up the fight and leadership for women's suffrage.

From 1848 to 1920, feminists made female suffrage the top priority. Even though one faction of the suffrage movement worked for a constitutional amendment while another worked for state-by-state suffrage, all feminists understood that suffrage was the key to both political and social reform. At the beginning of the 20th century, the founders of the women's suffrage movement were replaced by younger women. Carrie Chapman Catt led the liberal wing, while Alice Paul guided the radical faction toward active protests that included marches, pickets, parades, and hunger strikes.

Reproductive rights for women also remained a feminist issue in the early 20th century. Margaret Sanger emerged as the leader in this movement, arguing that birth control should be available to all women. Sanger had seen many women die in childbirth or from too many pregnancies. She ran into opposition from Anthony Comstock, who had succeeded in making it illegal to send "obscene" material through the mail. Birth control material met his definition of obscenity, and Sanger and other feminists were arrested for dispensing birth control material and devices.

The outbreak of World War I saw unprecedented numbers of women enter the labor market. Many women worked in jobs essential to the war effort, even though they were normally considered only suitable for males. As a result, in 1920, after the war, changed perceptions of women's roles provided the final push toward the passage of the Nineteenth Amendment, named for Susan B. Anthony. Once the vote was achieved, interest in feminism decreased, leading to what became known as a "feminist wasteland." Persistent feminists focused their attention on the passage of the Equal Rights Amendment (ERA), which was endorsed by both the Democrats and Republicans in 1940. However, the rejuvenation of domesticity after World War II relegated the issue to the backburner.

In 1949, feminists around the globe were galvanized by the publication of Simone de Beauvoir's *The Second Sex*, which identified woman as "the other," defined according to how woman differed from man rather than by her own nature. In the United States, feminists made only incremental progress toward equality. In 1961, President John Kennedy created the President's Commission on the Status of Women, chaired by former First Lady Eleanor Roosevelt. The group targeted sex discrimination and inequalities in a number of areas and called for reforms in politics, law, employment, and education.

## SECOND WAVE

The second wave of the women's movement began with the publication of Betty Friedan's *The Feminine Mystique* in 1963. Friedan, a white middle-class, college-educated woman, identified what she said had been "the problem without a name." Friedan believed that women were dissatisfied with their lives because they had lost their identities as a result of the post-World War II anti-feminism that pushed women back into the homes and made them feel that wife and mother were their only viable roles. Responding to feminist pressure, in 1963 Congress passed the Equal Pay Act, which mandated similar salaries for men and women in the same jobs. At the time, women made 64 cents for every dollar that men made. Unfortunately, changes in the law did not prevent employers, who were convinced that men deserved a "family wage," from rewriting male job descriptions and paying men higher wages.

When Congress voted on the Civil Rights Act of 1964, designed to ban racial discrimination in employment, feminists convinced Howard W. Smith, a supporter of women's rights but not of civil rights, to add the word "sex" to Title VII of the act. Smith thought his amendment would kill the bill. It did not, and sexual discrimination was banned also. The result was a plethora of sex-discrimination suits.

In 1966, Friedan and Gloria Steinem came together with a group of other feminists to found the National Organization for Women (NOW). As the voice of the modern women's movement, NOW focused attention on discrimination in the areas of law, employment, and education. They called for increased attention to women's issues, including reproductive rights, subsidized childcare, divorce, rape, domestic violence, sex discrimination, sexual harassment, and sexual orientation. Working with the National Women's Political Caucus, EMILY's List (Early Money Is Like Yeast), and the Congressional Caucus for Women's Issues, NOW promoted the election of women to political office and called for greater emphasis on women's issues by both males and females at all levels of politics.

Increased interest in the women's movement resulted in the resurgence of the Equal Rights Amendment. NOW forced ERA out of committee in 1971, and the amendment passed both houses of Congress. By 1978, 38 states had ratified the amendment, three short of the required number. Due to organized opposition, the amendment was never ratified. Despite the failure of ERA, bans against sexual discrimination were enacted by Congress and solidified by a number of landmark Supreme Court cases. In 1971, in *Reed v. Reed* (404 U.S. 71), the court banned arbitrary classifications by sex and began to carefully review sex discrimination cases.

The publication of Kate Millet's *Sexual Politics* in 1970 led to a call among some feminists for androgyny. The idea was to deemphasize gender differences by playing up the similarities in males and females. In 1975, Susan Brownmiller published *Against Our Will: Men, Women, and Rape*, which proposed the idea that rape was about power rather than sex. The book paved the way for legislation giving rape victims greater protection and generated calls for government funding of rape crisis centers. Some reforms were detrimental, as with "no-fault" divorce laws that led to the "feminization of poverty," leaving many divorced women and their children impoverished.

The most explosive issue of the Second Wave turned out to be abortion. In 1965, in *Griswold v. Connecticut* (381 U.S. 479), the Supreme Court held that the right to privacy gave married women the right to obtain birth control. *Griswold* paved the way for the constitutional right of women to obtain an abortion established in 1973 in *Roe v. Wade* (410 U.S. 113). From the beginning, the abortion issue pitted feminists who argue that women have a right to control their reproductive lives against those who give priority to the fetus. During the 1980s, Presidents Ronald Reagan and George H.W. Bush determined to appoint only Supreme Court nominees who opposed abortion. Feminists believed that conservatives would win the battle, but in 1992 in *Planned Parenthood of Southeastern Pennsylvania v. Casey* (505 U.S. 833), the court upheld *Roe* with some restrictions. However, the abortion battle was far from over.

## THIRD WAVE

Harking back to Wollstonecraft and Mill, Third Wave feminists continued to deal with the arguments while bringing new ideas to the concept of feminism. Opponents of feminism argued that nature had designed women to play a subservient role that centered on reproduction. Feminists argued that femininity was the result of socialization. The publication of Naomi Wolf's *The Beauty Myth: How Images of Beauty Are Used against Women* in 1991 called attention to the practice of forcing women to conform to the image of "feminine beauty." Feminists identified the so-called Barbie Doll syndrome that taught girls from an early age that they should look a certain way. Studies on the subject revealed that girls began dieting while in elementary school to fit the beauty mold. Carol Gilligan's studies dealing with the socialization of young girls suggested that parents and teachers enforced gender stereotypes that led to problems with self-confidence as girls reached puberty. Deborah Tannen's work on male and female communication explored the differences in the way males and females approached the workplace. Judith Wallerstein's studies on divorce provided significant understanding of the impact of divorce on American society.

Third Wave feminists pledged to fight the effects of Reagan's conservative policies and to mitigate the effects of his cuts to social programs that effectively decimated many programs designed to help poor women and their children. Sexual harassment became a major issue in 1991 amid allegation that George W. Bush Supreme Court nominee Clarence Thomas had sexually harassed Anita Hill, a law professor who had worked for him years before. Equal pay continued to be a rallying cry for feminists who developed the idea of comparable worth based on job rankings intended to eradicate the invalidation of female-dominated occupations. Feminists also called for flexibility in employment, family leave, and increased attention to childcare.

Feminists have often echoed the words of Henrik Ibsen's protagonist in *A Doll's House*. During a period of soul-searching in which the character begins to develop her idea of self, she tells her husband, "Before everything else, I'm a human being."

## SEE ALSO

*Volume 1 Left:* Friedan, Betty; Steinem, Gloria; Anthony, Susan B.; Civil Rights.
*Volume 2 Right:* Religion; Bush, George W.; Thomas, Clarence.

## BIBLIOGRAPHY

"Abigail Adams to John Adams, March 31, 1776," www.thelizlibrary.org/suffrage (May 2004); Susan Faludi, *Backlash: The Undeclared War against American Women* (Crown, 1991); Betty Friedan, *The Feminine Mystique* (W.W. Norton, 1963); Margaret Fuller, "Woman in the Nineteenth Century," www.vcu.edu (May 2004); Joanne Hollows, *Feminism, Feminists, and Popular Culture* (St. Martin's, 2000); Henrik Ibsen, *A Doll's House,* http://onlinebooks.library.upenn.edu (May 2004); Ethel Klein, *Gender Politics* (Harvard University Press, 1984); Wendy McElroy, *Liberty for Women: Freedom and Feminism in the Twenty-First Century* (Ivan R. Dee, 2002); Rebecca Merrill Groothus, *Women Caught in the Conflict: The Culture War between Traditionalism and Feminism* (Baker Books, 1994); John Stuart Mill, *The Subjection of Women,* http://cepa.newschool.edu (May 2004); Kate Millett, *Sexual Politics* (Doubleday, 1970); Judith S. Wallerstein and Sandra Blakeslee, *Second Chances: Men, Women, and Children: A Decade after Divorce* (Tichnor and Fields, 1990); Naomi Wolf, *The Beauty Myth: How Images of Beauty Are Used against Women* (Morrow, 1991); Mary Wollstonecraft, *A Vindication of the Rights of Woman,* www.bartleby.com (May 2004).

ELIZABETH PURDY, PH.D.
INDEPENDENT SCHOLAR

# First Amendment

DURING THE DEBATES in the Constitutional Convention in 1787 in Philadelphia, Pennsylvania, the 29 delegates were heatedly divided into two camps. These were the Federalists, like Alexander Hamilton of New York, who advocated a strongly centralized government, and the anti-Federalists, among the most influential, George Mason of Virginia, who preferred a more decentralized administration, such as had prevailed under the earlier 1777 Articles of Confederation. In terms of the relationship between the new government and its people, no area was of more importance than a Bill of Rights. Such a document was considered essential in protecting the rights of the people from usurpation by their own government. In the debates, Mason was concerned that an unfettered government could become a "monarchy, or a tyrannical aristocracy." Before the Constitution was signed on September 17, 1787, delegates like Elbridge Gerry of Massachusetts and George Mason of Virginia would not sign until they had received a promise that a Bill of Rights would follow.

In the debates that followed on ratifying the Constitution by the states, the need for a Bill of Rights attracted widespread support. During the Virginia debates, the concern was voiced that "there be a declaration or bill of rights asserting, and securing from encroachment, the essential and unalienable rights of the people." "Brutus" wrote in the New York Journal on October 18, 1787, that "in so extensive a republic, the great officers of government would soon become above the control of the people, and abuse their power to the purpose of aggrandizing themselves, and oppressing them." Even after Pennsylvania's ratification convention voted to approve the Constitution on December 12, 1787, some members were deeply concerned about its fundamental lack of a guarantee for individual freedom. On December 18, 1787, 21 of them signed a dissent, which appeared in the *Pennsylvania Packet and Daily Advertiser*. In the article, they stated, "the first consideration ... is the omission of a bill of rights, ascertaining and fundamentally establishing those unalienable and personal rights of men, without the full, free, and secure enjoyment of which there can be no liberty."

By July 1788, New Hampshire had ratified the Constitution, and the arena for debate about the Bill of Rights moved into the new United States Congress, with its upper chamber, the Senate, and lower, the House of Representatives.

Within the Congress, James Madison of Virginia, and a future president, had become convinced of the utter necessity of a Bill of Rights. The National Archives and Records Administration (NARA) web site on the Constitution states, "by the fall of 1788 Madison had been convinced that not only was a bill of rights necessary to ensure acceptance of the Constitution but that it would have positive effects. He wrote, on October 17, that such "fundamental maxims of free Government" would be "a good ground for an appeal to the sense of community" against potential oppression and would "counteract the impulses of interest and passion."

Elected as a delegate to the First Congress held under the new Constitution, Madison worked tirelessly for the passage of a Bill of Rights. Originally, 17 articles—or amendments—were debated. Eventually, 12 possible amendments were drawn up, as the framers had with great foresight provided a framework for amending the Constitution during the convention. On September 25, 1789, the 12 amendments were submitted to the states for a second ratification procedure. The National Archives observed that "The first two proposed amendments, which concerned the number of constituents for each Representative and the compensation of Congressmen, were not ratified."

At the time, the question of the "number of constituents" may have only served to undermine the public support for the Constitution and the new federal government it had created. The question of compensation—or salary—for the Congressmen was not considered because at that time it was not envisioned that Congressmen would serve that long within the legislative branch of the government. It was assumed they would serve, perhaps for only a brief period, and then, like the delegates who had worked on the Constitution itself, return to their previous occupations. On October 2, 1789, President George Washington, who himself had played a role in the Constitutional Convention, offered the 12 amendments for ratification by the states. The enthusiasm for a Bill of Rights was dramatically shown by the fact that by December 15, 1791, the necessary states had already cast their votes to ratify the nation's new Bill of Rights.

Therefore, the original Third Amendment of the bill now became the First, which states: "Congress shall make no law respecting an establishment of religion, or prohibiting the free exercise thereof; or abridging the freedom of speech, or of the press; or the right of the people peaceably to assemble, and to petition the Government for a redress of grievances." There have been few such simple paragraphs that have exerted such a profound impression on the course of human events than this First Amendment. Not only did it look forward to cast a bright light on freedom in the future, but it also cast a wary eye on the past, when such liberties did, in Mason's words, more often than not hinge on the whim of a "monarchy, or a tyrannical aristocracy."

Madison and Mason could look back on 150 years of constitutional struggle both in England and the United States over the very assurances for civil liberty that the First Amendment contained. Indeed, one could trace the constitutional history back further yet. From the time of the reign of King Henry VIII, the Anglican, or Episcopalian, Church had been considered the "established" church. All the subjects in England, and later in the English colonies in the New World, were supposed to contribute to its support, no matter what the dictates of their consciences in religious matters.

It was in the New World that the idea of real freedom of religion would take root in the 17th century, and then only gradually. The prohibitions against Roman Catholicism and the so-called Dissenters, like the Presbyterians, were carried over to the English colonies with the first settlers. Among the rigorous Puritans in the commonwealth of Massachusetts Bay, Dissenters, Catholics, and Quakers (members of the Society of Friends) could be severely beaten for attempting the exercise of their religion.

It was not until William Penn, himself a convert to George Fox's Society of Friends, founded his colony of Pennsylvania in 1682 that the colonies found a true haven for freedom of religious expression. When the first Pennsylvania legislature met in 1682–83, the remembrance of the persecution the Quakers themselves had suffered was fresh in the delegates' minds. Therefore heading the list of these fundamental statutes was Penn's law protecting freedom of conscience. Under this guarantee thousands of members of unpopular Christian sects were able to escape from the persecutions of the Old World. Unlike many people who have suffered restrictions on their freedoms, the Quakers had no wish to impose similar restrictions on others once they had the power."

Over the next century, the idea of religious tolerance gradually spread over the United States—but nowhere except in Pennsylvania was it enshrined in law. It would not be until the era of the American Revolution when the idea became truly broad-based. Gary Taylor and Helen Hawley wrote in "Freedom of Religion in America" in *Contemporary Review* in 2003 that "The American liberal perspective on religion, which is enshrined in the American Constitution, can be seen in the views of James Madison and Thomas Jefferson. Madison claimed in 1785 that our religious sensibilities must be left to our own conscience, and that we must have the right to live and believe according to its dictates. This was described as an 'unalienable right.'" Only with the ratification of the Bill of Rights in 1791 did the United States as a whole catch up to Pennsylvania in the essential right of religious freedom.

The rights of freedom of the press, of speech, and of assembly were only won after nearly 150 years of strife in England and the United States, an image that belies the conservative view that such freedoms evolved gradually, with peace, good fellowship, and Port wine.

King Charles I had attempted to rule without Parliament for some 11 years. In April 1640, Charles called it, needing it to raise funds for his war with Scotland. However, Parliament used its open forum to press for more civil rights for the English people and more say in the government of the kingdom. In March 1642, Charles entered with armed troops to seize the leaders of Parliament's press for more representation, Henry Pym and four others. Warned in advance, they had fled the king's wrath. The resulting English Civil War pitted those who championed the Crown against those who looked on Parliament as the better guarantor of their freedoms. However, when the war ended with the execution of King Charles in London in January 1649, those backing Parliament lost out. The Parliamentary Army, led by Sir Thomas Fairfax and Oliver Cromwell, effectively usurped Parliament. Under Oliver Cromwell's rule as Lord Protector, England effectively became the modern world's true military dictatorship, the "rule of the major generals." When Cromwell died in 1658, few mourned him. In May 1660, his son was called from exile in the Netherlands to rule as Charles II. During his 25-year reign, Charles II accustomed himself to ruling in conjunction with Parliament. He in fact, due to his personal affection for Roman Catholicism, attempted to introduce religious freedom into England but, as the BBC notes, "The King's desire for religious toleration ... was overwhelmed by the new parliament. Royalist in nature, they passed the Clarendon code, which ensured Anglicanism as the state religion and threatened non-conformists. Charles II tried to increase religious tolerance with his Declaration of Indulgence, but was forced to withdraw it."

When Charles II died, his brother, James, Duke of York, took the throne of England. Not only was he a Roman Catholic, but he had the absolutist tendencies of his father Charles II. In June 1685, James, Duke of Monmouth, Charles' Protestant son, invaded England.

Defeated at Sedgmoor by royalist forces in July, Monmouth asked his uncle for clemency, but the king had him beheaded. The trials and executions of those who supported Monmouth, the "bloody assizes" in September, marked James as a ruthless ruler.

The Declaration of Indulgence (1687) granted tolerance of Catholics and nonconformists. In response, both Tories and Whigs turned against the king in the Glorious Revolution of 1688. In November 1688, James's Protestant daughter, with her husband, William of Orange, the Stadtholder (ruler) of the Netherlands, invaded England. James was overthrown and William and Mary took the throne. However, they could not begin to rule until they gave their assent to Parliament's Declaration of Rights, which, according to the BBC, "stated that parliaments had to meet frequently, that elections should be free and fair, that the debates in parliament should be subject to freedom of speech and that parliamentary consent was required to levy taxation and maintain standing armies."

During the next century, the English colonies' public lives thrived on these freedoms, hard-won in England. The colonists considered themselves Englishmen, and endowed with the same constitutional rights. When King George III began to threaten those rights after the end of the French and Indian War in 1763, the colonists zealously defended them. In April 1775, the American Revolution began at Lexington and Concord in defense of them.

The Declaration of Independence was written, and enacted on July 4, 1776, because the colonists believed that George III had irrevocably taken away from them the rights that Englishmen had fought two other kings, Charles I and James II, to gain. As Thomas Jefferson wrote in the Declaration, "whenever any Form of Government becomes destructive of these ends, it is the Right of the People to alter or to abolish it, and to institute new Government."

The United States of America became truly independent with the Treaty of Paris in September 1783. The frame of its new government was established under the Constitution. But it was not until the Bill of Rights, with the powerful First Amendment, was ratified in December 1791 that Americans could rest assured that their own civil liberties had been truly won.

**SEE ALSO**

*Volume 1 Left:* Bill of Rights; Constitutional Amendments; United States; Liberalism.
*Volume 2 Right:* Conservatism; Second Amendment; United States.

**BIBLIOGRAPHY**

Pennsylvania Historical and Museum Commission, "William Penn in Pennsylvania," www.dep.state.pa.us (July 2004); Frederic Austin Ogg, *The Opening of the Mississippi* (Cooper Square, 1968); "The Bill of Rights: Archiving Early America," www.earlyamerica.com (July 2004); Ernest R. May, ed., *The Ultimate Decision: The President as Commander in Chief* (Braziller, 1960); Ralph Ketcham, ed., *The Anti-Federalist Papers and the Constitutional Convention Debates* (Mentor Books, 1986); The National Archives Experience, "The Charters of Freedom," www.archives.gov (July 2004); Christopher Collier and James Lincoln Collier, *Decision in Philadelphia: the Constitutional Convention of 1787* (Ballantine, 1986); Leonard Kriegel, ed., *Essential Works of the Founding Fathers* (Bantam, 1964); John A. Garatty, *The American Nation: a History of the United States* (Harper and Row, 1966); Richard A. Kohn, *Eagle and Sword: The Beginnings of the Military Establishment in America* (Free Press, 1975); Walter Millis, *Arms and Men: A Study of American Military History* (Mentor Books, 1956).

JOHN F. MURPHY, JR.
AMERICAN MILITARY UNIVERSITY

# First International

THE INTERNATIONAL Workingmen's Association, established under the leadership of English Trade Council activists in London, England, in 1864, was the first notable international socialist/communist organization. The association lasted for little more than a decade, and with the emergence of its successor movements, came to be referred to as the First International. In addition to Karl Marx, the leader of the association, notable figures of the First International included Mikhail Bakunin, Johann Becker, Friedrich Engels, Ernest Jones, Paul Lafargue, Wilhelm Liebknecht, William Morris, and Adolph Sorge.

Article 1 of its constitution declared that the International was "established to afford a central medium of communication and cooperation between Workingmen's Societies in different countries and aiming at the same end: the protection, advancement, and complete emancipation of the working classes." At the practical level, the association tried to accomplish solidarity between workers engaged in strikes, demonstrations, and other kinds of struggles with employers across different sectors and countries. The long-term aim, however, was much greater, hence more difficult to achieve: to establish a truly international class consciousness among the world's workers and to organize a permanent international class struggle against the capitalist system. Perhaps inevitably, the scale of this ambition would soon cause several disagreements among the International's membership as to appropriate methods and strategic priorities.

The first important ideological battle occurred between followers of Pierre-Joseph Proudhon and Marx. Proudhonists were opposed to trade unions and strikes. They propagated the principle of mutualism. Marx successfully made the case that the Proudhonist approach dangerously reduced the problem of emancipation into the question of wages and hours. While the Basel Congress of 1869 affirmed Marx's victory over Proudhonists, it also paved the way for a more significant controversy. Mikhail Bakunin, who had left the International following his brief membership in 1864, made a reappearance at this congress. He was not only the respected theorist of anarchism, but also a dedicated activist, hence a strong rival for Marx. In Bakunin's view, Marx exaggerated the importance of the working class as a revolutionary agent. Perhaps more fundamentally, Bakunin did not believe in organized "political" struggle, criticizing the necessity of proletarian conquest of power. Destruction, in his view, was inherently constructive. Once the existing social order was destroyed, everything would automatically take care of itself.

The Marx-Bakunin debate would change complexion in the early 1870s when the International's intellectual and material capabilities were put to a test in France. Home to the successful bourgeois revolution of 1789, France witnessed a proletarian revolution attempt in 1871 when a sizeable group of French activists tried to establish a commune in Paris. While the presence and efforts of the First International gave encouragement to the commune experiment, the organization's role in this entire episode remained limited. The ultimate failure of the Paris Commune triggered harsh debates in the International.

For Marx the commune experiment proved that the proletariat had to create its own state apparatus in order to achieve success. For Bakunin, it merely proved the necessity of making persistent and successive commune attempts. The Congress of 1872 not only gave overwhelming support to Marx's interpretation of events, it also expelled Bakunin from the International over multiple political and personal motives and incidents. The International's status had weakened considerably in this process. In addition, even simple membership in the International was arousing suspicion in several European capitals after the commune episode. In France, for instance, membership was held as a crime. Under these circumstances, the headquarters of the association were transferred to New York City, but this move would not suffice to prevent the International's eventual demise in 1876.

**SEE ALSO**

*Volume 1 Left:* Paris Commune; Marx, Karl; Communism; Second International; Third International (Comintern); Cominform.
*Volume 2 Right:* France.

**BIBLIOGRAPHY**

J. Braunthal, *History of the International, Vol 1: 1864–1914* (Praeger, 1961); H. Gerth, *The First International: Minutes of the Hague Congress of 1872* (University of Wisconsin Press, 1958); W. D. McClellan, *Revolutionary Exiles: the Russians in the First International and the Paris Commune* (Frank Cass, 1979); D. Riazanov, "Karl Marx and Frederick Engels: An Introduction to Their Lives and Work," http://csf.colorado.edu (March 2004).

ESREF AKSU
INDEPENDENT SCHOLAR

# Flynn, Elizabeth Gurley (1890–1964)

ELIZABETH GURLEY FLYNN was born in Concord, New Hampshire. Raised by socialist parents committed to activism, at the age of 16 she gave her first speech, "What Socialism Will Do for Women," at the Harlem Socialist Club, which resulted in her expulsion from high school.

In 1907, she became a full-time organizer for Industrial Workers of the World (IWW) and became active in campaigning for the rights of garment workers in Pennsylvania, silk weavers in New Jersey, restaurant workers in New York, miners in Minnesota, and textile workers in Lawrence, Massachusetts. During the Lawrence strike, she was instrumental in organizing women to participate and support the strike despite male prejudices that strike activity was not appropriate for women. She was arrested 10 times for her work, but never convicted. During this period of her life, the writer Theodore Dreiser described her as an "East Side Joan of Arc."

Flynn used every opportunity to spread the message about workers and women's rights. As a renowned orator, she saw the importance of labor court trials as an organizing medium and a way to spread the message about workers' rights to more people. She participated in free speech fights in Missoula, Montana (1908) and Spokane, Washington (1909–10). She also gave street-corner speeches and more formal presentations. She was an ardent defender of labor and political agitators facing deportation and organized the Workers' Defense League to fight for victims of the post-World War I Red Scare.

Flynn was also a founding member of the American Civil Liberties Union (ACLU). Ironically, given the focus of the ACLU on protecting civil liberties, she was later expelled from the group for her activities with the Communist Party, but the expulsion was rescinded in 1978. In 1936, inspired by achievements of the Russian Revolution, she joined the Communist Party and wrote a feminist column for the party paper, *The Daily Worker*. Two years later, she was elected to the national committee. In 1942, she ran for Congress in New York and received 50,000 votes, an unexpectedly large number.

In July 1948, 12 leaders of the Communist Party were arrested and accused of supporting the overthrow of the U.S. government through force, a violation of the Alien Registration Act (also called the Smith Act), which makes it illegal for anyone in the United States to advocate, abet, or teach the desirability of overthrowing the government. The main objective of the act was to undermine the Communist Party and other left-wing political organizations. Flynn actively campaigned for the release of the 12, but in June 1951, she was arrested in a second wave of arrests and charged with violations under the Alien Registration Act. She spent two years in a women's penitentiary, which she immortalized in *The Alderson Story: My Life as a Political Prisoner*. In 1961, she became the national chairperson of the Communist Party. She made several visits to the Soviet Union and died there in September 1964 while working on her autobiography. Flynn was given a state funeral in Red Square, and her remains were returned to the United States.

Flynn is remembered for her lifelong fight for women's rights and socialism, and particularly for the relationship between the two. She supported birth control and women's suffrage, and criticized trade unions for being dominated by male leadership and ignoring women's issues within the workplace. She argued for in-dustrializing domestic tasks though collective kitchens, dining places, nurseries, and laundries. Flynn believed that capitalism denied women equal opportunity. She believed that the state should provide for the care of children so that women are not dependent upon the support of men while they are in their child-bearing years. She challenged the opinions of some of the male activists who believed women should be supporting the men in their work, rather than fighting for workers rights. She was a tireless campaigner for the rights of women.

**SEE ALSO**

*Volume 1 Left:* Suffragists; Paul, Alice; Socialism; Russian Revolution; Communist Party.
*Volume 2 Right:* Capitalism; Ideology; McCarthyism.

**BIBLIOGRAPHY**

R. F. Baxandall, ed., *Words on Fire: The Life and Writing of Elizabeth Gurley Flynn* (Rutgers University Press, 1987); Elizabeth Gurley Flynn, *The Rebel Girl, an Autobiography: My First Life 1906–26* (International Publishers, 1973); Elizabeth Gurley Flynn, *The Alderson Story: My Life as a Political Prisoner* (International Publishers, 1963).

SHANNON K. ORR
BOWLING GREEN STATE UNIVERSITY

# Foster, William Z. (1881–1961)

THOUGH HE DID NOT join the American Communist Party (CPUSA or CP) until he was 40 years old, William Z. Foster rose quickly through the ranks. Already a veteran of class-war struggles, he was the CP's first-ever presidential candidate, in 1924; after World War II, and a series of ideological battles, he was named the party's top leader, only to face the threat of criminal prosecution for advocating the overthrow of the government.

Born in Taunton, Massachusetts, to poor immigrants who had 23 children (his father was Irish, his mother British) and raised in Philadelphia, Pennsylvania, Foster was selling newspapers on the street by age 7. He spent his youth working at a series of odd jobs; in each case, he later claimed, he organized the workers, only to be detected by company spies and fired. He joined the Socialist Party at age 19, only to quit because it was too moderate; other accounts say he was expelled for his membership in its left-wing faction. In any case, he joined the radical International Workers of the World (IWW, or the "Wobblies"), and became one of its top organizers, often participating in violent strikes and confrontations; at one point, he was nearly lynched in Montana—a fate that befell one of his fellow organizers.

Nationally known after mobilizing a steelworkers strike in 1919, he founded a propaganda organization, the Trade Union Education League, and was invited to an international trade-union congress in Moscow, Soviet Union. Upon his return, he joined the fledgling U.S. Communist Party. Despite early suspicion of his background, including willing testimony before a Senate committee during the steel strike, he soon became one of its stars—aided largely by his native birth and accent, which the party desperately needed to showcase. By 1930, he had risen to the position of general secretary; that same year, he was arrested after participating in a New York demonstration and served six months in prison.

His hard-line commitment to Stalinist ideology cost him influence within the party by the mid-1930s, when Moscow decreed establishment of the Popular Front, which called for cooperation with liberal, nonradical groups. He resumed a leadership post following the Nazi-Soviet pact of 1939, which he fervently defended, but was deposed again in 1941 after Hitler invaded the Soviet Union. Twice during the war, in 1939 and again in 1945, Foster was called to testify before the House Committee on Un-American Activities. Challenged during his first appearance to identify "any decision" that the Communist Party had taken that "conflicted with the decision of the [Soviet-led] Comintern," Foster was forced to confess, "Well, no, I cannot—no major decision."

In 1945, party leader Earl Browder was purged as the Comintern ordered a more hard-line, ideologically based struggle that was more in tune with Foster's policies and he was made the head of the party. In 1948, he and 11 other top party leaders were indicted for violating the Smith Act, charged with conspiring to teach and advocate the violent overthrow of the U.S. government; Foster was spared prosecution on medical grounds.

With the fall of Josef Stalin and the shift in Soviet line that denounced his policies, Foster again lost influence within the party and he finally retired in 1956. After a legal fight, he was finally given a passport in 1960 so that he could go to Moscow for medical treatment, and he died there of a paralytic stroke. Throughout his career, Foster made no claim to independent thinking. On the contrary: "I am for the Comintern from start to finish," he declared in 1925. "And if the Comintern finds itself criss-cross with my opinions, there is only one thing to do and that is to change my opinion to fit the policy of the Comintern."

**SEE ALSO**

*Volume 1 Left:* Cominform; Communist Party; Stalin and Stalinism.
*Volume 2 Right:* McCarthyism; Conservatism; Cold War.

**BIBLIOGRAPHY**

Theodore Draper, *The Roots of American Communism* (Ivan R. Dee, 1957, 1985); Irving Howe and Lewis Coser, *The American Communist Party: A Critical History* (Beacon Press, 1957); Walter Goodman, *The Committee* (Farrar, Straus and Giroux, 1968); Harvey Klehr and John Earl Haynes, *The American Communist Movement: Storming Heaven Itself* (Twayne, 1992); Herbert Romerstein and Eric Breindel, *The Venona Secrets* (Regnery, 2000).

ERIC FETTMANN
INDEPENDENT SCHOLAR

# Fourierism

FRANÇOIS-MARIE-CHARLES Fourier (1772–1837) is the epitome of an individual whose life is much less interesting than his ideas or the movement he inspired—Fourierism—in the United States and Europe in the middle of the 19th century. In fact, it is probably a compensation for his mundane life that Fourier's writings are pregnant with romantic impulses and nonsensical flights of the imagination (including a theory on the copulation of planets) alongside a penetrating critique of the bourgeois institution of marriage and the social consequences of *laissez-faire* capitalism.

The son of a provincial clothing merchant, Fourier held many jobs in retail such as bookkeeper, clerk, and salesman. Thus, he was exposed to the "crimes of commerce" and felt compelled to pen a social philosophy to overcome the vices of "civilization," a word he used in a pejorative sense. According to Fourier, human nature was driven—analogous to Isaac Newton's law of gravitational attraction—by "passionate attractions" such as taste, love, ambition, and the need for variety. Unbridled capitalism and middle-class conventions, however, distorted human passions in socially destructive ways,

*Charles Fourier and his followers sought to create a utopian society that eradicated social inequality.*

leading to warfare, poverty, and repressive moral codes such as the monogamous relationship. The solution Fourier advocated was to establish voluntary communal agricultural communities—so-called phalansteries or phalanxes—where the human passions would be emancipated and channeled toward socially productive activities. The phalanx was to be a cooperative of ideally 1,620 people in order to supply individuals of diverse natures with a suitable partner of the opposite sex. In his views on sexual freedom, the worth of children, and especially the emancipation of women, Fourier was a forerunner of his times and a precursor to radical feminism. Thus, he believed that "the degree of feminine emancipation is the natural measure of general emancipation."

Fourierism as a social movement was more influential and widespread in the United States than in Europe. In France, it shaped the philosophy of socialist feminists of the 1840s, such as Flora Tristan, whose goal was to attain gender equality and worker emancipation by creating self-governing labor unions. Fourier's principle disciple was Victor Considérant, who, until his exile from France in 1854 (he went to create a phalanstery in Dallas, Texas), advocated for a peaceful solution to the "social question" that would include the human right to work. Fourierism in the United States context flourished until the Civil War, because it built upon traditions and tendencies already embedded in the American social and political landscape.

American Fourierism set itself apart from other social movements of antebellum America for three reasons. First, Fourierists offered a critique of America's social problems from a sociological rather than a moralistic approach. Second, they sought to eradicate social inequality with a modern and rational blueprint for the ideal society, not simply an escapist agrarian utopia. Third, American Fourierists were committed to "universal reform," uniting all classes and creeds for the cause of societal harmony.

### SEE ALSO
*Volume 1 Left:* Feminism; New Left; Liberalism; Rousseau, Jean-Jacques; Socialism.
*Volume 2 Right:* Feminism; Capitalism.

### BIBLIOGRAPHY
Jonathan Beecher, *Charles Fourier: The Visionary and His World* (University of California Press, 1986); Doris and Paul Beik, eds., *Flora Tristan, Utopian Feminist: Her Travel Diaries and Personal Crusade* (Indiana University Press, 1993); Albert Fried and Ronald Sanders, eds., *Socialist Thought: A Documentary History* (Columbia University Press, 1992); Carl. J. Guarnieri, *The Utopian Alternative: Fourierism in Nineteenth-Century America* (Cornell University Press, 1991).

KEVIN J. CALLAHAN, PH.D.
SAINT JOSEPH COLLEGE

# France

THE MODERN HISTORY of France and its liberal heritage could be said to begin with the revolution in May 1789. For the first time in French history, the middle class and the common people began to mount an effective challenge toward the king, nobility, and clergy who had dominated their lives. In France, the first estate was the nobility, the second the clergy, and the third estate what Karl Marx in *The Communist Manifesto* (1848) called the bourgeoisie and the proletariat, the working class. Because of the way that the first and second estates, in alliance with the monarchy, controlled France, the real financial burden for the country rested upon those who could often afford it the least: members of the third estate. Vladimir I. Lenin, who founded Russian communism, quoted Friedrich Engels, Marx's collaborator in writing the *Manifesto*, "society has become entangled in an insoluble contradiction with itself, that it is cleft into irreconcilable antagonisms which it is powerless to dispel." This, in fact, would be the condition of France for much of its modern history.

King Louis XVI summoned the three estates to meet collegially as the Estates-General to help solve the growing French financial crisis. But the same "irreconcilable antagonisms" that had plunged the last meeting of the Estates-General into disarray in 1614 happened again. However, this time the third estate did not retreat meekly back into its shops and factories. It demanded a say in its own governing, something that successive kings had systematically denied it.

Alexis de Tocqueville wrote in *The Old Regime and the French Revolution* how any efforts at representative government were stifled even at the municipal level. Tocqueville observed that before 1789, "it was but an empty show of freedom; these assemblies had no real power." Rural society at large, commented Pierre Goubert, remained a society where "the struggle for daily bread remained the over-riding consideration."

Refusing to bow to pressure, the third estate met in defiance of royal authority on June 20, 1789, to declare in the Oath of the Tennis Court that it would not disband until representative government was granted to France. This was a direct challenge to not only the king, but to his supporters in the second and first estates.

However, as with the Russian Revolution of 1917 and the Mexican Revolution of 1910, the upper class still only sought its own advancement. Those at the lower levels of society were expected to remain content with their lot in life. Yet, as Marx and Engels noted, by raising itself up against the opposition of the feudal nobility, the bourgeoisie had also raised up its most obdurate opponents. Wrote Marx and Engels, the bourgeois had not only "forged the weapons that bring death to itself ... it also called into existence the men who are to wield those weapons, the modern working class or proletariat."

On July 11, the third estate (soon known as the Constituent, or later the National Assembly) had become the main legislative power in the country. On that day it passed the Declaration of the Rights of Man and of the Citizen, but still the document reflected the political needs of the bourgeois, not the very real material concerns of the working class.

Much like the Bolsheviks in revolutionary Russia, the Jacobin Club became the spokesman for the Parisian proletariat. On July 14, inspired by the orator Camille Desmoulins, an uprising of citizens destroyed the prison of the Bastille, which, towering over Paris, had become an emblem of royalist tyranny, an assertion of the will of the revolutionary common people. The Jacobins moved to consolidate their influence among the toiling Parisians starting in July 1789.

Throughout the critical years of 1789 to 1791, the nobility, clergy, and the upper class bourgeois continued to be unable to win common ground with the workers in Paris or the countryside. The result was that, as a revolutionary common ground was not found, the more progressive forces among the Jacobins began a press for power. Underlying the political ambitions of men like George Jacques Danton and Maximilien Robespierre was the view that any real compromise with the monarchists would inevitably bring about a surrender to them.

## GROWING EXTREMISM

During those critical years, the dissolution of the monarchy, with Louis XVI playing virtually no role in the greatest drama of his life (except suggesting that the guillotine have a triangular blade for a cleaner, sharper cut!), continued apace. On June 20, 1791, Louis XVI and Queen Marie Antoinette were apprehended at Varennes during an abortive flight to the French border. Any hopes for defense of the monarchy died when Louis's Swiss Guards were slaughtered at the Tuileries Palace on August 10, 1792, after Louis ordered the mercenaries to put down their guns—when they were on the verge of destroying the Jacobin Parisian street mob. The moderate Girondin faction in the assembly was swept away by the ruthless ascendance of the Jacobins.

It was during this period that the Jacobins sat to the left in the assembly and the Girondins to the right, thus beginning the association of leftism with radicalism and rightism with conservatism.

A National Convention was established in September 1792 to solidify the revolutionary movement and to give the revolutionaries recourse to defend it from the counterrevolutionaries, the royalist emigres, who sought to undo the revolution in collusion with the monarchies of Europe. Based on allegations of his complicity with the emigres in invading France, Louis XVI was sent to the guillotine he had improved on January 21, 1793; Marie Antoinette rode in the tumbril cart to the guillotine's blade on October 16, 1793.

However, a fratricidal power struggle broke out in the convention and its Committee of Public Safety that threatened to overwhelm the benefits of the revolution, such as the banning of the royal corvee, the required unpaid labor of the common people on public works projects, and the financial disestablishment of the Roman Catholic Church as the official church of France. The moderate Girondins were liquidated, although one of them left behind a phrase that has come to symbolize how revolutions can be killed by those who tried to save them. On his way to his death, the Girondin Pierre Victorien Vergniaud cried out, referring to the ancient Greek myth, "the revolution, like Saturn, devours its children."

On June 10, 1794, the power struggle between Robespierre and Danton finally ended with Danton condemned to the guillotine. Yet, the Jacobins begin to fear the "revolutionary justice" of Citizen Robespierre. Eventually on July 28, 1794, Robespierre was guillotined as well. After the death of Robespierre, the Reign of Terror, which caused some 15,000 deaths, drew to an end. But also did any real hope of the representative government that Robespierre and Danton had held out for the common people of France. A five-man Directory now ruled France, composed of members of the upper bourgeoisie, or middle class.

The organized terror of Robespierre had failed the revolution by providing the bourgeois foes of the proletariat with the excuse they needed to rein in the growing role of the working people in French government. As Burke commented, "very plausible schemes with very pleasing commencements have often shameful and lamentable conclusions." The situation by 1795 was chaotic as Parisian mobs continued their protests. The Directory summoned the most effective army general they had to restore order in the capital. On October 5, 1795, with his famous "whiff of grapeshot," General Napoleon Bonaparte crushed the final uprising of the popular movement. Yet Paul Barras and the other members of the Directory could turn to no one when Napoleon seized power in November 1799 as the first consul, effectively ending the Revolution.

Thus, France's great experiment in liberalism came to an end as Napoleon instituted a conservative dictatorship, stressing nationalistic principles. Napoleon's reforms were thorough. His attempts to institute a Bank of France on February 13, 1800, were marked with success, finally putting the country on a rational fiscal footing. He also oversaw the adoption of the Code Napoleon, an attempt to cut through the forest of judicial decrees enacted by the various parliamentary assemblies under the monarchy. However, his rule was marred by an imperialistic foreign policy that brought much suffering and loss to the French people. As a sign that he was the official undertaker of the French Revolution, Napoleon had himself crowned Emperor of the French on December 2, 1804. The end result of the Napoleonic Wars was Napoleon's final defeat at Waterloo in June 1815, with his French Empire returned to virtually the same boundaries it had had in 1789.

With Napoleon's exile to dismal St. Helena Island in 1815, Louis XVI's uncle, the Comte de Provence, ruled as Louis XVIII. (Louis XVI's son, considered Louis XVII by French royalists, died the victim of abuse in prison.) As the royalists returned to power, they were determined to root out the Revolution of 1789, but it turned out to be much more difficult than compelling Napoleon's former troops to replace the revolutionary red, white, and blue cockade in their caps with one of the Bourbon white.

While Louis XVIII remained careful in France, he showed his true autocratic disposition by sending a French army in 1823 to Spain to help King Ferdinand VII smash a republican uprising. In 1824, Louis would die, to be succeeded as king by the Comte d'Artois, who would reign as Charles X.

In July 1830, 41 years after the first French Revolution, Charles X was overthrown, to be replaced by Louis Phillippe, who ruled wisely as the Citizen-King. However, it was still government by the propertied classes; the urban workers laboring in the factories were still political mutes. In the France of the July Monarchy (1830–48), about one adult male in 30 could vote. Of course, the voting franchise for women was not even seriously considered as a political option.

## SECOND EMPIRE

After a bloody popular rising in July 1848, the French bourgeoisie, as in 1794, quickly tired of the revolution. They sought refuge this time in Napoleon's nephew, Louis Napoleon Bonaparte. As Marx wrote in *The Eighteenth Brumaire of Louis Napoleon*, "The French, so long as they were engaged in revolution, could not get rid of the memory of Napoleon, as the election of December 10 [1848, when Louis Bonaparte was elected president of the French Republic by plebiscite] proved. They longed to return from the perils of revolution to the fleshpots of Egypt, and December 2, 1851 [the date of

France has played a unique role in the history of the left, with a revolution against a monarchy and based on the principles of equality.
As a major, centralized country within western Europe, French liberal philosophy has spread throughout the region and the world.

the coup d'état by Louis Bonaparte], was the answer. Now they have not only a caricature of the old Napoleon, but the old Napoleon himself, caricatured as he would have to be in the middle of the nineteenth century."

However, the new emperor, now Napoleon III, was never able to rule with the absolutism of his uncle. The bourgeoisie by the 1860s had compelled him to accept, in a period historically called the Liberal Empire, the influence of the Legislative Body. But, raised on dreams of his uncle's imperial glory, Napoleon III committed the French people to imperialist adventures from Italy in 1859 to Mexico during the American Civil War. His promise in 1852, "the empire means peace," proved hollow. By 1871, his Second Empire came crashing down in ruins when he unwisely took on Prussia and its German allies. The result of this Franco-Prussian War was the abdication of Napoleon III and the proclamation of the new German Empire in the Hall of Mirrors at the Palace of Versailles, home of the greatest of France's kings, Louis XIV.

Even with a German army on French soil, the deep-seated class animosity prevented a truly united front within the country. A government of National Defense at Versailles, through negotiations by Jules Favre, negotiated an armistice with the Prussian Chancellor Otto von Bismarck on January 25, 1871; a formal peace was made on May 10, 1871. With peace made between Prussia, the leader of the German states, and the National Defense regime, the government at Versailles was freed to destroy the Paris Commune. This was a popular movement, formed largely from the proletarian neighborhoods, of Paris. The Versailles troops would kill some 20,000 *communards* in their violent counterrevolution.

## THIRD REPUBLIC

The government of the Third Republic was formed upon the wreckage of the Second Empire, beginning its fitful life with the slaughter of the Paris Commune. Ironically, the remaining monarchist feeling of the army caused Frenchmen in growing numbers to embrace the Third Republic, simply because there was no real alternative.

The failed coup of General Boulanger in 1889 cemented all classes of Frenchmen, except for extreme monarchists (supporters of the Bourbons) and Bonapartists (supporters of the Bonapartes), into a populist coalition in support of the republic. Socialism, inspired by figures like Jean Jaures, became commonplace on the

French political scene. Indeed, both socialists and republicans gained a firm foothold in French politics.

On August 4, 1914, World War I erupted in Europe, pitting France, England, and Russia against Germany and Austria-Hungary. While the war saw mutinies in the French Army in 1917 after the costly Nivelle Offensive, nevertheless the army held true to its loyalty to the republic, thanks in no small part due to the leadership of Premier Georges Clemenceau. In spite of class divisions, all Frenchmen rallied around *la patrie en danger,* "the country in danger."

On November 11, 1918, with communist rebellions erupting in Germany, the German Army was forced to sign an armistice with the victorious Western Allies. (The United States had joined the coalition in April 1917, while Italy had done so in 1915.) In May 1919, the Treaty of Versailles brought the long war officially to an end. However, the French idea of *revanchisme,* "revenge," against Germany for the human and material costs of the war poisoned any real opportunity for peace. A working-class spirit of communal socialism, which had been fractured by the war, never returned to Europe.

By the middle 1920s, political conditions in France, amid continuing financial scandals, had brought the country to political crisis again. William L. Shirer wrote in *The Collapse of the Third Republic: An Inquiry into the Fall of France in 1940* that "if parliament and government would not clean up their own houses then the people of Paris might have to take to the street, as they had in 1789, 1830, 1848, and 1871." In February 1934, the long scandal surrounding financial fraudster Serge Stavisky broke out with serious rioting in the city's Place de la Concorde. The Croix de Feu, "the Cross of Fire," a large fascist group, played a major role in fomenting the unrest, while the communists held lesser responsibility. By the time the firing stopped, Shirer recorded, "it was the bloodiest encounter in the streets of Paris since the Commune in 1871."

The political paralysis of the country, between left and right, prevented the Third Republic from being able to effectively face the greatest threat to French security since the war. In March 1936, in a triumph of sheer audacity, Adolf Hitler, the dictator of Germany's Nazi Third Reich, reoccupied the Rhineland territory neighboring France without a French bullet being fired. As Shirer wrote, "the whole structure of European peace and security set up in 1919 collapsed."

The Popular Front government, orchestrated by Socialist Leon Blum, was able to do little to close the chasm in French politics. On May 10, 1936, Blum described his Popular Front: "the majority is based on a coalition of the working class and the middle classes organized around the Popular Front Program." Indeed, Blum himself was beaten in Paris in April 1936 by thugs from Charles Maurras's fascist Action Francaise.

## WORLD WAR II

The ennui in French politics was epitomized by the Munich Conference of September 1938, at which Prime Minister Neville Chamberlain of Great Britain and Premier Edouard Daladier of France agreed to the severing of the German-populated Sudetenland from Czechoslovakia rather than confront the armed forces of Hitler's German Wehrmacht, or armed forces. For 20 years, France had operated on a basis of communal security with Czechoslovakia to hem in German territorial ambitions. Finally, when England and France went to war with Germany in September 1939 over Hitler's invasion of Poland, they did so alone. The rump part of Czechoslovakia had been absorbed by Hitler's Reich, and Yugoslavia and Romania were rendered powerless.

Josef Stalin, premier of the communist Soviet Union, had been so shocked by the capitulation of the French and English at Munich, that he signed a nonaggression compact with Germany in August 1939. On May 10, 1940, precisely four years to the day after Blum's Popular Front speech, the panzer (tank) divisions of Germany attacked France and the Low Countries. The defensive Maginot Line, the child of Defense Minister Andre Maginot, and symbolic of the lack of united action among the French, was completely circumvented by the Germans in the first days of their western offensive. By June 1940, France capitulated to German aggression and Marshal Philippe Petain and former Premier Pierre Laval took charge of a fascist French government in Vichy, which openly collaborated with the conquerors of Paris. Amazingly, the majority of French socialists gave their support as well to the Petain puppet government. The Third Republic officially died on July 10, 1940, replaced by Petain's Vichy regime.

The Vichy collaborators were challenged by a Free French movement, which had been established by General Charles de Gaulle in London after the surrender of France. Within France, the communists and socialists formed a major part of the ground forces of the FFI, the French Forces of the Interior, in a patriotic continuation of Blum's Popular Front. The fascist regime in Vichy even went so far as to put France's overseas empire at the disposal of the Germans in their war against

Great Britain in the Middle East and the Mediterranean Sea. In November 1942, Vichy's French North African territory was invaded and ultimately reconquered in Operation Torch. Within France, Vichy forces collaborated with the Germans both in fighting the FFI and in rounding up French Jews to be sent to the concentration camps.

When the Allies invaded France on June 6, 1944, the French responded with a heroic rising in Paris led by de Gaulle's FFI. On August 26, Paris was liberated by the Free French Army of Marshal Pierre Koenig and American forces. De Gaulle and his Free French exacted fierce retribution from the Vichy collaborators after liberation. Laval was shot by a firing squad in October 1945. Petain was only saved from the same fate by his advanced age and grudging recognition of his positive role in World War I. The personification of fighting France, de Gaulle formed a government with broad popular support in November 1945 by a Constituent Assembly, similar to the government of national salvation in 1792. However, he resigned in January 1946. The postwar period saw a resurgence of the French left, led by the existentialist philosophers like Jean-Paul Sartre and Simone de Beauvoir.

## FOURTH AND FIFTH REPUBLICS

When the Fourth Republic after the war began its campaign to reoccupy French overseas colonies, like those in Indochina (today's Cambodia, Laos, and Vietnam), the left, led by intellectuals like Sartre, rebelled against French imperialism. French efforts to reconquer Indochina from the communist Ho Chi Minh were crushed in the defeat at Dien Bien Phu, Vietnam, in May 1954. In November 1954, French Algeria broke out into a struggle for freedom led by the National Liberation Front, the FLN. The war brought down the shaky Fourth Republic (Guy Mollet, head of the Socialist Party, was prime minister from January 1956 to May 1957), and de Gaulle was brought back from private life to lead the Fifth Republic.

The French forces in Algeria carried on a savage war against the FLN, outraging progressive opinion at home. In March 1962, at Evian, France, an agreement was made with the revolutionary FLN and Algeria became independent. De Gaulle followed a uniquely French foreign policy much in keeping with traditional French politics. In 1965, he removed France from NATO, the North Atlantic Treaty Organization. A signal part of his French rearmament policy was building up France's own nuclear deterrent. He said, "no country without an atomic bomb could properly consider itself independent." Throughout his tenure in power, he followed a foreign policy often at odds with the doctrinaire anti-communism of London and Paris. De Gaulle was determined to keep open channels of communication with the Soviet Union, perhaps still remembering France's fate at the hands of Germany in 1940. However, as Shirer wrote, in April 1969 he resigned "after a defeat in a plebiscite over a relatively minor matter of constitutional reform."

RISE OF THE RIGHT

When Valerie Giscard d'Estaing became premier of France in the early 1970s, France began a new realignment with the Western allies, especially in the area of nuclear research. However, the growing number of immigrants from former French colonies led to a revival of the French right, which had been in retreat since the Vichy fiasco of World War II. Manipulating French working-class fears of job loss in an age of growing computerization and the dropping of trade barriers in Europe's Common Market (now the European Union), the right began a comeback.

The racism of the French right came to be symbolized by one man, Jean-Marie Le Pen, who founded his National Front Party (Front National, FN) in 1972, according to the British BBC. Le Pen was radicalized by his service in the French Foreign Legion, which he joined in 1954, in time to see active service in Indochina and Algeria. As the BBC observed, "His political career began in 1956, when he became a deputy for the shopkeepers' party of Pierre Poujade. In 1965 he helped run the election campaign of far-right candidate Jean-Louis Tixier-Vignancour, and in 1972 he set up the FN. With his dire warnings of the threat to French life from North African immigration, he pushed his share of the presidential vote up from 0.74 percent in 1974 to 14 percent in 1988 and 15percent in 1995."

Indeed, the entire social history of France for 30 years was affected by his extreme rightist views, making him a direct disciple of Charles Maurras and his Action Francaise. Against all immigrants from the former French colonies (which were colonized only so that the French could exploit their people and resources), he also carried on the anti-Semitism of the Vichy years.

In May 2002, President Jacques Chirac won a stunning electoral victory over Le Pen, bringing to an end one of the most polarizing political careers in the history of France. At the Chirac victory celebrations in Paris, Chirac supporter Sonia Guzik stated, "It's a true victory for Chirac, and a victory against the racism and xenophobia that Le Pen stands for."

Into the 2000s, the seeds of the liberal inspiration that led to the 1789 revolution still steer French politics. Experiments with socialism and governmental responsibility for French workers veer the country in one direction, while simultaneously the forces of the right, against immigration and for nationalism, zig the nation back to sometimes fascist tendencies. The country that helped create the political left by trying to enact human rights centuries ago would continue to be uncomfortable with the ramifications of its own creation.

**SEE ALSO**
*Volume 1 Left:* Paris Commune; French Revolution; Socialism; Communism; Liberalism.
*Volume 2 Right:* France; Conservatism.

**BIBLIOGRAPHY**
Michael Howard, *The Franco-Prussian War* (Collier, 1961); "Profile: Jean-Marie Le Pen," (BBC, April 23, 2002); Clare Murphy, "Chirac Supporters Revel in the Moment," (BBC, May 5, 2002); Karl Marx and Friedrich Engels, *Communist Manifesto* (Bantam, 1965); Karl Marx, *The Eighteenth Brumaire of Louis Napoleon,* http://digital.library.upenn.edu (July 2004); Thomas Carlyle, *The French Revolution* (Penguin, 2002); Alexis de Tocqueville, *The Old Regime and the French Revolution* (Anchor, 1955); George R. Havens, *The Age of Ideas* (Free Press, 1955); Crane Brinton, *Anatomy of Revolution* (Vintage, 1965); William L. Shirer, *The Collapse of the Third Republic: An Inquiry into the Fall of France in 1940* (Pocket Books, 1971).

JOHN F. MURPHY, JR.
AMERICAN MILITARY UNIVERSITY

# Freedom of Information

THE FREEDOM of Information Act (FOIA) is officially Section 552, Title 5, of the U.S. Code. It has been amended a few times through its history, but from the onset it has been the authority for any person in the United States to ask any government agency for information about virtually anything. If the government agency has the material, it must provide it to the requester at reasonable expense, either electronically or in hard copy. By 2002, requests numbered 2.4 million, of which 1.4 million were to the Veterans Administration alone.

On July 4, 1966, President Lyndon B. Johnson signed the FOIA into law. Johnson had reservations and was within a day of letting it die by pocket veto, but he had to sign to reduce the credibility gap generated by the war in Vietnam. He sought no publicity, so only a few journalists, lawyers, and legislators were at his Texas ranch to witness the event. From those hesitant beginnings, the Freedom of Information Act became the model for the sunshine laws now in effect in all 50 states and common in many other countries.

The original FOIA amended the Administrative Procedures Act of 1946, the law pertaining to public notice and comment on proposed rules and regulations. The legislation was so negligently written that its first 25 years generated over 3,000 lawsuits trying to make it compatible with privacy and copyright laws. Two dozen cases reached the Supreme Court by 1998. FOIA was a product of the legislative-executive conflict in 1955–58 during the Dwight Eisenhower administration. After Eisenhower fired alleged communists, a subcommittee of the House under John Moss (D-CA) asked for names and justifications. When the administration refused to provide the information, Democrats began what proved to be a 10-year fight to get inside the executive branch's cloak of secrecy. Hearings revealed that sometimes claims of national security were nothing more than efforts to conceal administration bungling. The press reported the disclosures, citing the right of the public to know. Still, three presidents, Eisenhower, John Kennedy, and Johnson, dragged their feet on FOI until 1966.

The FOIA initially required a response within 10 days, later extended to 20. That was the standard. In reality, replies could take months. Agencies rejected inquiries by citing the vagueness of a request or unavailability of the information. The requester had no recourse but to accept the decision. The act exempted documents pertaining to national security, personnel, trade secrets, privacy, and other information. In 1972, Moss held new hearings and not surprisingly found that enforcement of the act had been less than vigorous. In 1974, after Watergate, over Gerald Ford's veto, a stronger law came into being with stronger appeals process, tighter procedures, and set fees. Also, the law provided that a judge could overturn an agency's decision. Modifications occurred in 1986 and 1996.

The FOIA was unpopular with the bureaucracy because it was time-consuming and subject to abuse through frivolous requests. It also forced them to reveal things they did not really want journalists and other inquirers to know.

Jimmy Carter appointed judges supportive of the law. Ronald Reagan did not. Bill Clinton tried, but the Republican-controlled Congress held up most of his nominees. Supreme Court rulings became more conservative, more friendly to the agencies seeking to conceal than to FOIA requesters seeking to reveal government activity. The bureaucracy also fluctuated in its degree of responsiveness. It was slow under Reagan, better under Clinton, especially when his Justice Department stopped supporting slow rolling agencies and pushed for maximum release and minimal backlogs. In 1995, Executive Order 12958 ended the presumption of secrecy and declassified great volumes of material. Despite that, the agencies persisted in denying requests.

The events of September 11, 2001, led to tightening of restrictions. The Critical Infrastructure Information (CII) Act of 2001 exempted information about critical infrastructure from FOI disclosure as well as civil suits or antitrust action. The Department of Homeland Security Act of 2002 exempted CII as well. The Department of Justice under Attorney General John Ashcroft opposed the FOIA. In 2001, Ashcroft required agencies to withhold as much information as they could, a reversal of Clinton's Executive Order 12958. Ashcroft's memo alarmed FOIA advocates who feared that it would stifle the freedom of the law. In 2003, both the General Accounting Office and the National Security Archive found that the agencies ignored the memo as they had other White House guidance. Responses to FOI requests remained slow, muddled, lost, and otherwise bureaucratic. But the FOIA requests persisted.

## SEE ALSO

*Volume 1 Left:* Democratic Party; United States; Civil Rights. *Volume 2 Right:* United States.

## BIBLIOGRAPHY

Maarten Botterman et al., *Public Information Provision in the Digital Age: Implementation and Effects of the U.S. Freedom of Information Act* (Rand, 2001); Herbert N. Foerstel, *Freedom of Information and the Right to Know; the Origins and Applications of the Freedom of Information Act* (Greenwood Press, 1999); David G. Garson, ed., "FOIA and the Emergence of Federal Information Policy in the 1980s and 1990s," *Handbook of Public Information Systems* (Marcel Dekker, 2000); U.S. General Accounting Office, "Freedom of Information Act; Agency Views on Changes Resulting from New Administration Policy," www.gao.gov (September 2003).

JOHN BARNHILL, PH.D.
INDEPENDENT SCHOLAR

# French Revolution

WHEN THE FRENCH veterans returned from their service in the American Revolution, where they had aided the Americans under General George Washington in the decisive victory in October 1781, they brought their revolutionary ideals home. Their commander, the Comte de Rochambeau, would be spared during the French Revolution largely because of his contributions to the American Revolution, as would the Marquis de Lafayette, who had served as Washington's aide-de-camp.

The American Revolution had been greatly influenced, in fact, by the work of the Frenchman Charles-Louis de Secondat, the Baron de Montesquieu. His work, *De l'Esprit des Lois* (*On the Sprit of Laws*), published in 1748, worked as much as the writings of the Englishman John Locke to establish the ideas of separation of powers at the heart of the American system of government. Montesquieu had written, "in each state, there are three kinds of powers: the legislative power, the executive power which deals with international affairs, and the executive power [which in the American system would be called the 'legislative'], which has to do with civil laws." Yet, when writing of the English system of government, from which the American was directly derived, he was thinking as well of his native France. For the future of France, the monarchy proved unable—or unwilling—to reform itself.

Indeed, French society had changed little, at least on the surface, since the Middle Ages. As Karl Marx and Friedrich Engels wrote in *The Communist Manifesto* in 1848, "in the earlier epochs of history, we find almost everywhere a complicated arrangement of society into various orders, a manifold gradation of social rank." In France, society was ordered into three broad classes: the first estate, the nobility; the second estate, the clergy; and the third estate, what Marx called the bourgeoisie. However, more than just the middle class, the third estate imperfectly held all the rest of the society, including those Marx referred to as the lumpen-proletariat, those without any rooted occupations.

When the Treaty of Paris ended the American Revolutionary War in September 1783, French participation from the Treaty of Alliance in March 1778 had led to the French treasury being left with an unacceptable deficit of some 2 billion livres. Attempts by financiers like Jacques Necker to remedy the disastrous situation were met with little or no support from King Louis XVI and his pleasure-loving consort, Queen Marie Antoinette. Efforts to solve the problem finally led the king to summon the three estates as the Estates-General, a convention in Paris in May 1789. The scant esteem in which the kings held the Estates-General was shown by the fact that the last time it met to advise the king was in 1614, following the assassination of King Henri IV in Paris. Even then, dissension among the three estates had led to its disbandment.

Although the third estate had come to prominence economically during the long wars that France had fought since Louis XIV had invaded the Netherlands in 1672, the nobility had, unlike in England, conspired to keep them frozen out of the higher ranks of French government and society. Indeed, the only reason that King Louis XVI had summoned the Estates-General was that an Assembly of Notables, one of whom was Lafayette, had advised the king in 1787 that wider assent from the public was needed to vote on new taxes for France. Never did the king consider the Estates-General as a consultative body like the British king considered Parliament.

## ROOTS OF REVOLUTION

When the Estates-General met in May 1789, the lack of advancement which the French system offered to the urban middle class and rural gentry would assume crisis dimensions. Alexis de Tocqueville, in *The Old Regime and the French Revolution*, contrasted unfavorably the French situation with that in England. In France, the rich enjoyed exemption from taxation whereas, in England, it was the poor who were exempt, obviously favoring those economically least able to sustain the burden. Also, the clergy, the second estate in France, was virtually immune from taxation. Furthermore, since the members of the higher clergy were drawn from the aristocracy, it always tended to vote with the First Estate.

However, this time, animated in much part by the example of the American Revolution, the third estate insisted on a more democratic, proportional representation in which their topics of concern would be given a fair hearing. Finally, when their efforts met with no response, one of their leaders, the Abbe Sieyes, demanded in June 1789 that the third estate should reconstitute itself as a National Assembly. On June 20, as George Havens wrote in *The Age of Ideas*, the third estate met in a unused tennis court and, in what became known as the Oath of the Tennis Court, vowed "a solemn oath never to separate ... until the Constitution of the Kingdom shall be laid and established on secure foundations."

With the moderates of the third estate encountering opposition, a radical leftist movement began to take over what was increasingly a prerevolutionary situation in France. The members of the leftist Jacobin Club were already looking forward to revolution and beginning to form a political alliance with the common people of Paris, traditionally overlooked in French government.

Liberal nobles, some of whom had served in the American Revolution, chose to sit with the third estate. Among these was Lafayette, who had fought with the Americans in some of the major battles of their war. On July 11, inspired by the American Declaration of Independence (and the fact that its author, Thomas Jefferson, was then American ambassador to France), Lafayette proposed the Declaration of the Rights of Man and of the Citizen.

Camille Desmoulins was one of the few, along with Jean-Paul Marat, who styled himself the *ami de peuple*, "the friend of the people," who realized the utility of radicalizing the common people, the urban proletariat. Much as Vladimir Lenin and the Bolsheviks were able to channel the rage of the people of Russia in 1917 to support their party, Desmoulins and Marat were able to muster the *sans-culottes*, those who could not afford underclothing like the nobility, to support the Jacobins.

On July 14, the Parisians stormed the ancient prison of the Bastille in Paris, the towering symbol of royal absolutism in the capital. Thomas Carlyle, in *The French Revolution: A History*, wrote that "the fall of the Bastille may be said to have shaken all France to the deepest foundations of its existence." One month to the day after the fall of the Bastille, the clergy and nobility gave up their privileges, fearing the unleashed hostility of the common people. On October 10, a mob forced the king and queen to give up Versailles and move to the Tuileries Palace in Paris where they were kept virtually as prisoners.

## ROYALTY AND REVOLUTION

Power had moved swiftly from the hands of moderates like the Comte de Mirabeau, who had urged Louis to act as a constitutional monarch, under the same type of system that was evolving in England. Said Mirabeau to the king, "Sire, the very idea of monarchy is not incompatible with revolution." But the perspicacious Mirabeau would die on April 2, 1791, leaving the leftists in creative control of the rapidly evolving revolutionary situation. Realizing their uncertain fate, the royal family, now made tragic by the king's insensibility to the political crisis caused by his misrule, attempted to escape on June 20, 1791, but were discovered at Varennes near the French border.

A month later, the radicals attempted a coup under Marat on July 17, but their attempt to form a republic proved premature. They were crushed by Lafayette, who was in charge of the national guard. The National Assembly, or convention, was now split between the moderate Girondins and the Jacobin radical faction; in 1789, the first and second estates had joined the third out of a desire for preservation, not the liberalization of the political system. The Girondins, the increasingly ineffective moderates, were much like the sorcerer in *The Communist Manifesto* "who is no longer able to control the powers of the nether world whom he has called up by his spells." A month after Marat's aborted coup, the radicals reasserted their power in the streets when the Parisians, removing the last citadel of royalist opposition to the Revolution, seized the Tuileries Palace on August 10, 1792. In the assault they destroyed the mercenary Swiss Guards; the king's French Guards regiment had joined the revolution in time for the attack on the Bastille in 1789.

An allied army supporting the French monarchy, raised under the Prussian Duke of Brunswick, met with defeat at the hands of the new citizen army at Valmy, on September 20, 1792. Under General Kellermann, the professional troops were defeated by the celebrated "cannonade at Valmy." Two days later, Louis gave up the crown on September 21, 1792. The French First Republic was proclaimed.

The Jacobins under George Jacques Danton and Maximilien Robespierre were now in the ascendant. In the beginning, Danton had the upper hand: it was he who had set in motion the massacre of captive royalists during the bloody September Days of 1792. Paris was in a patriotic frenzy over the royalist refugees, or emigres, who were coming back to reclaim their estates under the banners of foreign armies. A third member joined Danton and Robespierre to make them an effective troika, Louis-Antoine de Saint-Just, who declared, "those who lead revolutions, those who wish to do well, must never sleep—except in their graves!"

Accusing the king of complicity in the foreign invasions smashed at Valmy and Jemappes (November 1792), Louis XVI, now "Louis Capet" under his nonroyal name, went on trial for his life on December 26, 1792. Louis was sent to his death on the guillotine on January 21, 1793; Marie Antoinette rode in the tumbril cart to the guillotine's blade on October 16, 1793. Of her death, Napoleon, who would be the ultimate heir of the revolution, commented, "this was not regicide [the killing of a king], it was much worse than that." Their son, Louis XVII, would die at the hands of his sadistic jailers on June 8, 1795.

Yet, before the young monarch died, others followed him. With the cry of "the fatherland is in danger," Danton and Robespierre turned on the moderate Girondins, who were seen as an obstacle to total mobilization of the people, which was being carried out magisterially by Lazare Carnot. This was the first act in the alienation of the moderates, who still could have been co-opted into supporting the goals of the revolution. Then, in what would be a fatal miscalculation for himself as well as the revolutionary radical left, Robespierre, with the aid of Saint-Just, would soon focus on removing Danton.

On July 13, 1793, Marat, tormented by a skin disease, was knifed to death in his bath by Charlotte Corday, a young French aristocrat. What followed has justly been called the Reign of Terror, when the Jacobins further drove away moderate support of the revolution. On June 10, 1794, Robespierre finally contrived to have Danton condemned to death—and sent to the guillotine where Danton had urged the king be put to death. Desmoulins was beheaded with him. But the Republic of Virtue proclaimed by Robespierre continued to claim its victims. Eventually, the surviving members of the convention and its Committee of Public Safety conspired against him to save themselves. Robespierre was to follow Danton to the guillotine within less than a month.

On July 28, 1794, a counterrevolution took place, provoked by the moderates who saw the revolution descending into anarchy. Robespierre was arrested. At his trial, the people had shouted out "the ghosts of Danton and Desmoulins haunt you!" Robespierre speedily followed them to the guillotine.

## END OF TERROR AND REVOLUTION

With the death of Robespierre, the Terror, which had claimed some 15,000 victims, entered a conservative phase, governed by a five-man Directory shocked at the excesses that had been unleashed in 1789. This conservative reaction soon took oppressive action against the Paris people, who had enjoyed a brief period of control of their own affairs.

The Directory called on one of the country's most promising generals, Napoleon Bonaparte, to put down the Parisian mobs. On October 5, 1795, with his famous "whiff of grapeshot," Napoleon crushed the final uprising of Desmoulins's *sans-culottes*, rendering them once more powerless to control their own affairs. Coming from an Italian noble family, Napoleon hated the expression of what Enlightenment philosopher Jean-Jacques Rousseau had called the *volonte generale*, "the will of the people." By 1797, aided by Director Paul Barras, Bonaparte became the leader of the army and crushed the Austrian armies sent against him at victories like Lodi and Arcola. Within a year, Napoleon would lead a French army to invade Egypt, leaving the counterrevolutionary forces to once again threaten the Revolution at home.

With the focus of the Directory on the threat from without, the Jacobins tried again to regain ascendancy in the revolution. As Georges Lefebvre wrote in *Napoleon from 18 Brumaire to Tilsit*, "the Jacobins wished to establish a democratic dictatorship by relying on the *sans-culottes*." The frightened Directors turned to Bonaparte for help. On November 10, they, with the help of Napoleon's soldiers, staged a coup. Napoleon, Abbe Sieyes, and Roger Ducos would rule as three consuls. Soon enough, Napoleon dominated France as first consul. Within five years of his coup, in December 1804, Napoleon crowned himself Emperor of the French.

The French Revolution was over and its liberal civil rights agenda (liberty, fraternity, equality) were put aside in favor of Napoleon's imperialism and the glory of France. Not until 1830 would the revolutionary spirit of 1789 be able again to assert itself in France.

## SEE ALSO

*Volume 1 Left*: France; Liberalism; Locke, John; Rousseau, Jean-Jacques.
*Volume 2 Right*: France; Monarchism; Conservatism.

## BIBLIOGRAPHY

Karl Marx and Friedrich Engels, *The Communist Manifesto* (Bantam, 1965); Thomas Carlyle, *The French Revolution: A History* (Penguin, 2002); Alexis de Tocqueville, *The Old Regime and the French Revolution* (Anchor, 1955); Edmund Burke, *Reflections on the Revolution in France* (Penguin, 1984); George R. Havens, *The Age of Ideas* (The Free Press, 1955); Georges Lefebvre, *Napoleon from 18 Brumaire to Tilsit* (Columbia University Press, 1969); Georges Lefebvre, *The French Revolution from Its Origins to 1793* (Columbia University Press, 1968); Crane Brinton, *The Anatomy of Revolution* (Vintage, 1965); Richard Deacon, *The French Secret Service* (Grafton, 1990); Erik Durschmied, *Blood of Revolution* (Arcade, 2001).

JOHN F. MURPHY, JR.
AMERICAN MILITARY UNIVERSITY

# Friedan, Betty (1921–)

THE "MOTHER" of the second wave of the American women's movement, Betty Friedan was born in Peoria, Illinois, to Harry and Miriam Horowitz Goldstein. Friedan was interested in writing from an early age. In high school, she wrote for the school newspaper and founded a literary magazine that was distributed to her fellow students. After graduating *summa cum laude* from Smith College in Massachusetts with a degree in psychology in 1942, Friedan began graduate work at the University of California, Berkeley. Upon graduation, she accepted the position of assistant news editor with the Federated Press, a left-wing news service.

In 1947, Friedan married Carl Friedan and gave birth to a son the following year. Friedan was fired from her job with UE News for taking maternity leave when her second son was born in 1952. For the next 10 years, Friedan devoted herself to freelance writing. During this period, she became introspective and unsettled, wondering why she did not feel more fulfilled in the role that society mandated for women of her generation. She questioned why she had spent years in school developing her intelligence and analytic abilities since they were rarely used in her circumstances.

Determined to discover whether similar, other college-educated women were experiencing the same sensations, in 1957 Friedan used her skills as a social scientist to develop a questionnaire that she distributed to Smith graduates. The questions were designed to identify how the women viewed themselves and their lives since leaving college. The responses to her questionnaire led Friedan to "the problem without a name," which she called "the feminine mystique." This became the title of the book that she published in 1963, in which she argued that the advertising industry had been instrumental in pushing women back into their homes after World War II. Friedan believed that those efforts had resulted in filling women with guilt because they could never meet the standards required of them. Instead of developing their intellect, she argued, women were worrying about having the smartest and best cared-for children and the cleanest clothes and houses.

Before publishing her findings in a book, Friedan submitted an article based on her questionnaire to *McCall's* magazine. In the article, she asked: "Are Women Wasting Their Time in College?" Convinced that the article would offend their readers, *McCall's* editors rewrote the article to take the opposite position. Friedan withdrew the article. She then extended her study by developing other questionnaires. Afterward,

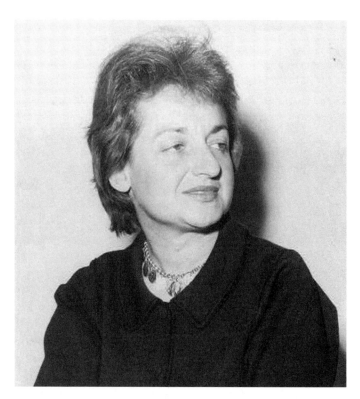

*Betty Friedan challenged the lives of modern women and helped usher in the second wave of the women's movement.*

she discussed her research and findings with psychologists and other experts.

In book form, response to *The Feminine Mystique* was overwhelming. Some people saw the book as a direct challenge to the American family, and Friedan received death threats. However, the book awoke a response in many women around the country who had experienced similar isolation and who were dissatisfied with their lives. Such women were gratified to learn that their feelings were shared by large numbers of other women. Younger feminists, such as Gloria Steinem, would later point out that this early stage in the modern women's movement was basically a response to the lives of white, middle-class American women. Historically, many reform movements have, indeed, been started by the middle class. As reform movements expand to include more members, they tend to become more responsive to the needs of a wider population. This was true of the women's movement. While the movement began from personal experiences, the result was a political response that changed the way that women as a whole saw themselves and their roles in society.

In 1966, along with Steinem and other feminists, Friedan cofounded the National Organization for Women (NOW), which became the largest women's organization in American history with chapters throughout the United States. NOW's Legal Defense Fund soon became involved with numerous cases of sexual discrimination. NOW successfully demanded greater political voices for women, expanded opportunities for education and jobs, and pursued an end to domestic violence, protection for reproductive freedom, and equality and justice under the law. In 1969, Friedan founded the National Association for the Repeal of Abortion Laws (NARAL), now known as the National Abortion Rights League. In 1971, Friedan, Steinem, along with Bella Abzug and Shirley Chisholm, two Democratic Congresswomen from New York, founded the National Women's Political Caucus to promote the election of political candidates who were supportive of women's issues.

In 1968, Betty and Carl Friedan divorced after years of marital discord. Over the next few years, Friedan also became alienated from the women's movement that had taken on a more radical character than any she had ever imagined. She blamed the media for becoming infatuated with Steinem because of her beauty, and for ignoring the more moderate wing of the women's movement. Friedan argued that Steinem and her cohorts had maneuvered her out of the organizations that she had founded. In the minds of the public, Steinem's more radical views represented the women's movement, resulting in the alienation of large groups of women who still saw marriage and motherhood as valid choices for their lives.

In 1981, the Ronald Reagan administration was not supportive of feminism and Friedan responded with the publication of *The Second Stage*, elaborating on what she saw as the new goals of the women's movement. Friedan argued that in the more advanced stage of feminism, feminists should be responsive to the ways that women's lives had changed since the birth of the modern women's movement. She maintained that feminists should work toward greater equality and implementation of the laws that had been passed against sexual discrimination. She also suggested that by concentrating on families and demanding such innovations as parental leave legislation and greater employment flexibility, feminism would appeal more to the women it was designed to help. Friedan turned her attention to age discrimination in 1993 with the publication of *The Fountain of Age*. After years of research, Friedan concluded that older people have become virtually invisible in American society. The book touched a chord with the American public, remaining on the bestseller list for six weeks. In the 2000s, Friedan has continued to teach college classes and lecture on women's issues.

**SEE ALSO**

*Volume 1 Left:* Steinem, Gloria; Abortion/Pro-Choice; Feminism; United States.
*Volume 2 Right:* Anti-Abortion/Pro-Life; Feminism; United States.

**BIBLIOGRAPHY**

Betty Friedan, *The Feminine Mystique* (W.W. Norton, 1963); Betty Friedan, *The Fountain of Age* (Simon and Schuster, 1993); Betty Friedan, *Life So Far* (Simon and Schuster, 2000); Betty Friedan, *The Second Stage* (Summit, 1981); Judith Hennessee, *Betty Friedan: Her Life* (Random House, 1999); Janann Sherman, ed., *Betty Friedan* (University of Mississippi Press, 2002).

ELIZABETH PURDY, PH.D.
INDEPENDENT SCHOLAR

# Fromm, Erich (1900–1980)

ERICH FROMM WAS a well-known German psychoanalyst and social psychologist. Born and raised in Frankfurt, Germany, Fromm's education was fostered by intensive religious studies, mainly Judaism. In 1922, at the age of 22, Fromm completed his doctoral studies at Heidelberg in sociology. Not too long after his graduation, at the age of 26, he denounced the Jewish roots that had shaped his young mind.

After completing his formal education, between 1929 and 1932, Fromm helped to establish the Frankfurt Psychoanalytic Institute. He was also invited to join the Frankfurt Institute for Social Research and began lecturing at the Institute and at the University of Frankfurt. By 1934, with the grip of Nazism taking over in Germany, Fromm moved to the United States. He continued to lecture between 1934 and 1950 at such prestigious institutions as Yale and Columbia universities. It was during this time that some of Fromm's most recognizable and influential works were written.

In his works and in his life, Fromm sought to combine the notions of Karl Marx and Sigmund Freud. While Freud held to the idea that human characteristics were crafted by biology and the unconscious, Marx saw people as products of their society. Fromm injected the notion of freedom, or as Dr. C. George Boeree stated, "He allows people to transcend the determinisms that Freud and Marx attribute to them. In fact, Fromm makes freedom the central characteristic of human nature!" In one of his earliest works, *Escape from Freedom* (1941; published in the UK as *The Fear of Freedom* in 1942), Fromm tried to explain why some individuals clung to the fascist regimes in Germany and Italy. It was a thorough examination of the growth of human freedom from the Middle Ages to modern times. He argued that while man seeks "freedom," he inversely seeks to belong to a larger group. A sense of freedom often leaves one with a feeling of isolation, at which time he or she seeks out a relationship with a larger group, thus surrendering freedom to the rules and mores of the larger social order.

When the highly democratic Weimar Republic was ousted by Adolf Hitler and Nazism in 1933, German citizens were left with the choice either to flee and establish their own form of freedom or adopt the patriotic attachment to the new ruling government. Many chose the inclusive option of submitting to the fascist regime in Berlin.

Fromm's works continued in the post-World War II era with *Man For Himself* (1947) and *The Sane Society* (1956). Combined, these two works argued that the modern capitalist society was yet another form of escape from freedom. Fromm sharply attacked the contemporary culture emerging at that time and, as Douglas Kellner noted, "popularized the neo-Marxian critiques of the media and consumer society, and promoted democratic socialist perspectives during an era when social repression made it difficult and dangerous to advocate radical positions."

As his career continued and his writings remained mainstays in Marxian and Freudian thinking, he penned several more books in the 1950s through the 1970s. Among these were *The Art of Loving* (1957), *Sigmund Freud's Mission* (1959), *The Heart of Man* (1964), and *The Anatomy of Human Destructiveness* (1973). Amid his writing, Fromm maintained an arduous lecturing regimen. After moving to Mexico in 1950, he helped direct the Mexican Institute of Psychoanalysis in Mexico City until 1976. His liberal humanist approach of mixing Freud and Marx kept him politically active as well.

Fromm's liberal ideology is also reflected in his politically motivated campaigns. Seeing it as the general good for all of humanity, as liberalism can be defined broadly, he participated in the anti-Vietnam movement in the 1960s and 1970s and argued vehemently for disarmament with SANE. He was an advocate of a more stringent liberal feminism, stating that the women's movement in the 1970s did not seek the full revolutionary aims it should have but rather only sought to share power and authority with men, thus keeping the patriarchical society intact. Up until his death in Switzerland in 1980, Fromm remained a liberal thinker and his works are still highly respected in political, psychological, and historical study.

## SEE ALSO

*Volume 1 Left:* Liberalism; Marx, Karl; Marxist Humanism. *Volume 2 Right:* Capitalism; Conservatism.

## BIBLIOGRAPHY

C. George Boeree, "Erich Fromm, 1900–80," www.ship.edu (July 2004); Daniel Burston, *The Legacy of Erich Fromm* (Harvard University Press, 1991); Douglas Kellner, "Erich Fromm: Biography," www.uta.edu (July 2004); Douglas Kellner, "Erich Fromm, Feminism, and the Frankfurt School," www.uta.edu (July 2004); Mark Smith, "Erich Fromm: Freedom and Alienation, and Loving and Being, in Education," www.infed.org (July 2004).

D. Steven Cronin
Mississippi State University

## Gandhi, Mahatma (1869–1948)

MAHATMA GANDHI will be remembered as the architect of India's independence and the pioneer of non-violence as a form of political action. Gandhi, a Hindu, was born in 1869 in the state of Gujarat, western India. His family sent him to London, England, to study law and, although he returned to Bombay, he left to live and work in South Africa in 1907. There, he worked ceaselessly to improve the rights of the immigrant Indians by taking part in passive protests against the government's discriminatory policies. It was there that he developed his creed of passive resistance against injustice or *satyagraha*, meaning "truth force," and began to be jailed as a result of his protests. Before he returned to India, he had radically changed the lives of Indians living in South Africa.

It can be argued that the independence movement in India was the inevitable result of the British Empire's own success in that it allowed the appearance of a highly educated Indian middle class. Indian nationals, however, were not given any political role in the administration of the British Empire. In 1885, educated middle class nationals had founded the Indian National Congress (INC). Their aim was to get a much greater say in the way India was governed. It was thus not surprising that on his return from South Africa in 1915, Gandhi joined the INC movement and soon emerged as

one of the party's prominent members, taking the lead in what would become his life-long struggle for Indian independence from Britain.

The Indian movement of independence intensified in the 1920s due to a combination of factors such as the lack of satisfaction with existing measures—the Morley-Minto reforms of 1909 had not redressed total political domination of a white elite—and the increasing currency of ideas of national self-determination that undermined the basic premise of the British Empire. As a result, Gandhi began to encourage Indians to boycott British goods and buy Indian goods instead. This helped to revitalize local economies in India while having deleterious consequences for the British economy. The other two names to emerge in the 1920s as key actors of the independence movement were Jawaharlal Nehru and Muhammad Jinnah.

Gandhi preached passive resistance, believing that acts of violence against the British only provoked a negative reaction, whereas passive resistance provoked the British into acting in ways that invariably pushed more people into supporting the INC movement. This tactic had the desired effect during the riots that broke out in Amritsar, where 379 unarmed protesters were killed and 1,200 injured by British soldiers. The incident shocked many in India but this was followed by outrage when the commanding British officer, General Rex Dyer, was simply allowed to resign with no more than a

*Mahatma Gandhi's nonviolent protests helped defeat the British Empire and move India toward independence.*

reprimand. As a result of Amritsar, many Indians rushed to join the INC and it very quickly became the party of the masses.

Gandhi started his second civil disobedience campaign in 1930, during the time the Simon Commission reported on India's suitability for self-rule. This included Gandhi deliberately breaking the law. After a 250-mile march to the sea, Gandhi started to produce his own salt, acting against a law stating that only the government could manufacture salt. This produced a violent clash with the British authorities and Gandhi was arrested.

By the early 1930s, a sympathetic British viceroy organized two roundtable conferences in London to discuss the future of India. Although nothing directly emerged from these talks (as many INC members were in prison), the British government eventually passed the Government of India Act, introducing limited self-rule and an elected Indian assembly. From then on, and until the final independence of India, the biggest challenge to be faced by Gandhi and the independence movement was the degree of religious division between Hindus and Muslims. Although Gandhi and the Congress Party under Nehru were determined to preserve Indian unity, the results of the 1937 regional elections gave the Muslim League under Jinnah enough popular support to demand a separate state of their own to be called Pakistan.

The situation of Indian independence came to a head soon after the end of World War II. Gandhi, realizing that the religious issues of India were too deep, collaborated with the British in the build-up to independence in 1947. This association with the break-up of India was to cost him his life. The last two months of his life were spent trying to end the appalling religious violence that ensued by means of a hunger strike that brought him to the brink of death. In January 1948, at the age of 79, Gandhi was assassinated by a Hindu for his tolerance towards Muslims.

Gandhi has passed to history as the political activist who could achieve his aims by nonviolent means and through civil disobedience. The power of nonviolence was particularly effective against the British colonial rulers. In the many occasions he was arrested, he coupled this strategy with hunger strikes. Due to his global popularity, Gandhi's death in prison would make international headlines and greatly embarrass a British government that was at the time condemning dictatorships in Europe. His beliefs and special type of activism would also become crucial to many other political movements across the world. For example, the 1960s civil rights movement in the United States and Martin Luther King, Jr., owe an enormous debt to Gandhi's political legacy.

In one sense, Gandhi can be viewed as an advocate of national self-determination, a view usually associated with the right. However, his adoption of *satyagraha*, his identification with the poor, and his advocacy of religious toleration put his views on the left of the political spectrum within the British Commonwealth and within India.

### SEE ALSO

*Volume 1 Left:* Civil Rights; India.
*Volume 2 Right:* Colonialism: United Kingdom; India.

### BIBLIOGRAPHY

Christine Hatt, *Mahatma Gandhi* (World Almanac Library, 2004); Ana Caybourne, *Gandhi: The Peaceful Revolutionary* (Hodder Wayland, 2003); Mike Nicholson, *Mahatma Gandhi*

(Merlin, 1989); Bhikhu Parekh, *Gandhi* (Oxford University Press, 1997).

KEPA ARTARAZ, PH.D.
UNIVERSITY OF DERBY, UNITED KINGDOM

# Gay and Lesbian Movements

BECAUSE HOMOSEXUALITY has historically been defined as "deviant" behavior, social, political, economic, and legal discrimination against openly homosexual individuals has been documented in most societies around the world. Several decades after gay and lesbian movements received public attention, the battle over why an individual is gay affects public attitudes toward homosexuality. Forty percent of the population now believes that homosexuality is a biological condition. They feel that no one should be punished for something beyond their control. Those who believe, as do the religious right and other ultraconservatives, that homosexuality is a life-style choice tend to be the most vocal critics of the extension of gay rights. Many conservatives justify their attack on gays and lesbians as attacks on atheists who reject biblical teaching. Some of the conservative animosity is also undoubtedly due to the fact that most gays and lesbians are Democrats. Liberals believe that the reason for being gay is irrelevant because the same rights should be extended to all people because of their humanity.

The gay rights movement officially began in Germany in 1896 under the leadership of Magnus Hirschfeld, who established the Scientific Humanitarian Committee to fight prejudice against gays. In pre-Hitler Germany, gay bars, nightclubs, and cabarets flourished, frequented by both gays and straights. However, the movement was virtually eradicated during the reign of the Third Reich, when homosexuals were forced to wear pink triangles for identification. Many were arrested and sent to concentration camps. Others were shot. Estimates of the number of homosexuals affected by Hitler's purges range from 10,000 to 600,000.

In 1924, the first secret advocacy group for homosexuals was founded in the United States as the Chicago Society for Human Rights. An underground gay rights movement spread around the country despite frequent raids and attacks by local police who were fond of entrapping homosexuals and charging them with vagrancy and lewd conduct. Another common police tactic was to suspend or revoke business licenses of known homosexuals. As hostility against homosexuals increased in small towns and rural areas, a mass urban migration followed. Secret gay societies were also established in Harlem (New York City), San Francisco (California), and New Orleans (Louisiana). The organized effort to win equal treatment for gays and lesbians surfaced in the United States only after World War II, partially in response to the fact that some 10,000 homosexuals were given dishonorable discharges from the military when the military belatedly began to enforce the 1943 ban on gays in the military. This issue was still highly volatile in 1993 when Bill Clinton attempted to deliver on a campaign promise to gays by announcing his "Don't ask, don't tell" method of protecting gays in the military.

A new wave of animosity toward homosexuals surfaced in the 1950s during the McCarthy area when Senator Joseph McCarthy added homosexuals to his list of "un-Americans." In 1951, the Mettachine Society was established as a legal front for the International Bachelors Fraternal Order for Peace and Social Dignity by gay rights pioneer Harry Hay. As the gay rights movement gained momentum, branches of the Mettachine Society opened in other large cities.

In 1955, Phyllis Lyon and Del Martin joined with a group of other women to form the first organized lesbian group in the United States. The group was named the Daughters of Bilitis after a French novel containing love poems between women. Lyon and Martin steered the group toward fighting for legal and social rights for lesbians. The two were also involved in the founding of the Council on Religion and the Homosexual, a group made up of gays and lesbians and religious leaders, designed to open a dialogue about California's sex laws. The publication of Del Martin's *Battered Wives* in 1976 lit a fire that led to the movement against domestic violence.

In the 1960s, as the attitudes and policies of the New Left gained prominence, the gay community recognized the concept of "gay pride" for the first time. Leaders of the movement began holding consciousness-raising meetings. As the civil rights movement gained momentum, "gay libbers," like "women's libbers," joined the battle to gain civil rights for all groups that had historically been discriminated against. A small group of extremist feminists claimed that all "true" feminists should be lesbians. Dissension within the gay and lesbian rights movement created deep divisions that brought an abrupt end to gay liberation. While groups continued to exist, they became more mainstream, working for the right to earn a living, to raise children, for fair access to housing, and for freedom from what became known as "gay bashing." In 1968, the Fifth North American Conference of Homophile Organizations (NACHO) agreed on a bill of rights that called for the repeal of all sodomy laws, an end to police entrapment of homosexuals, the elimination of discrimination against homosexuals in employment, and the right to serve in the military.

## STONEWALL RIOT

The Stonewall riot on June 27, 1969, was a major turning point in the gay rights movement. After police raided a gay bar in Greenwich Village in New York City, hundreds of people responded with violence. Media coverage of the event brought public attention to the issue of open hostility and discrimination of homosexuals, radicalizing gay/lesbian rights movements. In October 1973, gay activists founded the National Gay Task Force, later changed to the National Gay and Lesbian Task Force, to recapture unity in the fight for gay and lesbian rights. This group was instrumental in convincing the American Psychiatric Association (APA) to remove homosexuality from its list of mental illnesses.

During the conservative 1980s, gay and lesbian rights movements became rejuvenated. Leaders believed that it was necessary to establish a national gay identity that called for full citizenship rights through civil disobedience and organized efforts to effect legal changes at the state and national level. One of the motivating forces of the 1980s for lesbians and gays was the issue of AIDS (Acquired Immune Deficiency Syndrome). A backlash against homosexuals followed after it was announced that AIDS could be spread through sexual conduct and that gay men were the most likely group to contract the disease. Gay and lesbian rights organizations added AIDS education and support for AIDS victims to their agendas. As information about safe sex spread, the incidence of AIDS among gay males declined.

Members of the lesbian and gay rights movements received a major setback in 1986 when the Supreme Court handed down the decision in *Bowers v. Hardwick* (478 U.S. 186) that upheld Georgia's sodomy law. They were particularly galled by the fact that Justice Lewis Powell, who swung the vote toward the conservative position, later admitted that he made the wrong decision. In a scathing dissent to *Hardwick*, Justice Harry Blackmun refused to buy the argument that the case was about homosexual sodomy. He insisted that the issue

was about privacy and the fundamental right of individuals to lead their lives free of government interference. In 2003, in *Lawrence v. Texas* (02 U.S. 102), the Supreme Court overturned Texas's sodomy law and expanded constitutional protections for gays and lesbians by stating that discrimination based on a particular lifestyle is unacceptable.

Much of the work within gay and lesbian organizations is focused on dealing with the legal difficulties of same-sex unions. While one in every four gay and lesbian couple is raising children, most laws are not designed for same-sex parents. In Florida, for example, where adoption by homosexuals is illegal, gay partners may not have legal standing with regard to children of the other partner. Homosexuality has also been used to deprive gay parents of child custody in a number of states. Healthcare is a crucial issue for gay and lesbian couples. Many stay-at-home homosexuals have no health coverage. Even when companies include health insurance coverage for gay partners, the Internal Revenue Service (IRS) requires gay employees to count such benefits as income. The IRS also bans homosexual couples from filing joint tax returns and from claiming the marriage benefit, forcing gay couples to pay higher single tax rates.

As Baby Boomers grow older, the number of elderly gays and lesbians increases annually. Because two-thirds of gay and lesbian couples live in states where same-sex marriage is illegal, many gays and lesbians face major problems as they retire. Since the national government does not recognize such unions, gay partners cannot draw on the other's social security benefits. Depending on state laws, gay survivors may not qualify to inherit property without paying taxes, as do widows and widowers. If a gay partner dies without a will, the surviving partner may not be able to inherit at all.

## GAY MARRIAGE

The most volatile issue for gays and lesbians as the 21st century began was the issue of gay marriage. Gay couples demanded the right to legalize their unions, and California, Hawaii, Massachusetts, and Vermont complied by legally recognizing either gay marriage or same-sex unions. Bills to follow suit were introduced in state legislatures around the country. Conservatives responded by calling for a constitutional amendment to ban gay marriages. Well aware of the potential for votes in an election year, George W. Bush announced that he supported the amendment. Democratic candidate John Kerry stated that while he supports gay rights, he does not endorse gay marriage. While the amendment is not expected to gain the necessary support in the Senate, both parties have attempted to use the issue to their political advantage.

The number of gay and lesbian groups continues to grow yearly. While some groups are national, others are targeted at particular constituencies or issues. For instance, the Gay, Lesbian, and Straight Educational Network is concerned with educating the public about homosexuality. The Stonewall Democrats focus on a liberal agenda, while the Log Cabin Republicans adhere to conservative fiscal attitudes. The Gay Liberation Front and Queer Nation engage in more radical agendas, while Lamba Legal Defense and Education Fund targets civil rights and support for AIDS victims. Many mainstream liberal groups also support gay rights, including the National Organization for Women (NOW), the American Civil Liberties Union (ACLU), and Amnesty International.

## SEE ALSO

*Volume 1 Left:* American Civil Liberties Union; Civil Rights; Human Rights.
*Volume 2 Right:* Conservatism; Religion; New Right; Bush, George W.

## BIBLIOGRAPHY

Melvin P. Antell, "Should Homosexuality Ban Parents from Being Awarded Custody of a Child?" M. Ethan Katsh, ed., *Taking Sides: Clashing Views on Controversial Legal Issues* (Dushkin, 1993); Ari Bendersky, "The Peril of Online Polling, *Advocate* (March 2, 2004); Thomas C. Carmagno, ed., *Irreconcilable Differences? Intellectual Stalemate in the Gay Rights Debate* (Praeger, 2002); John D'Emilio, *Making Trouble: Essays on Gay History, Politics, and the University* (Routledge, 1992); Gary Gates, "Don't Ignore Gay Unions' Social, Economic Impact," *USA Today* (October 23, 2003); Aart Hendriks et al., *The Third Pink Book: A Global View of Lesbian and Gay Oppression* (Prometheus, 1993); George M. Kenna and Stanley Feingold, eds., "Does Government Have a Right to Prohibit Homosexual Acts?" *Taking Sides: Clashing Views on Controversial Political Issues* (Dushkin, 1989); Elizabeth Patterson, "Homosexual Rights and the Placement of Children," *Policy and Practice* (March 2004); Walter Shapiro, "Advances in Gay Rights Overtake Health Policy," *USA Today* (May 19, 2004); Ralph R. Smith and Russell R. Windes, *Progay/Antigay: The Rhetorical War over Sexuality* (Sage, 2000); Chuck Stewart, *Gay and Lesbian Issues: A Reference Handbook* (ABC-CLIO Publishers, 2004); William E. Symonds, "Gay Marriage Still Faces Long Slog," *BusinessWeek* (May 31, 2004); Suzanna Danuta Walters, "From Here to Queer: Radical Feminism, Post Modernism, and the Lesbian Menace," *Signs* (Summer 1996).

ELIZABETH PURDY, PH.D.
INDEPENDENT SCHOLAR

# Germany

THE GERMAN LEFT has been characterized as a phenomenon of the 19th and 20th centuries, however, it can be traced back to much earlier events that emphasized either theoretical or practical aspects of a political revolution. There are religious, philosophical, and social aspects that underlie the development of the left, which were later incorporated into political movements.

Already in the 16th century, there were religious elements and a tension between theory and practice that would later shape German politics. On the one hand, the Protestant Reformation led by Martin Luther adopted new doctrines in reaction against the submission to Rome, thus establishing independent reigns. On the other hand, other popular religious movements concerned with their daily situation of exploitation took that same moment to express themselves in a belligerent way, led by Thomas Muenzer in the so-called Peasants War (Bauernkrieg). Later on, the experiences of Muenzer and the peasants were rescued by Ernst Bloch, became a reference for the official Marxism of East Germany, and reached the Green Party.

There were also philosophical aspects that would later guide the German Left, such as the idea of "criticism" proposed in the transcendental philosophy of Immanuel Kant and the criticism of Kant by G.W.F. Hegel. The tension between theory and practice within philosophy and the need to resolve it by means of effective political action was a main concern for Hegel's disciples, such as Ludwig Feuerbach, Bruno Bauer, Max Stirner, and others. They had different opinions on how this could be done. As a result, there was a split between two groups: the Right Hegelians and the Left Hegelians. The latter turned to socialism.

It is at this point that one can find the origins of what can be properly called the German Left. The Left Hegelians adopted the socialism of Saint-Simon and argued for a revolution in Germany, because in their view, socialism was a coherent outcome of criticism. Accordingly, the first political moment in which the ideas of

*Immanuel Kant's philosophy of criticism was an early inspiration for the development of German socialism.*

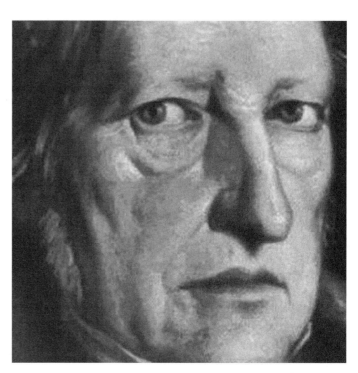

*G.W.F. Hegel built on Kant's criticisms and eventually Left Hegelian disciples turned to socialism as their practical guiding principle.*

the left were at play was during the revolutions of 1848, when different groups in Europe took arms in order to defend socialism.

After the attempt at a revolution in 1848, there was also the need to bring both the theoretical and practical tradition together, when the idea of a "dictatorship of the proletarians" was first mentioned. These discussions and initiatives provided the background for Karl Marx and Friedrich Engels to develop their proposals for a leftist philosophy. From a theoretical point of view, Marx and Engels adopted the philosophy of criticism, but enlarged it in order to move from an abstract "critique of pure reason" to a materialist "critique of political economy." According to Marx, one of the essential aspects of life was not the "Spirit" as Hegel claimed, but the concrete relation to nature and the work performed by humans. With this turn to the economical aspects of daily life, Marx was also able to understand and integrate the claims of the poor and the workers. In his view, poverty was a result of the alienation of their work by someone else, who would then accumulate capital at the worker's expense. While Marx turned to a "critique of Hegel's philosophy," Engels studied the history of revolutionary movements—including the movement led by Muenzer. Both Marx and Engels came to the conclusion that the revolutionary

theories were too abstract, while the revolutionary practices of peasant movements were too utopian.

In his famous thesis against Feuerbach, Marx stated that "the philosophers have only interpreted the world, [but] the point is to change it." This conclusion was crucial to the development of the left in Germany, because the differences between the theoretical and practical approaches to revolution were understood to be a result of class differences and their conflicting interests. Therefore, a "class conflict" (*Klassenkampf*) generated a series of other internal conflicts between bureaucratic work and manual labor, urban and rural workers, and men and women, as well as industrialized nations and colonies. This class conflict, according to Marx and Engels, had to be solved by the Left Hegelians in order to transform society.

The goal of social and political transformation had to be a classless society. Marx and Engels studied and supported a series of political movements, such as the workers' movement, the socialist party, the women's movement and the peasants' movement, among others. They also had an evolutionary conception of history, proposing a succession of stages in political and economic development, whereby socialism would be the inevitable and highest stage in the future. The impact of the ideas of Marx and Engels motivated new initiatives that were labeled Marxism. Under this label, there were several groups that advocated different means and strategies to attain the goal of a classless society. From a theoretical perspective, German thinkers and ideologues had several proposals. Orthodox Marxism followed the writings of Marx and Engels literally. Reformism held that the transformation of society would have to occur by means of improving already existing conditions of a given democratic society, since it would be impossible to have a new start in history. Among the advocates of this position were those who followed Vladimir Lenin's ideas in Western Europe.

Revisionism, in turn, suggested that the original tactics for a revolution, as proposed by Marx and Engels, had to be changed, because capitalism had reached some stages that were not previously envisaged by Marx and Engels. Klaus Kautsky and Edouard Bernstein were the most important defenders of this position. They still believed in original principles such as class struggle and the inevitability of socialism after capitalism reached its limits, but thought that some economic aspects needed better technical understanding. Austro-Marxism was a doctrine developed in Vienna, Austria, under the leadership of Max Adler and Otto Bauer around 1904. They adopted positivism, which was in vogue at the time, and argued that Marxism needed to be backed by rigorous science and concrete evidences. The position advocated by Rosa Luxemburg defended the revolutionary approach against the revisionists.

Other movements were more oriented towards practical life. Syndicalism, for instance, insisted that Marxism should be based on the organization of unions and syndicates in order to better prepare workers for the class struggle. Gustav Landauer was one of its main strategists and advocated the organization of strikes. Anarchism had its origins as an alternative to socialism, and was based on the ideas of Mikhail Bakunin, but at the beginning of the 20th century, it often merged with Marxism for mass strikes. Women's movements also had their inspiration in Marxism, starting with the involvement of Marx's daughter, Jenny Marx, and continuing with the participation of Clara Zetkin and others at the Second International in 1889.

Marxism became the most important doctrine for the German and the European left. In 1891, this doctrine was institutionalized through the creation of the German Sozialdemokratische Partei Deutschlands (SPD). Kautsky and Bernstein worked as editors of SPD publications, the *Sozialdemokrat* and *Neue Zeit*. Progressively, the party gained legitimacy and a steady share of the voters. As Donald Sassoon has argued, "The SPD influence grew as German industry grew," but it also began to have its internal differences with rightist and leftist groups within the party. After World War I, the German left was split into different parties, such as the Majority Social Democrats (MSPD), the Independent Social Democrats (USPD), the German Communist Party (KPD), and other smaller groups.

One of the important achievements of the SPD was the creation of the Weimar Republic in 1918, in which a democratic constitution was approved, the parliament gained power, social rights were implemented (granting voting, education, health, and freedom rights to all citizens), and workers had more guarantees, such as limited working hours, wage regulation, benefits, and other measures. With all these achievements, the task of implementing a social democracy occurred in a different way from what had happened in the Russian Revolution of 1917. However, the SPD began to lose its power, especially due to the difficult social situation in Germany after World War I. In this process, the left also lost part of its political influence, thus giving space for the advancement of the NSPD, the German National-Socialist (Nazi) Party led by Adolf Hitler. As the NSDP later implemented a new regime, it not only sealed the end of the Weimar Republic, but also the beginning of the internal policies and international politics that led to the Holocaust, the persecution of communists, the repression of civilians, and the beginning of World War II.

After the war, as Germany was divided among the nations that had led the Allied forces, the portion dominated by the United States, France, and England—West Germany—adopted the democratic system, while the portion conquered by the Soviet Union—East Germany—adopted communism. After the war, the SPD regained many voters in the part occupied by the Soviets and merged with the KPD to form the Sozialistische Einheitspartei Deutschlands (SED, Socialist Unity Party). With the Cold War, this was institutionalized as the official party of the German Democratic Republic. In this way West Germany was somewhat equated with the right, while East Germany was equated with the left.

Western Marxism in Germany was a revision of the Marxist doctrines in opposition to orthodox Marxism. This position was championed by the Frankfurt School, which proposed the turn to cultural, humanist, and aesthetical aspects of society. The Frankfurt School began when several intellectuals related to the University of Frankfurt and the Institute of Social Research began to develop a series of studies during the 1920s. Among them were Erich Fromm, Max Horkheimer, Theodor Adorno, Walter Benjamin, Herbert Marcuse, Sigfried

*Friedrich Engels steered Marxian philosophy away from abstract theory and toward practical application.*

*According to Karl Marx, one of the essential aspects of life was not the "Spirit" as Hegel claimed, but work performed by humans.*

Kracauer, and Leo Loewenthal, besides other Marxist thinkers who had indirect relations to the group, such as Ernst Bloch, and Gyorg Lukacs. One important heir to the Frankfurt School was Jurgen Habermas, who was involved in several debates concerning the future of the left in Germany, articulating Marxist ideas to language, society, psychoanalysis, and culture.

The impact of these ideas led to a new series of studies of the Marxist tradition, especially in the reappraisal of what had been neglected by the official partisan interpretation. As it emphasized culture, the theoretical ideas of the Frankfurt School had a direct and indirect influence on a series of socialist and leftist movements during the 1960s.

While the SPD regained its importance under the leadership of Willy Brandt during this time, there was also a new culture of resistance to the bourgeois values led by the women's movement, the workers' movement, and. most importantly, the students' movement. Rudi Dutschke and Daniel Cohn-Bendit were the most important leaders of the student movements that exploded during 1968 in Germany. Dutschke was born in East Germany, but was able to move to West Berlin in

1961, where he enrolled in the university to study sociology. In 1963, he began to take part in subversive actions by students and became very active in the German Federation of Socialist Students (SDS, Sozialistische Deutschen Studentenbund), which led a series of student revolts in the country, reaching its climax in 1968, when there were invasions of universities, the realization of an Anti-Vietnam Congress in Germany, and a series of manifestations. The radicalization of these times was also felt by Dutschke, who barely survived an assassination attempt and left the country. He died in 1979. Cohn-Bendit on the other hand, had both German and the French citizenship and was involved in movements in both countries, thus gaining international recognition as student leader.

Cohn-Bendit was also more realistic, as he did not believe in radical reforms or a revolution as the outcome of the student revolt. Later, he joined the Green Party and become a representative in the European Parliament. The manifestations of the students yielded a series of reforms in German universities, especially in opening them to more students and providing for student participation in decision-making processes. As an inheritor of the Frankfurt School, the philosopher Habermas tried to address the claims of the student movement, but later considered it to be violent and somewhat irrational. Indeed, the student movement also gave way to the radical left in the 1970s, which had one of its most belligerent expressions in the Red Army Faction, a group that committed a series of terrorist acts during the 1970s and was repressed by the German government. Later on, other groups such as the Young Socialists (JUSOS), the Autonomy (Autonomes), and the Anarchists inherited a certain radicalism but expressed it in terms of counterculture, attracting other groups such as hippies and angry youths to the left.

The future of the left in Germany is connected to the ecological or environmental movement. Although the beginning of the ecological movement in Germany was also connected to fascist and conservative ideas, the movement received the impact of the student protests, the support of the worker's movements, and the adhesion of the middle classes—especially after the pacifist protests against the installation of American nuclear missiles in Germany. These manifestations gave more power to the Green Party, which obtained more than 8 percent of the vote in the country in 1987.

During the 1990s, the Green Party also began to discuss association with socialist and communist groups, but always under the proviso that they could agree on basic principles. Accordingly, the party was divided between the Fundis (fundamentalists)—who, like Petra Kelly, opposed any alliance with working groups and considered the workers as allies of capitalism—and the Realos (realists)—who, like Joschka Fischer, were open to coalitions in order to gain more votes. The latter group won, and the Red-Green coalition was the result of the association of the Greens with the SPD and former members of the Communist Party in East Germany, after the reunification of Germany. In this way, the Greens were recognized as the New Left of the 1960s, but now with new clothes and mature perspectives. Moreover, by turning to questions of land and ecology, the Greens continue the tradition initiated by the peasants' revolts in the 16th century.

**SEE ALSO**

*Volume 1 Left:* Marx, Karl; Engels, Friedrich; Socialism; Communism; Green Party; Fromm, Erich; Anarchism.
*Volume 2 Right:* Capitalism; Fascism; Soviet Union; Germany.

**BIBLIOGRAPHY**

Werner Hofmann, *Ideengeschichte der sozialen Bewegungen* (Berlin, De Gruyter, 1966); Rolf Wiggershaus, *Die Frankfurter Schule* (Frankfurt, Fischer, 1989); Jürgen Habermas, *Die neue Unübersichtlichkeit* (Frankfurt, Suhrkamp, 1985); Werner Huelsberg, *The German Greens: A Social and Political Profile* (Verso, 1988); Donald Sassoon, *One Hundred Years of Socialism* (Free Press, 1996); Karl Marx and Friedrich Engels, *The German Ideology* (Moscow, Progress Publishers, 1983).

AMOS NASCIMENTO
METHODIST UNIVERSITY OF PIRACICABA, BRAZIL

# Gilman, Charlotte Perkins (1860–1935)

THE GRANDNIECE of Harriet Beecher Stowe, Charlotte Perkins Gilman grew up in Providence, Rhode Island. After the birth of her daughter, she experienced a severe depression lasting several years. She entered a sanitarium in Philadelphia, Pennsylvania, for a controversial rest cure that demanded no physical activity and no intellectual stimulation. One month later she returned home, and soon after suffered a nervous breakdown. In 1888, Gilman left her husband and moved to California, where she had a swift recovery from her depression.

In the early 1890s, she began writing and lecturing. Her most famous work, *The Yellow Wallpaper* (1892), told the story of a woman who suffers a mental breakdown after the birth of her child. The story has been interpreted commonly as either a semi-autobiographical account of her own experiences or as a metaphor for women's situation within society and within marriage. It is a story of women's confinement and escape. It details the oppression of the female artist within a patriarchal society and literary tradition. Repeated images of suffocation and confinement parallel the idea of women trapped within the domestic sphere. Gilman wrote the story not only to highlight the oppression of women in society, but also in hopes that the story would educate doctors about the perils of the rest cure she was prescribed.

Her cure involved lying down for an hour after each meal, limiting intellectual life, stressing isolation, immobility, overfeeding, and giving up writing and art for the rest of her life. She didn't see the work as literature, but rather a politicized piece of writing with a strong message about women's role within society. Gilman was a prolific writer throughout her life, and in 1898 she published the book *Women and Economics*, which was translated into seven languages and received critical acclaim. Her writing was expansive: she published in the areas of sociology, political science, economics, literature, and women's studies. The unifying theme, however, was society's need for reform. In addition to writing, she also engaged in activist work, as in 1915 when she cofounded the Women's Peace Party with activist Jane Addams. In 1932, she was diagnosed with breast cancer, and three years later committed suicide. In 1994, she was posthumously inducted into the National Women's Hall of Fame in Senecca Falls, New York.

Gilman is most known for her work on women's perspectives on work and family. She believed that men and women should share equally in housework responsibilities, a radical notion at the time. She argued that sex was a more fundamental social division within society than class, in contrast to Marxist beliefs. She argued that one of the sources of women's repression was their role as mothers, which limited their personal expression and creativity. She believed that childcare experts should raise children and that private housekeeping was inefficient and wasteful. She argued that households and the economy as a whole would be better off if women entered the labor force and communal kitchens were established for the mass production of food.

Many of these views can be found in her feminist utopian novel *Herland*, which tells the story of a visit by three male explorers to an island inhabited by a community of women. The men arrive with the expectations that the women will be grateful for male company, and in need of their expertise and control. Instead they find a community of women with strong social consciousness, sisterly affection, and social inventiveness.

She argued that society is structured so that men produce and distribute wealth while women receive it. This economic dependence disadvantages individuals and society as a whole, as keeping women at home and out of the workforce is a waste of economic contribution. She argued that suffrage was not enough. She demanded a radical shift in gender values and societal priorities and profound social restructuring of leisure, child rearing, work, and domestic responsibilities. Although advocates of women's rights were viewed by Marx as emphasizing a "false consciousness," Gilman directly assailed that view and cast her approach to feminist values in radical terms.

## SEE ALSO

*Volume 1 Left:* Feminism; Suffragists; Socialism; Civil Rights. *Volume 2 Right:* United States.

**BIBLIOGRAPHY**

Charlotte Perkins Gilman, *The Yellow Wallpaper and Other Writing* (Modern Library, 2000); Charlotte Perkins Gilman, *Women and Economics* (Prometheus Books, 1994); Catherine J. Golden and Joanna Schneider Zangrando, eds., *The Mixed Legacy of Charlotte Perkins Gilman* (University of Delaware Press, 2000).

SHANNON K. ORR
BOWLING GREEN STATE UNIVERSITY

# Gitlow, Benjamin (1891–1965)

ONE OF THE COFOUNDERS and most prominent early leaders of the Communist Party of the United States (CPUSA or CP), Benjamin Gitlow later broke with communism and became one of its harshest critics, allying himself with McCarthyite anti-communism. Today, he is best remembered for having instigated a landmark U.S. Supreme Court decision that expanded constitutional protection for freedom of speech—even though he lost the case.

The son of Russian-Jewish immigrants and ardent socialists, he worked as a cloth cutter while studying law at night and joined the Socialist Party. In 1917, he was one of ten Socialists elected to the New York State Assembly; by the end of his term, however, he had quit the party after an unsuccessful attempt, together with fellow Bolshevik supporters John Reed and Louis Fraina, to take control of the socialists.

In 1919, he, Jay Lovestone, and Charles Ruthenberg formed one of two competing U.S. Communist parties; they were eventually ordered by the Comintern in Moscow, Soviet Union, to merge, but Gitlow's group—known as the Goose faction, because its critics said "they cackle like geese"—remained dominant. Though its foreign-born leaders at first were disdainful of native communists, Gitlow later wrote, "they realized that without an English-speaking wing, it would be impossible to organize a Communist Party in the United States." That same year, Gitlow was one of many leftists arrested in a nationwide crackdown on alleged subversives. He was convicted of criminal anarchy by the state of New York for having published a pamphlet entitled *Left-Wing Manifesto*, saying it incited the overthrow of the government: It had demanded "mass strikes," as well as "expropriation of the bourgeoisie" and establishment of a "dictatorship of the proletariat." His case reached the U.S. Supreme Court, which upheld his conviction by a 7-2 vote, with Justices Louis Brandeis and Oliver Wendell Holmes dissenting; the latter declaring that "every idea is an incitement." But the majority decision, while ruling against Gitlow, established a critical precedent for all future First Amendment cases. For the first time, the court established that the Fourteenth Amendment's due process clause covered liberty of expression—meaning that freedoms and liberties, as well as personal property, were entitled to protection from state, not just federal, infringement.

Though sentenced to a term of five to ten years, Gitlow went free after serving less than four years, after receiving a pardon from New York's Governor Al Smith. During his imprisonment, the Communist Party's electoral arm, the Worker's League, tried to run him for mayor, but he was disqualified from the ballot when the Board of Elections ruled that he was a legal resident of Sing Sing, not New York. (He would appear on the ballot in 1924 and 1928 as the Communist candidate for vice president.) Meanwhile, the party distributed his speech to the trial jury in a pamphlet, *The Red Ruby*, taken from the prosecutor's accusation that Gitlow "would make America a red ruby in the red treasure chest of the red terror."

In 1929, the Comintern moved to cement its control of the U.S. Communist Party: Gitlow and Jay Lovestone were ordered to step aside for having committed "right-wing deviationism" and insisting that communist ideology in America had to be determined by domestic political events; they were also cited for failing to end factionalism within the CP. When the pair and their followers tried to resist Josef Stalin's directive, they were expelled from the party.

In his autobiography, *The Truth about American Communism*, Gitlow said he broke with the party because of its "enslavement of the human mind" and its "proscription of independent thinking." He became a fierce public opponent of the party, aligning himself with conservative anti-communists. In 1939, following the Hitler-Stalin pact, Gitlow testified against the party before Congress, providing details of Soviet funding for the U.S. party as well as espionage carried out by its members. More than a decade later, when the Justice Department moved to deport Louis Fraina, Gitlow was the chief witness against him.

### SEE ALSO

*Volume 1 Left:* Communism; Lovestone, Jay; Browder, Earl; Stalin and Stalism; Cominform.
*Volume 2 Right:* McCarthyism; United States.

### BIBLIOGRAPHY

Theodore Draper, *The Roots of American Communism* (Ivan R. Dee, 1985); Irving Howe and Lewis Coser, *The American Communist Party: A Critical History* (Beacon Press, 1957); Harvey E. Klehr, *Communist Cadre: The Social Background of the American Communist Elite* (Hoover Institution Press, 1978); Harvey Klehr, John Earl Haynes, and Friedrich Igorevich Firsov, *The Secret World of American Communism* (Yale University Press, 1995).

ERIC FETTMANN
INDEPENDENT SCHOLAR

# Goldman, Emma (1869–1940)

EMMA GOLDMAN WAS born in a part of what was then Tzarist Russia. She emigrated to the United States in 1885, where she got in contact with the anarchist Johann Most and the radical Robert Reitzel (both German-born). Whereas this older generation was still largely culturally bound to the Old World, Goldman tried to establish a sort of U.S. anarchism. She became a public figure when Alexander Berkman—her partner in life and politics—was convicted for a murder attempt on an especially brutal capitalist (Henry Clay Frick). While Berkman was in prison, Goldman embarked on a crusade as a speaker across the United States: She was imprisoned several times and at last deported during the Red Scare following the Russian Revolution. Goldman went to Soviet Russia, but soon fell out of favor with the dictatorial Bolsheviks. She left Russia in 1921, and spent time in several European states and Canada. During the Spanish Civil War, she strongly and personally supported the Spanish anarchists fighting the fascism of Francisco Franco. She died in Canada, but was posthumously granted entry to the United States to be buried in Chicago, Illinois (Waldheim cemetery, a famous final resting place for prominent left-wingers).

To get a picture of the views from the left on Goldman it is useful to compare Goldman to her contemporaries Rosa Luxemburg and Clara Zetkin. All three had an enormous impact on the left, especially in the early 20th century, and became female icons of diverging parts of the left. Biographically, both Goldman and Luxemburg shared a Jewish origin in parts of Eastern Europe then under Tzarist rule (Lithuania and Poland). Luxemburg stands for the pre-1914 German SPD (social-democratic party) and during the last days of her

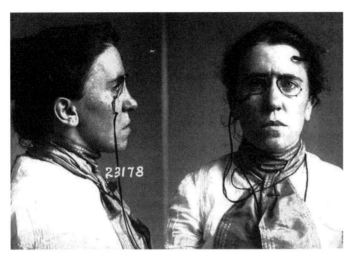

*Emma Goldman's radical anarchism did not fit well with Soviet communism, nor with U.S. authorities as this mugshot suggests.*

**SEE ALSO**
*Volume 1 Left:* Stalin and Stalinism; Communist Party, Soviet; Anarchism.
*Volume 2 Right:* United States; Capitalism.

**BIBLIOGRAPHY**
Peter Glassgold, *Anarchy! An Anthology of Emma Goldman's Mother Earth* (Counterpoint Press, 2001); Emma Goldman, *Living My Life: An Autobiography* (Gibbs Smith 1982); Emma Goldman Papers Project, ed., *Emma Goldman: A Guide to Her Life and Documentary Sources* (Chadwyck-Healey, 1995); Howard Zinn, *Emma* (Consortium, 2002).

OLIVER BENJAMIN HEMMERLE, PH.D.
CHEMNITZ UNIVERSITY, GERMANY

life, for the emerging (German) communist party; Zetkin symbolizes the post-1919 (German) communist party; and Goldman the (U.S., later European) anarchistic movement. All three share an unhappy fate, Luxemburg being murdered by an extreme right-wing soldier in 1919, and both Goldman and Zetkin dying in exile. Albeit, these three women inspired large parts of the left at certain times and continue to do so; this triplet also represents the bitter factions and infighting of the left from the late 19th century.

Goldman, seen from a social-democratic viewpoint, was an able agitator within the struggle for social and women's rights, but dangerously leaned to terroristic anarchism. Goldman, seen from a communist viewpoint, was an intolerable free spirit who never accepted the rule of the party as the only way of (communist) salvation.

It has to be mentioned that Goldman had admirers of her intellect not only in left circles, but appealed to others with her sexually explicit views on free love. As she pointed out in her memoirs, she was not always happy with those admirers translating her concept of free love into the idea of having sex with her. Goldman's theoretical concept of free love was a tool in the struggle for the emancipation of women, not a perversion.

Regardless of political viewpoints, Goldman is recognized for her expression of literary talent and her role as a humane fighter for the emancipation of women and for the rights of the underprivileged. Very early in the 1920s, she warned about the totalitarian dangers of Soviet Union-style communism that came about years later.

# Gorbachev, Mikhail (1931–)

MIKHAIL GORBACHEV is appreciated as one of the most distinguished and controversial leaders of the last quarter of the 20th century. He headed the Soviet Union (USSR) as the Communist Party general secretary beginning on March 11, 1985, and his policy brought an end to the 70-year experiment in constructing a social alternative to capitalism. The failure occurred at the time when "real socialism" seemed to achieve the greatest success and needed just more propulsion. In spite of lower living standards than in the West, the USSR was remarkable for impressive social guarantees and stability. The country that declared worldwide victory of communism as an official goal had a large zone of influence in East-Central Europe, Asia, and Africa and enjoyed military parity with the United States.

When Gorbachev, at age 54, received supreme power, the array of daunting problems was striking and included economic slowdown, losses in Afghanistan, destabilization in Poland, and the intention of the United States, headed by Ronald Reagan, to get an advantage in the Cold War by deploying new missiles in Europe and launching the Strategic Defense Initiative. International tension had reached a dangerous level.

Gorbachev was radically different from his authoritarian predecessors. Being able to search for political solutions and compromises based on dialogue, he represented another type of leader who aimed at popularity through active public policy; however, he only had a slight idea of what end he was going to achieve.

Gorbachev started the "revolution from above" by introducing *glasnost*— openness and publicity, which evoked rampageous debates on historical and sociopolitical issues in media and at meetings. Soviet society was split and baffled. The painful problem of a totalitarian past laid a trap at his every step. Gorbachev also launched *perestroika*—economic and administrative restructuring. Cutting subventions resulted in halting enterprises and whole manufacturing branches, especially in the military-industrial complex. Private entrepreneurship legalization, under the cover of supporting cooperatives, did not undermine the shadow economy, but led to rampancy of crime and rackets. Anti-alcohol prohibitionist arrangements resulted in budget shortages and people's discontent.

Gorbachev acquired a qualitatively new set of foreign policy beliefs and preferences expressed in the concept of the Unified European House. He rejected the Brezhnev Doctrine of firm control over satellites. "Each of Central-Eastern European peoples is the master of his own country and should be totally responsible for what is going on there," Gorbachev declared. The old *nomenklatura*, a significant part of the Communist Party, interpreted this as a lack of firmness, or as hesitation, while those from the hard-line camp called it a betrayal of Gorbachev vis-a-vis his former partners and "friends" from abroad. The foreign-policy reforms had a far-reaching impact on Soviet international behavior and did much to ensure that the Cold War came to an unexpected and peaceful end. Gorbachev and his allies had few opportunities to take advantage of his worldwide popularity, to build state capacity, or to institutionalize his new approach to foreign affairs. The give-and-take policy toward the West had turned into one-sided Soviet concessions from Gorbachev, who was awarded the Noble Peace Prize in 1990, some say as a sort of consolation.

Gorbachev's policy drew out destructive forces of criminality, extremist nationalism, and separatism which he was not able to control. In August 1991, he was blocked by putschists in his Crimean residence at Foros. Conspirators accused Gorbachev of "losing Eastern Europe and sacrificing world socialism." They demanded putting an end to destructive reforms and making order in the country. Boris Yeltsin, who played the major role in the failure of the coup, seized the reins of power in Moscow, tearing out the power of the Communist Party, and, personally, Gorbachev was reluctant to fight Yeltsin. After the December 1991 Belovezsky Agreement between Yeltsin, Leonid Kravchuk, and Stanislav Shushkevich, who represented major Soviet republics of the Russian Federation, Ukraine, and Byelorussia, the Soviet Union ceased to exist. Gorbachev was obliged to resign on December 25, 1991.

Though painful market reforms in Russia were put into practice by his successor, Yeltsin, Gorbachev is considered to be responsible for the backwash of hard times. He got only 0.5 percent of the vote when he ran for the 1996 presidency in Russia. One can still hear in the streets of Moscow tirades against the "the destruction brought by democracy and reforms prompted by Gorbachev who had been bought for 30 pieces of silver by the West."

Gorbachev became leader of the Social-Democratic Party of Russia, formed in 2001. The party didn't have any noticeable influence on Russian political life, but inside it, politics were boiling. In May 2004, the ex-general secretary and ex-president decided to leave the post without a struggle, as was his custom. Like many of the European left, Gorbachev accepts the post-September 11 realities, but he puts the blame on the United States for regarding the world through the prism of Cold War thinking. Gorbachev accuses America of pursuing a policy of world hegemony. Ironically, the new world order in which the global hegemony was assumed by the United States has been derived from his own policy, which brought one of the two poles of a formerly bipolar world to collapse. Political scientists in the former Soviet Union say that if you mean well to your people, whose interests you think to be protecting, you have no right to be actuated just with abstract principles of freedom and justice. You should consider what the declaration of those principles will lead to and how in the real world, they will affect people for whose sake those principles are declared. Deng Xiaoping of China fully possessed that political art. As for Gorbachev, it was *terra incognita*.

## SEE ALSO

*Volume 1 Left*: Soviet Union; Communism; Deng Xiaoping.
*Volume 2 Right*: Reagan, Ronald; Cold War; United States.

## BIBLIOGRAPHY

Mikhail Gorbachev, *Perestroika: New Thinking for Our Country and the World* (Harper & Row, 1988); Mikhail Gorbachev and Zdenek Mlynar, *Conversations with Gorbachev on Perestroika, the Prague Spring, and the Crossroads of Socialism*, George Shriver, trans. (Columbia University Press, 2002); Archie Brown, *The Gorbachev Factor* (Oxford University Press, 1996); George W. Breslauer, *Gorbachev and Yeltsin as Leaders* (Cambridge University Press, 2002); Janice Gross Stein "Political

Learning by Doing: Gorbachev as Uncommitted Thinker and Motivated Learner," *International Organization* (Spring 1994).

IGOR CHARSKYKH
DONETSK NATIONAL UNIVERSITY, UKRAINE

# Granger Movement

THE GRANGER MOVEMENT of the middle to late 19th century reflected a widespread movement toward workers joining together for better conditions and better lives. The Granger movement was the agrarian version of the new labor union movements, with a small difference. Where the labor movements focused on improved working conditions and better wages, this agriculturally based "union" was actually a secret society, the Order of Patrons of Husbandry, whose mission was to bring together farmers and their wives in various informative meetings and social activities in order to improve their lives in the midst of isolation and economic stress. Unlike labor unions, the Grangers focused on intellectual and social reform for farmers, but this ideal changed over time to include economics and politics, at least in practice if not in the Patrons' mission statement.

In 1866, under a commission from President Andrew Johnson, Oliver Hudson Kelley toured the farmlands of the recently defeated Southern states in order to assess the situation of the once agricultural backbone of the country. Appalled by the deplorable social and working conditions he found in the South, Kelley felt impelled to do something to improve the farmers' lot—not just those southern farmers affected by the Civil War, but all farmers in the United States.

His vision was to improve their intellectual and social state, and to do this, he decided to create a secret society, much like the Masons, which would offer informative lectures and social gatherings for its members. So on December 4, 1867, Kelley gathered a group of six men together and met in Washington, D.C., and founded the fraternal society of the Order of the Patrons of Husbandry and established the National Grange.

From this small beginning, the order and the resulting national movement reached hundreds of thousands of farmers in the south, midwest, and east. During the first few years, the Granger movement built slowly, but in the 1870s, it grew rapidly in response to the severe economic conditions of the 1873 depression. Adding to the economic problems, there was also a dawning recognition that the farmers' economic plight was due in part at least to the farmers' frustration in dealing with supposed unfair practices by middlemen, railroads, and others. By 1875, Granger enrollment reached over 875,000 nationwide, and the Grangers began to use the strength of their numbers to influence legislation affecting local agrarian interests.

As the membership grew and the agrarian economic situation worsened, the local meetings, although still officially nonpolitical in scope, often became political discussions once the main program ended.

The height of the Granger movement was not judged by just the numbers of membership. During the 1870s, several states passed the "Granger laws," which established regulations as to maximum railroad rates and state railroad commissions. Despite the railroads' attempts to overthrow the legislation, the Granger laws found support from the Supreme Court in the *Munn v. Illinois* ruling of 1876.

These attempts at controlling the unfair treatment of the railroads opened the way for the other economic and political innovations that would benefit the farmer. The Grangers became involved in buying cooperatives, grain elevators and mills, and other enterprises to eliminate the middleman. On the political side, the Grangers won several state legislator seats. The Grangers had learned the strength of numbers. As the popularity of third political parties increased in the late 1870s, the Grangers joined those that best met their individual needs, those with the strong agrarian platforms.

But the success and growth of the Granger movement was short-lived. By 1879, the enrollment of the Patrons of Husbandry started to decline, and by the mid 1880s, the membership had dropped to around 100,000. Several problems contributed to the decline and almost extinction of the order, including a dysfunctional organizational structure and forays into business enterprises.

Still in operation today, the Granger movement has returned to its original purpose of improving the intellectual and social life of the American farmer and the nonfarming rural citizen. Supporting education, legislation that improves the lot of the rural citizen, and economic development are still in the forefront of activities of the national and local offices.

**SEE ALSO**

*Volume 1 Left*: Unions; United States.
*Volume 2 Right*: United States; Globalization.

BIBLIOGRAPHY

Granger Movement, www.nationalgrange.org (May 2004); Solon J. Buck, *The Agrarian Crusade: A Chronicle of the Farmer in Politics* (Yale University Press, 1920); "Granger Movement," Readers Companion, http://college.hmco.com (May 2004); Solon Justus Buck, *Granger Movement* (University of Nebraska Press, 1963).

GLORIA J. HICKS
UNIVERSITY OF WYOMING

# Greece

GREECE, ONE OF the birthplaces of democracy, is home to powerful leftist political forces that ruled the country almost continuously from 1981 to 2004. Although ousted from government in the March 2004 general elections, the socialist-led Greek left remains a potent source of generous patronage and a controversial symbol of runaway social spending and virulent anti-Americanism. Analysis of the left's recent evolution reveals two primary strains: 1) the difficulties of building party democracy when the party is a quasi-family dynasty, and 2) the pressures of trying to stay true to leftist ideology while simultaneously meeting the strict economic requirements of membership in the European Union (EU).

Throughout its modern history, Greece has struggled to consolidate democracy. Indeed, democracy in this cradle of ancient democratic political thought is a remarkably recent phenomenon. The struggle for contemporary Greek democracy out of which the political left emerged dates from World War II. Invaded first by Italy and then occupied by Nazi Germany, Greeks turned to the communist-led National Popular Liberation Army to instigate their often-heroic resistance. With sovereignty returned upon the war's end, Greece nevertheless fell prey to internal divisions and eventually civil war (1946–49). Bolstered by extensive economic and military assistance from the British (and later the Americans), a precarious conservative Greek government battled communists in a conflict that took more than 100,000 lives. With victory, the post-conflict rightist regime repressed the left and effectively elevated anti-communism to the status of state ideology.

The succession of right-wing governments came to an end only in 1963, when an increasingly restive middle class threw its support behind the left-wing Progressive Center Union. Relying on communist support to cobble together a majority government after the 1963 elections, the Union secured an absolute majority on its own in 1965. Subsequent tensions over historical animosities with Turkey in divided Cyprus and the open hostilities among the governing left, the army, and the king led in 1967 to seven years of military junta and what became known as the "rule of the colonels." With competitive democracy restored in 1974, the left nevertheless languished. Conservative governments led by the New Democracy party of Konstantinos Karamanlis captured electoral victories and monopolized power until 1981.

The Panhellenic Socialist Movement (PASOK) is Greece's principal left-wing political party. PASOK's rise to power in 1981 coincided with Greece's accession to the European Community. The charismatic Andreas Papandreou, son of two-time prime minister George Papandreou, founded the party in 1974 and upon becoming prime minister aggressively pursued a successful brand of socialist populism coupled with anti-Americanism (a result of American support for the previous military regime). The socialists grew strong through the power of patronage—handing out civil service jobs generously and receiving electoral support in exchange. A governing ideology supportive of high levels of public spending to enhance social welfare stood consciously in contrast to American-style free-market capitalism. As a result, at least according to PASOK's critics, Greek government grew, the bureaucracy began to bloat, and corruption took hold.

Despite such charges, and perhaps as testament to the success of its patronage especially among blue-collar laborers and farmers, the socialists endured in power for two decades with only a brief interruption from 1990 to 1993. Andreas Papandreou served three terms as prime minister, finally yielding power in January 1996 shortly before his death. Assuming the party's (and country's) leadership upon the loss of PASOK's legendary founder, Costas Simitis gambled on early elections in September 1996 and held off the opposition conservatives. During his tenure as premier, Simitis struggled to rein in double-digit inflation and profligate spending.

With fiscal austerity demanded by its partners in the European Union, Simitis succeeded in getting Greece's finances in sufficient order to adopt the EU's euro as its currency. Such reforms came at no small cost, however; by injecting rationality into economic management, the socialists abandoned staples of their leftist ideology and drifted toward the political center.

This moderation, induced by the pressures of reaching economic parity with their EU neighbors, alienated traditional core constituencies. Simitis also earned domestic enemies—but international allies—by attempting to facilitate resolution of the Greek-Turkish conflict in Cyprus prior to Greek Cypriot accession to the EU in May 2004.

The Greek left reached another critical juncture at the outset of 2004. Party president and prime minister Simitis announced he was calling new general elections in March and that he would step down as both PASOK leader and premier. His appointed successor had a familiar surname: Papandreou. George Papandreou, grandson of a prime minister by the same name and son of Andreas Papandreou, won the party presidency and renewed his family's political dynasty with more than a million PASOK members' votes. Papandreou had been appointed foreign minister in 1999, and he was the minister responsible for advancing Greece's successful bid for the 2004 summer Olympic Games. Promising to renew a party now derided as complacent after a lengthy stay in power, Papandreou contested the 2004 election against New Democracy party leader Costas Karamanlis (himself the nephew of the former prime minister, who led Greece out of military dictatorship). In this clash of two political dynasties, Papandreou and the Greek left lost. Karamanlis's conservatives swept PASOK from power with a resounding five-percentage electoral victory, leaving the party of Papandreou to ponder its future in opposition after almost a quarter century in government.

PASOK is not alone on the Greek left. Competing, at least with modest success, in the electoral arena are the Communist Party (with 5.9 percent of the 2004 vote and 12 seats in the 300-member parliament), the Coalition of the Left and Progress (3.3 percent and 6 seats in 2004), and the Democratic Social Movement (1.8 percent but no seats in 2004). A host of other, often quite radicalized, leftist groups crowd the nonparliamentary Greek political spectrum. Chief among these—at least as measured by number of headlines captured—is the infamous November 17 ("N17") organization.

Formed in 1973 to protest the right-wing military dictatorship's brutal crackdown on a student revolt at the Athens Polytechnic University (resulting in the deaths of 20 students), N17 long embodied Greece's revolutionary left and continues to challenge the political establishment. Staunchly anti-American (because of a belief that the United States supported Greece's right-wing junta from 1967–74), the N17 group has killed at least 23 diplomats, politicians, and businessmen (in-cluding Richard Welch, CIA station chief in Athens, in 1975).

**SEE ALSO**
*Volume 1 Left:* Socialism; Democracy.
*Volume 2 Right:* Capitalism; Greece.

**BIBLIOGRAPHY**
Richard Clogg, *A Concise History of Greece* (Cambridge University Press, 2002); P. Nikiforos Diamandouros et al., eds., *Parties, Politics, and Democracy in the New Southern Europe* (Johns Hopkins University Press, 2001); Geoff Eley, *Forging Democracy: The History of the Left in Europe, 1850–2000* (Oxford University Press, 2002); Theodore C. Kariotis, *The Greek Socialist Experiment: Papandreou's Greece 1981–89* (Pella, 1992); Seraphim Seferiades, "Polarization and Nonproportionality: The Greek Party System in the Postwar Era," *Comparative Politics* (v.19/1, 1986); Charles R. Shrader, *The Withered Vine: Logistics and the Communist Insurgency in Greece, 1945–49* (Praeger, 1999); Michalis Spourdalakis, *Rise of the Greek Socialist Party* (Routledge, 1988); C. M. Woodhouse, *Modern Greece: A Short History* (Faber & Faber, 2000).

WILLIAM M. DOWNS, PH.D.
GEORGIA STATE UNIVERSITY

# Green Party

GREEN PARTIES WERE formed as a result of growing concern in the 1970s for the ecological sustainability of the planet and quality of life. Throughout the 1970s and 1980s, many countries formed green parties, and several preexisting parties renamed themselves as such (e.g., Ecology Party in Britain and the Values Party in New Zealand). The nuclear accident at Chernobyl (then part of the Soviet Union) in 1986 gave rise to increased environmental activism and helped many green parties gain election success in the late 1980s. However, during the 1990s, green parties in Europe experienced a significant decline. Part of the problem for the green parties is that they have attracted a wide range of ideological viewpoints, resulting in significant internal divisions that become particularly visible as party members reached legislative positions. While many supporters simply express concern for issues such as clean air or water, others within the party represented more extreme views, embracing libertarianism, feminism, neo-Marxism, paganism, and anti-industrialism.

United under an international agreement of common purpose, the Charter of the Global Greens states "We declare our commitment to nonviolence and strive for a culture of peace and cooperation between states, inside societies and between individuals, as the basis of global security." Many green parties subscribe to "10 key values" which serve as guidelines for their actions:

Grassroots democracy: Green parties believe that everyone deserves to have a say in decisions that affect them; as a result they work to expand public participation in government and ensure that government officials are held accountable for their actions.

Social Justice and equal opportunity: Citizens must commit to working to eliminate unfair treatment and unequal justice under the law.

Ecological wisdom: Human beings are part of nature and must work to achieve an ecological balance. It is important to live within the ecological and resource limits of our society and ensure that future generations will not be harmed by our present lifestyle. They support sustainable agriculture, an energy efficient economy, and respect for natural resources.

Nonviolence: There are alternatives to violence. Green parties support the elimination of weapons of mass destruction while recognizing the need for self-defense and the defense of others who may need assistance. They believe in working toward peace.

Decentralization: Decision making, where possible, should be brought to the individual and local level. They support a restructuring of social, political and economic institutions that move away from a system that is controlled by the privileged few, and instead empowers all citizens to be instrumental in the decision making process.

Community-based economics and economic justice: Citizens must support a sustainable economic system that offers meaningful work while paying a living wage that is reflective of the real value of work. Economic development must protect both the environment and the rights of workers and be based on broad public participation. Green parties support independently owned and operated companies that are socially responsible, as well as public corporations and cooperatives that encourage democratic participation.

Feminism and gender equity: Green parties support full participation of all citizens, and more cooperative styles of interaction that respect differences of opinion and gender.

Respect for diversity: Society must value and respect cultural, racial, sexual, religious, and spiritual diversity. Societal diversity should be reflected in our decision making bodies. The preservation of biodiversity is also valued.

Personal and global responsibility: People must work to improve their own lives while promoting ecological balance. We must join with people from around the world to promote peace, economic justice, and the health of the planet.

Future focus and sustainability: We must keep in mind the big picture and focus on long-term goals. Issues of concern are protecting natural resources, reducing waste and promoting sustainable development.

The following provides a brief overview of some of the most successful or otherwise noteworthy Green parties.

## UNITED STATES

In 1984, the first U.S. Green organizing meetings were held, which led to the creation of a national membership organization of Green local committees and individuals: the Green Committees of Correspondence. Greens were mostly concentrating on local community elections, with the first Green Party candidates on a municipal election ballot in 1985 in North Carolina and Connecticut.

In 1990, Alaska became the first state in which the Green Party appeared on the ballot, followed by California in 1992. The national level Green Party was formed in the United States after the 1996 election in order to help state-level parties expand their participation. State-level action is still the primary focus of the party. In the 2000 presidential election, Ralph Nader and Winona LaDuke ran for president and vice president; although unsuccessful, they received significant media attention and helped to energize the Green Party throughout the United States. As of February 2004, there were 206 Green Party members in various elected offices in 24 states.

## GERMANY

The German Green Party, Die Grünen, began as an "antiparty" party that slowly grew into a credible political force. In 1985, elected members of the Green Party to regional government were caught up in internal conflicts and the realities of party politics, which forced the Green Party members to compromise on their agenda, to the disappointment of many of their supporters and party members.

The Green Party had significant electoral success in 1998, resulting in a coalition with the Social Democrats

(SPD), popularly referred to as the Red-Green Coalition. However, the Greens were not really prepared to share power within a coalition, particularly with a party stronger in numbers. Rather than negotiating and making concessions for favored policies, they debated each issue in isolation, in the end losing ground in all policy areas. Greens were defeated on many of their core issues such as genetically modified food. They were able to make some significant political gains including plans to phase out nuclear power and changes to waste policy. In practice however, even these gains were lessened as the policies were significantly weakened at the implementation stage.

The war in Kosovo caused a significant divide among Green Party members, with some supporting German humanitarian intervention and most opposed. With the general population largely supportive of intervention, the Green Party suffered in the polls, and reports of their internal conflicts further weakened their public image.

In 2002, the Green Party campaigned on a platform of pacifism opposed to war in Iraq. They had their best ever election result, and the Red-Green Coalition was reelected with a slim majority.

## NEW ZEALAND

In March 1972, a group of activists formed the United Tasmania Group (UTG). In May, the Values Party was created out of the UTG as the world's first national Green Party. The Values Party ran in the 1972 general election in New Zealand on a radical platform based on Zero Economic Growth, Zero Population Growth, and reform of abortion/drug/homosexuality laws. Over the next few years, these policies were debated and expanded to form the 1975 Values Party Manifesto "Beyond Tomorrow," which was widely distributed internationally and contributed to the spread of the Green Party movement. The Values Party became active in numerous environmental campaigns throughout New Zealand, organizing for better public transport, recycling, and urban heritage preservation.

In 1989, the Values Party successfully contested several local elections throughout the country. In May 1990, the present Green Party of Aotearoa, New Zealand, was formed from a merger of the Values Party and the new Green groups that had independently formed. In the 1990 general election, the Green Party won 7 percent of the total vote, but no seats because of the "first past the post" electoral system. In 1991, the Green Party joined with other parties to form the five-party Alliance in response to the New Right direction of the National and Labor Parties. As part of the Alliance, Greens contested the 1993 and 1996 general elections, and in 1996, three Green Party members won seats in parliament. By the 1999 general election, the Greens had amicably split from the Alliance, and in the 1999 general election, they won seven seats and 5.2 percent of the vote under a new electoral system of mixed member proportional representation.

Since 2000, Green Party representatives have been elected to the national legislatures of Austria, Belgium, Cyprus, Finland, France, Germany, Ireland, Italy, Latvia, Luxembourg, the Netherlands, Portugal, Spain, Sweden, and Switzerland.

## SEE ALSO
*Volume 1 Left:* Environmentalism; Germany; United States; France; Nader, Ralph.
*Volume 2 Right:* Capitalism; Germany, United States; France.

## BIBLIOGRAPHY
Global Green Party, www.globalgreens.info (April 2004); Jon Burchell, *The Evolution of Green Politics: Development and Change within European Green Parties* (Earthscan Publications, 2002); Margrit Mayer and John Ely, *The German Greens: Paradox between Movement and Party* (Temple University Press, 1998); Gavil Talskir, *The Political Ideology of Green Parties: From the Politics of Nature to Redefining the Nature of Politics* (Palgrave Macmillan, 2002).

SHANNON K. ORR
BOWLING GREEN STATE UNIVERSITY

# Greenback Party

NAMED AFTER THE "greenbacks" (paper money) issued during the American Civil War, the Greenback Party found its way into national prominence in the mid 1870s. Formed in 1874, the party reflected the national trend of political and financial dissatisfaction among farmers, laborers, and even small businessmen with the national parties, Republicans and Democrats. Tied to the anti-monopolist movement that blamed the depression of 1873 in part on the tendency toward national banks and other monopolistic enterprises, the members of the first national Greenback platform opposed the return of specie payments and advocated continued and inflated issuance of paper money.

Growing out of a decade-old agrarian and laborer unhappiness with the old political parties, the monopolies of corporations such as railroads, and the sad state of the postwar economy, the Greenback Party was one of several small third parties founded amid the discontent of what party members perceived as abuses by those with political and monetary influence and position. Also known as the Greenback Labor Party and the National Independent Party, the party tied together a diverse group of constituents and actually garnered enough votes in several national elections to influence the control of Congress. The party's influence grew as the economic depression continued through the 1870s.

The first national convention of the Greenbacks, in Indianapolis, Indiana, in 1874, served to gather the various pockets of political and financial dissidents across diverse population groups and regional areas. Mostly comprised of (but not limited to) farmers and laborers from the midwest and the south, the party managed to gain national recognition and influence quickly.

Over the next two years, the fledgling party held three more national conventions and by May 1876, the Greenback Party was ready to enter the national election arena and held its national nominating convention. As to be expected based on the Greenbacks' founding principles, the party's primary concerns stated in its platform focused on financial issues: repeal of the Resumption Act (January 1875), which called for a return to the gold standard; support of the bond issue, which would adjust the volume of issued currency as the economy grew; promotion of the government's duty to aid the development and growth of new and existing business (agricultural, manufacturing, mining, and so on); and reform of the government's bond policies. The party nominated Peter Cooper, a New York businessman, and Samuel F. Cary of Ohio for president and vice president.

One reason the Greenback Party survives in the history books is its relative success compared to other third parties of the era. In the election of 1876, Cooper managed only a little over 80,000 votes, but his loss did nothing to discourage the party's growth. Between 1876 and 1878, more labor supporters gravitated toward the reforms espoused by the Greenbacks, aiding in even more national recognition. This increase in labor advocates induced a name change by 1878 to the Greenback-Labor Party, thus formally acknowledging its expanded platform and labor-heavy constituency. In the congressional election of 1878, the party garnered 13.8 percent of the national vote (over one million votes) and put 14 representatives in Congress.

In keeping with its 1878 success, the party expected great results in 1880 and expanded its platform to garner more electoral support. The expanded platform for 1880 included federal regulation of interstate commerce, a graduated income tax, and an endorsement for women's suffrage. Their presidential candidate was General James B. Weaver. Despite the party members' enthusiasm and high hopes, Weaver received only a little over 300,000 votes, a definite setback for the party. Several factors led to the poor showing at the polls: the recovering economy, the success of the Resumption Act, and the passage of the Bland-Allison Act, which encouraged increased coinage of silver.

Finally, after a dismal showing by the party's 1884 candidate, General Benjamin Franklin Butler, the Greenback-Labor Party dissolved. For the most part, the members returned to the Republican and Democratic parties, with a few joining the Union Labor party.

**SEE ALSO**

*Volume 1 Left:* Democratic Party; American Civil War; Civil Liberties.
*Volume 2 Right:* Republican Party; American Civil War; Capitalism.

**BIBLIOGRAPHY**

Gretchen Ritter, *Goldbugs and Greenbacks* (Cambridge University Press, 1997); Bernard Bailyn, et al., *The Great Republic: A History of the American People* (D.C. Heath, 1985).

GLORIA J. HICKS
UNIVERSITY OF WYOMING

# Greenpeace

In 1969, on the small island of Amchitka near Alaska, the U.S. Atomic Energy Commission announced plans for an underground nuclear bomb test. As the island lies in one of the most earthquake-prone areas of the world, and is home to numerous endangered species, many people were concerned about the possibly devastating effects of the blast on both the fault lines and the environment. An earthquake five years earlier in the area had killed 115 residents and caused massive waves as far away as Japan. On the day of the test 10,000 protesters blocked the United States-Canada border waving a banner that read, "Don't Make a Wave. It's Your Fault If Our Fault Goes." The U.S. government ignored the protests and detonated the bomb, and immediately announced plans for another test in 1971.

In 1970, the Don't Make a Wave Committee was formed to stop the second test. In order to emphasize the group's commitment to the planet and their opposition to nuclear arms, the committee was renamed Greenpeace. In 1971, a small group of activists sailed from Vancouver, Canada, in a fishing boat, the *Phyllis Cormack*, to Amchitka to "bear witness" (a Quaker tradition of silent protest) to the nuclear test. The boat did not reach Amchitka due to poor weather; however, the journey received significant media attention and public interest. The U.S. still detonated the bomb, however it was the last nuclear test on the island, which was later declared a bird sanctuary.

Greenpeace, now the world's largest international environmental campaign organization, is based in Amsterdam, Netherlands, with offices in 41 countries and more than 2.8 million supporters worldwide. In the words of their own mission statement: "Greenpeace has no permanent allies or enemies." The focus of Greenpeace is on nonviolence, political independence, and internationalism, and it has played a pivotal role in the following: a ban on toxic waste exports to less developed countries, a moratorium on commercial whaling, a United Nations convention providing for better management of world fisheries, a Southern Ocean Whale Sanctuary, a 50-year moratorium on mineral exploitation in Antarctica, bans on the dumping at sea of radioactive and industrial waste and disused oil installations, and an end to high-sea, large-scale driftnet fishing.

Greenpeace is frequently the subject of controversy and critique. With a worldwide budget of over $100 million dollars, and a staff that includes high-priced lawyers and lobbyists, Greenpeace has been accused of corporatization and detachment from its founding as a grassroots organization. In addition, the opposition of all genetically modified crops by Greenpeace has upset scientists in developing countries, who have seen much of their funding dry up as a result of Greenpeace campaigns. Greenpeace has been criticized for opposing all genetically modified crops; even those that appear to be entirely beneficial such as vitamin A enriched Golden Rice. In cases such as this, they have been accused of sacrificing scientific principles for media attention. Greenpeace has also had a history of insider feuds, not uncommon with activist organizations.

Greenpeace strategies include both traditional lobbying of government, as well as more attention-getting activities such as climbing nuclear smokestacks, spraying Newfoundland harp seals with paint, plugging industrial sewage pipes, delivering dead fish to annual meetings of corporations accused of polluting rivers and lakes, and sailing inflatable boats into nuclear test sites. In 1985, the Greenpeace ship *Rainbow Warrior*, in a campaign against nuclear testing, was sunk by French intelligence agents off New Zealand and a Greenpeace photographer was killed.

GREENPEACE CAMPAIGNS

Greenpeace has greatly expanded its mandate since its early roots in Alaska and is currently involved in the following campaigns:

Climate change campaign: Global warming or climate change is the result of the burning of fossil fuels by industry and consumers and is considered by Green-

A Greenpeace diver sends a message from the sea bottom to European governments to leave the Viking Bank in the North Sea alone.

A vessel sank with a cargo of toxic waste in 2000 and became a target for Greenpeace activism in Iskenderun port, Turkey.

peace to be the worst environmental problem facing today's society. The consequences of climate change include extreme weather events such as droughts and floods, the disruption of water supplies, melting polar regions, and rising sea levels. Greenpeace advocates the use of renewable energy and alternatives to climate-changing chemicals in order to reverse climate change.

Ancient forests: As a result of commercial clearing of ancient forests, plants and animals face extinction. Ancient forests are important for maintaining environmental systems as they influence weather by controlling rainfall and the rate of evaporation of water from the soil. Ancient forests also help to stabilize climate by storing large amounts of carbon that would otherwise contribute to the problem of climate change. In addition, ancient forests are home to millions of people who are dependent on the forests for their survival, as well as home to two-thirds of the world's land-based species of plants and animals. Greenpeace argues that commercial clearing of these forests must be controlled to prevent catastrophic effects.

Save the oceans: Species are driven to extinction due to over-fishing, pollution, pirate fishing, whaling, and intensive shrimp aquaculture. Greenpeace advocates the reduction of large-scale fishing fleets, a ban on the dumping of radioactive waste into waterways, bans on pirate fishing and commercial whaling, and controls on shrimp farms that release chemicals and fertilizers into local water sources.

Genetic engineering: Genetic engineering involves the creation of plants, animals and microorganisms through science. The biggest problem is that they can reproduce and interbreed with natural organisms, thereby spreading in unforeseen and uncontrollable ways. Greenpeace calls for bans on the release of genetically engineered organisms into the environment, interim measures such as food labeling, and bans on patents for plants, animals, humans, and genes.

Nuclear threat: Nuclear waste will be radioactive for tens or hundreds of thousands of years, and there is no safe solution for its disposal. The radiation released into the environment has resulted in contamination of rivers, air, soil, and oceans and caused cancer and other diseases. Greenpeace advocates the end of nuclear energy and nuclear weapons.

Sustainable trade: This campaign is primarily targeted at the World Trade Organization (WTO), which promotes free trade for the gain of private interests at the expense of health and the environment. Poorer countries repeatedly lose out to the economic interests of industrialized countries. Greenpeace argues that trade must not take priority over global environmental standards and sustainable development.

The driving force of the organization can be summed up in their own words; according to Greenpeace, "when the last tree is cut, the last river poisoned and the last fish dead, we will discover that we can't eat money."

**SEE ALSO**

*Volume 1 Left:* Environmentalism; Protests; Anti-Globalization; Green Party.
*Volume 2 Right:* Globalization; Capitalism.

**BIBLIOGRAPHY**

Greenpeace International, www.greenpeace.org (April 2004); Jim Bohlen, *Making Waves: The Origins and Future of Greenpeace* (Black Rose Books, 2001); Michael Harold Brown, *The Greenpeace Story* (Dorling Kindersley, 1991); David Fraser McTaggert, *Shadow Warrior: The Autobiography of Greenpeace International Founder David McTaggert* (Orion Media, 2002); Kieran Mulvaney, *The Whaling Season: An Inside Account of the Struggle to Stop Commercial Whaling* (Island Press, 2003).

SHANNON K. ORR
BOWLING GREEN STATE UNIVERSITY

# Guevara, Che (1928–1967)

KNOWN BY MANY simply as Che, Ernesto Guevara was the quintessential romantic revolutionary who died fighting for the liberation of Latin America. He was born to a middle-class Argentine family and became a medical doctor in 1953. Revealing a rebellious and adventurous spirit, Guevara then abandoned his medical career and began a motorcycle journey through Latin America, at a time when many roads barely accommodated cars, let alone motorcycles.

His travels exposed him to the stark poverty in which many Latin Americans lived and deepened his rejection of capitalist exploitation and U.S. intervention in the region. He arrived in Guatemala during the progressive government of Jacobo Arbenz and witnessed its 1954 overthrow in a U.S.-sponsored military coup d'etat. This experience intensified his political opposition to U.S. imperialism and strengthened his commitment to armed struggle and socialism as the method and goal of political struggle.

From Guatemala, he traveled to Mexico where he joined Fidel Castro and the July 26th Movement and embraced their plans to overthrow Cuban dictator Fulgencio Batista. In 1956, Guevara and 19 other men, out of an initial force of 86, survived the guerrilla movement's return to Cuba and initial skirmishes with Cuban government troops. The remaining members of the July 26th Movement retreated to the Sierra Maestra mountains, where they built a base among the area's impoverished peasants, some of whom joined the guerrilla movement while others offered it logistical support, food, and shelter. In January 1959, the guerrilla force marched triumphantly into Havana, Cuba, to the euphoric welcome of many Cubans, and Batista fled the country, taking much of the national treasury with him.

Guevara and Castro headed up the new Cuban government. Castro held senior posts in the Communist Party and the new government and Guevara concentrated on the economy. Determined to end Cuban economic dependency on sugar exports to the United States, Guevara devised a Four-Year Plan that called for "agricultural diversification (de-emphasis on sugar) and industrialization (the manufacture of light consumer goods," historians Thomas Skidmore and Peter Smith explain.

The plan failed, due to a shortage in consumer goods, a decline in foreign reserves, the lack of capital and skilled technicians needed to industrialize, and a drop in sugar production. U.S. opposition to the Cuban revolution and the embargo it imposed on Cuba effectively encouraged the Caribbean nation to look to the Soviet Union for support and supplies. Responding to both the plan's failure and Soviet opposition to his plan, Guevara resigned his position in 1963.

Guevara represented an idealistic interpretation of Marxism and the qualities needed to build a socialist society. He thought that in order to build a new society and successfully break with the capitalist past, it was essential to create *el hombre nuevo* (the new man). Guevara stressed the need for revolutionaries to sacrifice their material well-being, even their lives, in order to bring about the profound transformations that the construction of socialism demanded. He argued that moral incentives should replace material ones, thus people should work for the good of society, not for their individual advancement.

Guevara was an internationalist and believed that the model of guerrilla warfare successfully developed in Cuba could be applied in other countries. In order to educate and inspire other peoples to take up similar struggles, he published numerous texts on the subject, the most famous of which is *Guerrilla Warfare*. His writings and the Cuban revolution encouraged many revolutionaries throughout Latin America to attempt to replicate the Cuban example.

In the 1960s, many Latin Americans took up Guevara's call to "Create One, Two, Three Vietnams" and guerrilla movements developed in Brazil, Nicaragua, Venezuela, Guatemala, Mexico, and Peru. The U.S. government also paid close attention to Guevara's theoretical and political example and the emerging guerrilla movements throughout the continent. To prevent future guerrilla successes, the United States stepped up its training of Latin American militaries in counterinsurgency techniques and increased its military presence in the region.

In 1965, Guevara traveled to Congo to support the unsuccessful guerrilla movement there. He returned to Cuba briefly in 1966 and then slipped into Bolivia in an attempt to recreate in that Andean country the successful guerrilla movement that he had helped to lead in Cuba. News of the guerrilla troop's activities alerted the Bolivian and the U.S militaries to their presence. They tracked down the exhausted and isolated band of revolutionary fighters and, in October 1967, U.S.-trained Bolivian Ranger troops killed Guevara and most of the guerrillas.

Guevara's death only served to heighten his image as a heroic revolutionary who was willing to sacrifice everything for the sake of Latin America. Pictures of him, with long hair and a black beret perched on his head, adorn the walls and t-shirts of people, young and old, throughout Latin America. Numerous books, articles, and a movie, *Motorcycle Diaries*, produced by Robert Redford, tell the story of this romantic figure, ensuring that his legacy continues to inform and influence people who were not even alive when he died.

**SEE ALSO**
*Volume 1 Left:* South America; Socialism; Marx, Karl; Argentina.
*Volume 2 Right:* South America; Imperialism; United States.

**BIBLIOGRAPHY**
Jon Lee Anderson, *Che Guevara: A Revolutionary Life* (Grove Press, 1998); Jorge G. Castañeda, *Utopia Unarmed: The Latin American Left after the Cold War* (Vintage Books, 1993); James Cockcroft, *Neighbors in Turmoil: Latin America* (Harper & Row, 1989); Che Guevara, *Guerrilla Warfare*, J.P. Morray, trans. (Monthly Review Press, 1961); Brian Loveman and Thomas M. Davies, Jr., *Guerrilla Warfare* (Scholarly Resources Press, 1997); Thomas E. Skidmore and Peter H. Smith, *Modern Latin America* (Oxford University Press, 1997).

MARGARET POWER
ILLINOIS INSTITUTE OF TECHNOLOGY

# Gun Control

GUN CONTROL, OR THE monitoring and restriction of the public use of firearms, is thought by the left to be a useful tool in the control of crime. The history of gun control in the United States is both a matter of support and refutation of the assertion that gun control reduces crime and accidental deaths.

Since the writing of the Second Amendment to the Constitution (granting the right to citizens to bear arms), there has been much debate over how and if the government can regulate gun ownership. In 1813, the first state legislation prohibiting the concealment of weapons was passed. Since then, many states and towns have passed laws prohibiting the concealment of firearms. The federal government has also passed many acts to try to control the sale and possession of firearms. The Sullivan Law was passed in New York in 1911 after the shootings of Mayor William J. Gaynov and popular novelist David Graham Philips. This law, which is still in effect today, stood as a model for gun legislation for 50 years. The law requires people to acquire a license to possess or carry a firearm small enough to conceal. The law also made it illegal for aliens to possess firearms in any public place.

The Mailing of Firearms Act (MFA) was signed into law in 1927 by President Calvin Coolidge. The MFA, also known as the Miller Act, is also still in effect today. This law prohibits the sending of pistols and other firearms, which could be concealed on a person, through the mail. Representative Miller, who was a Republican representative from Seattle, Washington, wrote the bill and also a letter to President Coolidge stating that the ability to send firearms through the mail was tempting minors into criminal activity. The United National Association of Post Office Clerks also passed a resolution that supported the bill.

In 1938, the Federal Firearms Act was passed into law. This act regulated the interstate sale of firearms and other weapons. Manufacturers, dealers, and importers were required to become licensed and pay a registration fee. People convicted of a felony, fugitives from justice, persons under indictment, or those failing to meet local licensing requirements could no longer legally purchase a gun. However, the dealer was not responsible for selling a gun to those who were not allowed to purchase a gun, unless he/she did so knowingly, and in 1938 background checks were not performed. This act was replaced by the Gun Control Act of 1968.

Members of Congress began to write this act in 1963 with a bill to prohibit mail-order sales of handguns to minors. However, after John F. Kennedy was shot and killed in November 1963 with a mail-order rifle, the bill was expanded to include a ban on mail-order sales of shotguns and rifles. In 1968, Martin Luther King, Jr., and Robert Kennedy were both assassinated with guns.

The Gun Control Act of 1968 was passed as a response and included the following provisions: limiting foreign and interstate transportation of firearms to manufactures, dealers and importers; prohibiting interstate shipments of pistols and revolvers to private individuals; restricting gun purchases to a person's state of residency; imposing a licensing fee of $10; prohibiting minors from receiving a license or purchasing rifles, shotguns or ammunition; prohibiting sales of pistols and ammunition to anyone under 21; detailed record keeping requirement for dealers and collectors; restriction of the purchase of foreign military surplus firearms to those used in hunting; registration and transfer tax requirements on "destructive devices" such as bazookas, anti-tank guns, and mortars; prohibition of convicted felons, the mentally incompetent, and drug addicts from shipping or receiving weapons; and an extra punishment of a minimum of one year added to sentences of those who used a firearm to commit a crime that involved the breaking of any federal law.

The Brady Bill, passed in 1994, requires a background check before a gun purchase, using a national computer system on all purchasers of firearms. Assault weapons, such as civilian versions of the U.S. Army M-16 rifle and other automated guns, were banned in 1994. The ban, which was passed by Congress and signed by President Bill Clinton over the strenuous opposition of the National Rifle Association, was set to expire in 2004. Its effectiveness, according to the *New York Times*, "is fiercely disputed and statistically hard to determine." The *Times* noted, "One study, conducted for the Brady Center to Prevent Gun Violence by two former officials of the Bureau of Alcohol, Tobacco and Firearms, found a 66 percent drop in the use of assault weapons in crimes after the ban was enacted compared with the five years before it went into effect. The study, released this year, also concluded that had the law not been passed, approximately 66,000 more assault weapons would have been traced to crimes since 1994." Another study found "found only a small decline in crimes committed with semiautomatic assault weapons and said that it had been offset by a steady increase in crimes committed by other guns equipped with large-capacity magazines."

PROS AND CONS OF GUN CONTROL

The United States has one of the highest homicide rates in the world and some of the least strict gun control policies, which supports the gun-control-prevents-crime theory. But while availability of weapons in the United States has not changed significantly during the last 100 years, the homicide rate has fluctuated widely. The homicide rate was very high during the 1920s and during the 1970s and 1980s, but relatively low during the 1940s and 1950s and in the early 1900s. This behavior has caused some authors to speculate that America's crime problem is more related to violent black markets that arose from Prohibition in the 1920s and the War on Drugs in the 1970 and 1980s, than to the availability of firearms in the United States.

The prevention of accidental deaths is another reason commonly given for gun control, but according to the National Safety Council, Americans are far more likely to die from motor vehicle accidents, falls, certain types of poisons, drowning, and accidental fires than from firearm accidents. Organizations in support of gun control include the Southern Poverty Law Center and the Brady Center to Prevent Gun Violence; those opposed to gun control include the National Rifle Association and Jews for the Preservation of Firearms Ownership.

SEE ALSO

*Volume 1 Left:* Bill of Rights; Constitutional Amendments. *Volume 2 Right:* Second Amendment; National Rifle Association.

BIBLIOGRAPHY

Kirby R. Cundiff, "Homicide Rates and Substance Control Policy," Independent Institute List of Working Papers (Independent Institute, 2001); Pat Lewis, ed. "Gun Control," *West's Encyclopedia of American Law* (West, 1997); Mary J. Ruwart, *Healing Our World* (Sunstar Press, 1993); *Statistical Abstracts of the United States* (1900–2004); Glen H. Utter, *Encyclopedia of Gun Control and Gun Rights* (Greenwood, 2000); *World Almanac and Book of Facts* (World Almanac, 2004); Fox Butterfield, "As Expiration Looms, Gun Ban Debated," *New York Times* (September 10, 2004).

KIRBY R. CUNDIFF, PH.D.
NORTHEASTERN STATE UNIVERSITY

# The Left

# H

## Hall, Gus (1910–2000)

GUS HALL WAS BORN Arvo Kusta Halberg in Virginia, Minnesota, one of 10 children of Finnish immigrants. His father was a union activist and a founding member of the American Communist Party (CPUSA). Hall joined the Young Communist League at age 17 and, like many communists thought to have leadership potential, spent two years at the Lenin Institute in Moscow, Soviet Union. In 1934, he moved to Mahoning Valley, Ohio, where he worked as a union organizer for the Steel Workers Organizing Committee (SWOC). The same year, he met his future wife, Elizabeth, and, in fear of being blacklisted by employers, shortened his name to Gus Hall. Hall proved to be an effective grassroots organizer, leading the 1937 Little Steel strike in Youngstown, Ohio, and helping recruit more than 10,000 workers to the steel union in Mahoning Valley. His activism resulted in his being arrested several times on charges of incitement to riot. Hall was typical of a generation of communist activists whose dedication to the cause enabled the CPUSA to recruit numerous new members. In the 1930s, it was able to claim a membership of 100,000.

When the United States entered World War II, Hall joined the American Navy and served until 1946. At the same time, he continued to make his way up the CPUSA's hierarchy and was elected to its highest body, the National Executive Board, in 1946. The end of the wartime cooperation between the United States and the Soviet Union and the onset of the Cold War resulted in the persecution of American communists. Under the provisions of the anti-communist Smith Act, Hall was accused of advocating the violent overthrow of the American government and was sentenced to five years in prison. He fled to Mexico but was caught, and his sentence was lengthened. He was released from prison in 1957 and was awarded the Order of Lenin medal by the Soviet government.

Hall was elected general secretary of the party in 1959, but he was to preside over an organization in crisis. The revelations of Josef Stalin's crimes by his successor, Nikita Khrushchev, at the Soviet Communist Party's 1956 congress and the Soviet invasion of Hungary of the same year had rocked the party. Many members had resigned in protest. Years of underground activity and persecution had also taken their toll. Hall reaffirmed the party's pro-Soviet credentials and set about building up its membership and influence. Under his leadership, the CPUSA managed to recruit some of the new generation of civil rights activists that emerged in the 1960s. However, the CPUSA was increasingly seen as a staid, conservative organization by many young radicals. Hall stood five times as a presidential candidate, twice with the African American activist Angela Davis as his running mate. His best result came in the 1976 election when he received 36,386 votes. His last campaign was in 1984, after which the CPUSA ceased to stand candidates in presidential elections and supported the Democrats.

As an orthodox communist, Hall was a critical observer of Mikhail Gorbachev's reforms in the 1980s and expressed his disapproval at the turn of events that culminated in the disappearance of the communist regimes in Eastern Europe. These events, along with the publication of revelations concerning secret Soviet funding of the CPUSA, led to an internal party crisis. As a result, Davis and other leading figures left the party in 1992 and membership fell to around 15,000 in the 1990s. Despite the worldwide collapse of communism and the weakness of his own party, Hall remained optimistic. He was convinced of the inevitability of communism and took solace in the existence of communist regimes in North Korea and Cuba. He remained leader of the CPUSA until his death in 2000.

**SEE ALSO**

*Volume 1 Left:* Communist Party, Soviet.; Communism; Soviet Union.
*Volume 2 Right:* Capitalism; McCarthyism.

**BIBLIOGRAPHY**

Theodor Draper, *The Roots of American Communism* (Viking Press, 1957); Harvey Klehr, *The Heyday of American Communism: The Depression Decade* (Basic Books, 1984); Harvey Klehr, John Earl Haynes, Fridrikh Igorevich, *The Secret World of American Communism* (Yale University Press, 1995).

JEREMY TRANMER
UNIVERSITY OF NANCY 2, FRANCE

# Hammett, Dashiell (1894–1961)

THOUGH HE ONLY produced five novels, Dashiell Hammett became the most successful writer of detective fiction of the 1920s. In his books, which were soon defined as "hard-boiled fiction," he introduced tough heroes who fought against the corruption of an American society that had greed and violence as its main values. Hammett was also well known for his political militancy on the American left, and his association with the Communist Party caused him to be a target of the anti-communist hysteria that pervaded American society in the 1950s.

Hammett was born on a tobacco farm in St. Mary's County, Maryland, but grew up in Baltimore where he attended the Baltimore Polytechnic Institute. When he was 14, he was forced to leave school and work to help support his family. He held the most disparate of jobs, ranging from newsboy to advertising manager, before working as an operative for Pinkerton National Detectives. This experience was crucial to his future detective stories. During World War I, Hammett contracted tuberculosis while serving in the army, and the disease would plague him for the rest of his life.

In the mid-1920s, Hammett, who had moved to San Francisco, California, and had married nurse Josephine Dolan, began publishing short fiction in the pulp magazine *Black Mask* and quickly became one of the magazine's most successful contributors. The stories written for the *Black Mask* centered on an overweight detective known as Continental Op, considered the first believable private eye in American fiction.

In addition to appearing in these stories, Continental Op also became the protagonist of Hammett's first two novels, *Red Harvest* and *The Dain Curse*, both published in 1929 by Alfred A. Knopf. These were followed by three more books. *The Maltese Falcon* (1930) was most famously adapted for the screen by John Huston and starred Humphrey Bogart in the role of the detective Sam Spade. The *Glass Key* (1931), Hammett's favorite novel, centered on the partly autobiographical Ned Beaumont, a gambler and heavy drinker affected by tuberculosis. Finally, *The Thin Man* (1934) focused on a former playboy detective, Nick Charles, who has married a wealthy woman, Nora, loosely based on Hammett's new lover, the leftist playwright Lillian Hellman. With his novels and short stories, Hammett succeeded in the difficult task of satisfying readers and critics alike and his status soon outgrew that of a pulp writer. Hammett's works were not only adapted for the screen, but also became regular radio shows in the 1940s, contributing to the author's popularity.

In the 1930s, Hammett also worked in Hollywood, California, and committed himself to left-wing political activity together with Hellman. Both Hammett and Hellman were Communist Party members and actively fought fascism. Critics are far from being unanimous in their judgment of the degree to which Hammett's political stance influenced his fiction. Some scholars note that Hammett's most significant work was done during the 1920s, thus reflecting the decade's quest for intellectual artistry and sophistication and its pessimism about the intelligence of common people. Others, such as Michael Denning, not only point out Hammett's influence on left-wing culture of the Popular Front years, but also go as far as describing his works as displaced proletarian fiction. In Denning's reading of *Red Harvest*, the detective-story plot is firmly based on a strike story, one of the main features of proletarian literature. In addition, the novel clearly links gangsterism with local conservative politicians and capitalism. From the very title and through the obsessive color allegories that permeate the novel, Denning finds that the book promises a political Red harvest. Hammett's literary career declined in the 1940s and 1950s. Hammett had a severe drinking problem and, because of his political commitment, he became a target of McCarthyism, a witchhunt for communists. The popular radio shows based on his works were all suspended at the beginning of the 1950s, when the novelist was summoned before a court due to his vice-chairmanship of the Communist Party-affiliated Civil Rights Congress, a group that the Federal Bureau of Investigation considered subversive.

Hammett had to serve six months in prison for contempt of court as he refused to cooperate, and experienced the hardship of being on the blacklist (list of suspected communists ostracized and kept out of work). He was also attacked by the Internal Revenue, Service which claimed that he owed a huge amount in tax deficiencies. In the last years of his life, Hammett lived in New York City, where he taught creative writing at the Jefferson School of Social Science.

### SEE ALSO

*Volume 1 Left:* Popular Front; Socialist Party, U.S.; Communism.
*Volume 2 Right:* Hoover, J. Edgar; Capitalism; United States.

### BIBLIOGRAPHY

Michael Denning, *The Cultural Front* (Verso, 1997); Josephine Hammett, *Dashiell Hammett: A Daughter Remembers* (Carroll & Graff, 2001); Richard Layman, *Shadow Man* (Bruccoli and Clark, 1981); William F. Nolan, *Dashiell Hammett: A Life at the Edge* (Congdon & Weed, 1983).

LUCA PRONO, PH.D.
UNIVERSITY OF NOTTINGHAM, UNITED KINGDOM

# Harrington, Michael (1928–1989)

MICHAEL HARRINGTON was perhaps the most prominent American socialist from the 1960s until his death in 1989, both as a writer and political activist. Born into an Irish middle-class family in St. Louis, Missouri, Harrington graduated in 1947 from Holy Cross College, a Jesuit institution, and moved to New Haven, Connecticut, where he studied law at Yale University. After a year, he went to Chicago where he earned a master's degree from the University of Chicago. He started his activist career in New York in 1951, when he joined the Catholic Worker movement, an organization within the lay apostolate founded by Dorothy Day during the Great Depression.

After having rejected the Catholic theology, Harrington left the Catholic Worker movement two years later and joined the Young Socialist League. Throughout the 1950s, Harrington became more integrated within the American socialist movement, meeting leaders of several socialist groups, participating in demonstrations, and writing about Marxism and communism in journals such as *Dissent* and *Commentary*. In 1958, Harrington began a three-month journey that brought him to every corner of the United States. Following this experience, on the suggestion of the *Commentary* editor, Harrington wrote an article about poverty in America, entitled "Our Fifty Million Poor: Forgotten Men of the Affluent Society."

### AN ENDEMIC PLAGUE

This essay, together with the subsequent essay on urban slums, became the foundation for Harrington's book *The Other America: Poverty in the United States*. *The Other America* soon attracted an extraordinary amount of attention. Through statistics, straightforward analysis, and interviews, Harrington proved that not only was one-third of the entire American population (as many as 50 million people) living under the poverty line, but that poverty was still an endemic social plague in American society. *The Other America* showed how poverty was not limited to a small number of rural and economically depressed areas, or traditionally underprivileged segments of society, such as African Americans, as was assumed at the time. Poverty was instead hitting a "predominantly urban, white population" who, despite the "striking gains in productivity which have characterized the American economy since World War II, were left behind in the general economic advancement," Harrington wrote.

This new poverty was socially invisible, hidden in central urban areas where, even entering in those areas, it was very hard to detect the tragic reality behind the appearance. As Harrington argued, "America has the best-dressed poverty in the world." Despite his social content, Harrington refrained from using the word *socialist* in his book for fear that it would have alienated the readers and distracted them from the main themes and problems that he wanted to discuss.

*The Other America* was a wake-up call for many people who thought poverty had been virtually eliminated thanks to the unprecedented economic prosperity that American society had experienced since the 1950s. The book, read by President John F. Kennedy, inspired and helped to shape the War on Poverty policy declared by both the Kennedy and Lyndon Johnson administrations, through the development of social programs and structural reforms to education and welfare. Harrington became a participant in a presidential anti-poverty task force.

Unlike the socialists in the 1930s, such as Eugene Debs, who refused to collaborate with mainstream parties and opted to fight independently against the system, Harrington instead decided to collaborate with the American political establishment, and in particular with the Democratic Party.

Although this political choice made Harrington the object of fierce criticism by socialist movements in the United States, in his opinion, a purely socialist approach would have jeopardized his goal of transforming American society to free it from the logic of capitalism. According to Harrington, in fact, the strategy adopted by American socialists until that time was doomed to fail because of the anti-socialist sentiments historically expressed by the American worker. Although many disagreed with his political view, Harrington was able to earn great respect, both nationally and internationally, for his vociferous dedication to social and economic equality as well as civil liberties.

**SEE ALSO**

*Volume 1 Left:* Socialism; Communism; Democratic Party; Debs, Eugene V.
*Volume 2 Right:* Capitalism; Welfare and Poverty.

**BIBLIOGRAPHY**

Michael Harrington, *The Other America: Poverty in the United States* (Macmillan Publishing, 1963); Loren J. Okroi, *Galbraith, Harrington, Heilbroner: Economics and Dissent in an Age of Optimism* (Princeton University Press, 1988); Robert A. Gorman, *Michael Harrington: Speaking American* (Routledge, 1995).

PIETRO PIRANI
UNIVERSITY OF WESTERN ONTARIO, CANADA

# Hayden, Tom (1939–)

TOM HAYDEN HAS spent his adult life working for political, economic, and global change. Born in 1939, Hayden reached adulthood at the beginning of one of the nation's more activist periods, and he jumped right in. From his first anti-war demonstration through his years in the California state legislature and later as a retired legislator, Hayden has upheld his beliefs in democracy, specifically economic democracy.

Hayden first became interested in politics and activism in 1960 during the civil rights movement, when he joined the sit-in demonstrations against Woolworth stores. As he continued to work toward his degree in English, he also continued to explore political radicalism, eventually accepting his place in the student movements that spread across the nation in the mid-to-late 1960s. Hayden's involvement in the radical movement was more than joining the various student groups; instead, he formed two organizations of his own (VOICE, ERAP), staged demonstrations, and spearheaded many anti-war activities. Except for the anti-war demonstrations, Hayden's political activities and beliefs centered on the ideology of economic equity. He believed that the nation's problems were the result of economic oppression and the unregulated power of the federal government and large corporations. Through his Economic Research and Action Project (ERAP), Hayden organized a number of community action groups and was very active in the most successful of those groups, the Newark Community Union Project (NCUP). Under Hayden's sponsorship, NCUP managed to build a playground for the local children, helped terminate an urban renewal project, and got better garbage collection for the ghetto community.

Between 1966 and 1971, Hayden's militant anti-war stance grew until it culminated at a violent protest in Chicago, Illinois. He came to national attention in 1968 as one of the organizers of the demonstration and riot at the Democratic National Convention in Chicago, becoming a renowned leader of the national radical movement. A member of the infamous Chicago Seven, Hayden helped organize the various demonstrations, trained the youthful demonstrators in various military tactics and methods of self-defense, and recruited numerous students and others from the Students for a Democratic Society (SDS) and other student and anti-war organizations in which he was involved. The demonstrators hoped to prove to the political mainstream and the nation that the U.S. involvement in Vietnam was a conspiracy of the military-industrial complex and the fed-

Tom Hayden speaks to students in 1969 at an anti-war demonstration on the campus of the University of California, Berkeley.

eral government. After the riots, the Chicago Seven were indicted and convicted for conspiracy with the intent to incite a riot and contempt of court, charges that were overturned in 1973.

After the conviction in 1970 and throughout the early 1970s, Hayden began to move from overtly militant to more conventional methods of trying to influence the government. He continued to protest the war, but did so using traditional means such as supporting anti-war Democratic candidate George McGovern in 1972 and writing articles against the war. In 1971, he met activist-actress Jane Fonda, and together, they called for the immediate U. S. withdrawal from Southeast Asia. Once the Paris peace accords were signed ending the war, the couple continued their political involvement and solidified their commitment to their leftist politics and each other by marrying in 1973.

Finalizing his transition to more conventional methods to promote political and governmental change,

Hayden challenged John Tunney for the Democratic nomination for the U. S. Senate in 1976. Although he lost the primary, his campaign organization gave birth to still another Hayden-led organization, the Campaign for Economic Democracy (CED). Throughout the rest of his political career, the CED formed the basis of his many causes and projects. It was during the this time that he also began his work supporting the environmental and anti-nuclear movements.

With his failure to gain a national seat, Hayden turned his attention to his home state, California. Beginning in 1982, he began his career in California politics with his election to the state assembly. For 10 years, he represented his Los Angeles constituency in the assembly, and in 1992, he began an eight-year career in the state senate. Whether as an assemblyman or state senator, Hayden stood firm to his ideals espoused in the CED, as well as his defense of the disenfranchised. He has used his talent for organization and persuasion to influence many pieces of legislation, both statewide and locally, during his 17 years of service.

He worked for and helped to pass legislation to rectify economic and social inequalities for various minority groups: women, African Americans, Hispanics, the aged, and others. He became the environmental watchdog of the state senate, fighting for the protection of endangered species and against any abuse of power within his state. His interest in education found its voice in legislation that stopped university tuition increases, helped reform the public school system, and brought to light financial mismanagement in higher education.

Since 2000, this political activist and politician has continued to support special causes and joined the fight against the U.S.-led war in Iraq. In 2004, he was a codirector of the national campaign, No More Sweatshops! Over his some 40 years' involvement in social and political reform, Hayden has used a wide variety of weapons: from militant activism to legitimate political influence, but whichever overt weapon he used, he always used words. He is, and was, a columnist for various leftist organizations and the mainstream press. His publications range from the *Port Huron Statement* of 1962 to his most recent book, *Irish on the Inside*. He has written a total of eight books, including *Reunion: A Memoir*, *The Last Gospel of the Earth*, *The Zapitista Reader*, and *Rebel: A Personal History of the 1960s*.

## SEE ALSO

*Volume 1 Left*: Democratic Party; Johnson, Lyndon B.; Vietnam War.
*Volume 2 Right*: Nixon, Richard M.; Vietnam War.

**BIBLIOGRAPHY**

www.tomhayden.com (May 2004); John H. Bunzel, *New Force on the Left: Tom Hayden and the Campaign against Corporate America* (Hoover Institution Press, 1983); Tom Hayden, *Reunion: A Memoir* (Random House, 1983); Tom Hayden, *The American Future* (South End Press, 1980);William Spinrad, "Assessing the 1960s," *Sociological Forum* (v.5/3); Kathleen Adams and Tamala M. Edwards, "The Really Big Chill," *Time* (December 12, 1994); Tom Hayden, "The 'Kennedy Factor,'" *Nation* (November 10, 2003).

GLORIA J. HICKS
UNIVERSITY OF WYOMING

# Haywood, William D. (1869–1928)

WILLIAM D. "BIG BILL" Haywood was an atheist and a socialist. He was a physical presence with a thunderous voice, but more importantly, he was a radical labor leader who cared little for company bosses or the law.

Born in Salt Lake City, Utah, Haywood lost his father, a rider for the Pony Express, when he was three. He lost his right eye in a whittling accident at age nine, and he always offered his left profile for photographs. At age nine, he began working in the mines. He attributed his radicalism to the 1886 Haymarket riots, trials, and executions. His interest in unionism grew after the Pullman strike of 1893. Working as a silver miner in Idaho in 1896, he heard a speech by Western Federation of Miners (WFM) President Ed Boyce. Haywood threw himself into working for the WFM. He traveled the West as an organizer, often secretly to avoid arrest. By 1900, as secretary-treasurer, he was a member of the executive board. Boyce retired in 1902, recommending joint leadership by Haywood and Charles Moyer. Moyer was cautious and preferred negotiation to confrontation. The volatile Haywood preferred confrontation and violence if necessary.

As president, Haywood worked to improve workers' lives. His speeches rallied audiences to his campaign for the eight-hour workday. Before Haywood and the WFM campaign, miners worked 13 days with one day off, 10 hours a day, not counting travel time. Due to the WFM, Utah was the first state to enact the eight-hour day for miners. Haywood led the WFM in the Colorado Labor Wars against the operators and Colorado state government. Thirty-three union and nonunion workers died in the conflict, which included the June 4, 1904, explosion at the Independence train depot, costing 13 nonunionists their lives. Haywood was suspected, and, although no charges were filed, WFM members became targets of retaliation.

In 1905, just after Christmas, former governor Frank Steunenberg returned to his home after a day at his office in Caldwell, Idaho. When he opened his gate, a bomb blast shattered his body. He died within hours. Haywood was accused of ordering the Steunenberg assassination. Arrested with Moyer on murder charges in 1906, Haywood spent his time in the Idaho penitentiary reading Upton Sinclair's *The Jungle*, Thomas Carlyle's *The French Revolution*, and other works. He also ran for governor of Colorado on the Socialist ticket, took a correspondence course in law, and continued WFM work. After a highly publicized and lengthy trial, a jury acquitted him in July 1906, thanks to an effective defense by Clarence Darrow and, it has been suggested, a bit of jury tampering.

The friction between Moyer and Haywood grew during their time in the penitentiary. Moyer removed Haywood from the executive board in 1908, and Haywood began looking for a more radical labor organization. The most radical union in the United States was the Industrial Workers of the World (IWW), the "Wobblies." Haywood turned his efforts to the IWW and became its leader in 1915. The IWW advocated direct action, including sabotage. Under his leadership, the IWW struck at textile mills in Massachusetts and New Jersey. Membership grew rapidly, and at its peak the IWW claimed over three million mine, mill, and factory workers.

Haywood opposed World War I as a capitalist ploy to gain more wealth, and he spent a year in Leavenworth Prison for violating federal sedition and espionage laws by calling a strike during wartime. He also called for work slowdowns and resistance to the draft. In 1921, while out on appeal, he jumped bond and went to Moscow, Soviet Union, serving as adviser to the Bolshevik government and spokesman for the Marxism of Vladimir Lenin and others. Illness reduced his effectiveness, and some historians claim that he began to perceive the "worker's paradise" as nothing but an abusive police state. He died in Moscow in 1928. His ashes were split, with half being buried in the Kremlin close to John Reed, author of *Ten Days that Shook the World*, and near Lenin's tomb. The other half was buried quietly in Chicago, Illinois, near the monument to the Haymarket anarchists.

## SEE ALSO

*Volume 1 Left:* Reed, John; Unions; Industrial Workers of the World; Socialism; Soviet Union.
*Volume 2 Right:* Capitalism; United States.

## BIBLIOGRAPHY

Peter Carlson, *Roughneck: The Life and Times of Big Bill Haywood* (W. W. Norton, 1983); Melvyn Dubovsky, *"Big Bill" Haywood* (St Martin's, 1987); Melvyn Dubovsky, *We Shall Be All: A History of the Industrial Workers of the World* (University of Illinois Press, 1988); Doug Linder, "Bill Haywood Trial 1907," www.law.umkc.edu (May 2004); "William D. Haywood and the Radical Labor Movement," www.pbs.org (May 2004).

JOHN BARNHILL, PH.D.
INDEPENDENT SCHOLAR

# Healthcare

BECAUSE THE UNITED STATES does not have national health insurance, the discussion of healthcare in America tends to revolve around that issue. From the left-wing perspective, national health insurance for Americans is a dire and top priority: The United States is the only industrialized national government in the world that does not provide medical care to its citizens.

The movement for compulsory health insurance began in 1912 when Progressive reformers commenced a campaign to provide medical insurance for low income workers, paid for with employer, worker, and state contributions. Great Britain instituted insurance for laborers in 1911. The American Medical Association (AMA) undertook reform efforts as well, calling for regulation of medical education and licensure. The government established a presence in healthcare through the Pure Food and Drug Act of 1904 and workmen's compensation laws in 1914. AMA efforts to establish professional sovereignty, however, made doctors fear state regulation of their practices. Business leaders also opposed compulsory insurance since they did not want to pay for workers' health. Big business, organized medicine, and commercial insurance companies formed a successful alliance to prevent health reform. Although health insurance was a new concept in the Progressive era, insurers began to offer group-health policies to employers, who used them to prevent state mandates. It was in that atmosphere that reformers started their campaign for compulsory health insurance and alliances began to form right and left.

## THE NEW DEAL

The Great Depression brought a new wave of concern about the rising costs of medical care. Left-wing officials drafted national health insurance legislation for the New Deal, but AMA opposition dissuaded President Franklin D. Roosevelt from including it in his reforms. Roosevelt proposed national health insurance shortly before his death, leaving the issue for Vice President Harry Truman to pursue. Truman made the issue the centerpiece of his Fair Deal. His proposal for a cradle-to-grave program, again inspired by the newly revised British system, became the hallmark of Democratic liberalism. Predictably, the AMA joined with right-wing Republicans and launched an extensive advertising campaign to "educate" the public about the evils of socialized medicine. Truman's dream of universal coverage died as he left office in 1952. What remained from the healthcare debate was the enactment of the Hill-Burton Hospital Construction Act of 1946, which gave funding for infrastructure rather than for the actual provision of medical care.

## MEDICARE AND MEDICAID

Republican President Dwight D. Eisenhower embodied the right-wing doctrine against social insurance by maintaining a firm stance opposing national health insurance. A new proposal, Medicare, gained considerable popularity throughout the 1950s, however. John F. Kennedy, the new Democratic president, openly endorsed the program for medical care for the elderly, and Lyndon B. Johnson pushed the measure through Congress in 1965. The right won notable concessions, though, even as the left prevailed. Doctors were to set their own fee schedules, and hospitals based their payments on their own costs. Medicaid, medical assistance for the poor, relied on state operations.

The enactment of Medicare was a watershed moment in healthcare legislation. Proponents on the left viewed it as an incremental move toward universal coverage. Yet many right-wing politicians believed that in providing coverage for the most sympathetic groups—the poor and the elderly—universal coverage would be unnecessary. By the 1960s, many workers, particularly union members, received health insurance from their employers, further reducing the need for a government-mandated system.

## REPUBLICAN SHIFT

Healthcare costs rocketed as Medicare went into effect. Republican President Richard M. Nixon instituted wage and price controls on the medical industry, but once they were lifted, costs rose even more. This conundrum shifted the debate from providing healthcare access to controlling costs. Nixon surprised his right-wing constituency by proposing national health insurance. Far from the leftist ideal of a single-payer system, Nixon's proposal rested on an employer mandate and used commercial insurers as fiscal intermediaries. Liberal Senator Edward M. Kennedy, who sponsored the single-payer plan, negotiated a compromise with the Nixon administration. However, organized labor shunned Kennedy's efforts and derailed the proposal.

## DEMOCRATIC SHIFT

Democratic President Jimmy Carter revived the issue at the behest of organized labor, but like his Republican predecessor he shied away from any sweeping action

*Senator Edward Kennedy (right), a liberal proponent of healthcare reform, meets with President George W. Bush in the White House.*

that would upset the flagging economy. Carter attempted to enact hospital cost controls before releasing his insurance plan, but failed. His proposal, released late in his administration, closely resembled Nixon's effort. Labor leaders now stood behind a scaled-down insurance plan, but the administration could not rally enough support for congressional action.

A new wave of conservatism dominated the 1980s, but Republican President Ronald Reagan again blurred the right/left distinction in 1988 by expanding Medicare to include catastrophic illness and prescription coverage. Backlash from beneficiaries was surprising and extreme, however, and President George H. W. Bush repealed the law in 1989.

## THE CLINTON EFFORT

Democratic President Bill Clinton proposed national health insurance in 1992, based on a model of managed competition. This twist on the leftist ideal of single-payer coverage played to conservative beliefs in the power of the free market. Although committed to reform, he was wary of challenging the fiscal constraints that marred the efforts of his predecessor Jimmy Carter. Clinton's plan was unwieldy, though, and caused splinters among the liberal ranks. Without consensus, the effort failed. Clinton turned back to the incremental strategy, implementing the State Children's Health Insurance Program, which provided grants to states to provide insurance for low-income children who did not qualify for Medicaid. Additionally, he signed the bipartisan Kennedy-Kassebaum Act to launch an experimental program of Medical Savings Accounts, whereby individuals could save tax-deferred income for medical care, but could not roll it over from year to year.

## 21st CENTURY

Republican President George W. Bush signed a new Medicare expansion into law in 2003 that included prescription drug coverage. Although his action could be seen as a shift to the left, he maintained a stance on the right by including a provision for Health Savings Accounts (HSAs), interest-bearing savings accounts for medical expenses. These accounts could be rolled over year after year and interest earnings would be tax deductible. This move further illustrated the less than rigid delineations between right and left that characterized the late 20th century, although the tilt was clearly to the right. The HSAs would hopefully encourage small employers to buy accompanying high-deductible health insurance policies for their employees. Such a move would lower the number of uninsured workers and defer the need for national health insurance. As the 2004 presidential election drew near, cries for full-fledged national health insurance continued to come from the left.

## SEE ALSO

*Volume 1 Left:* Clinton, William J.; Carter, James E.; Roosevelt, Franklin D.; Democratic Party.
*Volume 2 Right:* Healthcare; Reagan, Ronald; Conservatism; *Laissez-Faire;* Republican Party.

## BIBLIOGRAPHY

Jonathan Engel, *Doctors and Reformers: Discussion and Debate over Health Policy* (University of South Carolina Press, 2002); Beatrix Hoffman, *The Wages of Sickness: The Politics of Health Insurance in Progressive America* (University of North Carolina Press, 2001); Jonas Morris, *Searching for a Cure: National Health Policy Considered* (Berkeley Morgan, 1984); Paul Starr, *The Social Transformation of American Medicine* (Basic Books, 1982) Kimberley Green Weathers, *Fitting an Elephant through a Keyhole: America's Struggle with National Health Insurance in the 20th Century* (Doctoral dissertation, University of Houston, 2004).

KIMBERLEY GREEN WEATHERS, PH.D.
UNIVERSITY OF HOUSTON

# Hillman, Sidney (1887–1946)

ONE OF THE AMERICA'S most powerful and influential labor leaders, Sidney Hillman cofounded the Congress of Industrial Organizations (CIO), which later merged with the American Federation of Labor (AFL) and mobilized its members into the first truly effective labor force in electoral politics. He was also one of the earliest trade-union advocates of constructive cooperation, recognizing that what helped an industry's workers benefited the industry itself. He was also a close confidante of President Franklin D. Roosevelt (FDR)—to the point where Hillman himself became a major issue during the 1944 presidential campaign, inspiring one of the most famous controversies, and slogans, in U.S. political history.

Born in Lithuania, Hillman abandoned rabbinical studies for a role in the struggle against Tzarist oppres-

sion: He took part in the abortive 1905 Russian revolution and was imprisoned for six months, freed in a general amnesty, then jailed again. Eventually released, he decided to leave Russia, immigrating first to England and then to the United States, where he arrived in 1907. Two years later, he began working in the men's clothing industry, where he organized an unsuccessful strike. Hillman persevered and eventually created a landmark series of cooperative agreements that provided for arbitration procedures; by 1914, he'd been named the first president of the Amalgamated Clothing Workers Union, a position he held for the rest of his life. While walking his first picket line, he met a young striker named Bessie Abramowitz, and they were married in 1916; she also became vice president of the union, whose membership rolls had reached 400,000 by the time of Hillman's death.

In 1935, Hillman took his union out of the AFL and joined with John L. Lewis to form the CIO, becoming Lewis's right-hand man and first vice president. There, he played a key role in organizing the steel and automobile industries, all with his trademark of avoiding violence and confrontation as much as possible. He and Lewis were often at odds, however, particularly over a merger with the AFL, which Hillman strongly favored. During the late 1930s, FDR turned to Hillman to represent the national mobilization in the face of the threat of war in Europe. His task was to keep the machinery of industry moving by using his influence to settle disputes and avert strikes and job walk-offs. He was successful enough that Roosevelt, in 1940, named him associate director of the Office of Production Management.

During the war, Hillman assumed control of the CIO's political action committee (CIO-PAC), which became a potent force aiding Democratic candidates and led to the controversy that increased his notoriety. When *New York Times* columnist Arthur Krock wrote that Roosevelt, in discussing the 1944 vice presidential nomination, had told a top aide to "Clear it with Sidney," a Republican campaign slogan was born, though it proved insufficient to defeat the president.

Adding to the controversy was Hillman's newfound willingness to work closely with communist-dominated unions. Though he had long fought communist attempts to take over his own union, Hillman reasoned that as the United States and Soviet Union were wartime allies, the latter's labor sympathizers should be encouraged to participate fully in the war effort. But Hillman moved from cooperation to outright advocacy: In 1944, communist and anti-communist factions, the latter led by David Dubinsky and Alex Rose, battled for control of the far-left American Labor Party, and Hillman interceded on behalf of the pro-communist unions, which won out. The losers then quit the ALP, which eventually disintegrated, and formed the New York State Liberal Party.

In his later years, Hillman pursued a dream of a worldwide labor federation in which Russian unions would cooperate on basic aims with the CIO. As a sign of the esteem in which he was held, the entire men's clothing industry shut down on the day of his funeral, which was held at Carnegie Hall in New York City.

### SEE ALSO

Volume 1 Left: Unions; Communism; Communist Party, Soviet; Roosevelt, Franklin D.;
Volume 2 Right: Capitalism; Conservatism; United States.

### BIBLIOGRAPHY

John C. Culver and John Hyde, American Dreamer: A Life of Henry A. Wallace (W. W. Norton, 2000); Walter Goodman, The Committee (Farrar, Straus, and Giroux, 1968); Murray Kempton, "A Great Labor Leader, a Fine Biography," New York Post (December 21, 1952); Arthur Krock, "The Facts At Last about 'Clear it With Sidney,'" New York Times (October 16, 1958).

ERIC FETTMANN
INDEPENDENT SCHOLAR

# Hillquit, Morris (1869–1933)

A SOCIALIST WRITER and thinker, Morris Hillquit was significant in defining socialism and the labor movement in the United States. Born as Moses Hilkowitz in Riga, Latvia, then part of Russia, he immigrated to the United States in 1886 when he was 17. He settled on New York's Lower East Side, a hotbed of immigrant radicalism. By day he worked in the garment industry and by night he participated in political discussions in English, Russian, and Yiddish on the Cherry Street rooftops. His interest in left-wing politics and labor unionism led him to establish the United Hebrew Trades, a Jewish garment workers' union, and to work with the well-established Socialist Labor Party (SLP).

He entered New York University in 1891, graduated in two years, and in 1893 established what turned into a successful law practice. He changed his name officially in 1897. In 1899, Hillquit was leader of the conservative, constitutional socialists, the Kangaroos, against the radical and authoritarian Daniel DeLeon in the faction-ridden SLP. Unable to oust DeLeon, in 1901 Hillquit's Kangaroos combined with the Social Democratic Party to form the Socialist Party of America. Hillquit was the party's first national secretary. Although the leadership included the more prominent Eugene Debs and Victor Berger, Hillquit was the party's leading tactician and theorist, and he represented it on the executive committee of the Socialist and Labor International.

Hillquit's socialism was similar to the centrism of Germany's Karl Kautsky rather than that of Rosa Luxemburg and Vladimir Lenin. Hillquit opposed the Industrial Workers of the World and wanted Bill Haywood expelled from the SP's executive committee. As an attorney, he defended unionists of all views, including Haywood. He was the first American socialist historian, producing The History of Socialism in the United States (1903) and Socialism in Theory and Practice (1909). He also wrote From Marx to Lenin (1923) after the socialists and communists split. Both Lenin and Leon Trotsky reacted and referred negatively to him, and Hillquit became anti-communist.

When the labor movement was defining its direction at the turn of the century, socialist unionists wanted unions to be the driving force in creating a more just and equitable society. Business unionists under the American Federation of Labor (AFL) and its president, Samuel Gompers, believed that labor had to work within the capitalist system for narrow bread-and-butter goals. When, in 1903, socialist AFL members agitated for public ownership of the means of production and political action, Gompers said, "Economically, you are unsound; socially you are wrong; industrially you are an impossibility." A decade later, in 1914, Gompers debated Hillquit about the goals of organized labor. The two spoke before the U.S. Commission on Industrial Relations, which Congress established to investigate what was causing so much industrial strife in the United States. Hillquit pinned Gompers down to admitting that he had no goals other than perpetual improvement in a business-owned system. Hillquit and other socialists had a goal, a worker-controlled society in the near future.

Hillquit opposed the entry of the United States into World War I, and he defended many socialists charged with espionage. He also provided legal advice to labor unions. Twice his party nominated him for mayor of New York City. Hillquit ran for mayor of New York in 1917 and many of the East Siders volunteered for his campaign. His mayoral race brought him some 250,000 votes. Five times he ran for the U.S. Congress. He brought his socialists into the camp of Robert M. La Follette and the Progressives in 1924. His autobiography is titled *Loose Leaves from a Busy Life* (reprinted 1971). Hillquit died of tuberculosis in 1933.

**SEE ALSO**

**BIBLIOGRAPHY**

Morris Hillquit, *Loose Leaves from a Busy Life* (Macmillan, 1934); "The Great Debate: Gompers Versus Hillquit," historymatters.gmu.edu (May 2004); Norma Fain Pratt, *Morris Hillquit* (Greenwood, 1979); "Morris Hillquit," Red Biographies, www.reds.linefeed.org (June 2004).

JOHN BARNHILL, PH.D.
INDEPENDENT SCHOLAR

# Hobbes, Thomas (1588–1679)

POLITICAL THINKERS are always products of their times. This is especially true with Thomas Hobbes, whose long life spanned the upheavals of the English Civil War (1642–51) and its aftermath, as well as the discoveries in science and math by contemporaries such as Francis Bacon, René Descartes, Galileo Galilei, Johann Kepler, and Marin Mersenne. Historians of political thought have long appreciated the importance of that context to the formation and nature of Hobbes's political philosophy, although they often disagree, considerably, about how exactly it played out.

Born in Malmesbury, England, in April 1588, Hobbes's earliest formal education was with Robert Latimer, who taught him Latin and Greek. In 1603, he attended Magdalen Hall in Oxford, an experience he wrote of disparagingly. Upon taking his B.A. in 1608, Hobbes began work for the Cavendish family, first as tutor to the son of William Cavendish, later Earl of Devonshire. His connections with that family were lifelong. Tutoring for a noble family gave Hobbes access to a good library, facilitated travel to Europe, afforded introductions to prominent men of letters, and also provided time to work on intellectual projects, such as his

translation and introduction for *Thucydides's History of the Peloponnesian War* (first published in 1629). During these years, Hobbes continued to read widely, in ancient and modern authors, giving for a time particular attention to Euclid's *Elements*. As an author on political subjects, Hobbes's first important writing was occasioned by the growing tensions between King Charles I and the parliament. *The Elements of Law, Natural and Politic*, like all of Hobbes's political philosophy, was sympathetic to absolutism, in part. It was not published, but circulated sufficiently in manuscript that Hobbes, fearing for his safety during the Long Parliament, fled to France in 1640. In Paris, Hobbes worked on scientific topics and had published, in 1642, his first book on political philosophy, *De Cive*, a work in Latin based largely on *The Elements of Law*. Hobbes later wrote of *De Cive* that it was the first ever book of "civil philosophy."

In his most famous political writing, *Leviathan, or The Matter, Forme, & Power of a Common-wealth, Ecclesiasticall and Civill* (1651), Hobbes again elaborated upon ideas first conceived many years earlier. Now, in a systematic treatise "occasioned by the disorders of the present time," Hobbes wrote that before the civil state, men lived in a "state of nature" where equal individuals engaged in a "war of every man against every man." All lived in "continuall feare, and danger of violent death," life was "solitary, poor, nasty, brutish, and short." Rational individuals naturally desired to quit that "state of war" and to unite for self-preservation.

The creation of a "common-wealth by covenant also resulted in "the Generation of that great Leviathan, or rather ... that Mortall God," who is "called Soveraigne, and said to have Soveraigne Power; and every one besides his Subjects." Hobbes considered that only a Leviathan was sufficient to guard against the factional strife he had witnessed in the England of his day. While, then, Hobbes might be seen as an apologist for royal absolutism, the foundation of royal power was a rational agreement among the people. In that sense, his writings might seem a rational basis for authoritarian or conservative rule, but Hobbes also made clear that the authority derived from the consent of the people. As he put it in a later work, "The power of the mighty hath no foundation but in the opinion and belief of the people."

In *Behemoth, or The Long Parliament* (completed in 1668 but only published posthumously, in 1682), Hobbes showed that analysis of the history of the English Civil War continued to occupy his mind. As he said, through the pupil of that dialogue, he was concerned with "the history, not so much of those actions that passed in the time of the late troubles, as of their causes, and of the councils and artifice by which they were brought to pass."

Hobbes's political thought met a varied reception from 17th-century contemporaries who read it more widely than scholars once thought to be the case. In England, he frequently was criticized, often for the anticlerical and secularizing undertone of *Leviathan*, which was considered a dangerous book. In 1666, the English Parliament even tried to pass legislation forbidding Hobbes from publishing. His early reception on the continent was equally varied, but more sympathetic. Hobbes died at Hardwick in 1679. His work was standard reading during the Enlightenment and later influenced utilitarian political thinkers, such as John Austin and Jeremy Bentham, among others. Today, *Leviathan* is considered a classic text of political theory.

**SEE ALSO**

*Volume 1 Left:* Liberalism; United Kingdom; Bentham, Jeremy; Hume, David.
*Volume 2 Right:* Conservatism; United Kingdom.

**BIBLIOGRAPHY**

M.M. Goldsmith, *Hobbes's Science of Politics* (Columbia University Press, 1966); C.B. Macpherson, *The Political Theory of Possessive Individualism, Hobbes to Locke* (Oxford University Press, 1962); Tom Sorell, ed., *The Cambridge Companion to Hobbes* (Cambridge University Press, 1996); George H. Sabine, *A History of Political Theory* (Henry Holt, 1973); Leo Strauss, *The Political Philosophy of Hobbes, Its Basis and Genesis* (University of Chicago Press, 1936); J.P. Summerville, *Thomas Hobbes: Political Ideas in Historical Context* (Macmillan, 1992).

MARK G. SPENCER
BROCK UNIVERSITY, CANADA

# Hollywood Ten

ALVAH BESSIE, Herbert Biberman, Lester Cole, Edward Dmytryk, Ring Lardner, Jr., John Howard Lawson, Albert Maltz, Sam Ornitz, Robert Adrian Scott, and Dalton Trumbo became known in the late 1940s and 1950s as the Hollywood Ten. They were all politically committed to the left, had been members of the Communist Party for various periods, and were involved with the movie industry either as successful and highly paid directors or screenwriters. In the previous decades, their films, such as *Hotel Berlin* (1945), *The Master Race* (1941), *Crossfire* (1947), *Sahara* (1943), *Pride of the Marines* (1945), *Destination Tokyo* (1944), and *Thirty Seconds over Tokyo* (1944), had contributed to fight fascism. With their resilient behavior, they came to symbolize left-wing resistance to the McCarthyist paranoia that engineered investigations in 1947 and 1951 and the consequent blacklist.

These investigations were carried out by the House on Un-American Activities Committee (HUAC), which charged that communists in Hollywood could use the film medium to place subversive messages in their movies and to discriminate against noncommunist colleagues. The HUAC also feared that left-wing artists could give negative images of the United States, which would have international resonance.

These concerns did not take into account the historical and production contexts in which some of the films targeted for their communist message were made. *Mission to Moscow* (1943), for example, the most pro-Russian film ever made, was not the result of Soviet *diktats*, but of orders from Franklin Roosevelt himself, who wanted to boost support for the Russian cause during World War II. In the 1930s and 1940s, Hollywood producers firmly controlled their studios due to fear of censorship under the Hays Code and supervised every stage of production, particularly for those few films that had a political edge.

At the end of the 1940s, the vast coalition that had supported the New Deal and fought fascism became suspect. The right-wing Republican Congressman John Parnell Thomas, a staunch opponent of the New Deal, was the chair of the HUAC in 1947 when it was decided to launch an investigation into Hollywood's allegedly subversive activities. The HUAC interviewed 41 people who were working in Hollywood and who voluntarily attended, gaining the benevolent status of "friendly witnesses.

During the hearings, the names of 19 people accused of holding left-wing views surfaced. One of them was the émigré Jewish playwright Bertolt Brecht, who agreed to testify, but left for East Germany soon afterward. Ten others of the group, later known as the Hollywood Ten, refused to cooperate with the committee claiming that the First Amendment of the Constitution gave them the right not to name names. The House of Un-American Activities Committee and the courts during appeals disagreed; all were found guilty of contempt of Congress, and each was sentenced to between 6 and 12 months in prison.

All of the Hollywood Ten were also added to the blacklist and were prevented from working again for many years; many of them emigrated either to Europe or Mexico.

Some of the Hollywood Ten, however, managed to continue writing screenplays under front names. Dalton Trumbo, for example, worked on the screenplays of the Academy Award-winner *Roman Holiday* (1953) and *The Brave One* (1956). Albert Maltz collaborated on the screenplay of *The Robe* (1953), while Adrian Scott wrote for TV series. The first of the blacklisted Hollywood Ten to write again using his proper name was Dalton Trumbo, who adapted the novel *Spartacus* by fellow blacklisted writer Howard Fast for the screen. Directed by Stanley Kubrick, the movie used the Roman Empire as the setting to analyze the spirit of rebellion and non-conformity. At the end of the film, when the Romans finally succeed in crushing the slaves' revolt, they ask the surviving slaves to identify their leader, Spartacus, and they crucify all of them after their refusal to do so.

After the blacklist was lifted, Ring Lardner, Jr. also resumed writing for Hollywood with his own name. He scripted critically and commercially successful films such as Norman Jewison's *The Cincinnati Kid* (1965) and the iconoclastic, anti-war satire *M\*A\*S\*H* (1970), which earned him a second Academy Award. As late as 1987, Lardner claimed that he had never regretted his association with communism: "I still think that some form of socialism is a more rational way to organize a society, but I recognize it hasn't worked anywhere yet."

The director Edward Dmytryk was the only one of the 10 to actively seek a pardon for his communism and, in the end, cooperated with the HUAC. Faced with financial problems because of his divorce, Dmytryk, who had emigrated to England, contacted the well-known anti-communist journalist Richard English. Together the two wrote the article "What Makes a Hollywood Communist?," which was published by the *Saturday Evening Post* in 1951.

In the same year, Dmytryk also agreed to appear again before the HUAC and to answer all questions that were put to him. He named 26 former members of left-wing groups. He also revealed how several of the Hollywood Ten, such as John Howard Lawson, Adrian Scott, and Albert Maltz, had forced him to make films that expressed the views of the Communist Party. Dmytryk's words were particularly damaging as several of the Hollywood Ten were at that time suing their previous employers for wrongful dismissals. Scott was willing to go before the U.S. Supreme Court, which rejected his case in 1957.

*From left, front row: Herbert Biberman, attorneys Martin Popper and Robert W. Kenny, Albert Maltz, Lester Cole. Second row: Dalton Trumbo, John Howard Lawson, Alvah Bessie, Samuel Ornitz. Back row: Ring Lardner, Jr., Edward Dmytryk, Adrian Scott.*

In one of those cruel ironies of history, John Parnell Thomas, the man who had curtailed the careers of many talented artists, would be himself investigated for financial fraud. Charges claimed that, from 1940 to 1945, Thomas had billed the government for the salaries of nonexistent staff members. This money had gone straight into his bank account. Though Thomas rejected the Hollywood Ten's appeal to the Fifth Amendment, his own strategy when questioned in 1949 was exactly the same. When he was found guilty of defrauding the government, Thomas was sent to the very same Danbury Prison where Lester Cole and Ring Lardner, Jr., were serving terms for their refusal to testify in front of Thomas's HUAC.

**SEE ALSO**

*Volume 1 Left*: Communism; Communist Party, Soviet; Media Bias, Left; United States.
*Volume 2 Right*: McCarthyism; Conservatism; United States.

**BIBLIOGRAPHY**

Bernard F. Dick, *Radical Innocence: A Critical Study of the Hollywood Ten* (University Press of Kentucky, 1989); Edward Dmytryk, *Odd Man Out: A Memoir of the Hollywood Ten* (Southern Illinois University Press, 1995); Ring Lardner, Jr., *I'd Hate Myself in the Morning* (Nation Books, 2001); Patrick

McGilligan and Paul Buhel, eds., *Tender Comrades: A Backstory of the Hollywood Blacklist* (St. Martin's Press, 1997); Victor Navasky, *Naming Names* (Hill & Wang, 2003).

LUCA PRONO, PH.D.
UNIVERSITY OF NOTTINGHAM, UNITED KINGDOM

# Hopkins, Harry (1890–1946)

HARRY LLOYD HOPKINS, known as an "ally of the poor and the defender of democracy," was born in Sioux City, Iowa. The fourth of five children born to David Aldona and Anna Pickett, Hopkins spent his childhood in Nebraska and Chicago, Illinois.

While still in high school, Hopkins demonstrated his political savvy. Opposed to the teachers fixing class elections in favor of the best student, he organized a ballot stuffing. Even though the vote was thrown out, Hopkins kept on electioneering. On the next supervised ballot, his candidate was elected with an even larger vote than the first time. Hence, at Grinnell College, Hopkins earned a reputation for brilliant political tactics and a "restless electric personality." After graduating from Grinnell College in 1912 he became a social worker in New York City.

Hopkins married Ethel Gross, a Hungarian Jew, in October 1913. They had three sons: David; Stephen, who was killed in action while serving with the U.S. Marines on Namur Island in the Pacific in 1944; and Robert, who accompanied his father as an army photographer at many of the wartime conferences. By 1929, Hopkins and Gross separated, and after 17 years of marriage, finally divorced in 1931.

*Jewish First Wife, Divorced: The Correspondence of Ethel Gross and Harry Hopkins*, a book by June Hopkins and Allison Giffen, the granddaughter and great-granddaughter, respectively, of Gross and Hopkins, furnishes the most diverse and dynamic exchanges between the couple, covering their work lives with various agencies and individuals as well as charting their dreams of a life together despite the difficulties of different faiths.

Politically, Hopkins was active in the Democratic Party and a strong supporter of Alfred E. Smith, who became the governor of New York for four terms and a Democratic Party presidential candidate. During World War I, Hopkins served as head of the Gulf Division of the American Red Cross for the relief of soldiers' families. In 1920, he headed the Department of Civilian Relief's Red Cross mission to Mexico. While campaigning for the 1928 Democratic presidential candidate, Alfred E. Smith, Hopkins met Franklin D. Roosevelt: "Governor Roosevelt liked him at once and Mrs. Roosevelt was very partial."

In 1931, Hopkins was appointed head of New York's Temporary Emergency Relief Administration by Roosevelt, then governor of New York. Two years later, after Roosevelt became president, Hopkins was recruited to implement his various social welfare programs. In 1933, Hopkins was appointed head of the Federal Emergency Relief Administration (FERA) and readily tackled the problem of providing immediate relief for the homeless and the hungry. As Civil Works Administrator (CWA) in the fall of 1933, he put 4 million men to work in less than one month, and in less than four months he spent $933 million. In 1935, he was appointed Works Progress Administrator (WPA) charged with the responsibility of putting 3.5 million people to work. As WPA head, Hopkins's drive and decisiveness earned him the acrimony of some and the admiration of many. Hopkins was appointed secretary of Commerce in 1938 after a fierce Senate battle over his confirmation. One year later, due to health problems and a strenuous workload, he resigned.

Hopkins not only held top administrative positions. He also served as a member on several committees, including the Industrial Emergency Committee; the Committee on Economic Security; the National Resources Committee; the Executive Council; the Re-employment Council; and the Central Housing Committee, to name only a few. An intimate friend of Roosevelt, Hopkins was a special assistant to the president during World War II. He administered the lend-lease program in 1941 and went on several missions to London and Moscow as the president's personal envoy. After Roosevelt's death, he went as President Harry Truman's representative to Moscow to settle problems that had arisen over Poland and the organization of the United Nations. In 1934, he met with Italian dictator Benito Mussolini to discuss the Italian public works programs.

During World War II, he met with Soviet leader Josef Stalin regarding Russia's need for war materiel and attended the 1943 Teheran Conference of the Allied wartime leaders. Hopkins helped arrange the Potsdam Conference for Truman but retired from public life soon afterwards. Truman presented the Distinguished Service Medal to Hopkins on September 4, 1945 for his "selfless, courageous and objective contribution to the war effort." Hopkins died in New York City on January 29, 1946.

Hopkins's unwavering loyalty to Roosevelt, his hard-driving enthusiasm for the New Deal, and his "piercing understanding" of war problems merited him an unparalleled position of power in 20th-century American history.

## SEE ALSO

*Volume 1 Left*: Roosevelt, Franklin D.; United States.
*Volume 2 Right*:Totalitarianism; Capitalism.

## BIBLIOGRAPHY

George T. McJimsey, *Harry Hopkins: Ally of the Poor and Defender of Democracy* (Harvard University Press, 1987); June Hopkins, *Harry Hopkins: Sudden Hero, Brash Reformer* (St. Martin's Press, 1999); Allison Giffen and June Hopkins, eds., *Jewish First Wife, Divorced: The Correspondence of Ethel Gross and Harry Hopkins* (Lexington Books, 2002).

JITENDRA UTTAM
JAWAHARLAL NEHRU UNIVERSITY, INDIA

# Human Rights

THE IDEA AND DEFINITION of human rights achieved universal characteristics after the Universal Declaration of Human Rights was adopted in 1948 by the United Nations (UN). Since then, the concept of human rights has become one of the most debated issues in both political and scientific arenas. To start, we apply the broader definition of the concept expressing all things belonging to human beings. Thus, the concept of human rights in its modern notion, are rights necessary for the survival and existence of human beings.

Since states on both the left and right have been guilty of suppression of particular human rights, conservatives have publicized the violation of various human rights within socialist regimes as a form of criticism of those regimes; while liberals have pointed to the violation of different types of human rights within capitalist countries and in some authoritarian regimes.

In its general terms, there exist two broad categories of human rights: negative rights determined through individual control and positive rights entitled by political and social structures that impose on others a restraint from action. The socially, economically, politically, and culturally diversified nature of modern society causes the definition of human rights to go beyond theories of natural rights, which are based on freedom defined neg-

atively as the absence of constraint. Thus, human rights, overall, expand the concept of rights, including positive rights as well as negative ones determined by individual choice, such as the right to shelter, food, education, and medical care.

In this respect, there are four main sub-categories of human rights: civil rights, political rights, social rights, and cultural rights. It is clear in the discussions on human rights that all these rights are defined at the level of the individual. Besides that, in recent decades, there has been a strong emphasis on rights of collectives such as rights of women, rights of workers, rights of minorities, and so on, but the group rights are also justified as belonging to individuals.

## LIFE, LIBERTY, AND PROPERTY

By the 17th century, some philosophers began to express the idea that all people are born free and equal and so have some natural rights, such as the right to life, liberty, and property. Thomas Hobbes (*Leviathan*, 1660) and later John Locke (*The Second Treatise of Government*, 1690) were the first of the natural rights theorists; for them, a person had rights by being human. In particular, Locke's formulation of rights constitutes the essence of the political and social thought of liberalism. For his formulation, each individual had some claims against both society and government, including the rights to life, liberty, property, and consent on how to be governed via a social contract. These rights were inalienable and needed to be protected by a proper political community. His views on natural rights were incorporated into the English Bill of Rights of 1689. The followers of natural rights theory saw the 17th-century development as a basis for civic, political, and religious rights. In the late 18th century, two revolutions, the American Revolution (1776) and the French Revolution (1789), used and made popular the notion of the inalienable rights of man.

One of the main outcomes of the French Revolution was the Declaration of the Rights of Man and of Citizens, which placed a strong emphasis on universal rights as inalienable ones in place of natural rights. On that basis, in the early 19th century, the idea of human rights began to be voiced by some philosophers. Among them were Thomas Paine (*The Rights of Man*, 1792), Henry David Thoreau (*Civil Disobedience*, 1849), and John Stuart Mill (*Essay on Liberty*, 1859).

Commonly accepted was the idea that all people had the right of self-determination and autonomous individuals had some civil rights (right to liberty, right to

*Mrs. Eleanor Roosevelt, wife of the former president, holds the Universal Declaration of Human Rights in November 1949 .*

expression, right to conscience, and so on) and political rights (right to elect and equal votes, right to representation, and so forth).

After the mid-19th century in the West, many issues like poor workplace conditions, serfdom, and racial and sexual discrimination gradually became a matter of human rights. Especially by the end of the 19th century and early 20th century, human rights activism was concerned in a large measure with political and social issues to meet socioeconomic changes. In that period, ideology was involved more and more in the search for expanding civil rights and human rights. Demanding better working conditions and wages, the right to strike, and rejecting the government's authoritarian measures, labor movements came to the fore as a driver of human rights activism. Women's rights movements began to find ground and gained some rights, such as the right to vote and equal access to public services. This period was a time for the development and rise of popularity of social and economic rights. All these rights became more accepted and were turned into practice by the rise of the idea of the welfare state in the Western world through the mid-20th century.

After World War II, the UN sought to bring about a global assertion on the definition and protection of human rights by providing both theoretical and ideological ground for human rights movements in the 1948 declaration. Later, this effort was followed by the other UN covenants and treatises, and the formation of many hundreds of human rights associations and solidarity organizations worldwide. Although they rely on a com-

mon ground, there exist several interpretations in ways that groups and organizations view human rights in their own political, socio-economic, and cultural contexts. Nevertheless, there is a common agreement on the basic idea of the declaration that all human beings are born free and equal in dignity and rights, and so should be treated in an equal way, disregarding their gender, racial, ethnic, social, and religious differences. Most democracies protect these rights by law.

## HUMAN AND CIVIL RIGHTS

The rising acceptance of human rights, especially in light of the efforts of the international human rights communities, began to broaden the analysis to make all social institutions accountable for rights. Parallel to that, in the second half of the 20th century, national liberation movements in the non-Western world and racial and religious minority movements in the West achieved some success, and brought the issue of human rights to a different area (for example, in India with Mahatma Gandhi and in the United States with Martin Luther King, Jr.). In this regard, the main development in the second half of the 20th century was that the scope of the concept of human rights was expanded to include cultural rights. This occurred in parallel with the rising demands of ethnic and religious minority, feminist, environmentalist, and gay and lesbian movements to gain equal access to public goods and services. It became obvious that the demand to express ethnic, religious, sectarian, gender, and conservationist claims was considered as belonging to cultural rights.

By the 1960s, the modern human rights movement came out in favor of peaceful expression of political, social, cultural, ethnic, religious, and sectarian beliefs and views. The most prominent organization to follow this pursuit was Amnesty International. The goal was to form a public opinion on human rights issues and persuade politicians and rulers to take into account these issues. In time, demands for human rights began to move beyond the scope of the Amnesty International, which gradually became insufficient, for example, to provide comparative human rights abuse analyses. The Amnesty International effort ignored some issues, such as the death penalty and abortion, and failed to criticize some authoritarian regimes. People with these concerns formed an organization called Human Rights Watch.

Besides the UN declaration, two covenants (International Covenant on Civil and Political Rights and International Covenant on Economic, Social and Cultural Rights, both adopted in 1966) aimed to create a universal standard among UN-member nations. The International Covenant on Civil and Political Rights set a global framework for the standards of civil and political rights. The covenant relies on the idea of the right of self-determination in a way that all autonomous individuals shall, as determined in Article 1.1, "freely determine their political status and freely pursue their economic, social and cultural rights." The states signing the covenant agree to promote the realization of that right in a way that each state shall respect and guarantee to "all individuals within its territory and subject to its jurisdiction the rights recognized in the present Covenant, without distinction of any kind, such as race, colour, sex, language, religion, political or other opinion, national or social origin, property, birth, or other status."

## INDIVIDUAL SOVEREIGNTY

It is the responsibility of each state to take necessary legislative and other measures within its constitutional mechanism for the functioning of the process of human rights. Law is given priority, because rights achieve legal status when law recognizes them. Among the basic civil and political rights emphasized in the covenant are the right to conscience, the right to think and express opinions, the right to association, the right to privacy, the right to security, the right to equal treatment and recognition as a person before the law, and the right of individual sovereignty over his or her body.

The UN 1966 International Covenant on Economic, Social and Cultural Rights recognized social and cultural rights as an integral part of human civil and political rights. Social rights include, for example, the right to an education, to healthcare, and to economic, social and personal security, or to a livelihood and to a socially acceptable level of food, clothing, and shelter.

In other words, the social claims that are essential to guarantee the legitimacy for the political order include minimum income, housing, education, and medical care. In general, social rights are justified in terms of protecting individual autonomy, as done for civic and political rights. Individuals are guaranteed access to the basic resources necessary for to maintain a decent life.

As socioeconomic rights, cultural rights are presented as necessary for being human. Among the basic cultural rights are the right to maintain and take part in culture, language, and, most importantly, access to education. The latter is seen as inevitable and an important tool to develop human potential and sense of dignity. In this regard, for example, the right to speak and learn in one's own language and to participate in one's own culture are also essential to the exercise of the right to conscience, since human thought is inconceivable without language.

One significant aspect of social and cultural rights is the rights of collectives and minorities. This is about the right to be a member of a collective within society. The concept of human rights is often thought of only within the framework of the rights of individuals, while collective rights are ignored. But, stressing human beings as social and cultural beings in a way that their ideas and opinions are shaped within society through education and culture, the advocates of collective and minority rights reject that view and emphasize the importance of society and culture for the realization of human dignity and human rights. Women or minority groups, as collectives, may make claims on society for rights essential to meet their needs.

In modern democratic and multicultural perspectives, there is a common perception that the issue of minority and group rights is considered part of individuals' free will and dignity. Regarding the question of cultural rights, the most discussed issue is about a possibility of the emergence of collectives and groups as hegemonic bodies, which threatens the human dignity and freedom of members. Thus, group and minority rights are usually treated as the rights of individual, which is guaranteed by a fundamental law that put a strong emphasis on being human as the ultimate virtue.

In conclusion, a contemporary definition of human rights goes beyond classical natural rights theory. The complex and more diversified nature of modern society makes it necessary to apply a broader concept of human rights. Regarding its global notion, it is obvious that equal protection against racial, social, sexual, ethnic, cultural, religious and linguistic discrimination by law at local, national, and international levels leads each individual to make claims on society and government. Thus, this equal protection comes to the fore as a basic principle in the defense of human rights.

**SEE ALSO**

*Volume 1 Left:* Civil Rights; Civil Liberties; American Revolution; French Revolution; Unions; Hobbes, Thomas.
*Volume 2 Right:* Colonialism; Imperialism; Capitalism.

**BIBLIOGRAPHY**

Ian Brownlie and Guy S. Goodwin-Gill, eds., *Basic Documents on Human Rights* (Oxford University Press, 2002); Jean-Marc Coicaud, *Globalization of Human Rights* (United Nations, 2003); Jack Donnelly, *Universal Human Rights in Theory and*

*Practice* (Cornell University Press, 2002); Walter Laquer and Barry Rubin, eds., *The Human Rights Reader* (Meridian Books, 1990); Robert McCorquodale, *Human Rights* (Ashgate, 2003); Michael J. Perry, *The Idea of Human Rights: Four Inquiries* (Sage, 2000); Christian Tomuschat, *Human Rights between Idealism and Realism* (Oxford University Press, 2004).

YILMAZ ÇOLAK, PH.D.
EASTERN MEDITERRANEAN UNIVERSITY, TURKEY

# Hume, David (1711–1776)

DAVID HUME WAS born in Edinburgh in 1711 and attended its university, where it seems he read classics. His attraction to philosophy and writing was marked from boyhood, and a brief attempt at law repelled him as a barren waste of technical jargon. He completed *A Treatise of Human Nature* at the age of 26 (although it "fell dead-born from the press").

Though he was the leading philosopher of the Scottish Enlightenment, allegations of atheism caused him to be turned down for chairs of philosophy in Edinburgh and Glasgow universities. His contemporary fame stemmed mostly from his contributions as an essayist and a historian, with his *History of England* (1754–62) serving as the principal such work.

Placid and phlegmatic by temperament, Hume was guided in his life as in his philosophy by moderation, and was thought gregarious and attractive by his many acquaintances. He obtained for Jean-Jacques Rousseau refuge and a pension in England during the latter's exile from Switzerland in 1766, but Rousseau quickly quarreled and scurrilously accused him of plotting to ruin his character. Hume secured appointments as secretary to the British ambassador in Paris, France, in the periods of 1763 to 1766 and from 1767 to 1768. He died in 1776.

As the foremost philosopher of the Scottish Enlightenment, Hume's empiricism followed upon and radicalized that of John Locke and George Berkeley—though the influence upon him of other thinkers from Isaac Newton to Pierre Bayle ought not be disregarded. His work in turn inspired the greater part of what would follow in the Enlightenment, spanning from Adam Smith's *Wealth of Nations*, Jeremy Bentham's utilitarianism, and James Madison's *Federalist No. 10*, to 19th-century deism and religious skepticism, and contemporary epistemology and scientific method.

A thoroughgoing nominalist in his handling of ideas of material objects as well as mind, Hume adduced arguments against the possibility of grounded, inductively derived expectations about the future, or the knowledge of causation apart from the customary conjunction of two impressions. He also put forth an instrumentalist view of reason as neutral as regards ends and a "bundle theory" of the self as an assortment of perceptions. Moreover, as a pragmatist, he asserted the irrelevance of such theoretical skepticism about the extent of knowledge to the practical concerns of daily life.

To ethics, he contributed a nontheological understanding of utility rooted in individual pleasure. He also observed that normative statements may not be deduced from empirical observations (that is, the is/ought distinction), instead grounding ethics upon human benevolence and "sympathy" rather than rationality. He would become most controversial for his writings on religion, in which he refuted the argument of design from divine existence, and argued that secondhand testimony for a miracle having taken place could never be sufficiently credible to countermand our cumulative experience of the immutability of the laws of nature. He suppressed two essays during his lifetime, "Of Suicide," which justifies the moral permissibility of its subject, and "Of the Immortality of the Soul," which rebuts arguments for human immortality.

Contrary to the prevailing mercantilist assumption that foreign trade represented a zero-sum game, based on the mercantilists' definition of a nation's wealth in terms of its stock of money, Hume argued the wealth of a country lay in its labor and commodities, rendering gains from trade possible. His price-specie flow theory perceptively argued against mercantilism that an inflow of specie into one country would unavoidably disperse to other countries, by changing the terms of trade against the first country, thus leading to increased demand for imports and reduced demand for its exports. Hume also produced a "loanable funds" theory of interest, relating interest rates to demand (for loans) and supply (of savings), and on its basis argued that lower interest rates, far from being indicative of excessive abundance of money, were instead symptomatic of a booming commercial economy.

An empiricist in his political as well as his philosophical work, Hume did not advance "natural law" or "social contract" theories of the state as did other Enlightenment philosophers. (Governments are, for Hume, established in human experience by violence and not contractual agreement; political allegiances are artificial and based on the interests of society.) Instead, Hume's political writings consist of a series of essay contributions dealing with momentary concerns. He generally enters disputes between British Whigs and Tories on the side of the latter, believing monarchy preferable to a republic. However, as usual, his opinions are nuanced: monarchies encourage arts, republics foster science and trade, and the mixed form of government in Britain is conducive to press liberties. Above all, moderation of partisan dispute is requisite for the avoidance of ruinous revolutions and civil wars, which arise generally from zealousness within party factions. Against both Whigs and Tories, he argues ("Of Passive Obedience," 1748) that resistance to the sovereign is justified "when the public is in the highest danger, from violence and tyranny," but not justified as a check to the power granted the sovereign under the Constitution.

With familiar moderation, he argues for the benefits of social position in the middle classes (the rich are immersed in pleasure, while the poor struggle for necessities; the middle classes are best able to acquire virtue, wisdom, and happiness). Likewise for his arguments "not to depart too far from the receiv'd Maxims of Conduct and Behaviour, by a refin'd Search after Happiness or Perfection" ("Of Moral Prejudices," 1742). For similar considerations, polygamy and divorce were to be avoided—the former undermining friendship and promoting jealousy, the latter provoking bad effects on children, insecurity, and hatred between divorcees. In the international realm, he argues the balance of power has been practiced since ancient times.

The role of Hume's writings in the development of the Enlightenment viewpoint of empirically orientated skepticism and pragmatic political moderation, which form at present the omnipresent cosmic background of modernity, is hardly capable of being overstated. In international economics, Hume's investigations into political economy inspired his friend Adam Smith to create modern economics with *The Wealth of Nations* (1776). Hume's moral philosophy in time triumphed over his conventional critics, whose objections attracted immense criticism to each of his works subsequent to "On Miracles." In the short term, many of the texts of moral philosophy used in the 19th century were written in opposition to Humean skepticism. Over the longer term, Hume's removal of traditional Thomistic bases for religious belief would prove seminal in the evolution of liberal and existentialist Protestantism. Bentham first discovered the force of utilitarianism upon reading Hume's *Treatise of Human Nature*, which caused him to feel "as if scales had fallen from [his] eyes."

Though James Madison drew quietly upon Hume's suspicion of faction in the *Federalist No. 10*, Hume's religious skepticism and Toryism made his political writings less influential in the United States. This is particularly true from the start of the 19th century onward, although his religious writings influenced 18th-century American Deists, such as Ethan Allen, Thomas Paine, and Elihu Palmer. From the middle 19th century onward, Hume's influence became indirect, indistinguishable from that point from the broader project of Enlightenment and modernity.

**SEE ALSO**

*Volume 1 Left:* Locke, John; Rousseau, Jean-Jacques; Liberalism. *Volume 2 Right:* Conservatism; United Kingdom.

**BIBLIOGRAPHY**

Duncan Forbes, *Hume's Philosophical Politics* (Cambridge University Press, 1975); Ernest Campbell Mossner, *The Life of David Hume* (Oxford University Press, 2001); David Fate Norton, ed., *Cambridge Companion to Hume* (Cambridge University Press, 1993); Mark Spencer, *Hume and Eighteenth-Century America* (Rochester University Press, 2004).

PATRICK BELTON
OXFORD UNIVERSITY, UNITED KINGDOM

# Humphrey, Hubert H. (1911–1978)

HUBERT H. HUMPHREY was perhaps the most important Democrat of the 20th century who never served as president. Humphrey was born in Wallace, South Dakota, second of four children of Hubert H. Humphrey, Sr., and Christine (Sannes) Humphrey. The elder Humphrey had served a term in the state legislature, and politics was a common topic in the household. Humphrey trained as a pharmacist and worked in the family drug stores in Doland and Huron, South Dakota, before entering the University of Minnesota in 1937. He married Muriel Buck in Huron, on September 3, 1936; to this union were born four children, Nancy, Hubert III (Skip), Douglas, and Robert.

Humphrey's appetite for elective office was whetted while at the University of Minnesota, where he also became a graduate student in political science. He made his first foray into practical politics in 1943, running as the Democratic candidate for mayor of Minneapolis. He lost, and although it was a two-way race with the incumbent Republican Marvin L. Kline, he blamed division of the vote between the Democrats and the Farmer-Labor Party, an agrarian-populist party with leftist aspirations. In 1944, Humphrey helped broker the merger of the two parties into the Democratic-Farmer-Labor Party (DFL). Under Humphrey's guidance, the party became one of the most successful political organizations in the country. Humphrey was elected mayor in a 1945 rematch, becoming the youngest mayor in the city's history to that time. He focused on eliminating corruption in the police department and securing passage of a civil rights ordinance. He was re-elected in 1947 by the biggest margin in the city's history to that time.

He next brought his civil rights agenda to the national stage, orating in favor of such a plank in the 1948 Democratic national platform, a move that led to the walkout of most of the Alabama and Mississippi delegations. The plank was adopted, and became the cornerstone of the Democratic Party for the next generation. Humphrey was elected to the U.S. Senate that year. (It was the last time he would run as Hubert H. Humphrey, Jr.; his father died the next year and Humphrey stopped using Junior.) He set a record for most bills introduced by a freshman senator. He was re-elected in 1954 and 1960. Humphrey ran for president in 1960 but was defeated by John F. Kennedy in key primaries. He was a key player in passing civil rights legislation, including the Civil Rights Act of 1964.

Lyndon B. Johnson tapped Humphrey that year as his running mate. When Johnson declined to seek reelection in 1968, Humphrey stepped into his campaign. Humphrey was perhaps unfairly painted with some of Johnson's unpopular policies, notably the Vietnam War. Humphrey's nickname, "The Happy Warrior," gained during his legislative days, was used against him. Feeling a duty to be loyal to Johnson, Humphrey declined to speak out against the administration's war policies until it was too late. Humphrey narrowly lost the popular vote to Richard M. Nixon. (The presence of a southern third-party candidate, Alabama Governor George C. Wallace, made a Democratic victory in the electoral college an impossibility.)

Humphrey returned to Minnesota and lectured at Macalester College and the University of Minnesota. (The political science department at Minnesota refused to let him teach there, because he had never finished his Ph.D. while a graduate student in the department 25 years earlier.) He won a return to the Senate in 1970 and

was re-elected in 1976. He ran for majority leader in 1977, but lost to Robert C. Byrd of Virginia. The Senate honored Humphrey by creating the post of deputy president pro tempore for him. In August 1977, Humphrey revealed he had terminal cancer. Over the next several months, Humphrey was accorded unprecedented tributes, including being the first nonmember in history to address the House of Representatives. Humphrey died at his home near Waverly, Minnesota, on January 13, 1978 and was buried in Minneapolis. He was succeeded in the Senate by his widow, Muriel.

Humphrey's long career in politics as a liberal Democrat found him consistently near or slightly to the left of the center of his party's positions on many issues of his time.

**SEE ALSO**
*Volume 1 Left:* Johnson, Lyndon B.; Vietnam War; Democratic Party.
*Volume 2 Right:* Nixon, Richard M.; Republican Party; United States.

**BIBLIOGRAPHY**
Hubert H. Humphrey, *The Education of a Public Man: My Life and Politics* (Doubleday, 1976); Carl Solberg, *Hubert Humphrey: A Biography* (Norton, 1984).

TONY L. HILL
MASSACHUSETTS INSTITUTE OF TECHNOLOGY

# Hungary

UNLIKE BRITAIN OR the United States, contemporary Hungary lacks a clear two-party political system. Moreover, the political divisions of right and left, applicable to western-style democracies, fail to capture the complexity and nuances of political and social movements in post-communist Hungary.

For most of the later 20th century, Hungarian politics was dominated by Soviet communism. Opposition to party lines was severely stifled, even before the Soviet occupation in 1956, during which student protests and rebellion were crushed. Although for much of the duration of Soviet occupation, Hungarians enjoyed considerably more personal freedom of travel, art, and culture than their counterparts in other Soviet satellite states; political participation was limited almost exclusively to Communist Party members.

Since 1990, Hungarian politics has settled down into a series of alliances largely comprised of four major political parties, along with smaller fringe parties. The parties themselves have in turn aligned around a somewhat discursive formation of right-leaning nationalism and populism, and left-leaning social welfare and market reform. However, these positions are neither as well defined nor as entrenched as their counterparts in Germany, Britain, and the United States, and many of the "traditional" concerns of the right and the left play out uniquely in Hungarian politics. The stability of the government overall has been strong since the fall of communism, especially when compared to other countries in the region.

Legislative representation in the form of the Hungarian Parliament has been in an almost constant state of flux since Hungary's first free election in 1990. Running on a right-leaning platform of free market economics and personal morality, these first elections resulted in a majority victory for the coalition of the anti-communist Hungarian Democratic Forum (MDF), the Independent and Smallholders and Citizens Party (FKGP), and the Christian Democratic Party (KDNP). The various socialist and leftist parties, including the Hungarian Socialist Workers Party (MSZMP) and the Hungarian Socialist Party (MSZP), received only 33 of the 386 seats in parliament in this first election. This right-leaning coalition lasted until 1994, when MSZP won an overwhelming victory in parliament. After four years of rightist politics, a majority of Hungarians were unsatisfied with economic conditions and the lack of any apparent prosperity, and many Hungarians expressed support for a return to state welfare programs and the higher standards of living under communism.

The Socialist coalition in 1994 thus represented a "middle ground" between the authoritarian and centralized economic programs of communism and the apparent failures and insecurities of radical market reform. The 1998 election brought, in turn, an unexpected victory for the reconstituted right-wing parties, led by Prime Minister Victor Orban. Although they did not win a majority vote, the breakdown of electoral districts provided this coalition with majority representation, and their message of cutting social services, reversing the devaluation of the forint, and revitalizing a more sophisticated market approach to the economy and particularly the growing entrepreneurial classes that supported market reform was well enough supported to win them the election.

Not surprisingly then, the 2002 Hungarian elections saw the ousting of Victor Orban and the somewhat radical right-wing government in favor of MSZP once again. The 2002 elections were particularly important for Hungary, as they determined which government would take the country into its slated European Union (EU) membership in 2004. In another sense, the 2002 elections represented a substantial solidification of party lines, including both economic and cultural platforms.

The constant fluctuation of party platforms and alliances suggests both the high levels of insecurity apparent for Hungarians in their rapidly changing country, as well as the relative inability of all parties to respond to the massive structural, cultural, and economic changes post-communist life has brought. This is clear in the ambivalence many Hungarians feel toward Hungary's entry into the EU itself. Many are suspicious that larger EU members will economically and culturally dominate Hungary.

At the same time, many Hungarians are reticent to be left behind, and in the case of the 2002 elections, fearful that increasing nationalism and radical market reforms will further disenfranchise a growing number of Hungarians and further divide an already growing discrepancy of wealth and insecurity.

## SEE ALSO

*Volume 1 Left:* Communism; Soviet Union; Stalin and Stalinism; Russia.
*Volume 2 Right:* Hungary; Capitalism.

## BIBLIOGRAPHY

Robert M. Jenkins, "Stabilizing the Democratic Transition: The 1990 Hungarian Parliamentary Elections," *Szelenyi* (v.60) http://hi.rutgers.edu/szelenyi60 (July 2004); Brigid Fowler, "ERSC: One Europe or Several," Centre for Russian and Eastern European Studies, University of Birmingham, www.one-europe.ac.uk (July 2004).

ANDREA MOLNAR WOOD
WILLIAM R. WOOD
BOSTON COLLEGE

# The Left

# I

## Ideology

IDEOLOGY IS A COHERENT system of ideas that orients collective conscience in relation to national, political, class, ethnic, or even religious affiliation. It is not simply a philosophy, a scientific doctrine, or a political program held by an individual, but a theoretical framework with a certain power to explain reality and motivate people to action whenever it is accepted by a collectivity and put into practice. As this set of ideas gains wider acceptability and a practical impact, it acquires political status and is recognized as valid. This, in turn, can be used to promote certain attitudes in the general population.

The term *ideology* has often been used, in a somewhat positive sense, to identify the way by which certain popular groups or movements embrace idealistic convictions and question the status quo by means of radical political activism. Thus, groups such as workers' unions, women's movements, student groups, and environmentalists have been characterized as ideological, since many times they equate their convictions to utopian ideals, religious beliefs, or aesthetic narratives.

However, the term *ideology* has also been used in a rather negative sense, which implies a form of manipulation. This perspective indicates that the acceptance of certain beliefs without question and the implementation of these ideas without reflection is nothing but blind activism that needs to be criticized. Such activism occurs, according to many analysts, both on the right and on the left, even though the term *ideology* has been used first and primarily to identify leftist movements. In both cases, however, ideology is expressed as a political behavior that has dogmatism as its main characteristic, often with obvious religious connotations. These movements hold only to certain general ideas that are affirmed in a radical way, without checking their sources or measuring their consequences.

The term *ideology* has been understood and applied in different ways and needs to be differentiated from utopian visions, religious doctrines or beliefs, party programs, or aesthetic attitudes. In order to understand the origins of the term, its applications, and how its use has changed over time, social and historical considerations are necessary.

### THE FRENCH IDEOLOGUES

The concept of ideology has its origins in the 19th century and was first used as a technical word by Destutt de Tracy. He was also considered the first ideologue, since he applied this word as a substitute for metaphysics. Following him is a whole generation of intellectuals in France who were also considered ideologues such as Benjamin Constant, Pierre Leroux, and Jean-Baptiste Say. During the first part of the 18th century, they formed a generation of very active political thinkers made up of politicians, economists and lawyers who influenced decision making in postrevolutionary France. Due to their involvement with politics, the term *ideology* gained the connotation of a political doctrine.

Another generation of French thinkers contributed even more to this connotation, since they were not only political thinkers, but also activists who created alternative communities or societies in which their ideas were to be applied. This is the case, for instance, of Charles Fourier, Étienne Cabet, Max Proudhon and, above all, Saint-Simon.

Fourier is known for having proposed a new communitarian thinking, by which he promoted the idea of creating alternative communities based on the principles of love and nature. His blending of cosmological, social, and sexual ideas became very popular, reaching also the United States, where many farms and communities were created that were based on his model.

Saint-Simon, one of the first French socialists, provides another example of how ideology could be understood at that time. Between 1817 and 1825, he studied the advent of "industrialism" and its influence on new work relations. He considered that the French Revolution had failed for not leading to an Industrial Revolution in that country. The reason, according to him, was that its leaders were metaphysicians, lawyers, and philosophers, who worked well with abstractions but could not lead a practical process of building a new society. Therefore, he worked out a scheme of class divisions to solve this problem. According to this scheme, most people would be workers, since they had the capacity for manual labor; others, in less numbers and with more rational capabilities, would be technicians and scientists; and a few—artists, religious leaders, and metaphysicians—would be their leaders. The function of these few, according to Saint-Simon, was precisely that of promoting the ideas of the new industrial society, thus inspiring and motivating the other classes to work. This last example explains why ideology was understood as promoting ideas onto a given group in order to motivate them to action.

## THE MARXIST CRITIQUE OF IDEOLOGY

At first, Karl Marx and Friedrich Engels came under the influence of French socialists such as Fourier and Saint-Simon and also dwelt on G.W.F. Hegel's philosophy. But later they developed their historical materialism and criticized both Hegel's idealism—that is, a philo-

sophical system based on concepts such as Spirit, Consciousness, and Idea—and the ideologies propagated by communists and socialists. At the same time, they did not limit themselves only to the debate about abstract philosophical ideas, but also took part in several political movements, including the revolutionary attempts in Germany and France around 1848. Therefore, their political thinking and action was an attempt to avoid two extremes: Hegel's idealism and Saint-Simon's ideology. As a result, the Marxist conception of ideology has a double negative meaning, being understood as a form of "false consciousness" imposed by the intellectual classes upon the workers.

The negative meaning of ideology was first expressed in the book written jointly by Marx and Engels and published in 1846, *The German Ideology*, an attack on a group of German thinkers who were both Hegelians and socialists. The book starts by stating that "up to now men have always formed false ideas about themselves, about what they are or should be" and goes on to criticize several revolutionary philosophers. It concludes by proposing a revolt against the empire of abstract ideas that mask reality. Based on this assumption, Marx and Engels developed their own point of view, affirming that one should not start by assuming arbitrary doctrines or dogmas, but rather take the real situation of real individuals, whose lives are based on specific material conditions and on the interaction with nature.

Out of this premise, they developed a new reading of history, showing the several economic stages and conditionings in human history, and affirmed that their analysis is a necessary point of departure for any political proposal. Finally, they criticize the emphasis on the representation of ideas, which they understood to be a tool that imposes the ideas of the hegemonic classes upon the working class, and they developed strategies to unmask this ideology.

Later on, Engels would complement this critique by coining the term *utopic socialism* to identify the abstract theories of certain socialist and religious groups and separate them from the form of political socialism he developed with Marx. Similar critiques were made in relation to anarchists, libertarians, and other groups. All these formulations and associations gave a negative connotation to the term *ideology*, which was maintained by later generations of Marxists. Lenin extended the meaning of ideology in order to define the "false science," which, in his opinion, was a set of ideas and methods of persuasion that could be used against proletarians. Karl Mannheim also proposed a connection between ideology and utopia. Furthermore, he stated that the concept of ideology reflects the discovery of political conflicts, in which the dominant position becomes blind and does not recognize reality. Moreover, Gyorg Lukacs rehabilitated the original ideas of the young Marx—whose manuscripts had become available around the 1920s—in his concept of class consciousness, which implied the need for the proletarians to recognize and overcome their alienation. In this way, ideology became equated with alienation, which was then understood as the control and manipulation of one's consciousness by external powers.

It is precisely in this negative and critical perspective that we can see the critique of ideology in several contexts during the 1960s. This critical perspective eventually gave birth to what became widely known as the New Left.

In Germany, Marxist tradition was combined with Freud's psychoanalysis, especially his method for interpreting dreams, in order to reveal the hidden structures and political interests that influence people's minds and behaviors. This led not only to the interpretation of ideology as culture, but also to the attempt to unleash repressed cultural elements through the action of several groups. The theoretical aspects of this process can be seen in the members of the Frankfurt School—Theodor Adorno, Max Horkheimer, and Herbert Marcuse—who developed a critique of ideologies aimed at unmasking the complex structure of the mass media, which was imposing a false view of totality upon the masses. Building on the tradition of the Frankfurt School, Jürgen Habermas centered his attention on language and proposed that the hermeneutic method could be used to critique ideologies. He defined as ideological those situations in which natural communication in daily life is distorted by technical and instrumental rationality.

In France, the association between psychoanalysis and politics was established already in 1924 by Georges Politzer, but it was during the 1960s that it became a tool to critique ideologies. Louis Althusser turned to Marx's mature work—*Das Kapital*—defining ideology as a "system of representations (images, rites, ideas or concepts) that have an existence and a historical role in a given society." Since Althusser emphasized the role of the state in imposing this system of representations upon several groups as a way of controlling them, he coined the term *ideological state apparatuses* and revealed how they are at play on a daily basis.

Accordingly, many structuralist and poststructuralist analysts began to reveal the disguised forms of social control in daily life. Michel Foucault and Jacques Derrida concentrated on the use of language, arriving at the conclusion that ideology was a type of political rhetoric. They also aligned themselves indirectly with the French feminists and revealed how politics can make use of sexual ideologies—such as machismo and phallocentrism—to control and repress the body. Furthermore, Jean-François Lyotard considered that by revealing the cultural impact of ideological apparatuses through art (theater, narratives, and other expressions), he could provide strategies to be used by oppressed groups as a form of resistance to the bourgeois values of the ruling classes. These various ways of bringing together a phenomenological view of Marx and Freud's psychoanalysis were indeed instrumental for the women's movement, the action of workers' unions, and the student revolts in 1968.

Similar experiences could be seen in the United States at the same time, due to the impact of the above views. In the same way that European immigrants founded many communities based on the ideas of the French ideologues during the 19th century, other European immigrants to the United States during the 20th century brought Marxism and other socialist ideas with them, including their views on ideology. Their actions around the 1920s were centered on the situation of workers and the opposition to authoritarianism. However, the negative impact of the Bolshevik Revolution resulted in a harsh critique of Soviet socialism and minimized the role of socialist debate in the United States. Nevertheless, German emigrés such as Adorno, with his studies on the authoritarian personality, Hannah Arendt and her analysis of totalitarianism, and Marcuse with his studies on the ideology of industrial society maintained the flame of socialism in theoretical discussions concerning the critique of ideologies.

However, by the end of the 1960s, this discussion had been clearly influenced by the categories of the Cold War, during which conservative groups identified communism as an ideology that could influence the population of Western democracies by means of political propaganda. Thus, the term *ideology* was used to criticize the repressive strategies of the Soviet Union as well as any discussions led by socialist sympathizers. On the other hand, leftist groups saw the efforts made by the United States to spread its influence to different countries after World War II as an ideological strategy of control as well. As a result, groups on both fronts accused each other of being ideological. Within this debate, any form of "ism" began to be understood and criticized as rigid ideology.

With all these events, ideology came to be defined as an erroneous philosophical or scientific doctrine, or as a set of ideas that were elaborated by intellectuals and political leaders and then put into practice through institutions, parties, and governments that imposed these ideas upon society as a strategy to maintain political power. Following the Marxist tradition, many intellectual, political, and social groups on the left criticized ideology and opposed it, mostly by means of what came to be called counterideology. On the other hand, groups on the right have claimed that the various forms of criticism of ideology by the left are nothing more but ideological expressions of a belief in Marxism.

THE END OF IDEOLOGIES

Already during the 1950s, the right used the term *ideology* to characterize what they considered to be radical groups sympathetic to Marxism, which had organized a series of actions aimed at questioning the hegemonic political power at the time. In this sense, ideology was conceived by the right as a belligerent attitude by popular movements such as the student movement, the women's liberation movement, worker unions, urban guerrillas, and several other groups that did not measure the consequences of their actions and acted, therefore, somewhat irrationally.

This label was then applied to popular movements, from workers, women, and students to radical and terrorist groups, as well as to distinct political views, such as libertarianism, egalitarianism, and environmentalism. By the 1970s, several groups and movements were criticized as being too ideological. Being overly ideological was a characteristic used to criticize the rise of the counterculture, the opposition to the Vietnam War, the criticism of corruption in politics, and the opposition to the Republican Party. As a result, the concept of ideology was being used by both fronts—the left and the right—against each other. Thus it gained a clear political character and lost its original meanings.

Daniel Bell turned his attention to both trends. Having studied the radical right during the 1950s and having witnessed the rise of the New Left in the 1960s, he published *The End of Ideology: On the Exhaustion of Political Ideas in the Fifties*. In his view, all the energy that was put into political activism by both sides was still there, but without a cause, since the categories of ideologies had become obsolete. Bell pointed to the origins of ideologies in the industrialism of the 19th century and observed that in a postindustrial age, those early motivations were out of place. Moreover, workers had

already secured many important rights by then and, according to Bell, there was no new motivation for social action. All that was left then was "rhetoric." Based on this view, he concluded that ideology functioned only as a rhetorical simplification, for "ideology makes it unnecessary for people to confront individual issues on their individual merits. One simply turns to the ideological vending machine, and out comes the prepared formulae."

A similar argument was brought out by Jean-François Lyotard in his book *La condition postmoderne* in 1979. According to him, postmodern was the situation in an information society, in which new forms of narratives and knowledge had arisen, leading to an epistemic crisis that brought about transformations in contemporary Western societies. This crisis, which occurred first in science and then appeared in several spheres of society, resulted in the critique of universal values and meta-narratives, which actually imposed just one set of values and provided one general historical analysis that abstracted from particular circumstances. Lyotard emphasized instead small projects and narratives. In his view, none of the great universal ideals of the French Revolution or the Enlightenment—such as *liberté, egalité and fraternité*—had the power to legitimize or provide authority to political action, for, in the end, the promotion of such ideals as universal would turn out to be nothing but a totalitarian ideology.

The questioning of this ideological framework also implies an end to the utopias. For Lyotard, however, this does not mean the death of politics, but rather the birth of new ways of acting politically at the local level, by means of small, singular, and localized linguistic, aesthetic, sexual, and marginal performances in everyday life. To be political and nonideological in this sense is, for him, to avoid the temptation of "representation" and thus the imposition or projection of one's experiences onto others.

In summary, we have shown that ideology is a modern concept coined during the 19th century, with origins in the peculiarities of the industrial era, that had an impact on class relations and influenced labor politics. Moreover, it is related to psychological views on consciousness. The history of the concept needs to be understood against this background. As Western societies came to experience what has been called the postindustrial or post-modern era, new forms of social relations have arisen, which cannot be seen according to the traditional views on ideology, especially when related to small-scale interactions between people. However, the problem and the danger of imposing certain ideas on the masses and promoting given attitudes by these means still remains.

## SEE ALSO

*Volume 1 Left*: Liberalism; Saint-Simonism; Socialism; Marx, Karl; Engels, Friedrich; New Left.
*Volume 2 Right*: Conservatism; Ideology; Religion; New Right.

## BIBLIOGRAPHY

Louis Althusser, "Ideology and Ideological State Apparatuses," *Lenin and Philosophy* (New Left Books, 1971); Daniel Bell, *The End of Ideology: On the Exhaustion of Political Ideas in the Fifties* (Basic Books, 2000 ); R. Boudon, T*he Analysis of Ideology* (Polity Press, 1989); Terry Eagleton, *Ideology: An Introduction* (Verso, 1999); Jürgen Habermas, *The Theory of Communicative Action: Vol. 1: Reason and the Rationalization of Society* (Heinemann, 1984) and *Vol. 2: Life-World and System: A Critique of Functionalist Reason* (Polity Press, 1987); Jean-François Lyotard, *La condition postmoderne* (Minuit, 1979); Herbert Marcuse, *One-Dimensional Man: Studies in the Ideology of Advanced Industrial Society* (Beacon Press, 1991); Karl Marx and Friedrich Engels, *The German Ideology* (Progress Publishers, 1968).

AMOS NASCIMENTO
METHODIST UNIVERSITY OF PIRACICABA, BRAZIL

# Immigration

IMMIGRATION IS A historical phenomenon, although it did assume some added characteristics after World War II. The simple portrayal of immigration is the movement of people who desire better life opportunities outside their place of origin. This definition comes with the stereotyping of the traditional actors involved in the process of migration, such as the sending country, the receiving country, and the socioeconomic migrant as opposed to the refugee. The catchword of globalization alerts us to some of the new conditions that were conducive for the novel shape of contemporary migration flows. In this altered context, however, one can also depict a strong undercurrent that portrays immigration at the global scale as a polarized affair: The massive movement of humans across international borders has come to be regarded as one of the most intractable problems by affluent, Western democracies, especially in the post-Berlin Wall era.

Furthermore, since the events of September 11, 2001, international migration and, in particular, immigration, assumed the status of a major security issue. This impending sense of crisis is compounded by the fact that international migration has both voluntary and forced aspects, as well as a large clandestine part to it that almost overshadows its legal and legitimate dimensions. Since the early 1990s, along with the adoption of draconian measures to protect national borders, humanitarian obligations such as those towards refugees and the displaced have gradually been pushed to the back burner as a result.

Immigration is further defined as the voluntary movement of residents of one country into another country for a long-term or permanent duration. Although some scholars wish to include internal migration in this definition, particularly movements from rural to urban areas, immigration is by and large understood as an interstate movement of peoples. It is also acknowledged that opportunities for voluntary migration for the citizens of developing and underdeveloped countries are limited, while globally, migrants leaving these countries constitute the largest category.

Immigration includes the movement of temporary workers, refugees, and clandestine and unauthorized migrants as well as permanent and legal immigrants. One explanation for this rather unwanted variety is related to the imbalances in wealth and resources that divide the north from the south in the global context. In this framework, Europe and North America emerge as the affluent "promised land" for those who have to take the flight for survival. The continents of Asia, South America, and Africa are thus painted with wide brush strokes in the image of poverty, backwardness, and anti- (Western) civilization. The language of push and pull factors traditionally used to explain migratory flows have thus become pointers that indicate the steady outpour of peoples to the West from the rest of the globe, aided further by environmental crises, civil wars, famines, and other kinds of scarcities that affect the poor masses.

In response, during the last two decades, academic literature on migration moved closer to the human/international security and sociopolitical as well as economic stability frame of analysis. The dominant conviction among Western nations is that unless effective, albeit drastic, countermeasures are adopted, immigration will substantially change the makeup of the receiving societies and turn them into "alien nations," according to Peter Brimelow (1995). In this debate, Western nations are seen as fragile lifeboats unduly towing the economy of the entire world and producing the wealth for all to consume. Accordingly, if they were to shoulder the burden of underclasses arriving at their door as unwanted immigrants, their ability to produce, invent, and pioneer further progress would be severely curtailed.

Such anti-immigration fervor is not a historical novelty. The fear of the "yellow-peril," voiced by the German emperor at the time of the Boxer Rebellion in China and the consequent banning of Asian immigrants from the "white world" is a typically cited example. Furthermore, the likelihood of massive immigration flows taking place between the global south and the global north is rather minimal, not only due to the militarization of border controls in the latter, but more so due to the fact that the nation-state continues to act as a possessive container for the populace residing within. Finally, unless due attention is paid to the need and ability of the labor markets in the north to accommodate the new arrivals, it is not possible to understand the absorption of particularly unwanted or self-selected immigrants at the current rate.

In other words, to a significant degree, there is an unspoken yet real demand for international migration in global economy, including un- and semi-skilled migrants. Meanwhile, there remains a gap between the goals of national immigration policies set by the governments of leading industrialized countries (not only the traditional Western ones but also countries such as the Asian Tigers), and the actual outcomes of these policies, as well as the numbers and kinds of immigrants received. One part of the problem is the denial of the needs of a given country for migrant labor due to populist concerns. Instead, emphasis is put on the native population's right to select and delimit immigration, a process within which decisions are primarily shaped by psychological, political, and cultural concerns rather than economic, demographic, or social ones.

The second, and equally important past of the problem, on the other hand, appears to be about the lack of full powers of selection on the part of the receiving countries' governments and the fear of too many unwanted immigrants and refugees arriving as part of a perceived endless global flow. This issue relates to primarily illegal networks of migration as well as controversial refugee acceptance procedures. Regarding the latter, the debate is mainly about how to define the right to asylum and the limits of the principle of nonrefoulment and of the regular resort to the safe third country options.

Indeed, one of the most troubling aspects of the international migration debate can be deemed to be what has been recently called the global refugee crisis. In reality, the vast majority of refugees and displaced people remain within their region of origin in the developing world rather than making the journey to Western, asylum-granting countries. In addition, supranational institutions involved in global governance schemes such as the UNHCR (United Nations High Commissioner of Refugees) have their mandate carved exactly to guarantee such an outcome. In this regard, the fear that the developed world is faced with millions of refugees and misplaced knocking at their door appears to be an unfounded one. The fact that only a small number of Western states constitute first-asylum countries by virtue of their geographical proximity to the center of an impending or ongoing crisis does not change the final outcome that a very small proportion of refugees in the world are actually directly taken care of by the industrialized north. For instance, from 1945 onward, refugee intake constituted at most 20 percent of the immigrant intake of the United States, according to Aristide Zolberg (1997).

## GLOBALIZATION AND IMMIGRATION

A new dimension of the debate on immigration emphasizes the phenomenon of globalization and the spiraling networks of communication and transportation as a result. However, again, this impressive-looking development affects only select groups of the population in the south. The presence of new networks does not automatically result in increased migratory flows. There are still economic, social, and political prohibitions exercised by the country of origin for the prospective migrant, as well as a host of stringent measures awaiting him/her at the country of destination. Immigration does not beget immigration when states at both ends intervene in full capacity. The result is more likely to be continuous trickles of clandestine population movements, and by definition, their size is destined to be limited. Instead, the south tends to create migrants who resort to south-to-south or east-to-east strategies of migratory movement. Only those who can afford more can make the move further to the north and the West. In this context, tightening of the procedures for immigration, asylum claims, and family reunion have indeed proven to be effective measures in terms of curtailing the possibility of a real and established interregional and international migration.

A more measured and statistically based study of migration therefore reveals that the bubble of crisis surrounding immigration is not to stand the test of close scrutiny. Finally, it is of utmost importance that immigration both as a matter of academic inquiry and as a matter of political controversy is attended in a global context, rather than as an issue that only troubles the developed north. In addition, how the factors of race, class, gender, and ethno-religious identity affect patterns of both voluntary and forced migration have to be taken into consideration in terms of determining the root causes as well as the magnitude of immigratory flows.

## SEE ALSO

*Volume 1 Left:* United States; Liberalism; Germany; France.
*Volume 2 Right:* Immigration Restrictions; United States; Germany; France.

## BIBLIOGRAPHY

Peter Brimelow, *Alien Nation: Common Sense about America's Immigration Disaster* (Random House, 1995); Stephen Castles and Mark Miller, *The Age of Migration: International Population Movements in the Modern World* (Guilford Press, 1993); Wayne Cornelius, Philip A. Martin, and James F. Hillifield, *Controlling Immigration: A Global Perspective* (Stanford University Press, 1994); Ted Robert Gurr, Ted Robert, *Peoples versus States: Minorities at Risk in the New Century* (United States Institute of Peace Press, 2000); Myron Weiner, *The Global Migration Crisis: Challenges to States and to Human Rights* (HarperCollins, 1995); Maura Toro-Morn and Marixsa Alecea, *Migration and Immigration: A Global View* (Greenwood Press, 2004); Aristide Zolberg, "Global Movements, Global Walls: Responses to Migration, 1885–1925," Wang Gungwu, ed., *Global History and Migrations* (Westview Press, 1997).

NERGIS CANEFE
YORK UNIVERSITY, CANADA

# India

INDIA IS THE WORLD's largest democracy. It is also a multiparty democracy, with a parliamentary system modeled after the Parliament of England. In addition, it also has a federal system of government with the states organized around ethnic and linguistic lines. Because of the enormous linguistic, religious, and cultural diversity in India, the major political parties tend to be coalitions. Some are ideological parties; others are personally led factions. Only a few political parties are large enough to be national in scope. Others are found only at the state level. And some others are minor factions. Overall India's election process is dynamic and the parties play a significant leadership role.

## CONGRESS PARTY

The Indian National Congress Party was organized in 1885. Its original members were Western educated Indian elites. Leading up to Indian independence, the Indian National Congress Party was a broad coalition fomenting a revolution. After independence, the majority of the Muslim leadership moved to form Pakistan. Today, the National Congress Party is called the Congress Party. Though dominating Indian elections since independence, it is also the party from which many splinter parties have emerged, some on the left and some on the right. For example, in 1947 an ideological disagreement led to the separation of elements from the Congress Party to form the Socialist Party.

The Congress Party, while the dominant party, has followed leftist policies throughout much of its history. It tried to institute a variety of socialist policies to establish and develop industry. It also, as a coalition, has promoted a more egalitarian society with policies aimed at eliminating the caste system.

During the Cold War, the Congress Party led India into joining with many third world countries in forming a bloc of nations that were aligned neither with the West nor with the communists. However, in foreign policy, it was often closer to the Soviet Union and welcomed military assistance from the Soviets. Today, it has moved more in the direction of free enterprise and closer to the Western democracies in foreign policy.

The Congress Party has been a mass movement that was nationalist in character and led by Jawaharlal Nehru and members of the Gandhi family. It has been able for much of its history to negotiate and manage social conflicts that are often ethnic and religious so that peace has prevailed. This is remarkable since India has over 500 languages and dialects. Forty-five of these are official languages. Hindi and English, in part for political reasons, have become major vehicles of communication, but tens of millions still speak other languages. While Indian parties originated as splinters of the Congress Party, the Communist Party is a notable exception.

The Communist Party of India began in 1925. Originally it belonged to the Third International. It also developed close ties with the Communist Party of Great Britain. Prior to independence, it joined with the Congress Party, especially with its socialist-oriented elements to press for independence. However, in World War II, it opposed the Congress Party's attempt to press for independence. It supported Great Britain and the Soviet Union in the fight against fascism. Prior to 1942, it was an illegal party.

While many in the anti-British Congress Party were in jail in World War II, it had an open field for organizing. After the war, the party was unable to decide whether to support or oppose the Communist Party. This is an issue that never really was resolved. During the Cold War, and especially after the death of Josef Stalin, the Communist Party turned to competing with the Congress Party in elections. It was very successful in a number of instances: In 1957, communists were the leading part of a coalition governing the south Indian state of Kerala. However, violence led to its removal from power and direct administration by the Indian president.

In 1964, the Communist Party split between a faction that kept close ties with the Soviet Union and a group that was more militant. The latter group became the Communist Party of India (Marxist). The moderate group, which retained the name Communist Party, followed the Soviet line that India was anti-imperialist and so should only be opposed on domestic issues, but with non-revolutionary intention. The Marxist group adopted the position of total opposition to the Congress Party.

The Marxists were led by Jyoti Basu and moved more toward a Maoist version of Marxism. It was able to win control of West Bengal and has remained a strong presence there ever since. In 1981, another split occurred within the Communist Party of India. Again the key issue was over how to relate to the Congress Party. This time a group left to form the All-India Communist Party. The remnant remained as the Communist Party.

The Communist Party is one of the six parties large enough to be national in scope. It has been able to sustain itself as a mass party despite several splits. However, the Communist Party is not as geographically widespread as is the Congress Party. The Communist Party has also been a significant power in several states. Along with over 20 other parties, it has been a significant presence in various Indian states; in its several forms, it has been successful in attracting some of the rural poor.

The All India Forward Block is an Indian communist party begun in 1939. It has continued to operate but with limited success. Other communists parties are the Communist Ghadar Party of India, the Communist

Party of India (Marxist-Leninist) and the Communist Party of India (Marxist-Leninist) Red Flag.

By the 1990s, the Congress Party was opposed by the National Front–Left Front Alliance, which was a major contender for a substantial block of seats in the government. The leftist alliance included parties such as the Janata Dal, different factions of the Communist Party of India, and a number of regional parties. The Peasants and Workers Party is a small party in Maharashtra state. It is radical and has had some success in attracting support from landless laborers.

In recent years, India has moved in the direction of open free enterprise with significant economic gain. However, leftists have made significant election gains in many places. In 2004, two communist parties won over 60 seats in the lower house of the Indian Parliament. Communist insurgency has committed violent acts in several places including the attempted assassination of Chief Minister Chandrababu Naidu (southern state of Andhra Pradesh.) These Maoists are known as the Naxalite movement. They are named after a 1967 peasant rebellion in West Bengal.

The "untouchables" (lower classes) in India have also formed parties to advance their interests. In 1956, a group of untouchables with others of lower castes formed the Republican Party of India. It achieved local success in Maharashtra in the 1950s and 1960s. However, it was then weakened by factionalism. In the late 1960s, the Dalit Panthers Party was organized in Maharashtra. It was more militant than the Republicans and was able to gather support from both rural and urban groups. Late in the 1970s, the All-India Backward and Minorities Communities Employees Federation began work organizing the untouchables and other lower caste members on a broad geographical basis.

**SEE ALSO**

*Volume 1 Left*: Communism; Stalin and Stalinism; Socialism. *Volume 2 Right*: India; Capitalism; Globalization.

**BIBLIOGRAPHY**

Paul R. Brass and Marcus F. Franda, *Radical Politics in South Asia* (MIT Press, 1973); Lewis P. Fickett, *The Major Socialist Parties of India: A Study in Leftist Fragmentation* (Syracuse University Press, 1976); Zoya Hasan, ed., *Parties and Party Politics in India* (Oxford University Press, 2001); Arun K. Jana, ed., *Class, Ideology and Political Parties in India* (International Academic Publishers, 2002); Surojit Mahalanobis, *What They All Said: Manifestos of Major Political Parties in India* (South Asia Books, 1997); Ross Mallick, *Development Policy of a Communist Government: West Bengal Since 1977* (Cambridge

University Press, 1993); Ross Mallick, *Indian Communism: Opposition, Collaboration, and Institutionalization* (Oxford University Press, 1994).

ANDREW J. WASKEY
DALTON STATE COLLEGE

# Indonesia

THE REPUBLIC OF Indonesia has had a troubled political history throughout much of its existence. As the fourth most populous country and the largest Muslim country in the world, Indonesia continues to be closely watched in the 21st century as it struggles to reassert itself as a democracy. Indonesia is made up of 17,000 islands, making it the largest archipelago in the world. Located between the Pacific and Indian Oceans, Indonesia was a prime target for imperialism in the 17th century, coming under the domination of the Netherlands. The Japanese occupied Indonesia during World War II. After the war, Indonesia declared independence in response to a growing nationalist movement. Indonesian independence was short-lived, however, for the Netherlands, aided by Great Britain, quickly reestablished its claim on the country. On December 27, 1949, Indonesia was declared officially independent. What became known as "guided democracy" was established in the 1950s, setting the stage for four decades of authoritarian rule. In 1998, amid rampant political scandal and economic collapse, a reform government began implementing changes aimed at establishing Indonesia as a true democracy. In July 2004, the country held its first direct presidential election in history. The People's Consultative Assembly had chosen the president in the past.

In 1959, Achmad Sukarno, Indonesia's newly established president, declared that he would govern under the "New Order," which, in fact, was almost oppressive as imperialism had been. Although Sukarno was never a communist, he began secretly meeting with Indonesia's Communist Party members (PKI) and representatives from Moscow, Soviet Union, and Beijing, China, in an effort to steer to the left. On September 30, 1965, Sukarno's activities erupted in what became known as the Night of the Generals. PKI members, with the full knowledge of Sukarno and his closest allies, launched a purge of military leaders who opposed Sukarno's activities and policies. Six generals were executed, but a sev-

enth escaped. The threat of communism in this strategic nation was a direct cause of United States involvement in Vietnam.

Response to the murders was immediate and brutal. The new Indonesian government, led by a coalition of military and Islamic leaders, chose General Suharto of the Golkar party as president. Prodded by intellectuals, academicians, and students, the government began to destroy the Communist Party by legislating it out of existence while conducting a massacre of PKI members and sympathizers. The new reform movement called for political liberty, general elections, freedom of thought and press, public meetings, and open political discussion. The Golkar party dominated Indonesian politics until Suharto's death in 1996. Despite its claim of democratic government, Suharto repeatedly tried to stamp out all resistance to his policies. For instance, when Indonesia's leading newsmagazine openly criticized the government, Suharto blocked its publication.

In November 1998, large student demonstrations resulted when outraged liberals demanded that President B. J. Habibie resign after being accused of using International Monetary Fund (IMF) monies for party purposes. Reformers created the Dewan Perwakilan Rakyat (DPR), also known as the People's Representative Assembly. Since its inception, six parties have dominated DPR. None of them has been able to form a governing coalition, which makes it difficult to institute much-needed reforms.

Tensions in Indonesia were further exacerbated in September 1999, when the legislature of East Timor voted to declare its independence from Indonesia. After the military engaged in a series of atrocities, the United Nations intervened by sending in peacekeeping troops. Former Defense Minister Wiranto, the third-place candidate in the 2004 elections, is still wanted in East Timor for war crimes. Abdurrahman Wahid was named president of Indonesia in October 1999, and Megawati Suhartoputri, daughter of former President Suharto, was named vice president. When scandal surfaced in 2001, Wahid resigned in disgrace. Megawati was officially named president on July 23, 2001.

Politics in Indonesia is complicated by the fact that it maintains a multiparty system made up of sectarian parties as well as modern and traditional Islamic parties. The military and police are also a constant presence in Indonesian politics. Since none of the three major parties won a clear majority in the July 2004 election, a runoff was scheduled for September 2004, pitting former security minister General Susilo Bambang Yodhoyono of the Golkar party against incumbent President

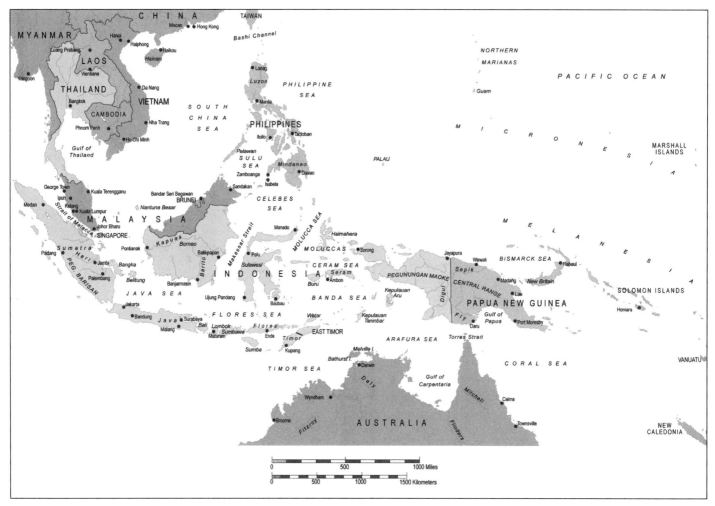

*As the world's most populous Muslim nation, the islands of Indonesia are governed by politics based on religion, regionalism, or social ties. All parties depend on powerful patrons and local leaders for success.*

Megawati Suhartoputri of the Indonesian Democratic Party (PDIP). Voting choices in Indonesian politics tend to be based on religion, region, or social ties, and all parties depend on powerful patrons and local leaders for success. None of the six parties presenting candidates for the 2004 election offered party platforms. Instead, they announced what they call "fighting programs," which different only slightly from one another.

While Golkar presents itself as a party of the center, PDIP represents the liberal element in current Indonesian politics. The main goals of PDIP are to defend the unity and integrity of Indonesia, to maintain secularism in government, to protect the interests of the common people, and to ensure separation of church and state. As a realist, Megawati has maintained close ties with the military in order to survive in the turbulence that makes up Indonesian politics.

Megawati has been criticized for not being able to take control of the problems facing Indonesia in the 21st century. In addition to facing discord within the Indonesian legislature, she has been faced with widespread poverty, endemic government corruption, unequal distribution of resources, a lack of legal recourse for contract disputes, the need for banking reform, and human rights abuses by both the military and the police. She has also been forced to try to find common ground among Indonesia's various political, religious, and social groups. Terrorism has been a major threat in Indonesia since October 12, 2002, when a radical Muslim group bombed a popular nightclub in Bali, killing 200 tourists from 21 countries. A second terrorist attack occurred on August 5, 2003, at a hotel in Jakarta. Megawati's supporters insist that she has brought liberal reforms and much-needed stability to Indonesia. Nonetheless, she has also arrested peaceful protestors and newspaper editors who have criticized her policies.

## SEE ALSO

*Volume 1 Left:* Communism; Vietnam War.
*Volume 2 Right:* Indonesia; Johnson, Lyndon B.

## BIBLIOGRAPHY

Jacques Bertrand, *Nationalism and Ethnic Conflict in Indonesia* (Cambridge University Press, 2004); Arnold Brackman, *The Communist Collapse in Indonesia* (Norton, 1969); Theodore Friend, *Indonesian Destinies* (Belknap, 2003); *CIA World Factbook,* "Indonesia," www.cia.gov (August 2004); "Indonesia: Political Conditions" www.countrywatch.com (July 2004); "Indonesia Puts on an Old Face," *Christian Science Monitor* (June 7, 2004); Florence Lamoureux, *Indonesia: A Global Studies Handbook* (ABC-CLIO, 2003); Jane Perlez, "Former General Wins Most Votes in Indonesian Election," *New York Times* (July 5, 2004); Angel Rabasa and John Haseman, *The Military and Democracy in Indonesia* (RAND, 2002); Stephen Sherlock, "The 2004 Indonesian Elections: How the System Works and What the Parties Stand For," www.cdi.anu.edu.au (July 2004).

ELIZABETH PURDY, PH.D.
INDEPENDENT SCHOLAR

# Industrial Workers of the World

AFTER THE VIOLENT confrontations of the Gilded Age, American craft unionism and big business established an uneasy truce. In return for toleration, the American Federation of Labor (AFL) accepted business dominance of the labor-management arrangement. The union worked to maximize benefits of its members within the system, tacitly acknowledging the death of the independent craftsman.

While the AFL was becoming a junior partner to business, the world of work in the United States was changing radically with cutthroat industrialization and the replacement of skilled unionists with unskilled sweat labor, often unassimilated recent immigrants. Although the new workers undercut the AFL's hard-won wage scales and benefits and wage levels fell, the AFL crafts structure was too inflexible to incorporate industry-wide unions that included unskilled workers. The exploited workers found a union that would work for them in 1905.

The Western Federation of Miners, an industry union, brought together 52 other small general unions into the Industrial Workers of the World (IWW), the "Wobblies." The IWW recognized that industrial organization required more than a handful of carpenters here, a handful of plumbers there, individual craftsmen within the industrial monolith. Behemoth monopolies needed a counterweight union including all workers, regardless of trade or skill. All of the industrial unions should combine into one big union against one big capitalism. The IWW took AFL rejects—Midwestern wheat workers, coastal dockworkers, miners, textile workers, and lumbermen. The IWW also accepted immigrants and African Americans into the leadership.

The IWW included the Irish-born union organizer Mary "Mother" Jones and the black Hubert Harrison from the Virgin Islands. Joe Hill was Swedish. The Dutch Daniel De Leon was one of the three major leaders of the IWW. The others were Eugene V. Debs and Bill Haywood.

The IWW had a strong propaganda corps. When Hill and Frank Little were martyred, IWW writers and speakers created sympathy with the downtrodden and oppressed working men and women of the IWW. Leading orators were Joseph Ettor, Elizabeth Gurley Flynn, and Haywood. The IWW benefited when its strikes provoked violent repression by the owners and "lapdog" local governments. Friends of the IWW included Clarence Darrow, Helen Keller, and Woodrow Wilson.

Debs and De Leon were both socialists, but like the movement in general at the time, they diverged in the type of socialism, the party they supported. They did agree that there was no need to overthrow the system. Unionism could bring about change to a worker's state through political activism and collective bargaining. Haywood repudiated accommodation, rejected the legitimacy of the state itself. Haywood's followers were the leaders in calling for and running strikes—even the general strike which was supposed to bring an entire economy to a halt—and boycotts. Critics accused them of sabotage and violence. In 1908, Haywood's syndicalists ousted De Leon's socialists from the IWW.

Direct action included 150 IWW-led strikes: Goldfield, Nevada, in 1906–07; Lawrence, Massachusetts, in 1912; Paterson, New Jersey, in 1913; iron miners struck in the Mesabi Range of Minnesota in 1916; lumbermen in the northwest in 1917. Other actions included the Seattle general strike of 1919 and a strike of miners in Colorado in 1927–28. During the radical years prior to World War I, IWW membership strength increased from 30,000 to 100,000 workers.

The establishment fought back. In 1914, Hill was convicted on circumstantial evidence of the murder of a Utah businessman. His execution over widespread protest in 1915 made him a martyr to the cause. Little had no trial; because of his unionism or his war opposition, he was lynched in Montana during World War I.

IWW opposition to war, militarism, and U.S. participation in World War I led some members to resist the draft and counsel others to do the same. It continued to strike during the war, leading critics to charge it with sabotage and being an agent of the enemy. The IWW violated the Espionage Act of 1917 and damaged its popularity with a war-rabid populace. The government arrested over 160 IWW leaders, including Haywood. Convicted and out on appeal, Haywood jumped bail, and fled to Russia, where he later died a hero.

The postwar Red Scare nearly finished the IWW. After the Russian Revolution of 1917, all socialist and communist groups in the United States were tarred with the brush of betrayal. The IWW was no exception. When the war ended, the anti-German fervor transferred to socialists, especially foreigners. The Red Scare included both official and unofficial harassment—the difference between lynching and deportation. The IWW survived, weakened.

Then, in 1924, the western and eastern wings of the IWW split over the degree of centralization the organization should have. By 1930, membership was under 10,000. Even though the total grew in the Depression and again in the 1960s, the IWW was a spent force. By the mid-1990s, it had less than 1,000 members. The IWW was a precursor of the Congress of Industrial Unions (CIO) of the 1930s, more violent and more radical but committed to a cohesive comprehensive union protecting all workers. It included too many transient workers, too much unskilled labor, too many who were easily replaced with "scabs," and was too mobile to be effective at organizing. It encountered opposition from government, industry, and the general public. It left the American counterculture the song "Casey Jones," the union movement song "I Dreamt I Saw Joe Hill Last Night," and its anthem, "Solidarity Forever."

**SEE ALSO**

*Volume 1 Left:* Debs, Eugene V.; Haywood, William D.; Socialist Party, U.S.; Unions.
*Volume 2 Right:* Capitalism; *Laissez-Faire*; United States.

**BIBLIOGRAPHY**

Melvyn A. Dubofsky, *We Shall Be All: A History of the Industrial Workers of the World* (University of Illinois Press, 1988); "Industrial Workers of the World," *The Columbia Electronic Encyclopedia* (Columbia University Press, 2002); William LeFevre, "In the Shadow of I.W.W. Revised 2002," Walter P. Reuther Library, Wayne State University, www.reuther. wayne.edu (January 2004); Patrick Renshaw, *The Wobblies: The Story of Syndicalism in the United States* (Doubleday, 1967); Fred Thompson, *The I.W.W.: Its First Fifty Years* (Industrial Workers of the World, 1955).

JOHN BARNHILL, PH.D.
INDEPENDENT SCHOLAR

# Iran

SINCE IT EXPERIENCED the Islamic Revolution in 1979, Westerners have developed an idea of Iran as a highly conformist, authoritarian state that is based on a conservative reading of Islamic teaching. In the decades before this revolution, Iranian politics, while predominantly authoritarian, were anything but conformist or dull.

Based on historian Fred Halliday's 1979 work, it is useful to see 20th-century Iranian history, before the 1979 revolution, as defined by five crises. The first was a Constitutional Revolution from 1905 to 1911, which established a parliament, the Majlis, in an effort to modify the power of the Qajar dynasty. Second, from 1919 to 1921, the Qajar dynasty was deposed and Reza Khan came to power and crowned himself shah. Third, as part of the wartime foreign occupation of Iran by British and Soviet forces, Reza shah was ousted and replaced as shah by his 22-year-old son, Mohammed Reza Pahlavi. Fourth, from 1951 to 1953, Mohammed Mossadeq became prime minister of Iran, attempted to expropriate Iranian oil from foreign control, and was overthrown by the U.S. Central Intelligence Agency in concert with some internal Iranian social forces. And fifth, in the early 1960s, the shah consolidated his regime and to some degree modernized Iranian society and economy.

Through much of this period, there was active competition between right- and left-wing forces, and the outcome of this struggle has had important long-term consequences for Iran. During much of the 20th century, Iran had an active Communist Party and/or the "Masses Party," commonly referred to in English as Tudeh (and probably most accurately transliterated as Téda). The Communist Party of Iran was formed in

The shah of Iran, Reza Pahlavi, persecuted the political left, which helped the rise of the religious extremism that deposed him.

able to the shah were legal, and the shah's secret police, SAVAK, had the right to examine and approve all candidates.

Under these conditions, dissident political movements, especially on the political left, could hardly survive, let along thrive. As early as 1932, 32 leaders of the Communist Party were arrested and tried and 27 were convicted for espionage, based on the belief that they were working for the Soviet Union. In fact, Western suspicion of communism and the Soviet Union, even during World War II, as well as the development of the Cold War after 1945, strongly informed the prospects of the Iranian left in the second half of the 20th century. As the 1930s wore on, the Communist Party largely disappeared as a result of the repression of its leadership and organization. But 1942 saw the establishment of the Tudeh Party, though there is significant scholarly disagreement about its origins and upshot. For example, Donald Wilber (1981) views Tudeh as nothing more than a Iranian front for the Soviet Union, designed to encourage a nationalist government like that of Mossadeq, with a plan to take over once conservative social forces were weakened. On the other hand, Homa Katouzian (1981) argues that Tudeh began as a broad anti-imperial, liberal, nationalist, and socialist movement and only eventually became aligned with the Soviets.

There is general agreement that Tudeh's political base was in Azerbaijan, as well as among intellectuals, students, and workers in the oil and other industrial sectors. Tudeh had participated, and even held cabinet posts, in the 1946 government of Ahmad Qavam, but by 1949 it, along with the communist-influenced trade union movement, had been banned. Once the Mohammed Mossadeq government was overthrown in 1953, the remnants of Tudeh were identified as an internal enemy to be eliminated. In September 1954, 600 officers and soldiers in the Iranian army were arrested for alleged Tudeh connections. Many were executed or imprisoned. By the late 1950s, much of Tudeh strategy and activities were developed outside of Iran, particularly in Europe. In April 1965, a failed assassination attempt on the shah was blamed on Tudeh influence. In this period, the United States was actively involved in Iran (seeing the situation through the lens of its Cold War competition with the Soviet Union), through arms sales and the operation of a number of military missions in the country.

The political left, as it is commonly understood, has had little influence in Iran since the early 1970s. Since 1979, a major Western concern, including for every

June 1920, inspired in part by the Russian Revolution and by the political tumult in Iran at that time. The Communist Party, like Tudeh later, however, attracted the negative attention of Reza shah and his son over their 70-odd year rule.

During the Pahlavi era, violations of human rights in Iran were common, especially after the deposing of Mossadeq and especially with regard to activists on the political left. In later years, the shah exercised widespread censorship, held political prisoners, engaged in torture, imprisoned people in harsh conditions, and engaged in summary executions and extra-judicial killings. The only trade unions tolerated were state-controlled. While there were elections in the 1950s through the 1970s, only the two political parties that were accept-

U.S. president since that time, has been the rise of Islamic fundamentalism in the Middle East. It is ironic that the Cold War liquidation of the political left in Iran meant that the only opposition to the pro-Western shah of Iran was found in the mosques and among small businesses. The Western world continues to live with the legacy of the rise of this conservative, anti-Western movement.

## SEE ALSO

*Volume 1 Left*: Communist Party, Soviet; Communism.
*Volume 2 Right*: Imperialism; United Kingdom; United States; Iraq.

## BIBLIOGRAPHY

Elton L. Daniel, *The History of Iran* (Greenwood Press, 2001); Fred Halliday, *Iran: Dictatorship and Development* (Penguin Books, 1979); Homa Katouzian, *The Political Economy of Modern Iran: Despotism and Pseudo-Modernism, 1926–79* (Macmillan, 1981); Donald N. Wilber, *Iran Past and Present: From Monarchy to Islamic Republic* (Princeton University Press, 1981).

GEOFFREY R. MARTIN
MOUNT ALLISON UNIVERSITY, CANADA

# Ireland

THE LEFT IN THE Republic of Ireland is consistently eclipsed by its conservative and centrist counterparts, at least when the measure used is electoral success. While Fianna Fáil (Soldiers of Destiny, a conservative populist party) and Fine Gael (Family of the Irish, a Christian democratic party) have captured first and second places in the country's last four parliamentary elections (as of 2004), an assortment of leftist forces—led principally by the Labour Party—scramble to constitute a coherent and effective opposition.

Laying claim to only a distant third place in Ireland's most recent (2002) parliamentary election, the Labour Party can nonetheless boast of being the oldest political party in Ireland and the only party that predates the country's independence in 1922. Established in 1912 by William O'Brien, James Larkin, and James Connolly as the political arm of the Irish Trade Union Congress, the Labour Party has sought throughout its history to advance a social policy agenda that targets unemployment, poverty, social exclusion, and emigration.

At the heart of Labour's programmatic message are four central principles: freedom, equality, community, and democracy. Yet because the "national question" (that is, the Republic of Ireland/Northern Ireland division) garners the lion's share of attention in Irish politics, the Labour Party's more conventional left-wing interests have at times languished.

Pushed aside by Fianna Fáil as the country's primary parliamentary opposition party in 1927, Labour fell prey to internal divisiveness through the 1940s. Five on-again, off-again coalitions with Fine Gael over the next four decades gave Labour important experience as a party of government. In 1990, Irish voters elected Labour's Mary Robinson as the country's first female president, a striking precedent for both Ireland and the party. Over the next two years, the Labour Party fused with the Democratic Socialist Party and the Independent Socialist Party, mergers that facilitated the party's best electoral performance (19.3 percent in the 1992 general election) and its sixth entry into a coalition government. In 1998, Labour expanded once again, this time combining with the much smaller Democratic Left. This latest merger failed to bear electoral fruit (winning only 10.4 percent of the vote in 2002) and prompted new leader Pat Rabbitte to consider strategically reorienting the party toward the ideological center.

Part of Labour's electoral troubles stem from the Irish left's division into multiple parties. While attempting to catch up with Fianna Fáil and Fine Gael on the right, Labour has simultaneously had to fend off challenges from its own left flank. Chief among these challengers are Sinn Féin (We Ourselves) and the Green Party. Sinn Féin advertises itself as a nationalist and labor-oriented party committed above all else to achieving a reunited 32-county democratic socialist republic free of British rule. With origins in the 1916 Easter Rising and subsequent civil war, Sinn Féin in the 1960s and 1970s staked out radical positions in demanding civil rights in Ireland and British expulsion from the six counties in Northern Ireland. Led by Gerry Adams, Sinn Féin later gained increasing consideration as a legitimate political force (and no longer just the political wing of the paramilitary Irish Republican Army) and earned its first parliamentary seat in 1997.

For their part, the Greens chisel away at Labour support by offering alternative ideas about how best to achieve grassroots, participatory democracy and wage security without being ecologically destructive. Founded in 1981 by Christopher Fettes, a Dublin teacher, the Greens made their breakthrough in 1994 by electing two members to Ireland's European Parliament delegation. Although it took eight years, the success at the European level finally translated into national-level success in 2002 when the Greens tripled their parliamentary representation from two seats to six (3.8 percent of the vote). Small in number, the Greens enjoy increasing success at selling their message of sustainable development, peace, and a redistribution of resources.

### SEE ALSO

*Volume 1 Left:* Labour Party, UK; United Kingdom; Green Party.
*Volume 2 Right:* Ireland; Conservative Party, UK.

### BIBLIOGRAPHY

Kieran Allen, *Fianna Fail and Irish Labour: 1926 to the Present* (Pluto Press, 1997); John Coakley, ed., *Politics in the Republic of Ireland* (Routledge, 1999); Michael Gallagher, *Irish Labour Party in Transition, 1957–82* (Manchester University Press, 1983); Peter Mair, "The Autonomy of the Political: The Development of the Irish Party System," *Comparative Politics* (v.11/4, 1979); Peter Mair, ed., *The Changing Irish Party System: Organization, Ideology, and Electoral Competition* (Palgrave Macmillan, 1987).

WILLIAM M. DOWNS, PH.D.
GEORGIA STATE UNIVERSITY

# Israel

THE MODERN HISTORY of the state of Israel began on November 29, 1947. The United Nations had been debating for months on the question that would likely lead to war: the partition of Palestine, which would give birth to the state of Israel. Then, on November 29, 1947, the United Nations voted on the momentous issue. The Palestine Broadcasting System recorded the decision: "the General Assembly of the United Nations, by a vote of 33 in favor, 13 against ... has voted to partition Palestine." On May 13, 1948, the British evacuated Jerusalem, having governed Palestine as a League of Nations Mandate territory since the end of World War I. On May 14, eight hours before the British Mandate officially ended, David ben-Gurion, the head of the governing Jewish Agency, proclaimed the establishment of the state of Israel. Fittingly, the historic meeting was held in the Tel Aviv Museum, where over 3,000 years of history looked down upon ben-Gurion and the other delegates assembled there. The delegates were drawn from the socialist Zionist movement, which had begun to settle in Palestine around 1904 to build the country based on socialism that the Zionist philosopher Moses Hess had envisioned in the 1840s.

At the same time, the Arab nations who had sworn to oppose the creation of Israel—Egypt, Lebanon, Iraq, Syria, Transjordan (now Jordan)—invaded the new nation. The Israeli Army, or Defense Force, had its origins in the militia of the labor movement Achdut Ha-Avodah, or Unity of Labor. The militia's name was the Haganah. On May 31, 1948, ben-Gurion, now Israel's first prime minister and minister of defense, issued the proclamation establishing the Israeli Defense Force (IDF): "with the establishment of the state of Israel the Haganah has left the underground to become a regular army."

The decisive factors were the centralized administration and combat experience of the forces of the Israeli Defense Force, drawing on its nearly 30 years (from 1920) of concerted action defending the Jewish agricultural settlements, or *kibbutzim*, from Arab attack. Finally, by January 1949, the fighting drew to a close. Israel signed an armistice with Egypt on February 24, 1949. Similar agreements were made with Lebanon on March 23, Jordan on April 3, and with Syria on July 29, 1949. Only Iraq, which contributed the least to the fighting, did not sign an armistice with the new Jewish State.

Within Israel, the socialist wing of the Zionist movement, the leftist side, maintained its sense of solidarity. Yossi Beilin writes in *Israel: A Concise Political History*, how "the left wing party workers ... prided themselves on their agricultural past, however brief." Until 1991, in fact, the Marxist hymn *The Internationale* would be sung at the convening of each congress of the Labour Party. Indeed, much of the internal history of Israel has really been the history of the Histradut, the Zionist labor group that had been founded in 1920. Beilin states that the Histradut was "devoted to the enhancement of Zionist goals through the infusion of Jewish labor and ownership of the land." The allied Mapai political party, formed in 1930, became the basis of power for David ben-Gurion. The Histradut still serves as the main force for labor in Israel and continues, in keeping with its socialist roots, to press for progressive social service programs within the nation.

Politically, the history of Israel has been dominated by offshoots of the Zionist labor movement as well. When ben-Gurion broke with the Mapai Party, he established in 1965 the Rafi Party with Moshe Dayan, the leading commander of the army in the Six Day War of

June 1967, and Shimon Peres. Ben-Gurion's rival from the 1948 War of Independence, Menachem Begin, who had led the opposing Irgun, established the Herut Party, which actually came in second in the 1955 elections. The Herut Party, as Charles D. Smith wrote in *Palestine and the Arab-Israeli Conflict*, claimed for Israel all territory that had been "Palestine in World War I, namely, that east and west of the Jordan River." Meanwhile, the struggle with the neighboring Arab countries erupted in war again in 1956, 1967, and 1973. It would be Begin, certainly one of the most innovative of Israeli leaders, who would sign the historic Camp David accord with Egypt's President Anwar Sadat in 1979, the first true treaty of peace with an Arab state.

From 1987, the main concern of Israel has been to find a satisfactory solution to the problem caused by the Palestinian Arabs who were displaced from their homes when Israel was founded. In December 1987, the Palestinian Intifada, or "uprising," began in the West Bank of the Jordan and the Gaza Strip, occupied by Israel. The result was the Oslo, Norway, agreement, which the cabinet of Israeli Prime Minister Yitzhak Rabin assented to on August 30, 1993. The agreement led to a Palestinian Authority under Yassir Arafat, long the chief of the main terrorist group fighting Israel, the PLO (Palestine Liberation Organization).

The Oslo Accords provided for a progressive program aimed at eventually a Palestinian State living in harmony with Israel. However, ten years later, that dream has yet to be realized. In 2004, Israeli Prime Minister Ariel Sharon pursued a policy of establishing a wall to create a *cordon sanitaire*—a protective zone—between Israel and the Gaza Strip and West Bank, where the Palestinian Authority rules. This was being done to block terrorist raids that are staged from these areas. In keeping with the Zionist nature of Israel, at stake in the ongoing crisis is the fate of some 7,500 Israeli settlers who now live in the Gaza Strip.

**SEE ALSO**

*Volume 1 Left*: Egypt; Middle East.
*Volume 2 Right*: Israel; Middle East.

**BIBLIOGRAPHY**

Yigael Allon, *The Making of Israel's Army* (Bantam, 1970); Walter Laqueur, *A History of Zionism: From the French Revolution to the Establishment of the State of Israel* (MJF Books, 1972); Charles D. Smith, *Palestine and the Arab-Israeli Conflict* (St. Martin's Press, 1992); John F. Murphy, Jr., *Pillar of Fire: The Spread of Weapons of Mass Destruction in the Middle East* (unpublished ms.), "The Early History of the Israeli Defense Force," (Israeli Defense Force College, 1997); David J. Goldberg, *To the Promised Land: A History of Zionist Thought from Its Origins to the Modern State of Israel* (Penguin, 1996); Yossi Beilin, *Israel: A Concise Political History* (St. Martin's Press, 1992); Tom Segev, *The Seventh Million: The Israelis and the Holocaust*, Haim Watzman, trans. (Henry Holt & Company, 2000); Matt Rees, "Prepare to Evacuate," *Time* (April 12, 2004); Avi Shlaim, *The Iron Wall: Israel and the Arab World* (Norton, 2001); Martin van Crefeld, *The Sword and the Olive: A Critical History of the Israeli Defense Force* (Perseus Books, 1998).

JOHN F. MURPHY, JR.
AMERICAN MILITARY UNIVERSITY

# Italy

DURING THE 20th century and into the 21s, the parties of the Italian left have been involved in countless dog-bites-man plots that have badly served their cause and marginalized their numerous votes into decades of opposition.

The first organized party of the Italian left was the Italian Socialist Party (PSI), which was founded in 1893 by trade unions and socialists. In the early decades of the 20th century, the radical left wing of the party clashed with the reformist wing. At the Livorno Conference in 1921, the left, which included important future leaders such as Palmiro Togliatti, Antonio Gramsci, Umberto Terracini, and Angelo Tasca, broke away to form the Italian Communist Party (PCI). During the fascist regime, members of the PSI and the PCI were persecuted and sometimes murdered. The Socialist deputy Giacomo Matteotti, for example, was killed in 1924 and Benito Mussolini admitted his responsibility in the action at the Chamber of Deputies in January 1925 with a speech that inaugurated the 20 years of fascist dictatorship. The communist leader and Marxist theorist Antonio Gramsci also died following his eight years in the fascist prisons.

In spite of the split consummated at the Livorno Conference, the PSI and the PCI were united in their fight against fascism and their alliance continued until the mid-1950s, when the PSI censured the Soviet Union after its invasion of Hungary. The two parties actually reunited under the common list of the Fronte Democratico Popolare (Popular-Democratic Front) in the 1948 election after they had been ousted from the government led by the Christian Democrat Alcide De Gasperi due to American pressure. Yet, the dawning of the Cold War, the paranoid rhetoric of the election, and the active anti-left propaganda of the Vatican contributed to the poor result of the Fronte Popolare led by Togliatti and Pietro Nenni. It barely obtained the 30 percent of the vote against the impressive 48.5 percent of the Christian Democrats (DC).

After the Soviet invasion of Hungary, the two parties progressively took separate political directions. In 1963, the PSI joined or supported center-left governments led by the Christian Democrats, although the following year its left-wing members abandoned the party to form the PSIUP (Italian Socialist Party of Proletarian Unity). The alliance with the DC caused a hemorrhage of votes in favor of the PCI, which became the major Communist Party in Western Europe. After the death of Togliatti and the brief leadership of Luigi Longo, the PCI was able to threaten the Christian Democrats as the largest Italian political party under Enrico Berlinguer's charismatic direction. Berlinguer, who as Longo's deputy had condemned the Soviet-led intervention in Czechoslovakia in 1968 and openly criticized Soviet Communism at a conference in Moscow the following year, led the party to its best electoral results in 1975 and 1976, when the gap between the PCI and the DC narrowed to a mere 5 percent.

Yet, Berlinguer's political line was not simply characterized by antagonism toward the Christian Democrats. On the contrary, in 1973, he launched the proposal for a coalition between the two parties to modernize and strengthen the Italian democracy. This proposal was soon called *compromesso storico* (historical compromise) and led the PCI to give its external support to Christian Democratic governments during the 1970s at a time when Italy was badly affected by terrorist actions from both right- and left-wing extremists. Though Togliatti and Longo had already distanced the party from Moscow, Berlinguer achieved a complete independence from Soviet communism and shifted the PCI to more pro-Western positions.

In 1971, he ended the party's stance against the European Economic Community and in 1976 he acknowledged the usefulness of the North Atlantic Treaty Organization (NATO). The Polish crisis at the beginning of the 1980s completely persuaded Berlinguer that the 1917 Russian Revolution had outlived its validity for Western socialism. In spite of Berlinguer's political far-sightedness and intellectual sharpness, after the mid-1970s, the PCI inexorably started to lose votes, although the emotional impact of Berlinguer's death during a

The Italian Communist Refoundation Party has been part of numerous left-wing coalitions, some more successful than others.

rally for the European elections of 1984 helped the party to overtake the DC for the first and last time.

The 1980s witnessed the rise in power of Bettino Craxi, the leader of the PSI, who became the first Socialist premier and shifted the party to centrist if not right-wing positions. Though Craxi was able to revive the electoral consensus of the PSI, he did so by inaugurating a rampant and ruthless political style that soon led to the political scandals of the 1990s, often grouped under the collective name of Tangentopoli. In 1992, the arrest in Milan of a local Socialist Party administrator, Mario Chiesa, uncovered the widespread system of kickbacks and corruption through which the DC and the PSI governed the country. The judicial enquiries that followed caused the dissolution of the PSI in 1994, and the creation of a new party, the Italian Socialists which in 1998 was renamed Italian Democratic Socialists (SDI).

The PSI was not the only party to come to its end in the 1990s. In the wake of the fall of the Berlin Wall and the poor result of the PCI under Alessandro Natta, the new communist leader, Achille Occhetto, proposed to reconsider the whole political line of the party and to change its name. In 1991, the last congress of the PCI gave way to the Democratic Party of the left (PDS, later only DS), from which, however, the far left split off to set up a new party, Partito Rifondazione Comunista (Communist Refoundation Party). The former trade unionist Fausto Bertinotti soon replaced Garavini as the party leader.

During the 1990s, the Italian left became the first victim of its successes and adopted a schizoid line that nullified its electoral victories. The crisis of the DC and the PSI and their allies following the Bribesville scandal caused a massive victory of the PDS in local elections in spring and autumn 1993. The same year, given the shock and fear in conservative circles, media magnate Silvio Berlusconi declared he was ready to enter politics to save Italy from the communist danger. In 1994, Berlusconi's coalition, formed by his own centrist party, Forza Italia, National Alliance (the former neo-fascist party), and the secessionist Northern League defeated the left-wing Progressive Alliance.

Yet, Berlusconi's blunders, his planned cuts to the welfare and pension systems, and the growing tensions in the coalition progressively weakened the government, which only lasted for six months. After an apolitical government of technocrats led by Lamberto Dini and supported by center-left parties, the Italian left finally found its unity and founded the Olive Tree Coalition, which, under the guidance of the moderate Romano Prodi, won the 1996 general election. Prodi became the first prime minister to lead a left-of-center government in 50 years with the PDS as the main partner and first national party.

Yet, after only two years, the Communist Refoundation Party withdrew its support, causing Prodi's downfall and an internal split within the party. The former Communist Party leader Massimo D'Alema became prime minister, but, despite his political ability, his two governments were marred by the numerous divisions in the coalition. In 2001, the general election witnessed the defeat of the Olive Tree Coalition (without the Communist Refoundation Party) and the return to power of Berlusconi with the largest parliamentary majority ever enjoyed by a postwar government. Whether the Italian left has learned its lesson from its many schisms or whether it will have to wait for another 50 years to regain power is one of the most challenging questions of the Italian political debate.

**SEE ALSO**

*Volume 1 Left:* Communism; Socialism.
*Volume 2 Right:* Italy; Fascism.

**BIBLIOGRAPHY**

John Baker, *Italian Communism: The Road to Legitimacy and Autonomy* (University Press of the Pacific, 2002); Roberto D'Alimonte and David Nelken, eds., *Italian Politics: The Center-Left in Power* (Westview Press, 1998); Alexander J. De Grand, *The Italian Left in the Twentieth Century: A History of the Socialist and Communist Parties* (Indiana University Press, 1989); Spencer M. Di Scala, *Renewing Italian Socialism: Nenni to Craxi* (Oxford University Press, 1988); Vassilis K. Fouskas, *Italy, Europe and the Left: The Transformation of Italian Communism and the European Imperative* (Ashgate Publishing, 1999); Stephen Hellman, *Italian Communism in Transition: The Rise and Fall of the Historic Compromise in Turin, 1975–80* (Oxford University Press, 1988); David Kertzer, *Politics and Symbols: The Italian Communist Party and the Fall of Communism* (Yale University Press, 1996).

LUCA PRONO, PH.D.
UNIVERSITY OF NOTTINGHAM, UNITED KINGDOM

# The Left

# J

## Japan

JAPAN SPENT CENTURIES in geographically induced and politically enforced isolation. When it opened up to the rest of the world in the second half of the 19th century, it embarked on the race to match the Western industrialized nations. With amazing speed, in less than a generation, Japan was transformed to reach this goal, and in the early 20th century, it was able to defeat Russia in war. This economic, political, and military success story had bad side-effects, as the Japanese society became very militaristic and jingoistic. What was celebrated as Samurai ethics played out as an Asian form of fascism starting in the late 1920s. Japan engaged in colonialist expansion politics and became the only Asian player in the concert of the European and U.S. imperialistic powers. Japanese neighbors, especially Korea and China, paid dearly for the ruthless expansion of Imperial Japan. Although Japan was something like a junior partner of Nazi Germany in World War II, the propagandistic indoctrination of the Japanese people and traditional warrior ethics prolonged the Japanese resistance at the end of the war. Only the use of atomic bombs forced the Japanese Emperor to surrender.

Examining the politics of Japan of today, from a left perspective, has to start with the past, as the idealization and mystification of the past are a forming element of the Japanese society. At the end of World War

II, when the Americans entered Japan, they wanted to remodel and democratize the country. But as General Douglas Macarthur kept the Tenno (Japanese emperor) in place, a symbol of the pre-1945 period was transferred into the new era. It is true that the Tenno was stripped of his role as a living god and had no real political power in the new constitution, but along with the keeping of the Tenno came tacit rehabilitation of the pre-1945 society as a whole. For example, kamikaze suicide missions of World War II are still regarded by a large percentage of the Japanese population as heroic and pure self-sacrifice, although it is by now well established by historians that brain-washing and sometimes even force induced the pilots to their brutal missions.

Democracy was never a project on which the Japanese society embarked voluntarily. The Americans forced it onto Japan after 1945, but large parts of the population stayed at least skeptical. This may have changed with the postwar generations, but it is certainly true for the period of de-facto one-party-rule from 1955 to the early 1990s (Liberal Democratic Party, LDP). Although Japan has had a democratic system since the constitution of 1946, this democracy was more formal than vivid for long periods. This led to large protest movements outside the democratically elected institutions, and both the extreme right and the extreme left use very violent measures to bring their political point to public attention. Whereby the left sometimes disturbs the traffic of Tokyo by attacks on transport systems, or attacks foreigners abroad (for example the assault by Japanese terrorists on an Israeli airport), the extreme right is much more powerful, because it had, at least from the 1950s to the 1970s, tacit approval of parts of the Japanese establishment.

A strange but symptomatic example is the attempted coup by the right-wing terrorist Yukio Mishima in 1970. Although it appeared like an operetta coup (Mishima performing the traditional Samurai suicide at the end), it showed the political inclinations of relevant parts of the Japanese society. Shinto, as a state religion, was banned by the Americans after World War II and only allowed for private worship, but the reestablishment of Shinto in its former role was a project of the Japanese extreme right ever since. On the fringe of the Japanese society are also dangerous religious sects like Aum Shinrikyo, which attacked the underground train system of Tokyo with poisonous gas in 1995.

The Aum Shinrikyo is symptomatic of the high industrialization level of Japan, as this terroristic sect produced poisonous gas in its own industrial facilities. The economic miracle of Japan after World War II (in fact the second industrial miracle of Japan after the first of the Meiji period) was possibly too fast to take the whole society to the new era. Although the Japanese state runs very successful programs to coordinate the research and development efforts of the Japanese industry, the social implications of such a dramatic change in society were left out. People economically and/or mentally left behind in the postwar success story tend to political or religious extremism. The economic problems since the 1990s have aggravated this situation. Probably the most dangerous aspect of Aum Shinrikyo was its membership, which comprised highly qualified scientists who seemed to have not found any sense in their life within the Japanese society, but instead embarked on producing weapons for obscure religious goals.

Japan after 1945 had a very splintered party system, especially on the left. Whereas the Liberal Party united more or less all nonsocialist groups within the Japanese society, neither the Socialist Party nor the Communist Party could ever lead the country. Indeed, for many years from the 1970s to the 1990s, the Liberal Party had an absolute majority in both houses, whereby any left opposition was marginalized. The Socialist Party grasped the feeling of participating in government on a junior partner level several times but was weakened by its internal feuds and rivalries. The Communist Party experienced rifts between supporters of the Soviet Union and of China. There are, at times violent, grassroots organizations of the extreme left. The major topics of the Japanese left were, apart of economic questions, the rearmament issue, relations with the United States, and the controversies over Japan's pre-1945 past.

The Japanese society and economy are still very hierarchically organized, and the Japanese forms of politeness are sometimes so overstressed, that these forms at least tend to prohibit the free exchange of opinions that is the basis of a democratic society. Pacifists would further argue that many governments have tried to erode the peaceful message of the Japanese constitution of 1946. Although Article 9 of that constitution prohibits any military forces, the so-called Japanese Self-Defense Forces have been strengthened since the attacks in the United States of September 11, 2001.

### SEE ALSO

*Volume 1 Left:* Japan; Asia; Communism.
*Volume 2 Right:* Asia; Xenophobia; Immigration Restriction.

### BIBLIOGRAPHY

Albert Axelbank, *Black Star over Japan: Rising Forces of Militarism* (Tuttle, 1988); Lawrence W. Beer and John M. Maki, *From Imperial Myth to Democracy: Japan's Two Constitutions, 1889–2002* (University Press of Colorado, 2002); Ruth Benedict, *The Chrysanthemum and the Sword: Patterns of Japanese Culture* (Mariner Books, 1989); Ian Buruma, *The Wages of Guilt: Memories of War in Germany and Japan* (Farrar, Straus, Giroux, 1994); Glenn D. Hook and Gavan McCormack, *Japan's Contested Constitution: Documents and Analysis* (Routledge, 2001); Gen Itasaka ed., *Japanese History: 11 Experts Reflect on the Past* (Kodansha International, 1996); Charles M. Overby, *A Call For Peace: The Implications of Japan's War-Renouncing Constitution* (Kodansha International, 2001); Edwin O. Reischauer, *Japan: The Story of a Nation* (McGraw-Hill, 1989); Koseki Shoichi and Ray A. Moore, *The Birth of Japan's Postwar Constitution* (Westview Press, 1997)

OLIVER BENJAMIN HEMMERLE, PH.D.
CHEMNITZ UNIVERSITY, GERMANY

# Jefferson, Thomas (1743–1826)

THE AUTHOR OF the Declaration of Independence, Thomas Jefferson led the first opposition party in the United States into becoming the dominant party, making the Democratic Party the oldest party in the United States. Jefferson's political contributions were substan-

*Thomas Jefferson's liberalism, more than other founders' philosophies, came to dominate politics in the young United States.*

tial. He served as president, vice president, secretary of state, foreign ambassador, congressman, governor, and state legislator. He was also a man of multiple talents.

In addition to founding the University of Virginia, Jefferson was a lawyer, philosopher, writer, architect, and scientist. He loved books and was known to read 15 hours a day at certain periods of his life. When the Library of Congress was almost totally destroyed by British troops in 1814, Jefferson donated his own library to Congress. With the purchase of the Louisiana Territory, Jefferson doubled the physical proportions of the United States. He also turned large areas of public land into private farmland. After Jefferson left office, he continued to influence national policy during the presidencies of his allies and fellow Virginians James Madison and James Monroe.

Jefferson was born in Shadwell, Virginia, on April 13, 1743, to Peter and Jane Randolph Jefferson. Peter Jefferson was a justice of the peace, a sheriff, a politician, a surveyor, and a mapmaker. Upon his father's

death, Jefferson inherited 2,700 acres of land and a large number of slaves. At 16, he entered the College of William and Mary. As a student, Jefferson often attended meetings of the Virginia House of Burgesses, obtaining a thorough grounding in the political process. In 1762, Jefferson entered the law office of George Wythe, a Williamsburg, Virginia, lawyer. Ten years later, Jefferson married a widow, Martha Wayles Skelton. After her death in 1782, Jefferson became vulnerable to rumors of a relationship with a slave, Sally Hemmings.

Ideologically, Jefferson was influenced by both 18th-century Enlightenment ideas and 19th-century Romanticism. As a prolific reader, his personal library included the works of Homer, Euripides, Cicero, Geoffrey Chaucer, John Milton, Alexander Pope, John Dryden, David Hume, Adam Smith, John Locke, Thomas Hobbes, Jean-Jacques Rousseau, the Baron de Monstesquieu, and Voltaire. As an Enlightenment thinker, Jefferson's philosophy was grounded in rationality, accepting the need for civil society and government. However, as a Romanticist, Jefferson understood the danger of governments that trampled on individuality, stripping humans of dignity and their oneness with nature. Throughout his life, Jefferson was shaped by his belief that agriculture should be the foundation of any society.

## DECLARATION OF INDEPENDENCE

In 1769, Jefferson was chosen as a delegate to the Virginia House of Burgesses where he argued against aristocratic methods of inheritance and limitations on individual liberties. As tensions between Virginians and the royal governor increased, the legislature was often dismissed. Jefferson was among those who regrouped at the Raleigh Tavern in Williamsburg, then the capital of Virginia, to develop strategies that ultimately led to the call for independence from England. In 1774, Jefferson articulated his political views, heavily influenced by John Locke and the Baron de Montesquieu, in *A Summary View of British America*.

At the age of 32, Jefferson was elected to the Continental Congress where he was appointed to a special committee to draft a statement of independence. On June 28, 1776, after 17 days of concentrated endeavor, Jefferson submitted the first draft of the Declaration of Independence. He opened the document with a justification for the right of the colonies to break free of the mother country: "When in the Course of human events, it becomes necessary for one people to dissolve the political bands which have connected them with another, and to assume among the powers of the earth, the separate and equal station to which the Laws of Nature and of Nature's God entitle them, a decent respect to the opinions of mankind requires that they should declare the causes which impel them to the separation."

Combining Lockean liberalism with his own interpretations of the natural rights philosophy, Jefferson established the foundation for the individual liberty of Americans by stating that some truths were so essential that they became "self-evident."

To Jefferson, those truths were "that all men are created equal, that they are endowed by their Creator with certain unalienable Rights, that among these are Life, Liberty and the pursuit of Happiness." Jefferson rejected Locke's prioritization of property, preferring the utilitarian idea that happiness, not property, was the ultimate goal of individuals.

As a contract theorist, Jefferson noted that government existed only through the "consent of the governed," insisting that the contract could be broken whenever the government became "destructive" of the ends established in the contract. Since the colonies refused to recognize the authority of the English Parliament, Jefferson listed the grievances that George III had in tyrannical fashion committed against the colonies. The grievances included the refusal to allow Americans to legislate for themselves; preventing passage of laws beneficial to the colonies; dissolving duly elected legislatures; interfering with population growth; obstructing justice; engaging in military harassment; blocking foreign trade; suspending charters; plundering of the lives, land, and seas of the American colonies; waging war against English citizens; and denying redress of grievances.

## THE CONSTITUTION

Jefferson served as the governor of Virginia from 1779 to 1781 when he resigned to serve as member of the House of Representatives. In 1784, Jefferson was appointed minister to France. In France, Jefferson spent a good deal of time with the revolutionary hero, the Marquis de Lafayette, the French philosopher Marquis de Condorcet, and other liberal thinkers of the day. Jefferson was in Paris, France, when the Constitution was written in Philadelphia, Pennsylvania, in 1787. His part in the construction of the document was indirect, mostly deriving from his influence on Madison, a major architect of the Constitution.

While Jefferson was never an Anti-Federalist, as some people have claimed, he was not inclined to accept the argument that the structure of the Constitution would protect liberty. Jefferson wanted written guarantees. In a letter dated December 20, 1789, Jefferson warned Madison that without a written guarantee against government intrusion, such basics as "freedom of religion, freedom of the press, protection against standing armies, restriction of monopolies, the eternal and unremitting force of the habeas corpus laws, and trials by juries" would be in jeopardy. Jefferson also believed that the office of the presidency should be rotated to prevent abuses of power. This did not happen until the passage of the Twenty-Second Amendment in 1951, after Republicans proposed the amendment to prevent any future Democratic presidents from winning four elections as Franklin Roosevelt had done.

## THE FEDERALISTS

By definition, liberals seek change. Once change has become the status quo, conservatives seek to protect it. Subsequent need for reforms is likely to result in the creation of a new, liberal party. This is exactly what happened in the early days of constitutional government. Proponents of the Constitution, known as Federalists, accomplished the change from a loose association of states under the Articles of Confederation to a strong central government separated into the executive, legislative, and judicial branches under the Constitution. As the only political party, the Federalists became conservative, seeking to protect the government they had created.

There was little question that George Washington, the hero of the American Revolution, would become the first president. Washington chose John Adams as his running mate, Jefferson as secretary of state, and Alexander Hamilton as secretary of the treasury. Almost immediately, Jefferson began to disagree with Adams and Hamilton over the role of the new government. Jefferson saw the Federalists as elitists who were unconcerned with the will of the people. In 1796, Jefferson became vice president of the United States, but he resigned over what he saw as irreconcilable differences with Federalist philosophy.

In an effort to control criticisms of Federalist policies, the Adams administration managed to convince Congress to pass the Alien and Sedition Act of 1789, which punished any criticism of the government that was considered "false," "scandalous," and "malicious." As France and England fought the Napoleonic Wars, the United States wanted to maintain trading relations with both countries, while remaining politically neutral. Neither England nor France accepted the right of America to do so.

Federalists were afraid that immigrants, particularly those from France, would incite a rebellion against the democratic government of the United States. The Alien and Sedition Act allowed the Adams administration to deport aliens and to prosecute newspapers and individuals for "seditious libel." Adams also saw the new act as a method to discourage the growth of the Democratic-Republicans, Jefferson's new political party. Twelve of the 25 people charged under the Alien and Sedition Act were ultimately convicted. Calling the Federalists' actions a "reign of witches," Jefferson pardoned them all when he became president. Congress later refunded all fines, plus interest.

## ELECTION OF 1800

In 1800, amid bitter controversy, Jefferson was elected the third president of the United States, becoming the first Democratic-Republican to serve in that office. The new party, also known as the Jeffersonians or the Republicans (which had no relation to the modern Republican Party), was a liberal party that had evolved as a response to the conservative Federalist policies of Adams. According to the original Constitution, presidential electors cast their votes for president and vice president at the same time. The candidate with the most votes became president, and the candidate with the next number of votes became vice president, as Jefferson had in the 1796 election. In 1800, however, the system failed, with Jefferson and Aaron Burr, the vice-presidential candidate, receiving 73 votes each. Since the House of Representatives, which had a constitutional mandate to choose the president under such circumstances, was controlled by the Federalists, representatives were opposed to both candidates. Hamilton (who was killed by Burr in a duel four years later) convinced members of the House to vote for Jefferson, who won on the 37th ballot. Delegates of two states refused to vote for Jefferson, preferring to submit blank ballots. Congress then proposed the Twelfth Amendment, which requires electors to vote for president and vice president separately.

The election of 1800 also enlarged the power of the Supreme Court. After losing the election to the Jeffersonians, the Federalists packed the federal courts with Federalist appointees with the idea that federal courts could overturn Jeffersonian reforms. Running out of time, the Federalists failed to deliver all official notifications of judicial appointments. When Madison, the new secretary of state, found these papers on his desk, he and Jefferson agreed that no more should be delivered. Deprived of his appointment, William Marbury sued Madison, leading to the landmark case *Marbury v. Madison* (5 U.S. 137, 1803). John Marshall, the new Federalist chief justice and a cousin of Jefferson's, changed the course of history by determining that the Supreme Court had the right of judicial review, allowing them to interpret the Constitution. The Court ruled that the Judiciary Act of 1789 was unconstitutional and upheld Madison's right to refuse to deliver the commissions.

## THE PRESIDENCY

Three years before becoming president, in a letter dated December 20, 1797, Jefferson expressed his views on aggressive government to his friend and protégé Madison: "I own I am not a friend to a very energetic government. It is always oppressive." Once in office, however, Jefferson became an active president, shaping both the politics and the geography of the new nation. Jefferson's liberalism was evident in his inaugural address in 1801. He promised to effect changes that included tax and foreign-debt reductions, cut-backs in governmental and military jobs and expenses, and a concentration on domestic rather than foreign affairs.

Calling his election "a second revolution," Jefferson saw his victory as a ratification of liberalism. Jeffersonianism moved the United States away from elitism toward popular democracy; created an alliance between the common people and the liberal intelligentsia made up of writers, scientists, planters, pamphleteers, and a group of lawyers; and implemented the concept of Manifest Destiny, which justified western expansion. Jefferson was also the first president to remove partisan government employees and replace them with his own supporters.

Jefferson believed in progress, and he was fascinated by technology. In 1803, Jefferson purchased the Louisiana Territory from France, paying about three cents an acre. On February 28 of that year, Jefferson launched the Lewis and Clark Expedition. Financed by a $2,500 appropriation, Jefferson's Corps of Discovery, led by Meriwether Lewis and William Clark, covered thousands of miles, paving the way for westward settlement that ultimately expanded the territory of the United States from western Missouri to the Pacific Ocean.

Foreign affairs required Jefferson's attention also. Almost immediately after taking office, Jefferson ordered the USS *Chesapeake* to patrol the West Indies to protect American ships from Barbary pirates. When the British attacked American ships, looking for deserters, Jefferson convinced Congress to pass the Embargo Act, banning trade with both England and France. When residents of northern New York rebelled against the subsequent loss of income from trade, Jefferson charged the rebels with treason.

## CIVIL RIGHTS AND RELIGION

Jefferson, like the other men who founded the United States, has been criticized for his hypocrisy because he accepted slavery while endorsing the concept that all men are created equal. Jefferson acknowledged this contradiction in the theory and practice of American equality. When writing the Declaration of Independence, he had included an anti-slavery plank. It was removed only after southern states refused to sign the document under those circumstances. In 1787, Jefferson supported efforts to include an anti-slavery provision in the Constitution. It was removed for the same reason.

In 1820, Jefferson warned decision makers that the Missouri Compromise would lead to civil war. A product of his times, Jefferson did not believe that equality would be possible after slavery was abolished because of ingrained prejudices in American society. Jefferson has also been faulted for his treatment of Native Americans. He ignored their "inalienable rights" by beginning the displacement that drove Native Americans further westward and away from the more settled eastern areas. To Jefferson's credit, he did convince Congress to make it easier for immigrants to become U.S. citizens, cutting the waiting period from 14 to 5 years.

To Jefferson, freedom of religion was the "most sacred of all human rights." In support of the Virginia Act for Religious Freedom, Jefferson introduced the concept of a "wall of separation" between church and state, arguing that government should be restricted to legislating actions rather than beliefs. In an 1802 letter to the Danbury Baptist Church, Jefferson contended that "religion is a matter which lies solely between man and his God, that he owes account to none other for his faith or his worship." While some people accused Jefferson of being anti-religion, that was never the case. He simply believed it was wrong for proponents of one religion to force their beliefs on others, and he objected to the practice of compulsory church attendance. Although his parents had been Anglican, Jefferson refused to tell people what religion he endorsed.

Jefferson's liberal belief in religious tolerance strongly influenced the Establishment and Free Exercise clauses of the First Amendment: "Congress shall make no law respecting an establishment of religion, or prohibiting the free exercise thereof." Historically, the Establishment Clause has prevented the government from establishing a state religion or from preferring any one religion to another. The Free Exercise Clause has allowed individuals to choose their own religions or to reject religion entirely.

The Supreme Court has generally interpreted freedom of religion as prohibiting government from subsidizing religious schools, from supporting the inclusion of religion in public schools, and from requiring members of some religions to engage in practices that violate their own beliefs. In 1972, William Rehnquist, then an associate justice, rejected Jefferson's wall of separation as a "misleading metaphor." As chief justice, Rehnquist tried to move the court toward the position of allowing government interaction with religion as long as it does not state a preference for one religion over another. He has been only partially successful, and Jefferson's wall of separation remains in place.

## SPEECH AND PRESS

Jefferson was an ardent supporter of freedom of speech, stating that he had "sworn upon the alter of God, eternal hostility against every form of tyranny over the mind of man." Jefferson argued that "Almighty God hath created the mind free and manifested his supreme will that free it shall remain." In Jefferson's view, repressing criticism of governments and their policies was unacceptable censorship. He believed that freedom of the press was essential to liberty, insisting that it was better to have newspapers without government than the other way around. Jefferson experienced censorship firsthand when he ordered a book in 1814 in which a French author discussed the creation of the world. Jefferson was outraged when the bookseller wrote him that the book was unavailable because it had been banned.

Jefferson saw education as a means of perpetuating democracy. He believed that as people became educated, they were less susceptible to having political and religious beliefs forced on them. After leaving the White House, Jefferson devoted himself to founding the University of Virginia and to developing model constitutions. In 1812, Jefferson and Adams renewed their friendship after a bitter 11-year hiatus. They spent many hours during the last years of their lives writing to one another, discussing their philosophical opinions and reacting to current events.

Jefferson died at Monticello, his Virginia estate, on July 4, 1826, the 50th anniversary of the Declaration of Independence. Adams died later that day. Thinking that his friend still lived, Adams's last words were "Jefferson lives." Jefferson had written his own epitaph, asking that these words become his memorial: "Here was buried Thomas Jefferson, author of the Declaration of American Independence, of the statute of Virginia for religious freedom, and founder of the University of Virginia."

**SEE ALSO**

*Volume 1 Left:* Liberalism; American Revolution; United States; Locke, John.
*Volume 2 Right:* Conservatism; American Revolution; United States.

**BIBLIOGRAPHY**

Joyce Appleby, *Thomas Jefferson* (Henry Holt, 2003); The Avalon Project at Yale Law School, "The Papers of Thomas Jefferson," www.yale.edu (1996–2003); James David Barber, *The Presidential Character: Predicting Performance in the White House* (Prentice-Hall, 1992); Carl L. Becker, *The Heavenly City of the Eighteenth Century Philosophers* (Yale University Press, 1978); Norman Cousins, ed., *The Republic of Reason: The Personal Philosophies of the Founding Fathers* (Harper and Row, 1988); Jerry Holmes, ed., *Thomas Jefferson: A Chronology of His Thoughts* (Rowman and Littlefield, 2002); Robert Isaak, ed., *American Political Thinking: Readings from the Origins to the Twenty-First Century* (Harcourt Brace, 1994); Adrienne Koch, *Jefferson and Madison: The Great Collaboration* (Oxford University Press, 1964); Max Lerner, *Thomas Jefferson: America's Philosopher King* (Transaction, 1996).

ELIZABETH PURDY, PH.D.
INDEPENDENT SCHOLAR

# Johnson, Lyndon B. (1908–1973)

LYNDON B. JOHNSON WAS one of only two persons to have held all four federal elective offices and the only one to have served as a legislative leader. Lyndon Baines Johnson was born August 27, 1908, near Stonewall, Texas, the oldest of the five children of Sam Ealy Johnson, Jr., and Rebekah (Baines) Johnson. Sam

Johnson was a rancher who had served in the legislature, as had his father. In 1913, the family moved to Johnson City, where Johnson graduated from high school in 1924. Johnson married Claudia Alta Taylor on November 17, 1934, in San Antonio. They had two daughters, Lynda Bird and Luci Baines. Since Johnson's wife was always known by the nickname "Lady Bird," all four had the initials LBJ. Johnson said he did this deliberately, to encourage the public to think of him by his initials the way they did of President Franklin D. Roosevelt (FDR).

In 1932, he was hired as a secretary in the Washington, D.C., office of U.S. Representative Richard M. Kleberg. This led to a position with the National Youth Administration in 1935. In 1937, Johnson won a special election to the U.S. House. He was reelected in the general election of 1938 and subsequently, through 1946. He lost a 1941 special election to fill a vacancy for the U.S. Senate. This was his only election defeat. After the attack on Pearl Harbor on 1941, Johnson became the first member of Congress to enter military service, keeping a promise he made to voters that if he ever voted to send troops to war, he would go too. However, he did not resign his House seat and needed the consent of the body in order to do this. He served as a lieutenant commander in the navy in the Pacific and was decorated for gallantry under fire.

In 1948, Johnson was elected to the U.S. Senate from Texas in a tumultuous and very close race. Johnson's margin was only 87 votes. From this, Johnson acquired the dubious nickname "Landslide Lyndon." It was only revealed after Johnson's death that the election had been fixed. Johnson had no trouble winning reelection in 1954 and 1960, the latter contest conterminous with his election to the vice presidency. Johnson advanced quickly within the Democratic ranks. He became minority whip after only two years in the Senate and minority leader two years after that. Johnson became majority leader, the most important person in the Senate, when the Democrats captured the majority in the 1954 election. Republican President Dwight D. Eisenhower found Johnson easier to deal with than did the Republican Congressional leaders. Rowland Evans and Robert Novak describe Johnson's method of persuasion, "the Johnson treatment," which he honed in these years and which proved most useful to him as president:

> Its tone could be supplication, accusation, cajolery, exuberance, scorn, tears, complaint, the hint of threat. It was all of these together. It ran the gamut of

human emotions. Its velocity was breathtaking, and it was all in one direction. Interjections from the target were rare. Johnson anticipated them before they could be spoken. He moved in close, his face a scant millimeter from his target, his eyes widening and narrowing, his eyebrows rising and falling. From his pockets poured clippings, memos, statistics. Mimicry, humor, and genius of analogy made The Treatment an almost hypnotic experience and rendered the target stunned and helpless.

Johnson was tapped as a vice-presidential running mate by John F. Kennedy in 1960. Kennedy's first choice was actually Minnesota Governor Orville L. Freeman. But Kennedy told his brother Robert to offer the post to Johnson, "and make sure he says no." But to everyone's surprise, Johnson accepted, and Kennedy insiders conceded that the Senate majority leader from Texas was a better balance to the youthful Kennedy than the Minnesotan was. The general election was closely fought, and the popular vote was one of the closest in history. Johnson also won reelection to his Senate seat, and he went so far as to be sworn in for the new term, only to resign minutes later. The vice presidency was a dull post for Johnson, and he did not perform the role Kennedy had hoped for as a legislative firebrand. However, he chaired the National Aeronautics and Space Council and the President's Committee on Equal Employment Opportunity.

Johnson's extended absence from Texas made the ongoing feud within the Democratic Party there harder to control. It was this rift that he and Kennedy hoped to heal when they visited Texas in November 1963. Kennedy was assassinated in Dallas on November 22, 1963, with Johnson several cars behind him in the motorcade. Johnson was sworn in as president upon Air Force One before the plane left Dallas for Washington. The oath of office was administered by Judge Sarah Hughes, making Johnson the only president sworn in by a woman. Johnson was the first Southerner to hold the presidency since Andrew Johnson nearly a century earlier.

One of Johnson's first acts as president was to install a blue-ribbon commission to investigate Kennedy's murder, authorized by an act of Congress. The circumstances of the murder were suspect since the killer, Lee Harvey Oswald, was a pro-Castro communist who had tried to defect to the Soviet Union, and because Oswald was himself murdered two days later by a terminally ill man with ties to organized crime. The President's Commission on the Assassination of President Kennedy,

As president, Lyndon Johnson steered the Democratic Party toward supporting racial desegregation in the U.S. south.

popularly called the Warren Commission after its chairman, Chief Justice Earl Warren, reported less than a year later that Oswald had not conspired with anyone. Johnson publicly accepted the conclusion, although privately he believed that there had in fact been a conspiracy.

The biggest initiative of his first year in office was the War on Poverty, which he emphasized in the State of the Union address preceding the launch of a major program. He signed a billion dollar anti-poverty program into law before the end of that year's legislative session.

One of the greatest legislative achievements of his presidency was the Civil Rights Act of 1964, which barred discrimination on the basis of race or gender in employment, public accommodations, and government. The principal legislative shepherd of the bill was Senator Hubert H. Humphrey, who was shortly named Johnson's running mate. In August 1964, responding to a putative attack on a U.S. vessel near the Vietnamese coast, Congress passed the Gulf of Tonkin Resolution authorizing the president to take military action to defend U.S. interests in the region.

Previously, the Vietnam War had been a low-key effort involving mostly military advisers and covert personnel. Although not much escalation on that front took place before the 1964 election—the first troops didn't land until March 1965—much of the rhetoric of the campaign focused on nuclear war with the Soviet Union. Johnson attacked his Republican opponent, Barry Goldwater, as a hawk on war with the Soviet Union. The Johnson-Humphrey ticket won a landslide victory in 1964, the last Democratic ticket to do so. As a result of the civil rights initiatives, Johnson lost most of the previously "Solid South," which formed the kernel of the Republican ascendancy that lasted the rest of the 20th century.

Even before being sworn in for a full term, Johnson launched a new series of initiatives in his 1965 State of the Union address. This program was called "The Great Society" and was the domestic hallmark of his administration. Congress established Medicare that year at Johnson's urging and doubled the anti-poverty program. The cabinet departments of Housing and Urban Development (HUD, 1965) and Transportation (1966) were created. These were only the most prominent expansions of the federal bureaucracy that happened in the 1960s, before "big government" became an unpopular phrase in Democratic circles and a dirty word in the Republican Party.

Johnson continued to support advances in civil rights, securing passage of another civil rights act in 1965. He also appointed the first black to the U.S. Supreme Court, Thurgood Marshall (whom he had previously appointed the first black solicitor general). Immigration law was overhauled for the first time since 1924, and U.S. immigration policy was essentially reversed. The large-scale third world immigration to the U.S. that continues into the 21st century was a result of the Immigration Act of 1965.

The Vietnam War escalated throughout the late 1960s. It became crucially unpopular by early 1968 after a Viet Cong military campaign known as the Tet Offensive (Tet is a Vietnamese holiday) caused a disproportionate number of U.S. casualties. The war was not going well for the United States, and daily news footage out of the battle zones proved a public relations disaster for the Johnson Administration. The consensus in the foreign affairs community—which had been that containment of communism was the central emphasis of U.S. foreign policy—was broken by the intractable failure of the Vietnam War. The U.S. could have won the war easily, had key dams and dikes been bombed in heavily populated areas of North Vietnam, but Johnson

felt it would be inhumane to kill so many innocent civilians. Johnson saw no way out of the war, and its unpopularity had spread to him and was spreading to the Democratic Party. Johnson was humiliated by the strong showing of anti-war Senator Eugene J. McCarthy in the New Hampshire primary. (Johnson won the primary, without even being on the ballot, but McCarthy's 23,280 votes to Johnson's 27,243 was seen as a slap in the face to the incumbent.) On March 31, 1968, Johnson announced he would not be a candidate for reelection.

Johnson lost the final political battle of his presidency. Chief Justice Earl Warren had announced his retirement in mid-1968, hoping to keep Republican Richard M. Nixon from naming his successor, in the event Nixon won the election. Johnson nominated Associate Justice Abe Fortas to fill the chief justiceship and an old friend from Texas, Homer Thornberry, to take Fortas's seat. The Senate was unable to break a filibuster over the Fortas nomination, and Johnson was forced to withdraw it. Johnson was again humiliated, and after the election, Nixon arrived at the White House with a chief justice to appoint. This illustrates the point judicial scholars often make that Supreme Court nominations are apt to fail in the fourth year of a president's term. The defeat of the Fortas nomination made little difference in the long run; the justice's financial improprieties were exposed the next year and he was forced to resign from the court.

Just before the election, Johnson announced a unilateral halt to the bombing of North Vietnam. This move did the Democratic nominee, Vice President Humphrey, little good, and with the Democratic base badly divided, Nixon swept to power.

On the whole, Johnson's political positions as president echoed and extended the liberalism of the New Deal. In particular, by declaring a War on Poverty and endorsing civil rights, Johnson altered the ideological party structure in the United States, by firmly committing the national Democratic Party to a policy of support for racial integration. This change broke the hold of the Democratic Party on the formerly "solid South"allowing conservative Republicans to build support among whites there.

Johnson embarked upon a retirement at his ranch. He worked on his memoirs but gave few interviews. He reportedly met with his ranch staff the way the president meets with his top advisers each morning. In late 1972, the Johnsons donated their ranch for use as a historic site, with a life interest. Johnson died of a heart attack at his ranch on January 22, 1973. A cease fire in the

Vietnam War came the next day. Johnson was buried at his ranch. A memorial to Johnson was erected on an island in the Potomac River in Washington, D.C. As of mid-2004, at age 91, Lady Bird Johnson still used her office at the Lyndon B. Johnson Library and Museum regularly.

## SEE ALSO

*Volume 1 Left:* Liberalism; Democratic Party; Kennedy, John F.; Vietnam War.
*Volume 2 Right:* Nixon, Richard M.; Vietnam War; Republican Party; Goldwater, Barry.

## BIBLIOGRAPHY

Robert A. Caro, *The Years of Lyndon Johnson* (Knopf, 1982–2002); Joseph A. Califano, *The Triumph and Tragedy of Lyndon Johnson: The White House Years* (Simon and Schuster, 1991); Robert Dallek, *Lyndon Johnson and His Times* (Oxford University Press, 1991–1998); Rowland Evans and Robert Novak, *Lyndon Johnson: The Exercise of Power: A Political Biography* (New American Library, 1966); Doris Kearns Goodwin, *Lyndon Johnson and the American Dream* (Harper and Row, 1976).

TONY L. HILL
MASSACHUSETTS INSTITUTE OF TECHNOLOGY

# The Left

# K

## Kefauver, Estes (1903–1963)

CAREY ESTES KEFAUVER was a lawyer, Representative, and Senator from Tennessee. As his later political career reflects, he was born and raised on a small farm community in Madisonville, Tennessee, in July, 1903. He attended the public schools in East Tennessee and graduated from the University of Tennessee at Knoxville in 1924. Kefauver then matriculated to the law school at Yale University from which he graduated cum laude in 1927. Admitted to the bar in 1926, he practiced law privately in Chattanooga until being elected on the Democratic ticket to the U.S. House of Representatives in 1939. Kefauver served in the House until his election to the U.S. Senate in 1948. He ran successfully for reelection in 1954 and 1960 and served until his death in 1963.

In his early years, Kefauver was exposed to populist politics. His father, Cooke Kefauver, was a life-long Democrat who served five terms as mayor of Madisonville in an extremely Republican area of Tennessee. Cooke was an enthusiastic supporter of William Jennings Bryan when he ran for president in 1896, 1900, and 1908. After hearing Bryan speak, young Estes recalled that it was one of the greatest memories of his younger years. The support that the Kefauvers had for the populist Bryan greatly influenced Estes's political ideology. When Governor Woodrow Wilson of New Jersey was nominated to be the Democratic contender for president in 1912, Cooke Kefauver took nine-year-old Estes campaigning for the progressive-minded candidate. Along with revering the speeches and ideas of Bryan, campaigning for Wilson gave Kefauver an introduction to formal politics and a taste of victory; Wilson won Kefauver's highly Republican home county, thanks in great part to the campaigning of the Kefauvers.

Upon completing his formal education at the University of Tennessee and Yale University Law School, Kefauver returned to his rural roots to practice law privately in Chattanooga in 1927. However, the early introduction to politics still resonated in the young attorney. Working for the law firm of Sizer, Chambliss & Kefauver, he was assigned to the legal account for the *Chattanooga News*, the city's local newspaper. The paper advocated strongly for liberal changes such as public electricity and reforms in the local government. Kefauver immediately took a leading role in aiding the paper and began shaping his political ideology as a liberal reformer. His activism led to his appointment as chairman of the local planning board. His political stock was climbing and in 1939 he served as Tennessee's Commissioner of Finance and Taxation. Kefauver's career in the political arena was just getting started.

The death of Congressman Sam D. McReynolds in July 1939 left a seat open in Tennessee's Third District, which included Chattanooga and Hamilton County.

Kefauver had recently left his post with the state and saw the vacancy as a golden opportunity. He ran successfully on the Democratic ticket in a special election and entered the U.S. House of Representatives on September 13, 1939.

Sticking to his liberal leanings, while in the House, Kefauver actively supported major New Deal-era programs like the Tennessee Valley Authority, federal aid to education, and significant congressional and electoral reform. His support of these New Deal initiatives put Kefauver at odds with many still-conservative Tennessee Democrats who still tended to shun President Roosevelt's liberal ideology. To Kefauver, however, they were the right programs to help bring Tennessee out of the economic crunch.

After announcing his plans to run for the U.S. Senate in 1948, Kefauver met with stern opposition. He faced B. Carroll Reece, the former national chair of the GOP. Reece had the ardent support of E.H. Crump, the long-time political boss and former mayor of Memphis. During the primary campaign, Crump attacked Kefauver as a communist sympathizer who worked in their interest with the "stealth of a nocturnal raccoon." The Kefauver camp relished the chance to capitalize on Crump's comment and quickly took on the raccoon as the campaign mascot, with Kefauver donning a coonskin cap out on the campaign trail.

In one of his most memorable lines, Kefauver commented, "I may be a pet coon, but I'm not Mr. Crump's pet coon." "The Keef," as he came to be affectionately known, solidly defeated Reece and the Crump political machine and took his seat in the U.S. Senate in January 1949.

Throughout his career in the House and Senate, Kefauver remained an outcast of the conservative South. Holding true to his liberal beliefs, he argued against a poll tax as a prerequisite for voting. He also refused to sign the Southern Manifesto in 1957, which was a reactionary response by the southern congressional bloc to the Supreme Court decision in *Brown v. Board of Education*. During the hysteria of the McCarthy hearings of the 1950s, Kefauver was an outspoken supporter of civil liberties and was the only senator to vote against a measure that made being a member of the Communist Party a crime. His belief and support of the "little people" helped shape his reputation as a populist and liberal in a time when it was politically detrimental to do so.

Kefauver gained national prominence during his time as the chair of the Special Committee on Organized Crime in Interstate Commerce. The committee's televised proceedings helped launch him to two unsuccessful presidential bids in 1952 and 1956 and a failed candidacy for vice president on the Democratic ticket with Adlai Stevenson in 1956.

His Democratic roots on the family farm in rural Tennessee shaped his populist and liberal leanings and help account for Kefauver's reputation as one of the most clearly defined liberal politicians of his time.

**SEE ALSO**

*Volume 1 Left:* Democratic Party; Truman, Harry; United States.
*Volume 2 Right:* Eisenhower, Dwight D.; Republican Party; United States.

**BIBLIOGRAPHY**

Robert B. Allen and Theodore Brown, Jr., "Remembering Estes Kefauver," www.populist.com (July 2004); "Biographical Directory of the United States Congress: Estes Kefauver," http://bioguide.congress.gov (July 2004); Charles L. Fontenay, *Estes Kefauver: A Biography* (University of Tennessee Press, 1980); Joseph Bruce Gorman, *Kefauver: A Political Biography* (Oxford University Press, 1971).

D. STEVEN CRONIN
MISSISSIPPI STATE UNIVERSITY

# Kennedy, John F. (1917–1963)

IN POPULAR MEMORY, the assassination of President John F. Kennedy remains a painful scar on the American past. A Democrat, narrowly elected after nearly a decade of cultural conservatism and Republican political dominance, he symbolized a new era in American politics and the American century. Though his administration lasted just over 1,000 days, Kennedy's personality and political initiatives had important, enduring effects for the American political and social landscape.

John Fitzgerald Kennedy was born on May 29, 1917, in Brookline, Massachusetts. The second son of Joseph Patrick Kennedy and his wife, Rose Elizabeth Fitzgerald, Kennedy enjoyed a privileged childhood within one of America's most prominent political families, known for their political liberalism and general allegiance to the Democratic Party. Educated at the Choate School, Kennedy then attended Princeton University until he was forced to withdraw for health rea-

*By reenergizing American idealism, Kennedy seemed to many to embody the best image of American liberal democracy.*

sons. He ultimately enrolled at Harvard University, graduating cum laude in 1940. Following his graduation, Kennedy joined the U.S. Navy and with America's entry into World War II in 1941, he was called into active service. While serving in the Solomon Islands in the Pacific in 1943, his boat was sunk by a Japanese destroyer. Although he suffered serious and permanent injuries to his back, he managed to lead his fellow survivors to safety.

Returning from the military, Kennedy's name and service record afforded him an easy entry into politics through the ranks of the Democratic Party. In 1945, he was elected to the House of Representatives, where he served until 1953, when he was elected to the Senate. A year later, he married Jacqueline Lee Bouvier, a socially prominent woman 12 years his junior. During his first term as Senator, Kennedy achieved national notoriety when his book, *Profiles in Courage*, won the Pulitzer Prize in History.

At the Democratic National Convention in 1960, Kennedy earned the nomination for president. Pro-

pelled by his success in the first nationally televised presidential debate, Kennedy defeated Republican opponent Richard M. Nixon in one of the closest popular votes in American history. His victory was in part due to his support from African Americans and minority voters. He was the first Roman Catholic elected to the office and at the age of 43, the youngest president. To many, he and his beautiful family seemed to bring a youth, charisma, and revitalized energy to politics.

With his inspirational inaugural address that told Americans to "ask not what your country can do for you—ask what you can do for your country," Kennedy reinvigorated the American spirit. Labeling the new age of scientific technology and social relations the New Frontier, Kennedy dared Americans to rise to the challenges of the 20th century. Many of Kennedy's initiatives, foreign and domestic, can be seen as functions of the international hostility known as the Cold War. The Cold War originated immediately after World War II as a contest between Western, capitalist nations, led by the United States, and the communist nations, led by the Soviet Union. To bolster American might in the event of military conflict, Kennedy supported the improvement of U.S. infrastructure through increased support of engineering education and corporations.

Given the prevalence of the Cold War, Kennedy's administration was particularly noted for its foreign affairs, specifically the incidents connected to the defensive struggle. His first foray into the international conflict occurred in April, 1961, when he authorized American-trained Cuban exiles to invade Cuba at the Bay of Pigs and overthrow Fidel Castro's communist regime. The invaders were quickly crushed and the invasion was considered an embarrassing failure.

In 1961, Soviet leader Nikita Khrushchev stepped up the Soviet Union's campaign against Western-controlled West Berlin. Kennedy responded to Khrushchev's aggression by offering support to West Berlin. The heightened hostilities between the Soviet Union and the United States over Germany culminated on August 13, 1961, with the erection of the Berlin Wall, which divided the communist bloc of East Berlin from West Berlin. The wall symbolized the ideological differences and sharp tensions between the two nations— tensions that were further played out through the 1962 Cuban Missile Crisis, in which American spy planes discovered that the Soviet Union was building missile sites in Cuba.

Kennedy ordered a naval quarantine on all offensive weapons bound for Cuba. For two weeks, the world teetered on nuclear war until Kennedy's aggressive stance forced the Soviets to remove their missiles from Cuba. Kennedy's leadership during the crisis was a pivotal moment in his presidency and also demonstrated his commitment to curtailing the threat of nuclear war. To this end, he negotiated the 1963 Limited Nuclear Test Ban Treaty in which the United States, Great Britain, and the Soviet Union agreed to ban all but underground nuclear tests.

Kennedy's policies in Southeast Asia, however, left a far less favorable effect. In an attempt to prove American might to the Soviet Union, Kennedy increased military aid to the government of South Vietnam, which was struggling against communist guerrillas. By late 1963, Kennedy's policies in South Vietnam had forced the country under the protection of the United States, an episode of historical contingency that had far-reaching effects. At home, Kennedy's support of civil rights met resistance from congressional conservatives and shook the southern stronghold formerly enjoyed by the Democratic Party.

But his concerns that the Soviet Union could use American internal strife as a form of propaganda intensified his desire to improve the status of African Americans. Moved by the brutal televised images of southern racism, Kennedy ordered federal troops to the University of Mississippi to end anti-black rioting in September 1962. And on June 11, 1963, on national television, he declared the segregation of the University of Alabama to be a "moral issue."

Kennedy's commitment to civil and human rights extended beyond domestic borders. In 1961, he created the Peace Corps, a program that sent skilled and idealistic Americans into third world countries to develop public health and agricultural procedures. Kennedy also introduced economic programs that helped launch the United States into its longest period of sustained growth since World War II. He expanded Social Security coverage and benefits, raised the minimum wage, furthered public housing initiatives, increased measures to clear the slums, and lowered tariff barriers. His 1961 Area Redevelopment Act directly benefited economically depressed areas and the 1962 Manpower Development and Training Act retrained destitute farmers and unemployed workers. Kennedy demonstrated bold leadership in the American space program as well, calling for the United States to land a man on the moon within the decade. Despite these legislative successes, Kennedy faced serious opposition from the conservative coalition in Congress on issues relating to tax reduction, federal aid to education, and medical care to the elderly.

On November 22, 1963, Kennedy was assassinated by a sniper in Dallas, Texas. Though the circumstances and motives behind his murder continue to arouse debate, his death resulted in an outpouring of grief across the globe. Although unflattering details about his private life and his health have emerged in recent years, contemporary politicians, particularly Democrats, continue to idealize him; indeed, historians have suggested that Kennedy was on the threshold of political greatness.

By reenergizing American idealism and committing the United States to the opportunities of the mid-20th century, Kennedy seemed to many to embody the best image of American liberal democracy.

**SEE ALSO**

*Volume 1 Left:* Democratic Party; Johnson, Lyndon B.
*Volume 2 Right:* Nixon, Richard M.; Republican Party; Conservatism.

**BIBLIOGRAPHY**

Robert Dallek, *An Unfinished Life: John F. Kennedy, 1917–63* (Little, Brown, 2003); Frank Freidel, *The Presidents of the United States of America* (White House Historical Association, 1985); Doris Kearns Goodwin, *The Fitzgeralds and the Kennedys: An American Saga* (Simon and Schuster, 1987); James M. McPherson, ed., "To the Best of My Ability," *The American Presidents* (Dorling Kindersley, 2000); Richard E. Neustadt, *Presidential Power and the Modern Presidents: The Politics of Leadership from Roosevelt to Reagan* (Free Press, 1990); Theodore C. Sorensen, *Kennedy* (Harper and Row, 1966); David Williamson, *Debrett's Presidents of the United States of America* (Salem House, 1989).

LINDSAY SILVER
BRANDEIS UNIVERSITY

# King, Martin Luther, Jr. (1929–1968)

THE FOREMOST ADVOCATE of peaceful resistance in the history of the United States and the leader of the civil rights movement of the 1950s and 1960s, Dr. Martin Luther King, Jr., was born in Atlanta, Georgia, on January 15, 1929, to Martin and Alberta King. Since 1983, King's birthday has been observed as a national holiday on the third Monday of January.

Even as a young boy, King demonstrated unusual intelligence. He skipped the first, ninth, and eleventh grades. In 1944, at the age of 15, King enrolled at Morehouse College, a predominantly black school in Atlanta, to study English and sociology. At Morehouse, King was exposed to Henry David Thoreau's *Civil Disobedience* and heard the issue of race debated for the first time. On the Intercollegiate Council, King learned that many whites were also opposed to racial discrimination. In 1948, after being ordained as a minister, King became one of six blacks in a class of 106 at the Crozer Theological Seminary in Chester, Pennsylvania.

During his years at Crozer, King read the words of Mahatma Gandhi, the famous advocate of passive resistance, who wrote, "Nonviolence is the greatest force at the disposal of mankind. It is mightier than the mightiest weapon of destruction devised by the ingenuity of man." While doing postgraduate work at Boston College, King met Coretta Scott. They were married on June 18, 1953. King received a Doctor of Philosophy (Ph.D.) degree in theology two years later.

King combined the teachings of Jesus with what he had learned from Thoreau and Gandhi, forming his own plan for using passive resistance as a means of advancing the goals of the fledgling civil rights movement. In "Nonviolence and Racial Justice," King established the major elements of his life creed on nonviolence: Never resist; never humiliate opponents, try to win friendship and understanding; attack principles not people; and avoid bitterness and internal violence of the spirit.

Many conservatives, including J. Edgar Hoover, the Director of the Federal Bureau of Investigation (FBI), were convinced that King was a left-wing radical who wanted to destroy America. They objected to his opposition to the Vietnam War as well as to his civil rights activities. He was called a "communist-dupe," a "troublemaker," and a "traitor." Hoover determined to "get" King and created a massive dossier that detailed King's every movement.

## MONTGOMERY

In Montgomery, Alabama, in 1955, African American passengers were required to sit in a section designated as "Colored." If the white section of a bus filled up, black passengers had to give up their seats. On December 1, Rosa Parks, a local seamstress, refused to move. She was arrested and fined. Black leaders in Montgomery decided to stage a boycott. They had used this tactic before, but this time they determined that it would succeed. When Rosa Parks, working with the NAACP, staged a protest in Montgomery, the time was ripe for civil right reforms. King was in Montgomery, having become the minister at Dexter Avenue Baptist Church. At the urging of Montgomery's black leaders, King accepted the position of president of the Montgomery Improvement Association and began to plan the boycott.

The Montgomery boycott proved to be more successful than most black leaders had dared to hope. On the first day of the boycott, the number of African-Americans riding buses dropped from 17,500 a day to 8. The boycott lasted for 361 days. On December 21, 1956, facing bankruptcy, city officials reached an agreement with boycott leaders, and buses were integrated. After the boycott, King was known throughout the United States.

In January 1957, in Atlanta, King joined with a number of black leaders from 10 states to found the Southern Christian Leadership Conference (SCLC) in response to growing protests among African Americans. The stated purpose of the group was to bring about political and social reform through nonviolent action. The group intended to bring an end to the Jim Crow practice of legal discrimination in the South and the less overt, but no less damaging, discrimination in the rest of the country. King was elected as president and his friend Ralph David Abernathy was chosen as program director. The SCLC became an integral part of the civil rights movement.

## BIRMINGHAM

In 1963, Birmingham, Alabama, the largest industrial city in the South, was the most segregated city in the nation. King and other black leaders maintained that 300 years of oppression were enough. It had been 100 years since the Emancipation Proclamation, and nearly that since the Civil Rights Amendments of the Reconstruction period guaranteed rights of citizenship to African Americans. It was time, they argued, to challenge the openly segregationist policies of city leaders. Much of the discrimination in Birmingham was due to "Bull" Connor, the commissioner of public safety, who had pledged to keep blacks in their "proper place." George Wallace, the segregationist governor of Alabama, offered no help in relieving the situation.

The Southern Christian Leadership Conference launched a campaign of passive resistance and turned to the federal courts for assistance. When King was arrested after disobeying an order forbidding the protestors to march, he was placed in the Birmingham Jail. From the cell where he was held in solitary confinement with no outside contact, King issued a passionate plea for other ministers to add their voices to the protests. Alarmed over his forced isolation, Coretta Scott King called Attorney General Robert Kennedy, who had contacted her during an earlier arrest. Both President John Kennedy and his brother responded to her call for help. King was allowed to call his wife and to see his lawyers, and the civil rights movement also received a lot of publicity.

In the Birmingham Campaign, black leaders asked for four things: the desegregation of lunch counters, fitting rooms, and drinking fountains in stores; the upgrading and hiring of blacks on a nondiscriminatory basis; dismissal of all charges against demonstrators; and the creation of a biracial committee to oversee the desegregation process. On May 19, an agreement was reached in which city officials agreed to desegregate store facilities over a three-month period and to comply with other stipulations immediately. Public reaction to the agreement led to federal troops being dispatched to Birmingham. The Connor gang was judicially removed from office.

## WASHINGTON, D.C.

An eloquent speaker, Martin Luther King, Jr., had the ability to inspire emotional responses in his listeners. King believed that God had given him a responsibility to speak for those who had no voice. One of his most inspirational speeches was given on the steps of the Lincoln Memorial in August 1963 during the March on Washington that brought tens of thousands of civil rights advocates to the nation's capital.

In ringing tones, King described an America free of prejudice, injustice, and oppression where "little black boys and black girls will be able to join hands with little white boys and white girls and walk together as sisters and brothers."

After the assassination of President Kennedy on November 16, 1963, Lyndon Johnson acted on initiatives begun by Kennedy and pressured Congress to pass major civil rights legislation in response to growing dissatisfaction over racial discrimination. Even though the Supreme Court had called for segregation in schools to end with "all deliberate speed" in *Brown v. Board of Education* in 1954, segregation continued in schools, employment, transportation, public places, and virtually every aspect of life, particularly in the South. While the new civil rights act brought about many changes, voting

rights remained elusive. King was determined to change this practice.

## SELMA

On October 14, 1964 at the age of 35, King became the youngest recipient to date to win the Nobel Peace Prize. King was only the second black to win the prize. The other was Ralph Bunche, an under secretary of the United Nations. King donated his $54,000 cash prize to the civil rights movement. After winning the Nobel Prize, King announced that a more militant stage in the civil rights movement was at hand. The campaign, he said, would begin in Selma, Alabama. King announced that African Americans were now demanding rather than asking for the vote. In response, white officials announced that they would uphold segregationist voter registration laws. The campaign was followed by a wave of violence against protestors, and hundreds were arrested.

Tensions in Selma came to a head on March 6, 1965, on what became known as "Bloody Sunday," when King gave Hosea Williams the go-ahead to lead a march from Selma to Montgomery, the state capital. As protestors neared a local bridge, local law officers met them. Both black and white marchers were beaten unmercifully as reporters filmed the action for national television audiences. Jim Reeb, a white Unitarian minister, died from the wounds received during the attack. Johnson responded with a plea for respect for human rights and guided the Voting Rights Act of 1965 through Congress. The act effectively banned all discrimination in voting on the basis of race, and the number of black voters increased immediately.

## MEMPHIS

On April 3, 1968, King traveled to Memphis, Tennessee, to support garbage workers who were on strike. The following day, when he stepped out onto a balcony of his room at the Lorraine Motel, he was shot. At seven o'clock that night, King was pronounced dead. His children heard about their father from a television news bulletin. The day before his death, King had, in effect, given his own eulogy when he told his audience that it did not matter what happened to him because "I've been to the mountain" and seen the "Promised Land." He also assured his listeners: "I'm happy tonight. I'm not worried about anything. I'm not fearing any man. Mine eyes have seen the glory of the coming of the Lord."

King's use of nonviolent tactics based on the methods of Mahatma Gandhi did a great deal to win over support of white liberals to the cause of racial justice. For the most part, King did not challenge the basic economic structure, nor did he accuse all whites of harboring racist values. Instead, by appealing to human rights arguments based on his restatement of the American creed, he explicitly sought to achieve his goals by gaining white support. Partly due to his efforts and approach, many white American liberals increased their awareness of the inequities of racial practices and policies.

### SEE ALSO

*Volume 1 Left:* Civil Rights; Human Rights; United States; American Civil War; Malcolm X; Gandhi, Mahatma; Desegregation.
*Volume 2 Right:* Segregation; American Civil War; Hoover, J. Edgar.

### BIBLIOGRAPHY

Lerone Bennett, Jr., *What Manner of Man: A Biography of Martin Luther King, Jr.* (Johnson, 1976); Stewart Burns, *To the Mountain Top: Martin Luther King, Jr.'s Sacred Mission to Save America, 1951–61* (Harper, 2004); Vincent Harding, *Martin Luther King: The Inconvenient Hero* (Orbis, 1996); Dexter Scott King, *Growing Up King* (Warner Books, 2003); Martin Luther King, Jr., "I Have a Dream" www.mecca.org (May 2004); Martin Luther King, Jr., "I See the Promised Land," James Melvin Washington, ed., *A Testament of Hope: The Essential Writings of Martin Luther King, Jr.* (Harper and Row, 1986); Martin Luther King, Jr., "Nonviolence and Racial Justice," James Melvin Washington, ed., *A Testament of Hope: The Essential Writings of Martin Luther King, Jr.* (Harper and Row, 1986); Martin Luther King, Jr., *Why We Can't Wait* (New American Library, 1963); "Mahatma Gandhi," www.engagedpage.com (May 2004).

ELIZABETH PURDY, PH.D.
INDEPENDENT SCHOLAR

# Korea, North

THE KOREAN WORKERS' Party (Chosun Nodong Dang) is the political party that controls North Korea, officially known as the Democratic People's Republic of Korea (Chosun Minju-jui Kongwa-guk). It was established in August 1946 from three groups of communists who had fought against the Japanese. Korean communists who had been in the Soviet Union during World War II composed the first group. Most of these had been in the Soviet Maritime Province along the Manchurian and Korean border. Another faction was close to the Chinese Communists. The third faction's members were resistance fighters who had fought the Japanese troops in Korea.

When the Korean Workers' Party was organized, it was modeled after the Soviet Communist Party. Many of the most prominent members of the party had been in the Soviet Union and had been members of the Soviet Communist Party. Rather quickly Kim Il-sung became general secretary. His close association with the Soviets aided his rise to party leadership. A master politician, he accepted the views of other party leaders from different backgrounds until he was able to purge all opposition.

Formally, the party congress, composed of delegates elected at provincial and city meetings, is the ruling body. It is supposed to meet every four years, but usually meets less frequently. When it does meet, it ratifies the decisions of its Central Committee. The Political Bureau (Politburo) is elected by the Central Committee. The Standing Committee of the Politburo has five members. The most powerful member was Kim Il-sung until his death and his son, Kim Jong-il since then.

The party has nine departments headed by party secretaries. The official organ of the party is *Nodong Sinmum (Workers' News)* which is a daily newspaper.

Other important mass organizations include the Socialist Workers' Youth League, which educates party members. The Young Pioneer Corps is for children. The organization, Democratic Front for the Reunification of the Fatherland includes many groups. Nearly a million Koreans live in Japan. Many belong to the North Korean party's front organization, the General Association of Korean residents in Japan.

North Korea appears to be a multiparty state. There are two parties besides the Korean Workers' Party: the Korean Social Democratic Party and the Chondogyo Chongu (Young Friends) Party. These are theoretically freely organized but are actually under the control of the Korean Workers' Party and are for presenting the image that Korea is a democratic multiparty state rather than a totalitarian one-party state.

An important element in the philosophy of the Korean Workers' Party is the philosophy of *Juche* ("self-reliance" or "independence"). *Kimilsungism*, the philosophy developed by Kim Il-sung, reflects Korean

The left in North and South Korea have one thing in common: both are subject to strong nationalistic governments.

values, especially that of stubborn resistance to foreign domination. Kim Il-sung was horrified by the sudden fall of communism in 1989. In response, he recalled all the North Korean students studying in communist East European countries. Intense indoctrination in North Korean beliefs was begun and maintained. He promoted a personality cult that was quasi-religious and focused on himself. The death of Kim Il-sung in 1994 was shocking to his country after 48 years of rule. His son and successor, Kim Jong-il, led the country in mourning for their Dear Leader. He seems to be supported in power by technocrats and party functionaries. He has a reputation for conducting "black operations," or covert action.

In the 1990s, it appeared that the United States had reached an agreement with North Korea on the issue of its nuclear arms program. However, it was a diplomatic opening that was quickly closed. In 2002, President George W. Bush named North Korea as part of an "Axis of Evil" in the War on Terrorism. The United States's war in Iraq in 2003 may have convinced the North Koreans that their security against invasion lay in having nuclear weapons. The United States, in response, attempted a multilateral diplomatic approach to resolving the North Korean nuclear threat. The regime in Pyongyang leads a totalitarian state, and it is intent on survival.

**SEE ALSO**
*Volume 1 Left:* Korea, South; Soviet Union.
*Volume 2 Right:* Korea, North; China; Bush, George W.

**BIBLIOGRAPHY**
John Fetter, *North Korea South Korea: U. S. Policy at a Time of Crisis* (Seven Stories Press, 2003); Samuel S. Kim. ed., *North Korean Foreign Relations in the Post-Cold War Era* (Oxford University Press, 1998); Leon Segal, *Disarming Strangers: Nuclear Diplomacy with North Korea* (Princeton University Press, 1997); Hazel Smith, ed., *North Korea in the New World Order* (St. Martin's Press, 1996).

ANDREW J. WASKEY
DALTON STATE COLLEGE

# Korea, South

UNTIL 1988, AUTOCRATS or military dictators usually governed South Korea. The left-oriented politicians were often ignored, imprisoned, or politically impotent. In 1988, Chun Doo Hwan, President of the Republic of Korea, retired as he had promised he would in 1980.

In the years of his administration, there were thousands of student protests across the country. The student demonstrations were so numerous and so frequent that many believe the Korean police became the most efficient in the world at riot control. Even while the Korean economy prospered enormously during the latter half of the 20th century, protests against the authoritarianism of the regime continued to the point of including numerous middle-class women.

In 1988, the year of the Seoul Olympic Games, Roh Tae-woo won election to the presidency through direct popular vote. Defeated were opposition leaders Kim Dae-jung and Kim Young-sam. The election and political events led to constitutional changes, and to the Korean Sixth Republic. The 1980s are often viewed as a period of democratization in South Korea.

In 1993, Kim Young-sam was elected president of the Republic of Korea. His election ended military and autocratic rule, or at least appeared to do so. He proclaimed an amnesty and released numerous political prisoners from Chun's time. In 1998, Kim Dae-jung was elected president and announced an amnesty for political prisoners and for everything from ordinary criminal offenses to parking tickets. The amnesty covered five million cases, suggesting that political repression still existed.

From 1993 on, democracy has grown to the point that student protests have not been met with tear gas or riot police. South Korea has during this period prospered despite significant economic problems associated with end of the growth of the previous decades. On February 25, 2003, No Mu-hyun was installed as president; however, he was impeached on March 12, 2004. Prime Minister Ko Kun became acting president.

Today in South Korea there are many political parties, however, the left-leaning parties are usually pushed to the fringes and excluded from the centers of power. In 1990, mergers among parties produced two major parties: the Peace and Democracy Party and the new Democratic Liberal Party. There are also a growing number of pressure groups that exercise influence that was formerly exercised only by politicians in offices.

Business groups reflect the growing power of economic interests. These and other important groups include the Federation of Korean Industries, trade unions, the student associations, farm groups, the Korean Council of Churches, and some professional groups. These voluntary associations are changing the old style individual leader politics, seeking to influence the political process by adding a layer of strength to Korean democracy that is apart from political parties. Also, the press is growing in importance as a channel for information that is independent. Intellectuals are increasing in influence, reflecting the Confucian basis of the country.

South Korea is also pursuing relations with North Korea over unification. The key problem is that unification is really a zero-sum game in which one regime must disappear. Increasing the contacts between the South and North has been favored by most Koreans in the South. Cases of families united, or of business contacts have been welcomed, but without welcoming the communism of the North. War is widely opposed, even though the military threat from North Korea is significant. North Korea has one of the world's largest armies. Its artillery alone could inflict terrible damage in the event of hostilities. However, many analysts believe that the poverty in the North is such that it lacks the supplies for a campaign that would allow it to conquer the South.

Despite the fact that the United States, the longtime ally of South Korea, views North Korea as a terrorist state, the South Koreans are making independent efforts to deal with issues between the two countries. Actions that are viewed from Washington as left-wing influenced. The confession of the North Koreans that they were building nuclear weapons shocked the South but most there opposed military action.

## SEE ALSO

*Volume 1 Left:* Korea, North; Communism; Clinton, William J.; United States.
*Volume 2 Right:* Korea, South; Bush, George W.

## BIBLIOGRAPHY

Soong Hoom Kil and Chung-in Moon, eds., *Understanding Korean Politics: An Introduction* (University of New York Press, 2001); Don Oberdorfer, *The Two Koreas: A Contemporary History* (Basic Books, 2001); Sung Chul Yang, *The North and South Korean Political Systems* (Westview Press, 1994).

ANDREW J. WASKEY
DALTON STATE COLLEGE

# The Left

# L

## La Follette, Robert (1855–1925)

THE UNITED STATES has experienced numerous periods of populism, reform, and progressive politics and one of the most famous and successful individuals associated with this in the last 100 years was Robert M. La Follette, Sr., of Wisconsin. "Fighting Bob," as he was known, was born in Primrose Township, Wisconsin, and would go on to establish a long and successful political career and a minor dynasty in the state. Known for his great oratory and boundless energy, the elder La Follette was educated at the University of Wisconsin, where despite a spotty academic record, he was granted a bachelor's degree in 1879. His wife, Mary Case, was also a graduate of the university and was the first woman to graduate from the law school in Madison, Wisconsin

After graduation, La Follette studied law for five months and was called to the bar, and his first major political victory was the district attorney's race in 1880, a campaign he succeeded in despite the opposition he faced from the dominant Republican Party machine. In this period, Wisconsin was virtually a one-party state, controlled by the Republicans, the party of Abraham Lincoln, but the party contained two wings within it, the stalwarts and the progressives. La Follette was elected to the House of Representatives in 1885, based largely on the support of the progressive wing, and during his six years in Washington, D.C., he became a member of the powerful Ways and Means Committee. He then moved home and was elected governor of Wisconsin in 1900. In 1905, he was elected to the U.S. Senate by the Wisconsin legislature, though he would spend almost a year finishing his work as governor before taking up the post. He served in the Senate for almost 20 years until his death in 1925. La Follette spent most of his public life as a member of the progressive wing of the Republican Party, but left the party and ran in the 1924 presidential election on the Progressive Party ticket, garnering 16.6 percent of the vote. After his death, he was succeeded in the Senate by his son, Robert M. ("Young Bob") La Follette. Another son, Philip, would also serve as governor.

La Follette was one of the best-known figures in Progressive-era America. Like the Progressive movement, La Follette accepted a set of ideas that were not always consistent. La Follette was a critic of capitalism, but never an open advocate of socialism. He was an advocate of reform, but had an ambiguous view of Democratic President Woodrow Wilson, and ultimately, of Teddy Roosevelt.

Certainly, like the Progressives generally, he was many years ahead of his time. As a legislator in the U.S. Senate, he sponsored successful legislation to provide an eight-hour work day for most women in the District of Columbia and to regulate hours and working conditions for U.S. sailors. He opposed the declaration of war against Germany in 1917, he voted against the Espionage Act and other legislation he regarded as oppressive, and he worked to protect the rights of conscientious objectors. For his critique of Woodrow Wilson and his position against the war, he was almost expelled from the Senate, though he was probably ultimately saved because of the close outcome in the 1918 mid-term elections, and the Republican majority needed his support to maintain control of the chamber. Throughout his life, La Follette was a strong supporter of democratic values and was suspicious of monopolistic corporations and their influence on mainstream politicians.

Like other Progressives, La Follette's popularity and influence peaked before World War I, and the Russian Revolution and the Red Scare that followed in the United States did not help his cause.

**SEE ALSO**

*Volume 1 Left:* Progressive Party; Populism; Democratic Party.
*Volume 2 Right:* Roosevelt, Theodore; Republican Party.

**BIBLIOGRAPHY**

Roger T. Johnson, *Robert M. La Follette, Jr. and the Decline of the Progressive Party in Wisconsin* (University of Wisconsin Press, 1964); Robert M. La Follette, *La Follette's Autobiography: A Personal Narrative of Political Experience* (University of Wisconsin Press, 1963); Patrick J. Maney, *"Young Bob" La Follette: A Biography of Robert M. La Follette, Jr.* (University of Missouri Press, 1978); Michael McGerr, *A Fierce Discontent: The Rise and Fall of the Progressive Movement in America, 1870–1920* (The Free Press, 2003).

GEOFFREY R. MARTIN
MOUNT ALLISON UNIVERSITY, CANADA

# Labour Party, UK

THE BRITISH LABOUR Party ended the 20th century with the largest landslide victory in its history. Through 100 years it rose from obscurity—forcing the ruling class to accept the legitimacy of political representation and participation of the working class—to command almost total control of Parliament. In 2004, the Conservative Party failed to dent the Labour government's majority in the polls. However, commentators might argue,

this dominance has taken place at the cost of the very values that have historically been embodied in the Labour Party.

The background to the emergence of the British Labour Party has to be found in the mid-19th century Victorian society and class division. In spite of Karl Marx having lived in London for three decades, no organized socialist movement existed in Britain at the time of his death in the early 1880s. However, very soon after, a number of socialist societies—the Social Democratic Federation (SDF) and the Fabian Society—had been formed by the end of that decade. Together with the Socialist League, itself the result of a secession from SDF, they formed the main pillars on which the future Labour Party would be formed. Young, intellectual, and dynamic, these societies fused English liberal intellectual tradition with Marx's view of history and capitalist society. The ideas espoused by these societies were strengthened by a new form of unionism among the working class that was militant, organized, class conscious, and socialist, fighting for better working conditions, such as the eight-hour working day. When this new form of unionism finally accepted the need for independent labor representation in Parliament, the seed of the Labour Party had been sown. The Labour Representation Committee (LRC) included trade unionists as well as members of SDF and the Fabians. In the 1906 general elections, they won 30 seats. The new parliamentary group decided to call itself the Labour Party; a new political party had been born.

In spite of being a deeply divided group of trade unionists, activists, and socialists, the Labour Party managed to hold together more successfully than the liberals. Immediately after World War I, it emerged united and confident in the future in a way that the Liberal Party was not. Having become the true opposition to the Conservatives, the Labour Party managed to win its first general election in 1924, a pretty remarkable achievement, making Ramsay MacDonald the first Labour prime minister in Britain. A moderate in charge of a government that needed liberal support, he could not go as far in radical policies as many of his followers would have liked.

The second Labour government of 1929 did not fare much better. Unemployment became the biggest issue of MacDonald's second premiership. Yet, although in the party's political language unemployment was the clearest indication of the ills of capitalism, the Labour government was unable to stem the flow of joblessness nor could it bring itself to challenge the capitalist system. Following the stock market crash, Britain soon reached the two-million unemployed figure. The economic crisis that ensued was associated by the voters with the government's inability to manage the economy properly, a suspicion that would see itself reinforced by Labour's performance in the 1970s, and one that would force a wholesale transformation of the party's ideals in the 1990s. For the time being, the Labour Party lost the 1931 election, returning to prewar levels of representation in the House of Commons. Labour would be in opposition for the rest of the 1930s decade and would only get a seat in a national government of unity when invited by the conservatives in 1940 as part of the war effort.

## THE GOLDEN ERA

The period after 1945 was the golden era of the British Labour Party. Not only did the party win the 1945 election unpredictably—the electorate having failed to reelect Prime Minister Churchill, who led the country to victory in World War II—but it did so with an overall majority for the first time in history. Besides, the new Labour government could count among its ministers a number of experienced politicians who had served in the previous national government of unity during the war. As such, Labour had government insiders with notable experience and proven political and economic competence. However, the 1945 Labour government was not devoid of problems. The country lay in economic ruin, with large parts of its basic infrastructure destroyed or seriously damaged, and with an industrial production that had been exclusively devoted to the war effort. The government faced the daunting task of reconstruction and of creating an economy capable of absorbing the large numbers of demobilized British soldiers spread over Europe and Asia. Britain's economy required the injection of investment in the form of loans that came mainly from the United States and were part of the Marshall Plan for the reconstruction of Europe. Added to this, the Labour government imposed a large degree of central economic planning, maintaining war time rationing. By 1950, it had also passed bills nationalizing key industries such as mining and gas and restraining consumer spending.

The economic reconstruction of the country was not the only great challenge faced by the postwar Labour government. It also faced enormous international responsibilities at the time. In 1948, the Labour government's mishandling of the situation in occupied Palestine and the rushed evacuation of troops led in part to the beginning of the conflict between Arabs and Jews that continues to this day. During this administration, Britain also had to contend with the loss of its imperial dominions in India, Pakistan, Burma (Myanmar), and Ceylon. The war had not only changed the map of the world; it had also changed Britain's identity, bringing into relief dominant and persistent socioeconomic divisions. This realization, coupled with Labour's socialist conviction, led an assault on these inequalities as the core of its political program. As a result, the 1945 Labour government was responsible for the creation of the welfare state the most important piece of which was the National Health Service (NHS). After tough negotiations with the biggest adversary of the NHS—the medical profession—the Labour government introduced a health system that offered universal health care on the basis of need that is free at the point of delivery. To this day and in spite of recurrent funding crises, the NHS remains one of the best-loved British institutions and a model of an efficient, equitable, and relatively cheap method of healthcare provision to every citizen.

Although the capitalist system has never been endangered in the hands of the British Labour Party, these victories for social justice and equality continued partly in the next Labour government in the 1960s. Spending in the social services continued to increase enormously between 1964 and 1970. The programs that made headway in this period were varied. The amount of social housing built did not reach the original target but exceeded anything previous administrations had achieved. Similarly, with education, the Labour government introduced a comprehensive system of secondary schools throughout the country and university education, the last remaining example of an elitist educational system, was expanded greatly to spread the benefits of higher education to sectors of the population beyond the upper middle classes. On the whole, this decade was characterized by the belief that the government had an important role to play in the country's social and economic affairs.

## LABOUR AND RECESSION

This belief in the government's role was maintained during the next Labour government between 1974 and 1979. However, the benign economic climate that had allowed such rises in public spending during the 1960s was not in place anymore, making these commitments more difficult to fulfill. The 1974 Labour government came to power in the middle of a global economic recession marked by the embargo on supplies imposed by oil-producing countries, a move that had made the price

The 1997 election of Tony Blair marked the beginning of New Labour, orienting the party more toward middle-class needs.

of oil rise more than threefold by 1973. Added to this, the Conservative Party was undergoing a tough confrontation with the mining industry over pay. The new government, through its contacts with the labor movement, managed to curb the demands of the miners in exchange for promises of higher social spending and a greater share of public ownership. By 1976, the heavy government borrowing necessary to finance public expenditure sent the value of the pound into freefall and the government had to seek economic assistance from the International Monetary Fund.

The subsequent pay- and public-finance restraint necessary to tackle this economic crisis led to a confrontation with the unions during the winter of 1978 that shattered the assumption that had brought the party into government in the first place, namely that the trade unions could be co-opted into supporting a Labour government. As a result, the Labour Party suffered a heavy defeat in 1979 that heralded the beginning of a new era in British politics. Tarnished with the reputation of being reckless with its economic manage-

ment, the Labour Party would be out of power for 18 years and would never be the same on its return.

The 1979 triumph of the Conservative Party in the general elections brought the first woman prime minister, Margaret Thatcher, and marked the introduction of neoliberal (conservative in American terminology) ideology in British political and economic life. Closely paralleled by the Ronald Reagan administration of the 1980s in the United States, neoliberalism stood for severely rolling back the state, limiting its social role, and promoting greater individualism and self-reliance (similarly pursued by Reagan as a conservative Republican). The future Labour government of 1997 would maintain many of the political and economic assumptions of Thatcherism. This was due in part to the accusation that Labour was the party of taxation and out-of-control spending.

## NEW LABOUR

The Labour Party's defeat in the 1992 general elections under Neil Kinnock's leadership and the loss of his replacement John Smith to a heart attack sparked a leadership crisis within a new generation of Labour members of parliament The victory of Tony Blair marked the beginning of New Labour, a more modern Labour Party, more electable, more in tune with the times and more economically responsible or at least better able to manage the country's economy without resorting to immediate tax increases. These characteristics also made it more able to convince the middle classes that this was the party that would dominate British politics for at least the next decade. Consequently, New Labour was young, dynamic, less infused with traditional values and more prepared to disengage itself from its trade union support

Since it was elected in 1997, the Labour Party has been accused of being obsessed by the media and a careful control of the party's image in a frenzy of self-presentation and political "spin" at the cost of true political debate. If the final years of the last Conservative government—in power between 1979 and 1997—were marked by constant accusations of improprieties and dishonesty, the Labour government that replaced it in 1997 will go down in history as the government of political "spin."

In particular, Blair stands accused of having exaggerated the case for war against Iraq in 2003, through careful control of the media, in order to fit in with the international policy priorities of the United States. Although he has taken a more prominent role in international politics than any other previous Labour leader, this has been done in tune with Britain's historic "special relationship" with the United States.

In the meantime, Blair might have alienated his European counterparts in France and Germany in exchange for a political alliance with the conservative governments in Spain and Italy. Bair's careful balancing act between being part of Europe while maintaining a special relationship with the United States is seen by many traditional Labour supporters with resentment. They might be tempted to argue that New Labour has lost its way, pandering to the middle classes and disassociating itself from the trade unions and its core voter support.

## SEE ALSO

*Volume 1 Left:* Unions; Socialism; United Kingdom.
*Volume 2 Right:* Reagan, Ronald; Thatcher, Margaret; Conservative Party, UK; United Kingdom.

## BIBLIOGRAPHY

Chris Cook and Ian Taylor, *The Labour Party: An Introduction to Its History, Structure and Politics* (Longman Publishers, 1980); Henry Pelling, *Origins of the Labour Party* (Oxford University Press, 1965); Paul Adelman, *The Rise of the Labour Party* (Longman, 1972); Keith Laybourn, *The Labour Party 1881–1951: A Reader in History* (Alan Sutton Publishing, 1988); Henry Pelling, *A Short History of the Labour Party* (Macmillan, 1982).

Kepa Artaraz, Ph.D.
University of Derby, United Kingdom

# Lenin, Vladimir I. (1870–1924)

LENIN, WHO WAS BORN Vladimir Ilyich Ulanov, emerged as the leader of the Bolshevik branch of the Russian Social Democrats in the decade before the Russian Revolution. A dedicated revolutionary, an incisive writer, and a compelling speaker, he brought his considerable powers of logic and legal training to bear on organizing an elite core of radicals to lead a successful revolutionary movement. After the revolution, he headed the Soviet Communist Party and was head of the Soviet State until his death in 1924. After his death, international communists regarded him as the father of the movement, recognition enshrined in the popular term *Marxism-Leninism.*

Lenin was born into a well-off family in the city of Simbirsk in central Russia, where his father was head of the provincial educational department. When Lenin was 17, his older brother was arrested and executed for his participation in a plot to assassinate Tzar Alexander III. Later the same year, Lenin entered a regional law school but was expelled for joining in a student demonstration. At home, he began studying revolutionary works, and was much impressed by the 1863 novel *What Is to Be Done?,* by the Russian writer, Nicholas Chernyshevsky. In that novel, a central figure, Rakhmetev, is portrayed as a brilliant and dedicated revolutionary, and Lenin consciously began to model his life on that character. He continued his study of law as an external student at St. Petersburg University and completed his degree in 1892. During this period, Lenin began to study the writings of Karl Marx and Friedrich Engels. After briefly working in a law office in the city of Samara, Lenin quit and moved to St. Petersburg. There he met with and began working with a group of radicals interested in the ideas of Marx and the Russian Marxist, Georgy Plekhanov.

In St. Petersburg, Lenin worked with other Marxists who distributed literature among the working class in the factories and tried to organize unions, which were illegal. While working in this group, Lenin met Nadezhda Krupskaya, who later became his wife. Lenin was arrested and was sentenced to exile in Siberia, where he spent three years. While in exile, he continued his studies and wrote his first major book, *The Development of Capitalism in Russia* (1899). In 1900, he moved briefly to Switzerland and then settled in Munich, Germany, where he became one of the editors of the revolutionary newspaper, *Iskra* (The Spark). In 1901, he adopted the revolutionary name Lenin, presumably after the river Lena.

He published a pamphlet, "What Is to Be Done?," repeating the title of Chernyshevsky's influential novel. Through his writings, Lenin became the unofficial leader of the Russian Social Democrat Labor Party (RSDLP). At a meeting of the party, Lenin emerged as the leader of a group arguing for an elite party that would act as a vanguard of the revolution, rather than as an extensive party open to all members who accepted the program. His position was held by a bare majority, and thenceforth, his wing became known as the Bolsheviks (Russian for "majority"). There was some irony in that fact as the Bolshevik wing stood for a very limited, rather than widespread membership in the party.

Lenin moved to exile again, living in Switzerland and France. After briefly working with opponents in the

RSDLP, the Bolsheviks organized a separate party conference in 1912 in Prague, and thenceforth, the Bolshevik Party was independent of the other Russian Social Democrat Labor factions. During the first years of World War I, Lenin remained in Switzerland. There he continued to write and published *Imperialism, the Highest Stage of Capitalism*, in which he argued that the war was a logical and inevitable consequence of capitalism and its expansion. He soon began to argue for the defeat of Russia in the war. He saw such a defeat as a step to bringing about revolution. His position, of course, was extremely unpopular among other Russian radicals, but when the defeat came amid revolutionary uprisings, he was seen as a brilliant prophet.

In March 1917, the Tzar abdicated and the Russian monarchy gave way to a provisional government. The next month, Lenin traveled by sealed train through Germany, Sweden, and Finland to St. Petersburg (renamed Petrograd), with the intent of organizing the revolutionary movement.

In October, armed workers, together with soldiers and sailors, seized government buildings in Petrograd and arrested members of the provisional government. A congress of soviets (workers and soldiers councils) proclaimed soviet rule. Working with another radical party, the Left Socialist Revolutionaries, the Bolsheviks formed a government, with Lenin as chairman. The government worked out a peace treaty with Germany in March 1918.

The Bolsheviks renamed themselves the Russian Communist Party (Bolshevik) and purged the Left Socialist Revolutionaries from the government early in 1918. In August 1918, Lenin was wounded in an assassination attempt, which left him weakened. During the civil war in Russia that lasted from 1918 to 1921, Lenin led the government in a period known as the Red Terror. As in the French Revolution, members of the old ruling class, together with moderate and centrist elements of the population, were ruthlessly exterminated.

Lenin's contribution to the left went far beyond Russia and the Soviet Union, however. In March 1919, he convened the Third International, or Comintern. Through the Comintern, the Soviet party was able to dominate Communist parties abroad. Not only did such parties support Soviet foreign policy, but they served as recruiting grounds for the overseas intelligence agents of both the state political police and the army's overseas intelligence organization.

After a series of strokes, Lenin died in 1924, leading to a long struggle for power among possible successors. Eventually Josef Stalin and Leon Trotsky emerged as the principal contenders, with Stalin ultimately successful by 1927. Under Lenin and his successors in the Soviet system, a very small group, later known as the Politburo, conducted analysis of the political situation. Lenin interpreted Marxism as a scientific system that could yield only one correct interpretation, and with such an understanding, it was only logical that the decisions of the leadership should be implemented without regard for dissenting or incorrect views. The certitude and singleness of purpose that characterized Lenin's personal approach to the revolution emerged as the style of the Bolshevik and later the international communist movement.

With a ruthless belief in the correctness of their approach and the error of those who opposed them, the leaders of the Soviet state sought to advance the cause of socialist revolution (as they defined it) over the next decades. However, rather than accepting a wide variety of socialist parties as collaborators in the establishment of Marxist-style societies, Marxism-Leninism became a constantly redefined orthodoxy.

In this fashion, those who at a particular period advocated a more violent or revolutionary course, such as Trotsky, would be defined by the Politburo and the Comintern as left-deviationists. Similarly those communists or socialists who happened to advocate greater cooperation with existing capitalist governments than official Politburo policy called for at a particular time, would be defined as right-deviationists, as was the American Communist leader Earl Browder, after World War II. For a period of at least three decades, from the early 1920s through the 1950s, Lenin and his successors imposed their views and labels on the political spectrum of the left.

**SEE ALSO**

*Volume 1 Left:* Third International (Comintern); Communist Party, Soviet; Stalin and Stalinism; Trotsky, Leon. *Volume 2 Right:* Soviet Union.

**BIBLIOGRAPHY**

Sheila Fitzpatrick, *The Russian Revolution, 1917–32* (Oxford University Press, 1984); Neil Harding, *Leninism* (Macmillan, 1996); Richard Pipes, *Russia under the Bolshevik Regime* (A.A. Knopf, 1993); Robert Service, *Lenin: A Biography* (Macmillan, 2000); James White, *Lenin: The Practice and Theory of Revolution* (Palgrave, 2000); Betram D. Wolfe, *Three Who Made a Revolution: A Biographical History* (Stein and Day, 1984).

RODNEY P. CARLISLE
GENERAL EDITOR

# Liberal Party, Australia

THE LIBERAL PARTY of Australia is a left-of-center party that has governed Australia for most of the period since the end of World War II. It was founded in 1944 in Canberra under the inspiring leadership of Robert Menzies. On October 16, 1944, the name "The Liberal Party of Australia" was deliberately adopted at the Albury Conference because of the associations the name had with 19th-century progressive political thinking. In 1946, the Liberal Party had some limited success. In 1947, it won elections in Victoria and other states. In 1949, it won national office in a coalition with the Country Party. Under Menzies's leadership, it governed Australia for the next 17 years.

Leaders of the party since its inception have been Robert Menzies (1944–66); Harold Holt, (1966–67) until he disappeared while swimming; John Gorton (1968–71); William McMahon (1971–72); Bill Snedden (1972–75); Malcolm Fraser (1975–83); Andrew Peacock (1983–85 and 1989–90); John Howard (1989–90 and 1995–2004); and Alexander Downer (1994–95). Menzies, Holt, Gorton, McMahon, Fraser, and Howard all served as prime minister, while the others were leaders of the opposition. For most of its history, the Liberal Party has governed Australia. It has also been very successful in governing in the state governments of Australia.

The Liberal Party's political philosophy combines individualist liberalism, conservatism, and practical action. It is oriented toward individual rights, free enterprise, high quality of life for all the citizens of Australia, environmental protection, and a sound foreign policy. It has tied Australia's security closely with both the United Kingdom and the United States in the post-World War II years. The party views the Menzies years as a golden era in Australian history. It was a period in which many policies of social welfare were instituted, but as the same time the period solidified defensive alliances with both the United Kingdom and the United States. These included the ANZUS (Australia, New Zealand, United States Security Treaty) and SEATO (South East Asia Treaty Organization) agreements. Other important achievements were improvements in education, transportation, old age assistance, and economic development.

The Liberal Party of Australia is organized on a federal basis, reflecting the federal system of government of Australia. The party has two basic wings—the Organizational and the Parliamentary. The Organizational wing is composed of the party's paid membership.

These are more than 80,000 in number and are organized into 2,000 local branches in the several Australian states. It develops the party's platform as a broad statement of the Liberal Party's beliefs. It also aids in the selection of candidates, manages elections, and conducts fund raising. The Parliamentary wing is composed of those who hold offices in the parliament. This group engages in the actual work of representation. It also develops specific policies, strategies, and priorities for implementing the party's political philosophy.

The Liberal Party of Australia is organized on a federal basis into separate divisions. The Federal Secretariat is the national headquarters of the Liberal Party. It is the national center for party administration, research, and election campaign coordination. It also gives assistance to the state parties. It is managed by the federal director and is located in R. G. Menzies House in Canberra. The Liberal Party is aided in its activities by a network of committees and by the federal council. The Liberal Party's major supporters are business and professional people. It has also allied with the National Country Party, which represents agricultural interests. The major opposition party is the Labor Party, which is supported by labor unions and allied often with the Australian Democratic Party, an environmental party.

**SEE ALSO**
*Volume 1 Left:* Australia; Liberalism.
*Volume 2 Right:* Australia.

**BIBLIOGRAPHY**
Brian J. Costar. ed., *For Better or Worse: The Federal Coalition* (Melbourne University Publishing, 1994); Ian Hancock, *National and Permanent?: The Federal Organization of the Liberal Party of Australia, 1944–65* (Melbourne Publishing, 2000); Gerard Henderson, *Menzies' Child: The Liberal Party of Australia 1944–94* (Allen & Unwin, 1995).

ANDREW J. WASKEY
DALTON STATE COLLEGE

# Liberal Party, Canada

THE LIBERAL PARTY has governed Canada for most of the country's existence. All of its leaders since the start of the 20th century have served as prime minister. The party has achieved this extraordinary level of success by following a formula honed by longtime leader (1919–48) W.L. Mackenzie King to stay as close to the political center as possible, allowing the party to appeal to either the Left or the Right by altering its position only slightly. The party has alternated between Anglophone (English-speaking) and Francophone (Frenchspeaking) leaders since the 19th century, partly by coincidence and partly by design. King, an Anglophone, succeeded Sir Wilfrid Laurier, a Francophone, and King was determined that a Francophone succeed him. This led to the election of his Francophone successor, Louis St. Laurent. The alternation continued with the elections to the Liberal leadership of Lester B. "Mike" Pearson, Pierre Trudeau, John N. Turner, Jean Chrétien, and Paul Martin. Liberal leadership contests are generational events, coming in 1919, 1948, 1957, 1968, 1984, 1990, and 2003. The other Canadian parties tend to have leadership contests more frequently.

The Liberal Party is flanked on the left by the New Democratic Party (NDP), formerly the Co-Operative Commonwealth Federation (CCF). The existence of a left-wing, social democratic party in Canada would theoretically be a bad thing for the Liberal Party, according to conventional political science, but the presence of a competitor on the left actually helps the Liberal Party maintain a firm grip on the center. With much of the political left busy in the NDP, the left wing of the Liberal Party has always been smaller than the left wings of the U.S. Democratic Party or the British Labour Party, for example. There have also usually been two parties to the right of the Liberal Party. The Conservative Party (known as the Progressive Conservative Party from 1942 to 2003) is Canada's oldest political party, although the names of the two parties are misnomers since the Conservative Party has also been a centrist party for most of its history.

The differences between the Liberal Party and the Conservative Party have usually been most pronounced in the ethnic, religious, and linguistic composition of the parties rather than ideologically. Since the election of Laurier in 1896, the Liberal Party has been the main party for Francophones, and this was cemented by the party's opposition to conscription during World War I. (Most Canadian Francophones did not support Canada's entry into what they perceived as England's war with Germany.) Most immigrants to Canada support the Liberal Party, as do the bulk of urban Catholics, and Jewish voters are the single most Liberal voting bloc. The Conservative Party, on the other hand, has traditionally been dominant among Canadians of Anglo-Celtic extraction. Socioeconomic status plays

*Prime Minister Paul Martin continues the long tenure of the Liberal Party maintaining political power in Canada.*

less of a role than in the divide between the parties in the United States, for both the Liberal and Conservative parties have done well in both wealthy and poor areas.

For most of the 20th century, the far-right party in Canada was the Social Credit Party, which formed the provincial governments in Alberta and British Columbia for decades and usually elected Members of Parliament from those provinces and also rural Québec, where the party's right-wing economic theses were supplemented with appeals to Québec nationalism. E. Preston Manning, son of a longtime Social Credit premier of Alberta, founded a new right-wing party in 1987, the Reform Party, which in 1993 supplanted the Progressive Conservative Party as the dominant party in western Canada and also eclipsed the NDP in that region. Renamed the Canadian Alliance in 2000, the party merged with the Progressive Conservative Party in 2003 to become the Conservative Party of Canada. It remains to be seen whether the party will be a centrist, nationally based party like the former Progressive Conservative Party or a hard-right party like the former Reform Party. Some speculate a new party on the right will emerge to fill the ideological gap that occurs.

The Liberal Party has thus been a vessel that accommodated the welfare liberalism of Mackenzie King, the nation-building of Trudeau, the pragmatism of Chrétien, and the fiscal conservatism of Martin. The party faces the first election of the 21st century with an uncertain ideology and disorganized rivals.

## SEE ALSO

*Volume 1 Left:* Canada; Liberalism.
*Volume 2 Right:* Canada; Conservatism.

## BIBLIOGRAPHY

Tony L. Hill, *Canadian Politics, Riding by Riding: An In-Depth Analysis of Canada's 301 Federal Electoral Districts* (Prospect Park Press, 2002); Christina McCall-Newman, *Grits: An Intimate Portrait of the Liberal Party* (Macmillan, 1982).

TONY L. HILL
MASSACHUSETTS INSTITUTE OF TECHNOLOGY

# Liberal Party, Hong Kong

THE LIBERAL PARTY of Hong Kong (HK) is an influential, conservative political force in the Special Administrative Region (HKSAR) of the People's Republic of China (PRC). It stands for Hongkongian business and is a strong proponent of compromise and cooperation with mainland China.

The Liberal Party (LP) was formally established on June 18, 1993, by tycoons, businessmen, bankers, and administration office-holders connected with HK Cooperative Resources Centre. "Focus on Economy; Concern for Livelihood" was adopted as the key political platform. Allen Lee Peng-fei became the first party chairman. The Liberal Party actively participated in the HK Legislative Council elections of 1995, 1996, 1998, and 2000, winning a total of 10 seats (from 60) as an average. The Liberal Party Manifesto (brief program, revised in 2003) focuses on the defending of liberty and developing the entrepreneurial spirit, and a fair and free market economy. It argues that Hong Kong's political structure must serve the economy's best interests. Freedom, democracy, economic and social progress, rule of law, equal opportunity and fair play, maintaining peace and order, and participation in governance are proclaimed as the party's values.

In 2003 and 2004, the LP position acquired a key significance in HK political life. HK government, being fully loyal to Beijing, decided to introduce the Hong Kong Basic Law Article 23 into the legal code in HKSAR. However, the unlimited power of the government and introduction of mainland China's concept of forbidden organizations deeply troubled the population. People believed the territory's freedoms and human rights were being eroded. On July 1, 2003, about half a million of Hong Kong citizens took to the streets to show their concern. Hongkongians came to conclude that they needed their own democratically chosen representatives to protect civil liberties acquired under British rule (relinquished in 1997)—not just against the Chinese central government, but also against the local "fat cats" who would govern in Beijing's name.

After the huge protest demonstrations, on July 6, 2003, James Tien, the leader of the Liberal Party, resigned from the executive council of HK and had his party members vote for a postponement. As a result, the government would have insufficient votes to pass the law on July 9 as first scheduled. It was a sharp turn from the LP's usual progovernment policy and was praised as heroic in temporarily relaxing a big conflict between the government and most Hongkongers. However, at almost the same time, LP decided to change its policy from "All legislation members should be directly elected in 2007" to "Hong Kong should become more democratic." The founder and ex-chair of the Liberal Party, Li Peng Fei, decided to leave the party since he believed the change was a turnaway from the people.

The limited democracy in HKSAR has a combined and tricky (partly multistage) voting system. It was devised (under the British rule and after) to make sure the democrats would always be outnumbered by the "yes" crowd. The LP shift of 2003 equalized the situation. The struggle on the issue of political reform will sharpen on the eve of 2007 elections. Although there is a strong voice among the people of HK demanding universal suffrage for electing the chief executive in 2007 and the entire legislature in 2008, the party's position on the matter remains deliberate. The method for forming the Legislative Council and selecting the chief executive should be specified in the light of the actual situation in HK, and in accordance with the principle of gradual and orderly progress, the HK liberals stress. They argue that "any changes to the political system, when deemed appropriate, should be gradual and orderly and, above all, should at all times preserve and protect economic prosperity and social stability. Such changes should be introduced only in a manner which would clearly bring about a better future for the people of HK."

Tien and his party took up a convenient station of facilitator in the dialogue between the Beijing government, HK administration, and the Hong Kong pro-democracy camp. His problem as the temporary master of the situation is how far to accommodate democratic demands in Hong Kong without damaging business with mainland China.

**SEE ALSO**

*Volume 1 Left:* China; Communism; Deng Xiaoping.
*Volume 2 Right:* China; Capitalism.

**BIBLIOGRAPHY**

"Liberal Party, Hong Kong," www.liberal.org.hk (July 2004); Christopher Patten, *East and West: China, Power, and the Future of Asia* (Random House, 1999); Jonathan Dimbleby, *The Last Governor* (Trafalgar Square, 2002); Hong Kong Basic Law Article 23, www.yourencyclopedia.net (July 2004); Opponents of Article 23, www.againstarticle23.org (July 2004).

IGOR CHARSKYKH
DONETSK NATIONAL UNIVERSITY, UKRAINE

# Liberal Party, UK

THE LIBERAL PARTY in Great Britain is a tiny remnant of the political power base it was in the 19th century. Then, it was one of the two major parties and dominated British politics for decades.

The Liberal Party in England developed from the the Whigs, who were a parliamentary faction in opposition to the religious policies of King Charles II. In the 18th century, they supported the Hanoverian succession. The Tories were their conservative opponents who supported the established system of church and aristocratic class, which controlled agriculture and rural areas. The Whigs were the party of reform in the 18th century and usually represented a medley of middle-class interests and the views of the industrial and commercial interests.

By the 1830s, political parties had developed from factions into organized groups of people sharing a common political philosophy. The organized groups, or parties, sought to take control of the government in order to put their philosophy into law. Their aim was to then make the laws and run the government on the basis of their political principles. The Whig political elements in this period represented the rising industrial and financial interests in the country. They were as a result in favor of free trade and free markets.

Growing uncomfortable with the aristocratic associations connoted by the name "Whig," they began to call themselves "liberals." The name was taken from French and Continental practice. This party dominated much of 19th-century politics. In 1868, the party officially adopted the name "Liberal" when William Gladstone became prime minister. The year 1868 was the high-water mark of the Liberal Party, when it captured 61.5 percent of the vote and 387 of the Members of Parliament. In 1877, the National Liberal Federation was formed, which is the direct predecessor of the Liberal Party of the 20th century.

From 1868 until 1894, Gladstone led the Liberal Party as a brilliant orator and debater, and his leadership gained the party many of its goals. However, when he retired, the party seemed unfocused despite contributions he made behind the scenes. In 1900, Henry Campbell-Bannerman led the party in opposition to the Boer War. Other leaders of the time were Herbert Henry Asquith, Edward Grey, Winston Churchill, and David Lloyd-George. The opposition gave the party a great victory in the "Khaki election." From 1900 until 1920, the Liberal Party fought for social, economic, political, and religious reforms. It pushed for disestablishment of religion, welfare reforms, limited working hours, national insurance, extending the vote to the working class and to the Irish, and for reform of the House of Lords.

The extension of the vote led to the rise of the Labour Party as this move brought into the electorate great numbers of people who did not vote for the Liberal Party. It also weakened the Liberal Party because it now needed the support of Irish nationalists. A major realignment of voter loyalties was the end result. In 1908 Asquith replaced Campbell-Bannerman as leader. By 1912, foment in Ireland led to the introduction of a bill on home rule. Tensions on this issue were high at the beginning of World War I in 1914.

World War I put the Liberal Party in a difficult position. As a party of free trade, limited government, and pacifist beliefs, it was not the party many desired for wartime. A number of its top leaders who were ministers in the government resigned. Ultimately, Lloyd-George and Churchill provided effective wartime leadership, but not before military failures in the early stages of the war sufficiently weakened the party that it was found necessary to invite the Conservative Party to share power.

Meanwhile, the Labour Party was growing in strength, especially as the leaders of the Liberal Party failed to address the Irish Question adequately and other issues as well. In the ensuing party realignment, the bulk of the strength of the Liberal Party went to the Conservative Party. In addition, the enfranchisement of working-class voters also realigned the struggle from a religious alignment to an alignment by classes.

In 1918, the Liberal Party appeared to be in a position of great strength, but it was very seriously divided. In the power struggle for leadership Lloyd-George bested Asquith. From 1920 until 1951, it experienced a steady decline in voter support when it took only 2.1 percent of the vote. Thereafter it increased in strength and flourished in the 1980s when it gained 25.4 percent of the vote.

Since the 1930s, the Conservative and Labour Parties have alternated in controlling the government. The Liberal Party and other minor parties have at times sought to be the balance of power in Parliament, but usually they were isolated. During World War II, Liberals held office as part of the National Coalition. Traditionally the Liberal Party was between the Labour Party on the left and the Conservative Party on the right.

During the 1950s and 1960s, the Liberal Party survived because of the traditional support it continued to enjoy in Wales and the Shetland Islands. But, as the decade of the 1960s advanced, urban middle-class voters began to take interest in the party. In 1962, a Liberal Party Member of Parliament was elected from a district in London for the first time in decades. In 1974, the Liberal Party won only 13 seats in Parliament. Then in March of 1977, it entered into a parliamentary accord with the Labour Party. This allowed the Labour Party to remain in office. However, the Liberal Party quickly reverted to its tradition of opposition.

In 1981, a number of Members of Parliament left the Labour Party. Led by Roy Jenkins, Shirley Williams, and others they formed the Social Democratic Party. In 1982, the Liberal Party formed an alliance with the Social Democratic Party. At the time it seemed the alliance would supplant the Labour Party. The percentage of the vote that the combination drew was gratifying because it was about 25 percent of the votes cast. However, the alliance gained few additional seats in Parliament.

In 1988, it seemed that the Liberal Party might recover and become a major party again. However, the Liberal Party split when many of its members joined with the Social Democrat Party to form the Social and Liberal Democrats Party. This new party is now usually called the Liberal Democrats. However, a remnant of politicians and activists organized a party with the old name of Liberal Party. These two parties, the Liberals and the Liberal Democrats, now have very different political platforms. After the merger of the Liberal Party and the Social Democratic Party, most of the leadership and supporters in both parties stayed with the Liberal Democrats. This group retained possession of the organization, its records, and the assets of the original Liberal Party. Today, its policy positions are near to the political philosophy of the original Liberal Party. Many believe that the Liberal Democrats are the true inheritors of the mantle of the old Liberal Party. In 2004, it was enjoying renewed success from its opposition to Prime Minister Tony Blair's support for the war in Iraq.

A remnant opposed the merger between the Liberal Party and the Social Democratic Party. This group was able to capture the Liberal Party label. Today, it is a loose federation of organizations. The basic units of the party are its regional organizations. It also has Scottish, Welsh, and Irish branches.

This new Liberal Party is far from the individualist ideology of its heyday. It is much more liberal than the Liberal Party was during much of the 20th century. It is seeking to create a "Liberal Society" that will be very egalitarian socially, economically, and politically. To this end, it supports an open society. It supports the United Nations and seeks a democratic world governing authority. It also supports European cooperation but opposes substituting the Euro for the British pound sterling. It promotes policies that are "green" and equality without discrimination. To further these and other aims, the Liberal Party seeks members and candidates who support them.

Political parties arise to gather and express the interests of groups in society at certain periods of history. If those interests are met, the party will be successful, but if not support will move to other prospects. Current events may be moving in a direction that will allow for a revival of the Liberal Party.

## SEE ALSO

*Volume 1 Left*: Labour Party, UK; Liberalism
*Volume 2 Right*: Conservative Party, UK; Conservatism; Thatcher, Margaret.

## BIBLIOGRAPHY

Vernon Bogdanor, *Liberal Party Politics* (Oxford University Press, 1983); Christopher Cook, *A Short History of the Liberal Party* (Palgrave Macmillan, 2002); Arthur I. Cyr, *Liberal Party Politics in Britain* (Transaction Publishers, 1977); Iain Dale, *Liberal Party: General Election Manifestos* (Routledge, 2000); Roy Douglas, *The History of the Liberal Party* (Fairleigh Dickinson University Press, 1971); Frank O'Gorman, *The Emergence of the British Two-Party System* (Edward Arnold Ltd.,

1982); G.R. Searle, *Liberal Party: Triumph and Disintegration* (Palgrave Macmillan, 2001).

ANDREW J. WASKEY
DALTON STATE COLLEGE

# Liberalism

A PROPER UNDERSTANDING of liberalism must include perceptions of the term within both a historical and a contemporary setting. Historical, or classical liberalism, has been used to describe both a political and an economic school of thought. The foremost proponents of classical liberalism were Thomas Hobbes, John Locke, Jean-Jacques Rousseau, Adam Smith, Thomas Jefferson, and John Stuart Mill. Politically, classical liberalism evolved as a response to tyrannical governments that attempted to control the beliefs and consciousness of individuals, going so far as to mandate particular religious beliefs. Economic liberalism grew in response to mercantilism, which dominated economic European policies with its goals of furthering the interests of property owners at the expense of the general population.

Classical liberalism was based on the assumption that human beings are rational, granting them the right to make decisions for themselves. This rationality allowed individuals to establish a social contract, thereby creating a *laissez faire*, or limited system of government. Hobbes believed that once a contract was negotiated, it became absolute. Locke disagreed, arguing that individuals retained the right to break a contract whenever government ceased to honor the terms of the contract.

Each individual was assumed to be the best judge of what makes him or her happy. Therefore, no government had the right to take away what Locke identified as the "natural rights" of life, liberty, and the right to own property. Locke argued that each individual owned the fruits of his own labors. As the founder of classical economic theory, Smith contended in *An Inquiry into the Wealth of Nations* (1776) that the interests of society were best served through a hands-off policy on the part of the government, allowing the economy to achieve a natural state of equilibrium.

Because resources were scarce, classical liberals believed that self-interested individuals were intent on controlling those resources. Rousseau believed that most crimes could be traced to the ownership of property and the struggle to amass resources. It became the responsibility of government to protect individuals from others who would take property by force and from outsiders who sought to drain the resources of a country. In the U.S. Constitution, these responsibilities were dealt with by insuring "domestic tranquility" and providing "for the common defense." Classical liberals also believed that government had a responsibility to provide public works and services that individuals could not provide for themselves.

As a 19th-century liberal, Mill went further than earlier liberals in extending individual rights, expressing great concern about government infringement on basic rights. For example, Mill defended the rights of citizens to criticize their governments. He also expanded concepts of equality by assuming that women deserved political rights. Unlike the European liberals, Jefferson had the opportunity to take part in creating a government grounded from the outset in liberal thought.

## 18th-CENTURY LIBERALISM

In 1776, classical liberal philosophy permeated the Declaration of Independence in which the American colonies declared that they had a natural right "to dissolve the political bands which [had] connected [them] with another, and to assume among the powers of the earth, the separate and equal station to which the Laws of Nature and of Nature's God entitle them." Jefferson's liberalism caused him to reject the authority of the British Parliament, in which the colonies had no representation. Instead, Jefferson announced the intention to rebel against the king by listing the grievances the colonies had suffered at his hands. American liberals did not fight a revolution to overthrow a form of government. They did battle to restore the rights that classical liberals claimed under social contract theory.

When the founding fathers met in Philadelphia in the spring of 1787 to create a system of government that would allow the new country to stand on its own, they were already well grounded in classical liberalism, particularly the works of Locke. The framers of the Constitution agreed that the new document would limit government while protecting individual rights. While their concept of equality was far from that of modern liberals, it provided the essential foundation for contemporary liberalism.

The classical liberals who designed the Constitution believed they had protected individual liberties through the entire structure of the document. By separating powers among three branches of government, designed to operate under a system of checks and balances, and by allotting specific powers to national and state governments, abuses of power had been checked at all levels. The Anti-Federalists who opposed the Constitution disagreed and refused to ratify the document without a bill of rights. The Bill of Rights was added at the first session of Congress.

American liberals distrusted factions, which James Madison defined in *Federalist Number 10* as "a number of citizens, whether amounting to a majority or a minority of the whole, who are united and actuated by some common impulse of passion, or of interest, adverse to the rights of other citizens, or to the permanent and aggregate interests of the community." They saw political parties and interest groups as deterrents to democracy.

However, the framers were realists. They understood that groups would form through competition for resources and power. Madison acknowledged that the only sure way to rid the country of factions was to abolish liberty. Since that was not an option to classical liberals, Madison contended that by controlling the "mischief of factions," the government could mitigate the threat to democracy. Factions were controlled, according to Madison, through pluralism, which allowed self-interested groups to compete, preventing any one group from gaining absolute governmental control.

Although the Constitution was created for men like the founding fathers, it was flexible enough to become more liberal and more inclusive through constitutional amendments, judicial decisions, and the political process. Jefferson, as well as Madison and James Monroe, the two Virginia Democrats who succeeded Jefferson, believed in the tenets of liberalism and believed that democracy should not be limited to an elite ruling class. He also believed that rights belonged to the people and not to government. Jefferson was appalled when the Federalists passed sedition laws that banned any criticism of the government.

Disagreements surfaced almost from the beginning of constitutional government. The first opposition party grew in response to conflicts with the Federalists over individual liberties and the role of government. The Democratic-Republican party, also known as the Jeffersonians, emerged as the party of the left. As the founder of the party, Jefferson went beyond classical liberalism to define a form of liberalism that would become associated with the Democratic Party. By definition, the Federalists, who were inclined to protect the status quo, became the conservative party, the party of the right. Over a period of years, the Republican party

became the dominant conservative party in American politics.

The presidential election of 1824 signaled a departure from the status quo. Two Federalists and three Democratic-Republicans had served as presidents, and all of them were of the founding generation. Andrew Jackson was a commoner rather than an aristocrat and a soldier rather than a thinker. Jackson won the popular vote in 1924 but lost the election to John Quincy Adams, the son of John Adams, when it was thrown into the House of Representatives. In 1828, Jackson became the first president to be seen as truly representative of the people. Jackson hated elitism and established a more liberal form of democracy that became known as Jacksonian democracy. Under Jackson, white middle-class males began to have a voice in government. Equality emerged as the dominant political value. In 1831, Alexis de Tocqueville, a French politician, came to the United States to observe the penal system. Tocqueville's commentary has become the classic description of early American democracy. He observed that equality was so important to Americans that they had rather be equal than free.

## 20th-CENTURY LIBERALISM

Like Madison, Woodrow Wilson hated group politics. In Wilson's view, partisan politics had no place in the battle against imperialists who were out to destroy democracy around the world. Wilsonian liberalism was articulated in the reforms of the New Freedom program, which expanded national power to protect individuals both politically and economically through agricultural aid, labor reforms, a central banking system, expanded free trade, increased internationalism, and the spread of liberal democracy. After World War I, a group of extreme conservatives known as the Merchants of Death tried to discredit both Wilson and liberalism by claiming that the president had engineered the war for his own purposes. The irony was that few people hated war more than Wilson.

It was Franklin Roosevelt who came to represent modern American liberalism by using the New Deal to turn the United States into a social welfare state. By enacting the liberal economic theories of John Maynard Keynes, Roosevelt moved away from classical liberal perceptions of limited government to justify an active governmental role. He had won the election of 1932 by promising to end the Great Depression. Therefore, he felt justified in using the extensive power of the national government to turn the economy around by hiring individuals to do everything from building roads to writing government pamphlets. Roosevelt established a welfare system, unemployment compensation, social security, agricultural aid, and mortgage assistance. He provoked animosity among conservatives by involving the national government in almost all aspects of American life. Roosevelt used emergency powers to fight an undeclared war when an isolationist Congress refused to declare war in the beginning days of World War II in Europe.

After Pearl Harbor, Roosevelt's brand of liberalism allowed him to aggressively attack enemies of democracy and to carve a solid place for the United States on the world scene. Roosevelt's social programs became so entrenched that not even the best efforts of popular president Ronald Reagan could dislodge them in the 1980s. Harry Truman expanded Roosevelt's policies and added his own brand of liberalism by integrating the military, expanding housing opportunities, promoting fair employment, and instituting slum clearance.

Under Wilson, Roosevelt, and Truman, liberals endorsed an internationalist view that completely changed the position of the United States in relation to the rest of the world. America emerged from both World War I and World War II with greater economic stability than did devastated European countries. As a creditor nation, the United States was able to set terms and to make demands. The creation of international bodies such as the United Nations and the World Bank and regional alliances such as the North Atlantic Treaty Organization (NATO) and the Organization of American States (OAS) provided the United States with a means of spreading liberal ideology around the world.

## CONTEMPORARY LIBERALISM

Ironically, in 1953, Republican Dwight Eisenhower promoted modern liberalism through the appointment of Earl Warren, the Republican governor of California, as chief justice of the Supreme Court. Under Warren's leadership, the Supreme Court established a course of liberal judicial activism that ended legal segregation, banned sexual discrimination, expanded criminal rights, and redefined the concept of political representation.

During the early 1960s, the administration of John Kennedy placed new emphasis on civil rights by interfering with the Jim Crow laws prevalent in the South. Women's issues were addressed in response to the emerging women's rights movement. After Kennedy's death, Lyndon Johnson's War on Poverty went further than any administration had ever done to reduce the in-

herent inequities of capitalism. In 1967, Johnson also appointed Thurgood Marshall, the liberal civil rights pioneer, as the first African American to serve on the Supreme Court. In 1971, Harvard philosopher John Rawls defined the goals of contemporary liberalism by explaining that the self-respect of individuals called for equal distribution of liberty, opportunity, and income. Rawls argued that the most disadvantaged in any society should receive priority in the distribution of resources.

Jimmy Carter continued to promote liberal policies, placing high priority on civil rights, women's rights, the environment, and social programs. A strong advocate of peace, Carter negotiated the Camp David Accord in 1978, leading to a historic agreement between Israel and Egypt. Carter wanted to be the first president to appoint a woman to the Supreme court but was not given the opportunity to fill a vacancy. In 1981, Ronald Reagan appointed Sandra Day O'Connor, a conservative Republican, as the first woman to serve on the court. In 1993, Bill Clinton appointed Ruth Bader Ginsburg, a strong supporter of women's rights, as the first liberal female justice.

While extreme liberal ideologies such as socialism and communism have achieved prominence in some parts of the world, liberalism in the United States has tended to be more moderate, with brief periods of radicalism in the 1920s to 1930s and again in the 1960s to 1970s. This is due in great part to the fact that the American public feels most comfortable around the center of the political spectrum, and neither the Democrats nor the Republicans vary from that position to any great extent. Furthermore, the two-party system has allowed the major parties to absorb both left and right reform movements, thereby remaining responsive to voters.

The turbulence of the 1960s and 1970s, which included civil rights marches, sit-ins, race riots, women's demands for equality, violent war protests, and campus takeovers, stained the reputation of modern American liberalism to such an extent that in the 1988 presidential campaign, candidate George H. W. Bush was allowed to turn liberalism into a "dirty word." In 1992, the election of Bill Clinton restored the reputation of liberalism to some degree by harking back to the liberalism of Jefferson, Roosevelt, and Kennedy.

## 21st-CENTURY LIBERALISM

Because the government of the United States was based on classical liberalism, most Americans may be defined as liberals in this sense. As classical liberals, both the

Democratic and Republican parties have maintained a respect for what Abraham Lincoln called "government by the people, of the people, and for the people," and for the right to "life, liberty and the pursuit of happiness."

However, modern liberals, embodied chiefly in the Democratic party, have extended the emphasis on individuals to encompass a strong sense of social justice, a demand for social reforms, and a belief that human beings have a right to basic human dignity. The role of government has, therefore, been expanded to ensure a basic standard of living for all Americans.

In the 21st century, the Democratic party endorses such liberal issues as civil rights, affirmative action, women's rights, reproductive rights, criminal rights, multiculturalism, minimum wage, welfare, social security, environmental protection, gun control, religious tolerance, healthcare reform, and expanded educational opportunities.

## SEE ALSO

*Volume 1 Left:* Locke, John; Hobbes, Thomas; Jefferson Thomas; Wilson, Woodrow; Roosevelt, Franklin D.; Johnson, Lyndon B.; Democratic Party; United States; Carter, James E.; Kennedy, John F.
*Volume 2 Right:* Conservatism; Republican Party; Lincoln, Abraham; Reagan, Ronald; United States.

## BIBLIOGRAPHY

Carl Becker, *The Declaration of Independence: A Study in the History of Ideas* (Vantage, 1992); Robert Brown, ed., *Classical Political Theories from Plato to Marx* (Macmillan, 1990); James L. Bugg, Jr., *Jacksonian Democracy: Myth or Reality?* (Holt, Rinehart, Winston, 1964); John Gray, *Liberalism: Concepts in Social Thought* (University of Minnesota Press, 1995); Russell Hardin, *Liberalism, Constitutionalism, and Democracy* (Oxford University Press, 1999); James Madison, *Federalist Number 10*, www.loc.gov (May 2004); Marcus G. Raskin, *Liberalism: The Genius of American Ideals* (Rowman and Littlefield, 2004); John Rawls, *Political Liberalism* (Columbia University Press, 1993); John Rawls, *Theory of Justice* (Belknap, 1971); David Steigerwald, *Wilson Idealism in America* (Cornell University Press, 1994); Alexis de Tocqueville, *Democracy in America* (Harper and Row, 1966); David F. B. Tucker, *Essays on Liberalism: Looking Left and Right* (Kluwer, 1994); James P. Young, *Reconsidering American Liberalism: The Troubled Odyssey of the Liberal Idea* (Westview, 1996).

ELIZABETH PURDY, PH.D.
INDEPENDENT SCHOLAR

# Lincoln, Abraham (1809–1865)

ABRAHAM LINCOLN's liberalism most clearly revealed itself in his belief that the federal government had an obligation to promote certain ideals in order to preserve republican government. His ideas on the role of government in its citizens' lives preceded that of the Progressives and Franklin Roosevelt's New Deal. Central to this ideology was faith in the individual, faith that, if all artificial barriers were removed and equal op-

*Abraham Lincoln's liberalism was evident in his beliefs in a strong government role and the freedom of slaves in the United States.*

portunity was fully employed, all Americans could experience unmitigated economic and social success. Lincoln revered the accomplishments of the founding fathers and marveled at the genius of the Constitution, but he also firmly believed that Americans could surpass the achievements of their ancestors by addressing the institution of slavery in a way that the founding fathers had felt impossible to do when attempting to create a nation out of diverse peoples. In this sense, Lincoln focused more on the promises of the Declaration of Independence than on the provisions of the Constitution, believing that the Declaration of Independence expressed more precisely the ideologies of the founders.

Personally, Lincoln loathed the institution of slavery. He believed it to be morally wrong and contradictory to the foundation upon which the Union existed. He supported enforcement of the Fugitive Slave Act and continued protection of the institution in the slave states because he felt that the Constitution mandated those provisions. His liberalism lay in his belief that the national government had an obligation to stigmatize the institution to prevent its expansion. To do so, the federal government should only adopt those policies that would eventually isolate and destroy it.

The end of slavery, Lincoln believed, would contribute to the ideal of equal opportunity in a number of ways. Most obviously, freedom for blacks would allow them an opportunity to pursue their own economic interests. Though Lincoln did not consider blacks to be equal to whites, he believed they should at least have an opportunity to compete and succeed even if they ultimately failed. More important than emancipation, however, was the opportunity for free white men to succeed economically, especially in the newly acquired western territories. The system of slavery had stifled the economic opportunities for southern whites who could not hope to compete with the minority of large slaveholders who held all the wealth and political power. This hindrance, in Lincoln's mind, violated the principle of liberty, a term he defined as the ability of any individual to reach his potential absent of any barriers. His vision of liberty was positive and dynamic; it allowed for change in the individual and society. The maintenance of slavery made change impossible not only for individuals but for the nation as a whole.

While in Congress, Lincoln voted in favor of the Wilmot Proviso every time the issue arose. He was outspoken about his opposition to the Kansas-Nebraska Act and the Dred Scott decision for many reasons, but his central concern was the moral effect the expansion of slavery would have on the nation's potential for positive change. The national government, he felt, must set the boundaries for morality when the future of the American people was at risk. Recognizing that the issue of slavery hopelessly divided North from South, Lincoln desired the federal government to take a clearer stand on the principle of right.

He had the opportunity to exercise this ideology when he took office in 1861. When war broke out, Lincoln expanded the powers of the presidency without consulting Congress on many occasions. He summoned and expanded both the army and navy between April and July of 1861, while Congress was out of session, despite the fact that no existing law gave him such authority. Over the course of the war, he also drafted soldiers, suspended habeas corpus, and freed slaves in Confederate held territories, all of which he did prior to congressional approval. In addition to circumventing congressional authority, he also bypassed the judicial system by placing certain Union-held territory under military authority.

Although all of these actions took place under the extreme circumstances of war, Lincoln's liberalism extended beyond wartime measures. Prior to the Civil War, Lincoln supported many policies that extended federal authority. He promoted federal funding of public works projects, public education for all children, and emancipation of the slaves in exchange for compensation. He supported the organization and activity of labor unions in order to maintain labor's independence from capital. He actively campaigned for congressional approval of the Homestead Act of 1862 and encouraged unlimited immigration.

All of these policies reinforced Lincoln's belief in equal opportunity for all men. He supported the establishment of government institutions and policies that would regulate this equality. His goals were not immediate, however. He wanted to establish institutions and policies that were best suited to work in the long term in moving the nation as close as possible to the principles set forth in the Declaration of Independence. The idea that "all men are created equal" could no longer remain ambiguous. Its meaning had to be clearly and unequivocally defined. The coming of war provided a unique opportunity to pursue that goal. Lincoln's liberalism lay in the Union's potential. His desire to remove all barriers from the right to pursue life, liberty, and happiness signaled a change in political ideology, a change that created a more active, regulatory state. This pursuit sought to allow all Americans the opportunities that Lincoln believed the founders had envisioned.

## SEE ALSO

*Volume 1 Left:* American Civil War; United States.
*Volume 2 Right:* Lincoln, Abraham; American Civil War; United States.

## BIBLIOGRAPHY

George P. Fletcher, *Our Secret Constitution: How Lincoln Redefined American Democracy* (Oxford University Press, 2001); J. David Greenstone, *The Lincoln Persuasion: Remaking American Liberalism* (Princeton University Press, 1993); J. G. Randall, *Lincoln: The Liberal Statesman* (Dodd, Mead & Company, 1947).

STEPHANIE R. ROLPH
MISSISSIPPI STATE UNIVERSITY

# Lippmann, Walter (1889–1974)

FOR OVER 60 YEARS, Walter Lippmann was one of America's most influential political commentators. As a journalist, his work influenced every president from Woodrow Wilson to Richard Nixon. Lippmann was born in Manhattan, New York City, and was an only child to privileged German-Jewish parents. He attended Harvard University where he studied philosophy and completed a four-year degree in three years.

His journalistic career lasted 35 years, and he authored 21 books. Lippmann was an associate editor of the *New Republic* from 1914 to 1917. He left this position to become an adviser to President Woodrow Wilson during World War I. As Wilson's assistant secretary of war, Lippmann had much influence over the president, especially with regards to Wilson's famous 14 Points, which formed the U.S. position at the Versailles Treaty concluding the war. Lippmann left his position with the president and became an editor for the *New York World* from 1921 to 1931. His journalistic career expanded to include writing for the *New York Herald Tribune* and gaining a national audience. His writing would continue through to the height of the Vietnam War, until he finally put his pen down for good in 1967 and retired at the age of 78.

One of Lippmann's main liberal contributions was his groundbreaking work on propaganda and the American public, especially during times of war. He believed that the public could be easily manipulated and that the masses often had difficulty in seeing the difference between the world around them and their perception of the world. In most cases, he believed people tended to respond more to fictions that they believe to be reality, than to actual reality.

Lippmann never simply followed party lines and always wrote based on his beliefs and feelings. While noted as a liberal thinker, he would change throughout his career from representing socialist-liberal views to conservative views. He would condemn American foreign policy in the Korean and Vietnam Wars and attack American policy with regards to McCarthyism and Harry Truman's role in increasing Cold War tensions with the Soviet Union.

In 1947, he published *The Cold War*, in which he criticized Truman's containment policy against the Soviet Union. He faced initial criticism from historians who, like Truman, believed that the Soviets had expansionist intentions. However, he has recently been the beneficiary of new studies that justify his early Cold War claims and further support Lippmann's place as one of America's most influential, important and insightful journalists.

For all of his great contributions, Lippmann was awarded two Pulitzer Prizes, in 1958 and 1962, for his syndicated column, *Today and Tomorrow*. He was also awarded honorary degrees from 19 different universities. He is best remembered for his amazing ability to foresee the long-term outcomes of American foreign policy, a quality that eluded many of the presidents that he wrote about. Lippmann died in December 1974.

## SEE ALSO

*Volume 1 Left:* Truman, Harry.; Wilson, Woodrow; Media Bias, Left.
*Volume 2 Right:* McCarthyism; Vietnam War; Media Bias, Right.

## BIBLIOGRAPHY

John Luskin, *Lippmann, Liberty, and the Press* (The University of Alabama Press, 1972); Pamela J. Shoemaker and Stephen D. Reese, *Mediating the Message: Theories of Influences on Mass Media Content* (Longman Publishers, 1996); Ronald Steel, *Walter Lippmann and the American Century* (Transaction, 1999).

DAVID W. MCBRIDE
UNIVERSITY OF NOTTINGHAM

# Lloyd, Henry Demarest (1847–1903)

HENRY DEMAREST Lloyd was a journalist best known for *Wealth against Commonwealth*, his exposé of John D. Rockefeller and the Standard Oil Company. Lloyd worked for years as an editor of the *Chicago Tribune* and supported various political causes including the rights of workers. Lloyd is widely considered to be one of the first crusading journalists who helping pave the way for later muckraking reporters such as Ida Tarbell and Lincoln Steffens.

Born in New York City, Lloyd's parents were Aaron and Marie; his father was a minister in the Dutch Reformed Church. As a child, Lloyd moved frequently as his father served as a minister in a variety of churches in New York, New Jersey, and Illinois.

In 1863, Lloyd began attending Columbia University. While excelling as a student, Lloyd developed the habit of overworking, producing health problems that would affect him for the rest of his life. In 1867, Lloyd graduated with a bachelor's degree, and moved on to Columbia Law School. In 1869, Lloyd passed the bar exam in New York. He then began working as an assistant secretary to the American Free-Trade League, which promoted the idea of free trade. At this time, Lloyd actively campaigned against the corruption of Tammany Hall and the corruption of William "Boss" Tweed. By 1872, Lloyd resigned from the American Free-Trade League.

That same year, Lloyd began working for the *Chicago Tribune* and a year later in 1873, he married Jessie Bross, the daughter of William Bross, one of the owners of the *Tribune*. In 1874, Lloyd became the financial editor and in 1880 was promoted to chief editorial writer for the *Chicago Tribune*. As editor, Lloyd attacked the business dealings of railroad magnates such as Cornelius Vanderbilt and Jay Gould. In 1881, Lloyd began writing about John D. Rockefeller and Standard Oil, and published in the *Atlantic Monthly* an exposé on Standard Oil titled "The Story of a Great Monopoly." The article was one of the first to draw attention to Rockefeller and Standard Oil. It described the behind-the-scenes dealings, including payoffs to politicians as well as ruthless business tactics. Lloyd asserted: "The Standard [Oil] has done everything with the Pennsylvania Legislature except refine it."

By 1885, Lloyd resigned from the *Chicago Tribune* as a result of differences with the primary owner of the newspaper, Joseph Medill. This was a crisis point in Lloyd's life; he traveled to Europe, where he suffered a nervous breakdown from which he never fully recovered. In the late 1880s, Lloyd became more actively involved in political causes. For example, he tirelessly defended those accused of implementing the Haymarket bombing in Chicago. In 1888, Lloyd wrote an article for the *North American Review* in which he advocated social and moral reform. During this period, he also became more interested in the issue of workers' rights. In 1889, Lloyd spoke at a number of labor rallies. In 1890, Lloyd published *A Strike of Millionaires against Miners*, a scathing critique of the coal industry. Throughout the 1890s, Lloyd worked with labor unions in the Midwest to create a political movement for reform.

In 1894, Lloyd wrote *Wealth against Commonwealth*, expanding upon his earlier article for *Atlantic Monthly* on Standard Oil. Some critics have declared *Wealth against Commonwealth* a polemical work rather than a scholarly study. What is indisputable is that *Wealth against Commonwealth* was an influential work, which helped to mobilize public sentiment against Standard Oil and other trusts. In 1890, Congress, in response to public opinion, passed the Sherman Antitrust Act. By the early 20th century, President Theodore Roosevelt, sensing the public mood, filed an antitrust suit against Standard Oil. By 1910, Standard Oil was split into multiple companies. *Wealth against Commonwealth* was also significant because Ida Tarbell built upon it when she wrote her pivotal book *The History of the Standard Oil Company* in 1904.

In 1896, Lloyd began investigating social reform in other countries, traveling to England where he investigated industrial cooperatives. In 1898, Lloyd wrote *Labor Copartnership*, which discussed his findings in Great Britain. In 1899, Lloyd traveled to New Zealand and Australia to investigate socialism and wrote *A Country without Strikes* and *Newest England*, which discussed his findings from his trip to New Zealand. In 1902, Lloyd became involved in the anthracite coal strike of the United Mine Workers in Pennsylvania. Along with Clarence Darrow, Lloyd was counsel to the United Mine Workers and argued vigorously on their behalf. On September 28, 1903, he died of pneumonia while participating in a labor campaign that called for the municipal ownership of street railways.

**SEE ALSO**

*Volume 1 Left:* Socialism; Unions; Sinclair, Upton.
*Volume 2 Right:* Capitalism.

**BIBLIOGRAPHY**

Chester McArthur Destler, *Henry Demarest Lloyd and the Empire of Reform* (University of Pennsylvania Press, 1963); Richard Digby-Junger, *The Journalist as Reformer: Henry Demarest Lloyd and Wealth against Commonwealth* (Greenwood Press, 1996); Jay E. Jernigan, *Henry Demarest Lloyd* (Twayne Publishers, 1976); Henry Demarest Lloyd, *Wealth against Commonwealth* (Harper and Brothers Publishers, 1894).

JASON ROBERTS
GEORGE WASHINGTON UNIVERSITY

# Lobbying

THE ROOTS OF the word *lobby* go back to the days when people, who wanted to meet and talk with Members of Parliament in Britain would gather in the entry hall, the lobby, of the British House of Commons.

Over time, the word has been most commonly used to refer to in-person contact between legislators and interest-group representatives.

While the most literal definition of lobbying would include only face-to-face contact with elected members, more generally it has come to also include contact with the bureaucracy, courts, and the president as well as the legislature. More broadly still, it has been used to refer to grassroots campaigns, mass media promotions, and the dissemination of research reports. The most basic definition then would be efforts to influence the formation or implementation of public policy. Most interest-group scholars consider lobbying to be an activity undertaken by professionals on behalf of a representative constituency. Thus, individuals contacting their government representative to comment on policy are not considered lobbyists.

The federal Lobbying Disclosure Act of 1995 defines lobbying activities as "lobbying contacts and efforts in support of such contact, including preparation and planning activities, research and other background work that is intended, at the time it is performed, for use in contacts, and coordination with the lobbying activities of others." It defines lobbying contacts as "any oral or written communication ... to a covered executive branch official or a covered legislative branch official that is made on behalf of a client...." Covered officials are those in a policy position including congressional and presidential staff. This definition excludes official testimony before Congress, indirect efforts through the media, filings before the court (such as amicus briefs), and responses to requests for comments published in the *Federal Register*.

Scores of studies of interest groups and lobbying have determined that the influence of a political interest group is a result of factors such as: group organization and structure; leadership skill; cohesion; its symbolic public status; its power status and bargaining potential vis-à-vis other interest groups; its political strategy; its ability to enlist political support; and its ability to influence mass opinion and/or mobilize members. Specific organizational factors include size, wealth and expertise. Sheer numbers are a contributing factor, perhaps in granting an organization moral authority when it claims that it speaks for an interest in society. Organizationally, the more staff that an organization can devote to its activities the better its capacity to lobby. A lobbyist acting on his or her own will be unable to contact more legislators than will a team of lobbyists. However, organizations may be able to overcome these deficiencies by operating within a coalition. Wealth is also considered to be key to success as the wealthier a lobby, the more likely it is that it has more access. Groups will differ significantly with respect to these qualities.

Decision makers need information in order to make policy, but what they need in particular is accurate, quality information. Credible information reduces the risk of pursuing inappropriate policy. The credibility of an interest group may be dependent upon the character of the group (bias and reputation), the character of the information (completeness), and the dissemination strategies (lobbying and protesting).

There are two kinds of lobby activities: inside lobbying and outside lobbying. Inside lobbying takes place within the halls of government and includes activities such as meetings with legislators, testifying before government committees, providing policy analysis directly to legislators, and negotiating with legislators or other interest groups. Inside lobbying typically requires access to decision makers and expertise. Making significant campaign contributions can be one way of gaining regular access to policy makers in order to lobby.

Outside lobbying is defined as attempts to mobilize citizens to contact public officials. Outside lobbying strategies might include letter writing campaigns, advertising policy positions, holding press conferences, protest demonstration or using a public relations firm.

While strategy choices are important, the decision about whom to lobby can be almost as important. An organization's choice of whom to lobby will vary depending on the characteristics of legislators (including their prior issue positions), the resources available to the interest group (i.e. its capacity for lobbying), and the context of the issue. By lobbying opposing or undecided legislators, lobbyists can affect overall support for or against legislation. By targeting allies, some lobbyists may be able to reinforce the preferences of allied legislators, as well as mobilize participation in the policy process.

There is a general consensus that interest groups have an incentive to lobby undecided or "swing" legislators. Presumably there is the chance for a high payoff because they may be the ones most susceptible to persuasion. Groups will in particular target influential legislators who may be able to sway other legislators to a particular way of thinking.

There exists in political science a general lack of consensus on the merits of interest groups in the political system. The concern about interest groups dates back to James Madison, who warned of the divisive consequences of what he called factions, or citizens organizing to pursue their own self-interest. He argued that the tendency to pursue self-interest was innate, and thus the formation of factions was inevitable. On the one hand, interest groups represent the freedom inherent in the system to join with others and to make demands on leaders; on the other, they represent a threat that certain groups will be able to mobilize more effectively than others, thereby creating and/or reinforcing disparities in political power.

Madison was particularly concerned that a powerful faction would rise to power and tyrannize others in society. He dismissed the idea of trying to eliminate factions, and advocated instead for controlling them through the structure of government detailed in the Constitution. A republican form of government would provide the necessary checks to curb the worst of the impulses of factions. He believed that, in a country as large as the United States, so many interests would arise that a representative government with its own system of checks and balances would not succumb to the power of any one faction.

Instead, government would deal with the views of all, thereby developing policy that would serve the common good. While Madison failed to foresee the unequal distribution of resources among groups and the fact that the least well-off in society have suffered through a failure to organize, the underlying beliefs of *Federalist Paper No. 10* have endured.

Many organizations on the left feel disenfranchised from government. Historically, organizations on the right have been funded by big business, and as such have more money at their disposal than those on the left. More money typically means more access to legislators who are dependent upon campaign contributions for reelection. Madison did not foresee that the unequal distribution of resources would lead to many organizations without access to government and unable to counter the lobby efforts of those more powerful and with more money at their disposal. This is of particular concern for those representing the poor or other marginalized groups in society who face additional challenges in trying to organize to make their voices heard by the decision makers of society.

Some top lobbyists on the left side of politics that have contributed substantial funds to electoral campaigns include unions like the United Steel Workers and the Communications Workers of America. Other leftists organizations are the National Committee for an Effective Congress, the National Association for the Advancement of Colored People, American for Democratic Action, the National Education Association, and the National Organization for Women.

**SEE ALSO**
*Volume 1 Left:* American Revolution; Think Tanks; Democratic Party; Media Bias, Left; Jefferson, Thomas.
*Volume 2 Right:* Lobbying; American Revolution.

**BIBLIOGRAPHY**
Frank and Beth Baumgartner, *Leech Basic Interests: The Importance of Groups in Politics and Political Science* (Princeton University Press, 1998). Steve John, *The Persuaders: When Lobbyists Matter* (Palgrave Macmillan, 2002); George W. Carey and James McClellan, eds., The Federalist by *Alexander Hamilton, John Jay, and James Madison* (Liberty Fund, 2001); Anthony Nownes, *Pressure and Power: Organized Interests in American Politics* (Houghton Mifflin, 2001).

SHANNON K. ORR
BOWLING GREEN STATE UNIVERSITY

# Locke, John (1632–1704)

KNOWN AS THE "father of classical liberalism" and often called the "unofficial Founding Father of the U.S. Constitution," John Locke was born in Somerset, England, to John and Agnes Keene Locke. At an early age, John's father, an attorney, exposed him to liberal and radical ideas and issues that challenged the status quo of 17th-century England. In 1646, Locke enrolled as an undergraduate at Oxford University's Christ Church College, where he became a tutor. In 1649, Locke published his *Essays on the Law of Nature*, and the following year he accepted the position of censor of moral philosophy at Oxford. Obeying his need as an empiricist to explain the physical world, Locke opened an experimental lab with David Thomas while at Oxford. The following year, Locke became the medical adviser to Lord Ashley, the future Earl of Shaftesbury, who became Lord Chancellor of England in 1672. In the Shaftesbury circle, which was composed chiefly of those who were determined to prevent James II from forcing Catholicism upon England, Locke was introduced to a world of power and intrigue.

Returning to Oxford yet again, Locke completed a bachelor's degree in medicine in 1674. After becoming ill, he spent three years in France, discussing philosophy and science with the major thinkers of France and the Netherlands. The Earl of Shaftesbury had escaped to Holland after being tried and acquitted on charges of treason, and Locke followed him. British authorities

*John Locke's theories about human behavior and government set the foundation of liberalism around the world.*

added Locke's name to a list of suspected traitors and threatened him with arrest. For a brief period, Locke was forced to use an alias. By 1686, however, Locke's freedom was no longer in jeopardy, and he returned to public life. Between 1689 and 1690, Locke published all of his major works: *Two Treatises of Government, A Second Letter Concerning Toleration*, and *An Essay Concerning Human Understanding*. With his legitimacy now restored, Locke played a significant role in the founding of the Bank of England in 1694 and was appointed to the Court of Trade two years later.

To explain his theories, Locke described man as being born into a state of nature where each person was born completely free and equal. Locke saw human nature in its natural state as a "blank slate," neither good nor evil. While Locke believed that people were capable of cooperation, he saw the state of nature as unreliable

because it forced man to be chiefly concerned with his own protection. To gain security, Locke suggested that rational men entered into a social contract with one another, creating a limited government. Once created, government bore the responsibility for protecting individuals from those who would "harm another in his life, liberty, or possessions." To Locke, "the great and chief end" of government was always "the preservation of property."

Locke is best known to the general public for his views on "natural rights." He believed that the "Law of Nature is God's rules for how his creation should operate." Locke argued that because property was God's gift to man, individuals have an inherent right to life, liberty, and property. While Locke believed that nurturing was the chief role of women, he conceded that woman was free to "overcome the natural limitations." If so, then she, too, was guaranteed those rights inherent to man. In Locke's view, each individual owned the fruits of his or her own labors; therefore, no one had a right to collect more property than could be individually used. In civil society, man discovered money, which could be hoarded, unlike the proceeds of hunting and gathering used as barter in the state of nature. Locke believed that money, like any property amassed in unequal amounts, led to conflicts.

Rejecting the absolutist theories of Thomas Hobbes, Locke argued that individuals retained an inherent right of rebellion if the government broke the terms of the contract. Government, though necessary, must always be limited, Locke wrote, because "unlimited power is and cannot be considered political power." Locke's sovereign, unlike that of Hobbes, was also subject to laws created under the contract. Locke expressly rejected the theory of "divine rights" purported by Robert Filmer in *Patriarchia*. According to Locke, the best form of government is one in which power is shared between an executive and an elected legislature, both chosen by majority rule, because "the greater force within each society shall rule it." In his view, the legislature, like the English parliament, should be supreme.

Religious toleration was also an important element of Locke's philosophy. He argued that if one set of religious rules was required for everyone, religious leaders were setting themselves in the place of the Divinity. Furthermore, forcing certain beliefs on a population would likely lead to religious hypocrisy. Locke insisted that sincerity and genuine worship were indispensable elements of the salvation experience. Locke thought that the choice between eternal heaven and unceasing hellfire kept true believers acting morally. Atheists, on the other hand, were hazards to humanity because they had no motivation to behave morally.

When Thomas Jefferson drafted the Declaration of Independence in 1776, he interpreted Locke's rights for Americans to mean: "We hold these truths to be self-evident, that all men are created equal, that they are endowed by their Creator with certain unalienable Rights, that among these are Life, Liberty and the pursuit of Happiness." Delegates to the Constitutional Convention in 1787 were also familiar with Locke's work as well as Jefferson's. Legend says that many delegates read Locke every day after leaving the convention hall in order to know what to argue at the next day's debates.

Although not specifically guaranteeing "life, liberty, and the pursuit of happiness," the concept of a limited government pledged to protect the rights of individuals was inherent throughout the U.S. Constitution. In the Preamble to the Constitution, the framers set out their Lockean goals: "We the people of the United States, in order to form a more perfect union, establish justice, insure domestic tranquility, provide for the common defense, promote the general welfare, and secure the blessings of liberty to ourselves and our posterity, do ordain and establish this Constitution for the United States of America." The ideas of limited government and individual rights were further strengthened by the addition of the Bill of Rights, proposed by James Madison in 1789 and ratified by the states in 1791.

Paradoxically, while Lockean thought was used to promote capitalism in the United States, Karl Marx used Locke's ideas on property to form the basis of his theories on communism. Marx, of course, believed that under communism alienated and exploited workers would rise up and destroy capitalism in order to regain the fruits of their own labors. Locke died at his home in England on October 28, 1704. Posthumously, the *Paraphrases on the Epistles of St. Paul* and the *Fourth Letter Concerning Toleration* were published in 1705 and 1706, respectively.

### SEE ALSO

*Volume 1 Left:* Liberalism; Hobbes, Thomas; Marx, Karl; United States.
*Volume 2 Right:* Capitalism; Libertarianism.

### BIBLIOGRAPHY

Carl Becker, *The Declaration of Independence: A Study in the History of Political Ideas* (Vintage, 1992); Robert Brown, ed., *Classical Political Thinkers from Plato to Marx* (Macmillan, 1990); Kevin L. Cope, *John Locke Revisited* (Twayne, 1999); John Locke, *Two Treatises of Government* (New American Library, 1963); Joseph Losco and Leonard Williams, *Political Theory: Classical Writings, Contemporary Views* (St. Martin's, 1992); H.B. McCullough, ed., *Political Ideologies and Political Philosophies* (Thompson, 1989); Andrzej Rapaczysnki, *Nature and Liberalism in the Philosophies of Hobbes, Locke, and Rousseau* (Cornell University Press, 1987).

ELIZABETH PURDY, PH.D.
INDEPENDENT SCHOLAR

# Locofocos

THE LOCOFOCOS was a moniker bestowed by the press on the Equal Rights faction of the Democratic Party in 1835. The Friends of Equal Rights, or the Equal Rights faction, was a comparatively moderate organization that revived that many of the goals and ideals of the more radical workingmen's parties, a labor-oriented movement that demanded a 10-hour workday, free public education, abolition of debtor imprisonment, and an end to competition from prison contract labor.

The Equal Rights Party platform was based on the advocacy of equal rights for every citizen, an opposition to bank notes as a circulating medium, an argument that gold and silver were the only safe and constitutional currency, and an opposition to all monopolies by legislation. The Equal Rights movement began its activity inside the New York City Democratic Party machine, known as Tammany Hall, and became particularly active in 1834, clashing with the Tammany monopolists over the issues of state banks, tariffs, and special interests. In the fall of 1835, the Tammany Democrats expelled William Leggett, the radical editor of the *New York Evening Post* from the party and the Tammany Nominating Committee and recommended for state offices a number of candidates who were not acceptable to the Equal Rights faction. A meeting was called on October 29 to ratify the nominations. The Equal Rights faction revolted. They voted down the proposed nomination of Isaac Varian, a mayoral hopeful and the newly chosen chairman. Before the meeting could be reorganized, the Democrats left the building and turned off the gas, leaving the assembly hall and the Equal Rights faction plunged into darkness.

However, the trick must have been anticipated, because everyone was prepared, carrying with them a can-dle and a self-lighting match, or "loco foco," and the group proceeded to work by candlelight and ratify a ticket featuring candidates who reflected the agenda of the Equal Rights faction. The next day, the Equal Rights men were dubbed "Locofocos," by the press (a name afterward applied by the Whigs to the entire Democratic Party). In 1936, the group reorganized itself as an official party and pushed forth with their opposition of the chartering of state banks and other forms of monopoly and exclusive privilege, as well as their advocacy of the suspension of paper money and legal protection for labor unions. In November 1936, they elected two of their representatives to the state assembly, which was a significant victory for a "fringe" party. The Locofocos was never a national party, nor did it intend to be a permanent one; rather the politicians wanted to shift the ideological center from the Tammany Democrats and to mainstream their platform. This agenda was largely realized after the Martin Van Buren administration adopted many of the Locofocos' policies, especially the fiscal ones. The Locofocos achieved one of their main goals in 1840 when Congress passed the Independent Treasury Act, which effected a separation of government and banking. By the beginning of the 1940s, the Locofocos were, for the most part, reintegrated into the Democratic Party.

As well as serving as an important example of successful intraparty dissent leading to progressive reform, the Locofocos movement would also contribute to the National Reform Association, organized in 1844, which consisted of the former members of the Workingmen's Party, the National Trades' Union, and the Locofocos. The National Reform Association carried on the project of advocating for progressive reforms in line with the Locofocos' ideals, such as federal homestead legislation to allow free settlement of the landless on public land and state adoption of the homestead exemption to preclude the seizure and sale of family farms for the nonpayment of debt. A sympathetic chronicle of the history of the Locofocos was recorded by their contemporary F. Byrdsall in *The History of the Loco-Foco, or Equal Rights Party*, published in 1842.

**SEE ALSO**

*Volume 1 Left:* Democratic Party; Civil Rights; Human Rights.
*Volume 2 Right:* Elitism; Conservatism.

**BIBLIOGRAPHY**

F. Byrdsall, *The History of the Loco-Foco, or Equal Rights Party* (Burt Franklin Publisher, 1965 reprint); G. Myers, *The History of Tammany Hall* (Best Books, 2001 reprint); A. Connable and E. Silberfarb, *Tigers of Tammany* (Holt, Rinehart, and Winston, 1970); M.R. Werner, *Tammany Hall* (Greenwood, 1970 reprint).

VERONICA DAVIDOV
NEW YORK UNIVERSITY

# Long, Huey (1893–1935)

HUEY LONG was a radical populist from the state of Louisiana who was determined to fight for the rights of the rural poor of his state. He took on big businesses, corporations, and Wall Street, determined to institute an economic system in which wealth was shared. Even though he was a Democrat, he famously broke allegiance from President Franklin Roosevelt, whom Long believed was failing the masses.

Long was born in Winnfield, Louisiana, and was the seventh of nine children. Long was a high school dropout, yet would later be accepted to Tulane University Law School. At Tulane, he received his law degree in just one year and returned to Winnfield to practice

*Huey Long was a liberal populist who is seen today as an alarmingly fascist demagogue by many historians.*

law. As a lawyer in Winnfield, he became known as a champion of the common people. Beginning in 1918, he embarked on his political career, which would culminate in his victorious gubernatorial campaign in 1928.

Long was governor of Louisiana from 1928 to 1932, and during that time was elected to the U.S. Senate in 1930. "Share Our Wealth" became the name of his political program, as it sought to lessen the gap between the rich and poor. Some of his recommendations included guaranteeing every family an income of $5,000 a year, while prohibiting any family from making over $1 million in a year. Under such a program he believed that "every man could be a king."

As governor, he built over 2,000 miles of paved roads and over 100 bridges for his state. Previously, Louisiana had only 300 miles of paved roads. He also instituted the state's first prison rehabilitation program and created an adult literacy program that greatly helped illiterate African Americans. This was an incredibly radical program considering the intensity of racism in Louisiana during the 1920s and 1930s. In addition, he ensured that every school child in Louisiana had free schoolbooks.

As a senator, he continued to push for his radical policies, including his restrictions on maximum family yearly incomes. He also supported policies that would give Depression-hit farmers bankruptcy privileges so they could keep their farms. It was as a senator that he turned his back on Roosevelt and began to support progressive Midwest Republicans.

Long was not free from criticism, though. Critics show how he selected family members for positions within the government. In addition, he was prone to giving state contracts to generous campaign donators. However, as Long admirers point out, these criticisms are not solely those of Long, but rather are in common with politicians both past and present.

Long always confidently believed that he would be elected president in the 1936 campaign, but he was never given the chance. On September 10, 1935, he died from gunshot wounds that he received two days earlier in Baton Rouge, Louisiana. His assailant, Carl Weiss, was a successful Louisiana doctor and son-in-law of one of Long's main adversaries. Long's sister recalled that his final words were "Don't let me die, I have so much to do."

No other politician has had a greater affect or made greater contributions to the political and social atmosphere of Louisiana than Long. His radical visions, and his implementation of these ideals, have yet to see their equal.

Long's ruthless machine politics in Louisiana and his publicity-seeking antics, such as "receiving" in his pajamas the ambassador from Germany, earned him many enemies. Some of his critics charged him with blending populist goals and dictatorial methods in a combination that resembled the careers of contemporary fascist dictators in Europe. When he joined with the right-wing Father Charles Coughlin in the Social Justice movement before his assassination, such charges gained further substance.

**SEE ALSO**

Volume 1 Left: Roosevelt, Franklin D.; Populism; Socialism. Volume 2 Right: Capitalism.

**BIBLIOGRAPHY**

Garry Boulard, Huey Long Invades New Orleans: The Siege of a City, 1934–1936 (Pelican Publishing Company, 1998); William Ivy Hair, The Kingfish and His Realm: Life and Times of Huey Long (Louisiana State University Press, 1997); Glen Jeansonne, Messiah of the Masses: Huey P. Long and the Great Depression (Longman, 1992).

DAVID W. MCBRIDE
UNIVERSITY OF NOTTINGHAM, UNITED KINGDOM

# Lovestone, Jay (1897–1990)

BORN JACOB LIEBSTEIN, he immigrated with his parents to the Lower East Side of New York City from Lithuania at age 10. At City College of New York, he was a student activist and a member of the Communist Party USA (CPUSA) from its inception in 1919. He was close to party leader Charles Ruthenberg and took over leadership of the party after Ruthenberg died. As leader of the CPUSA, he purged the Trotskyite followers of J.P. Cannon, who advocated a more "federal" communism, with autonomous national workers' movements rather than the centralized, Soviet-focused movement of the Leninist-Stalinist wing. Then in 1929, Lovestone himself was purged because he supported Nikolai Bukharin and the right-wing opposition, which wanted collectivization of industry and agriculture to progress more slowly in the Soviet Union.

The Lovestoneites were heretic communists because they called for collaboration among the classes, at least in the United States. They regarded America as an exceptional case, exempt from the capitalist economic laws that applied to the rest of the industrial world and the rest of the Communist Party. Their right-wing deviancy led to their expulsion in 1929. Ousted, the Lovestonites founded the Communist Party Opposition (CPO), which disappointed their expectations when it failed to draw more than a few hundred members. The CPO became the Independent Communist Labor League in 1939 and dissolved in 1941.

Lovestone turned to anti-communism, perhaps as early as the late 1930s but clearly by the end of World War II. He was a cofounder with Irving Brown of the Free Trade Union Commission (FTUC), also known as the American Institute for Free Labor Development (AIFLD), under the auspices of the American Federation of Labor (AFL). As head of the AFL-CIO Free Trade Union Committee, he was, in essence, foreign policy adviser to union president George Meany.

To an extent, the AFL-CIO was a covert arm of the U.S. foreign policy establishment through the AIFLD. The AIFLD operated from the position that the best way for working people to improve their lives was through collective bargaining, strong anti-communism, and cooperation with government and management. Irving Brown and Lovestone used the AIFLD to suppress the leftist unions in France and Italy after World War II. The need for funds to undermine the communist-led unions in Europe meant that Lovestone and Brown worked with gangsters and socialist and Catholic unionists.

The organization worked in Europe and Latin America to organize unions free of communist control. This occurred even before the establishment of the Central Intelligence Agency (CIA) in 1947. When the CIA came into being, Lovestone worked closely with it, using the FTUC as an intelligence-gathering organization and providing the CIA's counterintelligence chief, James Jesus Angleton, with information about communist labor union activity. Sources disagree about whether the Lovestone-Angleton relationship was one of equals—an independent FTUC assisting the CIA—or a matter of Lovestone being a subordinate, feeding information to the CIA. Either way, the arrangement persisted until the mid-1960s.

Some in the AFL-CIO disliked Lovestone. For instance, Victor Reuther, reputedly at one time on the CIA payroll himself, felt that the direction in which Lovestone led the AFL-CIO was tragic for international unionism. The context of Reuther's remarks is the AFL-CIO endorsement of the Vietnam War at a time when the membership and the movement were moving away from that support. At the same time as Reuther was reaffirming AFL-CIO support for the unpopular war, dissident auto workers from 14 countries were in Detroit, Michigan, to establish a different sort of unionism in the face of a globalizing world, one that sought to revitalize class solidarity.

Lovestone had undermined labor solidarity, and the dissidents sought to reestablish international unity. John Sweeney took over the AFL-CIO in 1995 and cut the budget of the International Affairs Department. And the AFL-CIO removed the long-standing anti-communist statement from its constitution. The AFL-CIO expelled Lovestone in 1974 when his CIA connections became known. Lovestone generated a Federal Bureau of Investigation file purportedly 5,700 pages long.

Lovestone was a private man who avoided the spotlight. He left that to more colorful colleagues such as Meany. His life was devoted to politics, both within the communist party and against it once he broke away. Although he was probably a sincere anti-communist, he also was a passionate intriguer, and it is arguable whether his love of intrigue or his dislike of communism was the more intense. His career is representative of the stifling of the communist labor movement by rigid doctrinal requirements, and by the antipathy of organized labor and the intelligence community to radical unionism.

## SEE ALSO

*Volume 1 Left*: Unions; Communism; Third International (Comintern); Cominform; Socialism.
*Volume 2 Right*: Capitalism; Hoover, J. Edgar.

## BIBLIOGRAPHY

Robert J. Alexander, *The Right Opposition* (Greenwood Press, 1981); Fred Hirsch, *An Analysis of Our AFL-CIO Role in Latin America or Under the Covers with the CIA* (n.p., 1974); Ted Morgan, *A Covert Life: Jay Lovestone, Communist, Anti-Communist and Spymaster* (Random House, 1999); Roy Rydell, "Jay Lovestone, an International Fink," www.pww.org/past-weeks-1999 (June 2004).

JOHN BARNHILL, PH.D.
INDEPENDENT SCHOLAR

# The Left

# M

## Malcolm X (1925–1965)

MALCOLM X is one of the most influential, important, and misunderstood civil rights leaders of all time. He became a prominent figure during the late 1950s and 1960s by preaching in northern American cities about the oppressive nature of institutional racism and the importance of black pride. He never received the acclaim of his peer, Martin Luther King, Jr., whose belief in nonviolence and civil disobedience were better received by white America, whereas Malcolm was accused of being a black militant who advocated violence, and thus instilled fear into the white masses. For African Americans in American cities, though, Malcolm became an icon whose message had more significance than King's movement.

Malcolm Little was born in Omaha, Nebraska, the son of Louise and Earl Little. His father was a Baptist preacher active in Marcus Garvey's Universal Negro Improvement Association. Growing up in Lansing, Michigan, Malcolm was introduced to racist attitudes at an early age. His father was killed in 1931, and much controversy persists as to whether he was killed by white supremacists. His mother, who could never come to terms with the death was eventually taken to a mental institution and her children were divided up by welfare agencies. Malcolm was sent to live with various foster families; he left school in the 8th grade and moved to Boston, Massachusetts, to live with his sister. In Boston, he became involved in petty crime, and in 1946 was sentenced to jail for burglary. It was while in jail that his life underwent a metamorphosis.

While in jail, he was introduced to the Black Muslim teachings of Elijah Muhammad and the Nation of Islam (NOI). When he left jail in 1952, he changed his name to Malcolm X to symbolize his abandonment of his slave name Little, and he entered the Nation of Islam organization. He officially became a minister of the NOI in November 1955, and his oratorical skills quickly elevated him as one of the Nation of Islam's most powerful and influential speakers. Malcolm spoke confidently and carefully, discussing how the white race continued to oppress the black race. He urged African Americans to embrace their heritage and to avoid becoming susceptible to such problems as alcoholism, drugs, and prostitution, which were not surprisingly uncommon in the poor inner-city ghettos. While King was influential throughout the South, Malcolm's message was embraced by inner-city African Americans, who faced different situations than southern, rural blacks.

Malcolm's criticism was not solely reserved for oppressive white treatment of African Americans, as he was very critical of certain black leaders whom he believed to be too passive. During Malcolm's early years as a speaker, King would be one of his primary targets, and he was greatly distressed by the famed March on

Washington, D.C., in 1963. He condemned the march as being organized by white politicians and for not calling enough attention to the problems of the black masses. He viewed King as being an "unwitting tool of white liberalism."

The year 1963 also marked the beginning of tensions between Malcolm and Muhammad. Some problems were a response to the amount of national attention that Malcolm was generating, as he was becoming a more prominent figure than the Nation of Islam. Further tension was caused by rumors of Muhammad's infidelities with his secretaries. What finally caused the relationship to sever, though, were comments that Malcolm made following the death of President John Kennedy, which went against Muhammad's directive for the Nation to remain silent on the subject. He was subsequently suspended from the Nation for 90 days, and during this time, his relationship with the Nation became nonreconcilable.

While apart from the NOI, Malcolm made his pilgrimage to Mecca, where his ideas underwent a slight transformation. He was around many white people whose attitudes helped to change his attitudes toward race relations, helping him to understand that positive relations between whites and blacks would best help to alleviate the problems of African Americans. At the same time, King was beginning to transform his policies as well, seeing many of the benefits and truths of what Malcolm had been advocating. Both influential leaders began to find a middle ground in their once contrasting ideas for ending black oppression. In June 1964, Malcolm announced the formation of the Organization of Afro-American Unity and immediately began to contact both King and other black civil rights groups to offer his assistance.

From 1963 onward, Malcolm received many threats on his life, most of which have been linked to the Nation of Islam. Nonetheless, he continued to speak out for his cause, both in America and abroad, where he was well received. On February 21, 1965, while giving a speech in Harlem's Audubon Theater, Malcolm was shot and killed by Talmadge Hayer, a black man in the audience. The Nation of Islam denied any connection with the death.

Malcolm's legacy remains as controversial as his life, and he has become a more prominent figure now than he ever was when alive. Black power and black pride were a lasting legacy of Malcolm, and can be seen by the formation of the Black Panthers following both his and King's assassinations. The Black Panthers helped to continue much of Malcolm's earlier beliefs, but like Malcolm, received negative attention, as they were associated with black militancy.

Although Malcolm was viewed by the white press simply as a militant, his ideology has defied classification by serious scholars. Some have viewed his support for nationalism as an extension of that essentially right-wing set of ideas; others have seen in some of his last statements an indication that he was beginning to broaden his critique of American society into one based on social and class concerns more typical of the left.

During the last years of his life, he worked on his autobiography with Alex Haley, which was published after his death and remains one of the most popular books on the civil rights movement. Movie director Spike Lee brought more mainstream attention with his biographical movie, *Malcolm X*, in the 1990s.

**SEE ALSO**
*Volume 1 Left:* Black Panthers; King, Martin Luther, Jr.; Civil Rights; Johnson, Lyndon B.
*Volume 2 Right:* Segregation; Muslim Brotherhood.

**BIBLIOGRAPHY**
Rodnell Collins, *Seventh Child: A Family Memoir of Malcolm X* (Carol Publishing Group, 1998); James Cone, *Malcolm & America: A Dream or a Nightmare* (Fount, 1993); William W. Sales, *From Civil Rights to Black Liberation: Malcolm X and the Organization of Afro-American Unity* (South End Press, 1994); Malcolm X, Alex Haley, ed., *The Autobiography of Malcolm X* (Ballantine Books, 1973).

DAVID W. MCBRIDE
UNIVERSITY OF NOTTINGHAM, UNITED KINGDOM

# Maoism

AFTER A BLOODY split in April 1927, Chiang Kai-shek of the Kuomintang, or Nationalist Party, ruling China broke with his allies in the Communist Party. He launched a series of "extermination" campaigns that gradually were destroying the communists and their Red Army. At that time, Wang Ming, the leader of the Communist Party, had been discredited when he had fled for his life to the Soviet Union in January 1931. Within China, the de facto leader of the party became Mao Zedong, who had become involved in progressive

*Chinese political prisoners, many of whom were labeled as spies, subversives, or traitors, are assembled for sentencing by Communist Party leaders in the early 1950s. Maoism put a high price on disloyalty to the changing nature of the revolution.*

politics while still a student at the First Normal School of Hunan in 1912, the year the Chinese Republic had been proclaimed by Sun Yat-sen. In October 1934, Mao and the communists set out upon their epic Long March to ultimate safety in Shanxsi.

At a critical moment in the Long March in January 1935, after heavy casualties, Mao won an important meeting at Zunyi, which established him as leader of the communists in China. Finally, by the time they finally reached Shanxsi province in the north in the autumn of 1935, little more than a tenth of those who had set out were still alive. But they had reached the sanctuary of the north, remote mountains and difficult terrain where they could regroup and launch new offensives. In December 1935, the Red Army was refreshed enough to march to Yenan where, for 11 years, Mao made his military base.

It was there in the caves at Yenan that Mao formulated the ideology that could be described as Maoism—the authentic voice of Chinese Communism. The relationship with the peasantry became the cornerstone of the Maoist world view—not that China lacked a working proletariat as had revolutionary Russia. Indeed, the Chinese Revolution had begun with workers' risings in Wuchang and Hankow. Indeed, Mao viewed the working proletariat as already radicalized, and thus an important ally of the Communist Party in awakening the peasantry. A major influence in Mao's thought was the "revolutionary literature" of China's past, including his favorite, *The Romance of the Three Kingdoms*.

In all of these tales, revolutionary bandits rebelling against unjust emperors had survived, and sometimes triumphed, with the help of the peasants who, in 1935, were still in the vast majority of China's population.

Indeed, they still are in 2004. Mao had astutely observed the alienation among the peasants that had accompanied the rampages of the armies of the warlords, like Chang Tso-lin, who had surrendered Beijing to Chiang in 1928. Mao realized correctly that if he were to win out against the superior Kuomintang forces of Chiang, he had to win the loyalty of the peasant masses. Chiang, of course, remained in power largely due to extortionate tax-gathering among the peasants.

As early as March 1926, Mao had written, "poor peasants [who] possess neither adequate farm implements or funds ... are among the most hard—pressed of the peasants, and very receptive to revolutionary agitation." Furthermore, "farm laborers find themselves the most oppressed in the villages, and hold a position in the peasant movement as important as the poor peasants." He saw potential allies already in those peasants he called the lumpen peasants—those who had lost everything and had formed gangs outside the Chinese economy. He wrote, "able to fight very bravely but apt to be destructive, they can become a revolutionary force if properly guided."

## THE RED ARMY

Much of Mao's time was spent in setting out what he thought would be the proper way for the Chinese Communists' Red Army to interact with the peasants. In giving conditions for a successful counteroffensive, Mao wrote that the first condition is that the "people give active support to the Red Army ... the first constitutes the most important condition for the Red Army." He would also declare that "the Red Army, though small, has great fighting capacity, because its men under the leadership of the Communist Party have sprung from the agrarian revolution and are fighting for their own interests, and because officers and men are politically united."

It was not hard to contrast the lot of the soldiers in the Kuomintang armies, who were brutalized by their officers, had their salaries stolen, and were forced to subsist on poor rations because the money apportioned to supply them went into the pockets of their commanders. Thus, as Mao wrote in December 1936 in Yenan, sometimes the best allies of the Red Army were the soldiers of the Kuomintang, who supplied them readily with weapons and would desert if possible. The Western powers delivered the best weapons they could to Chiang to help defeat the communists.

Mao wrote, "our basic directive is to rely on the war industries of the imperialist countries and of our enemy at home ... [the weaponry] is to be delivered to us by the enemy's own transport corps. This is the sober truth, not a joke."

Another important part of Maoism was a program of personal examination, either in an individual setting or in a communist group therapy session. While often used as a symbol of communist brutality in interrogations in the Korean War, it actually was grounded in Mao's thoughts on "remaking" citizens into communists. Indeed, according to Anne Freemantle, Li Lisan, historically the first major communist leader in China, was forced to resign from the ruling Central Committee of the party in September 1930 for ideological deviation from the party "line." However, he was readmitted to the Central Committee at the Seventh Party Congress in 1945, upon "rectifying" his mistakes. Such tactics were also used on former Kuomintang soldiers, according to Mao. "The Red Army is like a furnace," he wrote in November 1928, "in which all captured soldiers are melted down and transformed the moment they come over."

The Japanese had invaded China, occupying Manchuria in 1931–32 and turning it into the puppet kingdom of Manchukuo. Now, five years later, they began their attempt at taking over all the country. Chiang Kai-shek remained steadfast in his determination that the communists—not the Japanese who were invading and raping China—were his real enemy. Mao and the communists, however, retained hope in the United Front idea, which had proven to work well during the life of Sun Yat-sen.

Mao's philosophy served to give energy to the fight against the Japanese. Theodore H. White and Annalee Jacoby wrote in *Thunder out of China* how if "you present the peasant with an army and a government that help him ... he votes for that party, thinks the way that party wants him to think, and in many cases becomes an active participant." The United Front was already under severe strain before Japan would surrender in September 1945. Chiang kept some of his best Kuomintang divisions out of the war as a strategic reserve with which to resume the war against the communists.

## FROM THE PAST

A key part of Mao's strategy was also derived from China's past: an intimate knowledge of the famous *Art of War* by Sun Tzu, the Sun Tzu Ping Fa. As General Tao Hanzhang wrote in *Sun Tzu's Art of War: the Modern Chinese Interpretation*, many of the commanders of the Red Army, now formally the People's Liberation

Army, made use of the 6th-century classic, "under the guidance of Mao Zedong's military strategies."

After World War II ended, hostilities broke out again between the Communist Party and the Kuomintang, with the United States supporting the Kuomintang. However, no amount of foreign assistance could stop the massive defections from the Kuomintang or the Communist advance. In October 1949, Mao, with his eye on China's past, proclaimed the Communist People's Republic at the Imperial Tiananmen Square in Beijing. With all China conquered, Mao used his philosophy as the ideological foundation to rebuild a country that had not known peace since the first Chinese revolution of the 20th century in 1911. Into the 1950s, the period was characterized by efforts to achieve industrialization, collectivization of agriculture, and political centralization.

The First Five-Year Plan stressed the development of heavy industry on the Soviet model. Soviet economic and technical assistance was expected to play a significant part in the implementation of the plan, and technical agreements were signed with the Soviets in 1953 and 1954. For the purpose of economic planning, the first modern census was taken in 1953; the population of mainland China was shown to be 583 million, a figure far greater than had been anticipated.

Among China's most pressing needs in the early 1950s were food for its burgeoning population, domestic capital for investment and purchase of Soviet-supplied technology, capital equipment, and military hardware. To satisfy these needs, the government began to collectivize agriculture. Despite internal disagreement as to the speed of collectivization, which at least for the time being was resolved in Mao's favor, preliminary collectivization was 90 percent completed by the end of 1956.

## HUNDRED FLOWERS CAMPAIGN

In addition, the government nationalized banking, industry, and trade. Private enterprise in mainland China was virtually abolished. By 1956, Mao felt strong enough politically to launch the Hundred Flowers Campaign, in which he attempted to bring the country's intellectuals into the party camp as they had been in the days of the 1919 May Fourth Movement.

However, rough criticism of the party caused him to curtail the experiment and launch his Anti-Rightist campaign. In 1958, the Second Five Year Plan was announced as the Great Leap Forward, with the goals of fostering industrial growth and promoting industrializa-

tion. Yet, as the Library of Congress study wrote, "The Great Leap Forward was an economic failure. In early 1959, amid signs of rising popular restiveness, the CCP admitted that the favorable production report for 1958 had been exaggerated."

## CULTURAL REVOLUTION

By 1961, in fact, Mao had begun to lose power in the party to those who took a more rightist view of development, including Liu Shaoqi, and Deng Xiaoping. Yet Mao, having survived the political crisis during the Long March, struck back with the Socialist Educational Movement, taking strength from the generation of young Chinese who had grown up under communism. Mao opened the Great Cultural Revolution, in which he used young Red Guards to wrest back control of the country from the rightists. Deng was imprisoned, and his son was killed.

Soon, almost all Chinese youth seemed to be carrying the "Little Red Book," the *Quotations from Chairman Mao Zedong*. His policy, as chosen from selected quotations from his earlier works, put the revolutionary fervor into a new generation. "Our point of departure," he declared, "is to serve the people whole-heartedly and never for a moment divorce ourselves from the masses … the organs of the state must practice democratic centrism, they must rely on the masses and their personnel must serve the people."

In an evolution of the self-criticism that had begun at Yenan, urban workers and professors were sent out into the countryside to work with the toiling peasants. However, the program became unstable and seemed to be heading toward anarchy. The People's Liberation Army was called in to stabilize the situation but, as the Library of Congress recorded, "The radical tide receded somewhat beginning in late 1967, but it was not until after mid-1968 that Mao came to realize the uselessness of further revolutionary violence. Liu Shaoqi, Deng Xiaoping, and their fellow 'revisionists' and 'capitalist roaders' had been purged from public life by early 1967, and the Maoist group had since been in full command of the political scene."

By 1969, relations with the Soviet Union had deteriorated to the point that war almost erupted along the disputed Ussuri River. Mao, feeling confident in power again, made the last great gamble of his career. Using a political fluidity only seen among communist leaders in Lenin, Mao began normalization of relations with the United States. The process was greatly facilitated by Edgar Snow, Mao's old friend. Snow, an American jour-

Thus, political stability returned to China—Mao's last act as the country's Great Helmsman. In September 1976, Mao died, leaving a mixed legacy behind him. The "long march" to communism after 1949 had brought great suffering to the Chinese people in the Great Leap Forward, yet it had continued the economic modernization of China that has made it—as in the days of Manchu glory—the greatest power in Asia. What Mao wrote in 1945 might stand as an epitaph for himself and his ideology: "we stand for self-reliance. We hope for foreign aid but cannot depend on it; we depend on our own efforts, on the creative power of the whole army and the entire people."

**SEE ALSO**

*Volume 1 Left:* Deng Xiaoping; Soviet Union; China.
*Volume 2 Right:* China; Capitalism.

**BIBLIOGRAPHY**

U.S. Library of Congress Country Studies, "China," www.lcweb2.loc.gov (July 2004); Stuart R. Schramm, ed., *Quotations from Chairman Mao Zedong* (Bantam Books, 1972); Franz Schurman and Orville Schell, *Imperial China, Republican China, and Communist China* (Vintage, 1967); General Tao Hanzhang, translated by Yuan Shibing, *Sun Tzu's Art of War: The Modern Chinese Interpretation* (Sterling, 1990); Anne Freemantle, *Mao Zedong: An Anthology of his Writings* (Mentor Books, 1962); Winberg Chai, *Essential Works of Chinese Communism* (Bantam, 1972); C.P. Fitzgerald, *The Birth of Communist China* (Penguin Press, 1952); Harold R. Isaacs, *The Tragedy of the Chinese Revolution* (Stanford University Press, 1951); Don Lawson, *The Eagle and the Dragon: The History of US-China Relations* (Crowell, 1985); OTN, "Long March Was the Making of Mao," www.megastories.com (July 2004).

JOHN F. MURPHY, JR.
AMERICAN MILITARY UNIVERSITY

*Mao Zedong institutionalized his Marxist-Leninist beliefs in a cult of personality, Maoism, that repeatedly transformed Chinese society.*

nalist, had visited Mao in Yenan and had written *Red Star over China*, which had made Mao and the Communists known to thousands of Americans.

In September 1972, President Richard M. Nixon visited the People's Republic and in the Shanghai Agreement recognized the People's Republic as the authentic Chinese state, leaving the Kuomintang regime in offshore Taiwan in a political limbo. In April 1973, Deng Xiaoping was brought back to power in China.

# Marcuse, Herbert (1898–1979)

HERBERT MARCUSE was a German-born social philosopher and political activist. One of the founders of a school of critical social thought in the first half of the 20th century, he became famous during the tumultuous period of the 1960s and early 1970s as the "father" of the New Left movement, inspiring student radicals and other groups to advocate revolutionary social change. The aging professor (he was 70 years old in

1968, at the height of the protest era) became the unlikely intellectual guru to number of young radical groups such as the Students for a Democratic Society (SDS), a group that brought about many changes in the socially turbulent 1960s. To the disdain of the conservative establishment, he introduced his young followers to the idea of the Marxist-inspired possibility of revolutionary change through a concerted collective effort to resist the oppressive forces of society, an effort he referred to as the Great Refusal.

Marcuse was born in Berlin and educated in Germany. After World War I, in which he served with the German army, he received his Ph.D. in literature and worked for a short period as a bookseller. Marcuse possessed a desire to expand his knowledge of philosophy so he enrolled in studies at Freiburg University under the renowned philosopher Martin Heidegger. Soon afterward, he joined the Institute for Social Research at Frankfurt. Marcuse also joined the faculties at the institute's branches in Geneva, Switzerland, and at Columbia University in the United States. He worked with other social philosophers such as T.W. Adorno and Max Horkheimer on what came to be known as the Critical Theory of Society, or the Frankfurt School of thought. This perspective involved an examination of society using a Marxist foundation but also focused on cultural phenomena and the active participation of individuals to promote social change.

Marcuse drew heavily on the work of social philosophers Karl Marx, G.W.F. Hegel, and his own mentor, Heidegger. In the late 1920s and early 1930s, he published a number of works (essays and a book) that provided critical examinations of the works of these philosophers. Shortly after the Nazi takeover in Germany in 1933, Marcuse fled to Geneva and later to New York, continuing his employment with the Frankfurt Institute for Social Research. In 1933, Marcuse published the first major review of Marx's recently published *Economic and Philosophical Manuscripts* of 1844 and devoted himself to studying Marxist philosophy.

In 1941, Marcuse joined the U.S. Office of Strategic Services (OSS) and later worked with the State Department. It was also in 1941 that he published his ideas on critical theory in a work called *Reason and Revolution*, his first work in English. Marcuse continued his work with the institute at Columbia University, developing his philosophical theory. He also maintained his position with the U.S. government until the early 1950s. In 1955, Marcuse published the highly influential *Eros and Civilization: A Philosophical Inquiry into Freud*. In this work, he applied Marxist thought to the work of psychoanalyst Sigmund Freud. Using the position on social repression found in Freud's *Civilization and Its Discontents* as a point of debate, Marcuse described the potential of individuals to abolish the constraints of repression to lead lives of liberation and fulfillment in areas such as satisfactory work lives, sexual freedom, and leisure time. His somewhat radical notions and underlying critique of society in *Eros and Civilization* garnered the attention of many people (with both positive and negative reactions) and laid the groundwork of the controversial theoretical perspective that would gain him notoriety.

In 1958, Marcuse joined the faculty at Brandeis University where he became a distinguished and inspirational professor. He also published *Soviet Marxism* that year, a critical study of the Soviet form of socialism, using information that he had gathered during his government employment. In 1964, he published what is probably his best-known work, *One-Dimensional Man: Studies in the Ideology of Advanced Industrial Society*. In this book, which has a notably more pessimistic tone than its predecessors, Marcuse provided a critical examination of society and warned of the growing threat of unchecked technology and capitalistic corruption. He warned of a type of collective conformist ideology (one-dimensional thought) in which people blindly followed the dictates of an overly materialistic, media-driven social system. *One-Dimensional Man* gained Marcuse international recognition, along with much criticism from conservatives and a growing fan base among the new radical groups in America and Europe, especially college students alienated by the social conditions created by racial disharmony, gender oppression, the Vietnam War, and the widening gap between generations.

Marcuse accepted a professorship at the University of California at San Diego after Brandeis University refused to renew his contract. Despite his advancing age, he remained very politically active and spent much time promoting his ideas to student radicals. He became increasingly concerned about environmental issues and how those issues are closely related to human aggression and especially referenced the situation in the Vietnam War. During the 1970s, his attention also turned to feminism and to the efforts to promote gender equality. In addition to his activism, he continued to publish books and essays articulating his critical approach in such works as *Repressive Tolerance* (1965), *Negations* (1968), *An Essay on Liberation* (1969), and *Counterrevolution and Revolt* (1972). The "father" of the New Left retired from the University of California in the 1970s and died in 1979, the year that his last book, *The Aesthetic Dimension,* was published.

**SEE ALSO**

*Volume 1 Left:* New Left; Vietnam War; Feminism; Socialism; Marx, Karl; Environmentalism.
*Volume 2 Right:* Vietnam War; Capitalism.

**BIBLIOGRAPHY**

Joan Alway, *Critical Theory and Political Possibilities* (Greenwood, 1995); Maurice Cranston, ed., *The New Left* (The Library Press, 1971); Douglas Kellner, "Herbert Marcuse," www.gseis.ucla.edu (April 2004); Douglas Kellner, "Marcuse, Liberation, and Radical Ecology," www.gseis.ucla.edu (April 2004); Herbert Marcuse, *One-Dimensional Man: Studies in the Ideology of Advanced Industrial Society* (Beacon, 1991 reprint).

LEONARD A. STEVERSON, PH.D.
SOUTH GEORGIA COLLEGE

# Market Socialism

MARKET SOCIALISM DESCRIBES a range of models of political economy that combine aspects of free markets with elements of socialism. The necessary philosophical and political basis of market socialism is the belief that neither capitalism nor socialism is adequate or viable. While the dignity of human choice and autonomy is inherent in the free market principle, unregulated economies produce unjustifiable inequalities and injustices. Therefore, some collective standard of provision and guaranteed quality of life must modify and limit those very freedoms that permit choice. However, bureaucratic and centralized structures (associated with 20th-century command economies) are too domineering, inefficient, and restrictive of human freedom.

Market socialism is something of a compromise between the authoritarian excesses of a command economy and the cold injustices of an entirely free market. The historical genesis of market socialist ideals is the period of the late Cold War. Radical critics in both the west and the former communist world searched for models that rejected the worst features of capitalism—waste, greed and exploitation in the workplace and the marketplace—while retaining the attractive elements of relative economic prosperity, freedom, and consumer choice. The old models of socialism as they existed in Eastern Europe, the Soviet Union, and China were un-

acceptably authoritarian and rigid. Against capitalism, market socialism identifies the waste, inequality, workplace alienation, sexism, racism and environmental despoliation that are the normal, if not always inevitable, concomitants of an entirely unregulated free market. Against communist-style command economies, market socialists point to the oppressive controls, the bureaucratically driven waste, the overproduction of cheap and unwanted goods, the absence of innovation, and the dullness and indignities of life in a consumer market without freedom of choice. Too much power is placed in the hands of bureaucrats, managers, and producers.

In a market socialist political economy, freedom of market choice is combined with public regulation and the provision of certain goods and services through the state or nonprofit organizations. The principal manufacturing and resource industries might be under public control and/or ownership. Public enterprises could include the principal utilities, transportation networks, major manufacturers, and resource extractive industries.

The market socialist economy also advocates the widespread employment of workers cooperatives, a powerful degree of democratic decision making in private corporations, with codetermination (workers sitting on corporate boards) and profit sharing. This is a challenging structure, in that cooperatives do not respond in the same way as private corporations to market signals from without or organizational imperatives from within. Those who advocate market socialism recognize that the challenges of keeping cooperatives lean and responsive are substantial.

The characteristic fiscal strategy of market socialism places strong emphasis on redistributive and progressive taxation. Attention is paid to maintaining full employment, and inflation is controlled through measures of wage and price regulation. There is a strong welfare state and guaranteed provision of basic services from cradle to grave. Moreover, the collective provision of housing, health, safety-net support, education, and age-related needs is not incompatible with the development of strong voluntary networks of community activism in these fields.

Market socialism includes a measure of corporatism at the national and local levels (an arrangement in which the leading economic organizations in society are represented directly in the heart of government) and powerful state regulation of economic externalities. Democratic involvement, with citizens' forums and other consultative bodies, further shapes the decisional architecture of the state.

There may also be strong trends toward decommodification via strategic planning to reward successful enterprises and nurture poor ones back to economic health. If markets are to be taken seriously, the economic system must allow for risk and failure and for the closing down of inefficient or unresponsive enterprises. Holding companies could receive investment capital from various sources and then lend it at reasonable rates to promising enterprises. Risks and benefits might thereby be better socialized than in a purely capitalist economy. A market socialist economy can also promote choice and diversity in ways that meet the needs of its citizens and do so in ways that are currently difficult to achieve. In the field of media, for example, investment decisions might be structured so as to stimulate smaller and more specialized publications, web sites and programs.

On an individual level, there would be a substantial level of consumer choice, and market socialism incorporates modest and controlled incentives and disincentives with respect to reward for talent, risk and effort.

Market socialism is an ideal that has been more adequately theorized than realized in practice. Nonetheless, in the Cold War era and its aftermath, there were some limited variants of market socialism in both communist and capitalist countries. While the Swedish welfare state might better be described as fundamentally capitalist with social democratic characteristics, its commitment to social equality, rational planning, and income solidarity shares certain characteristics of market socialism. In many ways, the Swedish model comes closest in the real world to the abstract principles of market socialism. Further reforms to the Swedish model (those associated in particular with socially progressive and rational investment strategies and the decommodification of privately held capital) would prompt further developments along market socialist lines in Sweden.

In the current political economic environment, however, there is evidence that Sweden is turning away from market socialist principles rather than further embracing them. In the post-Stalinist world, a number of communist regimes experimented with marketization and decentralization of command economies. In the early 1950s, Marshal Tito's Yugoslavia broke with the Soviet Union, and in so doing implemented a cooperative system of decentralized planning and self-management, based upon Workers' Councils. A version of market socialism was also attempted in Hungary from the 1960s to the 1980s in the "New Economic Mechanism." However, neither it nor Soviet leader Mikhail Gorbachev's *perestroika* (liberalization) initiatives were sufficient to make the break from central command and control.

Following the Maoist era in Chinese politics, Deng Xiaoping's reforms of the late 1970s marshalled in a "socialist market economic system" that has been progressively decentralizing, marketizing, deregulating, and privatizing the Chinese economy. While contemporary China has been characterized by more open markets and less state control of the economy, the authoritarian state apparatuses have continued to dominate and little has been done to protect workers from alienation, exploitation and unequal opportunities. Therefore, China cannot be said to be a functioning market socialist regime.

### SEE ALSO

*Volume 1 Left:* Political Economy; Social Democracy; Socialism; Communism.
*Volume 2 Right:* Capitalism; *Laissez-Faire.*

### BIBLIOGRAPHY

N. Scott Arnold, *The Philosophy and Economics of Market Socialism: A Critical Study* (Oxford University Press, 1994); Jon Elster and Karl Ove Moene, eds., *Alternatives to Capitalism* (Cambridge University Press, 1989); Julian Le Grand and Saul Estrin, *Market Socialism* (Clarendon Press, 1989); David Miller, *Market, State and Community: Theoretical Foundations of Market Socialism* (Clarendon Press, 1990).

PAUL NESBITT-LARKING, PH.D.
HURON UNIVERSITY COLLEGE , CANADA

# Marx, Karl (1818–1883)

KARL MARX IS ARGUABLY one of the most influential persons of the modern historical era. Few other persons than Marx have had such a profound impact on the thought and actions of people, particularly national governments. It is with social philosophy and social theories that Marx has had his greatest effect, and even in the 21st century, he is still very much a champion of the political left and a source of derision for the political right.

Born in Trier, Germany, into a Jewish family headed by lawyer Hershel Marx (later renamed Heinrich Marx due to anti-Semitism), Marx was locally educated and was noted at his school for being a student of excellence. His senior school thesis, for example, entitled "Religion: The Glue That Binds Society Together," received a school prize. In 1833, Marx left school but continued his education and entered the University of Bonn to study law, but he was transferred by his father in the following year to Friedrich-Wilhelms-Universität in Berlin (now known as Humboldt University) due its perceived better atmosphere for study. Apparently, Marx had enjoyed the social life in Bonn a bit too much. However, to his father's dismay, Marx began to acquire an interest away from law while studying in Berlin, most notably in philosophy, particularly after joining a student/professor group called Young Hegelians, which group held strong opinions about the history, development, and future of Prussian society and included philosopher Bruno Bauer.

Bauer, a mentor of Marx, was to influence the young Marx by introducing to him the writing of philosopher G.W.F. Hegel, a professor who had worked in Berlin who had a major influence on academic thought at that time in Germany, particularly with regard to the evolution of historical process and dialectics (a way of understanding thoughts, actions, emotions, materialism, and so on). Due to his associations with this somewhat radical group, Marx was advised not to submit his doctoral thesis in Berlin as it might be poorly received by the conservative authorities, and, as a consequence, Marx submitted his work at the University of Jena in 1840.

Upon graduating, Marx returned to Bonn where he hoped to establish a career as an academic and to use Bauer's name to assist in the process of finding work. The need for work was heightened by his financial support being cut due to his father's death, and the years from 1840 to 1842 were a financial struggle for Marx. However, in 1842 events took a turn as Bauer was removed from the philosophy faculty. Marx, as a consequence, sought work outside of academic fields, in the field of journalism, and he quickly found employment as an editor of a radical magazine in Cologne, *Rheinische Zeitung*, despite his social leaning being too radical for many would-be employers. Through his journalistic abilities, Marx quickly received acclaim.

His article on the freedom of the press was well received in liberal circles in Cologne and subsequently he was promoted to editor of the journal. Under the guidance of Marx, the *Rheinische Zeitung* took a more radical perspective, in part due to frequent contact with Moses Hess, a self-proclaimed socialist. This led to problems of censorship with the authoritative Prussian government, and ultimately the closure of the journal

in January 1842 after the printing of Marx's article on the poverty of farmers in the Mosel Valley. Given warning that he may be arrested for his views and publishing activities, Marx quickly married girlfriend Jenny von Westphalen and escaped to Paris, France.

During his stay in Paris, Marx's life began to change as a result of a number of significant events: First, Marx began to socialize with working-class people for the first time; second, by mixing with working people, he began to witness at first hand the lives of people in conditions of poverty; third, he became the editor of a new political journal, *Franco-German Annals*, which gave him a platform to express his thoughts on broad matters such as philosophy, politics, and society at large; fourth, for the first time he came into contact with Friedrich Engels, the author of the classical work on laboring people in Manchester, England, *The Condition of the Working Classes in England in 1844*; fifth, Marx began to describe himself as a communist.

Similar to his life in 1840s Germany, Marx courted controversy in France. While editing the *Franco-German Annals*, he upset the journal's owner, Arnold Ruge, by writing a article on capitalism and also managed to get the journal banned in Germany due to its radical nature. However, as problems appeared in some areas of his life in Paris, other parts of his life bloomed, particularly due to his social and working activities with Engels. Upon discovering that he and Engels shared similar opinions regarding capitalism and other "theoretical fields," Marx began to write with Engels. The pair complemented each other to an incredible extent: Marx was able to work on his philosophical concepts, Engels had the ability to write them in a manner understandable to the wider audience. But again controversy arose while Engels and Marx worked on their first article, "The Holy Family," due to pressure from the Prussian government to expel Marx from France.

In January 1845, Marx was served with a deportation order and moved to Brussels, Belgium, the country with the greatest freedom of expression in Europe at that time. Living off money given to him by the royalties from Engels's 1845 book, Marx continued to write and concurrently the friendship with Engels grew stronger. In 1845, he visited Engels in England for the first time, staying in Manchester and London for more than a month. During the visit, he met with a number of political exiles and leaders of the left including George Harney, leader of the Chartists (a workers' movement). Upon the conclusion of his stay he returned to Brussels to finish *The German Ideology*, in which he began to examine the notion of human action as being fundamental to the development of history. Despite enjoying the freedoms of Belgium, Marx was unable to find a publisher for his work.

By early 1846, Marx established the Communist Correspondence Committee with the intention of bringing together all of Europe's socialist leaders. While this aim was never fulfilled, in London, socialists held a conference, and in so doing established the Communist League. Marx likewise established a similar organization in Brussels and in December 1847 he returned to London to attend a Communist League meeting. At this meeting, the Communist League changed its aims to overthrowing the bourgeoisie (capitalist class) and removing class antagonisms from society. Again, on returning to Brussels, Marx continued his writing. Using Engels's *The Principles of Communism* for inspiration, he and Engels began one of the most radical and influential books of the modern age, *The Communist Manifesto* (published February 1848). The impact of this book in the 19th century and beyond cannot be underestimated, for even decades later it helped inspire the Bolsheviks in Russia to overthrow the Tzar in 1917. The *Communist Manifesto* has maintained legendary status.

The central element of *The Communist Manifesto* is based on the relationship between two social groups, the bourgeoisie (the middle-class factory owners) and the proletariat (the laboring class). In Marxist thinking, the bourgeois have not only access to the means of production but they are both property-owning and exploitive in nature. The proletariat, on the other hand, are denied access to the means of production by the bourgeois, and it is with the work of Engels and Marx that attention was first given to the particular relationship—between who owns and who does not own the means of production and how that ownership affects social conditions

It is important to note that while his ideas are heavily revered they are also heavily criticized in many quarters: later interpretations of Marx's work (many hardly resembling Marx's original theses) have led to totalitarian communist states and numerous wars. Many people around the world have suffered at the hands of Marxists, that is, followers of Marxism. In simple terms, Marxism is the political ideas and social theories proposed by Marx. Famous followers include Edward Bernstein, Vladimir Lenin, Leon Trotsky, Josef Stalin, Max Horkheimer, Henryk Grossmann, and Mao Zedong. Yet, even a cursory historical analysis highlights that Marxism is a broad church of thought according to the perceived principles of these and other individuals.

Therefore, what is called Marxist and what Marx thought are often greatly different. Governments, for example, in the 20th and 21st centuries have often labeled themselves Marxist. Prominent examples include China, Cuba, and North Korea. But these labels are much like calling communist East Germany the German Democratic Republic (in reality, East Germany was the direct antithesis of a democratic republic).

Much attention has rightly been given to Marx due to the groundbreaking work of *The Communist Manifesto*. However, he also wrote another monumental piece, *Das Kapital* (1867), an economic criticism of capitalism originally penned in German. In this work, Marx focuses on the concept of surplus value and highlights that the fundamental injustice of capitalism is that it encourages employers to create profits at the expense of the employees. The economic theories outlined in *Das Kapital* influenced numerous followers and helped generate the science of economics. To economists, the name "Marx" has a wholly different meaning than it does to political scientists.

Marx died on March 14, 1883, and is buried in Highgate Cemetery, London, with a tombstone reading "Workers of all lands unite." In the years following his death, Engels edited and translated his work and in many ways continued their friendship beyond Marx's death. As a consequence, *Das Kapital* and other writing by Marx in German were translated by Engels into English. While Marx wrote a great deal about social and economic conditions endured by working populations during the 19th century, his legacy is still incredibly strong today in philosophical, sociological, and political thinking.

**SEE ALSO**

*Volume 1 Left:* Communism; Socialism; Soviet Union; China; Cold War.
*Volume 2 Right:* Capitalism; *Laissez-Faire.*

**BIBLIOGRAPHY**

Karl Marx, *Wage-Labour and Capital and Value, Price and Profit* (International Publishers, 1976); Karl Marx, *The Karl Marx Reader*, Robert Tucker, ed. (Friedrich Solutions, 1978); Karl Marx, *Capital: A Critique of Political Economy*, Ben Fowkes and J. M. Cohen, eds. (Penguin, 1992); J. Toews and F. Engels, *The Communist Manifesto and Selected Writings* (St. Martin's, 1999); David McClellan, ed., *Karl Marx, Selected Writing* (Oxford University Press, 2000).

IAN MORLEY
MING CHUAN UNIVERSITY, TAIWAN

# Marxist Humanism

DEFINING MARXIST Humanism is more than a linguistic task. It is a highly politicized task with important political implications. Marxist Humanism does not represent a single school of thought within Marxist scholarship nor does it enjoy a historical lineage that is either obvious or linear. A variety of philosophers have employed the term *Marxist Humanism*, or *Socialist Humanism*, to delineate a type of engagement with Marxist philosophy and post-Marxist theorists. These scholars have been as wide-ranging as Leszek Kolakowski, to Eric Fromm, Raya Dunayevskaya, the Yugoslav Praxis Group, and Chinese philosopher Wang Ruoshui—to name just a few.

The emergence of Marxist Humanism most directly corresponds to the appearance of a reinvigorated left in the 1960s across Western and Eastern Europe and North America. It does, however, also draw on the earlier works of a variety of post-Marx thinkers, such as Antonia Gramsci, Georg Lukács, Vladimir Lenin in his *Philosophic Notebooks*, and Herbert Marcuse on the first English translations of Marx's 1844 *Economic and Philosophic Manuscripts*. Importantly, those espousing a Marxist Humanist understanding of Marx's works also assert that a thorough understanding of Marx's use of the Hegelian dialectic, particularly in *Capital*, is key to recognizing the humanist content and revolutionary goal of Marx's critique of capitalism.

Although the philosophic and textual debates among those who draw upon the label "Marxist Humanism" is substantial, we can discern some common elements among the variety of approaches. First is the assertion that post-Marx Marxism, largely influenced by Stalinism, has become overly deterministic and reductionist. These so-called Orthodox Marxists draw heavily on Marx's economic theory but do not engage in either Hegelian dialectics or the notion that human subjectivity is itself the key to realizing revolutionary change. Second, Marxist Humanists dispute the notion that Marx's works can be divided as "early" Marxism, that is, Hegelian-influenced, and "late," that is, scientific or economic Marxism.

Instead, they assert that Marx's later works are strongly influenced by the Hegelian dialectic and, in Marx's own terms, advocate a "New Humanism." Finally, Marxist Humanists often reject vanguardism explicitly and instead focus on other subjectivities (for example, women's movements, youth movements, national liberation movements) as being important forces for realizing human emancipation.

Today, Marxist Humanism as both philosophic label and organization is most closely associated with the works of Raya Dunayevskaya. Drawing on Hegel's *Logic*, Lenin's *Notebooks*, and the *1844 Manuscripts*, Dunayevskaya asserted a humanist understanding of Marx's works in the early 1950s. In 1955, Dunayevskaya founded the News and Letters organization, which continues to publish a monthly newspaper and critically engages both world events and the international left from a perspective rooted in Dunayevskaya's writings on Marxist Humanism.

**SEE ALSO**

*Volume 1 Left:* Marcuse, Herbert; Praxis Group; Marx, Karl; Lenin, Vladimir I.; Stalin and Stalinism; Dunayevskaya, Raya. *Volume 2 Right:* Capitalism; Totalitarianism.

BIBLIOGRAPHY
Raya Dunayevskaya, *Philosophy and Revolution: From Hegel to Sartre, and from Marx to Mao* (Lexington Books, 1989); Leszek Kolakowski, *Toward a Marxist Humanism: Essays on the Left Today* (Grove Press, 1968); Herbert Marcuse, *Reason and Revolution: Hegel and the Rise of Social Theory* (Beacon Press, 1941); Gerson S. Sher, *Marxist Humanism and Praxis* (Prometheus Books, 1978).

SANDRA REIN
ATHABASCA UNIVERSITY

# Media Bias, Left

MOST PEOPLE believe the media are not objective or neutral. For example, one study found 90 percent of Americans believe reporters are influenced by their personal political views. The same media accused of being biased are responsible for reporting about the issue of media bias, one of the only institutions asked to be its own watchdog. Of those who believe the media is biased, the most frequent claim is that it leans left; in fact such claims outnumber claims of right bias four to one.

The loudest complaints about media bias have come from Republican politicians. Presidents as far back as Dwight Eisenhower have complained about the so-called liberal media. "Regular people," who are perceived by Americans as more credible than politicians, also seem to believe the media leans left. The argument that there is a liberal media includes more than just newspapers or television. Claims generally refer to the "seven sisters": television networks CBS, NBC, and ABC; newspapers the *New York Times* and the *Washington Post*; and news magazines *Time* and *Newsweek*. Some have also charged the entertainment media with leaning left as well. Sorting out which way the media leans is complicated by the fact that the terms *liberal, left, conservative,* and *right* are not clearly defined. Some people on the left feel many self-proclaimed liberals are actually more moderate than liberal.

The left generally responds to claims there is a liberal media that, in actuality, the media leans right. Although research generally shows that reporters describe themselves as liberals, the left asserts that those who own the media are much more important. In fact, there is really no consensus on whether journalists' beliefs are farther left than the general public. Some studies have shown that in regard to certain issues, including corporate interests and healthcare, journalists are more conservative than most. In general, journalists' beliefs seem to be more centrist than left. Regardless of their beliefs, while journalists may provide the labor, media owners have editorial control regarding what items are included in broadcasts and other media outlets.

Similarly, owners of entertainment media dictate what types of films are made and what types of television shows are aired. In entertainment media in particular, the profit motive drives action and skews coverage toward the conservative status quo. This is largely due to the importance of advertising, as executives cannot risk offending or dissatisfying advertisers with controversial content. Television programming is especially well suited to lean right because of its simple and quick style. It takes a great deal of time to delve into the complex concerns of the left, for example topics such as poverty, racism, sexism, and crime.

The left also points to the increased control of the media in a few hands in explaining why the media are more likely to be right-biased. There are more media outlets today than ever before, which would seem to offer the public greater diversity of opinion. Yet there are only six major companies that control what the public sees, hears, and reads: Time Warner, Disney, Viacom, General Electric, the News Corporation, and Bertelsmann. Each company owns a number of other companies, creating a very narrow flow of information. For instance, Rupert Murdoch's News Corporation owns: Fox Broadcasting Network; Fox Television, including over 20 U.S. stations and the largest station group reaching more than 40 percent of U.S. households; Fox News Channel; a major stake in several cable networks, including FX, Fox Sports Net, National Geographic Channel, and Fox Family Channel; film producers 20th Century Fox, 20th Century Fox International, 20th Century Fox Television, and 20th Century Fox Home Entertainment; more than 130 English-language newspapers, including the *London Times* and the *New York Post*; 25 magazines, including the widely read *TV Guide*; book publishers HarperCollins and Zondervan; Fox Interactive, News Interactive, and foxnews.com; Festival Records, and other nonmedia holdings, including the Los Angeles Dodgers baseball team.

Antonio Gramsci referred to the concentration of both resources and ideology in the hands of a few conservatives as hegemony. According to his theory of ideological hegemony, mass media are no more than a tool used by the ruling class to perpetuate their power, wealth, and status by spreading their own philosophy, culture, and morality. Other social groups having little or no access to the media cannot disseminate their viewpoints as easily, allowing for virtually complete ideological control by elites. Radical ideas typically only appear in underfinanced, noncommercial outlets, severely limiting the audience they reach. When far leftist viewpoints do appear in the mainstream media, it is often only to ridicule them.

Media can be biased in two primary ways; through emphasis and through omission. The left is concerned with the well-documented problems of race and gender bias in the media; both racial minorities and females suffer from undercoverage as well stereotypical emphasis. Historically, the media relied on stereotypes to attract the largest possible audience, thus they reinforced rather than challenged the attitudes of society. The left maintains stereotypical depictions and coverage emphasizing minorities are problems that remain. Studies show African Americans and Hispanics are still more likely to believe the media are biased in their coverage of race and ethnicity than whites, supporting the notion the media are skewed right.

Biased coverage is especially likely when a particular subgroup is perceived as a threat, as is the case with those of Middle Eastern heritage following the terrorist attacks of September 11, 2001. Even before September 11, coverage of Middle Easterners focused on terrorism, rich oil sheiks, and religious fundamentalism. Stories about African American criminals still dominate paper and television news coverage of crime. Blacks are still frequently portrayed in a negative light in entertainment media as well, often as criminals. Minstrelsy, or depicting whites in black face acting foolish, is not only a part of American history, but lives on in the depiction of African Americans as caricatures. For example, even

A news broadcast, such as above at WCPO in Cincinnati, Ohio, can be accused of left or right bias depending on the political perspective of the viewer. National broadcast media are perceived as liberal, while local broadcasts can be seen as conservative.

though Fox integrated more black perspectives in the mid-1980s into their programming, they did so using a white, conservative model. Topics that were "too black" were excluded, as were many black-centered dramas.

Native Americans are often portrayed as stoic warriors. News and entertainment coverage of Native Americans reinforces the notion that their cultures are almost dead, as current issues are rarely addressed and they are often depicted in traditional garb. Asian men are most often depicted as martial arts experts, while Asian women suffer from too-frequent portrayals as geishas.

News coverage of Asians reinforces they are the "model minority," overlooking the great diversity among Asians as well as the struggles they face in America. Despite the fact they are the largest and fastest-growing segment of the population, Hispanics are underrepresented and subject to stereotypical media coverage and portrayals as well. Hispanic men are often

seen as gangsters, while Hispanic women are too often depicted as sexually promiscuous.

Even media directed at children, such as Disney films, is not devoid of stereotypical coverage. A vast body of literature demonstrates that females and racial minorities are depicted in stereotypical fashion here as well. Even video games utilize racial and gender stereotyping. One study found heroes to be disproportionately white, with absolutely no Native American examples. Black characters are most often aggressive and Asians appeared as fighters.

Women in all media are portrayed as being in relationships rather than careers and as seeking romance more frequently than male characters on television and in film; in essence, the media stresses their domestic interests. The dominant ideology of gender coverage is patriarchal. Further, input in all types of media from females and racial and ethnic minorities is still limited. Studies have shown people of color are still underrepresented in newsrooms, and when they are given positions they are generally those with less power. In 2001, only 11.6 percent of employees at daily newspapers were nonwhite. Minorities are also underrepresented in TV news, in television programming, and in film, especially in decision making roles.

In addition, liberals point out that media pundits, both on television and radio, are almost exclusively conservative. The national television and print media·in particular is dominated by well-paid, upper-middle-class males whose politics are clearly right of center, giving the status quo a loud and expansive voice. Further, high-profile pundits who speak to a national audience often get large amounts of money for corporate appearances, making them unlikely to say anything that might alienate this lucrative source of funds. Most of the conservative pundits also reach millions through use of the internet.

The propensity to favor business and to promote a capitalist agenda further demonstrates the media's conservative bias. High incomes tend to be associated with conservative views, and while journalists are not paid as well as some professionals, those who work in Washington, D.C., and New York City fare pretty well. Polls demonstrate that journalists are generally supportive of corporations and are more sympathetic to free trade and globalization than most Americans. Similarly, the left points to the media's weak coverage of anti-war movements as further evidence of their slant to the right. The left argues conservatives, especially politicians, benefit from the claim there is a liberal bias. Even conservatives have admitted this is true. Merely asserting the claim serves to reduce the watchdog function of the media. The institutions revered by the right—the military, business, and organized religion—thus can often evade critique necessary for a functioning democracy. Additionally, conservative politicians have greatly benefited from the right bias of the media. For example, conservative radio talk show host Rush Limbaugh was integral in helping usher in a conservative Congress in 1994.

In sum, the media may not tell citizens what to think specifically, but they definitely guide what people think about. The left maintains that this guidance is in support of conservative beliefs and values, to the virtual exclusion of radical left viewpoints.

**SEE ALSO**
*Volume 1 Left:* Lippmann, Walter; Sinclair, Upton.
*Volume 2 Right:* Luce, Henry R.; *National Review*; Limbaugh, Rush; Coulter, Ann H.; Media Bias, Right.

**BIBLIOGRAPHY**
Eric Alterman, *What Liberal Media?* (Basic Books, 2003); Gail Dines and Jean Humez, eds., *Gender, Race, and Class in Media* (Sage Publications, 2003); Linda Holtzman, *Media Messages* (M.E. Sharpe, 2000); Yahya R. Kamalipour and Theresa Carilla, eds., *Cultural Diversity and the U.S. Media* (State University of New York Press, 1998); David Niven, *Tilt? The Search for Media Bias* (Praeger, 2002); Clint C. Wilson, Felix Gutierrez, and Lena Chao, *Racism, Sexism, and the Media* (Sage Publications, 2003).

LAURA L. FINLEY, PH.D.
INDEPENDENT SCHOLAR

# Mexico

THE POLITICAL AND SOCIAL development of Mexico, more than any other Latin American nation, has been shaped by the political left. The rise of the left, both radical and moderate, signaled the beginnings of a challenge to the hegemonic policies of a national elite in alliance with foreign capitalists. In the past 20 years, the left has challenged the legitimacy of the Mexican political system.

In seeking to explain the rise of the left in Mexico, the left's origins need to be carefully scrutinized and analyzed. In the early 20th century, Mexico underwent a social and political revolution. The goal of the revolution was to transform the exploitative social and political system, a system which had for centuries repressed the political demands of an urban proletariat and agricultural peasantry. Led by the middle class, the revolutionaries toppled the regime of Porfirio Diaz. Over the next seven years, the revolution would undergo phases.

In 1917, the different economic and political groups decided to write one of the most liberal and nationalistic constitutions in Latin America. Over the next 10 years, the left within the revolution assumed predominant power so that by the late 1920s, the political left, led by Alvaro Obregon, controlled the political and social system.

In 1934, one of the most leftist of the revolutionary leaders, Lazaro Cardenas, was selected to the presidency. Cardenas's policies, which have not been duplicated since, bordered for many on the political right as communistic. He nationalized a number of the most important economic sectors, including the petroleum industry. He nationalized the industry after a prolonged work stoppage by the oil workers' union against the exploitative practices in the oil field by Standard Oil. As a result, Cardenas was able to integrate the working-class unions and agricultural sectors into the main political party, the Revolutionary Institutional Party (PRI). The PRI ruled Mexico over the next 70 years, through World War II, the Cold War, and the post-Cold War period. The left had achieved, with its nationalism, hegemony within the political and economic sphere.

By 1988, the PRI had become an institution within the Mexican political system, essentially establishing a one-party state. The left within Mexico decided to act in a radical fashion. In 1988, the nation was slated for presidential elections. A former PRI senator and governor from the state of Michoacan, Cuauhtémoc Cardenas, decided to run for the presidency representing the leftist sectors of the political system who were vehement critics of the one-party rule of the PRI.

Organized as the FDN (National Democratic Front), Cardenas campaigned for the presidency against the PRI candidate, Carlos Salinas de Gortari. In the election results, Gortari claimed victory and was awarded the presidency. Cardenas and the left were astounded by the seeming corruption that the Gortaris victory symbolized. Essentially, Cardenas believed that the election had been stolen from him by the PRI. On May 5, 1989, spurred by his "loss," Cardenas and a host of left-of-center factions formed the Democratic National Party (PDN) to offer candidates at the national, state, and local positions.

The party essentially traces its political history to the influential Communist Party and Socialist Party that dominated the Mexican political left for decades. In the 1994 presidential election, Cardenas ran against the PRI candidate, Ernesto Zedillo, and lost the election. Cardenas and the left garnered 17 percent of the national vote and finished in third place. In 1997, Cardenas and the left were elected to the post that essentially served as mayor of Mexico City. However, it became evident that the left was losing its political base. Its socialist ideas were outdated in a modern world of globalization and transnational cooperations. In the elections of 2000, the left allied itself with the other opposition parties to finally rid Mexico of the corrosive PRI.

Allied with the conservative PAN's Vicente Fox, the opposition won the presidency. Cardenas ran and once again settled for third place. In this election, Cardenas also ran under an umbrella group called the Alliance for Mexico, which consisted of the leftist parties and moderate factions. Cardenas and the Alliance received 16 percent of the vote. In the Chamber of Deputies, the leftist PRD/APM garnered 95 seats while in the Senate, the PRD received 17 out of 128 total seats. Thus, the left in the Mexican political system decreased in power as the electorate became wary of radical change, which is the message that Cardenas and other leftists parties promoted. Moreover, the emergence of a militant, indigenous revolutionary group in the southern state of Chiapas also weakened the political support base of Cardenas and the left.

In 2000, a group of leftist revolutionaries started a military uprising. The group, the Zapatistas (EZLN) called for socialist revolution as well the government's recognition of indigenous rights in the southern state of Chiapas. Led by Subcomandante Marcos, the uprising made international headlines as the government sent in the military to unsuccessfully quell the rebellion. The left was virtually stunned by the revolution as for years, the PRD and Cardenas had represented the political ideals of the leftist movement. This changed as the media began to view the Zapatistas as the true descendants of the leftist and nationalistic revolution.

**SEE ALSO**

*Volume 1 Left*: Communism; Socialism; PRI (Mexico). *Volume 2 Right*: Mexico.

**BIBLIOGRAPHY**

John Mason Hart, *Revolutionary Mexico: The Causes and Process of the Mexican Revolution* (Berkley, 1996); W. Dirk Raat and William H. Beezeley, eds., *Twentieth Century Mexico* (University of Nebraska Press, 1986); Gilbert M. Joseph and Daniel Nugent, eds., *Everyday Forms of State Formation: Revolution and the Negotiation of Rule in Modern Mexico* (Duke University Press, 1994).

JAIME RAMÓN OLIVARES, PH.D.
HOUSTON COMMUNITY COLLEGE, CENTRAL

# Middle East

THE MODERN HISTORY of the Middle East begins with World War I, when the Ottoman Empire dissolved in October 1918. The Ottoman Turks had entered the war on the side of the Germans in October 1914. During the war, both Arabs and Jews had played significant roles in the victory of British General Sir Edmund Allenby. The Arab Revolt of June 1916 tied down thousands of Turkish troops and made possible a bitter guerrilla war against them. T.E. Lawrence, the legendary Lawrence of Arabia, had fought with the Arabs under Prince Faisal. The Jews helped with high-level intelligence-gathering and the efforts of the Jewish Legion allied with the British Army. The resulting postwar situation left a power vacuum in which many progressive reforms could have been made in a region that had been crippled by centuries of lax and corrupt Turkish rule.

The definition of those nations and regions constituting the Middle East has varied almost with every expert who has written on the topic. This article concentrates on the following countries, formerly part of the Ottoman Empire, which make up the core of the Middle East: Israel and Palestine, Egypt, Jordan, Syria, Saudi Arabia, and Iraq, with a glance at related events in Iran, Yemen, and Lebanon. The history of the left in the Middle East is the story of revolt, written again and again, of native peoples rising against the ruling power, whether it be Ottoman, British, French, or American.

Diplomacy during World War I had resulted in two agreements that, together, promised dynamic change in the embattled Middle East. In May 1916, Sir Mark Sykes of Great Britain and Georges Picot of France negotiated an agreement that effectively divided the Turkish Middle East *vilayets*, or provinces, between them. These included the modern countries of Israel, Jordan, Syria, and Iraq. The Treaty of San Remo in April 1920 made formal the Sykes-Picot compact. Since Theodore Herzl and the first meeting of the World Zionist organization in August 1897, the organization had decided on ancestral Palestine as the desired homeland for the Jewish people.

## BALFOUR DECLARATION

In recognition of Jewish aid during the war, on October 31, 1917, British Foreign Secretary Arthur Balfour wrote to England's Lord Rothschild in what would become known as the Balfour Declaration: "His Majesty's government views with favor the establishment in Palestine of a national home for the Jewish people." In January 1919, the Versailles Peace Conference opened to settle the issues of the Middle East. The San Remo Treaty was a result of the negotiations at the conference. In spite of the fact that Lawrence had brought Chaim Weizmann and Faisal into a personal meeting in London before the conference, no long-lasting agreement between the Arab and Jewish peoples came from the Versailles talks. European diplomacy, which had proven incompetent at preventing World War I in August 1914, proved to be equally inept in resolving the problems left at the end of the war in November 1918.

The result of the lack of a rapid settlement to the anarchy left by the war was first seen in Egypt. In March 1919, as Peter Masefield wrote in *The British in Egypt*, rioting broke out. Fortunately, British Prime Minister David Lloyd George sent Allenby, then at the Versailles Conference, to restore order. Allenby, after a show of imperial force, ended the uprising with minimum casualties. His tour as British proconsul was so successful that in February 1922 England gave Egypt its (conditional) independence.

Following his entry into Damascus in October 1918, Faisal had attempted to establish a home for Arab nationalism in Syria. Instead, the French invaded Syria and defeated Faisal's forces in July. After a brutal rule by General Maurice Sarrail, he was dismissed. In a conciliatory move, Henri de Jouvenel administered Syria. In keeping with the French idea of the "civilizing mission" of France, Jouvenel inaugurated the Constitution of 1926, which encouraged Chibli Mallat to write about Jouvenel, that "surely, the Constitution of 1926 is not exclusively the work of Henri de Jouvenel. But without him, however, it is probable that Sarrail's colonial military heritage would have prevailed against the adoption of a fundamental document established to provide for the rule of law" in Greater Lebanon, what the French, from their history in the Middle East going back to the Crusades, considered today's Lebanon and Syria.

However, the postwar period was marked by violence in Iraq, the most savage in the period. Iraq, formerly known by its ancient name of Mesopotamia, had been carved from the three Ottoman *vilayets* of Mosul, Basra, and Baghdad. In June 1920, a revolt broke out among the Iraqi tribes against the British occupying forces. The revolt occurred because it appeared the British were going back on the promises of independence made by Lieutenant-General Sir Stanley Maude when he entered Baghdad in March 1917. Maude had proclaimed in a declaration that "our armies do not come as conquerors or enemies, but as liberators."

The case of Faisal's brother Abdullah also testified to the problems inherent in postwar British imperial diplomacy. During the Arab Revolt, while Faisal had served as commander of the Arab forces, Sharif Hussein's brother had been the diplomat. It was intended that he receive land on the east bank of the Jordan after the war. As Philip Robins wrote in *A History of Jordan*, Abdullah "moved from Mecca to Maan in November 1920 with a retinue of some 300 men (and in possession of some six machine guns)."

The Middle East is not a natural geographic region, but rather a political one that includes Israel and Palestine, Egypt, Jordan, Syria, Saudi Arabia, Kuwait, Iraq, Iran, Yemen, Lebanon, United Arab Emirates, and Oman.

After much lost time, on March 12, 1921, the British opened the Cairo Conference, which attempted to settle the region they had received from the League of Nations as mandates and in which they were expected to promote self-government. The leading figures were Winston S. Churchill, then the British Colonial Secretary, Lawrence, Allenby, Gertrude Bell, one of the most distinguished of British Middle East experts, and Sir Percy Cox, the British high commissioner in what was then Mesopotamia. The conference created the land of Transjordan, on the east bank of the Jordan River, for Abdullah, the son of Sharif Hussein, who had been defeated in a power struggle with Abdul Aziz Ibn Saud. When Faisal entered Baghdad as king in 1921, the good will was from his role in the Arab Revolt, not because he was a friend of the British. Yet, on the whole, as Robins put it, "Cairo did not disappoint." However, when British Prime Minister David Lloyd George's government fell in October 1922, all hopes of the Cairo Conference leading to a fruitful Middle East policy were dashed when Andrew Bonar Law succeeded him, and Stanley Baldwin after Law.

In 1921, Haj Amin al-Husseini had been chosen the Grand Mufti of Jerusalem, the highest Muslim religious leader in Palestine, by the British proconsul Herbert Samuel. Yet, Samuel had known of Haj Amin's role in the Nebi Musa rioting and inexplicably chose him over the objections of other Muslim clerics. Yet, Abdullah had always been tolerant of all three of the desert faiths: Christianity, Islam, and Judaism. Indeed, before the 1948 war, the Jewish Agency in Palestine would make clandestine overtures to him to stay out of the fighting.

However, after the fall of Lloyd George, the British Foreign Office continually tried to degrade Abdullah and marginalize him from the affairs in Palestine. His final humiliation was at the hands of one of those British envoys who should have known better: Sir Percy Cox, the power behind the throne in Iraq and a delegate to the Cairo Conference. In August 1924, Abdullah was forced to accept the arrogant ultimatum that made clear that he did not capitulate to British demands, "His Majesty's Government [would] reconsider the whole position of Transjordan." This nearsighted political emasculation of Abdullah would cast a dark shadow over the future of the Middle East.

In the 1930s, severe political strain in the Middle East came from another quarter. In January 1933, Adolf Hitler's Nazi Party took power in Germany, unleashing latent anti-Semitism in Germany. As William L. Shirer wrote in *The Rise and Fall of the Third Reich*, "the so-called Nuremberg [Germany] Laws of September 15, 1935, deprived the Jews of German citizenship, confining them to the status of 'subjects.'" Reading the writing on the wall, many German Jews attempted to make their way to Palestine. This aggravated the situation between Arabs and Jews in Palestine.

As Tom Segev wrote in *One Palestine, Complete*, Mohammed Iz-al-Din al-Qassam, who had fought against the Italians in Libya in 1911, began to organize terror groups against the Jews in November 1935. Eventually, the Grand Mufti would throw himself into support, and what became known as the Great Arab Revolt would last until 1939. With the exception of World War II, the Arab-Jewish conflict would dominate Middle Eastern politics until today. Throughout the 1930s, the lack of an even-handed policy between Arabs and Jews by the British was the best guarantee of disorder in Palestine. Too often, anti-Semitism would be the rule in the corridors of power in Jerusalem and London.

## WORLD WAR II

During World War II, the entire region was drawn into the conflict. When the war began in September 1939, Egypt surprisingly declared its neutrality. This was as much due to England reasserting control after a 1939 independence treaty gave Egypt virtually complete freedom as it was to King Farouk's open admiration of England's enemy Benito Mussolini of Italy. Indeed, the behavior of Farouk did much to undermine the liberalism that had been the hallmark of much of British policy since the time of Allenby. British Ambassador Miles Lampson acted drastically.

On February 2, 1942, Lampson confronted Farouk in his study and forced him to make Nahas Pasha, the head of the Wafd Party and a supporter of the war effort, prime minister. From then on, Egypt served securely as a base against a far greater foe than British imperialism: Nazi totalitarianism. However, during the war itself, the Egyptian Army was thoroughly unreliable, because fascist groups like Young Egypt had infiltrated its officer corps. Indeed, Anwar Sadat, later the president of Egypt, would be interned for supporting the Germans.

In July 1952, King Farouk of Egypt was exiled from the country by a coup by the Free Officers Association, which soon formed the Revolutionary Command Council (RCC) to govern the country. The Free Officers Association was formed from those officers who had supported Young Egypt. According to Peter Mansfield in *A History of the Middle East*, the Free Officers had intended to hold off their coup until 1955, but the proven inability of the indolent monarch to govern hastened their plans. Major General Mohammed Naguib proclaimed the Egyptian Republic in June 1953, announcing that "the world's oldest monarchy became, for the time being, the world's youngest republic."

One of the main goals of the RCC was to improve the lot of the Egyptian peasantry, the *fellahin*. While only some 10 percent benefited from the land reform program, it would serve as a model for all developing countries. Yet, within a year, the new government showed the Bonapartism—the idea of the saving "man on the white horse"—which would doom so many other modernizing military elites. By April 1954, Naguib would lose an internal political power struggle to Gamal Abdel Nasser, who would rule until his death in 1970.

With no real political opposition in the "new" Egypt, any dissent was almost inevitably channeled into the Muslim Brotherhood, which had been founded by Hasan al-Bana in 1928. The idea of Muslim "brotherhoods," as either bandits or opposition groups, goes far back in Arab history; there are many similarities here to the bandits and triads in Chinese history. Nasser, in power, showed the same ruthlessness toward such opponents as Farouk, now relishing a sybarite's exile in Italy. Hassan al-Bana had been shot in 1949, most likely by agents of Farouk's secret police. Sayyid Qutb, who joined the Ikhwan, the Brotherhood, in 1951, would be hung in a Nasser prison in 1966. The failure of the secular government in Egypt to either permit open political opposition, or come to terms with the Brotherhood, would later reap a bloody harvest on the banks of the Nile.

At the same time, Nasser followed an adventurist foreign policy for which Egypt lacked the financial capital to underwrite. In 1956, in order to fund his grandiose schemes for development at home—which failed to materialize—and his expansionism abroad—Nasser took the fatal stroke of nationalizing the Suez Canal. For years, "liberation" gangs had mounted a guerrilla war against the Suez Canal Company, while Nasser, backing the campaign, forgot the canal was the golden goose that had hatched modern Egypt in 1869. On July 26, 1956, just after the third anniversary of Naguib's proclamation of the republic, Nasser announced the nationalization of the canal. In October 1956, Israel, Great Britain, and France attacked to seize the canal. Although a United Nations ceasefire ended the hostilities, the shocking Egyptian losses wiped out whatever gains Nasser could have achieved. Unwit-

tingly, he was becoming an Egyptian Benito Mussolini, who, ironically, had been Farouk's idol during World War I.

In order to try to save the Egyptian economy, and his foreign policy, Nasser entered into a Faustian bargain with the Soviet Union, which was anxious to find a compliant client in the Arab world. Walter Laqueur remarked in *The Struggle for the Middle East: The Soviet Union in the Mediterranean* that in 1963 Soviet "economic aid to the Middle East began to increase again and reached a new peak in 1964 and 1965—$530 million and $574 million respectively, most of it to Egypt." Not noted here is the vast amount of Russian military aid that Nasser would use to provoke the June 1967 war with Israel, again an economic disaster for the Land of the Nile.

In 1958, however, Nasser launched a foreign policy initiative that may have changed the face of Middle Eastern politics. He initiated the United Arab Republic with Syria, the UAR. The UAR, although it may have posed a new threat to Egypt, it also may have provided a parliamentary channel in time for Arab nationalism. However, the same landowning class in Syria that had blocked the land reform initiative in Egypt saw the same specter of Nasser's "socialism" in the UAR. Consequently, after a stormy marriage, the UAR dissolved in September 1961. An army coup sent the pro-Nasser Field Marshal Amer to Egypt, and the last attempt at a true Arab political federation ended.

## NASSER AND IRAQ

At the same time, Iraq suffered heavily because of Nasser's intervention in 1958. Already Nasser was heavily in debt to the Soviet Union for the military aid he had received for the 1956 Suez War. The pro-Western prime minister of Iraq, Nuri al-Said, had alienated the Soviet Union by supporting the Baghdad Pact in February 1955, a foreign policy initiative of American Secretary of State John Foster Dulles. The pact was designed to forestall Soviet influence in the region—but it could have also led to economic cooperation in an Arab version of the European Union. Instead, Nasser, according to some American intelligence reports, chose to back the Iraqi Free Officer coup to overthrow the Iraqi government. In July, the Free Officers struck under General Abd el-Karim Kassem. The palace was attacked, and later both the young King Faisal II and Nuri were murdered.

Within the same period, King Hussein of Jordan demonstrated his country's nationalism. Sir John

Bagot-Glubb, who had led the Jordanian Army, the Arab Legion, in the 1948 war with Israel, was removed from command and sent home to England in 1956. An admirer then of Nasser, the king attempted to cement fragile Arab unity in the Arab Solidarity Agreement, which was signed with Egypt and Saudi Arabia in January 1957. Later, Hussein would follow a short-lived diplomatic relationship with his Hashemite relative, Faisal II.

During the same time, political unrest rocked Lebanon, which, like Syria, had been granted independence by the anti-Vichy Free French government of Charles de Gaulle in 1941. Since then, the country had been governed by a political coalition of Muslims and Maronite Christians. Lebanon had achieved a degree of (apparent) political unity and a prosperity that caused Beirut to be called the "Paris of the Orient." However, the Maronites had remained in power by progressively denying the Muslims their proportional share in governing. When President Dwight D. Eisenhower announced the Eisenhower Doctrine in January 1957, with its aim of protecting the Middle East from communism, stability in Lebanon became essential.

When President Camille Chamoun asked for help while the Muslim Druze population revolted, 10,000 U.S. marines landed at Beirut. Robert Fisk said in his book, *Pity the Nation: The Abduction of Lebanon*, that Chamoun noted that "the Muslims were using the same pan-Arabic rhetoric as Nasser." However, Chamoun was replaced by General Fuad Chehab. But the long-standing problem of lack of adequate Muslim representation in the government would still remain.

In the midst of the chaos in the mid-1950s, Israel remained a steady example of representative government in the middle of failed constitutional examples like Egypt and post-coup Iraq. In 1930, David ben-Gurion was the driving force behind the Mapai labor political party, part of the Zionist movement. Throughout the 1930s and the independence war, the Zionist Jewish Agency, the governing office for the Yishuv (Jewish Community) in Palestine, was led by ben-Gurion and the Mapai Party. On May 14, 1948, David ben-Gurion declared the independence of Israel. Afterward, the Mapai Party remained the leading one.

However, in a truly functioning parliamentary system, opposition parties won seats in the Israeli Knesset, or parliament. To show the democratic inclusiveness of the Israeli system, in 1955, the Herut party led by Menachem Begin "had become the second-largest party in Israel," according to Charles D. Smith in *Palestine and the Arab-Israeli Conflict*. During the war of independ-

ence, Begin's Irgun Zvai Leumi (IZL) had fought virtually a civil war against the Haganah army of ben-Gurion's Jewish Agency.

In 1967, there took place a decisive event thatwould shape the history of the Middle East. Abetted by the Soviet Union, Nasser once again forsook the progressive development of his country for revenge against Israel. On May 27, Nasser declared: "our basic objective will be the destruction of Israel. The Arab people want to fight." On June 5, the Israel of Prime Minister Levi Eshkol launched a preemptive strike on the armed forces of Egypt, Syria, and Jordan. By the time that a United Nations ceasefire ended the fighting on the Golan Heights with Syria, the armed forces of all three Arab states were destroyed. Yet, the Six-Day War was a Phyrric victory for the Israelis. The thousands of new refugees went to fill the camps that were already established to hold the refugees from the wars of 1956 and 1948.

After the war, the refugees' plight stirred international concern. Edward W. Said wrote in *The Question of Palestine*, "the Palestinians have repeatedly insisted on their right of return, their desire for the exercise of self-determination, and their stubborn opposition to Zionism as it has been affected." Said added that "after 1967 ... it was no longer possible to avoid or ignore the occupied territories [seized by Israel in the war] or the Arabs there." Unfortunately, at the very time that the Palestinian cause was attracting serious interest, the Palestine Liberation Organization (PLO), ultimately led by Yassir Arafat, and the Popular Front for the Liberation of Palestine (PFLP) of Dr. George Habash embraced political terror as the weapon to make known their people's case.

Moreover, they allied themselves with similar foreign groups like the Basque separatist ETA group in Spain, the Irish Republican Army, the German Baader-Meinhof Gang, and the Italian Brigati Rossi, or Red Brigade. Their policy showed its ultimate futility when PFLP members, led by the freelance terrorist Carlos "The Jackal" Ramirez Sanchez attacked the Organization of Petroleum Exporting Countries (OPEC) meeting on December 21, 1975. It was Arab-dominated OPEC that had crippled the economy of the United States for supporting Israel in the 1973 Middle East War.

In 1978 and 1979, the Islamic Revolution under Ayatollah Khomeini broke out in Iran. In the early 1970s, Shah Reza Pahlavi, using increased oil revenues, had attempted to continue the modernization efforts of his father. In doing so, he demonstrated the same lack of

*The Israeli Army's 3rd Armor Division parades before dignitaries at the third anniversary of the nation's founding in 1951.*

understanding for the Shi'ite ayatollahs, or clerics, as did his father. His White Revolution was perceived as being a total Westernization of the country and a rejection of the values of Islamic society, especially the central place of the *sha'riah*, or law. As early as 1963, according to Sandra Mackey in *The Iranians: Persia, Islam, and the Soul of a Nation*, the shah's agents attacked a religious school in the holy city of Qum. She added: "those who managed to escape ran directly to Ayatollah [Ruhollah] Khomeini. Now it was the Ayatollah Khomeini, who from his French exile, continued to carry on a campaign against the shah, who continually appeared to rely on his brutal SAVAK security service instead of making substantive overtures to the religious leaders."

On September 8, 1978, the shah declared martial law and his troops fired on demonstrators. On the eve of the Shi'ite religious celebration of the month of Mo-

harram, on December 1, 1978, the ayatollah issued a call to his disciples for action against the shah. On January 16, 1979, the shah left the country as a National Front government under Shapour Bakhtiar became sole rulers of the country. On February 1, 1979, the ayatollah returned in triumph to Tehran. On April 1, 1979, Khomeini proclaimed Iran an Islamic Republic.

Meanwhile, generals and army officers had fled Iran to neighboring Iraq, where Saddam Hussein had risen to power in 1979, the same year as Khomeini. Anxious to have revenge on the ayatollahs, they convinced Hussein that the revolution had left Iran militarily weakened. Planning hostilities, as Judith Miller and Laurie Milroie wrote in *Saddam Hussein and the Crisis in the Gulf*, his "maximal aim was to precipitate the collapse of the Tehran [Iran] government."

Based largely on a Baghdad War College plan from 1941, Hussein attacked Iran on September 5, 1980. Iraq gained much support from conservative Muslim states like Saudi Arabia, who feared that their own populations might answer the call of the Islamic revolution. Saudi Arabia had a large Shi'ite minority in provinces along the Red Sea. The United States, of course, supported Iraq because Iranian students, remembering American support of the shah, had captured the American embassy in Tehran in November 1979. Finally, after nearly 1.5 million died, as Miller and Milroie stated, "on July 18, 1988, Khomeini suddenly accepted a United Nations-sponsored cease fire." Both nations had suffered incredible casualties—for almost no gain at all.

During the war, Iraq had incurred some $70 billion in war debt, and Saddam grew angry at Saudi Arabia and Kuwait for not giving what he thought was enough support for stopping the Islamic revolution of Iran. Using a large army, its spearhead veterans of the war with Iran, Saddam invaded the Gulf of Kuwait on August 2, 1990.

Although the ruling al-Sabah family had not realized promises for representative government, the Kuwaitis still viewed the invasion as a gross violation of their rights. During the months that followed, as Rick Atkinson wrote in *Crusade: The Untold Story of the Persian Gulf War*, "an outlaw nation had been confronted and then crushed by a world unified as never before by enlightened self-interest. If Saddam was no Hitler, the war ensured that he would not become one." President George H.W. Bush could proclaim to the American people on February 27, 1991, "Kuwait is liberated. The Iraqi army is defeated." However, completely deceiving the American negotiators under General Norman

Schwarzkopf, the coalition's chief, Saddam turned on his Kurdish and Shi'ite Muslim populations a true reign of terror.

In December 1987, after 20 years of Israeli occupation, Palestinians launched a dedicated *intifada*, or uprising, in the territories occupied by Israel since the 1948 war. Finally, in the interests of regional peace, in November 1988 Arafat announced that the Palestinians would finally accept the United Nations resolutions 242 and 338, in which, in return for leaving the occupied territories, the Palestinians and other Arabs would recognize Israel's "right to exist." In January 1993, secret negotiations began in Oslo, Norway, to open a dialogue between Palestinians and Israelis. A Palestinian Authority, the embryonic future government of a Palestinian state on the West Bank and in Gaza, was formed under Arafat as its chairman.

However, a dozen years later, the promise of Oslo remained unfulfilled. The Palestinian Authority seemed unable to restrain terrorist groups like Hamas, which launched attacks on Israel from its territories. Prime Minister Ariel Sharon was—in September 2004—building a wall to seal off Palestinian territory from Israel as a way to stop terrorist infiltration.

Yet, at the same time, the cause of the Palestinians was taken up by the Islamic extremist group al-Qaeda, led by the exiled Saudi Arabian Osama bin Laden. In 1998, bin Laden declared war on the United States for its support of Israel and for being *salibis*—crusaders—intent on destroying Islam. Osama bin Laden and his al-Qaeda extremist organization launched the attack on America on September 11, 2001.

Tragically, 600 Muslims were also killed in the attack on the World Trade Center, showing the ultimate nihilism of political terror. Bin Laden had made his home in Afghanistan with the extremist Taliban of Mullah Mohammed Omar; he had earned a reputation as a dedicated *mujahideen*, or holy warrior, in the war against Russia in the 1980s. When Afghanistan refused to surrender bin Laden, who was an honored guest, an American and British coalition invaded in October 2001. However, after severe fighting, by December it was believed that bin Laden and his senior lieutenants—like the Egyptian Dr. Ayman al-Zawahiri—were able to make their escape to the lawless Waziristan lands of Pakistan, where they were sheltered. They were most likely hidden by *ghazis*, Pashtun warriors dedicated to fighting for Islam. In March 2004, the Pakistani Army made an attack on the territory of the Waziri tribe, but neither bin Laden nor any other major figure was located.

At the same time, Hussein's Iraq still remained a source for concern, especially with suspicions that he was amassing again his arsenal of weapons of mass destruction (WMD): nuclear, biological, and chemical weapons. In the State of the Union Address in January 2004, President George W. Bush stated that Iraq had attempted to find fuel for the making of atomic bombs in Africa. In Operation Iraqi Freedom, on March 20, British and American coalition forces under American General Tommy Franks struck. The PBS show *Frontline* described the final attack on Baghdad: "U.S. forces secure Baghdad after final desperate resistance by Fedayeen and Ba'ath Party militias who are fighting almost alone. The regular Iraqi Army soldiers don't fight or even surrender en masse, as the Americans hoped; they simply go home. Late in the afternoon of April 9, in Baghdad's Firdos Square, the statue of Saddam Hussein is pulled down."

Though no WMD were found after the Iraqi invasion, Bush and his advisers remained adamant the Iraq war was necessary to preempt any possible action by Hussein.

## SEE ALSO

*Volume 1:* Asia; Iran; Egypt; Saudi Arabia; Israel; Palestine Liberation Organization.
*Volume 2 Right:* Middle East; Iran; Iraq; Saudi Arabia; Egypt; Israel.

## BIBLIOGRAPHY

Ahmad Gross, "Kaiser Wilhelm I: Deutschland und der Islam," www.enfal.de (July 2004); Wilfred Cantwell Smith, *Islam in the Modern World* (Mentor Books, 1957); Nicole and Hugh Pope, *Turkey Unveiled: A History of Modern Turkey* (Overlook, 1998); Philip Ziegler, *Omdurman* (Knopf, 1974); Robin Wright, *In the Name of God: The Khomeini Decade* (Simon and Schuster, 1989); Samir Raafat, "The Boutros Ghali We All Don't Know," *The Jordan Star* (September 26, 1996); John F. Murphy, Jr., *Sword of Islam: Muslim Extremism from the Arab Conquests to the Attack on America* (Prometheus Books, 2002); Gary Sick, *All Fall Down: America's Tragic Encounter with Iran* (Penguin Books, 1986); Albert Hourani, *A History of the Arab Peoples* (Harvard University Press, 1991); "Terrorists Plotted Attacks in Jordan," www.usatoday.com (July 2004); Albert Hourani, *A History of the Arab Peoples* (Harvard University Press, 1991); Charles Tripp, *A History of Iraq* (Cambridge University Press, 2002); Philip Robins, *A History of Jordan* (Cambridge University Press, 2004).

JOHN F. MURPHY, JR.
AMERICAN MILITARY UNIVERSITY

# Moore, Michael (1954–)

AMERICAN DOCUMENTARY filmmaker and director of TV series and music videos, Michael Moore is also the author of best-selling political books that critique U.S. domestic and foreign policies from a left-wing perspective and with scathing humor. Throughout his career, which was internationalized by the Academy Award-winning documentary *Bowling for Columbine* (2002), Moore has been praised for his investigations of corporate crimes and obscure international American dealings. Equally, he has been criticized for his alleged anti-Americanism, his aggressive style, and fabrication of facts.

Moore was born in Davison, a suburb of Flint, Michigan. Several of his relatives worked at the local General Motors factory, where Moore's uncle was one of the founders of the United Automobile Workers labor union. He received a Catholic upbringing and attended a youth seminary until the age of 14, when he went to Davison High School. Moore began his career as a polemicist at only 22 when he founded the unconventional weekly magazine *Flint Voice*, which he published for 10 years.

In 1989, with the money obtained through mortgaging his house and financial support from bingo fundraisers, Moore directed *Roger and Me*. The documentary, which became a surprising box-office hit, made him well known to the American public as a critic of neoliberal economic theories and of the globalization process. Through his distinctive combination of gritty reality and black humor, Moore shows the disastrous consequences on the local community of General Motors CEO Roger Smith's decision to close down several auto plants in Flint.

After directing the satiric movie *Canadian Bacon* (1995), in which an increasingly unpopular American president declares war on Canada to turn the public attention from domestic troubles, Moore returned to criticize corporate America in his best-seller *Downsize This! Random Threats from an Unarmed American* (1996). The book advocated more accountability for transnational conglomerates and targeted corporations such as Nike, which assigned orders to third world contractors whose focus was more on delivering on time and saving on the budget than on workers' rights.

Moore's longstanding critique of big corporations is also apparent in his 1999 and 2000 TV series, *The Awful Truth*, which was awarded the Hugh M. Hefner First Amendment Award for Arts and Entertainment. On the *New York Times* best-seller list for 50 weeks, *Stu-pid White Men* (2001) describes the shortcomings of U.S. foreign and domestic policies at the turn of the millennium, targeting, in particular, George W. Bush's administration.

Completed just before the terrorist attacks on the World Trade Center and the Pentagon, the book was initially held back by its publisher, HarperCollins, who asked Moore to rewrite it, toning down his critique of Bush. Yet, because of public pressure, HarperCollins finally agreed to publish the book in its entirety. Moore's critics pointed out his failure to sustain his accusations with evidence, a criticism to which the author responded with a more careful use of sources in his next book, *Dude, Where Is My Country?* (2003). The target is still the Bush administration, and chiefly its spurious motives for the Iraq War.

Moore's documentaries *Bowling for Columbine* (2002) and *Fahrenheit 9/11* (2004) definitely consigned their director to international fame, earning him respectively an Oscar for Best Documentary and the Palm d'Or at the prestigious Cannes Film Festival. *Bowling for Columbine* explores the culture of guns and violence in the United States, starting from the Columbine High School massacre. According to Moore, the United States is pervaded by a culture of fear, rooted in racial and economic concerns, which constantly pushes people to worry about their surroundings and thus turn to guns for security.

Such a culture of fear applies to both domestic and international situations and the film indicts America for its tendency to interfere in the political life of other countries whether with direct military interventions or with obscure diplomatic dealings. This tendency, the final part of the film suggests, backfired with the 9/11 terrorist attacks.

*Fahrenheit 9/11* controversially borrows its title from Ray Bradbury's novel *Fahrenheit 451* (1953), whose characters live in a dystopian society where censorship is pervasive and critical thought discouraged. Moore's film investigates the 9/11 terrorist attacks, concentrating on the business links between Bush, his associates, and many Saudi families, including Osama bin Laden's. Based on the evidence presented in Craig Unger's book *House of Bush, House of Saud* (2004), the documentary argues that the Bush administration was willing to overlook Saudi connections with terrorist groups, and examines the role of the American government in the evacuation of bin Laden's relatives from the United States immediately after the attacks. The film portrays Bush as an illegitimate president waging an illegitimate war against Iraq.

BIBLIOGRAPHY

Michael Moore, *Downsize This! Random Threats from an Unarmed American* (Crown Publishers, 1996); Michael Moore, *Stupid White Men* (HarperCollins, 2002); Michael Moore, *Dude, Where Is My Country?* (Warner Books, 2003); www.michaelmoore.com (July 2004).

LUCA PRONO, PH.D.
UNIVERSITY OF NOTTINGHAM, UNITED KINGDOM

# Mott, Lucretia (1793–1880)

AS A QUAKER MINISTER, women's rights advocate, abolitionist, peace activist, prohibitionist, educator, union supporter, and prison reform advocate, Lucretia Mott participated in most of the reform movements of the 19th century. She was born Lucretia Coffin on January 3, 1793, on the island of Nantucket, Massachusetts, to Thomas and Anna Coffin. The entire Coffin family was well known for their work with the Underground Railroad. Thomas Coffin, a ship captain, was furious when he learned that his daughters were only allowed to attend the local school for two hours in the afternoon after the male students had finished. He decided to send his daughters to a Quaker school in Nine Partners, New York. First as a student and later as a teacher, Mott questioned the differences in the way the sexes were treated. She discovered that although girls paid the same amount for tuition, they were given half as much instruction and that female instructors received only half the salary of their male counterparts.

On April 10, 1817, Lucretia Coffin married James Mott, a fellow instructor, and moved to Philadelphia, a city with a large Quaker population. In Philadelphia, Mott saw the realities of slavery for the first time, and she and James joined the Free Produce Society, pledging to refrain from using products made by slave labor. In 1821, Mott became a minister. After becoming a mother, Mott opened her own school to educate her own children and to promote education for women.

When the Quakers split in 1828 over theological issues and the reform tendencies of the followers of Elias Hicks, Lucretia and James Mott joined the Hicksites, the more liberal group. As a minister, Mott often preached about the evils of slavery and was considered radical even among this liberal group because she advocated immediate rather than gradual emancipation. She soon became known all over the world for her views on abolition and helped to launch the English women's rights movement. When the post office in Philadelphia received a letter from an English abolitionist addressed to an "unknown but fellow member of the same Christian society," it was delivered to Mott.

In 1830, William Lloyd Garrison was released from prison after being held for denouncing a Boston slave trader, and the Motts invited him to stay in their home. Both Garrison and Mott were appalled at the discrimination shown against women in a group that devoted their energies to fighting slavery. Nevertheless, when Garrison called an organizational meeting for the American Anti-Slavery Association in 1833, only four women were invited. As a result, Mott founded the Philadelphia Female Anti-Slavery Association.

On November 28, 1838, in Pennsylvania Hall at the first convention of the Philadelphia Female Anti-Slavery Association, mobs gathered outside the building. After the women left the building, mobs burned the hall to the ground while firefighters watched. The mob was angry not only over the abolitionist issue but also because women were daring to speak in public when it was illegal to do so in most sates. Mott, along with Sarah (1792–1873) and Angelina (1805–79) Grimké, feminist-abolitionist sisters from Charleston, South Carolina, were determined to ignore the prohibition, freely speaking out in public about slavery. The uproar over women's participation in the public arena led to a second split among the Quakers, and many former friends and allies shunned Mott.

In 1840, Mott and her husband sailed to London, England, to represent the American Anti-Slavery Association at a convention of the World Anti-Slavery Association. Mott was astounded to learn that the convention organizers were refusing to seat the women delegates from the United Sates. After an acrimonious debate, organizers agreed to seat the women in the balcony behind a curtain but allowed them no vote in the proceedings of the convention. Garrison joined the women.

At their London boarding house, the Motts met an American couple on their honeymoon, Elizabeth and Henry Stanton. Mott and Elizabeth Cady Stanton discussed their mutual outrage at the way the women were being treated and agreed to sponsor the first women's rights convention in America after they returned home. Both Mott and Stanton were influenced by *A Vindica-*

tion of the Rights of Women, published in 1792 by Mary Wollstonecraft, which promoted the education of women to free them of their dependency on men. Despite their best intentions to sponsor the convention, Mott and Stanton were busy, and plans were shelved for several years.

In late July 1848, Mott and Stanton saw their dreams realized when women and men gathered to discuss women's rights in Seneca Falls, New York. Most resolutions introduced at the Seneca Falls Convention dealt with improving the lives of women by abolishing the system of coverture that stripped married women of their rights and by promoting education and work opportunities for women. However, Stanton introduced the radical notion of women's suffrage, which ultimately passed by a narrow margin. Most newspapers vilified the women, but Frederick Douglass, a participant in the convention, defended them in his newspaper, the North Star. Along with Stanton and Susan B. Anthony, Mott worked for female suffrage through the National Woman's Suffrage Association (NWSA). She was instrumental in bringing about the 1890 merger of NWSA with its rival group, the American Woman's Suffrage Association (AWSA) to form the National American Woman's Suffrage Association (NAWSA). She also served as president of the Equal Rights Association for many years. Mott died on November 11, 1880.

### SEE ALSO

### BIBLIOGRAPHY

Margaret Hope Bacon, Valiant Friend: The Life of Lucretia Mott (Walker, 1980); Constance Brad Burnett, Five for Freedom (Greenwood, 1968); Miriam Gurko, The Ladies of Seneca Falls: The Birth of the Women's Right Movement (Macmillan, 1974); Lloyd C. M. Hare, The Greatest American Woman: Lucretia Mott (American Historical Society, 1937).

ELIZABETH PURDY, PH.D.
INDEPENDENT SCHOLAR

# Muste, Abraham J. (1885–1967)

A.J. MUSTE BEGAN his lifelong pursuit of Christian principles in 1909 when he was ordained a minister in the Dutch Reformed Church. He became increasingly uncomfortable with the church's rigid Calvinist preaching, however, and in 1914 left it to lead a Congregational Church. Muste was also inspired by the Quakers and became a pacifist with the outbreak of World War I. At that time, he also began working with the American Civil Liberties Union (ACLU), a nontypical union between a religious group and a civil liberties group. Three years later, he took a church post with the Quakers in Rhode Island.

In 1919, Muste became involved in the labor movement, a cause he would pursue for the rest of his life. His involvement began when the textile workers in Lawrence, Massachusetts, requested help with their strike. Muste saw the strike, involving some 30,000 workers, as an opportunity to demonstrate nonviolence truly works. He placed himself at the head of the picket line, where he was beaten to exhaustion by police and arrested. He convinced the workers to strike for 16 weeks. Muste next became director of Brookwood Labor College in Katonah, New York. The school's curriculum focused on the theory and practice of labor militancy. Muste also became chair of the Fellowship of Reconciliation (FOR) briefly in the 1920s, but began drifting toward a more revolutionary Marxist/Leninist position.

In 1929, he helped form the Conference for Progressive Labor Reform (CPLR), a group seeking to reform the American Federation of Labor (AFL) from within. In 1933, he helped form the American Workers Party. By this time, he had virtually abandoned his Christian pacifism and became a Marxist. He was also integral in the sit-in movement by striking workers in the 1930s. In 1936, he assisted the Goodyear Tire Workers in Akron, Ohio. Muste again shifted gears in 1936 after a visit with Russian communist revolutionary Leon Trotsky, returning to his prior Christian pacifism. Two constants remained: his involvement in the labor movement and his radicalism.

In 1940, Muste became the executive secretary of the FOR, a position he held until he retired in 1953. He also published a book in which he advocated a Christian pacifist approach to revolution. He called for an international police force, arguing that armies would be unnecessary if there was a political federation based on socialist principles of fair economic arrangements. He advocated the United States take a share of responsibility in building a world government, including investing in economic rehabilitation in Europe and Asia.

After World War II, Muste became the leader of the Committee for Nonviolent Action, a group that pushed for abolition of nuclear weapons. In 1961, Muste was part of a group of pacifists who walked from San Francisco, California, to Moscow, capital of the Soviet Union, carrying their anti-nuclear message into Red Square. Muste was also involved in the World Peace Brigade, an international group advocating world peace and including members from the African nations of Zambia and Tanzania.

Muste was a role model to many civil and human rights groups, reinforcing that they should use nonviolent techniques to end Jim Crow laws and attain justice. Socialists, unionists, and anarchists all trusted Muste, a feat not often accomplished by one person. Muste was especially active during the Vietnam War. In 1966, at the age of 81, he led a group of pacifists to Saigon, South Vietnam, where they were arrested and deported for trying to demonstrate for peace. Later that year, he met with North Vietnamese communist leader Ho Chi Minh to discuss peace. Less than one month after that meeting Muste died suddenly in New York. Muste is perhaps best remembered for the notion that peace is a verb, not a noun. His most famous quote is "There is no way to peace, peace is the way." He cautioned that pacifism is not a temporary tool but a way of life.

**SEE ALSO**

*Volume 1 Left:* Vietnam War; American Civil Liberties Union; Unions.
*Volume 2 Right:* Vietnam War.

**BIBLIOGRAPHY**

Nat Hentoff, *The Essays of A.J. Muste* (Bobbs-Merrill Company, 1963); Walter Wink, ed., *Peace Is the Way* (Orbis, 2000); "Who Is A.J. Muste?" www.ajmuste.org (April 2004).

LAURA L. FINLEY, PH.D.
INDEPENDENT SCHOLAR

# The Left

## NAACP

THIS ORGANIZATION, the National Association for the Advancement of Colored People (NAACP), has worked for African Americans' equality since 1909. Originally called the National Negro Committee until the first national conference in 1910, the integrated NAACP began its crusade to alleviate the conditions of the recently freed slaves in response to the race riot in Springfield, Illinois, in August 1908. During the years of its existence, the association has brought to the nation and its people a solid foundation of legal precedence and political influence to counteract the widespread prejudices reflected in the Jim Crow segregation decisions, which first appeared in the last decade of the 19th century.

The founding members of the association included black and white, men and women, progressives and militants. William English Walling, Mary White Ovington, Oswald Garrison Villard, and W.E.B. Du Bois came together in 1909 to begin what would be the most influential political organization of the 20th century.

With the aim of fighting for and securing the civil rights of African Americans and attacking all forms of disenfranchisement, segregation, and discrimination based on race, color, creed, or nationality, this group immediately began its long history of opposition to segregation. Although the U.S. Constitution had been

amended to insure citizenship, due process of law, and voting rights (males only) for all citizens, no matter their race, color, creed, or former status of slavery (Fourteenth and Fifteenth Amendments), many laws at the state and federal levels were worded in such a way as to deny African Americans just those rights.

During the first years of the NAACP's existence, the legal battles centered around fighting for due process of law for African Americans accused of crimes, an end to residential segregation, and equal treatment at the polls. With lawyers such as Clarence Darrow and Louis Marshall, the NAACP legal committee scored several successes, including the cases of *Guinn* and *Beal v. United States*, which overturned an Oklahoma law exempting white voters from the required literacy test, and *Buchanan v. Warley*, which forced the Supreme Court to acknowledge that states cannot segregate residential districts.

Protests during these first 10 years included one against the Woodrow Wilson administration for applying segregation in the federal government and a national protest of *Birth of a Nation*, a film that promoted racial segregation and bigotry. Another major concession the association won was a statement from Wilson against lynching.

After the 1918 statement by the president, the NAACP continued its campaign against lynching and against discriminatory racist organizations such as the

Ku Klux Klan. Although unable to secure legislation against lynching, the association campaigned against it, and mob violence in general, through protests and even ads in major newspapers. The period of the 1920s saw the NAACP rising to a national status as the primary vehicle for African Americans' civil rights. Beginning in the 1930s, the organization's protests expanded to include not only civil and personal rights issues but also to voice protest against Supreme Court justice nominees.

It was also in the 1930s that Thurgood Marshall and Charles Houston won the court case to admit African Americans to the University of Maryland (1935). Still another 1930s victory for equality came in 1939 when in response to the refusal of the Daughters of the American Revolution to allow Marian Anderson to perform in their Constitution Hall, the association booked her in the Lincoln Memorial and 75,000 attended her concert.

Although not as eventful as the previous decades, the 1940s saw several major gains in the fight for desegregation and equal rights. Partly thanks to pressure from the NAACP, President Franklin Roosevelt ordered nondiscrimination in war-related industries (1941) and President Harry Truman desegregated the federal government and the military (1948). It was also in the 1940s that the association took to court the issues of racial injustices in court procedures and discriminatory voting procedures and laws. The results of the court battles were mixed, but one major victory, *Smith v. Allwright*, in 1944 eliminated the all-white primary in Texas. Segregation laws and policies also began to feel the heat of the NAACP's influence. In 1946, in the case of *Morgan v. Virginia*, a Supreme Court win by the NAACP made it illegal to segregate facilities in interstate train and bus travel. But the big battles and victories were yet to come.

Amid the perceived complacency and normalcy of the 1950s, major changes were brewing for African Americans. The first major wins in the association's fight against segregation during this, the fourth decade for the NAACP, belonged to Marshall, who won three landmark cases desegregating graduate school programs. This was the beginning of a years-long process towards the national desegregation of public schools.

Over the period of the first two to three years of the 1950s, the NAACP accepted a number of cases across the South challenging the "separate but equal" ruling from the 1890s. Marshall took on the class-action suit of *Briggs v. Eliot* in South Carolina; the local Topeka, Kansas, chapter of the association filed on behalf of Oliver Brown. Other cases were filed in Virginia

For almost a century, the NAACP has followed a moderate left-wing path to secure the advancement of African Americans.

and Washington, D.C. For two years, the cases progressed through the appellate system until they all made it to the Supreme Court in 1952. Marshall and the NAACP's legal team consolidated all of the cases into one, *Brown v. Board of Education of Topeka*, and for the next two years, the court battle raged. The first decision was split, and the case was deferred for a year. Finally, the case again came before the Supreme Court, and in 1954, the court ruled in favor of Brown, declaring that "separate but equal" was unequal and unconstitutional. This victory for civil rights fostered a series of demonstrations, often led or supported by the NAACP, protesting the various segregated public venues and facilities.

A prime example was Rosa Parks, an NAACP member, who refused to give up her seat on a segregated bus in Montgomery, Alabama. This act of civil disobedience gave birth to other similar demonstrations across the country, putting civil rights at the top of the list of major national news events.

The *Brown* ruling signaled the overturning of the Jim Crow decisions, affecting not just schools but all aspects of the "separate but equal" rulings, providing the impetus for the stormy civil rights movement of the late 1950s and 1960s. For the next 20 years, the NAACP's main focus was racial integration, getting and enforcing severe penalties for civil rights violations, and strengthening African Americans' voting rights. Thanks to the persistence of the NAACP, the Civil Rights Act of 1964 made it through Congress and racial discrimination in public places was no longer legal. The next year saw the association leading and winning the fight for voting rights with the Voting Rights Act of 1965. Throughout the 1960s, 1970s, and 1980s, the NAACP campaigned across the South and the country to register as many African American voters as possible. The organization spearheaded numerous demonstrations and protests against various Supreme Court justices and reversals of previous pro-civil rights Supreme Court decisions and influenced over 850,000 African Americans to register and to vote.

The last 40 years have seen many successes, some failures, and even some reversals of earlier wins, and the NAACP continues to fight in the courts, in the media, and through protests and demonstrations for equality for all, no matter the gender, race, color, creed, or national origin. The association has 2,200 national and international branches in seven regions and 1,700 youth and college chapters, and each of the branches and chapters works toward equality in education, housing, voting, and all other civil rights. In 2001, shortly after the Cincinnati, Ohio, riots, the NAACP executive committee met and developed a five-year strategic plan of 10 initiatives, with objectives and goals for each. They include increasing membership, improving advocacy training programs, increasing the size of the organization's legal capacity, improving the quality of the advocacy programs and campaigns, and finally, focusing on five different civil rights issues.

As one of the oldest and largest civil rights organizations in the United States, the NAACP is uniquely qualified to wage the war against discrimination of any kind. They have proven that they can make a difference, legally and politically, no matter the opponent. With courage and dedication, the members of the NAACP have won many of its battles, but the war for equality continues. Leading people of all colors and all races towards its goal, the National Association for the Advancement of Colored People has maintained a moderate left-wing path, avoiding the more extreme advocacy of groups like the Black Panthers.

## SEE ALSO

Volume 1 Left: King, Martin Luther, Jr.; Malcolm X; Civil Rights; Desegregation.
Volume 2 Right: Segregation; Black Separatism.

## BIBLIOGRAPHY

NAACP, www.naacp.org (March 2004); Jake C. Miller, "The NAACP and Global Rights," The Western Journal of Black Studies (v.26/1, 2002); Kevern Verney, Black Civil Rights in America (Routledge, 2000); Manning Marable, Race, Reform, and Rebellion: The Second Reconstruction in Black America, 1945–90 (University Press of Mississippi, 1991); Minnie Finch, The NAACP: Its Fight for Justice (Scarecrow Press, 1981); Justin Ewers, "Making History," U.S. News & World Report (March 22, 2004).

GLORIA J. HICKS
UNIVERSITY OF WYOMING

# Nader, Ralph (1934–)

RALPH NADER, a consumer advocate, lawyer, and author, was born in Winsted, Connecticut, on February 27, 1934. In 1955, Nader received a B.A. magna cum laude from Princeton University, and in 1958 an LL.B. with distinction from Harvard University. His career began as a lawyer in Hartford, Connecticut, in 1959 and from 1961 to 1963 he lectured on history and government at the University of Hartford. In 1965 and 1966, he received the Nieman Fellows Award and was named one of ten Outstanding Young Men of Year by the U.S. Junior Chamber of Commerce in 1967. Between 1967 and 1968, he returned to Princeton as a lecturer, and he continues to speak at colleges and universities across the United States.

Nader's documented criticism of government and industry has had widespread effect on public awareness and bureaucratic power. He is the "U.S.'s toughest customer" as Time magazine noted. His inspiration and example have galvanized a whole population of consumer advocates, citizen activists, and public interest lawyers who in turn have established their own organizations throughout the country. Nader is opposed to corporate welfare and the dangerous convergence of corporate and government power. Nader first made headlines in 1965 with his book Unsafe at Any Speed, a scornful indictment that castigated the auto industry for producing unsafe vehicles. The book led to congressional hearings and a series of automobile safety laws passed in 1966.

In his career as consumer advocate, he founded many organizations including the Center for Study of Responsive Law, the Public Interest Research Group (PIRG), the Center for Auto Safety, Public Citizen, Clean Water Action Project, the Disability Rights Center, the Pension Rights Center, the Project for Corporate Responsibility, and a monthly magazine, *The Multinational Monitor*. He has built an effective national network of citizen groups that have had a major impact in areas ranging from tax reform to nuclear energy to health and safety programs. As the *New York Times* said, "What sets Nader apart is that he has moved beyond social criticism to effective political action."

In the mid-2000s, Nader lectures on the growing "imperialism" of multinational corporations and of a dangerous convergence of corporate and government power. With the passage of trade treaties like the North American Free Trade Agreement (NAFTA) and the new General Agreement on Tariffs and Trade (GATT), this merger of corporate and government interests is escalating. His magazine, *The Multinational Monitor*, tracks the global intrusion of multinational corporations and their impact on developing nations, labor, and the environment.

Nader's overriding concern and vision is presently focused on empowering citizens to create a responsive government sensitive to citizens' needs. The top of Nader's agenda has been defending the U.S. civil justice system. Corporate lobbyists and certain legislators have worked on both the federal and state levels to restrain consumers' rights to seek justice in court against wrongdoers in the area of product liability, securities fraud, and medical negligence. Nader recently coauthored a book on corporate lawyers and the perils of the legal system entitled *No Contest*.

Nader transformed consumerism into a movement that could effectively counter the power wielded by business in the marketplace and by government policy makers. Nader's leadership gave the consumer movement a proactive, visionary dimension. Through a process that he once described as "documenting your intuition," Nader spent the latter half of the 1960s investigating a host of abuses against individuals by American business and government. His reports spurred passage of new laws addressing unsanitary conditions in meatpacking and poultry production, the dangers of natural gas pipelines, radiation emissions from television sets and X rays, and hazardous working conditions in coal mines.

Nader argued that Thomas Jefferson did not envision how monied special interests, official secrecy, procedural complexities, and the sheer size of the nation would, by the mid-20th century, erode the sinews of government accountability. Nor, said Nader, could James Madison, author of the famous *Federalist No. 10* essay, have predicted how competing special-interest factions might not yield the public good. In this sense,

Nader's creation of a loose agglomeration of citizen groups to represent the people as a whole—"the public interest"—was a bold, innovative development in American politics. Nader sought to demonstrate the relevance of citizenship in modern mass society.

The savings and loan banks bailout has also been a serious concern for Nader. The deregulation of the banking industry in the early 1980s led to speculative real estate deals, which taxpayers must now unfairly finance. This is one of many examples of corporate subsidies taxpayers finance through a system that Nader calls "corporate welfare." Nader is also an advocate of insurance reform including loss-prevention activity and insurance consumer education. He coauthored the book *Winning the Insurance Game* and has been working with consumer activists in Massachusetts and California on improving the cost and coverage of automobile and health insurance in those states.

Nader's impact on the American political spectrum is enduring. He was Green Party nominee for president in 1996 (earned ballot status in 22 states: 685,000 votes or 0.8 percent of the vote). In February 2004, Nader announced his independent run for the presidency. Nader's reputation suffered in the 2000 and 2004 elections as Democrats felt Nader was taking votes away from the Democratic candidate, thus enabling the election of George W. Bush, at least in 2000.

**SEE ALSO**

*Volume 1 Left:* Liberalism; Anti-Globalization.
*Volume 2 Right:* Conservatism; Capitalism; Globalization.

**BIBLIOGRAPHY**

David Bollier, *Citizen Action and Other Big Ideas* (Center for Study of Responsive Law, 1991); Hays Gorey, *Nader and the Power of Everyman* (Grosset & Dunlap, 1975); Charles McCarry, *Citizen Nader* (Saturday Review Press, 1972); Ralph Nader and Barbara Ehrenreich, *Ralph Nader Reader* (Seven Stories Press, 2000).

JITENDRA UTTAM
JAWAHARLAL NEHRU UNIVERSITY, INDIA

# Nearing, Scott (1883–1983)

A PEACE ACTIVIST, conservationist, and writer, Scott Nearing was a leading American social critic whose career spanned most of the 20th century. Born in

Morris Run, Pennsylvania, in 1883, Nearing earned a Ph.D. in economics from the University of Pennsylvania in 1909. He taught at Pennsylvania until 1915, but was dismissed by university trustees for his vocal opposition to child labor. At the time, a number of trustees were wealthy industrialists whose factories employed children. Nearing's dismissal led to a nationwide letter campaign and a lengthy debate over academic freedom, however, Nearing was not reinstated. In 1916, he moved to the University of Toledo, but was again fired in 1917 for his public denunciations of America's entry into World War I.

Essentially blacklisted from higher education, in 1917 Nearing joined the staff of the Rand School of Social Sciences in New York, where he wrote an important anti-war pamphlet entitled *The Great Madness*. In 1918, Nearing unsuccessfully ran for Congress as a Socialist Party candidate against Fiorello LaGuardia. During the campaign, Nearing was under indictment for espionage for publishing *The Great Madness*, but defended himself in court and was acquitted of the charges in 1919. He was the only major World War I-era pacifist to escape prison.

From 1917 to 1922, Nearing was a member of the Socialist Party but quit when the party officially denounced the Soviet Union. (Nearing was a friend and colleague of John Reed and appeared in the 1981 film *Reds* depicting Reed's life). In 1927, Nearing joined the Communist Party, but left in 1930 when it refused to publish his book *Twilight of Empire* because it did not conform to Leninist theory.

In 1932, Nearing moved with his wife Helen to a small farm near Stratton Mountain, Vermont, where he embarked on a second career as a maple sugar producer. In Vermont, Nearing became a pronounced conservationist and proponent of self-reliant living. He and Helen grew their own food, practiced fasting, and abstained from habit-forming substances. They also devised a scheme for dividing the day's hours: one-third for "bread work" (livelihood), one-third for "head work" (intellectual endeavors), and one-third for "service to the world community." Feeling somewhat overwhelmed by their sugar business, in 1951 the Nearings moved to Harborside, Maine, where they built their own house and practiced subsistence farming.

In 1954, the Nearings wrote *Living the Good Life: How to Live Sanely and Simply in a Troubled World*. Initially self-published, *Living the Good Life* was reissued in 1970 at the height of the Vietnam War. The book was hugely popular and helped initiate a back-to-the-land movement among thousands of young Americans who wished to establish their own homesteads and live eco-friendly, ascetic lives. Sales from *Living the Good Life*, around 10,000 copies in the 1950s, climbed to 200,000 copies in the 1970s. The Nearings used the profits to publish Scott's other works on political and economic philosophy. Overall, Nearing published some 50 books and monographs and over 100 essays, including a "World Events" column, which appeared from 1953 to 1972 in the *Monthly Review*.

Nearing died on August 24, 1983, at age 100. Today, the Nearing homestead in Maine, known as Forest Farm, is owned and operated by The Good Life Center, a nonprofit organization dedicated to perpetuating the back-to-the-earth philosophy and lifestyle advocated by Helen and Scott Nearing.

**SEE ALSO**

*Volume 1 Left:* Socialist Party, U.S.; Communism; United States; Environmentalism.
*Volume 2 Right:* McCarthyism; United States.

**BIBLIOGRAPHY**

Scott Nearing, *The Making of a Radical: A Political Autobiography* (Social Science Institute, 1972); John Saltmarsh, *Scott Nearing: An Intellectual Biography* (Temple University Press, 1991); Steve Sherman, ed., *A Scott Nearing Reader: The Good Life in Bad Times* (Scarecrow Press, 1989).

JASON C. VUIC
OHIO STATE UNIVERSITY

# New Deal

THE NEW DEAL REFERS collectively to the domestic programs that President Franklin D. Roosevelt and his administration enacted in response to the Great Depression. The term is applied to the period of history from 1933, when Roosevelt's term in office began, until the onset of World War II in 1939.

New Deal programs involved a tremendous amount of federal legislation, government programs, bureaus, agencies, and commissions. Many of these programs had overlapping functions and jurisdictions, some of which had similar names. New Deal programs were often referred to by an alphabetical abbreviation, thus leading to the remark that an "alphabet soup" had been created. The extensive and multifaceted nature of the New Deal programs represent Roosevelt's willingness

*The huge construction projects of the New Deal's Tennessee Valley Authority were one example of the liberal recovery program.*

to utilize many approaches and to try anything that he thought might work. He was not, as was his predecessor Herbert Hoover, bound by a conviction that it was not the role of the government to involve itself in the economy. While Hoover opposed direct government aid to individuals in distress, Roosevelt felt that intervention was necessary. At one point in his presidency, he commanded one of his aides: "I don't care how you do it. Feed them damn it, feed them."

Roosevelt was elected president in November 1932, to the first of four terms. By March 1933, 13 million people were unemployed, and almost every bank had closed. In his first 100 days in office, he proposed and Congress enacted numerous programs to bring recovery to business and agriculture, relief to the unemployed and to those in danger of losing farms and homes, and reform programs that attempted to prevent another great depression from occurring and to cushion the economic effect in case one did. In an effort to organize New Deal programs clearly, historians usually di-

vide them into three main groups: relief, recovery, and reform.

Relief programs were designed to relieve economic suffering immediately by feeding those who were on the verge of starvation and by putting people back to work—working for the government if necessary. It included the Federal Emergency Relief Administration (FERA). This agency provided direct government aid, an outright government handout, to individuals in need. The Roosevelt administration felt people would have more self-respect if they worked for a living and preferred establishing federal projects in which a person might be employed by the government and paid wages or a salary. The program put people to work for the government as soon as possible by doing something that would benefit society. But the FERA was considered only a temporary measure.

People were put to work on a more permanent basis through other programs such as the Public Works Administration (PWA). Under this program, large sums of money were appropriated to be spent on giant public work projects such as building dams or large public buildings. The unemployed hired for such projects were paid by the government. Next, the Works Progress Administration (WPA) was similar in name and in concept to the PWA and employed people in a variety of public service tasks. Generally, WPA projects were not as large as PWA projects. For instance, WPA projects built college buildings while the PWA built great dams. Furthermore, WPA projects were much more varied than PWA. For example, WPA projects employed artists to paint pictures in post offices, historians to write history books, and actors to put on plays for the public. Many public buildings in use today were originally built as WPA projects. Finally, the National Youth Administration (NYA) and the Civilian Conservation Corp (CCC) employed young people in some kind of public service capacity.

Recovery programs were designed to return the economy to a normal, healthy state. Efforts were made to get business, labor, and agriculture back to a profitable basis. The first of these programs included the National Recovery Administration (NRA) as an effort to aid business and labor. Under the NRA, business and industrial firms dealing in the same area (for example, the steel industry as a whole, or the shoe manufacturing industry as a whole) were encouraged to cooperatively set certain prices that they might charge for their goods and still make a profit. Certainly, such price-fixing was a violation of the free-market concept and of anti-trust laws passed in the Progressive period.

Nonetheless, this became allowable in the early part of the New Deal through justification that emergency measures were needed. Participating firms displayed a blue eagle, the symbol of the NRA, at their business locations. Later on, the price-fixing aspect of the New Deal was terminated.

The Agriculture Adjustment Administration (AAA) also functioned as a recovery program. This program was designed to help agriculture become profitable again. Roosevelt recognized overproduction as a serious problem and felt that encouraging farmers to decrease their production would be the solution. To encourage them to do so, the government paid farmers a subsidy to reduce production, a practice that exists today began here. The government hoped to reach a point in which their intervention would be eliminated. This point never came. Current agriculture problems reflect the difficulty of dealing with overproduction with government controls but also highlight the political problems involved with federal intervention.

Finally, Roosevelt and his administration devised several reform programs. The first program, the Securities Exchange Commission (SEC), still exists today. It was established to regulate the sale of securities such as stocks and bonds. The program hoped to insure responsible dealings and the prevention of irresponsible practices that brought the stock market crashing down in the 1920s. The Federal Deposit Insurance Corporation (FDIC), also in existence today, is a government corporation created to insure bank deposits up to a designated amount. Should a bank fail, the government backs the deposits. This act seeks to prevent another failure of banks as happened in the Great Depression. Banks today often have signs on the door, "Member F.D.I.C." Finally, and perhaps the most well known program of the New Deal, Social Security began under Roosevelt. Social Security includes three parts: old age pension, unemployment insurance, and welfare. Old age pensions (commonly called social security today though the whole program is collectively called social security) provide a compulsory pension for elderly people over a certain age. Unemployment insurance provides income for those who have become unemployed with some limitations. Welfare payments are designated for individuals who, for various reasons, are unable to work or support themselves or their family at a minimum living standard.

Another part of the New Deal that does not easily fit into relief, reform, or recovery, is the Tennessee Valley Authority (TVA). During the New Deal, the government undertook a great project to develop and economically rehabilitate the valley of the Tennessee River. The river was harnessed by dams, and experts were sent in to help farmers learn better methods of agriculture in a great effort to transform the economy of the region from a depressed area to a thriving one. Under the TVA, dams produced electricity and the government sold, and still sells, the electricity to consumers at a cheaper rate than they could get it from private power companies. Those in the Tennessee area pay much cheaper electric rates today. New Deal supporters dreamed of doing the same thing in other river valleys such as the Missouri, Mississippi, Columbia, and Arkansas, but the TVA is the only one that was launched before World War II. After the war, public opinion did not favor more of these experiments. Thus, the TVA is the only one of its kind and represents a unique experiment in American history.

By 1939, the New Deal had run its course. In the short term, New Deal programs helped improve the lives of people suffering from the events of the Depression. In the long run, New Deal programs set a precedent for the federal government to play a key role in the economic and social affairs of the nation. Roosevelt's New Deal emphasized security rather than the redistribution of wealth, and the programs marked the United States government's first significant, direct investment in the everyday lives of Americans.

In establishing the New Deal, Roosevelt offered an alternative vision by presenting the government as an instrument of reform. In his view, the government represented a new order, one founded on hope rather than fear, and opportunity rather than dependence. The New Deal marked a critical departure in the governing principles, institutional arrangements, and policies that shaped modern American political life. Roosevelt reconstructed the definitions of American political parties and transformed the perception of the duty of the government as viewed by the people well beyond his years in office. As the successor of the Progressive Era and precursor to the Great Society, the New Deal stressed structural change rather than economic recovery; therefore, the birth of New Deal liberalism was a defining moment in the 20th century.

Although the New Deal was perceived at the time as a movement to the left in American politics, most of the permanent reforms and agencies established during the period were quite centrist from the perspective of social-democratic regimes in Europe. The National Recovery Administration had been built on an Associative State concept, in which code authorities would regulate the economy in the national interest. However, with the Supreme Court ruling that the code authorities represented unwarranted delegation of the power to legislate to administrative agencies in the *Schechter* case, that experiment ended.

The wide variety of other agencies, ranging from the TVA with its direct government financing of electrical power to provide a yardstick for power pricing and some development of rural Appalachia, to simple regulatory bodies, did not represent a challenge to the private enterprise, capitalist structure of American society. Indeed, by ameliorating some of the worst conditions of the Great Depression, the New Deal could be said to have preserved the American political economy from a more revolutionary approach.

**SEE ALSO**

*Volume 1 Left:* Roosevelt, Franklin D.; United States; Socialism; Welfare and Poverty; Liberalism.
*Volume 2 Right:* Hoover, Herbert C.; United States; Conservatism; *Laissez-Faire.*

**BIBLIOGRAPHY**

Roger Biles, *A New Deal for the American People* (Northern Illinois University Press, 1991); William H. Chafe, ed., *The Achievement of American Liberalism: The New Deal and Its Legacies* (Columbia University Press, 2002); M.J. Heale, *Franklin D. Roosevelt: The New Deal and War* (Routledge, 1999); Robert F. Himmelberg, *The Great Depression and the New Deal* (Greenwood Press, 2001); Hubert H. Humphrey, *The Political Philosophy of the New Deal* (Louisiana State University Press, 1970); Sidney M. Milkis and Jerome M. Mileur, eds., *The New Deal and the Triumph of Liberalism* (University of Massachusetts Press, 2002); Theodore Rosenof, *Economics in the Long Run: New Deal Theorists and Their Legacies, 1933–93* (University of North Carolina Press, 1997); Mark J. Rozell and William D. Pederson, eds., *FDR and the Modern Presidency: Leadership and Legacy* (Praeger Publishers, 1997).

DANA MAGILL
TEXAS CHRISTIAN UNIVERSITY

# New Left

THE NEW LEFT was both a product of, and contributed to, the tremendous political upheavals that shook the United States in the 1960s. The New Left derives its name in contradistinction to the Old Left, which consisted of established Marxist parties such as the Communist Party. Many young people who became active in the 1960s considered these parties dogmatic and irrelevant.

A variety of issues, most importantly the civil rights movement and the Vietnam War, gave rise to the New Left. In the early 1960s, the core of the New Left was noncommunist, anti-war, and anti-state. Young activists read C. Wright Mills, Herbert Marcuse, and Erich Fromm, not Karl Marx, Friedrich Engels, or Vladimir Lenin. However, by the late 1960s, their political experiences radicalized them; a significant sector of the New Left looked to Marxism to explain the world and the capitalist system they opposed.

## CIVIL RIGHTS

The civil rights movement inspired many young people to fight against racism and for racial equality. In the 1950s and 1960s, southern African Americans challenged segregation and the white supremacist system that oppressed them; they registered to vote, sat down at whites-only lunch counters, and took seats in the front of the bus. Their courage and the brutal repression that southern whites meted out to them outraged many people across the nation. Northern students went south on Freedom Rides and voter registration drives and came back to tell other young people about their experiences. Many of these young people thought that racism was not the result of bad individuals, but of a system that thrived on the economic exploitation, political disenfranchisement, and social marginalization of African Americans. This realization convinced them that in order to abolish white supremacy, they also needed to oppose the capitalist system they held responsible for it.

Beatnik poets decried the restrictive social and political views that had predominated in much of U.S. society during the 1950s and early 1960s as a result of the repressive political atmosphere that McCarthyism promoted. In Berkeley, University of California students spoke out against restrictions the university placed on their ability to voice freely their political opinions against racism and the Vietnam War, a protest that gave birth to the free speech movement in 1964.

## SNCC AND SDS

The two most important New Left organizations were the Student Non-violent Coordinating Committee (SNCC) and Students for a Democratic Society (SDS). SNCC began as a student-based civil rights organization that staged boycotts and sit-ins to end southern segregation. It developed into a multifaceted organization that sought political power for black people and fought economic inequality. Stokely Carmichael, an SNCC leader, epitomized the face of northern, urban African American militancy with his call for "Black Power." SDS, which began in 1960, became the largest student organization on U.S. campuses. It led the campus-based anti-draft movement, exposed connections between universities and the government, and protested Dow Chemical (which made the napalm the U.S. military dropped on the land and people of Vietnam) and ROTC (military recruitment on campuses). It published *New Left Notes* and mobilized hundreds of thousands of young people to act against the war.

## VIETNAM WAR

During the 1960s, U.S. intervention in Vietnam increased and so did opposition to it. In 1965, SDS organized the first major national demonstration against the war. Fifteen thousand people marched in Washington, D.C., to protest the war, and some even carried signs supporting the communist National Liberation Front (NLF) of Vietnam. As the U.S. government committed more troops to the war, and more and more Vietnamese and Americans died, opposition to the war permeated campuses and communities across the country. Nightly television broadcasts of the war starkly revealed how devastating the war was to the Vietnamese people and U.S. troops alike; they helped to convince many young people that the war was wrong and U.S. troops should be withdrawn. In response, many young people burned their draft cards, went to Canada rather than fight in what they considered an immoral war, and dedicated their lives to ending the war.

The numbers of people who protested the war grew. The 1968 Tet Offensive in Vietnam, a significant communist offensive, convinced many that the United States could not win the war. Then, in May 1970, the United States invaded Cambodia, after President Richard Nixon had promised to "Vietnamize" the war and withdraw U.S. troops. People poured into the streets to protest the invasion and the ongoing U.S. involvement in the war. Troops turned their guns on U.S. citizens, killing four white students at Kent State University and two African American students at Jackson State University. These attacks, the ongoing war, and the murders of black leaders Malcolm X and Martin Luther King, Jr., fueled many young people's anger and identification with the New Left; it convinced them the capitalist/imperialist system was the problem and fundamental, revolutionary change was necessary.

Other movements emerged both as part of and in response to the New Left; one of the most significant of which was the women's movement. Although part of the women's movement reflected the liberal political perspective of NOW (National Organization for Women), another, more radical sector, emerged from and identified with the New Left. This women's liberation movement rejected the NOW demand for equality and integration into the capitalist system. Instead, it called for an end to the oppression of women and the transformation of gender roles.

By the late 1960s and early 1970s, SDS had divided into a variety of leftist groups which defined themselves as Marxist. Many of these groups identified with the diverse struggles for national liberation then taking place in countries in Africa and Asia, opposed U.S. intervention around the world and capitalism in the United States, and preached the need for socialist revolution. Although the end of the Vietnam War in 1975 witnessed a decline in the numbers of people who were politically active, it did not end the New Left. During the 1970s, the New Left shifted its focus to the struggle for Puerto Rican independence; economic justice and the rights of people, especially mothers, living on welfare; and opposition to U.S. intervention in Latin America, especially the Nixon administration's involvement in the overthrow of Chilean president Salvador Allende in 1973. The women's movement expanded its analysis, membership, and impact on U.S. society. Following the 1969 Stonewall Rebellion, the gay and lesbian movement emerged to demand an end to the oppression of gays and lesbians.

From the 1970s into the 21st century, New Left activists have been involved in the political campaigns of an array of candidates, opposing U.S. military intervention in Central America and the Middle East; participating in solidarity movements, and working for women's rights, an end to racism, and an economically just society.

## SEE ALSO

*Volume 1 Left:* Socialism; King, Martin Luther, Jr.; Malcolm X; Student Non-violent Coordinating Committee; Desegregation; Feminism.
*Volume 2 Right:* Nixon, Richard M.; Capitalism; Cold War.

## BIBLIOGRAPHY

Paul Buhle, ed., *History and the New Left* (Temple University Press, 1990); Alice Echols, *Daring to Be Bad: Radical Feminism in America, 1967–75* (University of Minnesota Press, 1989); Max Elbaum, *Revolution in the Air: Sixties Radicals Turn to Lenin, Mao, and Che* (Verso, 2002); Chana Kai Lee, *For Freedom's Sake: The Life of Fannie Lou Hamer* (University of Illinois Press, 2000); Kirkpatrick Sale, *SDS* (Random House, 1973).

MARGARET POWER
ILLINOIS INSTITUTE OF TECHNOLOGY

# Niagara Movement

THE NIAGARA MOVEMENT was a social activism group formally organized on January 31, 1906, by the African American social reformer W.E.B. Du Bois. It began with a clandestine gathering in 1905 of 29 black men who wanted to form an organization that advocated for rights of black Americans. Since the group met on the Canadian side of Niagara Falls, they named the movement after the venue of the first meeting. The principles of the movement as provided in a declaration by Du Bois, coauthor William Monroe Trotter, and the other the members of the organization included a call for progressive advancement, political and civil rights, economic freedom, educational opportunity, egalitarian working conditions, social justice, healthy living conditions, solidarity, and, generally, an end to the oppression of black people. These principles were to be advanced through suffrage, free expression and criticism, and valiant and wise organizational leadership.

The means of achieving the organizational goals involved overt vocal and ideological opposition to any type of prejudicial, discriminatory, or oppressive practices. The declaration of the movement's principles left no doubt that the members were to "agitate" the powers that be in order to force the necessary changes for a totally egalitarian society. In this sense the movement was "radical," however, the group did not advocate violence as an acceptable means of bringing about this change.

After the formal organization of the group in 1906, the second meeting of the Niagara Movement took place that year overtly at Harper's Ferry, Virginia, on the site of John Brown's raid. This second conference included a dawn pilgrimage and a review of the organization's resolutions, which were delivered with a more forceful tone. The group met in Boston, Massachusetts, in 1907 and in Oberlin, Ohio, in 1908. Du Bois was severely criticized in the media for his involvement with this group, which was seen by many whites as being radical and threatening. During the early years of the movement, he began putting his thoughts in a small weekly magazine called *The Moon*, which would later become *The Horizon*. In 1910, this publication became the well-read periodical *The Crisis*.

The impetus of the group's formation had begun years earlier when the *Boston Guardian* journal editor William Monroe Trotter and a colleague heckled Booker T. Washington at one of Washington's presentations at a church. Washington, who was at that time America's highly respected and probably most famous black leader, was reportedly responsible for Trotter's incarceration. Du Bois, who was already critical of Washington's attempts at racial equality and what he saw as the unacceptable pacification of powerful white leaders, became infuriated when Trotter became jailed due to the disturbance (Du Bois himself was not present at the incident). The friction between Du Bois and his supporters and Washington and his supporters, a group Du Bois termed the "Tuskegee Machine," became legendary as the two camps verbally battled in an effort to sway the cultural ethos of race relations in America. For these reasons, Du Bois started the organization in an effort to more forcefully pursue racial equality.

The Niagara Movement itself lasted only a few years and had only five conferences. The organization had numerous problems to overcome, such as persistent financial problems, personality conflicts, and opposition from not only white leaders but also the Booker T. Washington camp. However, even with these disadvantages and barriers, the organization was one of the first to empower black Americans with the responsibility to aggressively promote demands for equality. In 1909, members of the Niagara Movement met for the last time. Later Du Bois himself stated that the movement progressed only slightly throughout its short life toward any meaningful change in race relations. However, looking at the experience of the movement in a larger historical context, the seeds of an ideology can be seen. Perhaps the greatest contribution of the small Niagara Movement is the fact that it was the precursor to a social organization that would be progressive and possess great longevity, the National Association for the Advancement of Colored People (NAACP), which was formed in 1909.

**SEE ALSO**

*Volume 1 Left*: Du Bois, W.E.B.; Civil Rights; Desegregation. *Volume 2 Right*: Segregation; Black Nationalism; Black Separatism.

**BIBLIOGRAPHY**

Frances L. Broderick, *W.E.B. Du Bois: Negro Leader in a Time of Crisis* (Stanford University Press, 1959); W.E.B. Du Bois, *Dusk of Dawn: An Essay Toward an Autobiography of a Race Concept* (Harcourt, Brace, and World, 1940); W.E.B. Du Bois, *The Autobiography of W.E.B. Du Bois: A Soliloquy on Viewing My Life from the Last Decade of Its First Century* (International Publishers, 1968); William M. Tuttle, Jr., *W.E.B. Du Bois* (Prentice Hall, 1973).

LEONARD A. STEVERSON, PH.D.
SOUTH GEORGIA COLLEGE

# Nigeria

NIGERIA HAS EARNED a reputation as a rogue state, a status blamed by left-wing opposition politicians on the right-wing *laissez faire* policies of the national government. Millions of internet subscribers worldwide have received email offers of fraudulent riches from a Nigerian cottage industry that rakes in millions of dollars annually—and has become a sore point between the Nigerian government and the U.S. State Department.

Believers in a strong centralized form of government are quick to blame this national embarrassment on Nigeria's 1999 constitution, which ordains a weak national government with limited authority in the nation's 36 autonomous states. The national government's policies are also blamed for Nigeria's international role as a major criminal center, specializing in financial fraud, money laundering, and drug trafficking. Nigeria is a major transit point for heroin and cocaine intended for European, East Asian, and North American markets and appears on the Financial Action Task Force's Non-Cooperative Countries and Territories List for its continued failure to address deficiencies in money laundering.

Nigeria's president has been widely criticized by opponents on the left for the way he has handled problems of racial and religious strife as well as widespread

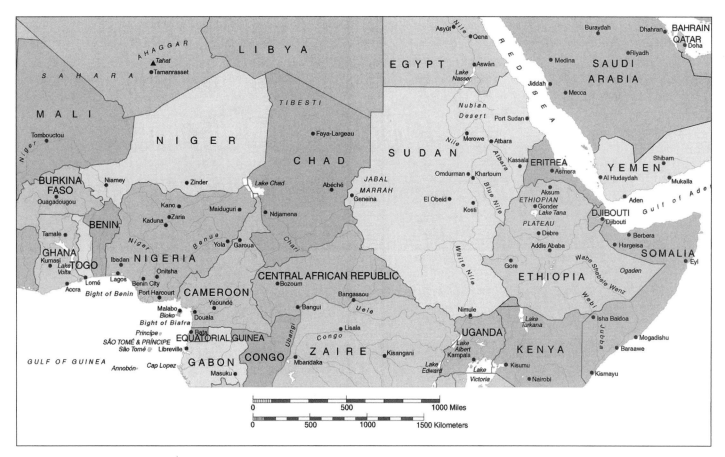

*Nigeria has the largest population in Africa, and like its third-world neighbors, the country's leftist politics are involved in the rise of Islamic extremism, as well as the effects of globalization and multinational corporations.*

criminal activity. He has adhered to the national constitution's mandate, which gives each province autonomy and a free hand in dealing with local issues. As a result, 12 of the predominantly Muslim provinces in 2004 had embraced Muslim *shari'a* religious law, which includes stern penalties for moral offenses, including beheading for blaspheming against the Muslim holy text or libeling Islam's founder, the Prophet Mohammed, and stoning to death for adultery.

What has been different about the rise of Islamist radicalism in Nigeria than in other countries in Africa or the Middle East is that it all happened in a period of democracy, which some critics say is perhaps better described as chaotic, free-for-all politics. Since the collapse of the latest military junta in 1999, Nigeria has had a weak, but elected government, led by a former military dictator, retired general and friend of Jimmy Carter, Olusegun Obasanjo.

The weak central government is also blamed for Nigeria's widespread corruption and the mismanagement of its petroleum industry. In 2003, some voting irregularities were reported in the first successful elections under civilian rule since independence from Britain in 1960, but the national balloting resulted in the leftist-centrist People's Democratic Party winning a 53.6 percent majority in the 107-seat national Senate and a 54.5 percent majority in the 346-seat House of Representatives. The left-leaning All-Nigeria People's Party took the next-highest margin—27.9 percent in the Senate and 27.4 percent in the House.

Although Nigeria is rich with oil, it has long been troubled by widespread poverty, years of political instability, and institutional corruption—all seemingly ignored by the national government due to its "hands-off" policies. Redistribution of vast oil riches is not on the agenda, although oil production provides 20 percent of the nation's GDP, 95 percent of foreign exchange earnings, and 65 percent of the government budget. The per capita income is only $800 with the majority of citizens subsistence farmers.

Once a large net exporter of food, in 2004 Nigeria was importing food, which has also been blamed on the government's refusal to take a central role in population control. Instead, it has had to borrow from international banks—and has experienced difficulty repaying those debts. In 2000, Nigeria received a debt-restructuring deal from the Paris Club and a $1 billion credit from the International Monetary Fund, both contingent on right-wing economic reforms. To the applause of Nigerian left-wingers, the government in 2002 pulled out of the IMF program amid criticism of such programs, which impose high interest rates and national austerity, including cutbacks in social services. That pullout rendered the country ineligible for additional debt forgiveness; however, the government made gestures signaling its willingness to submit. During 2003, for example, the government deregulated fuel prices and announced the privatization of the country's four oil refineries.

### SEE ALSO

*Volume 1 Left*: Africa; Anti-Globalization.
*Volume 2 Right*: Africa; Capitalism; Globalization.

### BIBLIOGRAPHY

Michael Radu, "The Nigerian Threat," *Front Page Magazine* (June 11, 2004); *National Geographic Atlas of the World* (National Geographic Society, 1999); Banjo Odutola, "2003: Our Checkmating Politics," www.lagosforum.com (July 2004); *The World Almanac and Book of Facts* (World Almanac, 2004); *The World Factbook* (CIA, 2003); William Tordoff, *Government and Politics in Africa* (Indiana University Press, 1997).

ROB KERBY
INDEPENDENT SCHOLAR

# The Left

## O'Neill, Thomas P. (1912–1994)

TIP O'NEILL served as Speaker of the U.S. House of Representatives for 10 years and was the leading Democrat in Washington, D.C., for the first six years of the presidency of Ronald Reagan, a time when the Senate was controlled by Republicans. Thomas Philip O'Neill, Jr., was born on in Cambridge, Massachusetts, the son of Thomas P. and Rose Ann (Tolan) O'Neill. His father ran the water department and had served on the city council. Tip's nickname derived from James O'Neill, a player with the St. Louis Browns baseball team who was reputed for his foul "tips." O'Neill's first foray into politics was in 1928, when at age 13, he campaigned for Democratic presidential candidate Alfred E. Smith.

O'Neill graduated from Boston College in 1936. While still a senior there, he ran for Cambridge city council and lost. This would be his only electoral defeat. The next year, 1936, he ran for and was elected to the lower house of the Massachusetts legislature. O'Neill married Mildred Anne Miller on June 17, 1941. To this marriage were born five children: Rosemary, Thomas III (who also served in the Massachusetts legislature and went on to be lieutenant-governor of the state), Susan, Christopher, and Michael O'Neill.

O'Neill served eight terms in the legislature, becoming minority leader in 1947 and speaker following the Democratic victory the next year. He was the youngest

*Speaker of the House Tip O'Neill provided a liberal counterweight to President Ronald Reagan's conservatism.*

speaker of the house in state history to that time. When U.S. Representative John F. Kennedy chose to run for the U.S. Senate in 1952, O'Neill ran for his house seat, which he won and held for 17 Congresses. O'Neill benefitted both from being a former state legislative speaker and from the tutelage of the Congressman from the neighboring district, John W. McCormick, who would also go on to be speaker. O'Neill was one of the few members of Congress who did not move his spouse and family to Washington, D.C., a practice that did not change until O'Neill became speaker 20 years later.

O'Neill was a loyal foot-soldier to the Democratic leadership and presidents Kennedy and Lyndon B. Johnson. His first major break with the leadership came over the Vietnam War. Owing in part to urging from his children (and in no small part to the liberal academic communities in his district, which included Harvard University and the Massachusetts Institute of Technology), O'Neill concluded that the Vietnam War was really a civil war, and that American interests were ill-served by American military participation. He supported Eugene J. McCarthy, the anti-war presidential candidate, in 1968.

O'Neill's rise to leadership began with his support of Hale Boggs of Louisiana for majority leader in 1971. Boggs appointed O'Neill majority whip. Boggs died in a plane crash the next year, and O'Neill was elected majority leader. When Speaker Carl Albert retired after the 1976 election, O'Neill was elected speaker without opposition. Jimmy Carter had become president by running as an outsider, against the Washington, D.C., establishment. O'Neill found the new president often unwilling to defer to O'Neill's advice about winning in the federal legislative process. When Carter and the Democratic Senate were defeated in 1980, O'Neill blamed Carter's ineptitude.

The election of President Ronald Reagan and a Republican Senate thrust O'Neill and the Democratic House into a new position. For liberals and Democrats, the House was the last bastion of progressivism in an increasingly conservative country. While O'Neill did not block Reagan's fiscal legislation entirely, he succeeded in hedging the turn to the right that the ascendance of Reagan and the Senate Republicans represented. To Republicans, O'Neill became the perfect symbol of the Democratic establishment in the capital, and one of their television ads in 1982 featured an actor who looked like O'Neill blithely ignoring national concerns. The campaign might have backfired, as the Democrats increased their House majority that year. O'Neill became a more fortified leader of the Democrats. He retired from elective office in 1986; the Democrats recaptured the Senate that year. O'Neill has been succeeded by a string of speakers whose tenure and prominence were of much less calibre.

O'Neill died in Boston, Massachusetts, on January 5, 1994. He was buried at Mount Pleasant Cemetery in Harwichport, Massachusetts, on Cape Cod.

**SEE ALSO**

*Volume 1 Left:* Kennedy, John F.; Johnson, Lyndon B.; Democratic Party.
*Volume 2 Right:* Reagan, Ronald; Republican Party.

**BIBLIOGRAPHY**

Paul R. Clancy, *Tip: A Biography of Tip O'Neill, Speaker of the House* (Macmillan, 1980); John A. Farrell, *Tip O'Neill and the Democratic Century* (Little, Brown, 2001); Tip O'Neill, *Man of the House: The Life and Political Memoirs of Speaker Tip O'Neill* (Random House, 1987).

TONY L. HILL
MASSACHUSETTS INSTITUTE OF TECHNOLOGY

# Orwell, George (1903–1950)

GEORGE ORWELL is the English author of several books, the most well known of which are *1984* and *Animal Farm*. The themes of his numerous writings, which range from essays to novels to memoirs, reflect his major political concerns and perspective. Although his writing style is clear and direct, he was a very complex character who experienced radical shifts in his political beliefs, thus making it hard to label him as a leftist or rightist.

Orwell was born in Bengal, India. He studied at Eton and then worked from 1922 to 1927 in the Imperial Police force in Burma, then part of the British Empire. He resigned and decided to become a writer. In 1934 he published *Burmese Days*, a fictional account of the lives of a group of English people living in Burma and their racist attitudes toward the Burmese population. The book offers a devastating critique of the effects of imperialism on the morals of the British people and the lives of the Burmese.

Like other young people who opposed fascism and supported the left, Orwell went to Spain in 1936 during the Spanish Civil War. Working as a journalist, he witnessed both the brutality of the fascist Francisco Franco forces and the efforts of the Spanish Communist Party, backed by the Soviet Union, to sabotage the anti-fascist work of the noncommunist left. The experience deepened his opposition to totalitarianism and made him very critical of the Soviet Union and the Communist Party; it also produced his gripping account of Spain during the civil war, *Homage to Catalonia* (1938).

*Animal Farm* (1945) and *1984* (1949) both reflect his deep-seated rejection of totalitarianism, be it on the left or the right. *Aninal Farm* is viewed as a parable about Josef Stalin and Stalinism in the Soviet Union. *1984* tells the dystopic (nonutopian) story of Winston Smith, who wages an ultimately futile rebellion against Big Brother and the party. Although some have interpreted the book solely as a criticism of communism, it can be more accurately understood as a critique of totalitarianism of all kinds.

*1984* warns the reader of the unprecedented power that science and technology offer to those who lust for domination and of the role technology can play in allowing totalitarian regimes to exercise control over the thoughts of citizens. The book also includes a discussion of how language can be a powerful tool that shapes how people think. In the hands of Big Brother, people learn and apparently believe such oxymoronic slogans as "War Is Peace," "Freedom Is Slavery," and "Ignorance Is Strength."

The key protagonists of Orwell's stories are men; his female characters frequently lack depth, strength of character, and moral complexity. One critical study of Orwell labels him as misogynist and anti-feminist. Another recent criticism of Orwell that surfaced in the 1990s was that he was an informer who provided the British government with the names of people he deemed "security risks, Communists or fellow travelers," according to journalist Alexander Cockburn. Orwell died in 1950 of a lung ailment.

**SEE ALSO**

*Volume 1 Left:* Communism; Communist Party; Soviet Union; Spain.
*Volume 2 Right:* Totalitarianism; Stalin and Stalinism.

**BIBLIOGRAPHY**

Alexander Cockburn, "St. George's List," *The Nation* (December 7, 1998); George Orwell, *1984* (New American Library, 1981); Daphne Patai, *The Orwell Mystique. A Study in Male Ideology* (University of Massachusetts Press, 1984); Richard Rees, *George Orwell: Fugitive from the Camp of Victory* (Southern Illinois University Press, 1961).

MARGARET POWER
ILLINOIS INSTITUTE OF TECHNOLOGY

# P

## Palestine Liberation Organization

FOUNDED ON Marxist-Leninist principles, the Palestine Liberation Organization (PLO) has become the longest-running revolutionary movement in the history of the world. The 1964 National Charter of the PLO was amended in 1968, and much of its far-left rhetoric has since been repudiated. From the time that Egyptian president Gamal Abdel Nasser conceived of the PLO, it was intended to protect Arab interests in relation to the Jewish State of Israel. By the late 20th century, the PLO had become a major player in global efforts to obtain peace in the Middle East. As both a political group and a paramilitary organization, the PLO is unique, having been granted observer status in the United Nations

When the Arab League founded the Palestine Liberation Organization in 1964, its goal was to establish an independent Palestinian state by eradicating Israel. During its 40-year history, the PLO has accepted more reality-based goals and is now reconciled to Israel's continued existence. Palestinian claims now focus on obtaining Palestinian control only over the West Bank and the Gaza Strip. Yasser Arafat, who died in 2004, was the president of the Palestine Authority, which governs Palestinian-controlled lands. Arafat was also the leader of the PLO and Fatah, the political party that obtained control of the PLO in 1969 under his decades-long leadership.

The PLO and its affiliates have been accused of causing the deaths of thousands of civilians, including the 1972 murders of 11 Israeli athletes during the Munich Olympic Games, the slaughter of 21 students in Ma'a lot in 1974, the deaths of 35 tourists, the wounding of several hundred others during the bombing of an Israeli tour bus in 1978, and the hijacking of the *Achille Lauro* cruise ship in 1985. In 1987, Palestinians launched the *intifada*, resulting in a new surge of violence and terrorism. Israel retaliated with more violence. In 1988, PLO leader Arafat publicly called for an end to terrorism and violence.

In 1970, Arafat created Force 17, a 10-member guard that expanded to a 1,000-member commando force. Force 17 is believed to be responsible for several suicide bombings. Al Aqsa Martyrs' Brigade, which has claimed responsibility for a number of suicide bombings, evolved from the PLO's militant wing after the September 2000 uprising. The uprising was sparked when Israel's Ariel Sharon, then the right-wing opposition leader, visited the holy Muslim site of Temple Mount. Sovereignty over several sites in Jerusalem is hotly debated because the city is home to areas considered sacred by Muslims, Jews, and Christians.

Despite its stated support for establishing a Palestinian state, the United States has traditionally viewed the PLO as an ongoing threat to America and its allies. This view is based in part upon the activities of Al Aqsa

Martyrs' Brigade as well as those of Iraq-based Abu Nidal. The latter group has claimed responsibility for terrorist attacks in at least 20 countries.

A number of American presidents have attempted to bring Palestine and Israel together. President George H.W. Bush failed in 1991. Bill Clinton was somewhat more successful, and Israeli President Yitzhak Rabin and Arafat signed the 1993 Oslo Accord. Unfortunately, the accord collapsed in 2000. Former president Jimmy Carter, who initiated the historic 1978 Camp David Accord, has expressed strong support for the 2001 Geneva Initiative, which evolved after a failed 2001 meeting at Camp David. It is believed that Arafat stonewalled the peace process by refusing to moderate his position. In 2002, Israel reclaimed much of the land it had previously conceded to Palestine. The Geneva Initiative focuses on creating a Palestine state in the West Bank and Gaza while protecting Israel's borders, conceding authority over disputed religious areas in Jerusalem, and guaranteeing the rights of Jewish settlers in Palestinian areas.

**SEE ALSO**

*Volume 1 Left:* Israel; Middle East; Egypt.
*Volume 2 Right:* Israel; Middle East.

**BIBLIOGRAPHY**

Anti-Defamation League, "Advocating for Israel," www.adl.org (August 2004); Jillian Becker, *The PLO: The Rise and Fall of the Palestinian Liberation Organization* (St. Martin's, 1984); Alain Gresh, *The PLO: The Struggle Within: Towards an Independent Palestinian State* (Zed Books, 1985).

ELIZABETH PURDY, PH.D.
INDEPENDENT SCHOLAR

# Paris Commune

THE HISTORY OF the Paris Commune, a short-lived socialist state in Paris, France, from March to May 1871, is closely tied to the Franco-Prussian War (1870–71). As the war ended in defeat for the French, the Prussians thus included in the details of the armistice the occupation of France's capital, Paris. In the face of the threat of foreign occupation, and given the fact that for six months prior the Parisians had withstood the Prussian troops, the local population was greatly defiant of this development—indeed the Parisians merely limited the Parisian occupation by the Prussians to a small section of the city.

The situation was far from suitable for the government of the Third Republic (1870–1945), headed by Louis-Adolphe Adiers, who feared the Parisians would use national guard weaponry to not only arm themselves for protection, but to also provoke the Prussian military forces. On March 18, 1871, French government troops thus entered into Paris with the intention of seizing arms but were met with much resistance. The national guard, for example, refused to hand over their weapons and so the French troops left empty-handed; in so doing forcing the French government to flee the city (to Versailles) and declare war on Paris. While the French government was obviously horrified by the resistance of the Parisian people, to others it was a time of great social hope (including future communists who viewed the events with interest).

The Paris Commune, a worker insurrection, came into being on March 28, 1871, two days after new local government elections were held in Paris. Louis-Auguste Blanqui, a communist who was frequently prepared to use violent means to meet his demands for social justice, headed the new municipal government and within the city much support was found (supporters and members of the regime being known as communards, that is, communists). In the face of war from the national government, the commune passed policies that ended conscription and replaced the previous security force with a new guard created by local citizens—all citizens under the new regime were given the right to bear arms. In addition, all unpaid prewar debts on rent were frozen and pawnshops were forbidden to sell any goods.

The French Revolutionary Calendar was reintroduced (it was previously abolished by Napoleon), all church property also became property of the state, religion was banned from Parisian schools, interest on debts abolished and as noted previously, debt payments suspended. The response by Adiers's government to these developments was to attack the city. The assault began on April 2, 1871, and despite consisting of a much weaker military force, the Parisians were able to maintain control of the city for a number of weeks.

Given their beneficial position, the national government refused to negotiate with the leaders of the Paris Commune and so fighting continued until the commune was forcefully removed. This decision not only meant that large numbers of soldiers (about 900 in total) would be killed, but civilians too. Furthermore, the city, which had received magnificent improvements under Georges Haussmann's scheme, was badly damaged. Fighting continued until each of the 600 or so barricades created by the Parisians fell. During the weeks of resistance by the commune and its supporters, Paris was constantly bombarded by the national government forces. Even though the city wall was breached by late May 1871, the working-class districts of the east still refused to drop their arms and the days from May 21 to May 29, 1871, when the districts of Belleville and Menilmontant continued to resist arrest, is known as *La Semaine Sanglante* (the blood-soaked week). Estimates of 30,000 deaths have been noted during the period of the Paris Commune as a result of the fighting between French troops and Parisians.

While the commune may have failed in its ends in France, ultimately it laid the path for subsequent worker rebellions such as the Russian Revolution of 1917 in Europe.

## SEE ALSO

*Volume 1 Left:* Communism; France; Russian Revolution.
*Volume 2 Right:* France.

## BIBLIOGRAPHY

Roger Gould, *Insurgent Identities: Class, Community and Protest in Paris from 1848 to the Commune* (University of Chicago Press, 1996); Alaistar Horne, *The Fall of Paris: The Siege and the Commune, 1870–71* (Macmillan, 1965); Euge Schulkind, *The Paris Commune of 1871* (Historical Association, 1998).

IAN MORLEY
MING CHUAN UNIVERSITY, TAIWAN

# Paul, Alice (1885–1977)

ALICE PAUL WAS BORN in Moorestown, New Jersey, to a Quaker family. She graduated from Swarthmore College in 1905 and worked briefly at the New York College Settlement. In 1906, she went to England for three years to work in the settlement house movement. Inspired by Christabel Pankhurst's dedication and passion for the suffrage cause, Paul joined the Women's Social and Political Union in London, England, and so at age 22 began her lifelong campaign for women's suffrage.

Back in the United States, Paul continued her work for women's right to vote by organizing protests and rallies. In 1912, she earned her Ph.D. in social work from the University of Pennsylvania, with a doctoral thesis

entitled "Toward Equality." That same year she was asked by Jane Addams to become the chairperson of the Congressional Committee of the National American Woman Suffrage Association (NAWSA) and to establish a Washington, D.C., headquarters. While in Washington, she wrote monthly editorials for *The Suffragist*, organized rallies, and created a "suffrage school" to train activists in law and public speaking. One of her most noteworthy accomplishments was a parade to draw attention to the issue of women's rights at the same time as inauguration festivities for President Woodrow Wilson. The parade attracted more than 1,000 marching women and resulted in near riots.

She withdrew from the NAWSA to form the Congressional Union for Woman Suffrage (CUWS), which evolved into the National Woman's Party in 1917. The CUWS was a more militant organization, engaging in demonstrations and daily picketing of the White House. She was imprisoned three times, and in October 1917 she was imprisoned for seven months.

After the passage of the 19th Amendment to the U.S. Constitution granting women the right to vote, she became active in trying to introduce and pass an Equal Rights Amendment (ERA). The ERA finally passed Congress in 1970 but was not ratified by enough states within the time limit. In 1938, she founded the World Party for Equal Rights for Women to argue for the rights of women around the world and particularly in Europe. This was not well received, particularly in Britain and France, with political attention directed more toward economic and political instability than issues of women's rights. Continuing her work on the international stage, she was also instrumental in ensuring that gender equality statements were included in the 1964 Civil Rights Act and the Preamble of the Charter of the United Nations. Paul died July 9, 1977, in New Jersey.

By her adoption of direct action tactics, Paul fell on the more radical side of the suffragist spectrum. However, after the achievement of the vote, she continued to advocate women's rights issues, rather than social and economic issues generally associated with the left.

## SEE ALSO

*Volume 1 Left:* Voting, Unrestricted; Suffragists; Constitutional Amendments.
*Volume 2 Right:* Feminism.

## BIBLIOGRAPHY

Amy Butler, *Two Paths to Equality: Alice Paul and Ethel M. Smith* (SUNY Press, 2002); Christine Lunardini, *From Equal*

*Suffrage to Equal Rights: Alice Paul and the National Woman's Party* (New York University Press, 1986); Virginia Bratfisch, *The Non-Violent Militant: Alice Paul* (Women's Heritage Series, 1971).

SHANNON K. ORR
BOWLING GREEN STATE UNIVERSITY

# Peru

IN 1924, TWO YOUNG Peruvian intellectuals, Jose Carlos Mariategui and Victor Raul Haya de la Torre, met in a crowded cafe in Mexico City and founded the Peruvian left. On that fateful day, May 7, the two met to discuss Mariategui's visit throughout Europe and his participation in the great industrial strikes in Turin, Italy. The two decided on a path to promote the working and rural underclasses in their native Peru. As a result, the American Popular Revolutionary Alliance or APRA was formed to address the needs of the Peruvian underclasses. The ideology of APRA reflected the ideological tendencies of its founder. De la Torre had a strong belief in the utility of the working class uniting in a regional manner. As a result, APRA promoted the idea of a system of Latin American solutions to specific Latin American problems. In addition, APRA promoted the notion of rejecting the capitalist political system of the United States while also rebuffing the ideological constraints of the Communist Soviet Union. Finally and most radically, APRA advocated universal democracy, equal rights, and respect for indigenous peoples, while also advocating a mild brand of economic nationalism.

APRA would become leader of the leftist movements throughout the 1930s, not only in Peru but more widely in Spanish-speaking South America. Its moderate tones and truly nationalist ideologies appealed to a working and rural underclass that was under economic strain from the Great Depression and industrialization. Indeed, between 1931 and 1945, APRA publicly advocated the overthrow of the military regime that had the support of the oligarchy. In 1945, the left and APRA participated in a political alliance and the party became legalized.

Unfortunately, the waning of the Peruvian system was unpredictable. In 1948, the military toppled the democratically elected government and once again outlawed any political opposition, including APRA.

The liberal ideology and popularity of the leftist APRA became a threat to the military regimes, which plagued the Peruvian political system until 1968. Significantly, the military that rose to power was socialist-oriented and sought to institute a serious number of social and agrarian reforms. APRA and the left found the reforms necessary and just in the political order. Unfortunately, De la Torre's drift to the right forced many of the APRA ideologues to change parties, specifically to the Socialists and the institutionalized Communist Party.

In 1985, popular democracy returned to Peru as the military relinquished control of the political system. After presiding over a free election, Francisco Belaunde turned the presidency over to the populist Alan Garcia Perez of APRA, who had swept to victory with 48 percent of the vote. Belaunde's party suffered a resounding defeat with a mere 6 percent of the vote, while the Marxist United Left (Izquierda Unida—IU) received 23 percent. The elections revealed a decided swing to the left by the Peruvian electorate. For the APRA, Garcia's victory was the culmination of more than half a century of political travail and struggle.

Unfortunately, Garcia's presidency suffered economic collapse, social chaos, and political corruption. The left suffered in the eyes of public opinion as a result of Garcia's inability to control his subordinates. In 1990, the left lost its hold on power to Alberto Fujimori who, within a year, would instigate an *auto-golpe* or self-coup, in alliance with the military to rid the country of the leftist influence.

In the 1980s, the country as well as the institutional left came under attack from a series of new and aggressive political actors. In the 1980s, the Shining Path or Sendero Luminoso was founded in the remote and impoverished department of Ayacucho by Abimael Guzman Reynosos, a philosophy professor at the University of Huamanga. Reynosos, in forming this new group, mixed the ideas of Marxism-Leninism, Maoism, and those of Jose Carlos Mariategui, Peru's major Marxist theoretician and a founding member of APRA. The movement, in the 1980s, launched a series of massive guerrilla raids against the government within the major cities.

At the same time, another guerrilla group, the Tupac Amaru Revolutionary Movement (Movimiento Revolucionario Túpac Amaru—MRTA), emerged in Lima to act as an urban guerrilla movement. The left thus also had to contend with the emergence of these new revolutionary groups that not only threatened Peruvian society but also threatened the left's long historical struggle to achieve legitimacy within the Peruvian political system.

## SEE ALSO
*Volume 1 Left:* Shining Path; South America.
*Volume 2 Right:* Peru; South America.

## BIBLIOGRAPHY
Robert Alexander, ed. *Aprismo: The Ideas and Doctrines of Víctor Raúl Haya de la Torre* (Kent State University Press, 1973). David Booth and Bernardo Sorj, eds., *Military Reformism and Social Classes: The Peruvian Experience, 1968–80* (St. Martin's Press, 1983); Jesús Chavarría, *José Carlos Mariátegui and the Rise of Modern Peru, 1890–1930* (University of New Mexico Press, 1979); Gabriela Tarazona-Sevillano, *Sendero Luminoso and the Threat of Narcoterrorism* (Praeger, 1990).

JAIME RAMÓN OLIVARES, PH.D.
HOUSTON COMMUNITY COLLEGE, CENTRAL

# Poland

TRADITIONAL UNDERSTANDING of political divisions into the left and the right have altered their meaning considerably in Poland due to communist rule after World War II. Changes after the Velvet Revolution of 1989 brought about the rebirth of political party life in Poland, but the division into the left and the right is sometimes very far from the understanding of these terms in the West. Also, barely a few of the newly formed parties manage to survive more than half a decade and still play an important role in the political life of Poland.

In the years from 1945 to 1989, the communist political model was in force in Poland (called the Peoples' Republic of Poland). Only three parties were legal: the Communist Polska Zjednoczona Partia Robotnicza—PZPR (Polish United Workers' Party); peasant Zjednoczone Stronnictwo Ludowe (United Peasant Party); and representing craftsmen, Stronnictwo Demokratyczne (Democratic Party). PZPR had its leading role confirmed in the Polish constitution and the two other parties were its satellites. All parties accepted the Marxist-Leninist principles of state, economic, education, social, religious, and cultural policy. At the same time, their functioning was based on nomenclature and statism, which in the long run proved an absolute fail-

ure and resulted in numerous crises and change of the political system in 1989.

Following the changes in 1989, the PZPR dissolved itself in January 1990. Its members formed the Social Democratic party, which created a leftist electoral coalition in the 1991 parliamentary elections (gaining over 10 percent). This new party, as well as other left groups established after 1989, claim to have nothing in common with the communist past, although they inherited all the possessions (real estates, cars, equipment, bank accounts) of the PZPR. They claim to defend workers' rights and work toward a social welfare state. Into the 2000s, there are four parties that can be considered left in the parliament and one outside it. The Polski Stronnictwo Ludowe (Polish Peasant Party) should also be considered left, although their focus is mainly on the struggle for the rights of farmers and the rural population.

The largest leftist party is Sojusz Lewicy Demokratycznej—SLD (Alliance of Democratic Left), established on April 15, 1999. Essentially, it is a party based on activists of the former PZPR. The same group changed the formula and structure of their party several times between 1989 and 1999, depending on the political situation and need of the electorate. The political formation that formed SLD won the 1993 parliamentary elections and formed a coalition government together with the Polish Peasant Party. After four years in power, SLD lost the 1997 elections to Akcja Wyborcza Solidarnosc—AWS (Solidarity Electoral Action). In 2001, it returned as the major player winning (together with Unia Pracy) 41 percent of votes in the parliamentary elections. The success was based on an electoral program that stressed equal rights for all, reducing unemployment, equal access to education and health service, equal rights for women, ethics and transparency in government, and the fight against corruption. SLD's leader, Leszek Miller, became the prime minister of the new, left government. The first two-and-a-half years of SLD's rule proved a complete failure; backing for the formation slid down to 10 percent, and approval of the prime minister was under 10 percent. SLD did not manage to meet any of its electoral promises and was involved in numerous political scandals and corruption. Leszek Miller had to step down as party leader (new leader: Krzysztof Janik) and prime minister. SLD itself split into SLD and the Polish Social Democratic Party on March 26, 2004, putting into question the existence of SLD in the future.

SLD's coalition partner, Unia Pracy—UP (Labor Union), was established as a party in 1992. It was formed from several smaller left-wing parties and organizations. UP based its tradition on the pre-World War II Polish Socialist Party. In its program, UP backed a political model based on a democratic parliamentary system with strong local governments. Its economic and social program promoted state interventionism and a welfare state for the poorest population. UP would also like to see the role of the Catholic Church diminished in Poland. Women's rights, including an almost unlimited right to abortion, are among its future priorities. In the 1993 elections, UP received a backing of 7.3 percent, while in 1997 this number dropped to 4.74 percent. In 2001, UP took part in the elections in a coalition with SLD, together gaining 41percent of the valid votes. UP formed the government together with SLD and the Polish Peasant Party. Its leader, Marek Pol, became the deputy prime minister.

Socjaldemokracja Polska—SdPL (Polish Social Democratic Party) was formed on March 26, 2004, when a group of activists from SLD decided to leave their former party and establish a new one. The leader of the new party was Marek Borowski. The new party states that it seeks to fulfill the electoral program of SLD from 2001. Their program is to be based on three pillars: a well-organized state with administration independent of party structures, social and democratic programs, and cooperation within the European Union. In particular, SdPL promises to separate the state from party politics, improve administration and civil service, improve social help for the poor, homeless and hungry, and promote education with equal access for all. Just distribution of Poland's gross domestic product is to be based on solidarity and social justice. The church is to be separated from the state. Equal rights are to be granted and realized for all: women and national and sexual minorities included.

The next representative of the left is Samoobrona (Self-Defense Party), which grew out of a farmers' labor union that contested the political and social system formed in Poland after 1989. From organizing blockades of roads by farmers, blackmailing or even beating those who opposed them, Samoobrona gained the backing of 10 percent of the vote and managed to become a strong parliamentary party with over 50 deputies. The number dropped down to 30 two years later, but Samoobrona was considered the second strongest party in Poland in spring 2004. Its program refers to pre-1989 Poland, a strong welfare state, and state interventionism. It is not clear how these aims should be achieved. Samoobrona is clearly a populist party promising fast changes for the poor and unemployed, yet very careful not to reveal how to bring about these changes. Andrzej Lepper, who is an undisputed leader of the party, is a very charismatic speaker for the poorest people in the society.

The only larger left party outside the parliament is Polska Partia Socjalistyczna—PPS (Polish Socialist Party). It has the longest tradition, dating back to 1880s, but does not have a large backing among the electorate. Their program aims at workers' rights, help for the poorest population, and establishment of a welfare state.

In general, the left-wing parties have been successful in winning half or more of votes in the parliamentary elections. Yet, this does not seem to be stable support, but more a reaction to specific electoral campaigns. SLD, which had the most stable electorate of at least 10 percent since 1989 (up to 35 percent), might even vanish from the political scene. However, the backing of leftist and populist electoral programs is bound to remain on the level of about 40 to 50 percent. It is closely connected with high unemployment (20 percent), poverty, and public sentiments after the welfare state of pre-1989.

**SEE ALSO**

*Volume 1 Left:* Soviet Union; Communism; Socialism; Solidarity.
*Volume 2 Right:* Poland, Globalization.

**BIBLIOGRAPHY**

M.B. Biskupski, *The History of Poland* (Greenwood Press, 2000); *Polityka* (v16, April 17, 2004); Jakub Basista, "Poland," G.T. Kurian, ed., *Encyclopedia of World Nations* (Facts on File, 2002); Polish political party websites: www.sld.org.pl; www.sdpl.org.pl; www.samoobrona.org,pl; www.pps.org.pl; www.psl.org.pl (April 2004).

JAKUB BASISTA, PH.D.
JAGIELLONIAN UNIVERSITY, POLAND

# Political Economy

POLITICAL ECONOMY is concerned with the relationship between democratic governments and capitalism. Classical liberal economists, beginning in 1776 with the publication of Adam Smith's *An Inquiry into the Nature and Causes of the Wealth of Nations*, argued that government should leave the economic system alone and allow it to seek its own equilibrium.

John Maynard Keynes (right) meets with Harry White of the U.S. Treasury at the inaugural International Monetary Fund meeting.

Classical liberalism, in the political sense, derived from the theories of British philosophers Thomas Hobbes and John Locke. Both Hobbes and Locke, known as the fathers of classical liberalism, endorsed the idea of government by contract. Hobbes's more authoritarian view suggested that men traded off any rights they possessed in a pregovernment stage (the state of nature) for the security of government. Locke, however, maintained that human beings possessed rights given by their Creator that could never be take away by government. The inherent rights were the right to life, liberty, and property ownership. Because classical economy derived from classical liberalism, the needs and desires of the individual retained their significance when translated into economic theory.

Classical economic theory evolved in direct response to mercantilism, the prominent political thought in Europe in the 17th century. Mercantilists maintained that governmental policy should be directed toward encouraging exports and discouraging imports in order to fuel the economy. They believed the "wealth of a nation" was measured by how much gold, silver, and metal it possessed. Because mercantilists used government policy to fill their pockets, while the general population suffered, classical economists, such as Smith, Jean-Baptiste Say, David Ricardo, Thomas Malthus, and Jeremy Bentham distrusted government. They believed that government was responsible for existing problems such as widespread poverty and political unrest during the early days of the Industrial Revolution.

John Stuart Mill stands alone among early classical liberals because his thinking has much in common with modern liberals. As a utilitarian, Mill was concerned with promoting the greater good; therefore, he accepted an active governmental role in the economy. While Mill agreed with Malthus that unchecked population growth was a constant threat to society because of a finite number of available resources, Mill's liberalism made him more optimistic about the ultimate outcome. He insisted that with education, female suffrage, and improved quality of life, most people would limit reproduction and solve the problems of rampant poverty. Like modern liberals, Mill was also an environmentalist and looked to government to protect valuable resources.

Keynes, the originator of macroeconomics, was a harsh critic of classical liberalism's *laissez-faire* approach. He argued that philosophers had provided the justification for businessmen to make as much profit as possible, regardless of the consequences. Classical liber-

This theory, which became known as *laissez-faire*, was adopted in both Europe and America. The Industrial Revolution proved an ideal testing ground, and *laissez-faire* flourished in the United States until the 1930s when the Great Depression called for drastic economic measures.

John Maynard Keynes's publication of *The General Theory of Money, Interest, and Employment* in 1936 signaled a move away from classical liberal economics to what became known as New Liberalism, or simply liberalism. Unlike classical liberals who accepted only a minimal role for government in capitalist economies, liberal economists contended that government had a responsibility to make economic decisions. Keynes's theories evolved to some extent from his fear of the growing shift toward the extreme left politics of communism and the extreme right politics of fascism. Keynes believed that the centrist theories of liberalism would check both moves, negating the need for totalitarianism by meeting the needs of those most vulnerable to extremism.

als endorsed the notion that such profits would benefit the nation and solve societal problems. In the 1980s, this argument was used by conservative economist Milton Friedman to influence Ronald Reagan. Liberals point out that the result of Reagan's "trickle-down economics," or "voodoo economics," as candidate George H.W. Bush called Reaganomics in 1988, was economic disaster that resulted in a trillion-dollar deficit.

During Franklin Roosevelt's first term, he applied active liberal economic planning to turn the economy around during the Great Depression. In 1936, Keynes published *The General Theory* and significantly influenced the economic views of many of Roosevelt's advisors, including a number of liberal academicians. During the recession of 1937, using Keynesian theory, Roosevelt turned the United States into a what some term a social welfare state.

Before Keynesian economics entered the American psyche, the concept of "government spending" to energize the economy was almost nonexistent. Roosevelt and his advisers endorsed Keynes's countercyclical argument, which stated that government should increase spending whenever the health of business declined and unemployment rose, even if it meant running a temporary budget deficit. Government, according to Keynes, should step back whenever prosperity was the order of the day. Friedman and the Chicago School of Economics led the conservative response to liberal economic theory by calling for a return to classical economic theory.

Economists such as Louis Brandeis, L.T. Hobhouse, John Dewey, John Kenneth Galbraith, Lester Thurow, and Robert Reich, the secretary of labor in the Bill Clinton White House, represent the modern liberal view. Liberal economists believe that the *laissez-faire* theory so dear to the hearts of conservative economists is based on faulty reasoning and that its narrowness of perspective makes it dangerous. Reich insists that classical economics has failed because it denies the integral relationship between politics and economics. To Reich, like most liberals, politics is more important because it encompasses a broader scope than economics, making it more responsive to reality. Liberal economists reject the classical economic decree that economic equilibrium should be the ultimate goal in a capitalistic society. Liberals argue that economic disequilibrium and depression are also normal characteristics of the economy. Because of this, they believe that policy makers are necessary to identify situations when government intervention is necessary. Democratic presidents from Roosevelt to Clinton have endorsed this philosophy.

**SEE ALSO**
*Volume 1 Left:* Liberalism; Hobbes, Thomas; Locke, John. *Volume 2 Right: Laissez-Faire;* Capitalism.

**BIBLIOGRAPHY**
Samuel Bowles and Michael Edwards, "Government: Capitalist or Democratic?" Bruce Miroff et al., eds.*Debating Democracy* (Houghton Mifflin, 1997); Omar F. Hamouda and John N. Smith, eds., *Keynes and Public Policy after Fifty Years, Volume I: Economy and Policy* (New York University, 1988); John Maynard Keynes, *The End of Laissez-Faire* (William C. Brown Reprint Library, 1927); Dean L. May, *From New Deal to New Economics: The American Liberal Response to the Recession of 1937* (Garland, 1981); Allan H. Meltzer et al., *Political Economy* (Oxford University Press, 1991); John Stuart Mill, *Principles of Political Economy* (Hackett, 2004); Alan Peacock, *The Political Economy of Economic Freedom* (Edward Elgar, 1997); Walter S. Salani, "The Spread of Keynesian Doctrine and Practices in the United States," Omar F. Hamouda and John N. Smith, eds., *Keynes and Public Policy after Fifty Years, Volume I: Economy and Policy* (New York University, 1988).

ELIZABETH PURDY, PH.D.
INDEPENDENT SCHOLAR

# Politically Correct

LIBERALS ARGUE THAT being politically correct is respecting the human dignity and personhood of other individuals and groups. Conservatives tend to use the term "political correctness" as a derogatory description of what they see as an attempt to ban anti-liberal speech. They insist that political correctness is an attempt by liberal professors to indoctrinate students with liberal thinking. The political correctness movement began on the campuses of colleges and universities among liberal academicians who were concerned about the effects of abusive speech on the ability of certain groups to receive an education. In response to that concern, many campuses defined abusive language as "hate speech" and instituted speech codes that banned such speech on the basis of race, color, sex, religion, ethnic/national origin, and sexual orientation. Conservatives claimed that such codes violated their First Amendment rights and claimed the right to censor whatever they found offensive such as material deemed sexually suggestive or critical of the United States, Christianity, or capitalism.

Despite conservative claims of absolute freedom to use abusive speech, Americans have never been granted that right. In *Chaplinsky v. New Hampshire* (315 U.S. 568, 1942), the Supreme Court identified several forms of speech that are never protected by the First Amendment: obscenity, slander, libel, seditious speech, and "fighting words." Fighting words, in the opinion of the court, were "those which by their very utterance inflict injury or tend to incite an immediate breach of the peace." Liberals maintain that all hate speech is classified as fighting words and is, therefore, illegal because it may lead to hate crimes. In 1990, Congress passed the Hate Crimes Statistics Act that requires the Federal Bureau of Investigation (FBI) to keep records of all hate crimes in the United States. In 2003 alone, the FBI investigated 7,462 alleged hate crime incidents, involving 8,832 separate offenses.

Most Western democracies have passed restrictions on abusive speech. As early as 1965, the United Kingdom passed the Race Relations Act, which punished threatening, abusive, or insulting language. Canada's comprehensive Hate Law was held as constitutional in February 1996. The Netherlands has criminalized public expression that is insulting on the basis of race, religion, or sexual orientation. Sweden and Australia prohibit public expressions of contempt on the basis of race, color, national or ethnic origin, or religious faith. International groups have also condemned abusive speech.

## POLITICAL DOGMA

Most scholars agree that the term *politically correct* was first used within the Communist Party to describe those who toed the party line. The assumption was that Vladimir Lenin would purge those who strayed from party dogma. During the 1960s, the New Left first used the term to establish lines between what was seen as offensive and what was not. It was not until the conservative 1980s that the term came to be used as an anti-liberal term. Conservative students began researching the voting records of college faculty to identify what they saw as liberal bias. Since liberalism is highly correlated with level of education and academic discipline, inquisitive students frequently found that liberal arts faculties were almost entirely liberal. They used their findings to launch the conservative backlash against political correctness.

Because Ronald Reagan and George H.W. Bush had filled the courts with conservative judges, conservative students were frequently able to successfully challenge speech codes and justify politically incorrect behavior. A good deal of the animosity of conservative students has centered on the issue of affirmative action, which they perceive as giving black students an unfair advantage.

As a justification for political correctness, liberals point to periods in world history where atrocities have occurred because of hatred and a lack of understanding and respect for certain individuals and groups. Adolf Hitler launched a massive effort to purge all Jews and homosexuals from Nazi Germany. In the name of progress, white European Americans relocated whole tribes of Native Americans westward. Because they believed that the African race was intellectually inferior but capable of enormous physical strength, white Americans and Europeans enslaved Africans for several centuries.

Numerous educational studies on children have demonstrated that when children are told they are smart and will succeed, they believe it. Contrarily, children who are told that they are worthless and inferior begin to view themselves as such. At the beginning of her autobiographical novel, *I Know Why the Caged Bird Sings* (1970), author and inaugural poet Maya Angelou writes of wanting to have blond hair and blue eyes because it was much more desirable than being black in 1930s rural Mississippi.

Likewise, Kenneth Clark's study of black children in South Carolina in the 1950s revealed that black children saw white dolls as "good" and black dolls as "bad." Clark's study was used in the preparation of *Brown v. Board of Education* (347 U.S. 483, 1954), which overturned "separate but equal" and redefined equality in America. To most young people in the United States, slavery happened a long time ago and is not relevant to their lives. In reality, slavery still exists. Approximately 27 million individuals are enslaved around the world. At least 100,000 of them live in Mauritania where slavery has flourished since the 12th century.

The issue of race continues to be the most controversial aspect of political correctness on campuses across the country, and racial conflicts are on the rise. One reason for this is the ubiquitous presence of hate groups such as the Ku Klux Klan and the White Aryan Resistance on the internet, distributing their hate-filled messages to new generations. Liberals contend that hate speech not only demeans the individual or groups involved but that it is also detrimental to society. Statistics have revealed that black students are five times more likely to drop out of predominately white schools than any other group. While predominately black schools make up only 19 percent of the nation's schools, they graduate 34 percent of all black students.

By the 21st century, the practice of political correctness had been somewhat discredited by conservatives. However, the reality of being politically correct has entered American consciousness. It could be argued, therefore, that political correctness has been a partial success because many people have begun to censor their own speech by thinking before they say something that may be offensive. In this context, "firefighter" is preferred over "fireman." "Mail carrier" is less offensive than "mailman." "Chair" is a better choice than "chairman." Overtly racist speech that once was taken as a matter of course has been struck from the socially conscious vocabulary.

### SEE ALSO

*Volume 1 Left:* Liberalism; United States; Civil Rights.
*Volume 2 Right:* Conservatism; New Right; United States.

### BIBLIOGRAPHY

Richard L. Abu, *Speaking Respect, Respecting Speech* (University of Chicago Press, 1998); "Campus Rules Overreach," *USA Today* (March 3, 2004); Charles S. Clark, Jr., "Is Political Correctness a Problem on College Campuses?" *Congressional Researcher* (February 16, 1996); Peter Collier and David Horowitz, *The Race Card: White Guilt, Black Resentment and the Assault on Truth and Justice* (Forum, 1997); Richard Dooling, "Unspeakable Names," *Our Times/5: Readings from Recent Periodicals*, Robert Atwan, ed. (Bedford, 1998); Frank Ellis, "Political Correctness and the Ideological Struggle from Lenin and Mao to Marcuse and Foucault," *Journal of Social, Political, and Economic Studies* (Winter 2002); Troy Ellis, "Disillusioned in the Promised Land," *Our Times/3: Readings from Recent Periodicals*, Robert Atwan, ed. (Bedford, 1993); Thomas Grey, "Responding to Abusive Speech on Campus, A Model Statute," *Our Times/3: Readings from Recent Periodicals*, Robert Atwan, ed. (Bedford, 1993); Garry Wills, "In Praise of Censure," *The Informed Argument: A Multidisciplinary Reader and Guide*, Robert K. Miller, ed. (Harcourt, 1992).

ELIZABETH PURDY, PH.D.
INDEPENDENT SCHOLAR

# Polls and Pollsters

WHILE POLLS HAVE been used in political campaigns since the early 1930s, major advances in technology have resulted in accurate polling that affects nearly every aspect of elections in the United States. By taking a relatively small sample of the public, pollsters are able to predict winners of most elections even before a single ballot is cast. Political polls also serve the dual purposes of informing political candidates about public opinion and providing politicians with "hot button" issues that need to be addressed. Once elected, politicians can use polls to gauge public reaction to policies and to follow public approval/disapproval of job performance. While media, academicians, and independent polling organizations conduct regular polls, political candidates also hire their own pollsters, who often serve as formal or informal advisers and strategists. Supporters of the polling process argue that polls advance the democratic process by giving all citizens an equal opportunity to be heard. Critics of polls contend that sophisticated techniques have provided politicians with a legitimate means of manipulating public opinion to their best advantage.

ELECTION TOOLS

Franklin Roosevelt (FDR) was the first to use opinion polls as an election tool. While the Democratic National Committee paid for polls conducted by Emil Hurja, FDR also used Hadley Cantril, a volunteer, to lead a secret polling operation. Since Congress refused to appropriate funds for public opinion polling, presidents have been forced to depend on funds from national committees or private sources. In the 1960 election, John Kennedy became the first presidential candidate to pay for private polling. Kennedy began using polls in 1958, hiring Louis Harris and Ted Sorensen to gather information on what the public thought about him and his policies. Kennedy was interested in learning what the public thought about his character, personality, image, and religion. He used the information produced by Harris and Sorensen to plan strategy for the 1960 presidential campaign, such as the focus on education. While the Harris polling operation has continued to build a solid reputation for conducting accurate opinion polls, Harris had been criticized for his liberal bias.

While both Harry Truman and Lyndon Johnson (LBJ) also used polls to provide information, neither ever trusted their accuracy. After the inaccurate prediction that Thomas Dewey would the 1948 election, Truman distrusted polls even more and refused to pay for a private pollster. Polls became more accurate after that election in large part because of the scientific methods developed by polling pioneer George Gallup. Democratic pollster Louis Harris noted wryly that Johnson only believed in polls that supported his position. LBJ hired Harris protégé Oliver Quayle to conduct secret polls.

In 1968, former Attorney General Robert F. Kennedy was the frontrunner in the campaign for the Democratic nomination. After he was assassinated in Los Angeles on June 6, 1968, hopes for a Democratic win in November fell apart. Vice President Hubert H. Humphrey, who had chosen not to run in any presidential primaries, was chosen by party leaders to head the Democratic ticket. The furor over Humphrey's nomination, coupled with violent protests outside the convention hall, led to a major overhaul in the way Democrats chose delegates to the national convention. Afterward, the people rather than party bosses chose the nominee. As a result, polling became even more important to presidential candidates because they identified issues of particular importance to voters and areas in which candidates were strong or weak.

In both the 1976 and 1980 presidential campaigns, Jimmy Carter depended heavily on pollster Pat Caddell, who became a de facto policy adviser, enjoying unlimited access to Carter. Caddell, who was best known for his ability to instinctively analyze poll data, honed the practice of designing poll questions to produce in-depth information. He often used follow-up questions to measure why a respondent answered a certain way on a previous question. During the 1980 campaign, Caddell advised Carter not to debate Ronald Reagan but to fall back on the "rose garden strategy" of being too busy to actively campaign. Carter ignored Caddell and gave Reagan the opportunity to use his acting skills to their fullest and push home the message that Carter had not been able to combat the economic downslide. Caddell also convinced Carter that the American people had lost confidence in America after Vietnam and Watergate, and Carter accordingly used that theme, and Reagan, who exuded confidence and optimism, easily trounced Carter in the November election.

Initially, the 1988 election was wide open because neither candidate was an incumbent. The Republican candidate, Vice President George H. W. Bush, had been labeled a "wimp" by Reagan image-makers, and the economy was in shambles after eight years of Reaganomics. Democratic candidate Michael Dukakis, governor of Massachusetts, surged ahead in the polls. Bush's campaign team responded with negative campaign ads that labeled Dukakis as a "Liberal" who furloughed vicious criminals and who hated the American flag. Dukakis was well aware that Bush's ads were lies,

but there is no mandate for truth in campaigning. Dukakis had supported the weapons Bush said he opposed, and the parole plan used in Massachusetts was similar to the one used by Reagan as governor of California. Dukakis's opposition to the Massachusetts pledge law was that it allowed no leeway to protect religious beliefs. Dukakis's pollster, Irwin "Tubby" Harrison, blamed Dukakis for refusing to follow advice based on poll data.

## 1992 ELECTION

Of all Democratic presidents, none depended on polls more than Bill Clinton. With an undergraduate degree in political science, Clinton was well aware of the influence of polls, which he read diligently. He used them to gauge public opinion and restructured his approach to policies in response to poll data. During the 1992 campaign, Clinton made pollster Stan Greenburg an integral part of his advisory team, even though some members of his staff resented Greenburg's influence on Clinton's decision making. Clinton reportedly paid Greenburg $2.7 million during the 1994 congressional campaign that gave Republicans control of Congress. Greenburg also served as pollster during Vice President Al Gore's unsuccessful bid for the presidency in 2000. Gore won the popular vote, but George W. Bush was given the electoral vote after contested votes in Florida were declared invalid.

The 1992 campaign turned vicious when rich Republican supporters went after Clinton with everything they could find, including his connection to the Whitewater financial scandal. With Clinton's history, Republicans had little trouble finding sexual incidents or women with a grievance who were willing, sometimes for money, to tell their stories. They also went after Hillary Clinton. Many conservatives objected to the fact that she was a feminist and a practicing attorney. Polls revealed that voters perceived Hillary as "hard" and "unsympathetic." The public frequently changes its mind, and a decade later, Hillary Clinton was a Senator from New York and had become one of "the most admired women in America."

After the terrorist attacks on September 11, 2001, approval ratings for newly elected President George W. Bush soared. Initially, polls revealed that the public as a whole supported Bush's decision to attack Afghanistan and Iraq. However, as the Iraq war dragged on, and scandals over intelligence-gathering and prison abuse surfaced, a Bush reelection seemed less certain. Democratic pollsters searched for key groups of people that might be expected to swing votes toward the party in a close election. Stan Greenburg and Celinda Lake determined that to win the White House in 2004, John Kerry needed to woo single women, who make up almost one-fourth of the voting population. They argued that some 6 million single women, including those who are divorced and widowed as well as those who have never been married, have been disillusioned with the direction that national politics has taken in recent years. Kerry's pollster and campaign manager advised Kerry to appeal to such voters by running only optimistic, positive ads and running on his record.

## SEE ALSO

*Volume 1 Left:* Roosevelt, Franklin D.; Democratic Party; Carter, James E.; Clinton, William J.
*Volume 2 Right:* Republican Party; Reagan, Ronald; Bush, George W.

## BIBLIOGRAPHY

Bruce E. Altschuler, *Keeping a Finger on the Public Pulse: Private Polling and Presidential Elections* (Greenwood, 1982); Adam J. Berinsky, *Silent Voters: Public Opinion and Political Participation in America* (Princeton University Press, 2004); Albert H. Cantril, *The Opinion Connection: Polling, Politics, and the Press* (Congressional Quarterly, 1991); Charles S. Clark, "Are Advisers and Handlers Harming Society?" *CQ Researcher* (October 4, 1996); Neal Conan, "Analysis: Unmarried Women Voters," Talk of the Nation, National Public Radio (May 18, 2004); "Dueling Pollsters," *Wilson Quarterly* (Spring 2002); Robert M. Eisinger, *The Evolution of Presidential Polling* (Cambridge University Press, 2003); Kathleen Hall Jamieson, *Dirty Politics: Deception, Distraction, and Democracy* (Oxford University Press, 1992); Mary Matalin and James Carville, *All's Fair: Love, War, and Running for President* (Random House, 1995); Nick Moon, *Opinion Polls: History, Theory, and Practice* (University of Manchester Press, 1999); David W. Moore, *The Superpollsters: How They Measure and Manipulate Public Opinion in America* (Four Walls Eight Windows, 1995).

ELIZABETH PURDY, PH.D.
INDEPENDENT SCHOLAR

# Popular Front

POPULAR FRONTS ARE ALLIANCES or coalitions that were formed primarily to counter the rise of fascism, and as such, are particularly associated with 1930s Europe, although a Popular Front government was elected in Chile in 1938. A popular front was also formed in Estonia in 1988 to campaign for independence from the Soviet Union. Usually, though, popular fronts predominantly comprise left and liberal, progressive, or centrist parties and politicians, each concerned with defending democracy and civil liberties from the political advance of fascism or other variants of right-wing authoritarianism.

The threat of fascism in interwar Europe was sufficient to persuade many such parties effectively to suspend their ideological differences and electoral rivalry, in order to secure cooperation and galvanize the defenders of liberal democracy and social reform. This pursuit of interparty unity was born of recognition that if fascism triumphed, not only would democracy and liberalism be destroyed, so too would the parties which, in their particular ways, espoused such principles.

The most famous popular front was formed in France in the mid-1930s, entailing an alliance between socialists and left-radicals—representing the working class and elements of the lower-middle class and peasantry, respectively—and which formed a government in 1936, supported by the French Communist Party. The same year also heralded the election of a popular front government in Spain.

Both of these popular front governments proved short-lived, however, and tragically illustrated the inherent tensions and contradictions within such broad-based political movements. Ideologically, crafting an agreed long-term program among communists, socialists, liberals, and sundry bourgeois reformists proved too difficult.

Beyond seeking to defend democracy and certain social reform from fascist aggression, there was little common ground among the partners in the popular front, certainly not enough to yield a stable, long-term government. For example, liberal or bourgeois participants in the popular front were naturally concerned with ensuring the defense of private property rights and liberal individualism, concerns that were clearly at odds with the ideological perspectives of leftist socialists and communists.

Although the popular fronts were able to agree on various short-term measures, including social reforms in France especially, these primarily pertained to shorter working hours, improved wages, and holiday entitlement for industrial workers and aspects of welfare reform. These measures were not only hampered by the stringent economic conditions that were themselves fueling the rise of fascism, these reforms also exacerbated the economic crises, thereby inadvertently boosting the advance of fascism. Indeed, the involvement of socialists and communists in popular front governments or movements (even where communist involvement was tacit or relatively marginal) was cited by fascists as incontrovertible evidence of the advance of communism in Western Europe, and the increasing proximity of communists to political power in countries such as France and Spain.

In certain respects, therefore, popular front governments provided a clear focal point and discernible enemy against which fascists could more readily mobilize, while concomitantly enhancing the ideological and organizational unity of fascism. This relative unity contrasted starkly with the heterogeneity of the popular front, whose disparate membership was essentially defensive and only able to agree on short-term measures and piecemeal reforms. As such, the popular front was unable to maintain long-term resistance to the apparent ideological certainties and political advances of fascism, particularly when these were articulated and promoted by various economic, military, and political elites in their respective countries. Indeed, the rise of the popular front, and the involvement (to varying degrees) of communists, served to persuade some on the right to disregard their previous unease or anxiety about aspects of fascism, and thus lend fascism their support, fearing that only fascism would now save them and capitalism from international (read: Soviet-backed) communism.

Furthermore, whereas the popular front was expressly formed to defend and abide by the principles and practices of liberal democracy, the fascists had few qualms about such constitutionalism and legality, readily proving instead their willingness to use direct action and violence to secure political power and thereafter crush their left-wing and centrist opponents. Consequently, the popular front government that had come to power in France in June 1936 fell in October 1938, while its Spanish counterpart, elected in February 1936—thereby inadvertently precipitating the outbreak of the Spanish Civil War—was defeated by Francisco Franco and the Nationalists in March 1939.

### COMINTERN

The popular front movements in Europe were stimulated in the 1930s by a decision taken in the Moscow-dominated Comintern (Communist International) to support such alliances. In the period 1929 to 1935, the Comintern urged party members to work within other party organizations by infiltrating them, in what was called a "united front from below." The policy engendered considerable hostility between communist party organizations and other parties and grass-roots organizations of the left in the period.

However, at the Comintern's Seventh World Congress, held in Moscow in August 1935, a new policy was endorsed, that of the "united front from above" or the Popular Front tactic. In that strategy, communist parties were directed to form political coalitions with the leadership of other parties on the left. There is some evidence that the pressure to make this change from hostile penetration to political cooperation was anticipated on a local level in the United States and elsewhere before becoming official doctrine. From 1935 through 1939, the policy of forming such alliances was sanctioned by the Comintern and had the limited successes noted above in Spain and France.

### SEE ALSO

Volume 1 Left: Socialism; Spain; France; Germany.
Volume 2 Right: Fascism; Spain, Germany; France; Hitler, Adolf.

### BIBLIOGRAPHY

David Blaazer, *The Popular Front and the Progressive Tradition* (Cambridge University Press, 1992); G.D.H. Cole, *The People's Front* (Gollancz, 1937); Theodor Draper, "The Popular Front Revisited," *New York Review of Books* (May 30, 1985); Helen Graham and Paul Preston, eds., *The Popular Front in Europe* (Macmillan, 1987).

PETER DOREY
CARDIFF UNIVERSITY, UNITED KINGDOM
RODNEY P. CARLISLE
GENERAL EDITOR

# Populism

THE TERM *POPULISM* HAS been associated with a set of different meanings that go from a political movement to a loose set of ideological principles. Originally, populism is an extensive and imprecise concept that first appeared in the vocabulary of political ideas during the 19th century in Russia. Based on a direct translation of the Russian *narodnik*, populism served to describe a political movement that brought a certain current of intellectuals closer to the peasantry, arguing that the true values of the ideal community were to be found in the village and the simple life.

The term *populism* has also been used to used to refer to a late-19th-century agrarian movement in the United States that expressed the political grievances of debt ridden farmers who felt let down by the political class. Having begun in the 1880s, the populist movement reached its zenith in the 1890s when its candidate, William Jennings Bryan, became the Democratic Party's nominee and came close to winning the presidential elections. Agrarian populism also fed the Progressive movement, a movement that had its roots

*Populist William Jennings Bryan came very close to winning the presidency in the 1890s, the height of populism in America.*

among the urban middle classes and that called for economic and political reform. In particular, the Progressive movement tried to push for the introduction of anti-trust legislation in order to attempt to break the link between political and economic power.

Later, it would become a term used to describe the political experiences of Brazil and Argentina in relation to the figures of Getúlio Dorneles Vargas and Juan

Peron. In general, populism makes a call to "the people," whatever this collective group might be, and uses it for the purpose of political mobilization. The basic ideas of mobilization and the people shape populism's vision of the role of the parties, its basic understanding of political action and of the nature of governments. This call to the people is characterized by the act of mobilization itself and need to abandon all actions leading to implementing a political program on the part of political actors. Political programs are instead substituted by empty discourses of what are called popular aspirations, destined to control the masses and to impose a political regime with varying degrees of authoritarian undertones.

Populism is thus essentially negative, as it opposes the so-called virtue of the people to enemies that can be as varied as the conspiratorial aims of the political system, the financial system, the intellectuals, capitalism, and even the imperialism of other nations. Given that populism has no clearly defined ideology and can even be hostile to ideologies, it feeds itself mainly from the charismatic virtues of its absolute leader or from the exaltation of those characteristics that are meant to define "the people." In this way, the national ideology can reach xenophobic extremes, proclaiming cultural and economic nationalist values and even ethnic purity.

In Latin America, populism has never referred to the popular agrarian movement that was in Europe or in the United States. Instead, it has always had the meaning of a particular doctrine of power. In this sense, the charismatic leader is the quintessential populist leader who instigates the masses for aims ultimately conservative even when these aims oppose themselves to the oligarchies and the "false" electoral democracies. The example of Peron serves to illustrate the meaning of populism. A military man who participated in the Argentine coup of 1930 and 1944, Peron showed strong admiration for the German and Italian fascist dictatorships of the prewar era. However, after retiring from the army and all previous government posts, he was also able to transform himself in order to contest and win the 1946 presidential elections as a democrat.

This charismatic leader's political genius was based on the realization of the political potential that lay in the unorganized Argentine working class. The masses of *descamisados* (the shirtless ones) became his solid political support, a support that was based on real wage advances for the majority. These gains were paid with blind devotion to the leader and high levels of labor organization. In exchange, the mass unions lost their independence and became a tool for controlling opposition

*Argentine leader Juan Peron helped redefine populism in relation to the fascisms of Germany and Italy of the 1930s.*

in defense of the leader's policies. His economic policy was based on heavy state intervention, nationalizing large parts of it in favor of a nationalist revolution that exalted a rediscovered Argentine identity in opposition to an alleged U.S. economic and political imperialism.

However, some movements (for instance, Carlos Menem in Argentina) have used the name of populism for themselves when, far from traditional populist instincts, they have imposed a neoliberal economic order. It would therefore be possible to talk of populism to refer to every form of political expression that creates itself based on a call to the people, a critique of the institutional aspects of power, and an identity based on a return to an alleged community, regardless of the details of the policies imposed.

Although populist candidates have often supported social and economic platforms usually associated with the left, the tendency of such candidates to appeal to nationalism, ethnic chauvinism, or to a reactionary tar-

geting of supposed internal enemies has often led to alliances with the political right.

**SEE ALSO**

**BIBLIOGRAPHY**

G. Ionescu et al., *Populism* (Weidenfeld and Nicolson, 1969); Paul Taggart, *Populism* (Maidenhead, 2000); Derek William Urwin, *A Dictionary of European History and Politics* (Longman, 1996); David Robertson, *The Penguin Dictionary of Politics* (Penguin, 1993).

KEPA ARTARAZ, PH.D.
UNIVERSITY OF DERBY, UNITED KINGDOM

# Postmodernism

POSTMODERNISM IS THE HISTORIC opposition to what is considered modern. In the discussion about postmodernity and postmodernism, reference is made to a rupture or critique of the political project of modernity (liberal democracy), its culture and science (Enlightenment), or its economic system (capitalism). In each of these terms, issues such as autonomy, freedom, and legitimization are at stake.

Postmodernism was initially found in the aesthetic debates on literature and architecture in the United States, France, and Italy. However, it was also applied to the fields of philosophy, sociology, economics, and politics. The idea of postmodernity was used by Arnold Toynbee in his book *A Study of History* to denote the last phase of Western culture, beginning around 1875. It then appeared in Latin America during the 1920s, identifying alternative groups of revolutionary artists and intellectuals. In the Anglo-American context, the term was used after 1940, first in literature and then in other areas, when Leslie Fiedler observed in the 1960s that a "futurist revolt" was its major tendency. This perspective became established in 1971, when Brian O'Doherty published his article "What Is Postmodernism?"

By 1977, it was used commonly and defined by Gerhard Hoffmann, Alfred Hornung, and Ruediger Kunow in the article "'Postmodern' and 'Contemporary' as Criteria for the Analysis of 20th Century Literature."

The postmodern social, economic, and political analyses run parallel to this development. The term was taken in the 1950s by Irving Howe in his *Mass Society and Postmodern Fiction*, and by Harry Levin in "What Was Modernism?" Amitai Etzioni discussed its sociological implications in his 1968 book, *The Active Society*, while the concept continued to be applied in Latin America, by Enrique Dussel in Mexico and Gustavo Gutiérrez in Peru. They discussed the socioeconomic meaning of this concept, seeing Latin America as "the underside of modernity." In Brazil, José Guilherme Merquior used it to describe a cultural movement after modernism.

In philosophy, the idea of modernity and its opposition by postmodernism is related to a debate between Jürgen Habermas in Germany and Jean-François Lyotard in France. Habermas defends the Project of the Enlightenment, affirming that it provided the basis for the development of Western societies, political liberalism, and human rights, as well as the ideal of reason (*Ideal der Vernunft*) proposed by Immanuel Kant in the 18th century. However, many of these assumptions were criticized in the 20th century, first by Martin Heidegger in his criticism of technique, later by Theodor Adorno and Max Horkheimer in their dismantling of a capitalistic "Dialectics of the Enlightenment" ("Dialektik der Aufklärung.") Based on this criticism, Jean-Francois Lyotard published the book *La condition postmoderne* in 1979 and launched a radical attack on the project of modernity. For him, Western societies had reached a postmodern condition under the capitalist system, which generated an incredulity in relation to any meta-narratives, such as those defended by Jurgen Habermas.

In its political application, the concept must be understood as an attempt to interpret the contemporary world beyond an almost obsolete characterization as modern. Postmodern politics is seen as an antidote to an oppressive modern society, giving room to the manifestation of several fragmented initiatives that were forgotten in mainline politics. Examples are the ecological movement, proposals for alternative communication, including cyber-activism, the struggle for human rights, feminist and minority movements, victims of the AIDS epidemics, and groups excluded from economic globalization. Postmodernism also denotes the crisis of the university and its relation to scientific knowledge, coming to characterize a series of new studies.

By the 1980s, the idea of postmodernism was definitely established as a concept and practical program. It changed the political-economic mode of production, allowing a move from fordism to flexible accumulation, as David Harvey showed in his 1990 book, *The Condition of Postmodernity*. Since then, the term is understood as a paradigm to understand the current social, political, and economic changes in contemporary societies.

**SEE ALSO**

*Volume 1 Left*: Anti-Globalization.
*Volume 2 Right*: Capitalism; Globalization.

**BIBLIOGRAPHY**

D. Bell, *The Cultural Contradictions of Capitalism* (Basic Books, 1978); H. Bertens, *The Idea of the Postmodern: A History* (Routledge, 1995); H. Dussel, *Historia de la Iglesia en América Latina* (Nova Terra, 1974); J. Habermas, *Der Philosophische Diskurs der Moderne* (Suhrkamp, 1985); D. Harvey, *The Condition of Postmodernity* (Blackwell, 1990); J.-F. Lyotard, *La condition postmoderne* (Minuit, 1979); A. Nascimento, "Colonialism, Modernism, and Postmodernism in Brazil," *Latin America Philosophy*, E. Mendieta, ed.(Indiana University Press, 2003).

AMOS NASCIMENTO
METHODIST UNIVERSITY OF PIRACICABA, BRAZIL

# Praxis Group

THE NAME Praxis Group, or Praxis Circle or Praxis Marxists as they were also known, refers to a group of philosophers in the former Yugoslavia who advocated a humanist interpretation of Marx's works. The praxis approach dominated the faculty of philosophy in Belgrade and the faculties of philosophy and sociology in Zagreb; a number of the key scholars of the approach gained prominence throughout the international academic community in the late 1960s and early 1970s. In addition to being key social critics within Yugoslavia, these thinkers also produced an academic journal, *Praxis*, which focused on engaging key questions around the humanist content of Marx's works. The philosophical work of the Praxis Group made an important and lasting contribution to post-Marx Marxist thought.

In essence, the Praxis approach challenged the Stalinist/authoritarian/reductionist readings of Marx prevalent at the time and instead argued that a humanist approach, or reading, was closer to Marx's own humanism, which clearly recognized the creative agency of individuals. Moreover, the reassertion that "men indeed make their own history" and are the creators, through labor, of their own futures opened up philosophical space for a renewed vision of what a revolutionary, democratic society should look like. As Gerson S. Sher notes in his introduction to *Marxist Humanism and Praxis*: "Underlying the humanist interpretation of Marxism is a radically dynamic view of man and his relation to nature, history and society. It is a view of man that stands in direct contrast to that of the orthodox Marxist school, for which man is merely a passive creature of objective forces—laws of movement of nature, history and society—which exist externally and independently of him. Man is a being of praxis, of practical activity which seeks to challenge, destroy, and transcend the limitations that everyday existence places upon his ability to develop as a free, creative being."

Not surprisingly, the philosophic orientation of the Praxis Group and its commitment to the "ruthless criticism of all that is existing" led to ongoing battles with Yugoslav authorities. Ultimately, the state imposed its own form of discipline on these intellectuals by restricting travel and employment opportunities, censoring publications, and, ultimately in 1975 terminating the publication of *Praxis* within Yugoslavia. Although these state-imposed restrictions were intended to limit both the domestic and international influence of the Praxis Group, the ideas being raised and debated did successfully reach a wider international audience. Erich Fromm's *Socialist Humanism: An International Symposium* (1965), for example, not only broadly engaged conceptions of humanist socialism, but included a number of essays by Yugoslav intellectuals associated with Praxis. Moreover, after the untimely demise of *Praxis*, a number of international scholars published a journal in solidarity with the Yugoslav dissidents entitled *Praxis International* (1981–92). Finally, the scholarship of Sher also ensured that important essays produced by the Praxis Group were translated and made accessible to a wider academic audience.

Key members of the Praxis Group included: Gajo Petrovic, Mihailo Markovic, Predrag Vranicki, Svetozar Stojanovic, Ljubomir Tadic, Rudi Supek, Danko Grlic, Milan Kangrga, Miladin Zvotic, and Zagorka Gulobvic.

**SEE ALSO**

*Volume 1 Left:* Marxism; Marx, Karl; Communism; Socialism; Fromm, Erich.
*Volume 2 Right:* Capitalism.

**BIBLIOGRAPHY**

Erich Fromm, *Socialist Humanism: An International Symposium* (Doubleday, 1965); Gerson S. Sher, *Praxis and Marxist Criticism and Dissent in Socialist Yugoslavia* (Indiana University Press, 1977); Gerson S. Sher, *Marxist Humanism and Praxis* (Prometheus Books, 1978).

SANDRA REIN
ATHABASCA UNIVERSITY

# PRI (Mexico)

THROUGH ITS HISTORY, the PRI, or Partido Revolucionario Institucional (Party of the Institutional Revolution), has evolved from its revolutionary origins, with each six-year presidential administration taking on a character that ranges from left of center to centrist.

In February 1913—during the Mexican Revolution of 1910—the military "man on horseback," General Victoriano Huerta, contrived in the murder of the duly elected President Francisco Madero. Reformist foment, which had aided Madero in ousting the aged strongman Porfirio Diaz in 1910, now rose up again to cast out the ruthless usurper Huerta. On March 26, 1913, one of the revolutionary *jefes*, or chiefs, Venustianzo Carranza, issued his Plan of Guadalupe, which promised (speciously) to carry out the progressive reforms for which Madero had gathered together his revolutionists in 1910. From that point on, the bearded Carranza became the de facto leader of the revolution, its *primer jefe*, or "first chief."

However, the commitment of Carranza to reform was only a matter of political calculation. Only leaders like Francisco "Pancho" Villa in the North of Mexico and Emiliano Zapata in the southern state of Morelos really hoped to champion the lot of the poor *campesinos*, the peasants who had rallied to the call for revolution. Inevitably, the revolution entered a second phase, in which Zapata and Villa challenged the rule of their first chief. However, those who wished to keep the established social order under Carranza possessed the best field general, Alvaro Obregon. In April 1915, Villa's celebrated Division del Norte, the Division of the North, was annihilated at Celaya. Emiliano Zapata was lured into an ambush by government forces and shot to death on April 10, 1919. Finally, the turn came for Carranza himself to die before the bullets of assassins in May 1920. He was succeeded in power by his own commander, Alvaro Obregon—the next "strongman."

With the coming of Obregon, it appeared that the violence of "la Revolucion" had come to an end. Anita

Brenner wrote in *The Wind That Swept Mexico* that Mexico "was new, it was a new world where fear was skewered." Yet it would prove deadly still for those who attempted to disrupt the peace that Obregon imposed on Mexico. On July 23, 1923, Pancho Villa, who like Zapata had kept to the original ideals of the revolution, was assassinated, reportedly at Obregon's insistence.

Nevertheless, the great problem of land reform still eluded solution since the great landowners, the *hacendados*, still backed the establishment, now headed not by Diaz but by the other former general, Obregon. Thus land reform, which had brought Zapata to the revolution, remained a serious threat to Mexican stability. Brenner wrote in *Idols behind Altars* that "insistently Mexico has died and killed for a phrase: Land and liberty." At the same time, the Mexican working class looked for political representation in industries where, as often as not, the ultimate say rested with absentee investors in the United States.

## STRUGGLE FOR REFORM

Luis Morones seized on the discontent of the laboring classes to make CROM, the national labor group, a power in the land. Later, the CTM organization would represent Mexico's burgeoning working class. The struggle for reform inevitably brought the new state into conflict with the old church: the Roman Catholic Church which had flourished and grown rich since the days when the Spanish under Hernando Cortez subjugated the Aztecs in 1521. Obregon's anti-clerical crusade brought forth an expected reaction, as superstitious villagers were urged by the priests to fight for "*el Cristo Rey*," "Christ the King." In 1928, in a restaurant appropriately called La Bomba, a zealot named Leon Toral killed Obregon.

When Plutarco Elias Calles came to power, in 1929 he established the PRI to consolidate the revolutionary settlement that he and the other *jefes* had made in Mexico. However, with the promises still unmet, revolutionary sentiment began to rise up among the people, and the laborers grew restive under the powerful Vincente Toledano. It was clear that Calles was no longer a popular candidate and the politicos, the powerful ones behind the scenes, chose Lazaro Cardenas to govern in his place. Cardenas proved to be the most effective of the PRI presidents and realized real reform for both the rural campesinos and the burgeoning labor force. He also gave Mexico great control over its future by nationalizing the petroleum industry, which had always been under foreign control. PEMEX, the Mexican oil organization, would later capitalize on an offshore production strike in the Gulf of Mexico, which aided modernization of the country. The promise of land reform was brought closer to reality. According to Eric Wolf in *Sons of the Shaking Earth*, "between 1910 and 1945, close to 76 million acres" were redistributed to "independent landowners" and the *ejidos*, landed communities for farmers.

Yet, the years after World War II saw the PRI becoming the government of a one-party state, where all political dissent was discouraged and those who disagreed were either co-opted or threatened into silence. Any real attempt at dissent could be met with as savagely as Obregon and the other *jefes* dealt with their enemies in the revolution. When Gustavo Diaz Ordaz was president, perhaps several hundred students were massacred by army units in 1968—just as the eyes of the world were on Mexico for the Summer Olympic Games that year. Furthermore, the growing importation of narcotics into the United States from Mexico provided an addictive source of income for policemen and other officials who had always been underpaid. Gradually, the power of the *narco-terroristas*, who trafficked in the narcotics, would reach to the highest PRI levels.

On January 1, 1994, the Zapatista Rebellion, named for the great revolutionary hero, broke out in Chiapas Province as a result of continued oppression of the *indios*, Mexico's Indian majority. On March 23, 1994, the PRI candidate for president, Luis Donaldo Colosio, was himself assassinated, inevitably bringing up allegations that the killing was part of Mexico's "*guerro sucio*," or "dirty war," being fought over the vast sums of money being gained by those involved in—or protecting those who were implicated in—the drug trade. The killing of Colosio in many ways was the death knell of the PRI. In elections in December 2000, Vicente Fox Quesada, the candidate of the reformist PAN, or National Action Party, brought an end to the PRI's one-party rule.

Through its history, the PRI veered left and centrist depending on the leader in office. The Cardenas regime, with its policies of land reform, support for the *ejidos*, its nationalization of petroleum, as well as its foreign policy of supporting the Loyalists in the Spanish Civil War, came closest to the social-democratic model of European states. Later regimes, although adopting some central reforms, including economic development programs, public health measures, and rural electrification, tended to be more centrist. As the government structure became more bureaucratic and PRI became more devoted to the retention of power, the party more and more resembled a simple political machine for retaining one-party power. Nevertheless, the preservation of the form of democracy and the tolerance of political parties on both the left and the right left the door open for the eventual transformation of the system into a multiparty state.

## SEE ALSO

*Volume 1 Left*: Mexico.
*Volume 2 Right*: Mexico; Conservatism.

## BIBLIOGRAPHY

Robert A. Rosenstone, *Romantic Revolutionary: A Biography of John Reed* (Vintage Books, 1975;) Charles W. Thayer, *Guerrilla* (Signet, 1963); John Reed, *Insurgent Mexico* (Penguin, 1983); Friedrich Katz, *The Life and Times of Pancho Villa* (Stanford University Press, 1998); Manuel A. Machado, Jr., *Centaur of the North* (Eaken Press, 1988); Anita Brenner, *The Wind That Swept Mexico* (University of Texas Press, 1971); Anita Brenner, *Idols behind Altars* (Beacon Press, 1970); "Mexico: History and Culture," www.geographia.com (July 2004); "Institutional Revolutionary Party, Mexican History," www.allrefer.com (July 2004); Eric Wolf, *Sons of the Shaking Earth* (University of Chicago Press, 1970); "Revisan asesinato de politico Colosio en Mexico," www.terra.com (July 2004); John Mason Hart, *Revolutionary Mexico* (University of California Press, 1987).

JOHN F. MURPHY, JR.
AMERICAN MILITARY UNIVERSITY

# Progressive Party

PROGRESSIVE PARTIES WERE a populist form of radical political organization that experienced some moderate successes in North America in the 20th century. Emerging as oppositional forces against the power of monopoly capitalism, these parties were anti-monopolistic without being anti-capitalist. They spoke on behalf of the interests of the small farmer and the independent small businessperson against the big banks and major manufacturing interests. Such independent operators were open to populist appeals of fairness in commercial dealings and a political voice for the "little guy." They held the belief—deeply resonant with the frontier mindset of American political culture—that the "fat cats" of industry and the venal political leaders needed to be kept in line. The political mechanisms chosen to effect such control were the popular referendum,

the initiative, and the recall. However, the Progressive parties that emerged in both the United States and Canada in the early 20th century were never entirely populist, incorporating elements of elitist bureaucratic reformism that favored social and political engineering over the simple espousal of the popular mood.

The most successful American Progressive party was created in January 1911, as the National Progressive Republican League following a series of defections from the Republican Party. Under the leadership of former president Theodore Roosevelt, these disaffected elements established the Progressive Party, popularly known as the Bull Moose Party. (Roosevelt stated that he felt as fit as a bull moose and therefore capable of fighting on behalf of those excluded from the Republican Party mainstream.) The party called for legislated regulation of big business interests, forms of direct democracy, and moderate social reform. The Progressive Party demanded the direct election of Senators and provisions for recall mechanisms, referenda, and popular initiatives. The party also argued for a level playing field in terms of trade and therefore for a reduction in the tariff. The Progressive Party also called for further restrictions on "industrial combination" (corporate concentration).

Roosevelt did well in the election, receiving over 4 million votes (27 percent of the popular vote), resulting in 88 electoral-college votes. Despite this, the initial momentum was unable to survive and support began to drift away by 1916. In that year, Roosevelt and many other Progressives renewed their memberships in the Republican Party.

The Progressive movement reemerged with some success in 1922 under the Conference for Progressive Political Action that sponsored candidates in the 1922 Congressional elections. The movement supported Robert M. La Follette, Sr., as presidential candidate in 1924, even though he ran as an independent. In this election, La Follette also enjoyed the support of the American Federation of Labor and other left-wing parties. The platform was not merely populist this time, calling for direct democracy, but was also pro-labor. The 1924 platform included demands for stronger state regulation of industry, public ownership, the breakup of monopolies, and recognition of collective bargaining rights. There were also calls for lower taxes on poor Americans and for a range of social assistance programs. La Follette won 5 million votes, but was only able to take the 13 electoral-college votes of Wisconsin. La Follette's sons, Robert M., Jr., and Philip F., continued the movement by forming a Wisconsin Progressive

*A panoramic photo of the National Progressive Convention in Chicago, Illinois, on August 6, 1912, shows the movement at its height. Progressive Party presidential candidate Theodore Roosevelt garnered 27 percent of the popular vote in the 1912 election.*

Party that enjoyed considerable success at the state level throughout the 1930s. The Progressive Party went into decline during World War II, and in 1946 La Follette, Jr., and the Wisconsin Progressive Party joined the Republicans.

The final version of the Progressive Party emerged following World War II as a challenge to the Democratic Party. Endorsed by both the Communist Party and the American Labor Party of New York state, the party contested the 1948 presidential campaign under the leadership of Henry A. Wallace. The party called for greater rapprochement with the Soviet Union and for a repeal of the Taft-Hartley Act, regarded as anti-labor. The Progressive Party of 1948 won just over a million votes (around 2.4 per cent of the total vote), but no electoral-college votes. As a viable political force, the Progressive Party suffered in the anti-communist environment of the early Cold War years. After a very poor showing in the 1952 presidential election, the party disappeared.

The Progressive Party in Canada was formed in 1920 as a political expression of the farmer movements of the west. Frustrated with their second-class constitutional status, economic oppression, and political impotence, the farmers demanded forms of direct democracy and political reform. As small independent producers, they called for free trade and an end to the power of the monopoly corporations. Inspired by American Progressivism, the movement was already spreading throughout western Canada by 1912 and continued to be popular throughout the teens. Riding a wave of popular support, the Progressive Party under Thomas Crerar won 65 seats in the federal election of 1921 and thereby became the largest single opposition party. However, the party soon collapsed through infighting and an incapacity to stand for anything coherent. They won relatively few seats in subsequent elections, as their members moved on to other political parties and movements. In 1942, what remained of the Progressive Party joined the Conservative Party.

Despite only modest successes at the polls, the North American Progressive movement exerted a powerful and long-standing impact on the development of political life and public policy in both Canada and the United States. In the United States, anti-trust legislation, the beginnings of a safety-net welfare state, recognition of the rights of organized labor, and—perhaps most importantly—the habit of supporting direct democratic initiatives and populist leaders changed the political landscape. Most significantly the Seventeenth Amendment, passed in 1913, realized the Progressive goal of instituting directly elected Senators—a major and lasting change in American democracy. In the contemporary United States, the upsurge of direct democracy and the election of charismatic independent candidates in gubernatorial elections reflect a continuation of the populist side of Progressivism. Renewed calls for sociopolitical reform from the liberal end of the political spectrum also celebrate the progressive traditions of grassroots democratic politics, calling for the democratization of American capitalist social relations and the market economy through a more equitable tax system, the removal of large-scale money from politics and positive action to empower the labor force.

## SEE ALSO

Volume 1 Left: La Follette, Robert; Populism.
Volume 2 Right: Roosevelt, Theodore; Republican Party; United States.

## BIBLIOGRAPHY

J.A. Gable, The Bullmoose Years: Theodore Roosevelt and the Progressive Party (1978); Thomas Goebel, A Government by the People (University of North Carolina Press, 2002); W.L. Morton, The Progressive Party in Canada (University of Toronto Press, 1950); Roberto Mangabeiro Unger and Cornel West, The Future of American Progressivism: An Initiative for Political and Economic Reform (Beacon Press, 2003).

PAUL NESBITT-LARKING, PH.D.
HURON UNIVERSITY COLLEGE, CANADA

# Protests

PROTEST IS A MEANS for the common people to assert power over their oppressors. People have protested against the ruling class at least since biblical times. The specific forms of protests are varied and range from aggressive riots to nonviolent acts. Taking to the street in unison for demonstrations or marches, insurgencies, coups d'états, industrial actions (strike, go-slow, work-to-rule), boycotts, petitions, taking over buildings, hunger strikes, and sit-ins are all forms of resistance that signify protest against any number of particular social conditions. Protesters congregate around an ideology or an individual who embodies an ideology, and their numbers can range from small groups to large masses.

Protest movements, as we know them now, first started to develop during the 19th century as the working classes became more educated. The spread of education made the boundaries between the working and the lower middle classes less clearly distinct. This brought with it a desire to have more say in the running of things. Inevitably, this led to various conflicts with the ruling classes. By the end of the 19th century, a number of different protest groups had emerged. Some complained peacefully, others used violence, sabotage, and threats to try and force change.

Resistance leads to protest on a myriad number of issues, both left and right. The bipolar viewpoints that dominated left and right during most of the 20th century were significantly challenged by the fall of communism and the breakup of the Soviet Union at the turn of the 1990s. As J.A. Laponce explains in his book Left and Right: The Topography of Political Perception, the boundaries of left and right shift across time and from country to country. However, he also argues that some contrasts are quite clear when a dualistic approach is applied. Thus, Laponce sees the left as egalitarian rather than hierarchical, concerned with poor people rather than the rich, and emphasizing free thought over religious dogma.

Each of these contrasting qualities has given rise to the most interesting moments of protest in history. Protest on the left embraces a sense of discontinuity over the weight given to tradition and continuity by conservatives. Whether we consider protest in an Old Left or a New Left context, political resistance increased substantially during the 20th century. Formal organized opposition to ruling elites before the twentieth century took the form of peasant revolts, slave rebellions, and the occasional ethnic uprisings.

## AGAINST THE ESTABLISHMENT

Before the 20th century, and into its first decades, the left was largely concerned with party organization and class consciousness. This became most evident by the adoption of the written works of Karl Marx by socialist, communist, and workers' parties in many countries. After the 1930s, this drive was displaced by the cultural agenda of what eventually came to be known as the New Left, when Marx was reinterpreted by Antonio Gramsci and the critical thinkers of the Frankfurt School. Disillusionment with the totalitarian policies of the Soviet Union gave rise to different ways of thinking about the issues at the heart of leftist ideology by many who considered themselves leftists.

The New Left is of great importance to the most radical of protest movements during and after the 1960s, primarily among university students. The New Left movement originated in the 1950s ban-the-bomb movement toward nuclear disarmament, but it was during the 1960s that the term *protest* as we have come to use it now entered the mainstream American vocabulary. Before this time, most protest focused on labor issues, but the New Left brought to the fore more personalized issues such as alienation and authoritarianism. These positions were mainly articulated by protests against the war in Vietnam, a heightened awareness about third world liberation issues, and by embracing a new movement for women's liberation. Resistance to the ever-growing affluent society in the post-World War II industrialized world gave rise to a counterculture, which incorporated the various protest movements that are still present in the economic, ethnic, feminist, and ecological demands by various protest movements in our times.

In the United States, the ideas of the New Left were first embodied most wholeheartedly by the Students for a Democratic Society (SDS), which was founded by Tom Hayden in 1962, when he wrote the Port Huron Statement calling for participatory democracy based on nonviolent civil disobedience. The main protest target of the SDS was the prevailing authority structures in society. Thus this rejection of authority came to be known as anti-establishment. By the late 1960s, the SDS produced at least two extremist splinter factions: the Weather Underground and the Progressive Labor Party. The Weather Underground was a terrorist organization that protested all forms of oppression arising from social inequality and the Vietnam war. Its members aligned themselves with the Black Panthers, dominating all other anti-establishment movements with their vio-

lent protest actions. Other similar left-wing violent protest movements at about the same period include the Red Army Faction of Germany, also known as Baader-Meinhof Gang, and the Brigate Rosse (Red Brigades) in Italy.

The New Left in Britain remained nonviolent, focusing their actions on the Campaign for Nuclear Disarmament and the double standards of the Soviet Union and other totalitarian regimes who hypocritically embraced socialism and communism while oppressing their citizens. Some students within the British New Left joined the International Socialists, which later became Socialist Workers Party (UK) while others became involved with groups such as the International Marxist Group.

## AGAINST OPPRESSION

Repression, be it from the government or from any other source of great power intimidates potential protesters. At the same time, one of the greatest driving forces for many protest movements is the understanding that rulers do not govern by divine authority and that socioeconomic inequality is not inevitable.

Most, if not all, protests can be labeled as acts against oppression. Using Laponce's contrast between egalitarian and hierarchical societies, we can see revolutions, such as the French Revolution (Paris in 1789), the American Revolution (Boston in 1774), and the Russian Revolution (St Petersburg in 1905 and Petrograd/Moscow in 1917), as large-scale protests.

Property damage, physical assaults, and assassinations are products of violent protest. However, violence is not a necessary component of all actions against the oppressive rule by state institutions or the economic elite. Most violent protest occurs when the suffering protesters either believe that they should govern themselves or feel that rather than voice their opinion against a particular issue they should eliminate the cause of their subjugation. In this way, terrorism (in the broadest sense of the word, since there is no universally accepted definition) is a form of violent protest. The violent tactics of terrorists who targets civilians, creating fear and/or political discord in the targeted society, have the intent of bringing about social change that favors the issue. Terrorists resort to individual or group terror acts when other avenues for change do not appear as effective. One way to reduce terrorism is to ensure that where there is a population feeling oppressed, some avenue of problem resolution is kept open, especially when dealing with minority groups. While terrorism is undoubtedly the most extreme and violent of all forms of protest, riots and lawless public assemblies are also extreme and violent. In contrast with terrorism, which is usually premeditated violence, riots are usually fairly spontaneous acts of violent protest from exasperated citizens.

Riots are violent versions of one of the most nonviolent forms of protest: mass congregation in public places for demonstrations or protest marches. The term *protest march* can be traced back to the 1913 march organized by Mohandas Gandhi to protest restrictions imposed on Indians in South Africa. Gandhi became famous for proposing nonviolent civil disobedience as a form of protest later in his life, when he used such tactics to promote the independence of India from British colonial rule. In turn, without Gandhi's direct involvement, South Africa became a place of radical protest for 40 years after 1955.

## AGAINST RACIAL DISCRIMINATION

The anti-apartheid movement embodied the desire for social equality by millions of oppressed black people in South Africa. It acted as an agent of change, seeking to influence policy at the Organization of African Unity (OAU), founded in 1963 to promote self-government, respect for territorial boundaries, and social progress throughout the African continent, as well as the British Commonwealth and the United Nations (UN). At the historic the 1977 UN-OAU conference in Nigeria, the UN suggested that the anti-apartheid movement should establish a World Campaign against Nuclear and Military Collaboration with South Africa, bringing international attention to the situation in the country.

Subsequently, in 1994, this movement managed to bring an end to official racial discrimination and saw the first black political leaders take charge of the country. In spite of this, the issue of economic inequality is still cause for protest in South Africa at the turn of the 21st century.

Centuries of racial discrimination in the United States led to the rise of the civil rights movement in the 20th century. Under the leadership of Martin Luther King, Jr., the civil rights movement used civil disobedience as its preferred protest tactic. The civil rights movement was most active between 1955 and 1965, starting with the Montgomery, Alabama, bus boycott and culminating with the follow-up to the 1963 March on Washington. Congress passed the Civil Rights Act of 1964 and the Voting Rights Act of 1965, guaranteeing basic civil rights for all Americans, regardless of

*A mother and son join a ban-the-bomb group in 1962, protesting President Kennedy's decision to resume atom-bomb testing.*

race, after nearly a decade of nonviolent protests and marches.

Characterized by the active refusal to obey certain laws and government regulations, civil disobedience is often used by protesters who choose not to resort to physical violence in their demands. Henry David Thoreau is credited with theorizing this practice in his 1849 essay, originally titled "Resistance to Civil Government." In the essay, Thoreau explains his reasons for having refused to pay his taxes as an act of protest against slavery and against the U.S.-Mexican War (1846–48).

## AGAINST WAR

Anti-war protests are not a modern phenomenon. In *Lysistrata*, a Greek comedy written by Aristophanes in 410 B.C.E., the women in the warring cities of Athens and Sparta conspire to deprive all men of sexual intercourse for the duration of the war. Moreover, the Athenean women stage one of the first recorded sit-ins by occupying the Parthenon, blocking access to the state treasury where the war chest is housed. While this play is a fictionalized version of something that may or may not have happened the way it is depicted, it certainly records a strong anti-war sentiment in the ancient world.

The first significant anti-war protest movement in modern times appeared before World War II. Eileen Eagan has chronicled an impressive account of the student peace movement of the 1930s in *Class, Culture, and the Classroom*. Thirty years before a new generation would follow in their footsteps, American students embodied the Marxist, pacifist, and reformist impulse that came from the Great Depression and international conflict, which eventually brought about World War II.

Thousands of students from schools as diverse as City College of New York and the University of Idaho took what was known as the Oxford Oath; swearing never to fight in any war conducted by the United States. On April 12, 1935, approximately 200,000 college students staged a one-hour strike protesting potential U.S. involvement in war. Similar sentiments were heard that day on about 140 college campuses in the 31 countries that participated in the event.

In the latter part of the 20th century, anti-war protests took on more than a message of peace as they had done in before. On January 17, 1961, President Dwight D. Eisenhower drew the world's attention to the military-industrial complex during his final speech as president. The military-industrial complex refers to relationship between the military and industrialists who profit by manufacturing arms and selling them to the government. This is also known as war profiteering. The concept of gave the anti-war left further reason to protest war beyond pacifist issues.

Most college campus activities in the United States involving the anti-war movement were organized around the SDS during the Vietnam War. Widespread opposition to the war made the SDS a prominent organization on a national level. Besides student protests in the United States, a wave of student protest movements broke out in many other countries, mainly across Europe and Japan. The effects of 1968 worldwide student protests were only really felt years later, when it became the reference point for many post-1968 student protest movement. When in June 3-4, 1989, students protested against the authoritarian Chinese government in Beijing's Tiananmen Square, they were frequently compared to the student protests of 1968 in places like Czechoslovakia and France, by the media and others who were familiar with the events of 1968.

## AGAINST RELIGIOUS DOGMA

Religion is at the heart of many protest movements. Most religious activism tends to be aligned with issues that are more in line with right-wing or conservative ways of thinking, but the left too has protest movements associated with religious beliefs. Historically, the most striking case is perhaps that of Protestant Christians in Northern Europe during the 16th century.

The 16th century saw great debate about Christian religious values leading to major reforms. The reformist movements occurred in conjunction with economic, political, and demographic forces that contributed to a growing hostility towards the wealth and power of the elite clergy. This movement was strengthened during the Enlightenment when many took a stance against the powerful Roman Catholic Church by embracing major scientific discoveries, such as the fact the earth was not flat and that it is not the center of the solar system.

The German theologian Martin Luther was one of the foremost Christian leaders to lead Protestant churches to part ways with the dogmatic ways of the Roman Catholic doctrines of the Vatican. Luther worked to change the church by making radical declarations, which he posted on church doors. He called for a return to the teachings of the Bible and insisted on making vernacular translations of the Bible available to all. These actions led to the formation of new traditions within Christianity, such as Lutheranism, Reformed churches, and Anabaptists.

Ironically, religious doctrine was often brought up in cases involving the civil rights of homosexuals and the reproductive rights of women during the final third of the 20th century. The gay rights movement began with the 1969 Stonewall riots, a series of violent conflicts between homosexuals and the New York City Police Department, which started after police raided the Stonewall Inn, a gay bar in Greenwich Village. This was the first time that a significant number of gays resisted arrest. Within months of the Stonewall riots, the Gay Liberation Front was formed, serving as a catalyst for other similar organizations in countries around the world, particularly Canada, most of Europe, Australia and New Zealand. Lesbian activism appeared at this time too, partly in relation to the radical feminism movement, which protested against the control of woman's rights over reproduction, also known as abortion rights. Large groups of lesbians came together to join many gay protests, and even organize their own.

## AGAINST THE SUBJUGATION OF WOMEN

Arguments against gender inequality and the promotion of women's rights, particularly the need for women's voices to be heard within a democratic society, were the issues that brought the oppression of women

*British anti-war demonstrators march on February 15, 2003, in London, protesting the impending invasion of Iraq by a coalition of American and British military forces.*

into mainstream consciousness. The international movement for women's suffrage, which first appeared in the mid-19th century, was the first social, economic, and political force to raise awareness about large-scale activism and advocacy about a woman's right to vote. In the United States, equal suffrage was first extended to women in the Wyoming Territory in 1869, but it was only in 1920 that a Constitutional Amendment ensured the right of all American women to vote. The earliest countries extending that right were New Zealand in 1893 and Australia in 1902. Women in United Kingdom were granted the right to vote in 1928. In Russia universal suffrage came with the 1917 revolution, but it was only with the Civil Rights Act of 1965 that all adults, without distinction as to race, sex, belief, or social status could vote in the United States.

Feminist political activists advocate such issues as women's suffrage, salary equivalency, and control over reproduction. Radical feminists, who were most vocal during the 1960s and 1970s, saw patriarchy as the rea-

son for most social problems. Some radical feminists argued that gender roles, gender identity, and sexuality are constructed by society as ways to wield power. For them, feminism is a primary means to liberation from other social problems. Other feminists emphasize other social problems, such as racism or class divisions, and see their movement as one of many working for liberation. Very few advances have been made in most non-Western countries by feminists, but many of the issues are also very pertinent all over the world particularly if seen as within the framework of freedom from oppression.

One of the reasons why expanded equality for women became so important throughout the 20th century is because different generations of feminists have also often aligned themselves with other low-income workers. Immigrants and children were also often exploited even more than regular workers, and unfortunately this issue remains quite pertinent in many countries even in our time. Socioeconomic equality

*Left-wing protests can overlap causes: The sign above protests against war and big business simultaneously.*

often gives reason for protest again capitalism and the economic structures that arise out of it.

## AGAINST CAPITALISM

Until the beginning of the 20th century, workers often labored for long hours and were paid very little. As people began to discuss how to improve their work conditions, the labor movement was born. There are now many laws protecting workers, but concerns about working conditions in many countries around the world. For various reasons, workers continue to seek higher wages, better health benefits, adequate pension schemes, and more vacation time.

In most industrialized nations during the 19th and early 20th centuries, employers could easily replace

workers because there was an abundance of labor. Many workers saw that one way to control this trend was for workers to join together to protect each other's employment. Large unions were formed to help workers bargain for their rights and requirements. Groups of workers have more bargaining power than individual employees. Employers are forced to listen to the concerns raised by unionized workers because if all their employees stop working at the same time, their business would suffer. The labor movement became a noticeable force in the United States by the 1930s, forcing Congress to pass the National Labor Relations Act of 1935 and other laws requiring employers to bargain with labor unions.

Protest by the labor movement in many countries around the world is divided in two categories: political action and direct action. Political action is achieved through membership in socialist groups and the trade union movement, emphasizing the dynamics of democracy. Direct action takes the form of strikes, propaganda, and boycotts. In both cases, arbitration and political affiliation play an important role.

Organized labor is not as powerful today as it once was. However, many people such as factory, construction, and industry employees are union members. In terms of protest, unions have relied on the premanaged economic and labor structure of syndicalism to enact direct actions often involving general strikes and even sabotage. Nonviolent civil disobedience has also been used by labor movements. An example of this is from the United Farm Workers (UFW), which was founded by Cesar Chavez and Dolores Huerta, and came to prominence almost overnight, when the National Farm Workers Association went out on strike in support of the mostly Filipino laborers in Delano, California, in 1965. Among several tactics, the UFW launched a boycott on table grapes and after five years won a contract with the major California grape growers. However, some of its public protest actions often became violent, with a number of UFW members killed on the picket line.

Boycotts are one of the preferred methods of protest for labor movements. This is quite clear from the actions of the American Federation of Labor and Congress of Industrial Organizations (AFL-CIO), the largest federation of labor unions in North America. The AFL-CIO has a Union Label and Service Trades Department, which organizes large-scale boycotts. For a number of reasons, a company's products or services can be put on the national list of AFL-CIO-endorsed boycotts, giving affiliated international and national unions a strong bargaining position to help the firm's employees protest against their company.

Boycott is also a form of protest favored by environmental activists. Environmentalists strongly believe that humanity should attain harmony with nature, rather than conquer it through technological exploitation. Prominent among environmental protest groups is Greenpeace, which has celebrated the power of the dissenting individual voice raised into direct action since 1985. The Greenpeace ship, the *Rainbow Warrior*, sails around the world protesting nuclear testing and dumping of nuclear wastes, whaling, and the devastation of the oceans by large corporations who lobby governments for decisions that will give them substantially greater revenues. In May 2001, Greenpeace's Stop Esso campaign, called on supporters to buy gas and other petroleum products from anyone but ExxonMobil (known as Esso in Europe), which the environmental movement sees as relentlessly campaigning against and subverting climate control initiatives such as the Kyoto Protocol. While boycotts and other nonviolent actions are the hallmark of environmental protest, there are also radical environmentalists, even within Greenpeace, who resort to violent or illegal forms of activism, which are termed ecoterrorism.

Labor, environmental, and racial/ethnic issues all come together in the protest actions of the anti-globalization movement, which is most visible whenever and wherever there is a meeting of the World Trade Organization or other similar body, such as the World Bank (WB), the International Monetary Fund (IMF). Rather than any of the traditional issues of the left, some anti-globalization activists are mostly concerned with what they see as the undemocratic workings of globalization, often calling it a new form of aristocracy, where government rule is in the hands of the wealthy upper classes of business people.

## SEE ALSO

*Volume 1 Left*: Civil Right; Human Rights; Suffragists; King, Martin Luther, Jr.; United States; Unions; Anti-Globalization; Greenpeace.
*Volume 2 Right*: Protests; United States; Conservatism; Capitalism; Globalization.

## BIBLIOGRAPHY

Charles F. Andrain and David E. Apter, *Political Protest and Social Change* (New York University Press, 1995); Michael Dorman, *Confrontation* (Delacorte Press, 1974); Eileen Eagan, *Class, Culture and the Classroom* (Temple University Press, 1981); Barbara Epstein, *Political Protest and Cultural Revolution* (University of California Press, 1991); J.A. Laponce, *Left and Right: The Topography of Political Perceptions* (University of Toronto Press, 1981); Gene Sharp, *The Politics of Nonviolent Action* (Porter Sargent Publishers, 1973); Henry David Thoreau, *Civil Disobedience and Other Essays* (Dover Publications, 1993 reprint).

TONI SANT
NEW YORK UNIVERSITY

# The Left

# Q-R

## Québec Separatism

FRENCH-CANADIAN SEPARATISM is a reflection of the uneasy position of French-speaking Québec in English-speaking Canada. Its historical roots date at least to the 1840s. Whether based on nationalist or economic motives, it seeks to restore special status and pride by either establishing total equality with English Canada or by actually separating and establishing a new sovereign nation.

Québec was largely independent from 1791 to 1841, at least it was free of other Canadian influences and direction. Confederation lessened Québec's status within Canada and fueled Québécois resentment. English Canada exacerbated the situation by executing Louis Riel in 1885 for leading the Metis uprising in the northwest and removing the Metis. The Manitoba Schools Question of 1890 eventually led to the end of French-language schools in Manitoba, further rankling French Canadians, who already felt slighted by the Metis crisis.

During the 1890s, French Canada was urbanizing and industrializing. Industrialization ended the French Canadian myth of the special Roman Catholic mission and the almost Jeffersonian cult of the virtuous agriculturalist. Québécois were increasingly obsolete and archaic in the modern industrial urban world. By 1921, Québec led the provinces in urbanization and industrialization. Government support of *laissez-faire* econom-

ics allowed abuses and excesses of French Canadian workers by owners, who tended to be English, Canadians, or Americans. The language of the businesses was English.

The pivotal events occurred under the leadership of Premier Maurice Duplessis. Economically conservative and strongly nationalist, Duplessis led Québec from 1936 to 1939 and from 1944 to 1959. He lost the 1939 election after challenging central government power over the provinces in wartime. He opposed much that came from Ottawa, the capital, after 1944 in education and social programs. He was anti-trade unions, pro-Catholic, and in favor of foreign investment. He was a founder of the Union Nationale (UN). But Québec continued urbanizing and industrializing in the late 1940s and 1950s. A French-speaking middle class emerged, and more students finished high school and entered college. When Duplessis died in 1959, the province was ready for a political change to match the economic and social ones. Jean Lesage and the Québec Liberal Party took power in June 1960 and began the Quiet Revolution, reforms that eliminated the corruption that had spread during the Duplessis era. The government removed the Catholic Church from secular involvement; invested in education, social infrastructure, and economic development; nationalized and consolidated the power companies; established a provincial pension; and created an investment capital fund.

In 1966, the Liberals lost power to the Union Nationale. Québécois labor and intellectual leaders believed that the economic problems of Québec were the result of the confederation. The only solution to the problems was either alteration or severing of ties with the central government and the English-speaking provinces. The UN and the Liberals polarized as public opinion hardened on their fringes. The parties accepted federalism, but differed on the degree of central control. The two parties shared the center while left extremists demands ranged from special status for Québec to outright separation and independence. A splinter group of the Liberals in Montreal were separatists, and their efforts laid the foundation for the secessionist Parti Québécois (PQ). The PQ, under Rene Levesque, a converted Liberal, won 24 percent of the vote in 1970, and outdated electoral districts allowed the Liberals to take 72 of 95 seats. The Liberals continued to work for reform of the constitution.

Terror was another element from 1963 on. Terrorists kidnapped British trade commissioner, James Cross, and Québec Labour Minister Pierre Laporte, the latter of whom they murdered. Québec called for federal assistance. Under the War Measures Act, civil liberties were suspended, federal troops entered Québec, and 500 arrests resulted. Although the murderers of Laporte were convicted, few others were.

In 1969, Canada declared that both French and English were official languages. Québec's official language became French in 1974. The separatists won the 1976 election and passed measures including a 1977 law limiting education in English-language schools. Other measures were the elimination of English place names and the mandatory use of French in courts, business, official documents and laws, government, and other public institutions.

The separatists were in power in 1980 when provincial independence was defeated in a referendum. The 1982 constitution called for freedom of language in education. The government opposed this measure and sought the power to veto constitutional change. The Canadian Supreme Court overturned the restrictions on schools in 1984. The Meech Lake Accord gave Québec status as a "distinct society." It also transferred powers from the central government to the provinces. Québec agreed to accept the 1982 constitution on condition that all other provinces accepted the accord. Although the House of Commons ratified Meech Lake on June 22, 1988, Manitoba and Newfoundland refused to ratify the accord on June 23, 1990. The accord died. New constitutional proposals developed by a committee of Parliament were agreed to in 1992. Québec was to have a special status, power would be decentralized, and the Senate would be elected. Canadian voters rejected the reforms in October 1992. Québec voters went to the polls in 1995 and narrowly rejected secession.

One stimulus for the cooling of the separatist impulse was the flight of English-speakers to Ontario and the United States in the 1970s and 1980s. The flight had generated economic dislocation, but it also helped spur accommodation by the remaining English speakers. The language and culture laws of the period also helped to pacify the French speakers. In 2003, the elections to the provincial assembly indicated that separatism, while still alive, was fading and quiescent—at least for the time being. The question of sovereignty was not even significant because the premier, Bernard Landry, recognized that another referendum would guarantee the Parti Québécois a losing poll in Montreal, home to 45 percent of the 7.2 million Québécois. The Liberal candidate was leading in the polls anyway. Other issues took primacy over independence for both French and English speakers: taxes, healthcare, and the economy, and the Liberals won 76 of the 125 seats in Parliament.

**SEE ALSO**

*Volume 1 Left:* Liberalism; Liberal Party, Canada; Canada.
*Volume 2 Right:* Canada; Xenophobia.

**BIBLIOGRAPHY**

Canadian Broadcasting Company, "Quebec Votes 2003," www.cbc.ca (June 2004); Charles F. Doran, *Why Canadian Unity Matters and Why Americans Care* (University of Toronto Press, 2001); Mike Fox, "Quebec Separatist Premier Quits," BBC News (January 11, 2001); Clifford Krauss, "In Quebec, Separatism Gives Way to Bicultural Spirit," *New York Times* (April 13, 2003); James M. McPherson, *Is Blood Thicker Than Water?* (Vintage Books, 1999); Kenneth McRoberts, *Misconceiving Canada* (Oxford University Press, 1997).

JOHN BARNHILL, PH.D.
INDEPENDENT SCHOLAR

# Rand School of Social Science

THE RAND SCHOOL of Social Science was established in New York City and was created by Carrie Herron and Morris Hillquit in 1917, using a trust fund left by Carrie's grandmother, Caroline Rand. Caroline Rand's socialist beliefs had been strengthened by her relationship with George Davis Herron, who eventually married her daughter, Carrie Herron. Carrie Herron, daughter of George and Carrie Rand Herron, acted upon her grandmother's wishes, establishing the school at the turn of the 20th century, and it soon became a center for labor and socialism in New York City until it closed its doors in 1956.

George Davis Herron was born in Montezuma, Indiana, on January 21, 1862. He was the son of William Herron, who was a teacher and newspaper publisher, and Isabella Davis. He received his only formal schooling as a student in the preparatory department of Ripon College in 1879, paying tuition by editing one of the college's most respected newsletters. However, his health problems returned and he was forced to drop out in 1881.

After returning to newspaper publishing, Herron married Mary V. Everhard of Ripon in 1883, with whom Herron had four children. Also in 1883, he decided to join the ministry and he was the pastor of a small Congregational church in the Dakota Territory. From this point, Herron rededicated himself to being a scholar, studying theology, philosophy, sociology, and economics. Throughout the religious community, his powerful preaching led to his rise to prominence.

Driven to spread his beliefs, Herron began to affiliate himself with the Social Christian movement, which had been first formed internationally on the basis that its members believed that the church could offer political solutions to the problems faced by the middle class. In 1891, Herron published a collection of his sermons titled *The Larger Christ*, which resulted in his appointment as pastor at the First Congregational Church of Burlington, Iowa, and his eventual reception of an honorary doctorate from Tabor College.

Within his new congregation, Herron took advantage of the opportunity to associate with Caroline Amanda Rand, a wealthy philanthropist. His relationship with Rand proved to be very beneficial. She arranged for him to become professor and the head of a new Department of Applied Christianity at Iowa College, which would later become Grinnell College. His classes soon became quite popular and Herron became one of the center components of the Kingdom Movement, which was an effort to place churches at the center of nationwide reforms to ameliorate labor strife and the ongoing Depression. With the acclaim and attention he received, Herron became more and more outspoken, which brought his position at the college under attack

for some of his more controversial views. In October 1899, Herron presented his resignation.

Taking advantage of the opportunity, Herron began to travel in Europe, accompanied by Caroline Rand and her daughter, Carrie Rand. During his time abroad, Herron became distanced from his wife, Mary. He demanded a divorce and the situation soon became quite a scandal. In March 1901, Herron was sued for cruelty and desertion by his wife and lost the suit. By May 1901, Herron was remarried to Carrie Rand and they moved to New York City, where Herron hoped to pursue his political activities. In June of the same year, he was defrocked as a Congregational minister as a result of the divorce and remarriage scandal.

Once settled in New York City, Herron and his new wife, Carrie Rand Herron, began to play an increasingly important role in the formation of the Socialist Party of America. He started to write for many socialist publications, but he could not escape the previous scandal, and decided to return to Europe with his new wife in 1902. He returned to the United States, having taken a more Marxist position from his experiences in Europe. By 1904, Herron nominated Eugene Debs for the presidency and arranged the party platform.

Still, criticism of the Herrons continued and they fled to Italy, living in Florence, where Caroline, mother of Carrie, died in 1905, leaving the funds later used to set up the Rand School of Social Science. Herron wrote extensively and made contacts throughout Europe, while trying to reconcile socialism with other reform movements. Carrie died in 1915 and Herron remarried again. With the outbreak of World War I, Herron disavowed socialism since he believed it was too pacifist. Then, Herron moved to Geneva, Switzerland, and helped with the Allies' coordination activities. After the war, Herron became a strong believer in Woodrow Wilson. Years later, Herron died in Munich, Germany.

His work had benefited socialists throughout the United States, who now had the opportunity to attend the Rand School for Social Science in New York City, as a result of Herron's relationship with the Rands. The school had a short, but often controversial history. In 1917, the school reestablished itself at 7 East 15th Street, near Union Square, where it remained until it shut its doors about 55 years later. It was modeled after the Socialist People's Houses in Europe, with which Herron had been very familiar. Faculty included Scott Nearing, Betrand Russell, and Charles and Mary Beard. Often, it evoked negative feelings from New York City police, who raided the school and seized some writings from the library which were never returned.

Following World War II, the Rand school was unable to continue operating due to finances. In 1956, a socialist summer camp located in the Pocono Mountains of Pennsylvania took control of the Rand school and its library. In 1963, New York University acquired the library, which remains one of the best collections of writings on the history of the New York City labor movement.

## SEE ALSO

*Volume 1 Left:* Debs, Eugene V.; Socialism; Socialist Party, U.S.; Nearing, Scott.
*Volume 2 Right:* Capitalism; United States.

## BIBLIOGRAPHY

"George Davis Herron," University of Central Oklahoma, www.libarts.ucok.edu (May 2004); "NYU Libraries," New York University, www.nyu.edu/library (May 2004); Norma Fain Pratt, *Morris Hillquit: A Political History of an American Jewish Socialist* (Greenwood, 1979).

ARTHUR HOLST, PH.D.
WIDENER UNIVERSITY

# Randolph, A. Philip (1889–1979)

IN THE 35 YEARS before the birth of the modern civil rights movement that he helped to spearhead, A. Philip Randolph was the most prominent—and the most effective—African American leader in the United States. His persuasiveness and adroit use of political pressure on two presidents led to creation of the first federal civil rights enforcement body as well as full integration of the armed forces.

The son of a Florida minister who impressed on his sons a love of the classics and an appreciation for black heroes of history, Randolph moved to New York City for a college education and in hopes of becoming an actor. But he forged a friendship with Chandler Owen, a law student and a socialist, and abandoned the stage for a lifetime commitment to leftist politics. In 1915, they cofounded *The Messenger*, billed as "the first radical Negro magazine," and Randolph gained fame in Harlem as a soapbox orator. Attorney General A. Mitchell Palmer tried to suppress the magazine during World War I, then arrested Randolph for urging blacks not to serve in the armed forces; the charges were later dropped.

Eventually, Randolph turned to labor organizing and joined the fledgling Brotherhood of Sleeping Car Porters, which he built into a union that was 8,000 strong—and the first with a membership that was almost exclusively African American. But it would take a dozen years before the railroad companies were willing to recognize the Brotherhood union and negotiate a contract with the workers, which they finally did in 1935.

It took Randolph longer, however, to force an end to racial discrimination within his own trade-union movement. For decades, he pressed the American Federation of Labor (AFL) to end segregation in its member unions; those efforts were rebuffed by AFL leader George Meany, who once indignantly demanded, "Who the hell appointed you as the guardian of all the negroes in America?"

In 1941, Randolph called for a national march of African Americans on Washington, D.C., the first mass protest of its kind, to demand an end to segregation in the military and discrimination in defense employment. The prospect so alarmed President Franklin D. Roosevelt that, after failing to pressure Randolph into canceling the event, he agreed to form the Fair Employment Practices Committee, which prohibited discrimination throughout the federal government, whereupon Randolph agreed to abandon the march. Threats of a similar march nine years later prompted Roosevelt's successor, Harry Truman, to integrate the armed forces.

Randolph did not openly oppose America's participation in World War II, as he had done in the previous global conflict. But he warned that "unless this war sounds the death knell to the old Anglo-American empire, it will have been fought in vain." Ever the dedicated socialist, he declared that "only a peace without imperialism will be a just peace that will endure."

By 1963, Randolph realized that mass protest was necessary to force a wholesale change in American racial attitudes, and he called for the March on Washington of 1963, where Martin Luther King, Jr., delivered his "I Have a Dream" speech. The event served as a symbolic passing of the torch from Randolph to a new generation of civil rights leaders. Illness prevented him from playing a key role in the activist politics of the 1960s, and his open denunciation of the militant black nationalist movement led younger activists to deride him as out of touch. But the movement he helped found continued to resound to his call that "We are the advance guard of a massive moral revolution for jobs and freedom."

SEE ALSO

BIBLIOGRAPHY
"A. Philip Randolph," Current Biography (October 1951); Paul Delaney, "A. Philip Randolph Is Dead; Pioneer in Rights and Labor," New York Times (May 17, 1979); John A. D'Emilio, Lost Prophet: The Life and Times of Bayard Rustin (Free Press, 2003); Kathleen A. Hauke, Ted Poston: Pioneer American Journalist (University of Georgia Press, 1998); James A. Wechsler, "A Tenacious Stoic against Prejudice," New York Post (May 18, 1979).

ERIC FETTMANN
INDEPENDENT SCHOLAR

# Reed, John (1887–1920)

JOHN SILAS REED was born in Portland, Oregon, to a middle-class family. His bourgeois origins gave no indication of the role he would play in two of the 20th century's most landmark revolutions. He matriculated at Harvard University, where he joined literary magazines in 1908. Here, the talents he would use in progressive thought were honed before an appreciative, yet discriminating audience. He joined the Harvard Lampoon and Monthly, becoming acquainted with the young poet Alan Seeger. Seeger's social consciousness and desire to fight oppression would lead him and other Harvard students to join the French Foreign Legion in 1914 to help defend against the German invasion in World War I.

After graduating from Harvard in June 1910, Reed took a tour through Europe, which was then de rigeur—an expected part of growing up—for those in the American upper- and upper-middle classes before World War I. While he enjoyed himself—a lucrative letter of credit assisted him, as Robert A. Rosenstone noted in Romantic Revolutionary: A Biography of John Reed—he began to develop the social consciousness that would characterize the mature part of his tragically short career. In the middle of enjoying Paris, France, Reed wrote that he would like to travel around the world, but only "when I have done something worth while myself." He went to New York City, where he became part of the intellectual ferment that made Greenwich Village a central location for progressive thought in the first third of the 20th century. Reed began working with Max Eastman on The Masses, a journal established in January 1911 that found itself becoming the voice of the socialists and other liberal thinkers who had been making New York City an intellectual hotbed since the 1880s.

Reed's first real social commitment came when he went to cover the silk workers' strike in Paterson, New Jersey. There, he met one of the most charismatic labor leaders of the period, William D. "Big Bill" Haywood of the International Workers of the World (IWW), or the "Wobblies." Arrested at the strike, after release Reed wrote of the strike in what could be seen as the inauguration of his career as a radical journalist. Writing of the oppression of the strikers by the police, Reed declared in The Masses, "the police club unresisting men and women and ride down law-abiding crowds."

Reed's pursuit of radical journalism led him to witness two of the most important upheavals of his time: the Mexican and Russian revolutions. On October 4, 1910, the Mexican dictator Porfirio Diaz, through manipulated elections, had been elected president for the eighth time. Resistance to Diaz coalesced around Francisco Madero, who became president after the people, dissatisfied with the Diaz oligarchs who had despoiled Mexico, overthrew Diaz. In a period of leaderless times, in the north of Mexico, the most charismatic leader was Francisco "Pancho" Villa, an outlaw turned revolutionary.

The Mexican Revolution had a profound effect on American journalism; the famous writer and Civil War veteran Ambrose Bierce would travel to Mexico, only to disappear. Reed was sent to the northern Mexico battle lines by the Metropolitan magazine in November 1913. Meeting with Villa, he reported a vivid picture of el centauro del norte, "the centaur of the north." Wrote Reed, "everywhere he was known as the Friend of The Poor. He was the Mexican Robin Hood."

However, events in Europe summoned Reed from seeing the revolution to its end, with its First Chief Venustianzo Carranza assassinated in 1920, and Villa meeting the same fate in 1923.

World War I had begun in Europe on August 4, 1914, frustrating the efforts of European socialists and other liberal thinkers to stop the mad race to war that the system of alliances had made perilously easy in the preceding years. Writing again for the Metropolitan, Reed saw the titanic battles of men and material on the Eastern Front, so often ignored in the writings of other war correspondents who filed their reports from Paris,

France. Reed arrived, in September 1917, in Russia, the main ally of France and England against Germany and the Austrian Empire. In November 1917, he watched as Tzarist Russia, ruled by the autocratic Tzar Nicholas II, collapsed into revolution and anarchy, having been overwhelmed by war and misrule. From the beginning of his Russian odyssey, Reed favored the Bolshevik Party of V.I. Lenin and Leon Trotsky. His friend Albert Rhys Williams, as Robert A. Rosenstone noted, spoke for both of them when he admired the Bolsheviks: "They want the sort of social justice you and I want."

As when he had followed Villa's fighting men, *la Division del Norte*, the Division of the North, into combat, so too did Reed become a participant—not just an observer—in the revolutionary ferment around him. Indeed, Trotsky lauds him in *The Russian Revolution* as "the observant John Reed," and again as "John Reed, who did not miss one of the dramatic episodes of the revolution." In 1919, Reed's classic *Ten Days That Shook the World* was published, giving a rare first-hand account of the Bolshevik takeover in November 1917. He wrote of the day when the Bolsheviks took power from the bourgeois provisional government of Alexander Kerensky, "in the name of the [Bolshevik] Military Revolutionary Committee, Trotzky [sic] had declared that the Provisional Government no longer existed." In August 1920, he went to Baku in Soviet Central Asia to take part in a congress dedicated to bringing the eastern peoples into the world revolutionary movement. On his return to Moscow, a weakened Reed contracted typhus. With his beloved Louise Bryant by his side, he died on October 17, 1920. At his funeral in historic Red Square in Moscow, a banner proclaimed his life of commitment to bettering the life of his fellow men and women through political and social action. The banner read: "The leaders die, but the cause lives on."

### SEE ALSO

*Volume 1 Left:* Communism; Media Bias, Left; Soviet Union; Russian Revolution.
*Volume 2 Right:* Soviet Union; Totalitarianism.

### BIBLIOGRAPHY

Robert A. Rosenstone, *Romantic Revolutionary: A Biography* (Vintage Books, 1975); Charles W. Thayer, *Guerrilla* (Signet, 1963); John Reed, *Insurgent Mexico* (Penguin, 1983); Friedrich Katz, *The Life and Times of Pancho Villa* (Stanford University Press, 1998); Manuel A. Machado, Jr., *Centaur of the North* (Eaken Press, 1988); Leon Trotsky, *The Russian Revolution*, Max Eastman, trans. (Anchor Books, 1959; John Reed, *Ten Days That Shook the World* (Boni and Liveright, 1919); John Mason Hart, *Revolutionary Mexico: The Coming and Process of the Mexican Revolution* (University of California Press, 1987).

JOHN F. MURPHY, JR.
AMERICAN MILITARY UNIVERSITY

# Rochdale Movement

THE ROCHDALE MOVEMENT gets its name from the Rochdale Society of Equitable Pioneers, which appeared in England in 1844. The original pioneers consisted of seven flannel weavers who quickly grew their society on Rochdale's Toad Lane in Greater Manchester into the Rochdale Equitable Co-operative Society Ltd. Common housing, production cooperatives, and common land for collective agriculture were among their ventures besides their original store. Production cooperatives and stores were owned and run by members of the society, who were also their primary consumers and customers.

The Rochdale pioneers based their society on the idea of a cooperative movement that was first proposed by Robert Owen (1771–1858), a Welshman who is known as the founder of socialism in Britain. Although Owen was originally a successful capitalist who traded in cotton, he also believed in worker control. He believed that it was good for businesses to provide a healthy environment to his workers and access to education for themselves and their families. His own attempts to create what he called "villages of co-operation" in Orbiston, Scotland, and in New Harmony, Indiana, failed. In these cooperative villages, workers grew their own food and made their own clothes while preparing ways to govern themselves.

The basis of the cooperative movement today comes from the Rochdale principles, which were established by the Rochdale pioneers back in 1844:

Open and voluntary membership
Democratic control (one member, one vote)
Fixed and limited interest on share capital
A surplus allocated in proportion to members' purchases (the dividend)
Provision for education
Cooperation amongst cooperatives
Political and religious neutrality
No credit
Quality goods and services

In the early 20th century, cooperatives formed the Co-operative Party to represent members of co-ops in the British Parliament. Eventually the Co-operative Party diverged from the Rochdale principles and merged with the Labour Party on condition that some Labour members of parliament should always come from within the Co-operative Party. In the United States, the Rochdale system became the dominant form of cooperative organization in the 20th century.

In 1979, Congress set up the National Consumer Cooperative Bank to provide technical and financial assistance to consumer cooperatives. President Jimmy Carter was a great supporter of this act, but the major force behind the bill was an organization called the Co-operative League, which was the main educational, coordinating, and lobbying organization of the Rochdale movement, and continues to be so into the 21st century. Under Carter, other agencies, such as the Urban Development Grant Program provided further federal government loans to co-ops.

Consumer cooperatives based on the Rochdale movement remain important. Almost one-third of all British people are now members of cooperatives. Cooperatives with Rochdale principles at their core can be found in many countries around the world, most notably in places where socialist politics form part of social life. In the United States, millions of people are members of farmer cooperatives, consumer goods cooperatives (mostly food stores), while thousands of others belong to other types of cooperatives dealing with health care, housing, (New York was the largest cooperative housing development), rural electricity and telephone, among many others. Most of the American cooperative movement uses the Rochdale system of selling at about market price and periodically refunding savings to members.

Cooperatives that operate in the tradition of the Rochdale Movement are among the most numerous in the International Cooperative Alliance (ICA), which has a membership of cooperatives from most countries in the world and is affiliated with the United Nations (UN).

Originally conceived as a variety of socialist organization to exist along side and in contrast to capitalist enterprises, Rochdale cooperatives have existed comfortably within largely capitalist societies, as well as within strongly social-democratic states such as Britain and the Scandinavian countries. The essentially left critique of capitalism implicit in the Rochdale movement has not received as much emphasis in the United States as it has in Europe.

SEE ALSO

*Volume 1 Left:* Socialism; United Kingdom; Carter, James E. *Volume 2 Right:* Capitalism; Laissez-Faire.

BIBLIOGRAPHY

Johnston Birchall, *CO-OP, the People's Business* (St. Martin's Press, 1994); Johnston Birchall, *The International Co-Operative Movement* (St. Martin's Press, 1997); J. Case and R. Taylor, eds., *Co-ops, Communes & Collectives* (Pantheon, 1979); Gunnar Svendsen and Gert Svendsen, *The Creation and Destruction of Social Capital: Entrepreneurship, Co-Operative Movements and Institutions* (Edward Elgar Publishing, 2004).

TONI SANT
NEW YORK UNIVERSITY

# Roosevelt, Eleanor (1884–1962)

ALTHOUGH ELEANOR Roosevelt earned her initial fame and influence through her marriage to President Franklin Delano Roosevelt, when she died in 1962 she was remembered as not just a former first lady, but as a speaker, writer, and activist. A symbol of American liberalism in the mid-20th century, Roosevelt was an important actor in the shaping of the modern Democratic Party and the American welfare state.

Roosevelt's commitment to liberal ideals stood in stark contrast to her conservative and privileged Victorian upbringing. Born in New York on October 11, 1884, Anna Eleanor Roosevelt was the daughter of Anna and Elliott Roosevelt, brother to the 26th president of the United States, Theodore Roosevelt, who was also Eleanor's godfather. Despite her auspicious beginnings, Roosevelt's childhood was marked by her parents' troubled marriage and the deaths of a brother and both parents, all before she turned 10.

A young orphan, Roosevelt lived with different relatives until she left for England in 1899 to attend the Allenswood School, a European finishing school. Upon her return to the United States, Roosevelt became involved with middle-class women's reform efforts to benefit women and child laborers. Through these activities, traditional for a white, upper-class woman during the Progressive era, Roosevelt realized the horrid working conditions for immigrants and the poor, many of whom were children. Thus, by the time she met Franklin Delano Roosevelt, her distant cousin, in 1902, the seeds of her political consciousness had already been planted.

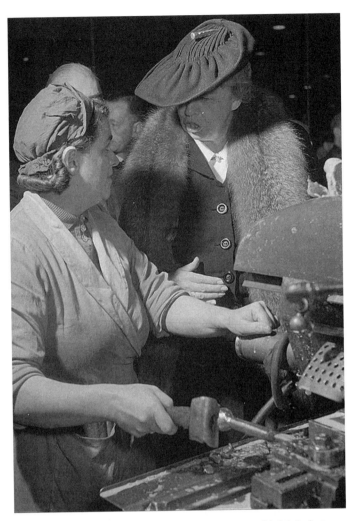

*Eleanor Roosevelt (right) meets with a woman machinist during a goodwill tour of Great Britain.*

Eleanor and Franklin Roosevelt were married on March 17, 1905, in New York City where President Theodore Roosevelt gave away the bride, his "favorite niece." In the years that followed, Franklin finished law school and began his public, political career in the Democratic Party while Eleanor tended to the couple's children and family life. Though during these years, Roosevelt ostensibly upheld the traditional roles for women, her personal tragedies, such as the loss of a young son, and public events forced a rediscovery of her strong character and convictions.

During the summer of 1921, Roosevelt's dormant political acumen was awakened when her husband was struck with poliomyelitis; he never recovered the use of his legs. Paralyzed, he encouraged his wife to travel on his behalf, to become his "eyes and ears" and a liaison between him and his constituents. By blending politics with her own intellect and empathies, Roosevelt proved to be not just a powerful partner to her husband, but an influential woman in her own right. When Franklin was elected president in 1933, the first Democrat elected to the office since Woodrow Wilson, Eleanor infused the role of first lady with her activist spirit and commitment to social justice.

Roosevelt was the most visible member of her husband's New Deal, the label for his administration's efforts to end the Great Depression and reform the American economy. As first lady, Roosevelt effectively used the media to reach the many Americans suffering from financial hardship. In 1936, she began a syndicated newspaper column entitled "My Day," which chronicled her daily activities and charted her public image. Similar to her earlier activist endeavors, Roosevelt became a particularly dedicated champion for women, children, minorities, and the disadvantaged. Even when World War II shifted her husband's attention away from his administration's social welfare programs, Roosevelt remained committed to the agenda and legislation that had given rise to the American welfare state. In addition, she became an active proponent of internationalism, or cooperation among the nations, world peace, and human rights during the war.

Though Franklin died in office in 1945, Roosevelt's political life continued to thrive. Consistent with her commitment to international peace and justice, she played an active part in the adoption of the United Nations' 1948 Declaration of Human Rights and was a member of the United Nations delegation until 1953. Unlike most liberals in the postwar era, Roosevelt was an outspoken advocate for civil liberties during the early years of the Cold War and she continued to use "My Day" as a forum to inspire the public on matters such as racial equality, an issue she took particular interest in during her post-White House years, as well as women's equal rights.

Though the Democrats would lose the White House in 1948 until 1960, Roosevelt remained a powerful presence in the party. When she died from illness on November 7, 1962, tributes poured in from across the globe. Roosevelt not only expanded the role of the first lady, but she left her mark on the international political and social landscape, earning the moniker, "First Lady of the world."

Roosevelt was not without her critics as a prominent first lady. She became a lightning rod for contemporary and later conservative criticism, and accusations flourished about her sexuality and friendships, loyalty to the United States, and supposed psychological problems.

SEE ALSO
Volume 1 Left: Roosevelt, Franklin D.; Democratic Party; Civil Rights; Liberalism.
Volume 2 Right: Roosevelt, Theodore; Republican Party.

BIBLIOGRAPHY
Maurine H. Beasley, Holly C. Shulman, and Henry R. Beasley, eds., The Eleanor Roosevelt Encyclopedia (Greenwood Press, 2001); Allida M. Black, Casting Her Own Shadow: Eleanor Roosevelt and the Shaping of Postwar Liberalism (Columbia University Press, 1996); Blanche Wiesen Cook, Eleanor Roosevelt, 1884–1933 (Penguin, 1993); Blanche Wiesen Cook, Eleanor Roosevelt: The Defining Years, 1933–38 (Penguin, 2000); Lois Scharf, Eleanor Roosevelt: First Lady of American Liberalism (Twayne Publishers, 1987).

LINDSAY SILVER
BRANDEIS UNIVERSITY

# Roosevelt, Franklin D. (1882–1945)

FRANKLIN D. ROOSEVELT (FDR) served longer as president than any other in history, and barring repeal of the 22nd Amendment, longer than anyone else ever will. He led the United States out of the Great Depression and into World War II, along the way becoming as close as the country ever had to a patrician king. Franklin Delano Roosevelt was born in Hyde Park, New York, January 30, 1882, the only child of James Roosevelt and Sara (Delano) Roosevelt, although his father had a son nearly 28 years Franklin's senior from his first marriage. Roosevelt's father was a wealthy railroad executive, and the family was distantly related to former President Theodore Roosevelt. Interestingly, Franklin's branch of the family pronounces their name Rose-e-velt, while Theodore's branch pronounces it Rooz-e-velt. Roosevelt attended Groton School and matriculated at Harvard University, graduating in 1904. He next received a law degree from Columbia University and went into private practice in New York City.

Roosevelt married his fifth cousin, Eleanor Roosevelt, on March 17, 1905, in New York City. Roosevelt was elected to the state senate in 1910 from Dutchess County and reelected in 1912. He chose instead to serve in the nascent administration of President Woodrow Wilson, as assistant secretary of the navy. He lost an election in 1914, a Democratic primary for the U.S. Senate. He made several trips to Europe during World War I and the period afterward. In 1920, he was the Democratic nominee for vice president on a ticket with James Cox of Ohio. The ticket lost to Republican Warren G. Harding and Calvin Coolidge. Roosevelt returned to New York to practice law and engage in the banking business. In August 1921, he was stricken with polio while vacationing at his summer home on Campobello Island, New Brunswick. Roosevelt adapted relatively quickly to his paralysis, and he pioneered the use of some devices for the disabled, including automobile controls. Roosevelt was an avid driver, and traveled throughout the country with his custom car. In 1928, he returned to the political sphere and was elected governor of New York.

In 1932, Roosevelt won the nomination of the Democratic Party for president. He was the first nominee to appear at a nominating convention and make an acceptance speech. When he wheeled to the podium in his wheelchair, it was the first time many of the delegates became aware that Roosevelt was disabled. Incumbent Republican President Herbert Hoover had made a much better reputation as an engineer than president, at least when it came to dealing with the economy. Voters did not know what Roosevelt had in mind to solve the Depression, but they knew he was not Hoover, and Roosevelt won the election in a landslide.

Before he even took office, Roosevelt was the victim of an assassination attempt. During a visit to Miami, Giuseppe Zangara, an anarchist, shot at the dais, missing the president-elect but fatally wounding Chicago Mayor Anton Cermak and wounding four others. Zangara was executed for the murder of Cermak.

Roosevelt's first term was a flurry of activity, and the start of it was the busiest time, known as the Hundred Days. Roosevelt announced the Good Neighbor policy toward Latin America at his inauguration. The administration was immediately confronted with the problem of bank failures. Roosevelt declared a "bank holiday," which lasted for eight days during which all banks were closed. Congress passed an unprecedented blank bill to deal with the crisis. Some of the New Deal agencies and acts created in the Hundred Days were the Tennessee Valley Authority (TVA), the National Recovery Administration (NRA), the Public Works Administration (PWA), the Federal Deposit Insurance Corporation (FDIC), the Civilian Conservation Corps (CCC), the Agricultural Adjustment Act (AAA), and the Federal Emergency Relief Act (FERA). It is perhaps fitting that the president who was the fountainhead of

*Franklin Roosevelt speaks into a microphone from his touring sedan in 1936. A victim of polio, Roosevelt was rarely photographed in a wheelchair. Despite his affliction, Roosevelt led a liberal revolution in American government.*

these agencies mostly referred to by their initials was himself the first of a series of presidents known by his initials, FDR.

Many scholars allege that there were in fact two New Deals. One was agencies like the NRA and the CCC, which were mostly formed to deal with the crisis of the Depression. Other agencies, such as the TVA, the FDIC, the FCC, and Social Security, were an institutionalization of a new way of doing government. Most of these permanent agencies were established later in the first term and not in the Hundred Days. Also, Roosevelt appointed the first woman to a presidential cabinet, Frances Perkins, who served as secretary of labor for his entire tenure as president; and the first woman ambassador, Ruth Bryan Owen. The public apparently approved of the New Deal, an unprecedented leaning to the left in American governance, to the point some programs were not far from outright socialism.

Among the agencies that were seen as the most radical in the period were the Resettlement Administration, which established whole communities and encouraged cooperativism in them; the Tennessee Valley Authority, which put the government in the busi-

ness of electrical power production; and the Rural Electrification Administration, which funded power-distribution cooperatives and provided power to them from Corps of Engineers-built hydroelectric dams. Other agencies such as the WPA became well known for employing artists and writers, many of whom were personally committed to the left.

Roosevelt was reelected in 1936 by the biggest landslide in the electoral college to that time. His Republican opponent, Alf Landon, carried only Maine and Vermont.

One entity that did not support the New Deal was the Supreme Court. Roosevelt sat completely frustrated as the court dismantled his handiwork piece by piece, mostly by 5-4 votes. Early in his second term—by which time Roosevelt had not yet had the opportunity to appoint a single justice—Roosevelt proposed a scheme whereby the president would appoint "supplemental justices" whenever a justice reached the age of 70. Conservatives attacked the plan as a "court-packing" scheme, and it was defeated. More significantly, it was the first time Republicans had formed a legislative coalition with Southern Democrats. The "conservative coalition," as it came to be known, grew in power over the years and did more damage to liberal ideals than the Supreme Court did. Nevertheless, one of the five conservatives on the court changed his vote, and the New Deal started meeting with the court's approval. Before the end of the year, Roosevelt made the first of his nine appointments to the court.

With the Depression seemingly in check, Roosevelt's second term was dominated by lesser economic concerns and the growing war clouds in Europe. When Germany invaded Poland in 1939, Roosevelt sided with those who supported the United States's traditional isolationist stance. The United States didn't join the war in Europe for two years. Roosevelt stunned many by running for a third term in 1940. Since George Washington retired after two terms, no president had sought a third term. No one was more disaffected than Joseph P. Kennedy, father of future President John F. Kennedy, who had expected to run in 1940. Republicans sported buttons declaring "No Third Term," "Force Franklin out at Third," and most memorably, "No Man Is Good Three Times." In spite of this, Roosevelt defeated Republican Wendell Willkie, by less of a margin than he had defeated Hoover and Landon, but solid nevertheless.

The third term started with alternatives to war. Roosevelt gave his famous Four Freedoms speech in January 1941. The Lend-Lease Act was passed in March to appease those who did not want America giving arms to warring allies but were able to stomach "leasing" arms to them. The Atlantic Charter for peace was proclaimed in August. But at the same time, there were rumblings leaning to war. When Japan attacked Pearl Harbor, Hawaii, Roosevelt proclaimed it "a day that will live in infamy."

With Germany declaring war on the United States within days, America was suddenly fully engaged in two theatres, the Pacific and European. By 1944, with the United States still completely occupied with the war, Roosevelt made the case, "Don't change horses in the middle of the stream." He was reelected to an unprecedented fourth term by a substantial margin over New York Governor Thomas E. Dewey. Roosevelt brought in a new vice president, his third, Senator Harry Truman of Missouri. Twelve weeks later, Truman would become president. The most significant act of Roosevelt's fourth term was the "Big Three" conference at Yalta with Winston Churchill and Josef Stalin.

Roosevelt died at his winter home in Warm Springs, Georgia, on April 12, 1945. News of Roosevelt's death came as a shock to most Americans. The younger generation could not even remember someone else being president. Roosevelt was buried at Springwood, his family home in Hyde Park. According to Roosevelt's stipulated wishes, a desk-sized block of granite was placed on Pennsylvania Avenue as a monument. His many friends and admirers in government realized that this was not enough of a monument, and a commission was appointed to establish a permanent monument. More than 40 years later, the best the commission could formulate was to rename the Washington Monument the Washington-Roosevelt Monument. (Signs to this effect were actually erected in the 1980s.) Finally, progress was made on a permanent monument in the 1990s, and the Franklin Delano Roosevelt Memorial, occupying eight acres between the Potomac River and the Tidal Basin, was dedicated in 1997.

**SEE ALSO**

*Volume 1 Left:* Democratic Party; Liberalism; Socialism; United States; Roosevelt, Eleanor; New Deal.
*Volume 2 Right:* Landon, Alfred M.; Supreme Court; *Laissez-Faire*; Conservatism.

**BIBLIOGRAPHY**

James MacGregor Burns, *Roosevelt: The Lion and the Fox* (Harcourt Brace, 1956); James MacGregor Burns, *Roosevelt: The Soldier of Freedom* (Harcourt Brace Jovanovich, 1970); Kenneth S. Davis, *FDR* (5 volumes, Random House, 1972–2000); Frank Freidel, *Franklin D. Roosevelt: A Rendezvous with Destiny* (Little, Brown, 1990); Otis L. Graham, Jr., and Meghan Robinson Wander, eds., *Franklin D. Roosevelt: His Life and Times: An Encyclopedic View* (G. K. Hall, 1985).

TONY L. HILL
MASSACHUSETTS INSTITUTE OF TECHNOLOGY

# Rousseau, Jean-Jacques (1712–1788)

PHILOSOPHER and writer Jean-Jacques Rousseau was born in Geneva, Switzerland. His mother died soon after he was born, and Rousseau's relationships with women were always somewhat unusual. For years, he was involved with Madame de Warens, who acted alternately as a mother figure and as a lover. In 1741, Rousseau moved to Paris, France, where he met and later married Thérèse Levasseau, a servant girl of questionable intelligence. He deposited all five of their offspring on the steps of foundling homes. Despite his eccentric personal life, Rousseau was a major figure in 18th-century political thought, and he has continued to influence political theory through his major works: *The Social Contract, Discourse on the Origin and Basis of Inequality among Men, Confessions,* and *Emile.*

From the outset, Rousseau's works were controversial. Calvinists in Geneva burned *The Social Contract* and *Emile.* In Catholic France, authorities confiscated all copies because they were perceived as rash, scandalous, impious, and seditious. When French authorities ordered his arrest, Rousseau was forced to flee the country. Settling temporarily in England, he quarreled with philosopher David Hume, then returned to his native Switzerland. By 1770, he had returned to France.

Much of the early controversy surrounding Rousseau stemmed from his rejection of the French Enlightenment. He accused Voltaire, a former friend, of corrupting Parisians with his "enlightened" ideas. Rousseau accused the Philosophes of being materialistic, hypocritical, immoral, and unrealistic. He insisted that they sought to free individuals from traditional morals and social customs without understanding the consequences. Through rejecting the Enlightenment, Rousseau played a significant role in the rise of romanticism, which transformed politics, literature, and art in the late 18th century, bringing about a new emphasis on individuality, spontaneity, emotionalism, and transcendentalism.

Philosophically, Rousseau was a classical liberal, and he accepted the idea of government by contract. Rousseau saw the contract as one in which citizens gave up the freedom of the state of nature to submit their individual wills to the general will. He perceived humans as rational beings who were capable of making their own decisions according to their perceptions of morality. Rousseau was also classical liberal in his belief that individuals competed for limited, available resources. Rousseau believed that humankind was ruled by two fundamental passions: the desire for self-preservation and the ability to feel pity or sympathy for others. Like John Locke, Rousseau accepted an inherent right to rebellion. He disagreed with Locke, however, on the issue of property.

While Locke saw property as a means of promoting citizenship and good government, Rousseau maintained that most crimes could be traced to the ownership of property. Unlike Thomas Hobbes, Rousseau argued that a sovereign must be bound by the laws of the social contract. Rousseau distrusted democracy, preferring a small body of aristocrats elected solely to implement laws directed toward ensuring equality and liberty.

Liberty was a significant concept to Rousseau. He wrote that "man is born free, and everywhere he is in chains." He saw government as the instrument of enslavement. Rousseau argued that the nature of humankind was formed not at birth but by the government that controlled every aspect of life. Rousseau heartily rejected the idea of representative government because he believed that sovereignty could not be represented. To him, the general will, not government, was the best protection against tyranny.

Influenced to a large extent by Plato, Rousseau identified the most desirable virtues as good citizenship, courage, self-sacrifice, and moderation. He saw good and evil as political rather than moral values. Individuals became corrupt, in his view, not because of any innate evil but because of the society that a particular form of government had created. A converted Catholic, Rousseau rejected traditional Christianity because he believed that it encouraged tyranny. He did, however, acknowledge the existence of an "almighty, beneficent, and tolerant divinity."

Rousseau, like other classical liberals, with the exception of John Stuart Mill, saw women as incapable of rationality because they were creatures of emotions. While men had inherent rights, in Rousseau's opinion, women had revocable privileges. Rousseau believed that educating women would give them power over men beyond the power they already exercised in the bedroom. In *A Vindication of the Rights of Women,* first published in 1792, English writer Mary Wollstonecraft responded directly to Rousseau, assuring him that what women needed was power over themselves and not over men.

Sometimes called the father of the French Revolution, Rousseau's views on property and the idea of human nature being shaped by government also inspired Karl Marx.

**SEE ALSO**

*Volume 1 Left:* Hume, David; Hobbes, Thomas; Locke, John; Liberalism; French Revolution.
*Volume 2 Right:* Conservatism; United Kingdom.

**BIBLIOGRAPHY**

Graeme Garrard, *Rousseau's Counter-Enlightenment: A Republican Critique of the Philosophes* (State University of New York Press, 2003); Joseph Losco and Leonard Williams, *Political Theory: Classical Writings, Contemporary Views* (St. Martin's, 1992); H.B. McCullough, ed., *Political Ideologies and Political Philosophies* (Thompson, 1989); Andrzej Rapaczysnki, *Nature and Liberalism in the Philosophies of Hobbes, Locke, and Rousseau* (Cornell University Press, 1987); Jean-Jacques Rousseau, *Emile* (J.M. Dent, 1974); Jean-Jacques Rousseau, *The First and Second Discourses* (St. Martin's, 1964); Jean-Jacques Rousseau, *The Social Contract* (Penguin, 1983).

ELIZABETH PURDY, PH.D.
INDEPENDENT SCHOLAR

# Russia, Post-Soviet

WHEN MIKHAIL GORBACHEV became general secretary of the Communist Party in March 1985, he was confronted with a system that had grown top-heavy with an unwieldy party bureaucracy. Since its beginnings under Vladimir I. Lenin in the Russian Revolution, the government had become more of a hindrance than a help in governing the 15 republics of the Union of Soviet Socialist Republics (USSR), also known as the Soviet Union. Unlike many in the party leadership, Gorbachev had become aware of the oppressive character of the regime. Gorbachev expressed in his memoirs that he realized, as well, that the foment of independence in Eastern Europe would also reach the USSR, and that he had to either be prepared to admit it—albeit in a controlled way—or resist it with the brutality with which Nikita Khrushchev had suppressed the Hungarian revolt in 1956.

In February 1986, Gorbachev initiated a complete leftist overhaul of the Soviet system at the Twenty-Seventh Congress. (Leftist, that is, in the noncommunist sense, as in the liberalization of Soviet society.) Robert G. Kaiser reflected on Gorbachev's dilemma in "The USSR in Decline" in *Foreign Affairs*, "the rhetoric of Soviet reform emphasizes renewal and progress, but the facts that made reform necessary describe failure—the failure of the Soviet system .... [Gorbachev] speaks of the need to democratize his country to make it work better. Economic reform, he has concluded, is impossible without political reform."

The Russian term for Gorbachev's anticipated reforms was *perestroika*, a total "restructuring" of the often repressive system that Josef Stalin had instituted in the 1930s. At the same time, he wanted to create a period of *glasnost*, not only a liberalization of Soviet society and culture, but an admission of the grave abuses that had happened in the Soviet past. In 1990, as an example of his doctrine, Gorbachev surrendered to Poland's Marshal Wojciech Jaruzelski sensitive files that proved Soviet complicity in the massacre of Polish officers at Katyn and other camps in World War II. The massacres had been designed to remove those whom Stalin saw as any opposition to Soviet control in the eastern part of Poland.

In September 1988, Gorbachev effected a dramatic reorganization of the Party Secretariat, which not only helped run the Communist Party but also the Soviet Union. As Kaiser stressed, Gorbachev "has proposed astounding changes to remove the Communist Party *apparat* [bureaucracy] from day-to-day administration of the economy and society, to replace it with new, elected bodies."

Yet, Gorbachev's main battle was still to be fought in the Soviet Union. He launched a gamble that harkened back to the days of the Russian Revolution of 1917 that brought the communists (then Bolsheviks) to power. At the July 1988 Party Congress, Gorbachev unveiled a plan to bring back the soviets. However, by attempting to marginalize the Party Central Committee and bureaucracy, he was also undermining the government that kept the Soviet Union together. In 1989, he attempted to open a Congress of People's Deputies, another step away from the centralism of the old Soviet Union. As the Library of Congress Country Study on Soviet Russia states, "In 1989 the Congress of People's Deputies stood at the apex of the system of soviets and was the highest legislative organ in the country. Created by amendment to the Constitution in December 1988, the Congress of People's Deputies theoretically represented the united authority of the congresses and soviets in the republics. In addition to its broad duties, it created and monitored all other government bodies having the authority to issue decrees."

In the rapidly changing world of the Soviet Union, still one of the most important indicators of political trends was the choice of who stood atop Lenin's Mausoleum with the general secretary on the anniversary of the October Revolution and on the Russian workers' holiday, May Day, May 1. David Remnick recorded in *Lenin's Tomb* that "the Kremlin announced that the liberal mayor of Moscow, Gavrili Popov, would be on the reviewing stand of Lenin's Mausoleum" along with the senior party members. However, the 1989 Congress of People's Deputies brought to national prominence the man who would become Gorbachev's nemesis: Boris Yeltsin of Russia, the most populous and richest of the Soviet Republics.

In 1990, the great secession of the republics began from the Union of Soviet Socialist Republics. The first would be those that Stalin had annexed brutally in 1940—the Baltic republics of Latvia, Estonia, and Lithuania.

In 1990, in an attempt to establish an alternate power base (not to champion reforms), Russia, under Yeltsin, would followed the lead of the Baltics. Gorbachev won the Nobel Peace Prize in 1990, but his image of peaceful methods was tarnished by a heavy-handed attempt to curb Lithuanian nationalist aspirations in January 1991. But, it became readily obvious that holding together Stalin's union could not be achieved by resorting to Stalin's methods. In fact, his liberalization of the Soviet Union, on his visit to China in the spring of 1989, inspired the Chinese democracy demonstrators who were crushed by the People's Liberation Army in Beijing in June 1989.

When the old guard of the Soviet party and armed forces attempted a coup against Gorbachev on August 19, 1991, while he was vacationing at Foros in the Crimea, he found an unlikely ally in Yeltsin. The rightists under KGB chief Vladimir Kryuchkov and Defense Minister Dmitri Yazhov were determined to prevent Gorbachev from convening a congress on August 21 that would mark the end of the old Soviet Union. After two days of near-chaos, the planned putsch collapsed, and its ringleaders, notably Kryuchkov and Yazhov, were arrested.

When the conservative elements attempted a desultory attack on the Russian White House, Yeltsin defiantly mounted a tank to demand their removal. As one observer wrote, Yeltsin's speeches and energetic opposition made him the hero of the hour. When Gorbachev returned to Moscow, Yeltsin had seized the initiative. He was quick to offer the presidents of the other republics full independence.

At the end of August, Gorbachev resigned as general secretary of the Communist Party. In September 1991, the Congress of People's Deputies would meet for the last time. The Union of Soviet Socialist Republics was officially dissolved, and in its place was created the Union of Sovereign States. In December 1991, the Commonwealth of Independent States replaced the union, and on December 25, Gorbachev resigned as president of the Soviet state. His last public statement reflected his commitment to reform, "we shall begin a new era in the history of the country with dignity, in conformity with the standards of legitimacy." Gorbachev's fall from grace was aptly summed up by American General William E. Odom, "by the time Yeltsin had made his comeback as leader of the RSFSR [Russia], Gorbachev had lost the democratic forces as well as the regional party apparatus and the senior military, leaving himself with virtually no domestic power base."

## RISE OF NATIONALISMS

Sensing a weakening of power at the top, the latent nationalism in the republics came to life, fanned by the nationalism now awakening the subjected peoples in the Soviet Union's sphere of influence in Eastern Europe. At the same time, the different nationalities of the Soviet Union were becoming restive, as they saw the populations of cities like Moscow seek a more open society. Nationalism was awakened throughout the Soviet Union.

In Soviet Central Asia, ethnic Russians were becoming surrounded by hostile native populations. Intimidated and feeling unprotected by the native party chiefs, many of them with progressive ideas were forced to return to the "Russian motherland." Ahmed Rashid noted that in Uzbekistan in 1994 "some 200,000 Russians have left Uzbekistan every year since 1988, because of the rise of Islamic fundamentalism and discrimination in favor of Uzbeks." Yet, ironically, in mapping a constructive future for the Central Asian states, Kazakhstan, Kyrgyzstan, Uzbekistan, Turkmenistan, and Tajikistan, the leaders were driving off the very people who could help most. Martha Brill Olcott wrote that the new nations were "beginning life with considerable disadvantages, not the least of which was the lack of an experienced elite capable of developing domestic or international policies independent of Moscow."

While Gorbachev had shown remarkable restraint in using the Russian Army to hold together the crumbling Soviet empire, Yeltsin's reformist zeal did not stop him from applying Stalinist methods against Chechnya, part of the Russian Federation. In 1994, with a ruthlessness not seen since the Soviet invasion of Afghanistan in December 1979, Yeltsin attacked Chechnya. However, the military forces were too few in number and too lacking in skill, and the Chechens carried out a fierce counterattack. Yeltsin, in 1999, launched a fierce offensive against the Chechens and neighboring Daghestan, which ranked with the most brutal of modern wars.

The same Stalinist ruthlessness also reappeared in Moscow itself. Keith Moon wrote in *American Diplomacy*, "in 1993, Yeltsin launched a full-scale military assault against the Russian parliament building in Moscow—killing hundreds—to dislodge rebelling members of the Congress of People's Deputies, whose political existence he had outlawed without any clear constitutional right to do so. He threatened to dismiss the Duma (parliament) when the members voted against his nominee for prime minister. Within months of this constitutional showdown, Yeltsin fired the minister himself. In his last years, all access to him, including by ministers, was tightly monitored by his bodyguard and his daughter. Yeltsin would disappear from Moscow for weeks at a time with various serious health problems."

In order to keep power, Yeltsin had made the bargain with the hard-liners in the armed forces that Gorbachev had refused to make. Robert Scheer wrote in the *Los Angeles Times* in November 1993: "Yeltsin owes his survival to the top military brass who backed him in the destruction of the Russian Parliament and Supreme Court. The payoff is that the generals now call the shots on arms control and intervention in regional as well as internal conflicts."

At the same time, Yeltsin, in an effort to win support, had helped create a new financial oligarchy, which had dark ties to the growing Russian Mafia. Assassinations of leading businessmen became regular news stories as the new alliance continued to sap Russians' belief that Yeltsin could ever really reform the economic system. Robert I. Friedman wrote, "Russian criminal groups penetrated virtually every level of the government, from Russia's parliament, the Duma, to President Yeltsin's inner circle. Even the immense arsenals of the Soviet armed forces were plundered." The Russian Mafia, with its Chechen allies, tried to smuggle out plutonium to be sold to the highest bidder from Russia's vulnerable defense sites.

By 1999, Yeltsin's record as a reformer had been indelibly tarnished. The memory of his standing on a tank in August 1991 to save the Russian White House, the Parliament, was destroyed by images of his tanks laying the building to waste two years later in 1993. Moreover, bombings in Russia in 1999 were blamed on the Chechens, severely undermining Yeltsin's claims to have won the war. Finally, on December 31, 1999, he officially handed over the reigns of power to Vladimir Putin, who had begun his public life in the KGB.

In 2001, Putin was elected president in his own right, with some 52 percent of the vote. The rise of Putin was only seen as a continuation of the tightening of state control that Yeltsin had begun. Indeed, the history of Putin's era is that of a gradual stifling of the freedom of expression that Gorbachev introduced during the period of *glasnost*.

Yet, even with enhanced political power, Putin was not able to stop the gradual disintegration of the old system, nor was he willing to countenance the freedoms

*Mikhail Gorbachev brought a liberalization to the Soviet system that ultimately helped bring about its collapse.*

that people had come to take for granted during Gorbachev's "Moscow Spring." A further omen of rightist movement was seen in early March 2004, when Putin chose Mikhail Fradkov to be the new Russian prime minister. Fradkov had gained a reputation as a new instrument of state repression when he served as chief of the Federal Tax Police Service for two years. As Mark McDonald wrote in the *Philadelphia Inquirer*, "its agents were notorious for wearing black ski masks and brandishing weapons when they would arrive for nighttime investigations of suspect companies and business people."

In March 2004, Putin easily won a second term in office, with the Russian electorate concerned over continued Chechen terrorism and no viable challenger. Putin had virtually recreated a one-party state in Russia. According to Oleg Shchedrov, "Putin's first four years in power have been marked by the silencing of most of

Russia's independent media and Kremlin pledges to restore strong powers to the state. The pro-Putin United Russia party won more than two-thirds of the Duma's seats in elections in December, and the opposition was reduced to little more than a symbolic presence." The same article reported that on March 31, 2004, "Russia's parliament gave initial approval to stricter rules on public protest that opposition leaders, already with little voice in the legislature, say could clear them off the streets as well."

After another massive terrorist attack by Chechen rebels, this time a school hostage-taking with some 150 deaths in September 2004, Putin declared that to fight terrorism, he needed to effectively cancel regional democracy in Russia. Regionally elected governors would be replaced with appointees, Putin explained, to strengthen central control. Both Gorbachev and Yeltsin publicly decried the loss of democracy. It seemed the leftism of the days of perestroika and glastnost was long gone.

## SEE ALSO

Volume 1 Left: Soviet Union; Gorbachev, Mikhail; Liberalism; Human Rights; Stalin and Stalinism; Communism.
Volume 2 Right: Soviet Union; Russia, Post-Soviet.

## BIBLIOGRAPHY

William E. Odom, The Collapse of the Soviet Military (Yale University Press, 1998); Robert G. Kaiser, "The USSR in Decline," Foreign Affairs (Winter 1988–89); Theodore von Laue and Angela von Laue, Faces of a Nation: The Rise and Fall of the Soviet Union, 1917–91 (Fulcrum, 1996); David Remnick, "Letter from Moscow: Post-Imperial Blues," The New Yorker (October 13, 2003); Mark McDonald, "A Surprise Russian Premier," Philadelphia Inquirer (March 2, 2004); David E. Mark, "Eurasia Letter: Russia and the New Transcaucasus," Foreign Policy (Winter 1996–97); Oleg Shchedrov, "Russian Opposition Decries Proposed Limits on Protesters," Boston Globe (April 1, 2004).

JOHN F. MURPHY, JR.
AMERICAN MILITARY UNIVERSITY

# Russian Revolution

THE RUSSIAN REVOLUTION had its origin in the Russian entry into World War I. The Russia of Tzar Nicholas II, who had ruled from November 1894, was a country terribly unprepared for the onslaught of modern war. Rural Russia, as Richard Pipes wrote in The Russian Revolution, could no longer offer its growing population arable land. Russian industries could not offer them work, with in Pipes's words, "an annual accretion of 1 million rural inhabitants" attempting to find employment. This formed, in Pipes's rueful judgment, "an unassimilable and potentially disruptive element" in Russian society. At the same time, neither Russian industry, nor the Russian high command, the STAVKA, were in any way prepared for the horrors of World War I.

In August 1914, two Russian armies had been annihilated before the end of the first month of the war by Russia's enemy, Imperial Germany. As A.J.P. Taylor wrote in A History of the First World War, "90,000 Russian prisoners were taken. One Russian army was broken; the other fell back in disorder. This was the battle of Tannenberg (August 29)." For three more years, Russian soldiers, loyal to their "Little Father," the tzar, were killed and wounded in the hundreds of thousands, as they charged the machine guns of the Germans and the empire of Austria-Hungary. In March 1916, in a response to the request of their French ally, the Russians launched an offensive at Lake Narotch. By the end of the month, the offensive had ground to a halt with 120,000 more casualties, an example of the horrendous losses endured by the peasant soldiers.

On February 23, 1917 (March 8 in our modern calendar), demonstrations broke out in the capital city of St. Petersburg. As Robert V. Daniels wrote, it was the International Women's Day, and "a hundred thousand striking factory workers, men and women, jammed the streets of [St. Petersburg] demanding bread and freedom." At the time, Nicholas was fatefully out of the capital at his military headquarters at Mogilev. He cabled the commander of the capital military district, General Sergius Khabalov, on February 25: "I command you to put an end as of tomorrow to all disorders in the streets of the capital." However, by this time, almost all of the intensely loyal soldiers were lying buried on the battlefields of the Eastern Front, in the war against Germany and Austria-Hungary, or in the war with Turkey, which had become Germany's ally in October 1914. Those left behind to garrison the capital had more in common with the striking workers. The first troops to rebel were from the Pavlovski Reserve Guards Regiment: the regiments of the Gvardia, or the Guards, the elite of the Russian Army.

The prime minister of the new Provisional Government was Prince Georgi Lvov, a liberal nobleman poorly suited to lead a government in the throes of revolution. By February 28 (March 12), as Orlando Figes notes, the casualties of the near-anarchy were "up to 1,500 people killed and about 6,000 wounded." On the night of March 13, the tzar, whose contact with his people was tenuous at best, boarded his imperial train for the passage back to the capital, not knowing the true extent of the disorders. However, revolutionary soldiers turned back the train as a new Provisional Government ruled in St. Petersburg, soon to be called Petrograd. The new government insisted on his immediate abdication. Nicholas first agreed to abdicate in favor of his brother Grand Duke Michael, who declined. The 300-year rule of the Romanov family was over, and the tzar who had presided over it was still only dimly aware of the poor conditions in Russia that had brought it about.

## REVOLUTIONARY IDEOLOGY

Meanwhile, the power was quickly being taken by those who were closest to the suffering that had provoked the revolution, the soldiers and workers. They formed soviets, or councils, throughout Russia, a movement begun during the premature Revolution of 1905. As Daniels wrote: "the soviets were evolving an organization that made them much more nearly a national popular government than the actual cabinet" of Prince Lvov's Provisional Government.

The revolutionaries who had made the Revolution in 1905 were all in exile when the outbreak began in St. Petersburg. Hastily, they returned. On April 3, Vladimir Lenin, who would prove the most important of all, debarked at the Finland Railroad station. Four days later, he would publish his *April Theses*, which would lay the ground work for his eventual conquest of the 1917 Revolution. Lenin trenchantly stated his position in the *April Theses*. He offered a direct challenge to the rule of the Provisional Government—and offered himself and his Bolshevik Party as the only realistic alternative for Russia.

The revolutionary core, or the workers, led by Lenin and his comrade Leon Trotsky, was about to come to power, a power that would quickly bear totalitarian consequences. In the swiftly shifting alignments of revolutionary Russia, the earliest days saw the rise of a liberal provisional government, before the advent of the Soviet Union when democratic efforts ended. From April 24 to April 29, 1917, Lenin held a conference of his Bolshevik Party to map plans for assuming control of not only the government, but of Russia as well. A few days later, Trotsky would arrive; earlier,

Josef Stalin had come to Russia. While working together under Lenin in the revolution, a later power struggle between them would threaten to destroy the revolutionary state that Lenin would build. In June, the first All-Russian Congress of the Soviets convened—an opportunity that Lenin did not miss as a means of exerting power over the armed workers, soldiers, and sailors, who he already conceived of as the fighting vanguard of his "proletarian revolution."

By May, Alexander Kerensky became minister for war in the Provisional Government. However, in spite of the hatred of the war that dominated the soviets, the Provisional Government went on with the offensive, attempting to keep Russia in the war. Kerensky's unsuccessful military efforts proved to the soldiers that Lenin and his Bolsheviks were the only party that could bring an end to the war.

Mutinous soldiers began to arrive back in the capital. Beginning on July 3, the turmoil known as the "July Days" broke out. Lenin and the Bolsheviks were caught totally surprised by the demonstrations but, desperate for an attempt to take control of events, put themselves at the head of the movement. The decision proved to have been taken hastily, and had—at least temporarily—disastrous consequences for the party. On July 7, Lvov resigned, and the energetic Kerensky became the new prime minister. General Lavr Kornilov, who had been commander of the (now) Petrograd garrison, assumed power over the armed forces, attempting to restore order in the ranks. Already, hundreds of officers had been executed by their own men. In fact, momentarily, Lenin was forced to flee back over the border to Finland on August 9 to escape arrest, a fate that had befallen Trotsky.

Yet, Kornilov became a Russian "man on the white horse," who attempted to subvert the revolution to make a military rule of his own. Belatedly, Kerensky realized the true nature of Kornilov's attempted putsch. On August 29, Kerensky appointed himself the new commander to deal with the uprising. The Bolshevik Party was able to take advantage of the situation and sent revolutionary agitators among the soldiers who were supporting Kornilov, which went farther toward ending the threat to the revolution than Kerensky's decrees. His rebellion collapsed, and on September 1, Kornilov was imprisoned.

With Trotsky (released from imprisonment) leading the party in Lenin's absence, the hold of the party grew stronger. It alone was able to harness the dynamic power of the soviets. Increasingly, Kerensky proved his inability to control circumstances. All other parties that clamored for power in the Duma, the representative assembly, like the rightist Kadets and the leftist Social Revolutionaries, seemed as incompetent as the Provisional Government. The only solution seemed for them all to form a coalition which, while leftist in orientation, would have blocked the militants of the Bolshevik Party from seizing power. On September 14, a Democratic Conference was held and debated whether it was possible for power to be shared between the revolutionary soviets and the middle-class bourgeoisie, which had supported the tzarist administration. Tragically for the future of Russia, the congress ended in an impasse: no real decision could be reached.

With the failure of the congress, Lenin began to plan with the Petrograd Bolsheviks, and with Trotsky the main strategist, to seize power in the vacuum left by the failed assembly. On October 7, he secretly returned to Petrograd. The next day, with incredible timing, a speech by the government expressing the possibility of surrendering the capital to the Germans was published, most likely with Bolshevik connivance. Thus, Kerensky's government further lost the confidence of all patriotic Russians—regardless of political persuasions.

By October 15, although all Petrograd papers were discussing the possibility of a Bolshevik coup, Kerensky still would take no action against them. Instead, he went to attend a conference at Pskov on the conduct of the war. Finally, on the night of October 18, he expressed a desire to strike at Lenin and his party. But, critically, the soviets were with the Bolsheviks, and Kerensky had to seek troops to support him back at the front. On October 25, the navy cruiser *Aurora*, supporting the Bolsheviks, fired blank rounds at the Winter Palace, home of the Provisional Government. Lenin issued a proclamation decreeing the end of the Provisional Government, and the Winter Palace was stormed by troops loyal to him and the Bolsheviks. The next day, supported by the Council of Soviets, Lenin took power.

## SEE ALSO

*Volume 1 Left:* Russia, Post-Soviet; Soviet Union; Lenin, Vladimir I.; Stalin and Stalinism.
*Volume 2 Right:* Soviet Union, Russia, Post-Soviet.

## BILBLIOGRAPHY

"Lenin's April Theses, April 1917," www.firstworldwar.com, (July 2004); Orlando Figes, *A People's Tragedy: The Russian Revolution* (Penguin, 1996;) Edvard Radzinsky, *The Last Tzar: The Life and Death of Nicholas II* (Doubleday, 1992); Robert V. Daniels, *Red October: the Bolshevik Revolution of 1917* (Scribner's, 1967); Richard Pipes, *The Russian Revolution* (Vintage, 1990); Leon Trotsky, *The History of the Russian Revolution*, Max Eastman,trans., www.marxists.org (July 2004); Henry M. Christman, ed., *Essential Works of Lenin* (Bantam, 1966); Robert K. Massie, *Nicholas and Alexandra* (Dell, 1978); Edmund Wilson, *To the Finland Station: A Study in the Writing and Acting of History* (Anchor Books, 1953).

JOHN F. MURPHY, JR.
AMERICAN MILITARY UNIVERSITY

# The Left

# S

## Sacco and Vanzetti

THE LIVES OF NICOLA Sacco and Bartolomeo Vanzetti changed forever on April 15, 1920. Seven years later, they were executed for their alleged roles in the events of that day. However, decades later the "case that will not die" continues to incite controversy over whether the two immigrants were even present when a paymaster and a guard were killed in the course of a robbery in South Braintree, Massachusetts. Around 3 P.M. on April 15, paymaster Frederick Parmenter and his bodyguard were delivering a payroll of around $30,000 in two boxes to two shoe factories. The two men were attacked, robbed, and murdered by two men carrying pistols. Witnesses later testified that at least five men were in the car that left the scene.

Sacco and Vanzetti, both Italian radicals, were known to openly endorse anarchy and atheism at a time when the United States was in the midst of a Red Scare. World War I had led to a new awareness of the threat of sabotage and sedition by resident aliens, and the U.S. Congress had passed the Espionage Act of 1917, and the Sedition Act and Immigration Acts of 1918. Overall, the national government had been given blanket authority to arrest anyone suspected of openly criticizing or trying to forcibly overthrow the government. Some idealists viewed the Bolshevik Revolution as an instrument of equality; and during this volatile period, some American liberals and radicals were flirting with far-leftist ideologies. While neither Sacco nor Vanzetti had been under investigation by authorities, a number of their associates were being closely watched as possible security threats.

A shoemaker, Sacco's family included his wife, Rosina, a young son, Dante, and a baby daughter, Inez, who was born after Sacco's arrest. Vanzetti, married with no children, was a fish peddler. Both men spoke broken English and were unable to understand some of the questions put to them by police and prosecutors. Witnesses at the trial testified that on the afternoon of April 15, Sacco had been obtaining a passport in Boston, and a number of witnesses had seen Vanzetti peddling fish.

Even though Sacco and Vanzetti asked for separate trials, their requests were denied. Prosecutors portrayed Sacco as a ruthless killer and insisted that Vanzetti was one of four accomplices. None of the others were ever brought to trial. Accusations centered on the fact that both Sacco and Vanzetti had been armed when police arrested them and that both had lied during detectives' questioning.

Civil libertarians and other supporters of Sacco and Vanzetti pointed out that neither had a record of prior arrest and that prosecutors had been unable to trace the money taken in the robbery to either of the two men. Committees were created to provide defense funds and to draw attention to perceived injustices. Writers who came forward to support Sacco and Vanzetti included Sir Arthur Conan Doyle, John Dos Passos, Upton Sinclair, and Katherine Anne Porter, who gave Dante Sacco a home after his father's execution. Indeed, the plight of Sacco and Vanzetti became a leftist cause not only in the United States, but all over the world.

Vanzetti was also tried in connection with a failed robbery that took place in nearby Bridgewater on Christmas Eve, 1919. Prosecutors believed the two crimes were connected. John Vahey represented Vanzetti in that case. Amazingly, Vahey entered into a partnership with the prosecutor, Frederick Katzmann, shortly after the trial. Observers pointed to Vahey's sloppy defense as evidence that he had made an agreement with prosecutors. He failed to subpoena witnesses and refused to call on those who came forward.

Amid a storm of publicity that generated attention around the world, the murder trial of Sacco and Vanzetti began on June 22, 1920. The prosecuting attorney, Katzmann, continued to coax and badger his own witnesses. Many of them gave contradictory evidence. Katzmann was later accused of withholding evidence from defense lawyers that might have helped to clear the defendants. During the trial, prosecutors played up the defendants' radical backgrounds to jurors. State troopers and local police allowed only a selected few to enter the courtroom during the trial, and Sacco and Vanzetti were placed in a steel cage to remind the jurors that they were dangerous criminals.

Labor lawyer Fred Moore represented Sacco and Vanzetti in the murder trial. The trial lasted six weeks. After five hours of deliberations, a unanimous jury found both Sacco and Vanzetti guilty as charged. After the trial, Moore declared that prosecutors had little evidence against Vanzetti, who had stood a chance of being acquitted. Moore reported that when he conveyed this information to Vanzetti, he had told him to save Sacco because of his family. At the sentencing, Vanzetti told listeners that he had never heard or read of anything as cruel as the treatment they had received before the court, and he accused Judge Webster Thayer of being the most prejudiced judge on earth.

Appeals in the Sacco and Vanzetti case lasted six years. Because all appeals were channeled in some way through Judge Thayer, all appeals were rejected. In 1925, Celestino Madeiros, a member of the Joe Morelli gang that many people believed had masterminded the South Braintree crime, confessed to the robbery. He positively stated that neither Sacco nor Vanzetti had been present at the time. Following the Madeiros confession, Governor Alvin T. Fuller appointed a committee chaired by Lawrence Lowell, the president of Harvard University. The committee subsequently announced that both men were guilty and that they saw no evidence that they had failed to receive a fair trial.

Subsequent investigations uncovered a number of illegalities. Investigators learned that out of the original pool of 500 potential jurors, only 7 were chosen. Judge Thayer had told the sheriff to bring in 175 new potential jurors, mostly farmers, except for a former chief of police who served as jury foreman. One juror was heard by witnesses to say that Sacco and Vanzetti should hang whether they were guilty or not. The gun owned by Sacco did not match bullets used in the murders. An eyewitness who was never called to testify swore that neither Sacco nor Vanzetti was in the automobile that drove away from the crime. Most legal scholars agree that the evidence used in the trial was incomplete and inconclusive.

On August 23, 1927, Sacco and Vanzetti were executed. Many people believed they were executed because they were anarchists and not because they were murderers. A wave of violence followed the executions, and explosions were set at the home of Judge Thayer and a juror. Meetings, parades, protest demonstrations, and strikes were held around the world, and American embassies in several countries received threats.

Despite a number of careful investigations into the Sacco-Vanzetti trial over a period of years, no one has ever been able to prove either guilt or innocence conclusively. On August 23, 1977, on the 50th anniversary of their executions, which was designated as the Nicola Sacco and Bartolomeo Vanzetti Memorial Day, Governor Michael Dukakis issued a proclamation acknowledging that the two immigrants had not received a fair trial from the state of Massachusetts. The proclamation stated in part: "Any stigma and disgrace should be forever removed from the names of Nicola Sacco and Bartolomeo Vanzetti, from the names of their families and descendants, and so, from the name of the Commonwealth of Massachusetts."

## SEE ALSO

*Volume 1 Left:* Sinclair, Upton; United States.
*Volume 2 Right:* McCarthyism; Dos Passos, John.

## BIBLIOGRAPHY

Paul Avrich, *Sacco and Vanzetti: The Anarchist Background* (Princeton University Press, 1991); Felix Frankfurter, *The Case of Sacco and Vanzetti: A Critical Analysis for Lawyers and*

*Laymen* (Little, Brown, 1927); "The Governor Dukakis Proclamation," www.saccovanzettiproject.org (May 2004); Brian Jackson, *Black Flag: A Look Back at the Strange Case of Nicola Sacco and Bartolomeo Vanzetti* (Routledge and Kegan, 1981); Joseph B. Kadane and David A. Schum, *A Probabilistic Analysis of the Sacco and Vanzetti Evidence* (Wiley, 1996); Eugene Lyons, *The Life and Death of Sacco and Vanzetti* (Da Capo Press, 1970).

ELIZABETH PURDY, PH.D.
INDEPENDENT SCHOLAR

# Saint-Simonism

ONE OF THE MOST eccentric and fascinating individuals of history is unquestionably Claude Henri de Rouvroy, Comte de Saint-Simon (1760–1825). Born into wealth and privilege as an aristocrat in Paris, France, in 1760, Saint-Simon felt himself destined for greatness from early on; his family claimed no less than to be direct descendants of Charlemagne. Apparently, he exhorted his valet to remind him upon awakening each day, "Remember, Monsieur le Comte, you have great things to do."

As a young man, Saint-Simon served in the French army as an officer in the American Revolution, distinguishing himself at the battle of Yorktown. Upon returning to France, Saint-Simon found himself caught up in the throes of the French Revolution. He welcomed the end of the French Old Regime but regretted the violence and anarchy the revolution had unleashed. In revolutionary France, Saint-Simon made himself a fortune, played the role as patron to a brilliant circle of scientists and artists, ingratiated himself unsuccessfully with Napoleon, and finally ended up in destitution and even briefly in an insane asylum. In post-Napoleonic France or the period of Restoration until his death in 1825, Saint-Simon styled himself a liberal aristocrat, a champion of bankers, economists, and publicists.

Saint-Simon's social and moral philosophy centers on three central tenets: his notion of a hierarchically managed society led by "industrialists"; his vision of European integration; and his proclamation of a New Christianity. First and foremost, Saint-Simon was a critic of *laissez-faire* capitalism for its social costs. Likewise, he opposed violent revolutionary change due to its anarchic tendencies and possible degeneration into authoritarian rule. Saint-Simon was also a modernist

dazzled by the potential of the application of rational planning and modern technology to society, a true child of the Enlightenment. Thus, the key to Saint-Simon was to design a rational social and economic order based on harmony, productive labor, and equality of opportunity in order to avoid rampant individualism and anti-social competitiveness.

At the apex of his society were to be "industrialists," or managers, which included scientists, philosophers, craftsmen, and various artists. According to Saint-Simon, society would function best administered by scientific technocrats who could bring about "the most rapid possible amelioration of the lot of the most numerous and poorest class." Saint-Simon envisioned a rational social organization to take root within a pan-European framework guided by Europe's two most productive powers, France and England. Saint-Simon's vision of a pan-European confederation was formulated as an antidote against European warfare, destructive nationalism, and popular unrest—three forces that undermined social stability and order and sparked senseless bloodshed and violence. Finally, Saint-Simon proclaimed the necessity of a new Reformation, the establishment of a New Christianity based on the principle that "all men must behave as brothers toward one another."

The legacy of Saint-Simonism is disputed, yet impressive. Saint-Simonism is most commonly explained as a form of utopian socialism, a forerunner to the scientific socialism of Karl Marx and Friedrich Engels. Some 20th-century philosophers, such as Hannah Arendt and Friedrich von Hayek, have seen in Saint-Simonism traces of communist and fascist totalitarianism, while other scholars have emphasized its peaceful, egalitarian, cosmopolitan, and feminist dimensions. After Saint-Simon's death in 1825, a small but influential group of his followers established Saint-Simonism as a religion. Eclectic individuals such as Prosper Enfantin founded a Saint-Simonian sect that delved into religious mysticism, cultic activity, eroticism, and the pursuit of the Great Mother, who would ostensibly reconcile the Orient and the Occident.

Saint-Simonian feminists in the 1830s agitated for greater social, economic, and political equality while believing in fundamental gender differences of the sexes. These initial utopian forays of Saint-Simonism gave way to a more practical and scientifically oriented generation of followers, who influenced greatly France's industrial, financial, and technological revolutions from the 1840s to the 1860s. Some of the achievements of these Saint-Simonian technocrats included the creation of a French national railway infrastructure, urban renewal in Paris, and the construction of the Suez Canal. In contemporary times, the European Union resembles in many ways the Saint-Simonian vision of a peaceful, pan-European technocracy with a European parliament.

**SEE ALSO**

*Volume 1 Left:* French Revolution; American Revolution; Socialism; Marx, Karl.
*Volume 2 Right:* Nationalism; Fascism; Feminism.

**BIBLIOGRAPHY**

Robert B. Carlisle, *The Proffered Crown: Saint-Simonism and the Doctrine of Hope* (Johns Hopkins University Press, 1987); Albert Fried and Ronald Sanders, eds., *Socialist Thought: A Documentary History* (Columbia University Press, 1992); George Lichtheim, *The Origins of Socialism* (Praeger Publishers, 1969); Claire Goldberg Moses and Leslie Wahl Rabine, *Feminism, Socialism, and French Romanticism* (Indiana University Press, 1993).

KEVIN J. CALLAHAN, PH.D.
SAINT JOSEPH COLLEGE

# Saudi Arabia

TODAY'S SAUDI ARABIA is the third kingdom created by the al-Saud and al-Wahhab families. In the mid-18th century, Muhammad ibn Abd al-Wahhab and Muhammad ibn Saud created the first Saudi kingdom. These two joined the sword of ibn Saud to the revival movement taught by al-Wahhab. The first kingdom was destroyed in 1818 by an Egyptian led Ottoman army.

In the mid-19th century, the second Saudi kingdom arose, based as before in central Arabia. It was suppressed by Muhammad ibn Rashid, amir of a Shammar tribe. In 1891, Abd al-Rahman, the head of the al-Saud dynasty, fled Riyadh in the night with his family. In 1902 his son, Abd al-Aziz ibn abd al-Rahman al-Saud, recaptured the city of Riyadh in a daring dawn raid. The young ibn Saud, dedicated to Wahhabi teachings, then began a series of conquests across Arabia with the aid of the Ikhwan (Wahhabi Brotherhood). In 1926, ibn Saud took the Hijaz region from the sherif of Mecca, Hussain ibn Ali, whose sons had led the Arab Revolt against the Ottoman Empire in World War I. Ibn Saud proclaimed himself king of Saudi Arabia. Not long afterward, oil was discovered in eastern Arabia.

Saudi Arabia is rather unique among Arab and Muslim countries. It was never a Western colony. It never developed an Arab nationalist movement of liberation. The oil industry is located in the Hasa province and the eastern part of the Rub al-Khali (Empty Quarter) and so is removed from the bulk of the population. Most of the people who work in the oil industry are foreigners or Shiites. The latter are willing to work with their hands unlike the dominant Sunni Saudis. Any dissent is repressed.

The outlook of the bulk of the people has, until recently, remained traditional and tribal as most Saudis are connected to the royal family directly or indirectly. Consequently the al-Saud dynasty has ruled through personal audiences in the traditional manner. Blood relationships that are tribal are very important and have added to the slow development of institutions associated with modern states. Saudi Arabia has no elective representatives. Political parties are illegal. Labor unions are also illegal. Human rights in the Western understanding are rejected for rule by Sharia (religious law).

The kingdom is a closed society, so information on secular political dissent is often scarce. But there has been opposition, both internally and externally.

King ibn Saud died in 1953, and was succeeded by his son, Prince Talal ibn 'Abd al-'Aziz al-Saud, leader of the reforming "free princes" against the "traditional princes." Eventually King Talal Saud was ousted by his brothers. The dispute reflects the political tensions within the extended royal family. In 1953, labor disputes in the oil fields led to the jailing of many people. One of those jailed was Ali Ghannam, an advocate of Ba'athist nationalism. In 1962, a dozen or more labor leaders disappeared. Nasser al-Said, who published a book critical of the kingdom, was kidnapped and returned to Saudi Arabia. In the 1970s, Saudi Arabia fought a border war with Yemen. Egyptians supporting the pan-Arabism of Gamal Nasser and the Saudi Communist Party were involved.

Opposition has come from military officers, many of whom were educated abroad. There have been at least two coups attempted. Also, several Saudi diplomats have sought political asylum. Reports in the 1990s claimed that opponents continued to disappear. In September 1994, Salman al-Awdah and Safar al-Hawali, both Muslim clerics, were arrested for publicly criticizing the government. Demonstrations on their behalf led to many more arrests.

The Committee for the Defense of Legitimate Rights (CDLR) has been very active in criticizing civil rights abuses by the Saudis. Many have been arrested for their criticisms. Exiled opponents have published critical magazines, newspapers, or books. In 1984, opposition leader-in-exile Shams Eddine Al-Fassi was nearly assassinated. Today exiles use radio, web sites, and other means to deliver messages of dissent.

## SEE ALSO

*Volume 1 Left:* Middle East.
*Volume 2 Right:* Middle East; Saudi Arabia; Egypt.

## BIBLIOGRAPHY

Madawi Al-Rasheed, *A History of Saudi Arabia* (Cambridge University Press, 2002); Nathan J. Citino, *From Arab Nationalism to OPEC* (Indiana University Press, 2002); Hassan A. El-Najjar, *The Gulf War: Overreaction & Excessiveness* (Amazone Press, 2001); David E. Long, *The Kingdom of Saudi Arabia* (University of Florida Press, 1997).

ANDREW J. WASKEY
DALTON STATE COLLEGE

# Schlesinger, Arthur M., Jr. (1917–)

ARTHUR MEIER SCHLESINGER, Jr., prominent historian and social critic, was born in Columbus, Ohio, son of a well-known historian of the same name. During his youth, he began to follow in the footsteps of his father, showing interest in American history and social issues. Schlesinger attended Harvard University and graduated in 1938. Almost immediately following his graduation, he became a member of the university's Society of Fellows. He remained with the Society of Fellows until 1942.

During World War II, Schlesinger's intelligence and talents were not ignored. He obtained a post in the Office of War Information, where he worked from 1942 to 1943. His efforts were well accepted and acknowledged throughout government, providing Schlesinger with many connections in Washington, D.C. Following World War II, he took a professorship in the history department at his alma mater, Harvard University. He continued his work there until 1961.

Throughout his life, Schlesinger was an active member of the Democratic Party. As part of his political efforts, he cofounded a political group known as the Americans for Democratic Action. In conjunction with the group he cofounded, Schlesinger assisted Adlai Stevenson with his two unsuccessful campaigns for the presidency in 1952 and 1956, losing both times to war hero Dwight D. Eisenhower.

Although Schlesinger had worked on two failing campaigns, he did not give up and assisted John F. Kennedy's presidential campaign. For his skills and his work, Kennedy appointed Schlesinger to the post of special assistant to the president for Latin American affairs. He only remained at his post during Kennedy's time as president and he resigned in 1964, soon after Kennedy's assassination.

Following his assignment in Washington, D.C., Schlesinger obtained the prestigious Albert Schweitzer Professorship of Humanities of the City University of New York. Soon after, his talents were once again recognized when he was appointed chairman of the Franklin Delano Roosevelt Four Freedoms Foundation, an organization that worked to achieve the goals outlined in Roosevelt's famous "Four Freedoms" speech. In 1994, he was awarded for his tenure at the City University of New York an emeritus professorship.

Throughout his life, Schlesinger has written prolifically and has been published in many popular periodicals and well-respected scholarly journals. He received his first public acclaim for one of his writings right after his graduation, when he published his honors thesis from Harvard, *Orestes A. Brown: A Pilgrim's Progress* in 1939. In 1945, his book *Age of Jackson*, which was an examination and reevaluation of the social, political, and economic aspects of the Jacksonian era, won him the Pulitzer Prize and led many other professors and writings in his field to reinterpret the times of Andrew Jackson.

Schlesinger continued his works on the U.S. presidents with a three-volume set titled *The Age of Roosevelt*, one volume published annually from 1957 to 1960. The set was an in-depth analysis of the New Deal in the fashion of sweeping narrative. Although it received much acclaim, some criticized it for being too strongly sympathetic.

Following his experiences in Kennedy's White House, Schlesinger wrote a study of the Kennedy administration, titled *A Thousand Days*, which was published in 1965. With the book's publication and positive reception, he won his second Pulitzer Prize. Continuing to write abundantly, his other popular works include *The Politics of Hope* in 1963, *The Bitter Heritage* in 1968, *The Imperial Presidency* in 1973, and *Robert F. Kennedy and His Times* in 1978. In 2000, Schlesinger completed an autobiographical work, *A Life in the 20th Century: Innocent Beginnings, 1917–50*. In

2004, he remained a prominent and passionate liberal historian and writer. In his writings, Schlesinger became known for being an "anti-communist liberal," defining democracy as a middle way between fascism and communism.

**SEE ALSO**

*Volume 1 Left:* Kennedy, John F.; Stevenson, Adlai E.; Democratic Party.
*Volume 2 Right:* Elitism; Goldwater, Barry.

**BIBLIOGRAPHY**

"Arthur M. Schlesinger, Jr., Biography," Swarthmore College, www.swarthmore.edu (March 2004); Arthur M. Schlesinger, Jr., *The Imperial Presidency* (Houghton Mifflin, August 2004); "Arthur Schlesinger, Jr.," HistoryCentral, www.multied.com (March 2004).

ARTHUR HOLST, PH.D.
WIDENER UNIVERSITY

# Second International

IN 1889, 13 YEARS AFTER the dissolution of the original International Workingmen's Association, a second international socialist/communist organization was formed in Europe. The Second International, as it came to be known, emerged out of a series of meetings convened under the auspices of Belgian, French, German, and Swiss communist/socialist parties. Especially noteworthy among these meetings were the Chur Conference (1881) and the International Labor Conference in Paris (1886). Eventually, the Second International Workingmen's Association was founded in July 1889 with the participation of delegates from 20 countries. Ironically, the new International would be initially headquartered in Paris, France, where the memories of the catastrophic "commune" experiment of 1871 were still alive.

While the Second International followed up on the work of its predecessor, there were notable differences between the two organizations. A new generation of intellectuals had now taken over from Karl Marx and Friedrich Engels, though the latter was elected honorary president of the International Socialist Congress in 1893. Leading figures of the new International included August Bebel, Karl Kautsky, Vladimir Ilyich Lenin, Karl Liebknecht, Rosa Luxemburg, Franz Mehring, and Georgi Valentinovich Plekhanov. These names brought along a considerable richness and diversity in the theorization and refinement of the socialist/communist worldview.

In addition, the new International was less centralized than its predecessor and would not even establish a formal secretariat until the turn of the 20th century. Such lack of centralization, however, did not necessarily signify any lack of effectiveness. In 1893, for instance, the International Metalworkers Federation was established under the International's auspices. Although the Second International was somewhat loosely organized, it comprised, unlike its predecessor, more properly designed political parties, with regularly elected leaderships and clearer political programs. Through its national chapters, the Second International managed to maintain a noticeable presence in each country. These chapters helped with the creation and development of various trade unions and encouraged the politicization of working classes. The International's Paris Congress of 1900 finally created a standing International Socialist Bureau, composed of representatives of all member parties. The bureau, presided by Emile Vandervelde, would set up its permanent secretariat in Brussels, Belgium.

Similar to the Marxist-Anarchist divide at the First International, the Second International was characterized by a major tension among its membership. Following especially Engels's death in 1895, the serious internal disagreements among the 28-member Russian delegation at the International Socialist Congress of 1900, and the eventual separation between the Bolshevik and Menshevik faction wings within the Russian Social Democratic and Labor Party in 1903, the socialist/communist movement split into what might be called roughly the socialist and communist camps. The actual difference between these two competing Marxian movements related more to strategy and tactics than the ultimate goal. Put crudely, the socialists (or social democrats) favored an evolutionary strategy, reminiscent of the British Fabian movement. Communism, on the other hand, insisted on revolution as the only viable means of political change.

The start of World War I in August 1914 marked, in Leon Trotsky's words, "the effective death of the International." Although the final session of the International Socialist Bureau in July 1914 resolved "unanimously that it shall be the duty of the workers of all nations concerned not only to continue but to further intensify their demonstrations against the war, for peace, and for the settlement of the Austro-Serbian conflict by international arbitration," several sections of the member parties, especially in England, France, and Germany, supported their governments' decision to wage war. The failure of the Zimmerwald Conference (September 1915) to reestablish unity meant, in practice, the end of the Second International. Following the successful Bolshevik Revolution in Russia, a more radical Third International was created in Moscow in 1919. Within two years, however, the Second International would be revived by leading European social democratic parties. An institutional expression of the socialist-communist divide was now firmly in place.

Henceforth, the Second International would be more frequently referred to as the Socialist International, underlining the clear distinction with the Third (Communist) International. The Socialist International still exists today as a network of communication among social democratic parties.

## SEE ALSO

*Volume 1 Left:* Socialism; Communism; First International; Third International (Comintern); Cominform.
*Volume 2 Right:* Capitalism; Imperialism.

## BIBLIOGRAPHY

R.P. Dutt, *The Two Internationals* (Labor Research Department, 1920); G. Haupt, *Aspects of International Socialism, 1871–1914: Essays* (Cambridge University Press, 1986); G. Haupt, *Socialism and the Great War: The Collapse of the Second International* (Clarendon Press, 1972); J. Joll, *The Second International, 1889–1914* (Routledge, 1974).

ESREF AKSU
INDEPENDENT SCHOLAR

# Sharecroppers' Union

FOUNDED BY TENANT farmers in Alabama in spring 1931 with the support of the Communist Party in Montgomery, the Sharecroppers' Union (SCU) was the largest communist-led mass organization in the South of the United States during the interwar period. The union was predominantly an African American underground organization of sharecroppers, initially established to improve wage and work conditions for black sharecroppers during the Great Depression.

Generally speaking, sharecroppers were mostly African American agricultural wage laborers who raised crops of farm plots owned by large landowners. Sharecropping substituted for slavery in southern states after the Civil War and was financially oppressive for most of the sharecroppers. Sharecroppers' conditions increasingly worsened during the Great Depression, when the Agricultural Adjustment Administration (AAA) was established by the Franklin Roosevelt administration in 1933. The purpose of the AAA was to reinvigorate the agricultural sector, which was in deep crisis mostly due to depressed prices for farm products and increasing crop surpluses. With the promulgation of the Agriculture Adjustment Act, the federal government decided to encourage landowners to reduce their production in exchange for government subsidies. However, because the AAA was heavily relying on local authorities and the same landowners for the redistribution of these payments, landlords rarely shared government subsidies with sharecroppers, forcing them to live in extreme poverty and, eventually, to migrate to urban areas after having been evicted from their land because of their inability to cope with an ever-increasing cost of living.

The SCU was immediately well received by the sharecroppers, counting 200 members after only two months. However, landlords and local authorities did not share the same enthusiasm for the union. In July 1931, the SCU (at the time known as the Croppers and Farm Workers Union, CFWU) was involved in violent fights with local authorities. Tommy Gray, one of the two founders of the union, was killed in Camp Hill, while the CFWU secretary Mack Coad was forced to flee Alabama. Eventually, the union was reestablished as the SCU under the leadership of Gray's daughter, Eula Gray.

In the period from 1932 to 1934, the number of new members skyrocketed from 600 to 8,000, and the SCU started to spread into other counties in Alabama, and to a few other areas along the border with Georgia. Despite the increasing number of new members, the SCU found itself isolated mostly because of the secretive nature of the organization, and for its incapacity to recruit white members. In the winter of 1934, Clyde Johnson, a white communist from Minnesota, became the new secretary. Johnson's main goal was to give a more transparent image to the union, transforming it from a secretive association into a legitimate agricultural labor union. During his leadership, the SCU spread to Louisiana and Mississippi, bringing its membership to 12,000.

The SCU's first public headquarters was opened in New Orleans, Louisiana, and its first newspaper, the

*Union Leader*, was founded. However, Johnson's goal to form a larger agriculture union based on the amalgamation of the SCU with the socialist-led Southern Tenant Farmers' Union (STFU) was fated to fail in 1936. Although attempts were initially made by both unions to overcome their political differences, STFU leaders eventually found that the demands made in the name of the Communist orthodoxy, endorsed by some SCU leaders, such as Donald Henderson, were not suitable for "cotton belt" realities. In particular, the STFU criticized the SCU idea of defining tenants from sharecroppers, based on the Marxist-Leninist credo, when in the Delta, it was very hard to determine sharecroppers' status given the rapid shift from one form of tenure to another.

The missed amalgamation convinced Johnson to liquidate the SCU as an autonomous body. The decision to divide the organization by tenure in 1937 (sharecroppers were sent to join the National Farmers Union while the agricultural wage workers were directed to the Agricultural Workers' Union) signaled the end of the SCU.

The failure of this grassroots union with its leftist goals can be directly traced to the fact that the American Communist Party during the 1930s had to strictly follow Soviet Comintern policy and could not readily adapt doctrine to local situations.

### SEE ALSO

*Volume 1 Left:* Unions; Southern Tenants Farmers' Union; Socialism; New Deal.
*Volume 2 Right:* Capitalism; *Laissez-Faire*; Hoover, Herbert.

### BIBLIOGRAPHY

Donald H. Grubbs, *Cry from the Cotton: The Southern Tenant Farmers' Union and the New Deal* (University of North Carolina Press, 1971); Robin D.G. Kelley, *Hammer and Hoe* (University of North Carolina, 1990); Howard Kestler, *Revolt among the Sharecroppers* (University of Tennessee Press, 1997).

PIETRO PIRANI
UNIVERSITY OF WESTERN ONTARIO, CANADA

# Shining Path

PERU'S SENDERO Luminoso, or Shining Path, was an organization on the Maoist left, which was founded by the university professor Abimael Guzman in the 1960s. It was the decade that saw the growth of leftist revolutionary movements among the Latin American peoples, and in 1967 the death of the revolutionary hero Ernesto "Che" Guevara in Bolivia. A faction of the Peruvian Communist Party, it began an armed struggle against the government in 1980, much like the FARC, the Revolutionary Armed Forces of Colombia. The ideology of the Shining Path resembled that of the Khmer Rouge of Pol Pot in Cambodia (Kampuchea); it desired to remove bourgeois institutions and rebuild Peru as a peasant society.

According to the *Bulletin of the Federation of Atomic Scientists* (FAS), "In the 1980s, SL [Sendero Luminoso] became one of the most ruthless terrorist groups in the Western Hemisphere, approximately 30,000 persons have died since Shining Path took up arms in 1980." The Shining Path pursued its own revolutionary course of development, being violently opposed to affiliation with any other leftist guerrilla movements. "It also opposes any influence by foreign governments, as well as by other Latin American guerrilla groups, especially the Tupac Amaru Revolutionary Movement (MRTA)," FAS explains.

The Tupac Amaru Revolutionary Movement, or in Spanish, the Movemiento Revolucionario Tupac Amaru, was formed in 1983 from the Peruvian Movement of the Revolutionary Left, which also was founded in the 1960s. The MRTA was largely destroyed in April 1997, when a siege of the Japanese embassy beginning in December 1996 ended when President Alberto Fujimori ordered a surprise attack. All 14 members present were killed; rumors persisted that they were shot without given a chance to lay down their arms.

With the eclipse of the Tupac Amaru movement, the Shining Path was the remaining Maoist guerrilla force in Peru. Its bloody tactics, however, terrorized the population as much as the soldiers sent by the government to hunt them down. Even American religious missionary nuns were killed by them in front of the villagers they served. Much like the FARC, however, the Sendero Luminoso has turned to trading in drugs to finance their operations, a grave strategic mistake that only further hurts the workers and peasants the organization ostensibly exists to help. While fighting an urban campaign, the Sendero Luminoso has also engaged Peruvian army and paramilitary police units in battle in the countryside, notably in the Upper Huallaga River Valley and the Apurimac/Ene River Valley.

In 2000, the government announced the arrest of Commandante Ormeno, Jose Arsela Chiroque, in a counterattack believed to be heavily aided by the United States anti-narcotics effort in South America. A sign of the movement's waning strength was its inability to disrupt Peru's presidential elections in April 2000, in which Alejandro Toledo was elected in the place of the discredited Fujimori. Charged with leading an increasingly harsh regime, Fujimori fled to Japan.

In 2002, eight members of the movement were arrested in connection with a bombing across the street from the American embassy. Strong action by Peru's new president, Alejandro Toledo, caused severe attrition in the Sendero Luminoso's ranks. According to one source, "membership is [now] unknown but estimated to be 100 to 200 armed militants" Sendero Luminoso's "strength has been vastly diminished by arrests and desertions."

## SEE ALSO

*Volume 1 Left:* Peru; South America.
*Volume 2 Right:* Peru, South America.

## BIBLIOGRAPHY

James Q. Jacobs, "Tupac Amaru: The Life, Times, and Execution of the Last Inca," www.jqjacobs.net (July 2004); "Tupac Amaru Revolutionary Movement (MRTA)," www.terrorismfiles.org (July 2004); Francois Sully, *Age of the Guerrilla* (Avon Books, 1963); James Fallows, *National Defense* (Vintage, 1981); "Sendero Luminoso (SL) Shining Path," *Bulletin of the Federation of Atomic Scientists*, www.fas.org (July 2004); "Shining Path," www.terrorismfiles.org (July 2004).

JOHN F. MURPHY, JR.
AMERICAN MILITARY UNIVERSITY

# Sinclair, Upton (1878–1968)

UPTON SINCLAIR was a renowned author and active political socialist. He was born Upton Beall Sinclair, Jr., in Baltimore, Maryland, in September 1878. His parents were far from wealthy, but a great deal of his childhood was spent with his rather affluent grandparents. This disparity in his family's financial stability guided Sinclair to adopt socialist ideology later in his life. He began writing early in life, scripting dime novels to pay his way through City College of New York and graduate work at Columbia University. It was during his formative collegiate years that Sinclair became a voice for liberal social change.

A very active writer, Sinclair's early works are hardly recognizable. He published his first novel in 1901, *Springtime and Harvest*, but it fell to the same fate as his next few books, *Prince Hagen* (1903), *The Journal of Arthur Stirling* (1903), *Manassas* (1904), and *A Captain of Industry* (1906), which all sold very poorly. Sinclair's most notable work came in the wake of these literary flops and was the result of his ties to socialism.

In 1904, the editor of the socialist journal *Appeal to Reason*, Fred Warren, called on Sinclair to investigate and write about immigrant workers in the Chicago meatpacking industry. After only a few weeks of research he penned his classic *The Jungle* (1906). The well-known novel detailed the horrid conditions and disgracefully unsanitary state of the business of meatpacking. The book was initially rejected by several publishers due to its controversial content. Sinclair made it known to readers of *Appeal to Reason* that he was going to publish the work on his own. When orders began pouring in, Doubleday decided to publish the book. Unlike his earlier works, *The Jungle* sold tremendously well and was eventually published in 17 languages around the world.

It was during the same time period that Sinclair developed ties to organized socialism. In 1905, he joined with fellow author and friend Jack London, Florence Kelley, Walter Lippmann, and Clarence Darrow to form the Intercollegiate Socialist Society (ISS). Along with being a socialist, Sinclair is noted in most history survey texts as a progressive muckraker. At the turn of the century, muckrakers in all venues of writing were exposing the disturbing social ills of American society. During the Progressive Era, authors like Ida Tarbell were divulging awful truths of business and industry that led to major reform legislation. After reading *The Jungle*, President Theodore Roosevelt ordered an immediate investigation of the meatpacking industry. The inquiry and the novel led to the passage of the Pure Food and Drugs Act (1906) and the Meat Inspection Act (1906). Using their literature to expose corruption, muckrakers during the Progressive Era like Sinclair and Tarbell were able to promulgate major social reform.

Besides being a prominent author and muckraker, Sinclair harnessed his socialist ideology into politics and activism. Soon after the success of *The Jungle*, he accepted the Socialist Party's nomination for Congress in New Jersey. It was a miserable defeat. He decided to establish a commune for radical left-wing writers called the Helicon Home Colony in Eaglewood, New Jersey, that would not survive a fire only months after its inception. Up until the 1940s, Sinclair continued to write with little critical acclaim but continued arguing his socialist point of view. He opposed World War I, arguing

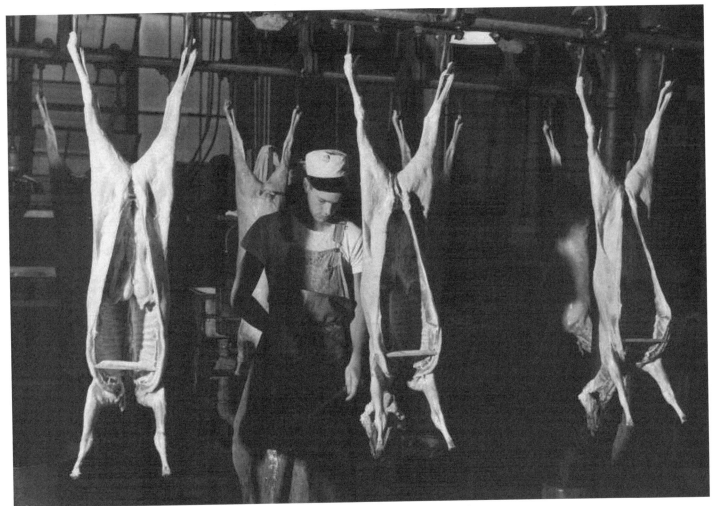

*A worker in the "Beef Kill" section of a Hormel meatpacking plant in 1938 in Minnesota was working in vastly improved conditions after the passage of meat inspection laws, which came about due to Upton Sinclair's investigative work.*

it was an imperialist venture, and later ran for governor of California in 1926 as the Socialist Party candidate and in 1934 as the Democratic Party candidate. He narrowly lost his bid in 1934 that was based on the socialist plan entitled End Poverty in California (EPIC).

Under that plan, bankrupt farms and industries would be taken over by the state of California for back taxes and operated as state enterprises, hiring the unemployed, who would be paid in scrip that would be used to purchase products so produced. By this device, a statewide socialist system would be able to co-exist, he claimed, alongside the capitalist system without disturbing it. His EPIC plan was characteristically introduced in a novel: *I, Governor of California*. He was defeated by a concerted effort of the major newspapers of the state working with the motion picture industry.

With unsuccessful political campaigns behind him, Sinclair once again turned back to writing, earning the Pulitzer Prize for fiction in 1943 for his depiction of Germany's fall to Nazism in *Dragon's Teeth* (1942).

Sinclair's liberal socialist ideology guided his careers in writing and politics. His radical positions are criticized by some and heralded by others. Nonetheless, Sinclair's effort to bring socialist concepts into the mainstream of American politics at the state level was striking for its near success in 1934.

## SEE ALSO

*Volume 1 Left:* United States; Socialism; Socialist Party, U.S.; Progressive Party.
*Volume 2 Right:* United States; Capitalism.

## BIBLIOGRAPHY

William A. Bloodworth, *Upton Sinclair* (Twayne Publishers, 1977); Max Horn, *The Intercollegiate Socialist Society, 1905–21: Origins of the Modern American Student Movement* (Westview

Press, 1979); R.N. Mookerjee, *Art for Social Justice: The Major Novels of Upton Sinclair* (Scarecrow, 1988); Upton Sinclair, *The Autobiography of Upton Sinclair* (Harcourt, Brace & World, 1962); Jon Yoder, *Upton Sinclair* (Ungar, 1984).

D. STEVEN CRONIN
MISSISSIPPI STATE UNIVERSITY

# Singapore

THE REPUBLIC OF SINGAPORE is a small city-state of 4.7 million people (2003) attracting outsized attention by its path of development and mode of government, which is reputed to be a most powerful challenge to the Western liberal model.

One of the earliest references to Singapore as Temasek, or Sea Town, was found in Javanese and Vietnamese sources of 1360s. Intermittently a pirate camp, it was a fortified city well connected to trade networks with China and other Asian countries. By the end of the 14th century, the Sanskrit name, Singapura (Lion City), became commonly used. Owing to its communicative and strategic importance, the city was traditionally a place of rivalry between Siamese and Javanese forces. Europeans came in the 15th century. Portuguese, Dutch, and French have been edged out by the English, whose Javanese governor Thomas Raffles, by tangling intrigues, gained for Britain the sole right to build a factory in Singapore in 1818. The status of the city as a British possession was formalized six years later.

In 1826, Singapore was joined to Penang and Malacca to become a distinct Straits Settlements protectorate in 1867. A decade later, the rubber planting began. Just at the same time that pneumatic tires were invented, a rubber trade boom began, contributing much to region's prosperity. During World War II, the region was occupied by Japan. After a short-lived postwar merger with Malaya, Singapore became an independent state on August 9, 1965, under the leadership of People's Action Party (PAP), which won 43 seats (of 51) in the Legislative Assembly. Since that time, and to date in 2004, PAP holds unalterable power, using it for creating an ever watchful political system, regimenting almost every aspect of Singaporean life and snuffing out sparks of political dissent, making Singapore the poster child for "soft" authoritarianism.

Meanwhile, the region experienced an economic boom. Singapore still benefited as the main seaport in Asia and as the world's premier rubber market. Singapore's gross national product (GNP) doubled every seven years on average up to and including the 1990s. Through a successful industrialization program, the city gradually became an industrial and financial center of Asia. The stable government led from 1959 to 1990 by Prime Minister Lee Kuan Yew and developed industry attracted ever more investments, changing the visage of the city-state, which has become not a less prosperous Asian country than Japan.

According to A.T. Kearney in *Foreign Policy* magazine's Globalization Index, Singapore is ranked as one of the most globalized nations owing to its trade-intensive economy, wide cross-border personal contacts, huge number of internet users and servers, and deep political engagement in international organizations. Singapore enjoys a successful free-market economy and one of the highest per capita gross domestic products in the world ($24,000 in 1997). Singaporean ethnic Chinese (77 percent), Malay (14 percent), Indian (7.6 percent), and others (1.4 percent) live together amicably using the English, Chinese, Malay, and Tamil languages interchangeably and proving the conventional wisdom that national wealth can successfully solve social and national problems.

Economically, Singapore is a relatively free, competitive market system, prospering greatly from global trade; however, politically and socially Singapore is a quasi-authoritarian state, an illiberal society with significant governmental controls over political, social, and cultural life. Being a Confucian society, it lacks a tradition of rights against the state. "To the extent that individual rights did exist, they were created by the state," S. Huntington explains in *Democracy's Third Wave*.

Although friendly to business, Singapore's government represses dissent and is far from transparent in its management of public funds. State authorities exert an almost legendary degree of social control. One will get into trouble with Singapore's police if he or she walks naked, has oral sex, or fails to flush a public toilet. Even chewing-gum is illegal to import or sell. There is a strict control on media and political expression. It is illegal to own a private satellite dish without obtaining a license. Offenders will lose their satellite dish and face a maximum fine of S$40,000 or a jail term of no more than three years. One must apply for a license to form a nongovernmental organization or to speak publicly. All groups or societies with at least 10 persons must be registered. An application may be rejected if the society is deemed prejudicial to public peace, welfare, or good order in Singapore. The government introduced a speakers' corner in 2000 to appease freedom-of-speech lobbyists. Speakers must register their names with the police.

The internet is regulated in Singapore through licensing and proxy servers. In 1991, an "Internet Code of Practice" was published as part of the Singapore Broadcasting Authority Act to ensure that "nothing is included in any broadcasting service which is against public interest or order, national harmony or which offends against good taste or decency." Political advertising that uses films or videos is banned, journalist Lisa Murray reports. Under an amendment to the Films Act in 1998, any person who imports, makes, reproduces, or distributes a film "made by any person and directed toward any political end in Singapore" could be fined or jailed up to two years.

Singaporean anti-narcotraffic laws are very strict, too. The country has the highest death-penalty rate in the world. Caning and execution by hanging in Singapore are widely criticized as inhuman. The reduction in perceived corruption and the growth of relative wealth are associated not with draconian law making but with the specific macroeconomic policy actions, which include lowering tariffs and other trade barriers; unifying market exchange and interest rates; eliminating enterprise subsidies; minimizing enterprise regulation, licensing requirements, and other barriers to market entry; privatizing while demonopolizing government assets; enhancing transparency in the enforcement of banking, auditing, and accounting standards; and improving tax and budget administration.

Being a small state, Singapore has no international ambitions and is seeking friends and partners all over the globe. It fully supports and is committed to regional cooperation. Singapore is a nonaligned state and has participated in United Nations peacekeeping/observer missions in Kuwait, Angola, Namibia, Cambodia, and East Timor. It also plays a positive role as a place of negotiations and agreements (1993) on the Divided China Problem.

**SEE ALSO**

*Volume 1 Left:* Socialism; Human Rights.
*Volume 2 Right:* Capitalism; *Laissez-Faire*; Singapore; Globalization.

**BIBLIOGRAPHY**

Larry Jay Diamond, "Hong Kong, Singapore, and 'Asian Values,'" *Journal of Democracy* (v.8/2, April 1997); Neil A. Englehart, "Rights and Culture in the Asian Values Argument: The Rise and Fall of Confucian Ethics in Singapore," *Human Rights Quarterly* (v.22/2, May 2000); Cherian George, *The Air-Conditioned Nation* (Landmark Books, 2000); Mahmood Monshipouri, "The East Asian Challenge for Human Rights," *Human Rights Quarterly* (v.22/1, February 2000); Garry Rodan, "Asian Crisis, Transparency and the International Media in Singapore," *The Pacific Review* (v.13/2, 2000).

IGOR CHARSKYKH
DONETSK NATIONAL UNIVERSITY, UKRAINE

# Social Democracy

IN THE 19th century, social democracy was widely associated with radical or revolutionary socialist parties and political movements, many of which actually included the term *social democracy* in their names. In Britain for example, a Social Democratic Federation was established in 1884, explicitly based on the theories of Karl Marx, as was the Social Democratic Party that was formed in Germany in 1875. Many other European social democratic parties, such as those formed in Austria and Scandinavia during this period, were also strongly imbued with Marxist ideology.

However, during the 20th century, social democracy dispensed with its Marxist precepts, and thereby consciously was transformed into a moderate, anti-revolutionary, ultra-constitutional, political philosophy, and array of left-of-center political parties. Indeed, so moderate has European social democracy become that many on the left alleged that 20th-century social democratic parties became devoid of any genuine socialist content and became, instead, bourgeois reformists merely seeking to humanize capitalism on behalf of the working class, rather than replace it with socialism through the active involvement of the working class.

Since eschewing its Marxist origins and outlook, social democracy has pursued avowedly socialist objectives: a fairer society with greater equality and the eradication of poverty, modest wealth redistribution (primarily via progressive taxation, whereby higher rates of tax are paid on higher salaries and other sources of income), equal treatment and respect for all citizens, including the eradication of all forms of discrimination, government regulation of the economy to ensure stability, stable growth and the creation of full employment, and a welfare state to provide free (paid for via taxes) education, healthcare, pensions, and other forms of social security for those in material need.

Crucially, however, social democracy has pursued these goals through parliamentary democracy, having totally rejected revolutionary or syndicalist means of effecting political change or overthrowing capitalism. Democratic elections, not direct action, became social democracy's chosen means of securing political power in order to create a fairer society. Only political power derived from winning a parliamentary majority through the ballot box is considered to be legitimate by social democrats.

Social democracy also maintains that the goal of establishing a fairer, more egalitarian society, should be pursued on an incremental basis, through policies and reforms that gradually, but peacefully, transform capitalism, without ever constituting an all-out direct assault on the capitalist system or bourgeoisie. In this respect, social democracy has accepted "the inevitability of gradualness," believing that social and economic reforms can be cumulative, each building on preceding reforms, and thereby becoming embedded, to the extent that they become virtually irreversible.

## SOCIAL REFORMISM

The extension of the franchise to the working classes during the late 19th century and early 20th century yielded a corresponding change of political perspective among many socialists in Western Europe. Whereas Marxist notions of class struggle and proletarian revolution had hitherto informed socialist praxis, the granting of the vote to increasing numbers of workers served to weaken the credence of arguments previously advanced for direct action and insurrection as the means of securing socialism.

The implications for socialists of the extension of the franchise was clearly recognized by the German Marxist, Eduard Bernstein, who actually spent the first decade of the 20th century living in Britain. His observations prompted him to revise (hence the term revisionists often applied to non-Marxist or post-Marxist socialists) his views about the attainment of socialism. Bernstein noted how the extension of the franchise led to the formation of explicitly working-class political parties, often closely linked to the trade unions, such as Britain's Labor Party, officially launched in 1906. Such developments imbued Bernstein with faith and optimism in the efficacy of constitutional and electoral channels as the means of securing power for socialist parties, thereby rendering revolution redundant.

Indeed, there was a moral and ethical dimension to this eschewal of socialist revolution, namely that a political doctrine or movement that sought to extend democracy to the economic and social realms could hardly be taken seriously if it rejected the recent extension of democracy to the political sphere. The extension of the franchise placed the onus on socialists to convince the majority of (working-class) voters that they ought to vote for socialist parties. If socialists could not persuade such a majority through rational argument, political education, and peaceful persuasion that socialism was in their interests, then they had no right seeking to impose socialism on the masses through insurrection and a Marxian "dictatorship of the proletariat." At both a theoretical and practical level, revisionists such as Bernstein recognized that electoral politics necessitated a clear rejection of the Marxist-Leninist model of a vanguard party seizing political power on behalf of the proletariat.

This revision of Marxist praxis in the context of political changes from the late 19th century onward was underpinned by wider changes in some of the economic and social aspects of 20th-century Western European capitalism.

## CHARACTER OF CAPITALISM

During the 20th century, three socioeconomic changes regarding Western European capitalism led social democrats even further away from Marxist precepts and prognosis. First, whereas Marx (and his acolytes) deemed capitalism to be inherently unstable and crises-ridden, due in large part to its inherent contradictions, and thus destined for eventual collapse, 20th-century social democrats pointed to the relative stability of capitalism overall, and thus its apparent durability. Of course, the economic problems afflicting much of Europe in the 1920s and 1930s—and which provided much of the context for the concomitant rise of fascism—were hardly redolent of a stable and smooth-functioning capitalism. Rather than view the economic slump as a vindication of Marxist theory about the inevitability of capitalist crises, social democrats tended to see it as a consequence of unfortunate circumstances and incorrect policies, not an intrinsic and unavoidable feature of capitalism per se.

The second socioeconomic change that social democrats interpreted as a refutation of orthodox Marxist analysis concerned the ownership and control of the means of production. Marxists deemed a single capitalist class to enjoy both ownership and control and predicted that this ownership and control would become concentrated in an even smaller number of hands (as larger or more successful capitalist companies took over or displaced their smaller or less successful rivals). By contrast, 20th-century social democrats noted that ownership and control were becoming increasingly separated, due to the expansion of joint-stock companies, along with the emergence of a new managerial class who controlled the routine or day-to-day activities of companies without actually owning them themselves; those in de facto control of industry were themselves employees paid a salary.

To social democrats, this trend indicated that ownership and control of the means of production were increasingly becoming both separated and more diffuse, and that managers themselves were often salaried employees. This development also meant, according to social democrats, that there was no longer a clearly defined capitalist class who could be identified as exploiting the working class and appropriating the proletariat's surplus value.

The third socioeconomic change discerned by 20th-century Western European social democrats in their rejection of Marxism concerned the apparently changing social structure of capitalist societies. Contrary to Marx's prophesy about the increasing immiseration of the working class under capitalism, and the extent to which there would be an ever-growing polarization between bourgeoisie and proletariat, social democrats pointed to the extent to which ordinary working people in general enjoyed steadily rising living standards during the 20th century, more especially after World War II. Moreover, instead of comprising two increasingly polarized social classes, working and upper class, the 20th century witnessed the enormous expansion of the middle class (which Marx had expected to disappear, merging with one of the two other classes).

POST-1945 SOCIAL DEMOCRACY

All of the above trends became more pronounced following the end of World War II and thereby yielded a further refinement of both the theory and the practice of social democracy. Indeed, some of the socioeconomic changes that characterized this period were, arguably, directly attributable to the application of social democratic policies. As such, the apparent success and efficacy of postwar social democracy further vindicated its rejection of Marxism

For example, during the 1950s and 1960s, many Western societies enjoyed unprecedented economic growth, prosperity, and stability. These developments, in turn, greatly reduced the number of citizens living in poverty and suffering other forms of socioeconomic deprivation. Marxist concepts pertaining to the allegedly irreconcilable conflicts and contradictions within capitalism, the increasing immiseration of the proletariat, and the disappearance of the middle class appeared totally inappropriate and inaccurate. Social democracy and its adherents thus exhibited considerable intellectual and political self-confidence and felt vindicated in their analysis of contemporary capitalism and its internal dynamics.

This confidence was particularly evident in the stance of some senior Labor politicians during the 1950s and early 1960s. For example, in his seminal 1956 book, *The Future of Socialism*, the Labor member of parliament (and a future education secretary) Anthony Crosland argued that Great Britain had become a "post-capitalist society," due to changes in both the economic structure of the economy and the ownership and control of industry, as well as rising living standards and growing prosperity, which were enabling an increasing number of workers to acquire middle-class consumer durables and lifestyles. This improvement in the material position of the working class had been further assisted by the attainment of full employment—via government regulation of the economy and the application of Keynesian methods of demand management—progressive (redistributive) taxation, the establishment of a universal welfare state, and an approximate parity of power between capital and labor, as trade unionism provided workers with a counterweight to the power of employers. These were deemed by social democrats such as Crosland to illustrate what could be achieved through benign government action on behalf of ordinary working people, which, in turn, seemed to render intellectually and politically redundant both the precepts of the Marxist left and the *laissez-faire* capitalism of the right.

This perspective virtually ruled out the need for further nationalization of industry, to the extent that the Labor leader, Hugh Gaitskell, sought formally to abandon the party's formal commitment to public ownership, although he was defeated due to opposition from the wider party membership. However, Tony Blair succeeded in 1995.

In West Germany, meanwhile, the Social Democrats' 1959 conference at Bad Godesburg approved a new political program, whereby the party would henceforth accept private enterprise and a market economy, whereupon the role of government would be to render capitalism more humane, efficient, and stable, so that it served the interests of all citizens. Probably the archetypal, and most successful, social democratic society, though, has been postwar Sweden.

One other key characteristic of 20th-century social democracy was its belief in the political neutrality of the state and its political institutions. Whereas Marxists alluded to a "bourgeois state" that was staffed by personnel who represented or served the overall interests of capital(ism), and who would therefore obstruct or undermine socialist governments, social democrats have insisted that the state is a neutral body that serves whichever political party has legitimately and democratically achieved political power through the ballot box.

In Britain, for example, mainstream Labor ministers have usually insisted that senior civil servants, who advise on policy matters and assist with policy implementation, faithfully serve governments irrespective of their political complexion or ideological orientation. More generally, social democrats have been able to cite the social and economic reforms and advances achieved in much of postwar Western Europe as evidence that the state is not the instrument of capital or the bourgeoisie (as Marxists claim), but that it genuinely serves the interests of society as a whole, via the democratically elected governing political party.

## SOCIAL DEMOCRACY IN CRISIS

By the 1980s and 1990s, the hitherto confidence and apparent hegemony of social democracy had been seriously undermined, as economic crises not only challenged some of its assumptions and policy solutions, but also led to a resurgence or renaissance of the right in parts of the Western world. In Britain, for example, Thatcherism represented a particular form of combative or aggressive conservatism that explicitly sought to discredit social democratic principles and destroy social democratic institutions and innovations.

Social democracy has also had to grapple with wider, longer-term changes during the 1980s and 1990s, particularly the development (or acceleration) of globalization, because social democracy tended, at least tacitly or implicitly, to be predicated upon national economies that could be regulated and partially controlled by domestic governments.

Social democrats have therefore had to acknowledge that globalization seriously constrains their ability to manage their economies in the national interest, so that former goals such as public ownership are rendered even more inappropriate and impractical. Similarly, social democrats have also needed to accept that many cit-

izens and companies are no longer willing to pay the levels of direct taxation that were necessary to finance a comprehensive welfare state. Consequently, the old model of the social democratic welfare state has increasingly been replaced by notions of a more targeted welfare state, one in which rights (to social security payments) are increasingly and explicitly linked to reciprocal responsibilities, including good behavior and active citizenship. These changes have been particularly apparent with the advent of New Labor and the election of the Blair governments in Britain (which have espoused a Third Way between old social democracy and the new right) and the notion of the Neu Mitte articulated by Gerhard Schroeder's Social Democrats in Germany.

Social democracy claims that its core principles remain largely unchanged—committed to economic stability, social justice, the eradication of poverty, tackling racial and sexual discrimination and social disadvantage, equality of opportunity, various employment rights and protection for ordinary workers against unscrupulous employers, a minimum level of income for all citizens, and a welfare system to help those who are genuinely unable to help themselves due to illness, infirmity, or other misfortune. However, economic changes and international obligations necessitate new means and methods to realize these principles.

## SEE ALSO

*Volume 1 Left:* Socialism; Marx, Karl; United Kingdom; Germany; Sweden.
*Volume 2 Right:* Capitalism; United Kingdom; Germany.

## BIBLIOGRAPHY

Eduard Bernstein, *Evolutionary Socialism* (Schocken, 1961); Anthony Crosland, *The Future of Socialism* (Jonathan Cape, 1956); Anthony Giddens, *The Third Way: The Renewal of Social Democracy* (Polity, 1998); S. Miller and H. Potthof, *A History of German Social Democracy* (Berg, 1986); Stephen Padgett and William E. Paterson, *A History of Social Democracy in Postwar Europe* (Longman, 1991); William E. Paterson and Alistair Thomas, eds., *The Future of Social Democracy* (Oxford University Press, 1986); Adam Przeworski, *Capitalism and Social Democracy* (Cambridge University Press, 1985); T. Tilton, *The Political Theory of Swedish Social Democracy* (Oxford University Press, 1991); Anthony Wright, "Social Democracy and Democratic Socialism," Roger Eatwell and Anthony Wright, eds., *Contemporary Political Ideologies* (Pinter, 1993);

PETER DOREY
CARDIFF UNIVERSITY, UNITED KINGDOM

# Social Security

SOCIAL SECURITY WAS a social insurance program created in 1935 as part of the second stage of the New Deal during the Franklin Roosevelt administration. Social Security was created in response to the more radical proposals by Senator Huey Long and Francis Townsend. Social Security has three main provisions: It provides aid to those with disabilities, survivor insurance, and a pension for the elderly and retired. Social Security is one of the most popular federal government programs and is considered so sacrosanct that has been dubbed the "third rail" (untouchable; derived from the electrified third rail of a railway) in American politics.

For decades, public officials advocated the creation of a social insurance program. As president, Theodore Roosevelt advocated the adoption of a social security program. He cited the fact that Germany, which implemented social insurance legislation in 1889, possessed more advanced social insurance laws than the United States. In 1909, the first old-age pension legislation was introduced in Congress. When Theodore Roosevelt ran for president as the head of the Progressive Party, he supported a social insurance program for those who were retired or with disabilities. In 1912, Isaac Rubinow wrote *Social Insurance*, which influenced Roosevelt. In 1915, old-age pension legislation was enacted in Alaska. In 1923, old-age pension legislation was enacted in Montana and held to be constitutional. In 1930, California enacted old-age pension laws.

It was not until 1935 that pensions for the elderly and retired were enacted at the federal level in the form of the Social Security Act of 1935. The bill passed with wide margins in both the U.S. Senate and House of Representatives. It became law on August 14, 1935. The Social Security Act of 1935 set up a system of compulsory saving in which both the employers and employees would pay a 3 percent payroll tax. The money would be paid to the employee once he or she turned 65. The Social Security Act also created a Social Security Board, whose members would be appointed by the president.

Social Security was attacked by critics on both the left and right. Franklin D. Roosevelt's opponent in the 1936 presidential election referred to the new program as a "cruel hoax." On the left, critics such as Townsend, who had a more radical pension plan of his own, believed that Social Security did not go far enough.

In 1937, Roosevelt proposed a number of amendments to the Social Security Act. In 1939, Congress amended the Social Security Act. Social Security now included both survivors' and dependent benefits. It also moved the date of dispensing monthly benefits to 1939. In 1940, Ida Fuller entered the history books as the first person to receive monthly benefits under Social Security. She received a check for $22.44, having paid $24.75 between 1937–39.

In 1946, the Social Security Act was again amended. Social Security was expanded to include monthly benefits to the families of deceased World War II veterans. In 1950, the Social Security Act was amended to include 10 million more people under the umbrella of Social Security. It also eased eligibility requirements as well as increased the amount of benefits. In 1952, Social Security benefits were increased and the requirements were eased further.

Upon entering office in 1952, President Dwight D. Eisenhower recommended that old age and survivor's benefits be extended to millions of Americans who were still excluded from the Social Security system. In 1954, Social Security benefits were extended to farmers, domestic workers, and other professions that were self-employed. By 1955, Social Security had over 7 million beneficiaries. In 1956, the Social Security Act was amended to give monthly benefits to middle-aged and elderly disabled workers in the 50 to 64 age range. It also provided disability benefits to disabled children and reduced the retirement age for widows to 62. In November 1956, benefits were paid out to women who were at least 62. In 1958, Social Security was amended and benefits were again increased.

## AMENDMENTS

In 1960, Social Security was amended in order to dispense Social Security disability benefits to people of all ages. The retirement and disability tests were further eased. In 1961, Social Security was amended during the administration of John F. Kennedy. The new amendments allowed male workers to retire earlier at the age of 62. It also increased the amount of benefits to aged widows, widowers, and surviving parents. That same year, Kennedy signed into law legislation intended to reduce tax fraud by assigning Social Security numbers.

In 1962, the payroll tax was increased to 3.125 percent for employers and employees and 4.7 percent for those who were self-employed. In 1965, beneficiaries began receiving lump payments, which were an increase over previous allotted payments.

Also in 1965, it became possible for widows aged 60 to receive benefits, albeit in smaller amounts. In 1967, Social Security was amended to increase benefits by 13 percent as well as expanded the earnings base to $7,800.

In 1969, the payroll tax for employers and employees was increased to 4.8 percent and 6.9 percent for the self-employed. Also in 1969, President Richard Nixon continued the bipartisan tradition of supporting Social Security. Nixon proposed increasing benefits across the board by 10 percent. That same year, Nixon signed the Tax Reform Act, which increased benefits by 15 percent. In January 1971, a 10 percent increase in Social Security benefits went into effect. It was under Nixon that the cost of living allowance (COLA) became law. In 1972, a 20 percent cost of living allowance became effective, which meant that benefits would increase with the rate of inflation.

In 1980, President Jimmy Carter signed a law that established tougher requirements for Social Security disability benefits. In 1981, Ronald Reagan set up a commission to look into reforming Social Security. Later that year, Reagan signed legislation that implemented a number of reforms including tougher penalties for Social Security fraud. It was in the 1980s that the issue of Social Security became politicized with Democrats charging that Republicans wanted to undermine Social Security and Republicans responding by accusing Democrats of attempting to scare the elderly. Ironically, reforms were implemented by both parties that helped to delay Social Security's bankruptcy. In 1983, Reagan created a bipartisan commission, that suggested solutions that helped to increase Social Security's longevity. It was believed in the 1980s that one of the reasons for the spiraling deficit was the unwillingness of both parties to contain the growing cost of Social Security, which along with Medicare consumed an ever increasing percentage of the federal budget.

In the 1990s, the issue of Social Security became even more politicized. In 1993, President Bill Clinton was attacked for raising the taxes on Social Security beneficiaries in the upper brackets. In 1995, the Republicans were accused of wanting to destroy Social Security, Medicare, and other entitlement programs. Clinton, in 1999, exploited the popularity of Social Security when he called for ensuring that the money from the Social Security Trust Fund was not used for other purposes. By the 1990s, Social Security had become the "third rail" of American politics that few, if any, politicians were willing to touch.

## SEE ALSO

*Volume 1 Left:* Socialism; Socialist Party, U.S.; Roosevelt, Franklin D.; New Deal.
*Volume 2 Right:* Capitalism; Welfare and Poverty; United States.

**BIBLIOGRAPHY**

Arthur J. Altmeyer, *The Formative Years of Social Security* (University of Wisconsin Press, 1966); Peter A. Diamond, *Social Security Reform* (Oxford University Press, 2002); John Dixon and Robert P. Scheurell, *Social Security Programs: A Cross-Cultural Comparative Perspective* (Greenwood Press, 1995); Peter A. Kohler and Hans F. Zacher, *The Evolution of Social Insurance: 1881–1981: Studies of Germany, France, Great Britain, Austria, and Switzerland* (St. Martin's Press, 1982); Social Security Administration, www.ssa.gov/history (May 2004).

JASON ROBERTS
GEORGE WASHINGTON UNIVERSITY

# Socialism

THE ORIGINS OF SOCIALISM are obscure. Historians have traced its roots to the religious utopias of the Old Testament, the principles of Mosaic Law, the anti-individualism of radical sects that emerged from the French Revolution, and the publication of the *Communist Manifesto.*

The word *socialism* made its first appearance in print in Italian in 1803, although its meaning at that time appeared to differ somewhat from current interpretations. For this reason, the origin of the term is usually attributed to a latter publication, in English. The word *socialist* was used in 1827 in the *London Cooperative Magazine* to designate followers of Robert Owen. In 1832, a French periodical, *Le Globe,* used it to characterize the writings of Saint-Simon. Despite such murky beginnings, by 1840 the concept was commonly used across Europe and was making its way across the Atlantic to the United States. By the early 1920s, the Soviet Union had already become a "socialist republic." Some 260 definitions of this term were available in the social-scientific literature. Since then, further refinement of the concept has appeared; for instance, we now differentiate among Chinese socialism, corporatist socialism, democratic socialism, radical socialism, and others.

Socialism was brought into existence by the rise of industrial production and the intensification of wage labor in handicraft enterprises. Prior to the large-scale existence of workshops, factories, and machines, most radical conceptions of reorganization of society were agrarian, as in Jean-Jacques Rousseau's constitution for an imaginary republic of Corsica. Socialist doctrines sought to organize society in order to replace the anarchy of the marketplace and large-scale poverty with an orderly system. Organization offered a rational solution to the social question, the problems of mass poverty and poor urban living conditions. Thus, most of the early socialists were middle-class reformers, concerned philanthropists who eagerly sought to improve the lot of the poor by changes in social organization rather than charitable activities.

It is hard to define what constitutes the common core of socialist doctrine. To be sure, all socialists were critical of the competitive and unequal nature of capitalist society and without fail they envisioned a more egalitarian and just future. At the same time, their visions regarding the organization of a socialist future were sufficiently diverse to render a single definition of the term practically impossible. It is assumed that the socialist doctrine demands state ownership and control of the fundamental means of production and distribution of wealth, to be achieved by reconstruction of the existing capitalist or other political system of a country through peaceful, democratic, and parliamentary means.

The doctrine specifically advocates nationalization of natural resources, basic industries, banking and credit facilities, and public utilities. It places special emphasis on the nationalization of monopolized branches of industry and trade. It views monopolies as inimical to the public welfare. It also advocates that smaller and less vital enterprises would be left under private ownership, and privately held cooperatives would be encouraged.

Given the nature of the doctrine, a single definition of socialism is likely to conceal more than it might illuminate. Thus, it may be better to analyze the best-known schools of socialist thought.

## UTOPIAN SOCIALISTS

This school of socialist thought considered socialism to be little more than a pleasant dream, a romantic vision whose purpose was not necessarily to be realized but to serve as an ideal against which the evils of capitalism could be compared. Though the scientific content of this vision, of course, varied from author to author, but two central themes united them. The first of them is the idea of community. Almost all utopian theorists championed a new social order, organized around the small communities. In most sketches of socialism this vision was realized in an agrarian setting, although some re-

quired advanced industrial development. In either case, it was assumed that these communities would be based on fellowship, harmony, and altruism—virtues that utopian theorists favored, on moral grounds, over bourgeois individualism.

Nostalgia for the past is the second common theme in utopian socialist thought. It frequently appeared in utopian novels and usually assumed one or two forms. In some versions the main characters are returned to the gaiety of their childhood times, while in others they reside in the Middle Ages or tell their stories against the backdrop of the less distant past. Their message was quite clear: In the transition to industrial capitalism, we have abandoned the "golden age" of social harmony and replaced it with a fragmented and competitive social order that is unable to provide the fulfillment and satisfaction of human needs.

## SCIENTIFIC SOCIALISTS

In the hands of scientific socialists, the romantic dream of utopian socialism vanished. Karl Marx considered scientific socialism to be a historically possible future for capitalism. He argued that the internal contradictions within capitalism would create some of the preconditions for socialism. According to the theory of historical materialism, the demands made by capitalist development will create increasingly grave crises for the ruling class. He maintained that with the mechanization of production and the concentration of capital in fewer hands, there will be greater polarization in class inequalities and an increase in the degree of exploitation of the working class. As capitalism enters its advanced age, the conditions of the working class will deteriorate and the struggle over the quality of their existence will intensify. At first the war between the "two hostile camps" of capitalist society—the bourgeois and the proletariat—will be waged within the boundaries of the particular nation state. However, as capitalism expands in the new markets in the international scene, workers across the world will be forced to unite in their efforts to overthrow capitalist society.

According to Marx, socialism will emerge out of this final instance of class struggle, though the details of the future were missing. However, he envisioned two stages in the evolution of socialism. In the first stage, what he referred to as socialism or the "dictatorship of proletariat," he foreshadowed two major improvements in the human condition. He predicted, for example, that private property would be abolished, the forces of production would be nationalized in the hands of state, rights of inheritance would be eliminated, universal suffrage would be introduced, state representatives would be elected from among the working people, and education would be accessible to all. At the same time, because Marx expected this to be a transitional stage, he believed that the some of the elements of the capitalist society would continue to prevail. Specifically, he mentioned that income inequalities would continue to exist in the first stage because workers would still be paid according to the amount of work that they would contribute.

Marx envisioned, at some point, this transition phase in the development of human history would evolve into the higher stage of socialism, a stage that he referred as communism. Under communism, work would no longer be an obligation but a free and creative activity, alienation would be transcended, the production process would be under direct control of the producer, and the distribution of rewards would be changed from "to each according to his ability" to "to each according to his needs."

## DEMOCRATIC SOCIALISM

Principles of scientific socialism gained considerable popularity among French, German, and British socialists during the 19th century. As the century progressed, however, and the Marxist scenario still appeared to be far away, some began to raise questions about the continued relevance of scientific socialism in the modern age. The main protagonist in this debate was Eduard Bernstein, a leading advocate of democratic socialism, which tried to question various elements of scientific socialism.

Bernstein (1961) noted that the standard of living at the turn of the century was improving rather than decreasing, class inequalities were far from polarized, and the ownership of capital, rather than being concentrated in the hands of a few, was in fact becoming diversified. In the light of these facts, Bernstein called for a revision of the Marxist program and offered a new interpretation of socialism. He argued that democracy was the most important feature of socialist society, and thus negated the concept of "dictatorship of the proletariat." Indeed, for Bernstein the importance of democracy was not solely that it guaranteed the representation of minority rights under socialism; it was also that it assured a peaceful transition from capitalism through a series of parliamentary reforms. This innovation earned the "revisionist" label for this school of socialist thought.

## RUSSIAN SOCIALISM

Similarly, during the early part of the 20th century, V. I. Lenin also amended the socialist concept by adding to it several new notions derived cautiously from his experiences with political organization in tzarist Russia. Taken together, these propositions comprise Russian Socialism, also known as Bolshevik theory. The most important contribution of this school of thought to socialist theory is the idea of "intellectuals' unity" or "vanguard party" that can help develop a revolutionary theory, to "go among classes, and to politically educate the proletariat." According to Lenin, Marx was unduly optimistic in his belief that the proletariat could develop the necessary class-consciousness to overthrow capitalism. A second feature of Russian socialism that sets it apart from the Marxist scheme is grounded in its claim that prospects of proletarian revolution can arise not only in advanced industrial societies but also in pre-capitalist economies.

However, it is important to mention that Lenin agreed with the Marxist idea that socialism will come in two stages. Though, according to his schema, the first stage, that is, the dictatorship of the proletariat, would not be a brief transitional period but would require a whole epoch in human history. During this time, the bourgeois state would be smashed, the class rule of the proletariat would be institutionalized, and the "special coercive force" of the proletariat state would suppress the opponents of the socialist regime. The second stage or higher stage of socialism, that is, communism, would be realized once the socialist state had "withered away" and democracy had become a "force of habit."

## CHINESE SOCIALISM

Another well-known attempt to innovate socialism was made by Mao Zedong, who argued that socialism could be appropriate also to the conditions of a peasant country. Unlike most interpretations of socialism, Mao is famous for his glorification of the peasantry. Earlier socialists, including Marx and Lenin, were skeptical about the revolutionary potential of agricultural labor. For the most part, they regarded the peasants as an inherently petty bourgeoisie, and consequently, as unlikely allies of the proletariat. Mao firmly believed that in the absence of an industrial class, as in the case of China, mass mobilization could be achieved by inciting the revolutionary spirit among masses of peasants. He insisted, therefore, that socialist revolution in China was a peasant revolution and had no reservations about organizing agriculture workers into revolutionary force on his side. One key feature that sets apart Chinese socialism is the lack of confidence in the guaranteed future of socialism. Mao believed that the socialist victories are not everlasting; even as the dust from the revolution begins to settle, old inequalities can resurface and new ones may emerge. Thus, the work of the revolutionaries is never completed—they must be constantly on guard against opposition and must be prepared to wage a permanent revolution.

## SOCIALIST EXPERIMENTS

In an effort to realize the socialist vision, a number of socialist communities were established. These included Etienne Cabet's Icaria in Illinois, Charles Fourier's Brook Farm in Massachusetts, William Lane's New Australia in Paraguay, and Robert Owen's New Harmony in Indiana. In nearly all of these cases, an attempt was made to isolate a small group of dedicated socialists from the rest of society and create a model environment for efficient production and egalitarian social exchange. These communities experienced varying degree of success, some even attracted a large number of followers (Icaria) and prospered for more than a decade (Brook Farm). Nevertheless, others were fraught with hardships from the beginning (New Australia) and some collapsed with in a few years (New Harmony).

However, in the end all these utopian experiments failed. They suffered from the lack of preparation and meager financial support, harsh living environments, the near absence of agricultural skills, heterogeneous membership, and the lack of long-term commitment to the socialist vision. The individuals who flocked to these communities were clearly adventurous but they were not trained to carry out the real tasks of building a new world.

Socialist experiments within the real world during the 20th century were much more successful and lasting than their utopian counterparts. With the Russian Revolution, 1917–23, the Soviet Union was the first country to call itself socialist. By the middle of the century, however, there were socialist regimes in Europe, Asia, Latin America, Africa, and the Near East.

The most prominent features of these socialist regimes were: 1) common ownership of the means of production and distribution; 2) centrally planned economic activities and the near absence of market forces in the allocation of resources; 3) single-party rule that legitimates itself by reference to some version of Marxism and Leninism; 4) all executive, legislative, and judi-

cial powers rested on the party with unitary ideology. Largely patterned after the Soviet model, many socialist regimes have secured a number of achievements. Within the decades of revolution they succeeded in industrializing their outmoded economies; guaranteed full employment and price stability; incorporated women in their labor force and expanded childcare services; developed their natural resources and fared well in the advancement of science and technology; strengthened their military power; and improved their education, healthcare, and social welfare systems. Along with these changes, socialist societies made strong commitments to reduce economic, educational, and occupational differentials following World War II. Furthermore, policies were also implemented by socialist states to reduce the intergenerational transmission of social inequalities—inheritance of wealth was eliminated.

Partially due to these changes, socialist societies carved out for themselves a position of considerable importance in the world system during the 20th century. During the 1960s, for instance, the Soviet Union competed head on with the United States in space exploration, the race for military power, and the development of science, technology, athletics, and arts.

Nevertheless, economic and social achievements in the socialist countries could not be sustained for long. In fact, by the early 1970s, centrally planned economies began to show multiple signs of strain. Bureaucratic blunders on the part of state officials resulted in poor investment decisions, frequent bottlenecks created breakdowns in production systems; chronic shortages of consumer items provoked anger and dissatisfaction among citizens; and curious managerial techniques, such as bribing, hoarding, and informal networking, had to be developed to mitigate the ineffective relationship between economic units and state.

The problems plaguing central management in the socialist economies were not restricted to the economic sphere alone, but adversely affected the social and political sector as well. Thus, by the 1970s many of these societies began to demonstrate substantial inequalities in their prestige hierarchy, patterns of social mobility, opportunities for educational attainment, and in the distribution of nonmonetary rewards. Socialist societies witnessed the rise of political inequalities. Many studies have shown that Communist Party functionaries enjoy definite social, political, and economic advantages: they attend party schools, shop at special stores, vacation at the most desirable holiday resorts, and have better access to decision making posts. Party members were also more likely to receive state-subsidized housing, purchase a car or vacation home, and frequently participate in cultural activities. Such differences in the allocation of resources have led many to conclude that the political sphere is central to the stratification system of socialist societies.

In the face of these problems, as well as the apparent failure of the egalitarian experiment, socialist states made serious efforts to reform their economies, however, the legacy of decades of overcentralization and the strong lobbies benefiting from these arrangements made these efforts inconsequential. In the spring of 1989, many of these conflicts came to head as a "gentle revolution" began to unfold within these countries. Most of the socialist countries formally accepted multiparty democracy and a clear policy framework to move in the direction of a market economy. The revolutionary idea of socialism lost its luster.

**SEE ALSO**

*Volume 1 Left:* Socialist Party, U.S.; Communism; United States; Sweden; Africa; Asia; South America.
*Volume 2 Right:* Capitalism; *Laissez-Faire;* Asia; Africa; South America.

**BIBLIOGRAPHY**

Eduard Bernstein, *Evolutionary Socialism,* Edith C. Harvey, trans. (Schocken Books, 1961); Daniel Bell, "Socialism," *International Encyclopedia of the Social Sciences,* David L. Sills, ed.(Macmillan and Free Press, 1968); Ivan T. Berend and Gyorgy Ranki, *Economic Development in East-Central Europe in the 19th and 20th Centuries* (Columbia University Press, 1974); George D. H. Cole, *A History of Socialist Thought* (Macmillan, 1959); Walter D. Connor, *Socialism, Politics and Equality* (Columbia University Press, 1979); Zsuzsa Ferge, *A Society in the Making* (M.E. Sharpe, 1979); Anthony Giddens, *Class Structure of the Advance Societies* (Hutchinson, 1973); John H. Goldthrope, "Social Stratification in Industrial Society," *Class, Status, and Power,* Reinhard Bendix and Seymour Martin Lipset, eds. (Free Press, 1966); F.D. Griffiths, *What is Socialism? A Symposium* (Richards, 1924); Alex Inkeles, "Social Stratification and Mobility in the Soviet Union," *Class, Status, and Power,* Reinhard Bendix and Seymour Martin Lipset, eds. (Free Press, 1966); V.I. Lenin, *Selected Works* (International Publishers, 1971); William Morris, *News from Nowhere* (Routledge and Kegan Paul, 1970); Karl Marx and Friedrich Engels, *Selected Works* (Progress Publishers, 1968); Mao Zedong, *Selected Readings from the Works of Mao Tsetung* (Foreign Language Press, 1971); Alec Nove, *An Economic History of the USSR* (Penguin, 1989); Domenico Mario Nuti, "Socialism on Earth," *Cambridge Journal of Economics 5*; Richard F. Starr, *Communist Regimes in Eastern Europe* (Hoover Institution Press, 1988).

JITENDRA UTTAM
JAWAHARLAL NEHRU UNIVERSITY, INDIA

# Socialist Party, U.S.

THE SOCIALIST PARTY in the United States is a viable, national organization that focuses on political, social, and economical reform. With a strong pro-labor platform, the party has worked toward equitable dispersion of monies and products, as well as for the rights of all workers—manufacturing, farming, and clerical. According to the Platform of the Socialist Party:

> The Socialist Party is the political expression of the economic interests of the workers. Its defeats have been their defeats and its victories their victories. It is a party founded on the science and laws of social development. It proposes that, since all social necessities today are socially produced, the means of their production and distribution shall be socially owned and democratically controlled.

Formed in 1901 by a merger of one faction of the Socialist Labor Party and the Social Democratic Party, the Socialist Party included as members both native-born citizens and immigrants. It drew socialists from all philosophical points of view, religions, and political stances. In part, this amalgam of political and philosophical views was to be expected, given the method of formation and the membership of the two groups. The Socialist Labor Party, founded in 1877, evolved from the American supporters of the Marxist First International and the Workingmen's Party of America. The other party of the merger, the Social Democratic Party, began its existence in 1898 and was led by Eugene Debs. Despite the disparity between the two groups, the new Socialist Party provided a solidarity and organizational unity previously unknown to the American socialist movement.

Like the majority of the new third-party groups of the late 19th century, the Socialist Party aimed toward national recognition as a political power and toward shaking up the established two-party system, which they thought was too easily swayed by big money and political influence. Also like many of the new parties, the Socialists impacted mostly local politics. Although longer lived than most, the Socialist Party suffered more from internal conflict than the inertia or lack of organization that afflicted other parties. Even with a solid pro-labor foundation, the party could not overcome its differences. Ironically, one of the major differences between party factions was whether to create a new workers' party or work from within the existing labor union, the American Federation of Labor.

Between 1901 and 1912, the Socialist Party grew to over 100,000 members, gained over 1,200 local political posts, and in 1912, Debs, the Socialist presidential candidate, received approximately 6 percent of the vote. However, given the eclectic membership within the Socialist Party of Marxists (with differing philosophies), Christian socialists, various groups of immigrants from Europe, single-taxers, and so on, internal rifts were inevitable. One of the major disagreements was between the revolutionaries (calling for drastic and immediate overthrow of the status quo) and the reformists (calling for change through education and building the new society upon the foundation of the old). Beginning in 1913, the growth and political influence of the party began to consolidate instead of grow.

Throughout its 100-plus years of history, the Socialist Party has withstood external and internal attacks. Many members battled various types of persecution during World War I, including incarceration and vigilante attacks. In 1917, the Bolshevik Revolution in Russia became the wedge between the far left and far right within the party lines, forever dividing the members into communists and socialists. Other national or world events destined to influence the party in one way or another included the Depression of the 1930s, Franklin Roosevelt's New Deal policy, and the Vietnam War. Once again, the Socialist Party protested the war, this time in Vietnam, and once again, this stance threatened the party's unity.

*Demonstrators in support of the U.S. Socialist Party march outside the Republican National Convention in New York City in 2004. With a strong pro-labor platform, the party has worked toward equitable dispersion of monies and products, as well as for the rights of all workers.*

Throughout the turbulent years of its first five decades as a political party, the Socialists continued to nominate presidential candidates; however, as of 1956, the party no longer tossed their hat into the ring with presidential nominees. Instead, they focused their considerable influence on education of the populace.

## SEE ALSO

*Volume 1 Left:* Debs, Eugene V.; Socialism; Communist Party, Soviet; Socialist Workers' Party, UK; Workingmen's Party. *Volume 2 Right:* Capitalism; *Laissez Faire*; Libertarianism.

## BIBLIOGRAPHY

Nelson Lichtenstein, "Socialist Movement," *Dictionary of American History* (Thomson Gale, 2003); Michael Kazin, "The Agony and Romance of the American Left," *American Historical Review* (December 1993); Socialist Party, http://sp-usa.org (April 2004).

GLORIA J. HICKS
UNIVERSITY OF WYOMING

# Socialist Realism

SOCIALIST REALISM WAS the aesthetic doctrine in the Soviet Union that was deemed compulsory practice for all revolutionary writers and artists during the mid-1930s. Because its proponents were mostly Soviet Stalinist intellectuals, socialist realism is associated with totalitarian art and has been condemned as stifling the artists' creative potential. Yet, the precepts of socialist realism and their concrete literary and artistic realizations did not always overlap as the practice often enriched the theory.

In his report to a committee that Communist Party leaders instructed in 1932 to form a writers' union and that was subsequently reprinted in *International Literature*, Valeri Kirpotin defined socialist realism as the artistic reflection of a society in its revolutionary development: "By socialist realism we mean the reflection in art of the external world in all its essential circumstances and with the aid of essential and typical characterization. We mean the faithful description of life in all its aspects, with the victorious principle of the forces of the socialist revolution. We set socialist realism against idealism, subjectivism, the literature of illusion in any form whatsoever, as an untrue and distorted reflection of reality."

Socialist realism was officially approved as the Communist Party's aesthetic doctrine in 1934 at the first All Union Congress of Soviet Writers, which took place from August 17 to September 1. Just before the congress, *Pravda*, the party's official newspaper, gave a definition of socialist realism that echoed and completed Kirpotin's, but which, in a move that is symptomatic of the political climate of the period, was attributed to Josef Stalin: "Socialist realism, the basic method of Soviet artistic literature and literary criticism, demands truthfulness from the artist and an historically concrete portrayal of reality in its revolutionary development. Under these conditions, truthfulness and historical concreteness of artistic portrayal ought to be combined with the task of the ideological remaking and education of laboring people in the spirit of socialism."

Since the Congress of Soviet Writers took place between the 17th Party Congress in January 1934, at which opposition to Stalin emerged, and the assassination of Sergei Kirov followed by the purges of many political opponents in December of the same year, it is only natural that pressure was put on writers to toe the party line. Both the domestic and the international situations were far from favorable for the Soviets. Millions of rural people had died in the famine that plagued the countryside for three years (1930–33) and urban living standards fell. Soviet foreign policy also resulted in evident failures. Communist revolutionaries were defeated in China, while Soviet directives to German communists only helped Adolf Hitler destroy the German Communist Party. In the face of national and international disasters, Stalin felt the need for writers to educate the masses about communism and to become engineers of the human soul.

Underlying the theory of socialist realism was the status of the artist not as a loner, but as a revolutionary militant, whose works gave voice to his social class and who advanced his party's vision of society through art and literature. This is the concept of partisanship, which built on an essay by Vladimir Lenin called "Party Organization and Party Literature" (1905). Lenin argued that, to revolutionaries, literature could not be a private matter, but "must become a component of organized, planned and integrated Social-Democratic Party work." Yet, he also recognized that writers must retain "personal initiative, individual inclination, thought and fantasy, form and content" as literature "is least of all subject to mechanical adjustment or leveling to the rule of the majority over the minority." According to socialist realism, artists should combine reflection and revolutionary praxis. The Statutes of the Writers' Union stressed the importance of combining the "veracity and historical concreteness of artistic portrayals," which derived from Karl Marx's and Friedrich Engels's commentaries on the typical, with "the tasks of the ideological remolding and education of toiling people in the spirit of Socialism."

In portraying the struggle for socialism, artists were granted freedom to exceed in what became known as "revolutionary romanticism," whose main sources were Lenin, particularly his essay "What To Do?," and the writer Maxime Gorky. Gorky stressed the author's freedom to exaggerate those elements of reality pointing to the future and Kirpotin stated that the future of the complete building of a socialist society "is actually among us, stands amid its scaffolding." Thus, writers

*A typical painting in the socialist realism style depicts Vladimir Lenin conferring with peasants.*

were performing a useful task in magnifying "the heroism, the exploits, the selfless devotion to the revolution, the fulfillment of our realistic dream" that were all basic characteristic of the revolutionary thrust. Revolutionary romanticism was legitimate as far as it showed the real forces of development.

Though later identified with Stalinist slaughter and with servile propaganda, socialist realism in its earlier formulations stressed the autonomy of the artist regarding the choice of form, style, and genre. Anatole Lunacharsky, speaking in front of the same committee to whom Kirpotin had given his definition of socialist realism, stressed that "socialist realism is a broad program which includes many different methods." He added that the aim to give "a picture full of truth" should also make clear "development, motion, and

struggle." Furthermore, given Marx's and Engels's preference for bourgeois authors such as Balzac, socialist realist writers were initially broadly defined. They included also noncommunist writers who were nevertheless sympathetic to the communist cause or who successfully conveyed the basic trends of development in a revolutionary society.

Socialist realism was expressed in paintings by Soviet artists who depicted idyllic scenes of Vladimir Lenin visiting with peasants or children offering roses to Josef Stalin, for example. Artistically, the hard realistic painting school or style was dismissed as bad art in Western circles, yet prints, posters, and original socialist realism paintings are today collected by galleries, museums, and private aficionados. While socialist realism was shaped in the Soviet Union, it also influenced many artists on the left outside Soviet borders.

**SEE ALSO**

*Volume 1 Left:* Soviet Union; Stalin and Stalinism; Communism.
*Volume 2 Right:* Soviet Union.

**BIBLIOGRAPHY**

Piotr Fast, *Ideology, Aesthetics, Literary History: Socialist Realism and Its Others* (Peter Lang, 1999); Velri Kirpotin, "Fifteen Years of Soviet Literature," *International Literature* (v.3/1, 1933): Vladimir I. Lenin, "Party Organization and Party Literature," *Soviet Socialist Realism: Origins and Theory,* C. Vaughan James, ed. (St. Martin's, 1973); Georg Lukacs, "Propaganda or Partisanship?" *Partisan Review* (April-May 1934); Anatole Lunacharsky, "Problems of the Soviet Theatre," *International Literature* (v.3/3, 1933).

LUCA PRONO, PH.D.
UNIVERSITY OF NOTTINGHAM, UNITED KINGDOM

# Socialist Workers' Party, UK

THE SOCIALIST WORKERS' Party in the United Kingdom emerged in 1977 from the International Socialists, whose weekly paper had been called *Socialist Worker* since 1968. Ideologically and intellectually, the Socialist Workers' Party is a Trotskyist party, deeming the Soviet Union to have become a "degenerated workers' state" in which socialism had been supplanted by a form of state capitalism, managed by a new privileged bureaucratic elite that effectively exploited the Soviet working class. The Socialist Workers' Party was thus emphatic that the Soviet Union was not a genuinely socialist society (even though the private ownership of the means of production had formally been abolished following the 1917 Bolshevik Revolution). Hence the party's de facto slogan: "Neither Washington nor Moscow, but International Socialism," which was clearly a riposte to those who equated the Soviet regime with socialism.

The Socialist Workers' Party was an avowedly revolutionary socialist party, insisting that the parliamentary road to socialism, as traditionally advocated by Britain's Labor Party, was ultimately a dead end. According to the Socialist Workers' Party, the social reforms achieved by Labor politicians through parliament do not liberate the working class from the alleged wage-slavery and exploitation of capitalism, but merely serve to integrate the workers further into that system, thereby beguiling them into believing that a fairer, more equal society can be pursued through general election victories and parliamentary majorities.

For the Socialist Workers' Party, the Labor Party has never been, and never will be, a vehicle for achieving socialism; on the contrary, it is deemed an obstacle to the liberation of the working class from the capitalist mode of production. Consequently, irrespective of the size of the parliamentary majorities variously obtained by the Labor Party in general elections, the Socialist Workers' Party is emphatic that Britain remains a capitalist state, in which the economic power of capital (even more so in the age of globalization) is infinitely greater than the political power of an election-winning Labor government, and in which the higher echelons or senior personnel of that state—judiciary, civil service, police, armed forces, and the ideological state apparatus—are instinctively and intrinsically hostile to anything more than the mildest of social reforms and workers' rights.

The Socialist Workers' Party also posits a distinction between potentially or actually militant rank-and-file workers and grassroots trade unionists, and a bureaucratic trade union leadership that is usually too eager to seek compromise solutions with employers. In this respect, both the Labor Party, and most trade union leaders, are deemed guilty of repeatedly selling out the British working class and of deliberately dissipating and dampening-down their radicalism.

Consequently, the Socialist Workers' Party sees its role as providing an independent and revolutionary socialist alternative to the Labor Party and class collaborationist trade union leaders. The first stage in this long-term process is tackling the "false consciousness" that allegedly keeps most of the working class wedded to the social reformism of the Labor Party and trade union bureaucrats, and concerned with achieving short-term, and sometimes short-lived, gains within capitalism. The Socialist Workers' Party therefore places great emphasis on direct and active involvement in the workplace and trade unions, particularly during industrial conflict such as strikes, where and when it can seek to mobilize and educate the more advanced sections of the working class, hoping to persuade them that their particular dispute is a manifestation of the irreconcilable conflict between capital and labor inherent within capitalism, and that their struggle should be seen as part of the wider struggle between the proletariat and the bourgeoisie.

Through such activism and agitation, the Socialist Workers' Party aims to instill a genuine socialist consciousness into sections of the working class, so that they will be primed and ready to follow revolutionary socialists in overthrowing capitalism when it eventually reaches its final, historically destined and inevitable (according to Marxist teleology) crisis and implosion.

However, the Socialist Workers' Party has not confined itself exclusively to involvement in industrial or workplace politics. It has also sought an active presence in other political struggles and social movements, through which it can similarly proselytize on behalf of revolutionary socialism and link the issue or grievance ultimately or in the last instance to capitalism. For example, the Socialist Workers' Party was instrumental in launching the Anti-Nazi League in Britain in the late 1970s, to counter the rise of the far-right National Front (since supplanted by the Britain National Party). However, although the Anti-Nazi League attracted members and supporters from across much of the mainstream political spectrum, the Socialist Workers' Party insisted that ultimately, racism could only be fully eradicated once capitalism, under which the bourgeoisie or capitalist class actively encouraged racism as a form of divide-and-rule among the indigenous working class, had been replaced by a truly socialist society, in which all men and women would be genuinely equal.

Similarly, the Socialist Workers' Party has supported feminism and women's campaigns against sexism and male violence, while remaining adamant that only the overthrow of capitalism will really secure women's liberation and emancipation from the inequalities and injustices that women continue to experience in contemporary Britain. Not surprisingly, the Socialist Workers' Party's involvement in various progressive campaigns has sometimes caused annoyance among other participants who have suspected the party of hijacking such causes for its own political and propaganda purposes.

Recently, the Socialist Workers' Party proved more willing to engage in electoral politics, most notably by participating and fielding candidates under the Socialist Alliance banner in such elections as those to the Greater London Authority. To date in the mid-2000s, however, the Socialist Workers' Party has struggled to secure appreciable support among the British working class and has also endured a fairly high turnover of members, many of whom—in spite of the party's romanticism about a revolutionary industrial working class—are resolutely white-collar professionals and middle class (students, academics, local government officers, journalists, and so on).

The Socialist Workers' Party also evinces an intrinsic, inherent tension between its espousal of the need for rank-and-file activism and "socialism from below," and the parallel necessity of a Leninist vanguard party to organize and mobilize the "more advanced" strata of the working class so that industrial struggles do not degenerate into mere short-term economism and social reformism. In this respect, the Socialist Workers' Party enshrines many of the debates over political strategy, and the appropriate relationship between class and party, which were so passionately rehearsed by revolutionary socialists such as Vladimir Lenin, Rosa Luxemburg, and Leon Trotsky a century earlier.

What is perhaps so remarkable about the Socialist Workers' Party is its relentless optimism in seeing virtually every strike or industrial dispute as potentially the catalyst for working-class radicalism and revolutionary activity. Furthermore, even when millions of ordinary industrial workers turn from the Labor Party to the Conservatives (as they did in the 1980s), the Socialist Workers' Party insists that this reflects disillusion with Labour's "betrayal" of socialism (rather than genuine serious support for right-wing policies), thereby providing further evidence of the apparent need to provide the British working class with a revolutionary socialist alternative.

**SEE ALSO**

*Volume 1 Left:* Socialism; Labor Party, UK; Lenin, Vladimir I. *Volume 2 Right:* Capitalism; United Kingdom.

**BIBLIOGRAPHY**

John Callaghan, *The Far Left in British Politics* (Blackwell, 1987); Alex Callinicos, *The Revolutionary Road to Socialism* (Bookmarks, 1998); Peter Mair, "The Marxist Left," *Multi-Party Britain*, H. M. Drucker, ed. (Macmillan, 1979).

PETER DOREY
CARDIFF UNIVERSITY, UNITED KINGDOM

# Solidarity

ON JULY 1, 1980, the communist regime in Poland announced price increases. With a centrally planned economy, no market control, and fictitious prices of products and wages, the government and the Polish United Workers' Party that ruled Poland had no other means to try and overcome the disastrous economic crisis. One week later, numerous factories in various parts of Poland went on strike. Initially, the western provinces and then later all of Poland stopped working. Strikes reached the biggest Polish seaport and shipbuilding industry towns: Gdansk and Gdynia. It was the Lenin Shipyard in Gdansk where a mass strike started at the beginning of August.

The local strike committee, led by an electrician, Lech Walesa, was soon transformed into an Interfactory Strike Committee, which took up the struggle against the communist authorities not only for the workers of the shipyard, but on behalf of all people employed in Poland. The committee, which was referred to as Solidarity (Solidarnosc), put forth a list of 21 demands to be met by the Communist Party and government. These included: the right to form independent unions, right to strike, freedom of speech and press, freeing of political prisoners, and numerous social and economic demands. On August 31, an agreement was signed between the committee represented by Walesa and Deputy Prime Minister Mieczyslaw Jagielski. As soon as the agreement was signed, workers at various factories and enterprises in Poland started to organize themselves into union groups. It should be added, that in the communist system, labor unions existed, but were not independent of the employer (the state) and were an extension of the Communist Party linked with the regime authorities.

On September 17, the emerging unions decided to band together and erect one central, general union called Solidarity. By this time (two weeks after the agreement was signed), the union rolls all over Poland numbered close to four million members and the decision to form one powerful union rather than hundreds of small, weak ones was a shock to the communist authorities. On November 10, following debates with the authorities and mutual threats, Solidarity was formally registered as a union.

The next 13 months saw a strange relationship between the ruling Communist Party and the union—which grew to number about 10 million members (about 70 percent of all professionally active people in Poland). Solidarity was gaining its demands through strikes or threat of strike. This was true both on a local and national scale. Solidarity's demands were, in most cases, limited to social conditions in factories, wages, and workers' rights. Theoretically, there was no unemployment in the communist system and all who wanted to work were employed; well over 95 percent of people were employed in state enterprises. The private sector was marginal. Thus, a communist regime, based on Marxist-Leninist theory and claiming it was a people's system of government, was challenged by a labor union demanding workers' rights be respected and work conditions be improved.

On December 13, 1981, the government, headed by Prime Minister General Wojciech Jaruzelski (who also held the posts of the first secretary of the Communist Party and minister of defense) introduced martial law and declared Solidarity illegal. Almost 10,000 Solidarity members were detained. Walesa, now president of Solidarity, was arrested as well. An 18-month-long struggle between the communist authorities (who had to report to Moscow, Soviet Union) and the independent labor union appeared to come to an end.

In April 1982, Solidarity activists who managed to avoid arrest formed a Solidarity Temporary Coordinating Committee to coordinate underground activity in Poland; in effect, the union went "underground." Four years later in 1986, Walesa called for an open, albeit illegal Solidarity Committee. The committee was not recognized by state authorities, and its members were closely observed by the secret police, but Walesa was not touched. After all, in 1983 he received the Nobel Peace Prize for his work with Solidarity.

## FUTURE OF POLAND

By the end of 1988, the communist authorities, together with the Catholic Church and underground Solidarity decided to start negotiations about the future of Poland. From February to April 1989, a Round Table brought together communists, opposition leaders, Solidarity members, and representatives of the Polish Catholic Church—which yielded considerable influence

since its leader was now Pope. In effect, the result of the talks allowed Solidarity to register again as a labor union. In the semi-democratic elections of June 1989, Solidarity candidates won all seats but one in the upper house.

With the dissolution of the Soviet Union and the end of the Soviet Communist Party, the Polish United Workers' Party (Communist Party) dissolved in 1990. It had ruled Poland since 1948. Walesa decided to step down as Solidarity leader and ran for the presidency. In December, Walesa became first Polish president elected in general election. Solidarity leadership fell to Marian Krzaklewski.

At this point, Solidarity was still a union, but also a political party taking an active part in politics. In the 1991 parliamentary elections, it gained 23 seats in the lower chamber. The following year, together with five other parties, Solidarity formed a coalition, center-leftist government. Ten months later, Solidarity overthrew the government it helped form. A no-confidence vote (a parliamentary process to recall government leadership) was proposed over social and employment matters that Solidarity found unacceptable. In this crisis, new elections took place in September 1993 bringing former communists to power. But support for Solidarity faltered: it did not pass the 5 percent threshold and did not enter the parliament.

In 1997, Solidarity's leader, Krzaklewski, led a turnaround for the party and managed to organize the Solidarity Electoral Coalition, which won the elections and formed a government. Thus, union activists reversed roles and became ministers, often facing their former colleagues protesting in the streets against the decisions taken in the government. The government, in spite of obstacles (also caused by Solidarity itself, critics point out) survived the whole term, but the electoral coalition did not. Solidarity leader Krzaklewski ran in the presidential elections in 2000, but lost. Neither he nor Solidarity itself could have changed the outcome of the 2001 elections. They received a vote of no-confidence from the electorate, didn't pass the necessary threshold, and did not enter the parliament. By the mid-2000s, Solidarity was one of two largest Polish labor unions, fighting for workers' rights and being consulted on all major changes concerning labor laws and employee codes by the government.

## SEE ALSO

*Volume 1 Left:* Unions; Soviet Union; Communism; Stalin and Stalinism.
*Volume 2 Right:* Soviet Union.

## BIBLIOGRAPHY

M.B.Biskupski, *The History of Poland* (Greenwood Press, 2000); Timothy Garton Ash, *The Polish Revolution: Solidarity, 1980–82* (Yale University Press, 2002); "Solidarity," www.solidarnosc.org.pl (April 2004); Arista Maria Cirtautas, *Polish Solidarity Movement: Revolution, Democracy, and Natural Rights* (Routledge, 1997).

JAKUB BASISTA, PH.D.
JAGIELLONIAN UNIVERSITY, POLAND

# South Africa

THE REPUBLIC OF SOUTH AFRICA is a constitutional democracy whose basic laws are enshrined in the Constitution of 1996. The constitution transformed an apartheid state based on racial segregation to an egalitarian democracy. Reflective of the will of the black African majority, South African government has a strong central bureaucracy with a powerful presidency. The president is both the head of state and government

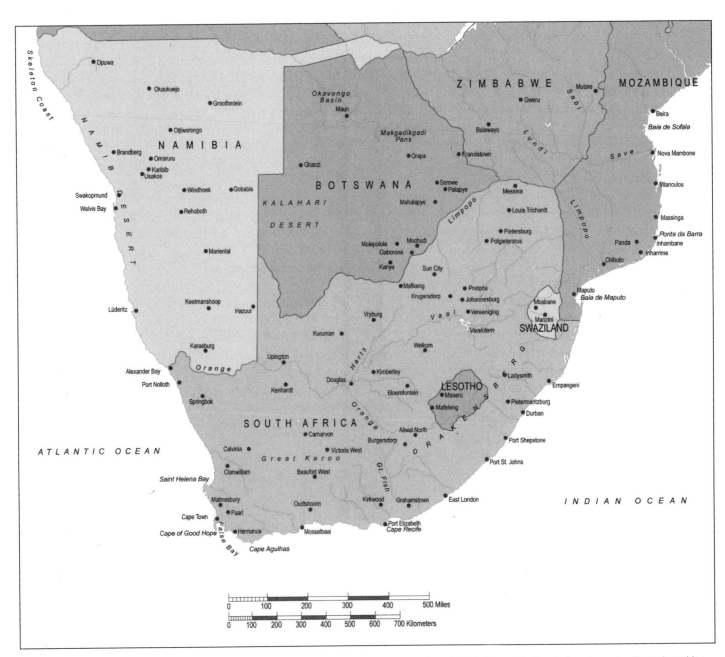

*South Africa employed a rightist apartheid or segregationist form of government and society that was challenged and eventually replaced by the leftist African National Congress, which brought an end to the apartheid regime.*

leader. Modern South Africa consists of an ethnically diverse population of 43,586,097 (2004). The constitution recognizes 11 official languages and specifies nine provinces with defined authority. The South African parliament is bicameral. Citizens vote directly for 400 members of the National Assembly, while their provincial legislators select representatives to serve in the 90-seat National Council of the Provinces.

The background to politics and government in South Africa is a tribal history of conflict, accommodation, and resolution. Much of the destiny of modern South Africa was shaped by the two principal white "tribes," the Afrikaners of Dutch origin and the British. The Dutch settled South Africa in 1652, and the British arrived in 1806. Conflict throughout the 19th century involving the Afrikaner, British, and indigenous populations culminated in the South African (Boer) War of 1899–1902. Following the war, the British and Afrikaner leaderships achieved a political settlement in the Act of Union (1910), the first formal constitution of South Africa. Establishing a racially exclusivist framework that was to continue until the end of apartheid, only whites were granted citizenship. An assertively nationalist Afrikaner leadership established the regime of apartheid in the late 1940s and early 1950s, introducing legislation to limit social, political, and economic advantage to the white minority and to segregate the races. The African majority engaged in sustained acts of protest, boycott, disobedience, and sabotage in order to press for change. In the end, the apartheid regime crumbled. A political deal between African National Congress (ANC) leader Nelson Mandela and South African President F. W. de Klerk marked the demise of apartheid in 1989.

The South African Constitution has certain federal characteristics, but with a strongly centralized presidency. The president and the assemblies are elected for five-year terms, with fixed election dates. However, the president, who is a sitting member of the National Assembly, can dissolve the National Assembly at any time after three years if a majority of members demand it. The president selects most members of the cabinet from the National Assembly, to which it is collectively and individually responsible. A simple majority vote of no-confidence in the cabinet causes the entire cabinet, including the president, to resign.

Regional government in South Africa is very important. Provincial governments spend most of the national budget and employ most of the public servants. Most provincial expenditure is on health, education, and social security and provincial politicians enjoy wide discretion. The leading political party in contemporary South Africa is the ANC. Banned in 1960, it reassembled in exile, where it continued to operate in the apartheid decades. The post-apartheid ANC regards itself as an inclusive popular front, representing a diverse coalition of voices in the new South Africa. The party was the runaway victor in the national election of April 2004, winning 70 percent of the vote in a national turnout of 77 percent. President Thabo Mbeki was elected for a second term.

The main opposition party is the centrist and post-apartheid Democratic Alliance, which picked up about 12 percent of the vote in 2004. It represents an increasingly liberal white electorate and hopes to generalize itself into the natural party of opposition. It has supplanted the New National Party (NNP), a reinvention of the dominant apartheid-era party. In the 2004 elections, NNP received less than 2 percent of the vote and seemed destined to disappear. The principal black alternative to the ANC is the Inkatha Freedom Party (IFP) that has its origins in the Zulu politics of KwaZulu Natal. While the IFP carries with it the taint of having accommodated itself to the apartheid regime and of having collaborated in the oppression of the ANC and its allies, the party has moved on to become a more moderate voice of black South Africa. In the 2004 election, it received less than 7 percent of the vote and was unable to defeat the ANC in its home territory.

**SEE ALSO**

*Volume 1 Left:* African National Congress; Africa.
*Volume 2 Right:* Apartheid; South Africa.

**BIBLIOGRAPHY**

Anthony Butler, *Contemporary South Africa* (Palgrave Macmillan, 2004); Tom Lodge, *Politics in South Africa: From Mandela to Mbeki* (Indiana University Press, 2003); Nigel Worden, *The Making of Modern South Africa: Conquest, Segregation and Apartheid* (Oxford: Blackwell, 1994).

PAUL NESBITT-LARKING, PH.D.
HURON UNIVERSITY COLLEGE, CANADA

# South America

THE LEFT IN SOUTH AMERICA can be described in two ways. First, it is an ideal that has been pursued by many political groups in the history of Latin America, according to several programs: anti-colonialism, independence, revolution and democracy. Second it is a form of reaction to the right, which has frustrated the aspirations of the left and posed continuous challenges by turning to colonialism, caudillismo, authoritarianism, militarism, and other forms of political power. Despite these two common elements, the left in South America cannot be understood as a block, since there are particularities to be accounted for. Therefore, we will use Latin America in reference to the Iberian American context in general, but also specify Central America in some cases, while concentrating on South American countries—since these regions have mutually influenced one another.

The countries in South America were impacted differently from Spanish and Portuguese colonialism. They suffered the common negative effects of economic disputes, but developed their democratic and political institutions at differing paces. Moreover, their responses to these situations varied, including peaceful resistance movements, opposition to the right by institutions such as the university or the church, development of new partisan platforms or also guerrillas with more or less violent strategies. Therefore, it is necessary to avoid generalizing the left, without recognizing the particular contexts and times in which it has emerged.

## REACTIONS AGAINST COLONIAL POWER

The impact of European colonization in South America was felt from 1492 until the beginning of the 19th century. While a great part of the continent was colonized by the Spanish crown, the Portuguese had their share in the colonization of Brazil. The origins of the South American right can be found in the agrarian structures of feudalism, slavery, and mercantilism, as well as the missionary work of the church and the establishment of a juridical elite. The origins of the left can be seen already in the 16th century, in several movements that opposed colonialism and its structures of power.

In Brazil, the basic institution in colonial times was the Portuguese monarchy, which never developed a strong army, but simply ruled by means of ideological tools. On the contrary, the countries of Spanish colonization implemented printing and universities: the university of Mexico was founded already in 1535 and its counterpart in Lima in 1584. The Portuguese, in turn, did not allow the growth of a middle class or an intelligentsia and centralized education in Portugal at the University of Coimbra, which trained bureaucrats to serve the Portuguese colonies in America, Africa, and Asia. Having eliminated the possibility of a middle class, colonial society was formed by a series of other social and political actors: landlords, priests, lawyers, small landowners, poor workers, slaves, and natives. The Spanish Crown had a larger military structure, responsible for controlling the colonies. Despite the plurality and complexity of the South American societies, it is possible to divide them according to the following structure: the landlords and the masses working for them; the controlling bureaucracy and the military power of the crown; normatively, the Church and the juridical institutions.

One of the first elements of opposition to colonialism was philosophical, as two representatives of Humanism were the first to criticize the colonizers. The Scot George Buchanan opposed the Spaniards and the Portuguese, writing two books in the 16th century in order to criticize the form by which Europeans were exploiting the people and natural resources of the continent. Bartolomé de Las Casas, who became famous after his series of debates with the philosopher Juan de Sepúlveda, defended of the rights of the Indians, arguing in favor of their humanity. These two initiatives, one related to the Portuguese empire and the other to Spain, mark a first reaction that would be later revived by independent movements and rebellions in South America.

Later on, similar initiatives were inspired by the Baroque culture and by the philosophy of the Enlightenment, especially in the 17th and 18th centuries. In the Spanish colonies, Carlos Sigüenza y Góngora and Francisco Xavier Clavijero were considered the exponents of emancipatory thinking before 1700, while in Brazil, the sermons of Padre Vieira between 1635 and 1683 were considered the first examples of original thinking about freedom and autonomy in Brazil. Sor Juana de la Cruz had a similar impact in Mexico with her poetry, while the Jesuit teachings had a strong cultural influence in the Americas at large.

## REVOLUTIONS FOR INDEPENDENCE

With the rise of an enlightened and anti-clerical absolutism in Spain and Portugal, around 2,200 Jesuits were expelled from Brazil in 1759 and from Spain and the Spanish colonies in America in 1767. Independently of these facts, however, European philosophers such as Jean-Jacques Rousseau and Thomas Reid were turning to American "Indians" in order to define the *bon sauvage* of the utopian missions of Jesuits among the Guarani natives in Argentina, Brazil, and Paraguay. It was under the impact of the Enlightenment that many groups would attempt to force a political Independence from Portugal or Spain.

The fundamental historical reference for the emancipatory movement in South America is Simón Bolívar, a *criollo* of European, Indian, and African origin known as El Liberador. As a soldier—inspired by Napoleon— statesman, intellectual, and political philosopher, he not only developed several ideas and texts defending the independence of South America, but also led a series of revolutions in Bolivia, Colombia, Ecuador, Peru, and Venezuela between 1810 and 1830. Under the leadership of San Martín, Argentina became an independent nation in 1810, while José Gervasio Artigas led the independence of Uruguay. Peru had its declaration of independence in 1824, after the famous Battle of Ayacucho. In what became known as the Second War of Independence from Spain in 1895, José Martí organized the independence of Cuba.

But independence was not enough to guarantee a liberation from the structures of power that were still in the hands of the aristocracy and landowners. Therefore, the new stage of disputes and tension between the left and the Right was party politics, with the constitution of a bi-partisan system in most countries, according to the scheme Conservative-Liberal.

Among the theoretical efforts of grounding socialism as an alternative in South America, one can find Esteban Echevarría and his book on socialism, published in Argentina in 1846, and the turn to Kant and Marx by Tobias Barreto in Brazil. Between the two extremes of authoritarian conservatism and an incipient socialism, the final choice was for positivism, a combination of liberal ideas with scientific rigorism, middle-class bureaucratic professionalism and militaristic strategies. From Mexico to Argentina, this would then become the hegemonic political position at the end of the 19th century.

Notwithstanding the results of these actions, it is important to mention that several resistance groups continued to exert political pressures and pursue their emancipation. In their view, the positivistic reforms only substituted the old colonial regime with new aristocracies and bureaucracies, without integrating the masses (peasants, workers, women, former slaves) into the political scenario. Accordingly, the 1880s marked the struggle for several rights, such as the abolition of slavery, constitutional autonomy, worker's rights, and the rights of women. It was amidst these processes that most South American countries entered the 20th century.

## THE 1920S AND MARXISM

The 20th century witnessed, from a more theoretical perspective, a greater influence of Marxism as a political philosophy. While Esteban Echevarría published his book on dogma, *Socialista*, in 1846, Juan B. Justo translated Karl Marx's *Das Kapital* in 1895, and Ricardo Flores Magón founded the magazine *Regeneración* in 1906. The most important Marxist in Latin America was José Carlos Mariátegui, who integrated Marx's theories and the Latin American reality (especially that of his home country, Peru) as he reflected on the "Indian Problem" in Latin America. As Enrique Dussel states, "When, in 1928, his publishing company, Amauta, published *Siete Ensayos sobre la realidad peruvia*, he was greeted as the most original and least dogmatic Latin American Marxist in the first part of the 20th century." Similarly, Aníbal Ponce published his *Educación y Lucha de Clases* in 1937, while Caio Prado Jr. became one of the main Marxist social thinkers in Brazil.

From a practical point of view, it is necessary to consider a series of crises and revolts between 1907 and 1913, when the social, economic and political situation that motivated the action of these groups was aggravated even more shortly later by World War I and the echoes of the Russian Revolution. But also within the very structure of the military there were reactions against traditional conservatism, such as the movement led in Brazil by Captain Luiz Carlos Prestes and promoted by a group of lieutenants between 1924 and 1929. Another reaction came from several immigrant groups from Germany, Italy, Poland, and Spain, which began to integrate into the politics of South American countries. Based on the impact of these groups, the workers' movement was also articulated in several countries. In Argentina, for instance, anarchists articulated their forces with several workers' groups to found the Workers Federation (FORA).

From a more institutional political view, attention can be given to political parties. The Cuban Revolutionary Party was founded by Martí in 1895, the Socialist Party was founded in 1896 in Argentina, the Liberal Fraternal Union in Mexico in 1906, the Socialist Workers' Party of Chile in 1912, and the Socialist Party of Chile in 1922. The Communist Party in Cuba was founded in 1925, the same year that the Communist Party was founded in El Salvador. During the first part of the 20th century, many of these groups and parties were able to gain power, not only through movements, coups, and so-called revolutions, but also through elections whose results favored the left. After the Mexican

Revolution led by Emiliano Zapata and Pancho Villa in 1910, echoes could be heard in other countries. In Argentina, the election of Hipólito Yrigoyen in 1916 was complemented by several reforms. Similar reforms were being made in Chile by President Arturo Alessandri and in Uruguay by President Battle y Ordonéz. In subsequent years, peasants and the worker classes were able to promote insurrections in El Salvador in December 1931—which resulted in the murders of 30,000 men, women, and children—as well as in Colombia, Peru, and Chile, while Augusto César Sandino led the revolution in Nicaragua.

Most of these initiatives were frustrated, however, by the effects of the Great Depression of 1929, by civil wars and conflicts within certain countries, and by military coups that tried to impose an authoritarian and unified rule after 1930. In Brazil, Getulio Vargas inaugurated the dictatorship of the Estado Novo. In Argentina, Uriburu took the office from Yrigoyen and established a military government. In Nicaragua, Sandino was assassinated in 1934. In all these cases, the military leaders were discontent with the way the civilian governments were dealing with social issues and were interested in speeding up the industrialization process in their countries. Thus, they adopted the ideology of nationalism to put the several pieces of their nations together. Such initiatives followed the fascism that was in vogue in Europe at the time of World War II.

## REVOLUTIONARY GUERRILLAS IN THE 1960s

The Cuban Revolution in 1959, the series of revolutionary movements in Central America, and the reaction of the United States to these events form the necessary point of departure for a series of initiatives by the left in South America during the 1960s.

No other movement of the Latin American left was as successful as the revolution initiated in Cuba by Fidel Castro and Ernesto "Che" Guevara. They ousted the dictatorship of Fulgencio Batista, challenged the support that the Cuban government was receiving from the United States, and gained the sympathy of several intellectual and political groups around the world.

The triumph of the Cuban Revolution had a great impact in Latin America, as many other movements tried to perform similar revolutions in their respective countries during the 1960s. At that time there was also a tension between two world powers that were trying to measure their influence on the continent: the United States and the Soviet Union. The history of the left during this period was expressed through the continental political alignment with either the Soviet Union or the United States, through rebellions against military governments in Central America, and through the impact of these initiatives in South American countries that received the support of the United States to combat the left. Clara Nieto documented all these facts in her book *Masters of War: Latin America and U.S. Aggression: From the Cuban Revolution through the Clinton Years.*

Central American countries continued to be inspired by the Cuban Revolution, which brought about a series of movements in South America. Still in 1959, there was an attempt at a revolution in Panama; while rebels also attempted to attack General Leonidas Trujillo in Santo Domingo and Anastasio Somoza in Nicaragua in 1960. Honduras had experienced massive strikes against American corporations working in the country in 1954 and 1957, but after the impact of the Cuban Revolution, the National Federation of Honduran Peasants was created and supported the social reforms promoted by the elected President Villeda Morales. Villeda was considered a communist by his opponents and suffered a coup in 1963, the last year of his mandate. El Salvador had similar experiences.

In 1961, Nicaragua tried to revive Sandino's legacy by organizing the National Sandinista Front of Liberation (FSLN) under the leadership of Carlos Amador, Tomás Borge, and Daniel Ortega. The FSLN endured decades of fights against the dictatorship of the Somoza family. Also in Guatemala there were similar events, which provoked the formation of several guerrilla groups, including the Revolutionary Movement of November 13 (MR-13) of Yon Sosa and the famous Revolutionary Armed Forces (FAR) of Luis Tucios Lima.

The majority of South American countries at the time were military dictatorships, while Argentina, Colombia, Peru, and Venezuela had civilian governments. While only Argentina and Mexico recognized the Cuban Revolution, the first South American country in which there was an attempt to apply the Cuban experience was Venezuela.

Fidel Castro visited Venezuela one year after the Cuban Revolution and expressed his sympathies for the government of Rear Admiral Larrazábal in Caracas. Soon thereafter, Brazilian President Jânio Quadros expressed his sympathies to Fidel Castro as well, visiting the Cuban leader in 1961, shortly before taking office in Brazil, thus provoking the United States. Quadros governed Brazil for only 11 months, and João Goulart, his vice president, was ousted by a military coup in 1964.

The climax of these initiatives occurred in Chile, with the election of the socialist candidate Salvador Allende in 1970. The reaction against the socialist reforms proposed by Allende also represented the climax of militarism and external intervention, as he was deposed on September 11, 1973, in an action led by General Augusto Pinochet. In this coup d'état many civilians were assassinated, while many others fled the country. It was in reaction to these events that guerrilla movements radicalized their action in South America, such as the Montoneros in Argentina, the Tupamaros in Uruguay, and the MR-8 in Brazil. However, no other group endured as long a time of conflict and had such a negative impact on civil society as the Sendero Luminoso in Peru and the FARCs in Colombia.

As a result of these actions, the United States exerted a growing influence in several countries. If this influence on internal affairs was exerted earlier on the basis of the Monroe Doctrine during the 19th century, it was later based on a reform plan that President Kennedy had proposed for Latin America in 1961, the Alliance for Progress, as he indicated that changes in the continent should not rely on violence as a condition for change. Nevertheless, at the end of the 1970s, the doctrine orienting the relationship between the United States and the South American countries was that of supporting militarism, the doctrine of national security and state terrorism. It is against this background that during the 1970s and well into the 1980s, the action of leftist groups, such as parties, NGOs, resistance movements, and even movements within other institutions, such as the church and the university system in several countries, was directed towards the civil opposition to militarism.

## THE ROLE OF LIBERATION THEOLOGY

Liberation theology and its principle of an Option for the Poor was one of the most important elements of a civil rights movement in the whole of Latin America. Between 1962 and 1965, the Catholic Church was experiencing a deep process of reform as a result of the Vatican Council. During those years, Pope John XXIII led the church to address social, cultural, political, and economic issues and this motivated the action of several priests who were working in Latin America. In 1968, the Latin American Episcopal Council held in Medellin, Colombia, marked the official position of the Catholic Church on issues of poverty and democracy in the continent. In the same way, Protestant churches were following the doctrine of the social

gospel, which defended the involvement of the church in social causes. Leaders of Jewish ecumenical groups adopted similar principles defending human rights. By the end of the 1960s, a series of events would mark what became known as the theology of liberation.

From a more theoretical point of view, there were two main books that served as orientation to liberation theology: the Catholic theologian Gustavo Gutiérrez published his *Theology of Liberation* in 1969, while the Presbyterian pastor Rubem Alves published *Theology of Human Hope* in the same year. Later, the writings of theologians such as Hugo Assmann, Jon Sobrino, Leonardo Boff, Julio de Santa Ana, Richard Shaull, and Elza Támez, among others, would complement the literature in this field and advance new reflections on how to interpret the Bible in light of the social struggles in Latin America and become involved in social action according to the gospel. Thus, liberation theology became one of the most important sources of leftist political reflection during the 1970s, at the same time it promoted the defense of human rights in several countries. In 1981, however, the book *Church, Charisma and Power*, by Leonard Boff, was censored by the Vatican, marking a new period of opposition to the left within the Catholic Church.

From a more practical point of view, many priests and pastors were deeply engaged in social actions, becoming involved with the revolutionary movement as well. In Colombia, priest Camilo Torres joined the revolutionary efforts and was later assassinated. In Brazil, an American Methodist missionary was assassinated, as well as the Presbyterian leader Paulo Stuart Wright. In El Salvador, Monsignor Romero denounced the abuses of military dictatorship and was assassinated, as well as a group of priests of the University of El Salvador. Also in Guatemala, priests were murdered due to their involvement with the revolutionary struggle. At the same time, Bishop Helder Câmara, Cardinal Paulo Arns, and Rabbi Henri Sobel criticized the military repression and publicly reported the crimes against human rights in Brazil, while Fernando Cardenal and Ernesto Cardenal led the resistance in Nicaragua and Franz Hinkelammert, Hugo Assmann, and Elza Támez in Costa Rica developed studies at the Ecumenical Department of Research.

The historical, theoretical, and practical dimensions of liberation theology had a profound impact on Latin America and were complemented at least by two fronts: the action of the Base Church Communities (CEBs) that spread throughout the poor urban and rural areas, and the expansion of liberationist thinking and practice to areas such as Paulo Freire's pedagogy of the oppressed, Enrique Dussel's liberation philosophy, and Augusto Boal's theater of the oppressed.

## THE ROLE OF THE LEFT IN DEMOCRACIES

At the beginning of the 1990s, the left had a relative success in ousting military dictatorships in South America. This was a result not only of its own efforts, but also of the times, which included *perestroika*, the fall of the Soviet Union, the acceleration of the globalization process, and the implementation of neoliberalism in several economies. One element for the success of the left in this process was the change in its discourse, as it gave up more radical measures and strategies in order to concentrate on issues related to human rights and democracy. In this process, the traditional ideals of the left were represented by NGOs and established parties that supported social democratic measures.

In Brazil, this social democratic agenda was defended by Fernando Henrique Cardoso, who was elected by the Social-Democrat Party of Brazil (PSDB) in 1994. As president, Cardoso did not follow the principles that he had once defended in his version of the dependência theory, but espoused a series of reforms that opened the country to neoliberal economics. He was reelected in 1998 and was substituted in 2002 by Luis Inácio "Lula" da Silva, from the Workers' Party (PT). Lula began his tenure by bringing together a leftist discourse and neo-liberal actions. In a similar way, Hugo Chavez came to power in Venezuela defending a type of populism and anti-Americanism that was typical of the left in previous years. However, his radical discourse brought him internal problems—with a tension between two groups within Venezuela, who either defended or opposed him—and external tensions, especially in relation to the United States.

Finally, another example of a turn to a populist left in Latin America was the election of Nestor Kirchner in Argentina. Kirchner inherited a country in a profound crisis and the pressure of several groups identified with the left, such as the *piqueteros*. Under these circumstances, he sided with these groups and maintained a strong discourse against the economic interests of the United States and of institutions such as the World Bank (WB) and the International Monetary Fund (IMF).

Finally, the left in South America also had a renewed expression in the actions of several NGOs. If at first the most important groups were related to human rights and environmentalist groups that were active during the times of the military dictatorship in several countries, later it was the World Social Forum that became the central arena for the left. Among the most important groups of civil society were the Madres de la Plaza de Mayo in Argentina and later the Landless Movement in Brazil, which kept some resemblance to the initiatives of the Zapatista Movement in Chiapas, Mexico. Moreover, women's groups, workers' unions, universities, and groups of environmental activists remained important arenas for the debates around the legacy of Marxism and other theories that had oriented the left in South America. The World Social Forum was organized a number of times in the city of Porto Alegre, in southern Brazil, which became the South American center for anti-globalization groups, thus complementing the action of critical movements that had organized anti-globalization manifestations in Seattle, Washington; Genoa, Italy; and other cities around the world.

**SEE ALSO**

*Volume 1 Left:* Brazil; Argentina; Guevara, Che; Chile.
*Volume 2 Right:* Brazil; Argentina; Chile; Fascism; Peronism.

**BIBLIOGRAPHY**

Amnesty International, *The 1992 Report on Human Rights around the World* (Hunter House, 1992); Barry Car and Steve Ellner, *The Latin American Left: From the Fall of Allende to Perestroika* (Westview Press, 1993); Jorge Castañeda, *Utopia Unarmed: The Latin American Left after the Cold War* (Alfred Knopf, 1993); Noam Chomsky, *Turning the Tide: U.S. Intervention in Central America and the Struggle for Peace* (South End Press, 1985); André Gunder Frank, *Latin America: Underdevelopment or Revolution* (MR, 1969); Irving Horowitz, *Cuban Communism* (Transaction Books, 1982); Eduardo Mendieta, ed., *Latin American Philosophy: Currents, Issues, Debates* (Indiana University Press, 2003); Clara Nieto, *Masters of War: Latin America and U.S. Aggression: From the Cuban Revolution through the Clinton Years* (Seven Stories, 2003).

AMOS NASCIMENTO
METHODIST UNIVERSITY OF PIRACICABA, BRAZIL

# Southern Tenant Farmers' Union

ON JULY 11, 1934, in the cotton country near Tyronza, Arkansas, socialists H.L. Mitchell, Clay East, and an integrated group (11 white, 7 black) formed the Southern

Tenant Farmers' Union (STFU) as a protest against the practices of the planter class and its associated political arm. The STFU sought to raise farm income through public protests and strikes. The initial focus was on getting the Agricultural Adjustment Administration (AAA) to keep its commitment to all farmers, not just farm owners.

Agricultural prices in the 1920s and early 1930s were low due in part to overproduction. One of the early New Deal programs, the Agricultural Adjustment Administration (AAA) paid some farmers to plow under crops and kill surplus animals. Fewer crops meant fewer acres in use. Acreage reduction led owners to evict tenants, and because the parity payments went to the property owners, some of the tenants received nothing.

Sharecroppers thought that they were going to get some AAA benefits. When 40 of them got termination notices instead of AAA payments in the fall of 1934, they sued the Fairview Plantation for violation of the AAA contract requiring owners to maintain the same number of tenants during reduction. The STFU sent a delegation to see Henry Wallace, secretary of agriculture. Wallace sent an investigator, whose unreleased report indicated that the AAA programs were resulting in evictions by the thousands.

Radicals in the AAA wanted to support the tenants against Fairview. Wallace purged them in early 1935. Then the court dismissed the suit because the contract in question was between the owner and the AAA, so the croppers had no standing. The union threatened owner power and generated conflict as owners and unionists confronted each other. Local law enforcement officials began arresting STFU leaders for enticing laborers, barratry, and other obscure charges. Mostly it was harassment. Then nightriders began shooting at homes, breaking up meetings, beating and killing and chasing members out of the state.

The STFU went on strike in the cotton fields in August 1935, when thousands of croppers struck. Owners fought back, but the onset of picking season forced them to agree to a wage increase. The union ended the strike, and the workers worked for 75 cents more in wages. The union had national recognition. By 1936, the STFU had 25,000 to 35,000 members in six states. The STFU allowed segregated locals, but many locals were integrated, as were its organizers. Black membership was between one-half and two-thirds of the total STFU membership.

Because the STFU publicized the difficulties that the AAA and the tenancy system created for sharecrop-

pers, it gained favorable publicity and moral and financial assistance from New Dealers, radicals, reformers, and liberal clergy. The stimulus for direct official action was, though, the shift in anti-STFU violence and harassment to its socially prominent white supporters. The STFU and its allies, including Eleanor Roosevelt, felt that the New Deal aimed its rhetoric at the tenants but put its resources behind the planters. In the aftermath of that shift, state and federal commissions explored the status of tenants.

The administration had been aware of unrest and problems in agriculture since 1935, when Rex Tugwell began the Resettlement Administration (RA), but the RA lacked much in the way of short-term relief, and the crisis was immediate. Still, there was only partial relief in the Farm Security Administration (FSA) programs under the Bankhead-Jones Farm Tenancy Act of 1937. The FSA included programs for loans to poor farmers for purchase of land. Sharecroppers were too poor, so they didn't benefit all that much from the FSA.

Mitchell and East were socialists, but the idea of land for the landless and farmers' cooperatives was consistent with the goals of New Deal programs such as the RA and FSA. After 1937, the STFU crumbled as socialists and communists disagreed and blacks became dissatisfied with the white leadership after the STFU affiliated with a cannery workers' union. A lot of the confusion was the intended result of the Communist Party of the USA (CPUSA) which had infiltrated STFU. The party worked actively to break up the union by way of the CPUSA-headed cannery workers affiliate of the CIO, or Congress of Industrial Organizations. The union survived until 1960 in various guises, but its constituency, the sharecroppers of the South, disappeared with postwar mechanization.

## SEE ALSO

*Volume 1 Left:* Unions; New Deal; Roosevelt, Franklin D.; Roosevelt, Eleanor; Sharecroppers' Union.
*Volume 2 Right:* Capitalism; United States.

## BIBLIOGRAPHY

M. Langley Biegert, "Legacy of Resistance: Uncovering the History of Collective Action by Black Agricultural Workers in Central East Arkansas from the 1860s to the 1930s," *Journal of Social History* (Fall 1998); Eleanor Roosevelt and Human Rights Project, "Southern Tenant Farmers' Union," www.gwu.edu (February 2004); Donald Grubbs, *Cry from the Cotton* (University of North Carolina Press, 1971); H.L. Mitchell, "The Disinherited: A Brief History of the Agricultural Workers Union (1934–59)," www.nathanielturner.com

(February 2004); Steve Schoenherr, "The Farm Security Administration," http://history.sandiego.edu (2003).

JOHN BARNHILL, PH.D.
INDEPENDENT SCHOLAR

# Soviet Union

THE SOVIET UNION (1922–1991), also called Union of Soviet Socialist Republics (USSR), was established with the 1917 October Revolution and with the ensuing civil war between the Bolsheviks (Russian communists) and the counterrevolutionary forces gathered in the White Army. The end of the civil war in 1922 witnessed the birth of the world's first communist state, a truly momentous achievement for the left.

Throughout the 1930s, the Soviet Union was considered a source of inspiration and leadership for communist and socialist parties throughout the world. Yet, the utopia of a classless society and the other lofty principles that the Soviet experiment set out to achieve were never really realized. In their place, Soviet leaders constructed a progressively bureaucratized and totalitarian regime, which could only be kept together through the use of violence and coercion, both physical and ideological. The long list of crimes, internal plots, struggles for power, and failed attempts to create a more open and democratic society that constellate Soviet history have led many to conclude on the incompatibility of communism and democracy. The collapse of the Soviet Union equally generated a sense of disorientation in leftist militants who saw the socialist alternative to market economy dissolve as a mere illusion.

At the beginning of the 20th century, Russia was still an industrially underdeveloped country governed by the autocratic regime of the tzars. This totalitarian regime was administered without any constitutional control or parliamentary body by a bureaucratic caste and kept in line by a powerful army and an ever-present security police. Radical opposition to the tzarist system gathered in the Socialist Revolutionary Party, of anarchist tendencies, and in the Russian Social Democratic Workers' Party, inspired more directly by the theories of Karl Marx and Friedrich Engels. The Social Democrats subsequently split into two parts: the Bolsheviks, led by Vladimir Lenin, who advocated immediate revolution, and the Mensheviks, who considered a revolution impossible in a largely peasant and preindustrial country. Though the constitutional norms passed after the massive demonstrations and strike of 1905 initially appeased popular discontent, World War I revived the hostility against the monarchy and the ruling dynasty, which seemed more intent on conserving its power than on effectively administering the country. Economic negligence plunged the country into food shortages with the effect of sharp price rises. The lack of a stable governing power led to the rapid disintegration of the country with local socialist-inspired soviets (councils) spreading throughout the nation and claiming to be the sole representatives of workers and soldiers.

In his essay "State and Revolution," Lenin identified the soviets as the basis of the revolutionary government that was to replace the tzarist system. Lenin's essay did not conceal a certain scorn for mere parliamentarism. The soviets were society, so there was no need of parliamentary representatives. Yet, the relationship between the self-organized communities of the soviets and the Communist Party began to dissolve very quickly as the party imposed its own diktats over the organization of grassroot communities.

Since its very start in October 1917, the Russian revolution departed from Marx's and Engels's ideal blueprint of a communist community. According to the two political thinkers, revolution was to take place simultaneously in all civilized and industrially advanced countries. Instead, a communist regime was being established in a single country where the industrial sector was still underdeveloped and the working class was a minority compared to the vast peasant masses. This contradiction would be a recurrent feature of all communist revolutions and, in spite of the Communist International, efforts to spread communism in more industrially advanced societies never succeeded.

In addition, following Marx's dictates in *The Communist Manifesto* that "communism deprives no man of the power to appropriate the products of society; all that it does is to deprive him of the power to subjugate the labor of others by means of such appropriations," collective ownership of the means of production was established in the Soviet Union. Yet, class differences were still visible. The precepts, known as "War Communism," designed by Lenin and Leon Trotsky to realize a socialist community also included the abolition of money and its replacement by tokens as well as free goods and services, the restructuring of the national economy according to a single plan, and the introduction of compulsory labor. These measures caused strong popular discontent and the outbreak of a civil war between the Bolsheviks and the counterrevolutionary forces, which, however, were finally defeated in 1922. That same year the Russian and Transcaucasian Soviet Federated Socialist Republics and the Ukrainian and Belorussian Soviet Socialist Republics formed the USSR. In subsequent years, the union was expanded to 15 socialist republics, which, although equal to Russia in theory, were heavily subjugated to it.

## LEFTISM TO RIGHTISM

Lenin and Trotsky's vision of a leftist, socialist government soon took on the trappings of rightist totalitarianism. In addition to military operations, the Bolsheviks consolidated their power by repressing with violence all forms of opposition, which were eliminated through assassination campaigns orchestrated by the Cheka, the Soviet secret police. As would happen in future communist countries, a vast cultural revolution was launched to replace bourgeois ideology with socialist dogmas. Hostile newspapers were shut down and publications were subjected to censorship, while artists were granted a certain degree of freedom of expression provided they did not criticize the system too overtly. Religious belief was considered mere superstition and all church properties were nationalized. The Orthodox Church was particularly targeted for its links with the monarchy and its capacity to influence vast sectors of the Russian population. Russian society started to be divided sharply into two categories of people defined by the party: the people and the enemies of the people.

The Bolsheviks, who had renamed their party the Russian Communist Party, based their power on a strong identification between party and state. The party-state maintained strict control and surveillance over the entire community. Though the Bolsheviks claimed to be representing workers' rights, all the power was concentrated in the hands of the Communist Party, the vanguard of the revolution and of the working class, against which little or no opposition was possible. Candidates for the Soviets were almost always taken from the Communist Party. The same Leninist method of managing the party, democratic centralism, was applied to the government of the entire nation. Democratic centralism, a political program embraced by many other Communist parties, even in Western countries, entailed an absolute party discipline and respect of party hierarchies. According to Lenin, the party and therefore the state had to be a highly centralized body structured around a small, ideologically homogeneous group of professional revolutionaries who would give directives to lower party organizations.

The Leninist precepts of War Communism brought about an unprecedented economic crisis in the early 1920s, which coincided with the beginning of Lenin's failing health and Josef Stalin's rise in power. From 1921 to 1928, NEP (New Economic Policy) allowed for a partial return to private property and landowning. NEP also included the reintroduction of money in Soviet economy. These new measures gave a certain degree of stability to Russian post-revolutionary society, but were complemented by further repression to prevent the partial economic liberalization from leading to a rise in counterrevolutionary sentiment. Concentration camps (*gulags*) were established and political dissidents were imprisoned there after farcical trials. These repressive methods became the distinguishing mark of Stalin, who had succeeded Lenin after the latter's death in 1924. Under the slogan "Socialism in one country," Stalin defeated the leftist faction of the party headed by Trotsky, who instead argued for the orthodox view that the revolution should be spread internationally. Stalin's idea appealed to party officials whose power would remain intact and would not be endangered by foreign conflicts.

Plagued by the constant problem of supplying enough grain to the urban population, Stalin abruptly ended the NEP and started a process of collectivization of the land. This agricultural policy forced the peasants to surrender their properties and join larger collective farms (kolkhozy). From independent producers, farmers became state employees and what they raised was thus considered state property. Stalin made the issue of collectivization a matter of class war, claiming that his goal was the elimination of the class of rich peasants, a minority exploiting the poorer countryside masses. Confiscation, arrest, and deportation to prison camps were the possible sanctions for those who refused to give up their land. The process was completed by 1936, finally establishing the firm hold of the party also on the countryside.

The same coercive methods were applied also to the other spheres of society and ideological conformity was required by literary authors, scientists, economists, and philosophers. Mass purges were conducted in all professional cadres throughout the Stalinist era and numerous trials and executions were displayed as public and educational events. A strong cult of personality led to vast historical falsifications to stress Stalin's role in Russian politics.

Stalin also introduced strict planning in the Soviet economy through five-year plans, which would become a constant of Soviet life, and stressed the importance of directing all resources to the process of industrialization of the USSR. This focus on industrialization, financed through the proceeds of grain sales, produced a strong movement of people from the countryside to urban centers and the emergence of the working class whose pay and rations were linked to workers' productivity. The successes of the industrialization process, which reached an unprecedented speed during the 1930s, however, caused the disruption of peasant villages and the annihilation of all forms of solidarity and community.

## SOVIET COMMUNISM AND FASCISM

Soviet foreign policy of the Stalin era was marked by the complete misjudgment of the phenomenon of fascism. Some of Stalin's directives, including the infamous purges of Trotskyites in the Spanish Civil War (1936–39) and the Nazi-Soviet Non-Aggression Pact (1939), actually helped to spread fascism throughout

A sixth-grade schoolroom in Latvia, when it was a republic of the Union of Soviet Socialist Republics.

A woman worker at a textile plant in the late 1930s whose photo was obtained by the U.S. Office of War Information.

Europe and alienated many left-wing militants worldwide. Yet, Hitler's 1941 aggression brought the USSR to fight on the Allies' side in World War II. Military victory brought several Eastern European countries (Czechoslovakia, Hungary, Bulgaria, Poland) into the Soviet sphere of influence, thus starting the ideological confrontation between the Eastern and the Western blocs known as the Cold War.

When Stalin died as a result of a stroke in 1953, he was succeeded by Nikita Khrushchev, who had been one of his staunchest supporters. Yet, Khrushchev shocked delegates to the 20th Party Congress in February 1956 by publicly denouncing the "cult of personality" that surrounded Stalin, and accusing Stalin of mass murder during the Great Purges. The speech, however, remained silent about those actions in which Khrushchev himself had been involved. The new leader set out to reform communism and announced his doctrine of peaceful coexistence with the West. His policy of de-Stalinization entailed a series of reforms that earned him the hostility of the conservatives led by Leonid Brezhnev. Yet, in spite of his liberal outlook, Khrushchev still repressed internal and international opposition. His own leadership was partly the result of the assassination of Stalin's most obvious successor, Lavrenty Beria.

During his 11 years as a leader of the USSR, Khrushchev crushed the reformist Hungarian government of Imre Nagy with the direct intervention of the Red Army. He allowed the publication of Aleksandr Solzhenitsyn's *One Day in the Life of Ivan Denisovich* in 1962, a harsh critique of Stalinist purges, but five years earlier he had censored Boris Pasternak's novel *Doctor Zhivago* (1957), forbidding the author to accept the Nobel Prize.

The failures of the Khrushchev administration in the agricultural sector, as well as the humiliating outcome of the Cuban Missile Crisis (1962), brought Khrushchev to his downfall in 1964 at the hands of his deputy Brezhnev. After a period of collective leadership, Brezhnev strengthened his position in the 1970s. Though the beginning of the Brezhnev era was marked by optimism and faith in economic growth, by its end the country was in steady decline, involved in a disas-

Soviet education reached deep into the heart of the country, such as this nurses' course in the Pamir region.

A nursery-on-wheels is part of a collective farm effort in the Soviet Union in the 1930s.

trous war against Afghanistan. The economic slowdown was further complicated by the increased defense spending to keep up the hard-won nuclear parity with the United States.

Brezhnev's foreign policy was marked by his authorization to direct military intervention against the Czech government headed by Alexander Dubcek and his "socialism with a human face" policy. This definitely alienated the sympathies of many leftists for the USSR, including those of the largest Western Communist Party, the Italian PCI. In his relationship with capitalist countries, Brezhnev inaugurated the so-called détente, which aimed at bringing the Soviet Union closer to the West. The economic, cultural, and social stagnation that characterized the Brezhnev years, spreading corruption and cronyism within the Soviet bureaucracy, was also the distinctive feature of Yuri Andropov's and Konstantin Chernenko's leaderships. Though Andropov tried to launch reforms to reduce corruption and absenteeism in the bureaucracy and more effective measures to counter the plague of alcoholism, the country was already in terminal decline. Andropov's agenda was too cautious and refused to come to terms with the contradiction of Soviet society and economy.

## THE LEFT RESURGENT

The most radical in his attempt to reform the system was also the last leader of the Soviet Union and the one who brought about its demise: Mikhail Gorbachev. Elected party secretary in 1985, Gorbachev expanded freedoms of expression and information under his policy of *glasnost* (openness). His *perestroika* (restructuring) encompassed political and economic organization, allowing some multicandidate elections and introducing some free-market measures in the Soviet economy. In his foreign policy, Gorbachev took equally unprecedented decisions, seeking less antagonistic relations with the West and supporting reforms in the countries of the Eastern bloc. In the end, this led to the democratic election of noncommunist governments in Poland, Hungary, and Czechoslovakia in the late 1980s and paved the way for the process of German reunification. Yet, Gorbachev's democratic reforms were also causing unrest within the USSR, where many republics started to advocate independence from Moscow.

Communist conservatives became increasingly worried about the party's loss of power and, in August 1991, effected a coup putting Gorbachev under house arrest for a few days. Though the coup, badly planned, failed in the face of popular resistance animated by Russian president Boris Yeltsin, it was clear that Gorbachev's leadership and the Soviet Union were over. On December 25, 1991, Gorbachev resigned as president of the Soviet Union, which ended the same day and was replaced by a commonwealth of former republics led by Yeltsin.

### SEE ALSO

*Volume 1 Left:* Communism; Marx, Karl; Lenin, Vladimir I.; Stalin and Stalinism; Gorbachev, Mikhail; Russia, Post-Soviet.
*Volume 2 Right:* Totalitarianism; Fascism; Capitalism; Soviet Union; Russia, Post-Soviet.

### BIBLIOGRAPHY

R. Conquest, *The Harvest of Sorrow: Soviet Collectivization and the Terror-Famine* (Oxford University Press, 1987); S. Fitzpatrick, *The Russian Revolution* (Oxford University Press, 1982); G. Hosking, *The First Socialist Society* (Harvard University Press); P. Kenez, *A History of the Soviet Union from the Beginning to the End* (Cambridge University Press, 1999); S. Kotkin, *Armageddon Averted: The Soviet Collapse* (Oxford University Press, 2001); M. Lewin, *Russian Peasants and Soviet Power* (Norton, 1975); M. McFaul, *Russia's Unfinished Revolution: Political Change from Gorbachev to Putin* (Cornell University Press, 2002); R. Pipes, *Russia under the Bolshevik Regime* (Vintage Books, 1995); R. Sakwa, *The Rise and Fall of the Soviet Union* (Routledge, 1999); A. Solzhenitsyn, *The Gulag Archipelago* (Harper and Row, 1985); K.M. Strauss, *Factory and Community in Stalin's Russia: The Making of an Industrial Working Class* (University of Pittsburgh Press, 1997); W. Taubam, *Khrushchev: The Man and His Era* (Norton, 2003); R.C. Tucker, *The Lenin Anthology* (Norton, 1975); V. Zubok and C.V. Pleshakov, *Inside the Kremlin's Cold War: From Stalin to Khrushchev* (Harvard University Press, 1997).

LUCA PRONO, PH.D.
UNIVERSITY OF NOTTINGHAM, UNITED KINGDOM

# Spain

A MAJOR IMPERIAL power from the 16th century to the Napoleonic era, Spain in the last 150 years has been riven by significant divisions in ideology, class, and ethnicity. The 19th century was a period of loss, in which the Spanish were driven out of their Latin American possessions, a process that largely ended in 1898, with the loss of Cuba and the Philippines. The first eight decades of the 20th century were a period of internal division and struggle, with the political left having its greatest influence during the Second Republic (1931–36), and in the 1980s, after the restoration of democracy provided for by the death of fascist Francisco Franco in 1975. Under the leadership of Felipe Gonzalez in the 1980s, Spain moved a great distance toward the European mainstream. The Socialists returned to power in 2004, resulting largely from the fallout of public opposition to Spanish participation in the invasion of Iraq, and the preelection Madrid bombing.

The first major period of the left influence in Spain was in the 1930s, with the founding of the Second Republic in 1931. There was a high level of conflict in this period, and a sizable portion of the population supported conservatism and other right-wing ideologies. This conflict boiled over in 1936, when General Franco led the military in an attack on the civil authority, based on his fear that the Republic was going to turn Spain into a Marxist or Soviet state. The Republicans were constituted by a broad coalition of liberals, social democrats, socialists, communists, and anarchists, each of which organized their own militias in opposition to Franco's military and fascist Falange movement. The Republic also had strong, nonstate international support, in the form of international volunteer brigades from the other Western countries. Many of those who fought in the war on the Republican side, like George Orwell and Ernest Hemingway, would write about those tragic events. After early successes by the Republic, the tables were turned because of the intervention of Nazi Germany and fascist Italy in support of Franco, while the Western liberal democracies maintained neutrality, or in the case of the Soviet Union, provided little or no help to the Republic.

Franco won that battle and would go on to rule from 1939 to 1975, the year of his death. By that time, Spain was well behind the rest of Europe. In something of a minor miracle, instead of falling back into authoritarianism, Spaniards wrote and ratified a democratic constitution in 1978, which walked a very fine line, by providing for a strong prime minister in a strong central government in a unitary state (a right-wing demand), while establishing "autonomous communities" which were de facto subcentral governments, on the other hand (a left-wing demand). During the 11-year rule of the Socialists under Felipe Gonzalez, which began in 1982, the military was modernized by reducing its role in domestic life and by professionalizing it. The Roman Catholic Church's position as the established church was altered, and censorship of the media was lifted. Spain joined the North Atlantic Treaty Organization (NATO) and the European Union (EU), which helped to rule out any return to fascism.

In early 2004, the left made a resurgence in Spanish politics. In March, al-Qaeda, the terrorist organization, simultaneously exploded several bombs around a Madrid commuter railway station, killing 200 people and injuring many hundreds more, just days before a scheduled election. Prime Minister José Maria Aznar, who led his right-of-center Popular Party government for eight years, had supported the 2003 U.S.-led invasion of Iraq despite Spanish public opinion, which ran strongly against the war. The voters responded by giving a surprise victory to the Socialist Party's José Luis Rodriguez Zapatero, by a margin of 43 percent of the vote to 38 percent for Aznar. The new prime minister promptly pulled Spanish troops out of Iraq.

## SEE ALSO

## BIBLIOGRAPHY

George Esenwein and Adrian Shubert, *Spain at War: The Spanish Civil War in Context, 1931–39* (Longman, 1995); Andrew Forrest, *The Spanish Civil War* (Routledge, 2000); G. Gunther, F. Sani, and G. Shabad, *Spain after Franco: The Making of a Competitive Party System* (University of California Press, 1988); Paul Heywood, *The Government and Politics of Spain* (Macmillan, 1995); Paul Heywood, ed., *Politics and Policy in Democratic Spain* (Frank Cass, 1999).

GEOFFREY R. MARTIN
MOUNT ALLISON UNIVERSITY, CANADA

# Stalin and Stalinism

JOSEF STALIN, known as "the man of steel," who led the Soviet Union from 1926 to his death in 1953, did more than any other Soviet figure to put his stamp on the Soviet Union. Born on December 21, 1879, he received a full scholarship to study in the Russian Orthodox seminary at Tbilisi in his native Georgia. However, as with many others in his generation, the young Iosif Vissarionovich Dzhugashvili entered the revolutionary movement of the Marxist Social-Democratic Party. In 1910, he adopted the shortened name, Josef Stalin.

From the beginning, Stalin's career diverged from those of his future mentor, Vladimir Lenin, and future rival, Leon Trotsky. While both of them spent many years in revolutionary exile outside the then-tzarist Russia, Stalin spent most of his formative years in the Caucasus Mountains and his native Georgia. Between the years 1902 and 1917, while Trotsky and Lenin were broadening their horizons, he was involved in guerrilla activities and periods of exile in Siberia. Instead of developing the progressive, internationalist views that Lenin would show in his classic "What Is to Be Done?" in 1902, Stalin associated with largely an ethnic culture little changed over the centuries.

When revolution came to Russia in 1917, the Bolshevik Party was led by Lenin and Trotsky. Significantly, Stalin did not support the revolution until Lenin came to Russia on April 16 from exile. Stalin only became active afterward, when Lenin had captured the revolutionary momentum with his control of the vital soviets, or councils, of the rebelling soldiers, sailors, and workers in St. Petersburg.

When, in the summer of 1917, Lenin had to flee to Finland during the counterrevolutionary campaign of Alexander Kerensky, head of the Provisional Government, it was Trotsky who served as the loyal lieutenant and strategist in St. Petersburg. When the October

Revolution brought Lenin to power, Trotsky again was his capable lieutenant.

When the counterrevolution of the White Russians (loyal to the Tzar) began, Stalin served as a political commissar with the revolutionary troops. He was present at the fighting for Volgograd, which he later had renamed for himself as Stalingrad. By now he had shown himself as a shrewd "party man," who would align himself with Lenin on the decision to make peace with the Germans at Brest-Litovsk in March 1918. Yet, still he was not in the leadership clique, which really would center around Lenin and Trotsky during the revolution and civil war. Trotsky, as commissar of military and naval affairs, would actually reforge a Russian Army decimated by war and revolution. Indeed, Stalin failed in his work as party commissar because as Roy V. Medvedev wrote in *Let History Judge: The Origins and Consequences of Stalinism*, Stalin's "arbitrary behavior" was one of the reasons that thwarted the "failure of the Soviet advance on Warsaw" in the 1920 war with Marshal Josef Pilsudski's Poland. Nevertheless, Trotsky's leadership would help the Red Army defeat the last of the Bolsheviks' opponents within Russia by March 1921. Lenin, speaking at the Tenth Congress of the Communist Party on March 8, 1921, could say, "The last of the hostile armies has been driven from our territories."

It was during the Bolshevik political reshaping of the country that Stalin, now an experienced party insider, or apparatchik, moved upward. He stuck closely to Lenin during the crises of the Ninth and Tenth Party Congresses, when Lenin's harsh "War Communism" came under the attack of his own party members. Yet again, while Trotsky saw brief service as commissar for foreign affairs, as well as his tenure as commissar of military and naval affairs, Stalin's expertise only remained in the area of the national groups that formed the majority of Russia's population, of which the so-called Great Russians formed only part. Indeed, the only provision he had been considered for was that of commissar for nationalities affairs.

However, his work as a party bureaucrat led to his appointment as the new general secretary of the Central Committee of the Bolshevik, now properly called Russian Communist Party, in April 1922. This was intended by Lenin to be an administrative position that would leave him to attempt to bring Russian out of the wreckage that was left behind by revolution and war. Instead, at the worst possible time, Lenin's health took a devastating turn for the worse in December 1921; the rigors of the past four years had physically ravaged him. During this period, he began to have serious doubts about Stalin's suitability as a successor, since he now was able to envision a Russia once again a member of the family of nations, and no more a revolutionary pariah. Lenin wrote of Stalin, "I suggest to the [party] comrades that they think of a way of transferring Stalin from [the general secretaryship] and assigning another man to it." Obviously, Trotsky would have represented a stimulating alternative to Stalin.

However, Lenin did not act on this secret memorandum and, before he could, he died in January 1924. Since Medvedev alleges that Stalin may have had a hand in the deaths of two potential rivals, Mikhail Frunze, who became Trotsky's successor, and Feliks Dzerzhinsky, the head of the V-Cheka, or secret police, it cannot be ruled out that Stalin hastened Lenin's death. Stalin's wife, Nadezhda Allilueva, could have let her husband know of Lenin's plans to remove him from party leadership. With Lenin gone, Stalin used his position to rapidly oust Trotsky from any positions of party influence. Lenin's state funeral took place on January 27, 1924. Significantly, Stalin had assured Trotsky it was not necessary for him to return for Lenin's funeral from the health resort where he was staying on the Black Sea, according to Robert Service in his *Lenin: A Biography*. By 1927, Trotsky was barred from the leadership of the party that he, next to Lenin, had done the most to make victorious in Russia.

Stalin continued his campaign against the "Old Bolsheviks" who had been around Lenin, and some of whom had more claims to prominence in the party than Stalin. Lev Kamenev, Nikolai Bukharin, and Grigori Zinoviev were all purged around the same time as Trotsky. As Theodore H. von Laue and Angela von Laue comment, "by April 1929 ... Stalin was the confirmed successor to Lenin. He was the socialist dictator in the largest country in the world, shaping in his own style an unprecedentedly novel political system." Stalin used the triumph over Trotsky, who increasingly had urged less centralized party leadership, to force upon Russia his drive for "collectivization" of agriculture. This, of course, frustrated the gradual move back to some form of capitalism, which had been an innovative part of Lenin's New Economic Policy (NEP). Basil Dmytryshyn stated in *USSR: A Concise History* that "at the end of May 1928 ... he called upon party members to choose between suicide and rapid collectivization of agriculture and development of heavy industry." From his narrow political experience, Stalin perceived the Soviet Union as surrounded by hostile countries, and the only way to survive was to ruthlessly drive the Russian people into an industrialized future. While modernization was necessary, the methods Stalin used unleashed a wave of brutality not even seen in Russia under Tzar Ivan the Terrible.

## THE GREAT PURGES

The combination of brutal repression by the state police, under changing names—V-Cheka, OGPU, NKVD—and economic dislocation killed thousands of Russians, especially among the peasants—those whom it had been the intent of the Bolsheviks to help. Stalin created a harvest of "dead souls," as dead peasants were called in tzarist times. David Remnick wrote about the region of Stavropol, where the future reformer Mikhail Gorbachev was born. "According to Western studies," Remnick cited, "more than 30,000 people in the Stavropol region died during the terror-famine of 1931–32."

On December 1, 1934, S.M. Kirov, the secretary of the Party Central Committee, was assassinated by a young Communist Party member, Leonid Nikolaev. While ultimate responsibility for the murder has never been definitely established, Kirov's murder was used by Stalin to begin what would be the era in Russian history known as the Great Purge. The campaign against anyone Stalin felt to be disloyal or a danger to his rule had, Medvedev notes, begun actually in 1928 with the Shakhty Affair, when engineers were accused of "bourgeois wrecking" in the coal industry. During this Purge period, thousands of party members, military, naval, and air force officers, and ordinary Russians were "liquidated" by Stalin's organs of state repression. Secret police killers ranged the world killing Stalin's enemies: in August 1940, Trotsky was assassinated in Mexico.

By the time the Stalinist frenzy had abated, perhaps the best idea of the total number of victims—executed or imprisoned—would come from Stalin himself. Basil Dmytryshyn said that at the 18th Party Congress in March 1939, Stalin admitted that membership in the party from 1934 to 1939 "dropped from 1,874,488 to 1,588,852" members. Some 300,000 people had "disappeared" in five years by Stalin's own accounting.

By 1941, Stalin appears to have been a leader whose own suspicions and fears of opposition had locked him in the worst type of prison: that of his own mind. In June 1941, disregarding information from many sources, Stalin's Soviet Union was massively invaded by the Nazi Germany of Adolf Hitler, who had signed a Non-Aggression Pact with the Russians in August 1939. Stalin was caught completely by surprise, as Lenin or

Trotsky may never have been. The Great Purge had wrecked the Russian armed forces, causing the country to lose the services of leaders like Marshal Mikhail Tukhachevsy and Vasili Blyukher. The massive losses suffered in the initial phases of the German attack can be in large part attributed to the gutting of the High Command, which would soon emerge as the STAVKA. Hitler's main thrust at Moscow would be stopped in December 1941. To attempt a counteroffensive, Stalin would be forced to invoke the military glory of the old tzarist regime, which he had spent his youth destroying. Brave fighters, along with receiving communist decorations like the Order of Lenin, also were presented with the Order of Alexander Nevsky, who had saved Russia from the German Teutonic knights some 700 years earlier.

In doing so, Stalin forged alliances with the "bourgeois" countries like the United States and Great Britain, led by President Franklin D. Roosevelt and Prime Minister Winston S. Churchill. At wartime conferences such as Tehran, Iran, in 1943, they decided the strategy to defeat the common German menace. For Russia, the decisive turn came at Stalingrad, when Germany's Sixth Army under Marshal Friedrich von Paulus was forced to surrender on January 31, 1943. Of the 91,000 taken prisoner, only 6,000 would survive captivity. Some Germans were not released from the Gulag until 1956, when Soviet Premier Nikita Khrushchev would denounce Stalin's excesses at the 20th Party Congress. By the time the war ended for Russia, on May 8, 1945, Stalin's Red Army soldiers, led by commanders like Marshal Georgii Zhukov and Vasili Chuikov, had fought their way into Berlin, Germany.

After the war, Stalin would extend his control into East Europe, locking countries like Czechoslovakia and Poland into the Soviet Union's sphere of influence to provide a buffer against further "aggression" from the West. The native East European communists who followed the Red Army used the same brutal methods to gain power that Stalin had begun to employ nearly 20 years earlier in Russia. Czech Foreign Minister Jan Masaryk, the son of Czechoslovakia's founding president, Tomas Masaryk, was most likely killed by the secret police of the Communist Premier Klement Gottwald in March 1948. By 1949, a full-scale Cold War existed between the Soviet Union and Stalin's former Western allies.

Five years after the death of Masaryk, Stalin died, apparently from natural causes, on March 1, 1953. A troika, or ruling triumvirate, now ruled Russia collectively, consisting of Lavrenty Beria, the surviving head of Stalin's secret police, Nikita Khrushchev, and Georgi M. Malenkov. In December 1953, Beria was executed, allegedly by Khrushchev himself. By 1956, Khrushchev, who had served his "boss" so well, was now supreme in Russia.

On the centennial of Stalin's birth in December 1979, the official Soviet assessment was given of Stalin and the system he created. The Soviet Union's Novosti Press Agency carried an article by Gennady Gerasimov. Gerasimov wrote "as time went on, Stalin found himself to be, in fact, beyond criticism, and his suspiciousness created a conducive climate for violations of legality. He made theoretical mistakes, committed acts of voluntarism and political blunders. The Soviet people knew Stalin as a defender of the USSR, fighting for the cause of socialism. But in this struggle he did not stop at resorting to unworthy methods, either." Estimates run that as many as 20 million Russians perished between 1930 and 1950 through Stalin's ruthless application of "unworthy methods."

Stalin's variety of communism came to dominate the Soviet Union, and through the Third International, much of the international communist movement through the 1930s and 1940s. Both domestically and internationally, Stalinism implied a monolithic support for the advancement of the Soviet state, in economic and military terms, and the establishment of Soviet hegemony. Stalin's ruthless control of the Soviet Party and through its domination of the International, control of communist parties around the world, represented the official definition of the left for a generation.

Those who disagreed with the policy at particular periods, by seeking more cooperation with democratic regimes, like Jay Lovestone in the United States, were viewed by the Stalinist structure as "rightist deviationist." Those, like Leon Trotsky, who argued for more immediate support of world revolution when Stalin was ordering cooperation with the bourgeois regimes, were viewed as "leftist deviationist." Thus, by control of the party and by defining the "correct line," Stalin in his own view and that of the official parties, established and defined his policies as the only proper Marxist-Leninist orthodoxy. Contrary views were simply portrayed as unscientific, mistaken, or worse, criminally misguided.

### SEE ALSO

*Volume 1 Left*: Soviet Union; Communism; Russian Revolution; Lenin, Vladimir I.; Trotsky, Leon; Third International (Comintern).
*Volume 2 Right*: Soviet Union; McCarthyism.

### BIBLIOGRAPHY

David Remnick, *Lenin's Tomb: The Last Days of the Soviet Empire* (Vintage Books, 1994); Robert Service, *Lenin: A Biography* (Harvard University Press, 2000); Roy V. Medvedev, *Let History Judge: The Origins and Consequences of Stalinism* (Vintage Books, 1971); Basil Dmytryshyn, *USSR: A Concise History* (Scribner's, 1978); Theodore H. von Laue and Angela von Laue, *Faces of a Nation: The Rise and Fall of the Soviet Union, 1917–91* (Fulcrum, 1996); Nikolai Gogol, *Dead Souls* (Airmont Press, 1965); Erik Durschmied, *Blood of Revolution* (Arcade, 2002); Orlando Figes, *A People's Tragedy: The Russian Revolution, 1891–24* (Penguin, 1996); Christopher Andrew and Oleg Gordievsky, *KGB: The Inside Story* (HarperCollins, 1990).

JOHN F. MURPHY, JR.
AMERICAN MILITARY UNIVERSITY

# Stanton, Elizabeth Cady (1815–1902)

AS A CHILD, Elizabeth Cady Stanton was exposed to reform movements through her cousin Gerrit Smith and received informal legal training from her father, a respected lawyer. In part due to these early influences she became active in the abolitionist movement at a young age, and later married anti-slavery orator Henry Stanton in 1840. Soon after their wedding, they traveled to London, England, for the World Anti-Slavery Convention where Henry was a delegate. When women delegates were denied official standing at the convention, Elizabeth Cady Stanton met with another delegate, Lucretia Mott, a Quaker teacher involved in temperance, the anti-slavery movement, and women's rights. Together, they decided to organize a women's rights convention in Seneca Falls, New York.

As part of the Seneca Falls Convention, Stanton wrote the Declaration of Sentiments, modeled after the Declaration of Independence. Together, the Declaration of Sentiments and the Seneca Falls Convention are credited with starting the movement for women's suffrage in the United States. After 1851, Stanton became closely allied with Susan B. Anthony, and together they founded the National Woman Suffrage Association (NWSA), with Stanton serving as president. Unable to assume an active travel schedule because of her seven children, Stanton wrote many of the speeches given by

Anthony as she traveled around the country educating women about the vote and organizing women to join the suffrage movement.

Stanton and Anthony, believing that suffrage for black men after emancipation should not take precedence over suffrage for women, were in conflict with the more conservative women involved in the movement. Along with Matilda Joslyn Gage, the two led the National Woman Suffrage Association, opposing the concept of the "precedence" that was accepted by the more conservative American Woman Suffrage Association. When the NWSA and the rival American Woman Suffrage Association merged in 1890, Stanton became president of the new National American Woman Suffrage Association. She became an outspoken commentator on social and political issues—speaking on maternity, drinking, child rearing, divorce laws, constitutional questions, and presidential campaigns.

In the 1880s, tired of travel and organizational leadership, Stanton began concentrating on her writing as a way to educate others about women's rights. She co-wrote three volumes of the *History of Woman Suffrage* (1880–85) with Anthony and Gage, which documented the history of activism associated with the suffrage movement.

Along with a committee of other women, she published a controversial critique of women's treatment by religion entitled "The Woman's Bible," as part of her lifelong study of the relationship between organized religion and women's subordination. The controversial religious commentary highlighted the parts of the Bible that focused on women and offered an alternative interpretation of biblical text that was deemed to be biased against women. She urged women to examine how religious orthodoxy and male-dominated theology was a source of women's oppression.

Thirty years after Seneca Falls, Stanton and Gage wrote the *Declaration of Rights of the Women of the United States*, which was presented by Anthony at the 1876 Centennial Celebration in Washington. Later in life, Stanton focused more on social reforms related to women's issues rather than just women's right to vote. She saw women suffering under the marriage laws of the time and advocated liberal divorce laws at a time when women did not even discuss the topic in private. She urged women to change their own thinking, to discard oppressive traditions, question religious doctrines that deemed women inferior, and to question supposed women's "virtues," which were used to justify inequality. She was active in winning property rights for married women, equal guardianship of children, and

liberalizing divorce laws so that women could leave abusive marriages.

Stanton believed in giving women educational opportunities and supported coeducation. She also believed in the need for women's economic independence, arguing that men and women were endowed with the same natural rights and rationality, and that as they were equals, they should be treated as such by law, government, business, and politics.

Stanton died in New York on October 26, 1902, nearly 20 years before women in the United States won the right to vote. She is remembered by students, scholars, and the public as a leader in the women's suffrage movement, and a powerful voice arguing for women's rights in society.

## SEE ALSO

*Volume 1 Left:* Suffragists; Flynn, Elizabeth Gurley; Civil Rights; Anthony, Susan B.
*Volume 2 Right:* Religion; Feminism.

## BIBLIOGRAPHY

Harriet Sigerman, *Elizabeth Cady Stanton: The Right Is Ours* (Oxford University Press, 2001); Ann D. Gordon, *The Selected Papers of Elizabeth Cady Stanton and Susan B. Anthony* (Rutgers University Press, 1997); Elizabeth Cady Stanton, *Eighty Years and More: Reminiscences of Elizabeth Cady Stanton* (Source Book Press, 1970).

SHANNON K. ORR
BOWLING GREEN STATE UNIVERSITY

# Steinem, Gloria (1934–)

A COFOUNDER OF Ms. magazine and a motivating force in the National Organization for Women (NOW), Gloria Steinem has been one of the foremost voices of the feminist movement since the late 1960s. Steinem was born on March 25, 1934, in Toledo, Ohio, into a line of determined women, beginning with her paternal grandmother, who had been a suffragist.

When Steinem was 10 years old, her father Leo moved out of the house, leaving Gloria and her sister to care for their mother, Ruth Nuneviller Steinem, who became increasingly emotionally fragile. The experience of accepting a parental role at such a young age affected Steinem for the rest of her life. She believed that her mother's depression was dismissed as "nerves" rather than understood as a physical condition because she was a woman.

While still a student at Smith College, Steinem's political views began to take shape. She worked on both the 1952 and 1956 presidential campaigns of Adlai Stevenson, the Democratic candidate who lost both elections to Republican Dwight D. Eisenhower. She later campaigned for Democrats Eugene McCarthy and Robert Kennedy. Steinem was graduated with high honors from Smith in 1956. Afterward, she broke her engagement, choosing instead to accept a scholarship to study in India. Temporarily stranded in London, England, on her way to India, Steinem discovered that she was pregnant and chose to have an abortion. She told no one for 15 years. The trip to India convinced Steinem that she had a responsibility to save the world, and she returned to the United States with a deep enthusiasm for political reform.

Settling in New York in 1960, Steinem accepted a position as an assistant at *Help* magazine. Later she turned to freelance writing for such magazines as *Show*, *Esquire*, *Glamour*, and *Ladies Home Journal*. In 1963, Betty Friedan published *The Feminine Mystique*, which ignited the modern women's movement. That same year, Steinem reluctantly went undercover for an assignment at the Playboy Club, a sexist yet popular men's club that was part of the *Playboy* magazine world, the magazine that pioneered showcasing nude women, including Marilyn Monroe. She described her experience in an exposé called, "A Bunny's Tale." By 1968, Steinem began to attract substantial attention as the editor of *New York* magazine, which she cofounded. Steinem remained actively political, demonstrating against the Vietnam War and the oppression of workers and for women's rights.

After familiarizing herself with the current literature on feminism, Steinem concluded that the women's movement as understood by Friedan and her supporters was basically a movement of white, middle-class women. Steinem began advocating a more extreme view of feminism and was accused of promoting "man hating" and "bra burning."

In 1970, Steinem received the Penney-Missouri Journalism Award for her article "After Black Power, Women's Liberation." Unfortunately, Steinem had also launched discord within the women's movement and begun a private feud with Friedan, who rejected what she saw as Steinem's radicalism. Undeterred, Steinem set out on a lecture tour of college campuses throughout the United States designed to educate young women on feminism.

In July 1971, along with Friedan and Congresswomen Bella Abzug (D-NY) and Shirley Chisholm (D-NY), Steinem cofounded the National Women's Political Caucus (NWPC) aimed at funding political candidates who are supportive of women's rights, particularly of reproductive rights. Motivated by the June 1966 Third Conference on Women's Issues, Steinem joined with other feminists to found the National Organization for Women, designed to advance women's interests through electoral mobilization, legislative lobbying, litigation, protest marches, and demonstrations.

Because the abortion issue had become so controversial since the *Roe v. Wade* decision in 1973, NOW began to focus a good deal of attention on protecting a woman's right to choose. In April 1992, NOW sponsored the March for Women's Lives that drew the largest number of protestors to date to the nation's capital. In 1972, Steinem was also heavily involved in gathering support for the Equal Rights Amendment (ERA), which had passed both houses of Congress after languishing since 1923. The amendment, which failed to win ratification, banned discrimination on the basis of sex by both federal and state governments.

Together with Brenda Feigen Fasteau, Steinem launched *Ms.* magazine to publicize ERA and to respond to the growing interest in the women's movement. Originally, only 300,000 copies of the new magazine were published. They sold out within eight days. Over the next two decades, Steinem and other feminists grew disillusioned with the magazine's dependence on advertising. In 1990, *Ms.* took a brief hiatus, returning in July 1993 with no advertising.

In 1972, Steinem, Pat Carbine, Letty Pogrebin, and Marlo Thomas founded the Ms. Foundation, designed to promote equality and fair treatment for women. Programs focused on the issues of employment, reproductive and health rights, violence against women, and socialization of young girls. Two decades later, the foundation launched the controversial Take Your Daughters to Work Day. Ultimately, the program was changed to Take Our Daughters and Sons to Work Day.

In 1993, Steinem's work for women's rights was acknowledged with her induction into the National Women's Hall of Fame in Seneca Falls, New York, where the first women's rights convention took place in 1848. Steinem surprised both her supporters and detractors by marrying at the age of 66. Some observers saw her marriage as a rejection of feminism, while others saw it as proof that feminists are free to make personal decisions about their own lives.

**SEE ALSO**
*Volume 1 Left:* Friedan, Betty; Stevenson, Adlai E.; Feminism; Civil Rights.
*Volume 2 Right:* Feminism.

**BIBLIOGRAPHY**
Carolyn G. Heilbrun, *The Education of A Woman: The Life of Gloria Steinem* (Dial, 1995); "Gloria Steinem," www.theglass-ceiling.com (March 2004); Gloria Steinem, *Outrageous Acts and Everyday Rebellions* (Henry Holt, 1995); Sydney Ladensohn Stern, *Gloria Steinem: Her Passions, Politics, and Mystique* (Carol Publishing, 1997).

ELIZABETH PURDY, PH.D.
INDEPENDENT SCHOLAR

# Stevenson, Adlai E. (1900–1965)

ADLAI E. STEVENSON WAS a public-minded Democrat and gifted orator who was twice nominated for president. Adlai Ewing Stevenson II was born February 5, 1900, in Los Angeles, California, son of Lewis G. Stevenson and Helen (Davis) Stevenson. He was named for his grandfather, Adlai E. Stevenson, vice president of the United States under Grover Cleveland in his second term.

An early event in Stevenson's life is believed to have shaped his humanitarianism. He accidentally killed a girl, Ruth Merwin, while playing with a gun at a Christmas party when they were both 12. Stevenson attended Choate School and graduated with a bachelor's degree from Princeton University in 1922 and a law degree from Northwestern University in 1926. He then practiced law in Chicago, Illinois. Stevenson married Ellen Borden in 1928 in Chicago. They had three sons, Adlai III (who served in the U.S. Senate from Illinois from 1970 to 1981), Borden, and John. The couple divorced in 1949. It is believed that Stevenson's divorce undercut his chances of being elected president at that time. Not until 1980 did the country elect a divorced president, Ronald Reagan (albeit one who had long since remarried).

In 1933, Stevenson was called to Washington, D.C., to join the Franklin Roosevelt's New Deal. He served as counsel to the Agricultural Adjustment Agency, and was chief attorney at the Federal Alcohol Control Administration, a body created to deal with the repeal of Prohibition. He was later an assistant to the secretary of the navy. Stevenson was part of the U.S. delegation to the United Nations when that body was founded after World War II. In 1948, Stevenson was elected governor of Illinois in the biggest landslide in the state's history.

Stevenson was nominated by the Democratic Party for president in 1952 on the third ballot, after trailing Senator Estes Kefauver of Tennessee on the first ballot. No major-party presidential nomination since has taken more than a single ballot. Although Dwight Eisenhower did not win the popular vote by a landslide, he won in most of the states; Stevenson won only the electoral votes of nine southern states. Stevenson claimed it was "better to lose the election than mislead the people." Stevenson sought a rematch in 1956. This time he was nominated on the first ballot, but he did not choose a vice-presidential running mate, preferring to let the convention choose one.

The convention chose Kefauver, although John F. Kennedy led the second ballot until Albert Gore (Sr.) and Hubert H. Humphrey withdrew in favor of Kefauver. Stevenson called for a "New America" and advocated programs that would in the next decade be implemented by Kennedy and Lyndon B. Johnson as presidents. "There is a New America every morning when we wake up. It is upon us whether we will it or not," Stevenson told the convention. This time, Eisenhower won a popular landslide, and Stevenson carried only six southern states and Missouri.

## IDEOLOGY

Stevenson's reputation and popular image as an intellectual and as a New Deal Democrat probably contributed to his defeat in the presidential elections of 1952 and 1956. He supported civil rights, a pro-labor position, and at the same time took a strongly anti-communist stand in international affairs. During the 1950s, his position and personality epitomized the core of American Democratic Party liberalism that was only slightly to the left of the position of the Republican Party on most issues. Stevenson chose not to run in 1960 but held out hope for a draft. He received about 80 votes at the convention. In 1961, Kennedy chose Stevenson to be U.S. Ambassador to the United Nations. By 1965, Stevenson was rumored to be interested in running for the U.S. Senate from Illinois or being tapped as Johnson's running mate. ("After four years at the United Nations I sometimes yearn for the peace and tranquility of a political convention," he quipped.) But these were not to be. Stevenson died suddenly in London, England, on July 14, 1965. He was buried in Bloomington, Illinois.

SEE ALSO
*Volume 1 Left*: Kefauver, Estes; Kennedy, John F.; Johnson, Lyndon B.; Democratic Party.
*Volume 2 Right*: Eisenhower, Dwight D.; Republican Party.

BIBLIOGRAPHY
Kenneth S. Davis, *A Prophet in His Own Country: The Triumphs and Defeats of Adlai E. Stevenson* (Doubleday, 1957); Edward P. Doyle, ed., *As We Knew Adlai: The Stevenson Story by Twenty-two Friends* (Harper and Row, 1966); Porter McKeever, *Adlai Stevenson: His Life and Legacy* (Morrow, 1989); John Bartlow Martin, *The Life of Adlai E. Stevenson* (Doubleday, 1976 and 1977).

TONY L. HILL
MASSACHUSETTS INSTITUTE OF TECHNOLOGY

# Students for a Democratic Society

THE HISTORY OF Students for A Democratic Society (SDS) can be traced to 1905 when writers Upton Sinclair and Jack London joined with lawyer Clarence Darrow and journalist Walter Lippmann to found the Intercollegiate Socialist Society (ISS), which aimed at motivating young people to adopt leftist philosophies. In 1921, the student arm of ISS (SLID) evolved into the League for Industrial Democracy (LID), which in turn became Students for A Democratic Society in 1959. In its heyday, Students for A Democratic Society claimed over 100,000 members with 400 chapters on college campuses across the United States. After the publication of the *Port Huron Statement* in 1962, which became the manifesto of America's New Left by calling for a commitment to "participatory democracy," SDS surfaced as the voice of young people who demanded substantive political rights.

The goals of SDS, which were often perceived in the 1960s as too far to the left to represent the views of America's college students, have become mainstream in contemporary American politics. Those goals included civil rights, women's rights, anti-poverty programs, military draft resistance, and unemployment measures. Internally, SDS reforms focused on making college campuses more responsive to the rights of students. The SDS call for an end to the war in Vietnam motivated anti-war protests around the United States. SDS also began the move toward disarmament of nuclear weapons that continued into the 1980s. The SDS-influ-enced anti-apartheid movement ended only when blacks were granted political and civil rights in South Africa in 1994.

Tom Hayden and his associates in SDS were influenced by philosopher and political activist John Dewey who had been introduced to them by their philosophy professor, Arnold Kaufman of the University of Michigan. The philosophy introduced in Hayden's *Port Huron Statement* also paid homage to the work of C. Wright Mills who endorsed Dewey's belief that the United States needed a well-defined political left-wing.

Students for A Democratic Society used a number of strategies to spread their leftist views throughout the United States: marches, rallies, sit-ins, teach-ins, picketing, vigils, conferences, leafleting, and education and research projects. On college campuses where SDS chapters favored militant action, members took over university buildings, frequently targeting the Reserve Officers Training Corps (ROTC) or blocking military recruiting stations. SDS militarism at Kent State University in Ohio had tragic consequences on May 3, 1970, when students set fire to the ROTC building. In the subsequent clash between students and the national guard, four students were fatally shot. SDS members frequently took over university buildings to achieve their goals. The most successful takeover was at Columbia University in New York, where in April 1969 SDS members led a month-long strike to protest racism and the Vietnam War.

SDS activities sometimes had an extensive political impact. SDS was responsible for much of the chaos of the 1968 Democratic Convention in Chicago, Illinois, that split the Democratic Party and propelled Republican Richard Nixon to victory. SDS attempted to influence foreign policy in the late 1960s by visiting the communist-controlled countries of Cuba and North Vietnam.

Despite attempts by the so-called establishment to abolish SDS, the organization ultimately fell apart because of opposing factions within the group. The infighting was concerned with ideological battles between leftists and radicals as well as with strategies for dealing with pressure placed on SDS by the Federal Bureau of Investigation (FBI) and the desire to bring an end to the war in Vietnam. By 1969, SDS had split into the traditional left wing and the more radical and violent Weathermen.

SEE ALSO
*Volume 1 Left*: Hayden, Tom; New Left; Democratic Party.
*Volume 2 Right*: Nixon, Richard M.; Republican Party.

**BIBLIOGRAPHY**

Tom Hayden, "Port Huron Statement of the Students for A Democratic Society, 1962," http://coursesa.matrix.msu.edu (November 2004); Tom Hayden and Dick Flacks, "The Port Huron Statement," *Nation* (August 5, 2002); G. Louis Heath, ed., *Vandals in the Bomb Factory: The History and Literature of the Students for A Democratic Society* (Scarecrow Press, 1976); Robert Pardun, *Prairie Radical: A Journey Through the Sixties* (Shire Press, 2001); Roger Rosenblatt, *Coming Apart: A Memoir of the Harvard Wars of 1969* (Little, Brown, 1997); Irwin Unger, *The Movement* (Dodd Mead, 1974).

ELIZABETH PURDY, PH.D.
INDEPENDENT SCHOLAR

# Student Non-violent Coordinating Committee

THE STUDENT NON-VIOLENT Coordinating Committee (SNCC) was established in April 1960 on the campus of Shaw University in Raleigh, North Carolina. It was formed in response to an event on February 1, when a group of African American students from North Carolina A&T University were denied service at a Woolworth's lunch counter in Greensboro, North Carolina. The students refused to leave the store, and instead simply sat at the lunch counter that was designated for whites only. Their protest marked the first of many sit-in protests in the South, and by April 1960, student-led sit-ins had been held in every southern state; nearly 50,000 students having participated. Ella Baker, a prominent activist who encouraged community-based civil rights protests, urged the early participants to hold a conference in which they could better organize their movement. Thus, SNCC was formed to help bring much-needed coordination as well as a strong central leadership for the movement.

While at first the formation of SNCC received little attention, it soon became an influential group in the civil rights movement and took part in many key initiatives, such as southern Freedom Rides. Many SNCC members participated in bus journeys throughout the South, beginning in May 1961, which protested against segregation. The protesters faced violent opposition on some of these trips, and in some instances were physically beaten by angry white mobs. Nevertheless, the protesters continued to partake in Freedom Rides, and

in doing so, gained the attention of President John F. Kennedy, who intervened to ensure that the state of Alabama ensured safe passage for the freedom riders.

SNCC also began to advocate for black voting rights, a movement that would be known as the freedom ballot. In the fall of 1963, SNCC helped to organize a mock election for African American voters in Mississippi, in which 80,000 black voters took part. The theory behind the freedom ballot was to show that if given the opportunity to vote, and if oppressive voting restrictions against black voters were barred, then African Americans would use their rights. Both black and white students helped make the mock election a success, although many of the white participants faced aggression from the local white populations.

The famous March on Washington in 1963 also witnessed the influence of SNCC, especially in the speech given by one of its leaders, John Lewis. Lewis was born in Alabama into a family of sharecroppers and joined SNCC during the 1961 Freedom Rides at the age of 21. During the March on Washington, Lewis's speech was a damning condemnation of the Kennedy administration. Many black leaders, including Martin Luther King, Jr., used the march as a celebration, to show the progress of the civil rights movement, and many of these leaders shared the attitude that the Kennedy administration was friendly toward the civil rights movement. Lewis challenged the Kennedy administration, claiming that they were not doing enough to help the civil rights movement. In particular, he used his position as one of the keynote speakers to emphasize that in the Deep South, conditions were still as bad as ever and challenged the president's administration to fulfill its duty to African Americans in the Deep South.

Another of SNCC's most important leaders was Stokely Carmichael. Carmichael joined the Freedom Rides, and in 1966 was elected as chairman of SNCC. He replaced Lewis, who would later emerge as a Congressman from Georgia, and this marked a transformation in SNCC from a group that advocated a policy of integration to a policy of black self-reliance and black pride. Carmichael joined fellow civil rights activist Malcolm X in being the first leaders to use the phrase "Black Power." A rift developed between SNCC members and those of another civil rights group led by King. SNCC members began to question King's insistence on nonviolence and also grew tired of King stealing all of the attention of the civil rights movement. These feelings helped to alienate various civil rights groups and would ultimately hurt the movement by splintering power. Carmichael joined the Black Panthers in 1968 after being dismissed from SNCC for promoting black violence in urban ghettos.

SNCC's major contribution was its work to help African Americans in the Deep South. Through sit-ins, Freedom Rides, and advocating black voting and working rights in the most racist of southern states, SNCC helped to bring national attention to the oppressive conditions facing African Americans in the South. In the end, SNCC's transformation from a group associated with nonviolence to one identifying with Black Power serves as a telling representation of the 1960s civil rights movement.

### SEE ALSO

*Volume 1 Left:* Civil Rights; Carmichael, Stokely; King, Martin Luther, Jr.; Black Panthers.
*Volume 2 Right:* Segregation.

### BIBLIOGRAPHY

Rhoda Lois Blumber, *Civil Rights: The 1960s Freedom Struggle* (Twayne Publishers, 1991); Stokely Carmichael, *Black Power: The Politics of Liberation in America* (Vintage Books, 1992); Clayborne Carson, *In Struggle: SNCC and the Black Awakening of the 1960s* (Harvard University Press, 1995); Cleveland Sellers, *The River of No Return: The Autobiography of a Black Militant and the Life and Death of SNCC* (Morrow, 1973).

DAVID W. MCBRIDE
UNIVERSITY OF NOTTINGHAM, UNITED KINGDOM

# Suffragists

SUFFRAGISTS FOUGHT for the vote for women in the United States, England, New Zealand and Australia. After the American Revolution's fervor faded, the initial impulse for expansion of rights gave way to a conservative retrenchment, then prosperity brought domestic complacency—for some. Women lost the right to vote in New York in 1777, Massachusetts in 1780, New Hampshire in 1784, and everywhere except New Jersey in 1787, when the U.S. Constitutional Convention empowered the states to determine voting qualification. New Jersey took the vote from women in 1807. Between 1820 and 1880, middle- and upper-class women were stereotyped under "The Cult of Domesticity." Working-class women were forgotten.

Men thought that woman's place was in the home, but some women thought they belonged in school.

Emma Hart Willard opened the first endowed school for girls, Troy Female Seminary in New York, in 1821. In 1833, Oberlin College became the United States's first coeducational college, awarding the first degrees to women in 1841. In 1837, Mount Holyoke College (Massachusetts) opened. It would eventually be the first four-year women's college. Vassar opened in 1861, Wellesley and Smith in 1875.

Women became active in other spheres too. In 1836, Sarah Grimké began speaking on abolition and women's rights; the Congregational Church of Massachusetts issued a Pastoral Letter in 1837 against women speaking against slavery in public. The National Female Anti-Slavery Society Convention of 1837 attracted 81 delegates. Women were barred from the 1840 World Anti-Slavery Convention in London. In 1844, Lowell, Massachusetts, textile workers organized the Lowell Female Labor Reform Association, an early women's labor organization. With that prelude, the movement began in 1848 at Seneca Falls, New York. On the legislative front, Mississippi enacted the Married Woman's Property Act in 1839.

The Seneca Falls Movement, the first women's rights convention in the United States, generated the Declaration of Sentiments and Resolutions, which outlined the goals and issues of the movement. After that, women's rights advocates met regularly. When Australian suffragists organized in 1889 they demanded equal rights for women, equal justice, equality in marriage and in divorce, child custody in divorce, and equal property rights—the Seneca Falls demands.

On the periphery, Amelia Bloomer began the dress reform movement in 1850, but "serious" suffragists rejected bloomers as a potential distraction from more important women's issues. African American women such as Harriet Tubman and Sojourner Truth joined the women's movement in the 1850s. Harriet Beecher Stowe published *Uncle Tom's Cabin* in 1852, relating the brutality of slavery to a wide audience. Vulcanization, successful in 1859, made condoms reliable and family sizes shrank from 5 to 6 children to 2 to 3 children by late in the century. Civil War work gave women additional organizational experience and work skills. Similarly, the memorial societies, popular with southern white women between 1865 and 1880, forced women into the public sphere. Southern black women at the same time organized uplift organizations.

Universal suffrage was the goal of the American Equal Rights Association, formed in 1866 by Susan B. Anthony and Elizabeth Cady Stanton. The 1868 Fourteenth Amendment defined citizens and voters as male.

The Fifteenth Amendment established voting rights for black men. The Fourteenth and Fifteenth amendments split the women's rights movement in 1869. Stanton and Anthony established the radical New York-based National Woman Suffrage Association (NWSA). Lucy Stone, Henry Blackwell, and Julia Ward Howe established the more moderate American Woman Suffrage Association in Boston, Massachusetts. Because the NWSA wanted an amendment giving universal suffrage, it refused to work for ratification of the Fifteenth Amendment, causing a break with Frederick Douglass's anti-slavery movement in 1870.

Between 1870 and 1875, all attempts to claim Fourteenth Amendment rights to vote or practice law failed. Anthony attempted to vote for Ulysses Grant in 1872. She stood trial in Rochester, New York, for doing so. Sojourner Truth demanded a ballot at Grand Rapids, Michigan, but she failed too. Out west, the Wyoming Territory was organized with women's suffrage, and it became a state with suffrage in 1890. Utah Territory granted suffrage in 1870 but revoked it in 1887.

The Woman's Christian Temperance Union, significant in the fight for suffrage, came into existence in 1874. The liquor industry opposed suffrage because it feared women would vote to restrict sales of liquor. Congress defeated the first Woman Suffrage Amendment in 1878. (The same wording would be in the 1919 Amendment that finally passed both houses of Congress.)

The two suffrage organizations merged in 1890 as the National American Woman Suffrage Association (NAWSA), led by Stanton. The settlement house movement began the same year. Ellen Gates Starr and Jane Addams founded Hull House in Chicago, and within the year there would be over 100 in the United States, mostly run by women. Social work and Progressivism in general gave women experience in work and politics. Ida B. Wells's national anti-lynching campaign began in 1891. Similarly in 1893 the National Council of Jewish Women began under Hannah Greenbaum Solomon. In 1893, Colorado amended its constitution to enfranchise women.

## THE NINETEENTH AMENDMENT

Wealthy and influential, Mrs. Arthur Dodge organized the National Association Opposed to Woman Suffrage in 1911. The liquor industry and some urban political machines, southern Congressmen, and capitalists funded the countersuffrage movement, but the momentum was building nevertheless.

In 1912, the Bull Moose Progressive Party, under Theodore Roosevelt, included women's suffrage in its platform. In 1913, the Congressional Union, which became the National Women's Party in 1916, took tactics from the Women's Social and Political Union of England. The Women's Party engaged in hunger strikes, picketing of the White House, and other civil disobedience. In 1914 the National Federation of Women's Clubs, two million members strong, endorsed suffrage. In 1916, NAWSA began coordinating all local and state organizations' activities. The same year, Jeannette Rankin of Montana won a seat in the U.S. House of Representatives, the first woman to do so.

World War I diverted many women to war work but validated their claim to the vote. After the war, on August 26, 1920, the Nineteenth Amendment finally granted women the right to vote in all the United States. The NAWSA went out of existence, but it left the structure that would become the League of Women Voters. The National Women's Party continued, introducing the Equal Rights Amendment for the first time in 1923.

Although men who were liberal or radical on other issues tended to avoid supporting suffrage for women in the early 19th century, by the early 20th century, the movement to restore the right to vote for women had become part of the Progressive left's panoply of ideas. Progressives shared the view that women as voters would support the international peace movement, prohibition of alcohol, immigration restriction, child labor laws, and other social legislation and for these reasons, men in such movements tended to endorse women's suffrage.

The fact that when women did vote, they divided their allegiance between left and right in approximately the same proportions as men, and that in the United States, national achievement of women's suffrage was followed by 12 years of conservative Republican administrations, suggested that the hopes of Progressives about the leftist orientation of women voters were somewhat illusory.

**SEE ALSO**

*Volume 1 Left:* Stanton, Elizabeth Cady; Anthony, Susan B.; Mott, Lucretia; Constitutional Amendments; Voting, Unrestricted.

*Volume 2 Right:* Elitism; United States.

**BIBLIOGRAPHY**

Australian Broadcasting Corporation, "Commonwealth Suffragettes" (1998), www.abc.net.au/ola (May 2004); Susan Barber, "One Hundred Years toward Suffrage: An Overview," http://uk.geocities.com/shyxy/Suffragists.html (May 2004); Lydia Bjornlund, *Women of the Suffrage Movement* (Lucent, 2003); Kristina Dumbeck, *Leaders of Women's Suffrage* (Lucent, 2001); Laurie Mann, "History of Woman Suffrage in the United States," http://dpsinfo.com/women (June 2004).

JOHN BARNHILL, PH.D.
INDEPENDENT SCHOLAR

# Supreme Court

THE FEDERALISTS responded to Anti-Federalist attacks on the U.S. Constitution written in Philadelphia, Pennsylvania, in 1787 by publishing *The Federalist Papers*. In *Federalist Number 78*, Alexander Hamilton sought to allay fears about the new judicial branch of government by promising that "the judiciary is beyond comparison the weakest of the three departments of power … it can never attack with success either of the other two." Hamilton reasoned that since the Supreme Court, which was the only court created by the Constitution, had neither the power of the sword like the president, nor the power of the purse like Congress, the judiciary would never challenge executive or legislative authority. Despite Hamilton's assurances, the Supreme Court gained its weapon in 1803 with *Marbury v. Madison* (1 Cranch 137, 163). Chief Justice John Marshall, who many consider the greatest justice of all time, forged the weapon of judicial review for the Court, allowing it to interpret the Constitution and paving the way for the liberal decisions of the 20th century.

With *Marbury*, the court overturned the Judiciary Act of 1789, establishing the right to overturn acts of Congress. The court has also proved its willingness to restrict presidential privileges, as it did in 1974 with *United States v. Nixon* (418 U.S. 683) when the court ordered the president to release the Watergate tapes. Information on the tapes contributed to Richard Nixon's resignation the following month. In addition, Marshall also began the practice of having the justices write majority and minority opinions, promoting greater understanding of constitutional law.

After the Civil War, the Supreme Court was concerned with individual rights; but as Reconstruction faded into history, the court moved away from that position. In the *Slaughterhouse Cases* (83 U.S. 36, 1873), the court held that the principles and immunities clause of the Fourteenth Amendment did not prevent states from exercising control over the civil rights of its citizens except in the narrow circumstances of extending civil rights to former slaves. Ten years later, in the *Civil Rights Cases* (109 U.S. 3, 1883), the court stated that the Fourteenth Amendment did not apply to private actions. In 1896, with only Justice John Harlan dissenting, the court handed down one of the most disastrous decisions in its history with *Plessy v. Ferguson* (163 U.S. 537), which legitimized the "separate but equal" doctrine.

Fears over espionage and sabotage during World War I brought a series of First Amendment cases to the court through challenges to the Sedition and Espionage Acts. In the years between World War I and World War II, the court became more open to protecting speech critical of the government. By the 1930s, the focus of the court had shifted from economic to individual liberties, earning it the nickname of "guardians of liberty." Since that time, America has looked to the Supreme Court for protection of constitutional rights.

The Constitution stipulates that the Supreme Court justices are appointed for life or "good behavior." Even though they are technically responsible to no one, ideology has frequently been the most important influence on the justices. In fact, only nine justices have not belonged to the party of the president who appointed them. At no time was the influence of ideology demonstrated more clearly than with *Bush v. Gore* (00 U.S. 949, 2000) when Republican justices chose to decide the highly contested presidential election in favor of the Republican candidate, even though the challenged votes were from Florida where the candidate's brother was governor. The Chief Justice later admitted that the court had saved the election for the conservatives.

## DEFENDERS OF LIBERTY

Several justices have been recognized as great protectors of individual rights. Oliver Wendell Holmes, known as the "Great Dissenter," was a strong proponent of free expression. In order to protect the right to criticize the government while defending national security, Holmes developed the Clear and Present Danger Test *in Schenck v. United States* (249 U.S. 47, 1919). A close ally of Holmes, Louis Brandeis was dedicated to preserving democracy, dissenting on decisions that limited free speech. Brandeis argued that the same speech protections should apply in wartime as in peacetime. Harlan Fiske Stone, author of the celebrated *Footnote Four of United States v. Carolene Products*, was an ardent support of Franklin Roosevelt's New Deal. He was instrumental in early attempts to protect racial and religious minorities and to expand constitutional protections for those accused of crimes. A brilliant legal scholar, Benjamin Cordozo joined with Brandeis and Stone in their support for the New Deal. Cordozo wrote the opinion in *Powell v. Alabama* (287 U.S. 45, 1932), overturning Alabama's illegal convictions of the Scottsboro Boys.

Although he was criticized for briefly belonging to the Alabama Ku Klux Klan, Hugo Black became a staunch defender of those who could not speak for themselves. He laid the groundwork for many of the liberal decisions of the Warren Court, including the move toward incorporation of the Bill of Rights. William Douglas was legal genius and a staunch defender of civil liberties and civil rights. He was adamant about First Amendment freedoms and wrote the opinion that recognized the right to privacy in 1965.

Earl Warren liberalized the interpretation of the Constitution to protect civil rights, civil liberties, and rights of the accused. William Brennan worked closely with Warren to liberalize the interpretation of the Constitution. Brennan was instrumental in expanding the meaning of due process and other rights and liberties. The first African American to serve on the court, Thurgood Marshall was a pioneer in helping to end racial discrimination. By the time he came to the high court, he had won most cases he had argued before the court.

A moderate Republican, Harry Blackmun never set out to become the foremost defender of a woman's right to choose. During his early days on the court, Chief Justice Warren Burger assigned Blackmun to write the majority opinions in two abortion cases, in part because of his experience with medical law and in part because he was a personal friend. Blackmun's decision in *Roe v. Wade* (410 U.S. 113) established a constitutional right to abortion. Along with Blackmun, Republican John Paul Stevens became a strong defender of civil rights as the court swung to the right.

The first Democrat appointed to the court since the 1960s, Ruth Bader Ginsburg was a pioneer in extending women legal protections that had long been enjoyed by men. Ginsburg was one of the lawyers in the landmark 1971 decision that ended arbitrary sexual classifications. Also a Democrat, Stephen Breyer has been openly critical of conservative attempts to limit established constitutional protections.

## THE ROOSEVELT ERA (1933–45)

Franklin D. Roosevelt (FDR) won the election of 1932 by promising to aggressively deal with the economic cri-

sis of the Great Depression. During FDR's first hundred days, Congress cooperated with Roosevelt by passing unprecedented legislation aimed at regulating the economy and bringing quick relief to those most in need. The conservative Supreme Court was reluctant to accept such broad interpretations of federal power and opposed to Roosevelt's efforts to turn the United States into a social welfare state.

During Roosevelt's first term, only Louis Brandeis, Benjamin Cordozo, and Harlan Fiske Stone were true liberals. The court was dominated by the "Four Horsemen": conservatives James C. McReynolds, Willis Van Devanter, Pierce Butler, and George Sutherland. The deciding votes on most issues were cast by Chief Justice Charles Evans Hughes, who was known for his ability to forge a consensus from deviating opinions, and right-leaning Owen J. Roberts. Over a 16-month period, the Supreme Court found a number of New Deal programs unconstitutional by five-four votes, with Hughes siding with the liberals and Roberts with the conservatives.

FDR was so infuriated by the court that in February 1947 he developed a court-packing scheme aimed at adding a new liberal justice for every justice over 70 who refused to retire. While the plan was unsuccessful, the Supreme Court recognized its vulnerability, and both Hughes and Roberts joined the liberal bloc. In what became known as "the switch in time that saved nine," the justices began reversing themselves. Between 1937 and 1946, the court had overturned 32 previous decisions.

Since the beginning of the 20th century, there have been only two major periods of liberal judicial activism. The first took place under the leadership of Chief Justice Harlan Fiske Stone between 1941 and 1946, and the second occurred during the Warren Court between 1953 and 1969. From the time that he took office in 1933 until his death in 1945, President Roosevelt was given the opportunity to place eight justices on the bench in addition to elevating Stone to the position of Chief Justice. As Chief Justice, Stone immediately allied himself with Hugo Black, Stanley Reed, Felix Frankfurter, William Douglas, Frank Murphy, James Byrnes, Robert Jackson, and Wiley Rutledge, the eight New Dealers chosen by Roosevelt.

In *Barron v. Baltimore* (32 U.S. 243, 1833), the court had held that the Bill of Rights had no application to the states, but in 1925 in *Gitlow v. New York* (268 U.S. 652), the court had incorporated freedom of speech and press so that states were obligated to protect those rights. In 1938, Justice Stone's often quoted *Footnote Four in United States v. Carolene Products* (304 U.S. 144) began the trend toward greater protection for individual liberties by questioning whether the Fourteenth Amendment mandated "more exacting judicial scrutiny" for laws that violated individual rights.

Liberals on the Stone Court began a slow attrition of the separate but equal doctrine in response to challenges by the National Association for the Advancement of Colored People (NAACP). For instance, in *Missouri ex rel Gaines v. Canada* (305 U.S. 337, 1938), the court declared that banning black students from state law schools was a violation of the Fourteenth Amendment. In 1935, in *Grovey v. Townsend* (295 U.S. 45), the court upheld white primaries that infringed on the rights of black voters, then reversed themselves in *United States v. Classic* (313 U.S. 299, 1941).

World War II and the Cold War ushered in new fears of seditious actions. Between the late 1940s and the early 1960s, the Supreme Court upheld individual rights in only 12 of 30 cases concerning alleged subversive or communist activity under the Smith Act of 1940 and the McCarren Act of 1954. William Douglas accused his conservative colleagues of riding roughshod over the rights of communists. Ultimately, the court upheld only a single conviction under the Smith Act and declared the McCarren Act a violation of the freedom of association guaranteed by the First Amendment.

The Fifth Amendment right to counsel was addressed by the court in *Betts v. Brady* (316 U.S. 455, 1942), in which the justices held that states were required to provide lawyers for those who could not afford them only under limited circumstances such as illiteracy, mental deficiency, and racial prejudice. In *Skinner v. Oklahoma* (316 U.S. 535, 1942), the court found an Oklahoma statute unconstitutional that mandated sterilization for "compulsory criminals," holding that the right to reproduce was a fundamental right.

The World War II decision to uphold the internment of Japanese Americans who lived on the west coast has been seen as a serious blot on the reputation of an otherwise liberal court. In 1941 in *Korematsu v. United States* (319 U.S. 432) and *Hirabayashi v. United States* (320 U.S. 81), the court chose to support Roosevelt rather than upholding civil liberties. Because the country was at war, First Amendment freedoms were vulnerable as the justices vacillated between the Preferred Position where those freedoms dominated all others to the Balancing Doctrine that weighed competing freedoms against one another. In 1940, in *Minersville School District v. Gobitis* (310 U.S. 586), the court upheld the right of Pennsylvania to force two children of the

Jehovah's Witnesses faith to salute the American flag, even though it was against their religious beliefs. Nearly 200 newspapers around the country joined Justice Stone in outraged disagreement. In 1943, in *West Virginia Board of Education v. Barnette* (319 U.S. 624), the court reversed itself.

Chief Justice Stone died in 1946, and President Harry Truman nominated Fred Vinson to replace him. Both the Stone and Vinson Courts had leaned toward incremental changes. When *Brown v. Board of Education* (347 U.S. 483) first came to the attention of the Supreme Court, the justices seemed unsure of how to deal with the situation. Even though the majority believed that the separate but equal doctrine was unconstitutional, the justices were loath to hand down a decision that invited open rebellion and potential violence. Justice Vinson died on September 8, 1953, leaving it to the Warren Court to hand down the decision that changed the very fabric of life in the United States.

## THE WARREN COURT (1953–69)

A military hero, Dwight Eisenhower was courted by both Democrats and Republicans. While he ran as a Republican, Eisenhower was never highly partisan. Given the opportunity to name a new chief justice in 1953, Eisenhower chose popular California Governor Earl Warren. Eisenhower later admitted that the Warren nomination was the worst decision of his presidency. Republicans accused Warren of catering to the interests of blacks, desegregationists, criminals, communists, aliens, atheists, free speechers, pornographers, and other "enemies" of the United States. Constitutional scholars, on the other hand, have called Warren the greatest chief justice since Marshall. Warren revolutionized the Supreme Court, turning it into an active body that expanded civil rights and civil liberties and made virtually the entire Bill of Rights applicable to the states.

Warren believed that the reapportionment decisions were the most important of his tenure on the court because they affected all Americans. Before the federal courts became involved in the redistricting process that takes place after every census, many states drew districts that were roughly equal geographically. The result was that urban districts where the population was greatest were vastly underrepresented while rural districts were overrepresented. As a result, politicians who represented rural districts had a disproportionate amount of power. The Warren Court implemented the concept of one-person-one-vote that had been devel-

*The liberal Supreme Court Justice Earl Warren instituted reforms that revolutionized criminal law in the United States.*

oped by Hugo Black in 1946, mandating that districts be drawn according to population, not geography. In 1962, *Baker v. Carr* (369 U.S. 186) applied the one-person-one-vote concept to elections for state houses. Two years later, the concept was applied to state senate elections in *Reynolds v. Sims* (377 U.S. 533) and to congressional districts in *Wesberry v. Connecticut* (376 U.S. 1).

While there is little doubt of the significance of the reapportionment decisions, most people believe that *Brown v. Board of Education* (347 U.S. 483, 1954) was the most significant decision of the Warren Court. Warren used his considerable leadership abilities to forge a unanimous decision in *Brown* that struck down the separate but equal doctrine in public schools and opened the door to overturning discrimination in all aspects of American life. In response to defiance and open rebellion, a series of subsequent decisions changed the "all but deliberate speed" of integration in *Brown* to "now" and gave federal courts the authority to oversee the desegregation process. Critics insisted that the Supreme Court had no right to make law, and the right-wing John Birch Society led an effort to "impeach Earl Warren."

By the 1960s, liberals on the court generally claimed victory on most cases involving individual rights. That is not to say that all liberals supported all decisions. In *Griswold v. Connecticut* (381 U.S. 479), for example, Hugo Black dissented from carving the right to privacy from several amendments by calling it "illegitimate judicial activism." In *Griswold*, the majority drew on "The Right to Privacy," an article coauthored by Louis Brandeis in 1919 for the *Harvard Law Review*, and the Brandeis dissent to *Olmstead v. United States* (277 U.S. 438, 1928) to determine that the right to privacy was derived from the right of the "inviolate personality," the right of individuals to be free from government interference. Before 1965, the court had only acknowledged the right to privacy in the limited areas of slander/libel and search and seizure cases, but *Griswold* signaled an openness to the idea that all individual rights were not specifically stated in the Constitution.

Civil liberties were also greatly expanded under the Warren Court. For example, *New York Times v. Sullivan* (376 U.S. 254, 1964) upheld the right of individuals to criticize government officials without fear of being charged with slander/libel. In 1969, in *Tinker v. Des Moines* (393 U.S. 503), the court upheld the essential right of symbolic speech as a means of political protest. A series of cases on separation of church and state led the court to ban required recitation of either the Lord's Prayer or a nonsectarian prayer, daily Bible readings, the posting of the Ten Commandments, and mandated teaching of the creation theory in public schools. In *Torcaso v. Watkins* (367 U.S. 488, 1961), the court struck down a Maryland law that required political candidates to swear to a belief in God. The court also dealt with freedom of expression in a number of significant decisions, including an attempt to define obscenity in *Roth v. United States* (354 U.S. 476, 1957), after which the court judged material on a case-by-case basis to look for "redeeming social value." In 1969, the court held in *Stanley v. Georgia* (394 U.S. 557) that individuals have a right to read anything they wish within in the privacy of their own homes.

No other court in history has done more to revolutionize criminal law than the Warren Court. Warren was in a unique position to understand the entire process of criminal law because he had spent 13 years as a district attorney and four years as an attorney general before becoming governor of California. The Warren Court was diligent in strengthening the rights of the accused. *Elkins v. United States* (364 U.S. 206, 1960), for example, banned federal agents from using evidence illegally seized by state agents. In 1961, in *Mapp v. Ohio*

(367 U.S. 643), the court applied the "exclusionary rule" to the states, stipulating that unconstitutionally obtained evidence could not be used against the accused in court. In 1965, the court used the case of a Florida indigent named Clarence Earl Gideon to clarify the Sixth Amendment's guarantee of the right to counsel. Overturning *Betts v. Brady* (316 U.S. 455, 1942), the court held in *Gideon v. Wainwright* (372 U.S. 335) that states were required to provide attorneys for those who could not afford them in all felony cases.

The court's 1966 decision in *Miranda v. Arizona* (384 U.S. 436) proved to be one of the most controversial because it led to the Miranda Warnings, requiring law officers to explain rights to those undergoing "custodial interrogation." The Miranda Warning states: "You have the right to remain silent. Anything you say can and will be used against you in a court of law. You have the right to speak to an attorney, and to have an attorney present during any questioning. If you cannot afford a lawyer, one will be provided for you at government expense."

Throughout the 1960s, the Warren Court continued to incorporate constitutional protections, making them applicable to state criminal trials. In *Malloy v. Hogan* (378 U.S. 1, 1964), the court held that the Fourteenth Amendment made the Fifth Amendment's protection from self-incrimination applicable to the states. The following year in *Griffin v. California* (380 U.S. 609), the court held that judges and attorneys were prohibited from negative comments about a defendant's refusal to testify. In 1965, the court applied the Sixth Amendment right to be confronted with a witness to state courts in *Pointer v. Texas* (380 U.S. 400). The right to a speedy trial was applied two years later in *Klopfer v. North Carolina* (386 U.S. 213). Fourth Amendment protections from "unreasonable searches and seizures" were clarified in *Katz v. United States* (389 U.S. 347, 351, 1968) and *Terry v. Ohio* (392 U.S. 1, 1968), and *Duncan v. Louisiana* (391 U.S. 145, 1968) required states to provide jury trials for all defendants accused of serious crimes. On Earl Warren's last day on the bench, the court applied the ban on double jeopardy in criminal trials to states in *Benton v. Maryland* (395 U.S. 784, 1969).

## THE BURGER COURT (1969–86)

Nixon entered office in 1969 with a concrete plan to overturn the liberal reforms of the Warren Court. In May, Lyndon Johnson's crony, civil libertarian Abe Fortas, was forced to leave the bench when it was discov-

ered that he had accepted a perpetual annuity to interfere in a Securities and Exchange Commission (SEC) case. Warren resigned due to illness, and Nixon appointed conservative Burger as chief justice and appointed Blackmun, Louis Powell, and William Rehnquist to fill other vacancies. Although Burger agreed with Nixon's conservatism in theory, he enjoyed being on the winning side, frequently switching sides to join the majority. As a result, the Burger Court did little to undo the legal decisions of the Warren Court. The Burger Court forged its own legal history in 1973 with its landmark decision in *Roe v. Wade* (410 U.S. 113) that legalized abortion.

The Burger Court also further expanded the scope of the equal protection clause of the Fourteenth Amendment in a number of race and sex discrimination cases. For example, in 1971, in *Reed v. Reed* (404 U.S. 71), the court overturned arbitrary classifications based on sex, stating that such designations were "subject to scrutiny under the Equal Protection Clause." Two years later in *Frontiero v. Richardson* (411 U.S. 677), a minority unsuccessfully called for sexual classifications to be treated with the same strict scrutiny given to race cases. In 1976 in *Craig Boren* (429 U.S. 190), the court stated that all classifications based on sex "must serve important governmental objectives and must be substantially related to achievement of those objectives."

Liberals on the Warren Court also led their colleagues into what Justice Brennan called "the opening shot in the modern due process revolution." Before *Goldberg v. Kelly* (397 U.S. 254, 1970), the court had interpreted the right of due process to mean that individuals were entitled to prior notification and hearings before rights were terminated only in cases involving personal property rights. The new meaning of due process extended rights to administrative hearings, giving individuals the right to be heard and to defend themselves. *Wisconsin v. Constantineau* (400 U.S. 433, 1971) extended due process before names could be posted on public lists of habitual drinkers. *Richardson v. Wright* (405 U.S. 208, 1972) mandated the right to oral defense and cross-examination in disability hearings. *Morrissey v. Brewer* (408 U.S. 471, 1972) applied due process before paroles could be revoked, and *Gibson v. Berryhill* (411 U.S. 564, 1973) applied the right before state boards could revoke professional licenses. *Weinberger v. Hynson, Westcott, and Dunning, Inc.* (412 U.S. 609, 1973) required due process before the Food and Drug Administration could remove approval for a new drug. In *Arnett v. Kennedy* (416 U.S. 134, 1974), the court extended due process to federal employees facing termination. By the following year, however, the due process revolution was over.

The Warren court had taken the position that the Eighth Amendment's ban on "cruel and unusual punishment" applied to the death penalty. Brennan and Marshall, in particular, were ardent critics of the death penalty and fought to have it declared unconstitutional. Three years after Warren retired, liberals on the Burger Court gathered enough votes in *Furman v. Georgia* (408 U.S. 238) to overturn the death penalty as written on the grounds that it violated the Eighth and Fourteenth Amendments, effectively overturning death penalty laws in 42 states. In 1976, the court accepted rewritten death penalty laws in *Gregg v. Georgia* (428 U.S. 153, 1976), *Proffitt v. Florida* (428 U.S. 242), and *Jurek v. Texas* (428 U.S. 262), agreeing that the new laws met the *Furman* standards by abolishing "arbitrary" decisions by juries in death penalty cases. The Burger Court subsequently backtracked from the Warren Court's position and declared that the Eighth Amendment's ban on "cruel and unusual punishment" prohibited only "barbaric" forms of punishment and not the death penalty when constitutionally applied.

## THE REHNQUIST COURT (1986–)

By the beginning of the 1990s, as liberals on the court grew older and retired and with no liberal appointees since the 1960s, George H.W. Bush was able to complete the trend started by Ronald Reagan and shape a conservative court. Bush appointees David Souter and Clarence Thomas joined Chief Justice William Rehnquist, named to the Court by Richard Nixon in 1972 and elevated to Chief Justice by Ronald Reagan in 1986, and Reagan appointees Sandra Day O'Connor, Antonin Scalia, and Anthony Kennedy. Although a Democrat, Byron White usually voted with the conservative bloc. Ironically, the new liberal bloc of the court was made up of John Paul Stevens, a Republican nominated by Gerald Ford in 1975, and Harry Blackmun, a Republican nominated by Richard Nixon in 1970. When Stevens was accused of becoming more liberal, he insisted that his position had not changed. Stevens said it only appeared so because the court had become so conservative.

Justice William Brennan led the liberal wing of the Supreme Court in holding firm for almost 34 years on the court, standing up for civil rights, women's rights, abortion, religious freedom, freedom of expression, criminal rights, and rights of the poor. His liberal lead-

*Conservative Supreme Court Justice William Rehnquist led renewed efforts to undo Warren Court decisions.*

ership was particularly significant between 1972 and 1990, as Republican presidents tried to reshape the court. Brennan argued that government interference in individual rights was acceptable only when the government could establish a compelling reason for doing so. He was also instrumental in the decisions of the conservative Rehnquist Court that upheld the right of Americans to burn the U.S. flag without prosecution and in standing by the "wall of separation" between church and state.

Liberals predicted that the conservative Rehnquist Court would overturn all the landmark civil liberties and civil rights cases of the Warren Court and the abortion decisions of the Burger Court. Both Reagan and Bush had used views on abortions as the "litmus test" for appointment to the court. Harry Blackmun, the author of *Roe v. Wade*, was so sure that his colleagues would back away from abortion rights in *Webster v. Reproductive Health Services* (492 U.S. 490, 1989) that he wrote in an unpublished dissent: "I rue this day. I rue the violence that has been done to the liberty and equality of women. I rue the violence that has been done to our legal fabric and to the integrity of the Constitution. I rue the inevitable loss of public esteem for this court." Although the court did turn control of abortion rights over to the states in *Webster*, it stopped short of overturning *Roe*. In *Planned Parenthood of Southeastern Pennsylvania v. Casey* (505 U.S. 833, 1992), Sandra Day O'Connor formed an alliance with David Souter and Anthony Kennedy to save *Roe v. Wade* (410 U.S. 113).

Conservative justices have succeeded in limiting the effects of desegregation rulings, restricting the application of affirmative action, and constraining criminal rights. Rehnquist has repeatedly led his conservative colleagues in trying to overturn *Miranda v. Arizona*; and in *United States v. Salerno* (481 U.S. 739, 1987), the conservative court upheld legislation that gave police the authority to hold accused criminals indefinitely without a trial based on the probability that other crimes may be committed. In a scathing dissent, Thurgood Marshall and William Brennan accused their conservative colleagues of disregarding "basic principles of justice ... established centuries ago and enshrined beyond the reach of governmental interference in the Bill of Rights."

The election of Bill Clinton in 1992 gave liberals two new seats on the court when Byron White and William Brennan retired. The balance of power shifted toward the center as Clinton appointees Ruth Bader Ginsburg and Stephen Breyer joined Stevens to make up a new liberal-leaning bloc, which was often joined by Reagan appointee David Souter, leaving centrist Sandra Day O'Connor to cast the deciding vote that saved many liberal decisions of the last several decades.

Liberals have charged that since September 11, the Bush administration has been rewriting constitutional law. In April 2004, the court heard arguments on a series of challenges to the USA Patriot Act (P.L. 107-56), which allowed the Bush team to ride roughshod over constitutional protections for those accused of so-called terrorist crimes. Chief Justice William Rehnquist went on record in *All the Laws but One: Civil Liberties in Wartime* that civil liberties should be suspended in wartimes. Liberal Stephen Breyer, on the other hand, contends that the Constitution is always relevant, particularly during emergencies.

**SEE ALSO**

*Volume 1 Left:* Civil Rights; Civil Liberties; Abortion/Pro-Choice; United States; Liberalism.

*Volume 2 Right:* Anti-Abortion/Pro-Life; Conservatism; Reagan Ronald; Nixon, Richard M.

**BIBLIOGRAPHY**

Joan Biskupic and Elder Witt, *The Supreme Court and Individual Rights* (Congressional Quarterly, 1997); David J. Bodenhamer, "Lost Vision, The Bill of Rights and Criminal Procedure in American History," David E. Kyvig, ed., *Unintended Consequences of Constitutional Amendments* (University of Georgia Press, 2000); Clare Cushman, ed., *The Supreme Court Justices: Illustrated Biographies, 1789–1993* (Congressional Quarterly, 1993); Michael O. Davis and Hunter R. Clark, *Thurgood Marshall: Warrior at the Bar, Rebel on the Court* (Carol, 1992); Charles Fried, *Saying What the Law Is: The Constitution in the Supreme Court* (Harvard University Press, 2004); Joel B. Grossman and Richard S. Wells, *Constitutional Law and Judicial Policy Making* (Longman, 1988); Alexander Hamilton, "Federalist Number 78, The Federalist Papers," www.constitution.org (May 2004); Peter Irons, *Brennan v. Rehnquist: The Battle for the Constitution* (Alfred A. Knopf, 1994); Peter Irons and Stephanie Guition, *May It Please the Court: The Most Significant Oral Arguments Made before the Court since 1955* (New Press, 1993); Leo Katcher, *Earl Warren: A Political Biography* (McGraw Hill, 1967); Philip B. Kurland, *Politics: The Constitution and the Warren Court* (University of Chicago, 1970); Frederick P. Lewis, *The Context of Judicial Activism: The Endurance of the Warren Court Legacy in a Conservative Age* (Rowman and Littlefield, 1999); William E. Leuchtenburg, *The Supreme Court Reborn: The Constitutional Revolution in the Age of Roosevelt* (Oxford University Press, 1995); Walter F. Murphy, "The Constitution and the Legacy of Justice William O. Douglas," D. Grier Stephenson, Jr., ed., *An Essential Safeguard: Essays on the United States Supreme Court* (Greenwood, 1991); David M. O'Brien, *Constitutional Law and Politics, Volume Two: Civil Rights and Civil Liberties* (Norton, 1991); David M. O'Brien, *Storm Center: The Supreme Court in American Politics* (Norton, 1990); Jack Harrison Pollack, *Earl Warren: The Judge Who Changed America* (Prentice-Hall, 1979); Joshua Rosenkranz and Bernard Schwartz, eds., *Reason and Passion: Justice Brennan's Enduring Influence* (Norton, 1997); James F. Simon, *The Center Holds: The Power Struggle inside the Rehnquist Court* (Simon and Schuster, 1995); James F. Simon, "Conflict and Leadership on the United States Supreme Court from Marshall to Rehnquist," D. Grier Stephenson, Jr., ed., *An Essential Safeguard: Essays on the United States Supreme Court* (Greenwood, 1991); "The Supreme Court and 9/11," *New York Times* (November 5, 2003).

ELIZABETH PURDY, PH.D.
INDEPENDENT SCHOLAR

# Sweden

DURING THE 20th century, Sweden was regarded as the archetype of the progressive industrialized country. Managing to find a true third way between capitalism and socialism, Sweden developed one of the world's highest standards of livings, while at the same time achieving a relatively high degree of egalitarianism among its population. The main means of achieving this was a cooperative nature among Swedes and the Social Democratic Party, which has ruled the country from 1932 to date in 2004, with the exception of the periods from 1976 to 1982 and 1991 to 1994.

Sweden is a constitutional monarchy and an ethnically homogeneous state that has produced public policy that seems to depend on certain commonly held values. As Donald Hancock notes, a large majority of Swedes appear to have a high level of respect for constitutionalism and law, veneration for established political institutions, receptivity to institutional and policy reform, and shared values of moderation and pragmatism. The 20th century was a tumultuous period in Europe, with ideologies like fascism and state socialism and everything in between competing for adherents, but none of these movements disrupted the Swedish consensus.

As Henry Milner has argued, social democracy is a distinctive system of human relations, different in degree from "competitive capitalism," exemplified by the United States, and "state socialism," still found in countries such as Cuba, North Korea, and a few others. As such, in Sweden it has been based on the principles of economic well-being, the importance of work, social solidarity, democracy, participation, and access to information.

Sweden's great achievement has been to implement a generous welfare state, based on high rates of taxation, and yet preserve a dynamic capitalist economy. Sweden's very existence and success seem to fly in the face of Anglo-American received wisdom regarding the desirability of a limited role for government along with an unregulated market economy. Of course, Sweden developed all of the usual welfare state policies in the 20th century, including "free" elementary, secondary, and post-secondary education, publicly funded healthcare, family support programs, public pensions, worker's compensation, and so on.

But perhaps Sweden's real success has been in its fully developed welfare state instead of the half-measures often found elsewhere in the world's economically advanced countries. Sweden has, for decades, had a high-wage policy, based on the idea that as a country of 8.8 million people, Sweden would drive up wages and minimize low-wage jobs, as a basis for building a wealthy society. To do this, the country would be highly engaged in the world economy as a trading partner. Sweden also developed an active labor market policy rather than the more passive ones found elsewhere in much of Europe and North America. This meant that when a traditional industry declined and people were thrown out of work, the state would not just settle for paying unemployment benefits or social assistance (passive support). Rather, the state would spend more money, not just to cushion the family that had lost work, but to retrain the worker so that she could find work in a "sunrise industry." With a high degree of social solidarity, the idea that a certain percentage of the population would be "written off" as unemployable or useless was simply not acceptable. Unlike many other countries, Swedish policies encourage work and do not provide perverse incentives to inactivity.

But Sweden recognized in the 1940s that it was in everyone's interest to avoid inflation, or the price increases that come with a currency declining in value. The union movement also recognized that it was not in the long-term interests of working people to hold on to existing jobs in declining industries. For its part, the government targeted spending in areas of high unemployment, through public works and special programs, rather than overheating the entire country's economy at the long-term cost of inflation and debt. The Swedish government also acted as referee with the national federations of labor and employers in a process of country-wide collective bargaining. This gave Swedish workers and employers clear future expectations, and it gave the country a remarkably strike-free economic environment.

More recently, there is some question whether the Social Democratic Party (SDP) still represents the left of the Swedish spectrum. According to its critics, the SDP has moved in a neoliberal direction, along with British Labor, the German Social Democrats, and others. The two cases that encourage this view are the recent experience with the SDP proposal for worker investment funds, as well as the failed 2003 referendum proposal to adopt the euro, the currency of the European Union, as the currency for Sweden. In the late 1970s, the Social Democrats developed a policy to encourage worker investment funds, which were intended to allow the working class to eventually take over ownership control of Swedish business. This has been perhaps the greatest controversy in the last 25 years, since the nonsocialist parties have opposed this, and they have used their brief periods in power to undermine the policy. These funds, designed to allow working people to peacefully take over private means of production, have never developed as proposed.

Since the 1980s, the Social Democrats have been reluctant to push any further in the development of the welfare state. In recent years, the Social Democrats have abandoned centralized wage negotiations, they have put more emphasis on monetary policy, and they supported (along with business interests) the unsuccessful "Yes" side in the 2003 euro referendum. Notably, much of organized labor, environmentalists, supporters of the welfare state, and opponents of globalization were lined up on the "No" side and they carried the day.

**SEE ALSO**

Volume 1 Left: Social Democracy; Socialism.
Volume 2 Right: Capitalism; Laissez-Faire; Sweden.

**BIBLIOGRAPHY**

Donald M. Hancock, "Sweden," Politics in Europe: An Introduction (Chatham House Publishers, 2003); Eric Lindstrom, The Swedish Parliamentary System: How Responsibilities Are Divided and Decisions Are Made (The Swedish Institute, 1982); Gregg M. Olsen, The Politics of the Welfare State: Canada, Sweden and the United States (Oxford University Press, 2002); David E. Woodsworth, Social Security and National Policy: Sweden, Yugoslavia, Japan (McGill-Queens University Press, 1977).

GEOFFREY R. MARTIN
MOUNT ALLISON UNIVERSITY, CANADA

# Switzerland

OVERSHADOWED BY the successes of the right-wing Swiss People's Party, the political left in Switzerland struggles to avoid increasing marginalization. As champions of working-class interests, generous welfare protections, gender equality, and environmental protection, the Swiss left resembles many of the socialist, social democratic, and ecologist forces found in most continental European polities. Although sharing some characteristics with their ideological brethren elsewhere, the Swiss left's successes and frustrations are nevertheless intimately linked to Switzerland's unique institutional configuration.

The primary vehicle for leftist interests in Switzerland is the Social Democratic Party (SP), which began to emerge from the labor movement in 1888 some 40 years after the country's founding. For much of its early history, the SP stood among the ranks of the parliamentary opposition. After the tumultuous General Strike of 1918, the Swiss House of Representatives introduced proportional representation, which helped the Social Democrats rapidly increase their seats and power. In 1943, the SP rose to become the single strongest party in parliament and for the first time captured a seat in the governing cabinet. Having earned the left an important entry into Swiss government, the SP then parlayed its way into the country's renowned "Magic Formula" in 1959. Forming the foundation of Switzerland's brand of consensus politics, this "2:2:2:1 formula" institutionalized the distribution of seats on the country's seven-person governing Federal Council (with a rotating presidency). In an arrangement that would endure for more than 40 years, the Social Democrats claimed two cabinet portfolios, as did the liberal Radical Democratic Party (FDP) and the conservative Christian Democratic Party (CVP); the avowedly right-wing Swiss People's Party (SVP) laid claim to a single portfolio under the formula.

In the 1980s, popular support for the Social Democrats waned, but the party reemerged as the country's strongest in the 1995 elections. In subsequent elections, the SP battled the increasingly extremist SVP for political primacy, ultimately falling behind the People's Party at the 2003 parliamentary elections that brought an end to 44 years of the Magic Formula (the SVP and CVP reversed roles, with the SVP holding two governing seats and the CVP but one). In 2003, the SP retained the support of only 23.4 percent of Swiss voters. As might be anticipated after a party witnesses a diminution in power, introspection and leadership crises have followed the 2003 electoral debacle.

In a European context, Switzerland's left wing as represented by the Social Democrats looks more like the Socialists in neighboring France than it does Britain's Labor Party or the Social Democratic Party of Germany. While traditional working-class parties in both Britain and Germany have moderated their ideological and policy positions and gravitated toward the center of the political spectrum, the Swiss left (as is the case in France as well) retains close ties with its traditional electoral constituencies and convictions. This can largely be explained by the country's institutional design, which allows the "big four" parties to take radical positions without being relegated to the opposition benches. The apparent permanence in power generated by Switzerland's consensual politics, however, also has its drawbacks—once in government left-wing members of the Federal Council are ultimately bound by the principle of collegiality, whereby the cabinet speaks with a single voice. Because only two of the seven Federal Council seats are likely ever filled by left-wing politicians, the Ministers are consistently pressured to endorse a more conservative public policy.

The divergence between a more ideologically pure party in the electorate and a more compromising party in the government is one of the reasons for the Swiss left's relative political decline. Another reason is simply that Switzerland is a comparatively wealthy country. The working class—a staple of left-wing support—has shrunk dramatically in the last half century and is today predominantly comprised of immigrants who have no right to vote. Joined by several much smaller forces on the political left (namely the communist Labor Party and the Greens), the Social Democrats face the challenge of countering the high-profile policies and pronouncements of the ascendant right-wing Swiss People's Party. Trumpeting their three central values—social justice, solidarity, and quality of life—the Swiss left seeks the preservation of social entitlements, policies to combat mounting unemployment, and eventual closer ties with the European Union.

### SEE ALSO

*Volume 1 Left:* Social Democracy; Socialism.
*Volume 2 Right:* Switzerland.

### BIBLIOGRAPHY

Michael Butler et al., eds., *The Making of Modern Switzerland, 1848–1998* (Palgrave Macmillan, 2000); Clive Church, *The Politics and Government of Switzerland* (Palgrave Macmillan, 2004); Hans Daalder, *Party Systems in Denmark, Austria, Switzerland, the Netherlands and Belgium* (St. Martin's, 1987); Carol Schmid, *Conflict and Consensus in Switzerland* (University of California Press, 1981).

WILLIAM M. DOWNS, PH.D.
GEORGIA STATE UNIVERSITY

# Symbionese Liberation Army

THE SYMBIONESE Liberation Army (SLA) began with Donald de Freeze, when he escaped from Soledad State Prison on March 5, 1973. De Freeze had been exposed to the progressive ideas of the Venceremos movement, whose name had been inspired by the hero of the Cuban revolution, the Argentine physician Ernesto "Che" Guevara. Thus, rather than being a mere thuggish group, as often portrayed, de Freeze's group was in keeping with the thought of the popular liberation movement in the Western Hemisphere. By now, de Freeze portrayed himself as "Field Marshal Cinque."

However, unlike the Cuban revolution and Guevara's ill-fated later Bolivian mission, where he was killed in October 1967, the SLA planned on a campaign of urban guerrilla war. On November 6, 1973, they killed the school superintendent of Oakland, California, Dr. Marcus Foster, for attempting to issue identity cards to the students. Foster had come from Philadelphia, Pennsylvania, where he had served as a caring school principal in one of the "inner city" schools. The SLA condemned his plan as "fascist."

On January 10, 1974, SLA members Joe Remiro and Russ Little were put on trial for the Foster killing, but only Remiro would eventually be found guilty of the crime. He was sentenced to life imprisonment. From the point of view of the progressive left, the execution-style slaying of Foster, who had devoted his career to helping poor youth, was incomprehensible. Even the Black Panthers and the Weather Underground, similar radical groups, condemned this political killing. Marshal Cinque had evidently never read what the Venceremos's hero, Guevara, had written: "the struggle is politico-military; so it must develop; so it must be understood."

After the killing of Foster, the SLA moved from its "safe house," the dwelling in Clayton, California. On January 11, 1974, the day after Remiro and Little were arrested for complicity in the Foster murder, the SLA left the house and attempted to burn it down to destroy evidence. However, the effort failed, and police discovered writings hinting at the proposed kidnapping of Patty Hearst, the heiress to the William Randolph Hearst publishing fortune.

Later, following the tactics of the Italian Red Brigade, the SLA staged a media sensation when it kidnapped Patty Hearst on February 4, 1974. Hearst's fiance, Steven Weed, was badly beaten during the attack. During her kidnapping, either through a genuine revolutionary conversion or some form of identification with her jailers, Hearst became a new recruit into the SLA as "Tanya." On April 15, 1974, in film shown to millions of television viewers in the United States, Hearst, now known as "Tanya," was seen on a bank videotape taking part in the armed robbery of the San Francisco branch of the Hibernia Bank.

On May 16, 1974, Bill Harris, his wife Emily, and Tanya traded fire with police outside Mel's Sporting Goods in Los Angeles. Although they made good their escape, they left behind their Volkswagen. In the Volkswagen, the police found the address of the new "safe house" in the Watts section of Los Angeles where Cinque was now living. The following afternoon, the authorities attacked the house at 1466 East 54th Street. The local population stated that—in spite of police assertions to the contrary—no effort was given to evacuate the people when a virtual military operation was now under way. All SLA members in the house, including Cinque, were killed. Watching on television as the house caught fire, Hearst recalled: "that final conflagration ... completely devastated me."

For a year, the FBI sought Hearst and the surviving members of the SLA. During that time, part of which was spent in a farm house in rural Pennsylvania, they had been sheltered by what had become an "underground railroad" of sympathizers for radicals in the United States. On April 21, 1975, Hearst took part in the SLA's revived assault, being involved in the robbery of the Crocker National Bank in Carmichael, California. During the robbery, a bank customer, Myrna Opsahl, was killed. Then, on September 18, 1975, Hearst and Wendy Yoshimura were arrested. Although sentenced to seven years for her participation in the Hibernia Bank robbery, President Jimmy Carter commuted Hearst's sentence to time served in January 1979.

Of the other members of the SLA, Emily and Bill Harris served eight years for their role in the kidnapping of Patty Hearst. Over the years, other SLA members emerged from the radical underground. Kathleen Soliah, who had lived under the alias of Sara Jane Olson, pled guilty in her trial on November 6, 2001. Her brother Steven Soliah had been acquitted in 1975 during a trial for bank robbery.

Then, the survivors were brought to trial in the murder of Myrna Opsahl. According to the *New York Times* (February 15, 2003), in an "agreement with prosecutors to each plead guilty to second-degree murder were William Harris, 58; his former wife, Emily, 56, who remarried and is now known as Emily Montague; Sara Jane Olson, 56; and Michael Bortin, 54. Judge Thomas M. Cecil of Superior Court sentenced Ms. Montague, who fired the shotgun that killed Mrs. Opsahl, to eight years, and Mr. Harris to seven years. Mr. Bortin and Ms. Olson were each sentenced to six years."

**SEE ALSO**
*Volume 1 Left:* United States.
*Volume 2 Right:* Hearst, William Randolph.

**BIBLIOGRAPHY**
"The Symbionese Liberation Army," www.claykeck.com (July 2004); George Lavan, ed., *Che Guevara Speaks: Selected Speeches and Writings* (Grove Press, 1967); "Ex-SLA Fugitive Reaffirms Guilty Plea," MSNBC, www.rickross.com (July 2004); Patricia C. (Patty) Hearst and Alvin Moscow, *Every Secret Thing* (Doubleday, 1982); "4 in Radical Group of 70's Are Sentenced in Murder," *New York Times*, February 15, 2003, www.rickross.com (July 2004); "Ernesto Che Guevara," www.che.islagrande.cu. (July 2004).

JOHN F. MURPHY, JR.
AMERICAN MILITARY UNIVERSITY

# Syndicalism

SYNDICALISM IS A politico-economic philosophy that flourished among French laborers prior to World War I. Syndicalism is taken from the French word for labor union, *syndicat*. Syndicalism was influential in France from the 1890s to the 1920s as the philosophy of a militant trade union movement.

There are several theoretical roots to the philosophy of syndicalism. In 1840, Pierre Joseph Proudhon, who was an impoverished printer's helper, wrote a short pamphlet, *Qu'est-ce que la Propriete? (What Is Property?)*. Proudhon declared that "property is theft." He wrote numerous works as a theorist of poverty and a champion of the poorer classes. Proudhon was the first political theorist to call himself an anarchist. In addition, he believed that control of the means of production should be in the hands of workers.

Another important theoretical root is the sociopolitical theory of George Sorel. Sorel espoused syndicalism but sought to combine it with anarchism into anarcho-syndicalism. This was syndicalism with violence added to achieve its goal. In 1908, Sorel wrote *Reflections on Violence*, in which he advocated using strikes and other forms of revolutionary labor activity. Syndicalist philosophy taught that the state should be abolished so that groups of producers could create self-governing cooperative enterprises run by the workers. To achieve this goal, a strategy of noncooperation with the capitalist-state system with opposing direct action should be followed. Syndicalists rejected collective bargaining or engaging in political activity to affect labor policies. Election reforms were seen as a form of revisionism or betrayal of the coming syndicalist anarcho-utopia.

In syndicalist theory, there would come a time when socioeconomic chaos would lead to the general strike. All of the workers would go on strike; then industrial capitalism and the state would collapse in just a few days. The workers, after abolishing both capitalism and the state, would gather into a peaceful anarchic society with workers' groups as the only form of organization.

From about 1890 until 1914, syndicalism was at its peak of influence in France and other countries. In 1906, the Charter of Amiens was issued with the basic claims of Syndicalism. After World War I, syndicalism declined in France as many workers preferred the "political" option of collective bargaining to revolutionary direct action. Also, many syndicalists joined the French Communist Party. Syndicalism has continued to influence the French labor movement ever since in limited ways.

In 1905, syndicalist philosophy guided the founding of the Industrial Workers of the World in Chicago, Illinois, by members of the Western Federation of Mines and 42 other labor organizations. Leaders included Eugene V. Debs and William D. Haywood. Nicknamed the "Wobblies," the movement spread to Canada, Australia, and elsewhere. Its opposition to American engagement in World War I led to its suppression. By the 1930s, it had fewer than 10,000 members. In the 1990s, only 1,000 or so remained. In 1912, the Syndicalist League of North America was organized in Chicago by William Z. Foster and Earl C. Ford. Together, they wrote *Syndicalism* (1912). This organization accepted shop-floor organization and direct action like the Wobblies. However, they advocated the strategy of boring within existing unions rather than the dual union approach of the Wobblies. It appealed most to those with anarchist tendencies. Syndicalism was very influential in Spain and Portugal. From there, it spread to the Latin American countries. Benito Mussolini's fascism was supposed to have been influenced by syndicalism, but this view is wrongly based on a brief association in 1915. Syndicalism appears today in many places at the margins of the labor movement or in association with anarchist groups. It has had some lasting influence, usually in the form of anarcho-syndicalism.

Because syndicalism advocates workers' control of the means of production, it is often view as a form of socialism. However, it rejects the socialist view that the society as a whole or the state should control the means of production and favors direct worker control.

## SEE ALSO

*Volume 1 Left:* Anarcho-Syndicalism; Debs, Eugene V.; Haywood, William D.; Industrial Workers of the World.
*Volume 2 Right:* Capitalism; France.

## BIBLIOGRAPHY

Marcel van der Linden, ed., *Revolutionary Syndicalism: An International Perspective* (Ashgate Publishing, 1990); Rudolf Rocher and Nicolas Walter, *Anarcho-Syndicalism* (Pluto Press, 1998); Kenneth Tucker, Jr., *French Revolutionary Syndicalism and the Public Square* (Cambridge University Press, 1996).

ANDREW J. WASKEY
DALTON STATE COLLEGE

# The Left

T

## Think Tanks

THINK TANKS CAN BE difficult to define, although they are usually nonprofit organizations with a significant research focus. Over time the boundary between objective policy evaluations, a traditional think tank activity, and policy advocacy have become blurred as think tanks have become increasingly involved in lobbying government. In order to receive tax-exempt status under the Income Tax Act in Canada and under the Internal Revenue Service Code in the United States, think tanks must be nonpartisan.

Although they do not claim to endorse the political positions of any parties, and thus meet the letter of the law, in fact many have openly acknowledged if not outright promoted their own political mandates. Think tanks are typically ideologically driven, espousing a particular perspective somewhere on the left-right spectrum.

Think tanks typically engage in a range of activities to fulfill their missions including: producing publications, holding open public forums and conferences, giving public lectures, and testifying before congressional and parliamentary committees. Public relations work including gaining access to political talk shows or doing media interviews are becoming increasingly important. Increasingly think tanks look a lot like traditional interest groups: taking out media advertisements about their positions, providing expert advice to individual legislators, and even engaging in lobby activities.

Think tanks fulfill multiple roles in society. They can be an important source of policy ideas, and can also be integral to popularizing new ones. They may engage in policy evaluation, writing critiques of proposed policies and analyzing potential impacts. They may be called upon to testify before Congress about policies. They may engage in program evaluation, determining if programs are operating efficiently and achieving their objectives. Increasingly think tanks are called upon by the news media to provide expertise and commentary on policy and current events.

Think tanks can be divided into three general categories:

*Universities without students:* Research-oriented think tanks produce objective policy analysis often accompanied by forward-looking policy prescriptions. Funding support usually comes from private foundations and institutional endowments. Additional support may come from contracts and corporations. These think tanks typically are staffed by academically trained scholars and produce books and scholarly articles. These think tanks tend to have more long-term research goals and are usually less reactive to current events. The research emphasis tends to be on rigorous academic research. Although of an academic bent, their work is distinct from that of most university research because the

447

first priority is on policy-oriented work, rather than the theoretically oriented work typical of most university researchers. Universities without students are also less likely to publish in the academic refereed journals preferred by university scholars. Their research also tends to include at least some prescriptive policy suggestions, unlike most university research.

*Contract researcher*: Contract researchers produce objective, often quite narrow and targeted policy analyses to satisfy government contracts. Funding support typically comes from government and private contracts, with some supplemental support from private foundations. The staff of these organizations often includes a mix of researchers with varying educational backgrounds, and they typically produce research reports and monographs. These think tanks often prepare reports for specific government agencies that are often not available to the general public. They may have strong ties to one particular agency, such as RAND and the Department of Defense. Contract researcher organizations are useful because they allow government agencies to involve experts in the field without having to deal with personnel restrictions imposed by Congress on their agency. These types of think tanks may be valued as outside opinions, particularly when dealing with internal policy disputes within an agency. They may also have more freedom to criticize the government because they are outsiders. However there is always a fine line in that respect, for agencies that are dependent upon government contracts may not wish to antagonize the source of their funding.

*Advocacy tanks*: Advocacy think tanks produce timely and accessible policy analyses targeted at specific policy making audiences in order to impact the policy making process. Support typically comes from individuals, corporations, and foundations. The staff members tend to be politically experienced professionals and they usually produce policy briefs and press releases. These think tanks may combine a partisan or ideological leaning with public relations activities to try to influence current policy debates. They tend to put a "spin" on existing research rather than doing original research, although some of these think tanks may also engage original research. These groups may also be affiliated with a particular interest, such as the American Association of Retired Persons (AARP), which combines advocacy with research to further their goals of representing the interests of those past retirement age. In general, there are more conservative think tanks than there are left-wing or progressive think tanks, and those with a conservative bent tend to be better funded.

## LEFTIST THINK TANKS

The following are some of the biggest left-leaning think tanks in the United States.

The Economic Policy Institute (EPI) was founded in 1986 with the aim of achieving a "fair and prosperous economy" with particular attention on the living standards of working people. The EPI was founded by a group of economic policy experts to bring attention to the interests of low- and middle-income workers, who are often left out of the political process. Their activities include research, making policy recommendations, and disseminating research. The five areas of interest include living standards and labor markets, government and the economy, globalization and trade, education, and retirement policy.

The Institute for Policy Studies is the nation's oldest multi-issue progressive think tank. Founded in 1963, the think tank was active in civil rights and the anti-war movement in the 1960s, women's rights and the environment in the 1970s, anti-apartheid, and anti-intervention movements in the 1980s, and fair trade and environment in today's era. The IPS has three main areas of focus. The first is democracy and fairness, which includes democracy and economic justice in the United States through research on issues such as migrant domestic workers' rights and activist training. The second area is global justice, looking at the flow of international capital and the burden of the world's poor in supporting the wealthy. Particular issues include free trade analysis, fossil fuels, and ecotourism. The third area is peace and security, which is intended to make the United States a responsible global leader and partner. Specific issues include nuclear policy and Middle East affairs.

Founded in 1974, the World Watch Institute focuses on the interaction among environmental, social, and economic trends. The mission is to work for an "environmentally sustainable and socially just society, in which the needs of all people are met without threatening the health of the natural environment or the well-being of future generations." The World Watch Institute focuses on four areas: people, nature, energy, and economy. Specific policy areas include population, food, water, urbanization, oceans, forests, infectious diseases, bio-invasions, pollution, materials use, energy, climate change, transport, consumption, globalization and governance, sustainable economy, and information technology.

A blue ribbon commission of government officials and civil leaders organized by President Lyndon Johnson in 1968 founded the Urban Institute. It was chartered as nonprofit, nonpartisan research institute to study America's cities. The focus is on social, economic, and governance issues broadly defined. Specific topics include: adolescents and youth development, children, cities, and metropolitan regions, crime and justice, data, District of Columbia, economy, education, the elderly, families, parenting, governing, health and healthcare, housing, immigration, international issues, labor market, nonprofit sector, race/ethnicity/gender, tax policy, and welfare reform.

## SEE ALSO

*Volume 1 Left:* Lobbying; United States.
*Volume 2 Right:* Think Tanks; Lobbying; United States.

## BIBLIOGRAPHY

Donald Abelson, *Do Think Tanks Matter? Assessing the Impact of Public Policy Institutes* (McGill-Queen's University Press, 2002); James McGann and R. Kent Weaver, eds., *Think Tanks and Civil Societies: Catalysts for Ideas and Actions* (Transaction Publishers, 2000); Diane Stone, *Capturing the Political Imagination: Think Tanks and the Policy Process* (Frank Cass, 1996); Diane Stone, Andrew Denham, and Mark Garnett, eds., *Think Tanks across Nations: A Comparative Approach* (St. Martin's Press, 1998).

SHANNON K. ORR
BOWLING GREEN STATE UNIVERSITY

# Third International (Comintern)

WHAT IS commonly referred to as the Third International is chronologically the third large-scale attempt of Marxian movements to get organized at the international level. Following the dissolution of the First International in 1876 and the near-collapse of the Second (Socialist) International during World War I, it did not take long for the socialist/communist world to create yet another organization. The formation of the Third International in March 1919 owed much to the efforts of the Russian Marxists. Interestingly, the two principal reasons for the erosion of the Second International acted precisely as the two major factors behind the creation of the Third International: the heated debate over revisionism and the chaotic environment of World War I. At the turn of the 20th century, a hard-line, revolutionary strand of the Marxist movement gradually distinguished itself from milder versions of socialism. The Bolshevik wing of the Russian Marxists was instrumental in this respect. Under Vladimir Lenin's leadership, the Bolsheviks pursued four different struggles simultaneously. As committed revolutionaries, they fought the imperial regime in Russia. As devoted internationalists, they supported the Second International's activism. As political strategists, they tried to gain the upper hand against their intellectual rivals within the Russian Social-Democratic and Labor Party, namely the Mensheviks. Finally, as theorists of a worldwide revolutionary project, they tried to discredit what they perceived to be revisionism, that is, social democracy.

In 1917, the successful Bolshevik Revolution in Russia caught the world by surprise. The new Russian regime would soon have to deal with the interventionist British, French, and American armies, not to mention the Japanese invasion in the east and the persistence of some Tzarist troops. Under these circumstances, the Bolsheviks found it necessary to attract as much support from their comrades in other countries as possible, both in material and intellectual terms. The Second International, though not abolished, had become totally idle since the break-up of the World War. In any case, from the Bolshevik perspective, the Second International had never been sufficiently revolutionary. For both pragmatic and intellectual reasons, then, Lenin decided that a new International should be created as soon as possible. Revolutionaries from all over the world were soon invited to Moscow to attend a preparatory conference.

The first step toward a Third International was taken in January 1919 with the adoption of a manifesto entitled *For the First Congress of the Communist International.* Fifty-two delegates from different countries attended the International Communist Conference in March 1919. Originally, the Third International was intended to serve the communist movement as a coordination mechanism for proletarian revolutions. Leading theorists of communism, including Lenin and Leon Trotsky, were convinced that the success of the Russian Revolution ultimately depended on the permanence of revolutions on a world scale. At the founding conference, Lenin formally introduced his thesis on bourgeois democracy and the dictatorship of the proletariat, which received unanimous approval from the participating delegations. On March 4, 1919, the conference decided to consider the Zimmerwald Association—a transitory association that had signaled the creation of a new International—dissolved and "to constitute itself as the Third International and adopt the name of the

Communist International." Despite its initial idealism, the Communist International (Comintern) moved swiftly away from its goals after Lenin's untimely death in 1924. Having managed to send Trotsky into exile, Josef Stalin turned Comintern into an arm of Soviet propaganda. In May 1943, he dissolved the Communist International altogether as a gesture of goodwill to the Western allies.

The Third International became a mechanism by which the Soviet state was able to dominate and control communist parties around the world, through financing and through the use of assassination and intimidation, to achieve the policy goals of the Soviet Union. For this reason, many foreign parties, particularly in democratic states like Britain, Canada, France, and the United States, had difficulty retaining members who joined their national party for idealistic reasons.

Furthermore, the use by the Comintern of local communist parties as recruiting grounds for spies for both the KGB and the GRU served to undermine the appeal of such parties to other members of the left. The exposure of the Comintern's role in such recruitment and in the control of the parties only fed into conservative claims that membership in communist parties represented a form of disloyalty for Americans, Canadians, and Britons.

**SEE ALSO**

*Volume 1 Left*: First International; Second International; Cominform; Socialism; Communism.
*Volume 2 Right*: McCarthyism; United States.

**BIBLIOGRAPHY**

M. Drachkovitch and B. Lazitch, eds., *The Comintern: Historical Highlights, Essays, Recollections, Documents* (Praeger, 1966); K. McDermott and J. Agnew, *The Comintern: A History of International Communism from Lenin to Stalin* (Macmillan, 1996); K. E. McKenzie, *Comintern and World Revolution, 1928–43: The Shaping of Doctrine* (Columbia University Press, 1964).

ESREF AKSU
INDEPENDENT SCHOLAR

# Third-Worldism

THE NOTION OF third-worldism is intimately linked to the term *third world*. According to Nigel Harris (1990), the third world first came to the fore in the mid-1950s, following the rapid decolonization process that began in the aftermath of World War II. The term itself was coined in 1952 by the French intellectual Alfred Sauvy and became institutionalized during the 1955 Bandung, Indonesia, conference, which brought together this group of newly decolonized countries to discuss their role in international politics.

Beyond the mere descriptive element in the label that referred to those newly independent countries, the term *third world* also gave these countries a new status in international politics by virtue of the fact that they amounted to more than half of the world's population. It could not be otherwise since the decolonization process took place in a world that was then divided between the capitalist first and the communist second worlds, both of which were poised to increase their influence on the decolonized nations. As a result, the third world grew partly to de-center and to provide a counterbalance to the increasing bellicose nature of the Cold War. The fear provoked by the original weapon of mass destruction—the atomic bomb—was clearly captured by Indonesian President Ahmed Sukarno in his speech at the Bandung Conference: "Not so long ago it was possible to take some little comfort from the idea that the clash, if it came, could perhaps be settled by what were called 'conventional weapons'—bombs, tanks, cannon and men. Today that little grain of comfort is denied us for it has been made clear that the weapons of ultimate horror will certainly be used, and the military planning of nations is on that basis."

The political emphasis on the third world's role was thus on world peace by advocating neutralism in the Cold War, the dominant conflict of the time. To this end, the third world was supported by large sectors of the left in the West, principally in Europe and the United States. This New Left was an assorted collection of intellectuals, activists, and students whose origins in Europe can be traced back to dissident sections of the communist parties who were critical of the Soviet Union's role in the Cold War, and of the political, economic, and military control it exerted over Eastern Europe. In particular, this New Left was united in the condemnation of the Soviet Union's crushing of the 1956 Hungarian revolt and of Josef Stalin's brutal political legacy.

However, the emphasis on peace and neutralism did not last in the third world. A number of major international conflicts altered both the meaning of the term and the support it received from the New Left. In France, the Algerian war of independence was perhaps the single most important formative experience of the

New Left and marked a radicalization of the intellectuals and of large sectors of the young, who would become the main actors of the May 1968 revolts in Paris. In the United States, however, the opposition to the Vietnam War acted as the catalyst for increasing the prominence of a new generation of activists. In the interim period, the terminology and conceptual understanding of the global political order had changed significantly.

What led to this change were the revolutionary movements that began to spread throughout large parts of the so-called third world. In Latin America, the Cuban Revolution advocated liberation from the new imperialism, or the political and economic domination of some countries by the West. As a result, the meaning of third world changed to refer to the less-developed countries and was generally associated with the vast majority of countries in Africa, Asia, and Latin America.

Third-worldism, on the other hand, became the belief that the world would be emancipated by means of the liberation of the poor peoples through revolutionary transformation in the style of Cuba and Vietnam. Thus, whereas traditional Marxist philosophy contended that revolution was class-based and the hallmark of industrialized societies, third-worldism argued instead for socialist revolutions in the poor countries. This belief became extended in the New Left during the late 1960s and appeared to be supported by international events and by developments in Marxist philosophy that grew to take account of these events. Even Jean-Paul Sartre and other distinguished intellectuals of the time, such as Frantz Fanon, called for this type of global transformation for a while.

The belief in third-worldism waned with the institutionalization of the Cuban Revolution and the end of the Vietnam War in the 1970s. However, the basic distinction between rich north and poor south, a distinction that stems from this period, is part of our basic understanding of global divisions today.

### SEE ALSO

*Volume 1 Left:* Asia; Africa; South America; Socialism; Communism; Soviet Union.
*Volume 2 Right:* Asia; Africa; South America; Capitalism; United States.

### BIBLIOGRAPHY

Gerard Chaliand, *Revolution in the Third World: Myths and Prospects* (Harvester Press, 1977); Frantz Fanon, *The Wretched of the Earth* (Penguin, 1967); Nigel Harris, *The End of the Third World: Newly Industrializing Countries and the Decline of an Ideology* (Penguin, 1990); Eric Hobsbawm, *Age of Extremes: The Short 20th Century 1914–91* (Abacus, 1994); Ives Lacoste, *Du Tiersmondisme à l'anti-tiersmondisme* (L'autre Journal, 1985).

KEPA ARTARAZ, PH.D.
UNIVERSITY OF DERBY, UNITED KINGDOM

# Thomas, Norman M. (1884–1968)

AMONG THE PROMINENT socialist leaders of 20th-century America, Norman Thomas has a unique place. He was born in Marion, Ohio, and after graduating from Princeton University in 1905 and Union Theological Seminary in New York City in 1911, he became the pastor of the East Harlem Church and accepted the chairmanship of American Parish, a settlement house in one of the poorest areas of the city.

Thomas entertained pacifist ideas and opposed the participation of United States in World War I. Increasingly, Thomas developed a liking for socialist ideology and finally in 1918 officially joined the Socialist Party. In the same year, he left the pastorship of East Harlem and was appointed secretary of the Fellowship of the Reconciliation, an international pacifist organization. In 1921 he joined the liberal weekly *The Nation* as an associate editor. In the following year, he was appointed executive codirector of the League of Industrial Democracy. His association with the league lasted for a decade. He was also one of the founders of the American Civil Liberties Union.

He ran for the governor of New York on the Socialist Party ticket in 1924. Twice (1925, 1929) he ran for mayor of New York City and he ran for president of the United States in six consecutive elections beginning in 1928. He polled his highest vote, about 880,000, in 1932. An advocate of evolutionary socialism, Thomas was a constant critic of the American economic system and of both major parties; he strongly opposed American entry in World War II while bitterly denouncing both fascism and Soviet Communism. He was openly critical of Franklin D. Roosevelt's Democratic New Deal administration, which espoused solution of the economic emergencies to the neglect of moral issues, according to Thomas.

In 1935, Thomas disengaged himself from the *New Leader*, a Marxist magazine dominated by "hard-liners" of the Socialist Party. Instead, he supported *Socialist*

*Call*, a newly founded magazine. His socialism became diluted by his advocacy of mixed economy. The internal factionalism in the party weakened his public influence, though for years he remained the party's de facto spokesman. After the war, he lectured and wrote extensively on the need for world disarmament and the easing of Cold War tensions. As the chairman of the Postwar World Council, he constantly devoted himself to unravelling the problems of international peace and strongly advocated a cessation of fighting in Indochina, though he backed the Korean War. Thomas passed away in 1968 at Huntington, New York.

From his busy public life, Thomas managed to find time to write several books, including: *The Conscientious Objector in America* (1923), *Socialism of Our Time* (1929), *Human Exploitation* (1934), *Appeal to the Nations* (1947), *Socialist Faith* (1951), *The Test of Freedom* (1954), *Mr. Chairman, Ladies and Gentlemen* (1955), *The Prerequisite for Peace* (1959), *Great Dissenters* (1961), and *Socialism Re-examined* (1963).

**SEE ALSO**

*Volume 1 Left:* Socialist Party, U.S.; Socialism.
*Volume 2 Right:* Capitalism; United States.

**BIBLIOGRAPHY**

Harry Fleischman, *Norman Thomas: A Biography* (Norton, 1964); W.A. Swanberg, *Norman Thomas, the Last Idealist* (Scribner's, 1976).

JITENDRA UTTAM
JAWAHARLAL NEHRU UNIVERSITY, INDIA

# Thompson, Hunter S. (1937/39–)

HUNTER STOCKTON Thompson, the journalist, author, and unsuccessful politician, was born in Louisville, Kentucky, on July 18, 1937, or 1939; questions remain about his birth year due to Thompson's habit of writing about himself as being either younger or older in his work. Thompson represents America's counterculture by openly advocating marijuana use, guns, and civil liberties. His unique style of journalism has seen him progress from a cult legend to a more mainstream fan base. Thompson espouses far right-wing opinions (gun rights, for example), but more often left-wing liberalism. His rebellious journalism weighs him in on the left side of politics.

His path into journalism was far from normal. While studying journalism at Columbia, he was forced to enlist into the air force after a crime-filled youth in which he was arrested in June 1956 for robbery. While in the air force (1956–58), he began writing for the base newspaper as a sports writer. Thompson first gained fame in 1966 for his book *Hell's Angels: A Strange and Terrible Saga*, an account of the year he spent traveling with the notorious outlaw bikers. However, he received nearly instant fame for his 1971 book, *Fear and Loathing in Las Vegas*, which has become a cult classic. Throughout the 1960s and 1970s, he also gained attention as a journalist for *Rolling Stone*. Prior to his long stint with the magazine, he wrote for the *New York Herald Tribune* and the *National Observer*. In 1971, he almost won the election for sheriff of Aspen, Colorado.

Often featured in his writings is his open use of illegal drugs and alcohol abuse. Persistent in his writings is both the feeling of society's degradation as well as his own near collapses, as portrayed memorably in *Fear and Loathing in Las Vegas*. His writing, while always humorous, is also often dark, and Thompson has a tendency to be attracted to places of violence and drugs, as can be seen in his early interest the Hell's Angels. In addition, he often paints a scathing picture of American society and has always done his best to show the ridiculous side of national politics in his coverage of the presidential elections.

Thompson is also famous for being the innovator of Gonzo Journalism, a journalistic style that is characterized by its subjectivity and highly personal accounts. It is both sarcastic and witty, and Thompson is notorious for his use of satirical devices in his work. His unique writing style makes no attempt to keep himself out of his stories, thus creating a subjective, insightful account of events based on Thompson's feelings rather than facts. Thompson does not believe that objective journalism can exist, and that when journalists try to write objectively, their readers will nevertheless associate the writer with a certain perspective. Thompson has always felt it better to acknowledge his subjectivity and has never shied away from its use, as is seen in his famous depiction of Richard Nixon as "a walking embarrassment to the human race."

Thompson's writing has covered many topics, but he is renowned for his social and political commentary, especially regarding presidential elections. His coverage of the 1972 election is depicted in his book *Fear and Loathing on the Campaign Trail*, and in 1992 he delved deep into the William Clinton and George H.W. Bush campaigns in his book *Better Than Sex*. His journalistic career and coverage of politics has both garnered the ire of his peers as well as brought him immense credibility as he is able to write the articles that other journalists see as wrong. His political affiliation is with the Democratic Party, as he abhors the politics of the conservative American right (though he shares many of their conservative views regarding gun control). In the 1992 election, he was in direct contact with the Clinton campaign officials, notably James Carville, and was always offering his perspectives and advice through the use of his famed fax machine.

Thompson's most recent writing is filled with loathing for the George W. Bush conservative administration. His belief centers on the premise that Secretary of Defense Donald Rumsfeld and Vice President Dick Cheney led America horribly astray with two wars that he believes America lost, as well as a ruined economy. Thompson believes this is the worst state that America has been in during his lifetime. He resides in Woody Creek, Colorado, where he has lived since 1967.

### SEE ALSO

*Volume 1 Left:* Carville, James; Clinton, William J.; Media Bias, Left.
*Volume 2 Right:* Bush, George H.W.; Bush, George W.

### BIBLIOGRAPHY

Hunter S. Thompson, *Better Than Sex: Confessions of a Political Junkie Trapped Like a Rat in Mr. Bill's Neighborhood* (Random House, 1994); Hunter S. Thompson, *Kingdom of Fear: Loathsome Secrets of a Star-crossed Child in the Final Days of the American Century* (Penguin Books, 2004); Hunter S. Thompson, "Page 2," espn.go.com (March 2004).

DAVID W. MCBRIDE
UNIVERSITY OF NOTTINGHAM, UNITED KINGDOM

# Titoism

TITOISM WAS A NATIONALISTIC ideology and practice of communism in Yugoslavia during the regime of Josip Broz Tito, officially knows as Marshal Tito, the president of Yugoslavia from the end of World War II until his death in 1980. This ideology took shape after Tito's quarrel with the Soviet Union, and Yugoslavia's subsequent expulsion from the Cominform, the Communist Information Bureau, an information agency organized in 1947 and dissolved in 1956,

*Josip Broz Tito broke with Stalin and formed his own brand of communism in Yugoslavia that came to be known as Titoism.*

consisting of the communist parties of Bulgaria, Czechoslovakia, France, Hungary, Italy, Poland, Romania, the Soviet Union, and Yugoslavia. Titoism was developed during the period of "Splendid Isolation" that lasted from the break with the Soviet Union until Nikita Khrushchev's reparatory visit to Belgrade, the Yugoslavian capital, in 1955. The Titoist paradigm was called "social democracy" and came about as a result of the Yugoslav communists' inability to sustain Stalinist Marxism after the dispute began.

The reforms of Titoism came out of practical considerations: As a result of the intensification of the bureaucracy, the experiments in collectivization, the reign of the secret police, and other classically Stalinist measures, the morale of the general population was low and weakened national defense efforts. In order to improve the living conditions in the country as well as to stabilize political and economic relationships with the West, the Yugoslav communists divested themselves of the rigid form of Stalinist communism, which they had been following as a blueprint before the crisis. As a result, Tito decentralized the economy, turning over economic controls from the state apparatus to the republics, limited the power of the secret police, and permitted a limited relationship with the West. Ideologically, these reforms signaled a break with the orthodox Marxist-Leninist doctrine, which mapped out the course of the communist revolution according to the scientific principles of dialectical materialism within history.

The Titoist doctrine went so far as to agree that small, poor countries have little or no chance to establish a viable capitalist system, sustained by the basic owner-worker relationships of capitalism, so it is impossible for such a society to progress to socialism by orthodox Marxist methods, that is, through a collapse of capitalism brought about by its internal contradictions, which, in turn, would serve as a basis for the new society. Thus, Titoism accepted that a Leninist-style revolution was the only way for a poor country to bypass the capitalist stage described by Marx in his evolutionary model of history. However, Titoism rejected the scientific rigidity of the Marxist-Leninist doctrine, claiming instead that the project of the revolution had to be practically adapted to individual national environments in order to avoid degeneration into Stalinism and state capitalism.

Titoism implied that, ideologically, a large difference between the Soviet Union and Yugoslavia was the historical role of the individual in both societies; the Soviet Marxist system that combined Marxism with the Russian tradition of placing the collective over the individual self was not an acceptable model to emulate for Yugoslavia, where historically the idea of an individual was a more important one. As a result of these differences Titoism was less ideologically militant than the other Soviet protégé ideologies, and thus has been generally perceived by historians as an authoritarian, rather than a totalitarian regime.

Because of the inherent flexibility adopted as a modus operandi by Titoism, it was necessarily more difficult for followers to articulate their specific theoretical tenets. Arguably, the best articulation of the theory of Titoism was the address entitled "Socialist Democracy in Yugoslav Practice" delivered in Oslo, Norway, in September 1954 by Edvard Kardel, considered the Yugoslav Marxists' leading spokesman, chief ideological theoretician, and second in importance only to Tito himself. Overall, Titoism was a systematic reconciliation of Marxist ideology with the national independence of the communist state of Yugoslavia from the Soviet Union. The decline and the end of Titoism signaled the rise of nationalism.

After Tito's death, the Socialist People's Republic of Yugoslavia lingered until 1991, at which point four out of the six constituent republics, Bosnia-Herzogovina, Croatia, Macedonia, and Slovenia became autonomous. The remaining republics of Montenegro and Serbia formed the Federal Republic of Yugoslavia, which eventually became a commonwealth named Serbia and Montenegro.

### SEE ALSO

*Volume 1 Left:* Stalin and Stalinism; Cominform; Soviet Union.
*Volume 2 Right:* Soviet Union; Totalitarianism.

### BIBLIOGRAPHY

Charles McVicker, *Titoism: Pattern for International Communism* (St. Martin's, 1957); Adam Ulam, *Titoism and the Cominform* (Harvard University Press, 1952); Stephen Clissonold, *Yugoslavia and the Soviet Union 1939–73* (Oxford University Press, 1975); Ghita Ionescu, *Communism in Rumania* (Oxford University Press, 1964).

VERONICA DAVIDOV
NEW YORK UNIVERSITY

# Trotsky, Leon (1879–1940)

LEON TROTSKY, one of the seminal figures in the history of the communist left, was born in the southern part of the Ukraine, then part of the Russian Empire. Named Lev Davidovich Bronstein, his father was a prosperous farmer, or kulak. It was an era when the Russian government was becoming increasingly oppressive toward the Jews. Often, in order to shift attention from the inequalities of Russian life, regime agents provocateurs (hired by the secret police to foment trouble) would stir up the Russian Orthodox Black Hundreds gangs to launch bloody pogroms, or genocidal riots, against the Jewish community. On many occasions, the anti-Semitic Cossacks would join in, using their swords and wicked whips, the knouts. Hence, liberal intellectuals soon said that the Russian tzars ruled by "the Cossacks and the knout." It was against this background, immortalized in Bernard Malamud's novel *The Fixer*, that Trotsky became a member of revolutionary groups dedicated to overthrow the autocratic tzarist regime. In fact, according to Avrahm Yarmolinsky in his *Road to Revolution: A Century of Russian Radicalism*, in the capital of St. Petersburg, "the nucleus of a revolutionary organization of a purely proletarian complexion: The Northern Union of Russian Workers" had already been formed late in 1878.

Seeing great potential in their son, Trotsky's parents sent him to primary school in Odessa, and then to Nicolayev, Russia, for his secondary education. In 1898, while not yet 20, Trotsky became one of the founders of the Russian Social Democratic Labor Party (RSDLP). Arrested by the regime, he was sent to internal exile to Russian Siberia, the "finishing school" for opponents of tzarist despotism since the Decembrists had been sent there after opposing the coronation of Tzar Nicholas I in 1825. In 1902, Trotsky managed to escape Siberia and flee to London, England, at which time he took the revolutionary name of Trotsky. London in Victorian times (1837–1901) had been hospitable to political refugees from troubled Central and Eastern Europe. Karl Marx, the founder of Marxism, had done much of his research in the British Museum.

It was in London that Trotsky met the fellow Russian refugee with which his name would forever be intertwined, Vladimir I. Lenin. When Lenin met Trotsky, according to David Shub in *Lenin*, Lenin observed, "the man is capable of learning and will prove very useful." In March 1903, Lenin invited Trotsky to join the staff of the progressive newspaper *Iskra*, or the *Spark*. However, as was common in Russian revolutionary politics, views diverged among the members of the movement. In 1903, at the RSDLP's Second Congress, the split led to Lenin siding with the Bolshevik, or majority wing, and Trotsky choosing the minority Mensheviks. However, the ideological disagreement did not affect their comradeship or working together.

Lenin and Trotsky both found themselves radicalized by the events of Bloody Sunday, January 22, 1905. On that day, incited by Father Gapon, a Russian secret police agitator, workers in St. Petersburg attempted to present their grievances to their "Little Father," Tzar Nicholas II, at his Winter Palace. The massacre that resulted set off the Revolution of 1905. Lenin attempted to get arms from his new haven in Geneva, Switzerland, to the rebels, but the shipment was lost. Trotsky arrived by subterfuge back in Russia in February, according to historian Edmund Wilson. Later, Wilson wrote, Trotsky "organized—the first meeting took place the night of October 13—a Soviet [Council] of Workers' Delegates." It was the first time that revolutionary soviets appeared in Russian revolutionary history. Both Mensheviks and Bolsheviks joined in supporting the Revolution. Lenin, however, would not arrive in Russia until November 1905.

The tzarist government reacted with predictable brutality. The Black Hundreds were summoned again. Wilson writes: "there were known to have been four thousand people killed and ten thousand mutilated" with "the Cossack and the knout." Trotsky was arrested with others of the St. Petersburg soviet and incarcerated in the forbidding Sts. Peter and Paul Fortress. Trotsky was sent again to Siberia and again managed to escape. At the Fifth Party Congress he met the revolutionary Josef Stalin, with whose life, like Lenin's, his would be tightly, and fatally, entwined.

When World War I broke out in August 1914, Trotsky was in Vienna, Austria. As an enemy national (Russia fought Germany and Austria in the war), he fled to Zurich, Switzerland. In November 1914, he moved to France, where his efforts against the war caused him to be arrested. The overthrow of Tzar Nicholas II found Trotsky in New York City with other revolutionaries such as Nikolai Bukharin, who, like Trotsky, would make his mark on Russia's future. Trotsky was not able to return to Russia until May 1917, when he was arrested by the Provisional Government of Prime Minister Alexander Kerensky. However, the monarchists in the armed forces, now known as the Whites (in opposition to the communist Reds), made an attempt to retake the capital of St. Petersburg.

General Lavr Kornilov attempted a military coup, and Kerensky was forced to release Trotsky to gain the support of what would now become the Red Army. Trotsky wrote in his book, *The History of the Russian Revolution*, "As early as the beginning of August, Kornilov had ordered the transfer of the Savage Division and the Third Cavalry Corps from the southwestern front to the sector of the railroad triangle, Nevel-Novosokolniki-Velikie Luki, the most advantageous base for an attack on Petrograd." In September, Trotsky organized some 25,000 volunteers to help defeat Kornilov; in October (November in the Western calendar), he helped coordinate the Bolshevik seizure of power under Lenin. Serving as commissar for foreign affairs, he helped negotiate the Treaty of Brest-Litovsk with the Germans, thus ending Russian participation in the war. Now faced with Allied intervention as well as the growing White movement, Lenin made Trotsky the commissar for war.

It was during the Russian Civil War that Trotsky made his greatest contribution to the Bolshevik triumph. As the commissar for war, he was able to take drastic steps away from party cant in order to win the struggle against the White Army, now nominally allied under Admiral Alexander Kolchak. On July 29, 1918, he issued his famous Order Number 228, which ordered up all former tzarist officers to help lead the Red Army. Orlando Figgis writes in *A Peoples' Tragedy: The Russian Revolution: 1891–1924* that "in the course of the civil war the number [of returning officers] rose to 75,000." These returning officers, to avoid hurting revolutionary sensibilities, were called *voenspets*, or "military specialists."

In November 1920, as W. Bruce Lincoln writes in *Red Victory: A History of the Russian Civil War*, the White armies of Baron Peter Wrangel evacuated the Crimea in the face of the attacks of Trotsky's best general, Mikhail Frunze. Frunze exulted: "Our triumphant Red standards are now firmly planted on the shores of the Crimea." By March 1921, all enemies of the Revolution had been crushed in the former Russian Empire by Trotsky's Red Army. Lenin, speaking at the 10th Congress of the Communist Party on March 8, 1921, could rightfully declare: "The last of the hostile armies has been driven from our territories."

However, just at the moment of triumph, Lenin began to grow feeble. The struggle for power began. Trotsky, as Lincoln points out, had never taken time to build a secure power base within the Communist (Bolshevik) Party: his time had been spent with the army. However, Stalin had spent the revolution and civil war years cultivating allies within the party. By 1922, Stalin was general secretary of the party, the most powerful political figure in the Soviet Union after Lenin. On May 26, 1922, Lenin suffered a stroke and gradually lost control of the state and the party; quickly, Stalin moved to fill the power vacuum.

On January 1, 1924, Lenin died, apparently from the massive stroke. However, in his last months, Lenin had begun to question Stalin's abilities to succeed him in power. According to Roy Medvedev in his *Let History Judge*, Stalin may have had a hand both in the deaths of Dzerzhinsky and Frunze, and it would not be idle speculation to surmise he may have abetted Lenin's as well. With the death of Lenin, Trotsky's fall came rapidly. At the 15th Party Congress, at the end of 1927, Stalin contrived to have Trotsky purged from the party. At first exiled to Central Asia, Trotsky left Russia for good in 1929.

The split between Trotsky and Stalin and the formation of the Fourth International by Trotsky's followers was characterized by the Comintern as a digression into leftist deviationism, and Trotsky's ideology was criticized as being to the left of the Communist Party.

Seeing a kindred spirit in the Mexico then ruled by the PRI, the Party of the Institutional Revolution, which had taken power in the Revolution of 1910, Trotsky ultimately settled there. But his old revolutionary talents still were feared by Stalin. On May 24, 1940, raiders likely sent by Stalin attacked Trotsky villa at Coyoacan. Although the attack was beaten off, the respite was brief. One of Stalin's agents, known to history as Ramon Mercader, had insinuated himself into Trotsky's inner circle. On August 20, Mercader took Trotsky by surprise, and struck him an assassin's blow in the head with an alpine pick axe. On August 21, 1940, Trotsky died.

## SEE ALSO

*Volume 1 Left:* Lenin, Vladimir I.; Russian Revolution; Communism; Stalin and Stalinism.
*Volume 2 Right:* Monarchism; Royalty; Elitism.

## BIBLIOGRAPHY

Avrahm Yarmolinsky, *Road to Revolution: A Century of Russian Radicalism* (Collier Books, 1962); David Shub, *Lenin* (Mentor Books, 1948); Orlando Figgis, *A People's Tragedy: The Russian Revolution: 1891–1924* (Penguin, 1996); W. Bruce Lincoln, *Red Victory: A History of the Russian Civil War* (Touchstone, 1989); Nicholas Berdyaev, *The Origins of Russian Communism* (University of Michigan Press, 1969); Richard Pipes, *The Russian Revolution* (Vintage Books, 1990); Leon Trotsky, *The History of the Russian Revolution*, F. W. Dupee, ed. (Doubleday, 1959); V.I. Lenin, *Essential Works of Lenin*, Henry M. Christman, ed. (Bantam, 1966); Christopher Andrew and Vasili Mitrokhin, *The Sword and the Shield* (Basic Books, 1999); Pavel Sudoplatov and Anatoli Sudoplatov, with Jerrold and Leona P. Schecter, *Special Tasks: The Memoirs of an Unwanted Witness—A Soviet Spymaster* (Little, Brown, 1994).

JOHN F. MURPHY, JR.
AMERICAN MILITARY UNIVERSITY

# Truman, Harry (1884–1972)

HARRY TRUMAN became the 33rd president of the United States on April 12, 1945, after the death of Franklin D. Roosevelt (FDR). Truman immediately encountered many monumental issues, especially with foreign policy. This was at first a daunting task for Truman, for as vice president, he was unaware of most of the important issues of FDR's presidency. He had no knowledge about the progress of the atomic bomb, nor was he fully appraised of the increasingly strained U.S. relationship with the Soviet Union. Roosevelt had largely ignored Truman, and the fact that Truman was able to step into the presidency and help guide America through one of its most momentous times is a credit to the strong will of his character. While historians remain largely divided over Truman's ability as a diplomat, he has become a mythological political figure of both the left and right who both credit him as being an everyday man who rose to meet the arduous demands of presidency.

The decision to drop the atomic bombs on Japan was Truman's first major decision as president. He was only made aware of America's secret operation to build an atomic bomb after he became president. The war in Europe ended in May 1945, but America was still engaged in fighting the Japanese. Truman learned that a successful test had occurred on July 16, 1945, and realizing that the weapon could bring a quick end to the war and save American lives, he decided to drop the bombs on Japan. On the August 6, 1945, barely four months into the Truman presidency, the first bomb was dropped on Hiroshima. Two days later, a second bomb was dropped on Nagasaki. Japan subsequently surrendered on August 14, signaling the end of World War II. The bombs were dropped primarily on civilians, and over 140,000 Japanese died immediately from both bombs. Some arguments contend that Truman decided to drop the bombs to show the Soviet Union, which Truman had begun to take a hard line against, the superior military power of the United States. However, admirers of Truman argue that the bombs saved countless lives of American soldiers and brought a decisive close to the most violent war in history.

The most significant issue that Truman faced was the growing Cold War tension with the Soviet Union. Following World War II, with the United States and Soviet Union as the world's lone super powers, problems arose over how to establish a global order. These differences were due to political and economic ideologies; the Soviets were a communist nation, while the United States was a democracy with a capitalist system. First and foremost, Truman wanted to ensure that communism did not spread worldwide, and he identified this as the greatest risk to American security. Truman thus took a hard line approach to the Soviets. In doing so, he played a major role in helping to rebuild Europe after the war. The Truman Doctrine provided military aid to countries opposing possible communist revolts, while the Marshall Plan gave economic aid to the war-torn countries of Europe in hopes of rebuilding them into strong U.S. allies. The aid that Truman gave to such countries was the key reason why Europe was able to rebuild following the war.

His hard-line approach has received mixed reviews, with some arguments claiming he helped to intensify the Cold War by overemphasizing Soviet intentions and capability to spread communism. His presidency was largely successful in containing communism, although in June 1950, when communist North Korea invaded South Korea, Truman brought U.S. troops to the aid of South Korea, thus beginning the Korean War.

One of the most significant decisions that Truman made as president occurred on May 14, 1948, when he formally announced the recognition of the Jewish state of Israel. The Holocaust resulted in many thousands of Jewish refugees left homeless after the war. With no willingness to return to their old homes where they faced anti-Semitic attitudes, and because neither the United States nor Great Britain would ease immigration restrictions to allow Jewish refugees to seek haven in their respective countries, Truman helped bring the Holocaust survivors, known as the Displaced Persons, to Palestine where Zionist leaders had begun a campaign for a Jewish state.

Palestine proved a difficult decision for the president as he knew that the Palestinians opposed Jewish immigration to what they perceived as their lands. At the time, Palestine was under a British mandate, and neither the Arabs nor the Jews had their own state. Moreover, the British Parliament urged Truman not to support Jewish immigration for fear of a potential Arab backlash. In the end, Truman believed that to deny the Displaced Persons the ability to immigrate to Palestine was unjust and immoral after the Holocaust. His policies helped bring the Jews to Palestine and thus allowed the Zionists to create a Jewish state. Much of Truman's legacy rests on his role in the establishment of Israel.

## CIVIL RIGHTS

Truman's greatest domestic liberal policy was arguably his desegregation of the armed forces. On July 26, 1948, Truman signed Executive Order 9981 that declared equality of treatment in the armed forces for minorities. While a very controversial issue of the time, Truman nevertheless failed to stray from his policy. While the policy took a few years to be incorporated, by 1953, 95 percent of African Americans serving in the armed forces were in integrated regiments. Truman also helped pass legislation that barred racial discrimination in federal employment and created the Committee on Civil Rights.

Through his civil rights work, Truman played an important role in shaping the government's eventual decision to help abolish segregation. While President Lyndon Johnson would officially abolish segregation in the 1960s, Truman took the first steps toward laying the foundation for Johnson's action. Truman left office in 1953 and retired to Independence, Missouri.

### SEE ALSO

*Volume 1 Left:* Roosevelt, Franklin D.; Desegregation; Johnson, Lyndon B.
*Volume 2 Right:* Segregation; Eisenhower, Dwight D.; McCarthyism.

### BIBLIOGRAPHY

Gar Alperovitz, *Atomic Diplomacy: Hiroshima and Potsdam: The Use of the Atomic Bomb and the American Confrontation with Soviet Power* (Pluto Press, 1994); Gar Alperovitz, *The Decision to Use the Atomic Bomb* (Vintage Books, 1996); Zvi Ganin, *Truman, American Jewry and Israel, 1945–1948* (Holmes & Meier, 1979); Alonzo L. Hamby, *Man of the People: A Life of Harry S. Truman* (Oxford University Press, 1995); Melvyn P. Leffler, *A Preponderance of Power: National Security, the Truman Administration and the Cold War* (Stanford University Press, 1992); David G. McCullough, *Truman* (Simon & Schuster, 1992); Arnold A. Offner, *Another Such Victory: President Truman and the Cold War, 1945–1953* (Stanford University Press, 2002).

DAVID W. MCBRIDE
UNIVERSITY OF NOTTINGHAM, UNITED KINGDOM

# Turkey

THE TURKISH LEFT HAS been represented by the center-left or social democrat parties in Turkey's mainstream politics. In the parliament there is one center-left party, the RPP (Republican People's Party) of Deniz Baykal that became the second party in the 2002 elections with 170 seats. From 1950 to 1980, the Turkish center-left was only represented by the RPP with a synthesis between statist-centralist perspective and social democrat policies. When the center-right Democrat Party won the 1950 elections, the RPP remained as the main opposition party until 1960. The RPP during that time tried to change its authoritarian party image and to reinterpret the principles of Kemalism (Turkey's state ideology) on the basis of social policies. But it maintained its connection with bureaucracy and the military. Except short-lived coalition governments it had remained in opposition until 1980.

The 1980 military intervention resulted in the polarization in left politics when it banned the RPP. In the 1983 elections, the Populist Party (PP) represented the center-left and won 30 percent of the votes. Later it merged with the Social Democrat Party (founded by former members of the RPP and headed by Erdal Inonu, the son of former RPP leader Ismet Inonu), becoming the Social Democrat Populist Party (SDPP). Bulent Ecevit, banned former leader of the 1970s RPP, returned to politics by the 1987 referendum and became the chairman of the Democratic Left Party (DLP). The SDPP (joined to with the RPP in the mid-1990s) and the DLP were the two main center-left parties of the 1990s. Thanks to its nationalist discourse in the face of the rising Kurdish separatist threat, the DLP became the leading party in the 1999 elections and became the leading partner in the DLP-led coalition government that remained in power until 2002. In the 2002 elections, its vote dramatically declined from 22 percent to 1.5 percent. This time the RPP became the representative of left politics with 19 percent of the vote.

There was not a considerable ideological difference between the SDPP-RPP and the DLP. However, the DLP leadership does not emphasize its connection with the pre-1980 RPP, although the RPP leaders stress the importance of the legacy of the old RPP for its survival. The other difference between them is that the DLP emphasizes nationalist and local values more than the RPP. Although among leaders of the two parties in the 1990s there was a belief in the necessity of a state role in the economy, throughout recent years both have seemed to move closer to British Prime Minister Tony Blair's understanding of the Third Wave. Less state intervention, private enterprises, joining the international market, individual rights, and so on are becoming the basic mottos of center-left politics in Turkey. Today's RPP is one of the passionate supporters for Turkey's joining the European Union and liberal social democracy. Nevertheless, the statist and bureaucratic values of the center are still dominant among the leaders of the RPP. It is very obvious in their attitude to the ruling Justice and Development Party (JDP) that represents a wide coalition of various segments, especially conservative ones, of the society that have been excluded from power. This seems to prevent the RPP from establishing healthy relations and alliances with the country's different social and cultural groups.

The Turkish left, as a form of radical or Marxist and socialist movements, became influential during the 1960s and 1970s. It was mainly a student- and worker-led movement, which culminated in large-scale demonstrations and political violence in the 1970s. The Turkish Labor Party (TLP) was the representative of this move in the 1960s, which was banned by the 1971 military intervention. Its vote was around 3 percent, not gaining political significance at the national level, though having a great ideological effect. Turkey's leftist groups have identified themselves with Kemalism, their interpretation especially relying on a centralist, laicist, statist model. In this model, the elite has a central role in monopolizing the decision making process, although they define their policies as populist.

**SEE ALSO**

*Volume 1 Left:* Socialism; Communism; Church and State Separation.
*Volume 2 Right:* Turkey; Religion.

**BIBLIOGRAPHY**

Feroz Ahmad, *The Making of Modern Turkey* (Routledge, 1993); Sibel Bozdosan and Resat Kasaba, eds., *Rethinking Modernity and National Identity in Turkey* (University of Washington Press, 1997); Metin Heper and Barry Rubin, eds., *Turkish Political Parties* (Frank Cass, 2002); Ergun Ozbudun, *Contemporary Turkish Politics* (Lynne Rienner, 2000); Erik J. Zürcher, *Turkey: A Modern History* (I.B. Tauris, 2001).

YILMAZ ÇOLAK, PH.D.
EASTERN MEDITERRANEAN UNIVERSITY
TURKEY

# The Left

## Uganda

UGANDAN POLITICS OFTEN follow ethnic, regional, and tribal lines with ideological differences being secondary. The country is roughly divided between two major peoples. In the north are the Nilotic; in the south are the Bantu, who have traditionally dominated the country and controlled the military. Uganda is landlocked in east-central Africa and was first populated by Bantu-speaking peoples more than 2,500 years ago. By the 1300s, three tribal kingdoms had emerged, but one dominated, Buganda. In 1862, John Hanning Speke, a British explorer searching for the source of the Nile, became the first recorded European to visit and by 1894 Uganda had been declared a British protectorate. A clerical error is blamed for dropping the "B" of Buganda and renaming the country, but the name stuck.

In 1962, Uganda became independent with the left-leaning Milton Obote as head of state. He was deposed in 1971 by Idi Amin, whose military rule was eccentric and brutal with an estimated 300,000 Ugandans killed for political reasons during the 1970s. He aligned the nation with some left-wing causes, making overtures to the Soviet Union and Communist China, but he did not follow a consistent ideological philosophy. In 1976, Amin declared himself President for Life and attempted to annex western Kenya and the Kagera region of Tanzania. That led to a series of military defeats and

Amin fleeing into exile, where he died in 2001. What followed was a struggle for power among varied political and ethnic rivals. One of the main contenders was the left-wing Uganda National Liberation Army (UNLA), which was successful in putting former President Obote back into power from 1980 until 1985. Repression continued during that period with an estimated 100,000 Ugandans killed and another 200,000 fleeing to political exile.

Despite the dangers of attempting political opposition during that time, the left-to-centrist Democratic Party (DP) decided to keep working within the system, while the more militant and leftist-radical Uganda Patriotic Movement (UPM) refused to accept the Obote government and left the political scene for guerrilla warfare. The UPM later developed a political wing, the National Resistance Movement (NRM), as well as a military wing, the National Resistance Army (NRA).

In 1985, Yoweri Kaguta Museveni became the sole leader of both the NRM and the NRA. Dissatisfaction with Obote's government grew amid political repression and nationwide economic hardship and instability. In 1985, a faction of Obote's military junta seized power and ousted Obote, who fled to Zambia. A military council was headed by General Tito Okello, but was deposed when Museveni refused to join the government and continued guerrilla warfare, capturing much of the countryside, then the capital—deposing Okello.

461

Museveni put into place a National Resistance Council (NRC), which named him as president. Under Museveni, political opposition was outlawed. Opposition political parties were allowed to exist, but were banned from supporting candidates.

Museveni's political ideology evolved into a pragmatic mix of state-run economics and free-market capitalism, particularly as he sought development loans. A period of relative prosperity and security ensued. Because political parties were not allowed to operate actively, election candidates had to stand as independents, even though they might belong to a registered political party. Museveni argued that what Uganda needed was stability and peace, not political division. Museveni was also strongly opposed to official corruption. Museveni won an easy victory in the presidential election held under this system, but voices started to be heard from the middle class about obtaining greater political liberty and power.

Among the many Ugandan political parties that exist but cannot promote candidates are the left-centrist Democratic Party, headed by Paul Kawanga Ssemogerere, who was Museveni's main contender in the 1996 elections; the leftist Uganda People's Congress, which is split between a faction that maintains Obote is the rightful leader of Uganda and another group that sees him as an embarrassment that belongs to the past; and the National Resistance Movement, the only party allowed to participate in the political process.

Some NRM supporters on the left have expressed concern over how Museveni has handled the economy, especially privatization of government operations. Government records show that 108 formerly state-owned operations have been sold off, but privatization has not led to the redistribution of wealth, as had been promised. Instead, Museveni insiders and senior army officers have become the owners of several companies.

**SEE ALSO**

*Volume 1 Left:* Africa.
*Volume 2 Right:* Africa.

**BIBLIOGRAPHY**

"Country Profile 2000: Uganda," (The Economist Intelligence Unit, Europa Publications Limited, 1999); *Keesing's Record of World Events 2000* (Keesing's Limited, 2000); William Tordoff, *Government and Politics in Africa* (Indiana University Press, 1997).

ROB KERBY
INDEPENDENT SCHOLAR

# Ukraine

UKRAINE, once commonly called "the Ukraine," has experienced a variety of challenges as it has undertaken self-rule upon the collapse of the Soviet Union. Officially it enjoys a right-wing market economy rather than a state-controlled system. However, a case can be made that the de-facto or real power remains in the hands of the left, those who believe in the need for a centralized government and a planned, state-run economy. That would be due to the fact that most of the wealth in Ukraine is controlled by former Soviet appointees and Communist Party faithful, who took advantage of economic reforms and emerged as entrepreneurs or "oligarchs," acquiring considerable wealth and power during privatization as they became the owners of formerly state-owned industries and operations.

Ukraine has experienced a difficult history. Dominated throughout much of history by outside rulers, Ukraine enjoyed a long period of local autonomy during the 10th and 11th centuries as the center of a large Slavic state. In the 12th century, it was incorporated into the Grand Duchy of Lithuania and then the Polish-Lithuanian commonwealth. During the 17th century, Ukrainians launched another 100 years of autonomy that ended when Russian tzars coveted the area's vast farmlands. Then, briefly, Ukraine was independent beginning with the 1917 fall of the Russian Empire until 1920 when Ukraine joined the Soviet Union. It then endured a brutal period that claimed as many as eight million Ukrainian citizens during Stalin-instigated famines designed to bring the Ukrainians into submission, then World War II, in which German and Soviet occupiers caused another seven to eight million casualties.

Memories of the abuse by outsiders and the prosperity and independence during periods of self-rule have instilled Ukrainians with a strong cultural and religious identity. In 1990, there were more than three million members of the Communist Party and an additional 66,000 were candidates for party membership. Independence was embraced in 1991 at the end of Soviet rule. Institutionalized corruption filled the vacuum left by the sudden disappearance of centralized control. In the 1998 parliamentary elections, more voters supported the Communist Party than any other, more than 6.5 million voters. Some legislators who chose to remain true to socialism joined the Socialist Party, or the more radically inclined Union of Ukrainian Communists. When the Communist Party was reregistered by the Ministry of Justice in 1993, it claimed 120,000 members. By 2002, it claimed 140,000 members and claimed popularity among the segments of the population who remembered the "good old days" of cheap vodka, sausages, and "full employment."

The national legislature is the 450-seat Verchovna Rada, which in 2004 was controlled by a right-leaning coalition government that enjoyed only a slight majority over the Communists and Socialists. Prime Minister Viktor Yanukovych, elected by the right-of-center majority, supported three different drafts submitted to the Supreme Court for a new constitution designed to strengthen the role of the Rada, resulting in a diminished role for the president. Under one of the proposed constitution's provisions, the president would be elected by parliament. Among the reasons cited for the need for such reforms were accusations by left-wing legislators against right-wing reformer President Leonid Kuchma, who was accused of abuses, corruption, and complicity in the murder of a journalist.

In 2004, during what became known as the Orange Revolution, opposition leader Viktor Yushchenko won the presidency after a contested election, in which he vowed to steer the strategic former Soviet republic on a new course toward the West and away from Russia.

### SEE ALSO

*Volume 1 Left*: Russia, Post-Soviet; Soviet Union.
*Volume 2 Right*: Russia, Post-Soviet.

### BIBLIOGRAPHY

Taras Kuzio, "Who Really Wears Pampers in Ukrainian Politics?" *Ukrainska Pravda* (June 25, 2004); N. Feduschak, "Ukraine's President Will Retire in 2004" *Washington Times* (August 22, 2001); "Ukraine," *World Factbook* (CIA, 2004); Catherine Lovatt, "Curtain Call for Kuchma," *Central Europe Review* (v.3/7, 2001); Agence France Press (December 27, 2004).

ROB KERBY
INDEPENDENT SCHOLAR

# Unions

UNIONS ARE A LOOSE or formal entity whose primary purpose is to promote the ideals and demands of a group of workers. Throughout history and to the present day, unions have acted as a supporting staff in defending the rights of their members, in the midst of economic and social pressures. Unions have mostly been given a reputation as radicals and agitators. This reputation has stemmed from business groups as well as government agencies. In the end, the somewhat leftist ideology of unions has on the whole aided workers to attain their economic and social demands.

A causal factor in the rise of unions is 19th-century industrialization, especially in Europe. In the latter half of the century, the Western European economies underwent a severe economic transformation. The process of industrialization made the production of goods more efficient, which led to an increase in consumption and economic expansion. The innovative means of production also led to the demand for new skills and workers able to accomplish those skills. The Industrial Revolution sparked a new economic and social system that had long- and short-term ramifications. As the European economies expanded, the urban proletariat also increased specifically in the area of first-time factory wage earners. The number of people who worked were employed in the shipping, building, and transportation fields. As a result, especially after the riots in the 1840s, workers began to rely less on the traditional guilds and mutualist societies and turned to trade unions and other forms of collective organizing.

In the second half of the century, workers increasingly turned to trade unions to express their grievances and demands. Governments began to extend legal protections to unions in the latter part of the century. A reason for this extension to a certain degree involved a concern by the governments that trade unions could be a political challenge to a government's hegemony. Trade unions became legalized in Britain in 1871 and were given permission to picket in 1875.

In France, Napoleon III allowed a weak trade union movement to exist as a political balance. In 1884, the French Third Republic fully recognized and legalized unions and in Germany, unions were allowed to exist after 1890. Trade unions made their demands and expressed these demands in the form of strikes and work stoppages. Clearly, the workers were venting their grievances. The emergence of unions at the height of the Industrial Revolution expressed worker reaction to the problematic situation of 19th-century Europe. The creation of a working-class mentality, based on nationalism and worker rights, was directly related to the rise of new technologies. These technologies, like the factory system, transformed not only the nature of work, but the way that workers identified their place in societies. With their labor devalued, workers became increasingly alienated from the larger society. They were alienated as well as increasingly impoverished as they did not benefit from the secondary effects of industrialization.

Union organizations, first in the form of mutualist societies, guilds, and federations, provided for the basic guidance of the worker. However, as the demands of business escalated on the worker, the organizations simply could not keep pace. The emergence of unions, organizations that protect the political and economic rights of the working class, answered the call for nationalistic defense of their rights. The first region that saw the emergence of unions was Europe, specifically, in England.

The Industrial Revolution played a major role in the social and economic development of worker grievances. Many felt that their labor was exploited by big business. Moreover, many informal collectives came to believe that the workers were psychologically weakened by a devalued sense of their labor. The result was England witnessing the growth of some of the most powerful labor organizations. In the 1860s, trades councils or informal labor unions were established in Britain's main industrial towns and cities. Concerned with the problems of industrial growth and its consequences, in 1868 leaders of these trade councils met in Manchester to discuss the possibility of forming an organization that might supply a cohesive tone for trade union rights. At the initial meeting, the 34 delegates established the powerful Trade Union Congress (TUC) and pledged to meet on an annual basis to discuss issues of vital importance to the labor movement.

In 1871, at the third Trade Union Congress in London, a parliamentary committee was appointed to bring pressure on Parliament to amend the repressive 1871 Trade Union Act. In the 1874 general election, the parliamentary committee asked candidates questions on their attitudes toward trade unions and urged members to vote for or against the candidates on the basis of their replies. Those Members of Parliament elected in 1874 surprisingly included two miners, Alexander Mac-Donald and Thomas Burt, who fully supported the policies of the TUC.

In 1896, Robert Smillie, president of the Scottish Miners' Federation, established the influential Scottish Trade Union Congress. His role was recognized when he was elected chairman at its first conference, a post he controlled until 1899. The Scottish TUC was more radical than the English TUC, with many of its leaders being members of the Independent Labour Party.

On February 27, 1900, the Trade Union Congress and representatives of all the socialist groups in Britain (the Independent Labour Party, the Social Democratic Federation, and the Fabian Society,) met at the Memorial Hall in Farringdon Street, London. After a debate,

the 129 delegates decided to pass a motion put forward by James Keir Hardie to establish "a distinct Labour group in Parliament, who shall have their own whips, and agree upon their policy, which must embrace a readiness to cooperate with any party which for the time being may be engaged in promoting legislation in the direct interests of labor." To make this possible, the conference established a Labour Representation Committee (LRC).

Established in 1900, the LRC committee included seven trade unionists and two members from the Independent Labour Party, two from the Social Democratic Federation, and one member of the Fabian Society. After the 1906 general election, the LRC became known as the Labour Party. Throughout the 20th century, and especially after 1950, the union movement became integrated into the Labour Party's political policies. In other words, it became fused into the political system.

Like many other political unions, the English trade union confederation became enmeshed in national politics and lost much of its ardor and glamour as it lost sight of the importance of nationalism. The notion of defending England against any foreign encroachment became secondary to attaining political power. In the Cold War era, the de-emphasis on unions led to a loss in working-class rights and privileges that were enjoyed during the period of greatest activity.

In other European nations, unions underwent a similar process of proletarianization and politicization. Essentially, many unions that started as labor activists intent on defending the rights of the workers increasingly turned to political parties and in some cases, to revolution.

In France, unions have succumbed to globalization and political power. The main French union confederation has put aside the concepts of defending national patrimony for political patronage. In the 20th century, French unions have joined in alliance with the leftist political parties and the United Front governments in return for governmental positions. The French believed that joining the political sphere was the most important way of controlling the increasingly volatile state of the working class.

The Russian example is the most fascinating of the union movements. In 1917, a social revolution led to the demise of the tzarist regime of Nicholas II. Leftist unions, in alliance with the working class-based Bolsheviks, sought to create a working-class paradise. The result was catastrophic in the long run. The subsequent communist governments essentially outlawed any form of unionization. Unionization, it was feared, would activate a dormant yet politically dangerous working class. The result was an absence of unions or any other form of political organization not subsidized by the governments. However, the consequence of the outlawing of unions led to the creation of a truly working-class and nationalistic mentality among members of the Communist Party. After the demise of the Soviet Union in 1991, unions were still outlawed. But workers increasingly used their political influence within the new regime.

## U.S. LABOR UNIONS

The trade unions in 19th-century United States were weak. Estimates vary but most scholars agree that approximately two percent of the total labor force and less than 10 percent of all industrial workers, became members of unions.

One American organization of this period was the National Labor Union. This was a delegate convention consisting of representatives from local, state, and national trade associations. At its height, membership was reported to approximate 640,000. Beginning in 1866, seven annual conventions were held by the membership. Initially, the influence of the national body was chiefly advisory and its aim essentially political. Its powers were strengthened somewhat as experience showed weakness. The convention was given authority to charter new locals and to exercise some degree of control over them. The organization was a vast umbrella organization which included both skilled and unskilled workers. However, the conflict between these two disparate groups would weaken the solidarity of the organization and would subsequently lead to its demise—opening the way for the rise of another more powerful organization.

As a result of an intense period of industrial production and business reorganization, in 1881 the Federation of Trades and Labor Unions was founded. In 1886, the organization changed its name to the American Federation of Labor (AFL). Based on the influential Trade Union Congress in England, the AFL's first elected president was Samuel Gompers. He had fairly conservative political beliefs and whispered that trade unionists should accept the fundamental tenets of the capitalist economic system, whether positive or negative.

In 1894, the Pullman Palace Car Company illegally reduced the wages of its workers. According to labor laws, labor and the company had to try to come to some type of agreement. The two groups had to engage in ar-

bitration, or the settlement of a labor dispute. When the company refused arbitration, the American Railway Union called a strike. Starting in Chicago, the strike spread to 27 states. The attorney general, Richard Olney, sought an injunction against the strikers under the Sherman Antitrust Act, which was a punitive measure against the labor unions. As a result of Olney's action, Eugene Debs, president of the American Railway Union and future leader of the Socialist Party, was arrested and imprisoned for a number of years.

Debs's case was argued before the Supreme Court in 1895, which refused the American Railway Union's appeal. This decision became an immense setback for the American trade union movement. The decision made some workers question the AFL's moderate approach. Debs, angered by the moderate tenor of the labor movement, converted to socialism and maintained that capitalism should be replaced by a new cooperative system, a system that bordered on being communistic.

With the weakening of the trade union movement, in 1905 representatives from 43 groups, opposing the conservative policies of the AFL, formed the radical labor organization the Industrial Workers of the World (IWW), also known as the Wobblies. The Wobblies wanted to organize all workers into "one big union." The IWWs were militant and fought when they were attacked. Some important leaders of this organization included William Haywood, Daniel De Leon, Debs, Elizabeth Gurley Flynn, Mary "Mother" Jones, Carlo Tresca, Joseph Ettor, Arturo Giovannitti, William Z. Foster, Joe Hill, Frank Little, and Ralph Chaplin. The radical ideology of the Wobblies centered on the usage of violence to attain political means. In other words, it was no longer necessary to utilize political means. Essentially, the Wobblies initiated a new form of political dialogue—a mixture of violence and radicalism. This was a formula that was not accepted by other sectors of American society.

After World War I, the police harassed the leaders of the IWW. The leaders suffered many legal prosecutions. Two important members, Little and Walter Everett, were lynched by local officials. This approach, along with the consequences of the repressive Red Scare that enveloped the nation after 1919, was highly effective and by 1925 membership had declined dramatically.

In 1921, John L. Lewis, leader of the United Mine Workers of America, unsuccessfully attempted to dispute Gompers's leadership for the presidency of the AFL. Lewis wrote that Gompers had led the AFL down the wrong road. In the process, he had bankrupted the AFL's constituency. After much political pressure, Gompers finally left in 1924 and was replaced by William Green. Gompers's replacement led the organization into the political sphere, as the AFL became more involved in the political process. Like other international unions, the AFL became embroiled in domestic political affairs, which to a certain degree weakened its ideological basis.

In 1932, in the midst of the Great Depression, the Democratic candidate, Franklin D. Roosevelt, was elected with the support of most trade unionists. Roosevelt, who promised a New Deal to the American public, sought to provide relief for the party's many constituents, including the working class. He immediately appointed Frances Perkins as secretary of Labor and Robert Wagner as chairman of the National Recovery Administration. Both Perkins and Wagner were widely known for their sympathy for the trade union movement.

## NATIONAL LABOR RELATIONS ACT

In 1933, Wagner introduced a bill to Congress that helped protect trade unionists from their employers' abusive and exploitative labor practices. With the support of Perkins, Wagner's proposals became the National Labor Relations Act. It created a three-person National Labor Relations Board to regulate labor relations in industries engaged in or affecting interstate commerce. The act also gave workers the right to join trade unions and, most importantly, to bargain collectively with their employers through representatives of their own choosing. Workers were now legally and constitutionally protected from their employers and as a result, union membership grew rapidly.

In 1935, John L. Lewis joined with the heads of seven other unions to form the Congress for Industrial Organization (CIO). Lewis became president of this new organization and over the next few years attempted to organize workers in the mass production industries. This strategy proved successful, as by 1937 the CIO counted more members than the AFL.

In June 1938, Perkins persuasively influenced Congress to pass the Fair Labor Standards Act. The main objective of the act was to eliminate "labor conditions detrimental to the maintenance of the minimum standards of living necessary for health, efficiency and well-being of workers." The act essentially instituted maximum working hours as 44 a week for the first year, 42 for the second, and 40 thereafter and minimum

wages of 25 cents an hour were established for the first year, 30 cents for the second, and 40 cents over a period of the next six years. The Fair Labor Standards Act also prohibited child labor in all industries engaged in producing goods in interstate commerce and placed a limitation of the labor of boys and girls between 16 and 18 years of age in hazardous occupations.

Another important act initiated by Perkins and Vice President Harry Truman was the Fair Employment Act. Passed in 1942, this act required that all federal agencies must include in their contracts with private employers a provision obligating such employers not to "discriminate against persons of any race, color, creed, or nationality in matters of employment." The act set up the Committee on Fair Employment Practice (FEPC), a body that was empowered to investigate all complaints of discrimination, take appropriate steps to eliminate such discrimination, and make recommendations to Roosevelt concerning discrimination in the war industry.

The Republican Party and right-wing elements in the Democratic Party objected to what they believed was the pro-trade union legislation of the Roosevelt administration. On June 23, 1947, the Republican Congress passed the controversial Taft-Hartley Act, over the veto of now President Truman, who denounced it as a "slave-labor bill" that sought to exploit the working class.

Specifically, the act declared the closed shop (that is, a worker could not be employed unless the worker belonged to the union) illegal and permitted the union shop only after a majority of the employees voted for it. Moreover, the act also forbade jurisdictional strikes and secondary boycotts, which would have been economically disastrous for a country involved in World War II. Other aspects of the legislation included the right of employers to be exempted from bargaining with unions unless they wished to.

In addition, the act forbade unions from contributing to political campaigns and required union leaders to affirm they were not supporters of the Communist Party. This aspect of the act was upheld by the Supreme Court on May 8, 1950.

Green remained president of the American Federation of Labor until 1952 when he was replaced by George Meany. In 1955, the CIO merged with the AFL. Walter Reuther, the president of the CIO, became vice president of the AFL-CIO. Meany became president of this new organization that now had a membership of 15 million workers. Eventually, the CIO would diminish in status as new technologies, innovations, and a general pro-business atmosphere prevailed during the Cold War, thus making unions a necessary yet outdated form of protest.

Certain features of the CIO endured. Mass production industries were organized on an enduring basis for the first time in America history. The CIO had lifted a whole section of working-class America out of poverty and integrated them, economically and culturally, into the nation. The CIO had helped to legitimate the idea of a welfare state. But the CIO's more ambitious schemes had been defeated.

## THIRD-WORLD UNIONISM

Unlike the partisan unionism of the Europeans and the politicization of the American labor movement, third-world unions have an entirely different set of issues and ideologies to contend with. Specifically, third-world workers not only have to deal with the travails of working class life, like low wages and exploitative living conditions, but they also have to contend with an intense nationalism, foreign intervention, and democratic systems that do not abide by democratic freedoms.

In Latin America, the concept of unionism consistently conflicted with the rise of powerful military and conservative groups, which viewed the unions as predominantly tools of the Communist International (Comintern). In two countries specifically, the main unions became labor confederations and acted as a challenge to the hegemony of the ruling classes. In Argentina, the General Workers Confederation acted as a counterbalance, especially during the Cold War, to the harsh repressive policies of the military regimes after 1950. In Mexico, the main labor confederation clearly has a dominant position within the political system, especially the dominant oil workers. Like Argentina and Mexico, unions in Latin America have acted as a pressure interest group constantly threatening a work stoppage whenever the political policies of the ruling classes exceeded their constitutional boundaries.

In the past few years, certain countries like Venezuela have seen the reemergence of a powerful labor confederation, acting independently of any political party. In 2001, President Hugo Chavez, who many political observers believe to be a socialist, experienced one of the greatest political work stoppages in both Latin American and Venezuelan history. Through an alliance of oil workers and anti-Chavez businesspeople, the work stoppage lasted for months and led to bloodshed and chaos in the streets of Caracas and Maracaibo. The strike showed the strength of the powerful oil

workers union, Fedepetrol, and more important, the idea that prevails in many Latin American unions, that when a national patrimony, in this case, petroleum, is believed to be under attack through a foreign ideology, the working class, through their respective unions, will be united in action.

## SEE ALSO

*Volume 1 Left:* Third International (Comintern); Socialism; Debs, Eugene V.; South America; United States.
*Volume 2 Right:* Capitalism; Globalization; United States; South America.

## BIBLIOGRAPHY

Harry Braverman, *Labor and Monopoly Capital: The Degradation of Work in the Twentieth Century* (Random House, 1975); Jeremy Brecher, *Strike!* (South End Press, 1979); Noam Chomsky, *World Orders Old and New* (Columbia University Press, 1994); Sidney Fine, *Sit-Down: The General Motors Strike of 1936–37* (University of Michigan Press, 1969); Mary Jones, *The Autobiography of Mother Jones* (Charles Kerr, 1925); Patricia Sexton, *The War on Labor and the Left* (Westview Press, 1994).

JAIME RAMÓN OLIVARES, PH.D
HOUSTON COMMUNITY COLLEGE, CENTRAL

# United Kingdom

THE BROAD POLITICAL beliefs, values, and ideals of the British people are set in the context of a constitutional monarchy that has evolved into a modern political system on the basis of democracy and the rule of law. Thus, while there is an ever-present strand of deferential and traditional conservatism in the British political culture, there is also a deep-rooted liberal tradition that underpins participatory democracy, human rights, and a range of freedoms. There is also a strong socialist heritage in the United Kingdom (UK), manifest in the longevity of the British Labour Party as well as the growth of the British welfare state.

Like other western nation-states, the UK (comprising England, Scotland, Wales, and Northern Ireland) has experienced major shifts in its political culture over the past 30 years. Increasingly better-educated citizens have become politically more self-confident and assertive, and at the same time decreasingly satisfied with the major political organizations, institutions, and lead-

The United Kingdom, comprising England, Wales, Scotland, and Northern Ireland, has a rich tradition and history of the left, including its Labour Party, which has been in and out of office in one form or another for 100 years.

ers. Their sense of political efficacy has increased as their levels of political trust have decreased. This era has also seen the reawakening of ideologies most of which had been latent in the immediate post-World War II era, including feminism, racism, anti-racism, nationalism, regionalism, and environmentalism.

Of greater importance than the overall British political culture is the proliferation of subcultural forces resulting from the principal sociopolitical cleavages. Of these, the most important is social class. While the class structure has changed in the United Kingdom since World War II, with a sharp diminution in the proportion of manual workers and the skilled working class, social class—as measured by occupation, education, and income—retains its political salience.

Ethno-racial differences are also important in the British context. Throughout its period of decolonization, the UK attracted nonwhite immigrants from the new Commonwealth countries. In 1996, racial minority Britons numbered 3.3 million, just under 6 percent of the population. Of these, 27 percent were of Indian origin, 23 percent were of Pakistani and Bangladeshi origin, and 26 percent were Afro-Caribbean.

## REGIONAL CONSIDERATIONS

While the United Kingdom is officially a unitary state, there is good reason to question this legal-constitutional status in light of recent political developments from below and above. Following a series of failed attempts, the UK finally joined the European Economic Community (now the European Union or EU) in 1971 under the Conservative government of Edward Heath. Both the Conservative Party and the Labour Party contained supporters and opponents of entry, and support for Britain's role in Europe has vacillated since the early 1970s. In a national referendum (1975), a two-thirds majority voted in favor of remaining in Europe. The UK has never been an entirely committed member of the European Union and held out against joining the European Monetary System in the 1980s and 1990s, retaining the British currency rather than adopting the euro. Despite some enthusiasm among the British for greater European unity, "Euro-skeptics" are dominant and UK policy remains cautious.

The UK has been called into question by three principal territorial fault lines in recent decades. The first is the ongoing issue of Northern Ireland. Following the partition of Ireland in 1922, the Protestant population became a majority in the six counties of Northern Ireland. The Catholics, now a minority, became increas-

ingly aggrieved at their loss of status and began to organize and mobilize for political change and civil rights in the 1960s. A series of conflicts arose and the two communities became entrenched in a protracted and bloody struggle between the Catholic Irish nationalists, who called for a reunification of Ireland, and the Protestant loyalists, who asserted the essentially British character of Northern Ireland. These communities formed armed militia, engaging in sectarian bombings and killings. A peace agreement, signed on Good Friday in 1998, offered a limited and contingent peace, but the intercommunity tensions remain and there is a climate of political volatility.

A solution to the regional and national aspirations of Scottish and Welsh citizens has been found in devolution. Devolution is a soft form of governmental decentralization that grants powers to legislate in certain fields to regional jurisdictions. Lacking the legal sovereignty of federal arrangements, devolution is nonetheless a serious decentralization of authority. A limited and yet persistent Welsh nationalism found expression in a Referendum in 1997, in which a bare majority voted in favor of devolution. There was more robust support for Scottish devolution in the same referendum. The new Welsh assembly had 60 members and passed secondary legislation—within the framework of laws passed in the English capital—over matters such as economic development, planning, health, education, and transport. The Scottish Parliament is altogether more powerful. Its 129 members possess the capacity to modify the Scottish tax rate, to pass primary legislation, and to shape the Scottish economy and society. Devolution has contributed to a renaissance of Scottish political identity and an increasingly independent approach to public policy in Scotland.

## THE POLITICAL ECONOMY

The modern British political economy can be traced back to World War II. The Great Depression that preceded the war, as well as the war itself, had created many hardships for the British people. Poverty, inequality, sickness, and insecurity were widespread among the British public. These facts persuaded many politicians and thinkers that a new relationship between the state and the free market was essential to achieve a just and stable order. Among the most notable thinkers was John Maynard Keynes, whose name has become synonymous with the rise of the British welfare state and mixed economy. Wartime politician W.H. Beveridge wrote a highly influential report that formed the basis of the postwar introduction of a National Health Service, universal secondary education, unemployment insurance, an expanded state pension scheme, and the provision of universal family allowances for mothers.

Both the Labour government of Prime Minister Clement Atlee and subsequent Conservative governments supported the basic provisions of the welfare state and favored an enhanced role for the state in economic planning through policy instruments such as nationalization, which took industries such as coal, steel, gas, electricity, and the railways under public ownership and control. Labour and Conservative governments also became more interventionist in attempting to use tax rates and interest rates to regulate the overall economy and thereby balance full employment with moderate inflation. Governments in this era also engaged in moderate forms of corporatism, in which the peak organizations of industry and the trade unions were brought into the heart of government itself for regular consultations on policy directions and to devise compromise solutions to wages and profit levels. The political economy of the welfare state and the mixed economy was crafted under the leadership of two chancellors of the exchequer (finance ministers), Hugh Gaiskell of the Labour Party and R.A. Butler of the Conservative Party. So closely were the economic policies of the governments associated that their policies came to be referred to as "Butskellism."

The broad consensus on macroeconomic steering policy came into question in the 1960s and 1970s. A globally overcommitted Britain discovered that its responsibilities as a former imperial power outstripped its capacity. The British economy was performing relatively poorly in comparison with its European neighbors, and the British currency, the pound sterling, was overvalued. By the early 1970s, declining productivity, combined with increasing public debt, was producing serious inflation, aggravated by the sudden quadrupling of oil prices by the OPEC (Organization of Petroleum Exporting Countries) oil cartel in 1973.

Contrary to the expectations of the time, a stagnating economy coincided with rising inflation, a situation referred to as "stagflation." The combination of stagflation, rising unemployment, and increasing burdens on the British welfare state caused governments to question the Butskellite assumptions of the Keynesian era. The Labour governments of 1975 to 1979 began to introduce wage controls, to limit the expansion of state spending, and to introduce monetarist economic policies to attempt to restrict the money supply and thereby to reduce inflation. The 1979 general election marked a

sudden turning point on the economic front. A revived Conservative Party under the leadership of Prime Minister Margaret Thatcher introduced radical economic surgery, including placing the top priority on "wrestling inflation to the ground," through a combination of direct assaults on organized labor as well as allowing unemployment rates to increase to levels that would have been unacceptable in the immediate postwar era. In this political economy, the Thatcher government attempted to inject stimuli to growth in the private sector through macroeconomic techniques known as supply-side economics. These measures included overall deregulation of the economy, tax cuts for the wealthy and for business, reduction in state spending on the welfare state, the ending of universal programs, the development of more selective benefits, and a series of privatization measures. The era of council housing (public housing) came to an end as the Thatcher government allowed long-standing state tenants to purchase their homes. A nation of new homeowners also became a nation of shareholders as the Thatcher government floated equities in newly privatized corporations. Schools, hospitals, and social service agencies were recreated as "quasi-markets," expected to show efficiencies and to operate profitably. The era of the mixed economy was over.

The election of the Tony Blair Labour Party government in 1997 did not alter the basic direction in political economy, despite a less confrontational attitude toward the trade unions, selective increases in public spending, and modest reregulation of privatized national utilities.

## THE CONSTITUTION

As a constitutional monarchy in which the principal revolutions occurred before the modern age of written declarations and constitutions, the British lack a written constitution. The 17th-century revolutions, notably the Glorious Revolution of 1688, ushered in the modern era of liberal-democratic and representative democracy in the United Kingdom in a way that modified the power of feudal institutions, such as the monarchy, the House of Lords, and the common law system, without supplanting them altogether.

Thus, there has been no formal written statement to usher in a new order. Following the Glorious Revolution, the authority of the crown was retained on the understanding that parliament would henceforth be supreme. The old order never died, it just faded away to some extent.

The contemporary constitution in the United Kingdom is grounded in a series of constitutional conventions. These conventions are commonly agreed-upon understandings that the constitution will be interpreted in certain ways and that key governmental actors will act in certain ways. Conventions are not legal agreements and have no force in law. Despite this, they are essential to the smooth functioning of the British constitution. A core constitutional convention is at the heart of the British constitution: that despite the formal constitutional authority of the crown, the "royal prerogative" will be used sparingly and in a restrained manner, leaving substantive policy decisions to the elected executive of the prime minister and cabinet (themselves entities only known through convention) and the parliament.

The authority of the "crown in parliament"—in practice, the prime minister and his government—is the basis of parliamentary or statute law, which is a further key element of the British constitution. Apart from conventions, the royal prerogative, and statute laws, the most important element of the British constitution is the accumulation of common law through centuries of court decisions in specific legal cases. The common law incorporates certain historically important precedents such as the writ of habeas corpus and the Magna Carta of 1215, which between them establish the basis of the Rule of Law. The principles of justice contained in the Rule of Law ensure that the law is applied in a manner that is fair, open, consistent, and equal. Since the 1970s, the British constitution incorporates elements of European law, notably as British law relates to Europe and also with respect to European human rights legislation.

Not everyone is happy with the unwritten British constitution and some, like the group Charter 88, are calling for a formal written document to deal with the ever-present possibility that basic rights of British people are denied.

## PARTIES, GROUPS, AND MOVEMENTS

Using a single member, simple majority or "first-past-the-post" principle, the British electoral system mathematically favors the existence of two major parties of the center-left and center-right that alternate in power. These two parties are, respectively, the Labour Party and the Conservative Party. The party that gains the plurality of votes in a general election is normally favored disproportionately in the eventual distribution of seats. Depending on the particular result, the second-place party may also gain a proportionate share of seats or better. Minor parties suffer from extreme disproportionality. It is for this reason that many in the United Kingdom have been calling for substantial electoral reform and why the Jenkins Report on the Electoral System (1998) called for an entirely new proportionate electoral system for the constituents of the United Kingdom.

The British Labour Party began its life outside parliament in the latter years of the 19th century as the Labour Representation Committee. Its purpose was to represent working men in the House of Commons. It made modest gains in the election of 1906 and by the 1920s was beginning to displace the Liberal Party as one of the two parties of government. The first minority Labour government was in 1924, and its first majority government was in 1945. The postwar Labour government created the welfare state and was still very much a party of the trade unions and traditional socialism. The modern party, under leaders Neil Kinnock and Tony Blair, has moved away from both of these pillars. The influence of the unions has diminished substantially, while the historical socialist "clause 4," sacred to many in the party for so long, has been abandoned. The modern New Labour Party is a mass membership, leader-centered, sophisticated marketing machine, which has been able to attract the electoral support of the moderate center in British political spectrum in recent years.

The British Conservative Party, began its life as a loose coalition of MPs in the House of Commons in the 18th century. Grounded in pragmatism, tradition, and adaptability, the party has successfully made the transition from the traditional Tory party of the 19th century to a modern party that incorporates elements of neoliberal fiscal beliefs with elements of social conservatism, notably a continued emphasis on British nationalism, law and order, and the social sanctity of the family.

The Liberal Democrats are the result of the union of the long-established Liberal Party and a former splinter group from the Labour Party, known as the Social Democratic Party. Officially established in 1988, the Liberal Democrats are a progressive party of the center left, whose nonsocialism initially separated them from the Labour Party. They have been sympathetic to a range of progressive causes, from regional and national aspirations to environmental integrity, constitutional reform, including most importantly reform of the electoral system, and a more positive approach toward European integration.

There is a range of small, but important, nationalist parties in Scotland and Wales and a series of unionist parties in Northern Ireland. While the official aspirations of both the Scottish National Party and Plaid Cymru (the Welsh nationalist party) continue to be for independence in Europe, both parties have benefited from the recent devolution of power from the capital, granting limited forms of self-rule.

There is a plethora of interest groups and social movements that, while not seeking elected office, nonetheless seek to influence government policy. These include major organizations such as the Trades Unions Congress, the Confederation of British Industry, and the National Farmers Union. There is also a series of nongovernmental organizations that represent the social movements. These include Greenpeace, Amnesty International, and Oxfam, all included in the left of center in Britain.

**SEE ALSO**

Volume 1 Left: Labour Party, UK; Socialism.
Volume 2 Right: Thatcher, Margaret; Capitalism; Reagan, Ronald; United Kingdom.

**BIBLIOGRAPHY**

Anthony H. Birch, *The British System of Government* (Routledge, 1998); Ian Budge, Ivor Crewe, David McKay, and Ken Newton, *The New British Politics* (Longman, 2004); Bill Coxall, Robert Leach, and Lynton Robins, *Contemporary British Politics* (Palgrave Macmillan, 2003); John Dearlove and Peter Saunders, *Introduction to British Politics* (Polity Press, 2000); Bill Jones and Dennis Kavanagh, *British Politics Today* (Manchester University Press, 2003); Bill Jones, Dennis Kavanagh, Michael Moran, and Philip Norton, *Politics UK* (Pearson, 2004); Dennis Kavanagh, *British Politics: Continuities and Change* (Oxford University Press, 2000); John Kingdom, *Government and Politics in Britain: An Introduction* (Polity Press, 2003).

PAUL NESBITT-LARKING, PH.D.
HURON UNIVERSITY COLLEGE, CANADA

# United States

THE UNITED STATES OF AMERICA is a liberal democratic country, and the basic elements of democracy (majority rule, government by popular consent, one person one vote, and competitive elections, to name a few) are revered. In this liberal democratic country, certain core values have persisted since America's founding. The American creed stresses such values as individuality, liberty, unity, self-government, diversity and equality.

At times, these values may be contradictory. For example, individuality may come under attack when segments of society feel they are disenfranchised or disadvantaged or discriminated against, and therefore these segments of society believe they are unable to equally compete with others in society. In a country as diverse as the United States, people will have different opinions regarding the core values of the country, the direction they believe the country should move toward, and the methods of governmental and societal change. To the left side of liberalism on the political spectrum is social democracy and socialism, and to the far left, communism. These ideologies have existed and persisted in the United States, although they have never dominated American political thought. However, a lack of political domination does not mean that these ideologies have not had an effect on American political thought.

The American party system is a two-party dominated system, and this means that only two political parties have a real chance of dominating either the House of Representatives or the Senate, or of having their nominee elected president. Except for a brief period known as the Era of Good Feeling (1820–24), there have always been two dominant parties in America, although it has not always been the same two parties. Since the Civil War, party politics in America have been dominated by the Democrats and the Republicans (and although these two parties have persisted, they have both altered in their ideologies). This does not mean that other parties have not formed and existed and had an impact on American political life. Other parties, usually referred to as third parties, may represent ideas from either end of the political spectrum. Currently, there are many third parties that are conservative. Current parties that are left of center include the Communist Party, the Freedom Socialist Party/Radical Women, the Grassroots Party, the Green Party, the Labor Party, the Light Party, the Natural Law Party, the New Party, the New Union Party, the Peace and Freedom Party, the Revolution, the Socialist Action, the Socialist Equality Party, the Socialist Labor Party, the Socialist Workers Party, the World Workers Party, and the Young Communist Party, to name a few.

Third parties differ broadly in their origins and their intentions. Some third parties have been literally imported into the United States. For example, European radicals fleeing persecution in Europe in the mid-

19th century found a haven in the United States and brought with them their socialists ideas. Other third parties arise from splits or factions within the dominant parties. Recognizing the dominance of the two-party system in the United States, most third parties have no intention of forming the government, but they do offer candidates as the most viable and visible way of garnering attention for their platforms. In a close election, such as the 2000 Presidential election, a third party may hold the balance of power. In rare instances, a third party may grandly claim to intend to win an outright electoral victory (for example, Ross Perot in both 1992 and 1996).

One of the first left-of-center third parties in America was the Populist Party, also known as the People's Party, and this third party, although short-lived, made an impact in the late 19th century. Following the collapse of agriculture prices and the Panic of 1873, various farmers' groups discussed their options and held a convention in 1892. As a result, the Populist Party was formed. The platform of the Populists included the abolition of national banks, a graduated income tax, the direct election of U.S. Senators, civil service reform, and the implementation of an eight-hour working day. In 1892, the Populists selected James B. Weaver as their presidential nominee and he collected over one million votes. Many of the policies of the Populists were adopted by the Democrats and this poaching of ideas hastened the demise of the Populist Party. However, the Seventeenth Amendment to the Constitution (1913), respecting the direct election of Senators, can be directly attributed to the ideas of the Populists.

## THE SOCIALIST PARTY

Formed in 1901, the Socialist Party has influenced American politics, albeit, at times, indirectly. A party of American radicals, the Socialist Party was formed following a unity convention in Indianapolis in 1901 that brought together Marxists, Christian socialists, unionists, Zionists, anti-Zionists, immigrants, and advocates of a single tax. One of the founders of the Socialist Party was the leader of the Social Democratic Party, Eugene Victor Debs. Debs ran for president five times (1900, 1904, 1908, 1912, and 1920). In 1912 and 1920, Debs received over one million votes (and in 1920, he was in jail, serving a sentence for espionage charges, when he ran for president). Prior to World War I, the Socialist Party was gaining recognition and acceptance across the country. Two socialists were elected to Congress, over 70 mayors across America were socialists, as were

countless city councilors, and the Socialist Party claimed to have over 100,000 members. The Socialist Party disagreed with American involvement in World War I and their protests led to the imprisonment of many socialist leaders, including Debs. There was a major split in the party in 1919. A segment of the party joined the Third (Communist) International and formed the Communist Party and the Communist Labor Party; these parties eventually became the United Communist Party, now the Communist Party USA.

The Socialist Party revived in 1928 under the leadership of Norman Thomas (a World War I opponent and a founder of the American Civil Liberties Union). The stock market crash in 1929 and the Great Depression that plagued the 1930s saw a revival of support for the Socialist Party. In 1932, Socialist Party presidential candidate Thomas garnered 896,000 votes. However, President Franklin Delano Roosevelt and his New Deal policies eroded socialist support. In the 1936 presidential election, the socialists only captured 185,000 votes. World War II and then the postwar period of economic prosperity further weakened socialist support. Although McCarthyism was specifically directed toward communist sympathizers, the nationwide anti-left sentiments affected all parties on the left. By the mid-1950s, the Socialist Party had dwindled to about 2,000 members.

In 1956, the Socialist Party and the Social Democratic Federation reunited and in 1958 the Independent Socialist league also joined forces. This reunion was short-lived; various factions within the party destabilized this attempt at a united socialist front. Within the Socialist Party, there was a strong push for a realignment strategy. This realignment strategy argued that the socialists should work within the politically dominant Democratic Party, and push the Democrats, from within, to the left. The labor movement is the key for social change for the socialists. However, labor would not come over to the Socialist Party, so many within the Socialist Party argued that the party had to go to labor, but labor was firmly aligned with the Democratic Party. Thus, socialists had to go to the Democratic Party. It was political realism. This realignment strategy, while intended to bring the Democrats further to the left, had the unintended consequence of toning down socialist policy. The youth within the Socialist Party (typically considered to be more left in attitude) were among the first to defect and they formed the Young People's Socialist League (although this league disbanded in 1963). Emotions in the United States were raw (for many reasons, including the assassinations of Martin Luther

King, Jr., and Robert Kennedy, the protests against the Vietnam War, and the continuing civil rights movement), and the riots at the 1968 Democratic National Convention in Chicago cast further doubts on the wisdom of the realignment strategy.

By the end of 1972, right-wing elements were in control of the Socialist Party and they decided to change the party name to the Social Democrats USA. Again, the early and mid-1970s saw many factions and splits within the party. In 1973, a conference on the future of democratic socialism in America led to the reconstitution of the Socialist Party USA. Countering the factions within the Socialist Party, another party, the Democratic Socialists of America, was formed in 1982.

The Socialist Party continues to offer candidates at the presidential level. In 2000, David McReynolds ran under the Socialist Party banner. His name was on the ballot in only seven states. He garnered only 7,746 votes nationwide, only 0.01 percent of the national vote, however this political segment of America continues to present their political ideas to a national audience.

## THE COMMUNIST PARTY

Further to the left is the Communist Party USA (CPUSA). Based on Marxist-Leninist ideals, the party was formed in 1919. The CPUSA believes that capitalism is fundamentally flawed and that capitalism abuses the working class to the benefit of the wealthy. Capitalism will eventually and inevitably give way to socialism. Although many argue that communism is flawed and the predictions of Marx proved incorrect (specifically, that the worldwide workers' revolution Marx predicted would begin in the industrialized countries), the CPUSA argues that many of Marx's predictions have, in fact, proved correct. For example, the internationalization of wealth, the concentration of wealth and power in the hands of a few, the inability of capitalism to avoid and/or handle repeated world economic crises, the growing gap between the wealthy and the poor, and the persistent drive for ever-increasing profits are all aspects of the world economy (and the American economy in microcosm). As long as these conditions exist, there will be people who are attracted to the tenets of both socialism and communism to combat these perceived disparities.

The goals of the CPUSA include: the creation of a life free of exploitation, insecurity, and poverty, including an end to unemployment, hunger, and homelessness; an end to racism, national oppression, anti-Semitism, discrimination in all its forms, prejudice, bigotry, and an end to the unequal status of women; and a renewal and extension of democracy, at least, a different conception of democracy, which would require both an end to the rule of corporate America and an end to the private ownership of the wealth of the nation, and in its place, there would be the creation of a truly humane and rationally planned society. These goals appear utopian, but the CPUSA argues that these goals can be realized when a socialist society replaces capitalism. The CPUSA argues that the United States is a country of revolution and is thus uniquely positioned to accept the revolutionary tenets of socialism and communism. As the United States was created following a revolution, how can being a revolutionary in the 21st century be deemed to be unpatriotic? The United States is unique in its history, traditions, and culture and thus socialism in the United States will also be a uniquely American phenomenon.

Communism in the United States came under vicious attack in the 1950s. Following World War II, Senator Joseph McCarthy spearheaded a communist witch-hunt that ruined the lives and reputations of many Americans affiliated with communism. Many leaders of the communist movement were persecuted and imprisoned. Ethel and Julius Rosenberg were convicted of conspiracy to commit espionage and they were executed in 1953. The Communist Party has never actually been banned by the United States government, however, many states prevented proclaimed communists from running for office.

Many of the policies advocated by communists have taken root in the United States. For example, in the 1930s, communists advocated for the creation of a national retirement program, and as the merits of this idea gained acceptance, today's system of Social Security can be attributed in part to the efforts of communists. Communist Americans fought in World War II against fascism, opposed the Korean War, the Vietnam War, and the two Gulf Wars, and participated in the civil rights movement. The ideas and attitudes advocated by communist Americans add another layer of richness to the social and political philosophy of the United States and force Americans to think about things in a different light.

## OTHER POLITICAL PARTIES ON THE LEFT

In the 2000 presidential election, the impact of the Green Party cannot be ignored. An environmentally based party, the Green party stresses community-based economics, decentralization, ecological wisdom, feminism, grassroots democracy, nonviolence, respect for diversity, and social justice. Consumer advocate Ralph Nader was the Green Party presidential nominee in 1996 and 2000. In 1996, Nader's name and party affiliation was on the presidential ballot in 22 states. He came in fourth and collected less than 1 percent of the total vote. In 2000, Nader's name appeared on the presidential ballot in 44 states. His anti-corporate campaign attracted considerable attention and many argued that his advocacy would nibble away at support for the Democratic candidate, Al Gore. As it turned out, the 2000 election was extremely close, with the Republican nominee George W. Bush narrowly defeating Al Gore (in electoral college votes, not the popular vote). Nader collected 2,858,843 votes (according to the United States National Archive and Records Administration), which amounts to only 2.7 percent of the national vote. However, this was sufficient to ensure Bush's victory (assuming that, if Nader had not been on the ballot, his votes would have found a home with the Democrats). Nader repeated his presidential run again in 2004, this time as an independent candidate.

The Grassroots Party advocates for the legalization of marijuana, the promotion of hemp farming, and the establishment of a national system of universal healthcare. The Labor Party, a liberal party formed in 1996, is a coalition of labor unions, including the United Mine Workers, the Longshoremen, the American Federation of Government Employees and the California Nurses Association. The Labor Party is concerned with issues important to working people. Their mandate includes trade issues, healthcare, and the rights to organize, bargain, and strike. The Labor Party formed out of a growing concern that the Democratic and Republican parties have failed working people and that these traditional parties neither listen nor respond to the concerns of working people.

## INTEREST GROUPS

When the Founding Fathers were creatively arguing about the design of the American government, debate arose over the natural proclivity of people to associate with others who share their concerns and interests. In *Federalist No. 10*, James Madison described the "mischiefs of factions," and he contended that there were only two ways to control the trouble that could arise from voluntary associations: one, remove the causes that lead to the formation of voluntary interests (and this Madison says is impossible, because it is in the nature of people to find other like-minded people and to

prohibit this would be to limit liberty); and two, controlling the effects of factions. The American system is an extremely fragmented political system. It is a federal system and it has a rigid separation of powers. A faction that might ultimately try to take over the government would have to take over both the national government and state governments and control many offices within these levels of government. Thus, the careful creation of an intricate and complicated government, in effect, controls factions. Despite this, in the past 200 years, an elaborate system of organized interests has developed.

Organized interests lobby (influence) both the state governments and the national government. It is estimated that there are well over 20,000 interest organizations that lobby the various states. Each of the 50 states requires that interest organizations register with the legislatures they lobby. In 1996, Congress enacted the Lobby Disclosure Act, and this legislation requires that all organizations both directly contacting legislators and spending at least $20,500 over a six-month period register with Congress. In 1996, nearly 6,000 interest organizations registered in compliance with the new act.

Organized interests fall into three general categories; governments (keep in mind that states lobby states, states lobby Congress, other countries lobby the United States); economic interests (including professional groups, agricultural groups, labor unions and business groups); and noneconomic (also known as citizens) interest groups. The most prolific category of interest groups are the economic interest groups (these groups tend to have both large memberships and access to large amounts of money), and although unions tend to be left of center, it is safe to say that the majority of the economic groups tend to be conservative in nature. Citizens groups, again speaking in generalities, tend to be more left of center in nature.

Many interest groups lobby on a wide range of issues; other interest groups are only concerned with one issue or at most, a narrow range of issues. Interest groups may target their message toward the American public, the political executive, the legislative branch of government, or the judicial branch of government, or any combination of these targets. One very well known, left-of-center organized interest is the American Civil Liberties Union (ACLU).

The ACLU was founded in 1920. This nonprofit and nonpartisan organized interest boasts nearly 400,000 members and supporters. With offices in nearly every state, the ACLU is involved in over 6,000 court cases annually. The ACLU defends the American Constitution and the Bill of Rights, and in particular, the First Amendment guarantees, equal protection under the law, due process rights, and the right to privacy. Issues of concern for the ACLU include voting rights, women's rights, immigrants' rights, disability rights, lesbian and gay rights, reproductive rights, students' rights, drug policy, free speech, racial equality, religious equality, criminal justice, and an end to the death penalty. The ACLU works to extend rights to segments of society traditionally denied their rights. Civil liberties have always been at the cornerstone of the ACLU mandate, and in the days since September 11, 2001, the ACLU has insisted that civil liberties must be respected, even in times of national emergency.

Another extremely well known left-of-center organized interest is the National Association for the Advancement of Colored People (NAACP). The NAACP was founded by a multiracial group of activists in 1909 (originally called the National Negro Committee). The NAACP broadly describes its mandate as a quest for civil and political liberty, more specifically, the pursuit of legal battles addressing issues of social injustice. Any issue of political, educational, social, and economic equality for both minority groups and individuals may attract the attention of the NAACP. The NAACP works to eliminate race prejudice, secure civil rights, inform the public, educate people with respect to their civil rights, and enact and enforce laws at all levels of government to secure civil rights. The NAACP works within the legal system to attain its goals.

Since its inception, the NAACP has fought to stop lynchings, sought the commission of African American officers in World War I, fought for equal access for African Americans, fought against segregation (the famous *Brown v. Board of Education* case in 1954 was argued by NAACP lawyers including Thurgood Marshall, who later became the first African American on the Supreme Court in 1967), and its members were at the forefront of the civil rights movement.

## SOCIAL MOVEMENTS

Social movements may be defined as both active and sustained efforts to achieve political and social change for groups who feel that the government and/or society has not respected their rights or responded to their concerns. There is an emphasis on group rights, as opposed to individual rights. Social movements tend to be more broadly based, loosely organized collections of individuals who advocate for the inclusion of interests traditionally outside of the political establishment. For example, the abolition of slavery, the civil rights move-

ment, and the women's movement are extremely well recognized, but other movements, for example, the gay/lesbian/bisexual/transgendered rights movement, the anti-nuclear movement, black nationalism, and the environmental movement are also examples of prominent social movements in the United States. Almost by definition, social movements tend to be left of center (there are exceptions, for example, fundamentalist Christian social movements would not be defined as left of center).

Social movements are an atypical type of political participation. However, just because a social movement is an unconventional type of political activism does not mean that it necessarily leads to violence or illegal activities. A social movement may be nonviolent. Martin Luther King, Jr., one of the most prominent leaders of the civil rights movement, advocated nonviolent civil disobedience.

The effects of a successful social movement may be profound. The abolition of slavery was propelled along by activists and the eventual Emancipation Proclamation indicates that a social movement can change the collective mind of a country. Direct consequences of the civil rights movement include the Civil Rights Act of 1964 and the Voting Rights Act of 1965. The women's rights movement promoted the Equal Rights Amendment, and despite the fact that this amendment to the Constitution failed to be ratified, its effects have been felt at all levels of American society.

The United States has had a rich history of politics on the left. While left-of-center parties have not dominated American politics, they have advocated changes that have been worked into the American system. The direct election of Senators, social security, union protection, and workers' rights (including minimum wages, maximum working hours, restrictions on child labor, unemployment insurance, workers' compensation) are all examples of the effects leftist parties have made on American society.

### SEE ALSO

*Volume 1 Left*: Communism; Socialism; Civil Rights; Debs, Eugene V.; Thomas, Norman; Green Party; American Civil Liberties Union; King, Martin Luther, Jr.; Democratic Party; Unions; Feminism.

*Volume 2 Right*: United States; McCarthyism; Conservatism; Republican Party; Bush, George W.; Capitalism.

### BIBLIOGRAPHY

Left-wing political party and interest group internet sites: www.sp-usa.org; www.cpusa.org; www.slp.org; www.socialdemocrats.org; www.dsausa.org; www.aclu.org; ww.naacp.org (May 2004); John H. Aldrich, *Why Parties? The Origin and Transformation of Political Parties in America* (University of Chicago Press, 1995); Clare Cushman, ed., *Supreme Court Decisions and Women's Rights* (Congressional Quarterly Press, 2001); Marjorie Randon Hershey and Paul Allen Beck, *Party Politics in America* (Longman Publishing, 2003); David Lowery and Holly Brasher, *Organized Interests and American Government* (McGraw Hill, 2004); Robert Nozick, *Anarchy, State, and Utopia* (Basic Books, 1974); Jonathan Rauch, *Gay Marriage* (Times Books, 2004); Michael J. Sandel, *Democracy's Discontent: America in Search of a Public Philosophy* (Belknap Press, 1996).

AMANDA BURGESS
WAYNE STATE UNIVERSITY

# The Left

## Vietnam War

THE VIETNAM WAR HAD its origin in American involvement in what was French Indochina in World War II. After the capitulation of France in June 1940 to Nazi Germany, the collaborationist regime of Marshal Henri Petain at Vichy took over the French colonial empire, including Syria and Lebanon in the Middle East and Indochina in Southeast Asia. When Japan went to war in December 1941, as an ally of Nazi Germany, it technically "occupied" French Indochina, rather than conquering it as the Japanese did the Dutch East Indies or the Philippines. This fiction was continued until March 9, 1945, when the Japanese struck at the Vichy authorities and took control militarily. France's French Foreign Legion soldiers who resisted were slaughtered at Ha Giang. Some 5,000 French troops, including those of the Fifth Foreign Legion Regiment, made a fighting retreat into friendly territory in China.

The Japanese coup had a direct effect on American intelligence operations in Southeast Asia, an outgrowth of the work of the American OSS (Office of Strategic Services) in China. American intelligence officers (those foreign nationals recruited are more precisely called the "agents") had entered French Indochina to help provide assistance for American airmen whose planes had been damaged on bombing flights against Japan. Among those who entered Indochina was the OSS officer

Archimedes Patti, who made contact with the Communist leader of the nationalist resistance to the French, Ho Chi Minh. (In Vietnamese, the name means "he who enlightens.") Ho had been born in about 1890 as Nguyen That Thanh, and had became a communist while in France during World War I. The Communist International (Comintern) had sent him to Moscow for training in 1923.

Ho became fully involved in support of the Americans and saved a large number of "downed" flyers, although exact figures are unclear. For the PBS series, *The American Experience: Vietnam*, Patti was interviewed. He recalled, "I first met Ho on the China border between China and Indochina in the last days of April of 1945. He was an interesting individual. Very sensitive, very gentle, rather a frail type. We spoke quite at length about the general situation, not only in Indochina, but the world at large. ... There, for the first time, we saw what kind of troops the Viet Minh were. They were a very willing, fine young nationalist, really what we used to say 'gung ho' type. They were willing to risk their lives for their cause, the cause of independence against the French."

When the Japanese surrendered on September 2, 1945, Ho issued a declaration of independence for the "Democratic Republic of Vietnam." In drafting it, Ho had been heavily influenced by the American Revolution against the British in 1775. Patti stated, "Of course, it was in Vietnamese and I couldn't read it and when it was translated for me, I was quite taken aback to hear the words of the American Declaration of Independence. Words about liberty, life, and the pursuit of happiness, etcetera. I just couldn't believe my own ears."

However, before long, the American involvement with Ho and his Viet Minh became entwined in the growing American concern over the advance of communism after the end of World War II. By 1947, the war had already been replaced by the Cold War. American President Franklin D. Roosevelt had followed an anti-colonialist foreign policy, which had led to Patti's encouragement of Ho. However, upon Roosevelt's death in April 1945, he was succeeded by his vice president, Harry Truman, who would become a "hard-liner," along with Secretary of State James Byrnes, against communism the world over. It was in 1947 that the career U.S. Foreign Service Officer George Kennan, wrote under the pseudonym "X" in *Foreign Affairs* his article on the "containment" of communism.

In March 1946, Ho, as President of the Democratic Republic of Vietnam, had reached an interim agreement with the French. The Japanese garrison troops had been disarmed in by Chinese Kuomintang (Nationalist) troops in the North and by the British in the South. Ho apparently had thought the French were returning for a brief period, but in fact they intended to restore their colonial rule. French efforts to recolonize Vietnam were now seen as part of the worldwide struggle against communism. This was especially true after Chiang Kai-shek and his Kuomintang were defeated, and China fell to the communists under Mao Zedong in October 1949. Chinese Communist troops appeared on Indochina's northern frontier. The fact that the Vietnamese had an antipathy toward the Chinese going back over 1,000 years was lost on Washington bureaucrats; as PBS noted, Vietnam's national heroes included "the Trung sisters, who led a rebellion against China in the first century [after] Christ."

By 1952, Truman was able to assure the French that their victory over Ho and his Viet Minh was "essential to the security of the free world, not only in the Far East but in the Middle East and Europe as well." According to Guenther Lewy in *America in Vietnam*, "U.S. assistance, which began with the modest sum of $10 million in 1950, in fiscal year 1954 reached $1.063 billion, at which time it accounted for 78 percent of the French war burden."

The French in their attempt to pacify the country only appeared to inspire alienation—or hostility—among the Vietnamese. On May 7, 1954, the French suffered a disastrous defeat at Dien Bien Phu at the hands of the Viet Minh under General Vo Nguyen Giap. For all practical purposes, the French had lost the war. Coincidentally, on May 8 a conference opened in Geneva, Switzerland, to decide the fate of Indochina. What resulted was a de facto partition with the North under Ho Chi Minh and the South under Ngo Dinh Diem, who effectively replaced the French choice, Emperor Bao Dai.

Almost immediately, American aid was given to Diem to make South Vietnam a barrier to communist expansion from the north, effectively making the North-South partition permanent. One of those sent was Edward Lansdale, who had had played an effective role in quelling the Communist Huk rising in the Philippines. Lansdale took a view of the Vietnamese situation that was not shared by the administration of President Dwight D. Eisenhower and Secretary of State John Foster Dulles. Lansdale noted that the "little guys, the rice farmers, know far more than the policymakers. [Theirs] is the simplified wisdom of the victim," as Cecil B. Currey quoted him in *Edward Lansdale: The Unquiet American*. The image of Vietnam as part of the global battlefield against communism remained throughout the Eisenhower administration and continued when John F. Kennedy became president in January 1961. Kennedy stated in September 1963 that "If we withdrew from Vietnam, the communists would control Vietnam. Pretty soon Thailand, Cambodia, Laos, Malaya would go."

Yet contrary opinion has stated that Kennedy privately intended to begin withdrawing American advisers in South Vietnam after he won the presidential election in November 1964. However, this was not to be, for Kennedy was assassinated in Dallas, Texas, in November 1963. Upon becoming president, Vice President Lyndon B. Johnson became a staunch supporter of American aid to South Vietnam. When North Vietnamese torpedo boats apparently attacked the American destroyers *Maddux* and *Turner Joy* in the Gulf of Tonkin in August 1964, Johnson obtained passage of the Gulf of Tonkin Resolution in Congress, using it effectively as a declaration of war. In March 1965, American Marines landed at Da Nang; the first American combat troops had been committed to support South Vietnam. Stated Johnson in August 1965, "If this little nation goes down the drain and can't maintain her independence, ask yourself, what's going to happen to all the other little nations?"

The American forces, led by General William Westmoreland, were more than capable of defeating the

*The toll at home: Anti-war protest reached a climax at Kent State University on May 4, 1970, when the National Guard shot four students. The demonstrations against the war helped give rise to the New Left political movement.*

enemy, the guerrilla Viet Cong and North Vietnamese "main force" regulars in combat. In November 1965, the North Vietnamese suffered heavy losses in the Ia Drang Valley in combat with the First Cavalry Division (Airmobile). Some of the most intense fighting took place in the tunnels at Cu Chi, which had been a Viet Minh/Viet Cong stronghold since the war against the French.

THE TET OFFENSIVE

However, beginning with the academic "teach-ins" in 1964, a protest movement was growing in the United States against the war. As American losses mounted, and continued expressions that "the light was at the end of the tunnel" proving erroneous, popular opposition mounted. It reached a crescendo at the time of the Tet

offensive, the Vietnamese New Year, on January 30, 1968. Indeed, the Tet offensive proved the turning point in the war. Although militarily defeated (it was Giap's last hurrah as a field commander), the North Vietnamese shocked Americans who had been lulled into a false sense of security by the Johnson Administration. From January to April 1968, the U.S. Marines and South Vietnamese troops underwent a terrible siege at Khe Sanh, which almost became an American Dien Bien Phu. Sensing growing dissatisfaction with the war, Johnson announced on March 31, 1968 that he would not run for reelection as president.

Although the United States could defeat the enemy in any battle, it proved almost impossible to win the war. As Sam M. Sarkesian wrote in *America's Forgotten Wars: the Counterrevolutionary Past and Lessons for the Future*, "the essence of manpower was not in the superiority of numbers by the counterrevolutionaries, but in the ability of the revolutionaries to mobilize superior numbers at any given moment." Even the massive "search and destroy" operations mounted by the Americans and South Vietnamese did not take away the enemies' option of refusing to fight if they felt nothing could be gained.

The Republican candidate Richard M. Nixon won in November 1968 on a platform of ending the war, and introduced "Vietnamization" as a strategy aimed at turning the war over to the South Vietnamese. American troop strength, which peaked at 543,000, would be gradually drawn down as the burden of the fighting—at least theoretically—could be safely entrusted to the South Vietnamese army, the ARVN. The military draft of the Selective Service system was replaced by a national draft lottery instead. In 1970, massive attacks were launched at Cambodia, in the "Parrot's Beak" area, and in Laos to attack North Vietnamese sanctuaries there. But the net result was only involving Cambodia actively in the war; in Laos, the CIA had been conducting a clandestine war while allied with the anticommunist General Vang Pao for some years already.

In April 1972, sustained American bombing helped the ARVN defeat the North Vietnamese Easter Offensive. Finally, in December 1972, Nixon ordered heavy bombing of the Northern capital of Hanoi and the bombing and mining of Haiphong harbor, the main port of North Vietnam, despite the danger of involving the Soviet Union in the war if Soviet shipping was harmed. After the heavy bombing, a peace treaty in Paris was signed on January 27, 1973, between the United States and the North Vietnamese. North Vietnam launched a heavy offensive against the South in March 1975, but Congress was against President Gerald R. Ford's desire to help the South Vietnamese: there had already been enough help, the Congress felt. The South Vietnamese Army virtually collapsed, and Saigon, the capital, fell on April 30, 1975. Laos and Cambodia fell soon thereafter.

A total of 2.5 million Americans fought in Vietnam. And 58,000 Americans died there. These figures, tallied daily in the American media, and the futility of the war, spurred the rise of the New Left in the United States. Draft-age activists against the war took on the reins of liberal protest, replacing the older generation of the Old Left who veered toward socialism earlier in the century. The New Left championed civil rights and antiestablishment doctrines of multiple sorts, from black power and women rights to the hippie back-to-earth movements.

**SEE ALSO**

*Volume 1 Left:* New Left; Hayden, Tom; United States; Liberalism; Johnson, Lyndon B.; Kennedy, John F.
*Volume 2 Right:* Eisenhower, Dwight D.; Nixon, Richard M.; United States.

**BIBLIOGRAPHY**

PBS, *Vietnam: A Television History: Roots of a War (1945-1953)*, Transcript, www.pbs.org (July 2004); John Steward Ambler, *The French Army and Politics* (Ohio State University Press, 1966); Guenther Lewy, *America in Vietnam* (Oxford University Press, 1978); Joe Havely, "Cu Chi: The Underground War," BBC News (April 25, 2000); Sam M. Sarkesian, *America's Forgotten Wars: The Counterrevolutionary Past and Lessons for the Future* (Greenwood Press, 1984); Douglas Porch, *The French Foreign Legion: A Complete History of the Legendary Fighting Force* (Harper, 1991); Anthony James Joes, *America and Guerrilla Warfare* (University Press of Kentucky, 2000); Cecil B. Currey, *Edward Lansdale: The Unquiet American* (Brassey's 1998); Marianna P. Sullivan, *France's Vietnam Policy: A Study in French-American Relations* (Greenwood Press, 1978); Lucien Bodard, *The Quicksand War: Prelude to Vietnam,* (Faber, 1965); Stanley Karnow, *Vietnam: a History* (Penguin, 1983); John S. Bowman, ed., *The Vietnam War: An Almanac* (World Almanac, 1985).

JOHN F. MURPHY, JR.
AMERICAN MILITARY UNIVERSITY

# Voting, Unrestricted

IN 1870, the Fifteenth Amendment guaranteed African Americans the right to vote, but state laws and local practice (intimidation, tax requirements, education tests, and so on), especially in the South, extremely restricted the voting possibility of nonwhites. It took the civil rights movement and the Voting Rights Act of 1965 to overcome these restrictions. Nevertheless unrestricted voting is a vision never to be realized, but always aimed at in a free society. Unrestricted voting must be at least universal, direct, equal, free, and secret.

"Universal" means that all voters in a given entity must have the right to vote. Universality is hampered in voluntary and involuntary ways. Voluntarily, certain groups are excluded, whereby the general acceptance for such exclusions has changed in history and is still in debate: Excluding women, nonwhite people, indigenous people, people of certain religious beliefs, non-nobles, or poor people from the right to vote was widely accepted in the 19th century, but is not today. Excluding children and juveniles up to a certain age and foreigners living in the country is still general practice in the 21st century. Really unrestricted voting would include all the people in a certain entity at a certain time. But still, in such a case, there would be involuntary restrictions, as people might not be able to express their vote due to youth, old age, disability, or illness.

"Direct" means that all voters can vote directly for the position or body. Therefore the U.S. presidential election system would not qualify, as it is an indirect voting system via electors. There are even more radical interpretations of "direct": One could argue that no representative system enables an unrestricted vote, as only direct involvement and participation of the voters in every decision is truly unrestricted. In this case, there would not be any institutions like the Congress, Senate, Parliament, and so on, as the voters would decide directly on every issue. But such a system is only practicable on a local basis or in very small entities (as in the polis of Ancient Greece or in some cantons in Switzerland today). An intermediary way between directness and practicability is the referendum, the possibility to decide on specific issues directly. Many countries practice referenda on a local or regional basis. In France, the president can put important decisions directly to the French people by the way of a referendum. Generally, at least new constitutions in emerging democracies are put to a direct vote by the people.

Equality means that all votes have the same value for the result. In a basic form, there must be equal access opportunities to polling stations (access in the form of the necessary time free from work or other duties, access in form of a reasonable distance to the polling station). Equality in a more sophisticated meaning is much more difficult to realize: equality in the information available to the voters or equality in the (basic) education of the voters to understand how to form an (educated) voting decision. In terms of voting systems, there are arguments for and against the contradicting systems of proportional representation or majority voting: In a proportional system small parties tend to get disproportionate influence, whereby the voters of small parties may have more influence than the voters of big parties, although a minimum percentage is required in many countries (for example 5 percent in the German system). In a majority vote, the winner takes all, whereby the voters of all other nonvictorious parties have no say at all (for example, in the British system). Some states have an obligation to vote for the pur-

pose of an equal participation (for example, Belgium). Vote-counting problems (as in the 2000 presidential election in Florida) raise serious doubts concerning the equality of the votes/voters in the outcome of a given election.

"Free" means that all voters can decide freely what to vote for or against. This means essentially freedom of fear of punishment for the vote by the ruler or an oppressive party (be it political, religious, or economic). Nevertheless, there are many occasions when a voter formally has a free choice, but by circumstances (especially by general economic pressures not aimed specifically at him or her, but applying to all) is forced to vote in a certain way. In any representative voting system, the voter is not really free, as he or she has to vote for a "package," that is, the political program of the party. He or she has to make a compromise decision, as the voter may like the economic program of one party and the foreign policy program of another party, but has only the choice to vote for one of the two parties. Terrorism is a new danger for free vote, as the Madrid, Spain, bombings of 2004 may well have had an influence on the result of the general election some days later.

Secrecy is a necessary safeguard for the voter to express his or her will in the election freely without any interference of a third party. In an ideal world, the secrecy of the vote would not be necessary, as any voter could express the choice publicly without fear of disadvantages. In the real world, the secrecy is an essential tool to allow unrestricted voting against possible pressure from employers, family members, political parties, the police, or the military.

It has to be mentioned that some left, mainly anarchistic circles, argue that voting in itself is an undemocratic process as any vote divides the people into winners and losers (politically, and economically). There have been many theoretical models of a democratic decision making process in the form of a consensual democracy, whereby no decision is reached without the consent of everybody. It seems, however, that no such consensual model has ever worked for a larger group of people. Other leftist critiques of voting would argue that even unrestricted voting does not touch on the real decisive economic factors in society, or that only a global democracy giving the possibility of vote to all human inhabitants of the planet would be a fair representation, as the nation-states of today can be seen as explicitly excluding people not belonging to the individual nation-state. Although there is without doubt no better alternative to voting, it has to be remembered that people like Adolf Hitler abused democratic elections to come to power. That means that even unrestricted voting has to be set in the frame of some fundamental human rights that cannot be changed—even by unrestricted voting.

## SEE ALSO

*Volume 1 Left:* Democracy; Electorate, African American; U.S.; Suffragists; Electorate, World Demographics. *Volume 2 Right:* Elitism; United States.

## BIBLIOGRAPHY

Michel L. Balinski and H. Peyton Young, *Fair Representation: Meeting the Ideal of One Man, One Vote* (Brookings Institution Press, 2001); Eleanor Clift, *Founding Sisters and the Nineteenth Amendment* (Wiley, 2003); David J. Garrow, *Protest at Selma: Martin Luther King, Jr. and the Voting Rights Act of 1965* (Yale University Press 1980); Dimitris Gritzalis, *Secure Electronic Voting* (Kluwer, 2002); League of Women Voters, ed., *Choosing the President 2004: A Citizen's Guide to the Electoral Process* (Lyons Press, 2003); Pippa Norris, *Electoral Engineering: Voting Rules and Political Behavior* (Cambridge University Press 2004); "Voting," Department of Justice, www.usdoj.gov (July 2004).

OLIVER BENJAMIN HEMMERLE, PH.D.
CHEMNITZ UNIVERSITY, GERMANY

# The Left

# W-Z

## Wallace, Henry A. (1888–1965)

HENRY A. WALLACE, secretary of agriculture, U.S. vice president, secretary of commerce, and presidential candidate, was born in Ames, Iowa, to a family of farmers, academics, activists, and newspaper editors. He was one of the leading progressives of the United States in the 20th century and held high office in an era in which people on the political left could directly influence public policy. Philosophically, Wallace believed in the "natural brotherhood" of humanity, the need for cooperation, the nobility of the those who worked the land, the importance of distributing fairly the bounty produced by working people, and the importance of using government to prevent the monopolization of eastern industrial interests.

His grandfather, Henry C. Wallace, was Pennsylvania-born and was ordained as a liberal Calvinist minister. He moved to Iowa, seeking fertile ground for his teaching, a combination of the Christian Social Gospel and Granger ideas. Henry A. Wallace studied at the institution now known as Iowa State University, having learned about livestock breeding and improving grains from his father, H. C. Wallace, the eldest son of Reverend Wallace and a professor at that college. In the 1920s, the third Henry Wallace engaged in business, specifically in the development and distribution of hybrid corn seed. He continued his studies informally past the bachelor's degree and became an expert in soil and crop management, genetics, and the application of statistical techniques to agriculture.

Initially a registered Republican, like his family Henry was a supporter of Teddy Roosevelt in the 1912 presidential election, of Robert La Follette in 1924, and Democrat Al Smith in 1928. In 1932, Wallace had come to the attention of the new president, Franklin Delano Roosevelt (FDR); Wallace followed in his father's footsteps and was appointed secretary of agriculture. From this position, Wallace implemented Roosevelt's New Deal provisions for rural America, principally through the Agriculture Adjustment Administration and the Rural Electrification Administration.

For eight years, Wallace served in the Agriculture Department. Then in 1940, despite his lack of support among the bosses of the Democratic Party, FDR chose Wallace as his vice-presidential running mate, displacing John Garner. The pair was easily elected, the third win for FDR, though Wallace would have difficulty coping with the inactivity imposed by the post. In one significant move, FDR appointed him as chair of the Board of Economic Warfare in 1941. Wallace also served as FDR's foil on the left, making speeches that were "trial balloons" for the administration. As vice president, Wallace made speeches advocating economic democracy through the idea of the "Century of the Common Man" and he alienated many Democrats, especially in the South, by advocating his idea of "genetic democracy," which reflected his own belief in the equality of the races and sexes.

By 1944, FDR arranged for Wallace to be dumped from the ticket, as easily as he had appointed him four years earlier. As secretary of commerce under Truman, Wallace found himself removed even further from the center of power than he had as Roosevelt's vice president. Wallace increasingly felt disquiet over the rightward direction in U.S. domestic and foreign policy, and he resigned from the Truman administration in 1946. He was among the last of Roosevelt appointees to do so. Wallace ran against Truman in 1948, as the candidate for a revived Progressive Party, but he fell far short in the national election.

Although Wallace's ideas sprang from his background as a Progressive and New Deal Democrat, his opposition to Truman's emerging anti-Soviet stand in 1948 marked him as the most left-leaning third-party candidate for the presidency since Robert La Follette in 1924.

**SEE ALSO**

*Volume 1 Left:* Progressive Party; Democratic Party; Truman, Harry; Roosevelt, Franklin D.; New Deal; Liberalism. *Volume 2 Right:* Republican Party.

**BIBLIOGRAPHY**

Mark L. Kleinman, *A World of Hope, a World of Fear: Henry A. Wallace, Reinhold Niebuhr, and American Liberalism* (Ohio State University Press, 2000); Karl M. Schmidt, *Henry A. Wallace: Quixotic Crusade 1948* (Syracuse University Press, 1960); Henry A. Wallace, *The Price of Vision: The Diary of Henry A. Wallace, 1942–46* (Houghton Mifflin, 1973).

GEOFFREY R. MARTIN
MOUNT ALLISON UNIVERSITY, CANADA

# Washington, George (1732–1799)

NICKNAMED "The Father of Our Country," George Washington profoundly influenced America in the late 18th century. A gentleman, landowner, surveyor, military leader, and politician, Washington dominated the Revolutionary War as commander in chief of the Continental forces and following the ratification of the Constitution, he was unanimously selected by the Electoral College to be the first president of the United States. Washington is remembered as one of America's greatest patriots.

Born to a well-off family of Virginia planters, Washington was the eldest son of his father's second wife. His father died in 1743 and the young Washington was sent to live with his half-brother, Lawrence, on Lawrence's Mount Vernon estate. Lawrence had married into a prominent Virginia family, the Fairfaxes, and Washington was welcomed into this extended family. His brother died in 1752 and Washington inherited Lawrence's Mount Vernon estate. Washington trained as a surveyor and surveyed the property of Lord Fairfax in the Shenandoah Valley. He made his reputation as a soldier and military leader during the French and Indian War. Promoted to the rank of colonel by the age of 23, he became the commander in chief of the Virginia militia.

Returning to Mount Vernon, Washington settled into the life of gentleman farmer, expanding Mount Vernon's farming operations. In 1759, Washington took a seat in the Virginia House of Burgesses (renamed the Virginia House of Delegates in 1776), the oldest representative legislature in the colonies. He retained his seat until 1774. His years in the Virginia legislature cemented his resolve to see representative government thrive in America.

Washington was a Virginia delegate to both the First Continental Congress and the Second Continental Congress in Philadelphia in 1775. On July 3, 1775, Washington became the unanimous choice of Congress to command the Continental forces. Washington did not accept pay for the position as commander in chief of the Continental Army, informing Congress that he had no intention of making a profit from his service. His troops lacked training and were poorly equipped and Washington suffered early defeats at the hands of the superior forces of the British, until his persistence and leadership changed the course of the Revolutionary War. Washington made sure the enemy was never aware of the inexperience and lack of supplies suffered by his troops. He carefully observed the actions of the British forces and realized they were rigidly attached to their European training. Washington determined not to act or react as the British anticipated, but worked hard to keep them off guard. He would do nothing to give them an advantage.

When the morale of the Continental Army was at its lowest point, Washington boldly planned a surprise attack on the Hessian fighters (British allies) encamped in Trenton, New Jersey. Washington surreptitiously moved his troops across the Delaware River in the middle of the night and attacked Trenton over Christmas 1776, taking the Hessians by surprise and scoring a huge victory for the Continental forces.

After the war, Washington returned to Mount Vernon, anticipating a quiet life as a farmer. However, the Articles of Confederation, the first constitutional document guiding the fledgling nation, did not seem sufficient and Washington was an advocate for the Constitutional Convention in Philadelphia in 1787, called to amend the Articles (although the delegates to the Convention abandoned the Articles and wrote a new Constitution in its place). Upon the ratification of the Constitution, Washington was unanimously elected by the Electoral College to be the first president of the United States (he remains the only president unanimously selected).

Sworn in as president on April 30, 1789, Washington moved his family (his wife Martha and two grandchildren they raised subsequent to the death of Martha's son during the Revolutionary War) to the temporary national capital in New York City. He was re-elected president in 1792 but weary of politics and the growing Jefferson-Hamilton factions within his cabinet, Washington retired at the end of his second term (starting a precedent of presidential service maintained until Franklin D. Roosevelt's four terms of office). During his presidency, he helped establish the financial system of the new government, and during the war between England and France, Washington advocated a neutral position for the fledgling nation. In his Farewell Address, Washington celebrated America's hard fought liberty. He discussed morality as a necessity for the nation's survival and growth and he referred to the sacred obligation of the people to obey the Constitution. Regarding America's place in the world, Washington both advocated the cultivation of peace and a wary involvement in the affairs of other nations.

Washington quietly retired to his beloved Mount Vernon. He succumbed to a throat infection and died on December 14, 1799. His impact on the new nation cannot be overstated: a man who loved the land and the country, a warrior when duty called to him, and a politician whose ideas guided the fledgling nation. Washington was also a man who questioned the sensibilities of the world he lived in; although a plantation owner and a slave-owner, he arranged for the freedom of his slaves in his last will and testament. That last act of emancipation and the fact that he refused to entertain any possibility of a Washington dynasty (in effect, making him king of America) stressed the liberal, leftist side of his political philosophies.

## SEE ALSO

*Volume 1 Left:* American Revolution; Jefferson, Thomas; United States.
*Volume 2 Right:* Monarchism; American Revolution; United States.

## BIBLIOGRAPHY

"George Washington," www.whitehouse.gov (May 2004); Barry Schwartz, *George Washington: The Making of an American Symbol* (Temple University Press, 1976); John E. Ferling, *The First of Men: A Life of George Washington* (University of Tennessee Press, 1988).

AMANDA BURGESS
WAYNE STATE UNIVERSITY

# Weathermen

INITIALLY KNOWN AS Weatherman, also known as the Weathermen and, later, Weather Underground, the group was a radical faction of the New Left that came into prominence in the United States during the early 1970s. The group, consisting mostly of young people from primarily white, privileged backgrounds, resorted to terrorist tactics, including the bombing of buildings, offices, police cars, and statues in an effort to begin a revolution in America. From the early years as a component of a larger radical, but primarily nonviolent, student collective to later as an underground revolutionary movement, well trained in Marxist-Leninist ideology, the group never ceased to be a highly controversial part of the social upheaval of the late 1960s and early 1970s.

Weatherman was initially part of the Students for a Democratic Society (SDS), a group of New Left students from colleges and universities throughout the United States that demonstrated in protest of racism, sexism, the Vietnam War, and other social conditions and events they considered oppressive. As the conflict between police and SDS members intensified into violence, SDS began to develop a more revolutionary approach. The group began to faction into separate units as conflict and disunity announced the end of the former organization. Three groups emerged to vie for leadership: the Marxist-Leninist-Maoist Progressive Labor Party later called Progressive Labor (PL); the Revolutionary Youth Movement (RYM) and its offshoot, RYM II; and Weatherman. In a 1969 conference, PL was ousted by Weatherman and RYM II due in part to its failure to support the struggles of radical African American groups such as the Black Panthers. Weatherman and RYM II controlled the new version of SDS.

Weatherman, the more radical of these two groups, split from RYM II. The group, who took their name from a Bob Dylan song that proclaimed, "you don't need a weatherman to know which way the wind blows," developed an organizational structure that was centralized in a unit called the Weather Bureau. The group members engaged in the 1960s counterculture activities such as use of hallucinogenics and group sex but, while these activities certainly added to their anti-establishment image, it was the violent political actions that became their trademark.

Although the Weather members had many protest items on their agenda, foremost was the escalating war in Vietnam. Operating under the slogan "Bring the War Home," they organized a series of violent altercations with police in Chicago in October of 1969 that were dubbed the Days of Rage. With a cache of speeches and demonstrations that coincided with the trial of the Chicago Seven (another group of New Left protesters, were also known as yippies), a faction of Weather people suddenly attacked a group of surprised police officers. Violence ensued over the next four days, producing serious injuries for police and Weathermen, 284 arrests, and over $1 million in damage to the city of Chicago.

After the Days of Rage, the Weathermen claimed victory in the altercation. Some outside groups and individuals supported the intensified rebellion, such as Eldridge Cleaver of the Black Panthers (although the majority of the black radicals did not). More people began to join the group primarily due to the Weathermen's newly achieved status as the premier revolutionary group in America. The same status also drew the attention of the Federal Bureau of Investigation (FBI), which was already tracking other subversive groups. In fact, the FBI placed one agent in the group as a spy.

As a result of the killing of two Black Panthers by the Chicago police, the group decided to increase the level of violent activity. In order to accomplish this, the Weather Bureau decided it would be best to depart from their confrontational style and "go underground" and use guerrilla-style attacks on symbolic targets.

To reflect the change in strategy, they changed their name to the Weather Underground. The group frequently sent out a series of public communiqués in which the anti-establishment rhetoric became increasingly threatening.

In March 1970, three Weather members were killed when a bomb they were making exploded in a New York townhouse. These three members became the martyrs of the organization. A few months later, the group began to hit strategic targets by bombing the New York City police headquarters, a San Francisco army base, and a bank in Manhattan. Immediately, federal indictments were issued for several of the Weather Underground members and the FBI beefed up its efforts to find and arrest the group members. In September 1970, some Weather members helped free, from a California prison, former Harvard professor and LSD advocate Timothy Leary, a high-profile counterculture figure. After the breakout, organization members drove him away, provided fake identification, and cleverly hid him in different locations before arranging for him to leave the country. This was seen as another victory by the mysterious underground organization.

The Weather Underground continued to send communiqués condemning "Amerikan [the misspelling was intentional] imperialism," and supporting the Vietnamese and other oppressed nations. Bombings continued in California at prison offices, and at a wing of the Pentagon. New indictments were issued for the arrest of the members. As the 1970s progressed, some revisions occurred in the group's administrative structure. There was, however, no change in revolutionary zeal as the group continued bombing symbolic targets such as an office in New York's Rockefeller Center, Salt Lake City's Kennecott's Corporate Office in 1975, and San Francisco's Immigration and Naturalization Service (INS) office in 1977, among others.

Some members of the group were found and others surrendered to the police in the 1980s. In 1981, an attempt by a few Weather members to rob a Brinks armored truck resulted in two police officers being killed and the members being arrested. In 1983, the U.S. Capitol was bombed after the invasion of Grenada, resulting in more arrests. In 1994, the last of the Weatherman group involved in the Days of Rage turned himself into police.

### SEE ALSO

*Volume 1 Left:* Protests; Vietnam War; Students for a Democratic Society.
*Volume 2 Right:* Justice; Nixon, Richard M.; Conservatism; United States.

### BIBLIOGRAPHY

Peter Collier and David Horowitz, *Destructive Generation: Second Thoughts about the 1960s* (Free Press, 1996); Todd Gitlen,

*The Sixties: Years of Hope Days of Rage* (Bantam, 1993); Harold Jacobs, ed., *Weatherman* (Ramparts Press, 1970); Ron Jacobs, *The Way the Wind Blew: A History of the Weather Underground* (Verso, 1977).

LEONARD A. STEVERSON, PH.D.
SOUTH GEORGIA COLLEGE

# Welfare and Poverty

WELFARE PROGRAMS may well be the most unpopular of all government initiatives. They are criticized by the social scientists who observe their effects, disdained by the taxpayers who pay the bills, and generally unappreciated by many of the people who go through the bureaucratic process required to collect the benefits. Yet, governmental support programs are as old as human civilization—with an ages-old realization that rulers have an obligation to look out for the welfare of the governed. The Bible teaches Paul's injunction to "do good to all men" by helping those in need by feeding the hungry, clothing the naked, housing the homeless, healing the sick.

Today, not all governments acknowledge such obligations. Canada and Denmark have wide-ranging social welfare legislation. Britain's National Health Service provides free medical treatment to citizens. Throughout the third world, on the other hand, few social services are available to help the needy. In the United States public assistance has increasingly come under fire. Thirty years and $3.5 trillion after President Lyndon Johnson fired the first shot in the War on Poverty, dramatic welfare reform measures in 1996 radically changed how the government provides public assistance.

From the left's perspective, these right-wing reforms were troubling, demonstrating a callous disregard for the needy. On the far left, the late Gus Hall, the U.S. Communist Party's repeated candidate for president of the United States called the 1996 welfare reform laws a "victory for the very rich."

He blamed the mass media for glossing over "the class nature" of the legislation. "They neglect to say it is a windfall for the rich and corporations. As a result, the very rich will get richer and the poor will get poorer. State after state is cutting food stamps. As a result, an increasing number of people are homeless, hungry and starving to death. Many of them are children, the elderly and disabled."

Governments have an obligation to champion the downtrodden, say proponents of public social programs; a lack of political power should not silence their voices. "Poor people are one of the least powerful groups in the United States and their civil liberties are therefore always in a precarious state," said the American Civil Liberties Union in a public statement. "Welfare laws and practices have often violated the rights of the poor, especially poor women and their children."

The federal welfare reform law passed in 1996 is no exception. Under the law, states can deny welfare to any child born into a family already receiving welfare. The promise of equal educational opportunity is a cornerstone of our democracy, but millions of poor and minority children in the United States are receiving an inadequate education. Poor people face a myriad of problems. The Hyde Amendment, passed by Congress in 1976, excludes abortion from the comprehensive healthcare services provided to low-income people through Medicaid. Poor people with HIV/AIDS are routinely denied access to homeless shelters. And the Supreme Court has ruled that a public housing tenant, who has committed no wrongdoing, can be evicted because a family member "engaged in drug related activities off the premises."

UNCONSCIONABLE

Such disregard by a government toward those in dire need is unconscionable, say voices on the left. Furthermore, public resentment toward those who need help the most is unreasonable, activist Jean Davidson wrote. She believes the resentment is fed by fallacies such as "Most welfare goes to minority women who never leave the dole."

The fact is, said Davidson, that more American whites receive aid than African Americans or Hispanics. Furthermore, two out of three welfare recipients are children, not adults who are refusing to work. Nor is the stereotype true of multigenerational families staying on welfare for year after year. Indeed, she said, nearly three out of four women receiving aid get off of welfare within two years; half of all families receiving Aid to Families of Dependent Children (AFDC) before the 1996 reforms got off within two years.

Isolated abuses are touted and stereotypes are highlighted as society shrugs off its responsibility to the poor, the downtrodden, and the disadvantaged—with the public believing such myths as that most welfare recipients are minorities. "The white women are invisible," says Nancy Lyman-Shaver, a former welfare mother and organizer of a social welfare organization in Springfield, Massachusetts. She cited statistics that non-Hispanic whites made up 39 percent of welfare recipients in 1992, non-Hispanic blacks totaled 37 percent, and Hispanics were 18 percent. Of the 13.6 million individuals who benefited from AFDC in 1992, she said, 9.2 million were children under 18—and only 15 percent of AFDC families stayed on welfare for five years or more.

Davidson disputed the claims that welfare encourages teen pregnancy and large, dependent families. "There is no evidence that welfare encourages more children," she wrote. "In fact, the states with the highest benefits have the lowest rates of additional births, and the states with the lowest benefits have the highest."

Davidson argued against the widespread belief that welfare has been a huge drain on the federal budget. "It's true that with state and federal expenditures, welfare programs cost a total of $24 billion annually," she wrote. "And yet welfare payments affect only 1 percent of the federal budget. The fact is, affluent Americans enjoy far greater benefits in the form of tax deductions for mortgage interest and property taxes, capital gains exclusions, and farm subsidies. The higher the household income, under current tax law, the greater the tax advantages."

What about assertions from the right that private charities were the traditional champions of the poor for hundreds of years—and that government needs to get out of the welfare business? "Some people argue that all social welfare work should be turned over to the churches and religious charities," said Father Fred Krammer, president of Catholic Charities USA. "No charity has the resources to be the long-term support of needy families."

## SOCIAL RESPONSIBILITY

Instead, the responsibility belongs to society as a whole, and government in particular. Social programs to meet needs of those who cannot help themselves "is a role which government fulfills through a complex web of social programs—from Social Security and Medicare to Supplemental Security Income, veterans' benefits, food stamps, and Medicaid. Charities just don't have the resources to do all this work," said Krammer, adding that a century ago, many more poor families simply died of hunger, sickness, and poverty. Society does not want to return to those dark times, he said. "Indeed, some things are better done by a more impartial government. Ultimately the churches cannot do a better job than the

government in meeting all the needs of low-income Americans. And we can't fix all of America's problems. Religious charities cannot pretend to replace government's responsibility for the common good nor assume its moral obligations."

A major flaw in welfare reform is the right's ignoring that there is a shortage of jobs paying a living wage available to the welfare recipient just entering the workplace, wrote Derrick Z. Jackson on the *Boston Globe*'s op-ed page. The result has been disastrous. "All of this was predicted by welfare advocates. They had studies to show there were nowhere enough jobs in large urban areas to lift people out of poverty. They warned that recipients needed far more education, training and child care. They produced data that showed there was not enough public transportation to get ex-recipients out to the suburbs, where the new jobs are." He said there is an ulterior motive on the part of conservative politicians: "There is clear evidence that New York's 33,000 workfare participants are nothing but cheap labor. They clean and maintain streets, parks, and buildings for between $5,000 to $12,000 in welfare benefits" replacing city workers who used to do those jobs for $20,000 to $40,000 a year.

Jackson said the media has ignored social welfare advocates' solid statistics, preferring to bash "welfare queens." He charged that conservatives have saturated the airwaves with apocalyptic visions of teenage mothers bearing babies to get a welfare check. "Informing the public of the failures of welfare reform is important," said Jackson. "But reform might not have failed so badly had the press been a fount of balanced information at the outset instead of a collapsed dam against a cascade of stereotypes."

As a result of welfare reform's cutbacks on public housing, communities of all sizes are facing the dilemma of where to house their neediest residents, according to Elsa Wenzel, writing in *Mother Jones* magazine. She described how in Birmingham, Alabama, housing officials passed out 3,000 applications to potential voucher recipients, some who camped overnight in cars by the housing office so they could be first in the line, which by mid-morning stretched five blocks long. Even after turning in the forms, they will wait again for months or longer to find out if they'll be awarded housing vouchers, she wrote.

In Chicago, Illinois, rather than build new homes or apartments, the housing authority demolished public housing, according to Angela Caputo, writing for a local advocacy journal, *The Chicago Reporter*. Since 1999, the Chicago Housing Authority has demolished 9,400 units, and the overhaul is accelerating, she reported. Plagued by poverty and lacking other options, many former residents have moved from the buildings slated for demolition and doubled up with family or friends, or seek refuge in homeless shelters.

Why would the government and American society shrug off the moral obligation to help the poor? Because of a failure of government and the public's loss of faith in government, *Mother Jones* reported. "Federal programs failed to heal our racial wounds, guarantee a good education for our kids, or protect us from factory closures. Watergate-style disclosures and lobbyist corruption have combined with Great Society failure to cause much of the public to lose faith in the government's competence—and its ability to act on behalf of ordinary Americans. The Republican Party capitalized on this anti-government sentiment and routed the party of Roosevelt."

As a result, "The basic rights of all human beings are being violated with the denial of food, shelter, free education, living wages and health care," according to Rocco Rosanio of the Poor People's Economic Human Rights March, an activist group in Philadelphia, Pennsylvania. "Now, more than ever, it is important that our voices be heard as we try to bring attention to, and remedy these violations. We recognize that there are many problems we face as a society. But we feel this is an issue that requires the public's and the media's undivided attention."

"While welfare 'reform' has moved people off the rolls, it has failed miserably at moving people out of poverty and into self-sufficiency," said Kim Gandy, president of the National Organization for Women in a news release. "It's high time the Senate catches on and passes the most family-friendly welfare bill this country has ever seen. A 2000 report from the Kellogg Foundation showed that 9 out of 10 people in the United States think that families moving from welfare to work should have access to education and/or training for jobs that would allow them to be self-sufficient."

Yet, she said, less than 1 percent of federal assistance to families was spent on education and training in 2000. The solution is "legislation that truly helps women and their families become self-sufficient by providing the education, fair job opportunities and programs that support work, including child care and transportation, that are essential for lifting poor women and their families out of poverty. After all, rhetoric about encouraging self-sufficiency for poor families is empty unless poor families can have access to an education that will guarantee equal opportunities. It's time to end the welfare debate once and for all. The only way to end the vicious cycle of poverty and welfare reform debate is to enact fair legislation that will yield real results. Educational opportunities and work supports, like child care and transportation, are key to real reform. This isn't rocket science, it's common sense."

**SEE ALSO**

**BIBLIOGRAPHY**

Angela Caputo, "Forgotten People," *The Chicago Reporter* (March 2004); Gus Hall, "New Budget a Good Deal—For the Rich," *The People's Weekly World* (April 9, 1997); Derrick Z. Jackson, "Op-Ed Column: Lazy Lies about Welfare," *Boston Sunday Globe* (May 3, 1998); Fred Krammer, "Churches Can't Pick Up the Welfare Tab," *Salt of the Earth* (Claretian Publications, 2004); P. Loprest, *How Families that Left Welfare Are Doing: A National Picture* (Urban Institute, 1999); Frances Fox Piven and Richard A. Cloward, *Regulating the Poor: The Functions of Public Welfare* (Vintage, 1998); "Poor Women Need Real Welfare Reform, Not Political Rhetoric; NOW Challenges Senators to Stop the Vicious Cycle of Poverty," Press Release (National Organization for Women, 2002); W. Primus, L. Rawulings, K. Larin, and K. Porter, "The Initial Impacts of Welfare Reform on the Incomes of Single-Mother Families" (The Center of Budget and Policy Priorities, 1999); "Rights of the Poor" (American Civil Liberties Union, 2004); A. Sherman, "Extreme Child Poverty Rises Sharply in 1997," (Children's Defense Fund, 1999); Holly Sklar, "Community or Chaos?," and Elsa Wenzel, "Slashing Section 8," *Mother Jones* (May 14, 2004); D. Zuckerman, "Welfare Reform in America: A Clash of Politics and Research," *The Journal of Social Issues* (Winter 2000).

ROB KERBY
INDEPENDENT SCHOLAR

# Wilson, Woodrow (1856–1924)

A PROGRESSIVE DEMOCRAT who hated war, Woodrow Wilson had the unenviable task of leading the United States through World War I. Wilson was born on December 28, 1856, in Staunton, Virginia, and was raised in Georgia and South Carolina. He was the first southerner to serve as president since the disastrous presidency of Andrew Johnson. National Democratic leaders groomed Wilson for national politics by supporting his candidacy for governor of New Jersey. In the presidential election of 1912, Wilson made individual liberties a national issue for the first time since the American Revolution. Under Wilson, the Democratic party, which had been struggling to redefine itself since the Civil War, became the symbol of American liberalism.

Wilson led liberals into establishing the twin goals of domestic reforms and a new world order. The Wilson coalition included die-hard Democrats, liberals, progressives, socialists, single-taxers, and intellectuals. Through increasing its strength in the west and in the Solid South, the Democratic party regained its status as the country's major party. Wilsonian liberalism survived through Wilson's impact on other liberals and through his 1916 appointment of Justice Louis Brandeis, the first Jew to serve on the Supreme Court, who provided a strong liberal voice on the Supreme Court until his retirement in 1939.

While Wilson worked well with Congress during his first administration, relations with Congress during his second term were often partisan and stormy, partially because of the conservative tendencies of many Southern Democrats who objected to what they saw as Wilson's increasing tendency to endorse internationalism. Wilson's New Freedom program resulted in a number of progressive reforms that included lowered tariffs, federal aid to farmers, a more sharply graduated income tax, federal oversight of bureaucracies, and protective labor legislation that encompassed bans on child labor and an eight-hour workweek for railroad workers. Wilson was also responsible for establishing the Department of Labor as a cabinet position, giving the federal government a voice in the labor movement that had grown up in response to American industrialization. In order to ensure fair trade, Wilson also created what is now the Federal Trade Commission.

In 1913, Wilson convinced Congress to pass the Federal Reserve Act, which established the Federal Reserve system that modernized the banking system and paved the way for federal management of the economy. Wilson deserved a good deal of credit for turning the American economy completely around. The United States entered the World War period as a debtor nation; but by war's end, the United States had become a creditor and a leading player on the world scene.

During the presidential election of 1916, Wilson was faced with international dilemmas stemming from rising tensions in Mexico and a concentrated assault on democracy in Europe. Wilson believed in a hands-off policy in South America, believing that Mexico should solve its own problems. The situation in Europe proved more troublesome. Even while technically neutral, the United States had provided money and resources to the democratic countries that were aligned against imperial Germany.

## WORLD WAR I

By the slim margin of 23 electoral votes, the Democrats won the election of 1916 by harping on the slogan, "He kept us out of war." Refraining from retaliation had not always been easy for Wilson, particularly after May 1, 1915, when German torpedoes sunk a British merchant ship, the *Lusitania*, resulting in the loss of 128 American lives. Wilson's claim that "There is such a thing as a man being too proud to fight" was ill received by American internationalists. Public reaction to the sinking of the *Lusitania* set the stage for Wilson's request to Congress to declare war on April 2, 1917, following the sinking of three American ships on March 27, 1917, as part of the German campaign of unrestricted submarine warfare.

During World War I, Wilson received Congressional approval for increased military funding and for the Selective Services Bill that enacted universal military service. In order to finance the war, Wilson convinced Congress to pass the War Revenue Act that enacted excess profits taxes, raised income taxes, particularly on the wealthy, and placed levies on everything from amusements to transportation. Liberty and Victory Loans further expanded the U.S. Treasury. Wilson also extended federal powers during World War I through the creation of the War Industries Board and the Food Administration, which were designed to oversee the production and distribution of essential war materials, establish prices, and cut down on war profiteering. The War Finance Corporation was created to provide credit to allied countries.

Despite Wilson's commitment to individual liberties, the World War I Congress enacted the Espionage Act and the Sedition Act of 1918, the most serious threats to civil liberties in the United States since the first Sedition Act under John Adams. The Committee on Public Information was created to control the flow of war information and propaganda. The establishment of the Office of Alien Property Custodian gave the government the authority to take control of U.S. property owned by citizens of enemy countries, and the Trading with the Enemy Act prohibited American businesses from interacting with enemy countries of the United States.

Liberal reforms of the Wilson presidency did not extend to ending the legal discrimination of African Americans and immigrants or to granting female suffrage. Wilson's position on woman suffrage shifted in response to the role of American women in World War I. His support was a significant factor in congressional approval of the Nineteenth Amendment, ratified in 1920. However, Wilsonian liberalism failed to solve the national dilemma of racial, ethnic, and sexual discrimination.

As a way to avoid future world wars, Wilson suggested the concept of an international body committed to working toward world peace and cooperation, capable of settling disputes through discussion and mediation. In January 1918, Wilson introduced his Fourteen Points before a joint session of Congress, laying out the basis of the League of Nations. Wilson's proposal included open diplomacy, arms reduction, freedom of the seas, reduced economic barriers, an end to imperialism, and the inclusion of the Soviet Union in the world community.

In 1918, Republicans gained control of Congress, in part by claiming that Wilsonian liberalism was akin to socialism. Partisans, egged on by former president Teddy Roosevelt and led by Henry Cabot Lodge, the chair of the Foreign Relations Committee, created a no-win situation for Wilson. Wilson's failure to include Republicans among the American delegation to Paris where the Treaty of Versailles was negotiated exacerbated an already volatile situation. Ultimately, Wilson's refusal to compromise on the terms of the Treaty of Versailles struck the final deathblow to the League of Nations.

Against the advice of his physicians, the president set out on a public relations tour to drum up support for the League of Nations, traveling a total of 8,000 miles over a three-week period and delivering 37 addresses. On September 15, in Pueblo, Colorado, Wilson suffered a major stroke. A subsequent stroke a few weeks later left him paralyzed on the left side. Broken and dysfunctional, Wilson survived until February 23, 1924. In 1932, Franklin Roosevelt, a Wilsonian Democrat, was elected as the 32nd president of the United States. In the closing months of World War II, Roosevelt reintroduced the idea of an international peacekeeping body. Like Wilson, Roosevelt never lived to see his dream realized. Instead, President Harry Truman, who became president after Roosevelt's death on April 12, 1945, guided the creation of the United Nations, which continues to serve as a memorial to the visions of both Wilson and Roosevelt.

Amid Wilson's liberal agenda was also the fact, as some biographers are reluctant to note, Wilson was a staunch segregationist. He and his cabinet members insisted on the maintenance of racial segregation, and rolled back some minor acts of integration that had taken place under Theodore Roosevelt and William Howard Taft.

**SEE ALSO**

*Volume 1 Left:* Roosevelt, Franklin D.; Liberalism; United States; Democratic Party.
*Volume 2 Right:* Roosevelt, Theodore; Republican Party; United States.

**BIBLIOGRAPHY**

H.W. Brands, *Woodrow Wilson* (Times Books, 2003); Kendrick A. Clements, *The Presidency of Woodrow Wilson* (University of Kansas Press, 1992); David L. Cohn, *The Fabulous Democrats* (Putnam, 1956); John Milton Cooper, Jr., "Wilsonian Democracy," *Democrats and the American Idea: A Bicentennial Approach*, Peter B. Kovler, ed. (Center for National Policy Press, 1992); Alvin M. Josephy, *The Congress of the United States* (American Heritage, 1975); Robert Allen Rutland, *The Democrats: From Jefferson to Clinton* (Missouri: University of Missouri Press, 1995); David Steigerwald, *Wilsonian Idealism in America* (Cornell University Press, 1994).

ELIZABETH PURDY, PH.D.
INDEPENDENT SCHOLAR

# Workers Party

The name Workers Party appears in the United States over three key historical periods in the development of the American left. In its first incarnation, the Workers Party was formed in December 1921 as the "legal organization" of the underground Communist Party. As James Cannon recounts in his *The History of American Trotskyism* (1944), "The Workers Party had a very limited program, but it became the medium through which all our legal public activity was carried on. Control rested in the underground Communist Party. The Workers Party encountered no persecution." By 1923, members of the underground communist movement in the United States, with the support and authority of the Comintern World Congress, chose to work through the legal party rather than continue a division between the "underground" and the legal organization. The rise of Stalin's authority and the expulsion of Trotsky from the Soviet Union also had repercussions in the United States.

In 1928, members of the Communist Party believed to hold "Trotskyist" sympathies were also expelled from the American Communist Party. These individuals, under the leadership of James Cannon and Max Shachtman (among others), formed the Trotskyist Communist League of America in 1934, which again used the name Workers Party after merging with the American Workers Party. Finally, in 1938, the Trotskyists formed the Socialist Workers Party (SWP), and in 1940 a number of members split with the SWP over the "Russian Question" (Soviet influence) to form a new Workers Party, this time, under the leadership of Max Shachtman.

This third incarnation of the Workers Party (WP), then, under the leadership of Shachtman, broke with Trotsky as a result of his defense of the Soviet Union as a "workers' state, though degenerate." Shachtman subscribed to the "bureaucratic collectivist" theory of the Soviet state. However, a minority within the Workers Party, led by Raya Dunayevskaya and C.L.R. James argued that the Soviet Union was premised on state capitalism. Dunayevskaya and James, and later Grace Lee Boggs, led what was to be known as the Johnson-Forest (James and Dunayevskaya's party names) Tendency within the WP. Wide-ranging theoretical and practical debates were carried out in the party's paper, the *New International*.

By the close of the 1940s, a number of debates, including the revolutionary role of African Americans and the perennial "Russian Question," were continuing to divide the Workers Party. Members of the minority, under the leadership of Dunayevskaya and James, left the party in 1947 and rejoined the Socialist Workers Party. In 1949, the Workers Party name was changed to the Independent Socialist League.

**SEE ALSO**

*Volume 1 Left:* Socialist Workers' Party, UK; Communism; Socialism; Dunayevskaya, Raya.
*Volume 2 Right:* Capitalism; *Laissez-Faire*; United States.

**BIBLIOGRAPHY**

James P. Cannon, *The History of American Trotskyism: Report of a Participant* (Pioneer Publishers, 1944); Peter Drucker, *Max Shachtman and His Left* (Humanities Press, 1994); Raya Dunayevskaya, *The Marxist Humanist Theory of State Capitalism: Selected Writings* (News and Letters, 1992).

SANDRA REIN
ATHABASCA UNIVERSITY

# Workingmen's Party

THE WORKINGMEN'S PARTY was one of the first organizations that represented the economic and political interests of the working class in the 19th century. There were essentially two phases in the development of the Workingmen's Party. Created in the early 19th century, the Workingmen's Party developed in Philadelphia, Pennsylvania, as a result of an increasing industrialization that enveloped the United States and its working people.

The Workingmen's Party organized to represent the interests of the working class, on both a political and social level. It aided workers to go to school to gain employment skills. As a result, it became increasingly a political party. Coupled with a migration into the major cities by farmers, the urban working class became increasingly dependent on this organization. In Philadelphia, journeymen house carpenters demanded less work hours and spoke out on other working-class issues. In 1829, at least 5,000 workers met in New York City in response to employers who were threatening to increase the working day. The workers promised that they would declare a strike against any employer who made them work in excess of 10 hours. The initial Workingmen's Party represented the regional interests of a class that felt alienated and disenchanted by a powerful political ruling class. The initial constituency of workers came primarily from journeymen, painters, bricklayers, and house carpenters.

On October 19, 1829, the party decided to run candidates in the elections in New York. They ran on a platform, considered radical for the time, of a free, tax-supported school system, abolition of debt imprisonment, shorter hours, better working conditions, and improved housing for workers. The result was that the Workingmen's Party became a viable political option between the Jacksonians and the the anti-Jacksonians. Essentially, the party offered serious and representative alternates to the dominant political parties of the era in America. By the 1830s, many within the Workingmen's Party abandoned the party and joined the Whig Party, primarily as a form of political protest against the Jacksonians.

The onslaught of the Industrial Revolution and the economic changes wrought by the rise of big businessmen like John Rockefeller and Andrew Carnegie as well as the rise of immigration led to the emergence of a new political party, patterned after the Jacksonian Workingmen's Party. This new party, emerging 1878 and created by Denis Kearney, was anti-immigrant and anti-foreign. Specifically, Kearney and others within the group believed that Chinese immigration had created a deplorable labor situation. Chinese workers worked longer hours and received less pay, thus making it difficult for American workers to effectively labor at a fair wage. Essentially, the party charged that the Chinese laborers had taken all of the natives jobs, thus creating a labor surplus. In response to the Workingmen's protest, Congress passed in 1882 the Chinese Exclusion Act. The act essentially banned Chinese immigration into the country, reflecting widespread xenophobia.

The Workingmen's Party had been formed in 1876 out of the American remnants of the First International and included a number of prominent labor leaders and radicals. In addition to Samuel Gompers, the party numbered among its members a number of Marxist leaders of the German-American and Irish-American communities. The party membership grew to more than 7,000, but by 1877, the party split, as many members, including Gompers, left the party to concentrate on labor organizing. The remainder of the group reorganized as the Socialist Labor Party, which went on to play a significant party in Illinois politics. Like the earlier Workingmen's Party of 50 years earlier, the party was less important for its direct impact on politics, and more significant for demonstrating to the major political parties that the discontents of the working class, unless represented politically, might take the form of separate political organization. For this reason, in both eras, the Workingmen's Party represented a pressure to move American politics in a left direction.

### SEE ALSO
*Volume 1 Left:* Socialist Party, U.S.; Socialism; Communism; Third International (Comintern).
*Volume 2 Right:* Capitalism; United States; Republican Party; Conservatism; Xenophobia.

### BIBLIOGRAPHY
Walter Hugins, *Jacksonian Democracy and the Working Class* (Stanford University Press, 1960); Edward Pessen, *Jacksonian America: Society, Personality and Politics* (Illini Books, 1985); Edward Pessen, *Most Uncommon Jacksonians* (State University of New York Press, 1990); Howard Zinn, *A People's History of the United States* (Harper Perennial, 1995).

JAIME RAMON OLIVARES, PH.D.
HOUSTON COMMUNITY COLLEGE, CENTRAL
RODNEY P. CARLISLE, PH.D.
GENERAL EDITOR

# Wright, Frances (1795–1852)

FRANCES "FANNY" WRIGHT, a woman ahead of her time, was a reformer, a radical free-thinker, a utopian, and devoted to the public good. She was born in Scotland to an upper-middle-class family. She and her younger sister, Camilla, were orphaned as children and sent to live with family in London, England. The death of an uncle left the young girls with a sizeable fortune. When Wright turned 18, she fled to the home of another uncle in Glasgow, Scotland. She was self-educated.

Wright first visited the United States from 1818 to 1820. Following this visit, she published *Views of Society and Manners in America*. She was a disciple of the English radical thinker Jeremy Bentham. During a trip to France, she met the Marquis de Lafayette, who became a close, life-long friend. She followed him to America in 1824 and became an American citizen in 1825.

Wright abhorred slavery. She sought to show the people of the United States how the country could extricate itself from its reliance on slaves. She planned to purchase slaves and then set them up in a remote area, on land she purchased on the Wolf River in southwestern Tennessee. She planned to educate the slaves morally and intellectually in preparation for a life of freedom. She believed the slaves would understand her good intentions and reward her by working extra hard on this farm, thus compensating her for the cost of their purchase. Any profit would be put toward expanding the project. The community she founded was called Nashoba.

Nashoba was little more than a shabby cabin, with no amenities and little food. Wright steadfastly believed others would copy her success and before long, slavery would come to an end. She compromised much of her fortune on this dream.

Unfortunately, Wright was not in good health. Malaria and other illnesses plagued her all her life. In

*Frances Wright was a free-thinker and the first woman to publicly oppose slavery and women's inequality in the United States*

1827 she decided to return to Europe to recuperate. The managers of Nashoba were nowhere near as tolerant as Fanny and abuse of the slaves became the norm. Wright eventually concluded that it would be best to only receive free blacks and educate them for possible colonization in Haiti. She believed they needed to be removed from the vicious white culture in America. However, attracting free blacks to Nashoba was not easy, nor was it simple, despite the hardships and prejudice they faced in America, to get free blacks to relocate outside America.

Wright subsequently became the coeditor of the *New Harmony Gazette* (later renamed the *Free Enquirer*) and she lectured all over the United States on topics such as sexual equality, universal education, free love, the abolition of marriage, the liberalization of divorce laws, birth control, the abolition of capital punishment, atheism, and communalism. Settling in New York, she purchased a church building and turned it into a combi-nation lecture hall, bookstore, museum, and headquar-ters for her causes. She became a central figure in the workingmen's movement, which included activism for factory workers. Her detractors called the working-men's movement, the Fanny Wright Party.

Traveling to Haiti with some free blacks, Wright turned to a companion, French physician William Phiquepal D'Arusmont, for comfort during the rough journey. Wright became pregnant and married D'Arus-mont in 1831, after their daughter was born. Subse-quent to her marriage, Wright became reclusive. D'Arusmont controlled her fortune and she lost a sec-ond child in a failed pregnancy. Finally, she left her hus-band and she returned to America in 1835. Although Wright still lectured, she never regained her previous popularity. She eventually divorced D'Arusmont and died in 1852. The inscription on Wright's tombstone reads: "I have wedded the cause of human improve-ment, staked on it my fortune, my reputation and my life." Despite Wright's progressive views, her daughter was an ardent Christian and a conservative who testified before a Congressional committee in 1874, arguing against women's suffrage.

**SEE ALSO**

*Volume 1 Left:* Suffragists; Anthony, Susan B.; Abolitionism; Stanton, Elizabeth Cady; Feminism.
*Volume 2 Right:* Feminism; Conservatism.

**BIBLIOGRAPHY**

"Fanny Wright," www.distinguishedwomen.com (May 2004); Annie Laurie Gaylor, *Women without Superstition: No Gods–No Master: The Collective Writings of Women Freethinkers of the Nineteenth and Twentieth Centuries* (Freedom from Religion Foundation, 1997); Margaret Lane, *Frances Wright and the "Great Experiment"* (Rowman and Littlefield, 1972).

AMANDA BURGESS
WAYNE STATE UNIVERSITY

# Zionism

FROM ITS BEGINNINGS, the political Zionist move-ment for a homeland for the Jewish people was heavily influenced by socialist thought. In the 19th century, dis-cussion groups among politically aware Jewish working men, usually from Reformed Judaism, gradually re-placed the older Orthodox Jewish Hasidic sects as the dynamic center of Jewish intellectual life. According to Walter Laqueur, Moses Hess, one of the ideological fathers of Zionism in the 1840s, believed that any Jewish state "was to be basically Socialist in character." Hess envisaged the establishment of voluntary cooperative societies.

David J. Goldberg wrote how after the Russian pogroms, or anti-Semitic rioting, in 1881, socialist societies began to organize to return to the Jews' traditional homeland of Palestine. However, they would leave behind the religious heritage of Judaism to create a modern secular society.

Theodore Herzl became head of the World Zionist Organization in 1897. Many of those who were delegates to its convention had religious motivation as well, but the idea of working together collectively put a socialist stamp upon their plans. Herzl was not inspired by any socialist thought, but by the revulsion against the Jews he saw in the Dreyfus Scandal in France in the late 19th century. Herzl was moved in 1896 to write *Der Judentstaat (The Jewish State)*, which could be considered the seminal document for political Zionism, but not its socialist thought. Ber Borochov was one of the clearest propagandists for Zionist socialism and was affiliated with the leftist Po'alei Zion, (The Workers of Zion), movement. At a conference in Poltava, Russia, in 1907, he and Isaac ben-Zvi unveiled a document called Our Platform, a coherent statement of their beliefs. Like Herzl's world Zionist movement, the Workers of Zion saw Palestine as the social laboratory in which to test their principles: "[Jewish] political territorial autonomy in Palestine is the ultimate end of Zionism. For proletarian Zionists, this is also a step toward Socialism."

Those of the First Aliya had come largely for religious reasons, but those now in the Second Aliya movement, roughly from 1904 to the onset of World War I in 1914, were ideologically inclined Zionist socialists like settlers from Borochov's Workers of Zion. The socialists were in a sense torn between two necessities: like the nonsocialists, they saw the need to defend themselves from Arab hostility to the new settlements.

But also, in the international spirit that had guided socialism from its beginnings in France after the Napoleonic Wars, they also felt a need to reach out to the Arabs as fellow laborers. As Yaacov N. Goldstein noted in *From Fighters to Soldiers: How the Israeli Defense Forces Began*, "this basic position became the heritage of the Jewish workers' movement in Palestine and of the Zionist movement, and its validity remains in force until the present day." Palestine was at this date part of the Ottoman Turkish Empire.

The Yishuv, the Jewish community in Palestine, supported the Western Allies after Turkey entered World War I on the side of Germany and Austria-Hungary in October 1914. Many began to fear a massive pogrom like the ruling Turks had visited on the Armenians after they had seized power in 1908. Estimates are that up to 1.5 million Armenians died, the victim of Turkish genocide. To help avert such a catastrophe, Aaron Aaronsohn, his sister Sarah, and some friends set up the NILI spy network to provide the British Army under General Sir Edmund Allenby with essential information that helped him in his conquest of Palestine in 1917 and 1918. Aaronsohn was a committed Zionist, whose agricultural work was of inestimable value to the Jewish kibbutzim [collective farms]. Aaron David Gordon summed up best the philosophy behind the kibbutz movement: "labour [is] the basic energy for the creation of a popular culture."

However, the 1917 Balfour Declaration, which promised "the establishment in Palestine of a national home for the Jewish people" led to unrest among the Arabs. Massive rioting began in Jerusalem in 1920, initiated by the anti-Semitic Grand Mufti of Jerusalem, Haj Amin al-Husseini. However, it was abetted by militaristic Zionists under Vladimir "Jabo" Jabotinsky, who had been instrumental in forming the Jewish Legion in the British Army in World War I. Jabotinsky went on to form Betar, an organization whose name was an acronym for that of Joseph Trumpeldor, a veteran of the Jewish Legion who had died fighting the Bedouins at Tel Hai in 1920. Jabotinsky's socialist thought was tinged with a fascism in keeping with the growing movement in Europe after World War I: In 1922, Benito Mussolini and his Fascisti had seized power in Italy. Betar stressed that the entire movement had been called into being by "the call of the one architect:" Jabotinsky. In the end, he would be repudiated by mainstream Zionism, which remained true to its socialist origins.

David ben-Gurion, who also had soldiered in the Jewish Legion, emerged early as a leader of Zionist socialism. He was a delegate at the Workers of Zion conference that had been held at Ramleh in Palestine in 1906. He was close friends with Israel Shohat, the organizer of the Hashomer movement that guarded the settlements from hostile Arab attack and also helped identify with peaceable Arabs as an example of putting their socialist philosophy to work. David J. Goldberg wrote of ben-Gurion in this period, describing how he worked without ceasing to form the "factions of the left into a semblance of unity in order to promote Zionist socialism."

After the war, in 1919, the Workers of Zion reformed into the Achdut Ha-Avodah, the Unity of Labor group. At the end of the war, the Third Aliyah brought many more committed socialists to Palestine. Histradut, perhaps the most important of all Jewish labor organizations, was founded in 1920 and continued to have an influence in Palestine (then Israel) even 30 years afterward. In 1930, ben-Gurion would be the driving force behind the Mapai labor political party in Palestine. In 1936, when anti-Jewish rioting became a virtual civil war in Palestine, the kibbutzim and other socialist settlements supplied members of their Haganah, or self-defense corps, to the Special Night Squads that the British Zionist Orde Wingate led against the terrorists inspired by the Grand Mufti. The Haganah had been founded in 1920 by the Achdut Ha-Avodah.

During World War II, labor Zionism under ben-Gurion actively supported the Western Allies as in World War I, knowing what was happening to their countrymen, or landsmen, in the death camps of the German Third Reich. The Zionist Jewish Agency, the governing office for the Yishuv (Jewish community) in Palestine, supplied not only troops from the Haganah, and its elite force, the Palmach (including future Israeli Defense commander Moshe Dayan) to battle the French Vichy forces collaborating with the Germans in Syria and Lebanon, but also helped form the Jewish Brigade with the British Army in Italy. On May 14, 1948, ben-Gurion declared the independence of the state of Israel, and the Achdut Ha-Avodah's Haganah would become the new nation's defense force, or army.

## SEE ALSO

*Volume 1 Left:* Israel; Middle East.
*Volume 2 Right:* Israel; Middle East; United Kingdom: United States.

## BIBLIOGRAPHY

Yigael Allon, *The Making of Israel's Army* (Bantam, 1970); Anthony Verrier, ed., *Agents of Empire: Anglo-Zionist Intelligence Operations* (Brassey's, 1995); Walter Laqueur, *A History of Zionism: From the French Revolution to the Establishment of the State of Israel* (MJF Books, 1972); David J. Goldberg, *To the Promised Land: A History of Zionist thought from Its Origins to the Modern State of Israel* (Penguin, 1996); Yossi Beilin, *Israel: A Concise Political History* (St. Martin's Press, 1992); Tom Segev, *The Seventh Million: The Israelis and the Holocaust,* Haim Watzman, trans. (Henry Holt, 2000); John F. Murphy Jr., *Pillar of Fire: The Spread of Weapons of Mass Destruction in the Middle East* (unpublished Ms.).

JOHN F. MURPHY, JR.
AMERICAN MILITARY UNIVERSITY